Windows® XP Home Edition: The Complete Reference

About the Authors

John R. Levine is the author of two dozen books, ranging from *Linkers and Loaders* to *The Internet For Dummies*. He also runs online newsgroups and mailing lists, hosts a hundred web sites, and consults on programming language and Internet topics. He lives in the tiny village of Trumansburg, New York, where in his spare time he's the water and sewer commissioner. John is also active in the anti-spam movement, is a board member of CAUCE (Coalition Against Unsolicited Commercial E-mail), and runs the **abuse.net** web site.

Margaret Levine Young is the co-author of over two dozen books with various co-authors, including *The Internet For Dummies, Internet: The Complete Reference, Millennium Edition*, and *Poor Richard's Building Online Communities*. She holds a B.A. in Computer Science from Yale University, helps run the Unitarian Universalist Association's online communities, lives near Middlebury, Vermont, and experiments in e-commerce at her family's Great Tapes for Kids web site at **www.greattapes.com**.

Doug Muder is a semiretired mathematician who has contributed to a number of books about computers and the Internet, including *Internet: The Complete Reference* and *Dragon Naturally Speaking For Dummies*. He is the author of numerous research papers in geometry and information theory, and dabbles in various forms of nontechnical writing. (Check out his fiction and essays at **www.gurus.com/dougdeb**.) Doug lives in Nashua, New Hampshire with his wife, Deborah Bodeau, whom he met while getting his Ph.D. in mathematics from the University of Chicago.

Alison Barrows has authored or co-authored books on Windows, the Internet, Microsoft Access, and other topics. In addition to writing books, Alison writes and edits technical documentation and training materials. She holds a B.A. in International Relations from Wellesley College and an M.P.P. from Harvard University. In real life she spends most of her time hanging out with her two young children, Parker and Mason. Alison lives with her family in central Massachusetts.

About the Technical Author

Diane Poremsky is a consultant who specializes in Microsoft Windows, Outlook, and Office training and development. She is a Microsoft Outlook MVP (Most Valuable Professional) in recognition for her technical support of Microsoft Outlook. She is a technical editor for a number of computer books and is a columnist, author, and technical reviewer for *Exchange and Outlook* magazine. Diane currently resides in East Tennessee with her family.

Windows® XP Home Edition: The Complete Reference

John Levine
Margaret Levine-Young

McGraw-Hill/Osborne

New York   Chicago   San Francisco
Lisbon   London   Madrid   Mexico City
Milan   New Delhi   San Juan
Seoul   Singapore   Sydney   Toronto

The McGraw-Hill Companies

McGraw-Hill/Osborne
2600 Tenth Street
Berkeley, California 94710
U.S.A.

To arrange bulk purchase discounts for sales promotions, premiums, or fund-raisers, please contact **McGraw-Hill/**Osborne at the above address. For information on translations or book distributors outside the U.S.A., please see the International Contact Information page immediately following the index of this book.

Windows® XP Home Edition: The Complete Reference

1234567890 DOC DOC 0198765432

ISBN 0-07-222664-1

Publisher
  Brandon A. Nordin

Vice President & Associate Publisher
  Scott Rogers

Acquisitions Editor
  Megg Morin

Project Editor
  Monika Faltiss

Acquisitions Coordinator
  Tana Allen

Technical Editor
  Diane Poremsky

Copy Editor
  Dennis Weaver

Proofreader
  Paul Medoff

Indexer
  Jack Lewis

Computer Designers
  Jean Butterfield
  Tara A. Davis
  Lucie Ericksen

Illustrators
  Melinda Moore Lytle
  Michael Mueller
  Lyssa Wald

Series Design
  Peter F. Hancik

This book was composed with Corel VENTURA™ Publisher.

Contents at a Glance

Part I   Working in Windows XP

1 Running Windows and Application Programs   3

2 Troubleshooting Windows XP and
Application Programs   35

3 Installing and Uninstalling Programs and
Windows Components   63

4 Running DOS Programs and Commands   83

5 Copying, Moving, and Sharing Information
Between Programs 107

6 Sharing Your Computer with Family Members
and Officemates 121

Part II Managing Your Files

7 Using and Customizing Windows Explorer 161
8 File Attributes, Searching for Files, and Burning CDs .. 189
9 Backing Up Your Files with the Backup Utility 217

Part III Configuring Windows for Your Computer

10 Setting Up Your Start Menu and Taskbar 253
11 Setting Up Your Desktop 275
12 Keyboards, Mice, and Game Controllers 307
13 Adding and Removing Hardware 325
14 Printing and Faxing 351
15 Running Windows XP on Laptops 371
16 Accessibility Options 395

Part IV Working with Text, Numbers, Pictures, Sound, and Video

17 Working with Documents in Windows XP 419
18 Working with Graphics 433
19 Working with Sound 457
20 Working with Video 507

Part V Windows XP Home on the Internet

21 Configuring Windows to Work with Your Modem 529
22 Connecting to the Internet 555
23 E-Mail and Newsgroups Using Outlook Express 593
24 Web Browsing with Internet Explorer and
    MSN Explorer 647
25 Internet Conferencing with Windows Messenger
    and NetMeeting 687
26 Using Other Internet Programs with Windows XP 709

Part VI   Home and Office Networking with Windows XP Home

27 Designing a Windows-Based Local Area Network 735
28 Networking without LANs 751
29 Adding Your Computer to a LAN 765
30 Sharing Drives and Printers on a LAN 799
31 Connecting Your LAN to the Internet 813
32 Network, Internet, and Web Security 829

Part VII   Windows and Disk Housekeeping

33 Formatting and Partitioning Disks 857
34 Keeping Your Disk Safe 883
35 Tuning Windows XP for Maximum Performance 893
36 Windows Update, Remote Assistance, and Other
      Windows XP Resources 905

Part VIII   Behind the Scenes: Windows XP Internals

37 Windows XP Configuration Files 925
38 Displaying and Editing the Windows XP Registry 939
A Installing or Upgrading to Windows XP 949

Index 985

Contents

Acknowledgments xxxiii
Introduction xxxv

Part I

Working in Windows XP

1 Running Windows and Application Programs   3

Objects on the Windows XP Screen   4
Choosing Between Single-Click and Double-Click   6
Starting Up and Stopping Windows XP   7
    Suspending, Shutting Down, and Restarting Windows . .   8
Methods of Starting Programs 10
    Starting Programs by Opening Documents 10
    Starting Programs Using Shortcut Keys 11
    Starting Programs from the Run Dialog Box 13
    Starting Programs When You Log In 14
Switching and Exiting Programs 15
    Switching Programs 15
    Exiting Programs 15

Controlling the Size and Shape of Your Windows 16
    Minimizing All Windows 18
    Arranging All Windows 19
    Moving and Resizing Restored Windows 19
Configuring Windows XP and Other Programs 20
Commanding Windows and Other Programs 21
    Tips for Choosing Commands from Menus 22
    Choosing Commands from Shortcut Menus 22
Tips for Using Dialog Boxes 24
Running Programs on a Schedule Using Scheduled Tasks 27
    Scheduling a Program 28
    Canceling a Scheduled Program 29
    Configuring a Scheduled Program 29
    Tracking Scheduled Programs 30
Running Programs in Compatibility Mode 31
    Configuring Compatibility Settings 31
    Troubleshooting Compatibility Issues 33

2   Troubleshooting Windows XP and
      Application Programs 35
An Overview of Troubleshooting Tools 36
Diagnosing Windows Problems with Troubleshooters 37
Returning Your System to a Predefined State with System Restore 37
    Automatic Restore Points 38
    Running System Restore 39
    Configuring System Restore 39
    Creating a Restore Point 41
    Restoring Your System to a Restore Point 41
    Undoing a Restoration 42
What To Do When Windows Won't Start 43
    Repairing Windows Using the Windows XP
      Setup Wizard 43
    Starting Windows in Other Startup Modes 44
    Using The Recovery Console 45
Creating Boot Floppy Disks 51
    Creating a Quick Boot Disk 51
    Creating Floppies from Which You Can Run
      Windows XP Setup 52
    Creating a DOS Boot Floppy 52
Dealing with Hung or Crashed Programs 53
    Killing Programs Using the Windows Task Manager 53
    Stopping Programs from Running at Startup 55

Diagnosing System Problems Using the Microsoft
   Management Console (MMC) 57
      Viewing Event Logs with the Event Viewer 57
      Logging Performance Data and Alerts 58
Reporting Problems with Dr. Watson 61

**3 Installing and Uninstalling Programs and
Windows Components** 63
What Happens During Program Installation and Uninstallation . 64
Installing Programs 65
      Installing Programs Using the
        Add Or Remove Programs Window 66
      Running an Install or Setup Program 67
      Installing Programs Without Installation Programs 68
      Finishing Installation of a Program 69
      Installing and Uninstalling Programs that Come
        with Windows 69
      Using the Add/Remove Windows Components Program 69
      Hiding Windows Middleware 71
Associating a Program with a File Extension 73
      Associating Files with Programs when Opening a File ... 74
      Associating Files with Programs by Using
        Folder Options 75
      Editing a File Association 77
Uninstalling Programs 78
      Uninstalling Programs Using the Add Or Remove
        Programs Window 78
      Running an Uninstall Program 80
      Uninstalling Programs Manually 80

4 Running DOS Programs and Commands 83
The Basics of DOS 84
The Command Prompt Window 85
      Opening a Command Prompt Window 86
      Issuing DOS Commands 87
Running DOS Programs 88
      Starting and Exiting DOS Programs 89
      Adjusting the Screen 89
      Using the Mouse and Clipboard 89
      Printing from DOS Programs 90
      Running Batch Files 91
Configuring the DOS Environment 92
      DOS Initialization Files: Autoexec and Config 92

Setting Command Prompt Window Properties 93
Setting Executable and Shortcut Properties 96
Installing and Configuring DOS Programs 104

5 Copying, Moving, and Sharing Information
Between Programs 107
Sharing Data Through the Windows Clipboard 108
Cutting, Copying, and Pasting 108
Dragging and Dropping 109
Using the ClipBook Viewer to Look at What's on
the Clipboard 109
Capturing Screens Using the Clipboard 111
Sharing Information by Linking and Embedding 111
Creating Linked or Embedded Objects 113
Editing a Linked or Embedded Object 115
Maintaining Links 117
Saving Small Bits of Data as Scraps 119

6 Sharing Your Computer with Family Members
and Officemates 121
User Account Basics 123
Types of User Accounts 124
User Accounts That Windows Creates 125
User Profile Configuration Settings 126
Simple File Sharing 127
Fast User Switching 128
Setting Up a Computer for Multiple Users 128
The User Accounts Window 128
Controlling How Users Log On 130
Logging On Automatically 130
Creating, Modifying, and Deleting User Accounts 131
Creating New User Accounts 131
Modifying User Accounts 132
Adding or Removing Passwords 137
Keeping Files Private 138
Enabling and Disabling the Guest Account 140
Deleting User Accounts 140
Using a Shared Computer 140
Logging On 141
Resuming Work after Locking Windows 142
Logging Off 142
Switching Users 142

Setting the Screen Saver to Require You to Log Back On . 142
Sharing Files with Other Users 143
Running a Program as Another User 143
Managing Multiple Users 145
Managing Logged-In Users 145
Setting Quotas for Disk Usage 146
Managing Users from the Command Prompt 149
Controlling File and Folder Permissions from Safe Mode 151

Part II

Managing Your Files

7   Using and Customizing Windows Explorer 161
The Structure of the File System 162
File Addresses 163
The Anatomy of Windows Explorer 164
Windows Explorer Toolbars 166
The Explorer Bar 169
The Task Pane 170
The Working Area 170
The Status Bar 176
Navigating the Folder Tree 177
Expanding and Contracting the Folders Explorer Bar 177
Navigating by Using the Address Box 178
Moving Up and Down the Folder Tree 178
Backtracking in the Folder Tree 178
Opening a New Window for Each Folder 178
Making and Working with Files and Folders 179
Creating Files and Folders 179
Selecting Files and Folders 179
Opening Files and Folders 180
Naming and Renaming Files and Folders 180
Deleting Files and Folders 181
Undoing Your Last Action 182
Moving and Copying Files and Folders 182
Using the Recycle Bin 184
Finding Files and Folders in the Recycle Bin 184
Retrieving Files and Folders from the Recycle Bin 184
Emptying the Recycle Bin 185
Resizing the Recycle Bin 186
Turning Off the Recycle Bin 187

8 File Attributes, Searching for Files, and Burning CDs . 189
    Types, Extensions, Properties, and Attributes of Files 190
        File Types and Extensions 190
        Properties of Files and Folders 192
        File and Folder Attributes 193
    Working With Special Types of Files 194
        Working With Shortcuts 194
        Working With Compressed Folders (ZIP Files) 196
        Working With Hidden Files and Folders 199
        Customizing a Folder 200
    Searching for Files and Folders 203
        Standard vs. Advanced Search Companion 204
        Search Criteria 206
        Using Indexing Service 209
        Saving and Retrieving a Search 209
    Making Your Own CDs 210
        CD-R and CD-RW Disks 210
        CD-Burning Basics 210
        Burning CDs from Windows Explorer 212
        Burning CDs from Windows Media Player 214
        Erasing Files From CD-RW Discs 214
        Troubleshooting Burning CDs 214

9 Backing Up Your Files with the Backup Utility 217
    Determining What to Back Up 218
        Types of Files to Back Up 218
        Backing Up a LAN 219
        Backup Media 220
        How Frequently to Back Up 220
        Storing Backup CDs and Tapes 221
        The Windows XP Backup Utility 221
        Backup Jobs 221
    The Removable Storage Service 222
    Backing Up with Windows Explorer 223
    Running the Backup Utility 224
        Installing the Backup Utility 224
        Running the Backup Utility 225
    Backing Up Files with the Backup Utility 225
        Creating a Backup Job with the Backup Or
            Restore Wizard 226
        Creating a Backup Job by Using the Backup Tab 232
        Running a Backup Job 236
        Excluding Files from Backups 237

Setting Other Backup Options 239
Running the Backup Utility from the Command Line 241
Restoring Files with the Backup Utility 244
Restoring Files Using the Restore Wizard 245
Restoring Files by Using the Restore And Manage
Media Tab 246
Managing the Removable Storage Service 249

Part III

Configuring Windows for Your Computer

10   Setting Up Your Start Menu and Taskbar 253
Anatomy of the Start Menu 254
Customizing the Start Menu 255
Reorganizing the Start Menu 255
Changing Start Menu Properties 259
Searching the Start Menu 264
Customizing the Taskbar 265
Enabling Taskbar Changes 265
Moving the Taskbar 265
Changing the Size of the Taskbar 265
Changing Taskbar Properties 265
Adding Toolbars to the Taskbar 268
Using TweakUI to Customize the Taskbar and Start Menu 272
Removing Microsoft Programs from the Start Menu 273

11   Setting Up Your Desktop 275
Display Properties 276
Choosing a Desktop Theme 277
Changing the Background 278
Selecting an Image or Pattern from the Background List . 279
Making Your Own Background Images 279
Selecting a Background Color 279
Using a Web Page as a Background 280
Setting Up a Screen Saver 284
Selecting a Screen Saver 284
Installing New Screen Savers 285
Configuring Your Screen Saver 286
Choosing a New Color Scheme 286
Finding the Perfect Color 287
Changing Windows, Buttons, and Fonts 289
Choosing Classic Style Windows and Buttons 289
Changing the Appearance of Individual Items 290
Changing Fonts 290

Changing Your Desktop Icons 293
  Changing Icon Size 293
  Arranging Icons on the Desktop 293
  Choosing New Desktop Icons 294
  Renaming Icons 295
  Deleting and Recovering Desktop Icons 295
  Using the Desktop Cleanup Wizard 296
Changing the Desktop's Visual Effects 296
Changing the Desktop's Sound Effects 297
Changing Display Settings 298
  Changing the Screen Resolution 299
  Changing the Color Quality 299
  Changing Color Profiles 300
  Changing Magnification 301
Getting Along with Your Monitor(s) 302
  Using Multiple Displays 302
  Diagnosing Display Problems 304

12   Keyboards, Mice, and Game Controllers 307
Configuring Your Keyboard 308
  Changing Keyboard Properties 308
  Changing Language Properties 309
  Determining Whether Handwriting and Speech
    Recognition Are Installed 312
Configuring Your Mouse 313
  Defining the Mouse Buttons 315
  Defining Your Double-Click Speed 316
  Configuring the Appearance of the Mouse Pointer 316
  Improving Pointer Visibility 316
  Setting the Mouse Speed 317
  Setting ClickLock 317
  Settings for Wheel Mice 317
  Mouse Tweaks 318
Configuring Your Game Controller 319
  Displaying and Changing Game Controller Settings 321
  Testing Your Game Controller 321
Windows' Regional Settings 322
  Telling Windows Where You Live 323
  Setting Number, Currency, Time, and Date Formats 323
Setting the Current Date and Time 323

13   Adding and Removing Hardware 325
Managing Your Hardware Components with the
  Device Manager 326
Types of Hardware 328

Integrated Versus Separate Peripherals 328
Connectors 329
Internal Adapter Cards 334
Hardware Parameters 335
Disk Controllers: IDE, EIDE, and SCSI Devices 337
Memory (RAM) 338
Hardware Drivers 338
Configuring Windows for New Hardware 339
Installing and Uninstalling PC Cards and Other
    Hot-Swappable Devices 340
Using the Add Hardware Wizard 340
Installing Modems 344
Troubleshooting Your Hardware Configuration 345
Solving Configuration Problems by Using the
    Device Manager 346
Booting in Safe Mode 348
More Diagnostic Tools 348
Adding Memory 349

14   Printing and Faxing **351**
The Printers And Faxes Folder 352
Types of Printers 353
Setting Up a Local Printer 354
Adding a Plug and Play Printer 354
Adding a Printer Without Plug and Play 354
Configuring a Printer 355
Testing and Troubleshooting Your Printer 357
Choosing Printing Options 357
Printing to a File 358
Managing Printer Activity 359
Pausing or Canceling Print Jobs 360
Changing the Order in Which Jobs Are Printed 360
Scheduling a Print Job 361
Typefaces and Fonts 361
TrueType Fonts 361
How Printers Handle Fonts 362
Installing and Using Fonts 363
Installing Fonts 363
Deleting Fonts 364
Finding Similar Fonts 365
Sending and Receiving Faxes 365
Configuring Fax Console 365
Sending a Cover-Page Fax from Fax Console 367
Sending a Fax from an Application 367
Automatically Receiving Faxes 368

Receiving Faxes Manually 368
Archiving Your Faxes 368

15 Running Windows XP on Laptops 371
Coordinating Your Laptop Files with Windows Briefcase 372
Printing Away from Home 376
Accessing Other Computers with Remote Desktop 377
Configuring the Client Computer for Remote Desktop .. 378
Connecting to a Remote Computer with Remote Desktop 379
Using the Remote Desktop Connection 382
Other Remote Desktop Options 383
Managing Your Computer's Power 384
Standby and Hibernate Modes 386
Power Schemes 387
Checking Your Battery Status 388
Using a Docking Station 388
Docking and Undocking 389
Creating and Using Hardware Profiles 389
Using DualView to Display on Two Monitors 393

16 Accessibility Options 395
What Accessibility Options Are Available in Windows XP? 396
Installing Accessibility Options 397
Making the Keyboard More Accessible 397
Making Your Keys Stick with StickyKeys 398
Filtering Out Extra Keystrokes with FilterKeys 399
Hearing When a Toggled Key Is Pressed 400
Displaying the On-Screen Keyboard 401
Configuration Settings for the Hearing Impaired 402
Configuration Settings for the Visually Impaired 403
Displaying in High Contrast 404
Controlling the Cursor's Size and Blink Rate 405
Magnifying the Screen 405
Listening to Microsoft Narrator Read the Screen
Out Loud 407
Configuration Settings for the Mouse and Alternative
Input Devices 409
Controlling the Pointer by Using the Number Pad 410
Configuring an Alternative Input Device 411
Turning Accessibility Options Off and On 412
Turning On and Off Magnifier, Narrator, and the On-Screen
Keyboard by Using the Utility Manager 413
Turning On and Off Other Accessibility Features 414
Making Internet Explorer Accessible 415

Part IV

Working with Text, Numbers, Pictures, Sound, and Video

17 Working with Documents in Windows XP 419
Reading Text Files with Notepad 420
  Running Notepad 420
  Files You Can Edit with Notepad 423
Simple, Free Word Processing with WordPad 423
  Formatting with WordPad 424
  Printing Your Document 426
  WordPad Extras 426
  Setting WordPad Options 427
Using the Windows Calculator 427
  Using the Standard Calculator 428
  Using the Scientific Calculator 428
Using Special Characters with Character Map 431

18 Working with Graphics 433
Images, Pixels, and Compression 434
Windows XP's Graphical Tools 434
Viewing Images on Your Computer 435
  Viewing Images in an Explorer Window 435
  Looking at Images with the Windows Picture And
    Fax Viewer 436
  Watching a Slide Show 438
Adding Information to Digital Images 439
  Adding Information to an Image File's Properties 439
  Annotating an Image with Windows Picture And
    Fax Viewer 439
Creating and Editing Images with Microsoft Paint 442
  Opening and Saving Files in Paint 442
  Selecting Objects 443
  Magnifying and Enlarging 444
  Drawing Lines and Curves 444
  Drawing Freehand 444
  Making Shapes 444
  Coloring Objects 445
  Adding Text 445
  Flipping, Rotating, and Stretching 446
  Cropping Images 446
Working with Digital Cameras and Scanners 446
  Setting Up a Scanner or Digital Camera 446
  Downloading Images from Digital Cameras 447

Downloading Images from Scanners 449

Linking Your Scanner or Digital Camera to a Program ... 449

Turning Images into Prints 450

Printing Your Pictures at Home 451

Ordering Prints of Your Pictures via the Web 451

Sharing Your Pictures over the Internet 453

Publishing Your Pictures on the Web 453

E-mailing Pictures to Your Friends 454

19 Working with Sound 457

Audio File Formats 458

Streaming Audio 459

MIDI Files 460

Configuring Windows to Work with Sound 460

Choosing and Configuring Audio Input and
Output Drivers 460

Displaying the Status of Your Audio Devices 463

Controlling the Volume and Balance 463

Choosing What Sounds Windows Makes 465

Playing Music and Other Audio with Windows Media Player 8
and 9 468

The Windows Media Player Window 468

Toolbar Buttons 468

The My Music Folder 471

Playing Audio Files Stored on Your Computer 471

Organizing Your Audio Files into a Media Library 474

Creating and Editing Playlists 478

Playing Streaming Audio Files from the Internet 480

Playing Audio CDs 483

Adjusting Volume, Graphic Equalization,
and Other Sound Settings 486

Ripping (Copying Music) from a CD to Your Computer 488

Configuring Windows Media Player to Rip CDs 488

Ripping CDs as WMA files 490

Ripping CDs as MP3 Files 491

Copying Music from Cassette Tapes or LPs 491

Moving Files to and from Portable Players 492

Creating Your Own Music CDs 493

Burning Audio CDs 494

Configuring Windows Media Player to Record
Audio CDs 496

Burning MP3 Data CDs 497

Troubleshooting Burning Audio CDs 497

Customizing the Windows Media Player Window   498
    Controlling How Windows Media Player Communicates
      over the Internet   499
    Switching Skins   499
    Specifying Which File Formats Windows
      Media Player Plays   502
Playing and Recording WAV Sound Files with Sound Recorder . .   502
    Playing Sounds   502
    Recording Sounds   503
    Editing Sounds   504
    Converting Sounds to Other Formats   505

20   **Working with Video** **507**
How Windows Works with Video Data   508
Playing Video Files with Windows Media Player   508
    Playing Video Files from Your Hard Disk   509
    Playing Streaming Video Files from the Internet   511
Creating and Editing Video Files with Windows Movie Maker . . .   512
    The Windows Movie Maker Window   513
    Importing Files   514
    Composing Your Movie   515
    Adding Sound   516
    Previewing Your Movie   517
    Editing Your Movie   518
    Saving Your Movie   519
Playing Video Disks (DVDs)   520
    Installing and Configuring a DVD Decoder   520
    Playing a DVD with Windows Media Player   521
    Controlling Rated Movies   521
Windows XP's Media Center   523
    My TV   524
    My Music   525
    My Pictures   526
    My Video and Play DVD   526

Part V

Windows XP Home on the Internet

21   **Configuring Windows to Work with Your Modem** . . .   **529**
Configuring Windows to Use Your Dial-Up Modem   530
    Modem Configuration Settings   531
Configuring Windows for Dialing Locations   536
    Displaying Your Dialing Locations   536

Creating a Dialing Location   536
Setting a Default Dialing Location   538
Using Dialing Locations   539
Setting Up Area Code Rules   539
Creating Area Code Rules   539
Configuring Windows to Use Calling Cards   541
Setting Up Calling Cards   542
Creating a New Type of Calling Card   542
Using Calling Cards   546
Troubleshooting a Dial-up Connection   546
Dialing Your Modem by Hand   547
Checking Your Modem's Log Files   549
Connecting to a DSL Line   549
Getting DSL   550
Configuring Windows for DSL   550
Connecting to a Cable Modem   551
Getting Connected   552
Configuring Windows for a Cable Modem   552
Connecting to an ISDN Line   552
Getting ISDN   553
Configuring Windows for Your ISDN Adapter   553

22   Connecting to the Internet   555
Types of Internet Accounts   556
Internet (PPP) Accounts   557
Cable Internet Accounts   558
Online Services   558
Types of Network Connections   559
Displaying Network Connections   560
Signing Up for a New Account   563
Running the New Connection Wizard   563
Letting Microsoft Recommend an ISP   564
Signing Up for an MSN Account   565
Creating a Network Connection for an Existing Account   565
Creating a Dial-up Connection   566
Creating a Network Connection for an ISDN Line   567
Changing Your Dial-Up Connection Settings   568
Configuring a TCP/IP Connection   573
Creating and Using Logon Scripts   573
Setting Additional Dial-Up Options   574
Renaming, Copying, or Deleting a Network Connection .   577
Other Dial-Up Connection Settings   577
Connecting to Your Internet Account   578
Dialing the Internet Automatically   578
Dialing the Internet Manually   580

Disconnecting Manually or Automatically 582
Enabling the Internet Connection Firewall Between Your PC and
    the Internet 583
    Turning On the Internet Firewall 584
    Configuring the Ports on Your Firewall 584
    Other Firewalls 585
Testing Your Connection 586
    Displaying Your IP Address 586
    Testing Communication with Another Computer by
        Using Ping 587
    Tracing Packets over the Internet 589
    Displaying Internet Connections Using Netstat 591

23 E-Mail and Newsgroups Using Outlook Express 593
Is Outlook Express Safe? 594
E-Mail Addresses, Servers, and Headers 595
Configuring Outlook Express 597
    The Outlook Express Window 597
    Setting Up Your Accounts 599
    Importing Messages from Other Mail Programs 601
    Importing Addresses from Other Mail Programs 602
    Choosing Where Outlook Express Stores Your
        Message Folders 603
    Choosing a Layout for the Outlook Express Window 604
Protecting Yourself from E-Mail Viruses 605
    Restricting Attachments in Outlook Express 605
    Preventing Other Programs from Sending E-Mail via
        Outlook Express 606
    Choosing Outlook Express's Security Zone 607
Sending and Receiving E-Mail 607
    Configuration Options for Sending and
        Receiving Messages 608
    Viewing Incoming Mail 609
    Composing Messages 611
    Saving and Filing Your Messages 619
    Sending Messages 620
Storing Addresses in the Address Book 620
    Running Address Book 621
    Entering Information into Address Book 621
    Looking Up Information in Address Book 624
    Contacting People 626
    Printing Information from Address Book 626
    Exporting Names and Addresses from Address Book ... 627
    Searching Additional Directory Services 627

Organizing Your Correspondence 628
    Working with Folders 628
    Finding Messages in Your Files 629
    Filtering Your Mail with Message Rules 630
Usenet and Other Newsgroups 636
Reading and Posting to Newsgroups 637
    Configuration Options for Reading and Posting
        to Newsgroups 638
    Subscribing to Newsgroups 639
    Reading a Newsgroup 641
    Participating in a Newsgroup 644

24   Web Browsing with Internet Explorer and
      MSN Explorer 647
Web Browser Concepts 648
    Browser Plug-Ins 649
    The Default Web Browser 650
    What's Going On With Java? 650
Which Browser Should You Use? 651
    Internet Explorer 651
    MSN Explorer 652
    Other Browsers You Can Use 653
Getting Started with Internet Explorer 654
    Explorer Windows in Internet Explorer 655
    Browsing the Web 656
    Opening Files on Your System 656
    Opening Web Pages 657
    Printing Web Pages, Frames, and Individual Images 658
    Saving Web Page Files 658
    Managing Internet Explorer's Windows 658
Getting Started with MSN Explorer 659
Remembering Where You've Been on the Web 660
    Examining History 662
    Using Favorites, Links, and Internet Shortcuts 664
Searching for Web Pages 665
    Search Engines 666
    Searching from the Address Box 666
    Using the Search Companion Explorer Bar 666
    Changing Internet Explorer's Default Search Engines ... 667
    Adding Custom Search Prefixes 667
Interacting with Web Sites Automatically 669
    Remembering Forms and Passwords Automatically 669
    Using Internet Explorer's Profile Assistant 671

Changing How Web Pages Look 672
    Choosing Fonts 672
    Choosing Colors 673
    Changing Language Preferences 674
    Choosing Whether to Download Images, Audio,
        and Video 675
Managing Internet Explorer's Behavior 676
    Choosing and Customizing Your Start Page 676
    Blocking Offensive Web Content 677
    Managing the Cache of Web Pages 677
    Changing the Default Browser 678
    Setting Your Mail and Newsreading Programs 678
Internet Explorer's Privacy Settings 679
    Controlling Cookies 679
    Displaying a Privacy Report About a Web Page 684
Creating Your Own Web Pages 685

25   **Internet Conferencing with Windows Messenger**
      and NetMeeting 687
Chatting Online with Windows Messenger 688
    Signing In to Windows Messenger with Your
        .NET Passport 690
    Configuring Your Contacts 693
    Starting a Windows Messenger Conversation 694
    Holding Voice Conversations 696
    Video Conferencing 696
    Sending Files to Others in a Conversation 696
    Sharing a Whiteboard 697
    Sharing Control of a Program 697
    Other Things You Can Do with Windows Messenger 700
Conferencing with Microsoft NetMeeting 701
    Running and Configuring NetMeeting 701
    Connecting to a Directory Server 702
    Making or Receiving a Call 704
    Once You Are Connected 705
    Hosting a Meeting or Joining an Existing Meeting 706
Using WinChat to Chat with Other Users on your LAN 708

26   **Using Other Internet Programs with Windows XP** 709
Logging into Text-Based Systems with HyperTerminal 710
    Running HyperTerminal 712
    Configuring HyperTerminal for Your Account 712

Connecting with HyperTerminal 715
Changing Information About a Connection 715
Transferring Files 717
Sending Text Files 719
Capturing Text from the HyperTerminal Window 720
Accepting Incoming Calls 720
Logging into Other Computers Using Telnet 721
Working with FTP and Web Servers Using Web Folders 722
Creating a Web Folder 722
Working with Web Folders 724
Transferring Files Using Ftp 725
Basics of FTP 725
Navigating the Folder Trees 726
Uploading Files 728
Downloading Files 729
Downloading, Installing, and Running Other Internet Programs . 730
Where to Get Internet Programs 730
Installing and Running Internet Programs 730

Part VI

Home and Office Networking with Windows XP Home

27 Designing a Windows-Based Local Area Network 735
Purposes of Networks 736
Sharing Hardware 736
Sharing Files 737
Sharing an Internet Connection 737
Peer-to-Peer vs. Domain-Based Networks 737
Peer-to-Peer (Workgroup-Based) Networks 738
Client-Server (Domain-Based) Networks 738
Steps for Setting Up a Peer-to-Peer LAN 739
Choosing Between Cabled and Wireless LANs 740
Ethernet Cable and NICs 741
Wireless LANs 742
Phone and Power Line Networking 742
Making the Choice—or Choosing More than One 743
Buying Network Hardware 744
Buying Network Interface Cards (NICs) 746
Buying a Hub 746
Buying Wireless LAN Adapters and Access Points 747
Buying Ethernet Cable 747
Buying Phone Line or Power Line Adapters 747
Installing Your Network Hardware 747
Installing Network Interface Cards or Wireless
LAN Adapters 748

Installing the Hub, Switch, or Wireless Access Point   748
Stringing Cable   748

28   Networking without LANs   751
Connecting Two Computers with Direct Network Connection . . .   752
Connecting Two Computers by Using a Dial-Up Connection   753
Connecting Computers with Virtual Private Networking   754
Configuring the VPN Client   755
Configuring the VPN Server   759
Networking Security Issues   762
Creating an Infrared Wireless Link   762

29   Adding Your Computer to a LAN   765
Windows Networking Components   766
Network Protocols   767
IP Addressing   767
Identifying the Computer   770
Adding Your Computer to a TCP/IP Peer-to-Peer LAN   771
Running the Network Setup Wizard   771
Viewing Network Resources with
the My Network Places Window   773
Viewing Your Network Connections   774
Reconfiguring Windows Me/98, 2000, and NT Systems
to Use TCP/IP   775
Adding Your Computer to a NetBEUI Peer-to-Peer LAN   775
Adding Your Computer to a Wireless LAN   776
Connecting to a Wireless Access Point   777
Connecting to an Ad Hoc Network   777
Wireless Network Properties   778
Connecting to a Phone Line or Power Line LAN   779
Installing and Configuring Network Components   779
Installing and Configuring an Adapter   781
Installing a Client   781
Installing a Protocol   783
Configuring the TCP/IP Protocol   786
Installing a Service   787
Changing the Computer Name, Workgroup, or Domain .   788
Displaying a LAN Icon in the Notification Area   790
Bridging Networks   790
Using Bridging with Internet Connection Sharing   791
Checking Your Network Connection   792
Checking Your TCP/IP Address   792
Testing Your TCP/IP Connection   794

Viewing LAN Resources with the Net Command 795
Viewing LAN Usage 795
Troubleshooting Your Network 796

30 Sharing Drives and Printers on a LAN 799
Enabling Hardware Sharing 800
User Accounts and LAN Security 800
Using Shared Drives from Other Computers 801
Using Network Drives with My Network Places 801
Opening and Saving Files on Shared Drives and Folders . 803
Mapping a Shared Drive or Folder to a Drive Letter 803
Tips for Mapping Shared Folders and Drives 806
Unmapping a Drive Letter 806
Sharing Your Disk Drives and Folders with Others 806
Making a Drive Sharable 807
Controlling Access to Files and Folders on NTFS Volumes 809
Sharing Printers on a LAN 809
Making Your Printer Sharable 809
Printing to a Network Printer from Another Computer .. 811

31 Connecting Your LAN to the Internet 813
Methods of Connecting a LAN to the Internet 814
What Does a Gateway Do? 814
Devices That Can Act as Gateways 815
Software and Hardware for a Windows-Based Gateway . 817
Installing and Using Internet Connection Sharing 817
Installing ICS on the ICS Server 818
Configuring the ICS Clients 822
Using Internet Connection Sharing 826
Troubleshooting ICS 827
Using NAT with Internet Applications 828
Deleting Internet Connection Sharing 828

32 Network, Internet, and Web Security 829
Protecting Your System from Viruses and Worms 831
Types of Virus Files 831
Preventing Infection by Viruses 832
Sources of Antivirus Information 836
Managing Which Files Internet Explorer Downloads 836
Java, JavaScript, VBScript, and ActiveX 837
Internet Explorer's Zones 837
Controlling Your Download Security 838
Managing Java and JavaScript 840
Managing ActiveX Controls 841

Securing Your Web Communication with Encryption
    and Certificates 842
        Browsing the Web Securely 842
        Using Object Certificates When Downloading Files 843
        Managing Certificates from Certificate Publishers 844
        Managing Your Personal Certificates 845
        Other IE Security Settings 846
Sending and Receiving E-mail Securely 848
        Getting a Certificate 849
        Sending Signed Mail 849
        Sending Encrypted Mail 850
        Receiving Encrypted or Signed Mail 853

Part VII

Windows and Disk Housekeeping

33   Formatting and Partitioning Disks 857
Partitions, File Systems, and Drive Letters 858
        Hard Disk Partitions 858
        The FAT, FAT32, and NTFS File Systems 861
        Why Divide Your Hard Disk into Partitions? 862
        Partition and Drive Letters 863
        Displaying Information about Drives and Partitions 864
Partitioning a Disk Using Disk Management 868
        Creating a New Partition 869
        Selecting the Active Partition 870
        Deleting a Partition 871
        Repartitioning a Disk 871
        Converting Partitions to NTFS 872
Choosing Your Own Drive Letters 872
        Changing Drive Letters 872
        Assigning Pathnames to Partitions 874
        Assigning Drive Letters to Folders 875
Formatting a Disk 876
        Formatting a Hard Disk 876
        Formatting a Removable Disk 877
        Copying a Floppy Disk 878
Checking Free Space 878
Configuring CD Drives 878
Configuring CD-R and CD-RW Drives 880

34   Keeping Your Disk Safe 883
Testing Your Disk Structure with ChkDsk 885
        Running ChkDsk 885
        Other ChkDsk Options 886

Defragmenting Your Disk 887
    Running Disk Defragmenter 888
Deleting Temporary Files with Disk Cleanup 889
    Types of Temporary Files That Disk Cleanup Can Delete . 889
    Running Disk Cleanup 891
    Disabling Low Disk Space Notification 892

35   Tuning Windows XP for Maximum Performance 893
Tuning Your Computer's Performance with the Performance
    Options Dialog Box 894
    Tuning Your Display Settings 894
    Tuning Your Processor and Memory Settings 897
    Tuning Your Swap File Size 898
Tracking System Resources 899
    Monitoring System Use with the Task Manager 899
    Viewing Graphs in the System Monitor 901
Tuning Your Hard Disk's Performance 902
Disabling Unnecessary Services 903

36   Windows Update, Remote Assistance, and Other
    Windows XP Resources 905
Updating Your Computer with Windows Update 906
    Scanning for Updates 906
    Downloading Updates for Multiple Machines 908
Updating Your Computer Automatically with
    Automatic Updates 909
    Configuring Automatic Updates 909
    Choosing Which Updates to Install 911
    Uninstalling Updates 912
Allowing a Friend to Control Your Computer 912
    Inviting a Friend to Help 913
    Responding to an Invitation for Remote Assistance 915
Microsoft's Support Resources 916
    The Help And Support Center 917
    Getting Help from Microsoft Online 918
    Microsoft's Web Resources 919
    Microsoft's Public Support Newsgroups 920
Other Online Information about Windows XP 920
    Web Sites 921
    Usenet Newsgroups 921

Part VIII

Behind the Scenes: Windows XP Internals

37 Windows XP Configuration Files 925

Types of Windows XP Configuration Files 926
    Making Configuration Files Visible 926
    Windows Initialization Files 927
    The Registry 928
Configuring Windows XP with the System Configuration Utility . 928
    Restarting Windows with Selected Startup Options 929
    Changing Your Services and Startup Settings 930
    Replacing a Corrupted Windows File 931
    Changing Your System.ini and Win.ini Files 932
    Changing Your Boot.ini File 933
    Changing Your Environment Settings 933
    Changing Your International Settings 935
Configuring DOS and Older Windows Programs to Run Under
  Windows XP 935
Disk Formats and Coexisting with Other Operating Systems 936
    Partitioning Disks 936
    Other Operating Systems and Windows Files 937

38 Displaying and Editing the Windows XP Registry 939

Registry Concepts 940
    Where the Registry Is Stored 940
    Registry Keys and Root Keys (Hives) 940
    Key Values 941
Restoring the Registry 942
Editing the Registry 943
    Running Registry Editor 943
    Finding Registry Entries 944
    Backing Up Registry Keys, Just in Case 945
    Adding and Changing Registry Entries 945
    Editing the Registry as a Text File 947

A Installing or Upgrading to Windows XP 949

Windows XP Installation Requirements 950
Installation Options 951
    Dynamic Update 951
    Choosing Your File System 951
Service Pack 1 (SP1) 952
Disk Space Requirements 952

Windows Product Activation (WPA) 953
    How Activation Works 953
    Reinstalling Windows after Activation 954
    Activation and Changes to Your PC's Hardware 955
    More Information on Windows Product Activation 956
Preparing to Install Windows 957
Starting the Installation 958
    Installing Windows on a Blank Hard Disk 958
    Upgrading to Windows XP 959
    Creating Dual-boot Installations 960
Windows Setup Wizard Versions and Command-Line Options .. 962
Answering the Windows Setup Wizard's Questions 963
Checking Your System After Installing Windows 971
Troubleshooting Windows XP Installation 973
Deleting the Backup of Your Previous Version of Windows 974
Transferring Your Data Files and Windows
  Configuration Settings 974
    What to Transfer 975
    Running the Transfer Wizard 975
    Answering the Transfer Wizard's Questions 977
    Transferring Files via Direct Cable Connection 977
Installing Additional Programs 979
Setting Boot Options 979
    Understanding the Boot.ini File 979
    Editing Boot.ini 981
    Checking Your Boot.ini Entries 983
Uninstalling Windows XP and SP1 984

Index... 985

Acknowledgments

The authors would like to thank the following people for valuable assistance in writing this book: Megg Morin and Tana Allen at Osborne/McGraw-Hill for making the book happen; Monika Faltiss, project editor; Dennis Weaver, copy editor; Paul Medoff, proofreader; Diane Poremsky, technical editor and general catcher of errors; Darrell Gorter, Kathy Ivens, Brian Knittel, Mark Miller, Rima Regas, Tyler Regas, Matt Ronn, Robert Schlabbach, Jordan Young, and everyone on the Microsoft Beta Support Team, for answering lots of questions. We also thank our friends and (most of all) our families for putting up with us during the seemingly endless process of updating such a long book.

Introduction

For years, Microsoft had two series of Windows versions: the Windows Me/9x series (which includes 95, 98, 98 Second Edition, and Me) for individual users, and the NT series (Windows NT and 2000) for corporate users and network servers. And for years, Microsoft tried to merge the two (slightly incompatible) series, so that everyone could run more or less the same version of Windows. With each new Windows release, Microsoft promised that the *next* release would be the one that combines these two strains of Windows.

Microsoft finally did it. Windows XP is the upgrade to both series of Windows, Me/9x and 2000/NT. Windows XP does away with the legacy architecture of the Windows 9x series. Windows 95 and its successors were based on DOS, the pre-Windows, non-graphical operating system that PCs started with. Windows XP removes the underlying DOS environment for increased reliability, and it uses the Windows NT/2000 file system for better security.

Why Windows XP Is Better

Windows XP is based on Windows 2000 and combines the technical core of NT/2000 with the ease-of-use of Windows 98 and Me. Because of its business-oriented lineage, Windows XP has some great new capabilities for Windows Me/9x users, including password-protected user accounts and system management programs. It's a more solid program, with far fewer crashes and hangs, because of its new Windows Driver Protection (which prevents you from installing flaky device drivers) and System Restore (which can rewind the system to an earlier, working state). But Windows XP also adds people-friendly features that were lacking in Windows NT and 2000, like Remote Assistance, a better help system, and a compatibility mode for running older programs, along with a completely redesigned (and spiffy-looking) screen design. This book helps you to make sense of the world of Windows XP, find your way through all the new and sometimes confusing options, learn the new interface, and make it work for you.

Initially, Windows XP came in two versions: Home Edition (for home use) and Professional (for small-office and workstation use). These two versions are intended for workstations—that is, computers that people sit in front of and use directly. Windows XP 64-Bit Edition is also available, but runs only high-end Itanium-based workstations, A new version, Windows XP Media Center Edition, turns a PC into a home multimedia center (see "Windows XP Media Center Edition" later in this Introduction). Additional versions are designed to run on servers—computers that provide services to other computers over a network. Windows .NET Server and .NET Advanced Server, will be available in 2003. This book describes Windows XP Home Edition as it is used on desktop and laptop workstations at home and in small offices.

Later in this Introduction are sections titled "New Features in Windows XP," an overview of Windows XP's features, and "Differences Between Windows XP Editions," which lists the major differences between Windows XP Home Edition and Professional.

Who This Book Is For

This book is for everyone who uses Windows XP Home Edition. You might already have Windows XP installed on your computer, or you might be considering upgrading a Windows Me or Windows 98 system to Windows XP. If Windows XP is your first exposure to computing, consider starting with *How to Do Everything with Windows XP*, by Curt Simmons (published by Osborne/McGraw-Hill) and using this book as a reference.

Your computer might be the only one in your home or office, or it may be on a local area network. You probably have a modem or network card, although Windows works perfectly well without either. Chances are, your computer is connected to the Internet, or will be soon.

If you're in a small office with two or three computers, we tell you how to set up a small, usable Windows network. Windows XP Home Edition includes all the software you need to set up a home, home office, or small office network, including sharing an Internet connection.

What's in This Book

This book is organized around the kinds of things that you want to do with Windows, rather than around a listing of its features. Each part of the book concentrates on a type of work you might want to do with Windows.

Part I: Windows XP Basics

Part I covers the basics of using Windows. Even if you have used Windows forever, at least skim through this section to learn about XP's new interface. If you are new to Windows, you'll want to read it carefully.

Chapter 1 starts with the basics of working in Windows and other programs that run on your Windows computer. Chapter 2 reviews the process of troubleshooting software problems. Chapter 3 explains how to install programs beyond those included with Windows—including using the new Compatibility Mode options that can run even the oldest DOS and Windows Me/9x programs. Chapter 4 covers the Command Prompt window in which you run DOS programs. Chapter 5 looks at the many ways to move and share information between and among programs. User accounts, which have been vastly improved in Windows XP, are described in Chapter 6.

Part II: Keeping Track of Your Files

All the information in your computer is stored in disk files and folders, and Part II helps you keep them organized and safe. Chapters 7 and 8 cover using and configuring Windows Explorer (also known as My Computer). Chapter 9 describes the backup program that comes with Windows XP, and how to set up a regular backup regime.

Part III: Configuring Windows for Your Computer

Windows is extremely (some would say excessively) configurable. Part III tells you what items you can configure and makes suggestions for the most effective way to set up your computer.

Chapter 10 covers how to configure the Start menu and taskbar. Chapter 11 details configuring the desktop, the icons, and other items that reside on your screen. Chapter 12 explains configuration options for your keyboard, mouse, and game controller, and Chapter 13 tells you how to add and set up additional hardware on your computer. Chapter 14 covers printing, including setting up printers and installing fonts, and using the built-in fax features. Chapter 15 highlights the special features that are useful to laptop computer users. Chapter 16 covers the accessibility features that make Windows more usable for people who may have difficulty using conventional keyboards and mice, seeing the screen, or hearing sounds.

Part IV: Working with Text, Numbers, Pictures, Sound, and Video

Chapter 17 discusses Windows' simple but useful text and word processing programs and calculator. In Chapter 18, you read about new features for viewing, printing, e-mailing, and making web pages with your pictures, including ordering prints over the Internet. Chapters 19 and 20 examine Windows' extensive sound and video multimedia facilities, including Windows Media Player.

Part V: Windows XP on the Internet

Windows offers a complete set of Internet access features, from making telephone or network connections to e-mail and the Web.

Chapter 21 explains the intricacies of setting up a modem to work with Windows, whether you use a dial-up account or a high-speed cable, ISDN, or DSL connection. Chapter 22 tells you how to set up and configure dial-up and high-speed Internet connections, including the Internet Connection Firewall. Chapter 23 describes Outlook Express 6.0, the Windows accessory program that handles your e-mail. Chapter 24 covers Internet Explorer 6.0, Microsoft's web browser, and MSN Explorer. Chapter 25 examines online chatting and conferencing with Windows Messenger and NetMeeting, and Chapter 26 discusses the other Internet applications that come with Windows, as well as how to find and install your own Internet programs.

Part VI: Home and Office Networking with Windows XP Home Edition

Like previous versions of Windows, Windows XP Home Edition has built-in peer-to-peer networking features. You can set up your Windows machine on a small network as a workstation, server, or both.

Chapter 27 introduces local area networks, including key concepts such as client-server and peer-to-peer networking. Chapter 28 describes ways to connect two computers without setting up a LAN, including by phone, cable, or infrared link. Chapter 29 walks you through the process of creating a small network of Windows systems or adding your computer to an existing peer-to-peer network. Chapter 30 tells you how to share printers and disk drives among your networked computers. Chapter 31 explains how to use Internet Connection Sharing to share one Internet connection among all the computers on a LAN. Chapter 32 covers the improved network security features that Windows XP provides.

Part VII: Windows and Disk Housekeeping

Windows is sufficiently complex that it needs some regular maintenance and adjustment, and Part VII tells you how. Chapter 33 discusses disk setup, including removable disks and new hard disks that you may add to your computer, as well as

NTFS and FAT32 partitions. Chapter 34 tells you how to keep your disk working well and how to use the facilities that Windows provides to check and repair disk problems. Chapter 35 explains how to tune your computer for maximum performance. Chapter 36 describes the newly revamped Help And Support Center; how to get assistance from friends, co-workers, and Microsoft over the Internet; and the other Windows resources available on the Internet and elsewhere, including Automatic Updates.

Part VIII: Behind the Scenes: Windows XP Internals

Part VIII covers internal Windows configuration files. Chapter 37 describes the configuration files that Windows uses, and Chapter 38 describes the Registry, the central database of program information that is key to Windows' operation.

Appendix

The Appendix describes how to install Windows XP as an upgrade to a Windows system, from scratch on a blank hard disk, or as part of a dual-boot configuration.

Conventions Used in This Book

This book uses several icons to highlight special advice:

 A handy way to make Windows work better for you.

 An observation that gives insight into the way that Windows and other programs work.

 Something to watch out for, so you don't have to learn the hard way.

When we refer you to related material, we usually tell you the name of the section that contains the information we think you'll want to read. If the section is in the same chapter you are reading, we don't mention a chapter number.

When you see instructions to choose commands from a menu, we separate the part of the command by vertical bars (|). For example, "choose File | Open" means to choose File from the Menu bar and then choose Open from the File menu that appears. If the command begins with "Start |," then click the Start button on the taskbar as the first step. See "Commanding Windows and Other Programs" in Chapter 1 for the details of how to give commands.

New Features in Windows XP

At first blush, Windows XP looks very different from its predecessors—the new interface can be a startling change, with its simplified desktop and Start menu. Windows is still under there, though—and, as we'll show in Chapter 11, you can switch the Windows desktop back to a more familiar style. But the new interface isn't the most important new feature. Here is a list of other new features:

- The **CD Copy Wizard** built into Windows Explorer makes it easy to copy your files (including music and graphics files) onto CDs (see Chapter 7).

- **Backup** is back! Microsoft used to provide a backup program with earlier versions of Windows, but recent versions have left it out (see Chapter 9). We're glad to see that it's back, as running backups regularly is vital to keeping your files safe. You'll need to install it from the Windows XP CD-ROM.

- **Internet Explorer (IE)** version 6.0 is an upgrade to Microsoft's powerful web browser, and **Outlook Express** 6.0 is the newest version of Microsoft's e-mail and newsgroup program (see Chapters 23 and 24).

- **Fast User Switching** and **password-protected user accounts** make it convenient to create and use a separate user account for each person who uses a single computer (see Figure 1): see Chapter 6. If you assign passwords to the accounts, users can have a private, password-protected folder for their files. Fast User Switching lets several people stay logged on at the same time, with a new keystroke—WINDOWS-L—to switch from one user to another.

- **Windows Messenger** challenges AOL Instant Messenger and other instant-messaging programs (see Chapter 25).

- **Windows Media Player 8** is a step up from the previous version, with DVD support, audio CD creation, and even automatic downloading of audio CD cover art from the Internet (see Chapter 19).

- **Photo printing** and **web publishing** are built in: when Windows encounters a folder that contains graphics files, it offers wizards that can upload your pictures to a web site or send them off to a photo-printing service (see Chapter 18, section "Printing Your Pictures at Home"). You can see your photos as a filmstrip or slideshow, too.

- The **Files And Settings Transfer Wizard** helps you move your files from one computer to another, including your documents and settings (see the Appendix, section "Transferring Your Data Files and Windows Configuration Settings").

- The **Internet Connection Firewall** protects your computer (or your whole LAN) from intruders on the Internet (see Chapter 32).

- **Web Folders** enable you to work with files and folders on FTP and web servers using Windows Explorer (see Chapter 26, section "Working with FTP and Web Servers Using Web Folders").

- The **Last Known Good Configuration** option lets you recover from Windows crashes by returning to a Windows configuration that worked (see Chapter 2, section "Starting Windows in Other Startup Modes").

- **Remote Assistance** enables you to ask a friend, coworker, or a support professional to take over your computer via the Internet and fix a software problem (see Chapter 36).

- **Windows Product Activation (WPA)** requires you to "activate" Windows over the Internet or phone within a grace period, or the program stops functioning (see the Appendix, section "Windows Product Activation"). Activation doesn't require personal information from you (it's not the same as registration) and is designed to stop software piracy.

Windows XP also removed a few programs that came with some earlier Windows versions. Windows XP doesn't come with FrontPage Express (an HTML editor for creating web pages), Microsoft Chat (an Internet Relay Chat program for chatting over the Internet), or Active Movie (which has been replaced by Movie Maker and Windows Media Player 8).

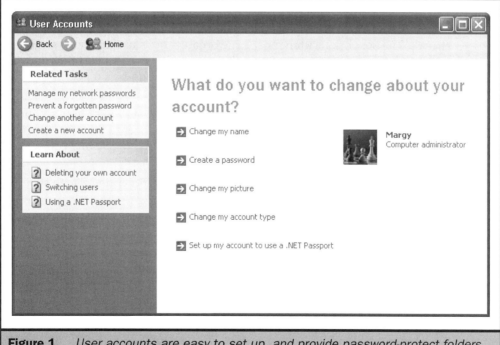

Figure 1.   *User accounts are easy to set up, and provide password-protect folders for each user's files.*

Differences Between Windows XP Editions

Windows XP comes in various versions: Windows XP Home Edition (for home and small-office users), Windows XP Professional (for corporate workstations), Windows XP 64-Bit Edition (for Itanium-based workstations), Windows .NET Server (for network servers), and Windows .NET Advanced Server (for network servers that need advanced features). Windows XP Media Center Edition, released in December 2002, comes preinstalled on PCs with special video and remote control hardware.

Windows XP Home Edition and Professional

Windows XP Home Edition and Professional are very similar: Microsoft has disabled a few features in Home Edition and made a few cosmetic changes. Generally, you need Windows XP Professional only if your computer needs to connect to a corporate (domain-based) network. Here are the major differences:

- **Backup**   The Microsoft Backup program comes with both editions, but must be installed separately in Windows XP Home Edition (see Chapter 9).

- **Multiprocessor support**   Home Edition supports only a single processor (CPU). Luckily, the vast majority of computers have only one processor. However, users of high-end scientific and analytical work need to install Professional.

- **Domain-based network support**   Home Edition cannot log onto a domain-based network. The networks within most large organizations use domains, so Home Edition won't suffice for corporate workstations. However, small-office and home users can use Home Edition on smaller workgroup-based peer-to-peer networks (see Chapter 27).

- **User administration**   Professional has a more flexible system of user accounts. Home Edition enables you to set up accounts for each user of the computer and choose whether they are administrative (with the ability to give any command) or limited (within all administrative privileges). See Chapter 6.

- **File Encryption**   Home Edition doesn't support the Encrypting File System (see Chapter 6, section "Keeping Files Private").

- **Remote Desktop**   Home Edition doesn't include this web-based application (also called Terminal Server client), which enables you to see the desktop of another computer on your own.

- **Offline Files And Folders**   Home Edition doesn't support this feature, which allows you to copy files from a server to a laptop before going on the road, and then synchronizing the files when you reconnect to the network.

- **Upgrades**   You can't upgrade from Windows NT or 2000 to Windows XP Home Edition, only to Professional. You can upgrade from Windows 98 or Me to either version of Windows XP.

Windows XP Service Pack 1

Windows XP Service Pack 1 (SP1) delivers a potpourri of fixes and updates. Here are the major changes:

- **Bug fixes**   Windows XP's AutoUpdate feature enables you to keep your version of Windows XP up-to-date by downloading and installing fixes over the Internet. SP1 combines all the most important box fixes in one big package. Especially crucial are the many security updates that Microsoft has had to issue to fix security holes in the Internet programs that come with Windows.

- **Windows Messenger 4.7**   This is an updated version of Microsoft's instant messaging program (see Chapter 25).

- **Set Program Access And Defaults**   This new feature (shown in Figure 2) enables you to hide Microsoft's bundled programs—Internet Explorer, Outlook Express, Windows Media Player, and others—if you prefer to use competitors' programs. See Chapter 3, section "Hiding Windows Middleware."

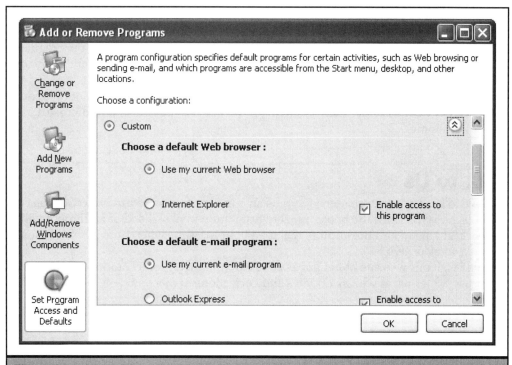

Figure 2.   *Service Pack 1 enables users or computer manufacturers to hide Microsoft's bundled programs.*

■ **Windows Program Activation updates**   If you have a pirated version of Windows XP, you may not be able to install SP1. It detects some product keys that have been widely used to install pirated versions (see the Appendix, section "Windows Product Activation"). If you upgrade your hardware with so many new components that Windows requires reactivation, SP1 gives you a new three-day grace period.

Windows XP Media Center Edition

Microsoft would like to take the computer out of the office and the den and bring it into the living room. Windows XP Media Center Edition (codenamed *Freestyle*) comes preinstalled on *media center PCs*, which come with special video hardware. You can watch television on your computer screen, use its Electronic Program Guide to see what's on, record TV shows off the air onto your hard disk, play DVDs, listen to music stored on your hard disk or streaming from the Internet, and view your digital photos. This version of Windows XP includes My TV, My Music, My Pictures, My Videos, and Play DVDs screens that you can choose from using a special TV-like remote control.

The media center PC that runs this version of Windows XP has an infrared sensor that allows the remote control, PC, and your cable or satellite box to communicate, a special graphics card, a TV tuner card, and a TV output that enables you to connect a regular TV screen to the computer. You can also hook your stereo to the outputs of the media center PC. You can't install Windows XP Media Center Edition on a regular PC—it requires this special hardware. Hewlett-Packard (Compaq), NEC, and Samsung plan to manufacture and sell media center PCs.

Chapter 20's section "Windows XP's Media Center" has more information about media center PCs. Also see Microsoft's Media Center web page at **www.microsoft.com/windows/ehome**.

Talk to Us

We love to hear from our readers. Drop us an e-mail note at **winxphometcr@gurus.com** to tell us how you liked the book or just to test your e-mail skills. Our mail robot will answer right away, and the authors will read your message when time permits (usually within a week or two.)

Also visit our web site at **net.gurus.com/winxphometcr** for a complete glossary of Windows XP terms, as well as updates and corrections to this book.

The
Complete
Reference

Part I

Working in Windows XP

The
Complete
Reference

Chapter 1

Running Windows and Application Programs

Before you can get any work done with your computer, you need to know how to make Windows XP and other programs do your bidding. Every computer user knows how to operate a mouse and keyboard and deal with windows, menus, and icons, but this chapter includes shortcuts and configuration options you may not be familiar with.

This chapter explains how screen objects work, how to start up and shut down Windows, and how to suspend Windows operation when you're not using your computer. We also review the many ways to run programs, including running them when Windows starts or on a regular schedule. Windows XP's new compatibility mode enables many older programs to run without problems. Because programs display information in windows, you also learn how the windows you see on your screen work, including resizing and moving them.

If Windows XP isn't installed yet on your computer, see the Appendix for instructions. Problems running Windows or programs are covered in Chapter 2.

Objects on the Windows XP Screen

The Windows *desktop* displays the work area in which you see your programs (see Figure 1-1). Windows XP's desktop is much less cluttered than those of previous versions of Windows, but it still tends to fill up with items that you use frequently and want to keep visible: icons and windows.

Note *Icons on your desktop that include a curved arrow in a little white box in the lower-left corner of the icon are shortcuts and represent files or programs on your computer (see Chapter 8). You can create your own shortcut icons.*

For readers who are new to Windows, here's a run-down of what the desktop can contain, in addition to windows and icons:

- **The taskbar** is a row of buttons and icons that usually appears along the bottom of the screen. You can display the taskbar along the top or side of your screen, hide the taskbar when you aren't using it, adjust its size, and configure it to include toolbars (see Chapter 10)—right-click a blank space on the taskbar to see a menu of options.

- **Task buttons** on the taskbar represent each program that is running. If a program displays more than one window, more than one task button may appear. If the taskbar gets too full to fit task buttons for all the open windows, Windows groups the buttons together, with one button for each application; click the task button to see a menu of the windows displayed by that program. Click a window's task button to make that window active (see "Switching Programs"). You can also right-click a button to see the System menu, a menu of commands you can give regarding that window, including opening and closing the window.

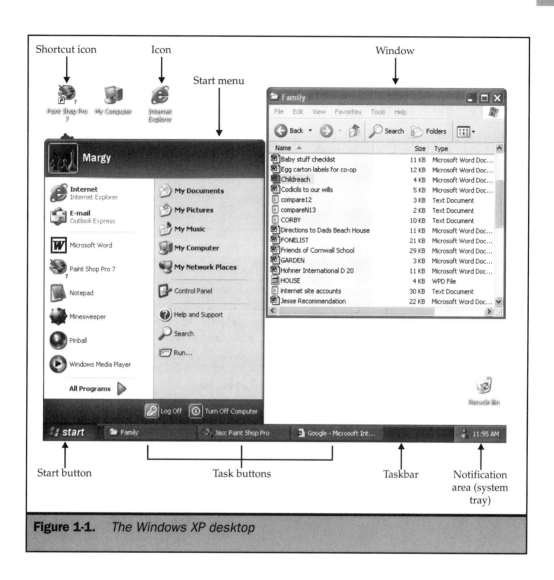

Figure 1-1. *The Windows XP desktop*

The task buttons used to be called the Task Manager in previous versions of Windows, but Microsoft has reassigned that name to a system management program (see Chapter 2).

■ **The notification area** (formerly called the system tray) at the right end of the taskbar contains the system clock along with a group of tiny icons. Windows XP displays fewer icons here than previous versions of Windows did, displaying them only when a program needs your attention. To find out the name of an icon, move the mouse pointer to the icon without clicking. After a moment, the icon's label appears. Some icons display information rather than a label (for example, the Power Management icon that appears on the system tray of most laptops displays how much charge is left in the laptop's battery). To change the settings for the program that displays the icon, or to exit the program, double- click or right-click the icon and choose a command from the menu that appears.

If there are too many icons to fit in the notification area, you see a left-pointing (<) button that you can click to see the rest of the icons. This button allows Windows to hide the icons that don't fit so they don't clutter up your taskbar.

■ **The Start button** displays the Start menu (you can also display it by pressing the WINDOWS key, if your keyboard has one, or pressing CTRL-ESC). The Start menu lists commands and additional menus that list most of the programs that you can run on your computer. You can customize which programs appear on the Start menu and how they are arranged (see Chapter 10)—right-click the Start button for a menu of options.

In this book, we indicate commands on the Start menu and its submenus like this: "Choose Start | Help And Support" means you should click the Start button and then choose the Help And Support command from the menu that appears.

Choosing Between Single-Click and Double-Click

You can choose how icons on the Windows desktop and in Explorer windows behave. Your choices are

■ **Single-click**   (web style) To select the icon without running or opening it, move your mouse pointer to the icon without clicking and wait a second. To run or open the icon, click it once. Icon labels appear underlined (like web page links).

■ **Double-click**   (Classic Windows style) To select the icon, click it once. To run or open the icon, click it twice. Icon labels are not underlined.

Follow these steps to choose between single- and double-click:

1. Choose Start | Control Panel. Click the Appearance And Themes category.

2. Click the Folder Options icon near the bottom of the Appearance And Themes window. You see the Folder Options dialog box, as shown in Figure 1-2. If the General tab isn't selected, click it.

3. In the Click Items As Follows box, click Single-click or Double-click. If you choose Single-click, choose whether you want icon titles to be underlined all the time (Consistent With My Browser) or only when your mouse pointer is on the icon (Only When I Point At Them).

4. Click OK.

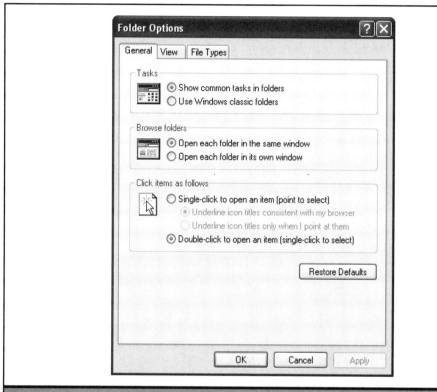

Figure 1-2.   *The General tab of the Folder Options dialog box, where you can specify how Windows icons work*

Starting Up and Stopping Windows XP

When you start most Windows XP computers, you see the splash (logo) screen and then the Windows desktop. However, if your computer is on a LAN or is set up for multiple users, you see the Welcome screen, showing the user accounts defined on the system (see Chapter 27). Click your user account name: if the account requires a password, type your password and press ENTER.

If your computer system has been suspended, Windows hasn't been shut down; instead, it is on standby or hibernating. To start up where you left off, just resume operation of your computer, which usually is accomplished by moving the mouse, pressing a key (such as the SHIFT key), or (if you use a laptop) opening the cover.

Another possibility is that someone locked the computer screen by pressing WINDOWS-L (that is, holding down the WINDOWS key, which not all keyboards have, and pressing **L**). If so, you see the same Welcome screen you saw when Windows started: click your user account name to continue.

If your computer's hard disk contains more than one bootable partition (that is, another section of your hard disk that contains an operating system), you may see the message "Please select the operating system to start," with a list of bootable partitions. Use the arrow keys to select the operating system you want and press ENTER. For information about partitions, see Chapter 33 and the Appendix.

Suspending, Shutting Down, and Restarting Windows

When you need to turn off the computer, shut down Windows first to allow it to close all its files and finish other housekeeping tasks—never turn the computer off without shutting down Windows. Choose Start | Turn Off Computer, click anywhere on the desktop and press ALT-F4, or press CTRL-ESC and choose Shut Down. The Turn Off Computer dialog box provides these options:

- **Stand By or Hibernate**   Some computers have a *Suspend Mode* or *Standby Mode* in which the computer remains on, but the disk drives, fan, and screen turn off. Others have a *Hibernate Mode* in which Windows stores the programs and data that are currently open—putting this information in a temporary file on the hard disk—and then shuts down Windows so you can turn the computer off; on laptops and other computers with power management, the computer turns off automatically. With either standby or hibernation, the next time you turn your computer on, you can pick up just where you left off. If Hibernate doesn't appear on the Turn Off Computer dialog box, try pressing the SHIFT key.

- **Turn Off**   Shuts down Windows. Windows displays a message when you can safely turn off the computer. Don't turn off the computer until you see this message. Computers with advanced power management shut off automatically.

- **Restart**   Shuts down Windows and then reloads it (useful if your computer starts acting funny). After installing some programs (or Windows upgrades) the installation program requires you to restart Windows.

If programs are running, Windows closes them before shutting down, switching to standby, or restarting. If a program has unsaved files open, the program should ask you whether you want to save your work before the program exits.

 With previous versions of Windows, restarting Windows every day or so was important. Windows' housekeeping wasn't perfect, and previous versions lost track of system resources over time (see Chapter 35). Windows XP is much better at remaining stable over long periods of time. However, to ensure that the maximum system resources are available for your use, restart Windows.

When Can You Turn Off the Computer?

We recommend you do not turn off the computer when you have finished using it.
Windows likes to perform housekeeping tasks when you aren't using the computer,
so leaving it on, even when you're not working, is a good idea. You can schedule
programs to run at specified times (see "Running Programs on a Schedule Using
Scheduled Tasks" later in this chapter)—for example, you can schedule Windows
to collect your e-mail at 7:00 every morning.

Many computers power down the screen, hard disk, and fan after a set time
of inactivity. The computer itself, however, is still running. If your screen doesn't
power off automatically, you should turn off your screen when you aren't using the
computer. Computer screens use the lion's share of the electricity consumed by
the computer (see Chapter 15).

Windows includes OnNow, technology that powers down the computer when nothing
is happening and powers back up when the computer is needed again, if the computer's
hardware permits. To use OnNow, choose Start | Control Panel, click Performance And
Maintenance, and then run the Power Options program (see Chapter 15). You can control
when the computer turns off its monitor and hard disks, as well as when it enters
standby mode or hibernates.

16-Bit Versus 32-Bit Applications

Older personal computers process data 16 bits at a time. These 16-bit computers are
based on older CPUs (central processing units), like the Intel 8088 and 80286. Newer
personal computers process data 32 bits at a time. These 32-bit computers are based
on newer CPU chips, like the Intel 80386, 80486, Pentium, and Pentium Pro.

DOS and Windows 3.1 run on both 16-bit and 32-bit computers. Windows 9x,
Me, NT, 2000, and XP, as well as Linux and OS/2, all require 32-bit computers.

Some programs are designed to run with DOS and Windows 3.1; these
programs are called *16-bit applications*. Other programs are designed to work
with later versions of Windows and are called *32-bit applications*.

As a Windows XP user, you can run both 16-bit and 32-bit applications.
When you have a choice, run the 32-bit version of a program, though; it takes
better advantage of your 32-bit computer, and it usually runs faster and has more
capabilities than the 16-bit version. If you have to run an older program, you can
use compatibility mode to simulate an older version of Windows (see "Running
Programs in Compatibility Mode" later in this chapter).

Methods of Starting Programs

Windows gives you many ways to start a program. Everyone knows the obvious ways:

- **Desktop icons**   You can control whether you need to single-click or double-click icons to run programs by setting your Folder options (see "Choosing Between Single-Click and Double-Click" earlier in this chapter).

- **Start menu**   When you install a program, it usually adds a command to the Start menu or a submenu (see Chapter 10). You might need to try several menus to find the one that contains the program you want. You can always press ESC to cancel the menu you are looking at (moving your mouse pointer off the menu usually cancels the menu, too). For example, WordPad appears on the Accessories submenu of the Programs menu. To run WordPad, choose Start | All Programs | Accessories | WordPad. If you've run a program recently, it may appear on the left side of the Start menu, with the frequently-used programs.

Caution   *You can change the order of the items on the Start and Programs menus by dragging them up and down on the menus. You can also drag an item from one menu to another, or "pin" a program to the top-left side of the Start menu by right-clicking it and choosing Pin To Start Menu. If you don't intend to reorganize your menus, don't click-and-drag the commands on them.*

- **WINDOWS key**   If your keyboard has a WINDOWS key, press it to display the Start menu; if not, pressing CTRL-ESC does the same thing. Press the LEFT-ARROW, RIGHT-ARROW, UP-ARROW, and DOWN-ARROW keys to highlight a command from the Start menu and press ENTER to choose the command. The same method works for choosing commands from submenus. The RIGHT-ARROW key moves from a command to its submenu (which is usually to the right on the screen). The LEFT-ARROW and ESC keys cancel a submenu and return to the previous menu.

- **Filenames**   Programs are stored in files, usually with the filename extension .exe (short for "executable") or .com (for "command"). Windows displays the names of program files in Explorer windows. To run the program, single-click or double-click the filename of the program you want to run.

The following sections describe other methods of running programs, including opening a document, pressing shortcut keys, typing commands in the Run dialog box, and running programs automatically when you log in.

Starting Programs by Opening Documents

Windows knows which programs you use to open which types of files. For example, it knows that files with the .doc extension are opened using Microsoft Word. When you install a program, the installation program adds a file association to Windows, so Windows knows what kinds of files it can open.

To run the program that can open a particular file, you can click or double-click the filename in an Explorer window—if the filenames are underlined, single-click the filename, and if the filenames are not underlined, double-click. Windows runs the appropriate program to handle that file (if the program isn't already running) and opens the file in that program. If an icon for a file appears on your desktop, clicking or double-clicking the icon tells Windows to do the same thing.

For example, if you double-click a file with the extension .mdb (a Microsoft Access database file), Windows runs Microsoft Access and opens the database file. Windows may be configured not to display extensions (the default setting is for extensions to be hidden); you can identify many types of files by their icons. To tell Windows to display full filenames, including the extensions, see Chapter 7.

If you try to open a file for which Windows doesn't know which program to run, you see a window asking what you want to do. Your options are

■ **Use The Web Service To Find The Appropriate Program**   Windows runs your web browser to display information about the type of file that you want to open, and helps you find a program that can open it.

■ **Select The Program From A List**   Windows displays the Open With dialog box, shown in Figure 1-3. Choose the program that can open the type of file you clicked; if the program doesn't appear on the list, click the Browse button to find the filename of the program. If you always want to run this program when you click this type of file, leave the check mark in the Always Use The Selected Program To Open This Type Of File check box. Optionally, you can type a description of the type of file: This description appears when you select a filename and choose View | Details. Then click OK.

You can control which program runs for each type of file, including which program to use when editing, viewing, or printing the file (see Chapter 3, section "Associating a Program with a File Extension").

 If you want to open a file using a different program from the one Windows automatically runs, right-click the filename and choose Open With from the menu that appears. Windows displays the Open With dialog box, and you can choose the program you want to run.

Starting Programs Using Shortcut Keys

If a shortcut—an icon with a tiny arrow in its lower-left corner (see Chapter 8)—exists for a program, you can define shortcut keys to run the program. *Shortcut keys* for programs are always a combination of the CTRL key, the ALT key, and one other key, which must be a letter, number, or symbol key. We like shortcut keys—they are much quicker than navigating the Start menu or finding an icon on the desktop.

To define shortcut keys for a program:

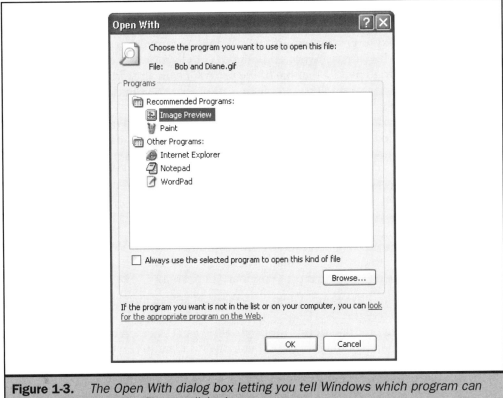

Figure 1-3. *The Open With dialog box letting you tell Windows which program can open the file you clicked*

1. Right-click the shortcut icon that launches the program and choose Properties from the menu that appears. You see the Properties dialog box for the shortcut.

2. Click the Shortcut tab, shown in Figure 1-4.

3. Click in the Shortcut Key box (which usually says "None") and press the key you want to use in combination with the CTRL and ALT keys. For example, press **M** to specify CTRL-ALT-M as the shortcut key combination. To specify no shortcut keys, press SPACEBAR.

4. Click OK.

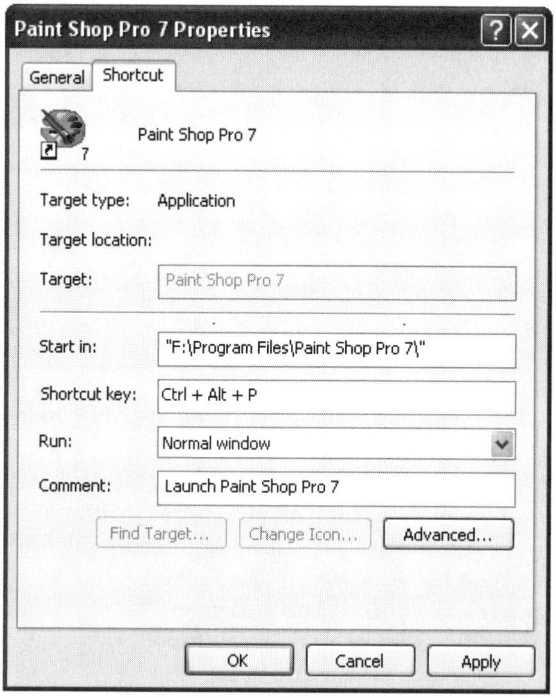

Figure 1-4.   *Defining a shortcut key for a program*

Once you define shortcut keys for a program, you can press the keys to run the program.

Note   *If another program uses the same combination of keys, that combination of keys no longer performs its function in the program; instead, the key combination runs the program to which you assigned the shortcut keys. However, few programs use* CTRL-ALT *key combinations.*

Starting Programs from the Run Dialog Box

Before Windows, there was DOS, which required you to type the filename of a program and press ENTER to run the program. If you prefer this method, it still works in

Windows—sometimes it's easier than finding the program in the maze of Start menu options. Choose Start | Run, and you see the Run dialog box:

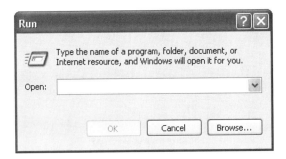

To run a program, type its full path and filename into the Open box (that is, the exact filename, including the folder that contains the file), or click Browse to locate the filename. Then press ENTER or click OK. Windows runs the program.

Depending on the program, you may need to type additional information after the filename. For example, to run the Ftp program (an Internet file transfer program that comes with Windows), type **ftp**, followed by a space and the name of a computer on the Internet (like **ftp.microsoft.com**). When you press ENTER, Windows runs the Ftp program by using the additional information you typed.

 If you've typed the filename in the Open box recently, click the downward-pointing button at the right end of the Open box and choose the filename from the list that appears.

A more arcane way to run a program from a dialog box similar to the Run dialog box is by using the New Task button on the Windows Task Manager. Press CTRL-ALT-DEL to display the Windows Task Manager (or right-click a blank place on the taskbar and choose Task Manager) and click New Task.

Starting Programs When You Log In

When you log into Windows (usually when Windows starts up), Windows looks in the Startup folder of your Start Menu for shortcuts to programs (see Chapter 8). This folder is usually stored in C:\Documents And Settings*username*\Start Menu\Programs (assuming that C: is the partition where Windows is installed). If any programs or shortcuts to programs are stored in this folder, Windows runs them automatically when it has finished starting up. You can bypass running these programs by holding down the SHIFT key while Windows starts up.

For example, you can use this Startup folder to run your word processor and e-mail programs automatically each time you start Windows. Just create shortcuts in your Startup folder (see Chapter 8).

The Windows Registry, which stores information about Windows and your applications, can also tell Windows to run programs automatically on startup and login. (The Registry is described in Chapter 38.) See Chapter 2 to diagnose problems with programs that run automatically on startup or login

Switching and Exiting Programs

Windows enables you to run many programs at the same time, each in its own window. You can exit from one program while leaving other programs running, and you can choose which program window is the active window—the window you are currently using.

Switching Programs

To *switch programs*—choose another window as the active window—you can click in the program's window or click the program's task button on the taskbar. If you prefer to use the keyboard, press ALT-TAB until the window you want is active, or press ALT-SHIFT-TAB to cycle through the open windows in the reverse order. Alternatively, press ALT-TAB and don't release the ALT key. A window appears with an icon for each program that is running, with the program in the active window highlighted, as shown here:

The name of the highlighted window appears at the bottom of the window. To switch to a different program, keep holding down the ALT key, press TAB to move the highlight to the icon for the window you want, and then release the ALT key.

Exiting Programs

Clicking the Close button in the upper-right corner of the program window is the easiest way to exit a program. (If a program displays multiple windows, close them all.) You can also choose the File | Exit or File | Close command from the menu bar, press ALT-F4, click the System Menu button in the upper-left corner of the program window and choose Close from the menu that appears, or right-click the program button on the taskbar and choose Close from the menu that appears.

If a program won't close in the usual ways, you can cancel it. Press CTRL-ALT-DEL to display the Windows Task Manger (shown in Figure 1-5, and described in more detail in Chapter 2). The Applications tab lists all the programs currently running.

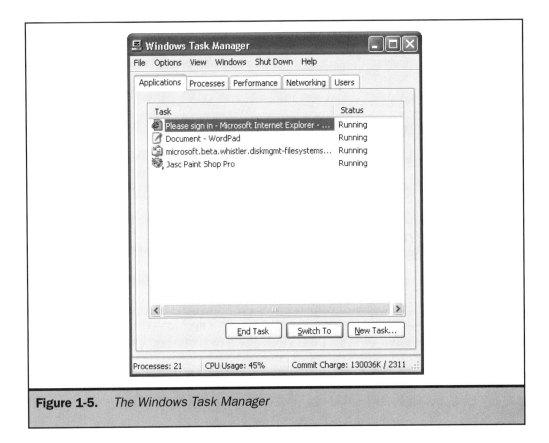

Figure 1-5.   *The Windows Task Manager*

To cancel a program, click the program name in the Windows Task Manager; then click the End Task button. If you were using the program to edit a file, you may lose some work.

The End Task button is designed for canceling programs that have "hung"—stopped responding to the keyboard or mouse. To avoid losing unsaved work, always try exiting a program by clicking its Close button, pressing ALT-F4, or choosing File | Exit before resorting to the Windows Task Manager.

Controlling the Size and Shape of Your Windows

Figure 1-6 shows the parts of a window. Some windows are divided into sections called *panes*. Although what's inside the window changes from program to program, most windows you see in Windows include the following components:

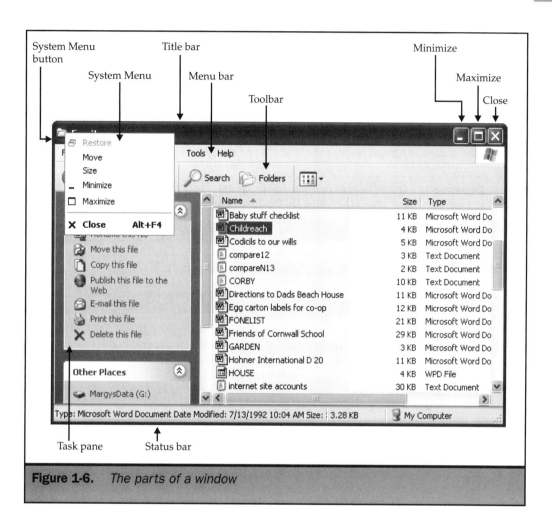

Figure 1-6.   *The parts of a window*

You can arrange your open windows to see the information you want to view.
A window can be in one of three states:

■ *Maximized*, taking up the entire screen, with no window borders. Click the
   window's Maximize button, the middle button on the right end of the title bar,
   or click the window's System Menu button and choose Maximize from the menu
   that appears. You can also press ALT-SPACEBAR to display the System menu and
   press X to choose the Maximize command, or right-click the window's button on
   the taskbar and choose Maximize from the menu that appears. When a window is
   maximized, its Maximize button is replaced by the Restore button, which returns
   the window to the size it was before you maximized it. Double-clicking a window's
   title bar switches between maximized restored.

■ *Minimized*, so all that appears is the window's task button on the taskbar. Click the window's Minimize button, the leftmost of the three buttons on the right end of the title bar, or click the window's System Menu button and choose Minimize from the menu that appears. You can also press ALT-SPACEBAR to display the System menu and press N to choose the Minimize command, or right-click the window's button on the taskbar and choosing Minimize from the menu that appears. To switch between minimized, and either restored or maximized, click the taskbar button for the program.

■ *Restored*, or *in a window*; that is, displayed with window borders—most windows are restored windows. You can change the height and width of restored windows. If a window is maximized, click its Restore button (the middle button on the right end of the title bar) to restore the window, click the window's System Menu button and choose Restore from the menu that appears, or press ALT-SPACEBAR to display the System menu and press R to choose the Restore command. If the window is minimized, click its taskbar button to restore it.

In the upper-right corner of almost every window is a red button with an X— the Close button, which performs the same action as choosing File | Close from the window's menu. If the program appears in only one window (the usual situation), closing the window exits from the program, the equivalent of choosing the File | Exit command. If you'd rather use the keyboard, you can close many windows by pressing CTRL-F4. To close a window and exit the program, press ALT-F4.

If the window is minimized, you can close the window without restoring it first. Right-click the window's button on the taskbar and choose Close from the menu that appears.

The choice between maximizing programs and running them in windows (restored) is a matter of taste. If your screen is small or low-resolution, maximize your windows, so you can see their contents as clearly as possible. If you have a large, high-resolution screen, you can run your programs in windows so you can see several programs at the same time.

Minimizing All Windows

You can minimize all the open windows on your screen by right-clicking a blank area on the taskbar and choosing Show The Desktop from the shortcut menu that appears. Using only the keyboard, you can press WINDOWS-M (using the WINDOWS key, which is next to the CTRL key on many keyboards). If the Show Desktop icon appears on your taskbar (it's on the Quick Launch toolbar, which may appear right next to the Start button), you can also click this icon to minimize all your windows. (See Chapter 10 for a description of the Quick Launch toolbar and how to display it.)

To reverse this command, right-click a blank area on the taskbar and choose Show OpenWindows from the menu that appears, press SHIFT-WINDOWS-M, or click the same Quick Launch button again.

Arranging All Windows

If you want to see all the windows on your desktop at the same time, you can ask Windows to arrange them tastefully for you. Right-click a blank area of the taskbar and choose one of the following commands from the menu that appears:

- **Cascade Windows** Opens all the windows so they overlap, with their upper-left corners cascading from the upper-left corner of the screen, down and to the right.

- **Tile Windows Horizontally** Opens all the windows with no overlap, with each window extending the full width of the screen and one window below another.

- **Tile Windows Vertically** Opens all the windows with no overlap, with each window extending the full height of the screen and one window next to another.

If you choose one of these commands by mistake, you can undo the command by right-clicking a blank area of the taskbar and choosing Undo Tile or Undo Cascade from the menu that appears.

Note *If four or more windows are open, Tile Windows Horizontally and Tile Windows Vertically arrange the windows the same way—in a grid.*

Moving and Resizing Restored Windows

Maximized windows always take up the entire screen, and minimized windows always appear only on the taskbar. When a program is restored (running in a window), you can move it or change its size and the shape (height and width) by using the *window borders*.

To move a window, click anywhere in the title bar of the window, except for the buttons, and drag the window to the place you want it to appear. You can also press ALT-SPACEBAR to display the System menu, press M to choose the Move command, press the cursor keys to move the window, and then press ENTER when the window is located where you want it or right-click the program button on the taskbar and choose Move from the menu that appears.

To change a window's height or width, click the window border and drag it. When your mouse pointer is over a border, it changes to a double-pointed arrow, making it easy to tell when you can start dragging. If you'd rather use the keyboard, press ALT-SPACEBAR to display the System menu, press S to choose the Size command, press cursor keys to adjust the window size, and press ENTER.

Configuring Windows XP and Other Programs

To use Windows and other programs effectively, you need to configure them to work with your computer's hardware and with each other. When configuring Windows and other programs, you use these Windows features:

■ **Properties** are settings for an object. Each object in Windows—the hardware components of your computer, software programs, files, and icons—has properties that affect how that object works. For example, a file has properties such as a filename, size, and the date the file was last modified. To display the properties of almost anything you see on the screen in Windows, right-click the item and choose Properties from the menu that appears. You see a Properties dialog box. Figure 1-7 shows the properties of a folder.

■ **The Control Panel** (shown in Figure 1-8) displays icons for a number of programs that enable you to control your computer, Windows, and the software

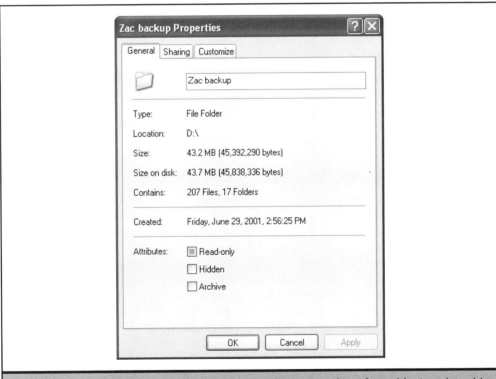

Figure 1-7.   *A Properties dialog box displays the properties of an object and enables you to edit some of them.*

WORKING IN
WINDOWS XP

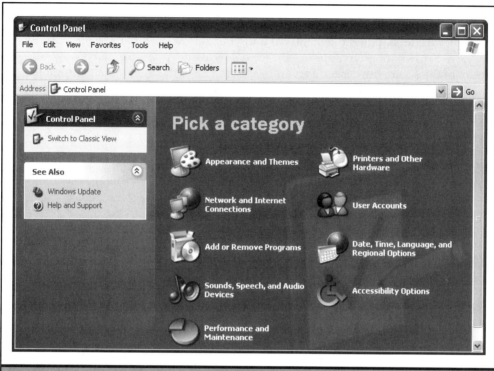

Figure 1-8.   *The Control Panel window*

you have installed. To see the Control Panel, choose Start | Control Panel. Windows XP displays a newly redesigned window with categories of tasks—Windows calls this *Category View*. Clicking a category in the Control Panel displays a list of tasks in that category.

Note   *If you are used to the "Classic" Windows 9x/Me Control Panel, click the Switch To Classic View option. You see most of the same Control Panel icons that appeared in earlier versions of Windows; double-click them to run them. These icons also appear in Category View, below the tasks.*

Commanding Windows and Other Programs

Almost every Windows program enables you to issue commands to control what the program does. Most programs provide several ways to issue commands, including choosing commands from the menu bar and clicking icons on the toolbar.

Tips for Choosing Commands from Menus

If you click a command on the menu bar and your screen doesn't have room for the entire drop-down menu to appear, you see a downward-pointing triangle at the bottom of the submenu; click the arrow to see the rest of the menu. Many programs use a Windows feature that displays only the most frequently used commands or the commands you've chosen recently. At the bottom of the menu is a double-*V* character (a double downward-pointing arrow) that you can click to see the rest of the available commands.

 If you are used to using a Macintosh, you can choose commands from menus the same way as you do on a Mac. Click and hold down the mouse button on the menu bar command, move the mouse down the drop-down menu to the command you want, and then release the mouse button.

Some commands have a keyboard shortcut. For example, many programs provide the key combination CTRL-S as a shortcut for choosing the File menu and then the Save command. Keyboard shortcuts appear to the right of commands on drop-down menus.

In most programs, you can use the ALT key to choose commands from menus. One letter of each command in each menu is underlined (for example, most programs underline the *F* in File). To choose a command, press the ALT key; the first command on the menu bar is selected and appears enclosed in a box. Press the underlined letter of the command you want; that menu drops down. Continue pressing letters to choose commands from menus. To cancel all the drop-down menus that appear on the screen, press the ALT key again. To back up one step, press the ESC or LEFT-ARROW key.

Choosing Commands from Shortcut Menus

Windows and most Windows-compatible programs display special menus, called *shortcut menus* (or *context menus*), when you click with the right mouse button. The shortcut menu displays commands appropriate to the object you clicked. For example, if you right-click a blank space on the Windows taskbar, the shortcut menu that appears contains commands you can perform on the taskbar or desktop:

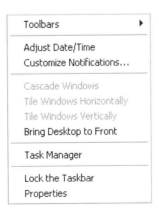

To cancel a shortcut menu, click outside the menu or press the ESC key.

You can't always guess where shortcut menus will appear or what will be on them. To use shortcut menus, right-click the item you want to work with and see what appears!

You can display a shortcut menu by using only the keyboard; select the item you want to right-click and press SHIFT-F10 to display the shortcut menu. Newer keyboards include an APPLICATION key that looks like the one shown on the left.

The APPLICATION key has the same effect as right-clicking at the mouse pointer location. Use the UP-ARROW and DOWN-ARROW keys to select the command you want, and then press ENTER to select it, or press ESC to dismiss the menu.

Using TweakUI to Change the Windows Interface

For years, Microsoft has provided an unsupported utility to change many aspects of the Windows interface that are stored in the Windows Registry. In older versions of Windows, TweakUI came on the setup CD, but Windows XP doesn't come with a copy. However, you can download and install TweakUI from the Microsoft web site, at **www.microsoft.com/windowsxp/pro/downloads/powertoys.asp**.

Once you've installed TweakUI using the instructions at the web site, you can run it by choosing Start | All Programs | PowerToys For Windows XP | TweakUI For Windows XP. The TweakUI window looks like this:

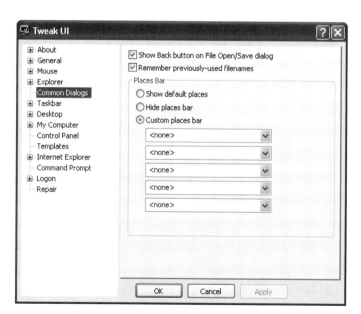

For more information on using TweakUI to configure your desktop and taskbar, see Chapter 10.

Tips for Using Dialog Boxes

A *dialog box* is a window that enables you to change settings or give commands in a program. For example, in most programs, when you give a command to open a file, you see an Open File dialog box that enables you to specify which file you want to open. You must exit the dialog box before continuing to use the program. Most dialog boxes include buttons to exit, with names like OK, Close, and Cancel. If you don't want to keep the changes you have made, click the Cancel button or press the ESC key. While a program is displaying a dialog box, the program usually won't accept any other input until you've closed the dialog box.

Tip *If a window has a question mark button in its upper-right corner, click it and then click the setting about which you want help. If the window doesn't have a question-mark button, click the Help button, if there is one, or press F1. Another way to obtain help is to right-click the setting you need information about and choose the What's This command from the shortcut menu, if it appears.*

The Open, Save As, and Browse dialog boxes in most programs have some special settings. All three dialog boxes provide you with a way of specifying a disk drive, a folder, and a file to work with, as shown in Figure 1-9.

Most (but not all) Open, Save As, and Browse dialog boxes have the following items:

- **Places bar**   Vertical bar down the left side of the dialog box with icons that usually include My Recent Documents (for files you've used recently, regardless of their location), Desktop (for the top-level view of the items in your computer), My Documents (for your My Documents folder), My Computer (for a list of the available disk drives and partitions), and (if your computer is on a network) My Network Places (for a list of network drives). Click one of these buttons to change the view in the folder tree to the right.

Tip *You can put different icons on the Places bar by using TweakUI, a Microsoft utility that is described in the sidebar "Using TweakUI to Change the Windows Interface." However, TweakUI limits you to using system folders like My Documents and History. To use any folder—like the Budget folder you store most of your files in—see the sidebar "Replacing Your Places Bar." Microsoft Office has its own Places bar; changing the Windows Places bar doesn't affect the Open and Save As dialog boxes in Office programs.*

- **Look In or Save In pull-down menu**   The Open and Browse dialog boxes contain a Look In pull-down menu that enables you to specify the folder that contains the file you want to open. The Save As dialog box contains a similar Save In pull-down menu that enables you to specify the folder into which you want to save a file.

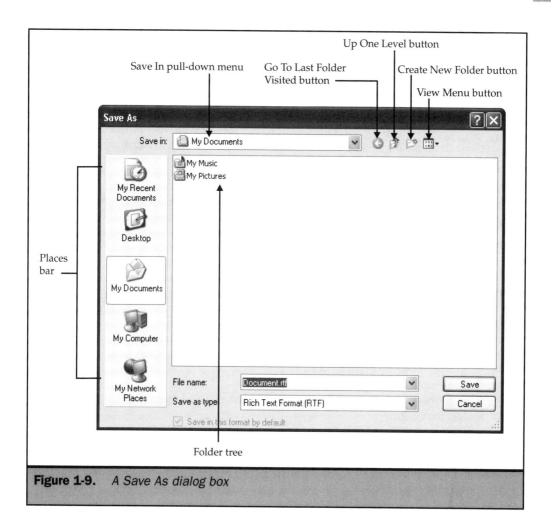

Up One Level button

Save In pull-down menu   Go To Last Folder   Create New Folder button
Visited button

View Menu button

Places bar

Folder tree

Figure 1-9.   *A Save As dialog box*

- **Folder tree**   This large list box displays the current contents of the folder you have selected (see Chapter 7). Press F5 to update the display if you think that the folder contents have changed.

- **Go To Last Folder Visited button**   Clicking this button goes back to the last folder you viewed.

- **Up One Level button**   Clicking this button changes which folder is named in the Look In or Save In box by moving up one level in the folder tree (to the folder's parent folder). The folder tree listing is updated, too. You can also press BACKSPACE to move up the folder tree one level.

■ **Create New Folder button** Clicking this button creates a new folder within the current folder (see Chapter 7).

■ **View Menu button** Clicking this button displays a list of the views you can choose: Large Icons, Small Icons, List, Details, and Thumbnails.

■ **Files Of Type box** Clicking in this box displays the types of files currently displayed in the folder tree. For example, in Microsoft Word, the Files Of Type box is usually set to display only Word documents, but you can choose to see all filenames.

Replacing Your Places Bar

The Places bar, which appears in most Open and Save As dialog boxes, usually contains icons for My Recent Documents, Desktop, My Documents, My Computer, and My Network. Wouldn't it be nice if there were icons for the folders that you most often use instead, like D:\Budget\Current Month? If you don't mind editing the Registry (as described in Chapter 38), you can create a new Registry key in which you store the icons that you want in your Places bar. This key replaces the usual Places bar; until you put values in it, your Places bar is empty.

First create the Registry key in which you can store the folders to want to appear in the Places bar. Follow these steps.

1. After backing up your Registry (as described in Chapter 38), run the Registry Editor.

2. Go to \HKEY_CURRENT_USER\Software\Microsoft\Windows\ CurrentVersion\Policies.

3. If there's no subkey named Comdlg32 (the name of the program that handles the Places bar), create one. (If you have run the TweakUI program, this key may already exist.) Right-click the Policies key, choose New | Key, type **Comdlg32**, and press ENTER.

4. In the Comdlg32 key, create a subkey named Placesbar by right-clicking the Comdlg32 key, choosing New | Key, typing **Placesbar**, and pressing ENTER.

At this point, if you use the Open or Save As dialog box from another program (try Notepad), the Places bar is empty. Now you can add string values (named Place0 through Place4) for the icons to appear in the Places bar. Each value can be a pathname (like D:\Budget\Current Month) or the system ID number for these special folders:

System ID	Folder Name
5	My Documents
17	My Computer
18	My Network Places
34	History
39	My Pictures

To add one of these special folders to your Places bar, right-click the Placesbar key, choose New | DWORD Value, and type the name (Place0, Place1, Place2, Place3, or Place4). Right-click this new value and choose Modify. In the Value Data box, type the system ID from the list (for example, **5** for the My Documents folder). Click OK.

To any other folder to your Places bar, right-click the Placesbar key, choose New | String Value, and type the name (Place0 through Place4). Right-click this new value and choose Modify. In the Value Data box, type the full pathname of the folder you want to add. Click OK.

After you add each folder to your Places bar, try the File | Save As command in Notepad to confirm that the special folder appears in your Places bar. If you want to return to the default Places bar, use the Registry Editor to delete the \HKEY_CURRENT_USER\Software\Microsoft\Windows\CurrentVersion\Policies\comdlg32\Placesbar key.

Running Programs on a Schedule Using Scheduled Tasks

Scheduled Tasks is the program Windows uses to check the files and folders on your hard disk automatically. You can also use the Scheduled Tasks program to run almost any program at a specified time on a regular basis. When you schedule a task, you must specify the following information:

■ What program you want to run.

■ How often you want to run it (daily, weekly, monthly, when your computer starts, or when you log on).

- What time you want the program to start running. For weekly and monthly schedules, you also specify what day to start the program.

- What user account you want to use when running the program. You enter the user's name and password (usually your own username and password).

When Scheduled Tasks is running, its icon appears in the notification area at the right end of the taskbar.

Scheduling a Program

To tell Scheduled Tasks to run a program on a regular schedule, follow these steps:

1. Look at the Scheduled Tasks window by choosing Start | All Programs | Accessories | System Tools | Scheduled Tasks; or choose Start | Control Panel, click Performance And Maintenance, and click Scheduled Tasks. You see the Scheduled Tasks window, shown in Figure 1-10.

2. Run the Add Scheduled Task item that appears in the Name column of the Scheduled Tasks window. (If it's underlined, click it once. Otherwise, double-click it.)

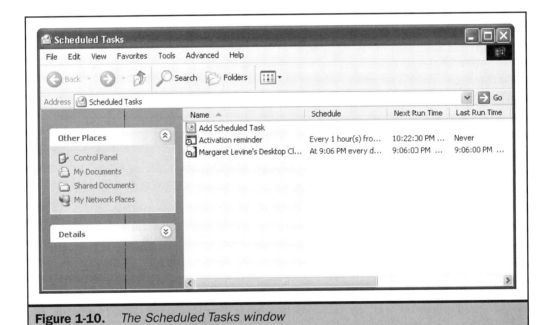

Figure 1-10. *The Scheduled Tasks window*

3. Windows runs the Scheduled Task Wizard, which takes you through the steps required to schedule tasks to run automatically. Follow the prompts on the screen, clicking Next to move to the next step.

4. When the Scheduled Task Wizard displays all the information you have specified about the program's schedule, including the name of the program and when you want it to run, click the Finish button. The program appears on a new line in the Scheduled Tasks window.

Be sure to leave your computer turned on all the time, so when the scheduled time arrives, Windows runs your program. If your computer is off (or Scheduled Tasks isn't running) when the time comes, the program doesn't run.

 When you schedule a task, Windows creates a file with the extension .job in the C:\Windows\Tasks folder (assuming that Windows XP is installed in C:\Windows).

Canceling a Scheduled Program

If you decide you no longer want Windows to run the program automatically, open the Scheduled Tasks window, right-click the line for the program, and choose Delete from the menu that appears. When Windows asks you to confirm that you want to delete the file for this job, click Yes.

To cancel running all scheduled programs, choose Advanced | Stop Using Task Scheduler from the menu bar in the Scheduled Tasks window. No scheduled programs will run until you choose the command Advanced | Start Using Task Scheduler. You can pause the scheduler program by choosing Advanced | Pause Task Scheduler to skip running scheduled programs temporarily and choose Advanced | Continue Task Scheduler to resume. Pausing Scheduled Tasks is a good idea while you are installing new software, for example, so installation isn't interrupted.

Configuring a Scheduled Program

You can configure other settings for a scheduled task. Click or double-click the line for the task in the Scheduled Tasks window (or select the line and click the Properties button on the toolbar or right-click the program name and choose Properties from the menu that appears). You see a dialog box with all the settings for the scheduled program (see Figure 1-11). The Task tab shows settings that determine which program runs. The Schedule tab controls when Windows runs the program. The Settings tab includes options to control how long the program can run (to stop runaway programs), whether the program runs if the computer is busy running other programs, and (for laptops) whether the program starts if the computer is running on batteries or is on standby.

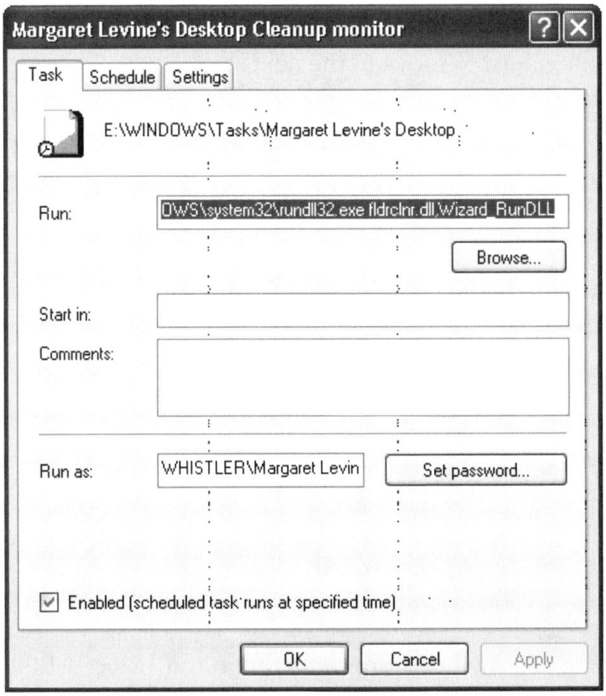

Figure 1-11.   *Settings for a scheduled program*

Tracking Scheduled Programs

You can ask Scheduled Tasks to let you know how its scheduled programs are doing. If you want to be notified when Scheduled Tasks is unable to run a scheduled program, choose Advanced from the Scheduled Tasks window's menu bar and make sure a check mark appears to the left of the Notify Me Of Missed Tasks option (if no check mark appears, choose the option from the menu).

You can look at a log file of the results of scheduled programs by choosing Advanced | View Log from the Scheduled Tasks menu bar. Windows runs Notepad to display the log file, which is stored in text format in C:\Windows\SchedLgU.txt (assuming that Windows is installed in C:\Windows). Log entries consist of several lines of text, as shown here:

```
"Activation reminder.job" (oobebaln.exe)
    Finished 4/3/2003 1:39:35 PM
    Result: The task completed with an exit code of (0).
```

The first line describes the program, and the subsequent lines report on the outcome of running the program.

Sometimes schedule tasks don't run. Here are two possible solutions:

- Give your user account a password (see Chapter 6). Scheduled tasks won't run if the current user account doesn't have a password, for security reasons.

- Make sure that the computer isn't starting in Selective Startup mode (see Chapter 2).

Running Programs in Compatibility Mode

Some older programs, especially games, don't run correctly under Windows XP. Windows XP has a new feature called *compatibility mode* that emulates previous versions of Windows—Windows 2000, NT 4.0, Me, 98, and 95. Compatibility mode can also set the display to the lower resolutions that were standard several years ago. If you have a program that used to run well but balks at Windows XP, compatibility mode may fix the problem.

 Don't use compatibility mode to run programs that are specifically designed for older versions of Windows. For example, a virus checker or disk cleanup program that is designed for Windows 95 won't work with Windows XP.

Windows XP comes with the Program Compatibility Wizard, which is part of the Help And Support Center. To run it, choose Start | Help And Support, search for Program Compatibility Wizard, and click its link. The wizard steps you through the compatibility settings you can use.

Configuring Compatibility Settings

To configure compatibility settings by hand, you can set all your compatibility mode options by creating or editing a shortcut for the program, or by working with the .exe (executable) file that you run to start the program (see Chapter 8). Right-click the shortcut or .exe file for the program that has compatibility problems, and choose Properties from the menu that appears. Click the Compatibility tab on the Properties dialog box (as shown in Figure 1-12). Your options are

- **Run This Program Using Compatibility Mode** Select this check box and select a previous version of Windows from the drop-down menu.

- **Run in 256 Colors** Some older programs look best in 256 colors (also known as *8-bit color*, a much smaller set of colors that are standard for Windows XP). This setting causes Windows to switch to 256 colors when you run the program and switch back when you exit.

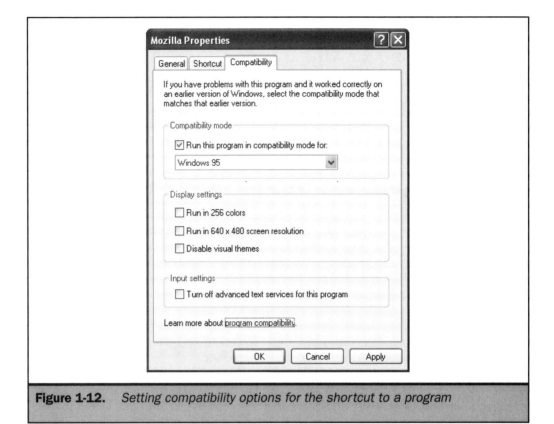

Figure 1-12.   *Setting compatibility options for the shortcut to a program*

- **Run in 640 × 480 Screen Resolution**   Some older programs are designed to run at a screen resolution lower than the usual 800 × 600 minimum for modern PCs. When the program runs, Windows adjusts the screen to the lower resolution, and reset it when you exit the program.

- **Disable Visual Themes**   If you use a desktop theme to dress up your screen, some older programs don't look right (see Chapter 11). This setting disables desktop themes while the program is running and switches them back on when you exit the program.

- **Turn Off Advanced Text Services For This Program**   Text services are part of Windows XP, and include hand-writing recognition, speech recognition, and handling for non-Roman alphabets. Older programs may not work with these services.

The Properties dialog box for the shortcut to a DOS program has several other tabs that you can use to configure the screen and keyboard; see the section "Setting Executable and Shortcut Properties" in Chapter 4.

Troubleshooting Compatibility Issues

Here are things to try if you are having trouble getting an older program to run with Windows XP:

■ Choose Start | Help And Support and click Find Compatible Hardware And Software For Windows XP in the Help And Support Center window. When you see the Product Search window, type the name of the program and click Search. Windows contacts Microsoft's database of compatible products over the Internet and displays a list of products that match the words you typed.

■ Check the Internet for upgrades or fixes. Go to the software publisher's web site, or start at Google (**google.com**) and search for the exact name of the program, along with the phrase "Windows XP."

■ If you upgraded your computer from an earlier version of Windows and the program was already installed before the upgrade, uninstall and reinstall the program.

■ Log in with an administrator account when you install the program. See Chapter 6 for the types of accounts; if your computer has only one user account, it's likely to be an administrator account. You can tell which account you are using by clicking Start—the user account name appears at the top of the Start menu. Also, some programs (especially games) run only when you are logged in as the same user that installed the program.

■ Log off all other users. If you have multiple user accounts (as described in Chapter 6), make sure that only one account is logged in: the administrator account you are using to install the program. Press CTRL-ALT-DEL and click the Users tab to see who is logged in.

■ If the program has an option to install the entire program or run part of the program from the CD, install the entire program (especially for games).

■ For games or other video-intensive programs, check whether you have an up-to-date video driver. Go to your video adapter manufacturer's web site to search for new drivers (see Chapter 13). Also check Microsoft's Game Support Center at **support.microsoft.com/default.aspx?PR=gms**.

The Complete Reference

Chapter 2

Troubleshooting Windows XP and Application Programs

E ven though Windows XP is more stable than its predecessors, it still hangs and crashes on occasion. Fortunately, Windows comes with a number of diagnostic tools that can help (most come from its Windows 2000 heritage). This chapter describes techniques for dealing with programs that hang or crash, stopping programs from running automatically, and what to do when Windows won't start.

Microsoft has also added a new tool, Remote Assistance, which allows Microsoft technicians (or knowledgeable friends of yours) to fix your computer over the phone (see Chapter 36).

An Overview of Troubleshooting Tools

When you run into trouble, you may need to look around inside Windows to search for anything that looks strange. We like to use the **System Information** program to look at the current system configuration (see section "More Diagnostic Tools" in Chapter 13).

The first programs to try if Windows or your programs appear to be damaged are Windows' built-in **Troubleshooters**, which are part of the Help And Support Center (see "Diagnosing Windows Problems with Troubleshooters," later in this chapter). If Troubleshooters can't track down the problem, try **System Restore**, a Windows program that can return you to a more reliable configuration (see "Returning Your System to a Predefined State with System Restore"). If you've made any changes to your computer's hardware lately, see the section "Hardware Drivers" in Chapter 13 to make sure that a bad device driver isn't your problem. Also check section "Diagnosing Display Problems" in Chapter 11.

If Windows won't start at all, other programs come into play. Dig out your Windows XP Setup CD and run the **Windows XP Setup Wizard** and choose its Repair option (see "Repairing Windows Using the Windows XP Setup Wizard"). Reinstalling Windows XP files from the CD may fix your problem. Alternatively, start up Windows in **Safe Mode**—a failsafe mode in which you can run System Restore, uninstall programs, or reinstall drivers (see "Starting Windows in Other Startup Modes"). If Safe Modem won't start, try the **Recovery Console**, a command-line interface that allows you to copy, rename, and delete files, copy files and folders from CDs, and fix your disk's boot sector and Master Boot Record (see "Using The Recovery Console").

With luck, Windows loads and your problem is with a program. You can use the **Windows Task Manager** to stop programs that have hung or crashed (see "Killing Programs Using the Windows Task Manager"). The System Configuration Utility (Msconfig) can help you prevent unwanted programs from loading when Windows starts up (see "Stopping Programs from Running at Startup"). The **Computer Management MMC** helps you view Windows system events and log system statistics to track down problems. If all else fails, **Dr. Watson** can store a "dump" of your system's state and the program that crashed, which may be useful when getting help from Microsoft or other software vendors. Chapter 13 describes another useful program, System Information.

When Windows crashes, won't start up, or acts strangely, the most likely culprit is the last program, Windows feature, or hardware component you installed. See Chapter 13 for how to solve hardware driver problems.

Diagnosing Windows Problems with Troubleshooters

Windows includes many *Troubleshooters*, step-by-step diagnostics that look for some of the most common problems and suggest solutions. The Troubleshooters, which are part of the Help And Support Center, start at a basic level and walk you through the details of system configuration changes.

Follow these steps to run a Troubleshooter:

1. Choose Start | Help And Support to display the Help And Support Center window. (Click the Home icon on the toolbar if this window is already open.)

2. Click the Fixing A Problem topic and select the topic that most closely matches the problems you're experiencing.

3. Follow its advice. Windows asks whether its suggestion solved the problem.

4. Click Yes or No and click Next to try the rest of the Troubleshooter's suggestions.

Returning Your System to a Predefined State with System Restore

Many people run into trouble with Windows right after they install a new program, upgrade a program to a newer version, or upgrade to a new version of Windows itself. When new program files interfere with the operation of other programs, you may wish that you could undo the installation and put your system back the way it was. Another common occurrence is that Windows' operation and performance degrades over time, and you may wish that you could return it to the way it ran a few weeks or months ago.

Windows XP contains a utility called System Restore, introduced in Windows Me. This program watches your system as you work, noting when program files are installed, changed, or deleted. It keeps a log of these changes for the last one to three weeks (depending on how many changes you make). You can also tell it to take a "snapshot"—a *restore point*—of the state of the system and store it away. For example, you might want to take a snapshot right after you have installed Windows from scratch, along with all the applications you rely on. Later, if you decide that an installation or some other fault has irreparably damaged your computer's stability, you can tell System Restore that you'd rather return your system to the way it was when you took the restore point snapshot.

When you tell System Restore to create a restore point, it makes copies of the critical files that define how the system works and what applications it is registered to use (the Registry, Windows program files, and other program files). It stores these copies, which are used later to restore the system to that state, in another location on your hard drive. The files that are stored include:

- The Windows Registry (described in Chapter 38)
- User profiles (described in Chapter 6)
- Files in the Windows system folder (usually C:\Windows)
- Boot files (files that Windows uses when starting up) like C:\Ntldr
- Program files (for example, .exe, .dll, and .com files)

System Restore restores programs, not documents. It doesn't restore Word documents, Excel spreadsheets, Access databases, text files, web pages, or files in the My Documents folder. To protect against major damage to your files, be sure to make regular backups.

Here are a few tips and warnings about using System Restore effectively:

- System Restore works best if you use it right away—as soon as possible after the system files develop a problem. If you've installed any programs since the restore point, System Restore restores old Registry entries and software files, effectively uninstalling your recently installed programs but leaving their files lying around. Installing restore points that are weeks or months old is risky.

- System Restore does *not* take the place of regular backups of the files you create and edit. System Restore does not take your computer back in time, as a product called GoBack from Roxio (**www.roxio.com/en/products/goback**) claims to do.

- If you want to make sure that restoring from a restore point won't affect a file, move the file to the My Documents folder.

- System Restore doesn't hold restore points forever. When it runs out of space, it deletes the oldest restore point on file. Most systems have room for restore points for only a week or so.

- If you start Windows in Diagnostic Startup mode (which you set using the System Configuration Utility, described in section "Stopping Programs from Running at Startup" later in this chapter), Windows deletes all your restore points. The same thing happens if you start in Selective Startup mode and deselect the Load System Services check box on the General tab of the System Configuration Utility's dialog box.

Automatic Restore Points

System Restore creates a number of restore points automatically:

- **Initial system checkpoint**   Created the first time you start your computer after installing Windows XP.

- **System checkpoints**   Created about every 24 hours that Windows is running (or as soon thereafter as you run Windows again).

- **Program installation checkpoints**   Created when you install a new program, it records the state of the system just *before* the installation.

- **Windows automatic update restore points**   Created when you install an update to Windows, it records the state of the system just *before* the installation.

In addition, you can create a restore point whenever you like, as described in the next two sections.

Running System Restore

System Restore is installed and running behind the scenes by default all the time that Windows is running. You can do only two things with it directly:

- Create a restore point for the current state of your system
- Return your system to a previously recorded restore point

To run the System Restore program, choose Start | All Programs | Accessories | Systems Tools | System Restore. You see the System Restore window, with two options: Restore My Computer To An Earlier Time and Create A Restore Point. If you've restored your system to a restore point recently, a third option also appears: Undo My Last Restoration.

Configuring System Restore

Although System Restore is running all the time by default, you can turn it off. To do so, to make sure that it's turned on, or to change its configuration, follow these steps:

1. Click Start, right-click My Computer, and choose Properties from the menu that appears. You see the System Properties window.

2. Click the System Restore tab, as shown in Figure 2-1.

3. Select the Turn Off System Restore On All Drives check box so it contains a check mark if you *don't* want to be able to use System Restore. Deselect it if you want System Restore runs in the background all the time, creating restore points to which you can return. (We recommend that you leave it running—leave the check box blank.)

Caution   *Turning off System Restore deletes all your existing restore points!*

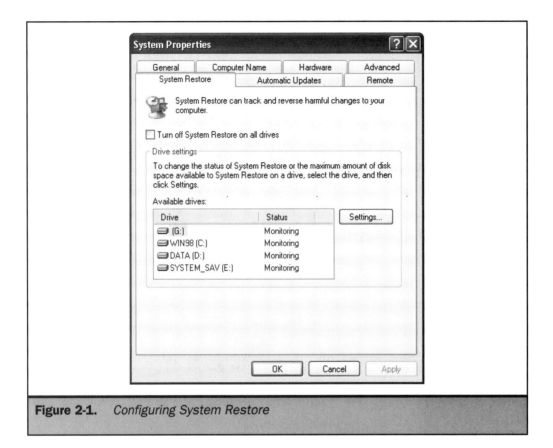

Figure 2-1. *Configuring System Restore*

4. You can control how much space System Restore uses for its restore points. Click a drive in the Available Drives box and click the Settings button to display the Disk Space Usage slider for that drive. Move the slider to specify how much of your hard disk (the disk on which the Windows program file is stored, if you have more than one) may be used to store restore points.

Tip *If you have a dual-boot computer, turn off System Restore for all disks or partitions for other operating systems, including other versions of Windows. When you are running Windows XP, you shouldn't be installing software on those disks or partitions. If you have disks or partitions that contain only data (no programs), you can turn off System Restore for them, too.*

5. Click OK on both dialog boxes to save any changes.

Note *System Restore won't run if you have less than 200MB free on your hard disk (the hard disk or partition that contains the Windows system folder, if you have more than one). It notifies you of the problem and offers to run Disk Cleanup.*

Creating a Restore Point

You can create a restore point any time you think you are about to make a change to the system that might be risky. It's a good idea to create a restore point when everything is working fine, so you can get your Windows system back to that state again later. A restore point you create is called a *manual checkpoint*. To create a restore point of your own, follow these steps:

1. Choose Start | All Programs | Accessories | Systems Tools | System Restore.

2. Select Create A Restore Point and click Next.

3. Enter a description of the save point for future reference. If you are installing software immediately after creating the save point, make note of it.

4. Click Next. System Restore creates the restore point and asks you to confirm the information about it.

5. Read the description to make sure you haven't missed anything. Click Back if you want to change the description you entered. Click OK.

That's it. You've finished. If you need to access System Restore when there's a serious problem that prevents you from restarting your computer normally, reboot into Safe Mode (see "Starting Windows in Other Startup Modes," later in this chapter).

Restoring Your System to a Restore Point

If your system starts acting strangely, if you get a virus, or if you delete a program file by accident, you can return the program files on your system to the way they were when System Restore created a restore point.

 Note   *If your system has a virus, the restore points may be infected too, unless the virus arrived after the restore point was made.*

Follow these steps:

1. Choose Start | All Programs | Accessories | Systems Tools | System Restore.

2. Select Restore My Computer To An Earlier Time and click Next.

3. You see a calendar of the current month. Days for which there is a restore point appear highlighted. Click a date to see a list of the restore points created on that day (as shown in Figure 2-2).

4. Click the restore point to which you want to return your system and click Next.

5. System Restore reminds you to close all other programs before continuing. Do so and click OK.

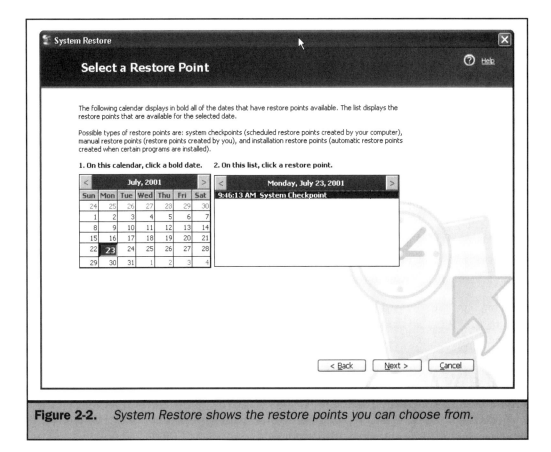

Figure 2-2. *System Restore shows the restore points you can choose from.*

6. System Restore shows the date, time, and description of the restore point you chose for your confirmation. Click Next. The restoration may take a few minutes and includes restarting Windows. When Windows is running again, you see the System Restore window, reporting whether the restore was successful.

7. Click OK.

Another way to return your system to a restore point is by starting your computer in Safe Mode (see "Starting Windows in Other Startup Modes" later in this chapter). After you log in and before you see the Windows desktop, Windows displays a dialog box about Safe Mode; click the Yes button to use Windows in Safe Mode or click No to start System Restore.

Undoing a Restoration

If you return your system to a restore point and it doesn't solve the problem you were facing, you can undo the restoration by following these steps:

1. Choose Start | All Programs | Accessories | Systems Tools | System Restore.

2. Choose Undo My Last Restoration and click Next.

3. System Restore prompts you to close all other programs and confirm the operation that you want to undo. In the process of undoing the restoration, it restarts Windows.

What To Do When Windows Won't Start

The worst problems prevent Windows from starting up at all. If this happens, don't despair. Windows comes with several programs that can fix your problem even when Windows itself can't run. The Windows XP Setup Wizard may be able to repair your program, or you can start Windows in an alternative mode, like Safe Mode or Diagnostic Startup mode. You can also start your system in the Recovery Console to repair Windows.

Repairing Windows Using the Windows XP Setup Wizard

The Windows XP Setup Wizard may be able to repair a corrupted Windows XP installation. Follow these steps:

1. Start the Setup Wizard from the Windows XP CD-ROM by putting the CD-ROM into your CD drive and choosing Install Windows XP. You may need to configure your computer to boot from the CD (see the Appendix for instructions).

2. Press ENTER each time that the Setup Wizard asks whether you want to install Windows XP (even though you don't want to!). Don't choose to run the Recovery Console, which is a different tool described later in this chapter.

3. After the first reboot, the Setup Wizard displays a list of existing installations of Windows XP and asks whether you want to repair it (see the Appendix).

4. Press R to attempt the repair. The Setup Wizard tries to repair the installation, and then reboots.

5. Choose the Windows XP installation that you want to repair and press F3 to restart. After you reboot back into the Windows XP Setup, you can quit the Setup Wizard without reinstalling Windows by pressing F3 each time the wizard asks whether to install Windows. You might want to remove the Windows XP Setup CD before the system reboots to try rebooting into Windows.

Some computers can't be configured to boot from a CD, preventing you from using the software on the Windows XP Setup CD. One solution is to use another computer to download and create a set of floppy disks from which you can start the machine and access the Windows XP Setup CD. Go to the Microsoft support web site at **support.microsoft.com** and search for article Q310994 or "Windows XP setup boot disks."

If Windows Hangs on Shutdown

If you use an Input Method Editor (a Windows add-on that handles Asian languages), Windows may occasionally hang when you try to shut the system down. An update is available to solve this problem. Go to the Microsoft support web site at **support.microsoft.com** and search for article Q307274. Click the link to download and install the "Restarting Windows XP" update.

Starting Windows in Other Startup Modes

If the Windows installation on your hard disk is intact, you can start Windows in one of several special *startup modes* that provide limited function and help diagnose problems. Nearly every mode has a purpose and the added options give you options when disaster strikes.

Press F8 during Windows startup (when you see the boot menu if you have a dual-boot system) to see a menu of startup modes:

- **Safe Mode** Windows starts by using the simplest possible set of drivers and hardware devices. All of Windows' basic functions are available, but the screen runs in basic VGA mode (640 × 480, 16 colors), and no devices are available beyond the screen, keyboard, and disks. You can edit, copy, and delete files; install or uninstall programs; update hardware device drivers; restore backed-up files; or run the Registry Editor (described in Chapter 38). You can also run System Restore (described in the section "Returning Your System to a Predefined State with System Restore" earlier in this chapter) to fix your Windows installation. If Windows still doesn't start, try Safe Mode With Command Prompt or the Recovery Console.

- **Safe Mode With Networking** Windows starts by using the simplest possible set of drivers and hardware devices but also includes simple networking components. This mode is helpful if you need to access files over a network *before* you can fix your computer, the tools you need to fix your computer are located on a remote machine, or you would like to be able to take advantage of the new Remote Assistance feature (see Chapter 36).

- **Safe Mode With Command Prompt** In addition to starting with the simplest possible set of drivers and hardware devices, Windows further reduces the overhead by not loading the Graphical User Interface—you communicate with it by typing DOS-style commands into a Cmd.exe window. Most DOS commands work here, along with many Recovery Console commands (described in the next section). See Chapter 4 for how to type commands in the Cmd.exe window. To restart from this mode, press CTRL-ALT-DEL to display the Windows Task Manager window and choose Shutdown | Restart from the menu.

■ **Enable Boot Logging**   Windows starts normally but logs all the drivers it loads in the file Ntbtlog.txt (usually stored in C:\Windows). Use this mode if you think that a device driver might be the problem.

■ **Enable VGA Mode**   Windows loads the standard, super-compatible Microsoft VGA driver, which can often assist in reducing conflicts until you can fix the problem. Use this mode if your video driver isn't working.

■ **Last Known Good Configuration**   Windows starts using the last configuration that did *not* to have known problems. It uses backup copies of your Registry and device driver files. This backup system isn't as reliable as System Restore. Each time you start Windows normally (rather than in Safe Mode), Windows assumes that the Windows configuration is good, so if you have doubts about your Windows installation, log on using Safe Mode until Windows is fixed.

■ **Directory Services Restore Mode**   This mode is not used in either Windows XP Home Edition or Professional: it is used on Windows servers.

■ **Debugging Mode**   Windows starts normally but sends debugging information through a serial cable to another computer (rarely used except by Windows system programmers).

■ **Diagnostic Startup**   This mode, which is similar to Safe Mode, isn't displayed on the Windows startup menu that appears when you press F8. Instead, you enable it by using the System Configuration Utility (see "Stopping Programs from Running at Startup," later in this chapter).

■ **Selective Startup**   You enable this by using the System Configuration Utility (see "Stopping Programs from Running at Startup"). You can choose which programs and services Windows loads at startup.

Note   *Windows XP doesn't run on top of DOS, as early versions of Windows did. As a result, Windows cannot start up in DOS mode. You can still start up DOS from a floppy disk, Zip drive (if your BIOS supports it), or bootable CD-ROM (see Chapter 4). When running DOS, you can't read disks formatted with NTFS.*

Using The Recovery Console

If you can't start Windows up, you can try to fix the problem using the Recovery Console, a DOS-like command-line system. To enter the Recovery Console:

1. Boot from the Windows XP CD-ROM and press **R** when the text mode part of the setup begins. You may need to configure your computer to boot from the CD (see the Appendix for instructions), and you may need to press a key or select options from a menu.

2. When Windows Setup runs from the CD, it loads a bunch of installation files and drivers. When prompted, press ENTER to start the setup (even though you don't want to set up Windows).

3. The Welcome To Setup screen prompts you to press **R** to run the Recovery Console.

4. If you have more than one version of Windows XP installed, choose the installation you want to fix by pressing its number from the menu and pressing ENTER.

5. A prompt asks you to enter your Administrator password. Type the password to your computer's Administrator user account and press ENTER. If your Administrator account has no password (which we don't recommend; see Chapter 6 to add a password once you get Windows running), just press ENTER.

6. When you see the command prompt (usually C:\WINDOWS>), type a command and press ENTER.

Now you are ready to try to fix your Windows installation. If you wrote down any names of files that were indicated as being corrupted or the cause of your systems recent demise, that's good.

When you are ready to leave the Recovery Console to see whether Windows can now start normally, type **exit**.

| Tip | *If you can start Windows, you can install the Recovery Console as a startup option by putting the Windows XP CD-ROM in the CD drive, choosing Start | Run, typing* **d:\i386\winnt32.exe /cmdcons** *(replacing d: with your CD-ROM drive letter if it's not D:) and clicking OK. After you give this command, a dialog box appears to ask whether you want to install the Recovery Console: click Yes. Now Recovery Console appears as an option on the boot menu that Windows XP uses for multiboot systems, which is described in the Appendix. Installing the Recovery Console takes about 7MB on your hard disk.* |

For more information about the Recovery Console, see the Microsoft KnowledgeBase article about it: start at **support.microsoft.com** and search for article Q307654.

Recovery Console File Management Commands

In the Recovery Console, you can use commands to look at or change files to fix your Windows problem. However, you are limited to the Windows program folder (usually C:\Windows), the root folder of the same partition (usually C:\), the root directories of other partitions or disks, and any folder on removable disks (like floppies, CDs, or Zip disks). If you have installed the Recovery Console program on your hard disk, you can also write files in that folder.

In Recovery Console commands, filenames can't contain spaces. To work with filenames that contain spaces, enclose the entire path or file name in double quotes.

Here are a few useful commands for looking around your hard disk (we shown them in uppercase, so that they stand out, but you can use uppercase or lowercase).

Listing Drives and Partitions with MAP   To see a list of the drive letters on your system with the drives and partitions to which they refer, type **MAP** and press ENTER. You see a listing like this:

```
E:    NTFS     3499MB        \Device\Harddisk0\Partition1
C:    FAT32    2165MB        \Device\Harddisk0\Partition2
D:    NTFS     3593MB        \Device\Harddisk0\Partition3
A:                          \Device\Floppy0
E:                          \Device\CdRom0
```

Listing Directory and File Contents with DIR and TYPE   This command displays a listing of the files in the directory you are currently in, with the modification date, modification time, attributes, size, and name, like this:

```
The volume in drive G is XP Pro
The volume Serial Number is 70f2-5ed8

Directory of G:\

02/08/02   02:17p   d-------              0   Documents and Settings
07/15/02   09:41p   -a-hs---      401752064   hiberfil.sys
03/12/02   02:32p   -a------            151   liprefs.js
02/20/02   11:04a   d-------              0   My Documents
05/24/02   09:41a   d-------              0   My Music
06/11/02   08:20a   d-r-----              0   Program Files
06/11/02   03:47a   d--hs---              0   RECYCLER
07/18/02   10:10a   d--hs---              0   System Volume Information
07/15/02   10:10a   d-------              0   WINDOWS
         10 file(s)    401752215 bytes
       414302208 bytes free
```

The attributes that appear to the right of the date and time are

- **d**   Directories (folders)
- **h**   Hidden

- **s**   System file or folder
- **e**   Encrypted
- **r**   Read-only
- **a**   Ready for archive (changed since the last backup)
- **c**   Compressed

You can use an asterisk to represent part of the filename. For example, to list all text files, type this:

```
DIR *.txt
```

You can display the contents of a text file on the screen by typing **TYPE** *filename* and pressing ENTER (replace *filename* with the name of the file). Don't try this with non-text files—the output looks like garbage. This command is useful for listing .ini and other text configuration files.

Moving to Another Folder with CD   To move to a different folder (directory), type **CD** and a space and the name of the folder. For example, to move to the System32 folder that is contained in the current folder, type:

```
CD system32
```

If you want to back out of a folder and return to the "parent" folder of the one you are in, type **CD ..** and press ENTER. The two periods indicate the folder one level up.

You can create a new folder in the current folder by typing **MKDIR** followed by a space and the name of the new folder.

*To move to the Windows system folder (usually C:\Windows), type **systemroot** and press ENTER.*

Copying Files with COPY and EXPAND   To copy a file from one location to another (one folder to another, one filename to another, or one disk to another), type **COPY** *sourcename1 targetname2*. You can't copy onto removable drives, only to your hard disk. Unlike the DOS COPY command, you can't use wildcard (* or ?) characters to copy multiple files, and you can't copy folders.

Most of the Windows XP program files on the Setup CD are contained in .cab (cabinet) files, which are compressed to save space. If you need to copy all the files from .cab files on the Windows XP Setup CD (or other sources), you can use the EXPAND command. Move to the drive and folder to which you want copy the files and type **EXPAND** *sourcename* and press ENTER (for example, type **EXPAND D:\SUPPORT\TOOLS\ SUPPORT.CAB** to extract all the files from this .cab file).

The COPY command can extract files from .cab files and expand them: use COPY to copy one file from a .cab, and EXPAND to copy all the files that the .cab file contains.

Deleting Files with DEL   To delete a file (or files), type **DEL** followed by a space and the name of the file to delete. You must indicate a file by name and extension. This can be dangerous, so be very cautious and always triple-check whatever it is you plan on deleting. For example:

```
DEL filename.txt
```

Changing File Attributes with ATTRIB   Files and folder can be marked as read-only (R), Windows system (S), hidden (H), or other attributes. If you need to turn a file attribute (usually to remove the read-only attribute prior to changing a file), type this command:

```
ATTRIB +x filename
```

Replace the *x* with the attribute (R, S, or H). To turn the attribute off, replace the plus sign with a minus sign. For example, this removes the read-only attribute from the Sample.mov file:

```
ATTRIB -R sample.mov
```

Checking Disk Integrity with CHKDSK   The Microsoft Check Disk utility has been upstaged by ScanDisk since Windows 95 shipped, but no more. CHKDSK is far more capable these days and can even work with NTFS-formatted disks. To get basic info and run a simple test, type **CHKDSK** and press ENTER. Windows checks the integrity of the current partition and lists the current space usage. If CHKDSK indicates that the drive has errors, type **CHKDSK /R** to fix the errors and recover information from the bad sectors.

   To get a listing of all commands in the Recovery Console, simply type HELP at the prompt and press ENTER.

Recovery Console Commands to Repair Windows

In addition to the family DOS commands in the previous section, the Recovery Console includes commands that may fix a non-booting system.

Editing the Boot.ini File with BOOTCFG   If Windows won't start, you may need edit or rebuild your Boot.ini file, the file that determines which versions of Windows appear on your boot menu. (See the Appendix for how to create a multiboot installation with more than one version of Windows.) To find out what Windows XP, 2000, or NT installations exist on your system, type **BOOTCFG /SCAN** and press ENTER. You see a listing like this:

```
Scanning all disks for Windows installations.
Pease wait, since this may take a while...
The Windows installation scan was successful.
Note: These results are stored statically for this session.
      If the disk configuration changes during this session,
      in order to get an updated scan, you must first reboot
      the machine and then rescan the disks.

Total identified Windows installs: 2

[?1?]: F:\WINDOWS
[?2?]: C:\WINDOWS
```

The **BOOTCFG /LIST** command lists the contents of the Boot.ini file, so you can compare it with the results of the installation scan. If a Windows installation is missing from your Boot.ini file, type **BOOTCFG /ADD** and choose which installation to add. To rebuild the Boot.ini file, type **BOOTCFG /REBUILD**. The Bootcfg program displays each Windows installation it found and asks whether to add include it in your Boot.ini.

Managing Your Disk Partitions with DISKPART   If you have more than one operating system (OS) installed, you probably have each in a separate partition. Even for single-OS machines, we like to put our data in a separate partition from Windows, so we don't have to disturb it when we reinstall or upgrade Windows. Chapter 33 explains how to create and manage partitions from within Windows.

However, if you can't start Windows, you may need to work with your partitions from the Recovery Console. The DISKPART command can create or delete partitions, like the FDISK command that comes with Windows 9x/Me. However, unlike third-party programs like Partition Magic, DISKPART can't resize or move partitions.

To see a list of your partitions, add new partitions, or delete existing partitions, type **DISKPART** and press ENTER. You see a text screen that lists the partitions on your system, along with the unpartitioned space. To create a new partition, select the unused space (by pressing UP ARROW and DOWN ARROW) and press **C**. To delete a partition, select it and press **D**. When you are done, press ESC.

If you create a partition, you need to format it before you can store files and folder in it. Type this command:

```
FORMAT d: /FS:filesystem
```

Replace *d* with the drive letter of the partition to format and *filesystem* with the file system to use (usually NTFS or FAT32). For example, to format drive E: as an NTFS partition, type

```
FORMAT e: /FS:ntfs
```

 Formatting a drive or partition deletes its contents!

Rewriting Boot Information with FIXBOOT and FIXMBR   The master boot record (or MBR, described in Chapter 33 contains the tiny program that gets the entire startup process going when you turn on or restart your computer. If the MBR is wrong, your computer can't find the Windows startup files. To rewrite your MBR, type **FIXMBR** and press ENTER.

Once the MBR loads, it runs programs in the system partition's boot sector to continue loading Windows. If this information is garbled, you can rewrite it by typing **FIXBOOT** and pressing ENTER. Your system knows which partition is the system partition; however, you can override this by specifying a drive letter (for example, FIXBOOT D:).

The system partition (from which your computer boots) must contain at least two files, Ntldr and Ntdetect.com. If these two files are missing you can copy them from the Windows XP CD-ROM with these commands:

```
COPY d:\i386\ntldr c:
COPY d:\i386\ntdetect.com c:
```

These commands assume that the CD is in drive D: and that your system partition is drive C:.

Creating Boot Floppy Disks

Historically, one of the steps in the Windows installation process created a startup floppy disk, or *boot floppy disk* (also called an *emergency boot disk* or *EBD*). The idea was that if the file system on your hard disk was damaged, you could start your computer from the startup floppy disk and repair the damage enough to make the hard disk bootable. With Windows XP, you can create three types of boot floppies: a quick boot disk, a set of floppies from which you can run the Windows XP Setup CD, or a DOS boot floppy.

Creating a Quick Boot Disk

You can create a floppy disk from which you can start a system whose master boot record is damaged. The floppy contains the hidden files needed to start a Windows XP system.

1. Open a Command Prompt window by choosing Start | All Programs | Accessories | Command Prompt (or choose Start | Run, type **cmd**, and press ENTER). See Chapter 4 for information about the Command Prompt window.

2. Put a floppy disk in the diskette drive (A:). (Be sure to format the floppy, even if it's already formatted, because this procedure requires a disk that is formatted by Windows NT, 2000, or XP.)

3. Type **format a:** and press ENTER. Windows formats the floppy, erasing whatever was on it.

4. Type each of these commands, pressing ENTER after each:

```
xcopy c:\ntldr a: /h
xcopy c:\ntdetect.com a: /h
xcopy c:\boot.ini a: /h
```

The three files you copied are hidden files, so the floppy appears to be empty. For more information, see **www.xxcopy.com/xxcopy/xxcopy33.htm**.

Creating Floppies from Which You Can Run Windows XP Setup

You can create a set of floppies from which you can boot from the Windows XP Setup CD; for instructions, go to the Microsoft support web site at **support.microsoft.com** and search for article Q310994.

Creating a DOS Boot Floppy

You can still make a boot floppy in Windows XP by using a single 1.44MB floppy disk. However, booting from this floppy starts the machine in DOS, which can't read NTFS-formatted disks, only FAT and FAT32 disks. Check how your hard disks are formatted before trying to access them from a boot floppy.

To make a boot floppy, follow these steps:

1. Write-enable the disk and put it in the disk drive.

2. Choose Start | My Computer.

3. Right-click the 3½ Floppy (A:) icon and choose Format from the shortcut menu that appears. You see the Format 3½ Floppy dialog box.

4. Select the Create An MS-DOS Startup Disk check box.

5. Click Start. Windows creates a bootable startup disk.

6. Remove the disk from the drive, write-protect it, label it, and put it in a safe place.

If you use this floppy disk to start your system, you see the DOS command prompt, described in Chapter 4. No drivers are loaded, so you can't use your CD-ROM or other hardware.

Dealing with Hung or Crashed Programs

Despite all the testing that software vendors do, Windows and the applications you run under it have bugs and sometimes *hang* (stop responding) or *crash* (fail altogether). When an application crashes, Windows displays a box telling you about it. There's not much you can do at that point, other than click OK. Windows may display a dialog box offering to send an error report to Microsoft about the problem, as described in the sidebar "Windows Error Reporting."

Tip *Restart Windows after a hang or crash in case the program damaged files or Windows' internal operations.*

Killing Programs Using the Windows Task Manager

If a program hangs, you generally can force Windows to stop the hung program. Press CTRL-ALT-DEL to open the Windows Task Manager dialog box, shown here:

On the Applications tab of the Windows Task Manager, a hung program usually has the notation "Not responding" in the Status column. (Healthy programs are designated as "Running.") Select the name of the program and click End Task. Normally the program exits.

If all else fails, press CTRL-ALT-DEL to display the Windows Task Manager and then choose Shut Down | Restart from the menu bar: Windows should restart. If the hang was particularly nasty, Windows runs ChkDsk so that disk errors can be repaired (see Chapter 34).

For more information about the Windows Task Manager, see Chapter 35.

Windows Error Reporting

Windows XP can call home when it has a problem. That is, Windows can use your Internet connection to send an error report back to Microsoft's developers. By collecting hang and crash information, Microsoft can fix problems with Windows more effectively.

When a program crashes or hangs, you see a dialog box asking whether to send a report. Microsoft promises that the information in the error report doesn't contain any personal information about you, just system configuration information about your computer, and that the information will be used only for software debugging. However, you also have the option of turning Windows Error Reporting off. Click Start, right-click My Computer, and choose Properties from the menu that appears. On the System Properties dialog box, click the Advanced tab. Click the Error Reporting button to display the Error Reporting dialog box:

You can choose whether to do any error reporting and whether to send reports only about Windows errors or about application program errors as well.

Stopping Programs from Running at Startup

When you start Windows, other programs may start up automatically, which can be very convenient (see Chapter 1). It's not always easy, however, to *stop* a program from running automatically when you start Windows.

Where Windows Stores Startup Programs

Here are three places to look for the entry that causes Windows to run the program:

- **Startup folder**   Make sure that a shortcut for the program isn't on the StartUp menu (Start | All Programs | Startup). If a shortcut for the program is there, delete it. (Choose Start | All Programs | Startup, right-click the item for the program, and choose Delete from the menu that appears.)

- **Registry**   Examine the Registry for an entry that runs the program (see Chapter 38). You can use the Registry Editor to remove the offending entry, after making a backup of the Registry. These Registry hives contain entries that run programs automatically:

  ```
  \HKEY_LOCAL_MACHINE\Software\Microsoft\Windows\CurrentVersion\Run
  \HKEY_LOCAL_MACHINE\Software\Microsoft\Windows\CurrentVersion\RunOnce
  \HKEY_CURRENT_USER\Software\Microsoft\Windows\CurrentVersion\Run
  \HKEY_USERS\.DEFAULT\Software\Microsoft\Windows\CurrentVersion\Run
  ```

- **Win.ini**   For older programs, look for a line in your Win.ini file that runs the program (see Chapter 37). The line would start with "run=" or "load=" in the windows section.

Choosing Which Programs to Run at Startup

To see and control what runs automatically, you can run the System Configuration Utility. Choose Start | Run, type **msconfig**, and press ENTER. Click the Startup tab, shown in Figure 2-3, to see a list of the programs that run at startup. You can use this program to display and edit the Win.ini file (but make a backup first). On the General tab, you can choose

- **Normal Startup**   Load all device drivers and start all Windows services specified in the System.ini, Win.ini, and Registry. When you choose this option, all the check boxes on the System.ini, Win.ini, Services, and Startup tabs are automatically selected.

- **Diagnostic Startup**   Load Windows with a minimum set of drivers and services. When you choose this option, all the check boxes on the System.ini, Win.ini, Services, and Startup tabs are automatically deselected.

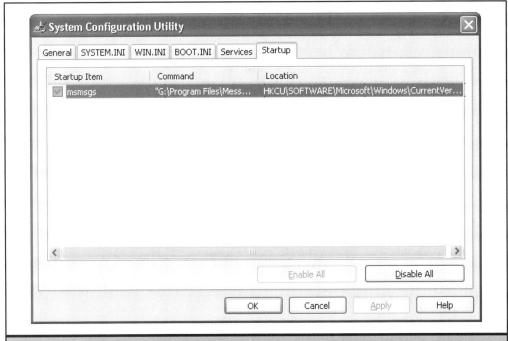

Figure 2-3. *The System Configuration Utility (Msconfig) displays programs that start automatically (in this case, Windows Messenger).*

- **Selective Startup** Loads Windows with only the services and programs that you specify on the System.ini, Win.ini, Service, and Startup tabs. When you deselect any checkbox on these tabs, this setting switches to Selective Startup automatically.

To stop a program from running at startup, follow these steps:

1. Choose Selective Startup on the General tab.

2. On System.ini, Win.ini, Services, and Startup tabs, click the Enable All button to select all the checkboxes.

3. On each of these tabs, deselect the items that appear to be part of the program that you don't want to run. Most programs appear only on the Startup tab; only old programs (those written before the development of the Registry) usually have entries in System.ini or Win.ini. Click the Hide All Microsoft Services checkbox on the Services tab to make finding non-Microsoft programs easier.

4. Click OK and Restart to restart your system. When Windows reloads, it omits the items for which you cleared the checkboxes. It displays a message to remind you that you are using Selective Startup.

5. If you plan to continue using Selective Startup to prevent programs from loading automatically, select the check box that prevents this message from displaying each time you start Windows. If you don't select this check box, you'll also see the System Configuration Utility window each time Windows starts.

Alternatively, you can choose Normal Startup on the General tab (which selects the checkboxes on the other tabs) and then deselect the check boxes for programs and services you don't want to run.

  To stop Windows Messenger from loading, see Chapter 25. Removing it from the Startup tab of the System Configuration Utility is only the first step!

Diagnosing System Problems Using the Microsoft Management Console (MMC)

Like Windows 2000, Windows XP collects lots of system tools into one place—the Microsoft Management Console (MMC). The window that displays the MMC is titled Computer Management, but the program that provides the information (what is referred to as a *framework*) is the MMC. The MMC can be the "frame" for a number of other "pictures." The pictures are called *snap-ins*, and each snap-in adds new capabilities to the MMC.

Note *Most snap-ins are targeted at systems administrators, information technology professionals, and all-around nerds. Though an integral part of Windows and its general health, you will not commonly find yourself poking around the MMC if you have a choice between that and playing a few rounds of Solitaire.*

To display the MMC, choose Start, right-click My Computer, and choose Manage from the menu that appears. The MMC is shown in Figure 2-4.

The Event Viewer and Performance Logs And Alerts icons may be useful in tracking down system problems. The Device Manager lists the hardware that makes up your system, along with the device drivers that allow Windows XP to work with the hardware. (See Chapter 13 for how to diagnose hardware problems with the Device Manager.)

Note *Windows XP Professional includes an additional System Tool that doesn't appear in Windows XP Home Edition: Local Users And Groups, which is used for managing advanced user profiles and profiles for groups of users (see Chapter 6).*

Viewing Event Logs with the Event Viewer

As Windows runs it makes notes of what's going on, and the Event Viewer displays these logs. The information contained in these logs may help determine the cause of system instability.

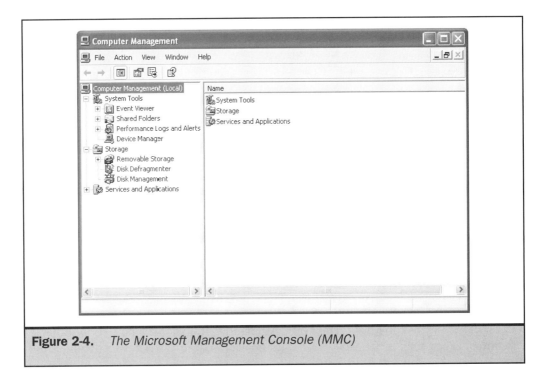

Figure 2-4.   *The Microsoft Management Console (MMC)*

In the Computer Management MMC window, click the Event Viewer's plus box to reveal three logs of recorded operational data:

- **Application**   Events generated by applications and programs.

- **Security**   Security-related events, anything from the number of bad logins recorded to when and where objects were added to or taken away from the computers file system.

- **System**   Events that are recorded by the operating system itself, including events, errors, and failures that occur in Windows XP's files, functions, or device drivers.

If you find an event that may have caused your system problem, double-click it (or right-click it and choose Properties) to see more information about the event, including the date, time, type of event, user (if any), computer name, and a description.

    If you want to see only certain types of events, choose View | Filter from the Computer Management MMC window's menu bar and choose the types of events to include in your display.

Logging Performance Data and Alerts

The Performance Logs And Alerts component of the MMC stores information about the state of the system. It records information about how well Windows performs and what tolerances, if any, it approaches or exceeds during normal operation. The logs are stored (usually in the Perflogs folder on the same disk on which Windows is installed), and you can configure Windows to store them in text files that you can import into a spreadsheet program, a database program, or a program designed specifically for analyzing logs. *Counter logs* record system statistics at regular intervals, *trace logs* record what was happening at the time of particular events, and *alerts* send a message or run a program when a counter hits a preset value.

By default, the logging and alert functions are not configured except for one sample Counter log that is installed with Windows. Logging is useful on large networks, where one network administrator is responsible for the functioning of many computers, but individual users rarely use them.

Most people never use the MMC Performance Logs And Alerts' logs, but if you want to try them, follow these steps:

1. In the Computer Management MMC window, click the Performance Logs And Alerts plus box.

2. Right-click Counter Logs and choose New Log Settings from the menu that appears.

3. In the Name box, type a descriptive name for your new log (for example, type **Disk Access** if you plan to log what percentage of the time the system is active that the disk is idle). Click OK. You see a Properties dialog box for your new log, like this one:

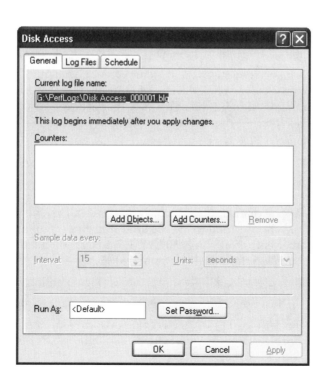

4. To specify which counter(s) to track, click the Add Counters button, which opens the Add Counters dialog box:

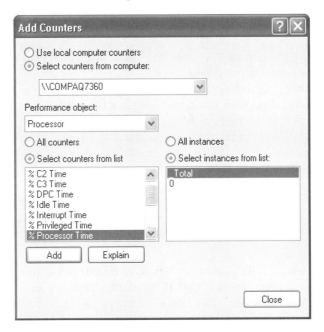

5. The Select Counters From Computer item is selected with your computer's name below it. Leave this setting, so that you are logging your own computer's performance. (Network administrators can log the performances of computers throughout the network they manage.)

6. Set the Performance Object box to the part of your system for which you want to see counters. (You can click the Explain button to get information on the selection option on this and the other lists.) For example, if you are tracking disk access, set it to PhsyicalDisk.

7. The Select Counters From List list displays counters about the performance object you choose. Choose the statistic that you want to track.

8. The Select Instances From List list enables you to choose whether to log the totals for all the instances of the performance object on your system, or separately for each instance. For example, if you chose PhysicalDisk for the Performance Object, you can choose Total to log the total statistics for all disks, or you can choose the other entry (ours says "0 C: F: D:" to include the three partitions on our hard disk) to log the statistic separately for each disk.

9. Click the Add button to add this counter to your log. (Nothing appears to happen.)

10. Repeat steps 6 through 9 for each statistic that you want to log.

11. Click Close. Back in the Disk Access dialog box, the Counters list now includes an entry for each counter that you added—something like this:

```
\\MORTICIA\PhysicalDisk(0 C:)\% Idle Time
```

12. Windows usually logs a sample every 15 seconds. You can change that interval by changing the value in the Interval box.

13. If you want to store the log file somewhere other than in the Perflogs folder on the same disk on which Windows is installed, click the Log Files tab and change the settings there.

14. If you want to store the log file in a format that you can import into a database or spreadsheet file, click the Log Files tab and change the Log File Type. (Windows defaults to a Binary File type, which can't be imported.) To import the data into a spreadsheet or database program, choose a text file, either comma-delimited or tab-delimited.

15. If you want to control when logging starts and stops (rather than just starting now and continuing indefinitely), click the Schedule tab and make your changes

16. Click OK to create your log. Now the log appears in the Counter Logs section of the Performance Logs And Alerts item in the MMC Computer Management window.

You can start and stop logging by selecting the log from the list and clicking the Stop The Selected Log button (a black box) on the MMC toolbar. To start it again, click the Start The Selected Log button (the right-pointing "play" arrow).

To view the log file after it has collected some data, you can open the log file, which is usually in C:\Perflogs and has the name you typed when you created the log, with a number at the end (for example C:\Perflogs\Disk Access_000001.blg). Double-click it to open the Performance window, a version of the Performance Logs And Alerts MMC snap-in with one additional component, System Monitor. This window is a live viewer into the operations that you have selected in your log.

Reporting Problems with Dr. Watson

Like detective Sherlock Holmes's trusty sidekick of the same name, Dr. Watson is a debugger program helps track down evildoers (in this case, malicious programs). When a program fails (crashes or hangs), Dr. Watson stores a log file that the program's support department can use to figure out what went wrong. Unlike the Dr. Watson program that came with previous versions of Windows, Windows XP's version runs automatically—you don't have to start it.

When a program fails, Dr. Watson creates a log file called Drwtsn32.log and stores it in the C:\Documents And Settings\All Users\Application Data\Microsoft\Dr Watson folder (assuming that Windows is installed on C:). The log file includes the system state and the program instructions that led up to the failure. When you contact your software vendor about the problem, they may ask you either to open the saved report and read them some of the saved information or, more likely, e-mail or upload the entire log file to them.

To configure Dr. Watson, choose Start | Run, type **drwtsn32**, and press ENTER. The Dr. Watson For Windows dialog box contains settings that control what information Dr. Watson stores in its log files, where logs files are stored, and how it notifies you that it has created a log file.

Previous versions of Windows came with a version of Dr. Watson named Drwatson.exe. Microsoft recommends using the updated Drwtsn32 instead.

The
Complete
Reference

Chapter 3

Installing and Uninstalling Programs and Windows Components

As you set up a new Windows XP system, you'll probably need to install new programs, or new features from the Windows XP Setup CD. Or, you may want to do just the reverse—uninstall programs that you no longer use or that are outdated. You can free up some disk space by uninstalling Windows components that you never use. Windows comes with a built-in system for installing and uninstalling programs. Windows XP Service Pack 1 includes a new feature that allows you to "hide" some of Windows nonuninstallable features, like Internet Explorer and Outlook Express.

When you install a program, Windows keeps track of what types of files the program can create and edit. You can change which program Windows uses to open each file type; for example, you might want to tell Windows to use a different graphics editor when opening your digital camera's photo files.

This chapter describes how to install and uninstall various kinds of programs, including Windows XP features, as well as controlling Windows' file associations.

 Windows XP omits a few programs that came with Windows 98 and Me, including FrontPage Express (a web page editor) and Microsoft Chat. If you upgraded your system from an older version of Windows, though, these programs may still be installed.

What Happens During Program Installation and Uninstallation

You may receive a program on a CD-ROM, as a stack of floppy disks or as a file downloaded from the Internet. A downloaded program usually arrives in the form of an *installation file* (also called a *distribution file*), which is a compressed file containing all the files required for a program to install and run. If your computer is connected to a local area network (LAN), the installation file may be stored on a network disk (see Chapter 30).

Once you have a program, you install it, usually by running an installation program to copy the program to your hard disk and configure it to run on your system.

Note *When installing programs, you must be logged on with a user account that is a member of the Administrator or Power user group (see Chapter 6). Limited and Guest user accounts can't install programs. If you haven't set up user accounts, you are probably logged on automatically as Owner or Administrator, both of which are members of the Administrator group.*

Most programs come with an installation program named Setup.exe or Install.exe. Many programs use the Windows Installer, an installation and software management program that comes with Windows XP and other recent versions of Windows. Programs that use Windows Installer come with an .msi file that contains information about how and where files must be installed. When you install a program, the installation program usually does the following:

- Looks for a previous version of the program on your hard disk. If it finds a previous version, the program may ask whether you want to replace the previous version.

- Creates a folder in which to store the program files. Most installation programs ask where you'd like this folder. Some installation programs also create additional folders within this folder. Windows creates a folder named C:\Program Files (if Windows is stored on C:). We recommend you install all your programs in folders within the Program Files folder.

Note   *Some software vendors have the bad habit of installing application programs in locations other than your Program Files folder. You can't do much about this; the additional folders may clutter up your root folder, but they don't do any harm. Don't move a program's files unless you know how to update the program's Registry keys to match.*

- Copies the files onto your hard disk. If the program files are compressed, the installation program uncompresses them. Usually, the installation program copies most of the files into the program's folder, but it may also put some files into your C:\Windows, C:\Windows\System32, or other folders.

- Checks your system for the files and hardware it needs to run. For example, an Internet connection program might check for a modem.

- Adds entries to the Windows Registry to tell Windows which types of files the program works with, which files the program is stored in, and other information about the program (see Chapter 38).

- Optionally, adds submenus or commands to your Start | All Programs menu and a shortcut to your Windows desktop. You can move or delete the command on the Start menu or create a command if the installation program doesn't make one (see Chapter 10). You can also create a shortcut icon on the desktop, if the installation program hasn't done so (see Chapter 8).

The perfect uninstallation program exactly undoes all the actions of the installation program, removing all the files and folders the installation program created, and putting back everything else where it was originally. Unfortunately, we've never seen a perfect uninstallation program, but most uninstallation programs do an acceptable job of removing most traces of a program from your system.

Installing Programs

The Add Or Remove Programs program on the Control Panel helps you find and start the installation program for a new program. However, you can skip this step and run the installation program yourself, if you know how. Some older programs don't come with installation programs, and you have to perform the actions of an installation program yourself.

What If You Run Out of Space for Programs?

Programs are usually installed in the C:\Program Files folder (assuming that Windows is installed on C:). If you run out of space on C:, and you have space on another hard disk, you can install programs there. Here's another approach: you can move the entire Program Files folder to a different drive (or partition), and "mount" that drive in place of the C:\Program Files folder. After making a complete backup of your system, move the contents of C:\Program Files to the root of another partition or drive (for example, E:). Then mount the drive in the C:\Program Files folder, following the instructions in the section "Assigning Pathnames to Partitions" in Chapter 33. Additional hard disks are cheap and fairly easy to install.

You must move the entire contents of the Program Files folder; you can't leave some programs in their original location. Because the pathnames of the files don't change—they still appear to be in C:\Program Files—no programs need to be reconfigured. And you must move the Program Files contents to the root of another partition or drive, because only entire partitions can be mounted in folders.

For most programs, putting the CD-ROM into the CD drive is all you have to do to start installing the program. An installation program usually runs automatically and steps you through the process.

Installing Programs Using the Add Or Remove Programs Window

Follow these steps to use the Add Or Remove Programs window to help you install a program:

1. Choose Start | Control Panel and double-click (or click, if you have configured Windows to run programs by single-clicking) Add Or Remove Programs. You see the Add Or Remove Programs window with four buttons down the left side. (The fourth button, Set Program Access And Defaults, is new in Windows XP Service Pack 1.)

2. Click the Add New Programs button so the window looks like Figure 3-1.

3. Regardless of whether you are installing a program from a floppy disk, CD-ROM, or a file on your hard disk or on a network drive, click the CD Or Floppy button. You'll have a chance to tell it where to look for the program in a minute. When you click Next, Windows looks on any floppy disk or CD-ROM in your drives for an installation program (that is, a program named Setup.exe or Install.exe). If Windows finds an installation program, skip to step 5.

4. If Windows doesn't find an installation program, you see the Run Installation Program dialog box, which asks for the full pathname of the installation program.

Click the Browse button and specify the installation program you want
to run. Click Open when you find the installation program.

5. Click Finish to run the installation program. Follow the instructions on the
screen to install the program.

Once you install a program, the program name usually (but not always) appears in the
list that the Add Or Remove Programs window displays when you click the Change Or
Remove Programs button.

Running an Install or Setup Program

If you know the pathname of the installation file for the program you want to install,
you can run the installation program directly—double-click its filename in Windows
Explorer or use the Start | Run command. Follow the instructions on the screen to
install the program. Programs that use the Windows Installer program may arrive
in .msi files. Run the .msi file (by double-clicking its filename in an Explorer window
or typing its filename in the Start | Run dialog box), and Windows Installer runs
automatically.

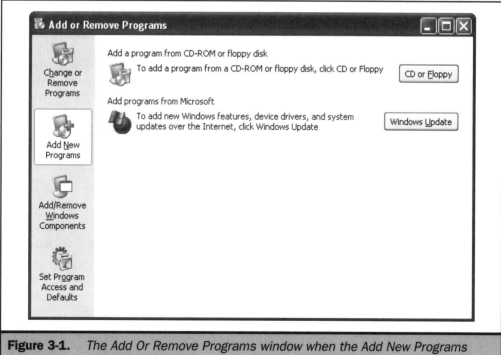

Figure 3-1.   *The Add Or Remove Programs window when the Add New Programs
button is selected*

Installing Programs Without Installation Programs

Older programs, such as those designed to run with Windows 3.1 or DOS, don't have installation programs. Instead, the programs are delivered as a set of files.

Some older programs arrive as a *ZIP* file, a file that contains compressed versions of one or more files (see Chapter 8). ZIP files have the extension .zip. (If you can't see filename extensions in Windows, see section "File Types and Extensions" in Chapter 8 to display them.)

To install a program from a ZIP file, you can use the Windows compressed folders feature, which treats ZIP files like folders (see Chapter 8). Alternatively, you can install an unzipping program such as ZipMagic (**www.ontrack.com/zipmagic**) or WinZip (**www. winzip.com**), which come with their own commands for unzipping (uncompressing) and installing programs from ZIP files.

To install a program that you receive as a set of files or as a ZIP file, using the Windows compressed files feature, follow these steps:

1. If you received the program as a ZIP file, open the ZIP file. In an Explorer window, it appears as a folder with a little zipper on it. Otherwise, look at the set of files in an Explorer window.

2. Look at the list of files to find files with the .exe or .com extension; these are executable programs. If one file is named Setup.exe or Install.exe, run it. Then follow the instructions on the screen. The installation program may ask you a series of questions to configure the program for your system. If one file is named Readme.txt (or some other name that suggests it contains instructions), read the contents of the file. If its extension is .txt, click or double-click the filename to see the file in Notepad.

3. Otherwise, look for an executable file with a name like the name of the program; this may be the program itself. For example, if you are installing a program called Spam Be Gone version 2.3, you might find a filename such as Spambg23.exe. To run the program, click or double-click the program name. The first time you run the program, it may ask you for information with which to configure the program for your system.

Other downloaded programs arrive in .exe files. Some .exe files contain self-extracting ZIP files—that is, the unzipping program is included with the ZIP file in one package. Run the .exe file to extract its files, and then follow the steps above starting with step 2. Other .exe files run a built-in installer or fire up the Windows Installer.

Older programs may need to use Windows XP's compatibility modes to run correctly. See the section "Running Programs in Compatibility Mode" in Chapter 1.

Finishing Installation of a Program

After you install a program, you may still need to configure it to work with your system. Many programs come with configuration programs that run automatically, either when you install the program or when you run the program for the first time.

If the installation program doesn't add the program to your Start menu, you can do so yourself (see Chapter 10). The installation program may also put an icon on the Quick Launch toolbar (a row of small icons on the taskbar you can click to run a program). If not, you can add an icon yourself.

You can also add a shortcut for the program to your Windows desktop, if the installation program didn't create one for you (see Chapter 8). You can create shortcuts on the desktop or in a folder.

Installing and Uninstalling Programs that Come with Windows

Windows XP comes with fewer optionally installed components than did previous versions of Windows. You get just as many features, utilities, and free applications, but you no longer have a choice about installing them. For example, you no longer have the option of saving disk space by uninstalling Outlook Express, NetMeeting, Windows Messenger, or other programs that you don't want to use—although you can hide these programs, they are still there.

 After installing a new Windows component, run Windows Update to download and install any available updates to the component (see Chapter 36).

Using the Add/Remove Windows Components Program

If you want to install or uninstall programs that come on the Windows XP CD-ROM, follow these steps:

1. Choose Start | Control Panel and run Add Or Remove Programs. You see the Add Or Remove Programs window.

2. Click the Add/Remove Windows Components button. You see the Windows Components Wizard with a list of the types of programs that come with Windows, as shown in Figure 3-2. The check box to the left of each type of program is blank (meaning none of the programs of that type are selected), gray with a check mark (meaning some, but not all, of the programs of that type are selected), or white with a check mark (meaning all the programs of that type are selected). The selections that appear (before you've made any changes) show which Windows programs are already installed.

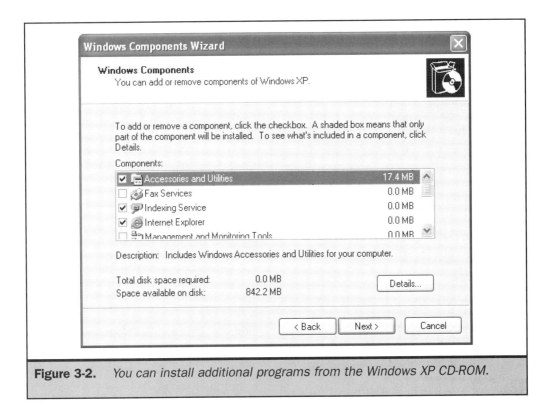

Figure 3-2.   *You can install additional programs from the Windows XP CD-ROM.*

3. To select additional programs, click the component's check box . A few items have only one program of that type, such as Fax Services. Most of the items on the Components list include a number of programs.

4. To select only some of the programs that make up a Windows component, click the Details button to see the list of programs of that type. In the window that appears, select the check boxes for the programs you want.

5. You can uninstall previously installed programs at the same time you install new programs. To uninstall a program, deselect its check box. Don't clear a program's check box unless you want to uninstall it.

6. After you select all the programs you want installed and deselect all the programs you don't want installed, click the Next button. Windows determines which programs you are installing and which you are uninstalling, and copies or deletes program files appropriately. The wizard may ask you to insert the Windows XP CD-ROM.

Uninstalling Windows Components That Don't Appear in the Windows Components Wizard

The Windows Components Wizard (which runs when you click Add/Remove Windows Components in the Add Or Remove Programs window) doesn't list all Windows components. Some are hidden. The list of uninstallable Windows components is stored in a file named C:\Windows\inf \sysoc.inf (if Windows is installed on drive C:). The file contains lines like this:

```
AutoUpdate=ocgen.dll,OcEntry,au.inf,hide,7
msmsgs=msgrocm.dll,OcEntry,msmsgs.inf,hide,7
WMAccess=ocgen.dll,OcEntry,wmaccess.inf,,7
```

Hidden items include the word "hide," which you can remove if you want to be able to uninstall the program.

Double-click the Sysoc.inf file in an Explorer window to open it in Notepad (but make a copy if it before you do, so you can replace the edited copy with the original if you run into trouble). Remove the word "hide" but leave the comma (you should see two commas in a row). Save the file. Go ahead and remove all the occurrences of "hide" (or globally replace "hide," with ","). The next time you run the Windows Components Wizard, many (but not all) of the unhidden programs appear on the list of components you can uninstall.

7. Depending on which programs you install, you may need to restart Windows when the installation is complete, and you may be directed to run Wizards or other configuration programs to set up the new programs.

 A few programs on the Windows XP CD-ROM don't appear in the Windows Components Wizard. Look in the /Valueadd folder on the CD-ROM for Microsoft programs (in /Valueadd/Msft) and programs from other companies (in /Valueadd/3rdparty). For example, the Microsoft Backup program doesn't appear as a Windows component: you have to install it yourself (see Chapter 9).

 Don't uninstall a program if you don't know what it does!

Hiding Windows Middleware

Windows XP Service Pack 1 added a new feature to Windows, probably in response to the antitrust case against Microsoft. Although you still can't remove *middleware*— programs like Internet Explorer, which Microsoft considers to be integral to Windows— you can hide them by using the new Set Program Access And Defaults icon on the Add

Or Remove Programs window. You can hide (that is, remove from menus and the desktop) five programs: Internet Explorer, Outlook Express, Windows Media Player, Windows Messenger, and the Java Virtual Machine (a browser add-on).

Few users will want to hide these programs; even if you don't usually use them on a day-to-day basis, you may need them from time to time. For example, even if you prefer to use Netscape's browser, you may need to use Internet Explorer to access Microsoft's own web site, which looks strange in any browser but their own. This new feature is mainly useful for computer makers, who now have the option of contracting with the makers of other browsers, e-mail programs, media players, and instant messaging programs to feature their programs on the Windows desktop and Start menu. Not all programs work with the Set Program Access And Defaults utility—Microsoft announced programming changes that would be needed, so versions of browsers, e-mail programs, and other programs from before the Fall of 2002 don't appear.

If you do want to hide Microsoft's programs, you first need to make your chosen non-Microsoft programs the defaults. When you first install most browsers, e-mail program, instant messaging programs, and media players, they offer to make themselves the default program of that type. Most browsers also have a command to make themselves the default browser. (In Mozilla, choose Edit | Preferences, expand the Advanced category, and click System. In Opera, choose File | Preferences and click Default Browser.) For the other types of programs, you can also set the default by choosing Start | Control Panel, clicking Internet Options, clicking the Programs tab, and setting the default. (This dialog box has no setting for your default browser.)

Once you have set your default programs to the ones you want to use, here's how to hide (or reveal) Microsoft's competing programs:

1. Choose Start | Set Program Access And Defaults or choose Start | Control Panel and click Add Or Remove Programs.

2. Click the new Set Program Access And Defaults icon in the lower-right part of the window, as shown in Figure 3-3.

3. If you want to use all of Microsoft's programs, choose Microsoft Windows in the Choose A Configuration box. Click the downward-pointing arrows button to the right of this option to see a list of the programs that will be enabled. Then skip to step 7.

4. If you want to use some non-Microsoft programs and hide some of Microsoft's, don't choose Non-Microsoft; instead, choose Custom so you can select each type of program.

5. Click the downward-pointing arrows button to the right of this option to see your options. For each type of program, you have two choices: Microsoft's program and the current default for that type. (You can't choose a program that's not already the default.) If Microsoft's program currently *is* the default, both choices have the same result.

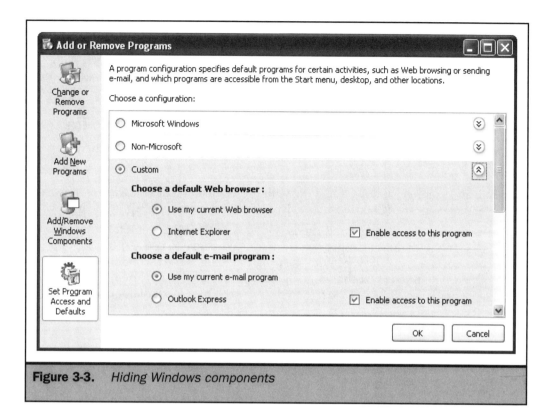

Figure 3-3.   *Hiding Windows components*

6. Make your choices. If you choose the current default program, choose whether to leave the Microsoft program visible; if you want to hide it, clear its Enable Access To This Program check box.

7. Click OK to put your choices into effect. Windows displays messages saying what programs it is hiding.

    You can remove the Set Program Access And Defaults command from your Start menu by right-clicking it and choosing Delete.

Associating a Program with a File Extension

Many programs create, edit, or display files of a specific type. For example, the Notepad program (a text editor that comes with Windows) works with text files that usually have the filename extension .txt (the extension is the part of the filename that follows the last dot in the filename). When you open a file with the extension .txt, Windows knows to run Notepad.

The Windows Registry stores *file associations*, information about which program you use to edit each type of file. Installation programs usually store this information in the

Registry, but you can, too. Chapter 38 describes how to view and edit the Registry with the Registry Editor program, but you can use other tools to change your file associations.

Windows offers three ways to create or change a file association: the Open With dialog box, the Folder Options dialog box, and the Edit File Types dialog box. The third method is rarely used.

Associating Files with Programs when Opening a File

You can tell Windows which program to use when opening files with a particular extension. Follow these steps:

1. In an Explorer window, find a file with the extension that you want to associate with a program. (Choose Start | My Computer to open an Explorer window.)

2. Right-click the filename and choose Open With from the menu that appears. (If Open With doesn't appear on the menu, you have to use another method of associating the file type with the program; see the next section.) You see the Open With dialog box shown in Figure 3-4. (If a small submenu of programs appears, select Choose Program to display the Open With dialog box.)

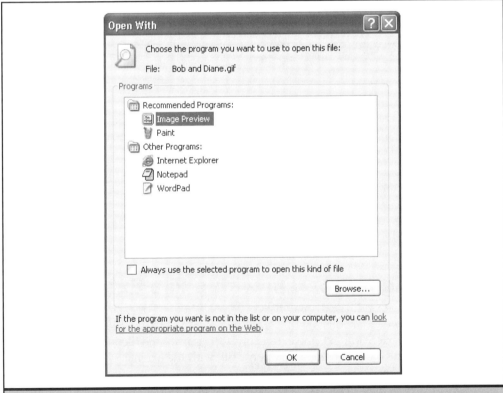

Figure 3-4.   *Which program do you want run to open this file (and files like it)?*

3. Select the program to run or click Browse to find the program file.

4. Click the Always Use The Selected Program To Open This Kind Of File check box and click OK.

Windows Explorer permanently saves the association of the filename extension with the program, and it opens the file you selected with the program you specified.

 Another way to display the Open With dialog box is to display the Properties dialog box for a file and click the Change button on the General tab.

Associating Files with Programs by Using Folder Options

Another way to associate a file type (file extension) with a program (or change the program associated with a file type) is to use the File Types tab on the Folder Options dialog box.

Editing an Existing Association

To edit a file association, follow these steps:

1. In an Explorer window, choose Tools | Folder Options. You see the Folder Options dialog box.

2. Click the File Types tab, shown in Figure 3-5.

3. In the Registered File Types list, click the type of file you want to associate with a program. (Scroll down the list—it's long.) When you select a file type, more information about that file type appears in the Details For File Type box. You also see two buttons: Change (to associate one program with the file type) and Advanced (to associate multiple programs with the file type).

4. To see or change which program Windows runs to open this type of file, click Change. You see the Open With dialog box (see Figure 3-4). Select the program to run. Then click OK.

Note *If you see a dialog box saying that Windows cannot open the type of file that you selected, click the Select A Program From A List option and click OK to display the Open With dialog box.*

5. Close the Open With and Folder Options dialog boxes.

Windows now knows to run the program you specified when you open a file of this type.

Tip *If you have no idea what type of file the file extension refers to, click the Look For The Appropriate Program On The Web link at the bottom of the Open With dialog box. A browser runs and displays a web page about that type of file, including some programs that can create or read the files.*

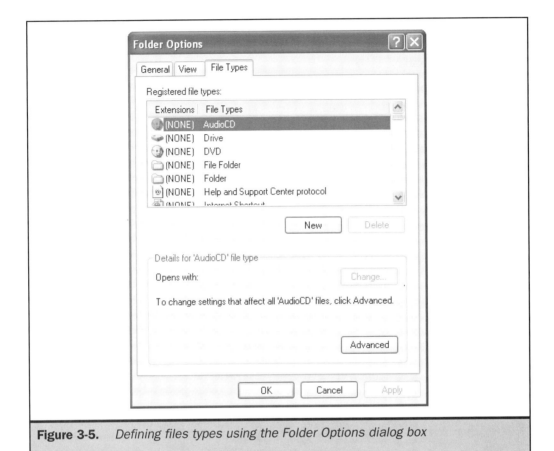

Figure 3-5. *Defining files types using the Folder Options dialog box*

Creating a New Association

You can create a new file type, with a new extension.

1. In an Explorer window, choose Tools | Folder Options and click the File Types tab (see Figure 3-5).

2. If the file extension doesn't appear in the list of Registered Files Types, click New to display the Create New Extension dialog box, shown here:

3. Type the extension in the File Extension box.

4. If you know the Windows file type (that is, the name of the Windows class or object that this file extension contains), click Advanced to expand the Create New Extension dialog box to include the Associated File Type list. Choose the file type from the (very long) list.

5. Click OK. Windows adds the new type at the top of the list (not in alphabetical order, unless you close and reopen the dialog box).

6. Select the program to associate with this new extension by following the steps in the previous section.

Editing a File Association

Rather than telling Windows that one program can handle a file type, you can specify different programs for different actions for example, you can use Internet Explorer to display .gif files, but use Paint Shop Pro to edit and print them. You rarely need to do this: installation programs use this facility when registering a new program to handle file types; human beings almost never need to change the details of file type association.

Follow these steps to specify the settings for a file type:

1. In an Explorer window, choose Tools | Folder Options and click the File Types tab (see Figure 3-5).

2. Choose a file type from the Registered File Types list. (You can click a column to sort the items into that order, to make file types easier to find.)

3. Click the Advanced button. You see the Edit File Type dialog box, shown in Figure 3-6. It displays the information that the Registry knows about this file type, including the icon to use for files of this type and a description of the file type. The Actions box lists the tasks that Windows knows how to perform for files of this type: open, print, edit, and other actions. For each action, you can tell Windows which program to use.

4. To change which icon appears for this type of file, click the Change Icon button. Windows displays the available icons. Click one and click OK.

5. To see the details of what Windows does when you choose a command like Open or Print from a shortcut menu for a type of file, choose the action from the Actions list and click the Edit button. You see the Editing Action For Type dialog box, which shows what command line Windows executes when you perform this action on this file type.

6. Click OK to store your changes to the way that Windows handles files of this type.

For details of how to tell Windows which programs to run for a file type, see the article "Understanding MS Windows Files Associations" by Brien M. Posey, at **www.microsoft.com/technet/prodtechnol/win98/maintain/assoc.asp**.

Figure 3-6.   *Specifying which programs open and print one file type*

Uninstalling Programs

If you have a program on your computer that you don't use, you can uninstall it to free up space on your hard disk (unless it's one of the many un-uninstallable components of Windows). You can also uninstall older versions of programs before installing new versions. The best way to uninstall a program is by using the Add Or Remove Programs window. If it doesn't appear on the Windows list of installed programs, run the program's uninstall program; if the program doesn't have one, you'll have to delete files manually.

Uninstalling Programs Using the Add Or Remove Programs Window

When you want to uninstall a program, first try using the Add Or Remove Programs window. Follow these steps:

1. Choose Start | Control Panel and click Add Or Remove Programs. You see the Add Or Remove Programs window. If the Change Or Remove Programs button isn't selected, click it, as shown in Figure 3-7. The Add Or Remove Programs window lists many of your installed programs (not including Windows components).

2. Click the program you want to uninstall. Windows tells you how much disk space the program occupies, how often you run the program, and when you last ran it. (This information isn't always very accurate; if you leave a program open all the time, Windows may think you rarely use it because you rarely *start* it.)

3. Click the Change/Remove button. Windows uninstalls the program, while messages appear to let you know what's happening.

If the program doesn't appear in the Add Or Remove Programs window, you have to uninstall the program another way (see "Running an Uninstall Program").

Note   *Sometimes Windows can't uninstall a program, usually because it can't find the files it needs to perform the uninstallation. You're stuck uninstalling it manually, and the program's name remains forever in the Change Or Remove Programs list of currently installed programs. You can remove a program's name if you don't mind editing your Registry; see the sidebar "Removing Orphaned Entries from the List of Currently Installed Programs."*

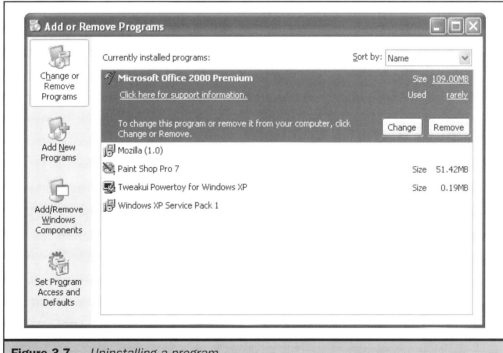

Figure 3-7. *Uninstalling a program*

Removing Orphaned Entries from the List of Currently Installed Programs

If Windows can't uninstall a program that appears on the Currently Installed Programs list on the Add Or Remove Programs window, you can usually uninstall the program manually, but it's annoying that the program's name remains on the list of installed programs. You can remove the program's name from the list by editing the Registry key that contains the list. After backing up the Registry (as described in Chapter 38), run the Registry Editor and location the \HKEY_LOCAL_ MACHINE\Software\Microsoft\Windows \CurrentVersion\Uninstall key. You see a list of installed programs, including many Windows components that don't appear on the Currently Installed Programs list. Some Microsoft products have long hexadecimal key names—look at the value of the DisplayName key to identify the program. When you locate the key for the program that is no longer installed, export it (so that you can reimport it later if you change your mind) and then delete it.

Running an Uninstall Program

Many programs come with uninstall programs, usually named Uninstall.exe. (Programs that use the Wise installation program come with an uninstall program called Unwise.exe.) Look for an uninstall program in the same folder where the program is stored. Run the uninstall program, and then follow the directions on the screen. The uninstall program may also be on the Start | All Programs menu on the same submenu as the program.

Uninstalling Programs Manually

What if a program doesn't appear in the Add Or Remove Programs window and doesn't come with an uninstall program? You can delete by hand the program files and the shortcuts to the program. You might not delete every last file connected with the program, but the remaining files usually won't do any harm. Before deleting anything, check the program's documentation for instructions. Be sure to back up your hard disk or create a System Restore checkpoint before uninstalling a program by hand, in case you delete a file your system needs (see Chapter 2, section "Returning Your System to a Predefined State with System Restore").

Rather than deleting a program, you might first want to rename the folder containing the program files, adding something like "deleted" to the end of the folder name. Wait a few days. If other programs are using those files, you'll see error messages when those programs run. If no programs report errors within a week, then you know it's safe to delete the folder containing the program files.

To delete the program files, determine which folder contains them. The easiest way to find out where the program is stored is to look at the properties of a shortcut to the program (see Chapter 8). Right-click a shortcut to the program on your desktop, on the taskbar, in a folder, or in the folder that contains your Start menu items (usually C:\Documents And Settings\All Users\Start Menu\Programs). Choose Properties from the menu that appears and click the Shortcut tab on the Properties dialog box for the program. The Target box contains the full pathname of the executable file for the program. Click Find Target to open an Explorer window for the folder that contains the program file.

To delete the program, delete the folder that contains the program files and all the files in it. After uninstalling a program, you might see shortcuts to the program lying around on your desktop, in folders, on the taskbar, or in your Start menu. Delete these shortcuts (right-click the shortcut and choose Delete).

Next, look in the Registry for entries for the program (see Chapter 38). Back up the Registry before making any changes. Look in the \HKEY_LOCAL_MACHINE\ Software hive for the program's key (most keys in this hive are organized by software publisher). Look at the values of the key's values for pathnames to other folders that you might want to delete (for example, the program may keep its configuration settings in a subfolder in C:\Documents And Settings). Export the key (and all its subkeys and values) for the program and then delete it. If Windows acts funny after these changes, reimport the keys you deleted.

Tip   *If at all possible, use a program's uninstaller instead of just deleting all the files because the uninstaller is safer and more comprehensive. Uninstallers remove files in C:\Windows, C:\Windows\System, C:\Windows\System32, and other locations in which the program might have installed them. Uninstallers also delete the Registry entries for the program (see Chapter 38).*

The
Complete
Reference

Chapter 4

Running DOS Programs and Commands

You may need to install and run older DOS programs on your Windows XP system. Windows provides ways to run DOS programs and commands; cut-and-paste between DOS and Windows programs; and configure how DOS programs work with the screen, mouse, and keyboard. If you're an old hand at DOS, you may also wonder what's happened to two files that were crucial to DOS: Autoexec.bat and Config.sys. This chapter covers all of these topics.

Windows 95 and 98 had a special version of DOS (version 7.0) to run DOS applications and games. Those versions could also be rebooted into a DOS mode, where the machine became a DOS-only computer until it was rebooted. In Windows Me, Microsoft finally removed all vestiges of DOS and replaced it with the *DOS Virtual Machine* (*DOS VM*). The only real difference was the absence of a DOS mode on startup, but the vast majority of DOS programs could still run successfully in the DOS VM.

Windows XP contains a similar DOS VM, which allows you to run those old, but still fun, DOS games of yore—at least a good percentage of them. Some old games just won't work because they don't have *real* access to the hardware, as they would under DOS.

The Basics of DOS

MS-DOS (or *DOS*, Disk Operating System, for short) is a simple operating system that was the predecessor to Windows. Early versions of Windows (through 3.11) were add-ons for DOS—first you installed DOS on your computer, then you installed Windows, and then you started Windows from the DOS command prompt. Windows 95, 98, 98SE, Me, and XP still have a version of DOS buried inside them, although Microsoft's engineers have integrated almost all of the DOS functions into Windows.

DOS provides only disk file management and the most rudimentary support for the screen, keyboard, mouse, timer, and other peripherals. As a result, interactive *DOS programs* (programs written to work with DOS rather than Windows) need to create their own user interfaces, usually by directly operating the hardware controllers for the screen and sometimes other devices. DOS supports only 640KB of memory, and the base functions of all DOS applications must fit inside of this limited space. Microsoft and other companies developed a variety of add-on drivers to allow DOS to handle larger amounts of memory, including *expanded memory* (EMS memory) and *extended memory* (XMS memory).

DOS doesn't have a graphical user interface (GUI) and usually doesn't display windows or work with a mouse. Instead, you type commands at the *DOS prompt*, a symbol that indicates DOS is waiting for you to type a *command line* (a command, optionally followed by additional information). The default DOS prompt is C:\>. This method of typing commands at a prompt is called a *command-line interface (CLI)*.

Windows, on the other hand, provides extensive facilities to handle the screen and keyboard, as well as sophisticated memory management, which all Windows applications use. These facilities make it difficult to run some DOS programs in Windows, because the DOS programs and Windows can't both control the same hardware at the same time. The DOS VM eliminates most of those hurdles and makes it easier to run DOS programs.

DOS Filenames

Pre-Windows 95 filenames were limited to eight characters (excluding spaces) followed by a dot and three more characters (the file extension). Each file and folder in Windows has a *DOS filename* (or *8.3 filename*), a short name that resembles its real name and that is legal in DOS. The DOS name exists for the purpose of backward compatibility; programs written for DOS or older versions of Windows might crash if Windows hands them files with long names and previously illegal characters. So, when dealing with pre-Windows 95 application programs, Windows pretends nothing has changed and gives the application the DOS filename rather than its real name. The DOS filename is usually the first six characters of the filename, followed by a tilde (~) and a number. The extension part of the DOS filename is the first three characters of the extension.

DOS names are invisible in Windows, but you still may see them if you run an older application. If the file you named My Summer Vacation.doc shows up later as MYSUMM~1.DOC, you'll know what happened.

Note *The Recovery Console, a startup mode you can use to repair Windows installations when Windows won't start, resembles DOS. Many DOS commands work in the Recovery Console (see the section, "Using the Recovery Console" in Chapter 2).*

The Command Prompt Window

Previous versions of Windows could run DOS programs in two different ways: as an application running in Windows or as a stand-alone program in a DOS environment. In Windows XP, the MS-DOS mode is no longer available, although you are welcome to boot your computer using a floppy disk that has DOS on it. However if you do so, most extended DOS services will not be available unless you have taken the time to prepare a bootable DOS floppy with all the necessary DOS programs or have a fully configured DOS hard disk and partition management software. Preparing such a boot floppy is a tedious process at best (see Chapter 2, section "Creating Boot Floppy Disks").

Tip *If you have an Emergency Boot Disk for Windows 98, hold onto it. You might want to use it to start your computer in DOS mode, although when running DOS, you won't be able to read any disks formatted with NTFS.*

The most convenient way to run most DOS programs is in a *Command Prompt window* (or DOS window), as shown in Figure 4-1. Windows creates a *virtual machine* for the DOS program—a special hardware and software environment that emulates enough of the features of a stand-alone environment to allow most DOS programs to run correctly. DOS programs that don't use extensive graphics can usually run within a Command Prompt window, sharing the screen with Windows applications. Programs that require

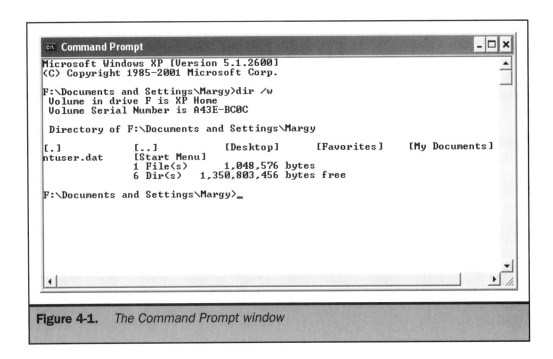

Figure 4-1. *The Command Prompt window*

full access to the screen hardware can also take over the screen while Windows continues
to run in the background.

Opening a Command Prompt Window

To open a Command Prompt window, choose Start | All Programs | Accessories |
Command Prompt. Or, you can choose Start | Run and type **cmd** and press ENTER.

*Windows XP comes with two programs that display a Command Prompt window:
Command.com and Cmd.exe. Command.com displays a Command Prompt window that
cannot handle long filenames (that is, filenames longer than eight characters and extensions
longer than three characters). Cmd.exe's window handles filenames the same way that
Windows does. There's no reason to use Command.com rather than Cmd.exe. When you
run Cmd.exe, its window's title is the program's pathname (usually C:\Windows\
System32\Cmd.exe) rather than "Command Prompt." We refer to both types of
windows as Command Prompt windows.*

You can use the Command Prompt window to type DOS commands (including
commands to look at or change the files on your disks) and to run DOS programs
(including some Windows utilities like Ping and Tracert). Since Windows doesn't give the
DOS program full control of the system, DOS programs running in a Command Prompt

window can run side by side with Windows applications, and even with other DOS applications. Some DOS programs are *Windows aware*, so that even though they don't run as Windows applications, they can check whether they're running under Windows and handle their screen and keyboard in a way that lets them run efficiently in Windows.

Issuing DOS Commands

In the Command Prompt window, you can type DOS commands as well as run programs. Just type the command (possibly followed by arguments or switches) and press ENTER. For some DOS commands, you can type arguments or switches on the command line after the program name, separated by spaces. An *argument* provides additional information (for example, the DOS COPY command accepts arguments that tell it what files to copy). A *switch* specifies a program option and usually consists of a slash (/) and a letter.

If a filename or pathname contains spaces, enclose it in quotation marks when you type it as an argument to a DOS command.

Table 4-1 shows a list of useful DOS commands. The Command Prompt displays the results of your commands, too.

DOS Command	Description	Example
cd *pathname*	(Or chdir) Changes the current folder (directory) to the one you specify.	cd \Budget\Current
copy *source target*	Makes a copy of the source file with the target name you specify. You can use the wildcard character * to specify a group of files. You can copy a folder by specifying the folder name as the source.	copy *.doc C:\Olddocs
del *pathname*	Deletes the file or folder. You can use * to delete groups of files.	del brazil*.gif
dir *pathname*	List the contents of the folder. If you omit the pathname, lists the current folder. Type **/w** at the end to see an abbreviated listing. Type **/p** at the end to pause after each screenful.	dir /p

Table 4-1.   *Useful DOS Commands*

DOS Command	Description	Example
help *command*	Listing instructions for using the command. Or, type a command name followed by /?.	help dir
md *foldername*	(Or mkdir) Creates a new folder in the current folder.	md Jan2004
start *filename*	Opens the file with the program that Windows associates with the file's extension (see Chapter 3, section "Associating a Program with a File Extension").	start readme.html

Table 4-1.   *Useful DOS Commands* (continued)

While the vast majority of DOS commands work, not all do. For a fairly complete list of commands accepted by the Command Prompt, type **help** and press ENTER.

To get help with a particular DOS command, type the command followed by /?. For example, type **copy /?** to get help with the COPY command. To stop the help text from scrolling off the top of the Command Prompt window, add | **more** to the end of the command line, like this:

```
copy /? | more
```

*If you can open a file by clicking or double-clicking it in Windows Explorer, you can open the file from the DOS prompt. Type **start** followed by a space and the pathname (address) of the file. If the pathname contains spaces, enclose it in double-quotation marks. The Start program opens the file (or folder) using the Windows file association.*

Running DOS Programs

DOS programs are stored in files with the extension .com or .exe. If you have a program that runs under DOS, you can run it in a number of ways. Once your DOS program is running, you can also adjust the way it looks on the screen, copy-and-paste material to and from the Windows Clipboard, print, and run batch files.

Starting and Exiting DOS Programs

You run a DOS program the same way you run a Windows program: by clicking or double-clicking its icon or filename in the Windows Explorer window or the Start menu, or by choosing Start | Run and typing its filename into the Run dialog box. A window opens in which the program runs.

Every DOS program has its own command to exit. Some use a function key, some use a text command (like "quit" or "exit"), and some use a menu command starting with a slash or another character. You can also force Windows to close a DOS program's window by clicking the Close button while the program is running. Windows may warn you that closing the program will lose unsaved information, but if you click End Now, Windows stops the program and closes the window anyway.

Adjusting the Screen

Windows normally starts each Command Prompt and DOS program window as a 25 × 80 character window, choosing a font to make the window fit your screen. You can select a different font from the Command Prompt Properties dialog box's Font tab (see "Choosing DOS Program Fonts," later in this chapter).

To switch between running in a window and using the full screen, press ALT-ENTER. Once in a full screen, ALT-ENTER is the only way, short of exiting and restarting the program, to return the program to running in a window.

Using the Mouse and Clipboard

Early versions of DOS provided no mouse support at all. Even in later versions, DOS provided only low-level mouse support, leaving it entirely up to each application which (if any) mouse features to provide. As a result, most DOS programs provide no mouse support, so the primary use of the mouse is to cut-and-paste material to the Windows Clipboard (see Chapter 5, section "Sharing Data Through the Windows Clipboard").

Using the Windows Clipboard

You can copy material from a Command Prompt window to the Clipboard. To do so, first click the System Menu button (with the C:\ icon) in the upper-left corner of the window and select Edit | Mark from the System menu that appears. Then use the mouse to highlight the area to copy and press ENTER to copy the selected area to the Clipboard.

Note   *DOS programs can place the screen (or the virtual screen emulated in a Command Prompt window) into either text mode (which can display only text) or graphics mode (which can display any pattern of dots, including text). Windows copies the marked area as text if the screen is in text mode and as a bitmap if the screen is in graphics mode. Some programs, such as word processors, use graphics mode to display text so that they can show font changes. If possible, tell the DOS program to switch back to text mode before copying to get text on the Clipboard.*

Windows lets you paste text from the Clipboard into DOS applications, too. The text is entered as though you had typed it on the keyboard. To paste, select Edit | Paste from the System menu.

Using the Mouse in DOS Programs

In those DOS programs that do provide mouse support, using the mouse in a Command Prompt window can be difficult. Since DOS provides no high-level mouse support, each application displays its own mouse pointer. In some Windows-aware applications, the DOS mouse pointer is synchronized with the Windows mouse pointer, but more often than not, it isn't. In the latter case, the best solution usually is to press ALT-ENTER to switch to full-screen mode, so no Windows mouse pointer appears at all.

Printing from DOS Programs

Windows provides limited support for printing from DOS programs. It offers a pass-through scheme that receives output from DOS programs and sends it directly to the printer. DOS programs have no access to Windows printer drivers, so each DOS application must have its own driver for any printer that it prints to.

Windows intercepts the DOS output and spools the output as it does printer output from Windows applications (that is, Windows stores the output and then sends it to the printer). This provides more flexibility in printer management and avoids the possibility that a DOS program will interfere with an active print job from another program.

Determining the Printer Port

DOS programs identify your printer according to the port to which the printer is attached (LPT1, LPT2, LPT3, COM1, COM2, COM3, or COM4). Network printers (that is, printers that are physically connected to another computer, and shared on a LAN) don't have ports; to print to one, see the next section. To find out what port a printer is attached to, follow these steps:

1. Select Start | Printers And Faxes (or Start | Control Panel | Printers And Other Hardware | Printers and Faxes) to open the Printers And Faxes window (see Chapter 14).

2. Right-click the desired printer and select Properties to open the printer's Properties dialog box.

3. Click the Ports tab to see a list of the ports, and look down the list for the first one whose check box is selected. If the dialog box has no Ports tab, look on all the tabs—the contents of the dialog box depend on the printer driver.

4. Click OK to close the printer Properties dialog box.

Printing to a Network Printer

DOS programs can also print to network printers (see Chapter 30). Windows captures the output from a simulated printer port and then spools the printer output through the network in the same way that printer output is spooled from Windows programs.

> **Caution**   *All printers are not created equal. Their capabilities depend both on the printer hardware and on the printer driver software. You may notice anywhere from subtle to enormous differences between the printer-related dialog boxes you see in this book and those you see on your computer. If you don't see a feature we mention here, your printer probably doesn't have it. Check your printer's manual to prevent yourself from wasting a lot of time on something that will simply not work.*

To print from a DOS program to a network printer, follow these steps:

1. Determine the pathname of the printer by displaying its Properties dialog box (as described in the previous section). If you see a Ports tab, look on that tab at the bottom of the list of ports for the pathname (you may need to drag the Port column divider to the right to make the entire name visible). The pathname is in the format \\computername*printername*, where *computername* is the computer's name on the LAN, and *printername* is the printer's share name (see Chapter 29).

2. Close the printer's Properties dialog box.

3. Choose Start | All Programs | Accessories | Command Prompt to open a Command Prompt window.

4. Type the following command and press ENTER. Replace *n* with the LPT number you want to use (if you already have a printer on LPT1, use LPT2), and *computername**printername* with the printer's pathname.

   ```
   net use lptn: \\computername\printername /persistent:yes
   ```

5. Now you can print from your DOS program to the LPT port you specified. When you are finished printing, type this command in the Command Prompt window:

   ```
   net use lptn: /delete
   ```

When you print from a DOS program to a spooled printer, either local or networked, Windows has no reliable way to tell when the DOS program is finished printing. If your program doesn't print anything for several seconds, Windows assumes that it's finished. This occasionally causes problems when an application prints part of a report, computes for a while, and then resumes printing, because Windows can interpret the pause in printing as the end of the print job. If this is a problem, use a locally connected printer and do *not* configure the printer to spool DOS print jobs.

Running Batch Files

DOS can run *batch files*, which are text files that contain a sequence of commands to be run as though they were typed at the DOS prompt. Batch files have the filename extension .bat. Windows treats a batch file as a DOS program and opens a Command Prompt window to run the batch file and any programs that the batch file runs. Since the Windows version of DOS lets you run any DOS or Windows program from the DOS prompt, you can use batch files as a low-budget scripting language, listing a sequence of programs you want to run.

For example, you can use a batch file as quick-and-dirty backup scheme for making copies of a few files on a Zip or other removable disk. Write a batch file that copies the files from their current location to the Zip disk. Then use the Scheduled Tasks program to run the batch file every night, and remember to leave a Zip disk in your Zip drive (see Chapter 1, section "Running Programs on a Schedule Using Scheduled Tasks").

Configuring the DOS Environment

Windows provides a long list of settings for customizing the environment for the Command Prompt window or for a DOS program. Nearly all the settings are parameters you can tweak to help a recalcitrant DOS program run in the Windows environment. For most DOS programs, adjusting these settings isn't necessary.

Earlier versions of Windows put the settings for DOS programs into separate *PIF files* (program information files, with filename extension .pif), and some programs still use them. Windows XP stores the settings in DOS initialization files, in Command Prompt properties, and in program properties.

Although you can edit a program's properties while the program is running, most changes do not take effect until you close the program and run it again. (The main exception is changing fonts.)

DOS Initialization Files: Autoexec and Config

DOS used a Config.sys file to load drivers and an Autoexec.bat file to run DOS commands before the program runs. Windows XP provides default versions of these DOS initialization files, called Config.nt and Autoexec.nt, which are located in the C:\Windows\System32 folder (assuming that Windows is installed in C:\Windows).

The Config.nt file contains DOS VM configuration commands, as well as commands to load real-mode device drivers. Autoexec.nt contains regular DOS commands to be run as soon as DOS has finished starting up. Although any DOS command is valid, the only command commonly used is SET, which defines environment variables used by some programs and drivers. Config.nt is read during the DOS startup process. Windows runs the commands from Autoexec.nt after processing Config.nt. These files can now be located anywhere, which improves DOS backward compatibility by allowing you to have several different versions of the files and selecting the one that best suits the program you want to run.

The Autoexec.nt and Config.nt files are text files, which you can edit with Notepad. Microsoft recommends that you leave the original Config.nt and Autoexec.nt unchanged, and create edited copies with other names, like Config.games and Autoexec.pcfile, for your various applications. See "Installing and Configuring DOS Programs" later in this chapter for how to create your own versions of the files for the DOS program you want to configure.

Read the Autoexec.nt and Config.nt files to start learning about how they work. They are both copiously commented.

Setting Command Prompt Window Properties

When a Command Prompt window is open, you can see and set its settings by clicking the System Menu button in its upper-left corner and choosing Properties. The settings on the various tabs of the Command Prompt Properties dialog box, shown in Figure 4-2, control the appearance and some operational aspects of a DOS program. Table 4-2 lists the settings by tab (left to right).

Depending on whether you start the Command Prompt from the Start menu (by choosing Start | All Programs | Accessories | Command Prompt) or from the Run command (by choosing Start | Run, typing **cmd***, and pressing ENTER), you see a different Properties dialog box. Changing the settings for one does not affect the other.*

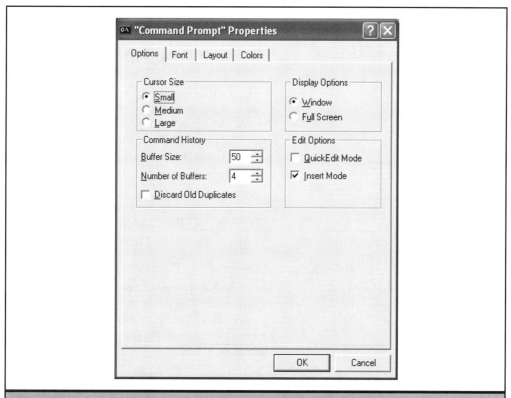

Figure 4-2.   *The Options tab of the Command Prompt Properties dialog box*

Tab	Setting	Description
Options	Cursor Size	Specifies the size of the cursor, the flashing marker that draws attention to where your typing will appear. Small appears as a line. Medium appears as a thick line. Large is a block.
Options	Command History Buffer Size, Number of Buffers, Discard Old Duplicates	Every time you type a command, Windows stores it in a buffer. Use the UP-ARROW and DOWN-ARROW keys on your keyboard to cycle through commands. The Buffer Size setting specifies the number of command lines stored. Number of Buffers controls how many different Command Prompt windows have buffers simultaneously. Discard Old Duplicates deletes duplicate commands from the buffer.
Options	Display Options	Specifies the default window size: Windowed or Full Screen.
Options	Edit Options	Selects either QuickEdit mode (in which you use the mouse pointer to select text and move the cursor) or Insert mode (in which you can place additional text wherever the cursor is instead of overwriting what's already there).
Font	Size	Specifies the font size in pixels (dots).
Font	Font	Specifies the font.
Font	Bold Fonts	Displays the selected font in boldface.
Layout	Screen Buffer Size	Specifies the virtual size of the window.
Layout	Window Size	Specifies the physical size of the Command Prompt window. If the Screen Buffer Size is larger, scrollbars appear to allow you access to the information that doesn't fit in the window.

Table 4-2.   *Settings in the Command Prompt Properties Dialog Box*

Tab	Setting	Description
Layout	Window Position	Specifies the position of the window on the screen. Let System Position Window enables Windows to choose the position. If you want the Command Prompt window to appear in the same place every time it opens, deselect the check box and set the coordinates of the upper-left corner of the window; 0 indicates the left or top edge of the screen. The limits are determined by what resolution you have your display set to.
Colors	Screen Text, Screen Background, Popup Text, Popup Background	Enables you to select which settings appear in the Selected Color Values section and the color bar.
Colors	Select Color Values	Specifies the color of the selected item (see the previous setting). The row of colors below this setting do the same thing.

Table 4-2.   *Settings in the Command Prompt Properties Dialog Box* (continued)

Choosing DOS Program Fonts

On the Font tab, the Window Preview box shows you how big your window will be relative to the Windows screen, and the Selected Font box shows what the text in the window will look like. First, choose a font from the Font box; then choose from the sizes that are available for that font.

Controlling DOS Program Window Settings

On the Layout tab, shown in Figure 4-3, you can set the virtual and actual sizes of the window. The virtual size (set using the Screen Buffer Size setting) controls the amount of text that Windows stores for the window. The Window Size setting controls the actual size of the widow on the screen. If the Screen Buffer Size is larger than the Windows Size (the default is for it to be several times taller, but the same width), you can scroll up and down the buffer using the window's scrollbars.

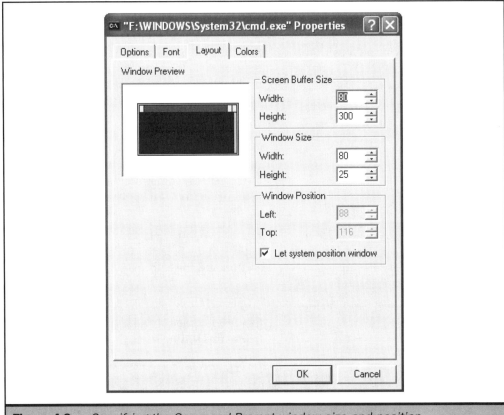

Figure 4-3. *Specifying the Command Prompt window size and position*

Setting DOS Program Colors

The Colors tab of the Command Prompt Properties dialog box, controls the foreground and background colors of the text in the window. Select the item for which you want to set the color (Screen Text, Screen Background, Popup Text, or Popup Background) and then select a color for it from the bar of colors running across the middle of the dialog box. Your choices appear in the preview panes below. If you don't like the colors listed, you can adjust the Selected Color Values boxes to get the colors you like.

Setting Executable and Shortcut Properties

Additional options for DOS programs are set in the program's Properties dialog box. To set them, find either the executable (.exe or .com) file for the program or a shortcut to the executable file (you may need to choose Start | Search to find it). Many DOS applications, especially games, come with more than one executable file. Along with the executable file that runs the program, other executable files may uninstall or configure the program. Once you've located the executable file that runs the program (or a shortcut to it), right-click the

Running a Command When the Command Prompt Window Opens

You can configure the Command Prompt window to run a command each time that the window opens. For example, you might want to see a list of the current folder each time you use the window. To set this up, you need to edit your system's Registry (see Chapter 38). After making a backup copy of the Registry, run the Registry Editor and move to the \HKEY_CURRENT_USER\Software\Microsoft\ Command Processor key. Create a new value by right-clicking the Command Processor key and choosing New | String Value. Type **AutoRun** as the name and press ENTER. Right-click the new AutoRun value and choose Modify. In the Value Data box, type the DOS command you want to run each time the Command Prompt window opens and click OK.

file or shortcut and choose Properties to see its Properties dialog box. Figure 4-4 shows the Memory tab of the dialog box.

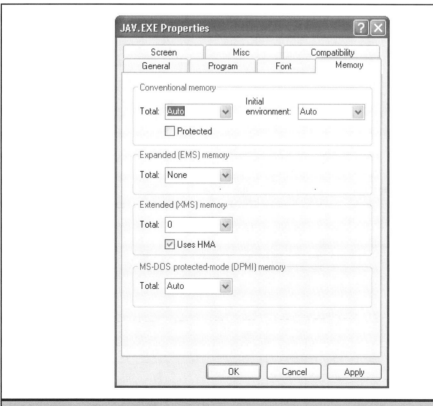

Figure 4-4.   *The memory options for a DOS program*

Table 4-3 lists settings in the dialog box, except for those on the Font tab, which is similar to the Font tab in the Command Prompt Properties dialog box, described in Table 4-2. The settings on the Compatibility tab are described in the section "Running Programs in Compatibility Mode" in Chapter 1. The Properties dialog box for a shortcut also includes a Summary tab, which isn't used for configuring programs.

Tab	Setting	Description
General	Attributes: Read-only, Hidden, Archive	Specifies the file attributes (see Chapter 8).
Program	Cmd line	Specifies the command line that you would type at the command prompt. The first thing on the command line must be the filename of the program. Many programs let you put parameters, switches, and filenames in the command line as well. If you type a space followed by a question mark in this box, Windows prompts you for command-line data when you start the program and replaces the question mark with the data you type.
Program	Working	Specifies the name of the folder to use as the program's *working folder*. The program reads and writes its files from this folder unless the program specifically names a different folder.
Program	Batch file	Specifies the name of a DOS batch file to run before the program starts. This is rarely used.

Table 4-3.   *Settings in the Properties Dialog Box for a Program or Shortcut*

Tab	Setting	Description
Program	Shortcut key	Specifies the key combination to start or activate the program (see Chapter 1, section "Starting Programs Using Shortcut Keys"). You can specify the CTRL or ALT key in combination with another key or a plain function key. Any combination you specify as a shortcut can no longer be used as input by any other program running on your computer, so choose a combination that isn't commonly used.
Program	Run	Specifies whether Windows starts the program in a normal, minimized, or maximized window (see Chapter 1, section "Controlling the Size and Shape of Your Windows"). Most DOS programs can't handle a maximized window.
Program	Close on exit	Specifies whether Windows closes the window in which the program appears when the program exits.
Memory	Conventional Memory: Total, Initial environment	Specifies the amount of memory (RAM) in kilobytes available to the program, up to DOS's limit of 640KB. For programs run in Windows 95 compatibility mode, the Initial Environment setting specifies the amount of memory reserved for the command-interpreter part of DOS itself. For most programs, leave these set to Auto.
Memory	Protected	Protects Windows' system memory from accidental modification by the DOS program and can keep a DOS program failure from crashing Windows. We recommend selecting this check box.

Table 4-3. *Settings in the Properties Dialog Box for a Program or Shortcut* (continued)

Tab	Setting	Description
Memory	Expanded (EMS) memory, Extended (XMS) memory, MS-DOS protected-mode (DPMI) memory	Specifies the amount of memory in kilobytes that Windows allocates as expanded, extended, or DPMI memory (three systems that DOS programs use to access more than 640KB).
Screen	Usage: Full-screen, Window, Initial size	Specifies whether the program starts full-screen or in a window. For some programs, you can select 25, 43, or 50 text lines on the screen by setting the Initial Size box. (If you select more than 25, be sure that the program can handle the size you select.) The program may override these settings.
Screen	Restore settings at startup	Specifies whether Windows remembers changes that the program makes to the screen setup from one run of the program to another.
Screen	Fast ROM emulation	Specifies whether the display driver provides video functions. Select this check box unless the screen display looks wrong.
Screen	Dynamic memory allocation	Maximizes the amount of memory available to other programs while this program is running.
Misc	Allow screen saver	Enables the Windows screen saver, even when this program is running.
Misc	QuickEdit	Causes any use of the mouse to mark text as though you had chosen the Mark command from the System Menu first. Check this box if your program makes no use of the mouse (though often Windows is able to automatically detect if the program can use a mouse or not and will disable the option appropriately).

Table 4-3.   *Settings in the Properties Dialog Box for a Program or Shortcut* (continued)

Tab	Setting	Description
Misc	Exclusive mode	Dedicates the mouse to this program. Not recommended, since it makes the mouse unusable as the Windows pointer until the program exits. If you select it, switch the Command Prompt window to full-screen mode instead (by pressing ALT-ENTER), which makes the Windows mouse pointer vanish.
Misc	Always suspend	Suspends this program whenever it's not the active window. Leave this box checked, unless the program does useful background activity.
Misc	Warn if still active	Specifies that Windows pop up a warning box if you try to close this program before it exits.
Misc	Idle sensitivity	Specifies that Windows attempt to detect when an active DOS program is idle and waiting for keyboard input, so that Windows can give more processor time to other applications. High sensitivity makes Windows give more time to other applications. Leave this alone unless keyboard response to the program is sluggish, in which case, make the sensitivity lower.
Misc	Fast pasting	Uses an optimized technique for pasting text into a Command Prompt window that fails with a few programs. If pasting doesn't work, turn this off.
Misc	Windows shortcut keys	Specifies which of the key combinations listed in this box perform Windows functions, even when Windows is running a DOS program. If your DOS application needs to use any of these combinations itself, uncheck the ones it needs.

Table 4-3.   *Settings in the Properties Dialog Box for a Program or Shortcut*
(continued)

Controlling the Amount of Memory the Program Can Use

The Memory tab of the program's Properties dialog box (shown in Figure 4-4) controls how much memory is available to a program using each of the DOS addressing schemes. In nearly all cases, Windows automatically allocates an appropriate amount of each kind of memory to the program when it runs the program. A few programs fail if given as much memory as Windows makes available (at the time many DOS programs were written, most people never imagined that anyone would ever put as much as 4MB in a single PC). If this is a problem, determine the kind of memory that the program uses—expanded (EMS), extended (XMS), or MS-DOS Protected-Mode (DPMI)—and try limiting it to 8,192KB (the program's documentation or help files may specify what types of memory the program can use and the maximum amount of memory that the program can handle).

 Be sure to select the Protected check box to prevent the DOS program from inadvertently changing the part of memory used by Windows itself.

Setting the Compatibility Mode

New to Windows XP is the compatibility mode, which attempts to present an environment for software that expects to be run in a particular version of Windows (see Chapter 1, section "Running Programs in Compatibility Mode"). For example, Ignition (the classic racing game from Unique Development Studios) refuses to install on Windows XP without the Windows 95 compatibility mode. You set the program's compatibility mode on the Compatibility tab of the Properties dialog box for the executable file or shortcut.

 You often must set the compatibility mode of both the installation program and the actual program for them to work properly. First, set the compatibility mode for the installation program and run it. Once the program is installed, find the installed executable program and give it the same compatibility mode. If it doesn't work the first time, try another mode.

Changing the Program's Icon

Windows uses an MS-DOS icon for DOS programs unless you configure it otherwise. If you want to use a different icon for a DOS program, display its Properties dialog box, click the Program tab, and click the Change Icon button. You see the Change Icon dialog box, shown here:

Windows displays a standard set of icons from which you can choose. If the program comes with an icon file, click Browse to select it.

DOS Programs vs. the Windows XP Desktop Theme

Applications written specifically for Windows XP use something called a *manifest* to work with the Windows XP theme. A manifest is a file that describes how the application is to appear while using the Windows XP theme. Most recent applications that comply closely with the Win32 API (Application Programming Interface—a set of tools that define how applications work with Windows) typically work fine without a manifest, but some do not. If an application behaves unexpectedly or does not appear correctly, try selecting the Disable Visual Themes check box on the Compatibility tab of the Properties dialog box for the program. For example, Macromedia's Dreamweaver 4.0 web site authoring program has custom toolbars that do not work well with the Windows XP theme (some buttons are covered by the swoopy new interface).

Installing and Configuring DOS Programs

DOS provides no standard way to install programs. Most DOS programs include a simple installation batch file that copies the program's files from the installation disks to your hard disk. Once a program's files are installed, you can create shortcuts to the executable file and put those shortcuts in the Start menu, on the desktop, or both, just like native Windows applications (see Chapter 1 for how to create shortcuts).

Since some DOS programs require that you install DOS drivers, Microsoft has included basic drivers for both sound cards and CD-ROM drives. These are loaded when Windows starts through lines in the Config.nt or Autoexec.nt files. For certain DOS programs, you may need to make changes to these files.

If you have a DOS program (or an older Windows program) that doesn't run properly under Windows XP, you can create revised copies of the Autoexec.nt and Config.nt files for use with the program and edit the properties of the program file (or a shortcut to it) to refer to the Autoexec and Config files you created. This method works if the documentation for the program specifies the lines that the Autoexec.bat (old name for Autoexec.nt) and Config.sys (old name for Config.nt) files need to contain. Follow these steps:

1. In an Explorer window, locate C:\Windows\System32\Config.nt and C:\ Windows\System32\Autoexec.nt (if Windows is stored on another drive, substitute the drive letter for C).

2. Select each file (Config.nt and Autoexec.nt) and press CTRL-C and then CTRL-V to place a copy of the file in the same folder.

3. Scroll down to the bottom of the list of files to find the copies. Select a file and press F2 to rename it. Name the copies Config.*ext* and Autoexec.*ext*, where *ext* is an abbreviation for the program you are configuring.

4. Right-click the program file or shortcut and choose Properties from the menu that appears. You see the Properties dialog box for the file or shortcut (described in the previous section).

5. Click the Program tab, which displays the name of the program file that the shortcut runs. Click the Advanced button to display the Windows PIF Settings dialog box:

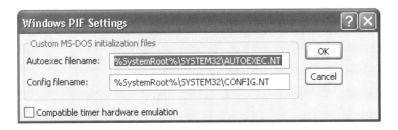

6. Change the contents of the Autoexec Filename and Config Filename boxes to the pathname of the file you created earlier. (If they are in the same folder as the Autoexec.nt and Config.nt files, change only the filename at the end of the pathname.) As you edit the filename, Windows shows you matching filenames.

7. If the program needs for the system clock to appear to run slower (that is, if it uses the computer's system clock for timing, and modern PCs make the program run too fast to be usable), select the Compatible Timer Hardware Emulation check box.

8. Click OK to return to the Properties dialog box for the shortcut.

9. For DOS programs that display information in the Command Prompt window, click the Font tab and choose a font size that looks good.

10. If the program uses expanded or extended memory, click the Memory tab and set the memory sizes, as described in the section "Controlling the Amount of Memory the Program Can Use" earlier in this chapter.

11. If you want the program to appear full-screen rather than in a window, click the Screen tab and choose Full-screen.

12. If the program needs to run in compatibility mode, so that Windows provides a software environment like a previous version of Windows, click the Compatibility tab, select the Run This Program in Compatibility Mode For check box, and select the version of Windows (see Chapter 1, section "Running Programs in Compatibility Mode").

13. Make any other changes to the properties of the file or shortcut and then click OK to save your changes.

14. Refer to the program's documentation and make whatever changes it suggests to the Autoexec and Config files you created for the program. When the manual or help file refers to the Autoexec.bat file, make the change to your copy of the Autoexec.nt file. When instructions refer to the Config.sys file, make the changes to your copy of the Config.nt file.

15. Test your changes by running the files or shortcut.

Tip   *If you want to see messages that let you know what Windows is doing when it processes your Config or Autoexec file, add the single word **echoconfig** as the last line of the file.*

The
Complete
Reference

Chapter 5

Copying, Moving, and Sharing Information Between Programs

Windows XP provides two methods of sharing data between different application programs (although each method has variations): You can cut or copy and then paste using the Windows Clipboard, or you can use OLE, object linking and embedding. In general, cutting-and-pasting (or its variant, drag-and-drop) works well for the simpler tasks—moving text from one application to another, for instance. OLE is useful when you want all the features of one type of program to work with an object in another program. For example, if you want to display an Excel spreadsheet in a Word document, and you want to be able to update a complicated formula and display the correct answer in the Word document, then you need to use OLE.

Sharing Data Through the Windows Clipboard

Copying or moving information from one location to another within or between programs is available in almost all Windows programs using the cut-and-paste commands. Cutting-and-pasting uses the Clipboard to store information temporarily. Some programs also let you use your mouse to drag information from one location to another.

| **Caution** | *The Clipboard can hold only one chunk of information at a time, so you either have to paste it somewhere else right away or not cut or copy anything else until you've pasted the information where you want it. If you cut or copy another chunk of information, it replaces the information already on the Clipboard.* |

Cutting, Copying, and Pasting

The following cut-and-paste techniques enable you to copy or move information within or between almost any Windows application:

- **Cut** Removes selected information from its current location and stores it (temporarily) on the Clipboard. From most programs you can choose Edit | Cut; press CTRL-X; right-click and choose Cut; or click the Cut toolbar button.

- **Copy** Copies selected information and makes a (temporary) duplicate of it on the Clipboard. From most programs you can choose Edit | Copy, press CTRL-C, right-click and choose Copy, or click the Copy toolbar button.

- **Paste** Copies information from the Clipboard to the location of the cursor in the active application. From most programs you can choose Edit | Paste; press CTRL-V; right-click and choose Paste; or click the Paste toolbar button.

To move information, you select it, cut it to the Clipboard, and then paste it in the new location. To copy information, you select it, copy it to the Clipboard, and then paste it in the new location.

| **Tip** | *If you're afraid you deleted something by mistake, press CTRL-Z to undo the change in most programs.* |

Once you cut or copy information onto the Clipboard, you can make multiple copies of it by pasting it as many times as you want.

Information on the Clipboard takes up RAM, limiting the resources your computer has available to do other things. Therefore, if you cut or copy a lot of information to the Clipboard, paste it quickly. Then, cut or copy something small—one letter or word, for instance—which replaces the large chunk of information on the Clipboard and makes most of the RAM available again. Some programs clear the Clipboard. You can also use the ClipBook Viewer to delete the information on the Clipboard.

If you use Microsoft Office 2000 or XP you may see the small Office Clipboard window (in Office 2000) or the task pane (in Office XP). The Office Clipboard stores up to 12 (for Office 2000) or 24 (for Office XP) "clips" from Office applications. Rest the pointer on a clip to see its contents. You can paste any clip by clicking its icon on the Office Clipboard. The Office Clipboard opens automatically after you cut more than one selection for Office applications.

Some programs don't completely support cut-and-paste. If you have trouble pasting into a program (pasting doesn't have the result you expect), first paste the information into Notepad. Then copy it from Notepad and try pasting into the program where you actually want the information to appear.

Dragging and Dropping

Drag-and-drop is another method of moving or copying information from one file to another, or to another location in the same file. To move information from one location to another, select it with your mouse and drag it to its new location.

Not all programs support drag-and-drop. Some programs copy the information you drag, rather than move it. Some programs enable you to choose whether to move or copy the information (for example, a program may enable you to copy the information by holding down the CTRL key while dragging).

Using the ClipBook Viewer
to Look at What's on the Clipboard

You needn't take for granted that the information you want is on the Clipboard—you can actually look at it by opening the ClipBook Viewer, a program that displays the current contents of the Clipboard. You can't edit what's on the Clipboard, but you can save it as a *Clipboard file*, with extension .clp. (Clipboard files are a form of HTML.)

ClipBook Viewer conflicts with Office XP, so it may not run if you have Office XP installed.

To open the ClipBook Viewer (shown in Figure 5-1), choose Start | Run, type **clipbrd** and press ENTER, or you can open a clipboard file (with extension .clp) from Windows Explorer. You can see two windows in the ClipBook Viewer, the Clipboard window (with the current contents of the Clipboard) and the Local ClipBook window (with your saved clips).

> **Note** *You might have to install the ClipBook Viewer (see Chapter 3, section "Installing and Uninstalling Programs that Come with Windows")—it isn't always automatically installed. Open the Control Panel, open Add/Remove Programs, click the Windows Setup icon, highlight Accessories And Utilities from the list of components, click Details, highlight Accessories, click Details again, and choose Clipboard Viewer.*

You can save the current contents of the Clipboard by using File | Save As on the ClipBook Viewer menu (but first make sure the Clipboard window is active). ClipBook Viewer saves the information in a clipboard file with extension .clp. Open a saved clipboard file by choosing File | Open. The ClipBook Viewer can open files saved in the Clipboard format only—you can give them a different extension, but the file is still in .clp format.

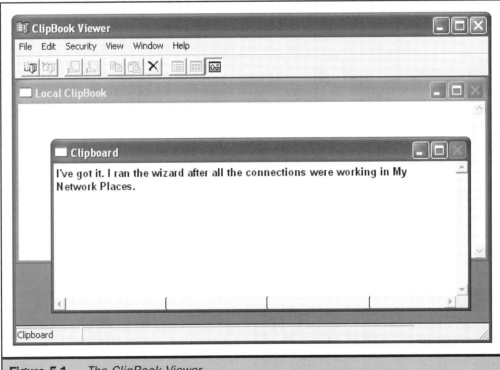

Figure 5-1. *The ClipBook Viewer*

When you open a clipboard file and the Clipboard already contains information, ClipBook Viewer asks you to confirm that you want to delete the current contents of the Clipboard.

To delete the contents of the Clipboard, choose Edit | Delete, press the DELETE key, or click the Delete (X) button. Deleting the contents of the Clipboard releases RAM for other uses. You can't cut-and-paste information from the ClipBook Viewer window—the information is already on the Clipboard!

The ClipBook Viewer enables you to save more than one clip at a time, by displaying the Local ClipBook window (with Window | Local ClipBook), pressing CTRL-V, and giving the clip a name.

Capturing Screens Using the Clipboard

Many products can take a *screen shot*, a picture of whatever is on the screen. This book is littered with screen shots that are used as figures. If you need to create a screen shot, you can use the Clipboard to create one. Use the PRINT SCREEN key that appears on your keyboard—it often is above the cursor control keys with the SCROLL LOCK and PAUSE keys. You can take two different kinds of screen shots:

- A picture of the whole screen by pressing PRINT SCREEN
- A picture of the active window by pressing ALT-PRINT SCREEN

Once the picture is on the Clipboard, you can paste it somewhere else. You may want to paste the picture into a graphics program such as Paint, so you can save it in a graphics file format and use it later (see Chapter 18). Or, you might want to paste it into a file, such as a word processing document containing an explanation of that screen or window.

Sharing Information by Linking and Embedding

OLE (Object Linking and Embedding) is far more flexible and can be far more complicated than cut-and-paste or drag-and-drop. OLE enables you to use all your software applications to create an integrated document. For instance, you might want to create an annual report that includes these components:

- Text you create and format by using a word processor, such as Microsoft Word or Corel WordPerfect.
- A company logo stored in a graphics file created by Adobe Photoshop, Paint, or some other graphics application.
- Data and calculations on operating costs stored in a Microsoft Excel or Lotus 1-2-3 spreadsheet.
- Graphs and charts, which may come from your spreadsheet package or another graphics package.

These components may not reflect exactly what *you* want to do, but the point is the same—if you want to combine the output of different applications, OLE offers many advantages over the Clipboard. Why? Because, when you use OLE, the original program retains ownership of the object, and you can use the program to edit the object. For instance, if you use OLE to embed a portion of a spreadsheet in a word processing document, you can always use the spreadsheet application to edit the object, and the spreadsheet in the word processing document will reflect those changes. If, instead, you use the Clipboard to copy the numbers from the spreadsheet and then paste the numbers to the word processor, they would just sit in the word processor, oblivious to their origins—you could use only the tools available in the word processor to edit the numbers. This means that if you later change the original spreadsheet, the numbers pasted in the word processing document won't change.

In OLE, an *object* refers to a piece of information from one application that is placed in a *container file* created by another application. For example, a spreadsheet or graphic is an object when it is included in a word processing document. OLE actually is two similar methods of sharing information between applications—embedding and linking. Sticking with the previous example, *embedding* means putting the spreadsheet object in the word processing document (container file) and asking the word processor to take care of storing the object. So, although the word processor enables you to edit the spreadsheet object by using the spreadsheet application, the spreadsheet object is stored with the word processing document. *Linking*, on the other hand, allows the object to retain a close relationship with its origins—so close, in fact, if the numbers in the original spreadsheet file change, the linked spreadsheet object in the word processing document changes to match. This occurs because the word processing document doesn't really contain the object it displays—it only contains a reference to the file where the information is stored.

You may also choose to insert a *package* into another file. A package is a small file that uses OLE, but instead of displaying content owned by another application, it displays an icon, which, when clicked, opens the owner application and displays the object. Packages can be either linked or embedded. Whether you choose to embed or link objects, the process is similar: You create an object in one application and then link or embed the object into another application.

Although using OLE to link files can be wonderfully convenient and can save you hours of revisions, it should be used judiciously. If you ever plan to move the file containing linked objects or to send it to someone, you must make sure one of the following occurs:

- The linked files also get moved or sent.
- The linked objects don't get updated. This means the host application won't go looking for the information in the linked file. To break the link, delete the object and paste in a nonlinked version instead.
- You edit the links so the host file knows where to find the source files for the linked objects.

Otherwise, your beautifully organized and time-saving document can become a complete mess. If you are going to move a document with linked objects in it, you need to know how to maintain links, a topic covered later in this chapter.

If you don't need the automatic updating you get with linked objects (for instance, if the source file isn't going to change, or if you don't want the object to reflect changes), or if you know you are going to move or send files, then stick with embedded objects—they're easier to maintain. However, embedding a large object may take more disk space than linking.

 Not all programs support OLE. Some applications enable you to link one file to another in a different way—by using a hyperlink (see Chapter 24). A hyperlink actually takes you from one file to another, opening the application for the second file, if necessary.

Creating Linked or Embedded Objects

The way you link or embed an object depends on the application programs you're using—the program into which you want to embed or link the object. Most programs have a menu command to create an object by using OLE, but you may have to use the online help system to find the command. In Microsoft Word, for instance, you can use Insert | Object to create an object by using OLE. When using Insert | Object in Microsoft Word or its equivalent in another program, you may see the Display As Icon option. This option allows you to create a package, an icon that when clicked, opens the object in its native application. The following two techniques may also work to link or embed an object: dragging-and-dropping and using Edit | Paste Special. Neither technique is supported by all applications.

Embedding an Object by Dragging and Dropping

The easiest way to embed an object is to drag the information from one program and drop it in the other program. For this method to work, both applications must support drag-and-drop embedding. Check the documentation for the program that contains the information you want to embed. When dragging the information you want to embed, use the same technique you use to copy selected information *within* the application: Some applications require you to hold down the CTRL key while dragging the information. For instance, in Excel, you have to click-and-drag the border of the selected area to move or copy it.

Follow these steps to use drag-and-drop embedding:

1. Select the information you want to embed.

2. Use drag-and-drop to drag the selected information to the other application; use the same drag-and-drop technique you use to copy information within an application. If the second application isn't visible on the screen, you can drag

the information to the application's Taskbar button—hold the mouse pointer there for a second, and the application window opens.

3. Drop the information where you want it—if the application supports OLE, you automatically create an embedded object.

You may be able to specify that the information be linked rather than embedded (the usual default when OLE drag-and-drop is supported) by holding down the SHIFT key—try it to see whether the application you are using supports this feature.

Linking or Embedding an Object Using Paste Special

You may want a little more control over the object than you have when you drag-and-drop it—to achieve more control over the object, use the Edit | Paste Special command found in many applications. The procedure is much like using the Clipboard to cut-and-paste, except you paste by using OLE instead, as follows:

1. Select the information you want to link or embed.

2. Press CTRL-C or CTRL-X to copy or cut the information (or use another method to copy or cut).

3. Move the cursor where you want the object to appear.

4. Choose Edit | Paste Special. You see a dialog box similar to the one shown in Figure 5-2. Choose the correct application from the choices displayed. Make

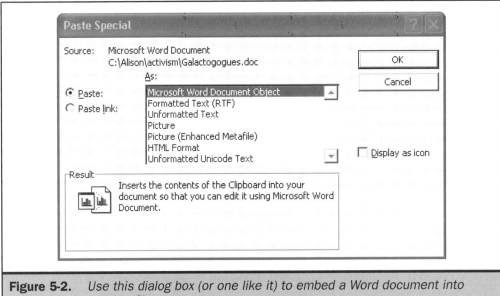

Figure 5-2.   *Use this dialog box (or one like it) to embed a Word document into another file.*

sure to choose the application you want to use to edit the object—in the figure, that is Microsoft Word. If you choose another option, you won't be using OLE—instead, you will be using the Clipboard to do a simple paste of information from one application to another.

5. Choose the correct setting either to embed the object in the new file or to link the two files together. To embed the object, choose the Paste option; to link the object, choose the Paste Link option. Figure 5-2 shows the settings to embed a Microsoft Word object into an Excel spreadsheet. Figure 5-3 shows the settings to link an Excel spreadsheet into a Microsoft Word document. Other applications may have Paste Special dialog boxes that look different from these.

6. Change the Display As Icon setting, if necessary. If you choose to display the object as an icon, you don't see the information itself. Instead, you create a *packaged object* that shows the information it contains only when you open its icon.

7. Click OK to link or embed the object. You see the object in the container file, as in Figure 5-4.

Editing a Linked or Embedded Object

Editing a linked or embedded object is simple—in most applications, you just double-click the object. For other applications, you may need to right-click the object to display a menu with an edit option or change modes so you are in Edit mode (if you're

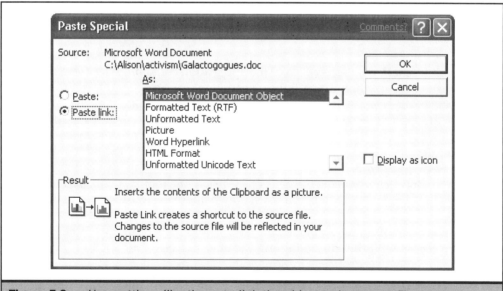

Figure 5-3. *Use settings like these to link the object to its parent file.*

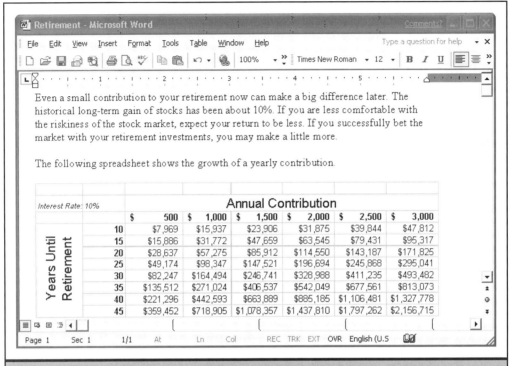

Figure 5-4.   *Part of an Excel worksheet embedded in a Word document*

having trouble, check the help system of the application containing the object). Once you figure out how to edit the object, the object's application opens. Next, the menu and toolbars of the window in which the object appears are replaced by the menu and toolbars of the application assigned by the registry to that file type (usually the application used to create the object). In other words, if you're editing an Excel object in a Word document, double-click the object to display Excel's menu and toolbars in Word's window, as in Figure 5-5. You can edit the object by using that application's tools. When you're done, click outside the object to reinstate the regular menu and toolbars, or choose File | Update or Exit. If you're asked whether you want to update the object, answer Yes.

If the object is linked, rather than embedded, you can also edit the object by editing the source file itself. If the file containing the object is also open, you may have to update it manually to see the new information in the object. Closing and opening the file containing the object may be the easiest way to update the object.

Delete an object by single-clicking it to select it—you'll probably see a box around it—then press the DELETE or BACKSPACE key.

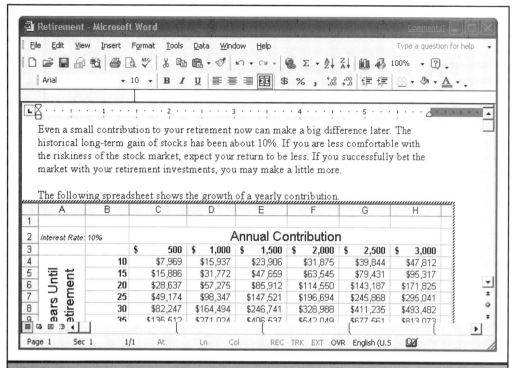

Figure 5-5.   *Edit an Excel object in a Word document by using the Excel menu and
toolbars that appear when you double-click the object.*

Maintaining Links

If you decide to use a link to put an object in a file, rather than embed the object, you
may have to do some maintenance if the linked file or the file containing the link moves
to a new location. A link is usually updated each time the file containing the object is
opened or printed. *Updating* means that the current information from the linked file is
brought into the object.

If the location of a file changes, you may need to "lock" the link so the last available
information is retained, break the link so the object becomes an embedded object rather
than a linked object, or edit the link so the correct path and filename are referenced. The
exact commands may differ by application (check the online help), but usually there's
one dialog box where all these tasks can be performed, like the following one.

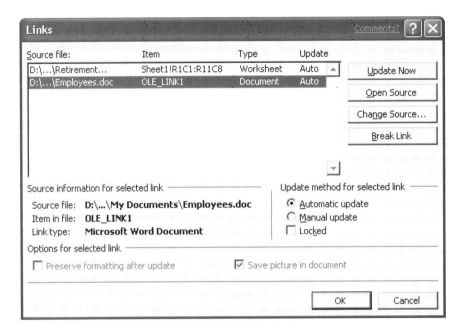

In most Microsoft applications, you can display the dialog box by choosing Edit |
Links. The following list explains how to do these three tasks in a Microsoft application.
Other applications work in a similar way, but may have different names for the dialog
box buttons and options.

- **Lock the link**   Use the Locked option on the Links dialog box to lock the
  selected link. You can select multiple links to lock by CTRL-clicking or SHIFT-
  clicking additional links. A locked link isn't updated. To check whether a link
  is locked, select the link and see whether the Locked option is checked.

- **Break the link**   Use the Break Link (or Cancel Link) button to break a link. When
  you break a link, the link disappears from the Links list, and you can no longer
  use the original application to edit the object. A better choice, often, is to lock the
  link or replace the linked object with an embedded object.

- **Edit the link**   Use the Change Source button to edit the link. This enables you
  to redirect the link to a different file or to the same file stored in a different location.

Another option is to set up the file to update the links only when you tell it to do
so by specifying manual updating. The Links dialog box has an Update Method option
that enables you to specify automatic or manual updating. If you set this option to
manual, the links are updated only when you display the Links dialog box and click
the Update Now button.

Saving Small Bits of Data as Scraps

Few people use scraps, but if you need them, they may be a lifesaver. *Scraps* are OLE objects that have been left on the desktop or in a folder. You can keep a scrap on the desktop or in the folder or, at some later point, drag it to another application. A scrap has an icon that looks like this:

Document
Scrap 'Scr...

Scrap icons all look the same, but their names give you a clue as to which application created them. For instance, a scrap from Word or another word processor is called a *Document scrap,* a scrap from Excel is a *Worksheet scrap,* and a scrap from Quattro Pro is a *Notebook scrap* (using the Quattro Pro terminology). Not all applications can be used to create scraps. For instance, Notepad, which doesn't support drag-and-drop, cannot be used to create scraps.

To create a scrap, drag some information to the desktop or copy it to the Clipboard, and then paste it to the desktop (by right-clicking the desktop and choosing Paste). When you open a scrap on the desktop, the application that created the information opens to display it. You can drag a scrap into a different application to create an OLE object out of it.

  Use only scraps that you have created. Sending scraps by e-mail is a clever way of distributing viruses, since scraps can executable programs.

The
Complete
Reference

Chapter 6

Sharing Your Computer with Family Members and Officemates

Because Windows XP is based on Windows 2000, it has security-oriented features that were never present in Windows Me/9*x*. Windows Me/9*x* (like the original DOS operating system on which they were based) had almost no built-in security, with no way to prevent one user from reading another user's files. For example, if you create multiple user profiles on a computer running Windows 98 Second Edition, you see a password dialog box when you start Windows. This suggests that the computer is secure, but you can simply click Cancel and get complete access. Windows XP can require a user name and password.

Windows XP also has a new feature, Fast User Switching, so that multiple people can be logged on and running programs at the same time. Once you have created separate user accounts for the people who will use the computer, you can set make folders private to prevent other users of the computer from seeing them. It also provides Simple File Sharing, which makes it easy to share access to files and folders with other people who use your computer. This chapter examines how to set up Windows for multiple users, including creating user accounts, assigning passwords, logging on, and switching users. We also describe how to log on and off and how to check who's logged on.

However, many of Windows XP's new user features aren't available in Windows Home Edition. If you need features listed in the sidebar "Windows XP Professional's User and Security Features that Aren't in Home Edition," you may have to upgrade. The last section of this chapter describes how to use Safe Mode to bypass some of Windows XP Home Edition's security limitations, but it's not for the faint of heart.

Windows XP Professional's User and Security Features That Aren't in Home Edition

Windows XP Home Edition omits the following user account features that are included in Windows XP Professional:

- **Encrypting File System (EFS)**   EFS enables you to encrypt files or folders so that other computer users can't open them without a password. However, you can prevent other users from reading the files stored in your My Documents folder.

- **Domain accounts**   Large organizations can stores account information in the Active Directory (AD) program running on a Windows NT, 2000, or .NET server. When you log in using a domain, your computer gets information from Active Directory about what your settings are and what you have permission to do. Domain accounts are used on larger networks where maintaining accounts stored in each individual computer would be impractical. Domain accounts can use *roaming user profiles*, which allow people to use their own user account from any computer on a LAN, and *mandatory user profiles*, in which only administrators can make changes.

- **Groups**   Each user account is a member of one or more *groups*, which define what the user can do. Each group comes with *rights* that allow members of that group to perform system-wide tasks, like installing or running programs. A user account has all the rights of all the groups to which it belongs. Groups also have permissions to use certain files and folders. Windows XP Home comes with two built-in groups that you can't change: Administrators (for Administrator accounts) and Users (for Limited accounts). Windows XP Professional enables you to edit the rights of existing groups and create new groups via the Microsoft Management Console.

- **Disabling Simple File Sharing**   If you want to control who has access to drives and folders, you have to disable Simple File Sharing. Windows XP Home doesn't allow you to disable this feature, except by starting in Safe Mode (see "Controlling File and Folder Permissions from Safe Mode" at the end of this chapter). Windows XP Professional enables you to control which users can read, modify, delete, create, and execute files in shared folders.

- **Policy settings**   These settings control many other security options, including whether user accounts need passwords, how often people need to change them, whether accounts are locked after a specified number of wrong passwords are entered, who can install printers, who can use the CD-ROM and floppy drivers, and other permissions.

Chapter 30 describes how to share files, folders, and printers with other people on a local area network (LAN), rather than users on a single computer. For network security topics, such as how to send secure e-mail, control what information Internet Explorer stores on your disk, or protect your computer from viruses, see Chapter 32.

User Account Basics

When two or more users share a computer, they don't have to argue about what color the background should be, what programs should be on the Start menu, or whether to use single-click or double-click style. Instead, each user can have a *user account* (called a *user profile* in previous versions of Windows). Windows creates a folder for each user account with files that describe each user's preferences, storing the folder in C:\ Documents And Settings. (Replace C with the appropriate drive letter if Windows isn't installed on C.) Each time a user logs on, Windows finds the appropriate user account and makes the appropriate changes. If you change any of your preferences (for example, choosing a new wallpaper), that information is stored in your user account, so that the change will still be there the next time you log on, but not the next time someone else logs on. Whenever your computer acquires a new user, you should establish a new user account (see "Setting Up a Computer for Multiple Users" later in this chapter).

User accounts enable several people to share one computer, or to share folders and other resources on a LAN.

Your *user password* is the password for your user account. You type it when you start up Windows or switch from one user to another, if your computer has user accounts for which passwords have been created. You can change your password at any time. Windows also stores a *password hint*—a word or phrase that would remind you of your password if you forget it, but that wouldn't give the password away to anyone else. If you are truly concerned about forgetting your password (we always are!), you can also create a *password reset disk*, a floppy disk that you can use to log on to your user account even if you forget your password.

You have the option to not have a password. Simply choose not to enter one when prompted by the Windows XP Setup Wizard, or remove the password later (see the Appendix). Regardless of your choice, if you plan on being the only user of your computer you can opt to automatically log into your machine. Just make sure you aren't offering free access to sensitive data to unauthorized individuals.

We recommend using a password, even a simple one (like your name, or the same name as the user account). Some programs (like Task Scheduler, described in Chapter 1) don't work with accounts that don't have passwords.

A new feature in Windows XP (new to Windows Me/9x users, anyway) enables you to password-protect the files in your My Documents folder, so that other people using the same computer later won't be able to read them. Each user's My Documents folder can be protected from view from the other users.

If you are wondering which user account you are logged on as, click the Start button. The user account name appears at the top of the menu.

Types of User Accounts

Windows XP Home Edition provides three types of user accounts:

- **Administrator** Enables access to all accounts. Each computer needs at least one administrator account at all times. You can have more than one, if you like. When using an administrator account, you can give commands to create, edit, and delete all user accounts, and you can install software. Windows comes with at least two administrator accounts named Administrator and either Owner or a user name you provided when you installed Windows XP. (When you install Windows XP, it asks you for the names of users, and Windows creates an administrator user account for each person). Microsoft recommends that you use administrator accounts only for installing programs and managing the system.

- **Limited** Enables access to your own account. When using a limited account, you cannot install software, open files in other people's My Documents folders, change system settings, or change other people's user accounts. You can run programs that are already installed, and you can modify your own user account (except that you can't change it into an administrator account). You should log on with a limited account for day-to-day work, to avoid viruses and other programs that might try to install themselves when you aren't looking.

■ **Guest**   Enables access only to programs that are installed on the computer. Windows has one guest account (named Guest). When using the guest account, you cannot change any user accounts, open files in other people's My Documents folders, or install software. The Guest user is disabled when Windows XP is installed, but you can enable it (see "Enabling and Disabling the Guest Account" later in this chapter).

> **Note**   *Some older programs, especially games designed to run under Windows 9x/Me, don't run in limited accounts.*

You can create as many administrator or limited accounts as you want. You can't create guest accounts.

We recommend that for a home computer, you create an administrator account for each adult (or one account that the adults share) and a limited account for each child (or one account that the children share). The adults can make their My Documents folders private and use them for billpaying, correspondence, and other files that you don't want the kids to tamper with. For a computer in a small office, consider whether you want to give some people access to all files while others have access only to their own files, and create administrator and limited accounts accordingly.

User Accounts That Windows Creates

When you install Windows XP, there are at least three accounts:

■ **Owner or a user name(s) you provided**   An administrator account. If you typed user names when the Windows XP Setup Wizard prompted for them during installation, you have administrator accounts for each user. For example, when you installed or upgraded to Windows XP, if you entered "Margy" and "Jordan" as the names of users, you have administrator accounts named Margy and Jordan. If you didn't enter names when you installed Windows XP, you have an administrator account named Owner.

■ **Administrator**   This account is hidden. (See the section "The User Accounts Window" later in this chapter for how to unhide this account.) You can log in only in Safe Mode or the Recovery Console (described in Chapter 2).

■ **Guest**   The guest account, which is usually disabled.

You can create additional administrative or limited accounts for each person who uses the computer, and you can rename or delete the accounts. Until you create other accounts and passwords, you automatically log on as Owner when you start Windows. For how to create new accounts, see "Creating New User Accounts" later in this chapter.

Caution   *If you are concerned about security (as you should be, if your computer connects to the Internet), make sure that the Guest account is disabled (see the section "Enabling and Disabling the Guest Account" later in this chapter). Also be sure to create passwords for each user account, as described in the section "Adding or Removing Passwords" later in this chapter. Change all but one or two rarely used accounts from administrator to limited accounts to reduce security holes.*

User Profile Configuration Settings

Table 6-1 lists the some of the files and folders that are stored separately for each user account. These items are stored in the user account's *user profile*—the folder that contains all the settings for the user. A user profile is usually in the C:\Documents And

Item	Contents
Ntuser.dat, Ntuser.dat.log, and Ntuser.tmp files	This user's configuration settings and other information.
Application Data folder	This user's application program configuration settings (some are also stored in the Local Settings\Application Data folder).
Cookies folder	The cookies stored by Internet Explorer while run by this user (see Chapter 24).
Desktop folder	The items that appear on this user's desktop.
Favorites folder	Items this user has added to the Favorites folder.
Local Settings\Application Data	This user's application program configuration settings (some are also stored in the Application Data folder).
Local Settings\History folder	Shortcuts to web sites this user has viewed recently.
Local Settings\Temporary Internet Files folder	Recently-viewed web pages.
My Documents folder	The files and folders that appear in this user's My Documents folder when the user is logged on. You can tell Windows to look in a different location for your My Documents folder: see "Modifying User Accounts" later in this chapter.
NetHood folder	This user's network shortcuts, which appear in the My Network Places folder when the user is logged on.
PrintHood folder	This user's shared printers.
Recent Documents folder	Shortcuts to files this user has opened recently.

Table 6-1.   *Information Stored in User Account Profiles*

Item	Contents
Send To folder	Shortcuts to folders and devices that appear on the Send To menu when the user right-clicks a file or folder.
Start Menu folder	The shortcuts and folders that Windows uses to display the Start and More Programs menus for this user.
Templates folder	Template files for word processors and other programs, used when this user creates a new document.

Table 6-1.   *Information Stored in User Account Profiles* (continued)

Settings*username* folder, where *username* is replaced by the name of the user account. (If Windows is installed on a partition other than C:, so is this folder.) You need to configure Windows Explorer to display hidden files and folders to see them (see Chapter 8).

User accounts have a number of configuration options:

Setting	Description
Name	User name that appears at the top of the Start menu and on the Welcome screen.
Picture	Graphic file that appears on the Start menu and welcome screen next to the user's name.
Account type	Administrator limited, or guest (see "Types of User Accounts" earlier in this chapter).
Password	The password should be at least seven characters, and ideally longer. You can include lowercase letters, uppercase letters, numbers, and punctuation. Don't use names or words that appear in the dictionary.

Simple File Sharing

Simple File Sharing (SFS) is a new feature of Windows XP. When Simple File Sharing is enabled (which it is when you first install Windows) and when you share a drive or folder, you share that drive or folder with all user accounts on your computer.

The advantage of Simple File Sharing is that you don't have to make a lot of choices when you decide to share files with other users of your computer, or with other people on your network (if your computer is connected to a local area network).

Windows XP Professional enables you to disable Simple File Sharing and use a more complex system of permissions. You can't disable Simple File Sharing in Windows XP Home Edition, except by starting in Safe Mode (see "Controlling File and Folder Permissions from Safe Mode" at the end of this chapter).

Fast User Switching

Fast User Switching is a new feature of Windows XP that allows you to switch from one user account to another without the first user logging off. For example, a user named Jordan might be running Outlook Express and Microsoft Access. Another user named Meg needs to check her mail and asks to use the computer. Fast User Switching lets Jordan step aside and Meg switch the computer to her user account. Jordan's programs are on hold until Meg is done using the computer. When Jordan switches back to his account, his programs are just where he left them.

Fast User Switching is enabled by default if your Windows system has at least 64MB of RAM. With less RAM, the system doesn't have enough space to store one user's environment, including its running programs and open files, while another user is active.

 You can't use Fast User Switching if you use the Classic logon screen instead of the Welcome screen for logging on (see "Controlling How Users Log On" later in this chapter).

Setting Up a Computer for Multiple Users

When you start using Windows XP, you are automatically logged on with an administrator user account named Administrator or Owner, unless you tell the Windows XP Setup Wizard the names of the people who will use the computer (which causes the Setup Wizard to create administrator accounts for each of them). Using this administrator account, you can create user accounts for the people who will use the computer, giving each person the appropriate type of account (administrator or limited) based on the person's level of use.

 We recommend creating a password for each user account, even if it's an obvious one. Passwords prevent toddlers or bored passersby from using your computer, even if the password is simply "xxx" or the same as the user name. Also, some programs (like Task Scheduler, described in Chapter 1) work only with accounts that have passwords.

The User Accounts Window

To make basic changes to user accounts or to create new accounts, choose Start | Control Panel and click User Accounts. You see the User Accounts window shown in Figure 6-1. The existing accounts appear in the lower part of the window.

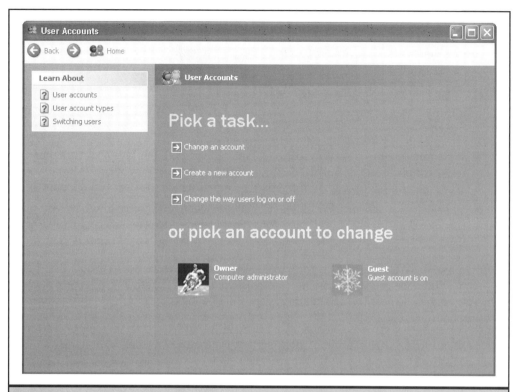

Figure 6-1. *Creating or changing user accounts (when logged on with an administrator account)*

If you want the User Accounts window to include the hidden Administrator user account, too, you can configure it to do so, as long as you don't mind editing the Registry (see Chapter 38). After backing up your Registry, follow these steps:

1. Find the HKEY_LOCAL_MACHINE\SOFTWARE\Microsoft\ WindowsNT\CurrentVersion\Winlogon\SpecialAccounts\UserList.

2. Right-click the UserList key and choose New | DWORD Value.

3. Type **Administrator** as the name of the new key and press ENTER.

4. Double-click the new key, type **1** in the Value Data box and click OK.

5. Close and reopen the User Accounts window to update its information.

After following these steps, take a look at the User Accounts window to see what appears.

We like to have the Administrator account visible so that we can set or change its password. However, making it visible still doesn't enable you to log onto it, except from Safe Mode or the Recovery Console (see Chapter 2).

Controlling How Users Log On

As the administrator of your PC, you can choose how Windows asks people to log on. You have two choices:

- **Welcome screen** The Windows XP Welcome screen displays a picture and name for each user account, so that users click the one they want. If the user account has a password, a white box appears in which the user types a password.

- **Classic logon screen** Windows NT/2000-style logon screen, in which you type the user account name and password. Fast User Switching isn't available if you use the Classic logon screen (see "Fast User Switching" earlier in this chapter).

If you use the Welcome screen, you can also choose whether or not to enable Fast User Switching. To choose between the Welcome screen and the Classic login screen, and to enable or disable Fast User Switching, you must be logged in with an administrator account. Follow these steps:

1. Make sure that you are the only user who is logged on (see "Managing Multiple Users" later in this chapter).
2. Choose Start | Control Panel, and click User Accounts to display the User Accounts window (see Figure 6-1).
3. Click Change The Way Users Log On Or Off. You see the User Accounts window shown in Figure 6-2.
4. Make your selections, using the Use The Welcome Screen check box and the Use Fast User Switching check box, and click the Apply Options button.

Logging On Automatically

If you want Windows to log onto a specific user account automatically when you start up Windows, so you don't have to type a password each time Windows starts, four things must be true:

- The Welcome screen must be enabled, as described in the preceding set of steps.
- The Guest account must be disabled. See the section "Enabling and Disabling the Guest Account" later in this chapter.
- Your computer must have only one user account (other than the Guest account and the hidden Owner or Administrator account).
- The user account must not have a password. See the section "Adding or Removing Passwords" later in this chapter.

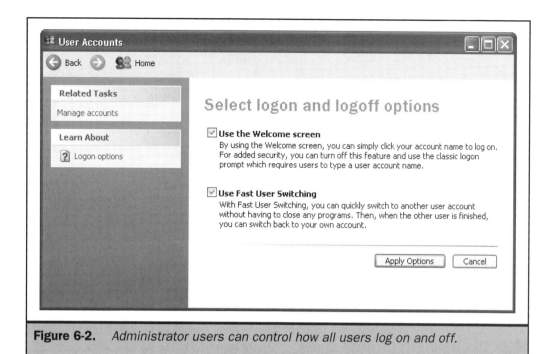

Figure 6-2.   *Administrator users can control how all users log on and off.*

Tip   *If you want to log on automatically even though not all of these four things are true, you can use the TweakUI program (see Chapter 1, section "Using TweakUI to Change the Windows Interface"). In the left pane of the TweakUI window, click the Logon plus box and click the Autologon category. Select the Log On Automatically At System Startup check box and specify the user name. Click the Set Password button to enter the password. You can also use TweakUI to control which user accounts appear on the Welcome screen.*

Creating, Modifying, and Deleting User Accounts

If you are logged in with an administrator account, you can change account settings for all user accounts. Limited account users can change only their own user account, and the Guest account can't change user accounts at all.

Creating New User Accounts

Follow these steps to create a new user account:

1. Choose Start | Control Panel and click User Accounts to display the User Accounts window (see Figure 6-1).

2. Click Create A New Account. Windows prompts you for the account name and the type of account. You have only two options: Computer Administrator or Limited.

3. Click Create Account. Windows creates the account.

4. Log in using the new account (by choosing Start | Log Off | Switch Users). Windows doesn't create all the configuration files until the first the new user logs in.

5. Adjust the desktop and Start menu for the new user, as described in Chapters 10 and 11.

6. If this user already has data files (word processing documents, spreadsheets, and so forth) stored on the computer, move these files into the My Documents folder for the new account. This step makes these files easily available when the person is logged on, because they appear in the My Documents folder.

New accounts start with the Windows default settings, as well as settings that have been stored for all users. For example, when programs are installed, they usually create desktop icons and Start menu commands in the C:\Documents And Settings\All Users folder so that all users, including new user accounts, can run the program.

Unless you don't care about security, be sure to modify the new account to have a password, as described in the next section.

Modifying User Accounts

You can change the name, picture, account type, and password from the User Accounts window. A few options, such as the locations of the My Documents and Favorites folders, are set in other ways.

To change user account settings, choose Start | Control Panel, and click User Accounts to display the User Accounts window (see Figure 6-1). In the lower part of the window, click the name of the account you want to change. You see a list of the settings that you can change. These are

■ **Name** Name that appears on the Welcome screen and at the top of the Start menu. It's also the name of the folder in C:\Documents And Settings that contains the settings for this user account. You can't rename the Guest account. When you rename an account, the renaming doesn't take full effect until you log off and log back on. Renaming a user account doesn't change the name of the user's folder in C:\Documents And Settings—Windows continues to use the folder with the old name.

■ **Picture** Picture that appears to the left of the user account name on the login screen and Start menu. Windows XP comes with a small selection of pictures you can use, or you can click Browse For More Pictures to specify a graphics file of your own. Click Change Picture when you have selected the picture you want to use.

Another way to change the picture of the currently logged-in account is by clicking the Start button and clicking the picture at the top of the Start menu.

- **Account type**   Administrator or limited. You can't change the type of the Guest account, and you can't change other accounts to be guest accounts.

- **Password**   Password that the user has to type when logging on. The Guest account has no password, and you can't create one. See the next section for how to create a password for an account. Once an account has a password, you can remove the password later.

If you are modifying your own account, you see another option: Set Up My Account To Use A .NET Passport. Clicking this option runs the .NET Passport Wizard, which asks a series of questions about your e-mail address, a password, a secret question and answer to be used to help you remember the password if you forget it, and your location. This passport enables Windows to identify you when you visit Microsoft-owned web sites such as **www.microsoft.com**, **www.msn.com**, and **www.hotmail.com**, as well as shopping sites that use the Microsoft Passport service. The Wizard suggests that you use a Microsoft-operated mailbox if you have an address there (addresses at hotmail.com and msn.com—Microsoft still uses Windows to sell its Internet services), but any e-mail address works. Once you've configured your account to use your .NET Passport, you can click Change My .NET Passport to switch to a different .NET Passport or to change information that is part of the Passport. You must be able to connect to the Internet to set up or change your .NET Passport, because Microsoft's servers store that information.

Changing the Location of the My Documents Folder

The My Documents folder for a user is normally in C:\Documents And Settings\ *username*\My Documents (assuming that Windows is installed on C:). You can tell Windows to use a different folder instead, by following these steps:

1. Click Start, right-click My Documents, and choose Properties from the menu that appears. You see the My Documents Properties dialog box, with the Target tab selected (see Figure 6-3). The Target box contains the current location of your My Documents folder.

2. To tell Windows that you want to store your files in another folder, click the Move button and browse to the folder in which you plan to store (or already store) your files. You can click the Make New Folder button if the folder doesn't exist yet. Click the My Network Places link if you want to choose a folder on another computer on your network. Click OK when you have selected the folder.

3. To switch back to the original (default) location of the My Documents folder (in C:\Documents And Settings*username*), click the Restore Default button.

4. Click OK. Windows asks if you want to move the files that are in your old My Documents folder to your new My Documents folder.

5. Click Yes or No.

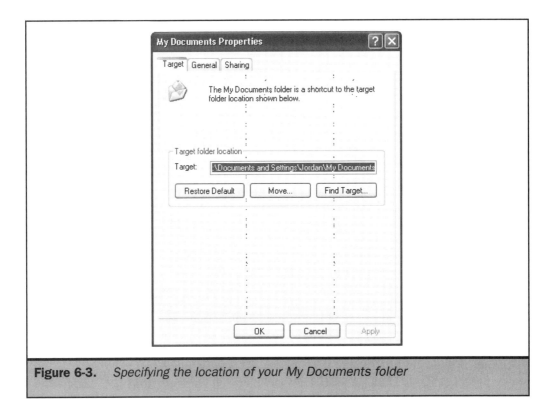

Figure 6-3.   *Specifying the location of your My Documents folder*

   Keeping your My Documents folder on a separate disk drive or partition makes it easy to backup or move your files separately from your programs. Wherever it is, be sure to back up your My Documents folder regularly if you store your files in it.

Changing the Location of the Entire User Profile

Domain-based LANS, such as those used by large organizations and run via Windows servers, enable you to store the entire user profile on another computer. For example, a corporation might set up all computers to store all user profiles on corporate servers that are backed up every night. This configuration makes software maintenance and backup easier, and Windows XP Professional's *roaming profiles* even allow employees to log in from any corporate computer to access their files.

What about Windows XP Home Edition users? This version of Windows doesn't support roaming files—it omits most corporate-oriented features, because it's designed for use on small (or no) LANs. However, you might still want to move your user profile— the contents of C:\Documents And Settings*username*—to another location. We like to create a separate partition (D:) in which we store all our files, separate from Windows and program files. We want our user profiles to be on D:, too, so that when we back up the files on D:, we back up all our program settings, Outlook Express messages, and other important files that are stored in our user profiles.

There are two ways to move your user profile to another location:

- **Hack the Registry.** Microsoft doesn't recommend this method, but we've used it successfully. For information, go to the **support.microsoft.com** web site and search for the KnowledgeBase article Q236621.

- **Mount a partition in its place.** As described in section "Assigning Pathnames to Partitions" in Chapter 33, you can tell Windows to assign a pathname (for example, C:\Documents And Settings\Margy) to a partition (for example, D:). This means that the contents of D:\ appear to be the contents of C:\Documents And Settings\Margy. Your Windows partition (usually C:) must be formatted using NTFS for this method to work.

If you'd like to try this last method, follow these steps to move the user profile for the account *username* (after making a backup of your system). These steps assume that your user profiles are currently stored in C:\Documents And Settings; substitute the actual pathname if they are elsewhere:

1. You need to be logged in as a different user when you mount the partition, and you need to be using an administrator account. If necessary, create a new administrator account to use during this process.

2. You need to be able to see all files, including hidden files, in order to move a user profile. In an Explorer window, choose Tools | Folder Options, click the View tab, scroll down the Advanced Settings list to find the Hidden Files And Folders settings, and choose Show Hidden Files And Folders. Click OK.

3. Log in as the *username* account. If the documents folder is private (which means that other user accounts can't see its contents), open an Explorer window (by choosing Start | My Computer), right-click the C:\Documents And Settings\ *username* folder, click Sharing And Security, and clear the Make This Folder Private check box.

4. Log off of the *username* account (Start | Log Off | Log Off) and log in using another account that is an administrator account.

5. Configure this account to be able to see hidden files, as shown in step 2.

6. Copy the contents of C:\Documents And Settings\ *username* to the root folder of another partition or drive. For example, copy all the file and folders from C:\Documents And Settings\Jesse to D:\.

7. Rename the C:\Documents And Settings\ *username* folder (for example, rename it as *Username* Backup). Then create an empty folder with the original name (*username*). You need a completely empty folder in the place where the user profile used to be.

8. Click Start, right-click My Computer, and choose Manage. You see the Computer Management window.

9. Click the Disk Management item that appears below the Storage heading in the left pane. Disk Management appears in the right pane.

10. Right-click the drive or partition to which you copied the user profile. Choose Change Drive Letters And Paths from the menu that appears. You see a dialog box showing the current name of the drive or partition (for example, D:).

11. Click Add.

12. In the Mount In The Following Empty NTFS Folder, type **C:\Documents And Settings***username* and close the Computer Management window. (Replace "username" with the actual account name.)

13. In an Explorer window, check that the user profile folders and files appear once again in the C:\Documents And Settings*username* folder (even though they are actually stored on a separate drive or partition).

14. Log in as *username* to test your moved user profile.

The first time you log in as *username*, you may see an error message telling you that it can't find your roaming profile, but the user account should work anyway. When you are sure that your pathname surgery worked, you can delete the backup copy of the user profile that you created in step 7.

Changing the Start Menu for All Users

Each user can customize her own Start menu, but an administrator user can customize everyone's Start menus at the same time. For example, you might want to add a command to display a program that everyone in your workgroup will use or a shortcut to a shared folder. Here's how:

1. Right-click the Start button and choose Open All Users from the menu that appears. You see the Start Menu window, which is an Explorer window displaying the files that make up the default Start menu for all user accounts. These files are usually stored in C:\Documents And Settings\All Users\Start Menu (if Windows is installed on C:).

2. If you want the command to appear in everyone's All Programs menu, open the Programs folder. Otherwise, stay in the Start Menu folder to create a command that appears on everyone's Start menu.

3. Choose File | New | Shortcut to run the Create Shortcut Wizard.

4. Following the Wizard's prompts, create a shortcut to the program, folder, or file that you want on everyone's Start menu.

The shortcut you create appears on each user's Start or All Programs menu the next time each person logs on. You can use the Start Menu window to move or delete shortcuts for all users, too.

Adding or Removing Passwords

If you don't want other people to be able to log on as you, assign your account a password. When you create a password for your own account, Windows also offers you the option of a private My Documents folder—one that other people can't open.

Another reason to assign passwords to user accounts is that some programs don't run on nonpassworded accounts. For example, Norton AntiVirus (**www.symantec.com**) won't run if the current account doesn't have a password. Scheduled tasks (described in Chapter 1 don't, either.

Follow these steps to add a password to your own user account in the User Accounts window (administrators can use the same steps to add a password to another user's account):

1. Choose Start | Control Panel, and click User Accounts to display the User Accounts window (see Figure 6-1).

2. Click the name of the account to which you want to add a password.

3. Click Create A Password. You see the window shown in Figure 6-4.

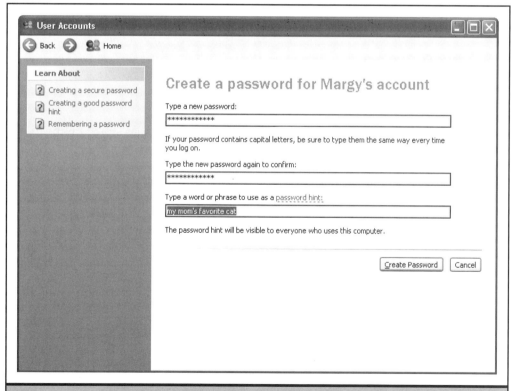

Figure 6-4.   *Changing the password for a user account*

4. Type the password into each of the first two boxes (you see only dots, in case someone evil is looking over your shoulder). You can also type a password hint (that is, a word or phrase that will remind you of your password without giving it away to anyone else) in the third box.

5. Click Create Password when you have typed the password and password hint.

6. If you are setting a password for your own user account, Windows asks, "Do you want to make your files and folders private?" Click Yes Make Private to create a private folder for your files, or click No not to. If you choose Yes Make Private, your My Documents folder can only be opened by you and by administrators. If you are adding a password for another user, Windows assumes that the other user wants private files and folders.

7. To create a password reset disk for use in case you forget your password, click Prevent A Forgotten Password on the Related Tasks list in the Task pane. (This link appears only when you are modifying the settings for your own account.) You see the Forgotten Password Wizard.

8. The Wizard steps you through creating a password reset disk. You need a blank, formatted floppy disk, and you need to know your current password.

Tip *We recommend that you create passwords for all your user accounts. If you're not worried about security, make all the passwords the same, but don't omit them altogether, unless your computer isn't connected to the Internet. We don't know of specific holes in Windows XP user account security, but why take a chance?*

Keeping Files Private

Windows XP Home Edition has three levels of security for the files stored on the local computer (rather than on other computers on a LAN):

- **Level 1: Private folders**   Each user's My Documents folder is accessible only by him or her.

- **Level 2: Private folders that administrators can access**   Each user's My Documents folder can be read only by the user or users with administrator accounts.

- **Level 3: Public folders**   Users store their documents in the Shared Documents folder.

Note *If your disk is formatted as FAT32 instead of NTFS volume, you can set up local user accounts and groups, but you can't make folders private (see Chapter 33).*

Each user account has its own My Documents folder in which the user can store files. Windows usually stores the My Documents folders for a user account in the C:\ Documents And Settings*username*\\My Documents folder. When you create a password for your account, Windows asks if you want a private documents folder (see the previous section). If you click Yes, your My Documents folder can only be opened by you and by administrative users. If you click No, anyone can open your My Documents folder. (If an administrator creates a new user account, Windows creates the private My Documents folder right away.)

When you are logged on, the C:\Documents And Settings*username*\My Documents folder appears as the My Documents folder in the folder tree of Explorer windows. Other users' folders also appear as subfolders of My Computer, with names like Zac's Documents and Jordan's Documents. My Computer\Shared Documents shows the contents of the C:\Documents And Settings\All Users\Shared Documents folder. If you try to open a private folder, Windows displays an error message instead.

 You can change the location of your My Document's folder; see the section "Modifying User Accounts" earlier in this chapter.

Making Your Documents Completely Private (Level 1)

Follow these steps to make your My Documents folder, or a folder within it, completely private:

1. Open an Exploring window (choose Start | My Computer).

2. Right-click your My Documents folder, or a folder within its folder tree, and choose Sharing And Security from the shortcut menu. If this option doesn't appear, choose Properties and click the Sharing tab on the Properties dialog box that appears.

3. Select the Make This Folder Private check box and click OK.

Now other users, including administrator users, cannot view the contents of this folder in an Exploring window, or open or save files in the folder.

 The My Documents folder must be stored on an NTFS volume (see Chapter 33).

Making Your Documents Private but Accessible to Administrators (Level 2)

This is the default setting for each user's My Documents folder. The Make This Folder Private check box on the Sharing tab of the Properties dialog box for the user's My Documents folder is not selected.

Making Your Documents Public (Level 3)

Store your documents in the Shared Documents folder, which appears as a subfolder of My Computer in the folder tree, below your disk drives.

 You can set folder access by user by starting in Safe Mode (see "Controlling File and Folder Permissions from Safe Mode" at the end of this chapter).

For more information on the three levels of Windows XP Home Edition security with Simple File Sharing, see the Microsoft Support web site at **support.microsoft.com** and search for article Q304040.

Enabling and Disabling the Guest Account

If you set up passwords for your accounts, you may also want to make sure that the Guest account is disabled (Windows disables it by default). If the Guest account is enabled, anyone can use your computer without a password.

To disable the Guest account, choose Start | Control Panel, and click User Accounts to display the User Accounts window. Click the Guest account and click Turn Off The Guest Account. You can turn it back on again by clicking the Guest account from the User Accounts window and clicking the Turn On The Guest Account button.

Deleting User Accounts

If someone with a user account on your computer will never, ever use the computer again, you can delete the user account. When you delete the account, Windows deletes the user's internal security ID (SID), and even if you create a new account with the same name, it will have a new SID, and a new profile and settings. So don't delete a user account if the person will be away temporarily—disable it instead.

In the User Accounts window, select the account name and click Delete The Account. Windows asks what you want to do with the files on the user's desktop and in the user's My Documents folder. Click Keep Files to move the files to a folder on the desktop, or click Delete Files to delete them. Either way, the user's folder in C:\Documents And Settings is deleted. You can't delete the account you are currently using.

Using a Shared Computer

Unlike Windows Me/9x, with Windows XP you are always logged on with a user account. If you haven't yet set up user accounts, you are logged on automatically as Owner. Once you set up additional user accounts, you can log on as any user (as long as you know the appropriate password), logging out when you are done. Using the new Fast User Switching feature, you can also switch from one user account to another in the middle of your work.

If possible, don't use Owner or any other administrator account for your day-to-day computer work. You can do less accidental damage from a limited account. However, some programs don't run from limited accounts, so you may be forced to use an administrator account.

Logging On

Once you have created user accounts, whenever your computer powers up or a user logs off, you see a logon screen. (The exception is if you have only one user account, it has a password, the Guest account is disabled, and Windows is configured to use the Welcome screen; in this case, Windows logs you in automatically.) You normally see the Welcome screen, as shown in Figure 6-5. If your system is configured to display the Classic logon screen, you see the Log On To Windows dialog box instead (see "Controlling How Users Log On" earlier in this chapter). Either way, click or type your user name and type your password, if your account has a password (and we recommend that it does). Windows loads your user account and you see your desktop.

When you see the Welcome screen, you can switch to the Classic logon screen by pressing CTRL-ALT-DELETE *twice. This trick, which works only if no other accounts are logged on, is useful if you want to log on using the Administrator or Owner account that Windows creates automatically but doesn't usually display on the Welcome screen.*

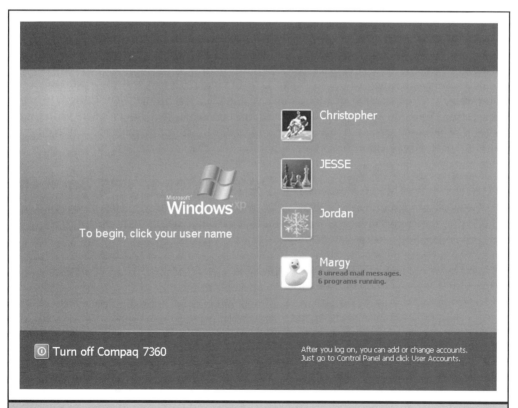

Figure 6-5.   *The Welcome screen greets you when you start up Windows, log out, or press* Windows-L *to switch users*

Resuming Work after Locking Windows

If your computer is configured to use the Welcome screen for logging on, pressing WINDOWS-L (that is, holding down the WINDOWS key and pressing *L*) to lock the computer also displays the Welcome screen (see Figure 6-5). Log back in to continue working. If your computer uses the Classic logon screen and you press WINDOWS-L, you see the Unlock Computer window, prompting you to enter your password to continue. Since Fast User Switching isn't available with the Classic logon screen, if you log on as another user, Windows logs off your original user account.

Logging Off

If you are done working, but you don't want to shut down the computer, you can log off. Choose Start | Log Off and click the Log Off button to confirm that you mean it. Windows exits all your programs, logs you off, and displays the Welcome screen or the Classic logon screen.

Switching Users

When Windows starts up, you choose which user to log on as by clicking or typing the user name in the Welcome screen or the Classic logon screen. If Windows is already running, you can switch users by logging off and letting the other user log on.

Fast User Switching provides a faster way to switch users: pressing WINDOWS-L. Alternatively, you can choose Start | Log Off and click the Switch User button. When you see the Welcome screen, log on as another user. When you switch users with this method, Windows doesn't exit the programs you were running: instead, they continue running in the background until you switch back to the first user account.

Setting the Screen Saver to Require You to Log Back On

If you are worried about someone using your computer when you step away from it, you can set the screen saver to require you to log back in using your user account name and password. Follow these steps:

1. Right-click a blank place on the desktop and choose Properties to display the Display Properties dialog box (see Chapter 11).

2. Click the Screen Saver tab and set the Screen Saver box to an option other than None.

3. Select the On Resume Display Welcome Screen check box.

4. Click OK.

Now when you return to your computer and click a key or move the mouse to wake Windows up, it displays the Welcome screen, and you have to enter a user password to continue.

Sharing Files with Other Users

If your My Documents folder is private, other users can't see its contents. To store
your files so that other users of your computer can read, edit, or delete them, store the
documents in the Shared Documents folder that appears under My Computer in
the folder tree. (This folder is actually called C:\Documents And Settings\All Users\
Shared Documents, assuming that Windows is installed on C:.) All users, including the
Guest account, can open the files in the Shared Documents folder. To see the Shared
Documents folder, choose Start | My Computer and click Shared Documents in the
Other Places part of the Task pane.

 *If you haven't disabled the Guest account, then files in the Shared Documents folder
can be opened by anyone who uses the computer (see "Enabling and Disabling the
Guest Account" earlier in this chapter).*

Running a Program as Another User

If you know the password for another user account, you can run a program as if you
were logged on as that user. Some older programs can't run unless the user account
has full rights on the system (for example, it insists on making system configuration
changes that would ordinarily be forbidden for your user account). The Run As dialog
box enables you to run a program and specify what user account to run it as.

To see the Run As dialog box (shown in Figure 6-6), hold down the SHIFT key while
you right-click an icon for the program (either on the desktop or in an Explorer window).

Figure 6-6. *You can run a program as if you were logged on as another user.*

Choose Run As from the menu that appears. In the Run As dialog box, click The Following User, type the user account name, enter the password (or leave the Password box blank if the user account has no password), and click OK.

 *Instead of typing the user account name, you can try clicking the down-arrow button at the right end of the User Name box to see a list of user accounts. If no accounts appear, type the computer name, a backslash, and the user account name to specify a user on your computer. For example, if your computer's name is GRACELAND and the user account's name is Elvis, type **GRACELAND\Elvis**.*

You can create a shortcut to a program that is set to run a program as another user. Follow these steps:

1. If the shortcut doesn't already exist, create it: Right-click the program's icon on the desktop or in an Explorer window and choose Create Shortcut from the menu that appears (or use another method to make the shortcut).

2. Right-click the shortcut and choose Properties to see the Properties dialog box for the shortcut.

3. Click the Advanced button on the Shortcut tab. You see the Advanced Properties dialog box, which offers the Run With Different Credentials option, as shown here:

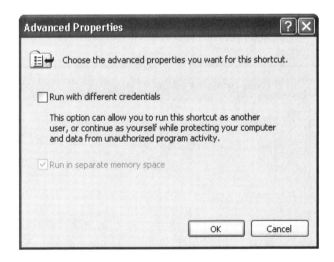

4. Click the Run With Different Credentials check box and click OK.

Each time you run the shortcut, Windows displays the Run As dialog box (shown in Figure 6-6) to ask you for the user name and password. Or, you can right-click the shortcut and choose Run As to see the Run As dialog box (no need to hold down the SHIFT key).

Managing Multiple Users

As an administrator user, you can keep track of who is logged on and who has programs running. You can also help users who have forgotten a password.

Managing Logged-In Users

In Windows Me/9*x*, the term "Task Manager" referred to buttons on the taskbar for the program that were currently running as well as to a program could who you what programs were running. In Windows XP, the Windows Task Manager is a program that can show you the tasks that the computer is currently doing, which users are currently logged on, and more.

Display the Task Manager by pressing CTRL-ALT-DELETE. You see the Task Manager, with tabs for Applications, Processes, Performance, Networking, and Users. To see who is using the computer, click the Users tab (see Figure 6-7).

Figure 6-7.   *The Task Manager's Users tab*

If you are an administrator, you see a list of the users who are logged on. (Other users just see an entry for themselves.) The user who is currently using the computer (you, presumably) has the status Active, while other logged-on users are Disconnected.

To switch to another user, click the currently active user and click Disconnect (because you've just logged yourself out, you see the Welcome or Classic login screen). To log a user out, click the user and click Logoff.

You can send a message to another logged-in user by selecting the user and clicking Send Message. When you see the Send Message dialog box, type the text of your message and click OK. The next time you switch to that user, the user sees a message box like this:

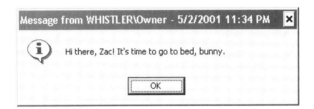

Setting Quotas for Disk Usage

For NFTS drives and partitions, you can limit users' files to a specified amount of disk space. Follow these steps:

1. In an Explorer window (choose Start | My Computer), find the drive or partition for which you want to set quotas.

2. Right-click the drive or partition and choose Properties from the shortcut menu. You see the Properties dialog box for the drive or partition.

3. Click the Quota tab, as shown in Figure 6-8. (The Quota tab doesn't appear for FAT32 and FAT drives.)

4. Select the Enable Quota Management check box. If you don't want to let people exceed their quotas, select the Deny Disk Space To Users Exceeding Their Quota Limit check box (otherwise, Windows displays a warning, but still allows the file to be stored).

5. Click the Limit Disk Space To *xx* radio button, and set the box to its right to the limit you want to set for new user accounts. Set the amount of space at which you want users to receive a warning, too. Be sure to change the right-hand box from KB to MB unless you are setting a *very* small limit.

WORKING IN
WINDOWS XP

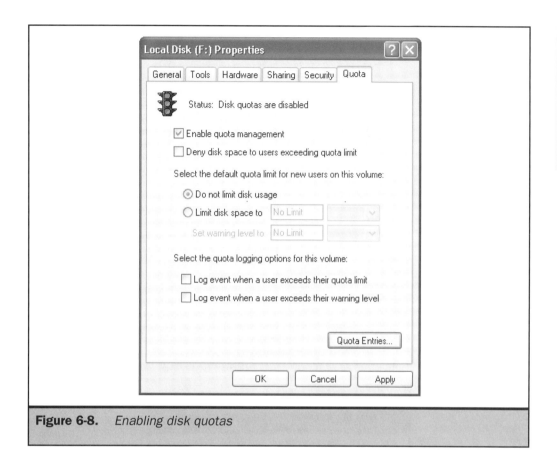

Figure 6-8.   *Enabling disk quotas*

6. If you want Windows to create a system log entry each time a user goes over quota, select one or both of the check boxes at the bottom of the dialog box.

7. To set limits for existing user accounts, click OK to close the Properties dialog box and enable quotas. Open the Properties dialog box again, display the Quota tab, and click the Quota Entries button. You see the Quota Entries dialog box, shown in Figure 6-9. Widen the Name and Logon Name columns by dragging the column header dividers rightward, so you can read the user account names. Listed users who are under their quotas appear with "OK" in the Status column. (These entries don't appear until after you have set up quotas.)

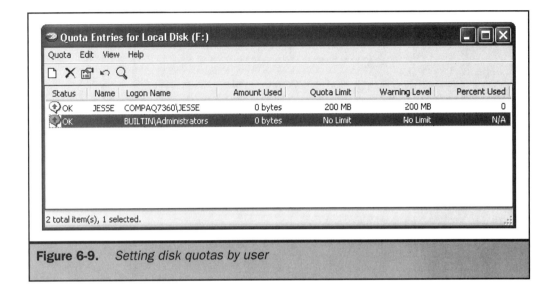

Figure 6-9. *Setting disk quotas by user*

8. The Quota Entries dialog box includes an entry for the Administrators group account (with no limit) and other system groups. To change the limit for a user account, right-click the user name and choose Properties. You see the Quota Settings dialog box:

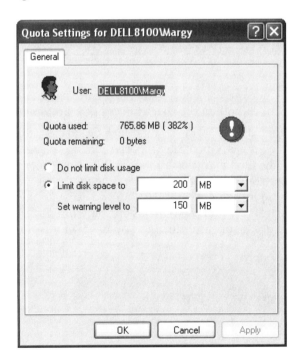

9. Click the Limit Disk Space To *xx* setting, and set the limit. Or, click the Do Not Limit Disk Usage setting to allow this user to use unlimited disk space. Click OK.

10. When you are finished setting quotas, close the Quota Entries dialog box and the Properties dialog box for the drive or partition.

If you don't want to limit how much space people use, but you want to track space usage, quotas are still useful. Enable quotas, but don't choose to deny disk space to people who exceed their quotas. Select the check boxes that cause Windows to log whenever people exceed their quotas, and watch your log files. To see when people have exceeded their quotas, click Start, right-click My Computer, and choose Manage to open the Computer Management window. Click the plus box to the left of Event Viewer in the list of items to see the types of logs available and click the System log.

Managing Users from the Command Prompt

If you don't mind typing commands, you can display and set options using the Command Prompt window that aren't possible using the User Accounts window. To open a Command Prompt window, choose Start | All Programs | Accessories | Command Prompt (see Chapter 4). Type commands at the DOS program, ending each command by pressing ENTER.

The NET USER command handles user accounts. To display a list of user accounts, type **net user** and press ENTER. You see a list like this:

```
User accounts for \\DELL8100


-------------------------------------------------------------------

Administrator           Guest                   HelpAssistant
Jordan                  Margy                   Meg
SUPPORT_388945a0

The command completed successfully.
```

This listing includes user accounts that are normally hidden, like Administrator, HelpAssistant, and Support.

To see detailed information about an account, type **net user** *username* and press ENTER. You see a listing like this:

```
User name               Margy
Full Name
Comment
User's comment
Country code            000 (System Default)
```

```
Account active            Yes
Account expires           Never

Password last set         7/29/2002 11:02 AM
Password expires          Never
Password changeable       7/29/2002 11:02 AM
Password required         No
User may change password  Yes

Workstations allowed      All
Logon script
User profile
Home directory
Last logon                7/29/2002 2:58 PM

Logon hours allowed       All

Local Group Memberships   *Administrators
Global Group memberships  *None
The command completed successfully.
```

Most of these settings are settings that you can display and change in Windows XP Professional by using the Microsoft Management Console (MMC), but that you can't otherwise see in Windows XP Home Edition. The NET USER command enables Home Edition users to display and set these additional settings. Table 6-2 lists some commands you can use. For more information, type **net help user** and press ENTER.

Command	Description	Example
net user *username*	Displays details about the user account.	net user meg
net user *username* *password*	Changes the password for *username* to *password*.	net user meg halibut3
net user *username* *password* /ADD	Creates a new user account with specified *username* and *password*.	net user zac zac8cookies /ADD

Table 6-2. *Some Arguments and Switches for the NET USER Command*

Command	Description	Example
net user *username* /DELETE	Deletes a user account name from the database but doesn't delete its settings from the Registry or its files from the C:\Documents And Settings folder. We recommend that you use the User Accounts window instead.	net user johnl /DELETE
net user *username* /ACTIVE:NO	Deactivates the account without deleting it. The account no longer appears on the Welcome screen and the user can't log in.	net user jesse /ACTIVE:NO
net user *username* /ACTIVE:YES	Reactivate an account.	net user jesse /ACTIVE:YES
net user *username* /PASSWORDCHG:NO	Prevent the user from changing the account password.	net user susan /PASSWORDCHG:NO
net user *username* /PASSWORDCHG:YES	Enable the user to change the account password.	net user susan /PASSWORDCHG:YES
net user *username* /PASSWORDEQ:YES	Requires the user account to have a password.	net user jordan /PASSWORDREQ:YES
net user *username* /PASSWORDEQ:NO	Enables the user account not to have a password.	net user jordan /PASSWORDREQ:YES

Table 6-2.   *Some Arguments and Switches for the NET USER Command* (continued)

Controlling File and Folder Permissions from Safe Mode

When Simple File Sharing is disabled, you see different options on the Sharing tab of the Properties dialog box for a drive or folder (see "Simple File Sharing" earlier in this chapter). You can control which users have permission to do what. The only way to disable Simple File Sharing in Windows XP Home Edition is by restarting the computer in Safe Mode. The changes you make while in Safe Mode remain in effect when you restart your computer normally (not in Safe Mode). Another method of setting permissions when you first share a drive or folder is described in the sidebar "Setting Folder Permissions by User."

Permissions tell Windows what a specific user account or user group is allowed to do with a specific folder. You can set permissions for everyone or set permissions for individual users (however it is preferable to set permissions for groups, rather than individual users, because groups are easier to manage as individuals come and go). The permissions that you can set depend on the file system of the disk on which the shared drive or folder is stored. NTFS disks (or partitions) support more security options than other formats (FAT32 and FAT). See the section "FAT, FAT32, and NTFS" in Chapter 33 for information about file systems.

Starting in Safe Mode to Set Permissions

To set permissions, start your computer in Safe Mode, which is described in more detail in the section, "Starting Windows in Other Startup Modes," in Chapter 2. Follow these steps:

1. Press F8 during Windows startup (when you see the boot menu, if you have a dual-boot system). You see a menu of startup modes.

2. Choose Safe Mode or Safe Mode With Networking. If you have a multiboot computer, choose the version of Windows to run. Windows starts up. Click Yes when Windows asks if you want to start in Safe Mode.

3. Run Windows Explorer (choose Start | My Computer) and display the drive or folder for which you want to set permissions.

4. Right-click the drive or folder and choose Sharing And Security from the shortcut menu that appears. Or, choose Properties from the shortcut menu and click the Sharing tab of the Properties dialog box that appears. You see a different Sharing tab than the one you normally see in Windows XP Home Edition. This tab includes additional sharing settings, as well as a Permissions button, as shown in Figure 6-10. Clicking the Permissions button displays the Permissions dialog box shown in Figure 6-11.

5. Make changes to your drive and folder permissions as described in the following sections.

6. Restart your computer to return to normal operation. The permission settings remain in effect.

 Windows XP Home Edition doesn't support the Offline Files feature of Windows XP Professional, so don't bother clicking the Caching button on the Sharing tab and making changes to the caching settings.

Setting User Permissions for FAT32 Drives

For a FAT32 drive or a folder stored on a FAT32 partition, you have limited options for setting permissions. You set permissions on the Permissions dialog box, shown in

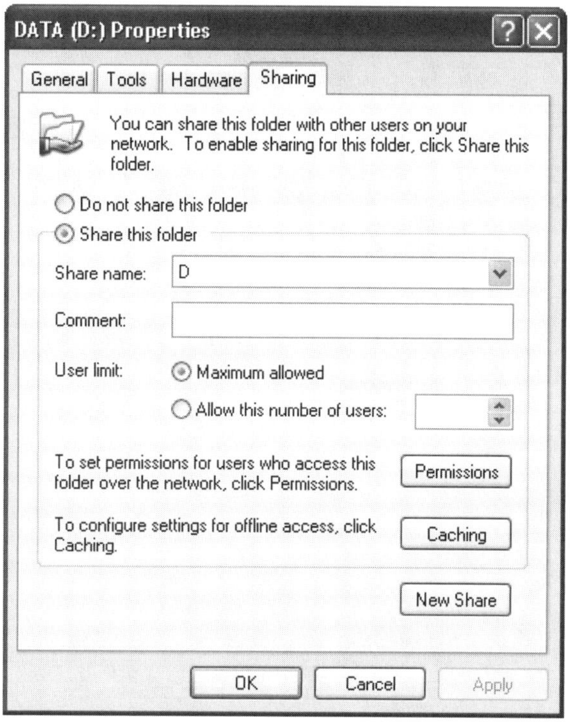

Figure 6-10.   *Sharing a disk drive with Simple File Sharing turned off, in Safe Mode*

Figure 6-11, which you display by clicking the Permissions button on the Sharing tab of the Properties dialog box for the shared drive or folder. In the Permissions dialog box, select the group or user and use the check boxes in the Permissions box to turn permissions on or off. You see the following permissions options:

- **Full Control**   Allows the user or group to read, create, change, delete files, and so on. If the computer is on a LAN, Full Control allows network users to do whatever the computer owner can do with the shared folder or drive.

- **Change**   Prevents users from deleting folders and files, changing permissions, or taking ownership for a file or folder.

- **Read**   Allows users only to open and read files.

Although each option has Allow and Deny check boxes, only three options are really available: Full Control, Change, or Read. If you click a Deny check box, other settings will change to reflect the option that is denied—for instance if you deny full control, then change and read are also denied.

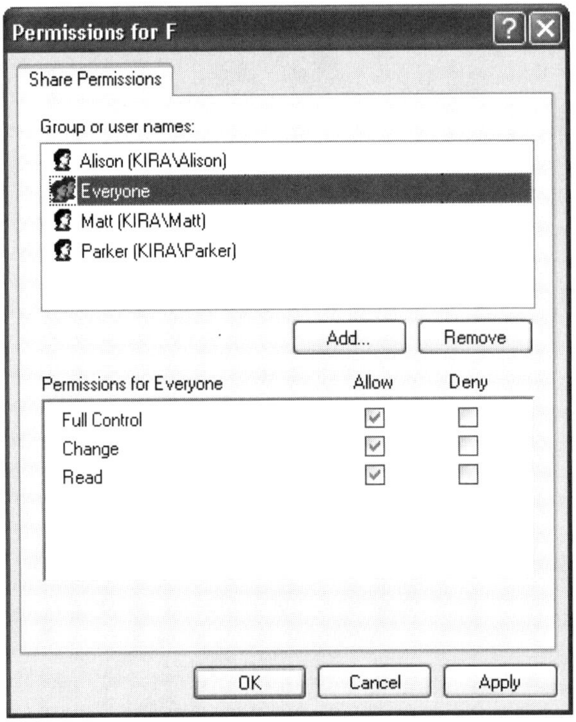

Figure 6-11. *Click the user or group in the Group Or User Names box to see the permissions for that user or group.*

You can add or remove users and groups listed by using the Add and Remove buttons. When you click Add, you see the Select Users Or Groups dialog box, shown here:

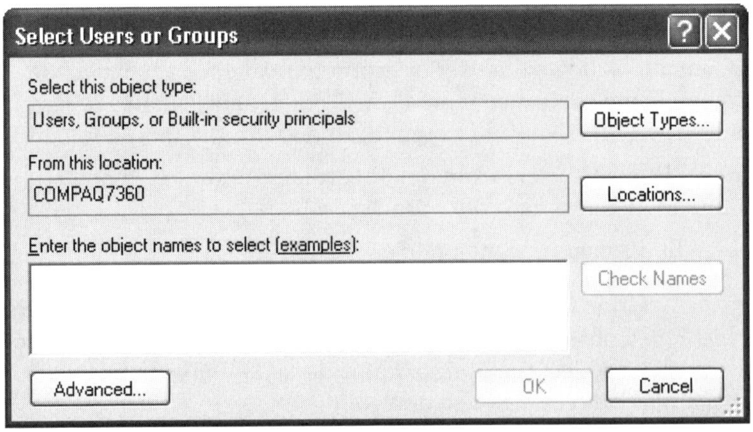

The From This Location box shows the name of your computer. Type a user account or group account name into the box at the bottom of the dialog box and click OK.

Setting User Permissions for NTFS Drives

For NTFS drives and partitions, and folders stored on them, you have more options. In Safe Mode, the Properties dialog box for the shared drive or folder includes a Security tab that you can click to set permissions, as shown in Figure 6-12.

 If the drive is formatted with NTFS, you should set permissions on the Security tab, rather than by clicking the Permissions button on the Sharing tab.

The Security tab allows more specific permissions settings but works the same way as the Permissions dialog box described in the previous section—first select a user or group; then define permissions. The following permissions are available:

■ **Full Control**   Allows the user or group to read, create, change, and delete files—whatever the computer owner can do with the shared folder or drive.

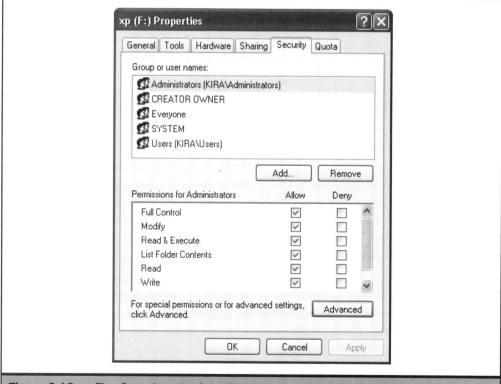

Figure 6-12.   *The Security tab of the Properties dialog box (for NTFS only)*

■ **Modify**   Prevents users from deleting folders and files, changing permissions, or taking ownership for a file or folder.

■ **Read & Execute**   Allows users to read and run files but not to change the contents of the shared drive or folder.

■ **List Folder Contents**   Allows users to see the contents of the folder.

■ **Read**   Allows users to see the contents of the drive or folder and open files but not to save changes.

■ **Write**   Allows users to write to the drive or folder but not to open files or see a list of files already there.

■ **Special Permissions**   Click the Advanced button to apply special permissions.

Setting Folder Permissions by User

Safe Mode isn't the only way to set folder permissions by user. Here's another way to set the permissions for a folder:

1.   Choose Start | Run to display the Run dialog box, Type **shrpubw** and press ENTER. You see the Create Shared Folder dialog box:

2. Click Browse to select the folder to share and type the share name and description. You can't type a share name that already exists. Click Next. You see this dialog box:

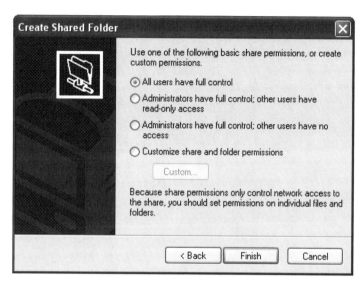

3. Choose one of the first three options for who can use the files in the shared folder or drive ("full control" means that people can read, edit, and delete files). Or choose Customize Share And Folder Permissions, click the Custom button to display the Customize Permissions dialog box (which looks like the Permissions dialog box shown in Figure 6-11), set permissions for users and groups, and click OK.

4. Click Finish to share the file or folder. The program asks whether you want to create another shared folder.

The Complete Reference

Part II

Managing Your Files

The Complete Reference

Chapter 7

Using and Customizing Windows Explorer

Windows Explorer is Windows' most fundamental application—it's where you do all the basic housekeeping of your files and folders. This chapter describes the anatomy of the Explorer windows that Windows Explorer creates, and tells you how to use the tools provided in Explorer windows to create, select, name, open, move, copy, and delete files and folders. It also explains how to reconfigure the elements of Explorer windows to your taste and habits. Finally, it describes the Recycle Bin, from which you can recover files and folders that you have deleted from your file system.

The Structure of the File System

Technically, a folder is just a special kind of file, one containing a list of other files. Opening a folder (for example, clicking the My Computer icon or choosing Start | My Computer) starts Windows Explorer, which opens an Explorer window to display the files the folder contains. Folders can in turn be contained in other folders, giving the whole collection of files and folders a tree structure, called the *folder tree*. You can see this structure in the Folders Explorer bar, shown in Figure 7-1. To display the Folders Explorer bar, click the Folders button on the toolbar or select View | Explorer Bar | Folders from the menu.

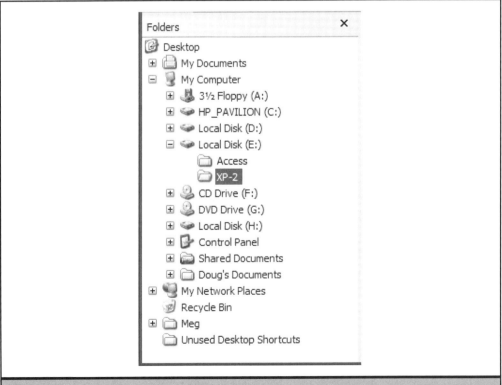

Figure 7-1.   *The Folders Explorer bar shows the structure of your file system.*

At the top of the tree is the Desktop folder. It contains any other files or folders that you (or whoever set up your computer) may have moved onto your desktop. In addition, it contains four special folders:

■ **My Computer** contains folders that you have access to on your computer. It always contains icons corresponding to the storage devices on your computer: hard disks, floppy drives, CD-ROM drives, and so on. It also contains two folders related to the users of your computer: Shared Documents, for files and folders that are available to all the users of your computer, and another icon for the My Documents folder, in which "My" has been replaced by your user name. (In Figure 7-1 it is Doug's Documents.) It also contains the Control Panel, a special folder that collects icons through which you control how Windows behaves.

■ **My Network Places** contains the folders that you have access to over your local area network (see Chapter 29).

■ **My Documents** is a folder into which you can store files that you create, though you may decide to put your files elsewhere. It, in turn contains two other folders that you may or may not use for the suggested purpose: My Music and My Pictures.

■ **Recycle Bin** contains files and folders that you have deleted.

Note   *Some of these icons may not appear on your desktop, but they still appear directly under the desktop in the Folder Explorer bar.*

File Addresses

An *address* is information that tells you (and Windows) how to find something. The three kinds of addresses are

■ **File addresses**   Tells you how to find files on your computer. A typical file address looks something like C:\Windows\Explorer.exe. Windows also refers to this as the *location* or *pathname* of the file.

Where the Desktop Is Stored

From a hardware point of view, every folder has to be stored somewhere: on a hard drive, a removable disk, or a network drive, but some folders like Desktop and My Documents seem to float above the hardware. In the folder tree the Desktop folder appears to contain all your disks, instead of being contained by one of them. So where are these folders stored?

Each user has his or her own Desktop and My Documents folders. Both of these folders are actually stored in the folder C:\Documents And Settings*username* (assuming that Windows XP is installed on C:).

- **UNC (Universal Naming Convention) addresses** Used when referring to files on some local area networks (LANs). UNC addresses are in the format *computername**drive**pathname*, where *computername* is the computer's name on the LAN, *drive* is the disk drive on that computer, and *pathname* is the file address on that drive. For example, if you needed to open a file called Budget03 in the C:\My Documents folder on a computer named DebB, you'd open \\DebB\C\My Documents\Budget03.

- **Internet addresses** More properly called *URLs*, specify how to find things on the Web (see Chapter 24). The URL of Microsoft's home page, for example, is **http://www.microsoft.com**.

The Address box in Windows Explorer handles all three kinds of addresses. Typing a file address into the Address box opens the corresponding file or folder on your computer, typing a UNC address opens the corresponding file or folder on your local area network (if your computer and the computer that has the file or folder are logged into the LAN and you have permission to open it), and typing a URL opens the corresponding web page on the Internet (if your computer is online).

File addresses, also called *paths* or *pathnames*, work in the following way: Each file or folder address begins with the letter of the drive on which the file or folder is stored. The *root folder*—the main, or top-level, folder on the disk—is designated by a backslash immediately after the drive letter and colon. (So C:\ is the root folder of drive C:.) The rest of the address consists of the names of the folders on the folder tree between the given file or folder and the drive that contains it. The folder names are separated by backslashes (\).

For example, the address C:\Windows\Temp refers to a folder named Temp, inside the folder named Windows, which is stored on the C drive. If the file Junk.doc is contained in Temp, Junk.doc's address is C:\Windows\Temp\Junk.doc.

Note *Both file addresses and UNC addresses use backslashes (\) to separate the pieces of the address, but URLs (for historical reasons) use slashes (/) for the same purpose.*

The Anatomy of Windows Explorer

Windows Explorer runs whenever you open a folder. It also appears on the Start menu as Start | All Programs | Accessories | Windows Explorer. The program has many features that you can display or hide, and several different views of the features it displays.

Windows Explorer is a twin of Internet Explorer, which is the Windows built-in web browser (see Chapter 24). Running either program opens an *Explorer window*,

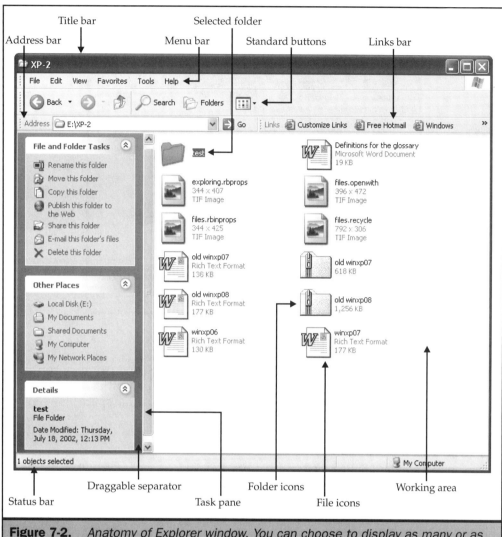

Figure 7-2. *Anatomy of Explorer window. You can choose to display as many or as few of these components as you like.*

which is extremely versatile and configurable. Figure 7-2 shows the many parts of the Explorer window other than the Explorer bar, which replaces the Task pane.

You can make the toolbars, Explorer bar, Task pane, or status bar appear or disappear from the View menu (see Chapter 8). When the Explorer window is stripped down to its absolute minimum, the same folder in Figure 7-2 looks like this:

Windows Explorer Toolbars

Windows Explorer has three toolbars: Standard Buttons, Links, and Address. You can display any collection of them you like by checking or unchecking entries on the View | Toolbars menu. You can display them in any order you like, allocate space between them, and even add or remove buttons.

Moving the Toolbars

The menu bar, Standard Button toolbar, Links bar, and Address toolbar are all movable. They always stay between the Title bar and the working area, but within that range you can put them anywhere you want. You may, for example, decide to put the Address toolbar on top of the Standard buttons or put the menu bar and the Links bar side by side. If you like, you can wind up with a very unconventional arrangement, like this one:

Before rearranging the toolbars, you must first unlock them by making sure that View | Toolbars | Lock the Toolbars is unchecked. When the toolbars are unlocked and ready to move, each toolbar has a column of dots on its left edge. When the toolbars are locked the dots vanish.

Move a toolbar by dragging and dropping. The place to "grab" a toolbar is just to the right of the column of dots on its left edge. (If you are too far to the left the mouse pointer turns into a two-headed arrow.) If you have hit the right spot, the cursor turns into four crossing arrows.

If two toolbars are on the same level, you can adjust the amount of space given to each toolbar by dragging and dropping the separator (the vertical line next to the column of dots on the left edge of the rightmost bar) between them. If the Explorer window isn't wide enough to contain all the toolbar elements you put on one level, a >> appears at the right edge. Click it to see a menu of the buttons that have fallen off the edge of the window.

The Standard Buttons Toolbar

In the default configuration, the Standard Buttons toolbar has six buttons: Back Forward, Up, Search, Folders, and Views, arranged left-to-right like this:

The Standard Buttons toolbar adds convenience to an Explorer window, but not functionality. The point of the buttons is to reduce frequent operations to a single click. The same actions can be performed using these menu or keyboard commands:

Button	Menu Equivalent	Keyboard Equivalent
Back	View	Go To	Back	ALT + LEFT ARROW
Forward	View	Go To	Forward	ALT + RIGHT ARROW
Up	View	Go To	Up One Level	None
Search	Start	Search	CTRL + E
Folders	View	Explorer Bar	Folders	CTRL + I
Views	View	None

These six are not the only buttons available to you. In fact, you can choose from a total of 23 buttons, and you can display any collection of them in any order you want.

Many of these buttons are Internet-related, and some appear automatically when the Explorer window playing its role as Internet Explorer rather than Windows Explorer. (You get to customize the Internet Explorer toolbar independently, so there is no need to add these to Windows Explorer.) You may find it convenient to add these buttons:

Button	Menu Equivalent	Keyboard Equivalent
Copy To	Edit | Copy To Folder	None
Move To	Edit | Move To Folder	None
Undo	Edit | Undo	CTRL + Z
Folder Options	Tools | Folder Options	None

The place to add, remove, or rearrange the buttons on the Standard Buttons toolbar is the Customize Toolbar dialog box, shown in Figure 7-3. To open this dialog box, select View | Toolbars | Customize, or right-click the toolbar itself and choose Customize from the shortcut menu. To add a button, select it in the left-hand window and click the Add button. To remove a button, select it in the right-hand window and click the Remove button.

You can change the order of the buttons you display by selecting a button in the right-hand window and clicking the Move Up or Move Down buttons. The top-to-bottom order of the buttons in the Current Toolbar Buttons window is the left-to-right order of the buttons on the Standard Buttons toolbar. Group buttons together by inserting a separator. You can have as many separators on your toolbar as you like; the separator is the only item in the left-hand window that doesn't vanish when you move it to the right-hand window.

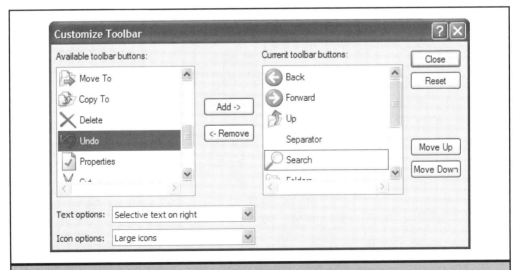

Figure 7-3.   *Clicking Add puts an Undo button to the left of Search.*

The amount of space the buttons take up on the toolbar is determined by the size of the button's icon and the text label. You can change either of these with the two drop-down lists at the bottom of the Customize Toolbar dialog box. The combination No Text Labels and Small Icons enables you to put a lot of small buttons on the toolbar, while Show Text Labels/Large Icons gives you a few big buttons.

The default settings are Selective Text on Right and Large Icons. The "selective text" labels enough buttons that you can probably guess the rest. For example, labeling the Back button gives you enough information to figure out where the Forward button is.

The Links Toolbar

The Links toolbar contains buttons that can link to the web sites, files, folders or programs that you use most often. However, to get much use out of the Links toolbar you'll need to customize it, because the Links that Microsoft puts on the toolbar for you aren't very interesting. A suitably personalized Links toolbar might look something like this:

To eliminate a link button, right-click it and choose Delete from the shortcut menu. To add a new link button of your own choosing, drag any file or folder icon to the Links toolbar and drop it where you want it. The file or folder stays where it was originally, and a shortcut is put on the Links toolbar (and in the folder C:\Windows\Favorites\Links, assuming that Windows is installed in C:\Windows). If you want to add the currently selected file or folder to the Links toolbar, you can drag the file or folder icon out of the Address box and drop it on the Links toolbar in the place where you want it to be. To rename a link button, right-click it and choose Rename from the shortcut menu.

The contents of the Links toolbar also appear in the Links folder of the Favorites menu, so you can also customize the Links toolbar via the Organize Favorites dialog box (see Chapter 24).

The Explorer Bar

The *Explorer bar* provides a variety of tools to help you find files and get a higher-level view of how your files are organized. To change what you see in the Explorer bar, select an option from the View | Explorer Bar menu or click the corresponding button on the toolbar. The choices are

- **Search** (see Chapter 8, section "Searching for Files and Folders") Helps you find files or folders on your computer system, web pages on the Internet, or people in a directory. In addition to the View | Explorer Bar menu, you can display the Search Explorer bar by clicking the Search button on the toolbar or pressing CTRL-E. You can open a new Explorer window displaying the Search Explorer bar by selecting Start | Search.

- **Favorites** (see Chapter 24) Shows you a list of favorite files, folders, and web pages. Clicking an object opens it. You can also open the Favorites Explorer bar by pressing CTRL-I.

- **Media** (see Chapter 19)   Puts Windows Media Player into the Explorer bar and displays some links to WindowsMedia.com.

- **History** (see Chapter 24)   Displays a daily list of whatever files or web sites you have opened in either Windows Explorer or Internet Explorer. You can also open the History Explorer bar by pressing CTRL-H.

- **Folders**   Displays the folder tree. In addition to using the View | Explorer Bar menu, you can display the Folders Explorer bar by clicking the Folders button on the toolbar. See the section "File and Folder Basics" earlier in this chapter.

You can make the Explorer bar disappear by clicking the X in the upper-right corner of the Explorer bar or by clicking the selected (pressed in) button on the toolbar. Resize the Explorer bar by dragging the boundary that separates it from the working area.

In the default configuration, only the Folders and Search Explorer bars have buttons on the toolbar. If you want other Explorer bars to have buttons, you can add them to the toolbar (see "The Standard Buttons Toolbar" earlier in this chapter).

The Task Pane

The *Task pane* (called the WebView pane in Windows Me) is a big blue column that sits on the left side of an Explorer window. It disappears if an Explorer bar is being displayed or if the window is too small. You can eliminate the Task pane for all Explorer windows by choosing Tools | Options to open the Folder Options dialog box and then clicking the Use Windows Classic Folders radio button. To reenable the Task pane, click the Show Common Tasks In Folders radio button in the Folder Options dialog box.

The Task pane has three major sections: Tasks (things you can do with objects in the right pane), Other Places (folders you might want to jump to), and Details (properties of selected objects in the right pane). Each has an arrow in its upper-right corner. An up arrow indicates that the box is currently expanded, and that you can contract it by clicking the arrow. A down arrow indicates that the box is contracted and that you can expand it by clicking the arrow.

The Working Area

Windows Explorer can display file and folder icons in the working area in five different views: Tiles, Icons, List, Details, and Thumbnails. You can find all these options on the View menu.

Folders that have been assigned a special folder template may have other view options (see Chapter 8, section "Folder Templates"). For example, a folder assigned a Pictures template (such as My Pictures) also has a Filmstrip view.

Tiles and Icons Views

Tiles view and Icons view are both graphical ways of presenting the contents of a folder—you can drag-and-drop the files and folders in the window in any way that makes sense to you, just as you might arrange objects on a desktop, piling up some and spreading out others.

Icons is the more compact view, Tiles the more informative. In Icons view the icons are smaller, text labels are under the file and folder icons, and no additional information is listed beyond the file names and icons, like this:

Party
Invitation

Tiles view gives you larger icons than Icons, text labels are to the right of the icons, and the types and sizes of files are given in the text labels, like this:

Journal
OpenOffice.org 1.0.1 Text Do...
8 KB

List and Details Views

List and Details views each are ways of putting the contents of a folder into a list. The difference between them is List gives only a small icon and a name for each file and subfolder. Details, as the name implies, gives a more detailed list that includes (usually) three more columns: the size of the file, its file type, and when it was last modified (see Figure 7-4).

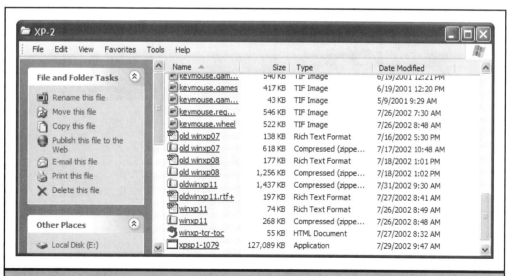

Figure 7-4.   *Details view shows you more information about your files.*

The number of columns and the column headings in Details view are different for special folders. (The columns displayed are specified by the folder template.For example, columns in My Computer are Name, Type, Total Size, and Free Space (see Chapter 8, section "Folder Templates"). In the Sample Music folder the headings are Name, Size, Type, Artist, Album Title, Year, Track Number, and Duration.

If you think Details view would be more informative if it had a different set of columns, select View | Choose Details. The Choose Details dialog box appears. Check or uncheck any of the attributes that you want. (Many of the headings are only appropriate for special types of files or folders; for other files or folders the corresponding column is empty.) To rearrange the columns of Details view, use the Move Up and Move Down buttons in the Choose Details dialog box. The changes you make apply to the current folder only, but will be remembered the next time you open that folder. You can also change Details view for all folders (see "Changing How the View Settings Work" later in this chapter).

You can adjust the width of the columns in a Details view by dragging and dropping the lines between the adjacent column heads. You can switch the order of the columns by dragging and dropping the column heads.

Thumbnails and Filmstrip Views

Thumbnails and Filmstrip views are good for looking at folders that contain image files or web pages saved on your disk. They are based on the idea of replacing the icon of an image file with a miniature version of the image itself, called a *thumbnail*.

Thumbnails view is shown in Figure 7-5. Graphics files are denoted by thumbnails of themselves, some files have been assigned special pictures, and all other files are

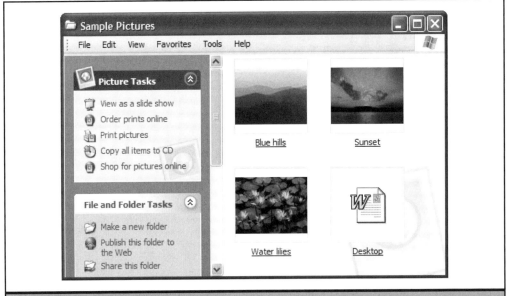

Figure 7-5.   *Thumbnails view uses miniature pictures to represent image files.*

denoted by squares surrounding their usual file icons. Folders that contain images are denoted by a folder icon with four of the folder's images shown on the icon, as the Email folder is in Figure 7-6.

In Filmstrip view, shown in Figure 7-6, thumbnails of the folder's contents are shown in a "filmstrip" across the bottom of the working area, and a larger view of the selected image is shown at the top of the working area. Underneath the selected image are four buttons: Previous Image, Next Image, Rotate Clockwise, and Rotate Counterclockwise. The Previous Image and Next Image buttons select the previous or next image in the filmstrip. Rotate Clockwise and Rotate Counterclockwise affect the display of the selected image. Clicking either of these buttons twice turns the image upside down.

Note *Filmstrip view does not appear on the View menu for folders that have a document template.*

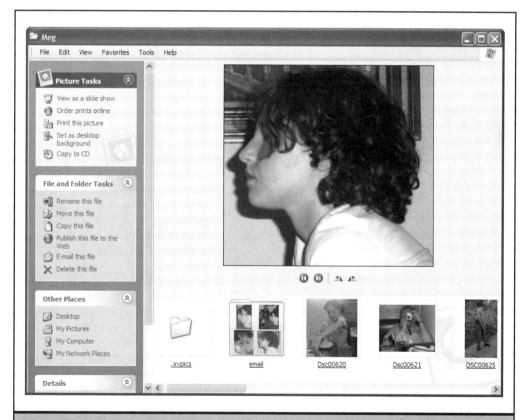

Figure 7-6. *Filmstrip view is convenient for examining a folder of pictures.*

Changing How the View Settings Work

By default, each folder has its own view settings. If you choose a new view from the View menu, you change the view for the currently displayed folder only. Windows remembers the new view the next time you open that folder, but all other folders are unchanged. However, another method enables you to change the view for all folders in one fell swoop.

Defining One View for All Folders   If you decide you like Details or Thumbnails (or some other) view and want to use it for all your folders, you can. Here's how:

1. Configure a folder the way you want all the folders to appear.
2. With that folder open, select Tools | Folder Options. The Folder Options dialog box appears.
3. Click the View tab of the Folder Options dialog box. Near the top of this tab is the Folder Views box. Inside this box is the Apply To All Folders button. Click it.
4. A confirmation box appears, asking you whether you really mean to change the default view settings. Click Yes and then click OK to close the Folder Options dialog box.

If you want to reset all folders back to the default settings, follow the previous instructions, except in step 4, click the Reset All Folders button.

 Changes that you make to the layout of columns in Details view can't be extended to all folders by this technique.

Defining a View that Stays with a Window   You may also decide you want the view settings to belong to the window, not to the folder. In other words, when you switch to, say, Thumbnails view, you want every folder you open from that window to come up in Thumbnails view until you change to something else. To change window settings:

1. Select Tools | Folder Options in Windows Explorer. The Folder Options dialog box appears.
2. Click the View tab of the Folder Options dialog box. The lower portion of the tab is the Advanced Settings box.
3. In the Advanced Settings box, find the line Remember Each Folder's View Settings. Uncheck the box next to this line.
4. Click OK.

To restore the default behavior, repeat the process, but check the box in step 3.

You can't set up Windows Explorer to open with a single click in one folder and open with a double click in another. Whatever decisions you make on the General tab of the Folder Options dialog box are applied automatically to all Explorer windows.

Sorting and Arranging the Contents of a Folder

Windows Explorer can sort the icons in an Explorer window automatically according to any column that appears in Details view for that folder. For most folders this means the icons can be sorted by name (alphabetically), by file type, by size (from smallest to largest), and by date (earliest to most recent). Even if you aren't in Details view, you can access the same choices by right-clicking in the pane and choosing Arrange Icons By or on the View | Arrange Icons By menu. Adding a column to Details view adds the same choice to the View | Arrange Icons By menu.

In any of these sort orders, folders are listed before files. Thus, in this Explorer window, the C Folder and the D Folder come before the A File:

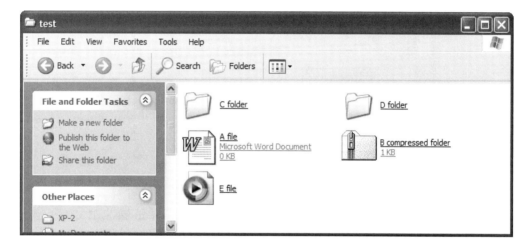

Compressed folders, however, are treated as files. So, for example, the B Compressed Folder comes after the D Folder and the A File.

In Tiles, Icons, and Thumbnails views, the contents of the folder are sorted in rows (if the window is wide enough for more than one column). The first element in the order is located in the window's upper-left corner, the second is to its right, and so on. In List, Details, and Filmstrip views, the contents are sorted in a list.

In Details view, sorting is particularly easy: click the column header to sort according to that column. Click it again to sort in reverse order (in which folders automatically go to the end of the list). The column by which the list is sorted displays a small arrowhead, which points up for a sort in ascending order and down for a sort in descending order.

In Tiles, Icons, or Thumbnails views, you can also arrange icons manually by dragging them. Here is a folder whose contents have been arranged manually—notice the irregular spacing and the overlapping icons:

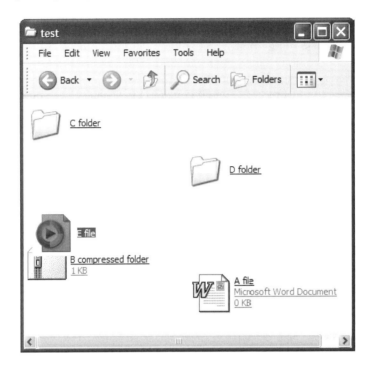

Metaphorically, manual arrangement is more like sorting stacks of paper on a table than sorting items in a filing cabinet. If Windows isn't letting you move icons where you want, make sure that View | Arrange Icons By | Auto Arrange is unchecked. Conversely, if you want to keep your icons in nice, neat rows, make sure View | Arrange Icons By | Auto Arrange is checked.

 If you overlap an icon too closely with a folder icon, Windows thinks you want to put the corresponding object inside the folder.

You can also group icons automatically according to any of the attributes that are columns in that folder's Details view (select View | Choose Details to add attributes). Make sure that View | Arrange Icons By | Show In Groups is checked. Then choose the appropriate attribute from the View | Arrange Icons By menu.

The Status Bar

The *status bar* is the bar at the bottom of an Explorer window (and many other windows, too). It displays information about any selected object. When a file is selected, for example, the status bar shows the file's type and size. When a drive is selected, it displays the free space and capacity of the drive. When a folder is open and no object is selected, it tells you the number of objects in the folder and how many of them are hidden. To display it, choose View | Status Bar.

When you are connected to the Internet or another network, the right end of the status bar tells you the security zone of the open folder (see Chapter 32, section "Internet Explorer's Zones").

Navigating the Folder Tree

Windows Explorer enables you to view the contents of any folder on your system. Once you find a folder in the Folders Explorer bar, you can click its icon there to display its contents in the working area. Here are some tips for setting up your Explorer window to make file management more convenient.

Expanding and Contracting the Folders Explorer Bar

You can expand or contract the Folders Explorer bar to whatever level of detail you find most convenient. A folder that contains other folders has a small box next to it, called a *plus box* if it contains a plus sign and a *minus box* if it contains a minus sign. A plus box indicates that the folder has subfolders, but that they are not shown. A minus box next to a folder indicates that its subfolders are listed below and slightly to the right of folder.

If the subfolders of a folder are not shown, you can display them (that is, expand or open the folder) by clicking the folder's plus box. Clicking the folder's minus box removes its subfolders from the list (contracts or closes it, in other words). Any portion of the folder tree can be expanded as much or as little as you like. The folders aren't affected—just your view of them.

Tip   *When the folder tree gets too wide to fit in the left pane, a scroll bar appears at the bottom. If you want to see the full width of the folder tree, drag the border between the right and left panes to the right.*

What Happened to the Dotted Lines?

If you've worked with previous versions of Windows, you may remember that the Folders Explorer bar was full of little dotted lines connecting folders to their subfolders. The lines made it easier to keep track of what was contained in what, but they also made for a lot of clutter. When Microsoft designed the Windows XP interface, they wanted everything to look clean and uncluttered, so the dotted lines went away.

You can put them back if you like them. From any Explorer window select Tools | Folder Options to open the Folder Options dialog box. On the View tab, uncheck the Display Simple Folder View In Explorer's Folder List check box. Then click OK to make the dialog box go away. Get rid of the dotted lines again by checking the Display Simple Folder View check box again.

Navigating by Using the Address Box

The Address box on the Toolbar displays the name of the folder whose contents appear in the working area. An abbreviated folder-tree diagram drops down from the Address box. It shows only the top layers of the folder tree, together with the folders between the open folder and the drive that contains it. You can use this diagram to jump to a new location in the folder tree by clicking any of the icons shown.

Another way to choose which folder to view is to type into the Address box the address of the file or folder you want to open. The Address box accepts file addresses, network addresses, and web addresses (see "File Addresses" earlier in this chapter). Your computer may automatically dial up your Internet provider if you type a web address (see Chapter 22).

Moving Up and Down the Folder Tree

The UP-ARROW and DOWN-ARROW keys move the cursor up and down the list of folders, while the RIGHT-ARROW and LEFT-ARROW keys expand and contract the currently selected folder. You can also select a folder by typing the first letter of its name.

The Up button on the toolbar (or the equivalent View | Go To | Up One Level command) "moves" the window up one level of indentation in the folder tree. The window then shows the contents of the folder containing the previously viewed folder. For example, if a window displays the contents of the C:\Windows folder and you click the Up button, your see the contents of the C: drive. Click Up again, and you see the contents of My Computer. Wherever you begin, if you click Up enough times, you reach the Desktop folder.

Backtracking in the Folder Tree

The Forward and Back buttons on the toolbar (or the equivalent commands View | Go To | Forward and View | Go To | Back) move the window back and forth among the previously displayed folders. The Back button returns to the previous open folder. Clicking the Back button again returns to the folder before that, and so on. The Forward button undoes the Back button: Clicking Back, and then clicking Forward leaves you where you started. Until you have clicked Back, there is no place to go forward to, so the Forward button is gray, indicating that nothing will happen if you click it. Similarly, once you have returned to the first folder you opened, the Back button turns gray.

Lists of folders to which you can go back or forward drop down when you click the arrows next to the Back and Forward buttons. Jump to any folder on the list by clicking its name.

Opening a New Window for Each Folder

You can decide you don't like the "navigating" metaphor at all, and go back to the original Windows 95 behavior: Every folder you open has its own window, which stays open until you close it. If you set things up this way, the Forward and Back buttons stop working, because there is nowhere to go forward or back to—any given Explorer window belongs to the folder it is displaying and has never displayed any other folder.

To make this change, open the Folder Options dialog box by selecting Tools | Folder Options from the menu. Select the Open Each Folder In Its Own Window radio button on the General tab of the Folder Options dialog box.

Making and Working with Files and Folders

The basic file and folder operations—creating, selecting, opening, naming, and deleting—are relatively unchanged from earlier versions of Windows.

Creating Files and Folders

Most of the time, you create new files and folders from within application programs, but you can create them from Windows Explorer, too. To create a folder or file, right-click any empty area on the desktop and choose New on the shortcut menu. In Windows Explorer, click the folder in which you want to create the new object and then choose File | New (or right-click any empty spot in the working area and choose New on the shortcut menu). All of these actions produce a submenu that lists the new objects you can create: folders, shortcuts, and a variety of types of files.

Selecting Files and Folders

Under the default settings, you select a file or folder by clicking its icon, and you open it by double-clicking. If you don't like all this clicking (or you're afraid of getting repetitive stress syndrome), you can adjust Windows Explorer so resting the cursor on an icon selects the corresponding object, and single-clicking opens the object (see Chapter 1, section "Choosing Between Single-Click and Double-Click").

To select more than one object, try these methods:

- **CTRL-click**   Select the first object, and then press the CTRL key while you select others. If you click a selected object while holding down CTRL, the object is deselected.

- **Click-and-drag**   If the objects you want to select are close together, move the cursor to an empty spot nearby, hold down the left mouse button, and drag the cursor. A rectangle forms, and any object inside the rectangle is selected. When you release the mouse button, the rectangle disappears, but the objects it contained continue to be selected.

- **SHIFT-click**   Select an object, and then hold down the SHIFT key and select another object. All objects between these two objects are selected.

- **Select All**   To select all the items in a folder, open the folder and choose Edit | Select All from the Explorer window's menu bar or press CTRL-A on the keyboard. To select all but a few objects in a folder, choose Select All, and then hold down CTRL while you deselect those few objects.

- **Keyboard**   To select consecutive files in a single list or column, select the first file; then hold down the SHIFT key and move to the last file by pressing arrow keys. To select files that aren't listed together, select one file, hold down the CTRL key, press the arrow keys to move to the next file you want to select, and press SPACEBAR to select it. Continue holding down the CTRL key, moving, and pressing SPACEBAR until you select all the files you want.

More complicated patterns of objects can be selected by combining these methods.

 If you want to select most of the files in a folder, select all the items you don't want to include. Then choose Edit | Invert Selection to deselect the selected items and to select the deselected ones.

Opening Files and Folders

You can open a folder—display its contents—by double-clicking its icon. To open files, you have many more methods.

Most people open files by choosing File | Open from within the program associated with the type of file. You can also open files from an Explorer window: Double-clicking a file opens the file using the default application for that file type. You can open a file in some other compatible application by right-clicking the file and selecting an application from the Open With menu, by dragging-and-dropping the file onto an application's icon, or by using the File | Open command from the application's menu (see Chapter 1, section "Starting Programs by Opening Documents").

If you double-click a file in an Explorer window and Windows doesn't recognize its file type, or if that file type has no associated application, an Open With box appears, asking you to identify an application to use in opening the file.

Some file types may have more than one application associated with them (see Chapter 3, section "Associating a Program with a File Extension"). To check, right-click the file icon and see if a command like Edit appears under Open in the shortcut menu. For example, in the default configuration image files open with Image Preview but are edited with Paint.

 You can change the settings of Windows Explorer so only a single-click is required to open a file or folder.

If both the file icon and the application icon (or shortcuts to either) are visible on your screen, drag-and-drop the file icon onto the application icon. If you do this frequently with a particular application, put its icon on the Links bar (see "The Links Toolbar" earlier in this chapter). Or, you can also create a shortcut to the application on the desktop (see Chapter 8, section "Making Shortcuts").

Naming and Renaming Files and Folders

File and folder names can be up to 255 characters long, and can include spaces. So if you want to name a folder Dumb Stuff I Gotta Do This Week, you can. You can use numbers and many punctuation marks in file and folder names, but not

\ / : * ? " < > |

or any character you make by using the CTRL key.

To rename a file or folder, select its icon and choose the Rename This File (or Rename This Folder) option from the Task pane or right-click the icon and choose Rename from the shortcut menu. You can also select the file and press F2 or click the file once to select it, and (after a pause) once more to edit its name. A box appears around the current name, and the entire name is selected. Type the new name in the box (or edit the existing name) and press ENTER.

 If you have set Windows Explorer to display file extensions, be careful not to change one unintentionally when you rename a file. Doing so changes the file type of the file and prevents Windows from finding the correct application to use when opening the file.

Deleting Files and Folders

You can delete a selected file, folder, or collection of files and folders by clicking the Delete This File (or Folder) option on the Task pane; choosing File | Delete from the menu bar; right-clicking the object and select Delete from the shortcut menu; pressing the DELETE key; or dragging the object to the Recycle Bin.

However you do it, a dialog box appears that asks whether you really want to send the objects to the Recycle Bin (if they are deleted from your computer's hard drive) or delete the objects (if they are on a removable disk).

Under the default settings, objects deleted from your computer's hard drives go to the Recycle Bin, from which they can be recovered. You can reset your preferences so objects are deleted immediately and don't go to the Recycle Bin (see the next section). Objects deleted from floppy drives or other removable disks don't go to the Recycle Bin. For this reason, be especially cautious when deleting objects from floppies or other removable disks.

 Even deleting a file from the Recycle Bin doesn't destroy the information right away. Windows makes the file's disk space available for reassignment but doesn't immediately write over that disk space. People with the proper tools could still read the file. To prevent this, you need file-deletion software that is not part of Windows.

Avoiding the Recycle Bin

If you want certain files and folders gone *right now*, with no shilly-shallying about Recycle Bins, or Undo buttons, hold down the SHIFT key while you click the Delete button, press the DELETE key, or drag the file to the Recycle Bin icon. (Of course, you should be *very sure* you want the files and folders gone, and that you haven't dragged along any extra objects by accident.) You have to click Yes in a confirmation dialog box, but the objects are deleted for real, not just sent to the Recycle Bin.

Eliminating Confirmation Dialog Boxes

The confirmation box that asks you if you really intend to delete something can be a real life-saver, but if you are deleting a lot of objects one-by-one, it can get tedious to confirm each decision. To eliminate the confirmation dialog box when you send something to the Recycle Bin:

1. Right-click the Recycle Bin icon on the desktop and choose Properties from the menu or select the Recycle Bin in a Folder or Windows Explorer window and click the Properties button on the toolbar. You see the Properties dialog box of the Recycle Bin.

2. From the Global tab of the Properties dialog box, uncheck the box labeled Display Delete Confirmation Dialog. Then click OK.

Even after carrying out these steps, deleting something from the Recycle Bin (that is, getting rid of it for good) still requires a confirmation. If you decide later that you've made the deletion process too easy, you can reinstitute Delete Confirmation Dialog; repeat the preceding steps, but check the check box in step 2.

Undoing Your Last Action

Windows Explorer has an Undo command that allows you to recover quickly from simple mistakes like deleting or moving the wrong file. Just press CTRL-Z on the keyboard or select Edit | Undo from the menu. Repeat either of these commands to step back through your recent actions. If you find yourself undoing mistakes frequently, you may want to add an Undo button to the Standard Buttons toolbar (see "The Standard Buttons Toolbar" earlier in this chapter).

Moving and Copying Files and Folders

You can move or copy files and folders via the Move or Copy option on the Task pane, by drag-and-drop, by cut-and-paste, or by using the Send To menu. All these techniques begin the same way: You open a source folder (the folder that contains the files or folders you want to move or copy) and select the items that you want to move or copy from the working area of the Explorer window.

Here are a few notes about how drag-and-drop and the Send To menu work.

Moving and Copying By Drag-and-Drop—But Watch Out

One method is to open both the source and target folders in separate Explorer windows. You can drag-and-drop objects from the source window to the target window.

 You can get away with using only one Explorer window if you display the target folder icon on the Folders Explorer bar.

Drag-and-drop has one unfortunate aspect. If you experiment, you soon notice it doesn't do the same thing in all circumstances—sometimes it moves an object, sometimes it copies it, and sometimes it makes a shortcut. The reason for this behavior is that the programmers at Microsoft have gone a bit overboard in trying to be helpful. Windows does what it guesses you intend to do, based on the file type of the objects being dragged, the locations of the source and target folders, and a few other things we haven't figured out.

Here's what happens when you drag-and-drop:

- **Objects to the same disk**   If you drag objects (other than programs) from one folder to another folder on the same disk, the objects are moved. (Remember, the desktop is a folder on the C drive. Anything else on the C drive is considered on the same disk as the desktop.)

- **Objects to a different disk**   If you drag objects (other than programs) from one folder to another folder on a different disk, the objects are copied.

- **Programs**   If you drag a program, it may behave like any other object but, for some programs, Windows makes a shortcut in the target folder and leaves the program file where it was in the source folder. We haven't come up with a firm rule describing this, although, in general, the more complex the program, the more likely it is that dragging and dropping it will create a shortcut. So, for example, you'll get a shortcut if you drag-and-drop Windows Media Player, but not Calculator.

Windows at least tells you what it's going to do with the objects you drop. When the object icons are in a droppable position, a tiny + appears next to them if they're going to be copied, while a tiny curved arrow (the same arrow that appears on shortcut icons) appears if a shortcut is going to be created. If nothing appears, the files are going to be moved.

Tip   *If you want to use drag-and-drop, but you neither want to memorize how it works nor trust Windows to guess your intentions, drag with the right mouse button rather than the left mouse button. When you drop in the target folder, select the action you intended from the shortcut menu.*

Copying Files Using the Send To Menu

Send To is a menu found on the File menu of Explorer windows and on the shortcut menu when you right-click a file or folder. The Send To menu enables you to copy files to preselected locations quickly and easily. To use Send To for this purpose, right-click the icon of a file or folder you want to copy, and choose a destination from the Send To submenu of the shortcut menu. (Alternatively, you can select File | Send To from the menu bar.)

The Windows installation program creates a default Send To menu that varies according to the resources available to your computer. A typical Send To menu offers you the following options:

- **Desktop** creates a shortcut on the desktop that points to the selected object.

- **Removable storage drives** Each removable storage drive on your system has its own entry on the Send To menu. Choosing it copies the selected item to that drive.

- **Mail recipient** opens your default e-mail application, creates a message, and attaches the selected item to the message.

- **Compressed (zipped) folder** creates a compressed folder containing the item. The new compressed folder has the same name as the item and appears in the same folder.

- **My Documents** copies the item to the My Documents folder.

To add a new destination to the Send To menu, create a shortcut to that folder or disk in the folder C:\Documents And Settings *username*\SendTo (assuming that Windows XP is installed on C:): see Chapter 8, section "Making Shortcuts," for instructions. To delete an item from the Send To menu, delete the corresponding shortcut from C:\Documents And Settings*username*\SendTo.

 By default, the SendTo folder is hidden. To access it you must display hidden files and folders (see Chapter 8, section "Working With Hidden Files and Folders").

Using the Recycle Bin

The *Recycle Bin* is a hybrid object that behaves like a folder in some ways, but not in others. Like a folder, it contains objects, and you can move objects into and out of the Recycle Bin, just as you do with any other folder. Unlike a folder, even an unusual folder like the Desktop, the Recycle Bin is not contained on a single drive. The Recycle Bin can contain deleted files and folders from any of your computer's hard drives.

Files that have been sent to the Recycle Bin aren't considered part of Windows' filing system, just as a wastebasket is not considered part of an office filing system. Folders in the Recycle Bin don't appear in the Folders Explorer bar, and they can't be opened. If you want to examine the contents of a folder in the Recycle Bin, you first must move the folder to another location. Likewise, files in the Recycle Bin cannot be opened or edited. Files and folders in the Recycle Bin show up searches, but files *inside* folders in the Recycle Bin do not.

The intention of the designers is clear: the Recycle Bin is not to be used as a workspace. Instead, it is a last-chance repository. You can put things in the Recycle Bin or take things out—that's all.

Finding Files and Folders in the Recycle Bin

When you double-click the Recycle Bin icon, an Explorer window opens to show you the files and folders that were deleted since the Recycle Bin was last emptied.

If the Recycle Bin contains only a few objects, you can easily see whether the file or folder you want is there. But the Recycle Bin can get quite crowded, and then you may want to switch to the Details view (shown in Figure 7-7) by choosing View | Details from the menu. In this view you can sort the list of files and folders by clicking on any of the column heads: Name, Original Location, Date Deleted, Size, Type, and Date Modified. You can also use Search to find files and folders in the Recycle Bin.

 If you delete an entire folder, then the contents of that folder are not visible in the Recycle Bin, though they will be restored if you restore the folder. The contents also will not show up in searches.

Retrieving Files and Folders from the Recycle Bin

When you find an object in the Recycle Bin and decide that you want to keep it, you should remove it from the Recycle Bin as soon as possible. The easiest way to do this

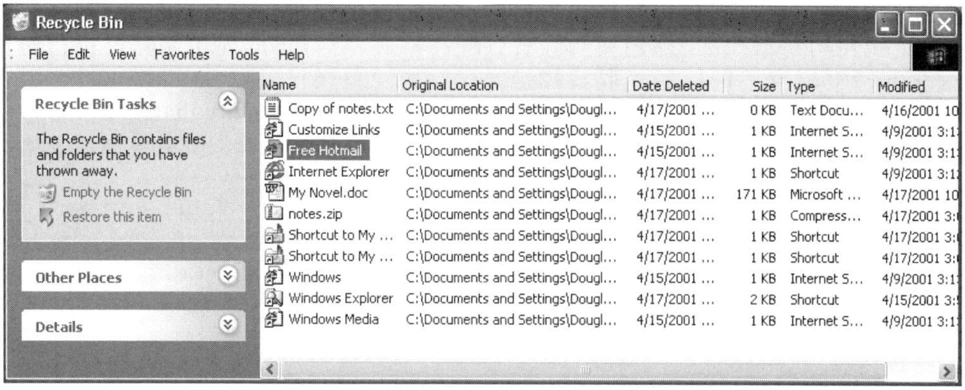

Figure 7-7. *The Recycle Bin in Details view*

is to right-click the object's icon and select Restore or choose File | Restore from the menu. The object returns to the folder it was deleted from—the address given in the Original Location column of the Details view. If the object is a folder, all its contents return with it. You can use Restore even if the object was deleted from a folder that no longer exists. A folder of the appropriate name is then created to contain the restored object. You can restore everything in the Recycle Bin to its original location by clicking the Restore All Items option on the Task pane.

Alternatively, you can remove an object from the Recycle Bin by moving it to another folder in any of the standard ways.

Emptying the Recycle Bin

Deleting old files serves two purposes: it clears useless files away so you don't confuse them with useful files, and it reclaims the disk space they occupy. The first purpose is served by deleting a file—once it's in the Recycle Bin, you aren't going to open it or work on it by mistake. However, a file in the Recycle Bin still takes up disk space: The space isn't reclaimed until the Recycle Bin is emptied.

To empty the Recycle Bin, right-click its icon on the desktop and choose Empty Recycle Bin from the shortcut menu. Confirm your choice by clicking Yes in a dialog box.

To purge selected files or folders from the Recycle Bin without completely emptying it, open the Recycle Bin folder and delete the files in the usual way. Objects deleted from an ordinary folder on a hard drive are sent to the Recycle Bin, but objects deleted from the Recycle Bin are really deleted.

If you're emptying the Recycle Bin in order to create space on a particular hard drive or hard drive partition, consider using Disk Cleanup to get rid of temporary files and other space-wasters while you're at it (see Chapter 34).

Tip *If you want to delete only items that have been in the Recycle Bin a long time, use Details view and sort according to the Date Deleted column.*

Resizing the Recycle Bin

By default, the maximum size of the Recycle Bin on any hard drive is 10 percent of the size of the drive itself. For example, a 10GB hard drive has a maximum Recycle Bin size of 1GB—a lot of space to use up for files you've decided to delete. If you delete an object that would cause the Recycle Bin to exceed that size, Windows warns you with an error message.

Having a maximum size for the Recycle Bin forces you not to clutter your hard drive with useless, deleted files, and 10 percent is as good a maximum size as any, but you may decide either to raise this limit (because you don't want to lose any of the files currently in the Recycle Bin) or lower it (because disk space is getting tight), either of which you can do by following this procedure:

1. Right-click the Recycle Bin icon on the desktop and choose Properties from the shortcut menu. You see the Properties dialog box of the Recycle Bin (Figure 7-8).

2. The Properties dialog box contains a Global tab, plus a tab for each hard drive on your system. If you want to change the maximum size setting for all the hard drives at once, set the new maximum size of the Recycle Bin (as a percentage of total drive space) by moving the slider on the Global tab. Then click OK. Skip the remaining steps.

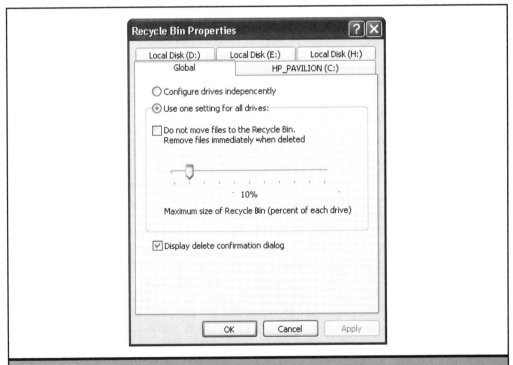

Figure 7-8. *The Recycle Bin properties*

3. If you want to reset the maximum Recycle Bin size for only a single drive, leaving the others the same, select the Configure Drives Independently radio button on the Global tab.

4. Click the tab for the drive you want to change.

5. Set the slider on that tab and click OK.

Turning Off the Recycle Bin

If you want to stop sending deleted files to the Recycle Bin

1. Right-click the Recycle Bin icon on the desktop and choose Properties from the shortcut menu. You see the Properties dialog box of the Recycle Bin (Figure 7-8).

2. On the Global tab of the Properties dialog box (or on the tab corresponding to the particular drive whose Recycle Bin you are turning off, if the Configure Drives Independently option is chosen on the Global tab), check the box labeled Do Not Move Files To The Recycle Bin. Remove Files Immediately When Deleted.

3. Click OK.

After you complete this procedure, files you delete from your hard drive are gone, just as are files deleted from floppy drives. Files that were already in the Recycle Bin, however, remain there until you empty the Recycle Bin, delete them, restore them, or move them to another folder.

You can turn the Recycle Bin back on by following the same procedure, but unchecking the check box in step 2.

 If you turn off the Recycle Bin, don't forget you did. The Recycle Bin remains off until you turn it on again. A more prudent choice might be to make your Recycle Bin smaller, but to leave it on.

MANAGING YOUR FILES

Chapter 8

File Attributes, Searching for Files, and Burning CDs

The previous chapter explained how to use and customize Windows Explorer. This chapter discusses issues that may not come up immediately as you work with files and folders, but that you should know about if you are going to have a long-term relationship with your computer.

Windows Explorer lets you ignore most of the technical aspects of files and folders most of the time. But ignorance is not always bliss, so this chapter briefly explains file types, file extensions, file attributes, and file properties. It also describes how to works with special types of files and folders: shortcuts, compressed folders, and hidden files and folders. Folders themselves are a special kind of file, and so this chapter describes how to customize a folder by choosing a new folder template.

Even the best-organized people occasionally forget where they put something, so you need to know how to use the Search Explorer bar. You can also speed up your searches with the Indexing Service.

Finally, this chapter explains how to use one of Windows XP's new features, the CD Writing Wizard, to create your own CDs.

Types, Extensions, Properties, and Attributes of Files

Windows keeps track of how to handle files by requiring that files have a file type. Every file has a properties box that you can open to see information about that file, or (depending on the file type) to enter information about the file. In addition, files can be assigned attributes to hide them or make it harder to change them.

File Types and Extensions

The *file type* tells Windows what icon to use for the file and what program to open the file with. (It also tells applications what to do with the file. For example, Microsoft Word handles both DOC and RTF files, but if you mislabel one as the other it gets confused.) The file type is coded into a three- or four-letter *extension* and added to the filename after a period. For example, most files created by Microsoft Word have the file type Microsoft Word Document and the file extension .doc, as in My Term Paper.doc. If you change the extension, you change the file type.

You may never notice these extensions because Explorer windows hide them under the default settings. Instead, the file type is listed under the name of the file (in Tiles view) or put in its own column (in Details view). In other views you can usually infer the file type from the icon used to represent the file.

Note *Windows always displays file extensions that it doesn't recognize. You can tell that Windows doesn't recognize a file's extension if the file has a generic icon like this:*

You can also create, delete, or edit a file type, and change the program that Windows uses to open or edit files of that type (see Chapter 3, section "Editing a File Association").

Making File Extensions Visible

You can do many things in Windows without paying any attention to file types; therefore, Windows hides the extensions of the file types it recognizes unless you ask to see them. Given that the file type is readily visible, the only reason to display the extensions is if you want to change them. To display file extensions in Explorer windows do the following:

1. From any Explorer window select Tools | Folder Options. The Folder Options dialog box appears.

2. Click the View tab. The Advanced Settings box contains a long list of options.

3. Uncheck the box next to Hide File Extensions For Known File Types and then click OK.

If you are displaying file extensions, you need to make sure to get the extensions right when you name or rename a file. Otherwise Windows won't know what to do when you open the file.

Changing a File's Type

In certain rare circumstances it is necessary to change a file's type. For example, you may receive a file via e-mail, and the file extension may be lost or wrong. In such a case you would want to give the file the appropriate file extension, and so tell Windows what type the file is.

Caution *Don't confuse changing a file type with converting a file from one type to another. Converting a file from one type to another involves rewriting the contents of the file, not just renaming it. To convert a file, you need an application that can open it as its current file type and save it as the new file type.*

To change a file's type, set Windows Explorer to display file extensions (as described in the previous section) and then rename the file with a different extension. (For example, if you rename the file Homework.doc as Homework.txt, you have changed its file type from Microsoft Word Document to Text Document.) Windows warns you that you are changing the file type and asks you to confirm your decision.

Don't change a file's type unless you know what you're doing. If you assign the file a type that Windows doesn't recognize, it won't know how to open the file. Unless you prepare the file in such a way that is appropriate for that application, the opening fails. (Consider, for example, the Paint program trying to open an audio file doesn't work.)

Properties of Files and Folders

Like almost everything else in Windows, files and folders have *properties*—information about a file or folder you can access and, perhaps, change without opening the file or folder.

To view this information and make changes, select the file or folder in Windows Explorer and then choose File | Properties (or right-click the file or folder and select Properties from the shortcut menu). The Properties dialog box appears, with the General tab selected (see Figure 8-1).

The General tab of a file's Properties dialog box displays information about the file, including the file type, the default application that opens files of this type, the location or file address of the file, the size (including both the actual size of the file and the slightly larger amount of disk space allocated to the file), and its attributes (described in the next section).

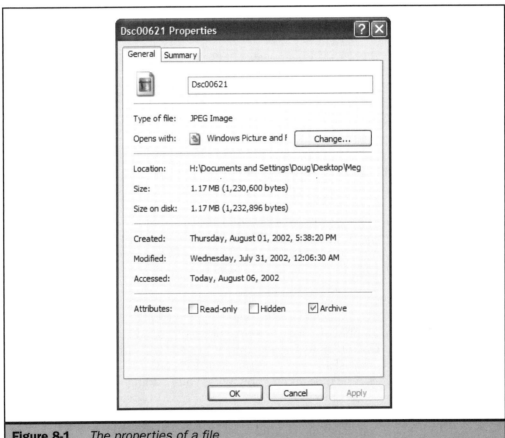

Figure 8-1.   *The properties of a file*

Depending on a file's type, it may have additional tabs of properties that you can access by clicking them individually. The properties of most image files, for example, include a Summary tab where you can enter the kind of information people write on the backs of photographs: who took the picture, who the people in the picture are, and so on.

Because a folder is technically a special kind of file, the General tab of its properties dialog box contains much of the same information: icon, name, type (File Folder), location, size (the number of bytes taken up by the folder and all its contents, including the contents of subfolders), date created, and attributes. The General tab for folders has one additional item: Contains, which reports the number of files and folders contained in the folder and all its subfolders.

For some folders (such as folders that people or programs create, rather than folders that come with Windows), the Properties dialog box includes a Customize tab, which enables you to control what the folder looks like, both when it appears as an icon and when you open the folder. See "Customizing a Folder" later in this chapter.

If your computer is on a local area network, folders also have a Sharing tab, with information about whether the folder (and the files and folders it contains) is shared on the network (see Chapter 30). Folders may also have a Security tab to control who may see its contents.

 To find the total size of a group of files and folders, select them all and then right-click anywhere in the selected filenames. Choose Properties from the shortcut menu. Windows displays the total number of files and folders, as well as their combined size.

File and Folder Attributes

The *attributes* of a file or folder include these settings, which can be selected or deselected for each file or folder:

- **Read-only**   You can read and even edit this file or folder; but when you try to save your changes, Windows reminds you this is a read-only file, and asks you to save your new version as a different file. If you try to delete a read-only file or folder, Windows reminds you it's read-only, but deletes it if you insist.

- **Hidden**   A file or folder that doesn't usually appear in Explorer windows, but can be made visible if you want to see it (see "Working With Hidden Files and Folders" later in this chapter).

- **Archive**   This setting may mean the file or folder has been changed since the last time it was backed up, depending on which backup program you use. Windows XP comes with Microsoft Backup (see Chapter 9). To see this attribute on an NTFS partition, click the Advanced button to see the Advanced Attributes dialog box, where it appears as the File Is Ready For Archiving attribute.

MANAGING YOUR FILES

- **Indexed**   Determines whether the file will be included in the Windows Indexing Service index, which is used when searching for files. You can set this attribute on for files stored in an NTFS partition.

- **Compressed**   Compressed to save space, available only on NTFS partitions. Compressed files and folders cannot be encrypted. This type of compression is different from the compressed folders described in "Working With Compressed Folders (ZIP files)" later in this chapter.

The attributes of a file or folder appear at the bottom of the General tab of the Properties dialog box. For files and folders stored on NTFS partitions, click the Advanced button to see additional attributes.

 In Windows XP Professional, files and folders on NTFS partitions also have an Encrypted attribute, which determines whether the file is Encrypted (encoded) so that only the user who created the file can open it later. Windows XP Home Edition doesn't support file and folder encryption.

Working With Special Types of Files

Several file types work with Windows Explorer to help you organize and display your filing system. Shortcuts allow you to have one copy of a file behave as if it were in two places in your filing system. Compressed folders let you store files in less disk space. Hidden folders keep you from accidentally deleting or changing system files, and folders, which themselves are a special kind of file, can be customized to display in a variety of ways.

Working With Shortcuts

Sometimes you want a file to be in two places at once: the place where it really belongs and somewhere like the desktop where you can easily get to it. Sometimes your filing system has two logical places to put the same file. Shortcuts enable you to deal with these situations, without the disadvantages that come from having two independent copies of the same file. (The concept of a shortcut is based on UNIX *links*.)

Technically, a *shortcut* is a file with a .lnk extension. Less technically, a shortcut is a placeholder in your filing system. A shortcut has a definite position on the folder tree, but it points to a file or folder that is somewhere else on the folder tree.

Most shortcuts point to program files. You usually should leave a program file inside the folder where it was installed, so you don't mess up any of the relationships between it and its associated files. At the same time, you might want the program to appear on the desktop, so you can conveniently open files by dragging them to the program's icon. Solution: Leave the program file where it is, but make a shortcut on the desktop pointing to it. When you drag a file to the shortcut icon, Windows opens the file with the corresponding program.

You may also want to create shortcuts to documents. Maintaining multiple copies of documents on your system is both wasteful of disk space and potentially confusing—when one copy gets updated, you could easily forget to update the others. And yet, files often belong in many different places in a filing system. If, for example, Paul writes the office's fourth-quarter report, the document may belong simultaneously in the Paul's Memos folder and in the Quarterly Reports folder. Putting the document itself in Quarterly Reports and a shortcut to it in Paul's Memos solves the problem, without creating multiple copies of the document. Clicking the shortcut icon opens the associated document, just as if you had clicked the icon of the document itself.

You can recognize a shortcut icon by the curving arrow that appears in its lower-left corner. A shortcut icon otherwise looks just like the icon of the object it points to: a document, folder, or application. A shortcut can be on your desktop or in a folder. A shortcut to the Word document To Do List looks like this:

Shortcut to To
Do List

 Windows also has shortcut keys and shortcut menus, which have nothing to do with shortcuts (see Chapter 1.).

Making Shortcuts

Shortcuts are created when you

- Drag-and-drop certain applications to a new folder or to the desktop
- Hold down the right mouse button while you drag any object to a new location and then select Create Shortcut(s) Here from the menu that appears when you drop the object
- Invoke the Create Shortcut Wizard either by selecting File | New | Shortcut in an Explorer window or by right-clicking an open space on the desktop or in an Explorer window and selecting New | Shortcut from the shortcut menu

In the first two cases, the original file or folder stays in its old location, and a shortcut to that file or folder is created in the drop location. In the third case, the shortcut is created in the folder from which the Create Shortcut Wizard was invoked.

Windows makes shortcuts automatically in certain circumstances. When you add a web page to your list of Favorites, for example, a shortcut is created and put in the folder C:\Documents And Settings*username*\Favorites (assuming that Windows is installed on C:).

Shortcuts can also point to web pages on the Internet. These shortcuts have file names that end with the extension *.url*, and you can also make them with the Create Shortcut Wizard. The procedure is the same, except you type the page's Internet address or URL (see Chapter 7, section "File Addresses").

Using Shortcuts

For almost all purposes, a shortcut to a file or folder behaves just like the target file or folder. Opening the shortcut, dragging and dropping the shortcut, or dragging and dropping something onto the shortcut produces the same result as performing the same action with the target file or folder.

The most convenient place to put shortcuts is on the desktop. Documents you are currently working on can reside in the appropriate place in your filing system, yet a shortcut on the desktop can make them instantly available. Programs you use frequently can remain in the folders they were installed into, yet be accessible with a single click. For programs you use frequently, you can add an icon to the Quick Launch toolbar on the taskbar (see Chapter 10, section "Editing the Quick Launch Toolbar").

 The structures of your Start and Start | All Programs menus are defined by the shortcuts that are stored in your C:\Documents And Settings folders—see Chapter 10.

Working With Compressed Folders (ZIP Files)

Everyone who has packed a suitcase knows the basic idea of a *compressed folder*—it's a trick for getting the same quantity of information to fit in a smaller space on a disk. Windows 98 and earlier versions of Windows required that you have a third-party application such as WinZip or ZipMagic to work with compressed folders (which everyone who doesn't work for Microsoft calls *ZIP files*). In many ways, these applications are still more useful and convenient than the Compressed Folders utility in Windows Explorer. If you are going to work with ZIP files every day, you probably want to acquire ZipMagic or some similar program; for occasional use, Compressed Folders work just fine.

The amount of disk space you can save by storing a file in a compressed folder varies depending on the kind of file it is; a Word document of 100KB, for example, might only take up 40KB in a compressed folder, while an Acrobat document of 100KB might still take up 80KB in a compressed folder. Many types of files (like Acrobat .pdf files and MP3 music files) already store their data in a compressed format.

Windows XP actually has two types of compressed folders: *NTFS compressed folders* and *ZIP compressed folders*. Here are the differences:

- **NTFS compression**, which is available for both files and folders, works only on NTFS partitions, and is completely invisible in operation. You compress or uncompress an NTFS compressed folder (or file) by changing its Compress Contents To Save Disk Space attribute on the Advanced Attributes dialog box (right-click the folder or file, choose Properties from the menu that appears, click the General tab, and click the Advanced button to see this attribute). When you turn on NTFS compression, Windows doesn't copy the file or folder—it compresses it in place.

- **ZIP compressed folders**, unlike ordinary folders, are actually files—in this case, ZIP files (with the extension .zip). All the files in this type of compressed folder are actually stored in the ZIP file. ZIP compressed folders are "virtual folders"— files that masquerade as folders in Windows Explorer. Most other programs see ZIP compressed folders as single files, though, and can't read or write the files contained in compressed folders. You can move or copy files to and from compressed folders.

Note   *Windows XP refers to both NTFS and ZIP compressed folders as compressed folders. In the rest of this chapter, when we talk about compressed folders, we mean ZIP compressed folders.*

The icon representing a ZIP compressed folder is a folder icon with a zipper on it:

July Photos

You pay a price for compression: files in compressed folders are harder to work with. They take longer to open than an identical uncompressed file, and most applications can't open them directly. If you open a document by single- or double-clicking its filename in an Explorer window, Windows makes an uncompressed copy of the file and runs the program associated with that type of file, but the copy is opened as a read-only file. Most applications can't save files in compressed folders at all. If you want to edit the document and save your changes, you must save the file in an ordinary folder. You can move the file into the compressed folder later.

Given their virtues and vices, compressed folders are best for archiving information that you don't access or change often. Compressed folders are also useful for sharing information with other people; they take less time to transmit and occupy less disk space. (For example, large files that you download from the Internet are frequently in .zip format.) The recipients can read the files, though, only if they have Windows XP, Windows Me, or a third-party utility like WinZip. If you want ZIP files to look like folders in Explorer windows, including opening and saving directly from ZIP files (compressed folders), get ZipMagic (**www.ontrack.com/zipmagic**), which combines the power of WinZip and the convenience of Windows compressed folders.

Compressed folders can also be encrypted. You can attach a password to the folder so no one else can open any of the files in the folder without knowing the password.

Creating a Compressed Folder

To create an empty compressed folder inside another folder, open or select the folder and choose File | New | Compressed folder. (To create one on the desktop, right-click an empty space on the desktop.)

To create a compressed folder with a specific file or files already inside it, select the files you want to include, right-click one of the selected files, and then choose Send To | Compressed Folder from the shortcut menu. The selected files remain unchanged, and a copy of them is created inside the compressed folder. The name and location of the folder is the same as the file (or one of the files) you right-clicked.

Working with Files in a Compressed Folder

To add a file to a compressed folder, drag it into the folder or use cut-and-paste. The file remains in its original location and a copy is created inside the compressed folder. To move the file without leaving the original behind, drag-and-drop it with the right mouse button, and then choose Move Here from the shortcut menu.

To many applications, a compressed folder appears to be simply a file of a type that the application doesn't know how to open properly. You can't, for example, use the File | Open command in Word to open a Word file that lives inside a compressed folder.

You can open a file in a compressed folder by double-clicking it, but the file usually lacks its full functionality. Windows uncompresses the file into a temporary location and then runs the program that handles the file. A Word file in a compressed folder, for example, opens in read-only mode. To regain functionality, you need to *extract* the file. The extracting process creates an uncompressed copy of the file outside the compressed folder.

To extract a file from a compressed folder, drag it from the compressed folder and drop it onto the desktop or into an uncompressed folder, or use cut-and-paste. One copy of the file is left behind in the compressed folder and a new, uncompressed copy appears in the new location. To extract the file without leaving a copy in the compressed folder, drag-and-drop with the right mouse button and choose Move Here from the shortcut menu.

To extract all the files in a compressed folder at once, select File | Extract All from the menu if the file is open, or right-click the folder's icon and choose Extract All from the shortcut menu. The Extract Wizard guides you in selecting a destination folder for the extracted files.

In many respects, the compressed folder and its files behave just as other folders and files. You can arrange and view the files within the folder in the usual ways, for example. However, Microsoft didn't completely integrate compressed folders into its filing system. Here is a short list of things Microsoft might want to fix:

■ Compressed folders don't show up in Browse windows. So, for example, you can't save a Word document into a compressed folder by choosing File | Save As from the Word menu bar. Most programs can't open a file that's stored in a compressed folder.

- You can't customize a compressed folder.
- You can't drag-and-drop or cut-and-paste a file from one compressed folder to another unless one of the folders contains the other.
- To most programs, they look like ZIP files instead of folders.

Adding a Password to a Compressed Folder

You can attach a password to a compressed folder so that Windows will ask for the password before opening or extracting any of the files in the folder. This technique encrypts the entire folder. If you want to encrypt some of the files in a compressed folder, but not other files, create a new compressed folder, move the files you want to encrypt to the new folder, and encrypt that folder. The password scheme used in compressed folders can be broken by a determined attacker and isn't a substitute for a serious encryption program, but it's adequate to deter casual snooping. It also stops mail server scanners from blocking zipped program files and other banned file types.

To encrypt a compressed folder, open the folder and select File | Add A Password. When the Add Password dialog box appears, type a password into the Password box, and then retype the same password into the Confirm Password box. (This retyping is to make sure you didn't mistype the password the first time, thereby creating a password that even you don't know.) Click OK to make the dialog box go away and close the folder (if it was open). The folder is encrypted.

Tip *Anyone can open an encrypted folder and look at the list of files. Windows doesn't ask for a password until you try to open or extract one of the files. In Details view, someone could learn the sizes and dates of the files without knowing the password. If you want even this information to be secret, put your files in another folder inside an encrypted folder. Then the password of the outer folder is required to open the inner folder.*

Opening and extracting files from encrypted compressed folders works exactly the same as opening and extracting files from ordinary compressed folders, except you have to type the password into the Password dialog box.

To decrypt an encrypted folder so that a password is no longer needed to access its files, open the folder, select Remove Password from the shortcut menu and then type the password into the Password dialog box.

Working With Hidden Files and Folders

As a safety feature, Windows' program files are *hidden*, which means, by default, they don't show up in Windows Explorer and can't be opened, deleted, or moved in Windows Explorer unless you choose to make them visible. If you want to display or hide all the hidden files and folders, follow these steps:

1. Choose Tools | Folder Options from the menu bar of any Explorer window. The Folder Options dialog box appears. (You can also open Folder Options from the Control Panel. It's part of the Appearances And Themes category.)

2. Click the View tab in the Folder Options dialog box. The Hidden Files section contains two radio buttons: Do Not Show Hidden Files And Folders and Show Hidden Files And Folders.

3. Click the Show Hidden Files And Folders radio button and click OK.

When hidden files and folders are shown, their icons appear as ghostly images like this:

PIF

Hidden files and folders usually don't play a significant role in the everyday life of the average computer user. For that reason, we recommend you leave them hidden whenever you are not working with one. This policy minimizes the chances you will alter or delete something important by accident.

Nonhidden files and folders contained in a hidden folder have an in-between status: they retain their original attributes and show up in Explorer windows if you move them to a nonhidden folder. But they are hidden in practice as long as they stay inside the hidden folder, because the path that connects them to the top of the folder tree includes a hidden link.

 A hidden file or folder shouldn't be considered secure. The Search command not only finds hidden files and folders, but anyone who finds your file by using this command can open it directly from the Search window (see "Searching for Files and Folders" later in this chapter). Also, you can see from the preceding discussion that viewing hidden files is not difficult. If other people use your computer and you don't want them to find particular files, you should encrypt those files, store them in your My Documents folder (assuming that your Windows user account has a password), or move them to a floppy disk you keep hidden in a more conventional way. See Chapter 6 for how to set up a private My Documents folder.

You can hide a file or folder by opening its Properties box (by right-clicking its icon and selecting Properties from the shortcut menu) and checking the Hidden check box on the General tab. To unhide the file, repeat the same steps, but deselect the Hidden check box.

Customizing a Folder

Technically, a folder is a file of type File Folder. It has properties like any other file, and you can change those properties in ways that affect the ways that the folder is displayed. In the previous chapter we described how to configure Windows Explorer to display folders in whatever way you find most convenient. In this section we describe changes you can make to the folder itself to allow even more display options.

You can select a new folder template for the folder, choose a picture to display on the folder's icon in Thumbnails view, or select a new icon entirely to represent the folder in any view.

These changes are made from the Customize tab of the folder's Properties dialog box, shown in Figure 8-2. You can display this tab either by opening the folder's Properties box and clicking the Customize tab, or by opening the folder and choosing View | Customize This Folder from the menu.

Folder Templates

How does Windows know to put Picture Tasks on the Task pane for a folder of pictures and add Filmstrip to the View menu? Or to put a musical note on the background of the working area when a folder of music files is open? Features like this are contained in folder templates. A *folder template* is a predefined set of features that you can choose to apply to a folder.

The default template for a new folder is the document template. Windows XP also offers six other templates. The photo album and pictures templates are discussed

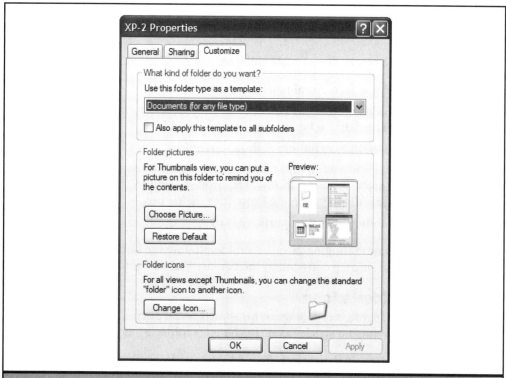

Figure 8-2. *Customize a folder from the Customize tab of the folder's Properties dialog box.*

in Chapter 18. The music, music album, and music artist templates are described in Chapter 19. The video template is used for the My Videos folder created by Windows Movie Maker, which is described in Chapter 20.

To change the template of a folder, open the folder and then select View | Customize This Folder. When the Properties dialog box appears, select the new template from the drop-down list in the What Kind Of Folder Do You Want box on the Customize tab of the Properties dialog box. Click OK or Apply to apply the new template.

Using a Picture as a Folder's Thumbnail Icon

The default icon for a folder in Thumbnails view is either a larger version of the ordinary yellow folder icon, or (if the folder contains image files) the first four image files from the folder arranged on the yellow folder icon like pictures pasted onto a manila folder. (You can change which four images are displayed by re-sorting the folder's contents.) You can make this icon more interesting and informative by choosing an appropriate image to be the folder's thumbnail icon. For example, if the folder contains music files from a particular album, you may be able to download the album cover from the Internet and use that image as the folder's thumbnail icon.

 The image on a folder's thumbnail icon doesn't have to be from an image file contained in the folder. The image can be stored anywhere on your computer or network.

To select a picture as a folder's thumbnail icon

1. Open the folder whose thumbnail you want to change.
2. Select View | Customize This Folder to display the Customize tab of the folder's Properties dialog box.
3. Click the Choose Picture button. A Browse window appears.
4. Use the Browse window to find the image file you want to use, then the Open button in the Browse window. The Browse window disappears, and the new image is displayed in the Properties dialog box.
5. Click the OK button in the Properties dialog box.

To restore the default thumbnail icon of a folder, follow the same steps, but click the Restore Default button in step 4 instead of the Choose Picture button.

Changing a Folder's Icon

If a folder has special content or you use it for some special purpose, you can remind yourself of that by giving it a special icon. To change a folder's icon

1. Open the folder and then select View | Customize This Folder. The folder's Properties dialog box appears with the Customize tab on top.
2. Click the Change Icon button on the Customize tab. The Change Icon box appears, as shown in Figure 8-3.

Figure 8-3. *Windows provides hundreds of icons.*

3. By default the Change Icon box shows the icons contained in the file C:\ Windows\System32\shell32.dll, where Windows stores its icons. If you want to look in another file or folder, click the Browse button and use the Browse window to select that file or folder.

4. Select an icon in the Change Icon box and Click OK to return to the Properties dialog box; then click OK to make the Properties dialog box disappear.

Searching for Files and Folders

Even with a well-organized file system, you can occasionally forget where you put a file or even what the file's exact name is. Fortunately, Windows provides the Search Companion Explorer bar to help you.

To start Search Companion, click the Search button on the Windows Explorer toolbar or select View | Explorer Bar | Search from the menu. Either action causes Search Companion to appear in the Explorer Bar. Answer the questions and click Search. When the search is done, the working area displays the files or folders that meet your criteria. From this Exploring window you can open, cut, copy, or drag-and-drop the files. If you have set the view to Details (the default, if you opened Search from the Start menu), you can sort by Name, Address, Size, and File Type by clicking the corresponding column header.

You can use as many different criteria as you want to narrow your search.

Standard vs. Advanced Search Companion

One of the new features in Windows XP is the Search Companion Wizard interface, shown in Figure 8-4. You begin by choosing an answer to the question What Do You Want To Search For? The multiple-choice style is maintained for as long as possible, and different responses lead to different follow-up questions. (This feature makes the interface hard for us to describe in detail.)

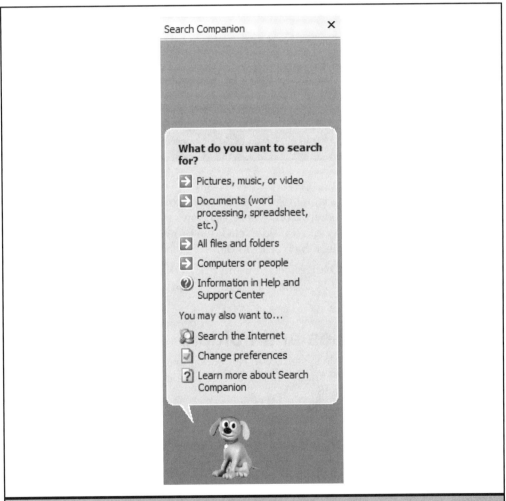

Figure 8-4. *Search Companion under standard settings, with the dog*

This behavior has the advantages and disadvantages of most Wizard interfaces: It's comfortable and unintimidating for beginners, but it's slow and frustrating for people who know exactly what they want to do—especially people who learned how to use Search under previous versions of Windows. If the designers of the Wizard have anticipated your desires, then you find a convenient button or link that does the job for you. If not, you end up studying the options given, guessing what follow-up options they lead to, and wondering if any of them is close enough to be worthwhile.

Fortunately, clicking the All Files And Folders option produces a window similar to the window in the old version of Search. If you like, you can skip the Wizard interface and make Search Companion go straight to this window when you start it up. In Microsoft's terminology, the Wizard interface is the "standard" version and the old interface is "advanced." If you search for files often enough to develop habits, we recommend switching to the advanced settings because they always put the same choices in the same places. To make this switch, follow these steps:

1. Choose the Change Preferences option in Search Companion. Scroll all the way down to the bottom of the Search Companion pane if you don't see this option.

2. Choose Change Files And Folders Search Behavior.

3. Select the Advanced radio button and click OK.

If you decide to go back to the standard settings, repeat the previous steps, but click the Standard radio button in step 3.

Putting Out the Dog

The folks at Microsoft have long imagined that computers are more friendly and less intimidating if the software includes cute animated characters. We have no idea why they believe this, but they do. (Personally, our anxiety level goes *up* whenever the computer display moves or makes noise on its own initiative.)

The latest offering from Microsoft's cartoon studio is the animated Rover in Search Companion. He serves no purpose other than to be cute. If you have other Microsoft programs installed (like Microsoft Office XP), other Search Companion characters may also be installed. Fortunately, Rover is easier to get rid of than some of Microsoft's earlier efforts (like Clippy, the animated paper clip in Microsoft Office). If you are using the standard Search settings, choose the Change Preferences option at the bottom of Search Companion's opening screen and then pick Without An Animated Screen Character. If you later decide that really miss Rover's big eyes and wagging tail, you can bring him back by choosing Change Preferences followed by With An Animated Screen Character.

If you decide you want a different cartoon character, you can switch to Earl (a surfing insect of some sort), Courtney (a girl with big glasses), or Merlin (a magician). Just click Change Preferences followed by With a Different Character. Then keep hitting the Next button until you see the character you want.

Under the advanced settings, Search Companion has a dialog-box interface, shown in Figure 8-5. You enter information into the dialog box by typing it into boxes, checking check boxes, or selecting radio buttons. The dialog-box format allows you to see all the search criteria at once, which gives experienced users a satisfying overview,

Search Criteria

With Search Companion, you can look for a file or folder by using any or all of the criteria listed next. The text boxes and radio buttons next all appear immediately in the advanced settings. If you don't see them under the standard settings, look for the Use Advanced Search Options button. Click the double-down arrows next to a question to see a list of possible answers.

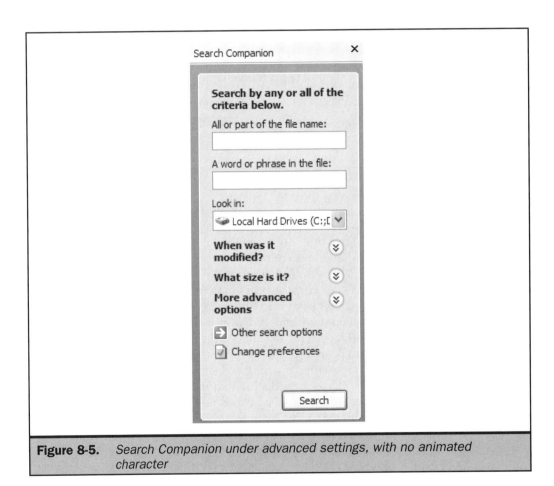

Figure 8-5. *Search Companion under advanced settings, with no animated character*

You can search for a file or folder:

- **By name or part of a name**   Type as much of the filename as you are sure of into the All Or Part Of The File Name box. In the advanced settings this box appears immediately. In the standard settings it appears as soon as you answer the What Do You Want To Search For question. Search Companion returns all the files and folders whose names contain the string. So "June" can net you both of the folders June 2003 and Juneau Alaska. You can take advantage of case sensitivity and wildcards, as described later in this chapter.

- **By a string of text contained in the file**   Type something into the box A Word Or Phrase In The File. You may need to click the Use Advanced Search Options button to make this box appear. A text search works just like a filename search, but now you are looking at the contents of the files rather than just their names. This is a much longer search than a filename search, but you can shorten it by taking advantage of the indexing service described later in this chapter. Unlike an Internet search engine, you only get to specify one word or phrase; you can't search for a collection of keywords.

- **By location**   Search only a particular drive or folder by using the Look In drop-down list. By default, the Look In box is set to the folder that was open when you pushed the Search toolbar button, or (if you opened Search from the Start menu) your local hard drives. If the folder you want isn't listed, select Browse and make a selection from the Browse For Folder window.

- **By file type**   The first question you are asked under the standard settings of Search Companion is essentially a question about file type. After you choose the Documents option or Pictures Music Or Video option, you have no opportunity to be more specific about file type, but in the All Files and Folders option a Type Of File drop-down list appears under More Advanced Options. (In any of the options, you can use the All Or Part Of The File Name box to enter a file extension, such as .doc for Word files.) Under the advanced settings, click the More Advanced Options button and then choose from the Type Of File drop-down list.

Note   *A document created by a non-Microsoft word processor in its own file type may not show up in a Documents search. Likewise, nonstandard or non-Microsoft media files may not show up in a Pictures, Music, or Video search. In these cases you either need to use the Type of File list to specify the exact file type or not use file type as a search criterion.*

- **By size**   Answer the What Size Is It question by choosing a radio button. The Specify Size radio button lets you search all files larger or smaller than a limit. Choose At Least or At Most from the drop-down list and then type the limit into the adjoining text box.

■ **By date modified, created, or accessed**   Answer the When Was It Modified question by clicking a radio button. If you want to search by date created or date accessed, click the Specify Dates radio button and choose Date Created or Date Accessed from the drop-down list. The Specify Dates option also allows you to pick a more precise range of dates than any of the radio button choices.

If all you know about a file is that you accessed it recently, you might do better to look on the History Explorer bar.

Wildcards

The asterisk (*) and question mark (?) characters play a special role in filename searches. Neither is allowed to be part of a filename, so when you include them in a filename search, Windows knows you intend for it to do something special with them. The asterisk and question mark are called *wildcards* because (like wildcards in poker) they can stand for any other character.

The question mark stands for any single character, so you can use it when you either don't know or don't want to specify a character in a filename. If, for example, you can't remember whether a file is named Letter to Tim or Letter to Tom, search for **Letter to T?m**—either Tim or Tom will match T?m. Similarly, you can find both Annual Report 2001 and Annual Report 2002, by using "Annual Report 200?" in your search.

An asterisk stands for any string of characters. Searching for **Letter to T*m** would not only find Letter to Tim and Letter to Tom, but also Letter to Travel Management Team.

Case Sensitivity

In filename and text searches you can insist that capital letters only be matched to capital letters, so that searching for "Bob" doesn't produce a file that contains "kabob." Such a search is called "case sensitive."

Case Sensitive is classified as an Advanced Search Option, so in the standard settings you find it by clicking links that contain the phrase "Advanced Search Options" or "Advanced Options" until the Case Sensitive check box reveals itself. In the advanced settings click the arrows-down button labeled More Advanced Options. The arrows on the button turn up and the Explorer bar expands to include more options, including the Case Sensitive checkbox.

Case sensitivity still doesn't work in Windows XP Service Pack 1, even though it worked in Windows Me and earlier versions of Windows.

Other Advanced Search Options

Clicking the double-down arrows next to More Advanced Options in the Search Companion Explorer bar gives you five check boxes. Case Sensitive is discussed in the previous section. The remaining four are self-explanatory: Search System Folders, Search Hidden Files And Folders, Search Subfolders, and Search Tape Backup.

If you are looking for a file you created yourself, chances are that it is not in a system folder, so you can leave that box unchecked. Ditto for hidden folders, unless you hid the folder yourself.

Most of the time you will want Search Subfolders to be checked, as it is by default. If it is unchecked, Search Companion searches only the folder specified in the Look In box, but not any of its subfolders.

Using Indexing Service

If you have ever searched through a book looking for a particular passage, you know what a difference it makes to have someone do the up-front work of making an index or concordance. That, in a nutshell, is what Indexing Service does: It is a utility that creates and maintains catalog files that keep track of the contents of the files on your computer. Having the Indexing Service enabled makes searches (especially text searches) much faster, at the cost of a certain amount of overhead: Indexing Service requires some time to construct an initial catalog, which it must update from time to time as you create new files and change old ones.

To find out whether Indexing Service is currently enabled or disabled, click the Change Preferences link in the Search Companion Explorer bar. The bar then displays the question How Do You Want To Use Search Companion? Click the response With Indexing Service or Without Indexing Service, whichever is offered. Search Companion then informs you whether Indexing Service is currently enabled or disabled and offers you the option of enabling it or disabling it.

If you administer a large, complex file system you may find it useful to create separate catalogs for various pieces of the system, so that the users on your system can do faster, better targeted searches. Catalogs are managed from the Indexing Service icon, which is in the Services and Applications section of the Computer Management console, but this topic goes beyond the scope of this book. See the "Using Indexing Service" topic in Windows Help And Support.

Saving and Retrieving a Search

After performing a search, you can save the search parameters by selecting File | Save Search. The list of files found with that search is not saved. The parameters are saved in a file of type *Saved Search* (with extension .fnd). To perform the search in the future, open the Saved Search file and click the Search Now button. Once a search has been saved, you can even share it with other people in the same ways you would share any other file—by copying it to a floppy, or attaching it to e-mail. Another way to rerun a search is by double-clicking its Saved Search file (which is usually stored in your My Documents folder, unless you specified another location).

Making Your Own CDs

All CD drives on computers can read CDs, but some CD drives can write CDs as well. Windows XP includes software for creating CDs: the CD Writing Wizard. If you are making music CDs, you should also see "Creating Your Own Music CDs" in Chapter 19 for how to burn music CDs using Windows Media Player. Also see the section "Configuring CD-R and CD-RW Drives" in Chapter 33.

CD-R and CD-RW Disks

You can create two different kinds of CDs:

- **CD-R** (compact disk recordable) disks can be written on once (they are *WORM*, or Write Once, Read Many). They can't be changed after they are written (though you can write on them many times until they are filled up). You can read CD-R disks in normal computer CD-ROM drives, as well as in audio CD players, so CD-R is the type of CD to use when creating music CDs or CDs to distribute to lots of people. Blank CD-Rs are relatively cheap (we've seen them for as little as ten cents apiece in the United States.).

- **CD-RW** (compact disk rewritable) disks can be written and rewritten many times, like a floppy disk. CD-RW disks can be rewritten about 1,000 times. You can use them as removable storage for sets of files that you want to update regularly (as a backup media). However, they are only readable in other CD-RW drives, and sometimes only by the same model drive. So, for example, you might put all your documents on a CD-RW and conveniently carry them to the other side of the world, where you could read and update them on another computer with a compatible CD-RW drive.

Both types of writable CDs hold approximately the same amount of data: about 650MB for 74-minute disks and about 700 MB for 80-minute disks.

 Don't bother buying high-priced blank CDs. Start with the cheapest CDs that you can find (we get ours at office supply stores) and see how they work in your CD-R or CD-RW drive. If you are burning audio CDs, test them in your audio CD players. If they don't work reliably, then try more expensive blank CDs.

CD-Burning Basics

There are two kinds of CD burners: CD-R drives and CD-RW drives. CD-R drives can write only CD-R disks, not CD-RW disks. CD-RW drives can write both types of disks.

Can I Write DVDs?

DVD-writing hardware and software exists and is supported by Windows XP, but Windows XP does not come with DVD-writing software. Usually, DVD-writing software is included with a DVD-writing drive. If your computer came equipped with such a drive, the software is probably preinstalled.

The DVD-writing market still has not settled on a single standard. DVD-RAM, DVD-R, DVD-RW, DVD+RW, and DVD+R are all different, and a drive that writes one may or may not read another. Before buying a DVD-writing drive, decide what devices you will be using to read the discs you write, and make sure you buy a drive that is compatible with those devices.

To create (or *burn*) a CD-R or CD-RW, you collect a group of files that you want to save on the CD and then write them in one *session*. You can write multiple sessions to both CD-R and CD-RW disks, but not all CD-ROM drives can read them: Audio CD players usually see only the first session on a CD-R disk, and some CD-ROM drives see only the last session. (Multisession CDs, packet-writing, and other more advanced CD topics are covered in the excellent CD-Recordable FAQ by Andy McFadden, on the Web at **www.cdrfaq.org**.)

Previous versions of Windows required third-party software to save files on CD-Rs and CD-RWs. If you do a lot of work with CD-Rs and CD-RWs you may still find it convenient to get software like Easy CD Creator (**www.roxio.com**) or Nero Burning (**www.ahead.de**). However, Windows XP integrates CDs into Windows Explorer. When you put a CD-R or CD-RW disk into your CD-R or CD-RW drive, Explorer recognizes what kind of disk it is and integrates it into the folder tree.

Before you store files on a CD, you decide what files to include in the session and how you want them arranged before you write any of them to the disk. For this reason, Windows provides a staging area on your hard drive that has the same capacity as the CD you plan to write. As you move files to and from the icon of your CD-R or CD-RW drive, the files are not actually written to the CD, but instead are copied to the staging area.

Tip   *Before trying to burn a CD, make sure you have enough space on your hard drive for the staging area. You'll need at least as much free space as is taken up by the files you plan to write to the CD. You can specify which drive or partition Windows uses for the staging area (see Chapter 33). It usually stores the staging area in C:\Documents And Settings\username\Local Settings\Application Data\Microsoft\CD Burning.*

Burning CDs from Windows Explorer

When you put a blank CD-R or CD-RW disc into your CD burner (CD-R or CD-RW drive), Windows takes a few seconds to recognize it. When it does, the follow dialog box appears:

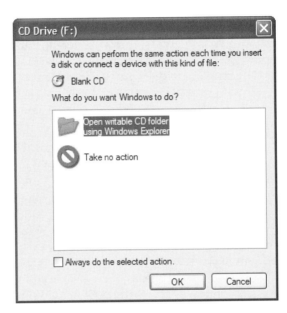

Selecting Open Writable CD Folder Using Windows Explorer creates an Explorer window with no icons in the working area. This is the staging area for your CD-writing session.

If your CD already has some files written on it, you see a different list of actions depending on the types of files that are on the disc. Select the Open Folder To View Files Using Windows Explorer option to open an Explorer window from which you can either examine the files already on the CD or add more files to it.

In either case (blank CD or partially full CD), the title bar and address bar of the Explorer claim to show you the contents of the disc in your CD-drive. This is only half true. The files that appear under the heading Files Currently On The CD are really there, but as you move new files into the working area they are not really being copied to the CD—at least not yet. These new files appear as ghostly images under the heading Files Ready To Be Written To The CD, as shown in Figure 8-6. These files are being copied onto your hard drive, and will not be written to the CD until you click the Write These Files To CD entry on the Task bar or select File | Write These Files To CD from the menu. (The advantage of this system is that you experiment with different ways of organizing the files and see just how many files you can get onto your CD before you run out of space.)

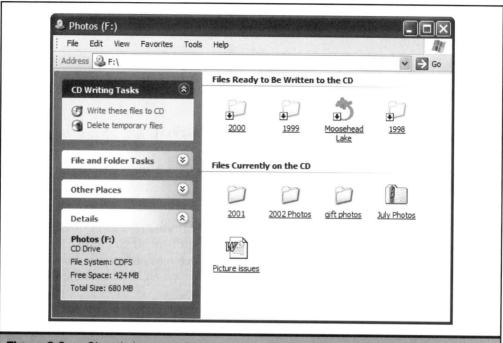

Figure 8-6.   *Ghostly images with arrows on their icons show you where files will be, not where they are.*

You can check the capacity of your CD by looking in the Details box on the Task pane, as shown in Figure 8-6. The free space listed is *before* including the files that haven't been written to the CD yet. Check the total size of the files you have in the staging area by selecting all of the ghostly icons, right-clicking one of them, and selecting Properties from the shortcut menu. The combined Properties box of the selected items tells you their total size. When you finally decide to write the files to the CD, the combined size of the files in the staging area has to be less than the free space listed in the Task pane.

You can also create folders inside the staging area, delete items, rename items, move items from one folder to another, and in general do whatever you need to do to get make your CD file system look the way you want it.

When you are satisfied, click Write These Files To CD on the task bar or choose File | Write These Files To CD from the menu. This invokes the CD Writing Wizard to guide you through the rest of the process. You don't have to do much: just give your CD a name and decide at the end whether you are finished or you want to write these same files onto another CD.

Expect the CD-burning to take several minutes, or even longer if you have a slow CD-burning drive.

Conversely, if you decide you want to leave the CD the way it was, click the Delete These Temporary Files option on the Task pane. The staging area is cleared and nothing is written to the CD.

Burning CDs from Windows Media Player

Windows Media Player 8, the audio and video program that comes with Windows XP, can also burn audio CDs (see the section "Creating Your Own Music CDs" in Chapter 19).

Erasing Files From CD-RW Discs

CD-RW discs can be erased and rewritten many times. (Industry standards call for 1000 times, but some companies claim much higher numbers.) If you have CD-writing software like Easy CD Creator you can delete files selectively, just as you do from a floppy disk. But Windows Explorer erases CD-RW discs on an all-or-nothing basis.

 Before you erase a CD-RW disc, make sure you have copied any files you want to keep.

To erase a CD-RW that is in your CD-RW drive, open the drive in an Explorer window and click the Erase This CD-RW option on the Task pane (or choose File | Erase This CD-RW from the menu.) The CD-Writing Wizard opens to ask if you really want to erase all the files on the CD-RW. If you have changed your mind, you have one more chance to click Cancel, but if you go forward the CD-RW will become blank and ready for reuse.

Troubleshooting Burning CDs

The most likely reason for failing to burn a CD is that the disc itself is bad. Try again with another disc.

If changing the CD doesn't help. Look at the Properties box of your CD-R or CD-RW drive. (Right-click the drive's icon in My Computer and select Properties from the shortcut menu.) It should have a Recording tab, as shown in Figure 8-7. If there is no Recording tab, then Windows doesn't recognize the recording capabilities of your drive. (In other words, it thinks you just have a CD-ROM drive.) You will need to reinstall the driver software for your CD-burning drive (see Chapter 13).

If your CD-RW drive's Properties box does have a Recording tab, the first and easiest thing to check there is that the Enable CD Recording On This Drive check box is checked.

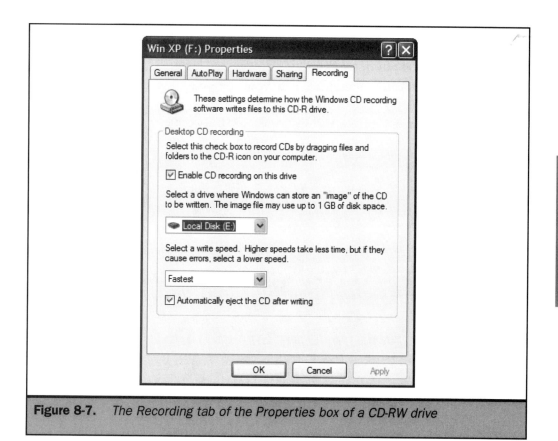

Figure 8-7. *The Recording tab of the Properties box of a CD-RW drive*

If you are running out of space in the staging area, the Recording tab tells you which hard drive Windows Explorer is using to store the files you have not yet written to a CD. You can choose a different drive from the drop-down list on the Recording tab.

If the CD-burning process completes, but the files have errors in them, try slowing down the recording speed. The default speed choice (shown in Figure 8-7) is Fastest. Pick a different speed from the drop-down list on the Recording tab of the Properties box of your CD-R or CD-RW drive. Lower speeds take longer, but produce fewer errors.

Here are some other things to try if you are having trouble burning CDs:

■ Reboot your computer before beginning to burn the CD, so that Windows starts with uncluttered memory and temporary files.

■ Exit all other programs. Press CTRL-ALT-DEL to display the Task Manager and end unnecessary processes.

■ Disable your screen saver. (Right-click your Windows desktop, choose Properties to see the Display Properties dialog box, click the Screen Saver tab, and set the Screen Saver drop-down menu to None.

■ If your printer can communicate with your computer (you use a bidirectional printer cable), unplug the printer.

■ If your computer is on a LAN, disconnect the LAN cable.

If you are creating audio CDs, see the section " Troubleshooting Burning Audio CDs" in Chapter 19 for other ideas.

The
Complete
Reference

Windows XP

Chapter 9

Backing Up Your Files with the Backup Utility

Backing up means making copies of your files so that you can get the information back should anything happen to the originals. The most important thing to say about backing up your files is this: **Back up your files!**

You can back up your files onto floppies, CDs, extra hard drives, Zip drives, Jaz drives, tapes, or whatever you happen to have. How you back up your files is much less important than that you do it. If you have only a few files or folders to back up, you can use Windows Explorer to make the copies. Just think how angry you'd be if you lost all the data files on your computer right now.

A backup program called the Backup Utility (written by Microsoft and Veritas Software) is included on the Windows XP CD-ROM. It installs as part of Windows XP Professional, but not as part of Windows XP Home Edition. However, Home Edition users can install the Backup Utility separately from the CD-ROM.

The Backup Utility makes backing up large numbers of files and folders reasonably painless. Your Zip drive, Jaz drive, CD burner, or tape drive may come with its own backup program; if it does, consider using that backup program instead, since it may have more features than Windows XP's Backup Utility.

Determining What to Back Up

Ideally, you should back up everything; but (depending on the speed of your machine, the size of your hard drive, and the type of backup medium you use) a complete backup can take a considerable length of time. Once you have a complete backup to work from, updating that backup takes considerably less time.

A backup of only files that are new or have changed is called an *incremental backup*. A complete backup of all files and folders is called a *full backup* or *baseline backup*.

Types of Files to Back Up

Backing up files is a little like flossing teeth: we all know it's good for us, but few of us do it as often as we know we should. If it takes you a month or two to get around to doing a complete backup, you should consider backing up the following parts of your system more often:

- **Documents you are working on**   Many applications put new documents in your My Documents folder or its subfolders. You may choose to put your documents anywhere you like, but for backup purposes, it is convenient to have them organized in subfolders of one easy-to-find folder.

- **Databases to which you regularly add data**   For example, if you use Quicken to balance your checkbook once a month, back up the file in which Quicken stores your checkbook data.

- **Correspondence, especially your e-mail files**   Letters and memos that you write are probably already in your documents folder(s). E-mail files, however, are usually stored in whatever folder you set up when you installed your e-mail program. Many Microsoft programs put your data in the C:\Documents And Settings*username* folder (replace *username* with your Windows user account name, described in Chapter 6).

If you back up these files frequently, a hard drive disaster is much less of an ordeal. Still, nothing beats the security of knowing that you have backups of *everything*.

Programs are not on the list of important items to back up because you (or the person who maintains your machine) should still have the CDs that you used to install the programs in the first place. Make sure you know where the CDs are, that they're in a safe place, and that the CD serial numbers are with them. If you have downloaded programs, you might want to reserve one backup CD for the downloaded installation files. If you lose your hard disk, reinstalling all of your software is a nuisance, but not a disaster. You would, however, lose all the special settings that you have made to personalize the software for yourself. If reselecting all of those settings would be an ordeal, then you need to either back up the entire program folder, or find out which specific files contain those settings.

 If you back up the C:\Documents And Settings folder (assuming that Windows XP is installed on C:), you have copies of everything in all users' My Documents folders, as well as everyone's program settings. Outlook Express also stores your message folders in a subfolder of C:\Documents And Settings.

If you like, however, you can back up all the files on your entire system, including your programs and Windows itself. If you do this, be sure to include the Windows Registry as part of the backup (see Chapter 38).

Backing Up a LAN

If your computer is on a LAN, you can back files up over the LAN (see Chapter 27). You can make backups on the hard disks of other computers, or on CD or tape.

For example, to back up a four-computer LAN, you could run the following backups:

- Weekly full backup of all data files, including the C:\Documents And Settings folders of all the computers, every Friday night. Make the backup files on a computer that has a CD burner and then burn these weekly backup files to CDs. Save these CDs for at least a month.

- Daily incremental backup of all data files, including only files that have changed since the preceding backup, Monday night through Thursday night. Store these daily backup files on the computer that has the largest hard disk. Save these files only until the weekly full backup is complete.

For this system, you need one computer with a large hard disk, big enough to store daily backups of the data from all four computers. Hard disks have gotten so cheap that a large hard disk is much cheaper than any tape drive. You also need a CD burner and enough CDs to store your weekly backup files. Depending on how much data your store on your computer, you may be able to fit the data from all four computers onto one CD per week, or you may need several CDs. Another good idea is to take your weekly backup CDs to another location from time to time (maybe monthly), so that if something happens to your entire office, you have a backup, even if it's not completely up-to-date.

Backup Media

Tapes are the traditional backup media, but tape drives are expensive and tapes are slow. The good thing about tapes is that they store a lot of data (as much as 30GB). Here are some alternatives to backing up to tapes:

- **Hard disk**   If you have two or more computers connected on a LAN, you can back up each computer's data files onto another computer. You might want to install a very large hard disk on one computer, create a separate, large partition, and back up the data files from all the other computers into that partition.

- **CDs**   If the amounts of data are small enough to fit on a reasonable number of CD-ROMs, you can burn the backup files onto CD-Rs or CD-RW. The Backup Utility can't back up directly to CD-R, so you need enough disk space to back up to hard disk, and then burn the backup files to CDs. Organize your backup jobs so that each backup file is small enough to fit on one CD-R, which can store about 650MB.

- **Zip disks**   Zip, Jaz, and other removable hard disks store less than CD-Rs, but they are reusable.

- **Floppy disks**   Floppies store very small amounts of data (1.2MB each), so unless you work with only a few small files, floppies are unlikely to provide a convenient way to back up.

How Frequently to Back Up

Different sources will tell you to back up your files daily, weekly, or monthly, but the real answer is that you should back up your files as soon as you have created or changed something that you don't want to lose. You need to balance the regular nuisance of backing up your files against the possible ordeal of regenerating your creative work.

If you work on a document daily, a single day's work can be a lot to lose. System files change when you reconfigure the settings of your system or when you install new hardware or software. Only you know how frequently your databases change or how much e-mail you are willing to lose in an accident. Backing up these frequently updated files need not be as involved as a full system backup (see "Determining What to Back Up" earlier in this chapter).

Storing Backup CDs and Tapes

Put your backup media in a safe place, preferably as far from your computer as practical. Backups that sit right next to your computer may be handy in a hardware or software crash—but they don't protect you at all in the event of fire, theft, or sabotage. If your backups are magnetically stored (tapes, removable disks, or hard drives— anything but CD-ROMs), keep them away from strong magnets. You may want to store an extra backup CD or tape off-site (in a different building).

The Windows XP Backup Utility

The Backup Utility is an updated version of the Windows Backup program that came with Windows 2000. The Backup Utility can make backups from all types of Windows-compatible partitions: NTFS, FAT32, and FAT (see Chapter 33). It makes a *volume shadow copy* of all the files you specify, including files that are open (many backup programs skip open files). You can continue to use your computer during a backup, even storing and editing files that are part of the backup. It can also spread your backup files across many floppy disks or other removable media without confusing itself.

Note   *The Backup Utility's Automated System Recovery (ASR) feature isn't available with Windows XP Home Edition. In Windows XP Professional, ASR saves and restores the system settings and configuration files that you would need if you had to restore your system from scratch. Windows XP Home Edition lets you create ASR disks, but doesn't let you restore from them!*

In order to run the Backup Utility, you need to be logged into Windows as an administrative user—Owner, Administrator, or another user account with administrative privileges (see Chapter 6 for an explanation of user accounts). If you are logged in as a non-administrative user, you can still run the program, but you can back up only your own files, and you can store the backup only on backup media that you have permission to use.

Backup Jobs

Making a backup requires you to make a series of decisions: what files to back up, what device to store the backup files on, and a number of more technical decisions, such as whether to use compression or not. Ideally, you would make these decisions once for each type of backup that you regularly do (complete backup, document backup, mail backup, system backup, and so on) and then have the computer remember those decisions so that you don't have to go through them again every time you back up.

The Backup Utility handles this situation by maintaining a list of *backup jobs*. Its Backup Or Restore Wizard helps you define a backup job by leading you through all the necessary decisions. In the course of that process, you give the job a name. The next time you want to back up those same files and/or folders, you need only tell the Backup Utility the name of the job.

If you schedule the backup job to run later and specify times for it to run, Backup stores your specifications as a backup job. If you tell the Backup Or Restore Wizard to run the backup job right away, it doesn't store your settings for reuse.

Backup jobs are usually stored in the C:\Documents and Settings*username*\Local Settings\Application Data\Microsoft\Windows NT\NTBackup\Data folder (we are not making this up). They have the extension .bks (for backup specification). Log files are stored in the same folder. Backup uses Scheduled Tasks to run backup jobs on a schedule (see Chapter 1, section "Running Programs on a Schedule Using Scheduled Tasks"). Once you've created a backup job, there's no easy way to modify it—instead, you recreate it.

The Removable Storage Service

Windows XP, like Windows 2000, includes Removable Storage, a service that can keep track of your tapes or other large-scale removable storage (but we refer to all storage media as tapes in this section for brevity). Removable Storage doesn't manage floppy disks or CD-ROMs, despite the name; however, it can label your tapes and keep track of which one you need to insert and when. It also works with the Backup Utility and other backup or storage programs that use removable media.

Removable Storage refers to a backup device (such as a tape drive) and its backup media (such as the tapes that work with the drive) as a *library*. A library can be robotic (with an automated media changer, like the 50-CD changer you can get for your music CDs) or stand-alone (manually operated). Only Windows servers usually have robotic backup devices. Removable Storage organizes them in a library into these media pools:

- **Import media pool** Media that have not yet been catalogued and labeled by Removable Storage. Before you can use them for backup, Removable Storage can import them into the Free media pool.

- **Free media pool** Unused, available media. When an application (like Backup) is done with a tape, it can return it to the free media pool.

- **Backup media pool** Media that have been reserved for use by the Backup Utility. When you use the Backup Utility to back up onto a new tape, Removable Storage moves the tape into the Backup media pool.

Before you can back up information onto tapes, the Removable Storage system catalogues your unused tapes and moves them to the Backup media pool. You can tell Removable storage to do this automatically when you back up onto a new tape. You can also turn the service on or off, and control which users can perform backups and restores (see "Managing the Removable Storage Service" at the end of this chapter).

 We find the Removable Storage service annoying and confusing, so avoid it unless you have large numbers of tapes. It doesn't work with CD-R or CD-RW drives.

Backing Up with Windows Explorer

Even if you can't get around to a complete backup, you can protect yourself against the worst without too much effort by backing up your most valuable files and folders each day that you work on them.

Even on a slow system, it usually takes only a minute or two at the end of each day to pop in a Jaz, Zip, floppy, CD-RW, or other removable disk and copy the files you worked on that day. It's a good habit to develop.

If you typically work on only a few files each day, put a blank Jaz, Zip, floppy, CD-RW, or other removable disk into the drive. Run Windows Explorer (choose Start | My Computer) and drag-and-drop the files onto the floppy or removable drive in the folder tree (see Chapter 7). Or, select the files, choose File | Send To (or right-click the file and choose Send To from the menu that appears), and choose your removable disk from the list of Send To destinations that appears.

 If the drive (or folder) that you use for storing backup copies isn't already available on the Send To menu, you can add it (see Chapter 7, section "Copying Files Using the Send To Menu").

If you work on a larger number of files, search for recently changed files to make sure that you don't miss any. Choose Start | Search to search for all files modified within the last day (see Chapter 8). You can drag-and-drop files directly out of the Search Results window onto a disk icon in Windows Explorer. Or you can right-click any file in the Search Results window and choose Send To from the menu.

 If you use Search to list the files you've worked on today, construct your search in such a way as to avoid finding all the temporary files that Windows creates in the course of a day. (If you do a lot of web browsing, there can be hundreds of them.) These temporary files are contained in subfolders of the C:\Windows folder (or whatever folder Windows is installed in).

A larger backup drive makes it less important to be selective about what you copy. A Zip disk is approximately 70 times larger than a floppy, a CD can contain up to 650MB, and a backup hard drive may be dozens of times larger yet. You probably can copy, without too much time or trouble, your entire documents folder (whether it is C:\My Documents or some other folder that you have chosen) at the end of each day. You probably can copy your entire e-mail folder as well (see "Determining What to Back Up" earlier in this chapter).

Running the Backup Utility

If you have large amounts of data, the Backup Utility has several advantages over Windows Explorer:

- It can copy files in a compressed form, so that they take up less disk space.
- It can spread a single backup job over several removable disks. This feature makes it possible to back up larger jobs.
- When you define a backup job, you decide once and for all what folders you want the job to back up. You don't have to go through the decision process every time you do a backup.
- It is automated. Once the job starts, all you need to do is feed it a new disk if it asks for one. If you are backing up onto a hard disk, tape drive, or some other medium with sufficient size, you don't need to do anything at all.
- It can back up files that are open. The Backup Utility takes a volume shadow copy—that is, what the files contain at the moment that the backup occurs.

However, the Backup Utility has a number of disadvantages, too:

- You must use the Backup Utility to retrieve the files you've backed up. You can't use Windows Explorer to get files and folders back.
- The Backup Utility can't store files directly on a CD-R or CD-RW. Instead, you have to create a backup file on a hard disk and then burn the backup file to CD.

Installing the Backup Utility

Although the Backup Utility comes with Windows XP, you may have to install it from the Windows XP Setup CD. If you don't find Backup on the Start | All Programs | Accessories | System Tools menu, follow these steps:

1. With the Windows XP CD-ROM in your CD-ROM drive, display the folder D:\ Valueadd\Msft\NTBackup in an Explorer window; substitute your CD-ROM's drive letter for D: if it's not drive D:. (If the Windows XP installation window appears, click Perform Additional Tasks, and click Browse This CD to see an Explorer window showing the files on the CD.) The folder contains two files: NTBackup.msi (the Backup installation program) and Readme.txt.

2. Run NTBackup.msi. Follow the instructions on the screen to install the Backup Utility files in your C:\Windows\System32 folder. The filename of the program is Ntbackup.exe.

3. Make a shortcut for the program. Right-click the desktop, choose New | Shortcut from the menu that appears, and type **C:\Windows\System32\ Ntbackup** into the box that appears. (Replace C: with the drive letter in which Windows is installed.) After you click Next, type any name for the shortcut (such as **Backup**). Click Finish, and the shortcut appears. If you want to add the Backup Utility to your Start menu, drag it to the Start button, to the All Programs option, and then to the location where you want it to appear.

Running the Backup Utility

Run the Backup Utility by running the shortcut you just created. You can also choose Start | Run and type **ntbackup** in the Open box. Or, right-click a disk drive in an Explorer window, choose Properties to display the drive's Properties, click the Tools tab, and click the Backup Now button.

Remember that you must be logged on as an administrative user (or with a user account that is a member of the Backup Operators group) to be able to back up or restore files (see Chapter 6).

The first time you run the Backup Utility, it checks your system for devices onto which you can copy files (backup devices). Then it runs the Backup Or Restore Wizard, which steps you through backing up files or restoring from a previous backup. If you'd rather not use the wizard, clear the Always Start In Wizard Mode check box on its first dialog box, and click the Advanced Mode link.

 Believe it or not, you can run three wizards from the Backup Utility: the Backup Or Restore Wizard, the Backup Wizard, and the Restore Wizard. You might think that running the Backup Or Restore Wizard and choosing Back Up Files And Settings would run the Backup Wizard, but it doesn't—the backup part of the Backup Or Restore Wizard is similar to the Backup Wizard, but it provides a few additional options. You can tell which wizard you are running by the name in the title bar of its window. We recommend using the Backup Or Restore Wizard if you must use a wizard at all—choose Tools | Switch To Wizard Mode form the Backup Utility's menu bar.

Backing Up Files with the Backup Utility

Backing up files is something you should do regularly, so it's worth taking some time to create backup jobs for the files that are the most important to you and to schedule them to run daily (or at least weekly). You can create a backup job with a wizard or from the Backup Utility window, and you can run backup jobs you've already created.

Creating a Backup Job with the Backup Or Restore Wizard

The Backup Or Restore Wizard may run automatically when you start the Backup Utility. Otherwise, choose Tools | Switch To Wizard Mode from the menu bar in the Backup Utility window. When the program runs, choose Back Up Files And Settings from the wizard's dialog box. Click Next to move from dialog box to dialog box, and click the Advanced button when it appears so that you have access to all the wizard's settings. You need to make the following decisions to create a new backup job (these decisions are described in more detail in the following sections):

- Whether to back up or restore files (if you need to restore files, see "Restoring Files with the Backup Utility" later in this chapter).

- Which files to back up (see Figure 9-1)

- Whether to back up only your files, the files of all the user accounts on the computer, or the files that you specify

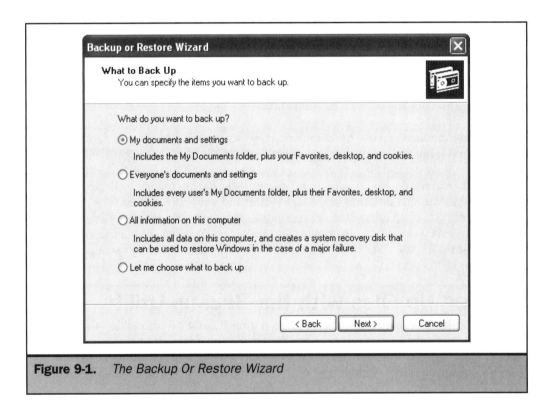

Figure 9-1.   *The Backup Or Restore Wizard*

- Whether to back up all the selected files or just the ones that have changed since the previous backup
- Where to store the backup data and whether to replace backup jobs that are already there
- Whether to verify the backup
- Whether to use compression to make the backup file smaller
- When to run the backup job—now or at a later scheduled time

When you click the wizard's Finish button, if you chose to back up now, the program begins copying files. You see a Backup Progress dialog box (shown in Figure 9-2) that shows how many files will be copied and how many have been copied so far.

When the backup is done, you can click the Report button to see a log of the files that were copied.

The following sections provide you with more detail about the choices you have to make when setting up a backup job.

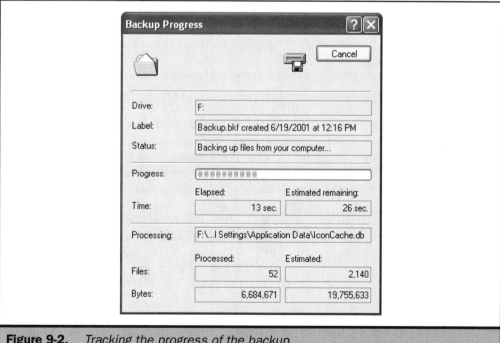

Figure 9-2.   *Tracking the progress of the backup*

Selecting Files to Back Up

The first decision you need to make is whether this backup job should be a complete backup or a backup only of selected files. You have four options:

- **My Documents And Settings** Includes the files in your Documents And Settings folder (usually C:\Documents And Settings*username*, where *username* is your user account name). This folder includes your desktop and Start menu settings, your My Documents folder, your Favorites, and other configuration settings. If you store all your data files in your My Documents folder and its subfolders, this option is an efficient way to back up your own files—program files can always be restored from CDs.

- **Everyone's Documents And Settings** Includes the Documents And Settings folders for all the user accounts defined on your computer (see Chapter 6).

- **All Information On This Computer** Includes all the files from all the drives on your computer. This option backs up Windows itself and all your application programs and data. Its offer to create a system recovery disk doesn't work on Windows XP Home Edition.

- **Let Me Choose What To Back Up** Displays a folder tree from which you can choose the files and folders you want to include.

If you choose the last option, you see a window (as shown in Figure 9-3) that works much like an Explorer window (see Chapter 7, section "The Anatomy of Windows Explorer"). When a folder in the left pane is selected, its contents appear in the right pane. The boxes with plus or minus signs denote whether a folder is expanded. Click a plus box to see the next level of the folder tree under a given folder. Click the My Computer plus box to see the disk drives on your system.

The difference between this window and an Explorer window is that each folder has a check box next to it. Clicking one of these puts a blue check mark in the box, indicating that the entire folder (and all its subfolders) has been added to the list of files and folders to be backed up. For example, clicking the check box next to the C drive icon adds the entire contents of the C drive to the backup job.

If you want to back up some of the files on a drive, but not all of them, click the plus box next to the drive icon to expand the folder tree underneath that drive. This gives you an opportunity to decide exactly which folders to back up. Select only those files and folders that you want to be part of this backup job. A gray check mark appears in the box next to a folder from which you have chosen to back up some, but not all, of its contents.

 To back up the Registry, boot files, and other system files, choose System State from the Items To Back Up list, which appears as the last item under My Computer. The System State option includes the boot files, too.

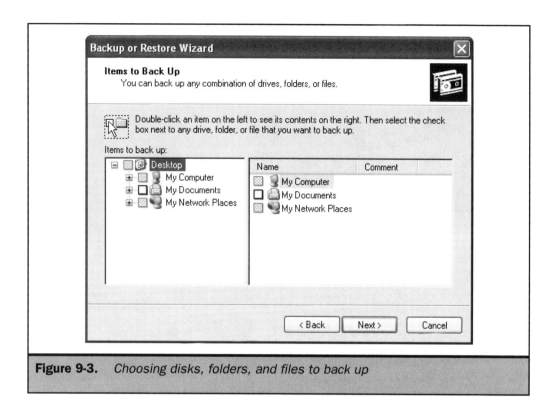

Figure 9-3. *Choosing disks, folders, and files to back up*

Choosing a Destination for the Backup File

The next screen of the Backup Or Restore Wizard asks where to store the backup files. The options you see depend on how you set the first setting, Select The Backup Type. You can set this to File or to a backup device—a tape drive or other mass storage device.

If you choose File, Backup combines the entire backup into one compressed backup file stored on the disk that you indicate. Backup files have the extension .bkf. When you restore one or more files from the backup file, the Backup Utility extracts the files you want from the backup file. When you choose File, you see these two settings, as shown in Figure 9-4:

■ **Choose A Place To Save Your Backup**   Select the drive on which to store the backup file. The drop-down box shows a list of your removable disk drives, but no CD burners. You can also store a backup file on a fixed hard disk—set the box to Let Me Choose A Location Not Listed Here and click the Browse button to see your hard disks and choose a folder. (We found that you have to put a formatted floppy disk in drive A: at this point, even if you don't plan to store your backup file on the floppy.) For example, if you want to make daily

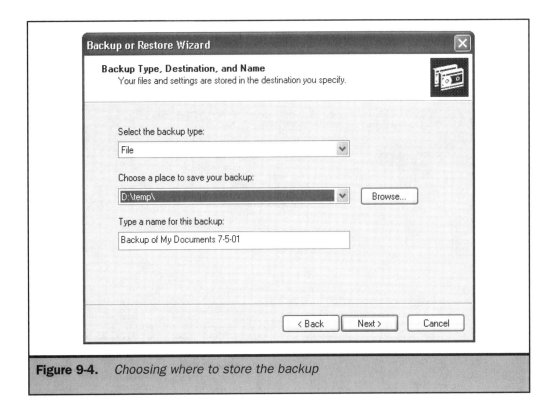

Figure 9-4.   *Choosing where to store the backup*

backups of a few important data files, you can store the files in a Backup folder on your hard disk. However, if your hard disk dies, all your backup files will be lost. The next time you create a backup job, the pathname you choose appears on drop-down the list of places.

- **Type A Name For This Backup**   This is the name of the backup file (you don't have to type the .bkf extension). The default name is Backup.bkf (the Backup Utility adds the .bkf extension).

If your computer has a tape drive, you can choose it from the Select The Backup Type drop-down menu, which includes an option for the type of backup tape you use (for example, miniQIC or Travan). Then, you have only one other option to set: Choose The Tape You Want To Use. Set this to New to use a tape that has not been catalogued by the Removable Storage program, or choose the name of an existing tape (see "The Removable Storage Service" earlier in this chapter).

The Backup Utility doesn't work directly with CD-R or CD-RW drives. If you want to back up to a CD-R or CD-RW disk, back up to a file first, and then burn the file onto the CD. This limitation prevents the Backup Utility from creating a backup that spans several CDs. One CD-R or CD-RW can hold up to about 650MB, so if your backup file is no larger than this, you can burn it onto a CD. For larger backup files, use a CD-burning utility that can split files over multiple CDs.

Choosing a Baseline or an Incremental Backup

After you have chosen which files to back up and where to store them, the wizard displays the Completing The Backup Or Restore Wizard dialog box, confirming the information you have specified so far, but you're not done yet—click the Advanced button to see some other settings.

The Type Of Backup setting controls whether to back up all the files you selected, or only files that are new or changed since the previous backup. (Windows tracks which files have been created or changed since your last backup.) You have five options for this setting:

- **Normal**   Copies all the files you selected and marks them as backed up.
- **Copy**   Copies all the files but doesn't mark them as backed up.
- **Incremental**   Copies only files that were created or changed since the last backup, and marks them as backed up.
- **Differential**   Copies only files that were created or changed since the last backup, but doesn't mark them as backed up.
- **Daily**   Copies only files that were created or changed today.

If this is the first time you are backing up files, choose Normal. If you have recently backed up files, choose Incremental to copy only the files that weren't included in your last backup.

Choosing How to Back Up

Next, you see the How To Back Up settings, which consist of these check boxes:

- **Verify Data After Backup**   After completing the backup, the Backup Utility reads the backup and compares it to the files it backed up to make sure that they match. This step lengthens the backup time, but it may be worth it. Verifying that the backup was successful takes only a little less time than the backup itself and may seem unnecessary, but remember: Paranoia is what backing up is all about. If you had faith that such things would always work properly, you wouldn't be backing up at all.

- **Use Hardware Compression If Available** Some backup devices can compress the backup information as it stores it. This check box is grayed out if your backup device doesn't support this feature.

- **Disable Volume Snapshot** The Backup Utility can include files that are open—files that programs are updating. If you don't want open files to be included, deselect this check box.

The next screen of the Backup Or Restore Wizard asks whether to Append This Backup To The Existing Backups or Replace The Existing Backups. For backups to tape, this setting determines what happens to the previous backup information that is already on the tape. Another option controls whether the backup is accessible only to administrative users or to all users.

If you are backing up to a new tape, the next screen of the wizard suggests labels to use for the tape. This label is stored on the tape and appears in the Backup window on the list of available backups. You may want to write the same information on a paper label and stick it to the tape.

Choose When to Back Up

Finally, the Backup Or Restore wizard asks whether to run the backup job Now or Later. If you choose Later, you specify the name of the backup job and when to run it, as shown in Figure 9-5. You can run the backup job once, or you can schedule it to run daily, weekly, monthly, or another schedule (see Chapter 1, section "Running Programs on a Schedule Using Scheduled Tasks").

This is the last information that the Backup Or Restore Wizard asks for. When you click Next, you see the Completing The Backup Or Restore Wizard dialog box again, with a summary window of all your settings (as shown in Figure 9-6). Click Finish to create the backup job and run it (now or whenever you specified).

If you are using a tape, you may see messages from the Removable storage program as it mounts the tape. When the backup job is finished, Backup exits.

If you plan to reuse these backup specifications—the files to include, the backup type, where to store the backup, and other settings—tell Backup to run the backup Later. This choice causes Backup to store the backup job so you can run it again.

Creating a Backup Job by Using the Backup Tab

You don't have to use a wizard to create a backup job. Instead, you run the Backup Utility and click the Advanced Mode link on its opening screen. You see the main window of Backup Utility, as shown in Figure 9-7. The Backup Wizard and Restore

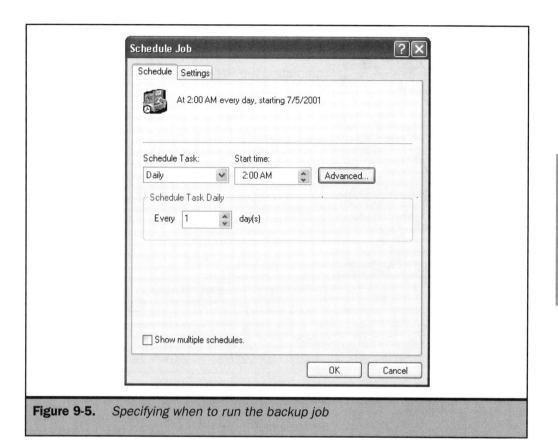

Figure 9-5.   *Specifying when to run the backup job*

Wizard buttons run limited versions of the Backup Or Restore Wizard that we describe in this chapter (we recommend that you run the Backup Or Restore Wizard instead by choosing Tools | Switch To Wizard Mode from the menu bar).

Tip   *If you rarely want to use the Backup Or Restore Wizard, deselect the Always Start In Wizard Mode check box on the wizard's opening screen.*

To create a backup job, click the Backup tab just below the menu bar. You see the window shown in Figure 9-8. The upper part of the window enables you to choose the files to include. The settings in the lower-left corner allow you to specify where to store the backup (see "Choosing a Destination for the Backup File" earlier in this chapter).

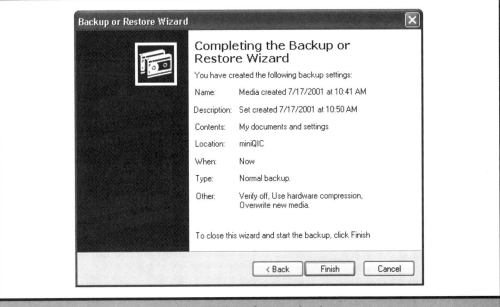

Figure 9-6. *Backup displays the settings for your backup.*

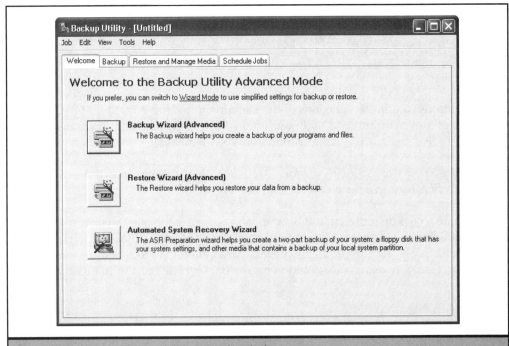

Figure 9-7. *The Backup Utility's main window*

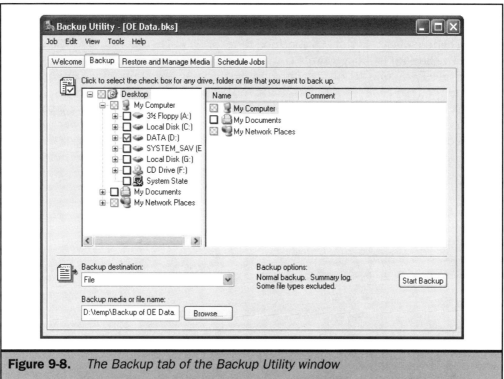

Figure 9-8. *The Backup tab of the Backup Utility window*

The rest of the options that the Backup Or Restore Wizard offers appear after you click the Start Backup button.

When you click the Start Backup button, you see the Backup Job Information window, shown here:

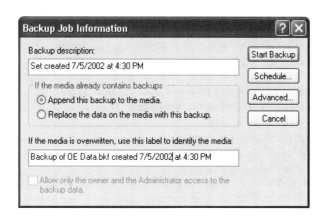

This window contains the rest of your backup options, as described in the "Creating a Backup Job with the Backup Or Restore Wizard" section earlier in this chapter.

To schedule the job to run at a specified time (or on a schedule), click the Schedule button. The Backup Utility prompts you to save your settings as a backup job, and lets you specify a name. If your user account has a password, it prompts you for the password (you have to type it twice). Then you see the Scheduled Job Options dialog box, as shown in Figure 9-5 (see "Choose When to Back Up" earlier in this chapter).

For other options, click the Advanced button to display the Advanced Backup Options dialog box, shown here:

In addition to the options described in the section "Choosing How to Back Up," you see these other settings:

- **Back Up Data That Is In Remote Storage**   Includes files that are stored in a *remote storage*, a special storage device that stores infrequently used files.

- **Automatically Backup System Protected Files With The System State** Includes the files in your C:\Windows folder (or whatever folder Windows is installed in). Choosing this option adds over 200MB to your backup job.

When you return to the Backup Job Information dialog box and click Start Backup, your backup job runs (or is stored to be run later).

Running a Backup Job

Once you have created and named a backup job, you can run it without going through the Backup Or Restore Wizard (in fact, the wizard doesn't include a way to rerun and existing backup job). The backup job is stored as a .bks file that you can reopen and rerun.

Running a Backup Job from the Backup Utility Window

To run an existing backup job, follow these steps:

1. Run the Backup Utility. If the Backup Or Restore Wizard runs, click the Advanced Mode link on its opening window. You see the Backup Utility main window, as shown in Figure 9-7.

2. Click the Backup tab (shown in Figure 9-8).

3. Choose Job | Load Selections from the menu bar. You see the Open dialog box showing the default location of .bks files.

4. Choose a backup job and click Open. If you've already selected some files, Backup asks whether it's okay to clear the current file selections and use the ones from the backup job instead. Click Yes. Backup shows the selected drives, folders, and files on the Backup tab.

5. Follow the instructions for creating a backup job from the main window in the preceding section.

Running a Backup Job on a Schedule

When you create a backup job, you can schedule it to run daily, weekly, monthly, or on some other schedule. The Backup Utility uses the Windows Scheduled Tasks feature to handle the scheduling (see Chapter 1, section "Running Programs on a Schedule Using Scheduled Tasks").

When you create a job using the Backup tab of the Backup Utility window, after you click the Start Backup button, click the Schedule button on the Backup Job Information dialog box to display the Scheduled Job Options dialog box (see Figure 9-5).

You can check the schedule of a backup job by clicking the Schedule Jobs tab in the Backup Utility window (as shown in Figure 9-9). Click a backup icon on a day on the calendar to see the Scheduled Job Options dialog box for that backup job. To change the schedule for the backup job, click the Properties button on the Schedule Data tab to see the Schedule Job dialog box, and click the Schedule tab. You can change the frequency, time, and day of the backups, as well as other settings (see Chapter 1, section "Configuring a Scheduled Program"). However, there's no easy way to change the files that are included—instead, open and rerun the job as described in the previous section.

Excluding Files from Backups

Some types of files don't need to be backed up, such as temporary files and files in a cache (temporary storage area). You can tell the Backup Utility not to include specific types of files by choosing Tools | Options from the Backup Utility's main window and clicking the Exclude Files tab (as shown in Figure 9-10). You can specify files that are in certain folders, files that have certain extensions, or both, and you can specify whether to exclude these files for backups made by all users or only backups made by the current user.

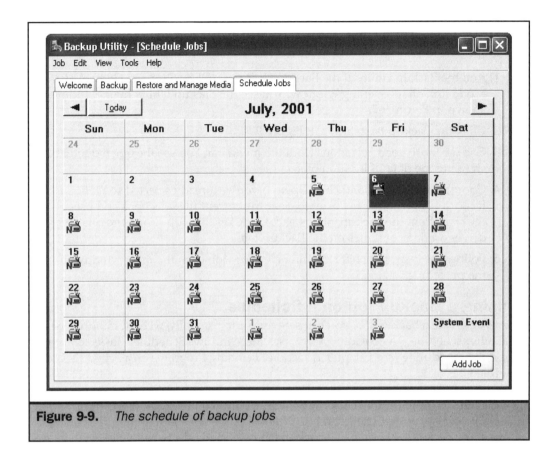

Figure 9-9. *The schedule of backup jobs*

The Backup Utility is preconfigured to ignore many temporary Windows files when making backups for any user. You can add files and folders to its exclusion lists by clicking the Add New button—choose the one below the Files Excluded For All Users or the Files Excluded For User *username* box. You can choose a file type (based on filename extension) or type in an extension, and you can type or browse to the folder to which the exclusion applies.

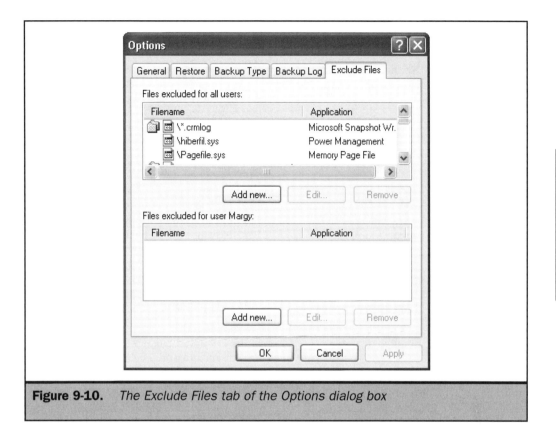

Figure 9-10. *The Exclude Files tab of the Options dialog box*

Setting Other Backup Options

The Backup Utility has a number of configuration options that you can set by choosing Tools | Options from the menu bar in its main window (shown in Figure 9-7). Table 9-1 lists the configuration settings and what they do.

Tab	Setting	Description
General	Compute selection information before backup and restore operations	Displays the estimated total number of files and total bytes to be backed up before the backup begins (ditto for restoring).

Table 9-1. *Backup Utility Configuration Options*

MANAGING YOUR FILES

Tab	Setting	Description
General	Use the catalogs on the media to speed up building restore catalogs on disk	When restoring from tapes, uses the file catalogs that are stored on the tapes when creating the list of files in the entire backup. This is faster than Backup scanning the tapes for files and creating a new catalog. However, if a tape is missing or damaged, its catalog may not be available, and you may need to turn this setting off to restore files from the remaining tapes.
General	Verify data after the backup completes	Specifies that after backing up the files, Backup compares the backup copies to the original files. Files that are in use and being updated during the backup may have changed between backup and verification, so not all verification errors indicate a problem.
General	Back up the contents of mounted drives	For mounted drives, includes the contents of the drive (see Chapter 33). If deselected, Backup includes only the pathname of the mounted drive and not its contents.
General	Show alert message when I start the Backup Utility and Removable Storage is not running	For backups to and restores from tape, displays a warning if the Removable Storage system isn't running. Backup can then start Removable Storage so you can use the tapes or other media that it manages. Select this setting if you back up to tapes. For backups to file or to removable disks (like floppies and Zip disks), this setting doesn't matter.
General	Show alert message when I start the Backup Utility and there is recognizable media available	For backups to and restores from tape, lets you know when new tapes are available. If you back up to tape, select this setting. Doesn't apply to backups to file or to removable disks.

Table 9-1.   *Backup Utility Configuration Options* (continued)

Tab	Setting	Description
General	Show alert message when new media is inserted	For backups to and restores from tape, lets you know when you insert a new tape. If you back up to tape, select this setting. Doesn't apply to backups to file or to removable disks.
General	Always allow use of recognizable media without prompting	For backups to tape, automatically moved a new uncatalogued tape in the tape drive into the Backup media pool and then uses it for backup.
Restore	Do not replace the file on my computer (recommended), Replace the file on disk only if the file on disk is older, Always replace the file on my computer	Specifies what Backup Utility does when restoring a file that already exists on your computer.
Backup Type	Default Backup Type	Specifies what type of backup appears as the default when creating new backup jobs (see "Choosing a Baseline or an Incremental Backup" earlier in this chapter).
Backup Log	Detailed, Summary, None	Specifies how much information to store in the log file for backups.
Exclude Files	Files excluded for all users	For all user accounts, specifies the list of file types to skip when backing up (for example, temporary and backup files, with extensions .tmp and .bak). Click Add to add a file type to the list.
Exclude Files	Files excluded for user *username*	Ditto, for the user who is currently logged in.

Table 9-1.   *Backup Utility Configuration Options* (continued)

MANAGING YOUR FILES

Running the Backup Utility from the Command Line

When you schedule a backup job, the Backup Utility creates a command line that runs the job with your settings—where to store the backup, what to call it, and other settings. (See Chapter 4 for how command lines work.) You can see the command line for a scheduled backup job by clicking the Schedule Jobs tab, clicking the icon for a backup job, and clicking the Properties button on the Scheduled Job Options dialog box that appears. You see the Schedule Job dialog box (see Chapter 1, section "Configuring a Scheduled Program"). The Run box on the Task tab shows the command line, which is something like this:

```
C:\WINDOWS\system32\ntbackup.exe backup "@C:\Documents and
Settings\Margy\Local Settings\Application Data\Microsoft\Windows
NT\NTBackup\data\OE Data.bks" /a /d "Set created 7/5/2002 at 4:12
PM" /v:no /r:no /rs:no /hc:off /m normal /j "OE Data" /l:s /f
"D:\Data\Backup OE Data.bkf"
```

To run the backup Utility from the command line (the Start | Run box, a Command Prompt window, or a shortcut), you type:

ntbackup backup [systemstate] *backupjob switches*

The systemstate switch is optional (don't type the brackets if you choose to include it). Replace *backupjob* with the name of the .bks file that contains the specifications for the backup job. Replace *switches* with the appropriate switches from Table 9-2. If you are backing up to tape (or any medium that is controlled by the Removable Storage service), also use the switches described in Table 9-3.

Switch	Description
backup	Specifies that you are performing a backup rather than a restore.
systemstate	Backs up the system state (Registry, boot files, and other system information). Omit this switch to avoid backing up the system state.
backupjob	Specifies the pathname of the .bks file that contains the backup job specifications.
/D *"label"*	Specifies a label for the backup set. Type the quotes around the label.
/F *"filename"*	Specifies the pathname of the backup file. Don't use this with the /G, /P, or /T switches when backing up to tape. Type the quotes around the filename.

Table 9-2.   *NTBackup Command Line Switches for All Backups*

Switch	Description
/J *"name"*	Specifies the backup job name, which appears as the Backup Identification Label on the Restore And Manage Media tab of the Backup Utility window. It also appears in the log file for the backup. Type the quotes around the backup job name.
/L:f or /L:s or /L:n	If "f," creates a full log file. If "s," creates a summary log file. If "n," doesn't create a log file.
/M *backuptype*	Specifies the backup type: "normal," "copy," "differential," "incremental," or "daily" (see "Choosing a Baseline or an Incremental Backup" earlier in this chapter).
/SNAP:on or /SNAP:off	If "on," includes open files, making a volume shadow copy (which used to be called a snapshot).
/V:yes or /V:no	If "yes," verifies the backup after it's finished.

Table 9-2.   *NTBackup Command Line Switches for All Backups* (continued)

Switch	Description
/A	Appends the backup to the end of the tape, rather than erasing what's already on the tape. Use with /G or /T, not with /P.
/G *"guidname"*	Specifies the tape by its GUID (globally unique identifier), and overwrites or appends to this tape. Do not use this switch in conjunction with /P. Type the quotes around the GUID.
/HC:on or /HC:off	If "on" and the tape drive supports hardware compression, uses hardware compression when backing up. If "off," doesn't use hardware compression.
/N *"newtapename"*	Specifies the name to give to the new tape used for the backup. Don't use with /A. Type the quotes around the tape name.

Table 9-3.   *NTBackup Command Line Switches for Backups to Tape*

Switch	Description
/P "*poolname*"	Specifies the media pool from which the tape comes. Backup uses any available tape from this pool, so you can't use /P with /A, /G, /F, or /T. Type the quotes around the media pool name.
/R:yes or /R:no	If "yes," only the user who created the tape, or administrative users, can use this tape.
/RS:yes or /RS:no	If "yes," includes the Removable Storage database in the backup. If "no," omits the database from the backup.
/T "*tapename*"	Specifies the name of the tape onto which to back up. Don't use with /P. Type the quotes around the tape name.
/UM	Backs up to the first available tape in the media pool that you specified with /P. Formats the tape before the backup.

Table 9-3.   *NTBackup Command Line Switches for Backups to Tape* (continued)

You can run the Backup Utility from the Command Prompt window or in the Start |
Run dialog box: type or copy the **ntbackup** command followed by the command line
switches or create a shortcut that contains the command line: right-click the Windows
desktop, choose New | Shortcut from the menu that appears, and type or copy the
ntbackup command line in the Type The Location Of The Item box. Once you've made
a shortcut for the ntbackup command, you can leave it on the desktop or copy it onto
the Start menu (see Chapter 10, section "Reorganizing the Start Menu").

Restoring Files with the Backup Utility

To restore files that you have backed up with the Backup Utility, you can use the Restore
Wizard or you can select options yourself.

*The Backup Utility stores backed-up files in a special format, and you need to use
Backup Utility to restore them. You can't just copy the files from an Explorer window
back to where you want to use them. The Backup Utility can't restore backups made
by other backup programs, either, including those made by the Windows Me/9x
backup utilities.*

Restoring Files Using the Restore Wizard

To run the Backup Or Restore Wizard to help you restore one or more files, follow these steps:

1. Start the Backup Utility. If the wizard doesn't start automatically, choose Tools | Switch To Wizard Mode from the menu bar.

2. When the wizard runs, choose Restore Files And Settings and click Next. You see the What To Restore window, containing two boxes: the one on the left shows the backup files and tapes available (Figure 9-11). Backups to file are listed under the File heading. Tape backups are listed under a heading that reflects the type of type (like miniQIC or Travan), and then by the tape.

3. Double-click an item on the left to see the files and folders that it contains on the right. Click the boxes next to files and folders to put a check mark by those that you want to restore. Click Next when you have finished. You see the Completing The Backup Or Restore Wizard, but you're not done.

4. Click the Advanced button to display the Where To Restore window.

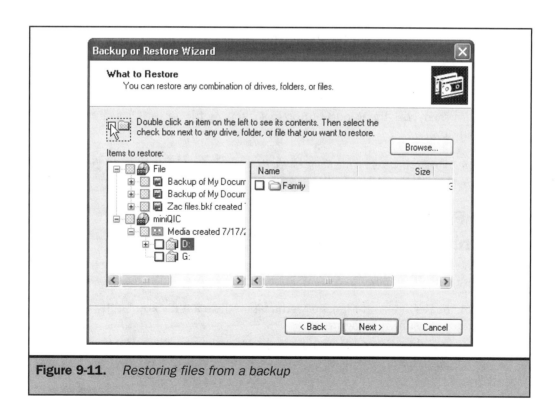

Figure 9-11.   *Restoring files from a backup*

5. Set the Restore Files To box to Original Location to put the files back where they came from; Alternate Location to put the structure of restored files and folders in a folder you specify; or Single Folder to put all the restored files into a single folder, without restoring the structure of the folders that they used to be in. Click Next.

6. In the How To Restore window, choose what to do if restoring a file would overwrite an existing file. Choose Leave Existing Files, Replace Existing Files If They Are Older Than The Backup Files, or Replace Existing Files. Click Next. You see the Advanced Restore Options window.

7. If you are restoring files that were stored on an NTFS partition, you can select the Restore Security Settings check box to restore the permissions and ownership for the folders and files. (See Table 9-4 in the following section for information about the settings in steps 7–9.)

8. If you are restoring a mounted drive, select the Restore Junction Points But Not The Folders And File Data They Reference check box (see Chapter 33).

9. If you are restoring files and folders that contain mount points for mounted drives, deselect the Preserve Existing Volume Mount Points check box. If you have already set up the mount points for mounted drives and you don't want to disturb them, select this check box. Click Next.

10. You see the Completing The Backup Or Restore Wizard window again. Click Finish to restore the files.

While the Backup Utility is restoring files, you see a Restore Progress window showing how many files have been restored and how many are yet to be restored. When it is finished, click the Report button to see the log file, or the Close button to close the window.

 If you are restoring from a file you can see in an Explorer window, double-click the .bkf file to start the Backup Utility.

Restoring Files by Using the Restore And Manage Media Tab

Alternatively, you can use the Restore And Manage Media tab on the main Backup Utility window to select what to restore. Follow these steps:

1. Click the Restore And Manage Media tab in the main Backup Utility window, as shown in Figure 9-12.

2. Choose the files and folders to restore, as described in step 3 of the previous section.

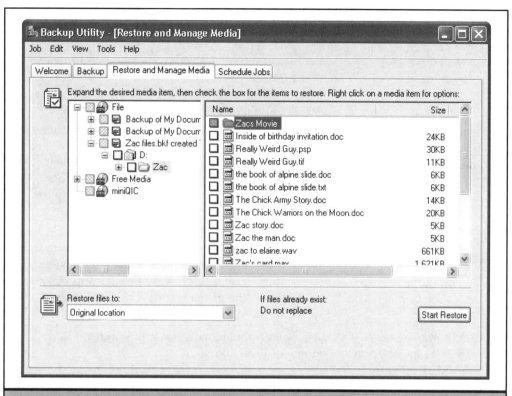

Figure 9-12.   *The Restore And Manage Media tab of the main Backup window*

3. The Restore Files To box is normally set to Original Location to restore the files and folders to the location from which they were backed up, in the same folder structure. You can change this setting to Alternate Location (to put the structure of restored files and folders in a folder you specify) or Single Folder (to put all the restored files into a single folder, without restoring the structure of the folders that they used to be in).

4. If you chose Alternate Location or Single Folder in the last step, set the Alternate Location box to the folder where you want to restore the files and folders.

5. Click the Start Restore button (you still have some other options to set). You see the Confirm Restore dialog box.

6. Click the Advanced button to choose other options for restoring files. Table 9-4 shows the advanced options available when restoring files. Click OK when you have finished.

Setting	Description
Restore security	For files and folders that were backed up from an NTFS partition and that are to be restored to an NTFS partition, restores the permissions and ownership information with the files and folders.
Restore junction points, and restore file and folder data under junction points to the original location	When restoring files to a disk with *junction points* (which are like mount points), restores the files and folders that are stored on the hard disk to which the junction point points (see Chapter 33). When restoring a mounted drive, restores only the folder that contains the mounted drive (unselect this option to restore the folders and files stored on the mounted drive).
When restoring replicated data, mark the restored data as the primary data for all replicas	When restoring files that are managed by the File Replication Service (FRS), specifies that this copy of the files is the primary copy. This applies only to Windows servers.
Restore the Cluster Registry to the quorum disk and all other nodes	A server option. Not available in Windows XP Home or Professional.
Preserve existing volume mount points	Doesn't restore mount points from the backup, leaving the existing mount points. If you want to restore backed-up mount points, deselect this check box.

Table 9-4.   *Advanced Options for Restoring Backed-Up Files*

7. Click OK to being restoring your files and folders. If you are restoring from a tape or other removable media, Backup prompts you to put in the necessary tape or disk; do so and click OK. Then Backup restores the folders and files.

8. When Backup has finished, the Restore Progress window displays information about how many files and folders were restored. You can click the Report button to see the log file. Click Close when you are finished.

Note   *When restoring files to a FAT or FAT32 partition, Backup may warn you that not all security features are available. FAT and FAT32 partitions don't allow you to set passwords for files (only NTFS partitions support this).*

Managing the Removable Storage Service

You can see a list of the library's set options for the Removable Storage service by opening the Computer Management window (also known as the Microsoft Management Console, described in Chapter 2). Click Start, right-click My Computer, and choose Manage from the menu that appears. When you see the Computer Management window, open the Storage item and then the Removable Storage item that it contains. You see a window that looks like the one in Figure 9-13.

You can set the Removable Storage options by clicking Removable Storage in the left pane and clicking the Properties button on the toolbar (or right-click Removable Storage and choose Properties from the menu that appears). On the General tab of the Removable Storage Properties dialog box, you can set these two check boxes:

- **Display Operator Request And Progress Dialogs**   Specifies whether to display dialog boxes to let you know what's happening—we keep this selected.

- **Use Status Area Icon For Pending Requests**   Specifies whether to display an icon in the notification area of the Windows taskbar when requests are pending.

Click the Security tab to see a list of the user accounts and groups that are defined on your system and to change their permissions. You can also change the permissions

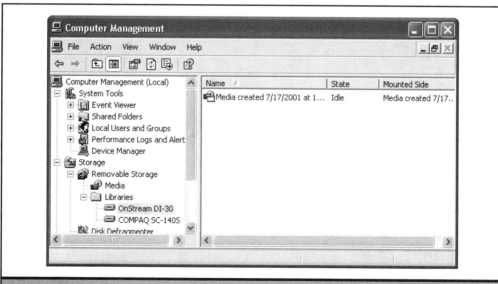

Figure 9-13.   *The Computer Management window displays your Removable Storage libraries.*

for a specific media library by right-clicking it, choosing Properties, and clicking the Security tab.

 For more information about the Removable Storage service, choose Help | Help Topics from the Computer Management window menu bar and click Removable Storage on the list of topics in the table of contents.

The Complete Reference

Part III

Configuring Windows
for Your Computer

Chapter 10

Setting Up Your Start Menu and Taskbar

The Windows XP Start menu was completely redesigned so that the programs you run most often are most easily accessible. Windows XP has Start menu features that move frequently used commands to the "front page" of the Start menu, and hide less-often used commands. Because of the Windows XP emphasis on keeping the desktop uncluttered, you'll probably use the Start menu more and desktop icons less.

Windows XP rearranges the taskbar slightly, combining the taskbar buttons for multiple windows displayed by the same program and shrinking the notification area (located on the right end, which used to be called the system tray). In addition to moving and resizing the taskbar, you can add toolbars on the taskbar—you can display any number or none at all of the four predefined toolbars, display toolbars on the desktop, and define your own toolbars.

Customize your Start menu so that it works for you. It doesn't take much time, and it saves you time in the long run. Also, if your computer is used by several people, provide them all with separate user accounts and let them all do their own customization (see Chapter 6). Each person sees a personally customized Start menu.

Anatomy of the Start Menu

The Windows XP-style *Start menu* is shown in Figure 10-1. If you prefer the classic style of the Start menu, you can switch back to it using the Customize Start Menu dialog box (see the next section). If your Start menu looks nothing like the one shown in Figure 10-1, you probably have the Classic Start menu configured (the old Windows Me/98 Start menu).

The All Programs option displays the *Programs menu*, a menu of programs you can run. This is the Start menu option that you are likely to use the most because you can use it to find and start programs. You can change the contents of the Programs menu by changing the contents of that folder, as described in the following sections.

With Windows XP, Microsoft has abandoned the feature that shrinks the Programs menu to only those items you have used recently. However, if you miss that feature you can have it back by using the Classic Start menu.

Your most frequently used programs appear above the All Programs command. Windows selects these programs based on how frequently and how recently you have run them. We've noticed that programs that you leave running all the time may not end up on this menu, because you don't start them often.

Pinned programs appear at the top of the left column. They always appear in this position so that they are easy to run. You can remove pinned programs and add new ones so that you see the programs that you use regularly.

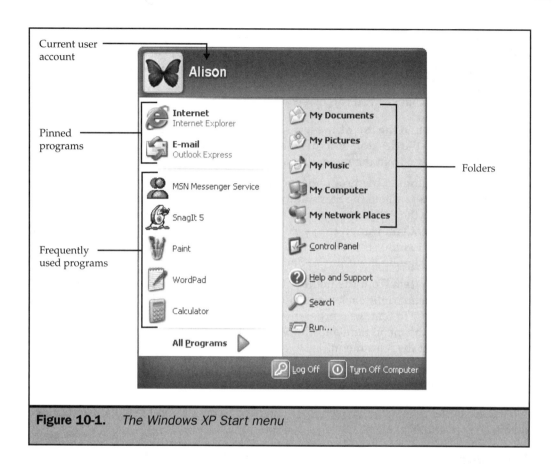

Current user account

Pinned programs

Folders

Frequently used programs

Figure 10-1.   *The Windows XP Start menu*

CONFIGURING WINDOWS
FOR YOUR COMPUTER

Customizing the Start Menu

Most of the Start menu and its submenus are customizable, with the following exceptions: Turn Off Computer, Help And Support, Search, and Control Panel. You can, however, add items to the top of the Start menu, and you have total control over the Programs menu and submenus.

    If your Programs menu has lots of submenus, getting to the item you want may take longer than you would like. If you find the Start menu cumbersome, reorganize it or explore the other methods of starting programs, which are covered in Chapter 1.

Reorganizing the Start Menu

You can organize those parts of the Start menu that you are allowed to edit in several ways—you can drag-and-drop items, cut-and-paste items, or use an Explorer window to edit the Start Menu folders in the C:\Documents And Settings folder. These folders and their subfolders contain shortcuts to the programs that appear on your Start menu, and the arrangements of these shortcuts and folders define what command appears on what menu.

Here are some changes you can make:

- **Add an item to the top of the left side of the Start menu**   Right-click a shortcut on the desktop or in the menu, or right click a .exe file. Choose Pin To Start Menu from the menu that appears.

- **Add a program to the Programs menu**   Drag a desktop shortcut or the program's .exe file to the Start button. Hold it there while the Start menu opens, hold it over the All Programs button until the Programs menu opens, and then drop it where you want it to appear. (Hold it over submenus to open them. You may prefer to move the item in two steps—first dropping it on the Start button, and then dragging it within the Start menu.)

- **Remove an item from the menu**   To remove a program from the left side of the Start menu, right-click it and choose Remove From This List from the menu that appears. To remove a program from the Programs menu (or its submenus), right-click the menu item and choose Delete. You can't remove items from the right side of the Start menu.

- **Rename a menu item**   Right-click the menu item and choose Rename. Type the new name and press ENTER.

If these bullet points don't cover what you need to do, or don't provide enough detail, keep reading!

Dragging and Dropping Items Within the Start Menu

The easiest way to reorganize items already in the menus is to drag-and-drop the commands where you want them. Find the item you want to move in the Start menu and drag it to a new position. The black bar shows you where the item you are moving will appear. You can open a submenu by highlighting it, and waiting for it to open.

 Dragging and dropping in the Start menu can be disabled (see "Customizing the Windows XP-Style Start Menu" later in this chapter).

Moving Commands and Submenus by Editing the Start Menu Folders

You can also customize the Programs menu and its submenus by using an Explorer window to add, remove, move, and rename shortcuts. You can also rename submenus and menu items and create new submenus by using this method.

The Programs menu displays the shortcuts stored in two separate folders—one contains the Programs menu shortcuts that all users see, and the other contains the shortcuts that are for the user account that is currently logged in. Windows combines the two sets of shortcuts and displays a single Programs menu. The C:\Documents And Settings\All Users\Start Menu folder contains most shortcuts (if Windows isn't installed on C:, substitute the correct drive letter); the other folder is in the folder for your profile, C:\Documents And Settings*username*\Start Menu (for example, C:\Documents And Settings\Alison\Start Menu).

Note   *Windows maintains a C:\Documents And Settings\username\Start Menu folder for each user account.*

When you install a program that adds commands to your Programs menu, Windows asks whether you want the new menu entries to appear only in your Programs menu or on the Programs menus of all users of the computer (you don't have the option of adding menu entries to specific users' menus—just your own or all). You can add, remove, and reorganize the Programs menu by adding, deleting, and moving shortcuts within the Start Menu folders. Menu items can be renamed by renaming the shortcuts.

The Start Menu folders (C:\Documents And Settings*username*\Start Menu and C:\Documents And Settings\All Users\Start Menu) contain the commands that appear at the top of the Programs menu. The Programs folder in each Start Menu folder contains the rest of the commands on the Programs menu. Each subfolder of the Programs folders corresponds to a submenu of the Programs menu. For example, the shortcuts in the C:\Documents And Settings\All Users\Start Menu\Programs\Games folder appear in the Start | All Programs | Games menu.

You can display the Start Menu folder for your user account—C:\Documents and Settings*username*\Start Menu—by right-clicking the Start button and choosing Open or Explore (Explore opens a window with the folder tree in the left pane). To display the Start Menu folder for all users, right-click the Start button and choose Open All Users or Explore All Users. Figure 10-2 shows the C:\Documents And Settings\All Users\Start Menu folder in Windows Explorer. If you display the folder tree, you can navigate to the Start Menu folder for any other user. All the customizable choices that appear on the Start menu also appear in the Start Menu folder. Commands you can't change (such as Help and Run) don't appear. Remember that what appears on the Start Menu is a combination of the shortcuts in the Start Menu folder for all users and the Start Menu folder for the logged in user.

Tip   *To edit any submenu of the Start menu, you can right-click it and choose Explore. Want to make changes to the Accessories submenu? Choose Start | All Programs, right-click Accessories, and choose Explore (for your user account settings) or Explore All Users. You see the C:\Documents And Settings\username\Start Menu\Programs\Accessories or C:\Documents And Settings\All Users\Start Menu\Programs\Accessories folder in Windows Explorer.*

CONFIGURING WINDOWS FOR YOUR COMPUTER

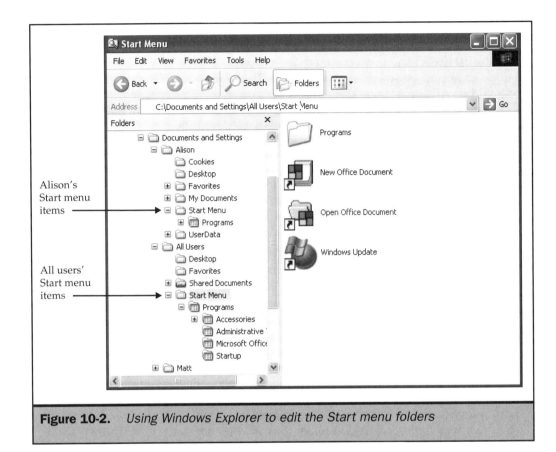

Alison's
Start menu
items

All users'
Start menu
items

Figure 10-2. *Using Windows Explorer to edit the Start menu folders*

Because the Start menu is stored as shortcuts within folders, it can be edited in the same way you edit folders and files:

- Move an item from one menu group to another by dragging or cutting and pasting the shortcut to another folder.

- Create a new menu group by creating a new folder: select the folder in which the new submenu will be stored and choose File | New | Folder from the menu bar.

- Rename a shortcut by selecting it and pressing F2 (or right-clicking the name and choosing Rename from the shortcut menu that appears). Windows highlights the name and shows a box around it. Type a new name or use the cursor to edit the name. Press ENTER when you finish (or press ESC if you change your mind).

Note Although you can edit the Start menu by changing the contents of the Start Menu folder and their subfolders, the Start Menu and Programs folders are not just regular folders. For instance, you can move the Programs folder out of its usual location, and you still see the Programs option on the Start menu (this can lead to complications that are hard to fix, though, so don't try it).

Changing Start Menu Properties

In addition to changing the programs that appear on the Start menu and the order in which they appear, you can customize the Start menu in other ways. Right-click the Start button and choose Properties to display the Taskbar And Start Menu Properties dialog box, shown in Figure 10-3.

The Start Menu tab on this dialog box enables you to choose between the Start menu (the new Windows XP design) and the Classic Start Menu (the old Windows 9*x*/Me

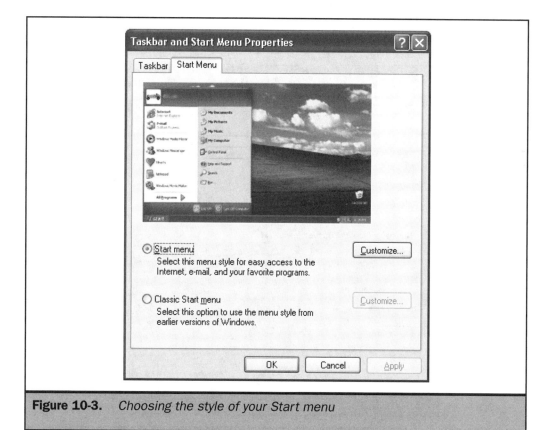

Figure 10-3.   *Choosing the style of your Start menu*

Start menu). Except for the section on the Classic Start Menu, this chapter assumes that you are using the Windows XP Start menu.

Customizing the Windows XP-Style Start Menu

To customize the standard Start menu, click the upper Customize button on the Start Menu tab of the Taskbar And Start Menu Properties dialog box to see the General tab of the Customize Start Menu dialog box, shown in Figure 10-4.

The General tab of the Customize Start Menu dialog box offers you the following options:

- **Select An Icon Size For Programs** By default, large icons are displayed in the Start menu. Choose the Small Icons option to make the first level of the Start menu take up less room on the screen.

- **Programs** By default, the six programs that you use most often are displayed on the first level of the Start menu. You can change the number of programs that appear by changing this setting—choose a number between 0 and 30.

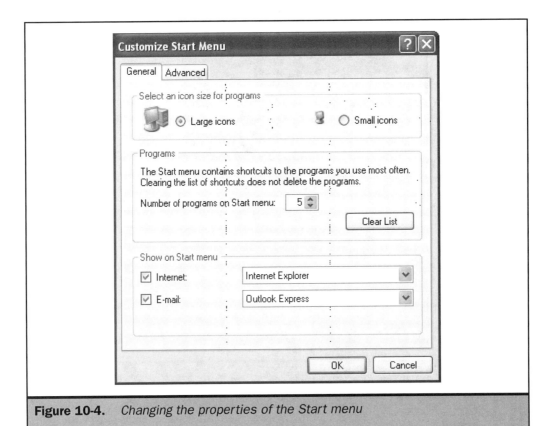

Figure 10-4. *Changing the properties of the Start menu*

■ **Show On Start Menu**   By default, a shortcut to a browser and a shortcut to
an e-mail program are displayed at the top of the Start menu. You can choose to
display a different program by choosing from the drop-down lists, or you can
choose not to display these programs by deselecting the check box. Remember,
you can put any program at the top of the Start menu by right-clicking it and
choosing Pin to Start menu. (Also see the section "Removing Microsoft Programs
from the Start Menu" at the end of this chapter.) Not all browsers and e-mail
programs appear on the lists; Windows displays most installed browsers and
e-mail programs, but some older programs may not appear.

Click the Advanced tab of the Customize Start Menu dialog box to see more options,
including those that allow you to choose the folder shortcuts that appear on the Start
menu. The Advanced tab has the following sections:

■ **Start Menu Settings**   You can have the Start menu open submenus when the
mouse is paused over them, or by deselecting this option, you can choose to have
the submenus open only when you click them. The other check box controls
whether new programs on the Start menu are highlighted in a different color.

■ **Start Menu Items**   This box gives you control over what is displayed and how
some items are displayed in the second column of the Start menu—the folder
shortcuts, the Control Panel, and the Run command. Many choices have three
settings: Display As A Link (opens an Explorer window to show this item), Display
As A Menu (opens a submenu), and Don't Display This Item (omits this item).
This box also contains two options that affect how the Start menu works: Enable
Dragging And Dropping (which controls whether you can edit the Start menu
by dragging commands around) and Scroll Programs (scrolls the contents of the
Programs menu if it gets too long to fit on the screen; otherwise, it appears in
two columns). You can control these items:

Control Panel	Displays the Control Panel (see Chapter 1, section "Configuring Windows XP and Other Programs").
Favorites	Displays your most frequently used files, folders, web pages, and programs. The menu displays the contents of the Favorites folder (usually C:\Documents And Settings\ All Users\Favorites or C:\Documents And Settings\ *username*\Favorites). The Favorites menu is easy to access, not only from the Start menu but also from Explorer windows and most Open and Save As dialog boxes.
Help and Support	Onscreen help.

CONFIGURING WINDOWS FOR YOUR COMPUTER

My Computer	Displays your disk drives and document folders.
My Documents, My Music, My Pictures	Displays your My Documents folder and its subfolders (usually C:\My Documents and C:\Documents And Settings*username*\Documents).
My Network Places	Displays your list of network drives (see Chapter 30, section "Using Network Drives with My Network Places").
Network Connections	Displays the Network Connections folder or a menu of your network connections. See Chapter 22 for Internet connections and Chapter 27 for LAN connections.
Printers and Faxes	Displays the Printers And Faxes folder (see Chapter 14).
Run command	Displays the Run dialog box, in which you can run programs by typing a command line (see Chapter 1, section "Starting Programs from the Run Dialog Box").
Search	Displays an Explorer window with the Search Explorer bar (see Chapter 8, section "Searching for Files and Folders").
System Administrative Tools	Displays a menu of Windows administrative utilities.

■ **Recent Documents** Selecting the List My Most Recently Opened Documents check box displays the My Recent Documents submenu on the Start menu, which displays the names of recently used files. You can select a file from this list to open it in its native program. Use the Clear List button to remove the list of recently opened documents—if the check box is still selected, Windows will build a new list as you open new files. The My Recent Documents command on the Start menu is similar to the Documents item on the Classic Start menu.

Customizing the Classic Start Menu

If you choose to use the Classic Start menu you have different customization options. To display the Customize Classic Start Menu dialog box, choose Classic Start menu on the Start Menu tab of the Taskbar And Start Menu Properties dialog box and click the Customize button to display the Customize Classic Start Menu dialog box, shown here:

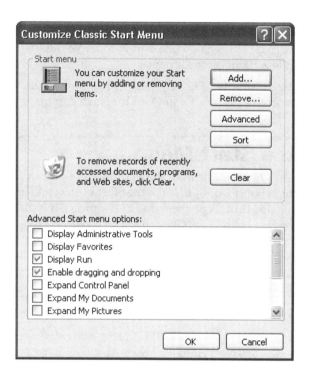

The buttons in the top half of the dialog box edit the programs on the Start menu. The Advanced button displays the Start Menu folder for your user account. Remember that most Start menu shortcuts are also stored in the C:/Documents And Settings/ All Users/Start Menu folder. The Sort button sorts the Programs menu alphabetically when you click it.

Most of the check boxes in the bottom half of the Customize Classic Start Menu dialog box are optional menu items—use the check boxes to select which items appear on your Classic Start menu. Use the Expand Control Panel, Expand My Documents, Expand My Pictures, Expand Network Connections, and Expand Printers check boxes to display the listed item as a menu rather than as a shortcut. Microsoft also included a few options that affect how the Start menu works:

- **Enable Dragging And Dropping**   The Start menu can be edited by dragging and dropping menu commands.

- **Scroll Programs**   Scrolls the contents of the Programs menu up and down when the list is too big to fit on the screen; otherwise, the Programs menu expands to more than one column.

- **Show Small Icons In Start Menu**   By default, large icons are displayed in the Start menu. Turn on the Small Icons option to make the first level of the Start menu take up less room on the screen.

- **Use Personalized Menus**   Displays only those commands you have used recently. Turn off this option if you want to see all commands all the time.

Searching the Start Menu

If you can't find the program you want in the Start menu, you can search the menu by using the Search Results window. Right-click the Start button and choose Search from the shortcut menu that appears. Type the name of the program you're looking for in the All Or Part Of The File Name box. Click the Search button.

The files that match the text you typed are displayed in an Explorer window. Windows displays the full pathname so that you can find the item in the Start menu, or you can open the item from the Search Results window. If you can't see the full path, increase the width of the In Folder column by clicking and dragging its right border to the right.

Note   *The Start Menu shortcuts are stored in two folders, both called Start Menu. One is C:\Documents And Settings\All Users\Start Menu; the other is in the folder for your user profile, for example, C:\Documents and Settings\Alison\Start Menu (for a user named Alison). (If Windows is installed on a drive or partition other than C:, these folders are usually on that drive or partition.) Search the entire C:/Documents And Settings folder for more complete results.*

Turning Off Balloon Tips

Many people find Windows XP's *balloon tips*—the pop-up messages that appear from icons in the notification area of the toolbar—annoying. You can turn them all off if you don't mind editing your Registry (see Chapter 38). After making a backup copy of part or all of the Registry, follow these steps:

1. Run the Registry Editor.

2. Move to the HKEY_CURRENT_USER\Software\Microsoft\Windows\CurrentVersion\Explorer\Advanced key.

3. Right-click the Advanced key and choose New | DWORD Value from the shortcut menu that appears. Type **EnableBalloonTips** as the name of the new value.

4. Double-click the new EnableToolTips value to confirm that it is 0 (zero).

5. Close the Registry Editor and either log out or restart Windows.

Customizing the Taskbar

Although most Windows users find no reason to customize the taskbar, a few do. You can move the taskbar around the desktop, and you can control its size and whether it is visible all the time. You may also see arrows on the taskbar—click them to see buttons or other information that Windows has hidden to keep the taskbar uncluttered.

 If you can't find your taskbar, try moving the mouse pointer to each edge of the screen. When the mouse pointer turns into a double-headed arrow, click-and-drag to increase the size of the taskbar.

Enabling Taskbar Changes

To disable or enable resizing the taskbar, right-click an unoccupied portion of the taskbar (try clicking next to the Start button if you're having trouble finding an unoccupied part) and choose Lock The Taskbar. To enable changes, repeat the same steps. When the taskbar is locked you can't edit it, move it to another edge of the screen, or change its size. You can still change the toolbars that the taskbar displays, though. (You can also lock and unlock the taskbar from the Taskbar And Start Menu Properties dialog box, which you display by right-clicking the taskbar and choosing Properties.)

 When the taskbar is not locked, you see "handles" (vertical columns of blue dots) that you can click and drag to move the taskbar or parts of it.

Moving the Taskbar

Move the taskbar to any edge of the desktop by clicking and dragging it to the desired position. You have to click an unoccupied area of the taskbar—not the Start button, or a program button—to drag it. An unoccupied area of taskbar is always available next to the Start button.

Changing the Size of the Taskbar

You can change the size of the taskbar by clicking and dragging its inside edge—that is, the edge that borders the desktop. (Be sure that the taskbar is unlocked before you try this.) You can size the taskbar back down by clicking and dragging the inside edge back toward the edge of the screen—make sure to release the mouse button when the taskbar is the desired size. You can even decrease your taskbar to a thin stripe along one edge of the screen by dragging the edge of the taskbar to the edge of the screen.

Changing Taskbar Properties

You can change some taskbar options by right-clicking an empty part of the taskbar and choosing Properties. You see the Taskbar tab of the Taskbar And Start Menu Properties dialog box, shown in Figure 10-5.

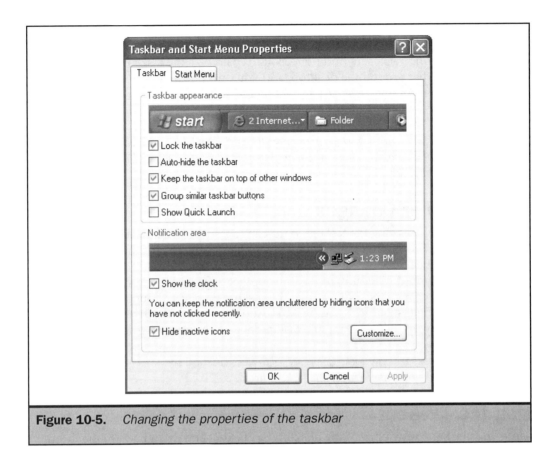

Figure 10-5. *Changing the properties of the taskbar*

Hiding the Taskbar

You can hide the taskbar in two different ways: by decreasing its size and by using the Auto-hide option. Changing the size of the taskbar is covered in the previous section—click-and-drag the inside edge of the taskbar to the screen's closest edge. The taskbar becomes a thin blue line on one edge of the screen. The other option is to use the Auto-hide feature to hide the taskbar. Auto-hide tries to determine when you need the taskbar and displays the taskbar only when you need it.

To turn on Auto-hide, display the Taskbar tab of the Taskbar And Start Menu Properties dialog box and select the Auto-hide The Taskbar check box. When Auto-hide is on, the taskbar disappears when it isn't being used. To display it, point to the edge of the screen where it last appeared. Or, you can press CTRL-ESC or the WINDOWS key (a key with the Windows symbol that displays the Start menu) to display the taskbar and open the Start menu at the same time.

If you can't find your taskbar, move the mouse pointer to each edge of the screen. If Auto-hide is on, the taskbar appears. If the taskbar is shrunk, the mouse pointer turns into a double-headed arrow—click-and-drag to increase the taskbar's size.

Allowing the Taskbar to Be Covered by a Window

You can choose whether you want the taskbar to be covered by other windows by selecting the Keep The Taskbar On Top Of Other Windows check box on the Taskbar tab of the Taskbar And Start Menu Properties dialog box. When the check box is selected, the taskbar always appears over other windows. When the option is off, windows may cover the taskbar. To use the taskbar when the Keep The Taskbar On Top Of Other Windows option is turned off, move or minimize windows until the taskbar is visible, or press CTRL-ESC or the WINDOWS key to display both the taskbar and open the Start menu (press ESC once if you want to use only the taskbar). We recommend that you leave this check box selected.

Grouping Taskbar Buttons

New in Windows XP is the option to group similar task buttons on the taskbar. This option, which is on by default, puts task buttons for files opened in the same program together on the taskbar. If the taskbar becomes crowded, the buttons are collapsed into a single button, like this (all four open Microsoft Word files appear on one task button):

A button for grouped windows has a downward arrow on its right side. Click the button to see the individual windows, and click the window you want. You can turn this option off by deselecting the Group Similar Taskbar Buttons check box on the Taskbar tab of the Taskbar And Start Menu Properties dialog box.

Some people don't like grouped task buttons, because it takes an extra click to switch from, say, one Word document window to another.

Hiding the Clock on the Taskbar

You can choose to display or hide the *system clock* that usually appears in the notification area of the taskbar. Display the Taskbar tab of the Taskbar And Start Menu Properties dialog box and then select or deselect the Show The Clock check box.

Hiding Notification Area Icons

The notification area where the clock appears also holds icons for programs and processes that are running in the background (that is, running without you realizing that they are running). In previous versions of Windows, this area filled up with icons. By default, Windows XP hides inactive icons (icons that don't require your immediate attention).

You can change this setting so that icons are visible all the time by deselecting the Hide Inactive Icons check box in the Taskbar tab of the Taskbar And Start Menu Properties dialog box. You can also customize the setting by clicking Customize to see the Customize Notification dialog box, which displays a list of the icons that are currently in the notification area (whether hidden or not). Select an item and then pick from the drop-down list. For each item you can select Hide When Inactive (the default), Always Hide, or Always Show. For your settings to take effect, be sure the Hide Inactive Icons check box on the Taskbar and Start Menu Properties dialog box is selected.

Adding Toolbars to the Taskbar

You can configure the taskbar to include toolbars, or you can display toolbars elsewhere on your desktop. Taskbar toolbars give you easy access to frequently used icons: you no longer have to minimize all open programs to display a desktop icon to open a program. Instead you can use a toolbar button. Or, you can use the toolbar button Show Desktop to minimize all open programs with one click. You can even edit the buttons that appear on a toolbar or create a completely new toolbar.

Adding and Removing Toolbars from the Taskbar

To add or remove toolbars, right-click an unoccupied part of the taskbar and choose Toolbars from the menu that appears. You see a menu of the available toolbars. Toolbars that are already displayed on the taskbar appear with check marks. To display a toolbar, click its name. To remove a displayed toolbar, follow the same procedure to remove the check mark.

Five taskbar toolbars come with Windows:

■ **Quick Launch toolbar**   Usually contains three buttons, from left to right: Show Desktop (minimizes all open windows to reveal the desktop), Launch Internet Explorer Browser, and Windows Media Player. You can change which buttons appear on this toolbar (see "Editing the Quick Launch Toolbar" later in this chapter). Here are the standard three buttons:

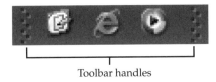

Toolbar handles

- **Address toolbar**   Double-click to see a text box where you can type a URL to open a web page or a file pathname to open a file. A drop-down list contains recently used URLs and pathnames:

- **Links toolbar**   Displays a drop-down list containing links to web pages Microsoft would like you to visit. Add new links by dragging them to the Links toolbar. This toolbar also appears in Internet Explorer. Click a button to open the web page.

- **Desktop toolbar**   Displays a drop-down list containing an item for each icon on the desktop and a menu for the My Documents, My Computer, My Network Places, and Recycle Bin folders.

- **Language bar**   Displays buttons for all installed languages and keyboard or input options that you have added using the Regional And Language options available from the Control Panel (see Chapter 12). This toolbar doesn't appear as an option unless you have installed support for additional languages and keyboard layouts.

Moving a Toolbar

You can move the toolbar to a different position on the taskbar or onto the desktop by clicking and dragging the toolbar handle, which looks like a vertical line of dots on the left end of the toolbar.

   Toolbar handles don't appear when the taskbar is locked. Right-click an empty spot on the taskbar and choose Lock The Taskbar to unlock (or lock) it.

To switch the order of the toolbars on the taskbar, move a toolbar by dragging its handle left or right. You may end up with a two- or three-row taskbar by the time you are done. If the individual toolbars are two or three rows high, you can then drag the top edge of the taskbar back down to the position where you want it.

You can also control how the taskbar is partitioned. You can make each toolbar wider or narrower by dragging its handle to the left or right. When many buttons are displayed and the buttons get small, scroll buttons appear, allowing you to view all the buttons for open applications.

To move a toolbar to the desktop, drag-and-drop its handle off the taskbar. Each toolbar looks different on the desktop, but they all appear with a title bar, a Close button, and icons, like this:

CONFIGURING WINDOWS FOR YOUR COMPUTER

Once the toolbar is on the desktop, you can no longer make it disappear by using the Taskbar shortcut menu—instead, you can use its Close button to get rid of it. You can move and change the size of the toolbar window by using the same techniques you use on any window.

You can move a toolbar from the desktop back to the taskbar, or to any edge of the desktop, by clicking-and-dragging the title bar—when the toolbar reaches any edge of the desktop, it changes shape to occupy the whole edge. If you move it to the edge with the taskbar, the toolbar is integrated back into the taskbar. If you move it to an empty edge, the toolbar takes up the whole edge of the desktop.

Controlling the Look of a Toolbar

You can control the way a toolbar works by right-clicking an unoccupied part of the toolbar (if you have trouble finding an unoccupied part of the toolbar, unlock your taskbar and right-click the toolbar handle). The following choices on the menu that appears control your toolbar (the rest of the choices that appear affect the whole taskbar):

- **View** Allows you to display either large or small icons. The default setting is Small.
- **Open Folder** Opens the folder where the toolbar shortcuts are stored, so you can edit the toolbar. Once the folder is open you can add and delete shortcuts to change the contents of the toolbar.
- **Show Text** Displays text on each button. Choose this option again to display icons with no text. Turning off this option makes a toolbar take up less space.
- **Show Title** Turns off or on the display of the name of the toolbar.
- **Close Toolbar** Removes the toolbar from the screen.
- **Toolbars** Allows you to display a new toolbar, hide a displayed toolbar, or create a new toolbar. This option is the same as the Toolbars option on the Taskbar shortcut menu.

When the toolbar is attached to an edge of the desktop but not in the taskbar, you see two additional choices:

- **Always On Top** The toolbar always appears on top of other windows.
- **Auto-hide** The toolbar disappears when not in use. Move the pointer to the edge of the screen where the toolbar is located to display it.

These additional two options work the same as the Always On Top and Auto-hide options for the taskbar.

Editing the Quick Launch Toolbar

You can easily add and remove buttons from the Quick Launch toolbar. To remove a button, right-click the button and choose Delete. To add a button, drag a shortcut or an

.exe file to the toolbar. If you want to make a copy of a shortcut from the desktop in the Quick Launch toolbar, hold down the CTRL key while you drag the shortcut from the desktop to the toolbar.

You can also edit the buttons on the Quick Launch toolbar by opening the folder that contains the shortcuts and adding and removing shortcuts. To open the folder, right-click the toolbar handle and choose Open Folder. The shortcuts for the Quick Launch toolbar are buried in the folder structure—you can find them in C:\Documents and Settings\ *username*\Application Data\Microsoft\Internet Explorer\Quick Launch: replace *username* with your own user name.

 Why does Microsoft store this information with Internet Explorer configuration data? Because they consider the whole desktop as a special Internet Explorer window.

Creating a New Toolbar

In addition to the existing toolbars, you can create your own toolbar to display the contents of a drive, folder, or Internet address. Depending on the options you choose for your new toolbar, it may look something like this one, which shows the contents of a folder called Consult:

In this example, the Consult folder contains three other folders and numerous files. On the toolbar, you can see the three folders—you can display the entire contents of the Consult folder by clicking the arrow at the right end of the toolbar. Notice that the subfolders are displayed as menus, so you can open a file directly from the toolbar. Clicking a folder button opens an Explorer window for that folder; clicking a file button opens the file.

CONFIGURING WINDOWS FOR YOUR COMPUTER

To create a new toolbar, right-click the taskbar or a toolbar, and choose Toolbars | New Toolbar from the shortcut menu that appears. You see the New Toolbar dialog box, shown here:

This dialog box enables you to browse available drives and folders. Click the plus box next to a folder name to expand that branch of the folder tree. You can open any folder or drive available to you in Windows Explorer—these may include drives and folders on the Internet. Click New Folder to create a new subfolder in the highlighted folder. Select the folder you want to use to create a toolbar and click OK in the New Toolbar dialog box.

Caution *If you create a new toolbar and then close it, it's gone. To redisplay it, you need to re-create the toolbar.*

Using TweakUI to Customize the Taskbar and Start Menu

TweakUI is a free, downloadable "PowerToy" available from the Microsoft web site (see Chapter 1, section "Using TweakUI to Change the Windows Interface"). It makes it easy to customize the taskbar and Start menu in ways that used to require editing the Registry.

In TweakUI, choose Taskbar to see the options available for the taskbar and Start menu. The Grouping option enables you to set preferences for how buttons on the taskbar are grouped. If you click the XP Start Menu option, you can choose which programs can be displayed in the Most Frequently Used Program section of the Start menu. Normally, Windows determines the programs that appear in this part of the menu according to the programs you use; however, if you don't want people to know that your most frequently used programs are Freecell, Solitaire, and Hearts, you can deselect them from the XP Start Menu list so that they will only appear in the Programs menu.

Removing Microsoft Programs from the Start Menu

A court order required Microsoft to add the ability to hide Microsoft "middleware" programs that come bundled with Windows: Internet Explorer, Outlook Express, Windows Media Player, Windows Messenger, and Microsoft's Java Virtual Machine. The resulting Set Program Access And Defaults feature is new in Windows XP SP1. Although this feature may be in compliance with the letter of the court order, it is generally agreed not to be in compliance with the spirit of the order. The options are not particularly self-explanatory. Also, the Microsoft programs are not removed from the system, only hidden—that is, removed from the desktop and Start menu and "other locations" (such as toolbars).

For how to hide these Microsoft programs that come with Windows, see the section "Hiding Windows Components That You Can't Uninstall" in Chapter 1.

CONFIGURING WINDOWS FOR YOUR COMPUTER

The
Complete
Reference

Chapter 11

Setting Up
Your Desktop

When your desktop is set up in a way that is right for you, everything flows more smoothly. Files and programs are where you expect them to be. The screen is attractive and doesn't hurt your eyes. Your desktop's background and screen saver are different from everyone else's, giving your computer a personal touch—homey, cool, or whatever fashion statement you want your computer to make.

This chapter describes how to configure your desktop to suit your own preferences, including choosing a desktop theme, background, screen saver, color scheme (using the Color dialog box), icons, other visual effects, and sound effects. Windows XP comes with the new Luna interface, but you can switch back to the classic Windows design if you prefer. It also tells you how to set your screen resolution, how to use multiple displays at the same time, and how to troubleshoot problems with your monitor.

Display Properties

You configure your desktop and monitor by changing Windows' display properties. You can dress up your desktop by changing the background color or image or change the size, color, or font of the individual elements that make up the desktop. You can even incorporate a web page or two into the background of your desktop. When you step away from your computer, you can tell it to display a screen saver or turn off your monitor until you get back.

The command center for anything having to do with your monitor or desktop is the Display Properties dialog box, shown in Figure 11-1. The easiest way to open it is by right-clicking any unoccupied spot on the desktop and choosing Properties from the shortcut menu. You can also access it by opening the Display icon from the Appearance And Themes category of the Control Panel.

The Display Properties dialog box has the following five tabs (your dialog box may have more tabs, if your system has any special display software):

- **Themes**   Controls desktop themes.
- **Desktop**   Lets you choose icons and background pictures.
- **Screen Saver**   Offers screen savers and automatic settings for turning off your monitor.
- **Appearance**   Controls the color, size, and font of every standard type of object Windows uses.
- **Settings**   Lets you set the size of the desktop (in pixels), number of colors displayed, and monitor performance

Note   *When you make changes on the Display Properties dialog box, the new settings are not applied until you click Apply or OK.*

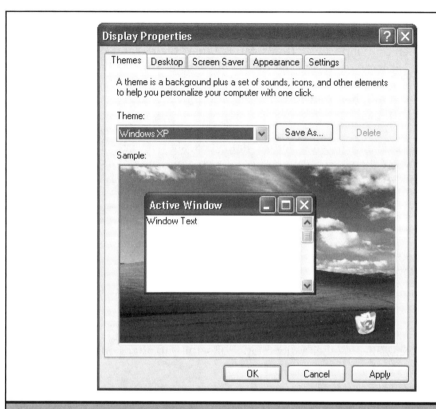

Figure 11-1. *The Display Properties dialog box controls the appearance of your desktop.*

Choosing a Desktop Theme

You can change the appearance of practically anything on your desktop. However, getting a collection of colors, icons, pictures, fonts, mouse pointers, screen savers, and so on that look good together takes more time and artistic talent than most of us have. A *desktop theme* is a complete "look" for your desktop. By changing themes, you can alter everything about the appearance of your desktop in one fell swoop. (A *color scheme* is more limited—it's a set of color and font settings.)

 Windows 98 and Me had both desktop schemes and desktop themes. Desktop themes were separate Windows components that you could install from your Windows Me/98 CD-ROM, while desktop schemes were selected from the Display Properties dialog box. Windows XP combines most of the elements of both into desktop themes.

A desktop theme provides not only a system of colors and fonts, but also sounds, icons, mouse pointers, a desktop background, and a screen saver as well. Windows XP ships with two themes: Windows XP (the default "Luna" theme) and Windows Classic (which looks like earlier versions of Windows). Other themes are available as part of Microsoft's Plus software package (information is at **www.microsoft.com/windows/plus**). You can download a number of third-party themes from C I NET's web site (at **download.cnet.com**).

To change your desktop theme, choose an entry from the Theme drop-down list on the Themes tab of the Display Properties dialog box, shown earlier in Figure 11-1.

After you choose a theme, you can modify it by changing any of its elements (as described in sections later in this chapter):

- The background image or color
- The screen saver
- The color scheme
- The windows and buttons
- The font or size of text used in title bars, message boxes, menus, and elsewhere
- The size or shape of icons
- Visual effects, like whether a menu fades or scrolls up after you're finished using it
- Sound effects

After you have modified a theme, it is listed as "modified" on the Theme drop-down list of the Themes tab of the Display Properties dialog box. To save your changes as a new desktop theme, click the Save As button on the Themes tab of the Display Properties dialog box. When the Save As dialog box appears, use it to name your theme and save it as you would any other file. Your new theme now appears on the Theme list in the Display Properties dialog box. To remove it (or any other theme) from the list, select it and click the Delete button.

Changing the Background

The *background* is the pattern, picture, or color that lies behind all the windows, icons, and menus on your desktop. (The background used to be called *wallpaper* before people noticed that wallpapering your desktop is a mixed metaphor.)

Your desktop background can be any color or image. Windows comes with several attractive photographs, as well as a number of abstract patterns, that you can use as a background. You can also use image files that you download from the Internet, copy from a friend, or get from your scanner or digital camera. Your background can even be a web page.

Selecting an Image or Pattern from the Background List

Select a background image or pattern from the Desktop tab of the Display Properties dialog box (shown in Figure 11-2). The Background box on that tab lists all the background image options that Windows knows about. Click a name in this list to see the image displayed in the preview box—the monitor-like graphic just above the list.

A background image is a file in an image format (with the extension .bmp, .jpg, or .gif) or HTML. That image has a size, which may or may not match the dimensions of your display. If the image is smaller than the display, the Position drop-down list (to the right of the Background list) gives you three choices:

■ **Center**   Puts the image in the center of the display, letting the background color of the desktop form a frame around the image. This is your best choice for photographs that are slightly smaller than the display.

■ **Tile**   Repeats the image to fill the display with the image. This works particularly well with patterns such as Coffee Bean or River Sumida, which are small images designed to be tiled.

■ **Stretch**   Stretches the image to fill the display. Photographs end up looking like fun house mirrors, but many abstract patterns like Vortec Space stretch well.

If the image you choose is larger than your display, Center and Tile both give you a single copy of the image, with the edges of the image off the screen. If this isn't satisfactory, you can use Paint to crop or shrink the image, or you can redefine the dimensions of your display (see "Changing the Screen Resolution" later in this chapter).

When the preview in the Display Properties dialog box looks the way you want, click either OK or Apply.

Making Your Own Background Images

You aren't limited to the backgrounds that come with Windows. You can use any image file—like a digital or scanned picture of your kids—as a background. Any image file that you move to your My Pictures folder automatically appears in the Background list on the Desktop tab of the Display Properties dialog box. If the file is somewhere else on your system, you can click the Browse button and find the file in the Browse dialog box that appears.

Selecting a Background Color

Any background image you select automatically covers the background color of your desktop. This means that you see the background color of your desktop only if your background image choice is None or is centered with the background visible around the edges.

To select a new background color, follow these steps:

1. Click the Color button on the Desktop tab of the Display Properties dialog box (shown in Figure 11-2). A palette of 20 colors appears.

2. If one of the colors on the palette is what you want, click it. The background of the preview box changes to the new color.

3. If you don't like any of the colors on the palette, click Other, and follow the directions in the section "Finding the Perfect Color" later in this chapter.

4. Implement your new background color by clicking Apply or OK.

Using a Web Page as a Background

Rather than a static decoration, your desktop background can be a page from the Internet, or it can contain accessories regularly updated from the Internet, such as a headline ticker or a weather map. (Microsoft used to call this idea the "Active Desktop," but it seems to have dropped the term.)

If you have a fast, always-on Internet connection, these Internet-updated options can be fun, but we have yet to find one that is worth tying up a phone line.

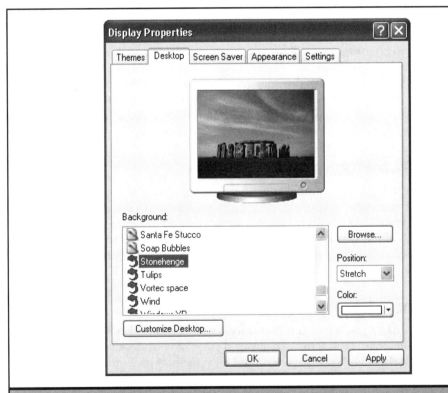

Figure 11-2. *The preview box in the center shows the effects of proposed changes before you apply them.*

In general, we recommend that you not bother with these web-based elements if you connect to the Internet via a modem attached to an ordinary telephone line; the connection is slow, and the benefit is not worth tying up the phone. But if you connect through an office LAN or an always-on home connection like DSL or cable, you may find that you enjoy having your desktop more closely integrated with the outside world. You can also display a web page that you've stored on your own hard drive, which doesn't depend on a connection to the Internet.

These possibilities are controlled from the Web tab of the Desktop Items dialog box, shown in Figure 11-3. Open this dialog box by clicking the Customize Desktop button on the Desktop tab of the Display Properties dialog box.

Adding Web Content to Your Desktop

The Web Pages list on the Web tab of the Desktop Items dialog box offers My Current Home Page, which is the page Internet Explorer displays when it opens—even if Internet Explorer is not your default browser. Other items may appear on your Web

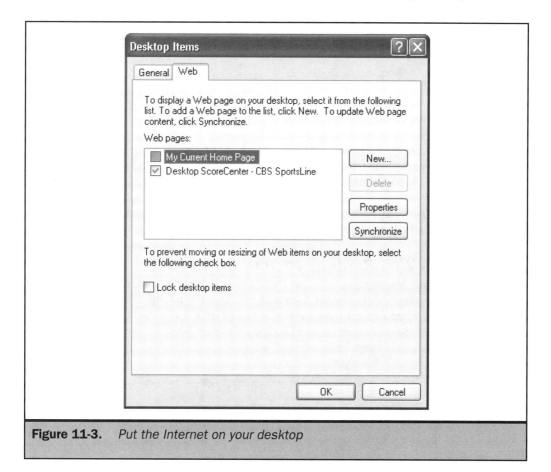

Figure 11-3. *Put the Internet on your desktop*

Pages list. To display a listed item on your desktop, check the corresponding check box, click OK to close the Desktop Items dialog box, and then click either OK or Apply in the Display Properties dialog box. Your computer will attempt to access the Internet and find the page you chose.

You can add any web page you want to the Web Pages list on the Web tab of the Desktop Items dialog box by clicking the New button on the Web tab of the Desktop Items dialog box. When the New Desktop Item dialog box appears, type the URL of the web page into the Location box. Alternatively, choose an item from your Favorites menu by clicking the Browse button and choosing a favorite from the Browse dialog box. After you click OK and confirm your choice, the new item appears on the Web Pages list with a check in its check box.

   If you add an image file to the list of Web Pages and choose to display it, the image floats over the desktop.

The New Desktop Item dialog box also contains a Visit Gallery button, which takes you to a Microsoft web site containing stock tickers, weather maps, and other items that you may find interesting to have on your desktop. Instructions for installing these items can be found on the web site. You may need to install the Java Virtual Machine before using these items.

   If you don't want web items to be accidentally moved or resized, select the Lock Desktop Items check box on the Web tab of the Desktop Items dialog box.

After you have added an item to the Web Pages list on the Desktop Items dialog box, you can add it or remove it from your desktop as often as you like by checking or unchecking its check box in the Web Pages list.

   When you display web content on the desktop, the transparent and shadow features no longer work on desktop icon text.

Working with Web Content on Your Desktop

Web pages that have become part of your desktop appear to have no definite boundary, especially if the background color of the page matches the background color of the desktop. However, if you rest the cursor at the top edge of the web page, a small frame appears around it. You can use this frame to drag the web page to another location or to resize it. The frame contains icons along the top border, like this:

Clicking the downward-pointing arrow in the left corner displays a menu of commands you can use to change the appearance of the web page—Microsoft calls this the Tools menu for the web page. The Tools menu contains commands that enable you to tell Windows whether to store the web page for use when your computer is offline, how much of the screen for the web page to occupy, and how often to update the web page from the Internet. You can choose Properties from the Tools menu to display the web page's Properties dialog box, which is described in the next section.

 If you are used to working with web pages inside browser windows, having a web page as part of your desktop takes some getting used to. For example, the web page stays behind any open windows on the desktop; you can't bring it to the front by clicking it.

Updating Your Desktop Web Pages

A web page on your desktop does not stay current automatically. You must either update it by selecting Synchronize from the Tools menu that drops down from the upper-left corner of its frame or by setting up a schedule to update it automatically.

To set up a schedule for web page updating, follow these steps:

1. Choose Properties from the web page's Tools menu to display the web page's Properties dialog box. (Another way to display this dialog box is from the Desktop tab of the Display Properties dialog box: click Customize Desktop, click the Web tab of the Desktop Items dialog box that appears, select a web page from the list, and click the Properties button.)

2. Click the Schedule tab of the Properties dialog box.

3. Click the Use The Following Schedule(s) radio button. If a schedule has already been defined but is not currently active, you can select it from the Schedules list.

4. If the schedule you want is not on the list, click the Add button. The New Schedule dialog box opens.

5. In the New Schedule dialog box, choose a number of days to wait before updating, a time of day when the update should happen, and a name for the schedule. A check box allows you to specify whether the computer should connect to the Internet automatically at the update time.

6. When you have finished entering information in the New Schedule dialog box, click OK. The new schedule now appears on the list of schedules. Click OK in all of the open dialog boxes.

You can change or remove an update schedule by repeating step 1 above, then selecting the schedule and clicking the Edit or Remove button. You can make the schedule inactive by selecting the Only When I Choose Synchronize From The Tools Menu radio button in step 3.

Setting Up a Screen Saver

A *screen saver* is a changing pattern that appears when your computer has been inactive for a while. A good screen saver is entertaining and discourages random passers-by from reading the document you were working on when you stepped out for coffee. The screen saver can also require you to log back in when you return, so others can't use your computer (without your password).

In homes or offices with multiple networked computers, the screen saver can display the computer's name, suitably colorized and animated. You can also download screen savers from the Internet, enabling you to display the latest *Harry Potter* images when you're not working. Or you can use the My Pictures Slideshow screen saver to cycle through pictures of your grandchildren or your vacation in Bali.

One alternative to a screen saver is to have your monitor turn itself off after a specified period of inactivity. You can do this (if your monitor supports this option) from the Power Options properties box, which you can open by clicking the Power button on the Screen Saver tab of the Display Properties dialog box.

Selecting a Screen Saver

To select and activate a screen saver, follow these steps:

1. Open the Screen Saver tab of the Display Properties dialog box, shown in Figure 11-4.

2. Select a screen saver from the drop-down list. The preview box shows a miniaturized version of what the screen saver displays. To see a full-size preview, click the Preview button. Move the mouse or click a key to stop the full-size preview.

3. When you find a screen saver you like, click either the Apply or OK button.

If you're sick of having a screen saver at all, choose None from the drop-down list on the Screen Saver tab of the Display Properties dialog box.

3D (DirectX) screen savers use the full CPU cycles of your computer and are known to cause computers to overheat. These screen savers have names that start with "3D." Stick with the simple screen savers.

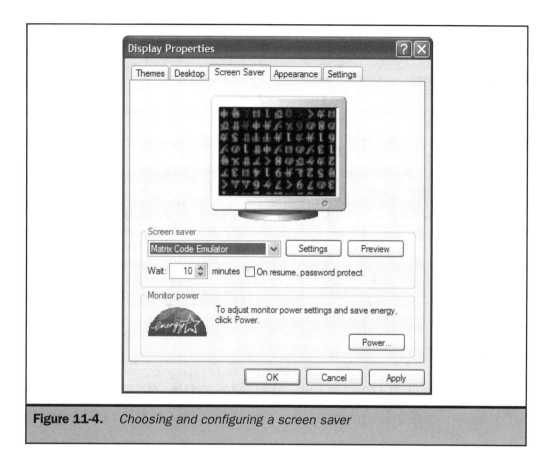

Figure 11-4. *Choosing and configuring a screen saver*

Installing New Screen Savers

Windows comes with a choice of several screen savers, but that's just the beginning. Additional screen savers are available over the Internet, and most of them are free. You can begin your search at C I NET's web site at **www.download.com**, which lists screen savers in the "Home and Desktop" department. You can also try looking on the web site of your favorite book, TV show, or movie to see whether there is a promotional screen saver.

A screen saver is stored in a file of type Screen Saver (.scr). After you have extracted the SCR file from the compressed folder you downloaded (almost all downloads arrive as compressed folders), move it to the C:\Windows\System32 folder (assuming that Windows is installed on drive C:). Now you should be able to select it from the list on the Screen Saver tab of the Display Properties dialog box, as described in the previous section.

Configuring Your Screen Saver

While you have the Screen Saver tab selected, you can make a number of choices about how your screen saver functions:

- **Change the settings.**   Click the Settings button. Each screen saver has its own list of settings; some let you change a handful of parameters; others offer an entire screenful of choices. In general, the settings of your screen saver control how fast the screen saver cycles, the colors it uses, the thickness of the lines it draws, and so forth.

- **Change the wait time.**   Enter a new number of minutes into the Wait box. The *wait time* is the length of time your system must be inactive before the screen saver starts up. Windows waits this long for keyboard or mouse input before starting the screen saver.

- **Require a password.**   Check the On Resume Display Welcome Screen check box. When the screen saver is displayed and you press a key, you will see the Unlock Computer window or Welcome screen, asking for your user account name and password (see Chapter 6).

Choosing a New Color Scheme

A *color scheme* is a coordinated set of colors for all the basic desktop objects. With a color scheme, you can change the color of everything at once and wind up with colors that look good together and provide reasonable visibility. (You don't want to wind up with black text on black title bars, for example.) You can change color schemes from the Appearance tab of the Display Properties dialog box, shown in Figure 11-5. Make a selection from the Color Scheme drop-down list and click OK.

Note   *The color schemes that are available to you depend in part on your choice of window and button styles. If you choose Windows Classic windows and buttons, all the Windows Me color schemes are available. The Windows XP windows and buttons only come in the default blue, olive green, and silver.*

Color schemes are not saved by themselves, but as part of the overall desktop theme. If you change color schemes or change the color of some object inside a color

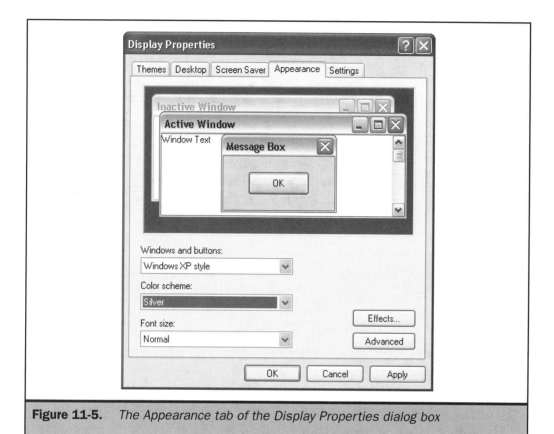

Figure 11-5.   *The Appearance tab of the Display Properties dialog box*

scheme, you have modified your desktop theme. If you like what you've done, give your modified theme a name and save it (see "Choosing a Desktop Theme" earlier in this chapter).

Finding the Perfect Color

When you choose to change the color of the desktop, the title bars, or any of the other basic objects, Windows offers a simple palette of 20 colors. If you want more choices, click Other on the color palette to display the Color dialog box, shown in woefully inadequate black and white in Figure 11-6.

The number of basic colors has now expanded to 48, shown in a palette on the left side of the Color dialog box. If the color you want is on this palette, click it and click OK. If even the 48 colors aren't enough for you, you can use the settings on the right side of the Color dialog box to get any color you want.

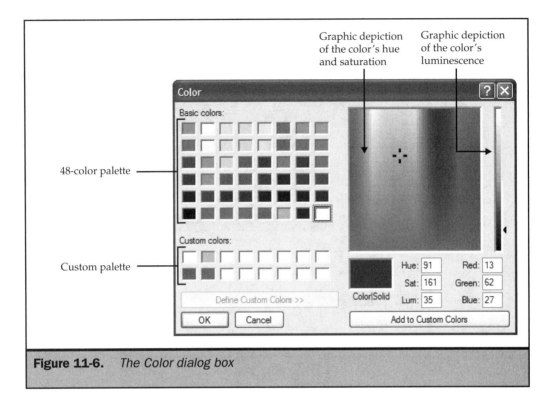

Figure 11-6.   *The Color dialog box*

The currently selected color is shown in the Color | Solid box. To the right of the Color | Solid box are two different numerical systems of describing the current color: its hue, saturation, and luminescence (known as *HSV coordinates*); and its red, green, and blue components (known as *RGB coordinates*). Above the Color | Solid box and the coordinates is a graphical representation of the current color's HSV coordinates. The horizontal position of the cross-hairs in the large square represents the hue, and the vertical position of the cross-hairs represents the saturation. The position of the vertical slider next to the square represents the luminescence. Thus, the same color is represented three ways: as RGB, as HSV, and as a position of the cross-hairs and slider. You can select a new color by manipulating any of the three descriptions:

■ Move the crosshairs and slider with the mouse.

■ Type new numbers (from 0 to 240) into the HSV coordinate boxes.

■ Type new numbers (from 0 to 255) into the RGB coordinate boxes.

When you use one of these methods to specify the color, the other two descriptions (and the Color | Solid box) change automatically to match.

If you think you might want to use this color again in the future, click Add to Custom Colors. The new color appears in one of the boxes in the Custom Colors palette on the lower-left side of the Color dialog box. If you like, you can define several custom colors, one at a time. Like basic colors, custom colors can be selected by clicking them.

When you have created all the colors you want, select the one you want to use and click OK. The color is applied, and the Color dialog box vanishes.

If you really want 256 colors, which Windows XP doesn't normally support, click the Settings tab on the Display Properties dialog box, click the Advanced button, click the Adapter tab, click the List All Modes button, and choose a display mode with 256 colors. Some older games require 256 colors.

Changing Windows, Buttons, and Fonts

You can configure the color, size, and font of almost anything—title bars, active windows, inactive windows, message boxes, and more. These choices are made all at once (along with changes in screen savers, background images, and many other items) when you choose a desktop theme (see "Choosing a Desktop Theme" earlier in this chapter). However, you may want to change the windows, buttons, or fonts while leaving the rest of your desktop alone, or you may want to change just one or two things, like the color of title bars or the font size of tool tips. The place to make changes to the windows, buttons, and fonts in Windows is the Appearance tab of the Display Properties dialog box (shown earlier in Figure 11-5). To get to this tab, right-click any open space on the desktop, choose Properties from the shortcut menu, and then click the Appearance tab when the Display Properties dialog box appears.

The Windows XP desktop theme overrides many of the choices you make in the Display Properties dialog box—especially color changes other than the desktop color. If this cramps your style, you can get more freedom by switching to the Windows Classic desktop theme.

Choosing Classic Style Windows and Buttons

The windows and buttons of Windows XP have a distinctive rounded look that is different from those in earlier versions of Windows. You can change back to the classic Windows look by displaying the Appearance tab of the Display Properties dialog box shown in Figure 11-5 earlier in this chapter, choosing Windows Classic Style from the Windows And Buttons drop-down list, and clicking OK. To change back to the new style, choose Windows XP Style from the Windows And Buttons drop-down list.

Choosing Windows Classic Style on the Appearance tab appears to us to have exactly the same result as choosing the Windows Classic theme on the Themes tab.

Changing the Appearance of Individual Items

You can edit the appearance of title bars, message boxes, and many other individual items from the Advanced Appearance dialog box, shown in Figure 11-7.

To display the Advanced Appearance dialog box, click the Advanced button on the Appearance tab of the Display Properties dialog box.

To change the appearance of an item, first find it on the Item drop-down list of the Advanced Appearance dialog box. (In Figure 11-7, Desktop is chosen.) After you choose an item, the text boxes and buttons relevant to that item become active.

Not all of the text boxes and buttons of the Advanced Appearances dialog box are relevant to all items. For example, a scrollbar has no text, so the second line of buttons and text boxes becomes inactive when Scrollbar is the selected item. Also, some changes apply only to programs that use the old-style controls rather than the new Windows XP design. For example, changing the title bar colors doesn't affect most newer programs. To explore which programs are affected by a setting, choose a bright, obnoxious color you'd never normally use, so that you can easily spot screen objects that use the setting.

The first line of text boxes and buttons (Size, Color1, and Color2) refer to the item itself. So, for example, for the Active Title Bar item, the Size text box on this line refers to the height of the title bar. Color1 is the color on the left side of the title bar, and Color2 is the color on the right side. The second line of text boxes and buttons (Font, Size, Color, Bold, and Italic) refers to the text (if any) displayed on the item.

As you enter the new information into the Advanced Appearance dialog box, the items in the dialog box's preview box change accordingly. When you are satisfied with your changes, click OK.

It's possible to make some dreadful choices in the Advanced Appearance dialog box. You can always go back to square one by choosing one of the built-in desktop themes (see "Choosing a Desktop Theme" earlier in this chapter).

Changing Fonts

You can fairly easily make an overall change in the size of the text that appears in menus, title bars, file labels, and other system contexts. With a little more effort, you can change not just the size, but the font as well. You also can make changes to the text used in specific contexts, rather than an overall change.

Changing the Size of Fonts

If the default fonts that Windows uses are not large enough for you, you can easily make them bigger. On the Appearance tab of the Display Properties dialog box

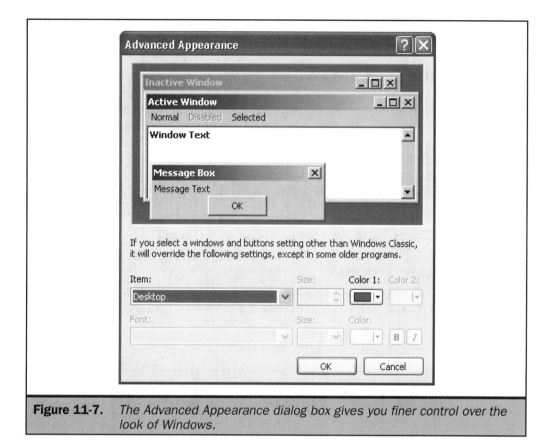

Figure 11-7.   *The Advanced Appearance dialog box gives you finer control over the look of Windows.*

(shown in Figure 11-5 earlier in the chapter), choose Large Fonts or Extra Large Fonts from the Font Size drop-down list.

 Another way to increase the size of text on your screen (as well as everything else) is to increase the magnification setting, as described in the "Changing Magnification" section later in this chapter.

The Advanced Appearance dialog box, shown in Figure 11-7, gives you much finer control over Windows' fonts. You can change the font, as well as the size of text, and you can change some items while leaving others alone. For example, you could choose one font for the text in menus and another for the text in message boxes. To change the font, size, or color of the text that Windows uses for a particular type of item, display the Advanced Appearance dialog box as described in the section "Changing the Appearance of Individual Items" earlier in this chapter.

Smoothing the Edges of Fonts

Fonts have a tendency to look ragged when displayed on a monitor. Windows offers a choice of two methods for combating this tendency: Standard and ClearType. The Standard method is the default. ClearType is a relatively new technique that Microsoft invented for use in e-books. We recommend taking a look at ClearType if you think that the fonts you're seeing look ragged, especially on LCD screens. (For more information, see **www.microsoft.com/typography/cleartype**.)

To change from one method to the other, follow these steps:

1. Click the Effects button on the Appearance tab of the Display Properties dialog box. The Effects dialog box appears, as shown in Figure 11-8.

2. Make sure that the Use The Following Method To Smooth The Edges Of Screen Fonts check box is checked.

3. Choose Standard or ClearType from the drop-down list, and then click OK in both the Effects dialog box and the Display Properties dialog box.

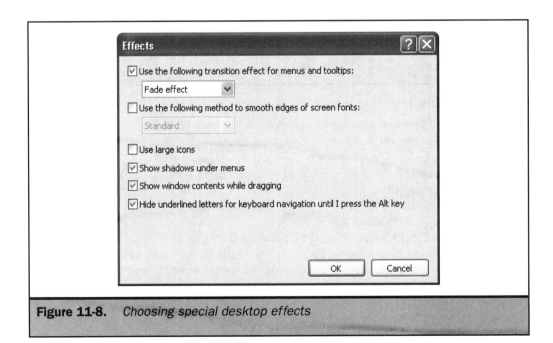

Figure 11-8. *Choosing special desktop effects*

Changing Your Desktop Icons

You can change the size or arrangement of the icons on your desktop. You can even define new icons for the various types of desktop objects.

Changing Icon Size

If your icons seem too small, you can switch from regular icons (32 points) to large icons (48 points), as follows:

1. Click the Effects button on the Appearance tab of the Display Properties dialog box. The Effects dialog box appears (see Figure 11-8).
2. Check the Use Large Icons check box.

You can make finer adjustments in icon size from the Advanced Appearance dialog box (shown earlier in Figure 11-7). Choose Icon from the drop-down Item list in the Advanced Appearance dialog box, and then type a number between 16 and 72 in the Size box. This represents the size of icons in points. The default size is 32 points. The second row of text boxes and buttons in the dialog box controls the font and size of the labels underneath your icons.

 Making your icons too large may cause them to look ragged. Rather than increase the point size of your icons, you may want to decrease the resolution of your desktop or increase the magnification setting of your display (see "Changing Magnification" later in this chapter). Icons in Explorer windows become more visible when you switch to Large Icons or Thumbnails view (see Chapter 8).

Arranging Icons on the Desktop

You can arrange your desktop icons manually by dragging and dropping them. If your system is set up for single-click opening, however, you may open the corresponding objects by mistake when you try to drag and drop icons. If you're having this problem, use right-click drag-and-drop. Select Move Here from the shortcut menu that appears when you drop the icon.

Arranging Icons Automatically

To arrange your desktop icons automatically, right-click any open spot on the desktop and choose Arrange Icons from the shortcut menu. Windows arranges the icons in columns, starting on the left side of the desktop. The Arrange Icons menu gives you the option of arranging by name, type, size, or date modified.

 Make sure that you really want the icons arranged in columns before you use an Arrange Icons option. There is no "undo" selection on the Arrange Icons menu.

Another option on the Arrange Icons menu is Auto Arrange. If Auto Arrange is checked, the icons are arranged in columns, and any new item is automatically ushered to the next open spot in the pattern. Auto Arrange prevents you from arranging your icons manually; any icon is whisked to the appropriate row or column as soon as you set it down.

Adjusting Icon Spacing

The spacing between icons is another of the many details controlled by the Advanced Appearance dialog box (see "Changing the Appearance of Individual Items" earlier in this chapter). To change the spacing, open the Advanced Appearance dialog box and choose Icon Spacing (Horizontal) or Icon Spacing (Vertical) from the Item drop-down list. Type a number (of points) in the Size box. Larger numbers create bigger spaces. Changing the icon spacing affects the icon arrangement of Explorer windows, as well as the icons on the desktop.

Choosing New Desktop Icons

You can choose new icons for any of the standard desktop objects. Make these changes from the General tab of the Desktop Items dialog box, shown in Figure 11-9.

Note   *You can change all your desktop icons at the same time by choosing a new desktop theme.*

To choose a new icon for My Computer, My Documents, My Network Places, or the Recycle Bin, follow these steps:

1. Click the Customize Desktop button on the Desktop tab of the Display Properties dialog box. The Desktop Items dialog box appears, with the General tab displayed.

2. Select the icon that you want to change from the box of icons in the Desktop Items dialog box. Scroll left and right to see them all.

3. Click the Change Icon button. The Change Icon dialog box appears, showing you the icons available for this item. If you don't see an icon you want and know that there are other icons elsewhere on your system, you can click the Browse button and look for another file of icons. (Windows normally looks in the file C:\Windows\System32\shell32.dll for icons; if you don't like any that you see there, click Browse and try the other .dll files in that folder. Some don't contain any icons.)

When you find the icon you want, select it in the Change Icon dialog box and click OK in all the open dialog boxes.

Tip   *If you'd like Run or Search icons on your desktop (the equivalents of Start | Run and Start | Search), drag these commands from the Start menu to the desktop. Windows creates a shortcut for the command.*

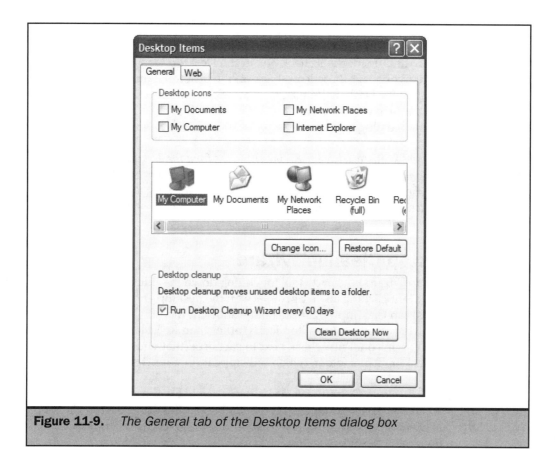

Figure 11-9. *The General tab of the Desktop Items dialog box*

Renaming Icons

You can rename most of the icons on your desktop by right-clicking, choosing Rename, and typing a new name. This method even works to rename some of the system icons, like My Computer and Internet Explorer. However, Windows doesn't let you rename some of the icons on your desktop, including the Recycle Bin.

Deleting and Recovering Desktop Icons

You can remove desktop icons in the same way that you delete files and folders: Select them and press the DELETE key. The only icon for which this technique fails is the Recycle Bin.

The My Computer, My Documents, and My Network Places icons represent capabilities of your system that you cannot delete; you can only stop displaying them on the desktop. The objects they represent continue to appear in Explorer windows, on the Start menu, and as links on the Task pane. To remove any of these icons from your desktop, open the General tab of the Desktop Items dialog box (Figure 11-9 in the previous section) and uncheck its check box in the Desktop Icons section.

If you decide that you want these icons back on the desktop, you can restore them from the General tab of the Desktop Items dialog box. Select the check boxes of the items whose icons you want to have on the desktop. Then click OK to close the Desktop Items and Display Properties dialog boxes.

The only way we know to delete the Recycle Bin icon from the desktop is to use the TweakUI program you can download from Microsoft (see Chapter 1, section "Using TweakUI to Change the Windows Interface"). Click the Desktop entry in the left-hand pane of the TweakUI window. The right-hand pane displays a list of desktop icons. Check or uncheck the boxes to display the icons you want.

Using the Desktop Cleanup Wizard

The Desktop Cleanup Wizard is a handy tool for cutting down the clutter on your desktop. Run this wizard by right-clicking any empty space on the desktop and selecting Arrange Icons By | Run Desktop Cleanup Wizard from the shortcut menu.

The wizard shows you a list of desktop icons (other than Recycle Bin) and the date when you last used each icon. Put a check next to each icon that you want cleared away into the Unused Desktop Icons folder, which will appear on your desktop instead of those icons.

You can run the Desktop Cleanup Wizard automatically by opening the Desktop Items dialog box (shown earlier in Figure 11-9) and clicking the Run Desktop Cleanup Wizard Every 60 Days check box. Conversely, if you are annoyed by wizards that pop up without an invitation, deselect the box.

Changing the Desktop's Visual Effects

Windows has a number of cute but inconsequential visual effects that create the illusion of motion or three-dimensionality on the desktop, like the thin shadow that surrounds the Start button. You can control these effects from the Effects dialog box (shown earlier in Figure 11-8). To open this dialog box, first open the Display Properties dialog box, then click the Effects button on the Appearance tab.

The check boxes in the Effects dialog box are self-explanatory. The effects themselves are harmless, so don't be afraid to experiment with them.

Changing the Desktop's Sound Effects

Many actions on the desktop are accompanied by a sound effect, and almost any desktop action can have a sound assigned to it if you want. You can change these sounds all at once (or turn them off entirely) by choosing a new sound scheme, or you can change only a few sounds and leave the rest alone. A *sound scheme* is a coordinated set of sounds for all the desktop actions.

Make these choices from the Sounds tab of the Sounds And Audio Devices Properties dialog box, shown in Figure 11-10. Open this dialog box by clicking the Sounds And Audio Devices icon from the Sounds Speech And Audio Devices category on the Control Panel, and then click the Sounds tab. Choose a sound scheme from the Sound Scheme drop-down list (Windows XP comes with only two sound schemes: No Sounds and Windows Default).

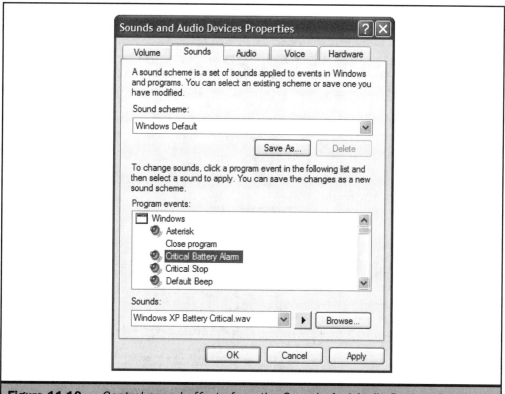

Figure 11-10.   *Control sound effects from the Sounds And Audio Devices Properties dialog box.*

You can also change sounds for individual events. To choose a new sound for a type of event, select the event from the Program Events list on the Sounds tab of the Sounds And Audio Devices Properties dialog box and then select a sound from the Sounds drop-down list. For more information about associating sounds with Windows events, see "Choosing What Sounds Windows Makes" in Chapter 19.

Changing Display Settings

Windows gives you control over the dimensions of your desktop, the color resolution of your display, and many other properties. Most of this power resides on the Settings tab of the Display Properties dialog box, shown in Figure 11-11. Open this dialog box by right-clicking any empty space on the desktop, selecting Properties from the shortcut menu, and then clicking the Settings tab.

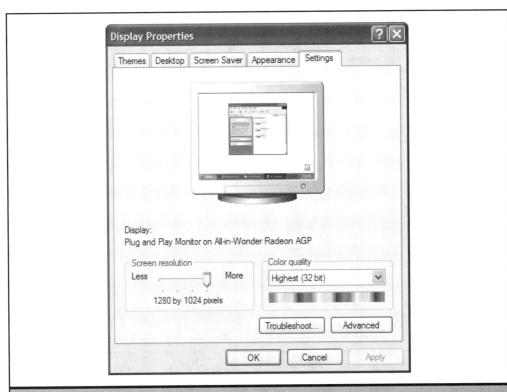

Figure 11-11.   *The Settings tab of the Display Properties dialog box*

Changing the Screen Resolution

The Screen Resolution slider on the Settings tab of the Display Properties dialog box controls the dimensions of your desktop in *pixels*, which are the colored dots on the screen. The current dimensions are stated under the slider. Increase the dimensions by moving the slider to the right; decrease them by moving the slider to the left.

Naturally, the size of your monitor doesn't change (the number of inches on your monitor is fixed); so when you increase the number of pixels on your desktop, each pixel gets correspondingly smaller, increasing the resolution. Icons and fonts shrink as well. As you increase the desktop area, you may want to increase font and icon size to compensate. (See the "Changing Fonts" and "Changing Icon Size" sections earlier in this chapter.)

The range of resolutions depends on what type of monitor you use. For a 14-inch monitor, your choices may range only from 800 × 600 to 1,024 × 768. For a 17-inch monitor, you can increase the resolution up to 1,600 × 1,200. Larger monitors support even higher resolutions.

Resolution is a trade-off. Setting the slider too low wastes the capabilities of your monitor. Setting it too high can give you eye strain. The following table contains our recommendations for screen resolution based on monitor size (that is, the size of the CRT tube that can display an image, measured diagonally):

Screen Size	Maximum Usable Resolution
14 inches	640 × 480
15 inches	800 × 600
17 inches	1,024 × 768
19 to 21 inches	1,280 × 1,024 or 1,600 × 1,200

Windows doesn't normally support resolutions of less than 800 × 600. However, if you really want a lower resolution, click the Settings tab on the Display Properties dialog box, click the Advanced button, click the Adapter tab, click the List All Modes button, and choose a display mode with 640 × 480.

Changing the Color Quality

The Settings tab of the Display Properties dialog box also controls the number of colors you display. The Color Quality drop-down list gives you choices that depend on the quality of your monitor and video card. Your options may include 16 colors, 256 colors, high color (16-bit, or 65,536 colors), 24-bit true color (16 million colors), and 32-bit true color (even more colors). Below the list is a color bar showing the spectrum of the selected color palette.

The choice to be made is a speed versus beauty tradeoff. Displaying fewer colors or pixels is less work for your computer and may help it run faster. On the other hand, displaying more colors and pixels provides a richer viewing experience, particularly if you are looking at photographs. Using 16-bit color or higher produces much-improved image quality.

> **Note** *Colors and pixels also trade off against each other, because increasing either one uses more of the portion of RAM your system devotes to the display. Windows accounts for this automatically. If you increase the desktop area beyond the capabilities of your RAM, it decreases the color palette to compensate. Likewise, if you increase the color palette beyond what your RAM can handle, Windows decreases the desktop size.*

A few programs don't work properly with the new color palette until you restart your computer. In general, we recommend restarting your computer to be completely safe; but, if you change the color palette frequently, this can get to be a nuisance. You may want to experiment to see whether the software you use has any problems when you don't restart after a color change.

You can set up Windows to restart automatically when you change the color palette, ask you whether to restart, or not restart. To make these choices, click the Advanced button on the Settings tab of the Display Properties dialog box. A dialog box appears whose title bar depends on your monitor driver and video card. The choices available to you are listed as radio buttons on the General tab of this dialog box.

Changing Color Profiles

Different monitor and printer drivers represent a color palette in subtly different ways. These representation schemes are called *color profiles*. For most purposes, the difference between color profiles doesn't matter. However, if you must be sure the colors you see on your monitor are exactly the colors you will get when you print, you can set the color profiles of your monitor and printer to reflect the exact way your monitor and printer render colors. Matching colors is especially important if you plan to edit and print photos.

Windows comes with profiles for many popular monitors. Its default profile, called the sRGB Color Space Profile, matches most monitors reasonably well. Unless you are a graphics artist, you probably won't notice the difference between the default profile and a perfectly tuned one. Most users do not need to change their color profiles.

To change the color profile of your monitor, click the Settings tab of the Display Properties dialog box and click the Advanced button. In the new dialog box that opens, click the Color Management tab (shown in Figure 11-12). Any profiles you have previously used are listed in the large window, with the current default profile in the box above the large window. To change to a new default color profile, select a new profile from the list and click the Set As Default button. To add a profile to the list, click the Add button and select from the color profiles listed. To remove a profile from the list, select it and click the Remove button.

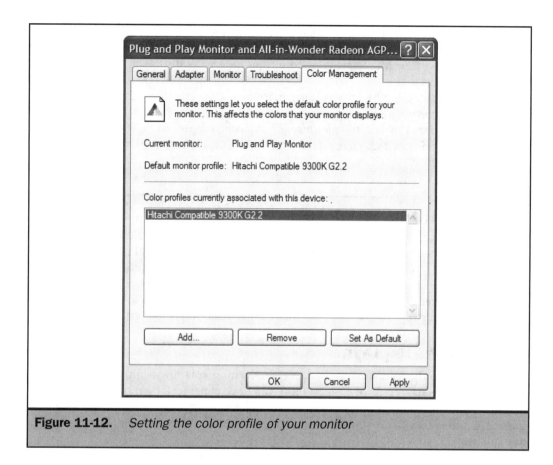

Figure 11-12. *Setting the color profile of your monitor*

Changing Magnification

To control font magnification, click the Advanced button on the Settings tab of the
Display Properties dialog box. You see a dialog box that displays properties of your
monitor. The title, tabs, and settings of this dialog box depend on the display driver.

 For higher magnification for the vision-impaired, see Chapter 16.

For most display drivers, the settings on the General tab include a magnification
setting (which may be called DPI Setting, for dots per inch). For a typical monitor, a
drop-down list gives you three choices: Normal Size (96 DPI), Large Size (120 DPI),
and Custom Setting. Choosing Custom Setting opens the Custom DPI Setting dialog box.
From this dialog box, you can type in whatever size you want as a percentage or change
the size by using the ruler as a slider.

After you've made your choice, click OK to return to the display driver's dialog box, where your chosen size is displayed under the Font Size box. If you like it, click Apply. If Windows doesn't restart your computer automatically, restart it yourself.

Be careful choosing very large font magnifications. Changing the size of fonts changes the size of everything that contains text, such as the Display Properties dialog box, for example. If you choose 200% font magnification and have an 800 × 600 desktop, the Display Properties dialog box gets so large that the Apply button goes off the bottom of the screen.

Getting Along with Your Monitor(s)

Windows can detect and install a driver for a Plug and Play monitor with little effort on your part (see Chapter 13). In addition, most monitors comply with Energy Star power-saving standards, enabling you to choose to have Windows turn off the monitor if you have been inactive for a certain period of time (see Chapter 15, section "Managing Your Computer's Power"). If you have two or more monitors hooked up to your computer, your desktop can stretch across all of them, and each can have its own settings.

Using Multiple Displays

Windows can handle four screens on a single system, displaying a single desktop that spans all the screens. A pair of 17-inch monitors have considerably more screen area than a single 19-inch monitor and can be a cost-effective alternative to a single larger screen. (On the other hand, you may not have much desk space left after setting up two monitors.)

There are three ways you can connect two or more monitors to your computer:

- **Dual display adapters**   *Dual display adapters* (or *dual video cards*) act like two adapters, with two IRQs and two sets of video memory addresses. Windows XP can support multiscreen displays with this type of adapter. However, not many people have dual display adapters, because they aren't cheap or commonly available.

- **Additional regular display adapters**   You can add a second regular display adapter to your system. For desktops, you can buy a display adapter for $40 and up, depending on the video quality, which you can install in an extra slot inside your computer. For laptops, PC Card display adapters are available from Margi (**www.margi.com**), but they cost over $200. Windows XP supports multiscreen displays on multiple video cards.

- **Laptops with external display jacks**   Almost all laptops have an internal LCD display and a plug to which you can connect an external monitor. With Windows Me, you can stretch your Windows desktop over the internal and external displays, but Windows XP may just show identical desktops on the two displays. Luckily, many display adapter manufacturers have updated their display drivers to work with Windows XP's less-powerful multiple-monitor support. Check your laptop manufacturer's web site to find out what type of display adapter it contains, and check the display adapter manufacturer's web site for updated drivers.

Configuring multiple screens to display one big desktop is straightforward once you install the new hardware (see Chapter 13, section "Configuring Windows for New Hardware"). Open the Settings tab of the Display Properties dialog box, which looks like Figure 11-13 if three display adapters are installed.

To configure an additional display, follow these steps:

1. Click the picture of the new monitor to highlight it. Windows may display a message box about extending the Windows desktop over multiple monitors. Click Yes and OK.

2. Drag the pictures of the monitors so they agree with the physical arrangement of your screens.

3. Configure the new display. If possible, configure all the displays to have the same number of colors and the same screen area, to avoid confusion when you move a window from one screen to another.

4. Click OK. Windows configures the new display.

Once configured, the additional display becomes part of the Windows desktop, and you can drag windows back and forth between the displays. You can even have a single window that spans multiple screens, which can be convenient for looking at spreadsheets with wide rows. If you want to change the color depth or resolution of one of the monitors, click the monitor on the Settings tab of the Display Properties dialog box, and then change the settings.

If you are taking your laptop on the road and need to disable all but the internal screen, open the Display Properties dialog box, click the Settings tab, click the box for the external screen(s), and deselect the Extend My Windows Desktop Onto This Monitor check box. When you reconnect your external screens, reselect this check box.

Windows considers one of your monitors to be the *primary display*, which is the monitor on which error messages and alerts appear. Some high-end DirectX graphics applications display correctly only on the primary monitor. If you have one AGP graphics card and one PCI graphics card, the PCI defaults to be the primary display, and the AGP is the secondary display.

Caution *Windows XP handles dual monitors differently from Windows Me/9x. If you are upgrading from Windows Me or Windows 98, you may need to buy a new display adapter for one or both monitors. Another approach is to switch which monitor is the primary display. Check your computer's documentation for the way to tell its BIOS which monitor is primary.*

CONFIGURING WINDOWS FOR YOUR COMPUTER

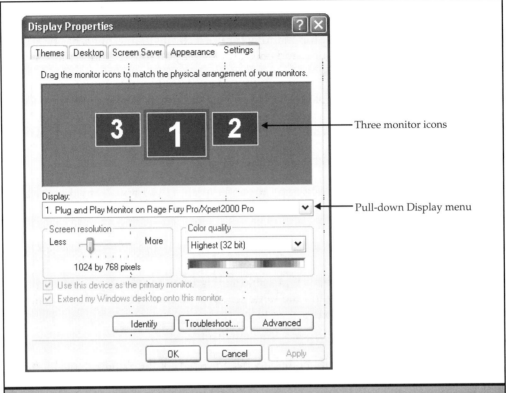

Three monitor icons

Pull-down Display menu

Figure 11-13.   *The Settings tab of the Display Properties dialog box with three monitors*

Diagnosing Display Problems

If your display is acting strangely, Windows offers several possible ways to fix the problem. This section describes the most common ways; also see Chapter 2 for how to use Windows' Troubleshooters.

If the screen is utterly unreadable, restart Windows in Safe Mode. After Windows is running in Safe or Normal Mode, open the Settings tab of the Display Properties dialog box and try the following:

■ Your screen might not be able to handle the display resolution your adapter is using. Try setting the Screen Resolution (number of pixels displayed) to a smaller value to see whether the screen clears. (The number of colors doesn't matter—all modern screens can display an unlimited number of colors. What you actually get, however, depends on your video card's capabilities.) When choosing Color Quality, choose 16-bit or 32-bit—not 24-bit, which takes more system resources.

■ Your screen might be able to handle the display resolution but might not be able to handle the adapter's *refresh rate*, the number of times per second the adapter sends the image to the monitor. Click the Advanced button to display the Properties dialog box for your display adapter and then click the Monitor tab. Try setting the Screen Refresh Rate box to the slowest available refresh rate, usually 60Hz. If that works, try faster rates until you find the fastest one that works reliably.

■ One final possibility is that the accelerator features in your display adapter aren't compatible with your computer. Symptoms typically are that the display is clear, but wrong, with lines or areas of the wrong color or pattern on the screen. Click the Advanced button on the Settings tab of the Display Properties dialog box to display the Properties dialog box for your display adapter. Click the Performance or Troubleshoot tab and look for the Hardware Acceleration slider ranging from None to Full. Try setting it to None; if this improves the display, try increasing the acceleration setting one notch at a time.

Note   *Once you change a setting and try to apply it, Windows makes the adjustment and then asks if you want to accept the changes. If you cannot see this dialog box, then your settings are not ideal. Wait 15 seconds, and the display returns to the currently saved settings.*

CONFIGURING WINDOWS FOR YOUR COMPUTER

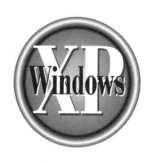

Chapter 12

Keyboards, Mice, and Game Controllers

Windows XP, like all operating systems, sits between the programs you run and the computer you run them on. Whenever a program accepts input from the keyboard, mouse, or a game controller or sends output to the screen or printer, Windows gets involved. As a result, when you configure Windows to work with your keyboard, mouse, or game controller, the settings you choose affect all the programs you run. You can choose the keyboard layout you want to use and set the sensitivity of the mouse. If you have installed a game controller or joystick, you can also check or change its settings.

Different countries use different currencies and formats for writing numbers, monetary amounts, dates, and times. Windows has regional settings that let it know about the formats used in most countries in the world (at least most of the countries where people are likely to use computers). By telling Windows which country you live in, you can cause Windows and most programs to use the date, time, and numeric formats with which you are comfortable.

Windows knows the current date and time (usually displayed at the right end of the taskbar) and understands time zones, U.S. daylight saving time, and leap years. If your system is on the Internet, Windows uses Microsoft's time server to set your system clock automatically, assuming that it knows what time zone you are located in.

Configuring Your Keyboard

Configuring your keyboard can mean two subtly different things:

- **Changing the way that your keyboard produces symbols,** for example, how long you have to press a key before it repeats. Microsoft considers these to be keyboard properties, and you control them from the Keyboard Properties dialog box.

- **Changing the way that symbols are mapped to keys,** for example, choosing a different alphabet or a different keyboard layout. Microsoft considers these to be language properties, and you control them from the Text Services And Input Languages dialog box.

Changing Keyboard Properties

Opening the Keyboard icon from the Printers And Other Hardware category of the Control Panel (or from the Control Panel itself if you are not using the category view) displays the Keyboard Properties dialog box, shown in Figure 12-1. From here you can control the following settings.

- **Repeat delay**   Delay between starting to hold down a key and when the key begins repeating

- **Repeat rate**   How fast the key repeats once it starts responding
- **Cursor blink rate**   How fast the cursor blinks.

 Additional keyboard settings are available if you have trouble using the keyboard (see Chapter 16, section "Making the Keyboard More Accessible").

You can test how your keys repeat by clicking in the text box and holding down a key.

Changing Language Properties

You can also control which language layout the keyboard uses. Different languages use different letters and assign the letters to different locations on the keyboard.

Figure 12-1.   *The Keyboard Properties dialog box contains settings for the keyboard and the cursor.*

If you use more than one language, you can choose a key combination that switches between two keyboard layouts.

For some languages, Windows offers a selection of *keyboard layouts*, which define the physical organization of the keys on the keyboard. For example, if you choose U.S. English as your language, you can choose among layouts that include the standard 101-key layout, the Dvorak keyboard, and even the left-handed Dvorak keyboard.

These choices are controlled from the Text Services And Input Languages dialog box, shown in Figure 12-2. To display this dialog box, open the Regional And Language Options icon from the Date, Time, Language, And Regional Options category of the Control Panel. On the Languages tab of Regional And Language Options dialog box, click the Details button.

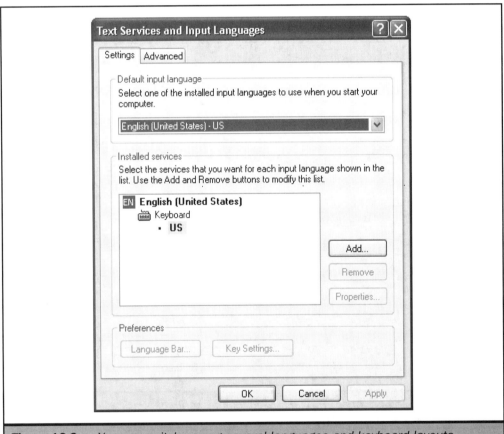

Figure 12-2. *You can switch among several languages and keyboard layouts.*

Configuring Your Keyboard for Another Language or Keyboard Layout

The languages and keyboard layouts that are installed on your computer shown in the Installed Services box on the Text Services And Input Languages dialog box. If the Installed Services box doesn't show the language or keyboard layout you want, click the Add button. When the Add Input Language box appears, select the language you want from the Input Language drop-down list or the keyboard layout you want from the Keyboard Layout/IME drop-down list and then click OK. The new service is added to the Installed Services box in the Text Services And Input Languages dialog box.

East Asian languages like Chinese or right-to-left languages like Hebrew might not appear, even in the Add Input Language box. In order to use these languages, do the following:

1. Open the Regional And Language Options icon from the Date, Time, Language, And Regional Options category of the Control Panel. The Regional And Language Options dialog box appears.

2. Check one of the two check boxes on the Language tab of the Regional And Language Options dialog box, depending on the language you want to use— either the Install Files For Complex Script And Right-To-Left Languages check box or the Install Files For East Asian Languages check box. Then click OK.

3. A confirmation box appears, listing the languages that will be added and the quantity of disk space required. (East Asian languages require 230MB of disk space, right-to-left languages only 10MB.) Click OK both in the confirmation box and in the Regional and Language Options dialog box.

4. Windows installs the necessary files. This takes a few seconds and you might need to insert your Windows XP CD-ROM. When all the files have been installed, a new confirmation box appears, asking whether you want to restart your computer. Click Yes.

5. After the computer restarts, the added languages will appear in the drop-down list on the Add Input Language box. From there you can add them to the Default Input Language drop-down list on the Text Services And Input Languages dialog box, as described earlier in this section.

To delete a language or layout you no longer plan to use, select that language or layout from the Installed Services box on the Text Services And Input Languages dialog box and click the Remove button.

Switching Languages and Keyboard Layouts

If you install more than one language or keyboard layout on your computer, you can switch from one to another in several ways. If you switch very rarely, make the switch by choosing the language you want from the Default Input Language drop-down list on the Text Services And Input Languages dialog box. Click OK and restart your computer.

Using the Language Bar   A quick way to change languages or keyboard layouts is to use the Language bar. To display the Language bar on your desktop or a language icon on the taskbar, go to the Text Services And Input Languages dialog box (shown in Figure 12-2) and click the Language Bar button. When the Language Bar Settings dialog box appears check the Show the Language Bar On The Desktop check box.

The Language bar is a small toolbar that sits just above the taskbar or can be dragged (by its left edge) anywhere on the desktop. (The Language bar that comes with Office XP works similarly to the one in Windows XP.) The Language bar has two buttons: one showing the keyboard's current language and the other its current layout. To change either, click the corresponding button and make a new choice from the menu that appears. The keyboard changes instantly; you do not need to restart the computer.

At the far right end of the Language bar is a small button to minimize the Language bar. If you click it, the bar disappears and is replaced by a small language icon on the taskbar next to the clock. Click the icon to change languages or restore the Language bar.

Keyboard Shortcuts for Switching Languages   You can also set a key combination for switching among languages and keyboard layouts. Your options are LEFT ALT-SHIFT, CTRL-SHIFT, or none. To set up such a key combination click the Key Settings button on the Text Services And Input Languages dialog box (shown in Figure 12-2). The Advanced Key Settings dialog box appears.

To set up or change a key combination for switching between languages or keyboard layouts, find the switching action on the Action list and select it. Then click the Change Key Sequence button. Use the Change Key Sequence box that appears to set up the desired key sequence.

Determining Whether Handwriting and Speech Recognition Are Installed

Microsoft Office XP includes handwriting and speech recognition features that come preinstalled on some Windows XP systems, too. To use handwriting to communicate with your computer, you need a mouse, stylus, or other handwriting device. To use speech recognition, your computer needs a microphone.

Not all programs accept handwriting input, but Windows and Microsoft Office XP do. For handwriting and speech recognition to work, Windows needs to know what language you are writing. These features currently work with only a few languages (English, Simplified Chinese, Traditional Chinese, Japanese, and Korean), but more may be added later.

To check whether handwriting recognition is installed on your system, follow these steps:

1. Choose Start | Control Panel, choose the Date, Time, Language, And Regional Options category, and open Regional And Language Options. (If you don't use Control Panel's category view, choose Regional And Language Options directly from the Control Panel.)

2. In the Regional And Language Options dialog box, click the Languages tab and click Details. You see the Text Services And Input Languages dialog box shown in Figure 12-2 (earlier in this chapter). The Installed Services box shows your installed languages and keyboards.

3. Click Add to display the Add Input Languages dialog box. If it includes Handwriting Recognition as an option, then this feature is enabled. Otherwise, you need to install it.

To determine whether your system has speech recognition enabled, look at the Language bar to see whether the Dictation or Voice Command settings appear.

If you don't have Microsoft Office XP, you can't install handwriting or speech recognition. If you have the Microsoft Office XP installation CD, install from the Office advanced Features | Alternative User Input category.

Note   *Windows XP comes with Microsoft Narrator, a rudimentary text-to-speech (TTS) translation system (see Chapter 16, section "Listening to Microsoft Narrator Read the Screen Out Loud").*

Configuring Your Mouse

You can control what the mouse buttons do and how fast the mouse pointer moves on the screen. You can define the shape of the mouse pointer, but not the cursor (the blinking element that shows where what you type will be inserted).

You can also choose the shape the mouse pointer assumes when used for pointing, when Windows is busy (the hourglass), when you are typing, when selecting text, when clicking a web link, when dragging window borders, and other functions. If you choose shapes other than the Windows default shapes, you can save the set of shapes you like to use as a *pointer scheme*. Windows comes with more than a dozen predefined pointer schemes from which you can choose. If you have a wheel mouse, you can also reset how the wheel works. These mouse settings are controlled from the Mouse Properties

The WINDOWS Key

Most new computer keyboards include a WINDOWS key, with the flying Windows logo on it. It's usually among the keys to the left of the SPACEBAR. The most convenient use of the WINDOWS key is to display the Start menu, but you can use the Windows key like a SHIFT key in combination with other keys. Here are the WINDOWS key combinations that work in Windows XP:

Key Combination	Action
WINDOWS	Opens or closes the Start menu.
WINDOWS-BREAK	Displays the System Properties dialog box.
WINDOWS-TAB	Makes the next application in the taskbar into the active window.
WINDOWS-SHIFT-TAB	Makes the previous application in the taskbar into the active window.
WINDOWS-B	Makes the notification area active.
WINDOWS-D	Shows the desktop (minimizes all windows).
WINDOWS-E	Opens Windows Explorer showing My Computer (like Start | My Computer).
WINDOWS-F	Opens Windows Explorer with the Search Explorer bar.
WINDOWS-CTRL-F	Opens Windows Explorer with the Search Explorer bar and with Search For Computers selected.
WINDOWS-F1	Opens Help.
WINDOWS-M	Minimizes all windows.
WINDOWS-SHIFT-M	Undoes minimize all windows.
WINDOWS-R	Opens Run dialog box (like Start | Run).
WINDOWS-U	Opens the Utility Manager for accessibility features (see Chapter 16, section "Turning On and Off Magnifier, Narrator, and the On-Screen Keyboard by Using the Utility Manager").
WINDOWS-L	Locks the computer, with the option to switch to another user (see Chapter 6).

dialog box, shown in Figure 12-3. Open this dialog box by clicking the mouse icon in the Printers And Other Hardware category of the Control Panel.

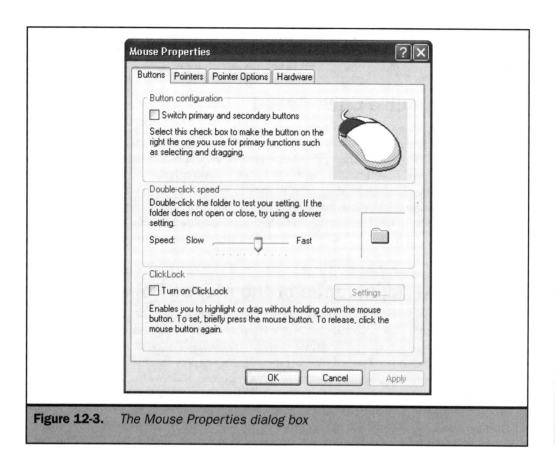

Figure 12-3. *The Mouse Properties dialog box*

You can further customize your mouse in two ways:

■ The TweakUI program gives you additional mouse settings: You can change the way Windows detects a mouse hover, or activate windows by moving the mouse into them (see Chapter 1, section "Using TweakUI to Change the Windows Interface").

■ Additional mouse settings are available if you have trouble using your mouse (see Chapter 16, section "Configuration Settings for the Mouse and Alternative Input Devices"). You might also consider installing a trackball or other pointing device.

Defining the Mouse Buttons

If you are left-handed, you may find it convenient to reverse the meanings of the two mouse buttons. In the Mouse Properties dialog box, click the Buttons tab and check the

Switch Primary And Secondary Buttons check box. To return to the default (right-handed) button configuration, uncheck the check box. Click OK to close the Mouse Properties dialog box and implement your changes.

Defining Your Double-Click Speed

Windows defines a double-click as two clicks within a specified time period, with no mouse motion during that period. That time period is called the *double-click speed*, and you can adjust it using the Double Click Speed slider on the Buttons tab of the Mouse Properties dialog box. If you have trouble clicking fast enough for Windows to realize you want to double-click, move the slider in the Slower direction. On the other hand, if you find two single clicks often get interpreted as a double-click, move the slider in the Faster direction. To test the setting, double-click the folder icon in the Double Click Speed box. If you can make the folder open and close, Windows is recognizing your double-clicks.

Configuring the Appearance of the Mouse Pointer

The mouse pointer changes shape depending on the context. For example, it appears as an arrow when you are selecting items, or as an *I* when you are editing text. You can choose the shape your mouse pointer assumes. In the Mouse Properties dialog box, click the Pointers tab to display a list of the current pointer shapes. To choose a different set of pointer shapes (mouse pointer scheme), choose a pointer scheme from the drop-down list. The pointers in the scheme are then shown in the Customize box.

You can mix-and-match to assemble your own pointer scheme. Click an item in the Customize box and click the Browse button. A browse window appears to show you the pointers in the folder C:\Windows\Cursors (if Windows is installed in C:\Windows). This folder contains two types of pointers: static cursors (with the extension .cur) and animated cursors (with the extension .ani). You can choose to display just one or the other in the browse window by selecting the corresponding file type in the Files Of Type drop-down list. Find the pointer you want and click the Open button.

If you want to go back to the default pointer for an item, click the item in the Customize box and click the Use Default button. When you have things the way you want them, click the Save As button and give your new pointer scheme a name.

 Installing a desktop theme is another way to change all your pointers (see Chapter 11, section "Choosing a Desktop Theme").

Improving Pointer Visibility

If you have trouble following the mouse pointer when it moves, you can give the pointer a *trail*. Trails are useful on laptops and other displays that redraw the screen slowly. To turn the pointer trail on or off and to set the length of the trail, click the Pointer Options tab of the Mouse Properties dialog box. Click the Show Pointer Trails check box to turn the trail on or off, and drag the Pointer Trail slider to the length you want. Click Apply or OK to implement your changes

If you have trouble finding the pointer, check the Show Location Of The Pointer When I Press The CTRL Key check box on the Pointer Options tab and click Apply or OK. When this box is checked, pressing the CTRL key causes Windows to draw a big circle around the pointer and then zero in on it with ever smaller circles.

Setting the Mouse Speed

You can adjust how far the mouse pointer moves when you move the mouse. For example, if you move the mouse in a small area of your desk, you can adjust Windows to make the mouse very sensitive, so moving the mouse one inch (2.5 cm) moves the pointer halfway across the screen. If you have shaky hands, you can make the mouse less sensitive, so small motions of the mouse result in small motions of the pointer.

On the Mouse Properties dialog box, click the Pointer Options tab and drag the Pointer Speed slider to adjust the mouse speed. To try out the new setting, click the Apply button.

 If your mouse or trackball is unresponsive, it may require a low-tech solution like cleaning. Pop the ball out and look for accumulations of dust on the contacts or the ball itself.

Setting ClickLock

ClickLock is a feature that allows you to drag objects without holding down the mouse button. To enable ClickLock, check the Turn On ClickLock check box on the Buttons tab of the Mouse Properties dialog box. After ClickLock is enabled, when you hold the mouse button down for a short time it "locks," and you can drag the selected object without continuing to hold the mouse button down.

You can adjust the length of time that you must hold the mouse button down before it locks. To make this adjustment, click the Settings button on the Buttons tab of the Mouse Properties dialog box. When the Settings For ClickLock box appears, adjust the lock time by moving the slider. Click OK to implement your changes.

Settings for Wheel Mice

A mouse that has a wheel between its buttons is called a *wheel mouse*. Turning the wheel scrolls through windows.

Your Mouse Properties dialog box has a Wheel tab, shown in Figure 12-4 to let you change how fast the wheel scrolls. You can set the wheel so that one notch on the wheel scrolls a set number of lines by clicking the The Following Number Of Lines At A Time setting and entering a number into the box underneath.

You can also click the One Screen At A Time radio button to cause the wheel to scroll down by screens rather than lines.

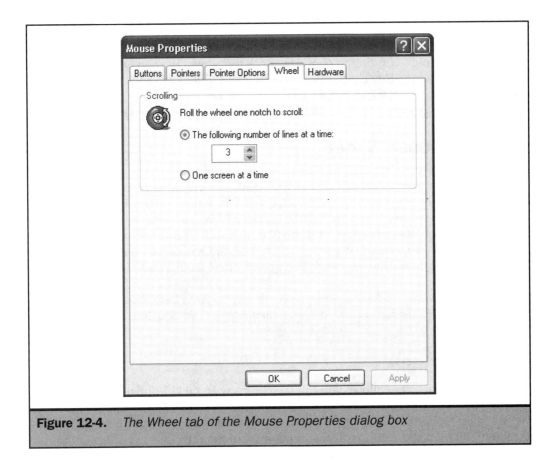

Figure 12-4.   *The Wheel tab of the Mouse Properties dialog box*

The TweakUI program gives you the option of turning off the wheel entirely. Expand the Mouse entry on left side of the TweakUI window and click Wheel. Now uncheck the Use Mouse Wheel For Scrolling check box.

Mouse Tweaks

The TweakUI PowerToy lets you make additional changes to the way your mouse works (see Chapter 1, section "Using TweakUI to Change the Windows Interface").

Changing the Hover Time and Sensitivity

A *mouse hover* occurs whenever the mouse pointer stays in a small region for a period of time. Mouse hovers effect the display of tool tips and (if you have Windows set to open files with a single click) hovers are used to select objects. TweakUI lets you change the size of the hover region and the length of time the mouse must stay there.

To make these changes, expand the Mouse entry on the left side of the TweakUI window and select Hover. Change the size of the hover region by entering a number of pixels in the Hover Sensitivity box. Change the hover time by entering a number of milliseconds in the Hover Time (ms) box.

Changing Window Activation

In Windows' default settings, you make a window active by clicking in it. You can change this behavior so that a window becomes active whenever you move the mouse into it. (This style matches the UNIX-based X Window system.)

To make this change, open TweakUI and expand the Mouse entry on the left side of the TweakUI window. Click X-Mouse and check the Activation Follows Mouse check box. You will probably also want to check the Autoraise When Activating check box, which causes the active window to rise above other windows that may have been covering it.

*If you check the Autoraise When Activating box, be sure to enter a number (try **500**) into the Activation Delay box. Otherwise, any window that the mouse pointer crosses rises immediately to the top, perhaps covering completely the window you want to be active.*

Configuring Your Game Controller

Game controllers and *joysticks* are devices that enable you to play arcade-style games on your computer.

To install a game controller, follow the instructions that come with it. Usually, you shut down Windows, turn off the computer, plug the game controller or joystick into the game port on your computer, and turn on your computer again. Windows should recognize the new device and install it. Have the floppy disk or CD-ROM that came with the game controller handy, and insert it when Windows is looking for the driver. If you've downloaded a driver, tell Windows where the driver file is stored (see Chapter 13).

To find out whether Windows has recognized your game controller or to change the settings for a game controller, look at the Game Controllers dialog box, shown in Figure 12-5. To see this dialog box, open the Game Controllers icon from the Printers And Other Hardware category of the Control Panel.

If no devices are listed in the Installed Game Controllers box, Windows didn't recognize your game controller. Click the Add button in the Game Controllers dialog box to see the Add Game Controller dialog box, shown in Figure 12-6. Select the line in the Game Controllers list that best describes your game controller and click OK.

If none of the descriptions on the Game Controllers list fit your game controller, click the Custom button on the Add Game Controller dialog box. Fill out the form on the Custom Game Controller dialog box to generate your own description.

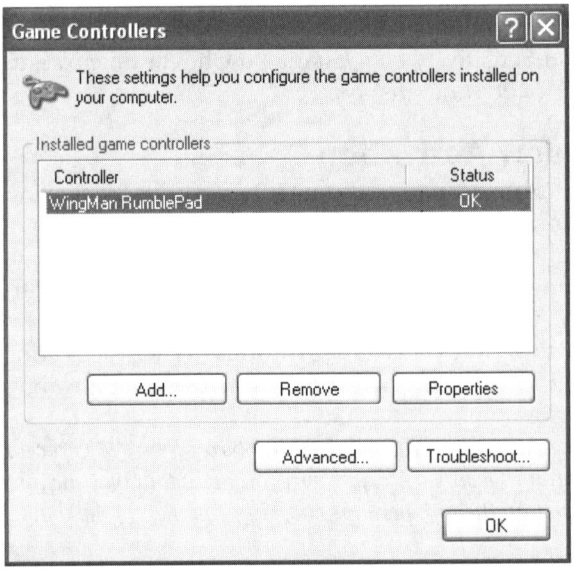

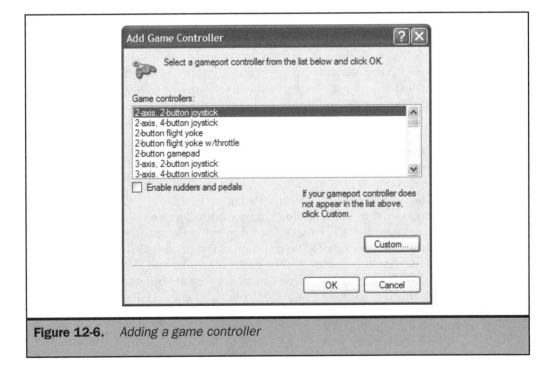

Figure 12-5. *The Game Controllers dialog box with a game controller installed*

Figure 12-6. *Adding a game controller*

Displaying and Changing Game Controller Settings

To see the settings for your game controller, select it from the list in the Game Controllers dialog box and click Properties. You see the game controller's Properties dialog box, shown in Figure 12-7. The dialog box for your game controller looks different if it has a different layout of buttons and other controls.

One computer can have several game controllers attached. Each controller has an ID number, starting with 1. You can see and change the controller ID numbers by clicking the Advanced button in the Games Controllers dialog box.

Testing Your Game Controller

To test your game controller, select it from the list in the Game Controllers dialog box, click Properties, and click the Test tab in the game controller's Properties dialog box (see Figure 12-7). Move the joystick or yoke and see whether the crosshairs in the Axes box move. Click the buttons on the game controller and see whether the button indicators light up. If not, calibrate the game controller by clicking the Settings tab, clicking the Calibrate button, and following the instructions.

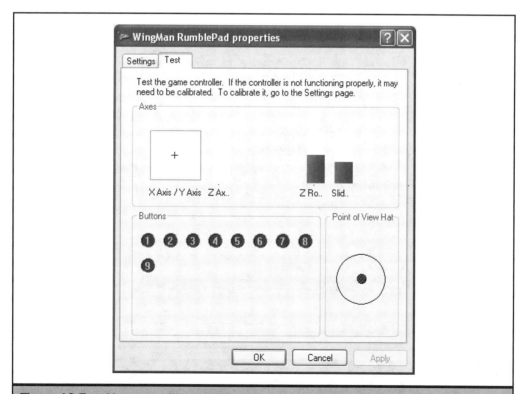

Figure 12-7. *You can calibrate and test your game controller from its Properties dialog box.*

Windows' Regional Settings

Windows comes with predefined regional settings for most of the countries in the world. *Regional settings* affect the format of numbers, currency, dates, and times. For example, if you choose the regional settings for Germany, Windows knows to display numbers with dots between the thousands and a comma as the decimal point, to use Deutsch marks as the currency, and to display dates with the day preceding the month.

Note *To reset your keyboard for other languages, see "Changing Language Properties" earlier in this chapter.*

To see or change your regional settings, look in the Regional And Language Options dialog box, shown in Figure 12-8. To display this box, open the Regional And Language

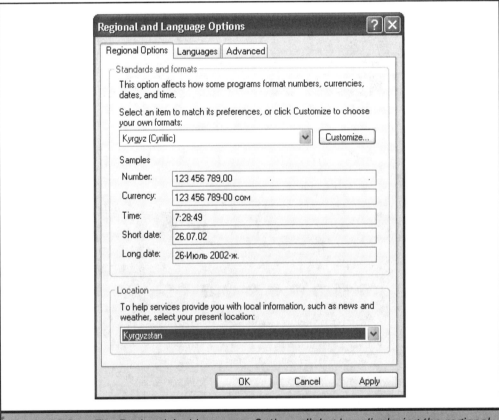

Figure 12-8. *The Regional And Language Options dialog box displaying the regional settings for Kyrgyzstan*

Options icon from the Date, Time, Language, And Regional Options category of the Control Panel.

Telling Windows Where You Live

Windows has predefined sets of regional settings, so you needn't select numeric, currency, date, and time formats separately. Choose the language you speak and the country where you live from the drop-down list in the Standards And Formats box on the Region Options tab of the Regional And Language Options dialog box. The list is arranged alphabetically by language, with the country in parentheses. There are, for example, 13 English entries, including English (Belize) and English (South Africa).

Setting Number, Currency, Time, and Date Formats

After you tell Windows which language you speak and where you live, it displays sample numbers, currency symbols, times, and dates on the Region Options tab of the Regional And Language Options dialog box. You will probably be happy with the way these samples are formatted. If not, you can change any of these items individually by clicking the Customize button. When the Customize Regional Options dialog box appears, click the Numbers, Currency, Time, or Date tab to see the corresponding settings. To change any of these settings, make another selection from the corresponding drop-down list and click the Apply or OK button.

Setting the Current Date and Time

Windows is good at keeping its clock and calendar correct. It knows about U.S. daylight saving time and leap years, but depending on where you live and the accuracy of your computer's internal clock, you might occasionally need to reset Windows' clock or calendar.

To display the Date And Time Properties dialog box, shown in Figure 12-9, double-click the time on the taskbar (usually displayed at the right end of the taskbar), or you can open the Date And Time icon from the Date Time And Language category of the Control Panel. You can set the date, time, and time zone.

If you want Windows to adjust the clock an hour for daylight saving time in the spring and fall, select the Automatically Adjust Clock For Daylight Saving Changes check box at the bottom of the window, so a check appears in the box.

Alternatively, Windows can update the time itself by synchronizing its clock with an Internet-based *time server*. (This feature is turned on by default.) To change this setting, click the Internet Time tab on the Date And Time Properties dialog box. The Automatically Synchronize With An Internet Time Server check box turns the feature on and off, and the Server box determines which time server you contact (the default is Microsoft's server at **time.windows.com**). Windows checks in with the time server every week and updates its clock.

Figure 12-9.   *The Date And Time Properties dialog box.*

Synchronization may fail for any of the following reasons:

- Your computer is not turned on and connected to the Internet at the proper time. You can request synchronization immediately by clicking the Update Now button on the Internet Time tab of the Date And Time dialog box.
- Your computer's firewall is blocking the synchronization request. (The firewall built into Windows XP doesn't block it.)
- The date is set incorrectly.

If you find Windows resetting your clock to the wrong hour, check that the time zone is set correctly.

Chapter 13

Adding and Removing Hardware

Windows XP lets you add new hardware to your computer relatively easily, but you still have a lot of details to get right. For a glossary of hardware terms, see this book's web site at net.gurus.com/winxphometer.

Plug and Play (PnP) is a feature of Windows and most modern hardware that allows Windows to configure itself automatically when the hardware is installed. Windows 95 was the first version of Windows to include Plug and Play, and Microsoft has been improving the feature with each new version. If your hardware is Plug and Play, Windows notices when you install a new device and tries to install and configure a driver for the hardware automatically.

This chapter describes the general steps for installing hardware, Plug and Play, the Device Manager, the types of hardware you may want to install, how to configure Windows to work with new hardware, troubleshooting hardware, and adding memory.

Before adding new hardware, make a backup of your important files, in case you can't restart your computer (see Chapter 9).

Managing Your Hardware Components with the Device Manager

To see a list of your computer's hardware, you use the *Device Manager* window, shown in Figure 13-1. The Device Manager lists all the devices that make up your computer and lets you see and modify their configuration. If the Add New Hardware Wizard detects a device conflict, it starts the Device Manager automatically.

To see the Device Manager, choose Start | Control Panel, click Performance And Maintenance, click the System icon, select the Hardware tab, and click the Device Manager button. (If you use Control Panel in Classic View, double-click the System icon.) You can view devices by type or by connection; by connection is usually better for driver debugging, since it displays each connected device separately. If hardware is having trouble, Windows displays the devices listed by type, with the type of the problematic device expanded.

Universal Plug and Play

Universal Plug and Play (UPnP), despite its name, has nothing to do with Plug and Play hardware. Instead, it is a set of networking software conventions that let computers and other devices on a network discover and control each other. If you have several Windows XP machines networked together, each machine automatically knows about all the printers attached to all the other machines, due to UPnP. In the future, Microsoft expects to use UPnP to control smart televisions and other appliances.

In the meantime, be sure to apply any critical or security updates related to UPnP, since a malicious or compromised device could use UPnP to attack all the XP systems on your network.

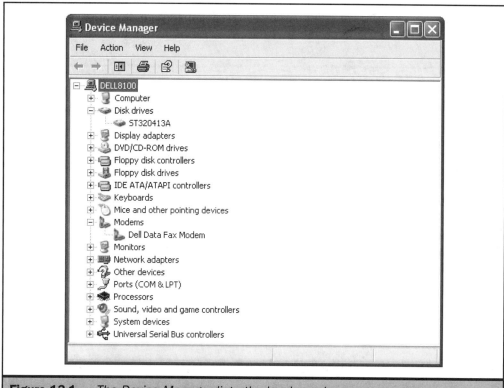

Figure 13-1.   *The Device Manager lists the hardware in your computer.*

Another way to see the Device Manager is within the Microsoft Management Console. Click Start, right-click My Computer, and choose Manage from the shortcut menu to see the Microsoft Management Console, which is described in Chapter 2. Then click Device Manager in the left pane of the window.

If you *really* plan on using the Device Manager often, you can create a shortcut to it on your desktop:

1. Right-click a blank place on your Windows desktop and choose New | Shortcut.

2. For the location of the item, type **C:\Windows\System32\Devmgmt.msc** (replacing C:\Windows with your Windows system folder) and click Next.

3. For the shortcut name, type **Device Manager** and click Finish.

4. You can move or copy this shortcut onto the Start menu: to add it to the left side of the Start menu, right-click the shortcut you just created and choose Pin To Start Menu.

Keep a logbook for your computer listing all the cards installed in your computer and the hardware parameters you've set on them. This makes troubleshooting a lot easier.

Types of Hardware

IBM-compatible computers, having evolved for over 20 years, offer many, often complicated, ways to attach new kinds of equipment. The details of PC hardware are beyond the scope of this book, but this section describes the basics of PC hardware that you need to know to get a recalcitrant Windows driver installed, including older types of PC components, in case you are upgrading an older computer. See Chapter 33 for more information about configuring hard disks. Chapter 11 describes how to configure your display, and Chapter 14 talks about how to print once you've installed a printer.

 *Windows XP can run on most PCs made in recent years either as is or with inexpensive upgrades, so long as the computer runs at 300 MHz or faster and has at least 128MB of RAM and 5GB of disk. See the Microsoft Windows Hardware Quality Labs (HCL) web site at **www.microsoft.com/hcl** to find out whether your hardware has been approved by Microsoft for use with Windows XP. Lots of hardware that Microsoft hasn't gotten around to testing also works, either because it's compatible with supported hardware or the vendor provides drivers.*

Integrated Versus Separate Peripherals

The original IBM Personal Computer contained nothing built into the computer beyond the *central processing unit* (*CPU*), memory, and keyboard. Everything else, including screens, floppy disk drives, hard disk drives, printers, modems, and serial ports, was provided by separate extra-cost add-in cards. (Hardware you add to your computer, other than processors and memory, is called a *peripheral*.) Over the years, manufacturers have found that, as the functions of the computer were combined into fewer and fewer chips, it became cheaper to build the most common peripherals into the computer's *motherboard*, *mainboard*, or *system board*, the printed circuit board that carries the CPU and memory. Modern computers typically include a parallel port, one or two serial ports, two PS/2 ports for keyboard and mouse, two Universal Serial Bus (USB) ports, controllers for up to two floppy disk drives and four IDE (Integrated Device Electronics) devices (hard drives, CD-ROM drives, CD-R drives, or DVD drives) on the motherboard, and often an Ethernet, 56K modem, and sound and video adapters as well. Windows usually can't tell whether these items are built-in or on separate cards, so Windows treats them all as though they are separate peripherals.

Connectors

The back of your PC is bristling with connectors for various sorts of devices (see Figure 13-2). If your computer has internal *expansion slots* holding adapter cards, each adapter card may have a connector or two, as well. Connectors to which you attach cables are also called *ports*. Most likely, the user's manual for your computer has a similar picture showing and labeling the connectors on your computer.

Serial (Com) Ports

Most PCs have one or two *serial ports*, which are D-shaped connectors with 9 or 25 pins (sometimes referred to as *DB-9* and *DB-25*):

Serial ports are used for serial external modems, serial mice, computer-to-computer cabling for "poor man's networking," and occasionally for printers. If you have a UPS (uninterruptible power supply), a cable may run from the UPS to the PC's serial port so that Windows can monitor the UPS, and knows to shut down when the power has failed and the UPS battery is almost dead.

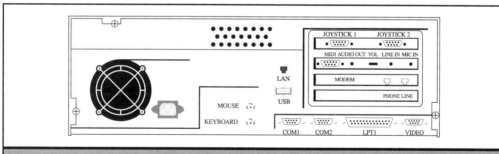

Figure 13-2.   *Connectors on the back of your computer*

Parallel Ports

Most PCs have a *parallel port*, a D-shaped socket with holes for 25 pins. Parallel ports are used for printers, and sometimes for other devices such as removable disk drives (such as ZIP drives).

 The 25-pin serial port is mechanically identical to the parallel port, except that the serial port is "male" and the parallel port is "female." Despite the similar connectors, you can't plug a device intended for one port into the other port.

Parallel ports can communicate unidirectionally (for sending information to a printer) or bi-directionally (for smart printers that send information back to the computer, as well as for devices that we think should never be connected to a parallel port in the first place, like ZIP drives and scanners). There are two bi-directional standards: ECP (Enhanced Capability Port, used mainly by printers and scanners) and EPP (Enhanced Parallel Port, used mainly by devices other than printers). When you look at your parallel devices in Device Manager, by clicking Ports (COM & LPT), Windows shows what kind of communication each parallel port uses.

 You set the communications standard for your parallel port in the BIOS setup for your computer. If you run into trouble connecting a device (especially one that requires bi-directional information), check your computer's manual for how to configure the parallel port.

Universal Serial Bus (USB)

The *USB* (*universal serial bus*) is a relatively new connector introduced in the late 1990s. It is a faster and simpler alternative to serial and parallel ports, as well as for low- to moderate-speed devices such as modems, printers, sound cards, networks, and backup tapes. Most new computers come with at least two.

USB lets you connect a *USB hub* to your USB port, so you can have a desk full of USB devices attached to the port. You can also *hot swap* USB devices—you don't have to turn off the computer, just plug the device in and turn it on.

USB printers and scanners are popular, and USB network adapters are a hit with high-speed Internet access installers (unlike network interface cards, USB network adapters don't require the installer to open up the computer).

If the device you are attaching has never been connected to the computer before, Windows will likely need to install a driver for it. The vast majority of drivers for Windows XP can be used without restarting the computer, thanks in no small part to XP's Windows 2000 heritage.

PS/2 (Keyboard and Mouse Ports)

All PCs new enough to run Windows XP either have two *PS/2 connectors*, for a keyboard and a mouse shown next, or they use USB.

The keyboard and mouse ports are identical—look at the little icons next to the connectors to determine which is which. Nothing terrible will happen if you plug a mouse into the keyboard port, or vice versa—Windows usually complains that it can't find your keyboard or mouse. On recent computers, the mouse connector is green, and the keyboard connector is blue or purple.

Display Ports

Display adapters (or video cards), into which you plug your monitor, all use a 15-pin (*DB-15*) connector that is similar in size to the 9-pin serial connector.

Display adapters are identified by acronyms like SVGA, XGA, Super VGA, and Ultra XGA, depending on their maximum resolution. All monitors made in recent years are compatible with almost all display adapters, at least at common resolutions. Common resolutions are 800 × 600 (the minimum required for Windows XP), 1024 × 768, 1400 × 1050, and 1600 × 1200.

The video display adapters that are built into new computers can support lots of colors beyond the original 256 colors (also known as 8-bit color); most can display 16-bit High Color, 24-bit True Color, and 32-bit True Color.

*Windows CE for Smart Displays (code-named "Mira" during development) is a display that can detach from the computer and be used separately. See **www.microsoft.com/ windowsxp/smartdisplay** for more information.*

Network Ports

Some PCs come with a built-in network adapter to enable the computer to connect to a local area network, DSL modem, or cable modem. Modern network adapters have *RJ-45* jacks that look like phone jacks, only larger. Old network adapters may have round coaxial cable connectors. See Chapter 29 for how to connect your computer to a network. See the "Installing Modems" section later in this chapter for more about installing DSL and cable modems.

Telephone Plugs

A *modem* connects your computer to a phone line. If you have a dial-up (analog) modem (the kind of modem that connects to a normal, old-fashioned phone line) the modem has one or two *RJ-11* telephone plugs that are identical to the plugs on the back of a U.S. telephone. (If you are outside the U.S., your modem should have come with adapters for your local phone plugs.) If there are two plugs, one is for the incoming phone line plugged into the wall, and the other is for a phone that shares the line with the modem. (The advantage to plugging the phone in via the modem is that you won't disconnect your modem call if you pick up the phone by mistake.) See "Installing Modems" later in this chapter for other types of modems.

FireWire

Some computers also have *FireWire* ports, also known as *IEEE 1394* or Sony *i.Link*. They are faster than USB ports and are typically used for digital video cameras, hard disk drives, and high-speed printers. FireWire was first developed by Apple for its Macintosh computers, but is now available on many Windows-compatible PCs, too.

FireWire cables are limited to about 15 feet in length. FireWire, like USB, can be hot-swapped—connected and disconnected—while the computer is running. FireWire is efficient, self-powered, flexible, and fast.

 Your FireWire port appears in the Network Connections window as a LAN port—choose Start | Control Panel, click Network And Internet Connections, and click Network Connections to see it.

Audio and Video Jacks

Most PCs have connectors for speakers or headphones, and sometimes a microphone. The speaker connector is a standard 1/8-inch stereo mini-audio jack. The microphone connector is usually also a mini-audio jack, so you have to be careful not to confuse the two. (Otherwise, your sound may play sdrawkcab. Well, not really.)

If your computer doesn't have speaker connectors, you can add an internal sound board. Many CD-ROM drives have headphone jacks so you can listen to audio CDs, even if your computer has no speakers.

Newer computers may have a digital audio jack (*S/PDIF* or Sony/Philips Digital Interface jack) to which you can connect digital audio equipment, like a DAT (digital audio tape) machine. Most S/PDIF ports accept standard RCA connectors, the same connector used for regular audio jacks.

 If you plan to use your TV to display information from your computer, check whether your PC has a TV jack or S-video jack, to which you can connect a television. Alternatively, your PC may come with a video card that includes a TV In plug so you can watch TV on your computer monitor. These video cards may include software for picture-in-picture (so that your TV picture appears in a window) and for capturing graphics from the video.

PC Cards

All laptop computers and a few desktop computers have one or two *PC card* slots (formerly known as *PCMCIA* slots). These take credit-card–sized adapter cards of many varieties, including modems, networks, and disk and tape controllers. PC cards can be hot-swapped, added or removed while your computer is running. To add a PC card, press it firmly into the slot until it seats. To remove a PC card, press the button next to the PC card to eject the card slightly and then pull out the card.

Before removing a PC card, you should first tell Windows, so that it can stop sending data to, or receiving data from, the card. When you have a PC card inserted, an icon for it may appear in the notification area of the taskbar. If so, click or double-click it to find a command to advise Windows that the card is about to depart.

Internal Adapter Cards

If you add a device to your computer that can't be plugged into one of the existing connectors on your computer, you have to add an *adapter card* that plugs into a slot inside the computer. As the PC has evolved over the past 20 years, the slots into which you can plug adapter cards have evolved as well.

PCI Cards

PCI (Peripheral Connect Interface) slots enable you to expand the capabilities of your computer by installing PCI adapter cards inside the computer. To install a PCI card, you need to turn off the computer, take off the cover, slide the PCI card into the slot, screw it down, replace the cover, and turn the computer back on. PCI cards include display adapters (for connecting to monitors), sound cards (for connecting to speakers), network adapter cards (for LAN and high-speed Internet connections), disk drive adapters (for connecting hard disks, CD-ROM drives, and floppy drives), and SCSI adapters (for connecting a wide variety of peripherals).

 Some older PCs have ISA (Industry Standard Architecture) slots, a predecessor of PCI. ISA cards are harder to install than PCI, because they are not self-configuring. You generally have to set jumpers on an ISA card to set its hardware parameters and then tell Windows what those parameters are when you install the card.

AGP Cards

AGP (Accelerated Graphics Port) slots are specialized slots for video cards, enabling faster screen updates. Most motherboards have a single AGP slot if the motherboard doesn't have a built-in video controller. Most video cards need an AGP slot, but some cheaper ones plug into regular PCI slots instead.

Other Kinds of Cards

Most computers have a few specialized slots and connectors for specific devices. There are usually two to four small slots for memory and a connector or two for IDE or EIDE expansion disks (see "Disk Controllers: IDE, EIDE, and SCSI Devices" later in this chapter). Your computer's manual should list the available slots and connectors.

Hardware Parameters

Every internal adapter card in your PC needs a variety of hardware parameters to be set so that the CPU can communicate with the card without interfering with other cards. Usually, these parameters are set automatically by Windows' Plug and Play feature, but ISA cards and a few early PCI cards require manual tweaking.

To see a list of your computer's hardware, you use the Device Manager window (see "Managing Your Hardware Components with the Device Manager" earlier in this chapter). Choose Start | Control Panel, click Performance And Maintenance, click the System icon, select the Hardware tab, and click the Device Manager button to see the Device Manager window (shown in Figure 13-1 earlier in this chapter). To see listings of the interrupts (IRQs), I/O addresses, DMA channels, and memory addresses, choose View | Resources By Type and click the plus box to the left of each item.

I/O Addresses

Every device attached to a PC has at least one *I/O address*, a hexadecimal number that the CPU uses to communicate with the device. All I/O addresses on a given computer must be unique; address "collisions" are the most common reason that a new I/O device doesn't work. A device's I/O address appears on the Resources tab of its Properties dialog box (right-click the device in the Device Manager window and choose Properties from the menu that appears, then click the Resources tab).

Devices on the motherboard have I/O addresses that either are permanently assigned or can be changed in the setup menus built into your motherboard (see the documentation that came with your computer). ISA cards have addresses set by moving jumpers on the card, while PCI cards have addresses that are set by software when you start your computer.

All traditional PC devices have well-known fixed addresses. These include up to four serial ports, a parallel port, floppy and hard disk controllers, and internal devices such as the clock and keyboard controller. Other add-in devices have more-or-less fixed addresses, depending on how popular the device is and how long it's been around.

See the troubleshooting section later in this chapter for advice on getting I/O addresses unscrambled.

 AGP, the Accelerated Graphics Port technology from Intel, is a derivative of PCI. AGP video cards appear in the hardware list as device 1 of PCI Bus 0. This is normal, despite the name AGP.

Interrupts (IRQs)

The PC architecture provides 15 *interrupts* or *IRQs* (interrupt requests), channels that a device can use to alert the CPU that the device needs attention. The interrupts are numbered 0, 1, and 3 through 15. (For historical reasons, interrupt 2 isn't available, and the few devices that used interrupt 2 on early PCs use interrupt 9 instead.) PCI devices all can, and usually do, share a single interrupt, but nearly every ISA device that uses an interrupt needs a separate unique interrupt number. The usual assignments are as follows:

Device	Interrupt
Motherboard devices	0 and 1
Built-in serial ports	3 and 4
Floppy disk	6
Parallel port	7
Clock	8
Built-in mouse	12
Floating-point unit	13 (even if you don't do any floating-point calculations)
Hard disk controller	15

Interrupts 5, 9, 10, 11, and 14 are usually available for other devices.

A device's IRQ appears on its Properties dialog box (right-click the device in the Device Manager window and choose Properties), on the Resources tab.

Assigning interrupts correctly on ISA cards is one of the most troublesome and error-prone aspects of hardware configuration. A few ISA cards can have their interrupt number set in software, in which case Windows sets the interrupt automatically, but most have jumpers you have to change. If you use ISA cards, use your motherboard's boot-time setup menu to mark the interrupt number(s) that the ISA cards use so the BIOS won't try to use those interrupts for PCI.

DMA Channels

DMA, which stands for *direct memory access*, is a motherboard facility used by a few medium-speed devices. There are six DMA channels, of which the floppy disk always takes DMA 2. Some ISA sound cards need a DMA channel, usually DMA 1. You set the DMA channel in the Properties dialog box for the device, on the Resources tab.

Memory Addresses

Each byte of memory in your computer has a unique *memory address*. A few devices, notably screen controllers and some network cards, use a shared memory region to transfer data between the CPU and the device. Those devices need a range of memory addresses for their shared memory. Screen cards generally use the ranges (expressed in hexadecimal numbers, or hex) 0xA0000 through 0xAFFFF, 0xB0000 through 0xBFFFF, and sometimes 0xC0000 through 0xCFFFF. The range from the end of the screen controller's memory to about 0xE0000 is available for other devices. PCI (and AGP) cards always have their addresses set in software.

To see a screen adapter's memory address range, display its Properties dialog box and click the Resources tab

Disk Controllers: IDE, EIDE, and SCSI Devices

A *disk controller* is a PCI adapter card or built-in board to which you connect hard disks, CD-ROM drives, or tape drives. Disk controllers present an extra configuration challenge, because you can attach more than one device to a single controller. See Chapter 33 for more information about configuring hard disks.

IDE and EIDE Device Numbers

IDE (Integrated Device Electronics) and *EIDE* (Enhanced IDE, also known as *ATA 2*) disk controllers support up to two devices, the first of which is usually a hard disk, and the second of which can be either a hard disk or a CD-ROM drive. The controller has two connectors into which drive cables are plugged, and which device is which depends on which connector each is plugged into. The first device is called the *primary* device, and is the second the *secondary* device. When the position on the cable determines which device is primary and which is secondary, this is called *cable select* (*CS*). Jumpers on the devices can also determine which one is primary and which one is secondary, regardless of where they are plugged in.

Most motherboards contain two IDE or EIDE controllers, each of which can have a primary and a secondary device, for a system total of up to four devices.

SCSI Device Numbers

SCSI (Small Computer System Interface) is a widely used standard for connecting high-speed devices to computers. SCSI is popular in server computers for connecting disks and tapes, since it can be faster than EIDE. SCSI comes in several versions with names such as SCSI 2 and Ultra SCSI. Each time a new version was incompatible with older versions, the SCSI committee defined a different connector, so you can be reasonably sure that if the connectors on your SCSI controller, cable, and devices match, they'll work together.

Each SCSI controller can connect up to 7 devices for older controllers, or 15 devices for more recent controllers. To identify devices attached to one SCSI controller, each device has a device number from 0 to 7, or 15.

The SCSI controller itself has a device number, usually the highest possible number—7 or 15. The first disk is invariably device 0, but other numbers can be assigned arbitrarily, as long as each device has a separate number. A few devices have subunits, such as tape or CD-ROM jukebox drives that can contain several different tapes or disks.

Caution *Due to some extremely bad planning in the early 1980s, older external SCSI devices use connectors that are physically identical to the DB-25 and Centronics connectors used on modems and printers on parallel and serial ports. Even if they fit physically, don't try connecting a SCSI device to a non-SCSI controller, or vice versa, because it won't work, and you may well cause expensive damage to the electronics.*

Memory (RAM)

Memory, or *RAM* (*random access memory*), is the temporary storage your computer uses for the programs that you are running and the files you currently have open. Most PCs have from two to four memory slots, and usually the computer is shipped with one or two of the four slots already containing memory. Memory comes in many different sizes, speeds, and types, so you must ensure that the memory you add is compatible with your particular computer (see the section "Adding Memory" later in this chapter). Memory chips are extremely sensitive to static electricity, so be sure to understand and follow the procedures needed to avoid static damage. (Some memory ships with an antistatic wrist strap and instructions on how to use it.)

Hardware Drivers

Many hardware devices—whether they come as part of your computer or are added later—require a *driver* or *device driver*, a program that translates between your operating system (Windows) and the hardware. For example, a printer driver translates printing requests from Windows (and through it, your applications) to commands that your printer can understand.

Windows comes with standard drivers for a wide range of monitors, printers, modems, and other devices. When you buy hardware, you usually receive a floppy disk or CD-ROM that contains the driver for the device, which you need to install during the configuring process to get the device to work with Windows. For some devices, Windows already has a driver on the Windows XP CD-ROM, so you never need to insert the driver disk.

Getting Updated Drivers

Many manufacturers provide updated device drivers on their web sites. If your device came with a driver for an earlier version of Windows on CD, check the manufacturer's web site for a Windows XP driver. (If a device doesn't have drivers for Windows XP, try the Windows 2000 drivers. Don't use drivers for Windows 98 or earlier.) Downloaded drivers are usually provided as an executable program or a ZIP file. If it's an executable, run it, and the drivers should install themselves. If it's a ZIP file, right click on the file and selecting Extract All to extract the contents of the file into a Windows folder.

Displaying Driver Information

To see information about the driver for a device, display its Properties dialog box— from the Device Manager window, right-click a device and choose Properties from the menu that appears. If there is a Driver tab, click it. Most Driver tabs contain a Driver Details button (for a list of files that make up the driver), Update Driver button (for installing a new driver), Roll Back Driver button (for reinstalling a previous driver), and Uninstall (to uninstall the driver, leaving the device with no driver).

Signed and Unsigned Device Drivers

A device driver may be *signed* by Microsoft. The signature is a small file of cryptographic data that Windows can check both to be sure that the signature is genuine and that the version of driver you have is identical to the one that Microsoft signed. All of the drivers that Microsoft distributes are signed. Hardware vendors can pay Microsoft to test and (assuming the tests pass) sign their drivers. Signing a driver doesn't make it work any differently—it just means the driver has passed Microsoft's tests. Since preparing and submitting the testing materials can be time-consuming and expensive, some reputable device makers don't bother to do so.

When you install a driver for a new device, if the driver hasn't been signed, you will see a warning like this:

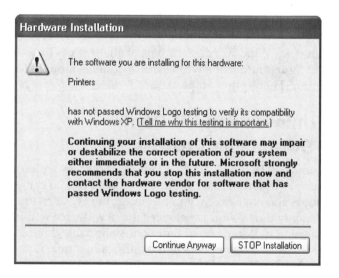

If the driver came on a CD with the device, or you downloaded it directly from the manufacturer's web site, click Continue Anyway to go ahead and install it. If you're unsure of the source of the driver, tell it to stop: you shouldn't be installing drivers of unknown origin in the first place.

Configuring Windows for New Hardware

Plug and Play helps Windows XP automatically detect and configure itself for a wider range of hardware devices. Follow these steps to install new hardware and configure Windows to use it (see the next section if you are installing a PC Card):

1. If the new device came with a CD, put the CD-ROM into the CD drive and see what happens. If an installation program starts, follow its instructions to install the drivers and other software that the new device needs.

2. Install your new hardware. This can involve opening up the computer and installing a card, inserting a card into a PC Card slot, or just plugging a new external device into a serial port, parallel port, SCSI adapter, USB port, or FireWire port. Follow the directions that come with the new hardware. (For PC Card, USB, and FireWire devices, you don't even have to turn off the computer before plugging them in.)

3. Turn on the device (if external), and turn on and start up your computer. Some devices have a BIOS setup routine that you have to enter when you turn on the computer and run one time to perform low-level configuration of your new device.

4. If you're lucky, Windows notices the new device as it starts and automatically configures it for you, displaying messages as it does so.

5. If you're less lucky, Windows just starts up. Run the Add New Hardware Wizard, described in the next section.

6. If you're unlucky, Windows doesn't start at all, or starts up in Safe Mode, and you have to figure out what's wrong (see "Troubleshooting Your Hardware Configuration" later in this chapter).

Installing and Uninstalling PC Cards and Other Hot-Swappable Devices

You can install or uninstall PC Card, USB, and FireWire devices without turning off your computer. For example, if you have a PC Card from your digital camera with memory containing the photos you have taken, you can insert the PC Card into the PC Card slot of your computer at any time. Windows notices the new device within a few seconds, and you can begin using it. When one or more hot-swappable devices are installed, a Safely Remove Hardware icon appears in the notification area of your taskbar.

Before you remove the device, though, you should tell Windows that you are going to do so. Click the Safely Remove Hardware icon on the taskbar to see a list of the devices you can remove. Choose the one you are about to remove. Alternatively, right-click the icon to display the Safely Remove Hardware dialog box, as shown in Figure 13-3. Choose a device and click the Stop button. If you want to see the properties of a PC Card, click the Properties button.

If a device doesn't appear in the Unplug Or Eject Hardware dialog box, don't disconnect it without first shutting down Windows and turning off your computer.

Using the Add Hardware Wizard

The Windows Add Hardware Wizard does a good job handling the details of installing new device drivers. After you've installed a new device, if Windows doesn't detect it, run the wizard by following these steps.

1. Choose Start | Control Panel, click Printers And Other Hardware, and click Add Hardware (it's under See Also in the Task pane to the left). The Add Hardware Wizard starts.

2. The first thing the wizard does after you click Next is search for new Plug and Play devices, devices that can provide with their own configuration information. Even if you know you don't have any new Plug and Play devices, you have to wait while Windows checks for them. If Windows finds the Plug and Play device you wanted to install and installed and configures it, you are done—click Finish.

3. If the wizard finds new devices (or old but unused devices), it shows you a list, as in Figure 13-4. If there are no new devices to be added, Windows asks whether you have already installed the new hardware. Assuming you have, click the Yes box and then Next to see a list of all installed hardware.

4. If one of the devices in the list is the one you want to install, check Yes, click the correct device, and then click Next.

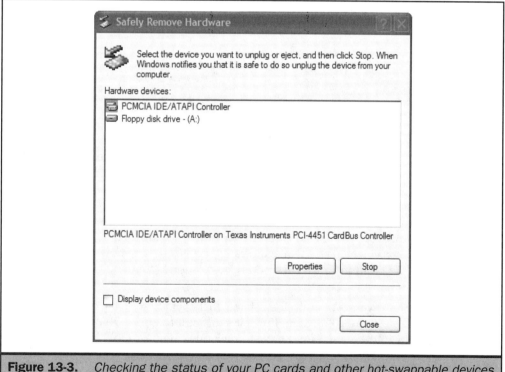

Figure 13-3. *Checking the status of your PC cards and other hot-swappable devices*

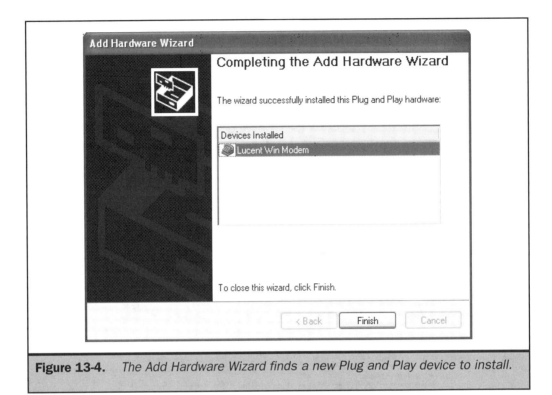

Figure 13-4.   *The Add Hardware Wizard finds a new Plug and Play device to install.*

5. Otherwise, click the Add A New Hardware Device item at the end of the list and click Next to proceed to the next screen. Windows then offers to search for non-Plug and Play devices, which it refers to as Other Hardware. Searching for non-Plug and Play is slower and riskier than searching for Plug and Play, and it sometimes crashes the computer. If you know what you just installed, you can select Install The Hardware That I Manually Select From A List (Advanced) and select the driver yourself. If you take the automated route, Windows attempts to find any new devices, which takes a while and rarely finds anything new. When it finishes, click the Next button to see a list of device categories that you can choose from (Figure 13-5).

6. Select the hardware type from the list and click Next to see a list of manufacturers and models (Figure 13-6). Sometimes it's difficult to guess which category a device falls into, so you might have to pick one category, look there, and then click Back and try another category or two before you find your device.

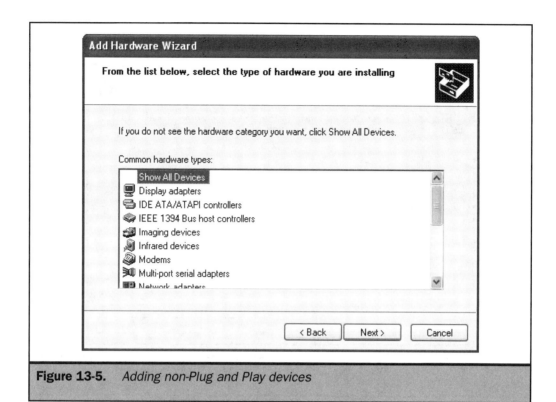

Figure 13-5.   *Adding non-Plug and Play devices*

7. Choose the manufacturer and the model of your device. If your device came with a driver on a floppy or CD-ROM and you want to use that driver, click Have Disk and tell Windows which drive contains the disk, which usually is drive A: (floppy) or D: (CD-ROM). If you downloaded a driver ZIP file from the manufacturer's web site, browse the folder of files you extracted from the driver ZIP file.

8. Click Next, and Windows finishes installing your device. You might have to insert your Windows XP CD-ROM if the device needs drivers that haven't been used before, and you might have to reboot Windows.

9. If you've installed a non-PNP device, Windows may not be able to figure out what the hardware parameters for the device are. If so, you have to set them yourself. Click View Or Change Resources For This Hardware to see the driver's Resources tab and then Set Configuration Manually to see a settings window. Double-click I/O range to set the I/O address and IRQ to set the IRQ. Once set, Windows usually offers to reboot to finish the driver installation.

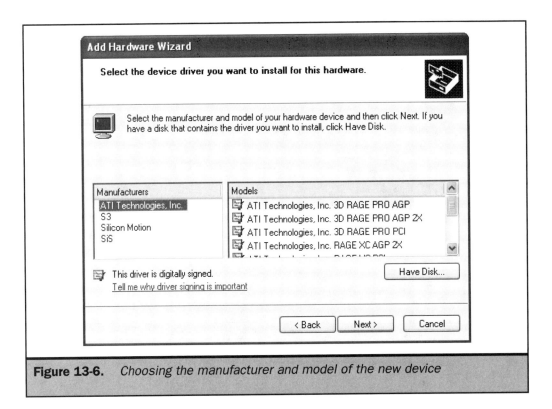

Figure 13-6.   *Choosing the manufacturer and model of the new device*

At this point, unless Windows has reported a configuration problem, your device should be ready to use.

Installing Modems

Originally, all modems connected to regular phone lines, but with the advent of high-speed Internet access, you may use one of three types of modems:

- **Dial-up modem**   Connects to normal voice-grade analog phone lines. Dial-up modems may be internal (adapter cards that install inside the computer) or external (boxes that connect to the serial port).

- **DSL modem**   Connects to a high-speed DSL phone line. DSL modems may be internal or external, and external DSL modems may connect either to a network adapter or to a USB port.

- **Cable modem**   Connects to a cable TV line. Cable modems connect to either a network adapter or a USB port in your computer.

> ## Windows Installation Glitch
>
> Windows installation files are stored in a compressed format in *CAB* or *cabinet files* (with extension .cab) on your Windows XP CD-ROM. When you install Windows, it may copy these CAB files to your hard disk, including standard hardware drivers.
>
> Sometimes, Windows can't find the component file that it is trying to install. When this happens, Windows says that it can't find the file where it is looking and asks for another location where the file might be. You need to find which CAB file Windows needs and tell it where to look for it.
>
> To find the missing file, click the Details button in the dialog box that appears and find the name of the CAB file that contains the file that Windows is looking for. Then search your hard disk (or your Windows XP CD-ROM) for this CAB by choosing Start | Search. For example, if Windows is looking for a file named Winsock.dll that is supposed to be in Net4.cab, search your hard disk or the CD for files with the filename *.cab. Then tell Windows to look in that folder for the CAB file.

Installing Dial-Up Modems

When Windows detects that you have installed a new dial-up modem (the kind you connect to a regular phone line), it runs the Install New Modem Wizard. You can run this wizard directly by opening the Phone And Modem Options icon in the Control Panel, select the Modem tab, and click Add.

If you haven't already set your location, Windows asks for the country and area code in which you are located, any digits you need to dial to get an outside line, and whether your telephone system uses tone or pulse dialing. Windows stores this information in your default dialing location (see Chapter 21).

The wizard offers to search for the modem, which you should let it do. The Install New Modem Wizard may call the Add Hardware Wizard described in the preceding section to find the modem, or you can choose the modem manufacturer and model from a menu.

Installing DSL and Cable Modems

DSL and cable modems are installed by telephone company or cable company installers. They usually connect to your computer's USB connector or network adapter. Once the equipment is in place, see sections "Connecting to a DSL Line" and "Connecting to a Cable Modem" in Chapter 21.

Troubleshooting Your Hardware Configuration

In a perfect world, every device installation would work the first time. In the real world, something goes wrong about one time in three, and you have to fix it. The most common problem is that an I/O device address or interrupt used by the new device conflicts with an older one (see "Hardware Parameters" earlier in this chapter).

Windows XP is smart when it comes to hardware, but it's not savvy about everything. Some older hardware may simply not work because neither Microsoft nor the hardware manufacturer have an updated driver for it. It's better to avoid potential conflicts when you install Windows by allowing the installation program to check system compatibility (see the Appendix, section "Answering the Windows Setup Wizard's Questions"). The Microsoft Windows Upgrade Advisor notifies you of any questionable software and drivers or hardware known to be problematic.

Windows is also good at allocating resources and dealing with conflicts, either real or looming. The most likely source for hardware conflicts is from older hardware (for example, an ISA or VESA Local Bus adapter card) that is not Plug and Play.

In the worst case, Windows doesn't boot at all after you add your new device. If you have an ISA adapter card, this invariably means that the settings on the card conflict with another device. Turn off the computer, take out the new device, turn on the computer, and reboot. Use the Device Manger to see what addresses and interrupts are currently in use, and use the card's documentation to find out how to change jumpers to addresses and interrupts that are available (the next section describes how). Then reinstall the card and try again. However, PCI cards almost never run into this problem because few have jumpers.

If you can't tell what the conflicts are, boot the computer in Safe Mode, described in the section "Booting in Safe Mode" later in this chapter.

If Windows does have a conflict with recently added hardware, the best thing to do is to locate the culprit in the Device Manager. If Windows is aware of the problem, it usually already has the device's listing in view and marked with an ugly icon. Highlight the gizmo and click Properties. There, you can access the devices specific Troubleshooter.

If you can't start Windows because of a device driver problem, press F8 while Windows is starting, and choose Last Known Good Configuration from the menu that appears. Windows restores the Registry and drivers from the last time that Windows started, effectively rolling back to a configuration that worked. Chapter 2 describes the Last Known Good Configuration and other startup modes.

Solving Configuration Problems by Using the Device Manager

You can use the Device Manager to deal with configuration problems by looking at the details of how Windows communicates with the device. The settings for each device are different, depending on the type of hardware and the specific model.

Display the Device Manager by choosing Start | Control Panel, opening the System icon, selecting the Hardware tab, and clicking the Device Manager button. (Figure 13-1 near the beginning of this chapter shows the Device Manager window.) If a device has a problem, its icon appears with a red or yellow exclamation point next to it (or a red X over it).

To see information about a particular device, right-click that device and choose Properties to see its Properties dialog box. Look at the General and Resources tab for information about its status (try the other tabs, too, if you can't find the information). If a device has resource conflicts, Windows displays them, as in Figure 13-7. In this case, the conflict is the interrupt number. To resolve a conflict, look at the settings that the device driver offers and try changing them.

Here are the two most common problems you can see in the Device Manager:

■ **Something wrong with the driver**   If the driver for the device doesn't work with Windows or is missing, you can right-click the device in the Device Manager window and choose Update Driver from the menu that appears. The Hardware Update Wizard runs and steps you through the process of installing a driver. If the device came with a CD-ROM, choose Install From A List Or Specific Location and put the CD-ROM into your CD-ROM drive. Be sure to check the manufacturer's web site for new drivers. If you have Windows 9x/Me drivers, they probably won't work with Windows XP.

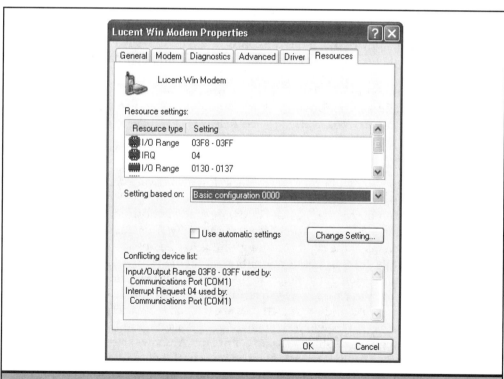

Figure 13-7.   *This modem has a hardware resource conflict, shown in the Conflicting Device List*

■ **Interrupt (IRQ) conflict** If two devices have an *X* on their icons in the Device Manager window, they may have conflicting interrupts (that is, they are both trying to use the same interrupt). Click the Resources tab on each device's Properties dialog box (if there is one) to see which IRQ the device uses to communicate with the rest of the computer (see "Interrupts" earlier in this chapter). To see a list of interrupts (IRQs) and which device uses each one, choose View | Resources By Type in the Device Manager window and click the plus box by the Interrupt Request (IRQ) item. Change the IRQ for one of the conflicting devices, restart the computer and see if the new setting works. Remember that several PCI devices can share an IRQ, but ISA devices each need a separate IRQ.

Booting in Safe Mode

Safe Mode provides minimal Windows functions by disabling all devices except the keyboard, screen, and disk. To cold boot (turn on your computer) into Safe Mode, start or restart your computer normally, but watch the screen carefully. As soon as you see the Starting Windows message, press F8 repeatedly. You should see a menu of startup options, one of which is Safe Mode. (Other options include Safe Mode With Network Support, which you can use if you're 100 percent sure that the problem isn't a network device, nor any other device that might be conflicting with the hardware resources used by a network device.) See Chapter 2 for more information on starting Windows in other modes.

Once you've booted in Safe Mode, you can use the Device Manager and other Windows facilities to figure out what's wrong. You can use System Restore to return Windows to a previous, working state. To leave Safe Mode, reboot the computer.

More Diagnostic Tools

Windows includes a variety of programs to track down hardware and driver problems. Choose Start | Help And Support. (If you are already running the Help And Support Center, click Home on the toolbar.) Click Hardware in the left column for a set of help topics about installing hardware, or click Use Tools To View Your Computer Information And Diagnose Problems in the right column for links to diagnostic tools.

One of the most useful is System Information. From the Help And Support Center home page, click Support on the toolbar, click Advanced System Information in the See Also section, and click View Detailed System Information (Msinfo32.exe) or choose Start | Run, type **msinfo32** and press ENTER. You can choose a variety of displays from the menu on the left side of its window, such as an IRQ list, Figure 13-8.

The System Configuration Utility lets you control the Windows startup process. Choose Start | Run, type **msconfig**, and press Enter. The most useful options are Diagnostic Startup on the General tab (which turns off all but the basic devices and drivers) and the Launch System Restore button to enable you to roll back your configuration to

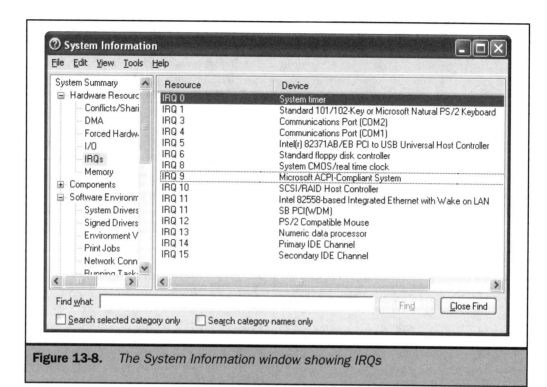

Figure 13-8. *The System Information window showing IRQs*

an earlier point. See Chapter 2 for how to use the System Configuration Utility and System Restore.

You can copy the information from the right pane of the System Information window into a text file for future reference. Select the items you want copy and press CTRL-C. *To copy the entire right pane, click in the right pane and press* CTRL-A CTRL-C.

Adding Memory

Adding memory is simple because no drivers are required. To add memory, follow these steps:

1. Shut down Windows, turn off and unplug the computer, open up the computer, and add the memory to available memory slots. Follow the instructions that came with your computer or with the memory. The memory must physically fit the slot, and in some cases must be the same as or compatible with any memory already installed.

Caution   *Either use an antistatic wrist band (or a wire clipped to your metal wristwatch and the grounded metal frame); at the very least, touch a piece of the metal frame of the case to discharge static electricity before handling RAM, to prevent static shocks from damaging the RAM chips. You can even plug the computer back in while you are installing the memory chips, so that the third prong of the AC outlet connects your computer chassis to ground.*

2. Unplug the computer if you plugged it back in, close it up, plug it back in, and start it up. Most PCs do an internal memory test, notice that the amount of memory has changed, and possibly display a message before Windows starts.

3. If your computer complains, enter the computer's low-level configuration setup (also called *BIOS setup* or *CMOS setup*), and adjust the configured amount of memory to reflect the total now installed. Then reboot. When Windows starts, it automatically takes advantage of all memory installed in your computer.

Tip   *The BIOS Setup programs of most computers can be accessed during the bootup process by pressing the DELETE or F1 key, as instructed. If Windows doesn't accept your new memory, the RAM card may not be seated properly or may be defective. Reinsert the memory card and try again. If you have another computer, test the RAM in that computer also.*

The
Complete
Reference

Chapter 14

Printing and Faxing

Y ou may not think of printing and faxing as having that much in common, but for Windows they are both ways of turning your document into a stream of dots and sending it somewhere, perhaps to a local printer six inches away, a network printer down the hall, or a fax machine in Ulan Bator.

After your printer is installed, you can manage your print jobs from the Printers And Faxes folder, holding or canceling documents you print. You can change the printer configuration including settings such as paper size and default fonts. If you run into printer trouble, you can use the Print Troubleshooter to find the problem (see Chapter 2, section "Diagnosing Windows Problems with Troubleshooters").

Windows handles the fonts that appear on the screen and on your printed pages. Windows itself comes with fonts, as do many application programs, and you can buy and install additional fonts. You can send or receive faxes using the Windows Fax Console, or you can use other faxing clients.

The Printers And Faxes Folder

The command center for printing and faxing is the Printers And Faxes folder, shown in Figure 14-1. To display the Printers And Faxes window, choose Start | Control Panel | Printers And Other Hardware | Printers And Faxes.

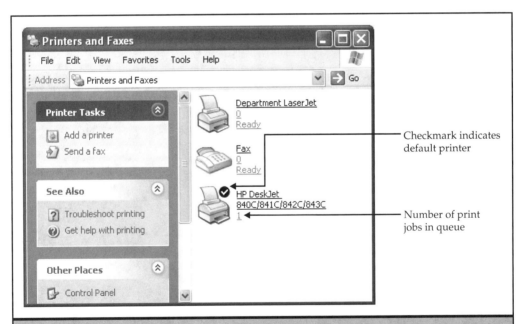

Figure 14-1.   *Windows keeps track of printers and fax devices in the same folder.*

To make the window more convenient to open, you can add a Printers And Faxes command to the Start menu as follows:

1. Right-click the Start button and select Properties from the shortcut menu. The Taskbar And Start Menu Properties dialog box appears (see Chapter 10, section "Changing Start Menu Properties").

2. Click the Customize button on the Start Menu tab. The Customize Start Menu dialog box appears.

3. Click the Advanced tab of the Customize Start Menu dialog box.

4. Check the Printers And Faxes check box. Then click OK to close each of the dialog boxes you opened.

Types of Printers

Printers come in three flavors:

- **Local printers** are physically connected to the printer port or USB port of your computer. Typically, a local printer is sitting right next to your computer.

- **Network printers** are connected to the same network as your computer (see Chapter 30).

- **Virtual printers** aren't really printers at all. When you "print" a document to a virtual printer, it doesn't put ink on paper, but it may send a fax or create a file in some compact, widely readable format like PDF. Adobe Acrobat, for example, sets up a virtual printer called PDF Writer.

When you print something from an application, a Windows *printer driver* (printer control program) for the current printer formats the material for that particular printer. As far as printer limitations permit, documents look the same no matter what printer they're printed on.

Each printer installed on your system has an entry in the Printers And Faxes folder. They may be different physical printers or different modes on the same printer. For example, a few printers handle both Hewlett Packard's PCL (Printer Control Language) and the Adobe PostScript language. You can have two printer drivers installed, one for PCL and one for PostScript. If your printer can print on both sides of the paper, you can have two drivers installed, one for single-sided printing and one for double-sided printing.

One printer is the *default printer*. Anything you print goes to the default printer unless you specifically tell your program to use a different printer. You can make any of your printers the default by right-clicking its icon in the Printers And Faxes folder and selecting Set as Default Printer from the shortcut menu.

Windows also provides *spooling*, a service that stores document data until the printer can accept it. When you print a document from an application, the information to be printed (the *print job*) is stored temporarily in the *queue* (storage for print jobs) until it can be printed. If you print a long document to a slow printer, spooling lets you continue working with your application while the printer works in the background. (Many years ago, "spool" stood for Simultaneous Peripheral Operation On-Line, but no one thinks of it as an acronym any more.)

Setting Up a Local Printer

Setting up a local printer can be as simple as plugging it in, connecting it to your computer, and waiting for Windows to notice it (see Chapter 13, section "Configuring Windows for New Hardware"). Or, you may need to answer a few questions for the Add Printer Wizard and insert the CD-ROM or floppy disk that came with your printer.

After the printer is set up, you may decide to share it over a network (see Chapter 30).

 If you have more than one user account on your computer, you need to install the printer from an account with administrator privileges (see Chapter 6).

Adding a Plug and Play Printer

Almost all new printers support Plug and Play, which makes them easy to install. If Windows XP already knows a driver for your printer, the process may be effortless. We installed an HP 842C printer just by plugging one end of a cable into the printer and the other into the appropriate port on our computer. Windows found the printer on its own and installed the appropriate driver in about the time that it took us to crawl out from under the desk. (Windows Help says to turn the printer on before connecting it to the computer, but we didn't even have to do that much.) If your printer connects wirelessly via infrared, turn the printer on and point its infrared port toward your computer's infrared port.

If Windows cannot identify your printer or find a driver for it, the Found New Hardware Wizard should appear. Answer its questions and be prepared to insert the floppy or CD-ROM that came with your printer if the wizard asks for it.

If Windows does not find your new printer at all, Plug and Play has fallen down on the job (or the printer is too old to support Plug and Play). See the instructions for installing a non–Plug and Play printer in the following section, or consult the printer's manufacturer.

Adding a Printer Without Plug and Play

To add a non–Plug and Play printer, follow these steps:

1. Make sure the printer is plugged in and turned on.

2. Connect the printer to your computer. The instructions that came with your printer should tell you what cable to use and which computer port to connect it to.

3. Display the Printers And Faxes folder (see "The Printers And Faxes Folder" earlier in this chapter).

4. Select Add a Printer from the Printer Tasks list or File | Add Printer from the menu. The Add Printer Wizard opens.

5. Answer the questions the wizard asks, clicking Next after each question. In particular, it asks what port you connected the printer to and the printer's manufacturer and model number. If you can't find the printer's make and model on the list the wizard gives, click the Have Disk button and insert the floppy or CD-ROM that came with your printer.

> **Tip** *If you have a disk for your printer and your printer also appears in the Windows list, you have a choice to make. In general, you want to use the newest driver you can. So use the Windows driver, unless your disk is dated 2001 or later. If your printer isn't listed and you don't have a recent disk, check the printer manufacturer's web site for up-to-date drivers that you can download and install.*

Configuring a Printer

After you install your printer or printers, you configure the driver to match your printer's setup. Some simple printers have little or no setup, while laser printers have a variety of hardware and software options.

To configure a printer, open the Printers And Faxes folder (see "The Printers And Faxes Folder" earlier in this chapter). Right-click the printer and select Properties from the menu that appears. You see the Properties dialog box for the printer, as shown in Figure 14-2.

Different printers have different capabilities, so their Properties dialog boxes are not identical. (A black-and-white printer, for example, doesn't have a Color Management tab.) Commonly used tabs include the following:

- **General** Comments about the printer and a button to print a test page.
- **Ports** Select the network connection or printer port, and change spooler settings.
- **Color Management** For color printers, select how color profiles work (making printed colors match screen colors).
- **Paper** Change the size of paper the printer is using; handle options such as double-sided, portrait, or landscape print orientation; and choose the number of copies of each page to print. (Some printers have a Printing Preferences button on the General tab that you use for setting paper size.)
- **Graphics** Change the dots-per-inch resolution of printed graphics (higher looks better, but prints slower); or use dithering, half-toning, and screening (techniques used to approximate shades of gray on black-and-white printers).
- **Fonts** Change which font cartridges are in use, control font substitution, control whether TrueType fonts are downloaded to the printer as fonts or graphics (which can be useful to work around flaky print position problems). Newer printers usually don't have a Fonts tab.

- **Device Options or Settings**   Change what optional equipment the printer has, such as extra memory, envelope feeders, and other paper-handling equipment, and change among various print-quality modes on ink-jet printers.

- **PostScript**   On high-end PostScript-compatible printers, select PostScript suboptions, and control whether PostScript header information is sent with each print job (important on printers shared with other computers) or only once per session.

- **Sharing**   If your computer is on a local area network, change whether other people on the network can share this printer (see Chapter 30).

- **Services**   Some printer drivers include procedures for maintenance, like cleaning print cartridges or aligning print heads.

The default printer's icon includes a checkmark. You can also set a printer to be the default printer by right-clicking it and choosing Set As Default Printer. If you want to remove an installed printer, just right-click the printer's icon in the Printers And Faxes folder and choose Delete from the menu that appears.

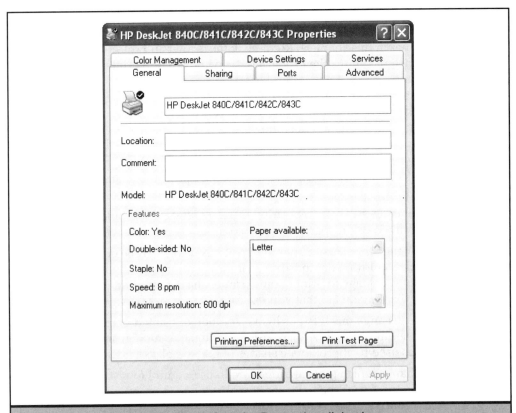

Figure 14-2.   *Configure a printer from its Properties dialog box.*

After you have the properties for your printer set to your liking, you'll find that you seldom need to change the properties. For most printers, you never need to change them.

 If you find that you frequently switch between two different sets of properties, such as single- and double-sided printing, install the printer twice and configure one installation for single-sided and one for double-sided printing. Windows lets you configure single-versus double-sided printing on a dialog box, but switching "printers" is a lot easier.

Testing and Troubleshooting Your Printer

After installing a new printer or changing its configuration, it's a good idea to print a test page. To do this, right-click the printer's icon in the Printers And Faxes folder and choose Properties from the shortcut menu. When the printer's Properties dialog box appears, click the Print Test Page button on the General tab.

After sending the test page to the printer (but before the printer has had enough time to do much with it) Windows asks you how the test page came out. Wait for the page to finish printing, and click OK if it looks good. If the page either does not print or looks wrong, click the Troubleshoot button to launch the Printer Troubleshooter. You can also launch the Printer Troubleshooter without printing a test page as follows:

1. Choose Start | Help And Support to display the Help And Support Center window.
2. Click the Fixing A Problem task in the Pick A Help Topic column.
3. Click Printing Problems. The Printing Problems screen appears on the right side of the Help and Support window.
4. Click Fix A Printing Problem.
5. Click Use The Printing Troubleshooter.

The Printing Troubleshooter asks you questions about your printer problem, so that it can identify the problem. Then it makes suggestions to fix the most common printer problems, such as no printing at all, slow or garbled printing, and distorted graphics. As with all such systems, the Printing Troubleshooter is hit-or-miss.

Choosing Printing Options

After you give the File | Print command to print a document from within an application program, the Print dialog box usually appears. The options this dialog box presents depend on the application and on the properties of your printer, so your Print dialog box may not look exactly like the one in Figure 14-3. Some of the choices you may be offered include

- **Printer name** The default printer is listed, but a drop-down list allows you to choose any of the printers whose icons are in the Printers and Faxes folder.

- **Pages range** You can print the entire document, specific pages, or a range of pages.

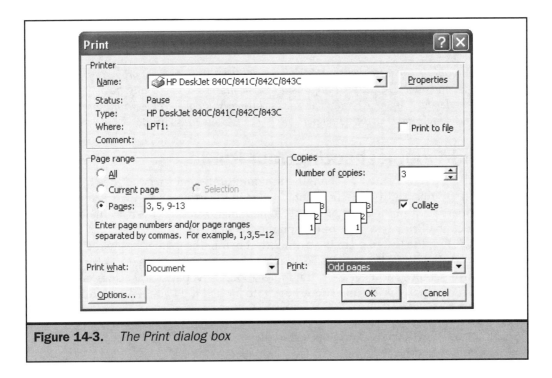

Figure 14-3.   *The Print dialog box*

- **Copies**   The dialog box in Figure 14-3 contains a Collate check box. If the box is checked, copies of the entire document are printed one by one. Otherwise, all the copies of a single page are printed before moving to the next page.
- **Print quality**   Low-quality printing is faster and uses less ink or toner.
- **Black-and-white or color**
- **Orientation**   Portrait orientation is taller than it is wide, while landscape orientation is wider than it is tall.
- **Paper tray**   If your printer has more than one paper tray, you can choose which to use.
- **Order of pages**   The default is to print page one first, but you may print in reverse order so that the document comes out properly ordered in the printer tray. You may also be able to choose to print only even or odd pages, which is handy if you are doing two-sided printing.

When you have made your choices, click OK to send the document to the printer.

Printing to a File

When Windows prints a document, it first converts it into a form that the printer can understand. You can decide to capture this printer-ready form of the document in a file (and not send it to a physical printer) so that you can print it later or transport it via e-mail or a floppy disk to a printer not connected to your computer. This is called *printing to a file*. You can do this in three ways:

- From the Print dialog box
- By changing the properties of an existing printer
- By creating a new printer icon

If you are printing only a single document to a file and will want to print subsequent documents directly to paper, issue the Print command from within the document's application and look for a Print To File check box in the Print dialog box. (Figure 14-3 has one, but yours may be in a different place or may be absent entirely. If you can't find it, you can still print to a file by changing the printer properties.) Make whatever other choices you want in the Print dialog box and click OK. A Print To File dialog box appears to let you choose what to call the file and where to save it. Click OK to begin producing the file.

If you are temporarily disconnected from your printer and want to print a series of documents to files, you may find it more convenient to change the printer properties so that documents sent to that printer go to a file automatically. To do this, find your printer's icon in the Printers And Faxes folder, right-click it, and select Properties. On the Properties dialog box, look for the tab on which the printer port is set. (In Figure 14-2 you would choose the Ports tab, but your printer's Properties dialog box may be different.) Choose File from the list of possible ports. Make a note of the port that the printer was connected to before you changed, so that you can change back.

If you frequently print to a file, create a new printer icon and choose File as its port. Follow the instructions for installing a non–Plug and Play printer (see "Adding a Printer Without Plug and Play" earlier in this chapter).

Managing Printer Activity

Occasionally, you need to communicate with a printer while it is in the act of printing. For example, you may realize that you have told the printer to print a full hundred-page document when you only intended to print one page of it. Or you may have queued several print jobs and realize that you want them printed in a different order or that you want to cancel a job and send it to a different printer.

You deal with these situations from the printer's Print Control window, shown in Figure 14-4. Open this window by double-clicking the printer's icon in the Printers And Faxes folder. (Or, if your Start menu displays the Control Panel as a menu, you can open the printer by selecting Start | Control Panel | Printers And Faxes | *printername*.) The printer control window shows you what job is currently printing, how that job is progressing, and which jobs are waiting to be printed.

CONFIGURING WINDOWS FOR YOUR COMPUTER

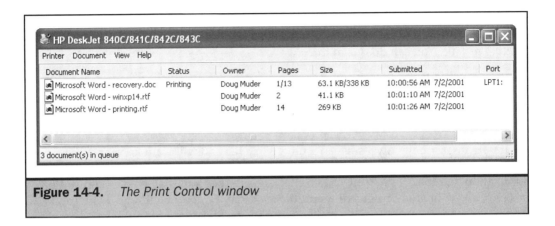

Figure 14-4. *The Print Control window*

Pausing or Canceling Print Jobs

To suspend the current print job until you can figure out what you want to do with it, choose Printer | Pause Printing from the menu of the Print Control window (or right-click the document in the Print Control window and choose Pause Printing from the shortcut menu). To resume the job where you left off, select Printer | Pause Printing again (or right-click anywhere in the Print Control window and choose Pause Printing). To delete a particular print job, right-click the job in the Print Control window and choose Cancel from the shortcut menu that appears. To get rid of everything waiting for that printer, choose Printer | Cancel All Documents.

Changing the Order in Which Jobs Are Printed

By default, print jobs are executed in a first-in-first-out manner. However, print jobs also have priority settings, and the highest priority jobs move to the front of the queue. If you are printing a number of jobs and want to move one of them in front of the others, change its priority as follows:

1. Open the printer's icon in the Printers And Faxes folder. The Print Control window appears, as shown in Figure 14-4. The jobs waiting to be printed are listed.

2. Right-click the print job whose priority you want to change and select Properties from the shortcut menu.

3. The default priority is 1, which is the setting for the least important jobs. (This takes some getting used to, as we usually think of "first priority" being the most important.) Move the priority slider to the right to raise the job's priority.

4. Click OK.

Scheduling a Print Job

If you have a very large print job that is going to take a long time, you can schedule it to print in the middle of the night or some other time when the printer is unlikely to be needed by anyone. To do this, submit your job to the printer as usual, but then do the following:

1. Open the printer's icon in the Printers And Faxes folder. The Print Control window appears, as shown in Figure 14-4.

2. Right-click the print job you want to schedule and select Properties from the shortcut menu. The Document Properties dialog box appears.

3. Click the Only From *xx* To *xx* radio button.

4. Select times from the drop-down lists so that the radio button corresponds to a complete sentence—for example: Only From 2 a.m. To 5 a.m.

5. Click OK.

 If you have scheduled a large print job for a time when the printer is unattended, make sure that it has plenty of paper and a fresh cartridge of ink or toner.

Typefaces and Fonts

Windows comes with a small but adequate set of fonts, but many programs and printer drivers include fonts of their own. Once a font is installed, any program can use it—no matter where the font came from. Thus, a typical Windows installation may have 50 to 100 fonts available, each in a wide variety of sizes.

 In addition to fonts that contain letters and numbers, Windows comes with several fonts of special characters. You can use the Character Map program to look at them and add them to your documents (see Chapter 17, section "Using Special Characters with Character Map").

TrueType Fonts

Computer printers and screens print and display characters by printing or displaying patterns of black-and-white (or colored) dots. The size of the dots depends on the resolution of the device, ranging from 72 to 100 dots per inch (dpi) on screens, to 300, 600, or even 1,200 dpi on laser printers. In early versions of Windows, each typeface was provided as a *bitmap* (dot picture) of the actual black and white dots for each character, with separate bitmaps for each size. The bitmaps were available only in a small variety of sizes, such as Courier 10-, 12-, and 18-point.

This scheme does not produce very good-looking documents, because the dot resolution of printers is rarely the same as that for a screen. In the process of printing, Windows had to rescale each character's bitmap to the printer's resolution, producing odd-looking characters with unattractive jagged corners. Even worse, if you used a font in a size other than one of the sizes provided, the system had to do a second level of rescaling, producing even worse looking characters.

TrueType solves both of these problems by storing each typeface not as a set of bitmaps, but essentially as a set of formulas the system can use to *render* (draw) each character at any desired size and resolution. This means that TrueType fonts look consistent on all devices, and that you can use them in any size.

Use only TrueType fonts in documents that you plan to print, to make your documents look their best.

How Printers Handle Fonts

Older printers had one or two fonts built in, and when you printed a document, those were the fonts you got. Modern printers can print any image that the resolution of the printer permits, so they can print all the fonts that are installed on your system.

Most printers have a reasonable set of built-in, general-purpose fonts, and some printers can accept font cartridges with added fonts. Occasionally, you may want to print a document that contains fonts your printer doesn't know, and then one of the following three things happens:

- Windows reverts to printing graphics, in effect turning your document into a full-page bitmap image that Windows can send (slowly) to the printer.

- If your printer is smart enough (most laser printers that use PostScript and PCL5 are), Windows can send the printer all the fonts that a particular document needs. This delays the start of the print job a little, but as soon as the printing starts it proceeds at a normal speed.

- To speed up printing, Windows uses *font substitution*, using built-in printer fonts where possible for similar TrueType fonts. For example, Microsoft's Arial font is nearly identical to the Helvetica font found in PostScript printers, so when Windows prints Arial text, it tells the printer to use Helvetica instead. This process of font substitution normally works smoothly, although occasionally on clone printers the built-in fonts aren't exactly what Windows expects and the results can look a little off. (You can tell Windows to turn off font substitution if you suspect that's a problem.)

Installing and Using Fonts

Windows provides a straightforward way to install and use fonts. To see which fonts you have installed, open the folder C:\Windows\Fonts in Windows Explorer (assuming that Windows is installed on drive C), like this:

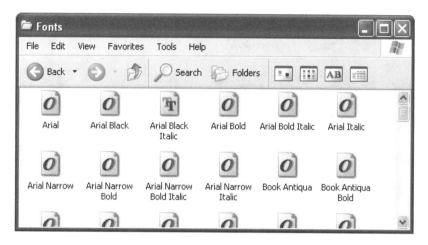

TrueType fonts have a TT icon, Open Type fonts have an O icon, and older fonts have an A icon. You can open any font to see a description and samples of the font in a variety of sizes. If you have a lot of fonts installed, choose View | Hide Variations to omit the icons for fonts that are bold or italic versions of other fonts.

 Windows can handle up to 1,000 fonts, but to avoid slowing down your applications, don't install more than 200.

Installing Fonts

If you buy new fonts, or they come with a program, you may receive font files with extensions .ttf or .fon. To install these new fonts from a floppy disk, CD, or network, follow these steps:

1. View the C:\Windows\Fonts folder in Windows Explorer (or the Fonts folder of whatever folder Windows is installed in).

2. Choose File | Install New Font. The Add Fonts dialog box, shown here, appears:

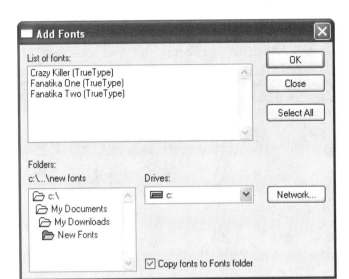

3. In the Drives and Folders boxes, select the drive and folder in which the files are located for the new font or fonts. Click the Network button if the font files are on a network drive that is not mapped to a drive letter on your computer. Windows displays the fonts it finds.

4. In the List Of Fonts box, select the font(s) you want to install.

5. Normally, Windows copies the font files into its font folder (C:\Windows\Fonts). If you are installing fonts from a networked folder, you can uncheck Copy Fonts To Fonts Folder to use the fonts where they are located, which saves space in exchange for some loss in speed.

6. Click OK, and Windows installs the fonts you want.

 You can also drag font files from the install disk or folder to the C:\Windows\ Fonts folder.

Deleting Fonts

To delete a font or fonts, display the C:\Windows\Fonts folder in Windows Explorer. Then select the fonts you want to get rid of and choose File | Delete. However, don't delete a font unless you are sure that none of the programs on your system use it. To be safe, move the fonts to a temporary folder for a few days to see if any programs display error messages when they try to use them. If your windows and documents continue to look and print normally, with no unexpected font changes, then delete the fonts.

Finding Similar Fonts

Windows offers an occasionally useful "font similarity" feature that lets you look for fonts that are similar to a particular font. When viewing the Fonts folder, choose View | List Fonts By Similarity and choose the target font at the top of the Fonts window. The font similarity feature depends on special information in the font files, so older fonts without this information aren't ranked for similarity.

Sending and Receiving Faxes

Most dial-up modems also have the ability to send and receive faxes, turning your computer into a fax machine. (DSL and cable modems cannot send or receive faxes.) You need to have a phone line connected to the modem and a fax client program installed on your computer. The client program allows you to compose, read, and archive faxes in the same way that an e-mail client handles e-mail.

*Another way to deal with faxes via your computer is to use an Internet-based fax service, like eFax (**www.efax.com**) or JFAX (**www.j2.com**). Both services can receive faxes for you and e-mail them to you, or allow you to send faxes from your computer for a monthly fee.*

Windows XP comes with a Fax Console accessory for sending and receiving faxes. Fax Console is not part of the default installation of Windows XP, so you may need to add it from the Windows XP CD-ROM (see Chapter 3). Choose Start | Control Panel, click Add Or Remove Programs, click Add/Remove Windows Components, and choose Fax Services from the list of components. Fax Console automatically detects fax-capable dial-up modems during installation and configures itself to send (but not receive) faxes.

When Fax Console is installed, run it by selecting Start | All Programs | Accessories | Communications | Fax | Fax Console.

Configuring Fax Console

The first time you run Fax Console, the Fax Configuration Wizard starts. It asks you to fill out the information (name, address, phone number, and so on) that you want to appear on the cover sheet of any faxes you send. You can choose to enable receiving faxes. If the wizard detects that Fax Console has upgraded Personal Fax for Windows, it offers you the option of importing your fax archives.

After the Fax Configuration Wizard has run, the Fax Console window appears, as shown here:

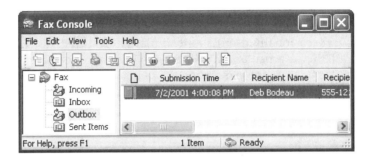

The Fax Console usually contains four folders: Incoming (faxes that are arriving), Inbox (received faxes), Outbox (faxes that you have scheduled to be sent, but have not yet been transmitted successfully), and Sent Items (sent faxes).

Windows treats a fax device as a kind of printer and creates a Fax icon for it in the Printers And Faxes folder. Opening this icon opens Fax Console. Right-clicking the Fax icon and selecting Properties is equivalent to choosing Tools | Fax Printer Configuration from the Fax Console menu bar. Either action produces the Fax Properties dialog box. From here you can do the following:

- **Adjust the size and quality of the fax images you send.**   From the General tab, click Printing Preferences and make your choices from the Fax Printing Preferences dialog box.

- **Share your fax printer over a network.**   This option is not supported for all fax devices, and Windows XP Home Edition doesn't support it (you'd need to upgrade to Windows XP Professional). Make your choices from the Sharing tab of the Fax Properties dialog box.

- **Set the properties of your fax devices.**   Use the Devices tab. This is where you configure a device to receive faxes (see "Automatically Receiving Faxes" later in this chapter). The options available here depend on the particular device.

- **Set the discount rate times.**   One option for sending faxes is for the fax to be held until the phone rates go down. Specify the discount rate times by clicking the Properties button on the devices tab. The Properties box for your fax device appears; set the discount times there.

- **Choose where sent and received faxes are filed.**   Use the Archives tab.

- **Decide how you will be notified about faxes that are sent or received.**
  Use the Track tab. An icon can appear in the notification area of the Windows taskbar or the Fax Monitor window can open, as shown here:

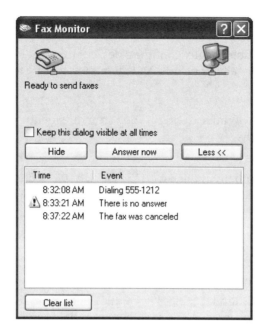

Sending a Cover-Page Fax from Fax Console

You can send a cover-page fax (consisting of a cover page with a subject line and a text note) from within Fax Console by selecting File | Send a Fax from the menu. The Send Fax Wizard opens to collect the recipient information, the subject line, and the text of your note. To send a longer fax, create the document you want to send with another application and send it from that application, as described in the next section.

The final page of the Send Fax Wizard is the Schedule page. Here you can choose to send the fax immediately, when discount rates apply, or during a specific time window (within the next 24 hours) that you set.

Sending a Fax from an Application

If you have a document open in an application (like Microsoft Word or Adobe Photoshop) you can fax that document to someone by selecting File | Print and choosing a fax printer from the drop-down printer list in the Print dialog box (see Figure 14-3 earlier in this chapter). The Send Fax Wizard appears and collects the information necessary to send the fax, such as the fax number of the recipient and the information you want to appear on the cover page of the fax. You can schedule the fax just as you would if had started the Send Fax Wizard from within Fax Console, as described in the preceding section.

Automatically Receiving Faxes

Fax Console does not automatically configure devices to receive faxes. To configure the Fax Console to answer all phone calls and attempt to receive faxes, do the following:

1. Open Fax Console.
2. Select Tools | Fax Printer Configuration from the menu. The Fax Properties dialog box appears.
3. Click the Devices tab.
4. Click your fax modem in the list on the Devices tab. The list tells you whether the device is already set up to receive. (If it says Yes, there is no need to continue.)
5. Click the Properties button. The Properties dialog box for the device appears.
6. Click the Receive tab of the device's Properties dialog box.
7. Check the Enable Device To Receive check box.
8. Enter your fax number into the CSID box.
9. You can make additional choices from this dialog box: You set whether the fax line should be answered automatically or manually, and whether faxes should automatically be printed or stored somewhere in addition to the Inbox folder of Fax Console.
10. Click OK in all open dialog boxes.

If you configured your fax device to receive faxes automatically, you need do nothing to receive an incoming fax—just leave the computer on. If you configured the fax device for manual receiving, select File | Receive Fax Now when a fax call is coming in.

Receiving Faxes Manually

If you use the same phone line for your modem and receiving voice phone calls, you may not want the Fax Console to answer every phone call to check whether it's a fax. Instead, you can tell the Fax Console to pick up only the next phone call. Click the **Receive Now** button on the Fax Console toolbar (the second button from the left). Or, choose File | Receive A Fax Now.

Archiving Your Faxes

The faxes you send accumulate in the Sent Items folder, and the faxes you receive accumulate in the Inbox. If you have a local fax device, the faxes stay in these folders until you delete them. For network fax devices, they may disappear after a period of time specified by the network administrator.

You cannot create additional folders for your faxes inside Fax Console, so if you want to organize your stored faxes you will have to translate them into some other format. To do this, select the Inbox (for received faxes) or Sent Items (for sent faxes) folder in the Fax Console window, choose a message from the message list, and right-click it. The shortcut menu gives you several choices. You can

- **Save the fax as a file.** Select Save As from the shortcut menu; then choose a file name and a folder in which to save your fax from the Browse window that appears.

- **Print it.**

- **Delete it.**

- **View it.** Selecting View from the shortcut menu opens the fax in a new window.

- **E-mail it.** Select Mail To from the shortcut menu. The fax appears in a message window of the default e-mail program. You can address it and send it as you would any e-mail message.

Note

Windows stores your faxes as images, with the extension .tif. You use Windows Explorer to copy these files from the Fax Console's folders into other folders. The Fax Console keeps its files in the C:\Documents And Settings\All Users\Application Data\ Microsoft\Windows NT\MSFax\Inbox (if Windows is installed on C). The fax file names are cryptic: to determine which fax is which, double-click to view the fax.

The
Complete
Reference

Chapter 15

Running Windows XP
on Laptops

You can use your laptop in two ways: as a secondary machine that you use when you need to be more mobile or as your main machine because you are always mobile. In either case, these Windows features may be useful:

■ You can coordinate files with those on a desktop computer by using the Windows Briefcase.

■ You can print a document to a printer other than your usual printer.

■ Power management can make your battery last longer.

■ If you use a docking station to connect your laptop to desktop devices, you should know about docking and undocking and hardware profiles.

■ You can use DualView to expand your display to a second monitor.

You may also want to explore connecting your laptop to a network or another computer to use its resources—see Chapters 27 and 28.

 Windows XP Professional has some additional features that may be useful for laptop users, such as Offline Files and Remote Desktop. Since this book is about Windows XP Home Edition, we don't cover them, but if you are a power laptop user and need to connect electronically to your home base, you may want to upgrade to Windows XP Professional.

Coordinating Your Laptop Files with Windows Briefcase

If you use files from more than one computer on a regular basis, Windows Briefcase can keep track of files that you use on your laptop but are normally stored on another computer. Windows Briefcase is a program that coordinates files you work on, so that you always use the most current version of the files. Windows Briefcase is useful if you use a laptop when you're on the road and a desktop machine in the office, but Briefcase is also useful for anyone who uses files from several computers.

The Windows Briefcase program creates and maintains *Briefcases*, which are folders containing files and subfolders that you can move between your laptop and another computer.

The easiest way to use Briefcase to coordinate files on different computers is to have the two computers connected by a network or another connection. However, you can also use Briefcase with a floppy disk or Zip disk, although that limits the total size of the files you can move from computer to computer.

You may see a Briefcase icon on the desktop. If it doesn't appear on the desktop, right-click the desktop and choose New | Briefcase from the shortcut menu. You can use this option to create multiple briefcases. The first time you open the My Briefcase window, you also see the Welcome To The Windows Briefcase window, with tips for using the program. Click Finish when you have read the tips.

You can rename the Briefcase by clicking the name on the icon once, clicking again, and typing a new name—the same method you use to rename any file or shortcut. Or click once and press F2 to change the name.

Synchronizing Files with Briefcase

The most common use of Briefcase is for transferring files from a desktop to a laptop for use while away from the office, and then transferring the updated files back to the desktop when you return. Using Briefcase to transfer files has four steps:

1. Move files to the Briefcase. Choose only the files you will use and update while you're away from your desktop computer.

2. Copy the Briefcase to the laptop.

3. Use files from the Briefcase while you are on the road using the laptop.

4. When you are ready to work at your desktop again, tell Briefcase to synchronize the files on the two computers, so both computers contain the latest version of each file in the Briefcase.

 Briefcase uses the system time and date to synchronize files—make sure the time and date on each computer is correct.

These steps are somewhat different, depending on whether a local area network (LAN) connects the laptop and desktop computers. Without a LAN connection, you have to use a floppy disk, CD-R, CD-RW, or other removable disks to move the Briefcase to the laptop. With a LAN, you can sit at the laptop and drag files from the desktop to the laptop's Briefcase.

Using Briefcase Without a LAN

If you don't have a LAN, you need to complete these steps:

1. Sit at the desktop and drag the files you need to the Briefcase icon on the desktop, or the Briefcase window if it's open. The easiest way to do this is to select files in Windows Explorer and drag them to the Briefcase icon or window. You can do this in several steps as you select files in different folders on your hard disk. You can also right-click a file and choose Send To | My Briefcase from the shortcut menu (the name of the briefcase will appear on the shortcut menu with the Briefcase icon).

 Make sure to drag actual files to the Briefcase, not shortcuts to files.

2. Drag the Briefcase to a floppy, Zip, Jaz, or other removable drive or right-click the Briefcase and choose Send To | Floppy (choosing the drive where you want to move the Briefcase). If you have a CD-R or CD-RW drive, you can burn the files onto a CD (see Chapter 8, section "Making Your Own CDs").

3. Copy the Briefcase to the laptop. Take the disk to which you copied the Briefcase, insert it in the floppy drive of the laptop, and view the contents of the drive. You see the Briefcase icon. Drag the Briefcase from the drive to the laptop's desktop.

If you want, you can use the Briefcase files from the floppy or removable disk. However, using a removable disk instead of the hard disk will slow you down noticeably if you are using large files. Briefcase files on removable disks tend to become corrupted, so we recommend copying them to your hard disk, editing, and copying them back to the removable disk.

 If the laptop already has an icon on the Desktop called My Briefcase, and that is the name of the Briefcase you are copying, rename the old My Briefcase, so the two don't have the same name.

Using Briefcase with a LAN

If you have a LAN connecting the desktop and the laptop, follow these steps to put files in the Briefcase on the laptop:

1. On the laptop, open the Briefcase.
2. Drag files and/or folders from Windows Explorer to the Briefcase icon or the Briefcase window. Normally, the files you move to the Briefcase will be stored on the desktop (that is, on a computer other than the laptop).

Now you're ready to disconnect the laptop from the LAN.

Using the Files in a Briefcase

While you're on the road (or not using your desktop computer), make sure to use the files from the Briefcase. To do so, simply open the Briefcase window (as shown in Figure 15-1) and double-click a file you want to use, just as you would a file in any other folder. You can use Explorer window commands to control how files in the Briefcase window appear (see Chapter 8).

If you use an application's File | Open command, display the files in the Briefcase by clicking the Desktop icon (or click the Up One Level button in the Open dialog box until you can't go up any more levels—the Briefcase is on your computer's desktop). Open the Briefcase to see the files it contains.

When you save a file from the Briefcase, use the Save button to make sure you save it back to the Briefcase. If you don't save the file back to the Briefcase, the Briefcase won't be able to synchronize files for you. If you create a new file that you want transferred back to the desktop, you can save it in the Briefcase.

 You should edit a file on only one computer before you synchronize the files with Briefcase, because you can keep only one version of the file—the one you took with you or the one you left behind. If you edit a file while you're on the road and someone back at home edits the same file, you won't be able to keep all the changes unless the program the file uses can show you what they are. However, if someone at home edits a file you took with you in your Briefcase but you didn't edit it, you can keep the most current version of the file.

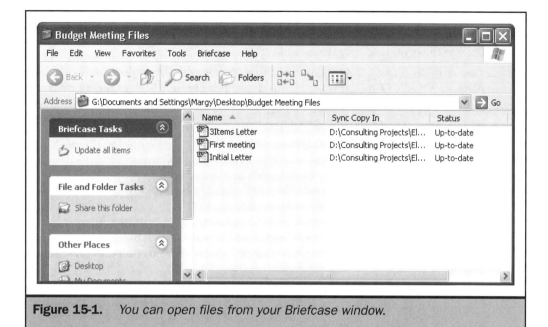

Figure 15-1. *You can open files from your Briefcase window.*

The Properties dialog box for each file in the Briefcase provides some useful options. To display it, right-click a file and choose Properties. Here are things you can do with files in the Briefcase window:

■ **You can see the update status of each file in the Status column in the Briefcase.** You can also check the status of a file in the Briefcase by displaying the Properties dialog box and clicking the Update Status tab.

■ **If you drag a file from another location into the Briefcase, you can find the original copy of this file.** In the Properties dialog box for the file, click the Update Status tab and click the Find Original button. Windows displays the folder containing the original file in an Explorer window.

■ **You can sever the connection between the original file and the copy of the file in the Briefcase.** For example, the copy in the Briefcase may have changed sufficiently that you also want to keep the original copy. Display the Properties dialog box, click the Update Status tab, and then click the Split From Original button.

Synchronizing the Edited Files in a Briefcase

When you return to your desktop PC, you need to synchronize the files on your laptop and your desktop. Follow these steps to synchronize the files:

1. Reestablish the connection between the two computers. If you have a docking station that supports hot docking (installing or removing the computer in the docking station without turning the computer off), the Briefcase may open automatically (see "Using a Docking Station"). If you don't have a LAN, move

Briefcase from the laptop's desktop back to the removable disk or burn it on a CD, take the disk or CD to the original computer, and then move the Briefcase back to the original computer's desktop.

2. Open the Briefcase window. You see the status of each file in the Status column. (Choose View | Details if this column doesn't appear.) A file's status can be one of the following three:

 - **Orphan**   The file exists only in the Briefcase and not on the source computer (in this example, the desktop computer is the source computer).

 - **Up-To-Date**   The file has not changed on either computer.

 - **Needs Updating**   The file has changed on either the desktop or the laptop (or both).

3. Click the Update All button on the Briefcase toolbar (the button with four sheets of paper and two arrows). The Update My Briefcase dialog box appears, showing how each file needs to be updated. A file can be updated in one of the following ways:

 - **Replace, with an arrow pointing to the right**   This is the most common action. It means the file in the Briefcase will replace the file of the same name on the desktop computer.

 - **Replace, with an arrow pointing to the left**   This means the file on the desktop computer is the most recent—it will replace the file of the same name in the Briefcase.

 - **Skip (both changed)**   This means both files (the one on the desktop and the one on the laptop) have been changed and Briefcase can't determine which file should be used. You need to determine which version of the file you want to use.

4. If you don't want a file updated as shown, right-click the file and choose a method from the shortcut menu that appears.

5. Click the Update button to update the files.

You can also update one file at a time—select the file and click the Update Selection button (the button with two sheets of paper and one arrow). The Update Briefcase dialog box appears with just the selected file.

Printing Away from Home

One frequent problem with traveling with a computer is you rarely have access to a printer. Even portable printers add more weight and cost to your electronic carryall than most people are willing to bear. So, instead, you survive without a printer.

You can print in several ways when you're away from home: you can connect someone else's printer to your computer; you can connect to a network and print on its printer; or you can fax your document to the nearest fax machine (assuming you have fax software and a fax modem). See Chapter 14 for more information about printing from Windows.

If you want to print your queued documents using a printer other than the one you usually use, you can temporarily change the printer. If the printer's drivers were included on the Windows XP CD-ROM, Windows can probably find it because Windows copies most of its files to your hard disk. If your printer's drivers aren't included with Windows (if you installed them from a CD or floppy disk that came with the printer), you might need to insert that CD or floppy when changing printer descriptions.

 If you use a wide variety of printers, you might want to install the Generic printer driver on your laptop to give you a basic printing option, no matter what kind of printer you're using.

Follow these steps to change the description of a printer temporarily:

1. Open the Printers folder by choosing Start | Printers and Faxes or by choosing Start | Control Panel | Printers and Other Hardware | Printers and Faxes.

2. Open the printer you printed to (the printer appears grayed-out to indicate it is offline). You see the Printer window with all your print jobs listed.

3. Right-click the printer window and choose Properties from the menu that appears. You see the Properties dialog box for the printer.

4. If necessary, change the port on the Ports tab.

5. On the Advanced tab, choose the Driver you need. If the printer you have available isn't listed (because you haven't used it before), click the New Driver button to choose the kind of printer you do have.

6. Close all the dialog boxes. You may be asked for your Windows XP CD-ROM.

7. If you change the driver for the printer, you need to repeat the preceding steps to change it back when you return to the office and connect to your regular printer.

 Windows uses a single driver for a variety of similar printers. If you already have a printer defined that's similar to the one you want to use, you'll probably find you can define the new printer and Windows won't need any extra files.

Accessing Other Computers with Remote Desktop

Remote Desktop allows you to have access to the desktop of one computer while you are running another. Not only can you see and use all the files on the remote computer, you can actually see the desktop and run programs as if you were sitting in front of the remote computer. If the remote computer is running Windows .NET, 2000, or NT Server, more than one person can use the remote computer at the same time. Remote

Desktop uses a LAN, a VPN (virtual private network), or the Internet to access the remote computer—the speed of response depends on the speed of your connection.

 *You can also access a computer remotely using NetMeeting (see Chapter 25, section "Conferencing with Microsoft NetMeeting"). Other remote-access programs have been available for years, including pcAnywhere (at **www.symantec.com/pcanywhere**) and the freeware VNC (Virtual Network Computing, at **www.uk.research.att.com/vnc**).*

The *server* is the computer that you take control of from a remote location. Usually, the server computer in the Remote Desktop application is the computer on your office desk—the one that you will not be taking with you. Or, the server can be a Remote Access Server (RA Server) on a Windows .NET, 2000, or NT machine. (Server systems call this feature *terminal services*.)

 A computer running Windows XP Home Edition can't act as a Remote Desktop server. That is, you can't remotely access a computer running Windows XP Home Edition using the Remote Desktop feature. Use VNC or pcAnywhere instead.

The *client* computer is the one that you will use while you are away to see the desktop of the server computer. You can use a computer running Windows XP Home Edition as the Remote Desktop client.

Remote Desktop comes in two flavors—regular Remote Desktop and Remote Desktop Web Connection. The first requires Windows XP's Remote Desktop Connection software on the client computer. The second needs only Internet Explorer on the client computer, but it requires more setup—IIS (Internet Information Services) with TSWeb (Remote Desktop Web Connection)—on the server computer.

You might want to use your Windows XP Home Edition laptop to connect to your Windows XP Professional desktop while you are away; if so, see *Windows XP Professional: The Complete Reference* for how to set up your desktop as a Remote Desktop server. Or you might need to work from home by using your home computer to connect to your office computer remotely; if so, contact your office's systems administrator for the information you need to connect. The following sections describe how to set up and use your Windows XP Home Edition computer as a Remote Desktop client.

Configuring the Client Computer for Remote Desktop

If the computer that you want to use remotely (the server computer) doesn't support Web Connection, then you use Windows XP's Remote Desktop Connection software on the computer that you will use while you are away (the client computer). On the client computer, check that this Windows feature is installed by choosing Start | All Programs | Accessories | Communications | Remote Desktop Connection (it's installed by default).

Note | *If the Remote Desktop Connection command isn't there, install it from your Windows XP Home Edition CD-ROM—insert the CD, click Perform Additional Tasks on the Welcome page, and then choose Set Up Remote Desktop Connection to run the Remote Desktop Connection InstallShield Wizard. You get to choose who can use the remote connection: anyone on the computer or just the logged-in user. Then the Wizard takes over. Once the Wizard has finished, you can close the installation program.*

If you are connecting to a server that supports Remote Desktop Web Connection, your client computer must have a TCP/IP connection to the server computer (usually over the Internet), and it must have Internet Explorer 4.0 or higher (Windows XP comes with Internet Explorer 6). No other configuration is necessary for Remote Desktop Web Connection.

Connecting to a Remote Computer with Remote Desktop

If the server is your own computer, make sure that the server machine is on and working and connected to whatever network you will use to access it—usually the Internet or a LAN (you need to do this before you leave). If you are connecting to a computer at your office, your system administrator is responsible for keeping the server running.

Sit at the client machine to test the connection. The next two sections describe connecting with the regular Remote Desktop and with the Remote Desktop Web Connection. Read the section for the type of connection for which the server is configured.

Connecting with Remote Desktop Connection

Start Remote Desktop Connection on the client computer (the one you will take with you) by following these steps:

1. Choose Start | All Programs | Accessories | Communications | Remote Desktop Connection. You see the Remote Desktop Connection window:

2. Type the domain name or IP address of the server computer in the Computer box.
3. Click Connect.

4. Enter your name and password in the Log On To Windows window: type the user account name and password that you use on the server computer. Click OK.

5. You see the remote desktop, which looks just like the computer screen would look if you were sitting at the server computer. There is a special toolbar at the top of the window—the *connection bar*. You can use it to minimize, restore, or close the Remote Desktop Connection window:

6. Click the Restore or Minimize button if you want to work on the client computer, but then return to the server computer. Clicking the pushpin icon locks the menu open.

You're ready to work on the server computer.

Connecting with Remote Desktop Web Connection

From the client computer, access the server computer by following these steps:

1. Open Internet Explorer.

2. In the Address box, type the URL for the home directory of the Remote Desktop computer. Generally, this URL takes the following form: **http://*servercomputer*/ *path***. Replace *servercomputer* with the address of the server computer, and *path* with the path containing the Remote Desktop Connection files (the default location is C:\Tsweb, if Windows is installed on C:). The computer address can be the name on the LAN, or the computer's numeric IP address. You can usually omit the **http://**. For instance, if you are connecting over a LAN to a server computer named Jadzia, type **Jadzia/Tsweb** in the Address box.

Note *To avoid typing this address again, add it to your Internet Explorer Favorites by choosing Favorites | Add To Favorites from the menu (see Chapter 24).*

3. Press ENTER to see the Remote Desktop Web Connection page (shown in Figure 15-2).

4. Type the server computer's name or numeric IP address in the Server box.

5. Choose the Size for the Remote Desktop window: Full Screen or one of the other available sizes. Remote Desktop is easier to use if the resolution of the client computer's screen is greater than size you choose (for example, you choose to display the server's screen at 800 × 600 on a client computer screen with a resolution of 1024 × 768).

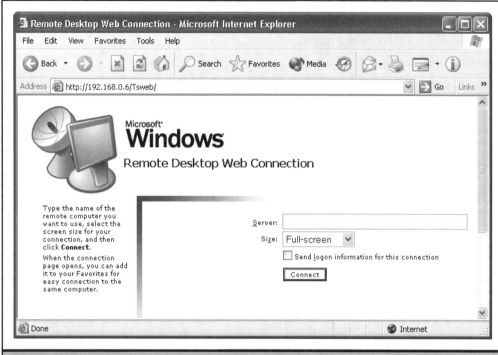

Figure 15-2.   *Logging into a remote PC using Internet Explorer*

6. Click Connect. The first time you use this feature, Windows may ask you whether you want to install and run the Microsoft Terminal Services Control program: if it does, click Yes. You see the Remote Desktop Connection Security Warning dialog box shown in Figure 15-3 with the following options:

■ **Connect Your Local Disk Drives To The Remote Computer**   Makes the drives on the local (client) computer available on the remote computer. So, for instance, if you are using Remote Desktop and opening a file in Word, you can see files on your local hard drives, network drives, and floppy drives. This option is automatically available in Remote Desktop Connection.

■ **Connect Your Local Ports To The Remote Computer**   Makes the ports on the local (client) computer available on the remote computer in the Remote Desktop Web Connection window.

Select or deselect check boxes as needed and click OK.

7. Log in to the server computer by typing the user name and password that you use on that computer.

CONFIGURING WINDOWS
FOR YOUR COMPUTER

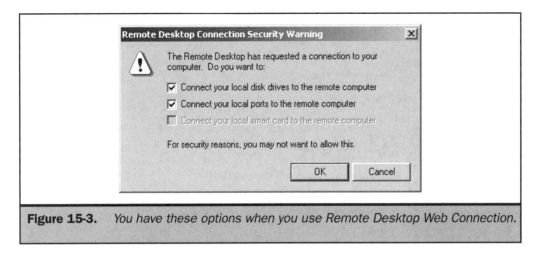

Figure 15-3.   *You have these options when you use Remote Desktop Web Connection.*

If you choose full screen, your screen looks the same as it would if you were sitting in front of the remote computer, with the addition of the same small connection bar shown in the previous section. If you choose another size, you see the remote desktop in an Internet Explorer window. Use the Minimize, Restore, or Close buttons to control the Remote Desktop Connection window. When you are done using the server computer, close the Internet Explorer window.

Using the Remote Desktop Connection

Once you have established the Remote Desktop Connection, you can work as if you were working on the server computer. You can also combine the capabilities of the remote server computer with the local client computer in the following ways:

- **Cut-and-paste**   You can cut information from the Remote Desktop window and paste it into an application on the local computer.

- **Use local files in the remote session**   If you are using the Remote Desktop Connection program, this option is available automatically. If you are using Remote Desktop Web Connection, you need to select Connect Your Local Disk Drives To The Remote Computer when you log in. Local drives appear in My Computer under Other, as shown in Figure 15-4. They will also appear in Open and Save dialog boxes in applications.

- **Use a local printer in the remote session**   When you print while you are using Remote Desktop, the print job automatically goes to the default local printer if the printer driver is available on the server computer.

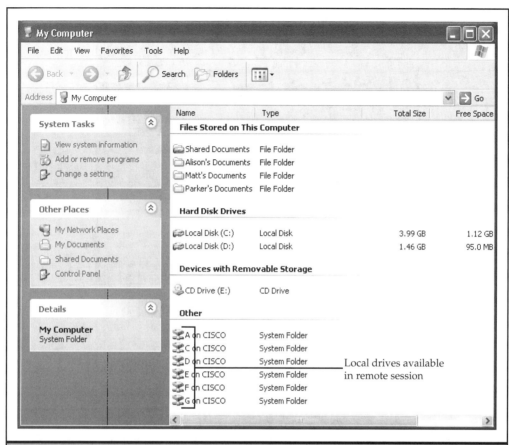

Figure 15-4. *Local drives are available in the remote session.*

Other Remote Desktop Options

When you connect to a computer using Remote Desktop, you see the Remote Desktop Connection dialog box (see "Connecting with Remote Desktop Connection" earlier in this chapter). You can click the Options button to see a larger version of this dialog box with many additional options, as shown in Figure 15-5. Table 15-1 lists the options.

Figure 15-5.   *Setting the options for your Remote Desktop connection*

> **Tip**   *Once you have configured the settings for your Remote Desktop connection, you can save them with a name by clicking the Save As button on the General tab of the Remote Desktop Connection dialog box. The next time you want to use these settings, click the Open button.*

Managing Your Computer's Power

If you often use your laptop when it isn't plugged in, you probably have had a battery die before you finished your work. Windows and some applications support power management, which eases this problem without actually solving it. Windows supports two power management standards: *Advanced Power Management* (*APM*) and *Advanced Configuration and Power Interface* (*ACPI*). To take advantage of Windows power management features, however, you must have a computer with hardware that supports one of these standards. (The computer needn't be a laptop).

Dialog Box Tab	Setting	Description
General	Computer	Name or IP address of the remote server.
General	User name and Password	User account information on the remote computer.
General	Domain	Domain name of which the remote computer is a part. For computers on peer-to-peer LANs, this setting is ignored.
General	Save my password	Specifies whether you have to type your user account password each time you connect.
Display	Remote desktop size and colors	Selects the size and color depth of the Remote Desktop window on your screen.
Display	Display the connection bar with in full screen mode	Specifies whether the small connection bar toolbar appears.
Local Resources	Remote computer sound	Specifies whether to play the sounds that the other computer would make on your computer instead.
Local Resources	Keyboard	Specifies whether ALT- key combinations apply to the local computer or the remote computer.
Local Resources	Local devices (Disk drives, Printers, and Serial ports)	Specifies which devices on the remote computer you connect to automatically.
Programs	Start the following program on connection	Runs a program automatically when you connect to the remote computer, and specifies which program.
Experience	Choose your connection speed to optimize performance	Specifies the speed of your connection to the remote computer.
Experience	Allow the following (Desktop background, Show contents of window while dragging, Menu and window animation, Themes, and Bitmap caching)	Specifies which desktop features appear in your Remote Desktop window. Deselect items to improve performance, especially if you have a slow connection.

Table 15-1.   *Settings on the Remote Desktop Connection Dialog Box*

Power management is handled from the Power Options Properties dialog box, displayed in Figure 15-6. To display the Power Options Properties dialog box, open the Performance And Maintenance icon on the Control Panel, and click Power Options. The options displayed on your Power Options Properties dialog box depend on what type of power management your hardware supports.

The most power-hungry component of your computer system is the monitor. Turning off the monitor when you won't be using it for several hours saves energy, in exchange for the relatively minor inconvenience of waiting a few seconds for it to come on again when you're ready to go back to work.

Standby and Hibernate Modes

Most laptops support Standby Mode, in which the disks stop spinning, the screen goes blank, but the memory and CPU continue to run, using much less power than full operation. To switch to Standby Mode, choose Start | Turn Off Computer, and then choose Stand By.

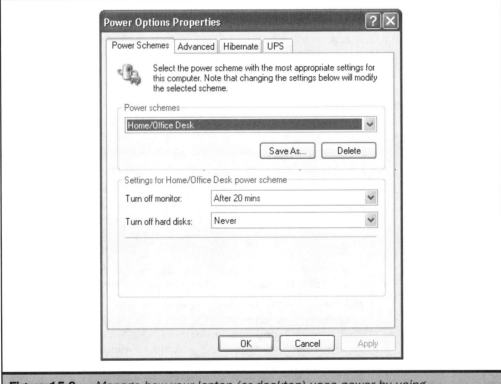

Figure 15-6.   *Manage how your laptop (or desktop) uses power by using these settings.*

Many laptops (and some desktops) also support hibernation, in which the computer stores the contents of its memory in a temporary file on your hard disk and then shuts itself down completely, so it stops using power. When you reopen the laptop, click the computer's power button and press keys or move the mouse. The computer wakes up again, restoring the contents of its memory from the temporary file. If your computer supports Hibernate Mode, the Power Options Properties dialog box includes a Hibernate tab. Click it and select the Enable Hibernation Support check box. The dialog box shows how much disk space will be required to store the contents of your computer's memory during hibernation, as well as the amount of free disk space currently available—be sure that you have enough space! When hibernation is enabled, an additional choice—Hibernate—appears when you choose Start | Shut Down.

Your computer can switch to Standby or Hibernate Mode automatically after a specified number of minutes of inactivity.

 Many laptop manufacturers add extra power management drivers to take advantage of special power-saving features—such as running the CPU slower when the computer is working on batteries than when it's plugged in, or turning off serial and parallel ports when you're not planning to use them. Consult your laptop's documentation to see whether your computer has any extra features you can enable.

Power Schemes

You can choose a *power scheme*, which is a group of settings that define when and if Windows should turn off the power to parts of your computer or switch to Standby or Hibernate Mode. Power schemes enable you to create and use different power management profiles for use under different circumstances.

Click the Power Schemes tab in the Power Options Properties dialog box and then click the Power Schemes drop-down list (the topmost setting). Choose the power scheme that reflects the type of hardware you're using:

- **Home/Office Desk**   Turns off the monitor after 20 minutes. On battery, goes into power-saving mode in less than half an hour.
- **Portable/Laptop**   Goes into power-saving mode fairly quickly whether plugged in or on battery.
- **Presentation**   Monitor never turns off. Goes into power-saving mode when running on battery without turning off monitor.
- **Always On**   Turns off monitor and hard drives (when on battery) but never goes into Standby or Hibernate.
- **Minimal Power Management**   Similar to Home/Office Desk, but takes much longer to hibernate.
- **Max Battery**   Goes into power-saving modes very quickly, especially when running on the battery.

You can see the specifics by selecting the power scheme. Once you've chosen the scheme that most closely matches your needs, you can edit the power management settings. If you've made changes you can save the settings as a new power scheme by clicking the Save As button, typing a new name for the power scheme, and clicking OK.

Note *The Advanced tab may have some additional settings for laptop power management.*

Checking Your Battery Status

To see the status of an individual battery in your computer, click the Power Meter tab in the Power Options Properties dialog box, make sure the Show Details For Each Battery check box is selected, and click the battery icon. You can also set alarms to beep when your battery charge drops to a preset level: click the Alarms tab on the Power Options Properties dialog box to set alarms.

Tip *You can display the Power Meter in the notification area of the Windows taskbar. Click the Advanced tab on the Power Options Properties dialog box and select the Always Show Icon On The Taskbar check box. The Power Meter shows whether the computer is connected to AC power or is running on batteries. Double-clicking the Power Meter in the notification area displays the Power Meter dialog box, which shows the status of your batteries.*

Using a Docking Station

Docking stations enable laptop users to avoid resource limitations that most laptops have. A docking station lets you connect to a better monitor, a real mouse, a full-sized keyboard, and possibly a network. Some docking stations give you access to additional hardware, such as a hard drive or CD-ROM drive. In addition to these resources, docking stations are convenient—by simply clicking the laptop into the docking station, you have access to these additional resources, without having to plug cables into the laptop.

Note *Port replicators are a kind of simple docking station that contain no resources except additional ports. A port replicator can be used to give you immediate access to a full-sized screen, keyboard, mouse, printer, and network connection, without having to plug each cable in separately. Port replicators don't have hard drives or other internal resources.*

Windows provides some features that are useful to users of docking stations:

■ **Hot docking**   If your hardware supports it, you can plug your laptop into its docking station *without turning off the laptop* and gain access to the additional resources provided by the docking station.

■ **Hardware profiles**   Enables you to create profiles so your laptop works properly, whether it's connected to the docking station or not.

Docking and Undocking

If your laptop supports hot docking, you can usually undock it by choosing Start |
Eject PC. Windows automatically adjusts to the change in hardware, notifying you of
open files and loading or unloading any necessary drivers. When you're ready to dock
the laptop again, simply put it in the docking station. Windows again adjusts automatically
to the change in hardware. Some laptops support hot docking, but no Eject PC command
appears on the Start menu.

If your laptop doesn't support hot docking (check the laptop's manual or online help
to find out for sure), you need to shut down Windows and turn the laptop off before
docking or undocking. You can benefit from creating two hardware profiles—one to
use when the laptop is docked and one to use when you work away from the docking
station. Multiple hardware profiles can save you time. When you undock your laptop,
you needn't change each hardware setting that needs to be changed; instead, you can
choose the correct hardware profile when the machine boots.

Creating and Using Hardware Profiles

A *hardware profile* is a description of your computer's hardware resources. Creating
multiple hardware profiles gives you an easy way to tell Windows to what hardware
the computer is connected. If the laptop is attached to a network, you want to be able
to use the network printer. If it's in a docking station, you want to be able to use the
docking station hardware—extra drives or sound card—and you may want to change
your screen resolution to take advantage of a regular monitor. Hardware profiles can
save information about the available hardware and the drivers used by the hardware.
You create one hardware profile for each hardware configuration you use.

Hardware profiles store information about printers, monitors, video controllers,
disk controllers, keyboards, modems, sound cards, network cards, pointing devices,
and ports.

Hardware profiles are useful when you have more than one way you commonly
use a computer. Your computer might sometimes be connected to a network and use
shared drives and printers. At other times, your computer might be disconnected from
the network and not have access to the network's shared resources. Or, you may have
a laptop you sometimes use with and sometimes use without a docking station. Hardware
profiles easily enable you to load and unload the drivers needed for the resources to
which your computer has access.

Creating a New Hardware Profile

The following are the steps for creating a new hardware profile. We recommend that
you first configure your hardware to get all your peripherals and network connections
running (see Chapter 13). Also, it's a good idea to make a copy of your original profile
in case you have trouble with the new profiles.

CONFIGURING WINDOWS FOR YOUR COMPUTER

Follow these steps to create a new hardware profile:

1. Open the System Properties dialog box by choosing Start | Control Panel | Performance And Maintenance | System. (Or, click Start, right-click My Computer, and choose Properties.)

2. Click the Hardware tab and then the Hardware Profiles button to see the options shown in Figure 15-7.

3. Select the hardware profile that is current. (At this point you may want to use the Copy button to create a copy of the working profile.)

 Making a copy of the original configuration profile is a good idea. Leave the original configuration profile as is, in case you have problems with the other profiles.

4. Click the Copy button to display the Copy Profile dialog box.

5. Type the new profile name in the To box. Use a name that is descriptive, such as "Networked," "No Network," or "Not Docked" as the name of the profile. Click OK.

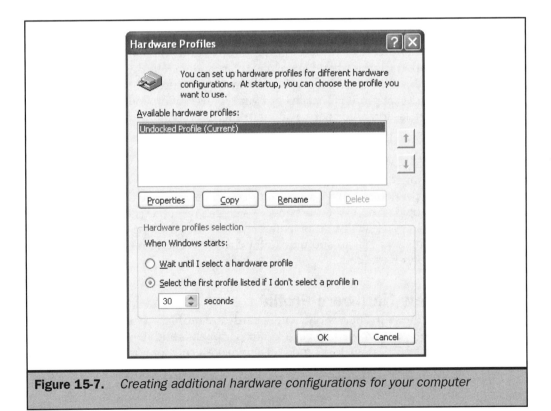

Figure 15-7.   *Creating additional hardware configurations for your computer*

6. Select the Hardware Profile that you are going to edit—in other words, the profile that will be for the computer when hardware connections are different than when you initially set the computer up.

7. Click OK to close the Hardware Profiles dialog box.

8. Click the Device Manager button on the Hardware tab of the System Properties dialog box to see the Device Manager window shown in Figure 15-8.

9. Expand the category that you want to change in the selected profile, and look for the hardware device(s) you want to disable

10. Right-click the device and select Properties button to see the properties for the device. The dialog box you see looks like the one displayed in Figure 15-9.

11. At the bottom of the General tab, choose Do Not Use This Device In The Current Hardware Profile as the Device Usage setting. When Remove is selected, the hardware is removed from Device Manager.

12. Repeat steps 10 and 11 as necessary to disable or remove additional hardware from this profile.

13. Click OK.

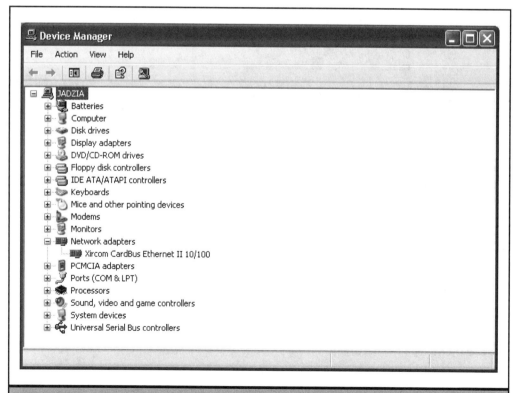

Figure 15-8.   *The Device Manager shows the hardware components of your computer.*

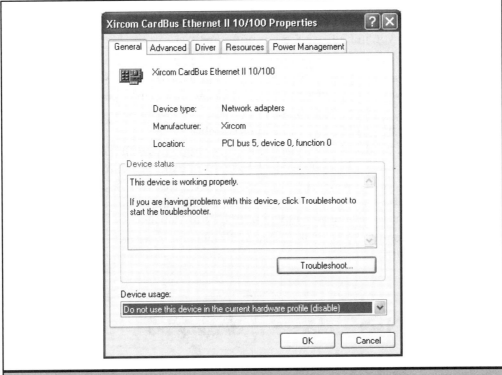

Figure 15-9. *Disabling hardware in the current profile in the Properties dialog box*

Switching Hardware Profiles

When the computer reboots—and whenever it starts from now on—you see a menu similar to the following:

```
Windows cannot determine what configuration your computer
is in.
Select one of the following:
1. Original profile
2. Networked
3. No Network
```

The menu lists the hardware profiles you created. Pick the configuration you want to use.

Modifying and Deleting Hardware Profiles

If you decide not to use a hardware profile any more, you can delete it by selecting it on the Hardware Profile tab of the System Profiles dialog box and clicking Delete.

To reenable a hardware device in a hardware profile, start the computer using the hardware profile. Then open the Add New Hardware icon in the Control Panel to add the drivers for this device to the hardware profile.

Using DualView to Display on Two Monitors

Windows XP allows you to use up to 10 monitors in order to increase your monitor "real estate." Many people find that one monitor is plenty, but for some applications, having multiple monitors can be useful. A similar feature is the DualView feature that allows laptop users who have two video ports on a single video card to expand the display to a second monitor. The laptop display remains the primary display, and a second monitor becomes the secondary display. This feature can be useful for presentations and other applications when you may want one monitor to display PowerPoint while you use the other monitor to do another task.

To use DualView, turn off your computer, attach the second monitor, and turn the computer on. Choose Start | Control Panel | Appearance And Themes | Display. For more about using multiple monitors, see the section "Using Multiple Displays" in Chapter 11.

CONFIGURING WINDOWS FOR YOUR COMPUTER

Smart Displays

Smart displays are a series of new products that will increase your mobility while you use your computer. A smart display (code-named Mira during development) is a portable monitor with a touch screen. You can use it as a secondary monitor or pick it up and take it with you around the house or office. The display interacts with the base computer via a wireless network and comes with a stylus and touch screen.

Some smart displays will come with portable keyboards. Of course, with a smart display, your mobility is limited by how far you can go and still be connected via your wireless network. This technology looks very interesting for home use—taking online recipes to the kitchen, surfing the Web while watching TV, and other activities.

The first versions will allow only a single person to use the computer at a time (either via the smart display or in the usual way—with the keyboard and mouse). However, later versions will allow two users to use one computer at the same time. See **www.microsoft.com/windowsxp/smartdisplay** for more information.

The Complete Reference

Chapter 16

Accessibility Options

L ike previous versions of Windows, Windows XP includes a number of options to help people who have disabilities that make using a computer difficult. In some cases, people without disabilities may also find the accessibility options useful. The options include settings for your keyboard, sound, display, and mouse.

To set your accessibility options, you can use the Accessibility Wizard, described in this chapter. (You may need to install the options from your Windows XP CD-ROM first.) After you set your options, you can turn them on and off by using the Accessibility Options dialog box, the icons that appear in the notification area on your taskbar, or the Utility Manager. Internet Explorer (Windows's web browser) has additional accessibility options.

What Accessibility Options Are Available in Windows XP?

Windows includes the accessibility options for people who have difficulty typing, reading the screen, hearing noises the computer makes, or using a mouse.

Keyboard aids for those who have difficulty typing include

- **StickyKeys**   Enables you to avoid pressing multiple keys by making the CTRL, WINDOWS, SHIFT, and ALT keys "sticky"—they stay in effect even after they have been released.

- **FilterKeys**   Filters out repeated keystrokes. Good for typists who have trouble pressing a key once briefly.

- **ToggleKeys**   Sounds a tone when the CAPS LOCK, SCROLL LOCK, and NUM LOCK keys are activated.

- **On-Screen Keyboard**   Displays a keyboard on the screen that enables you to type by using your mouse.

   For sloppy typists of all abilities (and for those with small laptop keyboards), ToggleKeys can be convenient to guard against accidentally pressing CAPS LOCK and typing capitalized prose by mistake.

Visual translation of sounds for those who have difficulty hearing include

- **SoundSentry**   Displays a visual warning when the computer makes a sound.
- **ShowSounds**   Displays a caption when the computer makes a sound.

Display options for those who have trouble reading the screen include

- **High Contrast**   Uses a high-contrast color scheme and increases legibility wherever possible.

Do Applications Use the Windows Accessibility Settings?

Although accessibility options are built into the Windows operating system, software applications must be designed to work with them. Microsoft maintains standards, including standards for accessibility that developers must meet to put the Designed for Windows logo on their product. The standards include support for high-contrast and enlarged displays, keyboard use with a single hand or device, adjustable timing for the user interface, and keyboard-only operation. If you need to use accessibility options with new software, make sure the software supports Windows accessibility options before you buy. Microsoft maintains an accessibility web site at: **www.microsoft.com/enable**.

- **Cursor Options**   Makes the cursor easier to see.
- **Magnifier**   Displays a window that magnifies part of the screen.
- **Narrator**   Reads text on the screen aloud.

Mouse options for those who dislike or have trouble using a mouse or trackball include

- **MouseKeys**   Enables you to use the numeric keypad to control the pointer.
- **SerialKey**   Turns on support for alternate input devices attached to the serial port.

Installing Accessibility Options

Most of Windows accessibility options are found on the Accessibility Options dialog box. Choose Start | Control Panel | Accessibility Options, and then click the Accessibility Options icon.

You can also use the Accessibility Wizard to guide you through the accessibility settings that make using a computer easier for you. All the accessibility options changed by the Accessibility Wizard appear on the Accessibility Options dialog box and are covered in detail in the rest of this chapter. To run the Accessibility Wizard, choose Start | All Programs | Accessories | Accessibility | Accessibility Wizard. Or, choose Configure Windows To Work For Your Vision, Hearing, And Mobility Needs on the Accessibility Options screen of the Control Panel.

Making the Keyboard More Accessible

Most of the options to change the way the keyboard accepts input are found on the Keyboard tab of the Accessibility Options dialog box, shown in Figure 16-1. Choose

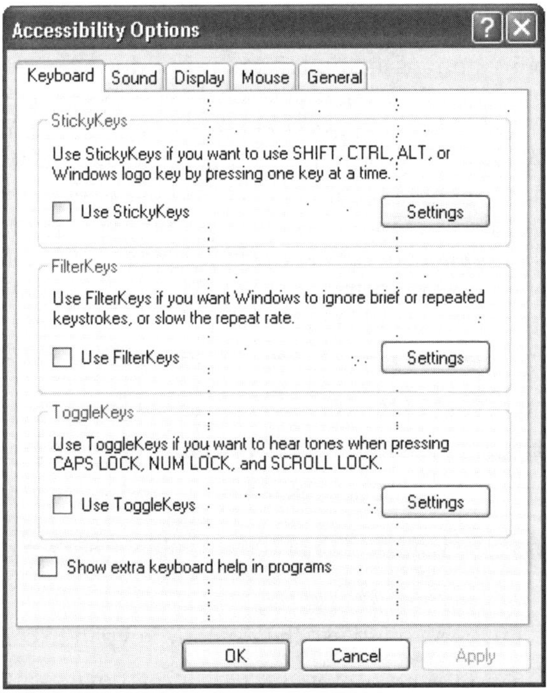

Figure 16-1.   *The Keyboard tab of the Accessibility Options dialog box*

Start | Control Panel | Accessibility Options, run the Accessibility Options program, and click the Keyboard tab if it's not selected.

Note   *Other keyboard settings, including character repeat settings and language, are available on the Keyboard Properties dialog box (see Chapter 12). To ask programs to display all available help information about the keyboard when you use their online help systems, select the Show Extra Keyboard Help In Programs check box on the Keyboard tab of the Accessibility Options dialog box.*

Making Your Keys Stick with StickyKeys

If you have trouble holding down two keys at once, activate *StickyKeys*, so you can press the keys separately and still get the same effect. When StickyKeys is on, you can save a document (for instance) by pressing the CTRL key, and then pressing the **S** key—you needn't press them at the same time. Pressing a second key turns off (or unsticks) the first key. StickyKeys works only with the *modifier keys*: SHIFT, WINDOWS, CTRL, and ALT.

 The ALT key is sticky all the time—to choose a command from a menu bar, you can press and release the ALT key before you press the letter for the command.

To turn on StickyKeys, select the Use StickyKeys check box on the Keyboard tab of the Accessibility Options dialog box. Then, click the Settings button to see five check boxes that define exactly how StickyKeys works:

- **Use Shortcut**   Turns StickyKeys on or off when you press SHIFT five times.
- **Press Modifier Key Twice To Lock**   Lock on a modifier key when you press it twice. Turn off the key by pressing it once again.
- **Turn StickyKeys Off If Two Keys Are Pressed At Once**   If two keys are pressed at once, StickyKeys turns off. To make a modifier key sticky again, StickyKeys must be turned on again by using the shortcut (if the Use Shortcut option is selected) or by displaying the Keyboard tab of the Accessibility Options dialog box and selecting the Use StickyKeys option. This option can be annoying if you ever want to press two keys at the same time.
- **Make Sounds When Modifier Key Is Pressed**   Beeps when a modifier key is struck. This is particularly useful when the previous option is turned on— it lets you know when StickyKeys is turned off.
- **Show StickyKeys Status On Screen**   Displays a small graphic to the left of the time in the notification area of the taskbar, as shown in the following illustration.

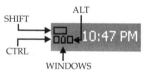

The four blocks represent the four modifier keys: SHIFT at the top, CTRL at the bottom left, WINDOWS in the bottom middle, and ALT at the bottom right. When a modifier key is stuck, its block is shaded on the diagram. You can double-click the icon to display the Accessibilities Options dialog box and make changes to your settings. When StickyKeys is off, the diagram is removed from the taskbar.

Filtering Out Extra Keystrokes with FilterKeys

If you have trouble typing each letter only once, you may want to turn on *FilterKeys*— which "filters out" extra keystrokes—rather than spending time editing them out yourself. You can configure FilterKeys to ignore repeated keystrokes repeated too quickly and to slow down the repeat rate (the rate at which a character is repeated when a key is held down).

To turn on FilterKeys, select the Use FilterKeys check box on the Keyboard tab of the Accessibility Options dialog box. Then, click the Settings button to define exactly how FilterKeys works:

- **Use Shortcut**   Turns FilterKeys on or off when you hold down the right SHIFT key for eight seconds.

- **Ignore Repeated Keystrokes**   Ignores keys repeated without a sufficient pause (sometimes called *BounceKeys*). When you choose this option, click the Settings button next to it and then define the interval within which repeated keys should be ignored. Getting the right interval is crucial to avoiding frustration, so use the Test Area box to type words with repeated letters to see whether the setting works for you.

- **Ignore Quick Keystrokes And Slow Down The Repeat Rate**   This option enables features called SlowKeys and RepeatKeys. *SlowKeys* enables you to filter out keys that are pressed only briefly. When SlowKeys is on, you must type more methodically, but Windows ignores keys touched lightly or quickly. *RepeatKeys* enables you to change the way keys are repeated (see Chapter 12)— normally, if you hold down a key, it repeats at a certain rate after it has been held down for a certain interval. The settings for SlowKeys and RepeatKeys are on the same dialog box. Choose the radio button and click the Settings button next to it to configure them—if holding down a key causes it to repeat; if so, after what interval and at what rate should it repeat; and how long a key should be held down to register.

- **Beep When Keys Pressed Or Accepted**   Tells Windows to beep when a key is pressed, and beep again when a key is accepted.

- **Show FilterKey Status On Screen**   Displays a small graphic to the left of the time on the system tray, as shown in the following illustration:

You can double-click the icon to display the Accessibilities Options dialog box and make changes to your settings. When FilterKeys is off, the diagram is removed from the taskbar.

Hearing When a Toggled Key Is Pressed

ToggleKeys is useful if you accidentally press keys that change the behavior of the keyboard. When ToggleKeys is turned on and you press CAPS LOCK, NUM LOCK, or

SCROLL LOCK, a tone sounds—a high-pitched tone when you turn CAPS LOCK, NUM LOCK, or SCROLL LOCK on, and a low-pitched tone when you turn it off.

To turn on ToggleKeys, select the Use ToggleKeys option on the Keyboard tab of the Accessibility Options dialog box. Click the Settings button to turn on the Use Shortcut setting, which enables you to turn ToggleKeys on or off by holding down the NUM LOCK key for five seconds.

Displaying the On-Screen Keyboard

If using the mouse or other pointing device is easier for you than typing on the keyboard, Windows can display a picture of a keyboard on the screen. You can use a mouse, joystick, pointing stick, or other pointing device to choose characters from the On-Screen Keyboard:

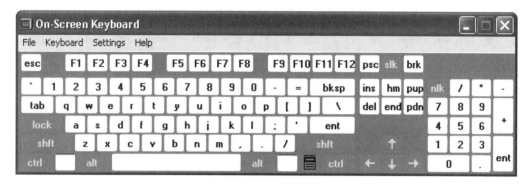

To display the On-Screen Keyboard, choose Start | All Programs | Accessories | Accessibility | On-Screen Keyboard. The program displays an explanatory dialog box along with the On-Screen Keyboard. After reading it, click Do Not Show This Message Again, and then OK to dismiss the dialog box.

You can type by choosing the keys on the On-Screen Keyboard with your mouse in one of three ways (typing modes):

- **Click To Select**   Click an on-screen key.

- **Hover To Select**   Rest the mouse pointer on the on-screen key for the specified period of time. You can choose the amount of time the mouse pointer must "hover" before the key types.

- **Joystick Or Key To Select**   Windows automatically moves the highlight from key to key on the On-Screen Keyboard, cycling endlessly across the keys. When the highlight gets to the key you want, press a key, click the mouse, or activate the joystick to select that key. You can choose how fast the highlight moves, what key or click chooses the selected key, and how your selection device is connected to the computer.

Choose your typing mode by choose Settings | Typing Mode from the menu bar at the top of the On-Screen Keyboard window.

The characters you "type" using the On-Screen Keyboard appear in the active window—be sure to select the window into which you want to type first. When you choose the "shft" button on the screen, it remains on until you choose the next button (for example, choose "shft" and then *a* to type a capital *A*). ALT-TAB is the keystroke combination to choose the active window: from the On-Screen Keyboard select "alt," select "tab" repeatedly until Windows highlights the icon for the window you want, and then select "alt" again).

You can choose:

- Whether the keyboard appears "on top" of other windows that it overlaps, by choosing Settings | Always On Top

- Whether the on-screen "keys" make a sound when chosen, by choosing Settings | Use Click Sound

- What font appears on the keys of the On-Screen Keyboard, by choosing Settings | Font

- Whether to display the standard or enhanced keyboard (the enhanced keyboard includes the numeric keypad and more cursor movement keys), by choosing Keyboard | Enhanced Keyboard or Keyboard | Standard Keyboard

- Whether to arrange the keys like a real keyboard, or in a grid, by choosing Keyboard | Regular Layout or Keyboard | Block Layout

- How many keys to display, by choosing Keyboard | 101 Keys, Keyboard | 102 Keys (which adds a backslash key to the left of Z), or Keyboard | 106 Keys (which adds Japanese-language characters).

Configuration Settings for the Hearing Impaired

Windows includes options to help translate the sounds programs make for people who have difficulty hearing. The sound accessibility options don't work for all sounds, but they do work for most sounds generated by Windows and for some sounds generated by applications. The options are found on the Sound tab of the Accessibility Options dialog box, shown in Figure 16-2. Choose Start | Control Panel | Accessibility Options, run the Accessibility Options icon, and click the Sound tab.

The two sound options are SoundSentry and ShowSounds:

- **SoundSentry** tells Windows to use a flashing element on the screen to tell the user a sound has been made. Set the Choose The Visual Warning box to choose a screen element to flash. We recommend choosing either the Flash Active

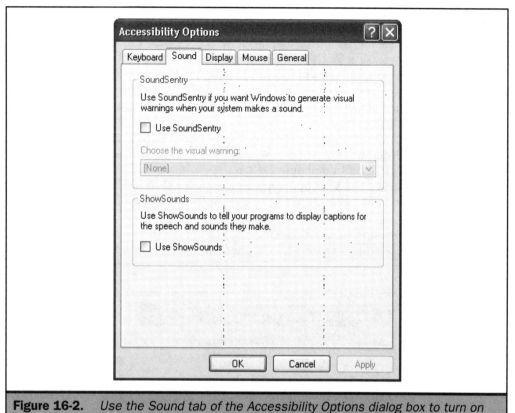

Figure 16-2. *Use the Sound tab of the Accessibility Options dialog box to turn on the accessibility options for the hearing-impaired.*

Caption Bar or the Flash Active Window option—otherwise, it's impossible to determine which application caused the sound.

- **ShowSounds** option displays a caption on the screen each time Windows (and some other programs) makes a sound.

Configuration Settings for the Visually Impaired

Windows has four features that make the screen easier to read: a high-contrast color scheme, configurable cursor appearance, Magnifier (which can magnify part of the screen), and Narrator (which reads the screen out loud).

 Other display settings—including colors and fonts—are available on the Display Properties dialog box (see Chapter 11, section "Display Properties").

Displaying in High Contrast

High Contrast changes the Windows color scheme and increases legibility wherever possible, often by increasing font sizes. Not every program uses font sizes controlled by Windows, so not everything on the screen gets bigger. You control High Contrast from the Display tab of the Accessibility Options dialog box, shown in Figure 16-3. Choose Start | Control Panel | Accessibility Options, run the Accessibility Options icon, and click the Display tab.

Turn on the High Contrast feature by clicking the Use High Contrast check box. Click the Settings button to turn on the Use Shortcut setting, which enables you to turn High Contract on or off by pressing LEFT ALT-LEFT-SHIFT-PRINT SCREEN (that is, hold down the ALT and SHIFT keys that appear on the left side of the keyboard near the X and Z keys, and also press the PRINT SCREEN button). You can also choose a color scheme.

When High Contrast is on, your screen looks like Figure 16-4—the High Contrast White (Large) color scheme is shown. (High Contrast Black is the default, but the white

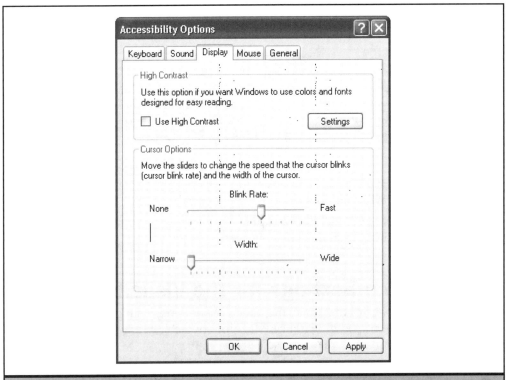

Figure 16-3. *Turn on the High Contrast option by using the Display tab of the Accessibility Options dialog box.*

version is more readable when printed in this book.) Using bigger fonts results in less information fitting on the screen, so you see more scroll bars than usual. Also, the different color scheme may take some getting used to.

Controlling the Cursor's Size and Blink Rate

The Display tab of the Accessibility dialog box (shown in Figure 16-3) also contains the Cursor Blink Rate and Cursor Width settings. Move the sliders to control how quickly the cursor blinks and how wide it appears on the screen.

Magnifying the Screen

The Magnifier is an alternative to High Contrast mode—it enables you to magnify only a part of the screen at a time. One section of the screen (usually a strip along the top of the screen) shows a highly magnified version of one area of the screen—the area where you are working.

Turn on Magnifier by choosing Start | All Programs | Accessories | Accessibility | Magnifier. (From the keyboard, press WINDOWS or CTRL-ESC to display the Start menu, press **R** to choose Run, type **magnify**, and press ENTER.) Windows displays an explanatory message the first time you run Magnifier: Click the Do Not Show This Message Again check box after you've read it and click OK. You see the magnification

Figure 16-4. *The desktop and Windows Explorer in High Contrast*

window at the top of your screen and the Magnifier Settings dialog box, as shown in Figure 16-5.

You can control the magnification level, which part of the screen is displayed in the magnification window, its color scheme, and its location on the screen:

■ **Magnification Level**   Determines how much larger things appear in the magnification window. Use the Magnification Level setting on the Magnifier Settings dialog box. The larger the level, the more the contents of the magnification window are magnified.

■ **Tracking**   Determines what part of the screen is shown in the magnification window. You can choose to Follow Mouse Cursor, Follow Keyboard Focus, and Follow Text Editing. These three options are not mutually exclusive—

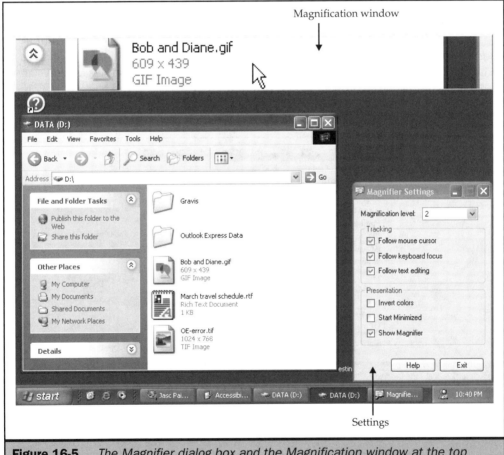

Figure 16-5.   *The Magnifier dialog box and the Magnification window at the top of the screen*

if you select all three, the display in the magnification window is determined by what you are currently doing—in other words, Windows does its best to display the part of the screen you're working with in the magnification window.

- **Colors** Controls colors in the magnification window. Click the Invert Colors check box to use the opposite of the colors in the rest of the screen. Inverted colors make it easier to see that the magnification window is a special part of the screen, but they may also make the display more confusing.

- **Size and Location** You can change the size of the magnification window by dragging the lower window border up or down. You can change the position of the window by clicking inside the window and dragging. You can "dock" the window along any edge of the desktop or put it somewhere in the middle of the screen. If the magnification window appears as a window rather than a wide border, you can control its size and position in the same way you'd change them for any window. Your ideal magnification window may be a small square near one corner of the screen. The magnification window always appears on top—it cannot be covered by another window.

When you have adjusted the settings in the Magnifier Settings dialog box, click its Minimize button to shrink it to a button on the taskbar. (You may want to select the Start Minimized check box first to tell Windows to minimize the Magnifier Settings dialog box whenever you start Magnifier.) Don't click Exit unless you want to stop seeing the magnification window on your screen. You can redisplay the Magnifier Settings dialog box by right-clicking the magnification window and choosing Options from the shortcut menu or by clicking its button on the taskbar. Close the magnification window by closing the Magnifier Settings dialog box or by right-clicking the magnification window and choosing Exit.

 Deselect the Show Magnifier check box to turn off the magnification window temporarily; click it again to display the window again.

Listening to Microsoft Narrator Read the Screen Out Loud

For vision-impaired users, a screen-reader can be the best way to find out what's on the computer display. Windows XP comes with a rudimentary screen reading program called Microsoft Narrator. Narrator is designed to work with most parts of Windows XP itself, but may not work with other programs. The program says the items in the active window, including text, buttons, lists, and other things, using a computer-generated voice.

To start it, choose Start | All Programs | Accessories | Accessibility | Narrator. (From the keyboard, press WINDOWS or CTRL-ESC to display the Start menu, press **R** to choose Run, type **narrator**, and press ENTER.) Read (or listen to) the explanatory dialog box, select the Do Not Show This Message Again check box, and click OK. You see (and hear) the Narrator dialog box, shown here:

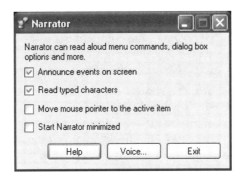

You can control these aspects of narrator from the Narrator dialog box:

- **Voice**   Click the Voice button to choose which preprogrammed voice to use and how fast, high, and loud the voice speaks.

- **What to read**   Select the Announce Events On Screen check box to hear when something changes on the screen and the Read Typed Characters check box to hear what you type.

- **Mouse movement**   Select the Move Mouse Pointer To The Active Item check box to make the mouse pointer follow the "focus" (that is, what item on the screen is active).

You can also use the following keyboard shortcuts with Narrator:

Keyboard Shortcut	Action
CTRL-SHIFT-ENTER	Hear information about the active item.
CTRL-SHIFT-INSERT	Hear details about the active item.
CTRL-SHIFT-SPACEBAR	Hear all the information in the active window.
ALT-HOME	Hear the title bar of the active window.
ALT-END	Hear the status bar of the active window. (This feature does not work for all programs).
CTRL	Silence the Narrator.

Once you have Narrator configured as you like it, select the Start Narrator Minimized check box in the Narrator dialog box to minimize it in future. Also take a look at "Useful Keyboard Shortcuts" sidebar in this chapter.

Useful Keyboard Shortcuts

If you prefer using the keyboard to the mouse, you may want to try the following key combinations, which many but not all programs support:

- **ALT-SPACEBAR** Displays the system menu, from which you can choose to close, minimize, restore, maximize, or move the current window.

- **ALT-F4** Closes the current program.

- **ALT-TAB or TAB** Switches to another running program. Keep pressing TAB or ALT-TAB to cycle through all the programs that are running.

- **CTRL-C** Copies the selected information to the Clipboard.

- **CTRL-V** Copies the current contents of the Clipboard to the current position of the cursor.

- **CTRL-A** Selects all the information in the window.

- **CTRL-F4** Closes the current window. CTRL-W performs the same task in some programs.

- **SHIFT-F10** Displays the shortcut menu (the same menu you would see if you right-clicked at the current position of the mouse).

- **ESC** Cancels the current dialog box (the same as clicking the Cancel button).

- **ENTER** Click the currently selected button.

- **WINDOWS or CTRL-ESC** Displays the Start menu.

- **WINDOWS-L** Locks the computer.

- **WINDOWS-U** Displays the Utility Manager (see "Turning On and Off Magnifier, Narrator, and the On-Screen Keyboard by Using the Utility Manager" later in this chapter).

CONFIGURING WINDOWS
FOR YOUR COMPUTER

Configuration Settings for the Mouse and Alternative Input Devices

If you have difficulty using a mouse or other pointing devices, if your pointing device is broken, or if you don't like to use it, turn on MouseKeys. If you have trouble using a keyboard and mouse for input, you can let Windows know you use an alternative input device. Windows also includes a number of keyboard shortcuts for giving commands from the keyboard (see "Useful Keyboard Shortcuts").

Other mouse settings—including button configuration, double-click speed, and mouse pointer speed—are available on the Mouse Properties dialog box (see Chapter 12). See Chapter 13 for information on installing other pointing devices.

Controlling the Pointer by Using the Number Pad

MouseKeys enables you to control the mouse pointer by using the numeric keypad on your keyboard. The regular mouse or other pointing device continues to work as well. To turn on MouseKeys, choose Start | Control Panel | Accessibility Options, run the Accessibility Options icon, click the Mouse tab, select the Use MouseKeys check box, and click the Settings button to display the Settings For MouseKeys dialog box, shown in Figure 16-6. You can set these options:

- **Use Shortcut** Turns MouseKeys on or off when you press LEFT ALT-LEFT SHIFT-NUM LOCK (hold down the ALT and SHIFT keys that appear on the left side of the keyboard near the X and Z keys, and also press the NUM LOCK key). When you turn MouseKeys on using the keyboard shortcut, Windows displays a little dialog box.

- **Top Speed** Sets the pointer's top speed when you hold down keys to move it.

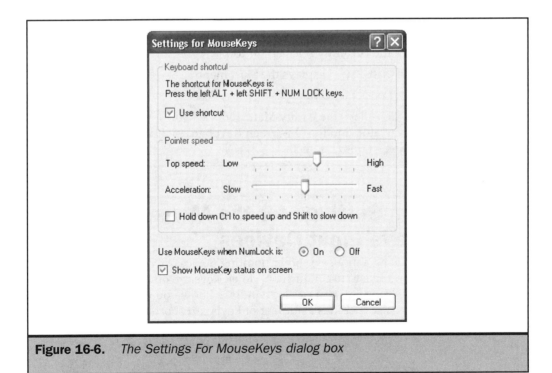

Figure 16-6. *The Settings For MouseKeys dialog box*

- **Acceleration**   Sets the speed at which the pointer accelerates when you hold down a key to move it. A faster rate of acceleration means the pointer reaches its top speed sooner.

- **Hold Down Ctrl To Speed Up And Shift To Slow Down**   Gives you more ways to control the speed of the mouse pointer. When this option is selected, you can hold down CTRL when you want the pointer to move in big jumps across the screen and hold down SHIFT when you want the pointer to move in smaller-than-usual increments.

- **Use MouseKeys When NumLock Is On/Off**   Determines when the number pad keys move the mouse pointer—when NUM LOCK is on or off. If you choose the Off setting, then you can enter numbers by using the number pad when NUM LOCK is on. However, you need another set of arrows to move the cursor. (Most keyboards have a separate set of cursor motion keys.)

- **Show MouseKeys Status On Screen**   Displays a small graphic in the notification area on the taskbar to the left of the time, as shown here:

The following list shows how to use the number pad to control the pointer when MouseKeys is on (be sure to use the keys on the numeric keys, not the equivalent keys elsewhere on your keyboard):

- Press the arrow keys to move the pointer.

- Press the – key to set MouseKeys to click the right mouse button whenever you press the 5 key.

- Press the / key to set MouseKeys to click the left mouse button whenever you press the 5 key.

- Press the * key to set MouseKeys to click both mouse buttons whenever you press the 5 key.

- Press the 5 key to click (with left or right mouse button, depending whether you last pressed – or /) whatever the pointer is on.

- Press the + key to double-click whatever the pointer is on.

- Press the 0 or INSERT key to begin dragging (the equivalent of holding down the mouse button). Move the item by pressing the arrow keys on the number pad. Drop the item (release the mouse button) by pressing the "." or DELETE key.

Configuring an Alternative Input Device

If you're using an alternative input device (something other than the keyboard and a mouse), and you want to connect that device to a serial port, turn on the Use Serial

CONFIGURING WINDOWS FOR YOUR COMPUTER

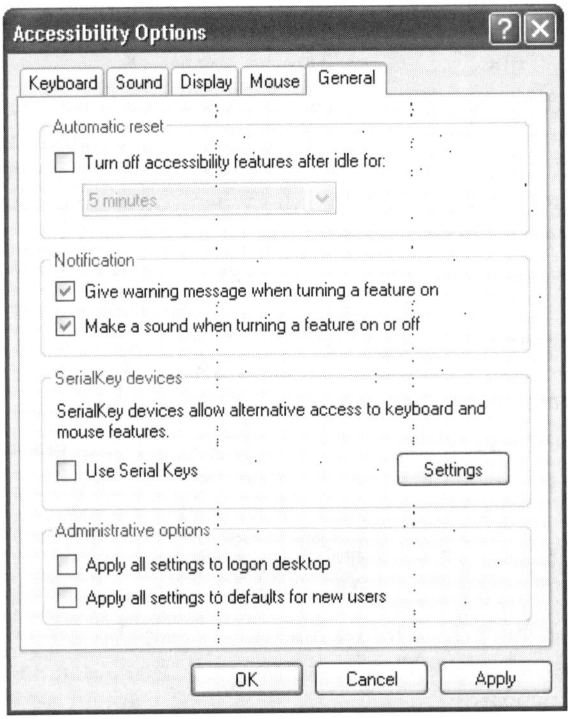

Figure 16-7. *The General tab of the Accessibility Options dialog box*

Keys option on the General tab of the Accessibility Options dialog box (shown in Figure 16-7). Choose Start | Control Panel | Accessibility Options, run the Accessibility Options program, and click the General tab if it's not selected. Use the Settings button to choose the serial port and baud rate for the device.

Turning Accessibility Options Off and On

In general, you probably want to turn on whichever accessibility options you find useful, and leave them turned on but, if you share your computer, you may want the capability to turn them on and off easily.

Turning On and Off Magnifier, Narrator, and the On-Screen Keyboard by Using the Utility Manager

Windows XP has a new way to turn the Magnifier, Narrator, and On-Screen Keyboard on and off: the Utility Manager. Press WINDOWS-U to see it:

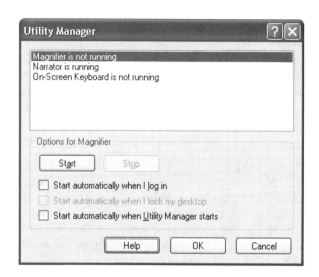

You can also start the program by choosing Start | All Programs | Accessories | Accessibility | Utility Manager. You can turn on your accessibility options by pressing WINDOWS-U when you see the Welcome To Windows logon screen, before you even log on.

The Utility Manager shows which of the three programs are running. You can stop or start a program by clicking it and clicking the Start or Stop button. You can also use check boxes in the Utility Manager window to start each of the three programs when you log in, when you lock the desktop (by pressing WINDOWS-L), or whenever you run the Utility Manager. Click a program and then select the options for that program.

   Narrator is usually configured to start automatically when you open the Utility Manager window, so don't be surprised when your computer starts reading the screen to you. You also see an informational Microsoft Narrator dialog box. Click OK in the Microsoft Narrator dialog box and then click Exit in the Narrator dialog box.

Turning On and Off Other Accessibility Features

The General tab of the Accessibility Options dialog box (shown in Figure 16-7) has some options for turning accessibility options off and on. Choose Start | Control Panel | Accessibility Options, run the Accessibility Options program, and click the General tab if it's not selected.

- **Turn off after the computer is idle**   If more than one person uses the computer, you may want the accessibility options turned off when it has been idle for a certain interval. The Turn Off Accessibility Features After Idle For option on the General tab enables you to choose how long the computer must be idle before all accessibility options are turned off. If you always want accessibility options to remain on, make sure this option is not selected.

- **Beep when settings change**   You may also want notification when accessibility options are turned on or off. The Notification options enable you to see a message when an accessibility feature is turned on and to hear a sound when an accessibility option is turned on or off.

- **Turn on accessibility options for Welcome logon screen**   If you need accessibility options, you'd probably like them to be available during Windows logon (unless you don't use a logon screen—see Chapter 6 for logging into a multiuser computer, and Chapter 27 for logging into networks. You must be logged on with an administrative account to change this setting.

- **Apply settings to new users**   If your computer is set up for multiple users, apply the same accessibility settings to any new accounts. You must be logged on with an administrative account to change this setting.

After you activate an accessibility option and enable its shortcut by using the Accessibility Options dialog box, you can turn the option on and off by using these keys:

Setting	How to Toggle On and Off
FilterKeys	Hold down SHIFT for eight seconds
High Contrast mode	Press LEFT ALT-LEFT SHIFT-PRINT SCREEN
MouseKeys	Press LEFT ALT-LEFT SHIFT-NUM LOCK
StickyKeys	Press SHIFT five times
ToggleKeys	Hold down NUM LOCK for five seconds

Making Internet Explorer Accessible

Internet Explorer 6.0, which comes with Windows XP, has additional accessibility features you can use:

- **Keyboard**   Press TAB and SHIFT-TAB to cycle among the active parts of the Internet Explorer window, including links and buttons. The selected item is highlighted with a dotted-line box.

- **Display**   Internet Explorer can use the font sizes and formatting you choose, even if they are different from those specified in the web page (see Chapter 24).

To choose other accessibility options, choose Tools | Internet Options on the Internet Explorer menu bar and click the Advanced tab. In the list of settings that appears, you can select or deselect these settings:

- **Always Expand ALT Text For Images**   (in the Accessibility section) Turn this setting on to display the entire ALT (alternative) text supplied on some web pages as captions for pictures, so a screen reader can read the caption.

- **Move System Caret With Focus/Selection Changes**   (in the Accessibility section) Turn this on so the cursor moves along with the mouse pointer and a screen reader or magnifier program can read or display the right part of the Internet Explorer window.

- **Enable Page Transitions, Use Smooth Scrolling**   (in the Browsing section) Turn these off to make screen readers and voice recognition programs work better.

- **Play Animations In Web Pages, Play Videos In Web Pages, Show Pictures** (in the Multimedia section) Turn these off if your vision is impaired and you want to speed up web browsing.

- **Play Sounds In Web Pages**   (in the Multimedia section) Turn this off if sounds are annoying or interfere with your screen reading program.

- **Print Background Colors and Images**   (in the Printing section) Turn this off for clearer printouts.

CONFIGURING WINDOWS FOR YOUR COMPUTER

The Complete Reference

Part IV

Working with Text, Numbers, Pictures, Sound, and Video

The
Complete
Reference

Chapter 17

Working with Documents in Windows XP

Although word processing isn't glamorous, it is, and probably forever will be, one of the most popular uses for a computer. Many computers come with Microsoft Word or Works preinstalled, so you are equipped with a word processor. However, Windows XP itself comes with two tools for working with text documents—the first is the unsophisticated Notepad, and the second is the surprisingly powerful WordPad. This chapter discusses both.

This chapter also covers two other useful utilities: Calculator and Character Map. The Calculator provides all the scientific functions you may need from a calculator, and Character Map gives you access to a variety of special characters.

Reading Text Files with Notepad

Notepad is a holdover from Windows 3.0. Back in the Windows 3.0 era, configuration information was stored in text files that regularly needed to be edited, and Notepad could edit those files. In subsequent releases of Windows, editing configuration files has become a task more often done either automatically by installation programs or manually by system administrators and hackers than by people simply trying to make their computers work the way they want.

Notepad, however, remains available in Windows XP and using it is the simplest way to edit a text file. Sure, you can use a full-fledged word processor, but doing so is often more trouble than it's worth. Use Notepad to edit any *text file* (also called an *ASCII file*)—that is, files that contain only letters, numbers, and special characters that appear on the keyboard. Notepad can't format your text with bold, italics, or anything else pretty, but we've been known to use Notepad to edit web pages, and it's invaluable for storing little snippets of text you might need later. Unlike the Notepad in previous versions of Windows, Windows XP Notepad can handle large text files (as large as your computer's free RAM).

Running Notepad

To run Notepad, choose Start | All Programs | Accessories | Notepad. (Or, you can choose Start | Run to display the Run dialog box, and then type **notepad** and press ENTER.) Notepad looks like Figure 17-1: just a window with a menu.

Here are some tips for using Notepad:

- **Print Settings, Headers, and Footers**   To change the setup of the document when you print it, choose File | Page Setup (this command isn't available if you haven't installed a printer). Use the Page Setup dialog box (see Figure 17-2) to change margins, page orientation, and paper size. (In the Orientation box, Portrait prints on paper in the usual way; Landscape prints sideways on the page, with the lines of text parallel to the long edge of the paper.) If you have more than one printer, you can select the one to use. Use the Header and

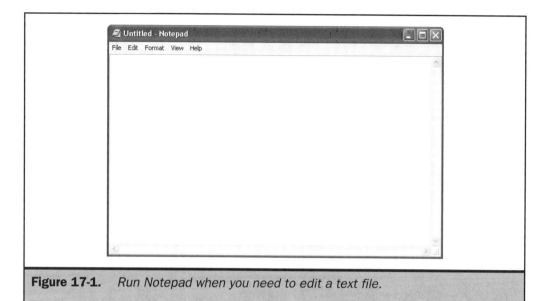

Figure 17-1.   *Run Notepad when you need to edit a text file.*

Footer text boxes to add headers and footers to your documents. You can type plain text, or you can use these codes:

Code	Meaning
&f	Displays the name of the file
&p	Displays the page number
&d	Displays the current date
&t	Displays the current time
&&	Displays an ampersand
&l	Left-justifies the text after this code
&c	Centers the text after this code
&r	Right-justifies the text after this code

- **File Types**   Choose File | Open to see the Open dialog box. Change the Files Of Type option to All Files if the file you want to open does not have the .txt extension.

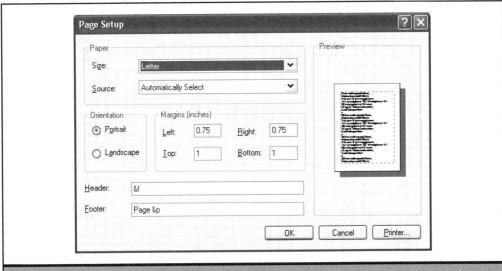

Figure 17-2. *Notepad options for printing a text file*

■ **Fonts** Notepad normally uses a fixed-pitch font to display text files. You can change the font by choosing Format | Font to display the Font dialog box and then setting the font, style, and size.

■ **Log Files** Create a log file by typing **.LOG** in the upper-left corner (the very beginning) of your Notepad file (be sure to use capital letters). Each time you run Notepad and open the file, Notepad enters the current time and date at the end of the file. You can then type an entry for that time and date.

■ **Moving Around Large Text Files** You can move quickly through a large file by using the Go To option—choose Edit | Go To or press CTRL-G to display the Go To Line dialog box.

■ **Time and Date** You can insert the current time and date (according to your computer's clock) at the cursor by choosing Edit | Time/Date or by pressing F5.

■ **Undo** If you make a mistake, you can reverse your last edit by choosing Edit | Undo or pressing CTRL-Z.

■ **Word Wrap** As you work with a document, you might want to turn on the *Word Wrap*, so that Notepad breaks long lines to fit in the Notepad window. When Word Wrap is off, each paragraph appears as a single long line (unless it contains carriage returns). Turn on (or off) Word Wrap by choosing Format | Word Wrap. Notepad then wraps lines the way a word processor wraps lines, so no line is wider than the Notepad window. The Notepad Word Wrap feature doesn't add carriage return characters to the text file when you save it and it doesn't affect the way the file appears when printed.

Files You Can Edit with Notepad

The standard file extension for text files is .txt. When you click or double-click a .txt file in Windows Explorer, Windows runs Notepad to view the file.

Windows associates a number of other types of files with Notepad, too, because these files contain only text. These file types include

- Configuration files, such as files with the extension .ini (see Chapter 37).

- Log files, such as the logs that the Backup program creates (see Chapter 9). Many log files have the extension .log.

- Setup information files, which come with many installation programs and have the extension .inf.

Simple, Free Word Processing with WordPad

WordPad is a great little word processor if your needs are modest—and the price can't be beat! Open WordPad by choosing Start | All Programs | Accessories | WordPad. (Or, you can choose Start | Run to display the Run dialog box, type **wordpad**, and press ENTER.)

WordPad (shown in Figure 17-3) does not offer many of the advanced features that you get in Microsoft Word or Corel's WordPerfect—notably missing is a spell check. But WordPad does offer many of the formatting tools you need to create a spiffy letter, memo, or essay. Many of the commands and keyboard shortcuts are the same as those in Microsoft Word, which makes them easy for many people to remember. And, because WordPad is a small program, it loads quickly.

WordPad can open documents that are saved in any one of a variety of formats, including Word 97, 2000, and 2002 (WordPad cannot preserve all of Word's formatting, however). Choose File | Open, and use the Files Of Type option on the Open dialog box to choose the type of document you want to open.

When you save a document to pass on to a friend or coworker, choose File | Save to use the existing filename, or choose File | Save As to specify the filename. Be sure to save the document in a format that your friend's or coworker's software can open. Here's a rundown of the file formats WordPad can use to save a document:

- **Rich Text Format** If you want to preserve any formatting you've done in your WordPad document, save it in Rich Text format. *Rich Text Format (.rtf)* is compatible with just about anything.

- **Text Document** When you save a file in text format (with the extension .txt), you lose all formatting, but you preserve all text in the *ANSI* character set (a standard set of codes used for storing text).

- **Text Document—MS-DOS Format** When you save a file in MS-DOS text format (also with the extension .txt), you lose all formatting, but you preserve all text in Microsoft's extended ASCII character set, which includes various

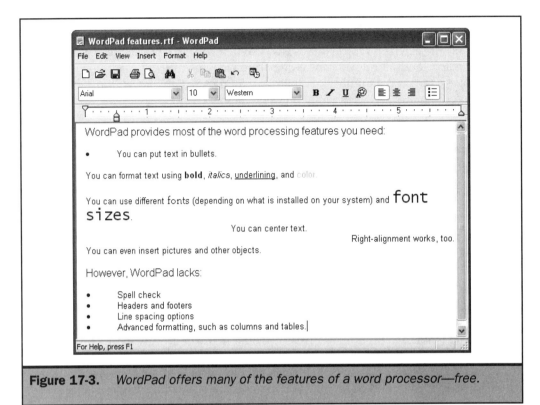

Figure 17-3.   *WordPad offers many of the features of a word processor—free.*

accented characters and smiley faces. Use this format only if you want to use the text in a Windows or DOS application, but not if you plan to send the file to a Mac, UNIX, or other non-Microsoft system.

■ **Unicode Text Document**   *Unicode* enables you to use characters from practically every language on Earth, from Latvian to Japanese, but make sure your recipient has a Unicode-compatible program before you save Unicode documents.

Formatting with WordPad

Use the options on the format bar (the row of buttons below the toolbar) to format a document in WordPad. If you don't see the format bar (or WordPad's other bars—the toolbar, ruler bar, or status bar), use the View menu to display them.

Like Word, formatting in WordPad works like this:

■ Select the text you want to format, using your mouse. Or, choose Edit | Select All (or press CTRL-A) to select the entire document.

■ Click the button or give the command for the type of formatting you want to apply.

Here are some formatting options in WordPad:

■ **Bullets**   Click anywhere in the paragraph and click the Bullets button at the very end of the format bar, or choose Format | Bullet Style. To format more than one paragraph, select the paragraphs before clicking the Bullets button.

■ **Indents**   Click in the paragraph (or select several paragraphs) and choose Format | Paragraph to display the Paragraph dialog box. You can type a measurement from the left or right margin, or for the first line only. You can also specify that the paragraph is left aligned, right aligned, or centered. When you click OK, the margin indicators on the ruler bar move to show the current margins for the paragraph in which your cursor is located.

■ **Tabs**   You can set tab stops by clicking the ruler bar. If the ruler bar isn't already displayed, choose View | Ruler to display it. Be sure to select the text for which you need the tabs (press CTRL-A to select all text in the document) before you create tabs, because the tabs you create only apply to the paragraph the cursor is in if no text is selected. To set tab stops, click the ruler where you want a tab stop. L-shaped markers appear at each tab stop. Drag the L-shaped tab markers left or right on the ruler bar to adjust the tab stops. To delete a tab stop, drag it down off the ruler bar.

Alternatively, choose Format | Tabs to display the Tabs dialog box. Set a tab stop by typing a measurement from the left margin and clicking the Set button (if you're not sure what to use, every 0.5 of an inch is pretty standard). The tab stop appears on the list of tab stops that are set for the current position in the document. Type additional measurements from the left margin and click Set to set more tab stops. To delete a tab stop, select it from the list and click the Clear button. When you click OK, little L-shaped tab indicators appear on the ruler bar to show the location of tab stops.

■ **Fonts, Size, and Color**   To change the font, font size, or color of the selected text, click the Font or Font Size box on the format bar and choose the font or font size from the list that appears. Or, choose Format | Font to display the Font dialog box. If you have installed multilanguage support, you can also choose the script (alphabet). You can also choose settings from the Font dialog box without selecting text, before you type the text you want to format; use the Font dialog box again to turn the formatting off.

You can also format text by using keystroke combinations: CTRL-B to bold, CTRL-I to italicize, and CTRL-U to underline. You can use these keystrokes after you select text or before you type the text you want to format (press the key combination again to turn off the formatting).

Printing Your Document

To print your document, click the Print button on the toolbar, choose File | Print, or press CTRL-P. You see the Print dialog box, in which you can select the printer, which pages to print, and the number of copies.

You may want to preview (see exactly what it will look like on paper) the document before you print it so you'll know exactly how it will look on paper. To preview your document, click the Print Preview button (the fifth button on the toolbar) or choose File | Print Preview. The WordPad window shows approximately how the printed page will look. You can click the Zoom In button to get a closer look, click Print to begin printing, or click Close to return to the regular view of your document.

You can also format the page by choosing File | Page Setup to display the Page Setup dialog box. Use the Page Setup dialog box to change margins, paper orientation, and paper size.

WordPad Extras

WordPad has a few additional features you may find useful.

- **Date and Time**   Insert the current date and time into your document by clicking the Date/Time button, the last button on the toolbar, or by choosing Insert | Date And Time. The Date And Time dialog box appears, from which you can choose the format for the date, time, or both.

- **Inserting Objects**   Insert an object (such as a picture) into a WordPad document by dragging the object into the WordPad window from Windows Explorer; using Insert | Object and choosing the type of object you want to insert; or pasting an object from the Windows Clipboard. You can see the properties of an object by clicking the object and choosing Edit | Object Properties or by pressing ALT-ENTER. If you insert a picture, you can use WordPad's simple graphic editing commands by double-clicking the picture; the annotation toolbar appears at the bottom of the WordPad window. You can also move an object in your document by clicking-and-dragging it to a new location.

- **Find and Replace**   You can replace specific text with other text throughout your document by choosing Edit | Replace or pressing CTRL-H. You see the Replace dialog box. In the Find What box, type the text to be replaced. In the Replace With box, type the text to be inserted. You can select the Match Whole Word Only and Match Case check boxes to tell WordPad which instances of the text to match. Click Find Next to find the next instance of the text in the Find What box, and then click Replace to replace this instance with the Replace With text. To replace all the rest of the instances in your document, click Replace All.

- **Undo**   Undo your last action by clicking the Undo button on the toolbar by choosing Edit | Undo, or by pressing CTRL-Z.

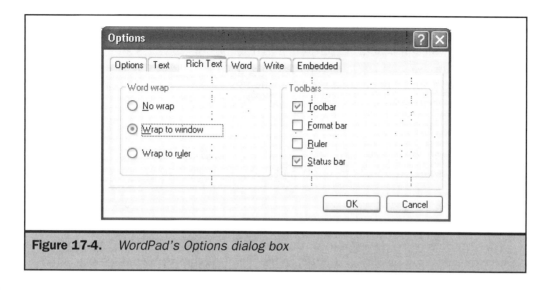

Figure 17-4. *WordPad's Options dialog box*

Setting WordPad Options

You can configure WordPad by choosing View | Options to display the Options dialog box (shown in Figure 17-4). Five tabs of this dialog box, the Text, Rich Text, Word, Write, and Embedded tabs, have the same options. Choose the tab for the type of document you're editing—most likely, Word, Rich Text, or Text. Use the Options tab to choose measurement units and automatic word selection. WordPad knows what kind of document you are editing based on the type of file you open.

Using the Windows Calculator

The Windows Calculator is actually two calculators: the unintimidating Standard Calculator that does simple arithmetic, and a more complicated Scientific Calculator. To use either of them, choose Start | All Programs | Accessories | Calculator. Switch from one calculator to the other by using the View menu.

Note *Calculator usually installs as part of Windows. If Calculator doesn't appear on the Start | All Programs | Accessories menu, you can install Calculator from the Windows XP CD-ROM (see Chapter 3, section "Installing and Uninstalling Programs that Come with Windows"). Calculator is in the Accessories And Utilities category, in the Accessories subcategory.*

In addition to entering number by clicking buttons or typing, you can use cut-and-paste to copy numbers from a document into the Calculator, do a calculation, and then cutting-and-pasting paste the result back into a document (see Chapter 5, section "Cutting, Copying, and Pasting"). The CE button stands for Clear Entry (clear the current entry) and the C button stands for Clear (clear the current calculation).

Using the Standard Calculator

The Standard Calculator (which you switch to by choosing View | Standard) adds, subtracts, multiplies, divides, takes square roots, calculates percentages, and finds multiplicative inverses. It has a one-number memory.

Enter a calculation as you would type it, left to right, as in

3 + 5 =

To compute a percentage, make the percentage the second number in a multiplication and don't use the equal sign. For example, to figure 15 percent of 7.4, enter

7.4 × 15%

The $1/x$ button computes the multiplicative inverse of the displayed number.

The four buttons on the left side of the Standard Calculator control its memory. To store the currently displayed number in the memory, click the MS (memory store) button. An M appears in the box above the MC button to show the memory is in use. The memory holds only one number, so storing another number causes the calculator to forget the previously stored number. Clicking MC (memory clear) clears the memory. To recall the number stored in memory, click MR (memory recall). Clicking the M+ button adds the displayed number to the number in memory and stores the result in the memory.

Note   *Use the memory to transfer a number from the standard to the scientific calculator or vice versa. The current display is cleared when you switch from one calculator to the other, but the memory is not cleared.*

Using the Scientific Calculator

The Scientific Calculator (shown in Figure 17-5) is considerably larger, more powerful, and more complex than the Standard Calculator. Switch to it by choosing View | Scientific. Anything you can do on the Standard Calculator works exactly the same way on the Scientific Calculator, except the Scientific Calculator has no % or sqrt button. (Compute square roots by clicking x^2 when the Inv box is checked.) In addition, you can perform calculations in a variety of number systems, do logical operations, use trigonometric functions, and do statistical analyses.

Why Don't All the Buttons Work?

Some buttons on the Scientific Calculator only make sense in certain situations; in other situations, they are grayed out and clicking them does nothing. For example, the A–F buttons are numbers in the hexadecimal number system, so they don't work unless the Hex radio button is selected. The hexadecimal, octal, and binary number systems are set up for whole number calculations only, so the trigonometric function buttons are grayed out when the Hex, Oct, or Bin radio buttons are selected. The statistics buttons are grayed out when no data is loaded in the statistics box.

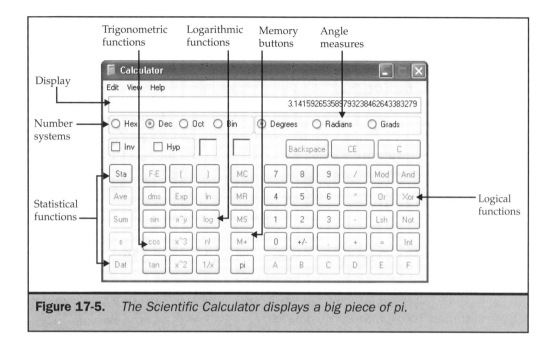

Figure 17-5. *The Scientific Calculator displays a big piece of pi.*

Number Systems and Angle Measures

The Scientific Calculator can work in Dec (decimal, the default), Bin (binary), Oct (octal), or Hex (hexadecimal) number systems. Choose among number systems by using the radio buttons on the left side of the top row. When you are working in the decimal number system, you can use the radio buttons just to the right of the number-system buttons to choose among the different ways of measuring angles: degrees (the default), radians, and gradients. When using degrees, the DMS button converts a decimal number of degrees into degrees-minute-seconds form. To convert back, check the Inv box and click DMS again.

When you are working in the binary, octal, or hexadecimal number systems, the radio buttons just to the right of the number system buttons enable you to select the range of whole numbers with which you will work. (In geek terms, this is the register size.) The choices are Byte (from 0 to 255, or 8 bits), Word (16 bits), Dword (double word, or 32 bits), and Qword (quadruple word, or 64 bits). The arithmetic in these systems is modular, so in hexadecimal with Byte register size

    2 - 3=

yields the answer FF rather than –1.

The F-E (fixed-exponential) button toggles between fixed-point notation and scientific notation. When entering a number in scientific notation, click the Exp button before entering the exponential part.

Trigonometric Functions

Trigonometric functions are computed with the Sin, Cos, and Tan buttons. Use the Inv and Hyp check boxes to compute inverse or hyperbolic trigonometric functions. The pi button (below the memory buttons) enters the first 32 digits of π. Because trigonometric functions almost never yield whole numbers, these buttons are grayed out in any number system other than decimal.

Logarithmic Functions

The Ln and Log buttons compute natural logarithms and base-10 logarithms, respectively. The Exp button *does not* compute exponentials. (It is used for entering numbers in scientific notation.) Compute exponentials by using Ln with the Inv box checked.

Statistical Functions

To use the statistical functions of the calculator, you must first enter a list of numbers, which constitutes the data. To enter a data list:

1. Enter the first number in the calculator display.
2. Click the Sta button. The statistics buttons are activated and a statistics box opens.
3. Click the Dat button. The number in the calculator display appears in the statistics box.
4. Enter the rest of the data, clicking Dat after each entry.

Once you enter a data list, Ave computes the average of the entries, Sum computes their sum, and S computes their standard deviation.

You can see the statistics box at any time by clicking Sta. To edit the data list, use the buttons at the bottom of the statistics box: LOAD copies the highlighted number back to the calculator display, CD deletes the highlighted number from the data list, and CAD clears the data list.

Logical Functions

When the Bin radio button is chosen, the calculator works in the binary (base-2) number system and the buttons And, Or, and Not perform the bitwise logical operations their names suggest. The Xor button does exclusive or, and Lsh does a left shift. Perform a right shift by clicking Lsh with the Inv box checked.

Other Functions

The Int button finds the integer part of a number. When Inv is checked, the Int button finds the fractional part of a number.

Compute squares and cubes with the X^2 and X^3 buttons. Compute other powers with the X^y button.

The N! button computes factorials of integers. If the displayed number has a fractional part, N! computes a gamma function.

The Mod button does modular reductions, for example:

12 Mod 5 = 2

Using Special Characters with Character Map

Do you need to use unusual characters, like Æ, Ö, or ô? The Character Map accessory can help you find them and copy them to the Clipboard for pasting into other programs. Open Character Map by choosing Start | All Programs | Accessories | System Tools | Character Map. Or, choose Start | Run and type **charmap**. You see the Character Map window shown in Figure 17-6.

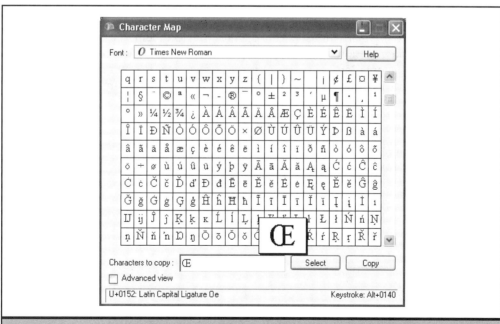

Figure 17-6. *The Character Map lets you use unusual characters.*

If Character Map doesn't appear on the Start | All Programs | Accessories | System Tools menu, you can install Character Map from the Windows XP CD-ROM (see Chapter 3, section "Installing and Uninstalling Programs that Come with Windows"). It's in the Accessories And Utilities category, in the Accessories subcategory.

To use a character from the Character Map:

1. Select a font from the Font list. The characters available in this font appear in the Character Map window, arranged in a 20-column grid.

2. Double-click the character you want to use or single-click it and click Select. The selected character is magnified and a copy of it appears in the Characters to copy box.

3. When you have displayed all the characters you want from this font in the Characters to copy box, click Copy. Character Map copies the characters to the Windows Clipboard (see Chapter 5).

4. Paste the characters into a document using a command in the program you use to edit that document. (Most programs use Edit | Paste or CTRL-V to paste from the Clipboard.)

You can remove characters from the Characters To Copy box by clicking in the box and either backspacing over the characters or deleting them.

Another way to use many unusual characters is to select them in Character Map and notice the keystroke notation in the bottom right corner of the Character Map window. Once you know this notation, you can produce the character in any document without running Character Map. For example, using the information in Figure 17-6 you could type a Œ character in any document as follows:

1. Open the document in a word processing program.

2. Set the font to Times New Roman.

3. Press the NUM LOCK on your keyboard.

4. While holding down the ALT key, type **0140**.

The
Complete
Reference

Chapter 18

Working with Graphics

Windows provides many tools for working with pictures and other images. Some are built into Windows Explorer, and some are bundled applications. This chapter tells you how to use these tools to view images on your monitor; add information to the images; create or edit image files; download images from digital cameras or scanners and print them, order prints of them over the Internet, publish them to the Web, or e-mail them to friends.

Images, Pixels, and Compression

For a computer to display, edit, or otherwise work with an image, that image is transformed into an array of small rectangles called *pixels*. Each pixel has only one color. If the pixels are small enough, the human eye doesn't notice this transformation. The color of each pixel is represented numerically, and the list of all these numbers is then turned into a file.

A file created in this way is very large, but fortunately much of this information is redundant. (Very often, for example, pixels next to each other have similar colors.) This fact allows an image file to be compressed into a smaller file from which a computer can re-create the original image file when needed. This compression can be done in a variety of ways, depending on whether the purpose of the compression is to create the smallest possible file, to represent the image most accurately, or to perform the compression as quickly as possible. Each compression method produces a different image file format. The most popular image formats are .bmp, .pcx, .gif, .jpg, and .tif.

Windows XP's Graphical Tools

Windows XP gives you more tools for working with images than any previous version of Windows.

- **My Pictures folder** is a subfolder of My Documents. It is the natural place in the Windows filing system to keep digital photos, pictures, graphics, and other images. Microsoft has preconfigured the viewing options in the My Pictures folder to make it easy for you to sort through pictures.

- **Windows Picture And Fax Viewer** is the default application for viewing image files (see "Looking at Images with the Windows Picture And Fax Viewer" later in this chapter). You can also use it to annotate images stored in .tif files.

- **Microsoft Paint** is an application for drawing and coloring (see "Creating and Editing Images with Microsoft Paint" later in this chapter). It also allows you to crop photos or transform images from one file format to another.

- **Scanner And Camera Wizard** sets up Windows to work with a scanner or digital camera (see "Downloading Images from Digital Cameras" later in this chapter). This wizard starts automatically when you plug a digital camera into your computer's USB or other port.

- **Photo Printing Wizard** leads you through the process of printing pictures on a printer (see "Printing Your Pictures at Home" later in this chapter). It produces pictures in all the standard photo sizes and arranges them on a page so that you get as many pictures as possible on each sheet of paper. Start this wizard by selecting Print Pictures from the Picture Tasks section of the Task pane of the My Pictures folder, by right-clicking any image file and choosing Print from the shortcut menu, or by clicking the Print button on the toolbar of the Windows Picture And Fax Viewer.

- **Web Publishing Wizard** helps you upload your pictures (or other files) to a web site where your friends and family anywhere in the world can view them (see "Sharing Your Pictures over the Internet" later in this chapter). Start this wizard by displaying the file(s) you want to publish in an Explorer window and then selecting Publish This Folder To The Web from the Folder Tasks list on the Task pane.

- **Online Print Ordering Wizard** leads you through the process of choosing an online photo service, sending them your image files, and placing an order for prints (see "Ordering Prints of Your Pictures via the Web" later in this chapter). Start this wizard by selecting Order Prints Online from the Picture Tasks list of the Task pane of the My Pictures folder or any folder containing the pictures you want made into prints.

Viewing Images on Your Computer

Windows gives you two ways to view images: Windows Explorer and Windows Picture And Fax Viewer. Either application lets you start a slide show of the images in a folder.

Viewing Images in an Explorer Window

Explorer windows have two views that are convenient for examining folders of image files: Thumbnails view and Filmstrip view. See "Thumbnails and Filmstrip Views" in Chapter 7.

Either of these views can be selected from the View menu of an Explorer window. Thumbnails view is available for any folder, while Filmstrip is available only for folders that have the Photo Album or Pictures template. Most of the time Windows recognizes when a folder contains a large number of image and assigns it a Photo Album or Pictures template, but if Filmstrip is listed on a particular folder's View menu, you can change the folder template (see Chapter 8). The Pictures template is recommended for folders with a large number of image files and has Thumbnails as its default view. Photo Album is recommended for folders with a smaller number of pictures—say, less than a dozen—and has Filmstrip as its default view.

 You can change the size and quality of thumbnail images using TweakUI (see Chapter 1, section "Using TweakUI to Change the Windows Interface"). Expand the Explorer entry and select Thumbnails, then move the slider to change image quality or enter a new value between 32 and 256 in the size box. (Default size is 96 pixels.) The size of existing thumbnails doesn't change, but new thumbnails are created whenever you move files to a new folder.

Both Pictures and Photo Album templates display Picture Tasks in the Task pane. (If you don't see a Task pane in an Explorer window, close the Explorer bar and/or enlarge the window.) To start a slide show, click the View As Slide Show option in the Picture Tasks section of the Task pane.

 If you want to use an image as your desktop background, right-click its icon in an Explorer window and select Set As Desktop Background. Or, select the icon and choose Set As Desktop Background from Picture Tasks.

Looking at Images with the Windows Picture And Fax Viewer

Unless you have installed other graphics applications that have claimed image file types as their own, Windows opens image files using the Windows Picture And Fax Viewer, shown in Figure 18-1. The image resembles what you would see in the Filmstrip view in an Explorer window but is larger and inside its own window. You also have a few more toolbar buttons to work with.

Picture And Fax Viewer can open files in a large number of formats: bitmap (.bmp), tagged image file or TIFF (.tif), JPEG (.jpg), GIF (.gif), Fax (.awd), PCX (.pcx), DCX (.dcx), XIF (.xif), and WIFF (.wif).

In addition to having the same Previous Image (left-arrow) and Next Image (right-arrow) buttons as Windows Explorer's Filmstrip view, Windows Picture And Fax Viewer gives you several tools to help you examine an image:

- **The Zoom In and Zoom Out tools** (represented on the toolbar by magnifying glasses) adjust the magnification of the image. To enlarge a portion of an image, click the Zoom In tool button and then click the part of the image that you want to see closer.

- **The Best Fit tool** (represented by a rectangle with arrows pointing outward from its corners) adjusts the size of the image to fill the window.

- **The Actual Size tool** (represented by a rectangle with arrows pointing inward to its sides) makes each pixel of the image equal a pixel on your monitor. This gives you the most accurate view of the image file.

Figure 18-1. *The Windows Picture And Fax Viewer*

■ **The Rotate Clockwise and Rotate Counterclockwise tools** (triangles with a clockwise or counterclockwise arrow above them) rotate the image 90 degrees. To turn an image upside down, click either button twice. Unlike the zoom and size tools, the rotation tools change the image itself, not just your view of it. (The program saves the rotated picture automatically.)

The toolbar also contains Delete, Print, Copy To, and Edit buttons. Print starts the Photo Printing Wizard; Copy To opens a dialog box that lets you pick a folder to copy the file into; and Edit opens the default graphics editing application, which may be Microsoft Paint (see "Creating and Editing Images with Microsoft Paint" later in this chapter).

Tip   *You can use the Copy To tool to convert an image file to a different file type—for example, to change a BMP file to TIFF or vice versa. Click the Copy To icon on the toolbar (it's a picture of a floppy disk) to display the Copy To dialog box. Change the Save As Type setting to the file format you want.*

To start a slide show of all the pictures in the same folder as the currently displayed picture, click the Start Slide Show button or press F11.

Watching a Slide Show

One of the best ways to view a collection of pictures on your computer monitor is to start a slide show. In a slide show the entire monitor is used to display images against a black background. You can scroll through the collection by clicking a toolbar button or you can automatically display each image for a fixed length of time.

Selecting Images for a Slide Show

Either Windows Explorer or Windows Picture And Fax Viewer can start a slide show of all the pictures in a folder. In Windows Picture and Fax Viewer, open the image that you want to view first and click the Start Slide Show button on the toolbar or press F11. In Windows Explorer, either select the file's icon and click the View As Slide Show option in Picture Tasks, or open the folder and click View As Slide Show.

To view some (but not all) of the images in a folder:

1. Open the folder in Windows Explorer.

2. Select the images you want to display, using the techniques from "Selecting Files And Folders" in Chapter 7 as needed.

3. Open the selected images simultaneously by clicking (or double-clicking) one of their icons. The image whose icon you clicked appears in a Windows Picture and Fax Viewer window.

4. Click the Start Slide Show button on the Windows Picture and Fax Viewer toolbar. The slide show cycles through all the selected images.

To view all the images from several subfolders of the same folder (the My Pictures folder, for example), select the all the subfolders and click the View As Slide Show option in Picture Tasks.

Controlling the Slide Show

By default the slide show cycles through its pictures automatically. If you move the mouse while the slide show is on, this small toolbar appears in the upper-right corner of the screen:

Left to right the buttons are Play, Pause, Previous Image, Next Image, and Stop. You can take control of the timing of the show by using the Next Image and Previous Image buttons to change images when you want. If you click Next Image or Previous Image while the slide show is playing, it continues cycling automatically from the next or previous image. If you use Next Image or Previous Image while the show is paused, it freezes on the next or previous image.

You can also control the slide show from the keyboard. Use the space bar to switch between Play and Pause modes. The left and right arrow keys substitute for the Previous Image and Next Image buttons. The ESC key stops the slide show. Use CTRL-K to rotate the image clockwise and CTRL-L to rotate counterclockwise.

Adding Information to Digital Images

For as long as people have been taking photographs, they've also been writing on the backs of their prints so that they can keep track of information, such as where and when the picture was taken, who the people are, and so on. You can't write on the back of an image file, but Windows gives you two ways to attach extra information to a digital image: You can include this information in the file's properties, or (if the image is in TIFF format) you can add annotations to the image itself. (Using Paint, you can add annotations in other formats, too.)

Adding Information to an Image File's Properties

Like any file, an image file has a properties box that you can open by right-clicking its icon and selecting Properties from the shortcut menu. The General tab of the Properties dialog box contains the same kind of information that is in any file's properties: the file's name, type, size, and so on. But the Summary tab of an image file's properties contains spaces you can use to record other important details about the picture. See the example in Figure 18-2.

 It's especially valuable to enter details about a photo into its properties page if you are planning to e-mail the file to other people.

Your camera or scanner may already have recorded quite a bit of technical information about the image without telling you. To see this information, click the Advanced button on the Summary tab of the image's Properties dialog box. Return to the simple view of the Summary tab by clicking the Simple button.

Annotating an Image with Windows Picture And Fax Viewer

Windows Picture And Fax Viewer can add annotations to images in TIFF format. When you open a TIFF file in Windows Picture And Fax Viewer, the toolbar grows (as shown in Figure 18-3) to include annotation tools that let you draw on an image, highlight portions of the image, and add text comments. While you are annotating, the rest of the

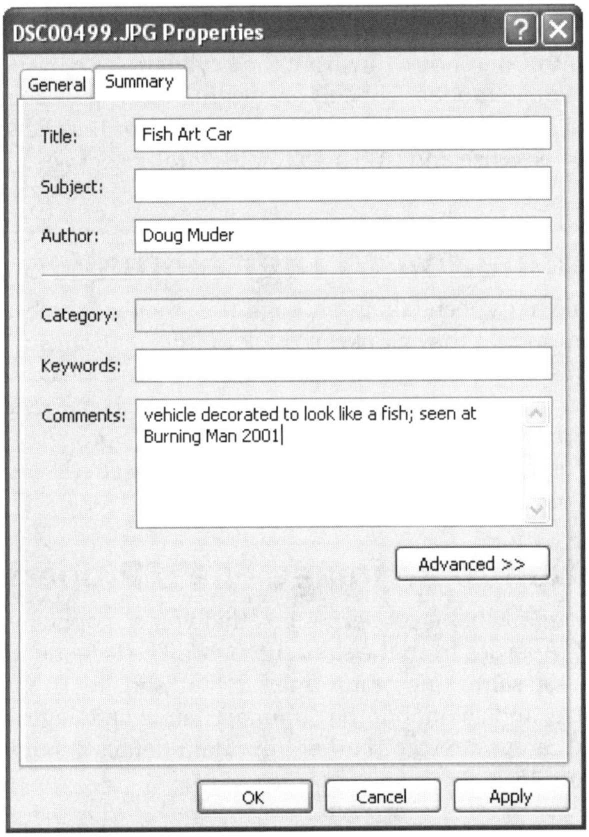

Figure 18-2. *Typing information into the Summary tab of an image file's Properties is like writing on the back of a print.*

toolbar works exactly as described in section "Looking at Images with the Windows Picture And Fax Viewer" earlier in this chapter.

The Select Annotation (arrow icon), New Freehand Annotation (curved line), and New Straight Line Annotation (straight line icon) tools are almost identical to the corresponding Paint tools (see the next section).

Windows Picture And Fax Viewer has three rectangle-making tools: New Highlight Annotation (highlighter icon), which produces a translucent rectangle; New Frame Annotation (rectangle outline icon), which makes a hollow rectangle; and New Solid Rectangle Annotation (solid rectangle icon), which makes a filled rectangle. Two tools add text annotations: New Text Annotation adds text with a transparent background,

Figure 18-3.   *Adding annotations to your pictures*

and New Attached Note Annotation adds text with a colored background. Both work similarly to the Text tool of Paint: click the tool button; then drag a rectangle on the image to create a box in which the text will appear. Click inside the box and start typing. The note in Figure 18-3 was made with the New Attached Note Annotation tool.

The annotations that Windows Picture And Fax Viewer adds to an image can be moved, edited, or deleted, even after they have been saved to a file. To change an existing annotation, click the Select Annotation (arrow icon) button on the Windows Picture And Fax Viewer toolbar and click in the annotation. A box appears around the annotation and the cursor changes to four crossing arrows. You may use the cursor to drag the annotation to another location on the image or to resize the annotation by dragging a corner of the surrounding box.

To edit a Text or Attached Note annotation, select the annotation using the Select Annotation tool as in the previous paragraph. When the annotation has been selected, click inside the surrounding box to make an editing cursor appear.

Creating and Editing Images with Microsoft Paint

Microsoft Paint is to images what WordPad is to text documents—a simple but versatile tool for creating and editing files. You can use it to make diagrams for presentations or to crop your online vacation photos; your five-year-old can use it as a coloring book, or your ten-year-old can use it to draw moustaches on the Mona Lisa.

For more advanced editing of image files, as well as for converting files to different graphics formats, we recommend Paint Shop Pro (**www.jasc.com**). You can download a shareware version from TUCOWS (**www.tucows.com**. You may also want to consider the Windows version of the open-source graphics application GIMP (GNU Image Manipulation Program), which you can obtain free at **www.gimp.org/~tml/gimp/win32/**. Other graphics editing and conversion programs are available from the Consummate Winsock Applications web site at **cws.internet.com**.

Paint runs in a variety of situations, depending on how your system is configured. It may be the default application for editing images, in which case you can run it by right-clicking an image file and selecting Edit from the shortcut menu or by clicking the Edit button on the toolbar of the Windows Picture And Fax Viewer. You can also find it on the Start | All Programs | Accessories menu.

 If Paint doesn't appear on the Start | All Programs | Accessories menu, you can install Paint from the Windows XP CD-ROM (see Chapter 3, section "Installing and Uninstalling Programs that Come with Windows").

Figure 18-4 shows the parts of a Paint window. The tool box buttons are labeled with shapes that suggest their use. For example, the button that draws lines has a line on it. When the cursor passes over a tool button, a short description of the tool appears on the status bar.

Opening and Saving Files in Paint

Paint opens files in most popular image formats, including bitmap (.bmp), TIFF (.tif), JPEG (.jpg), and GIF (.gif). Files created or edited by Paint can be saved as bitmap files in a variety of color schemes (monochrome, 16 color, 256 color, and 24-bit color), as well other image formats.

 By default, most image file types open in Windows Picture And Fax Viewer. Even if you have just created a file in Paint, opening its icon will open it in Windows Picture And Fax Viewer. To open an image file in Paint, right-click its icon and select Open With | Paint from the context menu.

By default the File | Save command saves new files in the My Pictures folder inside My Documents, and it saves other files to the location from which they were opened. To save elsewhere, choose File | Save As.

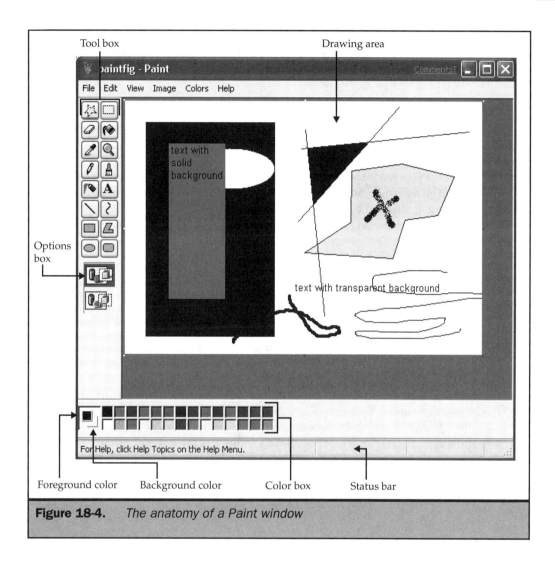

Figure 18-4. *The anatomy of a Paint window*

Selecting Objects

With the Select tool chosen (by clicking the dotted rectangle button in the Tool box), you can select objects inside the drawing area, just as you select objects inside an Explorer window: by enclosing them in a rectangle. Move the pointer to one corner of the rectangular area that includes the objects you want to select, hold the mouse button down, move to the opposite corner of the area, and release the mouse button.

The Free-Form Select tool (the dotted star button in the Tool box) enables you to select objects and parts of objects inside a region of any shape. Drag the cursor to trace out any shape. Either close up the shape, or Paint closes it up automatically with a straight line. The enclosed region is now selected, and can be moved by dragging or copied by cutting-and-pasting—useful for creating repeated patterns.

Magnifying and Enlarging

To zoom in on a portion of the drawing area, click the Magnifier tool (the magnifying-glass button in the Tool box). A rectangle appears in the drawing area, which represents the portion of the drawing that will be visible after magnification. Position the rectangle to enclose the area you want to zoom in on and then click. The portion of the drawing that was inside the rectangle now fills the entire viewing area. To zoom back out, click the Magnifier tool again, and then click anywhere in the viewing area.

When the Magnifier tool is selected, the Options box displays four magnification levels: $1x$, $2x$, $6x$, and $8x$. The current level of magnification is highlighted. To change to another level of magnification, click that option in the Options box.

To enlarge or shrink the drawing area (the "sheet of paper"), drag its corners.

Drawing Lines and Curves

Clicking with the Line tool (the straight line button in the Tool box) nails down one end of a line; the other end moves with the cursor. When the line is where you want it, click again to fix the other end. To make a curved line, click the Curve tool (the wiggly line button in the Tool box) and begin by drawing a straight line, as you would with the Line tool. Then, click-and-drag a point on that line to make a curve. You have the option of dragging a second point to make another kink in the curve.

When the Line or Curve tools are selected, different line thicknesses appear in the Options box, just below the Tool box. Select a new thickness by clicking the line thickness you want.

When you click with the left mouse button, the Line and Curve tools draw in the foreground color. To draw lines and curves in the background color, use the right mouse button.

Drawing Freehand

Paint has four tools in the Tool box that make freehand marks as you drag them: Pencil, Brush, Spray Can, and Eraser. Pencil makes thin lines, Brush makes thick lines, and Spray Can sprays a pattern of dots. You can choose among three densities of Spray Can dot patterns by clicking the pattern you want in the Options box. As its name suggests, the Eraser erases anything in its path, replacing it with the background color.

Making Shapes

These four tools in the Tool box make shapes: Ellipse, Rectangle, Rounded Rectangle, and Polygon. The simplest shape to make is a rectangle:

1. Click the Rectangle tool (the solid—not the dotted—rectangle button).

2. Click in the drawing area where you want one corner of the rectangle located.

3. Drag to where you want the opposite corner of the rectangle located. When you release the mouse button, Paint creates the rectangle.

You use the Ellipse and Rounded Rectangle tools in a manner similar to the Rectangle tool.

The Polygon tool makes figures with any number of sides:

1. Click the Polygon tool (the L-shaped polygon button).

2. Click inside the drawing area where you want one corner of the polygon located.

3. Each click defines the next corner of the polygon. For the first side, you must click-and-drag; for subsequent sides, just click.

4. Double-click the last corner. Paint closes up the polygon automatically.

Coloring Objects

Control the colors of objects by using the Color box at the bottom of the Paint window. The two colored squares at the far left of the Color box show the current foreground and background colors, with the foreground square on top of the background square. Any object you construct using the left mouse button has the foreground color, whereas objects made using the right mouse button have the background color.

To choose a new foreground color, left-click the square of the new color in the Color box. To choose a new background color, right-click the square of the new color. You can match the color of any object in the drawing area by using the Pick Color tool (the eyedropper button in the Tool box). Select the tool and click the object whose color you want to match. Left-clicking changes the foreground color to match the object; right-clicking changes the background color to match the object.

To color within an outlined area, such as a rectangle or an ellipse, select the Fill With Color tool (the tipped paint can button) and click within the area. Right-click to fill with the background color. Using the Fill With Color tool on an area that is not outlined colors the whole "sheet of paper"—the area outside of any enclosed region.

Changing the foreground or background color does not change the color of objects already created. To change an object to the new foreground (background) color, select the Fill With Color tool and click (right-click) the object whose color you want to change. You can invert the colors in a region (that is, make a negative of the original) by selecting the region choosing Image | Invert Colors.

Adding Text

Click the Text tool (the button with the *A*) and drag across the part of your picture where you want the type to appear. Paint displays a rectangular text box for you to type in. A font selection box appears above the text box so you can select the font, size, and style of the text. The color of the text is the foreground color. Click inside the text box and type. Click outside the text box when you are done typing.

The Options box below the Tool box gives two choices for using the Text tool. The top choice makes a solid background for the text box, using the background color. The bottom choice makes a transparent background.

Flipping, Rotating, and Stretching

Commands on the Image menu flip, rotate, or stretch the entire image or a selected part of the image. Choosing Image | Flip/Rotate opens a dialog box from which you can choose to flip the image horizontally or vertically, or you can rotate it by any multiple of 90 degrees. Choosing Image | Stretch/Skew opens another dialog box from which you can stretch the image horizontally or vertically by any percentage or slant it by any number of degrees.

Elements that you add to a flipped, stretched, slanted, or rotated drawing are normal. This feature allows you to mix elements of various types in a single drawing, as in Figure 18-4.

Cropping Images

You can crop an image—remove unwanted material around the edges of a picture. To crop an image, use the Select tool to enclose the area of the image that you want to keep. To save the selected area as a new file, choose Edit | Copy To. Type a new filename and click Save. The original image is unaffected.

Working with Digital Cameras and Scanners

From a user's point of view, scanners and cameras have little to do with each other. It would never occur to you, for example, to point your scanner at the Grand Canyon. But to a computer, scanners and digital cameras are very similar: Both turn visual information into image files. This is why these two types of devices share a Control Panel icon (Scanners And Cameras, which lives in the Printers And Other Hardware category) and a wizard (the Scanners And Cameras Wizard) for installing them.

Setting Up a Scanner or Digital Camera

In order to work with a scanner or digital camera, Windows needs to have a driver program that tells it how to communicate with the device (see Chapter 13, section "Hardware Drivers"). Windows XP comes with drivers for most popular devices, so your installation process may be as simple as plugging your scanner or camera into the appropriate port (usually a USB or serial port), turning it on, and waiting for Windows to notice it. Installing a Sony DSC-S70 camera was just this easy when we tried it; Windows noticed the camera immediately and had it ready to go in less than a minute.

If the plug-in-and-wait technique doesn't work with your camera or scanner, put the CD that came with the camera or scanner into your CD-ROM drive and see whether a program runs that steps you through installing the drivers and related software.

If you still don't have drivers installed, try this:

1. Open the Scanners And Cameras icon from the Printers and Other Hardware category of the Control Panel.

2. Select Add An Imaging Device from the Imaging Tasks section of the Task pane. The Scanner And Camera Installation Wizard starts.

3. The wizard asks you the manufacturer and model of your camera or scanner. If you can't find your camera or scanner on the wizard's list, click the Have Disk button and be prepared to insert the floppy or CD that came with your hardware.

4. Tell the wizard which port the device is connected to. The rest of the installation happens automatically. You may have to restart the computer before using your device.

You can test your scanner or digital camera by clicking its entry in the Scanners And Cameras window, clicking the Properties button, and then clicking the Test Scanner Or Camera button.

Many cameras and scanners come with additional software, beyond the drivers needed to allow Windows to work with the device. These additional programs may provide a "front panel" for the device (one of our scanners comes with a program that looks like the front of a photocopying machine) or graphics editing. You usually don't need this additional software to use your camera or scanner: you do need the drivers.

| **Note** | *Even after you install your scanner or digital camera and it works fine, the Scanners And Cameras icon may not appear in the Control Panel. If you open the Scanners And Cameras window, your scanner or camera may not appear in the list of installed devices, either. The device may appear, however, in your System Properties dialog box: Choose Start | Control Panel | Performance And Maintenance | System, click the Hardware tab, and click the Device Manager button to display the Device Manager window (see Chapter 13, section "Managing Your Hardware Components with the Device Manager"). Look down the list of all installed devices—scanners and cameras appear in the Imaging Devices category. Older cameras and scanners may not be on the list, and you can't add them.* |

Downloading Images from Digital Cameras

A digital camera is also a disk drive in disguise. As you take pictures, the image files are stored on some device like a CompactFlash card, a Smart Media card, a floppy disk, or a Memory Stick. When you connect the camera to your computer, Windows assumes you want to do something with the files the camera is holding, so it displays the following box:

The default choice is to open the Scanner And Camera Wizard, which helps you download the pictures to a folder on your computer. If you want the wizard to start automatically whenever you connect your camera to the computer, check the Always Do The Selected Action check box.

The Scanner And Camera Wizard takes you through the process of selecting which pictures to download and what folder to store them in. You can tell the wizard to automatically delete the pictures from the camera after you download them, or you can leave them on the camera and deal with them later. After the pictures have been downloaded, you are given a choice to close the wizard, publish the pictures to the Web using the Web Publishing Wizard, or order prints over the Web using the Online Print Ordering Wizard (see "Sharing Your Pictures over the Internet" later in this chapter). If you don't want to go straight into another wizard, you lose nothing by waiting—you will get the same publishing and ordering options when you open the folder that you download the prints to.

If you would rather avoid the Scanner And Camera Wizard, you can select the Take No Action option when you plug in the camera. Instead, open My Computer; the camera should be listed among your disk drives. You can open its icon and move files to and from the camera as you would any other disk drive.

If you're on the road with nothing but a laptop and a digital camera, you can use the camera as a disk drive to back up a few important files. Strange, but true!

You can also copy pictures out of a camera by removing the storage media from the camera and inserting it into some appropriate device attached to your computer. Most forms of camera media have adapters that fit into a floppy drive, as well as drives that attach to your computer's USB port or PCMCIA card slot.

Downloading Images from Scanners

When you first connect your scanner to your computer, you may see the illustration shown in the preceding section, asking what you want Windows to do with images that arrive from the scanner. The preceding section also describes how you can use the Scanner And Printer Wizard to copy files from your scanner to your computer.

Alternatively, graphics programs can use your scanner to create images. Most scanners come with a *TWAIN* driver that adds an Acquire command to your graphics editor (for example, the Paint Shop Pro program gains a File | Import | TWAIN | Acquire command after you install a scanner driver). You can give this command to bring information from the scanner or camera into the program.

Run your favorite graphics editor (but not Microsoft Paint, which doesn't support TWAIN) and check whether it can acquire pictures directly from a scanner. Some programs start scanning as soon as you give the command, others display a dialog box in which you can set scanner parameters before you click a Scan button. When the scanner finishes, the picture appears on your screen. Use the graphics program's usual commands to edit and save the scanned image.

Linking Your Scanner or Digital Camera to a Program

In addition to graphics programs, some other types of programs accept digital graphic information directly from a scanner or camera. For example, a database program may accept a digital picture of a person for storage in a personnel database, and pressing the button on the camera can send the picture directly into the database. If both your scanner or camera and your program support this feature, you can tell Windows to run a program whenever you scan an image or take a digital picture. Follow these steps:

1. Display the Scanners And Cameras window (see "Setting Up a Scanner or Digital Camera" earlier in this chapter).

2. Click the device and then the Properties button to display the Properties dialog box for that scanner or camera, as shown in Figure 18-5. Click the Events tab. (If the Events tab does not appear, your scanner or digital camera does not support linking to programs.)

3. In the list of events to which the camera or scanner can respond, click an event.

4. In the Start This Program box, click the name of the program that will receive the image from the scanner or camera. Only programs that can accept digital images appear on the list.

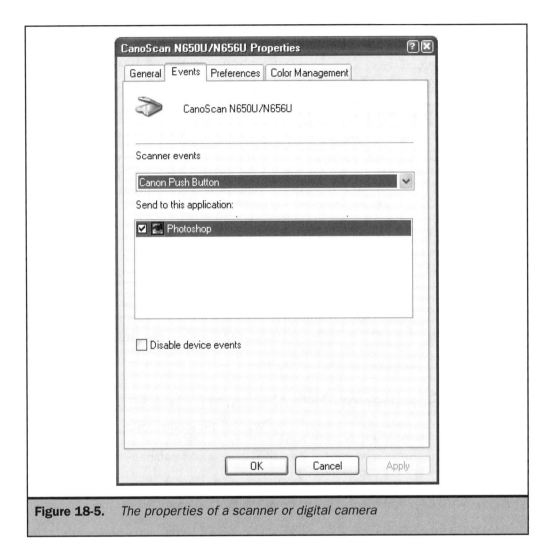

Figure 18-5. *The properties of a scanner or digital camera*

Turning Images into Prints

A digital image file is convenient in many ways, but it's not very satisfying to carry one around in your wallet. For some purposes you still can't beat printing a picture on paper. An ordinary color printer can produce adequate pictures, especially if you use paper made for photographs. If you print a lot of photos and want high quality, you can get a special photo printer. Or, you can send your image files to a photo shop to be printed. You can even use the Online Print Ordering Wizard to order your prints over the Web.

Printing Your Pictures at Home

You can use any local or network printer to print your pictures. The quality of your prints depends on three factors:

- **The image file**   Paper is a more demanding medium than a computer monitor. Flaws in your pictures that don't seem significant on the screen are much more visible when you print. A rule of thumb is that you need about 2 megapixels (2 million pixels) to make a high-quality 5×7 print, and about 3 megapixels to make an 8×10.

- **The printer**   Printers that do a perfectly good job on documents may not be adequate for pictures. A good general-purpose color printer will print your photographs reasonably well, but won't rival the prints you get from a photo shop. If you want photo-shop quality, you need a special photo printer.

- **The paper**   Paper makes a huge difference in printing photos, particularly if you have an ink-jet printer. Ink spreads as it soaks into low-quality paper, and that makes your pictures fuzzy. You can find good photographic paper at any camera, office supply, or large computer store.

Windows includes a Photo Printing Wizard to help you print your pictures. Start the wizard in any of these three ways:

- Right-click the icon of an image file in an Explorer window and choose Print from the shortcut menu,

- Select an image file in an Explorer window and choose Print This Picture from the Picture Tasks area on the Task pane, or

- Display an image with the Windows Picture And Fax Viewer and click the Print button on the toolbar.

The Photo Printing Wizard leads you through a process of selecting which pictures to print, choosing a printer (or installing one if none is installed), setting the number of copies to make of each picture, selecting print size, and laying out the pictures on the pages you print. Figure 18-6 shows how the wizard arranges pictures on a sheet of paper.

Ordering Prints of Your Pictures via the Web

The most obvious way to get photo-shop quality prints is to order them from a photo shop. Most photo shops will print your pictures if you bring in a disk, and you can even do it at most Wal-Marts. But you can also use the Online Print Ordering Wizard to order prints from an online photo service. The wizard leads you through the process of selecting the pictures you want, then connects you with one of several online photo-printing services so that you can complete your order. The cost of the prints

WORKING WITH TEXT, NUMBERS, PICTURES, SOUND, AND VIDEO

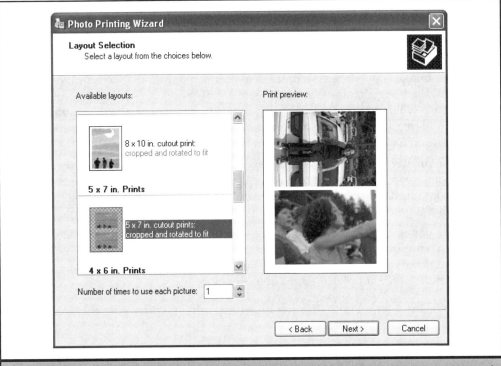

Figure 18-6. *The Photo Printing Wizard arranges your pictures to use each sheet of paper efficiently.*

(plus a shipping fee) is charged to your credit card, and the prints are mailed to you or delivered by a courier service.

 Rather than mail a large number of prints to a friend or relative, have an online print service ship your order directly to them.

To order prints online, first assemble the pictures you want printed in a single folder. Then open that folder and select Order Prints Online from the Picture Tasks section of the Task pane. (We don't know of any way to start this wizard if you don't have the Task pane displayed.)

The wizard leads you through the following steps: selecting which pictures in this folder you want printed, choosing a printing service, and connecting you to that service. You select the number and size of prints you want, give a mailing address (not necessarily your own) and a credit card number. The image files are then uploaded to the service's computer.

Photo files are often in the 1–2MB range, which means that they can take a minute or so each to upload even on a broadband Internet connection. If you have an entire vacation's worth of photos and a dial-up connection, take your pictures to a photo shop on a CD.

When we tried it, the wizard offered a choice between Kodak's Ofoto (**www.ofoto.com**), MSN Photos (which uses Fuji, at **photos.msn.com**)), and Shutterfly (**www.shutterfly.com**). Prices were similar on the three sites. MSN Photos charges your credit card through Microsoft's .NET Passport, which has its good and bad points.TIP: You can probably find prints at cheaper prices elsewhere on the Web (see Chapter 24). In late 2002, Ofoto, MSN Photos, and Shutterfly were all charging $0.49 for each 4×6 print, while Wal-Mart (**www.walmart.com**) and Snapfish (**www.snapfish.com**) were charging $0.26 on their web sites.

Sharing Your Pictures over the Internet

The Internet is a great way to share photos. Making print copies of photos for all your friends and relatives can be terribly expensive, but it costs nothing to e-mail an image file to 20 people or to upload a picture to the Web where anyone who is interested can see it.

E-mail and the Web each have their advantages as a way of sharing pictures. In general, if you have a picture that you know a few people will want to see, e-mail it to them. On the other hand, if you have many pictures that many people may or may not want to see, put the pictures on a web site and e-mail the web address to people who you think are interested.

 Be careful about sharing sensitive or confidential pictures over the Internet. When you give someone else a digital copy of a picture, for all practical purposes, you lose control of it. Your picture can spread like a rumor, and you have no way of knowing who ultimately will see it.

Publishing Your Pictures on the Web

You can store pictures or other files on web servers and use a browser to retrieve them from any computer that is online. You can also give the web address (and possibly a password, if the files are password protected) to other people so that they can see the files also.

You can get a small amount of web storage space free from MSN or Yahoo, and you can rent more space if you need it. Kodak's Ofoto service (at **www.ofoto.com**) and Snapfish (**www.snapfish.com**) also provide free password-protected photo sharing along with photo-printing services. Go to the web site and follow the site's instructions.

To upload files to the Web, do the following:

1. Collect the files and move or copy to a single folder.

2. Open that folder and click Publish This Folder To The Web in the File And Folder Tasks section of the task pane. The Web Publishing Wizard starts.

3. Answer the wizard's questions.

The wizard leads you through the process of choosing a web-hosting service for your files, and setting up how others will access them. Each service does this differently.

E-mailing Pictures to Your Friends

You don't need Windows XP to e-mail pictures to friends. You can use your e-mail program to create a message and then attach the picture to the message (see Chapter 23). But Windows XP has a neat feature that can compress one or more pictures into a single file and e-mail it. Follow these steps:

1. In an Explorer window, select a picture or a folder of pictures. Or, select some pictures from a folder (click the first picture and CTRL-click the other pictures to add them to the selection).

2. In the File And Folder Tasks section of the Task pane, click E-Mail This File, E-mail This Folder, or E-Mail The Selected Items. Or, right-click the file(s) or folder and choose Send To | Mail Recipient from the shortcut menu that appears.

3. You see the Send Pictures Via E-Mail dialog box, asking whether you want to compress the files so that they transfer more quickly over the Internet:

4. Click Make All My Pictures Smaller if you are sending the files over a dial-up line, if the recipient uses a dial-up line, or if you are sending a lot of pictures. Otherwise, click Keep The Original Size.

5. If you want to choose the exact size of the pictures, click Show More Options and click a size.

6. Click OK. If you chose to resize or compress the files, Windows does so. If you are sending a folder, Windows compresses the files into a compressed folder (see Chapter 8).

7. Windows passes the files to your default e-mail program (Outlook Express or another e-mail program) and you see a new, blank message with the file(s) attached.

8. Address the message, type a subject line and text, and send the message as usual.

The Complete Reference

Chapter 19

Working with Sound

L
ike Windows Me/9x, NT, and 2000, Windows XP contains built-in support for
audio devices—hardware that enables your computer to record and play sounds.
In addition to better drivers for audio devices, Windows XP also comes with
Windows Media Player 8 for playing audio files, video files, CD, DVDs, and streaming
audio and video files from the Internet. You can also use the Sound Recorder to record
your own audio files with your computer's microphone. If your PC has a CD-R or
CD-RW drive, you may also want to create your own audio CDs using Windows
Media Player or other programs.

Note   *Chapter 13 describes how to install hardware, including audio hardware; this chapter
explains how to configure and use these devices.*

Audio File Formats

Table 19-1 lists some commonly used file formats for the audio data you can play or record.
(For a more complete list, see the Sonic Spot's File Format List at **www.sonicspot.com/
guide/fileformats.html**.)

Medium	Input Device	Output Device	File Extensions for Popular Formats
Audio	Microphone, MIDI keyboard, synthesizers, line input	Speakers, headphones	.aif (Apple's Audio Interchange Format); .wax, .wma, and .wvx (Windows Media); .avi and .wav (Windows audio);.mp3 and .m3u (MP3); .rmj (RealAudio)
Streaming audio	Microphone, MIDI keyboard, synthesizers, line input, usually downloaded from the Internet	Speakers, headphones	.ram and .ra (RealAudio); .asf and .asx (Microsoft's Advanced Streaming Format)
MIDI	MIDI-compatible instrument	MIDI-compatible instrument, speakers, headphones	.mid, .midi, or .rmi

Table 19-1.   *Audio Devices and File Formats*

To see the properties of any audio file, right-click the filename and choose Properties from the menu that appears. You see a Properties dialog box like the one shown in Figure 19-1.

The information on the General tab parallels that provided for almost any file: type, size, and attributes. The Summary tab displays the bit rate, audio sample size, and other formatting information.

Streaming Audio

Streaming audio is audio stored in a format for use over a network, usually the Internet. Because audio files can be large, it's annoying to have to wait for an entire file to download before you can start playing it. With streaming audio files, your computer can start playing the file after downloading only the beginning of the file, and can

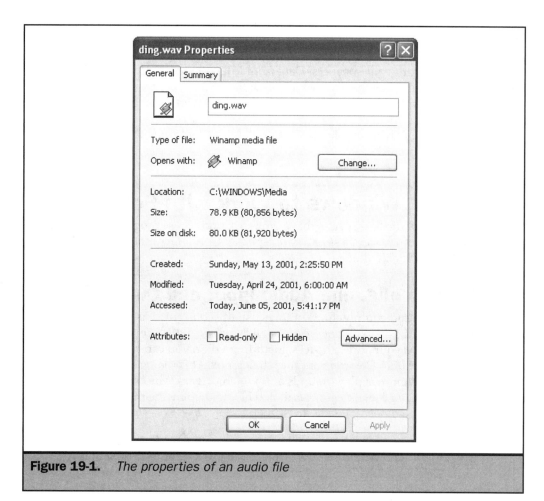

Figure 19-1. *The properties of an audio file*

continue to play the audio while the rest of the file downloads—optimally, downloading stays a step ahead of the player (the audio yet to be played is stored in a *buffer*.

Two incompatible streaming audio formats are used on the Internet: RealAudio (the original streaming format, with extensions .ra and .ram) and Microsoft's Advanced Streaming Files format (also called Windows Media format, with extensions .asf and .asx). To play Windows Media format files, run Windows Media Player (see "Playing Music and Other Audio with Windows Media Player 8 and 9" later in this chapter). To play RealAudio format files, run the RealOne Player (see "Listening to RealAudio Files" later in this chapter). For instructions for playing streaming video files, see the next chapter.

MIDI Files

A specialized type of audio data is called *MIDI* (Musical Instrument Digital Interface), a format for transmitting and storing musical notes. MIDI devices are musical instruments or recording devices that have digital inputs and outputs and can transmit, store, and play music using the MIDI language. For example, if you connect a MIDI keyboard to your computer, you can view the music you play on the MIDI keyboard on your computer screen and hear it from your speakers. Data from MIDI devices is stored in MIDI files. Windows includes software that can "play" MIDI files; that is, software that can translate the musical notes in the files into sound that can be played through speakers or headphones.

Windows Media Player can play MIDI files. You need additional MIDI software to edit and mix MIDI inputs.

Configuring Windows to Work with Sound

Many applications, particularly games, have built-in sound. Those programs automatically take advantage of your system's sound card, speakers, and microphone, once Windows is configured to work with them.

Choosing and Configuring Audio Input and Output Drivers

When you install sound equipment, Windows usually configures itself automatically to use the proper sound drivers. If you need to tell Windows which sound drivers to use, or choose settings for your audio devices, including voice, you can configure Windows in the Sounds And Audio Device Properties dialog box. This dialog box has tabs for configuring when Windows plays sounds and which drivers Windows uses to play and record sounds. You can also use this dialog box to display the properties of all your audio and video devices. Follow these steps:

1. Choose Start | Control Panel, click Sounds Speech And Audio Devices, and click Sounds And Audio Devices. (In Classic view, double-click Sound And Audio Devices on the Control Panel.) You see the Sounds And Audio Devices Properties dialog box.

2. Click the Audio tab, as shown in Figure 19-2, if it's not already selected.

3. Choose the driver used to play sounds by selecting the device from the list of available devices in the Sound Playback section of the Audio tab.

4. Tell Windows more about your speakers or headphones by clicking the Advanced button in the Sound Playback section of the Audio tab. You see the Advanced Audio Properties dialog box, as shown in Figure 19-3. (You can also display it by clicking the Advanced button in the Speaker Settings part of the Volume tab.)

5. Click the Speakers tab if it's not already selected. Click the Speaker Setup box and choose your computer's arrangement of speakers or headphones.

6. To set the amount of computing power your computer devotes to playing audio, click the Performance tab. Then, set the Sample Rate Conversion Quality slider. If your computer has a fast processor, move the Sample Rate slider

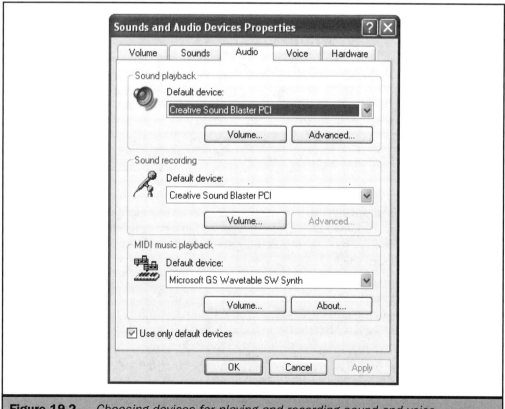

Figure 19-2. *Choosing devices for playing and recording sound and voice*

WORKING WITH TEXT, NUMBERS, PICTURES, SOUND, AND VIDEO

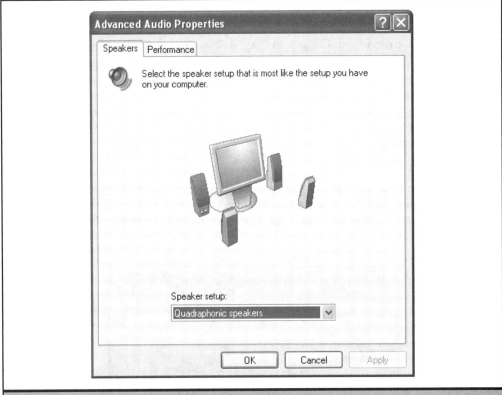

Figure 19-3. *Use the Advanced Audio Properties dialog box to set the properties of your speakers or headphones.*

toward the Best setting; otherwise, move it leftward to sacrifice sound quality for performance.. Leave the Audio Playback Hardware Acceleration slider alone unless you're having trouble with the sound acceleration features of your sound card. Click OK.

7. To control the volume of your speakers or headphones, click the Volume button in the Sound Playback section of the Audio tab of the Sounds And Audio Devices Properties dialog box. You see the Volume Control window (see "Adjusting Volume, Graphic Equalization, and Other Sound Settings" later in this chapter). Close the window when you've adjusted the volume.

8. Choose the driver used to record sounds by clicking in the Default Device box in the Sound Recording section of the Sounds And Audio Devices Properties dialog box and choosing a driver from the list that appears—to record sound from a microphone, choose the driver for the sound card into which the microphone is plugged.

9. To set the amount of computing power your computer devotes to recording audio, click the Advanced button in the Sound Recording section of the Audio tab (unless it appears gray—some sound cards don't support advanced settings). Then set the Sample Rate Conversion Quality slider. Click OK.

10. To control the volume when recording, click the Volume button in the Sound Recording section of the Audio tab. You see the Recording Control window (see "Playing and Recording WAV Sound Files with Sound Recorder" later in this chapter). Close the window when you've set the recording volume.

11. If you use voice applications (for example, to dictate into a voice-recognition system such as Dragon Naturally Speaking, or to talk to other people over the Internet), click the Voice tab on the Sounds And Audio Devices Properties dialog box. You see sections for Voice Playback and Voice Capture, which you can set as described in steps 3–10.

12. Click OK to save your changes and exit the Sounds And Audio Devices Properties dialog box.

Displaying the Status of Your Audio Devices

To see all the audio devices installed on your system, choose Start | Control Panel, click Sounds, Speech, And Audio Devices, and click Sounds And Audio Devices. You see the Sounds And Audio Devices Properties dialog box. Click the Hardware tab to see the dialog box shown in Figure 19-4.

To display or change the settings for some devices, click the device and click the Properties button. Many of the devices are software only, notably the audio and video codecs (compressing and decompressing schemes) that determine the scheme used to encode sounds in audio and video files (see Chapter 20, section "How Windows Works with Video Data").

 If you have trouble getting sounds to play, try the Windows Sound Troubleshooter by selecting a device from the list on the Hardware tab of the Sounds And Audio Devices Properties dialog box and clicking the Troubleshoot button (see Chapter 2, section "Diagnosing Windows Problems with Troubleshooters").

Controlling the Volume and Balance

You can control the volume and balance of the sound that goes into your microphones and comes out of your computer's speakers or headphones. You can also choose to mute (suppress) the sound for any audio device.

If you don't see a Volume icon (a little gray loudspeaker icon) in the notification area on your taskbar, then open the Sounds And Audio Devices Properties dialog box as described in the preceding section, click the Volume tab (if it's not already selected), and select the Place Volume Icon In The Taskbar check box so that a check appears.

Figure 19-4. *The Hardware tab in the Sounds And Audio Devices Properties dialog box displays audio devices with their properties.*

To adjust the volume of your speakers, click the Volume icon on the taskbar once; you see a Volume slider and a Mute check box: Most sound applications such as the Windows Media Player also have volume controls you can adjust.

Drag the Volume slider up for louder volume or down for softer volume. Select the Mute check box to suppress audio output completely (such as when you are using your laptop on a train). Click outside the window to make it disappear.

To adjust the volume and balance of any audio device, double-click the Volume icon. You see the Volume Control window:

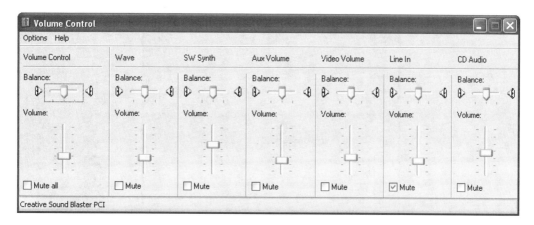

Another way to display this window is by clicking any of the Volume buttons on either the Audio or Voice tab of the Sounds And Audio Devices Properties dialog box.

The Volume Control window can display a volume, balance, and mute setting for each audio input and output device on your computer, depending on your sound card's capabilities. To choose which functions are included in the window, choose Options | Properties from the Volume Control menu bar to display the Properties dialog box, as shown in Figure 19-5. Click the Playback setting to include audio output devices, the Recording setting to include audio input devices, or the Other setting to include other audio devices. (The only other audio device is Voice Commands, which allows you to use software that interprets your voice input as commands to control programs). You can also click check boxes for individual audio devices in the Show The Following Volume Controls list. Leave the Mixer Device setting alone—it's usually a feature of your audio card. Then click OK to return to the Volume Control dialog box.

 Some sound cards come with their own mixer application. To use all of the features of your installed device, use the mixer program that comes with the sound card.

When you display volume controls for playback devices, the window is called Volume Control; when you display recording devices, it's called Recording Control.

 If your speakers or headphones have a physical volume control knob, it's generally simpler to leave the Windows volume set fairly high, sending a strong signal through the wires, and just turn the knob to change the volume.

Choosing What Sounds Windows Makes

Windows comes with an array of sounds that it makes when certain *events* (Windows operations) occur. When you start Windows, for example, a rich, welcoming sound

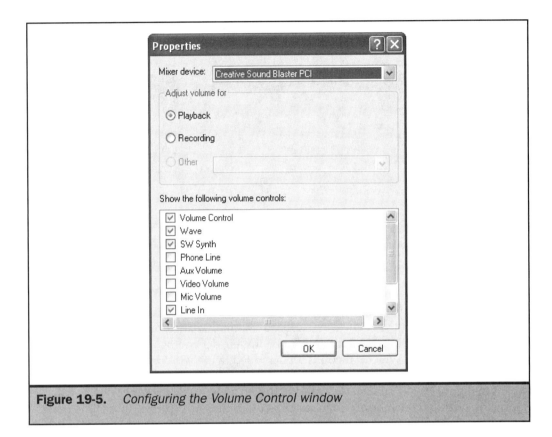

Figure 19-5. *Configuring the Volume Control window*

occurs; however, you might prefer the sound of a child yelling "Hello!" You can control which sounds Windows plays when specified events occur by clicking the Sounds tab on the Sounds And Audio Devices Properties dialog box, as shown in Figure 19-6.

The Program Events box lists all the events that you can associate with a sound, including events that happen in Windows and other programs that use sound, such as Windows Messenger. If an event has no speaker icon to its left, no sound is currently assigned to that event. To change the sound for an event:

1. Click the event name in the Program Events box.

2. Click the down-arrow button at the right end of the Sounds box and choose a sound stored in a WAV file on your computer. You see a list of the sounds that come with Windows XP. Click the Browse button to find other WAV files, such as the ones you recorded yourself (see "Playing and Recording WAV Sound Files with Sound Recorder" later in this chapter). To assign no sound to an event, choose (None) from the Sounds list.

3. To test out the sound, click the right-pointing triangle Play button to the right of the Sounds box.

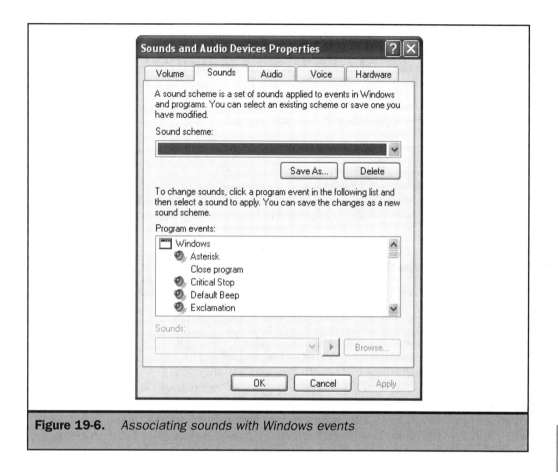

Figure 19-6.   *Associating sounds with Windows events*

The list of sounds in the Sound box is the list of WAV files (with extension .wav) in the C:\Windows\Media folder (assuming that Windows is installed on C:). If you want to add your own sounds to the list of sounds, record or edit a WAV file and store it in this folder. You can test sounds in the Open dialog box that you see when you click the Browse button. Select any sound that appears in the window and click the Play button at the bottom of the dialog box—the sound plays. If the sound is too long, click the black square to stop it.

You can save the set of sound associations as a *sound scheme*. Windows comes with a Windows Default sound scheme, which associates sounds with many events, and a No Sounds sound scheme, in which no sounds are associated with events. Load an existing sound scheme by selecting it on the Sounds tab of the Sounds And Audio Devices Properties dialog box. You can create your own sound schemes, too; simply associate the sounds you want to hear with the events that you want to prompt those sounds. If you create your own sound scheme, save it with a name by clicking the Save As button.

Playing Music and Other Audio with Windows Media Player 8 and 9

Another program that can play sound files, and many other types of files, is Windows Media Player. Windows XP comes with version 8, and version 9 came out in late 2002. The two versions are very similar; this chapter describes both.

 Windows Media Player 9 is a newer version of the program, but it doesn't come with Windows XP. You can download version 9 separately from the Microsoft web site. Windows Media Player 9 has improved playlists, can fade from one song to the next, and can configure the player not to share information with media web sites. However, version 9 still omits the ability to create MP3 files or play DVDs—as with version 8, you need to buy add-ons to get these features.

The Windows Media Player Window

Start Windows Media Player by choosing Start | Windows Media Player (if the program appears on the left side of the Start menu, as it does when you first install Windows), choosing Start | All Programs | Windows Media Player, or clicking the Windows Media Player icon on the Quick Launch toolbar (if it appears on your taskbar). You see the Windows Media Player window shown in Figure 19-7.

The program has buttons on the left, top, and bottom of the Windows Media Player window. The area in the center of the window is the "video screen" on which videos and other pictures appear. You can also choose to display other information on the video screen. Playlists or lists of Internet radio stations may appear on the right side of the window. (Windows Media Player 9 looks similar, but a few of the buttons are in different locations.)

Note *The program doesn't update its video screen until a file is loaded, and the video screen might end up displaying bits and pieces of the windows and dialog boxes that you have displayed in that area. Don't worry—the Windows Media Player program is fine.*

Toolbar Buttons

Windows Media Player has its own toolbar that runs down the side of the window. (The program calls this the Features Taskbar, but we reserve the term "taskbar" for the Windows taskbar.) If the Windows Media Player window isn't tall enough to display all the buttons, double-chevron buttons appear at the top and bottom of the toolbar so that you can scroll the toolbar buttons up and down. You can hide the toolbar by clicking the tiny right-pointing arrow button in the middle of the right side of the toolbar. Display the toolbar again by clicking the same arrow button.

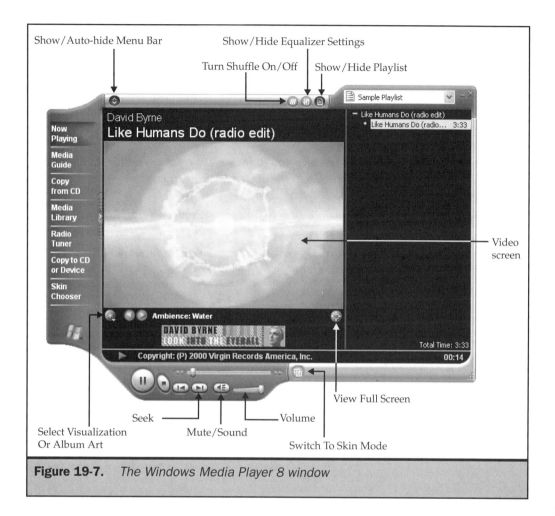

Show/Auto-hide Menu Bar

Show/Hide Equalizer Settings

Turn Shuffle On/Off   Show/Hide Playlist

Video screen

Select Visualization Or Album Art

Seek

Mute/Sound

Volume

View Full Screen

Switch To Skin Mode

Figure 19-7. *The Windows Media Player 8 window*

The toolbar contains these buttons:

- **Now Playing**   Displays the currently loaded file. If the file is a video, it appears on the video screen. If an audio file is loaded, you see a visualization of the music (see "Playing Audio Files Stored on Your Computer" later in this chapter).

- **Media Guide**   Connects to the Windows Media web site over the Internet, from which you can view video files content that is updated on a daily basis (see "Controlling How Windows Media Player Communicates over the Internet" later in this chapter).

- **Copy From CD**   Copy music from an audio CD inserted in your CD-ROM drive to the computer's disk (see "Playing Audio CDs" later in this chapter).

- **Media Library**   Enables you to organize your audio and video files (see "Organizing Your Audio Files into a Media Library" later in this chapter).

- **Radio Tuner**   Plays Internet radio stations—that is, radio stations that are available over the Internet as streaming audio files (see "Listening to Internet Radio Stations" later in this chapter).

- **Copy To CD Or Device**   Enables you to move audio files to and from a portable audio player or create audio CDs (see "Moving Files to and from Portable Players" later in this chapter).

- **Services**   Premium music and video services that you can sign up for. This button appears in Windows Media Player 9 but not in 8.

- **Skin Chooser**   Enables you to choose a different look (appearance and controls) for the program (see "Customizing the Windows Media Player Window" later in this chapter).

Note   *Windows Media Player has an Auto Update feature that tells you when updates to the program are available from Microsoft over the Internet. When you exit Windows Media Player, a dialog box may appear offering to download and install updates. Read the information about the update and decide whether you want it. You can check for updates any time you are online by choosing Help | Check For Player Updates from the menu bar.*

Windows Media Player 9 has a teeny version that can appear on your Windows taskbar, like this:

To display it, right-click a blank spot on the taskbar and choose Toolbars | Windows Media Player from the shortcut menu that appears. Repeat this command to remove the mini-player.

Microsoft's Older Media Player

If you don't like all the bells and whistles of Windows Media Player 8, Windows XP comes with an older version of the program, version 6.4. To run it, execute the file C:\Program Files\Windows Media Player\Mplayer2.exe. It doesn't include the Media Library or Radio Tuner features, it can't copy to or from CDs, and it doesn't use skins. It can play the same file formats as the newer version, but it's smaller and takes up fewer system resources.

The My Music Folder

Windows XP comes with a folder called My Music in your My Documents folder:

The idea is for you to store your music files there for replay with Windows Media Player. The folder can contain subfolders for different types of music—Windows Media Player automatically creates new folders when you copy sound files from audio CDs. When you display the My Music folder in an Explorer window, the Task pane includes two links just for sound files:

- **Play All** Plays all the music in the folder (or just the selected files).
- **Shop For Music Online** Displays the shopping section of Microsoft's WindowsMedia.com web site in Internet Explorer. The site contains links to selected music e-tailer's web sites.

Playing Audio Files Stored on Your Computer

To play a sound file stored on your computer or on a shared drive on a LAN, choose File | Open set the Files Of Type box to Audio File (to skip other types of files, such as video files), choose the filename, and click Open. (If you don't see the menu bar, click the Show/Auto-hide Menu Bar button above the upper-left corner of the video screen part of the Windows Media Player window.) Windows Media Player can play sound files in a variety of formats, including WAV, MP3, MIDI, and streaming audio files. You can stop playback by clicking the Stop button near the bottom of the window.

| Note | *Another way to play files on your computer is to create a Media Library, as described in the next section.* |

Click the Now Playing button on the toolbar to see the video that goes with the audio. If the file you are playing doesn't include video images, Windows Media Player creates them for you. As the music plays, the video screen shows *visualizations*, graphical representations of the sound. Forty-six kinds of visualizations come with Windows Media Player—all are interesting, and some are positively mesmerizing. You can change the visualization that appears by clicking the Previous Visualization and Next Visualization buttons (the small gray arrow buttons underneath the visualization). The name of the visualization appears to the right of the buttons. You can also surf through them all by choosing View | Visualizations from the menu, selecting the name of a group of visualizations, and choosing the specific visualization.

When the file is over, you can click the Play button in the lower-left corner of the Windows Media Player window to play the sound file again.

> **Tip** *You can remove visualizations that you never watch, change the properties of some visualizations, or add new visualizations that you download from the Internet. Choose Tools | Options from the menu and click the Visualizations tab to display a list of the available visualizations.*

You can add other information to the video screen by using three buttons that always appear along the top of the Windows Media Player 8 window (we list them as they appear from left to right):

- **Turn Shuffle On/Off** Click this to tell Windows Media Player whether to play the available tracks randomly (on) or in order of appearance (off). In Windows Media Player 9, this button appears in the center bottom of the window.

- **Show/Hide Equalizer And Settings In Now Playing** Displays controls along the bottom of the video screen when Now Playing is selected (see "Adjusting Volume, Graphic Equalization, and Other Sound Settings" later in this chapter). In Windows Media Player 9, choose View | Settings | Graphic Equalizer to display these controls, and click the controls' Close button to hide them.

- **Show/Hide Playlist In Now Playing** Displays your current playlist down the right side of the Windows Media Player window. In Windows Media Player 9, click the Maximize Display Panel button near the lower right corner of the visualization to hide the playlist; click the Restore Display Panel to display it again.

Windows Media Player 9 can display additional information in the video screen by choosing View | Settings and choosing one of these commands:

- **Quiet Mode** Enables you to reduce the difference between loud and soft sounds, which is useful when playing music in a noisy place (like a car).

- **Crossfading And Auto Volume Leveling** For MP3 or WMA format files, fades from one track to the next and adjusts the volume of tracks in a playlist so that the volume matches from one track to the next.

■ **Play Speed Settings** Enables you to adjust the speed at which tracks play (without affecting the pitch of the music).

 See the section "Playing Video Files with Windows Media Player" in the next chapter for details about playing video files with Windows Media Player.

Getting Music Files

Where can you get audio files to play? Here are some sources:

■ Copy the tracks from CDs that you own. See "Ripping (Copying Music) from a CD to Your Computer" later in this chapter.

■ Download them. We don't encourage trading in illegal music files, but there are many web sites with legally licensed music files—it's a great way for new bands to get known. Start at the MP3.com site (**www.mp3.com**).

■ Read the audio-related newsgroups. The largest is **alt.binaries.sounds.mp3**. The Outlook Express program that comes with Windows XP enables you to subscribe to these newsgroups and read the postings, but Outlook Express doesn't help you download the many MP3 files that are posted on these groups. You'll need a better newsreader program to assemble and store binary files (including audio files) from newsgroup postings; we recommend Agent, an inexpensive program you can download from **www.forteinc.com**.

■ Use a file-trading service. Because of legal issues (most of the files that are traded on these services are in violation of copyright), these services come and go. The original music-trading service, Napster, was shut down several years ago, but others have sprung up, including Kazaa (**www.kazaa.com**), Scour (**www.scour.com**), and WinMX (**www.winmx.com**).

 Watch out when using file-sharing services! They require you to download file-sharing software, which may contain viruses or spyware.

If you play an MP3 or other audio file from a web site, Windows stores it in your C:\Documents And Settings*username*\Local Settings\Temporary Internet Files folder (where *username* is your user account name). If you want to keep the file, open this folder in an Explorer window. Sort the files to show the most recent files first by clicking the Last Accessed column header. You can usually recognize the file by its name. Drag or copy the file to your My Music folder, or wherever you keep your music files.

WORKING WITH TEXT, NUMBERS, PICTURES, SOUND, AND VIDEO

Organizing Your Audio Files into a Media Library

The Media Library is a storehouse for all of your audio and video files (see Figure 19-8). To organize these files (also called tracks), Windows Media Player can search your drives (local and shared network drives) for files. It organizes them into lists of audio files, video files, and the addresses of radio stations on the Internet. You can then organize the files into playlists, described in the next section.

Creating Your Media Library

The first time you click the Media Library button, Windows Media Player offers to perform the search, or you can follow these steps at any time:

1. Choose Tools | Search For Media Files from the menu (or press F3). You see the Search For Media Files dialog box:

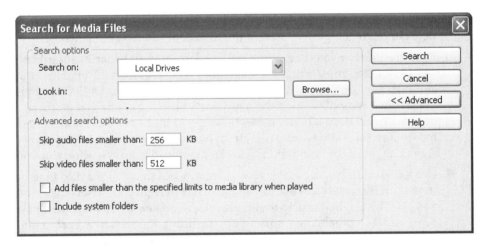

2. In the Search Options section, specify whether to search Local Drives (disk drives on your own computer), Network Drives (shared drives on a LAN), All Drives, or a list of individual drive letters. If you select a specific drive by drive letter, you can choose a folder to start in (the program searches only that folder and its subfolders).

3. Click the Advanced button to display the Advanced Search Options section of the dialog box. (In Windows Media Player 9, check the Show Advanced Search Options check box.)

4. The previous version of Windows Media Player had the annoying habit of including the small sound event files that come with Windows. Now you can specify that small files be skipped and not added to your media library—just leave the Skip Audio Files Smaller Than *xx* KB settings large enough to skip the small "beep" and "ding" event sounds (set it to at least 200KB). Windows

Media Player 9 put this option on the Media Library tab of the Options dialog box (see "Configuring the Media Library" later in this chapter).

5. Unless you want to include the audio files that come with Windows (unlikely, if you are making a catalog of music files), leave the Include System Folders check box deselected. Windows Media Player 9 omits this option.

6. Click Search. A dialog box appears telling you the progress of the search. When it has finished, it tells you how many files it found. Click Close.

7. Click Close again to dismiss the Search For Media Files dialog box

8. Click the Media Library button (if it's not already selected) to see all your audio and video files.

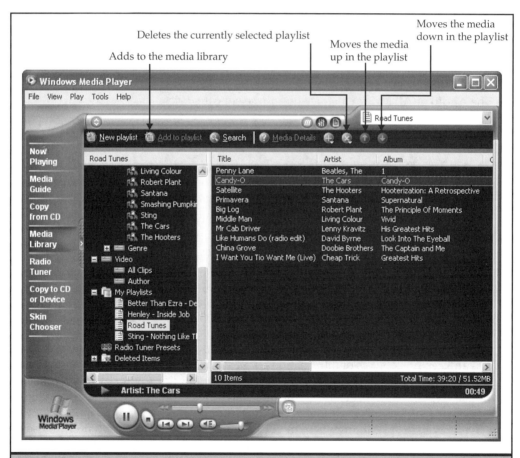

Figure 19-8. *Playlists of audio files in the Media Library*

The list on the left shows the files by category, and the list on the right shows the contents of the selected category. The major categories are:

- **Audio**   (In Windows Media 9, this is called All Music)
- **Video**   Described in the next chapter (Windows Media Player 9 calls this My Video)
- **Other Media**   (Windows Media Player 9 only)
- **My Playlists**   Described in the next section
- **Auto Playlists**   Playlists that the program creates for you (Windows Media Player 9 only)
- **Radio Tuner Presets**   Internet radio stations, described in the section "Listening to Internet Radio Stations" later in this chapter
- **Deleted Items**   (Omitted in Windows Media Player 9)
- **Subscriptions**   Premium services to which you have subscribed (Windows Media Player 9 only)

The Audio or All Music category lists these subcategories:

- **All Audio**   Displays all audio files in alphabetical order, no matter where they are stored.
- **Album**   Displays audio files by the album of which they are a part (if any). Windows Media Player identifies albums by information from audio CDs (see the next section), or from the MP3 ID3 tags for MP3 format files.
- **Artist**   Displays audio files by artist. If you have songs from more than one album by a single artist, the albums appear as sub-subcategories.
- **Genre**   Displays audio files by genres and styles. Since genres and styles are primarily determined by personal taste (ever argue with someone as to whether Steely Dan is jazz, rock, or progressive?), this is an unreliable way to sort music—unless you go through each album and assign each album to the genre where you think it belongs.

You can click a file to play it and the files that follow it on the list. Windows Media Player can keep track of lots of information about each file—use the horizontal scrollbar at the bottom of the list of files to see the title, artist, computer, genre, length, file size, file format (type), creation date, file pathname, and other items. To see more information about a file, right-click it and choose Properties from the menu that appears. If you don't want a file to appear anywhere in your Media Library, right-click it and choose Delete From Library from the shortcut menu that appears.

Updating Information about Albums and Tracks

If Windows Media Player doesn't recognize an album, it appears as "Unknown Album" by "Unknown Artist." You can replace these labels with information you enter yourself. Right-click the album name in the Album list (Album appears in the Audio category). Choose Get Names. Windows Media Player offers to search the Windows Media database for the album, but you can also click Type The Information For A Personally Created (Burned) Album.

You can also update the information about a file. Right-click a piece of information about a file and choose Edit. Windows Media Player enables you to edit the field you clicked (this feature doesn't work on all fields). You can also make the same change to the information about a group of files (for example, change the Genre of a group of files). Select a group of files, click a field (like Artist or Genre), choose Edit Selected, edit the text, and press ENTER. Windows Media Player makes the change to all the files you selected.

You can also click the Search button along the top of the video screen to search for a field by a word or phrase in its title, as shown here:

Click the Media Details button along the top of the video screen to ask Windows Media Player to get details, if any, about the selected file.

 Windows Explorer displays cover art for folders that contain music (at least for albums for which it can identify the album). You can replace the image that Windows displays, using any JPG file instead. Rename the .jpg file as Folder.jpg and store it in the folder that contains the music files. For example, if you have a folder that contains several recordings of your children singing, store a picture of them in the folder so that it appears as the "album cover."

Configuring the Media Library

You can configure other Media Library settings. Choose Tools | Options from the menu and click the Media Library tab to set these options in Windows Media Player 8:

- **Access Rights Of Other Applications**   Sets the level of access other programs have to your Media Library and playlist information.

- **Access Rights Of Internet Sites**   Sets the level of access that web sites have to your Media Library and playlist information.

- **Media Files**   If you uncheck this check box, Windows Media Player asks whether you want the program to manage that media or not. This setting is only useful if you use other digital media applications, such as Liquid Audio.

Windows Media Player 9's Media Library options include settings for automatically adding new files to the Media Library, skipping small files, and updating information about media files.

Creating and Editing Playlists

A *playlist* is a set of audio files that you plan to play as a group. You can create a playlist, give it a name, and put audio (or video) files into it. Then you can play that group of files any time, either in the order in which they appear on the playlist or in random (shuffled) order.

Click the Media Library button on the toolbar to see, create, and edit playlists. In the list of categories on the left side of the video screen, one category (near the bottom of the list) is My Playlists. Windows Media Player 8 comes with one playlist, named Sample Playlist. Windows Media Player 9 creates playlists for your music when it adds it to the Media Library.

To create a new playlist, click the New Playlist button at the top of the video screen area. Type a name for the new playlist and click OK. Windows Media Player adds your

---

Playing Music Files on Your Stereo

There are two ways to play your music files on your stereo: connecting the computer to the stereo, or burning the music files to a CD that your stereo can play. To connect your computer to your stereo (assuming that they aren't too far apart), get an audio cable with a one-eighth inch stereo plug on one end and two RCA jacks on the other. Plug the stereo plug into the Line Out jack on your sound card. Plug the two RCA jacks into the Aux In (or other input) jacks on your amplifier, equalizer, or mixer. Use shielded extension cable rather than cheap speaker wire to avoid interference and hum.

For instructions on burning audio CDs, see the section "Creating Your Own Music CDs" later in this chapter.

new playlist to the My Playlists category. (In Windows Media Player 9, click the Playlists button, choose New Playlist, type a name in the Playlist Name box, and click items in the lefthand list to add them to your new playlist.)

You can add files to a playlist in several ways:

- Look in the All Audio, Album, Artist, or Genre categories for the track you want to add, and click the track in the right side of the Windows Media Player window. (You can select multiple tracks by SHIFT-clicking or CTRL-clicking.) Click the Add To Playlist button at the top left of the video screen when the Media Library button is selected. You see a menu of your playlists.

- Right-click a file (or select a group of files and right-click it), and choose Add To Playlist from the shortcut menu that appears.

- Drag the file (or files) to the name of the playlist in the My Playlists category on the left side of the video screen when Media Library is selected.

When you add a file to a playlist, Windows Media Player doesn't copy the file to the playlist—the audio file remains where it is stored. Instead, it creates a shortcut to the file. This capability allows you to include one file in many playlists. When you delete a file from a playlist, Windows doesn't delete the audio file; it just deletes the shortcut to the file from the playlist. To delete a file from a playlist, right-click the file and choose Delete From Playlist from the shortcut menu that appears (or click the Delete Media From Playlist Or Library button along the right top of the video screen).

You can adjust the order of the files in the playlist by dragging them up and down the list. Or, select a file and click either the Moves The Media Up In The Playlist button or the Moves The Media Down In The Playlist button along the right top of the video screen. Click the Turn Shuffle On button along the top of the Windows Media Player window to play the files in random order.

You can also save your playlists in files in various formats, including Windows Media types (with extensions .asx, .wax, and .wvx), as well as the WinAmp format (.m3u). To export a playlist, do the following:

1. Click the Media Library button.

2. Click the My Playlists item to show your available playlists on the right.

3. Select a playlist.

4. Choose File | Export Playlist To File or File | Save Playlist As to open the Save As dialog box.

5. Type a name for the file in the Save As box.

6. Add one of the file extensions to have it saved as a particular type (usually .m3u).

7. Click Save.

Tip *To play a playlist you've heard recently, choose it from the drop-down list in the upper-right corner of the Windows Media Player window.*

Playing Streaming Audio Files from the Internet

Windows Media Player can play streaming audio and video files in the Windows Media Advanced Streaming Formats (with extensions .asf and .asx). It can't play the more widely used RealAudio format (with extensions .ra and .ram). (See the sidebar "Listening to RealAudio Files.")

To play a streaming audio file if you know the exact URL of an audio file on the Internet, choose File | Open Location or File | Open URL and enter the URL of the file to play it. However, it's usually easier to use the Media Guide button to help you find the file you want.

When you click the Media Guide button, the program connects to Microsoft's WindowsMedia site at **www.windowsmedia.com**. This site, as shown in Figure 19-9, changes often, usually lists links to television, movies, or new music, and often has neat stuff to look at or listen to.

Windows Media Player's Media Guide feature acts like a browser to show you the WindowsMedia home page, which you can also view with Internet Explorer. Some

Figure 19-9.   *Microsoft's Media Guide web site*

links may display pages in your browser rather than on the Windows Media Player's video screen.

Configuring Windows Media Player to Communicate over the Internet

If your PC connects to the Internet through a firewall, you might not be able to use Windows Media Player's Media Guide or Radio Tuner buttons. The port numbers used when connecting to streaming audio material on web sites aren't standard, and the system that connects your LAN to the Internet might not be configured to handle them. If you have a problem, choose Tools | Options to display the Options dialog box. The Network tab controls how the program receives audio and video data over the Internet:

- ■ **Protocols** Defines which network access protocols the program uses to communicate with servers and (optionally) which ports to use (useful if you communicate with the Internet through a firewall).

- ■ **Proxy Settings** Specifies whether your PC communicates with the Internet over a LAN, using a proxy server program (see Chapter 31). The default is not to use a proxy server. If your PC connects to the Internet over a LAN, get the configuration information from your LAN administrator.

Three other configuration settings affect the quality of streaming files from the Internet. The Performance tab of the Options dialog box enables you to set them:

- ■ **Connection Speed** You can let Windows Media Player detect the speed at which your computer communicates with the Internet, or, if you know for sure, you can set it yourself.

- ■ **Network Buffering** Defines how much data is stored in RAM before it actually plays. If you have trouble getting smooth playback, click the Buffer radio button and put up to 60 seconds in the field (30 to 45 seconds is typically adequate).

- ■ **Video Acceleration** Allows you to set how much of the video rendering is performed by your video card. Cryptically advanced controls and options are available by clicking the Advanced button, but we do not recommend altering anything unless specified by a technical support agent or other experienced source.

Listening to Internet Radio Stations

Many radio stations use the Internet to broadcast their signal to parts of the world that their antennas could never reach. In addition to large-scale commercial stations, hundreds of little operations are cropping up (although some have had to stop broadcasting due to issues of artist royalties). Window Media Player brings all of the stations that use the Windows Media streaming technology to you in the form of a searchable database.

WORKING WITH TEXT, NUMBERS, PICTURES, SOUND, AND VIDEO

Listening to RealAudio Files

The most widely used format for streaming audio files (including Internet radio stations) is RealAudio, which Windows Media Player can't handle. You can download the RealOne Player program for free from the Real.com web site at **www.real.com**; this program works with your browser to play both RealAudio and RealVideo files from the Internet. (You may need to look around on the Real.com site for a link to the free player; they'd prefer for you to pay for a more powerful player.)

When you install the RealOne Player, it usually configures Windows to make it the default player for MP3, AIFF, and AVI audio files; MPEG and AVI video files; and audio CDs. You can choose to leave Windows Media Player as the default player for these types of files.

An example of Internet radio on a small scale is radioIO (at **www.radioio.com**), where a small cadre of people handles all aspects of the operation of one streaming station. On the other end of the scale is Live365 (at **www.live365.com**) which has 100 streaming stations all going at the same time. Both are professionally programmed radio stations.

Note
The Recording Industry Association of America is trying to charge Internet radio stations high royalty fees—fees far higher than those for over-the-air stations. If implemented, these fees would probably put all but a few Internet radio stations out of business. Stay tuned!

To listen to Internet radio, click the Radio Tuner button. Windows Media Player shows the list of presets and radio stations shown in Figure 19-10. You see information from the WindowsMedia.com web site.

The left side of the video screen lists your preset stations (these stations also appear when you click the Media Library button in the Radio Tuner Presets category). A number of presets are already there, but you can remove or edit them. Those presets appear in the Featured Stations preset list. Click an entry to see your options: Add To My Stations (that is, to your My Stations preset list), Visit Website (the radio station's web site), or Play. You can make your own preset list using My Stations.

To find stations that aren't on a preset list, click Find More Stations. Set the Browse By Genre box to a category, or type a name or keyword into the Search box and click the arrow button to its right. You can also search by ZIP code to find stations in an area you're interested in. Windows Media Player searches for stations that match. The stations that Windows Media Player finds appear in the Search Results list. To listen to a station, click it and click Play. You may have to wait a minute or two until the music (or talk) begins. You may see a dialog box asking whether to install a downloaded codec (compressing and decompressing schemes).

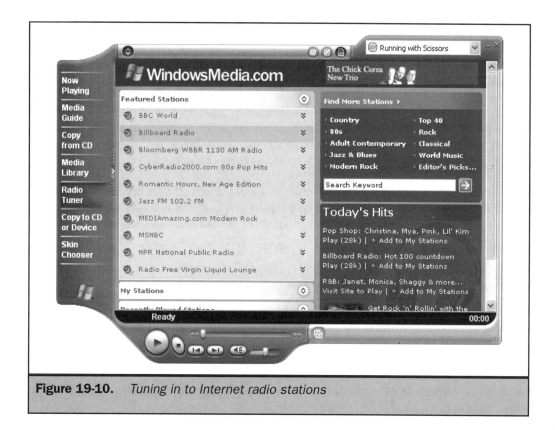

Figure 19-10. *Tuning in to Internet radio stations*

If you like a radio station, you can add it to your My Stations lists. Highlight the station and click the Add To My Stations button.

 Another way to listen to an Internet radio station is to display its web site in your browser. Click a link to listen to the Windows Media-format streaming audio. Links to RealAudio-format streaming files don't work with Windows Media Player—you need the RealOne Player instead.

Playing Audio CDs

When you insert an audio CD into your CD-ROM drive, the Windows Media Player program runs automatically. If AutoPlay is turned on, the music begins playing (later in this section there are instructions for turning AutoPlay off).

Every audio CD has a serial number that identifies the artist, the album title, and the list of tracks (songs) on the CD. Thousands of these serial numbers are stored in a database called the *Compact Disc Database* or *CDDB*, which is accessible over the

Internet. The CDDB began as a cooperative effort of the community of music lovers, entering information about their CDs, but has since become a commercial venture.

Windows Media Player reads the number from the audio CD and sends that number to the CDDB over the Internet. If the audio CD number is in the CDDB, the list of songs and artists is usually already in the CDDB, unless you have a truly obscure album. Windows Media Player downloads this information to your computer automatically. The list of tracks appears in the playlist that appears when you click the Now Playing or CD Audio button. If the CD is not in the CDDB database (perhaps because it's just been released) you have the option to type in the titles of the tracks yourself.

 If you have installed another program that can play audio CDs (such as the RealOne Player, which is described in the sidebar "Listening to RealAudio Files" earlier in this chapter), that program may run when you insert an audio CD. You can choose what program runs (if any)—see the section "Controlling CD AutoPlay" later in this chapter.

Playing Selected Tracks

To play a specific track, double-click or right-click a song title and select Play; or select the song title and click the Play button at the bottom of the window. You can edit the information about a CD track the same way you edit information about a track in a playlist: right-click information about the track and choose Edit from the shortcut menu that appears; or, select a group of tracks, right-click the information about one track, and choose Edit Selected to make the same change to all the selected tracks. For more information about a track, right-click it and choose Properties. In Windows Media Player 9, you can click the Album Info button.

Choosing What Order to Play Tracks

You can change the order in which Windows Media Player plays the tracks on the CD. Right-click a track and choose Move Up or Move Down from the shortcut menu, or simply drag them up or down with the mouse. A gray line tracks your movement, indicating where the track will be placed when you let go. Click the Shuffle button along the top of the Windows Media Player window to play the files in random order. (In Windows Media Player 9, the Shuffle button is along the bottom edge of the window.)

 The check boxes to the left of the tracks are used for selecting tracks when copying a CD; they don't affect which tracks Windows Media Player plays.

Configuring How Windows Media Player Plays CDs

You may be able to improve the playback quality of CDs by choosing Tools | Options from the Windows Media Player's menu bar, clicking the Devices tab, selecting your CD drive from the list, and clicking Properties. (Click the Show Menu Bar button above the upper-left corner of the video screen if the menu bar doesn't appear.) In the Playback section, try switching between Digital and Analog. You can also turn on error correction, which increases the amount of RAM used to buffer the audio data, but minimizes noise. Digital playback with error correction usually provides the best sound.

 If your CD-ROM drive doesn't support digital playback, and you set the Playback setting to Digital, Windows may hang or display an error message.

Controlling CD AutoPlay

Windows Media Player is configured to start playing an audio CD as soon as you put it in the drive. However, you can turn the AutoPlay feature off. Follow these steps:

1. Choose Start | My Computer to open an Explorer window.

2. Right-click the CD drive and choose Properties from the menu to display the Properties dialog box for the drive.

3. Click the AutoPlay tab (as shown in Figure 19-11), which enables you to choose how Windows responds when you insert a CD in the drive, depending on the type of files on the CD.

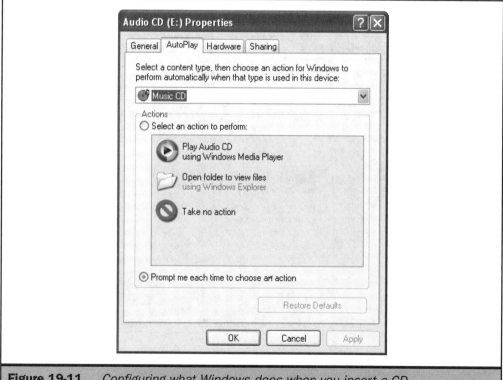

Figure 19-11. *Configuring what Windows does when you insert a CD*

4. Set the dropdown menu to Music CD.

5. In the Actions section of the dialog box, choose what you want Windows to do.

Adjusting Volume, Graphic Equalization, and Other Sound Settings

If you want to adjust how your audio files sound, click the Show Equalizer And Settings In Now Playing button at the top of the Windows Media Player window and then click the Now Playing button. The equalizer and settings appear in the bottom part of the video screen. Click the Show Equalizer And Settings In Now Playing button again to remove these tools from the screen. You can also start or stop displaying these tools by choosing View | Now Playing Tools from the menu, and choosing the tool. (In Windows Media Player 9, click the Info Center View button below the video screen and choose Settings, or choose View | Settings from the menu bar to choose these options.)

Using Another Audio Player

The first time you insert an audio CD into your CD-ROM drive, you may see a dialog box like this:

You can decide whether to use Windows Media Player or another program to play your audio CDs.

Several sets of tools can appear in this area. The gray menu button in the lower-left corner of the area selects which of the following tools appears.

- **SRS WOW Effects** Includes several special effects: TruBass, WOW Effect, SRS WOW Effect, and Speakers. TruBass adds more bass to your music the farther to the right you slide it. WOW Effect adds more separation between the stereo channels. The On/Off button enables or disables all these effects. Clicking the SRS logo takes your browser to the SRS Technologies web site at **www.srstechnologies.com**, in case you are interested in files that use the SRS WOW technology. The Speakers button switches among Normal Speakers, Large Speakers, and Headphones.

- **Graphic Equalizer** Enables you to adjust the treble and bass balance, and left and right speaker balance. The ten vertical sliders adjust the volume of the high treble notes (at the right end) through the low bass notes (at the left end). The On/Off button enables or disables the effects of any modifications you make to the equalizer. Turning it off means you get the sound exactly as it was recorded. Rather than setting them individually, you can click the button below the On/Off button, which cycles through preset bass/treble settings that work for many common musical genres. The Balance slider adjusts the relative volume of the left and right speakers. If you like to adjust the equalizer yourself, the three buttons on the left end of the controls define whether you can adjust each frequency individually, adjust them in a loose group, or adjust them in a tight group.

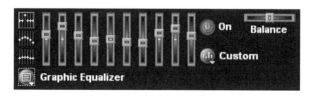

- **Video Settings** Enables you to control the color and brightness of the video images.
- **Media Information** Displays any information that the program can glean about tracks or albums you are listening to. If it's available, it even shows a picture of the album cover. When you are playing MP3 files downloaded from the Internet, no information appears.

MP3 files have their own way of identifying the file's contents to MP3 players. They are called ID3 tags, and they embed the information about artist, album, title, length, genre, track number, and notes.

- **Captions**   Displays captions, if the file includes them.
- **Lyrics**   Displays song lyrics if the file includes them or if they are available via the CDDB.
- **DVD Controls**   Displays the other controls that Windows Media Player needs if you are playing a DVD. These additional controls include the Variable Play Speed slider, Rewind, Play, Fast Forward, and Next Frame buttons. Even more controls are available during playback by right-clicking the video.

Ripping (Copying Music) from a CD to Your Computer

Music is stored on audio CDs in an uncompressed format. Windows Media Player can copy CD tracks to your computer and encode them in WMA files. If you want to store your music in another format, like the popular MP3 format, you need to use another program—either a MP3 Creation Pack that plugs into Windows Media Player, or a standalone program. (The RealOne Player, which is described in the sidebar "Listening to RealAudio Files" earlier in this chapter, rips CDs to its own .rmj format, which Windows Media Player can't play.) Once you've copied them, you may want to edit your audio files to convert the tracks to other formats, eliminate noise, or make other changes (maybe you're tired of listening to the applause at the end of a live recording).

When you rip tracks from a CD, you use an *encoding rate* or *bit rate* at which the program encodes (stores) the audio information. The higher the encoding rate, the higher the quality of the sound, but the larger the file. Audio programs may use encoding rates of 64 Kbps, 96 Kbps, 128 Kbps, 160 Kbps, or 320 Kbps—128 Kbps is considered by many to be close to the quality of a CD.

 Not all CD drives enable you to rip CDs; the drive must support Digital Audio Extraction (that is, sending the digital data on the CD to your computer, rather than sending an analog signal to your computer's sound card).

Configuring Windows Media Player to Rip CDs

Windows Media Player includes several configuration settings for copying tracks from audio CDs. Before you start ripping, configure the program by choosing Tools | Options to display the Options dialog box. (Click the Show Menu Bar button above the upper-left corner of the video screen if the menu bar doesn't appear.) Then check these configuration settings:

■ **File location**   Click the Copy Music tab to see the dialog box shown in Figure 19-12. In the Copy Music To This Location section, click the Change button.

■ **Digital rights management protection**   The Protect Content check box controls whether Windows Media Player keeps track of whether you have a license for the music files on your hard disk. When you rip a track from a CD, the program records license ownership for the file, but allows you to copy this file only a limited number of times and won't let you burn it on a CD. We recommend that you deselect this check box; we know of no user benefit to leaving it selected. If you do leave the Protect Content check box selected, you'll need to worry about backing up your licenses and not accidentally deleting them. Microsoft provides the Personal License Update Wizard for this purpose, at **www.microsoft.com/ windows/windowsmedia/WM7/DRM/pluwiz.asp**.

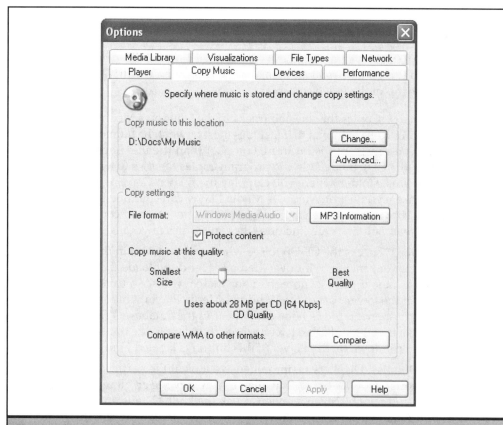

Figure 19-12.   *Configuring Windows Media Player to copy files from audio CDs*

■ **Quality**   The Copy Music At This Quality slider enables you to set the encoding rate. You can choose between small file size (and lower quality) and highest quality (with larger files). The default is 64Kbps, but you may want to increase it.

■ **Filenames**   You can choose how Windows Media Player names the files that it creates when you copy tracks from audio CDs. Click the Advanced button on the Copy Music tab to see the File Name Options dialog box, in which you can choose what information makes up file names: track number, sing title, artist, album title, genre, and bit rate.

■ **Digital vs. analog copying**   Click the Devices tab, select your CD drive from the list, and click Properties to control how audio CDs play On the Audio tab, in the Copy section, you can choose between analog and digital copying, and you can turn error-correction on and off. For some CD-ROM drives, you can set the quality level that you want to use when copying music from CDs to your hard disk—the higher the quality, the bigger the file.

Ripping CDs as WMA files

With Windows Media Player running, put an audio CD in your CD drive and click the Copy From CD button on the toolbar. If an audio CD is in the CD drive, these buttons appear across the top of the video screen:

■ **Copy Music**   Copies the selected tracks to the Windows Media (WMA) digital format at 128 Kbps (a format that includes most of what the human ear can discern from digital music, but is far more compact than the uncompressed format stored on the CD). By default, the program copies the files to a new folder in your My Music folder, where you can play them later. Copying tracks from a CD can take a while, but Windows Media Player can continue to play the CD while it's copying: click the Stop Copying button to interrupt copying. Windows Media Player automatically includes these new files in your Media Library.

■ **Get Names**   Checks the CDDB to see whether your CD is in the database. If there is only one match, Windows Media Player downloads the list and stores it for reuse later. If there is more than one match, you see a list of the located matches in the lower part of the Windows Media Player window and you can select the best one. If the CD doesn't appear in the database, Windows Media Player asks if you would like to contribute that data to the database for others to see. (In Windows Media Player 9, this button is labeled Find Album Info.)

■ **Album Details**   Displays a comprehensive look at the particular title you have in your CD-ROM drive, if available. You may see an album cover, a list of songs, and possibly even a review. Click the Hide Details button to remove this information from the window. (In Windows Media Player 9, this button is called View Album Info.)

When you click the Copy Music button to begin copying tracks from a CD, you may see a dialog box warning you that the music is copyrighted. This dialog box reminds you that you shouldn't play tracks from this CD on other computers (see "Licensing Issues for Digital Music" later in this chapter).

If you are having trouble getting good quality when you rip CDs using Windows Media Player, you might want to try one of the standalone programs mentioned in the next section.

Ripping CDs as MP3 Files

You may want to store your music in MP3 files rather than WMA files, even though MP3 files are much larger. Most portable MP3 players play only MP3 files, not WMA files. (See the section "Moving Files to and from Portable Players" later in this chapter).

Windows Media Player doesn't copy music directly from CDs to MP3 files. You need another program. You have two options:

- **MP3 Creation Pack** This is a small program that plugs into Windows Media Player, enabling you to use Windows Media Player to rip music from CDs directly to MP3 files. Several are available, and they all cost about $10. To see a list of available MP3 Creation Packs, choose Tools | Options, click the Copy Music tab, and click the MP3 Information button. Or use your browser to display the MP3 Creation And DVD Decoder Packs web page at **www.microsoft.com/ windows/windowsmedia/windowsxp/buypacks.asp**.

- **Standalone program** A number of free or reasonably priced MP3-ripping programs are available. Go to **download.com.com** and search for Windows MP3 software to see a list. RealNetworks at **www.real.com** has programs that can encode MP3 files. Our favorite MP3 encoding program is CDex, at **www.cdex.n3.net**, a small, free program that can play audio CDs and rip all or selected tracks to WAV or MP3 files. Another good program is MusicMatch Jukebox, available at **www.musicmatch.com**.

Copying Music from Cassette Tapes or LPs

Ripping CDs gives you good quality music, but what about your old cassettes and LP records? You can copy music from them, too, but the quality won't be as good.

To record from a cassette tape or LP record, you connect a stereo cable to your computer's sound card's Line In jack. For cassettes, connect the cable to your cassette deck's Output jack. For records, connect your record player to your amplifier, and connect your computer's cable to the Output jack on your amplifier.

Windows Media Player doesn't record from your sound card's input. Instead, you will need to use a program that can record incoming sound as WAV files. You can play these WAV files with Windows Media Player or convert them to other formats using the standalone audio programs listed in the preceding section. Windows comes with

Licensing Issues for Digital Music

In order to protect music transferred from audio CDs or the Internet from being copied, Microsoft has integrated some protection features that prevent you from copying *unsigned* files to a portable device. A file is *signed* if you copied the music from an audio CD using Windows Media Player. When you copy music from an audio CD, Windows Media Player assumes that the music is licensed to you to use at your discretion (as long as you don't resell it or otherwise redistribute the media to the general public). All files that you copy are encoded in Microsoft's proprietary .wma format by default, so you need a device that can play them (some portable MP3 players can also play WMAs) You can also get signed music files by buying and downloading them from the WindowsMedia.com web site. The Acquire Licenses Automatically check box on the Player tab of the Options dialog box tells Windows Media Player to download licenses whenever available.

Note *You are fairly safe from getting improperly licensed music from unknown online sources as long as you patronize the WindowsMedia.com web site (and maybe a few select partners). Any music purchased through the WindowsMedia.com site or from one of its partners is likely to be properly licensed.*

If you need to move your media licenses from one computer to another, go to the Microsoft support web site at **support.microsoft.com** and search for article Q308638.

Most people who use Windows Media Player simply turn off its license-tracking features when ripping CDs. Choose Tools | Options, click the Copy Music tab, and clear the Protect Content check box.

a WAV-recording program—Sound Recorder, which is described later in this chapter—but it can record only short files. GoldWave (at **www.goldwave.com**) is a good, inexpensive WAV recording program, and it can also convert your WAV files to MP3s. dBpowerAMP Music Converter (at **www.dbpoweramp.com**) is a free file converter that can also record WAV files. Other popular audio-editing programs are Cool Edit (at **www.syntrillium.com**) and Sound Forge (at **www.sonicfoundry.com/home.asp**).

Moving Files to and from Portable Players

Once you've assembled a collection of audio files you like, you can take your music with you in a portable MP3 player. Your PDA (personal digital assistant) and cell phone may be able to play MP3 files, too. Today's portable digital music players can hold many hours of music and connect to your PC's USB or FireWire port. All portable players can play MP3 files, and some can also play WAV files (the uncompressed format that Sound Recorder creates) and WMA files (the format in which Windows

Media Player stores files ripped from CDs). Some portable players can also record MP3 files with a microphone.

Here's how to copy music from your PC to a portable player:

1. Make a playlist of the music you want to copy, in the order in which you want the tracks copied.

2. Connect your portable player to your PC with its FireWire, USB, or serial cable.

3. Click the Copy To CD Or Device button. The tracks on a playlist appear on the left side (Music To Copy). Any existing tracks appear on the right side (Music On Device).

4. Select which files will be copied by checking or unchecking the tracks on the Music To Copy list. If no tracks appear, choose or create a playlist.

5. When you have selected all of the tracks to copy (assuming that they do not exceed the storage capacity of your portable player), click the Copy Music button in the upper-left corner of the window.

The serial connections with which many portable players connect to the PC are slow, but many portable music players come with USB or FireWire connections that are much faster.

You can control how Windows Media Player copies files to portable players—choose Tools | Options and click the Device tab of the Options dialog box to see a listing of your devices. If an installed device does not appear, it is either not supported or not correctly installed.

Note	*Some portable players come with their own software that makes it easier to "sync" the player with your PC's music files.*

Creating Your Own Music CDs

CD-R and CD-RW burners can record using one of two formats: audio (CD-DA, or Compact Disk Digital Audio) or data (CD-ROM, or Compact Disk Read-Only Memory). Here are the differences:

- **Audio CDs** The tracks of an audio CD are stored in an uncompressed format that is equivalent to WAV (.wav) files on your PC. This is the format used in music CDs that you purchase. Any CD player can play audio CDs that were burned on a CD-R burner, although they usually can't play CD-RWs. (If you have a CD-RW drive, use CD-Rs when burning audio CDs.) Audio CDs are limited to about 74 or 80 minutes of music (depending on the type of blank CD you record on).

- **Data CDs** A few recent CD players can also play data CDs that contain MP3, WMA (the format in which Windows Media stores tracks ripped from CDs),

WORKING WITH TEXT, NUMBERS, PICTURES, SOUND, AND VIDEO

and ASF (Microsoft's Advanced Streaming Format) files. The advantage over audio CDs is that a data CD can contain almost 10 times as much data as an audio CD—up to 650MB or 700MB. The average audio CD recorded at 128Kbps takes about 60MB of space.

For more information about burning CDs, see "Configuring CD-R and CD-RW Drives" in Chapter 33 and "Making Your Own CDs" in Chapter 8.

 It's not worth paying more for blank "audio CDs"—instead, use the cheapest blank CDs that work in the machines in which you want to play the CDs.

Burning Audio CDs

Windows Media Player can create audio CDs using the files and playlists that you've already created and imported. Follow these steps:

1. Make a playlist of the music you want on the CD, in the order in which you want the tracks copied.

2. Put a CD-R in your drive. (Don't use CD-RWs, which many CD players can't play.)

3. Select the playlist and click the Copy To CD Or Device button. The tracks on a playlist appear on the left side (Music or Items To Copy), as shown in Figure 19-13. The right side shows any tracks that are already on the CD. (There should be no tracks, because audio CDs must be recorded in one session.) If you haven't already put a blank CD in your drive, Windows Media Player displays the status "Will not fit" for each file.

4. Select which files to burn by checking or unchecking the tracks on the Music (or Items) To Copy list. Windows Media Player shows the side and length of the files, so you can see whether they exceed the storage capacity of your CD, which is 74 or 80 minutes of music depending on the type of blank CD you use.

5. Exit all other programs so that Windows Media Player has the complete attention of your computer, to reduce the possibility that the recording process will fail due to data being sent to the CD-R drive too slowly.

6. Click the Copy Music button in the upper-left corner of the window. Windows Media Player converts the files to WAV files and then copies them to the CD. The WAV files are stored temporarily; if there isn't enough room (the files are usually stored on the disk on which Windows is installed), you can specify another location (see the next section). Windows Media Player displays its progress by showing the status of each of the files it is burning.

7. When Windows Media Player is finished, it displays "Closing disc" as the status of the last file and ejects the CD. Until you put a new, blank CD in the drive, the files appear with the status "Will not fit," indicating that you can't burn them again on the same CD.

Figure 19-13. *Ready to burn an audio CD*

WORKING WITH TEXT, NUMBERS, PICTURES, SOUND, AND VIDEO

If Windows Media Player encounters a problem converting your files or copying them to the CD, you see an error message asking whether to burn only some of the files or abort the operation. Cancel burning, because you can't add songs to the CD later. The files that caused problems have the status "An error occurred." Right-click the file and choose Error Details to find out what the problem is.

Alternatively, you can use another program to burn CDs. Windows includes the CD Writing Wizard which can write both audio and data CDs (see the section "Making Your Own CDs" in Chapter 8). Easy CD Creator is a popular program than comes free with many CD-R and CD-RWs. Be sure to specify that you want to create an audio CD, not a data CD.

Note *You can also transfer your audio files to cassette tape. Connect your computer's sound card's Line Out jack to your cassette deck's Aux In jack with a stereo cable. Start recording and pause your tape deck after a few seconds, to skip the blank tape at the beginning. Start Windows Media Player playing the playlist of songs you want to record, and immediately unpause the tape deck. You may need to experiment with volume levels to get the right volume on tape.*

Configuring Windows Media Player to Record Audio CDs

Choose Tools | Options, click the Devices tab, select your CD-R or CD-RW drive from the list, and click Properties. (Click the Show Menu Bar button above the upper-left corner of the video screen if the menu bar doesn't appear.) On the Recording tab (shown in Figure 19-14) are these settings:

- **Enable CD Recording On This Drive**   Governs whether you can use the drive to create CDs or not. This option is purely subjective, because if the drive were not capable of recording, the Recording tab would not have appeared in the first place.

- **Location of CD Image**   Before Windows Media Player copies the files to the CD, it makes an image of what it plans to copy, converting files from WMA, MP3, and other formats to the format used on the CD. This CD image is usually stored on the same hard disk where Windows is installed, but you can change

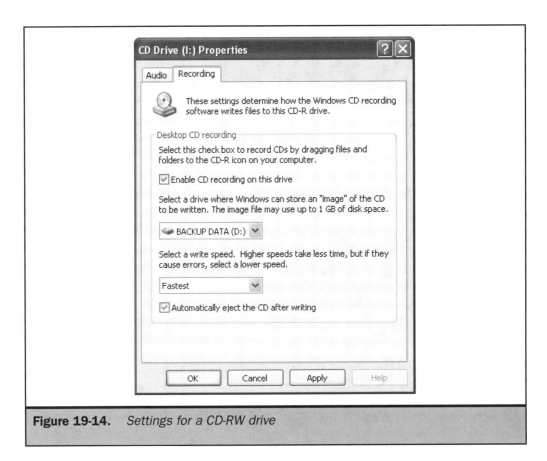

Figure 19-14.   *Settings for a CD-RW drive*

this location. Be sure to choose a local drive (one installed on your own computer), not a network drive, because the data may not arrive over the LAN fast enough to be burned on the CD.

- **Speed Selection**   Controls how quickly Windows can write to the drive. You can't select a speed that is faster than your drive actually supports. If you are using older CD blanks that support only slower speeds and you have trouble getting CDs that play well, burn the CDs at a slower speed than the drive is capable of handling.

- **Automatically Eject The CD After Writing**   The sound of your CD burner spitting out the new CD is your signal that the CD is done.

Burning MP3 Data CDs

When you store music on a CD, you choose which format to use for the files:

- **MP3**   Some CD players can play MP3 files from data disks. You can use this method to store MP3 files to play on your computer or to move to an MP3 player.

- **WAV**   We don't know of any CD players that can play WAV files, and WAVs are much larger than MP3 or WMA files, so you can't fit as many on a CD. But you can burn them to a CD to transport the files to another computer.

- **WMA (Windows Media Player)**   When Windows Media Player copies tracks from a CD, it converts them into .wma files to store on your hard disk. These .wma files are compressed, so they take up less space on your hard disk. But if you store .wma files on a CD, few CD players can play them. However, you can use this method to transport .wma files to another computer.

To create a data CD, you can use Windows Explorer. See the section "Making Your Own CDs" in Chapter 8 for how to copy any set of files to a data CD.

Troubleshooting Burning Audio CDs

See the section "Troubleshooting Burning CDs" in Chapter 8 for troubleshooting CD burning problems. Here are two ideas that are specific to audio CDs:

- If you are burning WAV files, they may use a sampling rate and sample size that is different from that required by audio CDs. Use an audio editing program like GoldWave to convert the WAV files to stereo, with a sampling rate of 44.1 KHz and a sample size of 16 bits.

- If your CD player won't play the CDs that you burn, make sure that you choose to burn them as audio, not data CDs. Make sure you aren't using CD-RWs. You might also want to try another brand of blank CDs.

More Information about MP3s and Burning Audio CDs

If you want to know more about storing music on your computer, finding and purchasing music online, and burning audio CDs (as well as data CDs that are readable by some CD players), you'll need programs beyond those that come with Windows XP. For more information, go to these web sites:

- Andy McFadden's CD-Recordable FAQ at **www.cdrfaq.org**
- The Sonic Spot at **www.sonicspot.com**
- Xory's MP3 FAQ at **webhome.idirect.com/~nuzhathl/mp3-faq.html** (or search Google for the title)
- MP3.com at **www.mp3.com**
- The Alt.binaries.sounds.mp3 Newsgroup FAQ at **www.mp3-faq.org**

Customizing the Windows Media Player Window

You can configure Windows Media Player by choosing Tools | Options to display the Options dialog box. The Player tab of the Options dialog box controls the program itself:

- **Automatic Updates** Specifies how often you want Windows Media Player to check the Microsoft web site for updates. You can also enable or disable automatic codec downloads.
- **Internet Settings** Controls whether your player is individually recognized on the Internet and whether to get media licenses. The first option allows web sites to store something like a media cookie on your PC. (In Windows Media Player 9, these settings have moved to the Privacy tab.)
- **Player Settings** Specifies how Windows Media Player looks when it starts.

You can also change when the program connects to the Internet, how the program's window looks, and what file formats it plays, as described in the next three sections.

Windows Media Player 9 has a Change Player Color button near the lower right corner of its window; click this button repeatedly to cycle through a number of tints for the program's window.

Controlling How Windows Media Player Communicates over the Internet

When you click the Media Guide button on the Windows Media Player toolbar, Windows connects to the Internet to display the WindowsMedia.com web site. When you put an audio CD in your CD drive, Windows connects to the Internet so that Windows Media Player can consult the CDDB database of CD titles and tracks. But what if you don't want Windows to connect to the Internet at these times?

Here are settings that control when Windows Media Player connects to the Internet and what information it transmits. Choose Tools | Options to display the Options dialog box, which contains most of these settings:

- **Automatic updates**   On the Player tab, the settings in the Automatic Updates section control how often Windows Media Player checks for program updates, and whether it downloads them automatically when it finds them.

- **Privacy**   On the Player tab, the Allow Internet Sites To Uniquely Identify Your Player check box controls what information Windows Media Player transmits about you when you insert an audio CD into your CD drive or listen to streaming audio or video. (In Windows Media Player 9, a similar Send Unique Player ID To Content Providers check box appears on the Privacy tab.)

- **Startup mode**   On the Player tab, in the Player Settings section, clear the Start Player In Media Guide check box if you don't want to display the WindowsMedia.com web site each time you start Windows Media Player.

To prevent Windows from connecting to the Internet when you insert an audio CD, choose File | Work Offline from the Windows Media Player menu. However, this command affects your connection for other programs, too, including Outlook Express and Internet Explorer.

Switching Skins

WinAmp, a popular shareware MP3 player, popularized the ability to *skin* an application—that is, offer a variety of user interfaces so that you can choose among a number of window, menu, and button designs (or even create your own). In a complete turnaround from Microsoft's typical functional look, the company had integrated skins into Windows Media Player. Full mode has only a single look, but in Skin mode, customization can run rampant.

When you run Windows Media Player, it appears in Full mode, with all the buttons and controls we've described so far. The other option is Skin mode, in which you see one of the included skins.

To switch from Full mode to Skin mode, click the Switch To Skin Mode button that appears at the right end of the Seek slider. (In Windows Media Player 9, it's near the lower right corner of the window.) How the Windows Media Player window looks depends on which skin you chose. You usually see something like this:

<table>
<tr><td>**Caution**</td><td>*Changing skins changes the locations of all the controls and the overall appearance of Windows Media Player, often drastically. Don't try changing the program's skins until you feel confident with the application as a whole. To return to Full mode, hover your mouse over buttons until you find one called Return To Full Mode. If you do get stuck here's how to get back to Full mode in Windows Media Player 8, click the anchor window— the large Windows Media logo button that appears in a floating window—or the same logo wherever it appears in the Windows Media Player window. Then choose Switch To Full Mode from the menu that appears:*</td></tr>
</table>

To switch to another skin, starting in Full mode:

1. Click the Skin Chooser button on the toolbar down the left side of the window. In the video screen, you see two lists: on the left is a list of available skins and on the right is a picture of the selected skin (see Figure 19-15).

2. Select a skin name from the list on the left side. An image appears in the right pane showing you what the skin really looks like.

3. Click the Apply Skin button at the top of the list to activate the skin and switch to Skin mode. If you want to change skins without changing modes, just leave the new skin selected and click a different button on the toolbar.

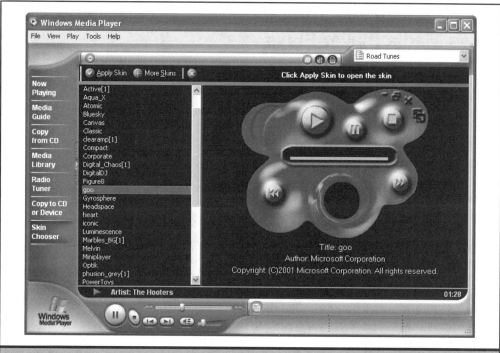

Figure 19-15. *Choosing a different skin for Windows Media Player*

You can get more skins from the WindowsMedia.com web site at any time. Skins are stored in files with the extension .wmz in the C:\Program Files\Windows Media Player\Skins folder (assuming that Windows is installed on C:). Click the More Skins button at the top of the list and your browser goes to the Skins pages on the Microsoft Windowsmedia.com web site. When you click the picture showing the skin, Windows Media Player downloads it and asks if you would like to activate your new skin now.

Switching back from a new skin can be trickier, since the new controls may be unrecognizable. Hover your mouse pointer over anything that looks like it might be a button until you find one with the label Return To Full Mode. If nothing appears familiar or your hover search reveals no clues, you may also right-click anywhere on the skin and select Full Mode from the menu that appears.

 Some skins consume lots of memory. If your computer's performance slows when you are using Windows Media Player, switch back to the default skin.

Specifying Which File Formats Windows Media Player Plays

You can choose which file formats Windows Media Player plays (which file formats the program is associated with). Choose Tools | Options from the Windows Media Player menu bar and click the File Types tab to see a list of audio and video file formats. If you want another program to play files of a specific format, uncheck the check box for that format. If you can't live without Windows Media Player, click the Select All button to make it the default player for practically everything.

Playing and Recording WAV Sound Files with Sound Recorder

If your computer has a microphone, you can record your own sound files. Most sound cards have a microphone jack into which you can pug a standard microphone. Wouldn't your dad be thrilled to get a recorded message from your kids by e-mail?

To play or record very short WAV files (with the extension .wav), you can use the built-in Sound Recorder program. (It's the same program that came with Windows Me/9x.) Sound Recorder is limited to files up to one minute long. For longer files, you'll need a more powerful audio editing program like GoldWave (at **www.goldwave.com**).

Choose Start | All Programs | Accessories | Entertainment | Sound Recorder. You see the Sound Recorder window, as shown in Figure 19-16.

Playing Sounds

To play a WAV file, choose File | Open, choose the filename, click Open, and click Play. Use the Stop, Seek To Start, and Seek To End buttons to stop playback or to play all or part of the file.

The Position slider tracks your current position in the sound. To change your current position, drag the Position slider left or right to move forward or backward in the sound file, or click Seek To Start or Seek To End. For example, to hear the second half of the sound, drag the Position slider to the middle and then click the Play button. To discover other interesting ways that you can play back a sound (such as slower or backward), see the section "Editing Sounds" later in this chapter.

Note *Some sound files come with information about who created the sound; choose File | Properties to see the properties of the file.*

Windows comes with lots of sounds in WAV files in C:\Windows\Media folder (assuming that Windows is installed on C:). To play these sounds, you can also use Windows Media Player, described earlier in this chapter.

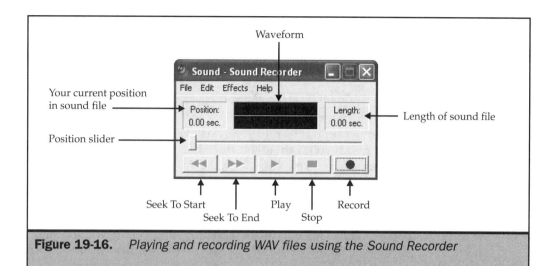

Figure 19-16.   *Playing and recording WAV files using the Sound Recorder*

Recording Sounds

If your computer has a microphone, you can record sounds and store them in WAV files. Follow these steps:

1. Choose File | New to record a new file. If you are editing a WAV file and haven't saved your changes, Sound Recorder asks whether you want to save them now.

2. Click the Record button in the Sound Recorder window.

3. Start the sound you want to record (for example, start talking).

4. When the sound you want to record has finished, click the Stop button.

5. Play back the sound by clicking the Play button.

6. Edit the sound as necessary (see the next section).

7. If you want to save your recording, choose File | Save As, type a filename, and click Save.

If a file is already open in Sound Recorder when you record a sound, the recorded sound records over part of the existing sound or is added to the end of the existing sound, depending on the location of the Position slider. To add on to the end of a sound, move the Position slider to the right end (or click the Seek To End button) and then record. To replace part of any existing sound, move the Position slider to the beginning of the sound you want to record over, and record.

Editing Sounds

Once you've opened or recorded a sound file, you can fool around with it in the following ways:

- **Copy**   To copy the entire sound to the Windows Clipboard so that you can paste (insert) it later, choose Edit | Copy or press CTRL-C.

- **Insert**   To insert another sound file into your existing sound, move the Position slider to the point at which you want to insert the file, choose Edit | Insert File, and choose the filename. To insert a copy from the Windows Clipboard, choose Edit | Paste Insert or press CTRL-V.

- **Mix**   To mix another sound file with your existing sound, move the Position slider to the point at which you want to mix the other sound, choose Edit | Mix With File and choose the filename. To mix a sound from the Windows Clipboard, choose Edit | Paste Mix. Sound Recorder mixes the two sounds together so you hear both at the same time. For example, you can record your voice several times and then mix the sounds together to sound like a crowd.

- **Cut**   You can omit parts of the sound, either from the beginning of the sound to your current position, or from your current position to the end of the sound. Move the Position slider to the point before or after the part that you want to delete. Then, choose Edit | Delete Before Current Position or Edit | Delete After Current Position. Click OK to confirm that you want to delete part of the sound.

- **Speed up or slow down**   To speed up the sound, choose Effects | Increase Speed. Sound Recorder plays the sound in half the time and raises the pitch. To slow down the sound, choose Effects | Decreases Speed; the sound plays in twice the time at a lower pitch.

- **Change volume**   To make the sound 25 percent louder, choose Effects | Increase Volume. To make the sound softer, choose Effects | Decrease Volume.

- **Play backward or add echo**   To play the sound backward, choose Effects | Reverse. To add an echo, choose Effects | Add Echo. (There's no way to remove the echo, so you might want to save the WAV file first.)

Note   *You can't edit a sound if it is stored in compressed format. You can tell that a sound is stored in a compressed format, because no green waveform appears in the Sound Recorder window.*

Editing a sound changes the sound in memory but doesn't affect the sound file; to save your changes, choose File | Save or File | Save As. Until you save a sound, you can choose File | Revert to return to the previously saved version of the sound.

Converting Sounds to Other Formats

WAV files can use one of many different formats, which offer tradeoffs between audio fidelity and disk space, and are designed for different kinds of sounds, such as music or voice. You can also change the attributes of the sound, such as the sampling speed in hertz (Hz), the number of bits used to store each sample, and whether the sound is stereo or mono. Some formats are compressed; if you convert a sound to a compressed format, you can't edit the sound in Sound Recorder. Confusingly, all of these formats are stored in files with the .wav extension.

To change the format of your WAV file, choose File | Properties to display the Properties dialog box for the file, as shown in Figure 19-17. The top half of the dialog box shows information about the sound, including its format. In Figure 19-17, the format is PCM, the format that Sound Recorder uses when recording sounds from your microphone.

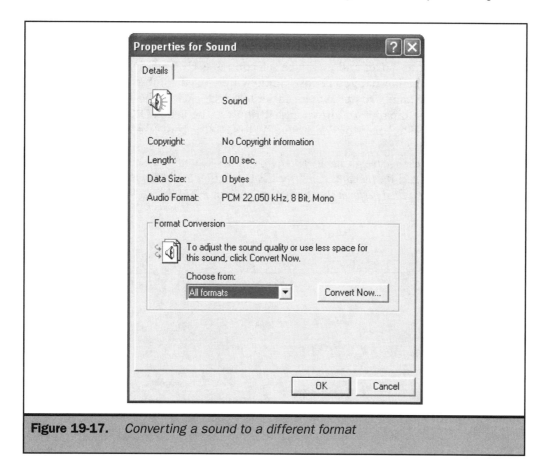

Figure 19-17.   *Converting a sound to a different format*

The Format Conversion section of the Properties dialog box for a WAV file enables you to convert the sound to a different format; however, all the available formats are still stored as WAV files. Click the Convert Now button to see the Sound Selection dialog box, shown here:

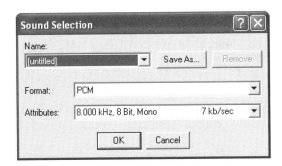

You can choose the format and the attributes you want to use by clicking in the Format and Attributes boxes and making a selection in each. The list of Attributes changes based on the Format you choose. Some widely used combinations of formats and attributes have names to make them easier to select; click in the Name box to choose a named combination of format and attributes. Then click OK twice to convert the sound. Choose File | Save or File | Save As to save the converted sound in a file.

You can also change the format when saving a file. Choose File | Save or File | Save As and type or select the filename. Click the Change button to display the Sound Selection dialog box, and then perform the conversion as described in this section.

The
Complete
Reference

Chapter 20

Working with Video

Computers have been able to handle video data for decades—after all, when you use a computer you are already sitting in front of a video screen. Windows XP supports video output on the screen, and video input if you add the necessary hardware to your computer. Now that many people have fast Internet connections (DSL or cable Internet connections), downloading video from the Internet is more convenient and more popular.

This chapter describes what formats video data is stored in, how to play video files using Windows Media Player, and how to make your own video files using the Windows Movie Maker program. The new version of the Windows Media Player that comes with Windows XP can also play DVDs. If you'd like to be able to participate in video conferences using webcams, see Chapter 25 for how to use Windows Messenger.

How Windows Works with Video Data

You can use various *video capture* devices, such as digital video cameras, to get video information into your computer. See Chapter 13 for instructions on how to install video capture devices. To display video, Windows uses your screen, and to play the accompanying audio it uses your sound board and speakers.

Because the amount of data coming from a digital video camera is so immense, your computer can't process and store it fast enough. Instead, video data is compressed on its way into the computer from the camera and is then stored in a compressed format. A very fast *DSP* (*digital signal processor*, a kind of specialized computer) chip in your video capture hardware does the actual compression. Windows comes with a number of *codecs*, programs for video compression and decompression, so that it can decompress and recompress video data when you want to display or edit it. Windows also includes *DirectX*, a feature that enhances video playback. Windows stores most video in *AVI files*, files with the filename extension .avi. Other popular formats for video files are QuickTime (.qt) and MPEG (.mpg).

To see a list of your installed video capture devices, along with a list of the available codecs, choose Start | Control Panel; click Sound Speech And Audio Devices; click Sounds And Audio Devices; and click the Hardware tab. You see the list of audio and video devices your computer can use (see Figure 19-4 in the previous chapter). To see a list of video capture devices, click the Legacy Video Capture Devices entry, click the Properties button, and click the Properties tab. To see a list of codecs that are available, click the Video Codecs list item, click the Properties button, and select the Properties tab.

Playing Video Files with Windows Media Player

As described in the previous chapter, the Windows Media Player program that comes with Windows can play many different types of multimedia files, including video files. This chapter describes Windows Media Player 8 and 9, which are very similar.

*Windows Media Player can't play all types of video files. To play Apple QuickTime files (.qt), you'll need the QuickTime viewer, available at **www.apple.com/quicktime**. Windows Media Player can play the popular MPEG format.*

Playing Video Files from Your Hard Disk

You have several options for selecting a file to play. The easiest is for you to have Windows Media Player scan your disk drives for audio and video files of all types (see Chapter 19, section "Organizing Your Audio Files into a Media Library"). If you have already scanned for files, click the Media Library button, click Video in the list of categories, and click the All Clips subcategory. (In Windows Media Player 9, click the All Videos plus box.) Windows Media Player displays all available video files. When you double-click a file in the Media Library, Windows Media Player plays the file, followed by the rest of the files on the list. If the file requires a codec to tell Windows Media Player how to read its format, the program connects to the Windows Media web site (at **www.windowsmedia.com**) and tries to locate the appropriate codec.

 If you access the Internet via a dial-up connection, Windows Media Player tries to connect. If you are already connected, Windows Media Player connects to the Windows Media web site through the existing connection. You may be required to validate the installation of the new codec.

To play a video file that is not in your Media Library, choose File | Open from the Windows Media Player menu bar, or press CTRL-O. In the Open dialog box that appears, navigate to your video file and click Open. You can also drag the video file (or any multimedia file) from the desktop or an Explorer window into the Windows Media Player window.

Make sure to set the Files Of Type box to All Files, so that you see all types of video files.

When you open a file, either by choosing File | Open or by using the Media Library, Windows Media Player loads the video file, switches to the Now Playing view, and displays the video in the video screen part of the Windows Media Player window. If it's not already playing, click the Play button to start the video, which appears in the video screen (middle) section of the Windows Media Player window.

While you are playing a video file, you can also perform these actions:

- Stop the video by clicking the Stop button.
- View the image full-screen by pressing ALT-ENTER or by choosing View | Full Screen from the menu bar. To return from full-screen display, press ESC or ALT-ENTER.

WORKING WITH TEXT, NUMBERS, PICTURES, SOUND, AND VIDEO

■ Move forward or backward in the file by clicking the Skip Forward, Skip Backward, Fast Forward, or Rewind buttons (the VCR-style buttons along the bottom of the window); or by dragging the Position slider.

■ Adjust the volume by clicking and dragging the Volume slider or by choosing Play | Volume from the menu bar.

If you are experiencing video problems and suspect your video card, you can change your acceleration setting. Choose Tools | Options from the menu and click the Performance tab, as shown in Figure 20-1. Reduce the Video Acceleration (that is, slide it to the left) to solve some hardware-based video problems.

In Windows Media Player 9, you can also adjust the program's video settings by choosing View | Settings | Video Settings to display hue, brightness, saturation, and contrast settings.

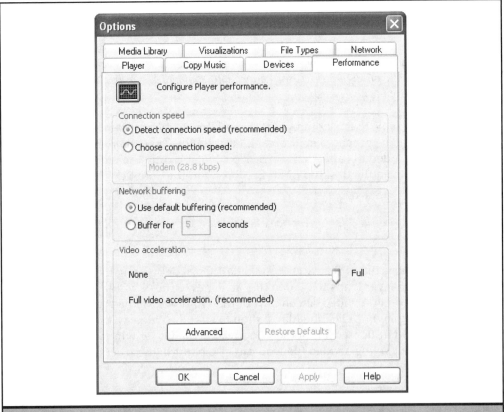

Figure 20-1. *The Performance tab of the Windows Media Player Options dialog box*

Playing Streaming Video Files from the Internet

Video files tend to be huge because each frame of a video requires many thousands of bytes of information. Viewing video over the Internet can involve long waits for video files to complete downloading. The advent of streaming video improved matters: you can begin playing a streaming video file after only a portion of the file has arrived (see Chapter 19, section "Streaming Audio"). The streaming video player continues to receive parts of the file at the same time that it is playing earlier parts. As long as the program can receive information at least as fast as it can play it, you see uninterrupted video. Streaming audio files and players work the same way.

The most popular streaming video format is RealVideo (with extension .rv). You can download the RealOne Player program for free from the Real web site at **www.real.com**; this program works with your browser to play RealAudio and RealVideo files from the Internet (see Chapter 19, section "Listening to RealAudio Files").

Microsoft has its own streaming video format, called *Advanced Streaming Format*, or *ASF*. Files in this format have the extension .asf or .asx. *ASF files* with the .asf extension contain the actual streaming video data. *ASX files* with the .asx extension contain a single line of text, with the URL of a continuously updating video newsfeed. Windows Media Player can play both ASF and ASX files. Normally, Windows Media Player runs automatically when you start to download an ASF or ASX file from the Internet. You can also run Windows Media Player and then open the streaming file by choosing File | Open URL from the menu.

When you see a link on a web page for an ASF or ASX file, click the link. Depending on how your browser is configured, you may see a message asking whether to open the file or save it; choose to open the file. Your browser downloads the first section of the file, runs Windows Media Player, and begins to play the file. The video may appear in your browser window or in a separate window.

> **Note**   *Strangely, if you use the Media Guide button and the Windowsmedia.com web site to find streaming video, your browser window may pop up to play the video, rather than Windows Media Player displaying the video.*

To find video to watch on the Internet, you can use the Media Guide button on the Windows Media Player toolbar, as shown in Figure 20-2 (see Chapter 19, section "Controlling How Windows Media Player Communicates over the Internet"). If you have Windows Media Player 9, click the Services button to find out about added-cost video-on-demand services (see Chapter 19, section "Playing Music and Other Audio with Windows Media Player 8 and 9").

Figure 20-2. The Media Guide button offers links to online video—some appear in the Windows Media Player window, but most play in your browser.

Creating and Editing Video Files with Windows Movie Maker

Windows Movie Maker is essentially the same program that came with Windows Me. It enables you to edit graphical, audio, and video files into movies that are stored in video files that you can play with Windows Media Player.

Windows Movie Maker creates files called *projects*, with the extension .mswmm. Each project can contain one or more *collections*, which are lists of items to include in the movie. A collection contains *clips*, which can be video, audio, or still-graphics files. Information about your collections is stored in your My Videos folder, which Windows Movie Maker creates in your My Documents folder. Once you've created your movie, you can save it as a video file in Windows Media format with the extension .wmv.

If you want to edit video on your computer, make sure it has lots of memory (512MB or more of RAM) and lots of free hard disk space—you'll need it!

The Windows Movie Maker Window

To open Windows Movie Maker choose Start | All Programs | Accessories | Windows Movie Maker. The Windows Movie Maker window has four areas and several toolbars, as shown in Figure 20-3. The parts of the window are

- **Collections list** Lists the collections in this project. One collection is selected.
- **Clips** Shows icons for each clip in the currently selected collection. Clips can include graphics files, audio files, or video files. For graphics files, you see a small version of the file (a thumbnail). For audio files, you see a speaker icon. For video files, you see a thumbnail of a scene from the video.

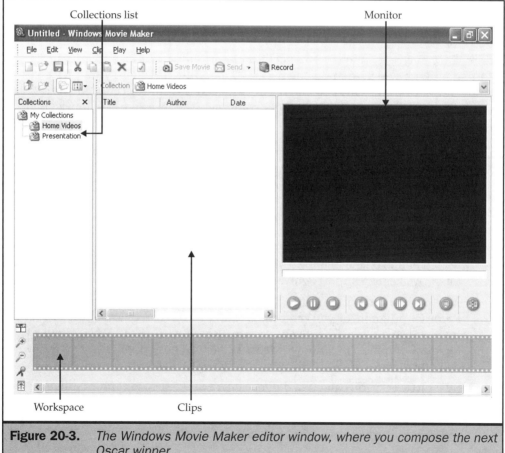

Figure 20-3. *The Windows Movie Maker editor window, where you compose the next Oscar winner*

- **Monitor**   Displays the current clip, if it's a graphic or video file. If the current clip is an audio file, you see a speaker icon. Below the Monitor are VCR-style buttons to play the current clip.

- **Workspace**   Displays the timeline or storyboard of your movie, as explained in the section "Composing Your Movie," later in this chapter.

If you've already been working on a movie, Windows Movie Maker opens the last project you opened. You can open any existing project by choosing File | Open Project from the menu or clicking the Open Project icon on the toolbar.

 We've had a lot of trouble getting Windows Movie Maker to work properly on computers with limited memory. It sometimes can't export your project as a movie that you can play with Windows Media Player, and other times it can't reopen files that it saved only moments before.

Importing Files

Before you can create a movie, you need to import video, audio, and graphic information with which to make the movie. Depending on where your picture, sound, and video information come from, you need the appropriate hardware or access to get that information onto your computer. The three types of information you can import are

- **Video**   Some video equipment stores can copy your videotapes to CD-ROM, which you can then import into Windows Movie Maker. If you want to import your own video from a regular (non-digital) video camera or VCR, you need a video capture card. Both ATI (**www.ati.com**) and Creative Labs (**www.creativelabs.com**) make reasonably priced video capture cards. If you have a digital video camera, you can attach the camera to your computer through a USB or FireWire port (see Chapter 13, section "FireWire")—once the video camera is connected, click the Record button on the Windows Movie Maker toolbar to begin recording. Windows Movie Maker can import .wmv, .asf, .avi, .mpg, and other video format files.

- **Audio**   You can capture audio with your computer by running the Sound Recorder program, or you can use Windows Media Player to capture music from audio CDs (see Chapter 19, section "Ripping (Copying Music) from a CD to Your Computer"). Windows Media Player can import .mp3, .asf, .wma, .wav, and other format audio files.

- **Still pictures**   You can use a digital camera or scanner to capture still pictures in graphics files. You can also create drawings or titles using Microsoft Paint or another graphics editor (see Chapter 18). Windows Movie Maker can import .gif, .jpg, and other types of graphic files.

Once you have graphic, audio, or video files, you can import them into Windows Movie Maker. Follow these steps:

1. Run Windows Movie Maker and open your project if it's not already open. To create a new project, choose File | New | Project from the menu bar.

2. Select the collection into which you want to import the files. You can create a new collection for them by selecting the top-level collection (My Collections) and choosing File | New | Collection from the menu.

3. Choose File | Import or press CTRL-I. You see the Select The File To Import dialog box.

4. Select the file or files to import. You can select more than one file by holding the SHIFT or CTRL keys while selecting files.

5. After a potentially grueling wait, the files are added to the active collection.

Another way to import files is to drag-and-drop them into the Windows Movie Maker window.

After you import information into the program, Windows Movie Maker shows each clip as a little icon in the current collection. You can find out more about any clip by right-clicking it and choosing Properties from the shortcut menu that appears. To play a single clip, select it and click the Play button on the VCR-style buttons just below the Monitor (the leftmost button).

When you import a video file, Windows Movie Maker automatically breaks it into clips, based on where it thinks the scenes start and end. To turn this feature off, choose View | Options and deselect the Automatically Create Clips option.

You can organize your clips into collections by dragging the clips from one collection to another, or by using cut-and-paste (CTRL-X to cut and CTRL-V to paste).

If you don't have any video, just place all of your still pictures in a collection and make a slide show with still pictures and a soundtrack or narration.

Composing Your Movie

The Workspace area at the bottom of the Windows Movie Maker window displays either the Storyboard or the Timeline. To create a movie out of your clips, you drag them to the Storyboard or Timeline in the order that you want them shown.

The *Storyboard* is like a book, in which each blank square is like the page of a book, and you decide what appears on each page and in what order. Find the first clip— either video or graphic file—and drag it to the first space in the Storyboard. This clip becomes the first page of your story, and the first part of your movie. Continue dragging video and graphic clips to the Storyboard in the order in which you want them to appear. You can always switch the order later. With clips, the Storyboard looks like this:

 To move clips around after you've placed them in the Storyboard, just drag them left or right. When a line appears between the clips where you would like to place the clip to be reordered, drop it.

The *Timeline* gives you another view of the same movie. Display it in the Workspace area by clicking the Timeline icon at the left end of the Workspace (switch back to the Storyboard by clicking the Storyboard icon that takes the Timeline icon's place), or choose View | Timeline from the menu (View | Storyboard takes you back to the Storyboard). The Timeline shows the timing of the clips in the movie, displaying how many seconds each clip takes:

You can add, delete, and rearrange the clips on either the Storyboard or the Timeline—the effect is the same. If you delete a clip from the Storyboard or Timeline, it disappears from the movie, but remains in the project available for reuse. If you don't think you'll use a clip after all, you can delete by selecting it in the Clips area and pressing the DELETE key—this action deletes the information from the project.

Adding Sound

To provide a soundtrack, you can drag an audio clip to the Timeline (not the Storyboard). The audio clip runs along the bottom of the Timeline, showing where the audio starts and ends. You can control the balance between the sound portion of the video clips and of the audio soundtrack by choosing Edit | Audio Levels from the menu and sliding the slider between Video Track and Audio Track:

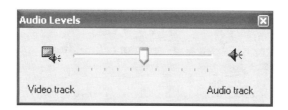

You can record a narration to go with your slide show or video. The idea is to synchronize what you're saying with what's appearing on the screen. (Note: Your computer needs a working microphone to record the narration.) Follow these steps:

1. Choose File | Record Narration to display the Record Narration Track dialog box.

2. If you want to mute the audio track during the playback of the movie, click the check box marked Mute Video Soundtrack.

3. When you're ready, click the Record button. Be prepared—as soon as you click the Record button, Windows Movie Maker begins recording and playing the video at the same time.

4. Talk along with the movie.

5. When you're finished, click the Stop button. Windows Movie Maker prompts you to save your narration and imports it into your project.

  Run through your video a few times, clicking Pause and making some notes. Then spend some time rehearsing. Don't try to be Marlin Perkins, but you'll gain appreciation if you do a well-timed job.

Previewing Your Movie

After you add the clips for your movie, you can see how it looks. Choose Play | Play Entire Storyboard/Timeline from the menu, or right-click the Storyboard or Timeline and choose Play Entire Storyboard/Timeline from the shortcut menu that appears. You can also play a section of the movie by selecting a series of clips from the Storyboard and clicking the Play button below the Monitor. Or, select all of the clips on the Storyboard (right-click any clip and choose Select All) and then click the Play VCR button below the Monitor. The VCR-style controls look like this:

Editing Your Movie

Windows Movie Maker includes many commands for editing your movie. Here are a few neat things you can do:

- **Slide shows** If you put a graphic file in your movie, Windows Movie Maker shows it for five seconds. You can make a good-looking slide show that you can send to people through e-mail, just by adding your still photos to the Storyboard of a movie. You can change the five-second length to speed up or slow down your slide show. On the Timeline, select the clip for the still photo. A pair of triangles appears along the top of the clip, one on each end. Drag the right-hand triangle to the right to add time to the clip, or to the left to subtract time from it.

- **Transitions** You can create a fading transition from one video or picture to the next. Click the first clip of the pair. A pair of triangles appears along the top of the clip. Drag the right triangle into the next clip, so the clips appear to overlap:

The wider the overlap, the longer the transition will be. The resulting fade-in looks like Figure 20-4.

 Windows Movie Maker does not have integrated transition effects as other consumer-grade video editors do. You can't add special transitions other than the fade effect.

Figure 20-4. *Overlapping two clips results in a fade-in.*

- ■ **Titling** Windows Movie Maker does not have commands to create titles (as some other video edition programs do). To add titles, choose Start | All Programs | Accessories | Paint to run Microsoft Paint (see Chapter 18, section "Creating and Editing Images with Microsoft Paint"). Choose Image | Attributes and change the document size to a width of 320 pixels and a height of 240 pixels. Add anything to your title page or pages that you like. A basic black background with white lettering goes well with video presentations and is also easy to read. Save your document or documents using descriptive filenames in a folder to import them into Windows Movie Maker.

Saving Your Movie

Once your movie shines, click the Save Movie button on the toolbar or choose File | Save Movie from the menu. You see the Save Movie dialog box. The Setting box in the Playback Quality section gives you four choices for quality: Low Quality, Medium Quality (Recommended), High Quality, Other (then choose a format in the Profile drop-down menu).

As you set the Play Quality Setting, the File Size shows how large the resulting movie will be. The default is Medium Quality, which gives reasonable clarity and excellent sound. A collection of photographs and music that runs 30 seconds took a mere 791Kb of space at High Quality. It was 94Kb at Low Quality and 343Kb at Medium Quality, all of which are reasonable sizes when sending movies via e-mail. If you plan to make large movies with video, be aware that they can take up anywhere from several megabytes to several hundred megabytes of disk space.

Fill out the other information on the dialog box with as much or as little detail as you wish and click OK. In the Save As dialog box that appears, enter a name for the file. Windows Movie Maker saves the movie in a file with the .wmv extension.

If you have a CD-R or CD-RW drive, create a CD-ROM to send your family and friends, rather than e-mailing huge files.

You can e-mail your movies or send them to your web server directly from Windows Movie Maker. To send a movie via e-mail or the Web, click the Send button on the toolbar or choose File | Send Movie To from the menu. Select E-mail or Web Server from the menu that appears. Choose the quality for the resulting video and fill out the other information on the dialog box. When you click OK, Windows Movie Maker asks which e-mail program to use. Select either Default E-mail Program at the top of the list or the name of the program you typically use from the items below. If you plan to send the videos using a different program another time, leave the Don't Ask Me Again item unchecked. Click OK. Your e-mail program opens and a new message appears, waiting for you to enter the addresses of those you wish to send it to.

 Be sure to check that your intended recipients have Windows Media Player before sending them a movie.

Playing Video Disks (DVDs)

A *DVD* (*Digital Versatile Disk* or *Digital Video Disk*) is like a large CD—it's a digital disk that can contain video material. If you buy movies on DVDs and you have a DVD drive connected to your computer, you can play DVDs on your computer by using the Windows Media Player program (previous versions of Windows came with a separate DVD Player program). Before you try this, make sure that your DVD drive has the appropriate decoder card and software drivers to play DVDs.

 You cannot play a DVD movie with just a DVD drive and a disc. You must also have a decoder, either built in to the drive, on a separate card (or integrated into your systems video card), or from a software package like WinDVD or PowerDVD. Windows comes with the program—Windows Media Player—but not with the decoder. The next section includes a source for decoders if your DVD drive didn't come with one. Your DVD player may have come with its own player program that you can use for playing DVDs—you don't have to use the Windows Media Player program.

Installing and Configuring a DVD Decoder

If your computer has a DVD drive, you probably got it in one of two ways: preinstalled in your computer or as a third-party add-on. If the DVD drive was part of your computer system, it should have been tested and properly configured from the get-go, so no additional configuration should be needed.

If you installed a third-party DVD drive, you need a decoder to read the DVD media. There are two kinds of DVD decoders: hardware and software. Hardware decoders are uncommon (we were only able to locate a single PCI-based DVD decoder card in two hours of searching). Software decoders, however, are easy to find and inexpensive. WinDVD (**www.intervideo.com**) is the most popular package, retails for $50 and ships with various third-party DVD drives, and installs in seconds. We found it capable and easy to use, though we recommend at least a 500 MHz Pentium III with 128MB of RAM for reasonable playback performance (an 800 MHz Pentium III with 256MB of RAM and an 8MB video card works about as well as a hardware DVD player).

Another option is PowerDVD from CyberLink (**www.gocyberlink.com**), which also costs $50. It has some compelling pluses, such as smoother playback and better color even on slower machines. An 800 MHz PC becomes a powerful multimedia center when PowerDVD is at the helm.

 Either WinDVD or PowerDVD installations allow Windows Media Player to play DVD titles, as they provide the decoder. However, the DVD support in Windows Media Player has resulted in crashes and in most cases does not work as well as the third-party player.

With such high entrance stakes, DVD on the desktop has not taken off. Another reason, of course, is that most people prefer to watch movies on larger screens in the comfort of their living rooms, rather than on computer screens at their desks—although they are great for long trips. We do know people who use their computers to show the kids DVDs on long car trips or plane rides, although playing DVDs uses a lot of power and can run down your laptop's battery before a full-length movie is over.

Playing a DVD with Windows Media Player

To play a DVD, insert the DVD in your DVD drive, and Windows Media Player starts automatically. If it doesn't, choose Play | DVD Or CD Audio from the menu bar. If you have more than one CD drive (i.e., CD-RW, DVD, CD), you see a list. Select the drive letter assigned to your DVD player.

When you are playing a DVD, the Windows Media Player works like a VCR (as shown in Figure 20-5). Additional controls may appear for the advanced features that a specific DVD offers: consult the DVD itself. These advanced features may play video clips, alternative edits, different endings, or the ever-popular outtakes. Windows Media Player has a few added DVD interface options. To view them, click Now Playing on the toolbar and make sure that the Equalizer And Settings pane is displayed. Click the Select View button and select the DVD Controls item. If there is a problem with your DVD drive's installation or if you are missing a DVD decoder package, this item doesn't appear.

Controlling Rated Movies

One popular feature with parents is Parental Control, which is amazingly simple and effective. The Parental Control feature uses the already existing and well-established MPAA ratings system. Each DVD movie has a lot of additional information encoded into the DVD, including the movie's rating, so the decoder software can tell a G-rated movie from an NC17-rated movie.

Figure 20-5. *Windows Media Player playing a DVD—it's like an onscreen VCR.*

Before you can use parental controls, you must set up user accounts for yourself and other users of the computer (see Chapter 6). Assuming that you are a parent, give yourself and other adults administrative user accounts, and make any children's accounts limited accounts. Once you set a maximum DVD rating in Windows Media Player's parental controls, only administrative users can play DVDs with higher ratings.

To control which DVDs people can play on Windows Media Player, choose Tools | Options from the menu, and click the DVD tab (shown in Figure 20-6). Select the Parental Control check box, and select the highest rating that you want nonadministrative users of the computer to be able to play.

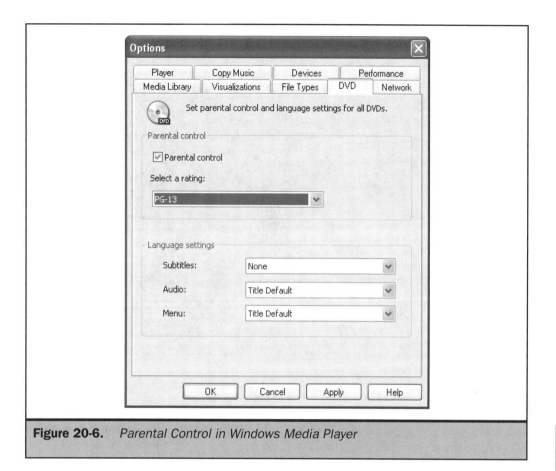

Figure 20-6. *Parental Control in Windows Media Player*

Windows XP's Media Center

A new version of Windows XP includes the Media Center, which turns a computer into a multimedia home entertainment center. The Media Center is available only as part of Windows XP Media Center Edition, which comes preinstalled on new computers and requires specialized hardware, including a TV card and remote control, a high-quality video card, and a very large hard drive. For more information about Windows XP Media Center Edition, see its web site at **www.microsoft.com/windows/ehome**.

Media Center, shown in Figure 20-7, puts TV, DVD, music, and pictures together in one interface, optimized for remote control use.

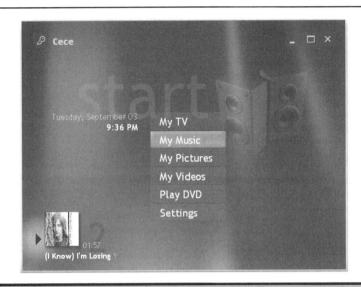

Figure 20-7.   Windows XP Media Center Edition, with a thumbnail of the currently playing album displayed in the lower left corner, along with the current song title.

Note   *Windows XP Home Edition doesn't come with Media Center, and as of the end of 2002, no upgrade is available. To get Media Center, you need to buy a computer on which it is preinstalled (Hewlett-Packard and Samsung manufacture them). The following pages give you an overview of Media Center's features in comparison with Windows XP Home Edition.*

The Media Center's startup screen has buttons you use to select My TV, My Music, My Pictures, My Videos, Play DVD, or Settings. Selecting My TV starts the TV tuner. Once the TV has finished initializing, you can watch TV, check the Media Guide, set up or play back recordings, search for programs to watch, or adjust TV and recording settings. The default screen size is a medium-sized window within the Media Center interface; the TV screen shrinks to a thumbnail in the lower-left corner when you select one of the options and you expand it to fill the Media Center window or monitor.

When you first start Media Center, you select the signal type: cable, satellite, or antenna. Once you enter your ZIP code or other geographical identifier, the Media Guide uses this information to download and update the TV listings each day, getting only the listings for your signal type and location.

My TV

Windows XP Media Center Edition's Media Center turns your computer into a digital VCR and recording your favorite shows is easier than it is with a traditional VCR (see Figure 20-8). All you need to do to record the program is select it in the Media Guide,

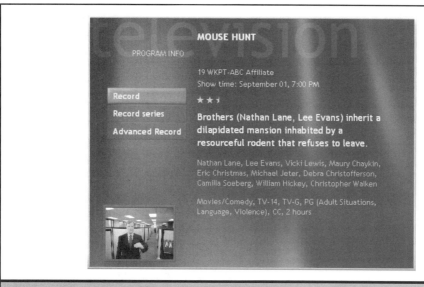

Figure 20-8. *Recording from the program guide is as easy as pressing the Record button. The TV thumbnail is in the lower-left corner.*

then select the Record or Record Series button. As an added bonus, you don't have to remember to use a fresh videotape, because the video is stored on your hard disk. You'll need plenty of free hard drive space, though, since a one-hour recording easily exceeds 2GB.

You can search by category, title, or keyword to find a program to watch or record. The extensive list of categories includes education, kids, lifestyle, movies, specials, and sports.

Recording with Media Center adds copy protection code to the recording. You can play the recorded programs only on the computer they were recorded on. Media Center will not record copy-protected DVDs.

My Music

Media Center's My Music plays music that you previously indexed in Windows Media Player (see Chapter 19). The My Music screen lists your recently played music and has buttons for you to select music by album, artist, playlist, song, or genre, as shown in Figure 20-9. You can search My Music by typing letters from the remote control keypad—the search begins with the first letter typed and finds all songs, artists, and genres that contain any word beginning with that letter. You'll want to narrow the search by entering at least the first two letters of a word in the artist's name, song title, or genre category.

Media Center can't copy music from CDs or create playlists. You need to use Windows Media Player for these tasks.

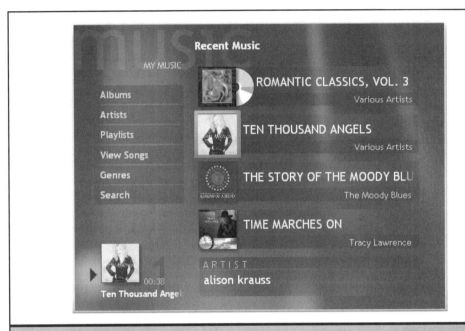

Figure 20-9.   *My Music with the most recently played albums or songs*

My Pictures

If you have a digital camera or a large collection of images, Media Center's My Pictures can display them in a slideshow. Pictures in subfolders of My Pictures and the Shared Pictures folders are included in the slideshow. You can sort the pictures by name or date, adjust how long the pictures display during the slideshow, and choose whether the slideshow is in random or alphabetical order. If you want to rename or move images to different folders or even e-mail them, you'll need to do those tasks in Windows Explorer.

My Video and Play DVD

You use Media Center's My Video screen to play videos stored in your My Video folder. Use Play DVD to play DVDs. Media Center doesn't offer any features that Media Player lacks, but you can use a remote control to choose the scenes or control the sound. Windows XP Media Center Edition, unlike Windows XP Home Edition, includes the decoders you need to play back DVDs.

The Complete Reference

Part V

Windows XP Home on the Internet

The Complete Reference

Chapter 21

Configuring Windows to Work with Your Modem

Before you connect to the Internet (or any other computer) using a modem, you must install your modem, whether you use a conventional modem and phone line, a high-speed *broadband* DSL (Digital Subscriber Loop) line, cable modem, or ISDN (Integrated Services Digital Network) line; see Chapter 13, section "Installing Modems" for instructions.

This chapter describes how to configure Windows dial, your dial-up modem, or communicate over your broadband modem. Once your modem is working, you're ready to read Chapter 22 to connect to an Internet account.

Note *If you connect to the Internet over a local area network (LAN) rather than by using a modem, see Chapter 31.*

Configuring Windows to Use Your Dial-Up Modem

If you connect to the Internet via a dial-up modem that attaches to a regular phone line, Windows needs to know exactly which make of dial-up modem you have, so it can send the appropriate commands. You can also tell Windows from which area code you usually dial, from what other locations you make calls (if you have a portable computer), and to which calling cards you want to charge your calls.

Winmodems and Real Modems

Modern dial-up (analog) modems do a remarkable amount of computing to turn digital data into the beeps and hisses that the modem sends down the phone line, and at the other end to extract the data from the beeps and the hisses. In external modems and some internal modems, the modem itself contains a computer chip (usually a specialized one called a digital signal processor or DSP) to do the computing. But low-cost internal *winmodems* punt the job to the Windows device driver, using the computer's own CPU. On slower computers (300MHz and below) the modem processing can take most or all of the available CPU time, leaving nothing for other programs. On more recent machines, keeping up with the modem isn't a problem, but you can still notice slowdowns if your other programs do a lot of computing, as graphics-intensive games do.

Another important difference between regular modems and winmodems is that regular modems all work about the same as far as Windows is concerned, so even if your modem doesn't have a specific driver; the generic "standard modem types" driver will work. A winmodem needs a driver for the exact model of modem, since there's no standardization in the way that a winmodem communicates with its driver.

Modem Configuration Settings

You can look at or change your modem configuration settings by choosing Start |
Control Panel, clicking Printers And Other Hardware, and then clicking Phone And
Modems Options. (If Windows doesn't know you have a modem, the Add New
Hardware Wizard runs. If your modem is external, make sure it is turned on, and
then follow the Wizard's instructions to set up the modem.)

You see the Phone And Modem Options dialog box. Click the Modems tab to see
a list of the installed modems, as shown in Figure 21-1. Select the appropriate modem
from the list, and then click the Properties button to see the Properties dialog box for
the modem, shown in Figure 21-2. (The exact appearance of the dialog box depends
on which modem driver you select.) To find out which modem driver Windows uses
for your modem, click the Driver tab in the modem's Properties dialog box.

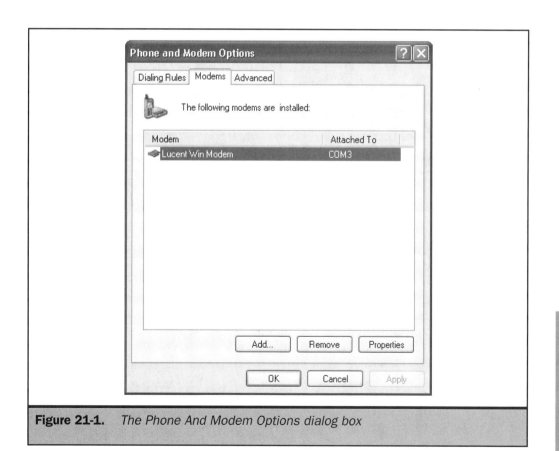

Figure 21-1.   *The Phone And Modem Options dialog box*

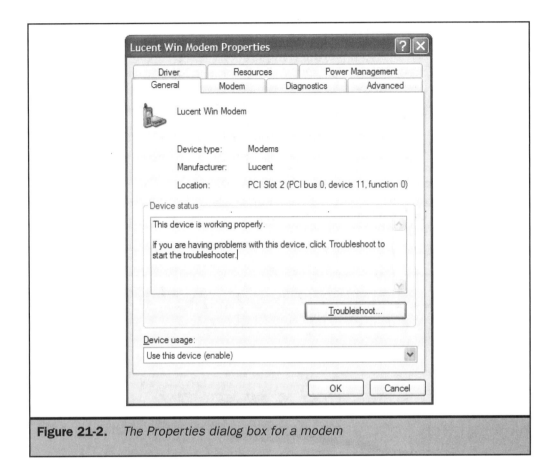

Figure 21-2.   *The Properties dialog box for a modem*

Table 21-1 lists the modem properties that appear in the Properties dialog box for most modems. Table 21-2 shows additional settings that appear on the Default Preferences dialog box for the modem, which you display by clicking the Advanced tab on the modem's Properties dialog box and then clicking the Change Default Preferences button. Except where noted, don't change these settings unless you are sure your modem is configured incorrectly. Most people never have to change these settings except in consultation with their modem manufacturer, communications software publisher, or Internet service provider.

Dialog Box Tab	Setting	Description
General	Device usage	Enables or disables the modem. For example, if your computer's built-in modem is broken, you can disable it and use an external modem.
Modem	Port	Specifies how your modem is connected to your computer. PCs have serial communications ports named COM1, COM2, COM3, and COM4, or your modem may connect to a USB or FireWire port. Even if your modem is internal (installed inside the computer), it is assigned a port.
Modem	Speaker volume	Specifies how loud the modem's speaker is set, or how loud the system speaker plays modem sounds.
Modem	Maximum Port Speed	Specifies the maximum speed at which your modem can communicate over the cable to your computer (not over the phone to another modem), in *bps* (*bits per second*) (usually 115,200bps). Leave at the highest available speed.
Modem	Wait for dial tone before dialing	Specifies whether to wait for the modem to detect a dial tone before sending commands to dial; if the modem can't detect a dial tone, this should be deselected. Outside North America, many modems require this to be deselected.
Diagnostics	Modem Information	Displays identifying information about your modem, such as its serial number. Click Query Modem to see the responses to standard modem commands (refer to your modem's manual for the meanings of the commands and responses).
Diagnostics	Append to Log	Specifies whether to store information sent to and from the modem in a log file—usually in C:\Windows\Modemlog_*modemname*.txt. The log file is useful for troubleshooting; to see the log file, click View Log.
Advanced	Extra initialization commands	Lists additional commands to send to your modem after Windows sends the standard initialization commands. Consult your modem's manual for a list of commands your modem understands.

Table 21-1.   *Modem Properties on the Properties Dialog Box*

Dialog Box Tab	Setting	Description
Advanced	Country/Region Select	Tells the driver where you are, so it can adjust country-specific settings appropriately.
Advanced	Advanced Port Settings	Lets you change the COM port an internal modem is assigned to and limit or disable the modem's internal buffering.
Driver	Driver Provider, Driver Date, Driver Version, Digital Signer	Displays information about the software driver for the modem. Click Driver Details for more information, including the names and locations of the driver files. Click Update Driver to install a new driver. Click Roll Back Driver to reinstall a previously installed driver. Click Uninstall to remove the driver.
Resources	Resource settings, Conflicting device list	Hardware settings (I/O, Memory, and IRQ) used by the modem.
Power management	Allow the computer to turn off this device to save power	Normally checked, lets the computer turn off the modem when it's in standby or hibernating mode.
Power management	Allow this device to bring the computer out of standby	Let the modem turn on the computer if the phone rings. Useful if the modem is configured for incoming faxes or voice mail.

Table 21-1. *Modem Properties on the Properties Dialog Box* (continued)

Dialog Box Tab	Setting	Description
General	Disconnect a call if idle for more than *xx* mins	Specifies whether to hang up the phone connection if no data is transmitted for a specified number of minutes (usually not selected). Choose this setting if you want to avoid leaving the phone off the hook when you remain online by accident.

Table 21-2. *Modem Properties in the Default Preferences Dialog Box*

Dialog Box Tab	Setting	Description
General	Cancel the call if not connected within *xx* secs	Specifies whether to time-out after this number of seconds if no connection occurs (usually selected, with a time-out period of 60 seconds).
General	Port speed	Same as the Maximum Port Speed in the modem Properties dialog box (see Table 21-1).
General	Data Protocol	Specifies what type of error correction to use. Removing error correction may allow modems to make a connection at the cost of undetected data errors.
General	Compression	Specifies whether to compress data before transmitting it (usually enabled). Not all modems support data compression.
General	Flow control	Specifies whether to use *flow control* to manage the flow of data between your modem and your computer. If selected, you have two options: Xon/Xoff or Hardware (preferred).
Advanced	Data bits	Specifies the number of *data bits*, the number of bits of information included in each byte sent (must be 8 bits).
Advanced	Parity	Specifies whether the modem uses *parity*, a primitive error-detection scheme. Select None.
Advanced	Stop bits	Specifies how many extra *stop bits* are sent after each byte (must be 1 bit).
Advanced	Modulation	Specifies the *modulation*, which is how your modem converts the digital information from your computer into analog "sound" information for transmission over the phone.

Table 21-2.   *Modem Properties in the Default Preferences Dialog Box* (continued)

You can also display your modem's Properties dialog box from the Device Manager: select the modem and click the Properties button on the toolbar.

Windows displays another dialog box about your modem—the Modem Configuration dialog box—when you click the Configure button from the Properties dialog box of a dial-up connection. The settings on the Modem Configuration dialog

WINDOWS XP HOME
ON THE INTERNET

box control how the modem works when used for that dial-up connection (see Chapter 22 for more information).

Configuring Windows for Dialing Locations

If you have a laptop computer, you may connect to the Internet or your online service from different locations using different phone numbers. A *dialing location* defines a location from which you use your modem. Windows stores information about the area code and phone system from which you are dialing, including whether to dial extra digits to get an outside line. It also remembers whether the phone line at that location uses *call waiting*, a phone line feature that beeps when another call is coming in on the line. The call waiting beep disrupts most connections, so you should tell Windows to turn off call waiting before dialing the phone if you don't want your online session interrupted.

Displaying Your Dialing Locations

To define or change your dialing locations, choose Start | Control Panel, click Printers And Other Hardware, and click Phones And Modem Options. On the Phone And Modem Options dialog box that appears, click the Dialing Rules tab (if it's not already selected), which lists your existing dialing locations, as shown in Figure 21-3.

The Dialing Rules tab enables you to create area code rules to tell Windows when to dial 1 and enables calling card definitions to tell Windows the access number, account number, and PIN you use when charging phone calls to a calling card.

Creating a Dialing Location

To make a new dialing location, follow these steps:

1. Click the New button in the Dialing Rules tab of the Phone And Modem Options dialog box. You see the New Location dialog box, shown in Figure 21-4. (If this is the first dialing location you create, you can skip this step and edit the New Location dialing location that already appears.)

2. Type a name for the dialing location in the Location Name box (using any name you'll find helpful), choose the country from the list, and type the area code or city code from which you are dialing.

3. If you need to dial extra digits before dialing local or long-distance phone numbers, type the digits into the two To Access An Outside Line boxes.

4. The Use This Carrier Code To Make Long-Distance Calls/International Calls boxes are rarely used.

5. If the phone line has call waiting (that is, if incoming calls cause a beep on the phone line), select the check box to disable call waiting and select the number

to disable it. Unless your phone is connected to an office PBX, the number is invariably *70 (that is, the star key and the number 70).

6. If your phone line doesn't accept tone dialing, set Dial Using to Pulse.

7. If you have to dial the area code or 1 and the area code for some or all exchanges in this area code—even in your own area code—click the Area Code Rules tab to tell Windows exactly what to dial (see "Setting Up Area Code Rules" later in this chapter).

8. If you use a calling card to charge the calls made from this phone line, click the Calling Card tab to select a card (see "Configuring Windows to Use Calling Cards" later in this chapter).

9. Click OK to return to the Phone And Modem Options dialog box, where your new location appears.

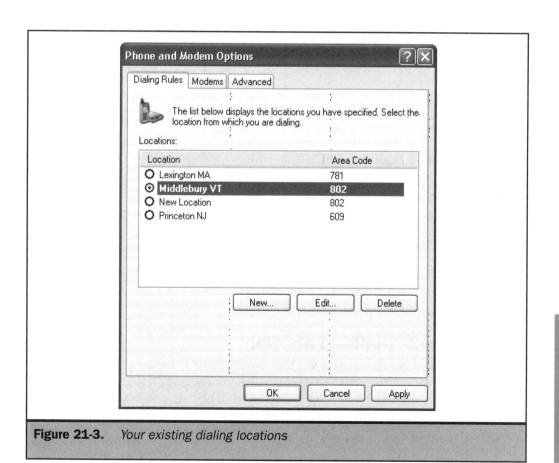

Figure 21-3. *Your existing dialing locations*

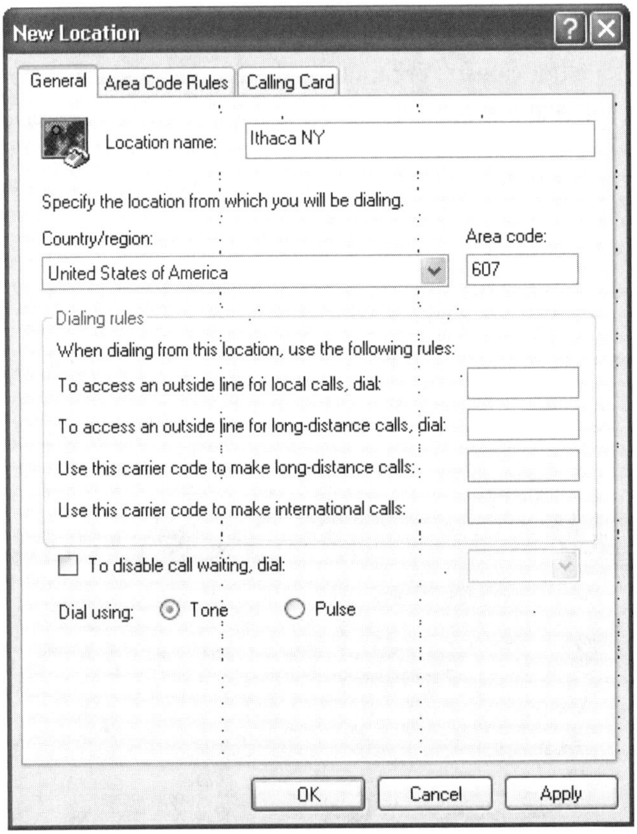

Figure 21-4. *Creating or editing dialing locations*

To delete a dialing location, choose the dialing location from the Locations and click Delete.

Setting a Default Dialing Location

Before you exit from the Phone And Modem Options dialog box, select the dialing location you use most often, so that a dot appears in the radio button to its left. Windows displays this dialing location in dial-up connections, and Fax Console as the default dialing location.

> **Tip** *When you go on a trip and arrive at your destination, create a dialing location for the phone from which your computer will be dialing. Select this dialing location before exiting the Phone And Modem Options dialog box to make this location the default. When you return from your trip, display the Phone And Modem Options dialog box again, select the dialing location for your home or office and click OK. This resets the default to your usual dialing location.*

Using Dialing Locations

Dialing locations come in handy when connecting to the Internet and when sending faxes.

- **Dial-up Internet connections** You can use dialing rules when calling your ISP with a dial-up connection. In the Connect dialog box, you select your dialing location by clicking the Properties button to display the properties of the dial-up connection, clicking the Use Dialing Rules check box, clicking the Dialing Rules button and choosing another location (see Chapter 22).

- **Sending faxes** In the Windows Fax Console, you can use dialing locations when sending a fax (see Chapter 14, section "Sending and Receiving Faxes"). In the Send Fax Wizard, select the Use Dialing Rules check box and choose a dialing location.

Setting Up Area Code Rules

In the old days, you probably had to dial 1 and the area code only for numbers outside your own area code. Now, you may have to dial 1 and the area code for some or all phone numbers, even within your own area code. You can tell Windows exactly when it has to dial what numbers, so when you type a phone number to dial, Windows can dial the correct sequence of digits. Windows stores this information as an *area code rule*, which defines what Windows should dial when calling from one dialing location to one area code (for example, when dialing 617 area code numbers from your Lexington, Massachusetts dialing location).

Creating Area Code Rules

To tell Windows the dialing rules for an area code

1. Choose Start | Control Panel, click Printers And Other Hardware, and click Phones And Modem Options. On the Phone And Modem Options dialog box that appears, click the Dialing Rules tab (if it's not already selected).

2. Choose the dialing location for which you want to create area code rules, click the Edit button to display the Edit Locations dialog box, and then click the Area

Code Rules tab. You see a list of the area code rules that apply to calls made from dialing location (the list starts out empty).

3. Click the New button. You see the New Area Code Rule dialog box, shown in Figure 21-5.

4. Type the area code to which this rule applies (that is, Windows follows this rule when dialing numbers in this area code from this dialing location).

5. In the Prefixes section, specify whether the rule appears to all numbers in the area code or only to certain prefixes (or exchanges; that is, the three digits that come after the area code). If the rule applies to certain prefixes, click Add and type the prefixes.

Note   *You can't tell Windows that a rule applies to all prefixes except the ones you list (which would be handy in some area codes).*

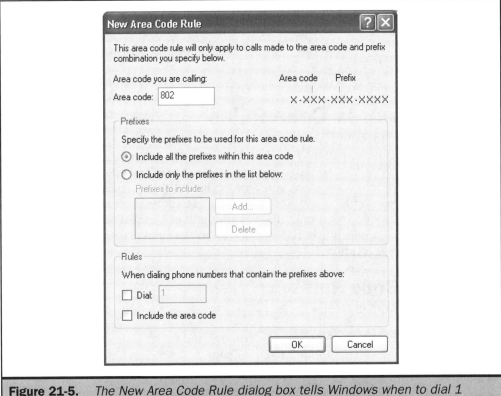

Figure 21-5.   *The New Area Code Rule dialog box tells Windows when to dial 1 and the area code.*

6. If you must dial 1 (or another set of digits) for these phone numbers, click the Dial check box and type the digit (usually 1, which already appears there).

7. If you must dial the area code for these phone numbers, click the Include The Area Code check box.

8. Click OK to return to the Edit Locations dialog box, where your rule now appears. Click OK again to return to the Phone And Modem Options dialog box.

You can change an existing area code rule (or delete it) by selecting the dialing location to which it applies from the Dialing Rules tab of the Phone And Modem Options dialog box, clicking Edit, clicking the Area Code Rules tab of the Edit Location dialog box that appears, clicking the area code rule, and clicking Edit or Delete.

> **Tip** *In most parts of the U.S., you can simply configure Windows to dial all calls with 1 and the area code, and they'll be handled correctly. In a few areas (Texas, notably) local calls must be dialed without the 1, so you'll probably have to create a dialing rule for nearly every prefix you call.*

Configuring Windows to Use Calling Cards

If you use a telephone calling card to charge your phone calls, especially when you are away from your home or office, Windows can dial all the extra digits for you.

A *calling card* is a telephone credit card to which you charge toll calls. To use a calling card, you dial several series of digits in addition to the phone number you want to call, usually including some digits to identify your calling card account. Windows can store information about your telephone calling cards; so when you need to connect to an Internet account via a calling card, Windows can dial the special digits for you.

Windows needs to know the following to place calls using a calling card:

■ **Account number**   The number you dial to identify yourself to the calling card company. Windows predefined calling cards don't use the account number at all, so we recommend leaving this box blank unless you are setting up your own calling card.

■ **Personal ID Number (PIN)**   The number that identifies you to the calling card company, usually your phone number plus four additional digits.

■ **Long-distance access number**   The digits you dial to connect to your calling card company before you dial the phone number you want to call or your calling card number. Windows doesn't let you type punctuation, such as dashes—just the digits to dial. For example, to use AT&T from most locations in the United States, you dial 10288, followed by 0; so you would type **102880**. You can also include pauses to wait for a prompt from the calling card company.

- **International access number** The digits you dial to connect to your calling card company when you want to place an international call.
- **Local access number** The digits you dial to connect to your calling card number when you want to place a local call.

Setting Up Calling Cards

To create, edit, or delete your list of calling cards, Choose Start | Control Panel, click Printers And Other Hardware, and click Phones And Modem Options. On the Phone And Modem Options dialog box that appears, click the Dialing Rules tab (if it's not already selected). Choose the dialing location for which you want to work with calling cards, click the Edit button to display the Edit Locations dialog box, and then click the Calling Card tab. You see a list of the calling cards you can use from this dialing location (Figure 21-6). Windows comes with calling cards for several large, pricey phone companies predefined.

Windows already knows about dozens of widely used calling cards, including their access numbers and the sequence of numbers to dial when placing a call. To set up a calling card that Windows already knows about, choose it from the Card Types list. Windows displays the default properties for that type of calling card. Only the Account Number and Personal ID Number (PIN) boxes are blank; you must type these numbers before Windows can use the calling card. Also check that the access numbers are right (these are the numbers that Windows tells your modem to dial when making long-distance, international, and local calls using the calling card). When you click OK, you return to the Phone And Modem Options dialog box.

 To delete a calling card, choose the calling card you no longer want to use from the Edit Location dialog box for the dialing location and then click Delete.

Creating a New Type of Calling Card

If your calling card doesn't appear on the Calling Card tab of the Edit Location dialog box for your dialing location, you can create one. You need to know not only the access numbers, account number, and PIN number, but also in what order to dial them and how long to wait between them. Most calling cards use your phone number, followed by a secret four-digit code as the PIN. A few use your phone number or a random ten-digit number as the account and a separate four-digit PIN. The standard set of steps for dialing a calling card number is

1. Dial the access number.

2. Wait for a moment (10 seconds is usually enough).

3. Dial the PIN.

4. Wait a moment more (about 5 seconds).

5. Dial the area code and phone number that you want to call.

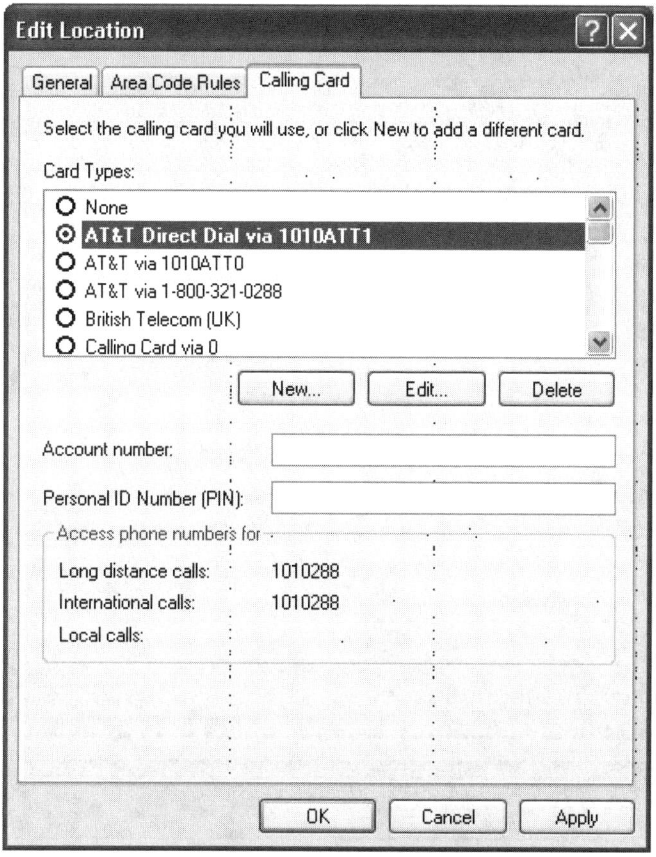

Figure 21-6. *Many calling cards are predefined in Windows.*

When setting up a new calling card, you tell Windows what to dial and when to pause. Follow these steps:

1. Make a note of what you dial and what you wait for when you place a call by hand. If you dial your PIN, followed by the number you want to dial, that's all you have to enter. But if there are additional steps, with additional prompts, make a note of them so you can tell Windows how to follow the same steps.

2. In the Edit Location dialog box for the dialing location, click the Calling Card tab and click the New button. You see a dialog box that looks like Figure 21-7. The settings for a new calling card are blank, so you have to enter them.

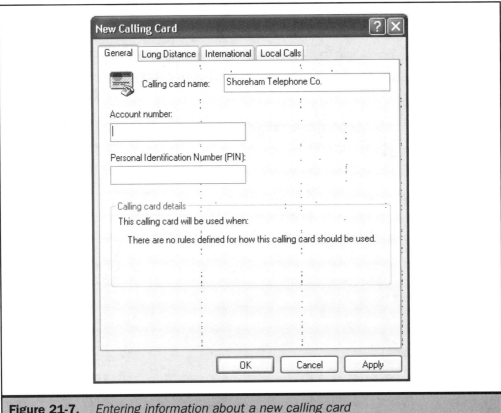

Figure 21-7.   *Entering information about a new calling card*

3. Type the name of the calling card, your account number (if your calling card uses one—most don't, so you can leave it blank), and your PIN (usually your phone number followed by a four-digit number).

4. Click the Long Distance tab (shown in Figure 21-8), in which you tell Windows the sequence of steps to follow when dialing a long-distance number using the calling card. Each step includes dialing a number or pausing for a prompt.

5. In the Access Phone Number For Long Distance Calls box, type the digits you would dial, omitting any punctuation (Windows allows only digits in this box).

6. Consult the notes you made in step 1 and click the button in the lower part of the dialog box to indicate what Windows should do first when dialing the number. For most calling cards, this usually means dialing the access number you typed in step 5, so click Access Number. The step appears in the Calling Card Dialing Steps box.

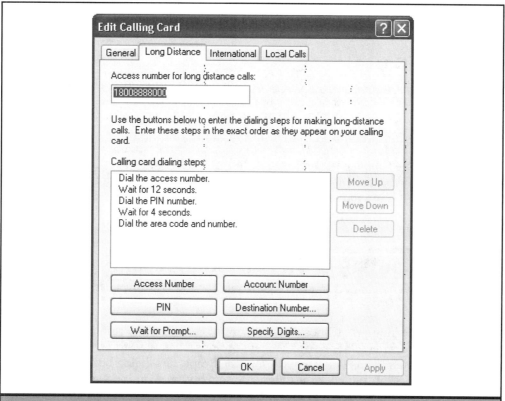

Figure 21-8.   *The Long Distance tab shows the steps for dialing long-distance numbers using the calling card.*

7. Continue clicking buttons to specify what to dial or how long to wait. If Windows needs to wait before continuing to dial, click Wait For Prompt and specify whether to wait for a dial tone, wait for a message to play, or wait for a specific number of seconds. Each step you specify appears in the Calling Card Dialing Steps box. If you enter a step by mistake, remove it by selecting the step and clicking Delete. You can also change the order of the steps by selecting a step and clicking Move Up or Move Down.

8. When the series of steps looks right, click the International tab to see an identical dialog box for specifying how to dial international calls with the calling card. Then click the Local Calls tab to specify how to dial local calls.

9. Click OK to save all the sequences of steps for the calling card.

If your calling card *does* appear but the access numbers or other information is wrong, you can change it by selecting the calling card and clicking Edit on the Calling

Card tab. You see the Edit Calling Card dialog box with the same settings as the New Calling Card dialog box.

Using Calling Cards

When placing calls using a dial-up connection, in the Properties dialog box for the connection, click the Use Dialing Rules check box, click the Dialing Rules button, choose a dialing location, click Edit, click the Calling Card tab, and choose a calling card to use (see Chapter 22).

When sending a fax with the Windows Fax Console, you can use calling cards when dialing the call (see Chapter 14, section "Sending and Receiving Faxes"). In the Send Fax Wizard, select the Use Dialing Rules check box, choose a dialing location, and click the Dialing Rules button to see or change the calling card used when making calls from that dialing location.

Troubleshooting a Dial-up Connection

If your modem won't connect or otherwise doesn't work, Windows has a few diagnostic aids:

- **Query the modem**   Choose Start | Control Panel, select Printers And Other Hardware, select Phone And Modem options, click the Modems tab, click your modem, and click Properties. In the Properties dialog box, click the Diagnostics tab and click the Query Modem button. Windows sends a set of requests to the modem to report on which of a large set of features the modem supports, listing the command that it tried and the modem's responses in the Command-Response section of the dialog box. If the Command-Response list fills up with messages, your modem is connected to the computer and working. (A few messages like "command not supported" are OK; these mean that your modem doesn't provide some optional feature.)

- **Make sure the correct driver is installed**   Look on the Modems tab of the Phone And Modems Options dialog box to make sure the correct modem is listed. Remove any modems that are no longer installed. If the wrong modem is listed, click Add to run the Add New Hardware Wizard and install the correct driver.

- **Make sure the driver is enabled**   Choose Start, right-click My Computer, choose Manage, and choose Device Manager from the list at the left side of the Computer Management window. Choose View | Devices By Type, and then click the plus (+) sign next to the Modems entry on the list of devices. Your modem should appear in the list—if it appears with an exclamation point or *X* on it, something is wrong. Click it and click the Properties button to display the Properties dialog box for the modem. On the General tab, make sure that Device Usage is set to Use This Device (Enabled).

■ **Make sure the modem is connected to the correct port**   Display the Properties dialog box for the modem as described in the preceding paragraph. On the Modem or General tab, check that you see the port to which the modem is connected (see Chapter 13, section "Connectors").

■ **Make sure the modem speed is right**   On the Modem tab in the Properties dialog box for the modem, check the Maximum Port Speed setting. If you have an external modem, choosing a lower speed may solve your connection problem.

■ **Check for device conflicts**   In the Device Manager (described in Chapter 13), be sure that there are no resource conflicts between the modem and other devices.

■ **Reset the modem**   If you have an external modem, turn the modem off, wait a few seconds, and turn it on again. If you have an internal modem, shut down and turn off the computer, wait a few seconds, and turn it on again.

■ **Check the cables**   Be sure the phone cables are plugged in correctly. If your modem has two jacks, be sure the phone line cable is plugged into the Line and not the Phone jack.

You can also use the Windows XP Modem Troubleshooter to help pinpoint the problem. To start the troubleshooter, click the General tab in the modem's Properties dialog box, and then click the Troubleshoot button. Follow the instructions in the Help And Support Center window that appears.

Tip   *If you have an external modem, be sure the modem is turned on.*

Dialing Your Modem by Hand

If you still can't figure out why more modem doesn't connect over the phone, try the HyperTerminal program to type commands directly to the modem, so you can see whether it's connecting to the other computer (see Chapter 26 for a full description of HyperTerminal). Follow these steps:

1. Run HyperTerminal by choosing Start | All Programs | Accessories | Communications | HyperTerminal.

2. Cancel out of its initial connection menu.

3. If you have an internal modem, its default settings are probably OK. If you have an external modem, select File | Properties to see the connection properties where you can select the COM port to use under Connect Using, then click the Configure button to open the Connection Preferences window. There you can set the port speed to 9600, a speed that every modem made in the past decade supports. Then dismiss the settings windows.

4. Press ENTER to connect to the modem; the status line should switch from Disconnected to Connected, as in Figure 21-9.

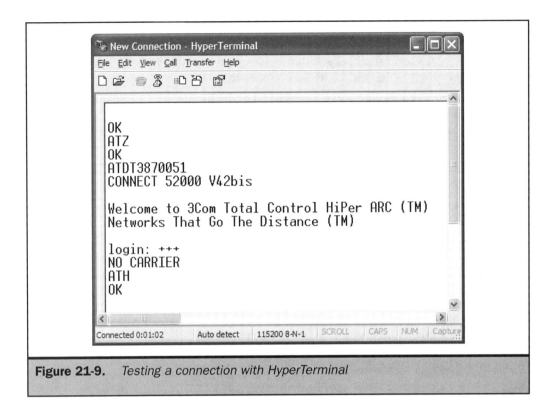

Figure 21-9. *Testing a connection with HyperTerminal*

5. Type **ATZ** and press ENTER a few times (this is the reset command). The modem should respond with OK.

6. To dial the modem, type **ATDT** followed by the phone number (just the digits, no hyphens) and press ENTER. You should hear the modem connect to the phone line, dial, and then hisses and whistles, then see a CONNECT message with the connection speed. Depending on your ISP's setup, you may see a text welcome message, or just unreadable binary text. Either is OK.

7. To hang up, type **+++** (don't press ENTER) to get the modem's attention, and when it says OK, type **ATH** and press ENTER.

If this procedure works, you can be confident that your modem is installed and working correctly. If you still can't connect to your ISP, the problem is most likely a mistyped password, or possibly one of the security options in the dial-up connection's properties (see Chapter 22).

Checking Your Modem's Log Files

When Windows tries to install your modem, it logs its attempts to detect your modem in C:\Windows\ModemDet.txt (assuming that Windows is installed on drive C:). If the installation fails, this file can contain hints about what went wrong.

When you use your modem, Windows logs the modem control messages (but not the data) in C:\Windows\Modemlog_*xxx*.txt, where *xxx* is the modem name. If Windows is unable to connect to your ISP, this file shows the setup messages it sent to the modem, and the responses from the modem.

Connecting to a DSL Line

DSL (*Digital Subscriber Line*) is a special phone line that communicates digitally. With a dial-up phone line, your modem converts the digital information from your computer into an analog signal for transmission. At the other end, another modem converts the analog signal back into digital information. Along the way, your phone company may perform additional conversions. With a DSL line, your digital information never has to be converted. Unlike dial-up lines, DSL lines stay connected all the time—there's no waiting for your computer to connect. Data transmission is also much faster than on a dial-up line: downstream (downloading) speeds range from 384 Kbps to 8 Mbps, and upstream (uploading) speeds range from 90 Kbps to 640 Kbps.

DSL comes in several varieties:

- **ADSL**   Asymmetric DSL, because it downloads faster than it uploads. Permits simultaneous computer and voice use
- **SDSL**   Symmetric DSL
- **IDSL**   ISDN (Integrated Services Digital Network) emulating DSL
- **HDSL**   A modern replacement for a T1 line

ADSL, the most common type of DSL line, supports faster communication to your computer (downloading) than from your computer (uploading), which matches the way most people use the Internet. When people talk about DSL, they usually mean ADSL.

There are two ways that your PC can connect to the Internet using your DSL line:

- **DHCP (Dynamic Host Configuration Protocol)**   Your computer is online all the time, with a numeric IP address assigned to you by your ISP's DHCP server (a server that issues IP addresses as needed). Chapter 29 describes how IP addresses are issued.
- **PPPoE (PPP over Ethernet)**   Your computer must log on each time you want to use the Internet, as if you were dialing in (but faster). Once you log in, your

ISP issues your computer a numeric IP address that works until you log out (or the connection times out).

Which method you use depends on your DSL provider; you don't get to choose. Windows XP can work with either method. You can find out more about DSL from the xDSL web site at **www.xdsl.com**.

Because DSL is high speed, it's well suited for allowing a LAN (like a group of networked computers in a home or small office) to share one Internet account (see Chapter 31 for how to share an Internet connection).

Getting DSL

DSL is available from most (but not all) phone companies and depends on your distance from the phone companies central office. Prices and speeds vary. You can call your local phone company for pricing and availability in your area. Better yet, call your ISP and ask them to order the DSL line for you. You may also be able to get a DSL line from a local or national ISP or (in areas where AOL Time-Warner owns the cable system) AOL.

To connect your computer to a DSL line, you need a *DSL modem*. DSL modems may be internal or external, and external DSL modems may connect either to a network adapter or to a USB port. Order the DSL line from your ISP when you check whether they offer DSL service; your ISP can probably order the line for you from your phone company. Ask for the phone company or ISP to provide the DSL modem, too—some phone companies don't support DSL modems purchased elsewhere. If the DSL modem requires a network adapter (network interface card, or NIC), get one from a computer store and install it in your computer before the installer arrives (see Chapter 13, section "Network Ports"). The ISP or phone company should provide the software and instructions for configuring Windows to work with the DSL modem. Your phone company or other DSL provider usually installs the DSL modem and configures your computer to use it. They usually configure your network interface card to work with the cable modem (see Chapter 22).

Not all DSL modems work with all DSL lines. Get your DSL modem from your phone company or ISP. If you already have a DSL modem, check with your DSL provider to find out whether it will work with their phone lines.

Configuring Windows for DSL

To see your DSL configuration, choose Start | My Network Places, click View Network Connections in the Task pane, right-click your DSL connection, and choose Properties to see the Properties dialog box. Click Internet Protocol (TCP/IP) and click the Properties button to see the configuration for the connection. Don't change the settings without information from your ISP.

Sharing a Line Between DSL and Voice

DSL (specifically, ADSL, the most common type of DSL) can and usually should share a physical phone line with your regular voice phone service. You have to install small filters between your phones (as well as answering machines, faxes, and anything else that plugs in like a phone) and the DSL phone line to prevent interference between the phone and ADSL. If you're lucky, the installer can split the DSL from the phone service at the place where the phone line enters your house and put one filter there. Otherwise, you have to plug a filter into each jack that's used for a phone and plug the phone into that. The filters are small boxes about an inch square that are available from your DSL provider and from electronics stores.

In some areas, the phone company won't share a line between phone and DSL, usually because the DSL provider and the phone provider aren't speaking to each other, so they can't figure out how to send you two bills for one line. In that case, you have to get a second physical line for DSL, even though there's no technical need to do so.

Tip   *On the Properties dialog box for the DSL connection, make sure that neither the Client For Microsoft Networks nor the File And Printer Sharing For Microsoft Networks check boxes are selected. If they are, deselect them—otherwise, you may be giving other people on the Internet access to your files and printer!*

Connecting to a Cable Modem

Most cable television companies offer *cable Internet accounts*—cable connections to the Internet over the same cable that your television uses. Not all cable companies can do so—they must upgrade the cable system to support two-way transmission. (A few older cable Internet systems require a phone line to dial in for uploading information; the cable connection is for downloading only.) Downloading speeds can be fast, sometimes 10MB per second or faster. Uploading usually isn't as fast, but cable connections are almost always faster than dial-up lines. Cable Internet accounts have several advantages over dial-up Internet accounts:

- **Speed**   Cable modems can communicate much faster than dial-up modems. Expect downloading speeds of 1 to 2 Mbps or more, and uploading speeds of between 500 Kbps and 1 Mbps.

- **Separate line**   If you use a cable account, you don't tie up your regular phone line. If you currently pay for a separate phone line for your Internet connection, the cost of a cable Internet account usually won't be much more than you're paying for your dial-up ISP and a second phone line.

Call your local cable company to find out if it offers Internet service.

Getting Connected

To connect your computer to the cable system, you use a *cable modem*. It connects to a network interface card (also used for connecting to a LAN—see the section "Buying Network Interface Cards" in Chapter 27) or less commonly to a USB port. Your cable company usually supplies the modem, along with the software and instructions for installing the cable modem and configuring Windows to use it. Some cable companies give you the option to buy or lease the cable modem. If the cable company uses standard DOCSIS modems, buying one is a good deal, since you can reuse it or sell it if you move. If not, lease one that's compatible with their system. The cable installer usually configures your network interface card to work with the cable modem (see Chapter 22).

Configuring Windows for a Cable Modem

When your cable installer connects your PC to the cable modem, she or he usually also configures Windows to work with the cable modem. Windows communicates with the cable modem using the TCP/IP networking protocol, which you can configure. Choose Start | My Network Places, click View Network Connections, right-click your cable Internet connection, and choose Properties to see the Properties dialog box. Click Internet Protocol (TCP/IP) and click the Properties button to see the configuration for the cable connection. Don't change the settings without information from your cable company.

 On the Properties dialog box for the cable Internet connection, make sure that neither the Client For Microsoft Networks nor the File And Printer Sharing For Microsoft Networks check boxes are selected. If they are, deselect them—otherwise, the other people in your neighborhood with cable Internet accounts may have access to your files and printer!

Connecting to an ISDN Line

ISDN (Integrated Services Digital Network) is an all-digital phone line that is less widely used in the United States, but quite common, for example, in Europe, where an ISDN line is typically cheaper than two analog phone lines. The type of ISDN service for residential customers is Basic Rate Interface (BRI). A BRI consists of two 64 Kbps (or 56 Kbps on some older systems in the United States) channels, each of which can be used independently for phone, fax, or data connections. Both channels can be combined (bundled) in a single data connection, allowing you to connect at 128 Kbps—over twice the speed of a fast dial-up line. Unlike DSL and cable modems, ISDN is not connected directly to the Internet, but rather to the telephone network, so you connect to the Internet by making a phone call to an ISP that offers ISDN access.

If your phone company offers DSL, choose it over ISDN, as DSL is much faster and usually cheaper, particularly in areas where ISDN connections are charged by the minute.

For more information about how ISDN works, see the ISDN Zone web site at **www.isdnzone.com**.

Getting ISDN

You can order an ISDN line from your local telephone company, but you should call your ISP first to confirm they can also provide ISDN service. ISDN lines are more expensive than normal phone lines, and not all phone companies can provide them. Even companies that do provide ISDN lines often have trouble installing them correctly; so if your ISP can arrange to set up the line, order it through them.

You also need an *ISDN terminal adapter* (also called an *ISDN adapter, ISDN TA,* or *ISDN modem*) to connect your computer's serial port to the ISDN phone line. Better yet, get an external ISDN adapter with a USB (Universal Serial Bus) interface or an internal ISDN adapter card that installs inside your computer for faster communications (external ISDN adapters that connect to the serial port are limited by the 115-Kbps speed of the serial port). Your ISP (or whatever computer you are connecting to) must have ISDN phone numbers for you to connect to (see Chapter 22).

Configuring Windows for Your ISDN Adapter

Your telephone installer usually installs the ISDN adapter and configures Windows to use it, but here is information about how to do so yourself. See Chapter 13 for how to install an internal ISDN adapter. If you have an external ISDN adapter that connects to the serial port, connect its serial cable to a serial (COM) port on your PC (shut down Windows and turn your PC off first). If you have an external USB ISDN adapter, plug it into a free USB connector on your PC (you don't have to turn off your PC first).

When you turn your PC back on or when you plug in an USB ISDN adapter, Windows should detect the new hardware and run the Add Hardware Wizard automatically. If it doesn't, choose Start | Control Panel | Printers And Other Hardware and choose Add Hardware from the See Also list. If the wizard doesn't detect the ISDN adapter, choose Add A New Device.

When Windows has installed the drivers for the ISDN adapter, you (or your telephone installer) configure Windows to use it. The Add Hardware Wizard usually displays a dialog box asking for configuration information: if it doesn't, choose Start | Control Panel | Printers And Other Hardware and choose System to display the System Properties dialog box. Click the Hardware tab and click the Device Manager button. (You can also see the Device Manager from the Computer Management window.) Your ISDN adapter appears in Modems if it is external or Network Adapters if it is internal. Right-click the

ISDN adapter and choose Properties from the menu that appears. Click the ISDN tab and select the Switch type or D-channel protocol your phone company uses (ask your phone company for this information). Then click the Configure button and enter the requested information, which you need to get from your phone company or ISP:

- **Phone Number**   The phone number(s) of your ISDN line for U.S. and Canada switch types. Your ISDN line may have one or two phone numbers.

- **Service Profile Identifier (SPID)**   Your ISDN phone number, plus a few extra digits that identify the ISDN connection. If your SPID isn't entered exactly right, your ISDN connection won't work at all. (SPIDs are used only in North America.)

- **Multi-Subscriber Numbers (MSN)**   The phone number(s) of your ISDN line for European ISDN (DSS1)—this has nothing to do with MSN, Microsoft's ISP. European ISDN allows multiple phone numbers on an ISDN line. You only need to enter the MSN(s) you actually intend to use with your computer—the MSNs you want your computer to accept calls for, and the MSN to which you want outgoing calls to be billed. Note that outgoing calls you make with your computer will be billed to the first MSN in the list, which will always be the lowest number, since Windows sorts the list. If you enter no MSN, the calls will be billed to the primary MSN of your line.

Tip   *You must be logged on using an administrator account to configure your ISDN adapter.*

See "Creating a Network Connection for an ISDN Line" in Chapter 22 for how to create and configure a dial-up connection for your ISDN line.

Two-Way Satellite Connections

Another option for connecting to the Internet is by two-way satellite. For example, Starband (at **www.starband.com**) and DirecPC (at **www.direcpc.com**) offer a satellite dish, satellite modem, Internet account, and optional satellite television service. It's more expensive than a DSL or cable Internet, but it's available anywhere in the continental United States where you can see the southern sky.

The satellite dish mounts on your roof, and connects using a coaxial cable and a satellite modem to either the USB or network adapter on your computer. A Starband or DirecPC installer does the installation of both the disk and the modem.

Chapter 22

Connecting to the Internet

Once your modem is installed (as described in the previous chapter), you need to configure Windows XP to connect to your Internet account. How you connect depends on the type of account. Windows can have network connections to dial-up, ISDN, DSL, and cable Internet accounts, as well as connections to local area networks (LANs). Whatever your connection, be sure to enable Windows XP's Internet Connection Firewall to protect your computer from malefactors.

If your computer is connected to a local area network, you can connect to the Internet over the LAN if another computer (or a router) serves as an Internet gateway. If you have a small LAN at home or in a small organization, Windows XP comes with Internet Connection Sharing that allows a computer running Windows to act as an Internet gateway for all the computers on the LAN (see Chapter 31).

If you dial in to your Internet account, you can tell Windows either to dial direct or use a telephone calling card, and you can specify whether to dial the area code or not (see Chapter 21). These features are especially useful when you take your laptop on a trip.

For all types of accounts, the built-in Ping, Tracert, and Netstat programs can help you test your connection. This chapter describes all these programs.

Types of Internet Accounts

How Windows XP connects to the Internet depends on the types of account: Internet PPP account (using a dial-up, ISDN, or DSL line), cable Internet account, or online service. You can also use an old-fashioned text-based account (see the "UNIX Shell Accounts" sidebar in this chapter). Cable Internet accounts are described in "Connecting to a Cable Modem" in Chapter 21.

Note

If you connect to America Online (AOL), you must use the software that AOL provides—you can't use the Windows network connections. AOL connection software may come with your Windows XP installation. If you use a UNIX shell account (where you type UNIX commands), bulletin board system, or other text-based system, you can connect to the Internet by using HyperTerminal, the Windows terminal program (see Chapter 26, section "Logging into Text-Based Systems with HyperTerminal").

TCP/IP

TCP/IP is the acronym for Transmission Control Protocol/Internet Protocol, the way computers communicate with each other on the Internet. All Internet accounts use TCP/IP. Windows XP also uses TCP/IP for communication over local area networks (see Chapter 22, section "TCP/IP").

Internet (PPP) Accounts

A *PPP (Point-to-Point Protocol)* account is an Internet account that uses the PPP communications protocol. PPP is the standard type of dial-up Internet account. Occasionally, you may run into *SLIP* (Serial Line Internet Protocol), an older, less-reliable predecessor of PPP, but which works the same way. This book refers to PPP and SLIP accounts as *dial-up Internet accounts.*

Internet service providers (ISPs) provide Internet accounts, usually PPP accounts, but occasionally UNIX shell accounts. All ISPs provide dial-in accounts using regular phone lines, and many also provide ISDN and DSL connections.

Dial-Up Internet Accounts, Including ISDN

To connect over a dial-up phone line, you need a PPP- or SLIP-compatible communications program, such as the built-in Windows Network Connections program (see "Displaying Network Connections" later in this chapter). Network Connections can dial the phone by using your modem; connect to your ISP; log into your account by using your user name and password; and then establish a PPP or SLIP connection, so your computer is connected to the Internet. While connected, you can use a variety of Winsock-compatible programs to read your e-mail, browse the Web, and access other information from the Internet. When you are done, you tell Windows to disconnect from your Internet account. You configure your network connection by using the New Connection Wizard (see "Creating a Network Connection for an Existing Account" later in this chapter). You can also create and edit network connections manually (see "Changing Your Dial-Up Connection Settings" later in this chapter).

 Dial-up connections that appear in the Network Connections window were called Dial-Up Networking (DUN) connections in previous versions of Windows.

ISDN phone lines are a high-speed type of dial-up line; see the section "Connecting to an ISDN Line" in Chapter 21 for instructions on how to configure Windows to connect to an ISDN line. Then see "Creating a Network Connection for an ISDN Line" later in this chapter.

 You can have several network connections on one computer. For example, your laptop computer might have one network connection for the DSL account you use at home and another for the nation-wide ISP you dial into when you are traveling.

DSL Accounts

If you want to use a high-speed Internet account, check with local and national ISPs to find out which ones offer DSL in your area. If your ISP offers ISDN or DSL accounts, they can work with your telephone company to get the high-speed phone line installed and tell you the type of ISDN or DSL modem you need. See the section "Connecting to a DSL Line " in Chapter 21 for how to connect Windows to DSL network hardware.

UNIX Shell Accounts

Before the advent of PPP and SLIP accounts, most Internet accounts were text-only *UNIX shell accounts*. You run a *terminal-emulation program* (a program that allows your PC to pretend it's a computer terminal) on your PC to connect to an Internet host computer. Most Internet hosts run a version of UNIX, a powerful operating system with commands that can be terse to the point of bafflement. (Common UNIX variants include Linux, Sun Solaris, and BSD.) You have to type UNIX commands to use a UNIX shell account. To send and receive e-mail or browse the Web, you run text-only programs, such as Pine, a popular UNIX e-mail program and Lynx, a text-only web browser. UNIX shell accounts don't let you see graphics, use a mouse, or easily store information on your own computer.

Some ISPs give you both a PPP account and a UNIX shell account; you use the PPP account for your regular Internet work, and the UNIX shell account only when you need to use a facility on the ISP's UNIX server.

Windows comes with HyperTerminal, a terminal-emulation program you can use to connect to UNIX shell accounts and other text-only systems (see Chapter 26, section "Logging into Text-Based Systems with HyperTerminal").

DSL providers use two primary schemes to connect your Windows machine. Some simply configure their network as a large LAN, using the standard DHCP network service to configure your connection (Chapter 29 describes how DHCP works). Others use PPPoE (PPP over Ethernet) which, as its name suggests, treats the Ethernet-like DSL connection as a PPP dial-up account that you have to log into in order to use.

Cable Internet Accounts

With a cable Internet account, your cable television company is your ISP, and you connect to the Internet over your cable. Contact your cable company to find out whether it offers Internet accounts. The monthly fee usually includes the rental of a cable modem. See "Configuring Windows for a Cable Modem" in Chapter 21 for an explanation of how to connect Windows to work to a cable Internet equipment. Once you're connected, the cable Internet usually appears to Windows to be a large LAN.

Online Services

An *online service* is a commercial service that enables you to connect and access its proprietary information system. Most online services also provide an Internet connection, e-mail, web browsing, and sometimes other Internet services. Online services usually require special programs to connect to and use your account.

The two most popular online services in the United States are America Online (AOL, at **www.aol.com**) and (a distant second) CompuServe (CIS, at **www.compuserve.com**), which is owned by AOL. The Microsoft Network (MSN) started out as an online

The Microsoft Network (MSN)

Microsoft Network (MSN) was Microsoft's entrant in the world of online services in 1995. Although MSN has gained a lot of users because of the easy-to-click icon on the Windows 9*x*/Me desktops, it's never been as highly rated as AOL or CompuServe. Microsoft changed MSN from an online service to a regular Internet service, so you now use network connections to connect to MSN and Winsock-compatible programs to access its services.

When you start Internet Explorer, you usually start at the MSN web site (**www.msn.com**), which is accessible no matter what kind of Internet account you use.

service, but was relaunched as an ISP, and has grown in popularity (see the sidebar "The Microsoft Network" in this chapter). AOL and CompuServe let you use most Winsock-compatible programs while you are connected to the account. For example, you can use the Internet Explorer, Mozilla, or Netscape Navigator web browsers with any of these accounts. However, AOL doesn't support standard e-mail programs— you have to use their software (or Netscape 6, Mozilla, or the AOL web site) to read your mail.

Types of Network Connections

A *network connection* tells Windows how your computer is connected to another computer, whether over the phone or via a cable. Windows supports these types of network connections:

- **Dial-up connection**   Connection using a modem and phone line, either a regular phone line or an ISDN line. Dial-up connections to the Internet are described throughout this chapter. Dialing one Windows computer from another is described in section "Connecting Two Computers by Using a Dial-Up Connection" in Chapter 28.

- **Local area network (LAN) connection**   Connection over a cable or wireless LAN adapter to other computers in the same building. LAN connections are described in Chapter 29. Always-on DSL and cable Internet accounts appear as LAN connections, because they don't have to dial in.

- **Broadband connections that need a user name and password**   (also known as PPPoE) A DSL connection that's physically always connected but needs a user name and password to log in.

- **Virtual Private Network (VPN) connection**   Connection to a private LAN over the Internet. See Chapter 28 for details.

- **Direct network connection**   Connection to another computer over a cable or infrared link. See the section "Connecting Two Computers with Direct Network Connection" in Chapter 28.

- **Incoming connection**   Connection that allows other computers to dial in to your computer (or connect via a cable, infrared link, or over the Internet as part of a VPN). See Chapter 28 for how to set up an incoming connection.

- **Gateway connection**   Connection through another computer. For example, if you connect to the Internet via Internet Connection Sharing on another computer on a LAN, you see a Residential Gateway connection on your computer (see Chapter 31).

- **Network bridge**   Connection among two or more LANs (see Chapter 29, section "Bridging Networks").

Displaying Network Connections

To see network-related tasks you can perform, such as creating and editing network connections, display the Network And Internet Connections window shown in Figure 22-1 by choosing Start | Control Panel | Network And Internet Connections. You also use this window to manage your LAN connections, as described in Chapter 29.

To see your existing Internet and LAN connections, click the Network Connections icon to display the Network Connections window, shown in Figure 22-2. (You might think to click the Internet Options icon instead, but the dialog box that this icon displays pertains mainly to Internet Explorer rather than connecting to the Internet.) The Network Connections window lists every way that your computer connects to other computers:

Network Connection Type	Types of Connections
Broadband	Broadband connections that require a user name and password
Dial-Up	Dial-up connections (including ISDN connections)
Direct	Outgoing direct cable connection (see Chapter 28)
Gateway	Internet Connection Sharing connection (see Chapter 31)
Incoming	Incoming dial-up or direct connection (see Chapter 28)
LAN Or High-Speed Internet	LAN, cable Internet, and DSL connections

Network Connection Type	Types of Connections
Other	Shared disks on the server computer to which you are connected using Remote Desktop Connection (see Chapter 15)
Virtual Private Network	VPN connections (see Chapter 28)

You can right-click a connection in the Network Connections window and choose Properties from the menu that appears to see or change the properties for that LAN or Internet connection.

Another way to display the Network Connections window is by choosing Start | Connect To | Show All Connections (if Connect To appears on your Start menu) or Start | All Programs | Accessories | Communications | Network Connections.

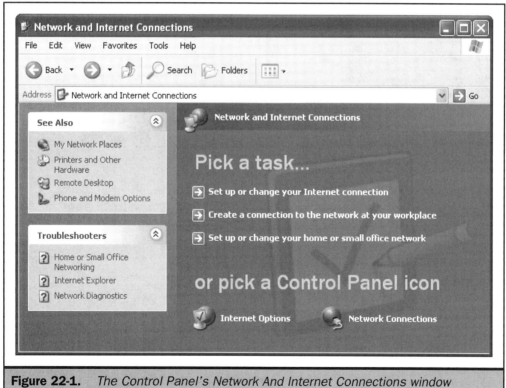

Figure 22-1.   *The Control Panel's Network And Internet Connections window*

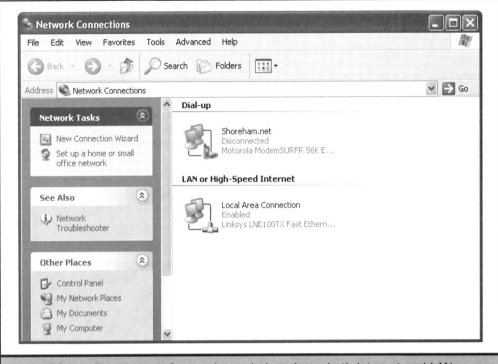

Figure 22-2.   *The Network Connections window shows both Internet and LAN connections.*

    If you look at the Network Connections window often, add it to your Start menu: see the sidebar "Displaying the Network Connections Window" in Chapter 29. Then you can display the Network Connections window by choosing Start | Network Connections.

Winsock-compatible Applications

Winsock (short for *Windows Sockets*) is a standard way for Windows programs to work with Internet connection software. Any Winsock-compatible program can work with any Winsock-compatible connection software. Windows network connections are Winsock-compatible; if you use them to connect to your Internet account, you can use almost any Winsock-compatible program with your account. All Windows Internet programs are compatible with the Winsock standard.

Windows comes with many Winsock-compatible programs, including Internet Explorer (see Chapter 24) and Outlook Express (see Chapter 23). See Chapter 26 for descriptions of other Winsock-compatible programs.

Signing Up for a New Account

We recommend that you choose an ISP by talking to people you know and determining which ISP your friends and coworkers are most satisfied with. However, you can also use the New Connection Wizard to look for ISPs with phone numbers in your area or sign up for an MSN account. Whether you have already chosen an ISP or want use the Microsoft Internet Referral Service to select an ISP, you start by running the New Connection Wizard.

Running the New Connection Wizard

The New Connection Wizard starts automatically when you run an Internet application (such as Internet Explorer or Outlook Express) with no Internet connection configured. You can also start the New Connection Wizard clicking Create A New Connection in the Task pane of the Network Connections window, or by choosing Start | All Programs | Accessories | Communications New Connection Wizard. The New Connection Wizard gives you four choices (shown in Figure 22-3):

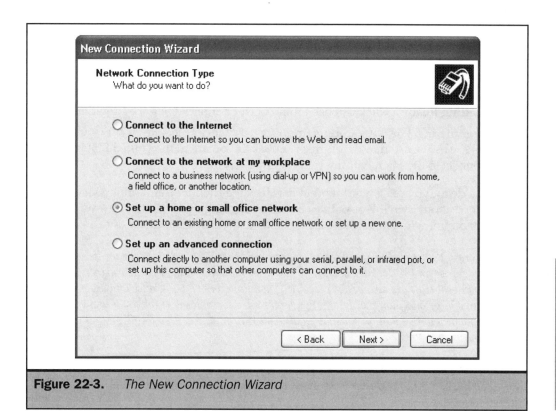

Figure 22-3.   *The New Connection Wizard*

- **Connect To The Internet** Helps you sign up for a new Internet account and configures a network connection to connect to it. The rest of this chapter describes how to use this option.

- **Connect To The Network At My Workplace** Helps you create a Virtual Private Network (VPN) connection via the Internet. VPN is described in Chapter 28.

- **Set Up A Home Or Small Office Network** Runs the Network Setup Wizard to help you set up a LAN (see Chapter 29, section "Adding Your Computer to a TCP/IP Peer-to-Peer LAN").

- **Set Up An Advanced Connection** Helps you create an incoming connection so that other people can connect to your computer or a direct network connection for a computer that is directly cabled to yours (described in Chapter 28).

Previous versions of Windows came with the Internet Connection Wizard, which has been replaced with the New Connection Wizard. If the Internet Connection Wizard is still lurking on your system (for example, if you upgraded from Windows 9x/Me), close this Wizard if it runs, and use the New Connection Wizard instead.

Letting Microsoft Recommend an ISP

Follow the instructions in the previous section to run the New Connection Wizard. Make these choices, clicking Next after each:

- **Network Connection Type** Click Connect To The Internet.
- **Getting Ready** Click Choose From A List Of Internet Service Providers (ISPs).
- **Completing The New Connection Wizard** Click Select From A List Of Other ISPs. The wizard dials a toll-free number (if you are in the United States) to connect to the Microsoft Internet Referral Service.

After a delay, you see a window that lists its suggested ISPs and online services. You can read about each ISP or online service by clicking its name. If you want to sign up for an account with one of these ISPs, click Next. Otherwise, click Cancel.

Microsoft's list of ISPs includes only large ISPs that have paid to be in the list. Before you choose an ISP, look for ads in the business section of your local newspaper to see what local ISPs are available. A local ISP usually gives better service and support than a large one, along with having a better selection of local numbers. If you travel frequently with a laptop, consider a national ISP, or stick with a local ISP and use a national ISP when you're on the road.

If you choose to create a new account by using one of the ISPs listed by Microsoft, the wizard asks you to provide information about yourself, including a credit card to which you want to charge your account. The sign-up procedure varies by ISP. During the sign-up, be sure to write down all the information the sign-up program displays, including technical support phone numbers, account numbers, and passwords.

 Before using your account, check that the number your modem will dial to connect to the account is a local call. If not, you should probably cancel the account because the long-distance charges for using the account will be many times more than the cost of the account itself. Instead, find a local ISP with a local phone number.

Signing Up for an MSN Account

The New Connection Wizard gives you the option of signing up for an MSN account. Follow the instructions in the section "Running the New Connection Wizard" earlier in this chapter to start the wizard. Click Next to move from screen to screen, answering its questions:

- **Network Connection Type**   Choose Connect To The Internet.
- **Getting Ready**   Click Choose From A List Of Internet Service Providers (ISPs).
- **Completing the New Connection Wizard**   Choose Get Online With MSN.
- **Use MSN Explorer**   The wizard offers to set up MSN Explorer as your web browser and e-mail program (see Chapter 24).
- **Welcome to MSN Explorer**   Whether you choose Yes or No, MSN Explorer runs and steps you through setting up an MSN account.

Creating a Network Connection for an Existing Account

To create a new network connection to a dial-up Internet account, you use the New Connection Wizard. For ISDN accounts, see "Creating a Network Connection for an ISDN Line" later in this section. For DSL accounts, your DSL installer should already have set up Windows to work with your account: some DSL accounts appear as dial-up-like connections in the Network Connection window, and you use this connection to log in.

 If you installed Windows XP, the Setup Wizard may have created a network connection for your Internet account during Windows setup. Check the Network Connections window to find out.

WINDOWS XP HOME
ON THE INTERNET

Creating a Dial-up Connection

The New Connection Wizard can create a network connection, with much more straightforward questions. Run it by following the instructions in the section "Running the New Connection Wizard earlier in this chapter. Click Next to move from screen to screen, answering the following questions:

- **Network Connection Type** Choose Connect To The Internet.

- **Getting Ready** Choose Set Up My Connection Manually.

- **Internet Connection** Choose the type of phone line (or cable Internet connection) you use.

- **ISP Name** Type the name that you want to use for this connection. It doesn't have to be your ISP's name—it's the name that Windows will assign to the connection icon.

- **Phone Number** Type your ISP's access phone number (for dial-up accounts only).

- **Internet Account Information** Type the user name and password for the account (your ISP provides this information).

- **Use This Account Name And Password When Anyone Connects To The Internet From This Computer** If you want all user accounts on your computer to be able to use this Internet account, leave this check box selected.

- **Make This The Default Internet Connection** If you want to use this network connection to connect to the Internet whenever you run an Internet program and you're not already online, leave this check box selected.

- **Turn On Internet Connection Firewall For This Connection** Unless you have a specific program (for example, a chat program or interactive game) that doesn't work through a firewall, leave this check box selected (see "Enabling the Internet Connection Firewall Between Your PC and the Internet" later in this chapter).

- **Add A Shortcut To This Connection To My Desktop** A shortcut to your ISP connection used to be handy, but no longer. Now Windows can connect to your account automatically when you run your browser, e-mail program, or other Internet program, so you rarely need to start your ISP connection yourself.

The wizard creates a new icon in the Network Connections window, and you see the Connect window described in "Connecting to Your Internet Account" later in this chapter.

Creating a Network Connection for an ISDN Line

To create a dial-up connection for an ISDN line, run the New Connection Wizard by following the instructions in the section "Running the New Connection Wizard" earlier in this chapter. Click Next to move from screen to screen, answering the following questions:

- **Network Connection Type**   Choose Connect To The Internet.
- **Getting Ready**   Choose Set Up My Connection Manually.
- **Internet Connection**   Choose Connect Using A Dial-Up Modem
- Windows shows a list of available devices that contains the individual ISDN channels of your ISDN adapter, as well as an entry named All Available ISDN Lines Multi-linked, which is selected by default.
- Keep this selection if you want to bundle both channels of your ISDN line (for 128 Kbps speed), or clear it and select only one of the channels if you always want to connect with a single channel at 56/64 Kbps.

The wizard creates the dial-up connection for the ISDN line. Now you can configure the ISDN line type to use. Follow these steps:

1. Right-click the dial-up connection icon in the Network Connections window. Choose Properties from the menu that appears. You see the Properties dialog box for the ISDN connection.

2. On the General tab, select the ISDN channel that you want to configure. Click the Configure button to display the ISDN Configuration dialog box.

3. Set the Line Type, Negotiate Line Type, and other settings according to the instructions you receive from your phone company or ISP.

Some phone companies charge "data" calls by the minute, while "voice" calls are free. For that reason, some ISPs allow you to connect with the "56K Voice" line type, which disguises the connection as a "voice" call" to the phone company. This method is called Data Over Voice (DOV).

If you create a multilinked ISDN connection that bundles both of your ISDN channels, you can also configure the bundling. Click the Options tab of your dial-up

WINDOWS XP HOME
ON THE INTERNET

connection's Properties dialog box and select the bundling behavior under Multiple Devices:

- **Dial Only First Available Device**   Uses only the first free ISDN channel and leaves the other one available, so you can still make or receive phone calls.

- **Dial All Devices**   Creates a "static" 128 Kbps connection that uses both ISDN channels all of the time.

- **Dial Devices Only As Needed**   Allows dynamic use of the ISDN channels, which you can configure by clicking the Configure button. With this setting, Windows initially uses only one ISDN channel, and starts using the second one when you fully exploit the bandwidth of this channel for an extended time period (for example, when you start downloading a big file). When the download is finished, Windows automatically disconnects the second ISDN channel again.

(Thanks to Robert Schlabbach for these instructions.)

Changing Your Dial-Up Connection Settings

Once you have created a network connection, you can change its settings, copy it, rename it, or delete it. You can also choose which network connection is the default for connecting to the Internet.

Note   *Previous versions of Windows didn't come with TCP/IP (the communications protocol used on the Internet) preinstalled. Instead, you chose it from a list of popular network protocols. Windows XP comes with TCP/IP installed, and you can't uninstall it. (It's unlikely that you'd want to do so, since TCP/IP is used for both the Internet and LANs.)*

To configure a network connection or to change an existing connection's configuration, open the Network Connections window by choosing Start | Connect To | Show All Connections (if Connect To appears on the Start menu), choosing Start | Network Connections (if Network Connections appears on the Start menu), clicking View Network Connections from the Task pane of the My Network Places window, or choosing Start | Control Panel | Network And Internet Connections | Network Connections. Right-click the icon for the connection and choose Properties from the menu that appears, or select the connection icon and choose File | Properties. Either way, you see the Properties dialog box for the network connection. Different types of connections display different Properties dialog boxes. Figure 22-4 shows one for a dial-up connection, and Table 22-1 lists dial-up connection properties. For the properties of LAN connections (including DSL and cable Internet connections), see section "Installing and Configuring Network Components" in Chapter 29.

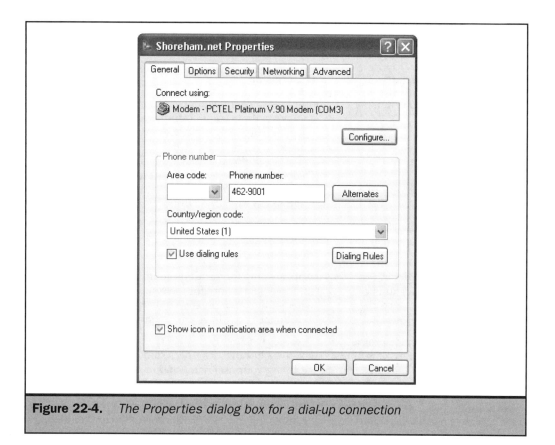

Figure 22-4. *The Properties dialog box for a dial-up connection*

Tab in Properties Dialog Box	Setting	Description
General	Connecting using	Specifies which modem to use to connect. Click the Configure button to check or change the configuration of the modem (see Chapter 21).

Table 22-1. *Settings for a Dial-Up Connection*

Tab in Properties Dialog Box	Setting	Description
General	Phone number	Specifies the phone number your computer dials to connect to the account. Composed of the area code, telephone number, and country code (you choose from a list of countries). Click the Alternates button to enter additional phone numbers. Select the Use Dialing Rules check box to use area code dialing rules and calling cards (see Chapter 21, section "Setting Up Area Code Rules").
General	Show icon in notification area when connected	Specifies whether to display an icon at the right end of the taskbar. You can click the icon to see the status of the connection.
General	All devices dial the same number	Appears only for multilink connections (which use multiple phone lines for the connection). Specifies whether the same phone number is dialed when additional phone lines are used for this connection.
Options	Display progress while connecting	Specifies whether to display the Connection dialog box, which shows whether Windows is dialing or verifying your user name and password before the connection is made.
Options	Prompt for name and password, certificate, etc.	Specifies whether to display a dialog box that prompts for your user name and password (or other security information if your account requires it) before connecting.
Options	Include Windows logon domain	Specifies that if the preceding check box is selected, Windows also prompt for your logon domain. This setting isn't used by most ISPs.
Options	Prompt for phone number	Specifies whether to include the phone number in the Connect dialog box displayed before connecting to the account. This setting allows you to check or change the phone number each time you dial the account.
Options	Redial attempts	Specifies how many times Windows redials the connection if it can't connect.
Options	Time between redial attempts	Specifies how long Windows waits before dialing again.

Table 22-1. *Settings for a Dial-Up Connection* (continued)

Tab in Properties Dialog Box	Setting	Description
Options	Idle time before hanging up	Specifies whether Windows disconnects if the connection is idle for a specified length of time. Choose Never to disable auto-disconnect.
Options	Redial if line is dropped	Specifies whether Windows reconnects if the connection is lost (for example, if the ISP hangs up).
Options	X.25	If you're dialing into an X.25 network, displays the X.25 Logon Settings dialog box, in which you specify the X.25 network provider and the X.121 address of the server to which you are connecting.
Security	Validate my identity as follows	Specifies how your ISP determines who you are. For most ISPs, choose Allow Unsecured Password (that is, passwords are sent unencrypted). For corporate networks, you may need to choose Require Secured Password or Use Smart Card.
Security	Automatically use my Windows logon name and password (and domain if any)	Specifies what user name and password to use (available only if you set the preceding setting to Require Selected Password or Use Smart Card). Usually not selected for Internet accounts.
Security	Require data encryption (disconnect if none)	Specifies that the computer to which you are connecting must support encryption for all information transmitted, and to disconnect otherwise (available only if you set the preceding setting to Require Selected Password or Use Smart Card). This setting is rarely used.
Security	Advanced (custom settings)	Click the Settings button to display the Advanced Security Settings dialog box, on which you can specify EAP (Extensible Authentication Protocol) or other advanced protocols, if your ISP supports them.
Security	Show terminal window	Specifies whether to display a terminal window that shows the interaction between the network connection and the account while the logon script is running. During debugging, select this setting so you can see the terminal window.

Table 22-1.   *Settings for a Dial-Up Connection* (continued)

Tab in Properties Dialog Box	Setting	Description
Security	Run script	Specifies the name of the file containing the logon script for this connection (see "Creating and Using Logon Scripts" later in this chapter). Click Edit to edit a script file or Browse to select an existing file.
Networking	Type of dial-up server I am calling	Specifies the type of account; all ISPs now provide PPP. Your other choice is SLIP. Click Settings to display the PPP Settings dialog box, in which you can choose: whether to use LCP (Link Control Protocol) extensions, which are not supported by older PPP accounts; whether to enable software compression, which enable most PPP accounts to speed up throughput; and whether to use *multilink* negotiation (that is, use multiple phone lines for the connection if they are available).
Networking	Components checked are used by this connection	Specifies how to communicate over the network. Most connections use TCP/IP and QoS Packet Scheduler. See Chapter 29 for information about other protocols.
Advanced	Protect my computer and network by limiting or preventing access to this computer from the Internet	Specifies whether to use the Internet Connection Firewall when connected (see "Enabling the Internet Connection Firewall Between Your PC and the Internet" later in this chapter). We recommend that you select this option unless you have another firewall or the connection is to another computer on a LAN.
Advanced	Allow other network users to connect through this computer's Internet connection	Specifies whether to run Internet Connection Sharing on this PC, allowing other computers on the LAN to access the Internet through your connection (see Chapter 31).

Table 22-1.   *Settings for a Dial-Up Connection* (continued)

You can set a few more items by clicking the Configure button on the General tab of the Properties dialog box for the connection: you see the Modem Configuration dialog box. Most of the settings on this dialog box are the same as the settings in the modem's

Properties dialog box (see Chapter 21, section "Modem Configuration Settings").
One is not: the Show Terminal Window setting specifies whether Windows displays
a terminal window before dialing, to enable you to type modem commands.

 *Make sure that file and printer sharing are not enabled for your Internet connection,
unless you want to allow everyone on the Internet to access the files on your computer.
On the Networking tab of the Properties dialog box for your Internet connection, make
sure that the check boxes are not selected for these two components:*

- *File And Printer Sharing For Microsoft Networks*
- *Client For Microsoft Networks*

Configuring a TCP/IP Connection

For a connection to an Internet account, you may also need to configure the TCP/IP
protocol. On the Properties dialog box for the connection, click the Networking tab,
select Internet Protocol (TCP/IP) in the list of components, and then click the
Properties button. You see the Internet Protocol (TCP/IP) Properties dialog box,
shown in Figure 22-5.

When your computer is connected to the Internet using TCP/IP, it has its own
IP address (*IP* is the acronym for Internet Protocol). An IP address is in the form of
xxx.xxx.xxx.xxx, where each *xxx* is a number from 0 to 255. (That is, an IP address
consists of four eight-bit numbers.) An example of an IP address might be 204.71.16.253.

In addition to IP addresses, computers on the Internet have *domain names*, alpha-
numeric names like **www.microsoft.com** or **net.gurus.com**. A *domain name server* or
DNS is a computer on the Internet that translates between domain names and numeric
IP addresses. Your ISP usually provides two DNS servers to share the load.

On the Internet Protocol (TCP/IP) Properties dialog box, make these entries:

- **Your IP address**   Almost all ISPs assign you a temporary IP address when you
  connect, so choose Obtain An IP Address Automatically. If your ISP has given
  you a static IP address (unlikely) enter it here.

- **DNS Server Address**   If you have a PPP account, choose Obtain DNS Server
  Address Automatically unless your ISP tells you otherwise.

 *For more settings, click the Advanced button to see the Advanced TCP/IP Settings
dialog box. Few ISPs require you to change these settings.*

Creating and Using Logon Scripts

Nearly all ISPs use one of a few standardized logon sequences known as PAP
(Password Authentication Protocol) or CHAP (Challenge Handshake Authentication
Protocol). If your ISP is one of the few that doesn't, Windows can use *logon scripts* to

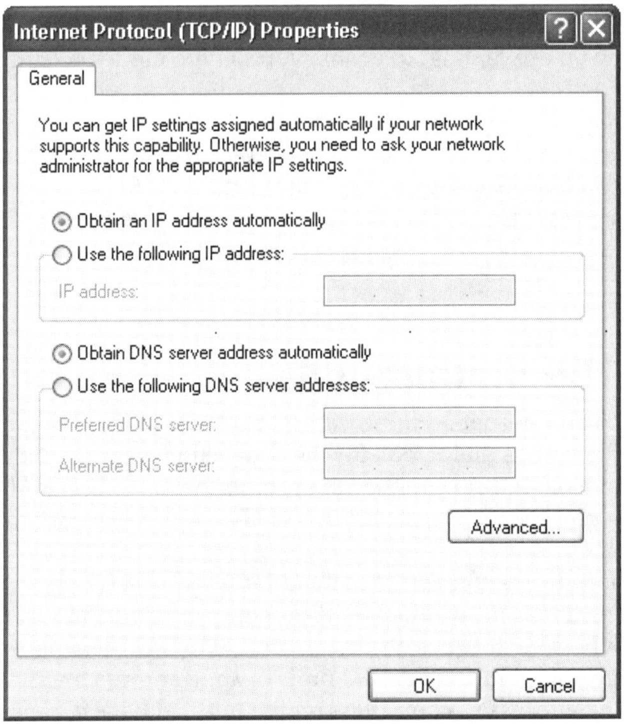

Figure 22-5.   *Configuring the TCP/IP settings for a connection*

automate the sequence of sending logon information to the ISP. If your ISP requires a logon script, they should be able to provide you with one that works. If not, Windows comes with a set of well-commented sample scripts that explain the scripting system. Customizing one of the sample scripts is usually easier than writing your own from scratch. These sample scripts are stored in C:\Program Files\Accessories (assuming that Windows is installed on C:) with the extension .scp.

Setting Additional Dial-Up Options

You might think all the properties of a dial-up connection would appear on the connection's Properties dialog box (shown earlier in the chapter in Figure 22-4), but they don't. Most of the settings on the (ill-named) Internet Properties dialog box pertain to the Internet Explorer browser, rather than to your Internet connection, but a few additional settings appear on its Connections tab. (This dialog box is called Internet Options when you display it by choosing Tools | Internet Options from Internet Explorer.)

To display the Internet Properties dialog box, choose Start | Control Panel | Network And Internet Connections and run the Internet Options program. Figure 22-6 shows the Connections tab of the Internet Properties (or Internet Options) dialog box. The other tabs of this dialog box apply to using Internet Explorer, and are covered in Chapter 24. Most of the settings on the Connections tab control your Internet connection:

- **Dial-up settings** Lists your dial-up connections, so you can enable those to use, disable those not to use, configure them, and set the default connection.

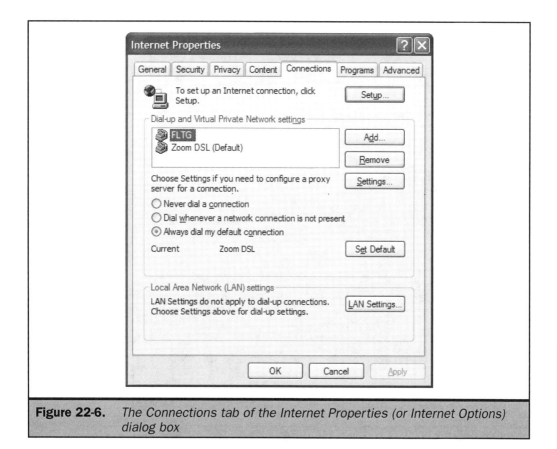

Figure 22-6.   *The Connections tab of the Internet Properties (or Internet Options) dialog box*

- ■ **Never dial a connection, Dial whenever a network connection is not present, and Always dial my default connection**   Specify what Windows does when a program tries to connect to the Internet (for example, an e-mail program tries to connect to a mail server, or a browser tries to retrieve a web page) and there's no connection active.

- ■ **Current default**   Displays the name of the connection Windows uses unless you specify another connection. To change the default, select a connection from the Dial-Up Settings list and click the Set Default button.

Click the Setup or Add button to create a new connection: both buttons run the New Connection Wizard, but you see a different series of screens (it looks like two slightly different Wizards with the same name!). The Settings button displays a Settings dialog box (shown in Figure 22-7) that contains settings for the selected connection: you

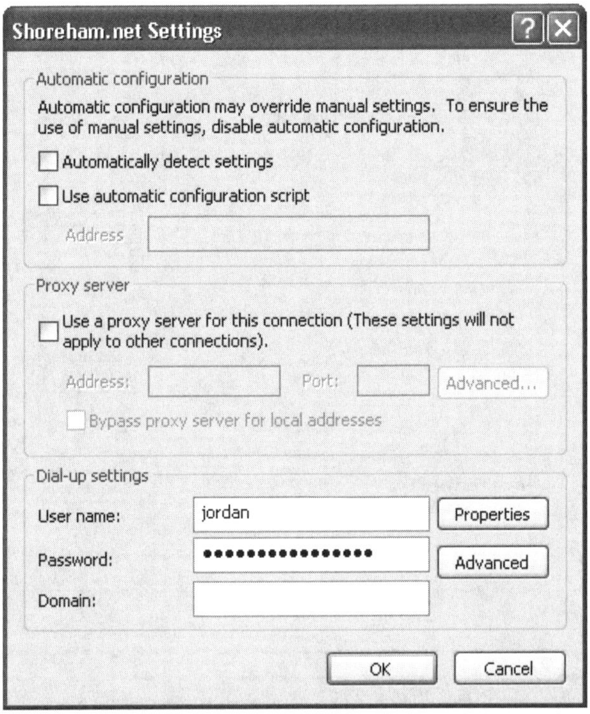

Figure 22-7.   *Settings dialog box for a dial-up connection*

see the same settings that appear on the Properties dialog box for the connection, but arranged differently. A few items on the Settings dialog box pertain to connecting to the Internet over a LAN. The LAN Settings button displays the LAN Settings dialog box, which also contains LAN-related settings (see Chapter 31, section "ICS Server Configuration Details").

Renaming, Copying, or Deleting a Network Connection

You can rename a network connection by right-clicking the connection and choosing Rename from the menu that appears. This action changes the name that appears on your computer for the connection; it doesn't change any of the information sent to the ISP.

Sometimes you want two or more versions of the same dial-up connection. For example, you might dial into your ISP from different numbers depending on where you take your laptop. To copy a connection, right-click its icon in the Network Connections window and choose Create Copy. A new icon appears. Rename the new copy and change its settings by right-clicking it and choosing Properties.

If you don't expect to connect to a particular account in the future, delete its connection from the Network Connections window by selecting the icon for the connection and pressing DELETE (or right-click the connection icon and choose Delete). Be sure you also delete any shortcuts to the connection.

Other Dial-Up Connection Settings

Two other settings are available for dial-up connections, although not usually used for regular Internet accounts:

- **Autodial**   Windows automatically dials an Internet connection if you are not connected to the Internet and you ask for Internet information (for example, you run your browser or e-mail program, or click a web address in a document). You can turn autodial off, or control which dialing locations it works from, by choosing Advanced | Dial-Up Preferences from the Network Connections window menu bar. Click the Autodial tab if it's not already selected, and choose which dialing locations from which you want Windows to autodial.

- **Callback**   Some Internet hosts offer to call you back to continue the connection. Callbacks ensure that you are who you say you are (or at least that you are at the phone number that you're supposed to be at). If an Internet host offers to call you back, Windows usually displays a dialog box that asks whether you want to do so, but you can configure how Windows responds to the offer. Choose Advanced | Dial-Up Preferences from the Network Connections window menu bar and click the Callback tab.

Streamlining Your Internet Connection

Your Internet connection uses TCP/IP, not NetBEUI (Microsoft's file- and printer-sharing protocol) or IPX/SPX (Netware's protocol). You can speed up the process of connecting to your ISP, and make sure that your computer isn't open to intruders, by following these steps:

1. Display the Network Connections window.

2. Right-click the connection you use to connect to your ISP. Choose Properties from the shortcut menu that appears. You see the Properties dialog box for the connection.

3. Click the Networking tab. If NetBEUI or IPX/SPX appear among the installed components, make sure that their check boxes are cleared.

4. On the Networking tab, deselect the File And Printer Sharing For Microsoft Networks check box and the Client For Microsoft Networks check box. These are not needed (or wanted!) on dial-up Internet connections.

5. Click the Options tab. Deselect the Include Windows Logon Domain check box, unless your computer is on a domain-based LAN (check with your LAN administrator).

6. Click OK.

7. Connect to your ISP to make sure that changing these settings doesn't prevent you from connecting. (If so, repeat the steps and reverse your changes.)

Connecting to Your Internet Account

You can tell Windows to connect to your Internet account automatically when a program asks for information from the Internet, or you can tell Windows when to connect.

Some Internet connections, such as LAN connections and many DSL and cable Internet connections, are connected all the time, so you don't need to connect— you're online all the time.

Dialing the Internet Automatically

What happens if you aren't connected to the Internet and you tell your e-mail program to fetch your mail, or you ask your browser to display a web page? Windows usually tries to dial up and connect to your Internet account automatically when you request Internet-based information.

To set Windows to connect automatically, follow these steps:

1. Choose Start | Control Panel | Network And Internet Connections | Internet Options (or choose Tools | Internet Options from Internet Explorer) to display the Internet Properties (or Internet Options) dialog box, shown earlier in this chapter in Figure 22-6.

2. Click the Connections tab and make sure the Always Dial My Default Connection setting is selected. (If your computer is sometimes connected to the Internet over a LAN, choose Dial Whenever A Network Connection Is Not Present instead.)

3. Click the dial-up connection you want to use and then click the Set Default button to make this connection the one Windows will use.

4. With the dial-up connection still selected, click Settings to display the settings dialog box for the connection (see Figure 22-7 earlier in this chapter).

5. In the Dial-Up Settings part of the dialog box, type your user name and password.

6. Click the Advanced button to display the Advanced Dial-Up dialog box, shown here:

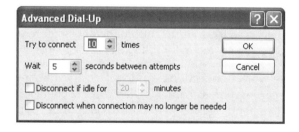

7. Set the number of times to try to connect, how long to wait between dialing attempts, whether to disconnect if the Internet connection has been idle, and whether to disconnect when the program that originally triggered the connection exits.

8. Click OK to dismiss the Advanced Dial-Up dialog box and OK again to dismiss the Internet Properties dialog box.

When you use an Internet program and Windows detects you are asking for information from the Internet, Windows dials your default connection. You don't see anything at all if you have configured the connection not to display the progress of the connection (using the Display Progress While Connecting check box on the Options tab of the Properties dialog box). If the connection is configured to display its progress, you see this Connecting dialog box, which displays the progress of your connection:

The dialog box displays messages as it dials, connects, and logs in to your Internet account using the information in the Dial-Up Settings dialog box.

Automatically dialing the Internet can be annoying, too. For example, if you are reading your e-mail offline and open a message that contains a link to the Web, you might not want your computer to dial into the Internet. If you no longer want Windows to connect automatically to the Internet, display the Internet Properties (or Internet Options) dialog box, click the Connections tab, and click the Never Dial A Connection option.

Dialing the Internet Manually

Usually, Windows connects to the Internet automatically (as described in the preceding section). However, you can also dial in by following these steps:

1. Display the Network Connections window (see "Displaying Network Connections" earlier in this chapter). Then run the connection icon (click or double-click it, depending on how Windows is configured). If a connection icon appears on your desktop, you can run it instead. You see the Connect dialog box, shown in Figure 22-8.

   If the user name, password, or phone number doesn't appear, fill it in. (See "Configuring Windows for Dialing Locations" in Chapter 21 for instructions on how to set up dialing locations, if you use a laptop computer in more than one location.)

3. Unless you are worried about someone else using your computer to connect to your account, select the Save This User Name And Password For The Following Users check box so you needn't type your password each time you connect. Choose whether Windows saves this information only for when you are logged in to the computer or for all user accounts (see Chapter 6).

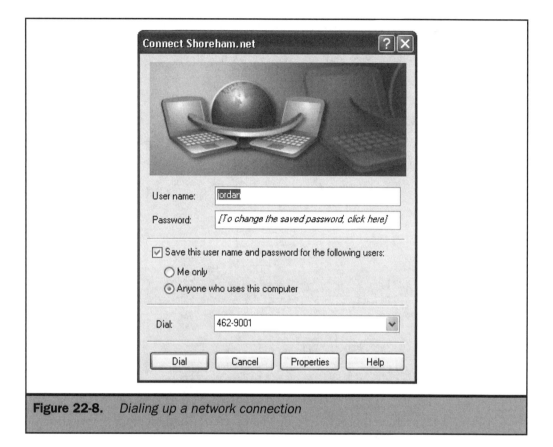

Figure 22-8. *Dialing up a network connection*

4. Click the Dial button. Windows dials your account and logs in. You may see a window telling you that you're connected to the account. If your modem has a speaker, you should hear the progress of the call as it dials and connects.

If you see a window confirming that you are connected, click the Do Not Display This Message In The Future check box, so you needn't see this confirmation dialog box each time you connect to the Internet.

5. Click the Close button.

While you are connected, the dial-up connection icon—two overlapping computer screens—may appear in the notification area at the right end of the taskbar. (It appears if you have selected the Show Icon In Notification Area When Connected check box on the General tab of the Properties dialog box for the connection.) Move the mouse pointer to the icon (without clicking) to see the name of the connection, your connection speed, and how many bytes have been sent and received. Click the icon to see more details, as shown here:

Click the Details tab on the status dialog box to see the modem name, connection type, IP address, and other information.

If you need to make an operator-assisted call to connect to the Internet (for example, from a hotel phone), choose Advanced / Operator-Assisted Dialing from the menu in the Network Connections window. Open (click or double-click) the connection as usual, pick up the phone, and talk to the operator as necessary. Click Dial on the Connect dialog box when you are done. Don't hang up the phone until you hear the ISP and your modem exchange tones. Choose Advanced / Operator-Assisted Dialing again to turn off this feature.

Disconnecting Manually or Automatically

When you are done using the Internet, you can disconnect. Or you can configure Windows to disconnect automatically when the connection isn't being used.

You can disconnect your Internet connection in several ways:

- If a dial-up connection icon appears in the notification area of the taskbar, right-click it and choose Disconnect from the menu that appears.

- Click the dial-up connection icon in the notification area to display the status dialog box for the connection and click the Disconnect button.

- Choose Start | Connect To and choose the dial-up connection to display its status dialog box. Click Disconnect.

If you are connected to your Internet account and don't use it for a while (usually 20 minutes), Windows or your ISP may disconnect you automatically. You may see a dialog box asking whether you want to disconnect. You can't control whether your ISP hangs up on your after a period of inactivity, but you can configure Windows whether and when to disconnect. Follow these steps:

1. Choose Start | Control Panel | Network And Internet Connections | Internet Options (or choose Tools | Internet Options from Internet Explorer) to display the Internet Properties (or Internet Options) dialog box, shown earlier in this chapter in Figure 22-6.

2. Click the Connections tab.

3. Click the dial-up connection for which you want to configure auto-disconnection and click the Settings button. You see the settings dialog box for the connection.

4. Click the Advanced button to display the Advanced Dial-Up dialog box.

5. To tell Windows to hang up after a specific time during which no information is transmitted, select the Disconnect If Idle For *xx* Minutes check box and set the number of minutes.

6. To tell Windows to hang up when no Internet programs are running, select the Disconnect When Connection May No Longer Be Needed check box.

7. Click OK three times to dismiss all the dialog boxes.

Enabling the Internet Connection Firewall Between Your PC and the Internet

A *firewall* is a program that stands between your computer (or your LAN) and the Internet. Each packet on the Internet is addressed to a specific *port number* on a specific computer. Each computer connected to the Internet "listens" to packets addressed only to certain ports. As a general rule, most computers use only a few ports for incoming connections: 21 (for FTP, or file transfer), 25 (for outgoing e-mail), 80 (for web pages), 110 (for incoming email), 119 (for newsgroup messages), and sometimes 443 (for secure web connections).

The Internet Connection Firewall (ICF) comes with Windows XP and controls what ports are open, refusing to respond to packets addressed to other ports.

 Don't enable the Internet Connection Firewall on connections within your local area network, because it will block file and printer sharing.

Turning On the Internet Firewall

We recommend that you enable the Internet Connection Firewall on all your Internet connections to the outside world, unless you have another firewall between you and the Internet. Follow these steps:

1. Open the Network Connections window (choose Start | Control Panel | Network And Internet Connections | Network Connections).

2. Right-click the Internet connection and select Properties. You see the Properties dialog box for the Internet connection.

3. Click the Advanced tab. You see the Internet Connection Firewall and Internet Connection Sharing settings.

4. Select the Protect My Computer And Network By Limiting Or Preventing Access To This Computer From The Network check box.

5. Click OK to put the changes into effect.

 ICF may block using FTP to transfer files. If you use FTP and can't transfer files using Internet Explorer after enabling ICF, run Internet Explorer, choose Tools | Internet Options, click the Advanced tab, and select the Use Passive FTP check box in the Browsing section of the settings.

Configuring the Ports on Your Firewall

If you run servers on your computer, you'll have to adjust the firewall to permit connections to the servers. Return to the Advanced tab in step 3 in the previous section, and click the Settings button to open the Advanced Settings window, shown in Figure 22-9. If your service is in the lists of popular services, select it and click OK in the window that pops up, checking to be sure you have the correct service. If your service is not in the list, click Add and enter the name of the service and its port number in the pop-up window.

Tip *Once you have enabled the Internet Connection Firewall, go to Steve Gibson's web site at **grc.com**, click the link to his Shields Up free firewall-testing service, and follow the directions on the web page. Shields Up can tell you whether the firewall is working correctly.*

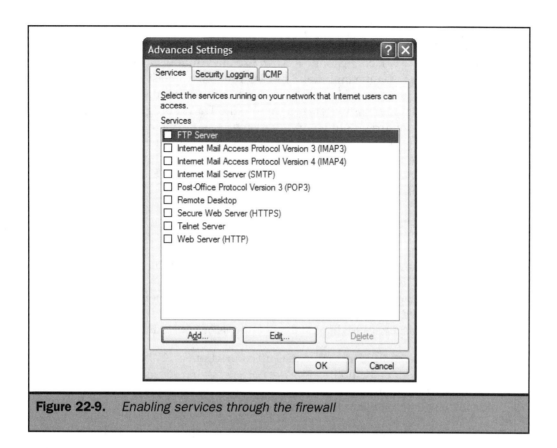

Figure 22-9. *Enabling services through the firewall*

If your home or office contains a LAN that is connected to the Internet, the entire LAN needs a firewall between it and the Internet. The computers on the LAN don't need firewalls within the LAN—the Internet Connection Firewall blocks file and printer sharing on a LAN. See Chapter 31 for details.

Other Firewalls

We recommend that if you have no other firewall, you enable Internet Connection Firewall. If you are connecting a LAN to the Internet, the router may include a firewall (see Chapter 31).

Many other firewall programs are available, with features that ICF doesn't have, like monitoring both incoming and outgoing packets and displaying an alarm when packets are discarded. Zone Alarm (**www.zonelabs.com**) has a free version you can download. Outpost Firewall (**www.agnitum.com**) also blocks banner and pop-up ads.

Testing Your Connection

After dialing up a network connection, you can use the Windows Ipconfig command to find out the IP address of your computer. The Ping program can test whether packets of information can make the round trip from your computer, out over the Internet to another computer, and back to your computer. You can use the Tracert program to trace the route packets take to get from your computer to another computer, and you can use the Netstat program to find out to which computers your computer is talking.

Some of these commands are usually run from the Command Prompt window (see Chapter 4). Open a Command Prompt window by choosing Start | All Programs | Accessories | Command Prompt.

Displaying Your IP Address

Your computer can have more than one IP address at the same time: each network connection can have a separate IP address. For example, your computer can have the address 204.135.25.67 on the Internet (via a dial-up, cable, or DSL account, assigned by your ISP) and the address 192.168.0.1 on your LAN (see Chapter 27 for how IP addresses are assigned on the LAN).

There are three easy ways to display the IP address of your Internet connection:

- **Dial-up connection icon**   For a dial-up connection, click the dial-up connection icon on the notification area of the taskbar (described earlier in this chapter, in the section "Dialing the Internet Manually"). In the status dialog box that appears, click the Details tab, as shown in Figure 22-10.

- **View Status Of This Connection**   For all connections, display the Network Connections window (shown in Figure 22-2 earlier in this chapter). Select the connection and click View Status Of This Connection in the Network Tasks section of the Task pane. You see the status dialog box for the connection. For dial-up connections, click the Details tab (shown in Figure 22-10). For LAN connections, click the Support tab.

- **Ipconfig program**   The Ipconfig program displays information about your TCP/IP connection. To run Ipconfig, open a Command Prompt window by choosing Start | All Programs | Accessories | Command Prompt. Type **ipconfig** and press ENTER. You see a listing of your network connections that communicate using TCP/IP (including dial-up Internet connections, DSL and cable Internet connections, and most LAN connections), like this:

```
Windows IP Configuration

Ethernet adapter Local Area Connection:
```

```
        Connection-specific DNS Suffix  . :
        IP Address. . . . . . . . . . . : 192.168.0.1
        Subnet Mask . . . . . . . . . . : 255.255.255.0
        Default Gateway . . . . . . . . :

PPP adapter Shoreham.net:

        Connection-specific DNS Suffix  . :
        IP Address. . . . . . . . . . . : 208.144.253.8
        Subnet Mask . . . . . . . . . . : 255.255.255.255
        Default Gateway . . . . . . . . : 208.144.253.8
```

The IP address of your Internet connection is likely to change each time you connect to your ISP because most ISPs assign IP addresses dynamically.

Testing Communication with Another Computer by Using Ping

Sending a small text packet on a round-trip is called *pinging*, and you can use Windows' built-in Ping program to send one. (Think of old submarine movies, with the sonar

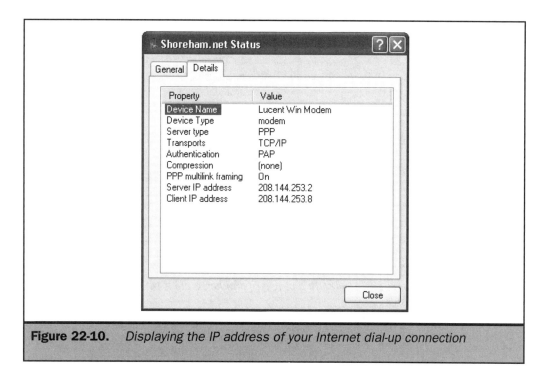

Figure 22-10.   *Displaying the IP address of your Internet dial-up connection*

pinging in the background. Some people imagine one computer sending a "ping" and the other replying "pong.") To run Ping, open a Command Prompt window by choosing Start | All Programs | Accessories | Command Prompt, and then type the Ping command, as follows:

```
ping system
```

Replace *system* with either the numeric IP address or the host name of the computer you want to ping. Choose any Internet host computer that you're sure is online, such as your ISP's mail server. Then press ENTER.

*To see a listing of all the command-line options for the Ping program, type **ping /?** at the DOS prompt.*

For example, you can ping the Internet Gurus' host computer by typing

```
ping net.gurus.com
```

Ping sends out four test packets (pings) and reports how long the packets take to get to Yahoo and back to yours, like this:

```
Pinging net.gurus.com ]208.31.42.79] with 32 bytes of data:

Reply from 208.31.42.79: bytes=32 time=204ms TTL=248
Reply from 208.31.42.79: bytes=32 time=220ms TTL=248
Reply from 208.31.42.79: bytes=32 time=200ms TTL=248
Reply from 208.31.42.79: bytes=32 time=210ms TTL=248

Ping statistics for 208.31.42.79:
    Packets: Sent = 4, Received = 4, Lost = 0 (0% loss),
Approximate round trip times in milli-seconds:
    Minimum = 200ms, Maximum = 220ms, Average = 208ms
```

For each packet, you see both how long the round-trip takes in milliseconds and summary information about all four packets' trips. If ping doesn't receive the response it is waiting for within a time limit, you see an error message. It's OK for it to report a few lost packets when pinging a distant system.

If one system doesn't respond with a ping, try another. Not all Internet servers respond to pings.

Ping has a number of options (we've omitted some arcane options that are rarely used):

Option	Description
-a	Reports numeric addresses rather than host names.
-f	Specifies that packets contain a Do Not Fragment flag, so packets aren't fragmented en route. (Useful to test very slow dial-up connections.)
-i *ttl*	Specifies the *Time To Live* for the packets (how many times the packet can be passed from one computer to another while in transit on the network).
-n *n*	Specifies to send *n* pings. (The default is four.)
-r *n*	Specifies the outgoing and returning packets should record the first *n* hosts on the route they take, using the Return Route field; *n* is a number from 1 to 9.
-t	Specifies to continue pinging until you interrupt it. (Otherwise, it pings four times.)
-w *n*	Specifies a time-out of *n* milliseconds for each packet.

Tip *First try Ping with a numeric IP address (for example, 216.32.74.50 for a Yahoo web server, or 208.31.42.79 for our web server), to see whether packets get out to the Internet and back. Then try Ping with a host name, to see whether you successfully contact your DNS to convert the name into an IP address. If the first test works and the second doesn't (failing with an "Unable to resolve target system name" error), your connection isn't set up properly to contact a DNS.*

Tracing Packets over the Internet

Packets of information don't usually go directly from one computer to another computer over the Internet. Instead, they are involved in a huge game of "whisper-down-the-lane," in which packets are passed from computer to computer until they reach their destination. If your data seems to be moving slowly, you can use the Tracert (short for *trace route*) program to follow your packets across the Internet, from your computer to an Internet host you frequently use. The technique Tracert uses doesn't always work, so it's quite possible running Tracert to a remote computer can fail, even though the computer is working and accessible.

If Ping returns errors, it's likely that Tracert will return an error in reaching the destination server, too. But the servers along the way should respond, and you can see where communication breaks down.

To run Tracert, open a Command Prompt window by choosing Start | All Programs | Accessories | Command Prompt. Then type the Tracert command:

```
tracert system
```

Replace *system* with either the numeric IP address or the Internet name of the computer to which you want to trace the route. Then press ENTER.

 *To see a listing of all the command-line options for the Tracert program, type **tracert** at the DOS prompt, with no address.*

For example, you can trace the route of packets from your computer to the Internet Gurus host at **net.gurus.com** by typing

```
tracert net.gurus.com
```

You see a listing like this:

```
Tracing route to net.gurus.com ]208.31.42.79]
over a maximum of 30 hops:

  1    *        *        *      Request timed out.
  2   148 ms   149 ms   139 ms  rtr.shoreham.net ]208.144.253.1]
  3   149 ms   149 ms   149 ms  shoreham253.greenmountainaccess.net ]208.144.253.253]
  4   149 ms   139 ms   149 ms  richmond-1.greenmountainaccess.net ]208.144.252.13]
  5   190 ms   179 ms   189 ms  sl-gw20-nyc-6-1-0-TS8.sprintlink.net ]160.81.215.241]
  6   216 ms   189 ms   229 ms  sl-finlak-7-0.sprintlink.net ]160.81.228.18]
  7   220 ms   199 ms   219 ms  208.31.47.5
  8   229 ms   199 ms   209 ms  net.gurus.com ]208.31.42.79]

Trace complete.
```

The listing shows the route the packets took from your computer to the specified host (sometimes Tracert reports a different host name from the one you specified, which means the host has more than one name). For each hop (stage of the route),

Tracert sends out three packets and reports the time each packet took to reach that far. It also reports the name and numeric IP address of the host. The time is reported in milliseconds, 1/1000 sec. On a LAN, the times should be under 5ms, while the time to a distant system can normally be up to 500 ms.

Here are the options you can use with the Tracert program (type them before the host name or address). A few other arcane options are not listed:

Option	Description
-d	Specifies not to resolve addresses to host names, so the resulting list of hosts consists only of numeric IP addresses
-h n	Specifies a maximum number of n hops to trace before giving up
-w n	Specifies that the program wait n milliseconds for each reply before giving up

Displaying Internet Connections Using Netstat

Netstat is a network diagnostic program you can use for any TCP/IP connection—Internet connections or LANs. You can run Netstat to see which computers your computer is connected to over the Internet—not the ISP to which you dial in, but other Internet hosts to or from which you are transferring information.

To run Netstat, open a Command Prompt window by choosing Start | All Programs | Accessories | Command Prompt (see Chapter 4). Then type the following:

```
netstat
```

When you press ENTER, you see a listing of the TCP/IP connections currently or recently running, like this:

```
Active Connections

Proto   Local Address         Foreign Address          State
TCP     inspiron7000:4683     ftp1.us.dell.com:ftp     ESTABLISHED
TCP     inspiron7000:4684     wx.iecc.com:pop3          SYN_SENT
TCP     inspiron7000:4687     pop.vip.sc5.yahoo.com:pop3   TIME_WAIT
TCP     inspiron7000:4689     smtp.america.net:smtp    ESTABLISHED
TCP     inspiron7000:4690     books.iecc.com:http       SYN_SENT
TCP     inspiron7000:4431     msgr-ns9.msgr.hotmail.com:1863
ESTABLISHED
```

This listing shows that the computer is connected to other computers for receiving web pages (the 80 or http at the end of the address signifies the port commonly used for web page retrieval), for file transfer (ftp), for sending mail (smtp), for receiving mail (pop3), and for instant messaging.

 *To see a listing of all the command-line options for the Netstat program, type **netstat /?** at the DOS prompt.*

The Complete Reference

Chapter 23

E-Mail and Newsgroups Using Outlook Express

Windows XP comes with Outlook Express 6, Microsoft's free e-mail and newsreading program. You can also install and use any number of mail and newsreading applications, whether they are Microsoft products or not.

Outlook Express is not the same program as Outlook, the e-mail program that comes with Microsoft Office. If you want to use the Exchange Server calendar system, you have to use Outlook, not Outlook Express.

This chapter describes how to use Outlook Express to send and receive e-mail messages, organize the messages you decide to keep, and read and post messages to Usenet newsgroups. If you correspond with people whose software can read messages written in HTML (the language in which web pages are written), you can compose HTML messages using Outlook Express. This chapter also describes how to use the Windows XP Address Book, either with or without Outlook Express.

*If you'd like to test your e-mail program, get news about updates to this book, or just say "Hi" to the authors, send a message to **winxphometcr@gurus.com** (our mail robot will send an automatic response, and we read all our messages).*

Is Outlook Express Safe?

If you are a happy user of Eudora, Netscape Messenger, or another e-mail program, Outlook Express doesn't contain any gotta-have features that would make you want to switch. The hassle of importing your messages (which never seem to come through perfectly) isn't worth it. However, if you are a new user who doesn't have a lot of message files, or if you have used other e-mail programs and have been unhappy with them, Outlook Express is worth a try.

The case for using Outlook Express gets a little better with each new version. Outlook Express has a number of advantages: It's free, already installed, and easy to use; it has a nice collection of features for handling e-mail and newsgroups; it lets you import messages and addresses from most other popular e-mail programs; and it works well with Hotmail, Microsoft's free web-based e-mail provider.

In the past, the main reason not to use Outlook Express was security. Outlook Express 6 includes some new features for handling attachments safely and avoiding spreading e-mail viruses to others. These features help resolve Outlook Express's most obvious security problems. However, the sheer popularity and ubiquity of Outlook Express (along with its cousin Outlook, which is part of Microsoft Office) makes it an inviting target for hackers. The people who write viruses (like the people who write any other kind of software) want to write for the largest possible market, so they target Microsoft products. And the problem is exacerbated by Microsoft itself, which has historically taken a lax attitude toward security. (Recently Microsoft's management has been giving security a higher priority, but it is too soon to tell what the ultimate effects of this change will be.)

*Our favorite e-mail program, Eudora, is available at **www.eudora.com**. If you use Netscape Navigator or Mozilla as your web browser, you may want to use its corresponding e-mail programs, Netscape Messenger and Mozilla Mail. See Netscape's web site at **home.netscape.com/products** or Mozilla's web site **www.mozilla.org**. Other popular programs you might try are Pegasus (**www.pmail.com**), The Bat (**www.ritlabs.com/the_bat**), and Becky (**www.rimarts.co.jp/becky.htm**). Agent (**www.forteinc.com/agent**) is primarily a newsreader, but a competent e-mail program, too. If you want to handle your mail without using your mouse any more than minimally necessary, consider PC Pine (**www.washington.edu/pine**).*

Microsoft's antitrust agreement with the U.S. Government makes it possible for computer manufacturers to set up their machines with a *default e-mail program* (the program that runs when another program tells Windows that you want to send e-mail) other than Outlook Express and hide Outlook Express, but so far we know of no manufacturers who plan to do so. Unless you've installed another e-mail program, Outlook Express is probably your default e-mail program. When you install another e-mail program, its installation program usually asks whether to make it the default e-mail program. If you plan to use it regularly to send and receive e-mail, choose Yes. If Outlook Express isn't your default, all you have to do is run it from the Start | All Programs menu. The first thing it will do is ask you if you want it to be the default.

 *For news and tips about Outlook Express, check out Tom Koch's web site at **www.tomsterdam.com/insideOE**.*

E-Mail Addresses, Servers, and Headers

Oversimplifying somewhat, e-mail addresses and servers work like this:

1. Using an e-mail program, such as Outlook Express, the sender creates a message and decides who the recipients should be.

2. The sender lists the e-mail addresses of all the recipients. (The sender can specify a long list of recipients, but for simplicity, we'll pretend there is only one.) The e-mail address specifies two things: a computer on the Internet on which a recipient receives mail (called an *incoming mail server*), and the name that the incoming mail server uses to designate the mailbox of the recipient. So, for example, the e-mail address **president@whitehouse.gov** specifies the incoming mail server whitehouse.gov and a mailbox on whitehouse.gov called president.

3. The sender connects to an *outgoing mail server*, a computer connected to the Internet (usually a computer owned by the sender's Internet service provider) that runs a mail-handling program that supports *SMTP* (Simple Mail Transfer Protocol), which is used for Internet mail. These servers are usually called *SMTP servers*. The message is sent from the sender's computer to the outgoing mail server.

4. From the outgoing mail server, the message is passed across the Internet to the recipient's incoming mail server.

5. The recipient's incoming mail server files the message in the recipient's *mailbox*, a file or folder containing all the messages that the recipient hasn't downloaded to her own computer yet.

6. Using an e-mail program (which need not be the same as the one the sender used to create and send the message), the recipient looks for new mail by logging in to the incoming mail server. Incoming mail servers use one of three protocols for receiving mail: *Post Office Protocol 3* (abbreviated *POP3* or *POP*), *Internet Message Access Protocol (IMAP)*, or *Hypertext Transfer Protocol (HTTP)*. The incoming mail server uses POP, IMAP, or HTTP to deliver the message to the recipient's computer, along with any other messages that may have arrived since the recipient last checked for mail.

7. The recipient uses the e-mail program to read the message.

Every e-mail message consists of a *header* (lines containing the address, the return address, the date, and other information about the message) and a *body* (the text of the message).

To send messages right away to people who are logged in at the same time you are, and receive answers in seconds, use an instant messaging program like Windows Messenger (see Chapter 25, section "Chatting Online with Windows Messenger").

Microsoft's Hotmail Service

Hotmail (at **www.hotmail.com**) is Microsoft's web-based e-mail service—an e-mail service that you can access with your browser rather than with your e-mail program. After you identify yourself by giving a user name and a password, the Hotmail web site shows you your messages and allows you to send e-mail to other people. A Hotmail account is set up for you automatically if you get a .NET Passport, and the e-mail component of MSN Explorer also works through Hotmail. Many other free web-based accounts are available: the most popular alternative to Hotmail is Yahoo Mail, at **mail.yahoo.com**.

Web-based e-mail accounts are handy to use when you are on the road, because the messages are stored on a web server, rather than on the computer you are using. You can use a web-based e-mail account from many different computers and not worry about transferring files from one to the next. The disadvantage of having your messages on the web server, however, is that you can't read your messages offline. When you read your Hotmail messages with a web browser, messages remain on the Hotmail web server until you delete them; with POP mailboxes, messages are usually deleted from the mail server as soon as you download them to your computer.

Microsoft has gotten around this difficulty by designing Outlook Express to work neatly with Hotmail. You can easily set up Outlook Express on the computer you usually use so that it downloads and stores messages from your Hotmail account automatically (as it would from a non-web-based e-mail account). But when you access your Hotmail account from any other computer via a browser, the messages are stored on the web server until the next time you sign in from your usual computer using Outlook Express. See "Setting Up Your Accounts" later in this chapter.

Configuring Outlook Express

When you run Outlook Express for the first time (Start | All Programs | Outlook Express, or Start | E-mail if Outlook Express is your default mail program), you may be greeted with a dialog box asking if Outlook Express should be your default e-mail client (the program Windows launches when you give a command to send mail from some other application, such as your browser). If you intend to choose No, uncheck the Always Perform This Check When Starting Outlook Express check box so that you are not nagged.

The New Connection Wizard may start to help you set up a mail and/or newsreader account (see Chapter 22, section "Running the New Connection Wizard"). If you choose to set up your accounts right away (you can always do it later), skip to "Setting Up Your Accounts" later in this chapter. Otherwise click Cancel, click Yes when the verification box asks if you are sure, and then the Outlook Express window appears, as shown in Figure 23-1.

The Outlook Express Window

The Outlook Express window resembles an Explorer window. Below the toolbar, the window is divided into three panes. The right pane contains links that you can click to do the things that the text describes, such as set up a newsgroup account or create a new mail message. The upper-left pane is a folder list, similar to the Folder Explorer Bar described in Chapter 7. Outlook Express is at the top of the list and is highlighted, indicating that it corresponds to what is currently shown in the right pane.

The folders in the Local Folders section of the folder list are necessary parts of the mail system:

- **Inbox**   Where Outlook Express puts the messages that it downloads from your incoming mail server. The messages remain there until you delete them or move them to another folder.

- **Outbox**   Contains the outgoing messages that you have completed and chosen to send, but have not yet been sent. You can choose to send messages immediately after you complete them, or to store in the Outbox until you decide to send them. This feature is handy if you like to compose messages offline, and then connect to the Internet later to send them.

- **Sent Items** Contains messages that you have sent. Messages remain in this folder until you delete or move them.

- **Deleted Items** Contains the messages (both incoming and outgoing) that you have deleted. Like the Recycle Bin, it is a last-chance folder that gets unwanted messages out of the way, but from which they still can be retrieved. Outlook Express can be set up to clean out the Deleted Items folder automatically, or you can delete messages from it manually (see "Saving and Filing Your Messages" later in this chapter). Outlook Express cannot retrieve messages deleted from the Deleted Items folder.

- **Drafts** Contains unfinished messages that you have chosen to save and work on later. Any time you are composing a message, you can choose File | Save to save the message in the Drafts folder.

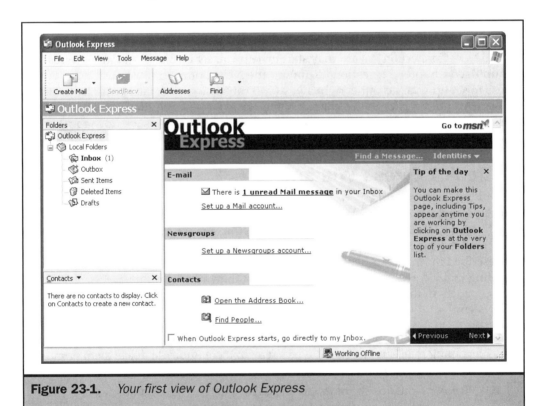

Figure 23-1. *Your first view of Outlook Express*

As you begin sending and receiving messages, you can set up other folders to keep track of your correspondence (see "Organizing Your Correspondence" later in this chapter). You don't have to do so, but if you plan to keep copies of messages, they will be easier to find if you sort them into folders by topic or by correspondent.

Setting Up Your Accounts

Before Outlook Express can send or receive mail, or allow you to interact with newsgroups, it needs to know what accounts you have and how it can access them. If you installed Windows XP as an upgrade to an earlier Windows system, any mail and news accounts that your previous version of Outlook Express knew about are preserved. Also, if you used the Files And Settings Transfer Wizard to move your settings from another computer, any mail or news accounts Outlook Express knew about on your old computer should appear on your new one (see the Appendix, section "Transferring Your Data Files and Windows Configuration Settings").

If you need to tell Outlook Express about a mail or news account, have the following information handy:

- **The name you want attached to any message you send**
- **Your return e-mail address**
- **The names of the servers your account deals with**   For an e-mail account that is not web-based, you provide two names: one server for incoming mail (a POP or IMAP server) and one server for outgoing mail (an SMTP server). (Your ISP—Internet service provider—should have given you this information—if you don't have it, check their web site or call them.) Outlook Express can deal with web-based e-mail accounts if they either offer public HTTP mail access (so far, Hotmail is the only one that does), or if they also have POP or IMAP servers. To set up a Hotmail account, choose HTTP as the incoming mail server type and then select Hotmail from the HTTP mail service provider list. Outlook Express already knows Hotmail's servers, so you don't have to enter their addresses. For a *news account* (which lets you read newsgroups), this is an NNTP server with a name like *news.serviceprovider.com* (see "Reading and Posting to Newsgroups" later in this chapter).
- **Your user name and password (if any) for logging into the servers**   This information also comes from your ISP.

To configure Outlook Express for your account, choose Tools | Accounts. When the Internet Accounts dialog box opens, click the Add button and select the type of account you want to define: mail, news, or directory service. Choose Mail for an e-mail account. Outlook Express runs the Internet Connection Wizard, which collects the necessary information about your e-mail account.

Outlook Express can handle multiple e-mail accounts. You go through the preceding process for each account you want to establish.

Identities

You can define separate *identities* to separate your various accounts. For example, you can define a work identity that contains your business e-mail and newsgroup accounts and a home identity for your personal e-mail and newsgroup activity. Or, you can define separate identities for different family members. Each identity has its own accounts and the message files of one are not visible to the others.

Creating and Removing Identities   Identities are created or destroyed from the Manage Identities dialog box. Open this box from Address Book by choosing File | Switch Identity and clicking the Manage Identities button, or from Outlook Express by selecting File | Identities | Manage Identities.

To create a new identity, click the New button in the Manage Identities dialog box. Type a name for the identity in the New Identity dialog box and click OK.

To remove an identity, select the identity from the list in the Manage Identities dialog box and click Remove.

A password prevents other household members from logging in to your accounts. To establish a password for your identity, choose File | Switch Identity, and then click the Manage Identities button in the Switch Identities dialog box. Select your identity from the Identities list in the Manage Identities dialog box and click the Properties button. Click the Require A Password box in the Identity Properties dialog box. Choose a password and type it in the Password and Confirm Password lines of the Enter Password dialog box. Click OK or Close in all the open dialog boxes.

To change the password on your identity, follow the same instructions as in the previous paragraph until you see the Identity Properties dialog box. Click the Change Password button. Enter your old and new passwords into the Change Identity Password dialog box. Type your new password a second time in the Confirm New Password line.

Switching Identities   You can tell which identity is currently logged in by looking at the right side of the folder bar in Outlook Express or at the title bar of the Address Book. To switch to a different identity, select File | Switch Identity. The Switch Identities dialog box appears, as shown here:

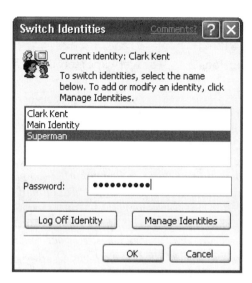

Select the identity you want to switch to, enter that identity's password (if any), and click OK.

Importing Messages from Other Mail Programs

If you've been using e-mail for a while, your message files are a valued asset. Continuity can be an important reason to stay with whatever mail program you've been using. Outlook Express 6 lets you convert your message files from these other mail programs:

- Previous versions of Outlook Express. Only Outlook Express 4 and 6 are on the list of options the Outlook Express Import Wizard gives you, but if you are importing from Outlook Express 5, don't despair—just use the Outlook Express 6 setting. If the import doesn't work, check the Outlook Express FAQ at **www.tomsterdam.com/insideOE**.

- Eudora Pro or Eudora Light, versions 1 through 3. For later versions, the import program runs but the results may be inaccurate. (When we imported messages from Eudora Pro 4.1 plain text messages appeared with HTML codes embedded. In previous versions of Outlook Express, the importation program got the messages right, but sometimes garbled the dates.)

■ Microsoft Exchange, Outlook, Internet Mail for Windows 3.1, or Windows Messaging.

■ Netscape Mail (versions 2 or 3) or Netscape Communicator.

Migrating into Outlook Express is easier than migrating out. The Outlook Express export feature only exports to other Microsoft e-mail clients. If you decide to go back to your old e-mail client later on, you'll be relying on that client's ability to import Outlook Express messages. Or, save your messages in text files by selecting the messages and choosing File | Save As in Outlook Express (you can read the messages in Notepad even if you can't import them into another e-mail program). If you plan to try Outlook Express for a few days before choosing between it and your old mail program, set Outlook Express to leave your incoming messages on your incoming mail server, and collect your mail using both programs until you make up your mind. Choose Tools | Accounts from Outlook Express' menu bar, click the Mail tab, select your e-mail account, click Properties, click the Advanced tab, and select the Leave A Copy Of Messages On Server check box. Above all, you should inspect your imported files for completeness before throwing away the originals, or just archive the originals somewhere.

To import messages from one of these mail applications, select File | Import | Messages from the menu, and then answer the questions asked by the Outlook Express Import Wizard. The wizard needs to know the application from which it is importing, and where the files are located. If your old e-mail program isn't installed, you may need to install it for the import to work (for example, if you are moving your e-mail files to a new computer). Folders of imported messages show up in the Outlook Express folder list, from which you can move them into whatever folders you like (see "Organizing Your Correspondence" later in this chapter). The imported folders retain their names and structure. For example, say you import a folder from Eudora named People At Work, with subfolders Bob and Jenny. When it arrives in Outlook Express it should still have the subfolders it contained, and those subfolders should contain all the messages they had in Eudora. (However, in our experience, subfolders don't always import correctly.)

Importing Addresses from Other Mail Programs

Outlook Express can import addresses in these formats:

■ Eudora Pro or Eudora Light address books, versions 1 through 3

■ LDIF (LDAP Data Interchange Format) directories

■ Microsoft Exchange Personal Address Book or Internet Mail for Windows 3.1 Address Books

- Netscape Address Book (from Netscape version 2 or 3) or Netscape Communicator Address Book (version 4)

- Text files created by any program, with one line per entry and fields separated by commas

If you want to import a Windows Address Book (.wab) file select File | Import | Address Book from the menu. If you are importing addresses from another program, select File | Import | Other Address Book. Then answer the questions asked by the Outlook Express Import Wizard. If all goes well, the addresses wind up in the Windows Address Book (see "Storing Addresses in the Address Book" later in this chapter).

You can import your Windows Address Book from another computer. The Files And Settings Transfer Wizard can do this automatically (see the Appendix, section "Transferring Your Data Files and Windows Configuration Settings"). But you can also find your address book (.wab) files in the folder C:\Documents And Settings\username\ Application Data\Microsoft\Address Book (replace username *with your Windows XP user name, which appears at the top of your Start menu) on the other computer. Transfer these files to your computer, and then open Address Book and select File | Import | Address Book. When the Select Address Book File To Import From window opens, browse to find the file you want to import and click Open. If the other computer is on your LAN, you can skip the step of transferring the file to your computer, and browse through the other computer's files over the LAN.*

Choosing Where Outlook Express Stores Your Message Folders

Outlook Express stores your message folders in a *message store*, which is usually C:\ Documents And Settings*username*\\Local Settings\\Application Data\\ Identities\\ *GUID*\\Microsoft\\Outlook Express, assuming that Windows is installed on drive C:. (We are not making this amazingly long pathname up.) *Username* is your Windows XP user account name, and *GUID* is your user account's *globally unique identifier*, a long unintelligible code.

You can change this location to one that will be easier for you to back up. We like to move our message store folder onto drive D:, the partition on which we store all our data files. (See Chapter 33 for reasons to separate your programs and data into separate partitions.)

To change the location of your message store, follow these steps:

1. Create an empty folder in which you'd like your message store to be stored (for example, D:\Email). The folder must be on a local disk, and it must be empty.

2. In Outlook Express, choose Tools | Options, click the Maintenance tab, and click the Store Folder button. The Store Location dialog box appears, displaying the current location of the message store.

3. Click the Change button, browse to the folder you created in step 1, and click OK.

4. Click OK in the Store Location dialog box and exit Outlook Express.

5. Run Outlook Express again. Before it displays its window, it copies your message store to its new location.

Choosing a Layout for the Outlook Express Window

Like Windows Explorer, the Outlook Express window provides a number of features that you can choose to display or not display. When all the features are made visible, you get a busy, complicated window, as shown in Figure 23-2.

You can display or hide any of these features (other than the working area). Choose View | Layout to display the Window Layout Properties dialog box, check the features that you want to have in your Outloo k Expr ess window, and click OK.

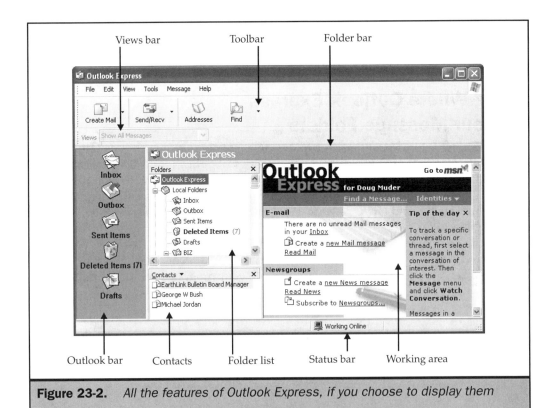

Figure 23-2. *All the features of Outlook Express, if you choose to display them*

We recommend displaying the folder list, toolbar, and status bar. You might also find the Contacts list useful. If you like the Views bar, you can drag it up to the right end of the menu bar. If you don't use Windows Messenger, close the Contacts pane.

Protecting Yourself from E-Mail Viruses

E-mail viruses spread by e-mailing copies of themselves to other computers. (Technically, such programs are *worms*, not viruses, but the popular press does not usually make this distinction.) If an e-mail virus gets into your computer, it may try to send infected e-mail to everyone in your Address Book, addresses on web pages in your browser's cache, and addresses in text files on your hard disk. The e-mail will look like it is coming from you—which won't make you popular with the people in your Address Book.

The most common (but not the only) way for e-mail viruses to spread is through file attachments, especially attachments that are executable (.exe) files or that invoke applications or macros. The text of the message is a lure to get you to open the attachment. (The message comes to you from someone who has you in his address book, so it looks like your good friend Bob has sent you a mysterious attachment with a message saying something like "Try this. It's fun.") Once you open the attachment, your computer is infected.

Because Outlook and Outlook Express are so widely used, they are the most popular targets for the hackers who create e-mail viruses. Outlook Express 6 contains two features for decreasing your vulnerability to e-mail viruses: restricting attachments and warning you if any other program attempts to send e-mail from your computer using your identity. In addition, you have a choice of whether Outlook Express uses the rules of Internet Explorer's Internet zone, or the much safer Restricted Sites zone (which we recommend). (See Chapter 32, section "Internet Explorer's Zones.")

These features and options are far from a panacea. The file types that are blocked are the most popular ones for e-mail viruses, but far from the only ones. And blocking HTML attachments does nothing to protect you from viruses that may be embedded in e-mail messages written in HTML. Whether you use these features or not, we recommend that you continue to be cautious: Do not open unexpected attachments from strangers, or even from friends if the accompanying message does not convince you that they are genuine.

 For more about viruses in general and what you can do to protect your system, see the section "Protecting Your System from Viruses and Worms" in Chapter 32.

Restricting Attachments in Outlook Express

When you open a file attached to an e-mail message, the file is opened by the application appropriate to its file type, not by Outlook Express. In other words, if you don't know the file type of an attachment, you can't be sure what program will run when you open it. If the attachment is itself a program, opening the attachment turns the program loose to do whatever it was designed to do. Some types of files are more dangerous to open than others, because the applications that run them have the power to make fundamental changes to your system. In particular, executable (.exe) files, scripting files (such as .vbs for Visual Basic or .js for JavaScript), or files that contain links to other files that could contain executable code (like .htm or .url).

Some viruses try to disguise the file type of their attachments by giving the files two extensions (for example, Loveletter.doc.vbs). If Windows is configured not to display all extensions, you might be fooled by the filename, which would appear without the last extension (for example, you'd just see the filename Loveletter.doc). For this reason you should never open an attachment if Outlook Express is displaying the wrong icon for it. To display all extensions, choose Start | My Computer, choose Tools | Folder options from the menu bar, click the View tab, and deselect the Hide Extensions For Known File Types check box.

By default Outlook Express blocks attachments that it judges to be of a dangerous file type. When you receive a message with a blocked attachment, the paper clip icon still appears next to the message in the message list. Clicking the icon reveals a list of attachments, but any attachments that are blocked appear dimmed, so that they cannot be selected. If you decide you want to open the attachment anyway, click the Forward button on the toolbar to see a message in which you can access the attachment. (Then close the forwarded message without sending it.)

Note *Even if you are blocking some attachments, image file attachments still get through and are displayed appended to the end of the message they are attached to.*

Preventing Other Programs from Sending E-Mail via Outlook Express

By default, Outlook Express is set up to allow other programs to use it to send e-mail automatically. A virus program could use this feature to send itself to other people. You can alter this behavior so that Outlook Express blocks such e-mail until you have confirmed that you want to send the message. Make this change as follows:

1. Select Tools | Options from the menu bar. The Options dialog box opens.
2. Click the Security tab.
3. Check the Warn Me When Other Applications Try To Send Mail As Me check box and click OK.

To undo this change, repeat these steps but uncheck the box in step 3.

Choosing Outlook Express's Security Zone

Outlook Express borrows its security zones from Internet Explorer. See the section "Internet Explorer's Zones" in Chapter 32 for more details about security zones and how to change the rules that apply to them. Outlook Express offers you a choice between the two most conservative zones: the Internet zone and the Restricted Sites zone. The Restricted Sites zone is more conservative and we recommend it.

To choose your security zone, follow these steps:

1. Select Tools | Options from the Outlook Express menu. The Options dialog box appears.

2. Click the Security tab of the Options dialog box.

3. Select the radio button of the security zone you want, and then click OK.

Sending and Receiving E-Mail

After you set up one or more mail accounts, you can check your mail by clicking the Send And Receive button on the toolbar, choosing Tools | Send And Receive | Send and Receive All, or pressing CTRL-M. Outlook Express goes through the following process.

1. Connects to your mail servers. If you are not already online, it establishes a connection to the Internet first.

2. Sends all the messages in your Outbox. (Messages you aren't ready to send should be stored in the Drafts folder, not in the Outbox.)

3. Downloads all the incoming messages from the server into your Inbox (or into other folders if you have defined message rules that sort your incoming correspondence)—see "Filtering Your Mail with Message Rules" later in this chapter.

By default, the Send And Receive button sends all queued messages and checks for mail in all of the e-mail accounts it knows about. If you want to be more selective, click the down arrow next to the Send and Receive button. A drop-down menu offers you the following choices:

- **Send and Receive All**   The default.
- **Receive All**   Checks for incoming mail in all known accounts, but doesn't send queued messages.
- **Send All**   Sends all queued messages, but doesn't check for incoming mail.
- **Individual Listings Of Your E-Mail Accounts**   Choosing an account sends and receives for that account only.

The same choices are available from the Tools | Send And Receive menu.

While messages are downloading, a dialog box may appear if you connect to the Internet on a dial-up connection. You may click the Hang Up When Finished box if you want Outlook Express to close the Internet connection when it is done.

Configuration Options for Sending and Receiving Messages

Table 23-1 shows some of the most important configuration options for sending and receiving messages. (We omit those that are self-explanatory.) Choose Tools | Options to display the Options dialog box that shows these settings. See Table 23-2 for settings that control how messages are composed and the section " Reading and Posting to Newsgroups" later in this chapter for settings that affect reading newsgroups.

Tab	Setting	Description
General	Send and receive messages at startup	When you start Outlook Express, it sends messages in your Outbox and downloads messages from your incoming mail server.
General	Check for new messages every *xx* minutes	Specifies how often Outlook Express connects automatically to the mail servers to download incoming messages and upload outgoing messages.
General	If my computer is not connected at this time	Specifies what to do if your computer is not connected to the Internet when Outlook Express tries to check for new messages. Your options are Do Not Connect, Connect Only When Not Working Offline, and Connect Even When Working Offline.
Read	Mark message read after displaying for *xx* seconds	Specifies that Outlook Express mark a message as read after displaying it in the preview pane for the specified time.

Table 23-1. *Send/Receive Settings of the Options Dialog Box*

Tab	Setting	Description
Send	Save copy of sent messages in the 'Sent Items' folder	Specifies that Outlook Express keep copies of your outgoing messages. You can move them from the Sent Items folder to another folder after the message is sent.
Send	Send messages immediately	Specifies that Outlook Express connect to your outgoing mail server and send messages whenever a message is in your Outbox.
Security	Select the Internet Explorer security zone to use	Specifies which security zone to use when deciding whether or not to let ActiveX controls and other potentially dangerous scripts and programs run (see Chapter 32, section "Internet Explorer's Zones").
Connection	Ask before switching dial-up connections	Should Outlook Express break an existing dial-up connection to use its default connection, or should it ask you what to do?
Connection	Hang up after sending and receiving	Specifies that after sending and receiving messages, Outlook Express disconnect from the Internet.

Table 23-1. *Send/Receive Settings of the Options Dialog Box* (continued)

Viewing Incoming Mail

New mail accumulates in your Inbox and stays there until you delete it or move it to another folder. To see your new mail, click Inbox in the folder list of the Outlook Express window. The window has three panes, as it does when you look at any mail folder: the folder list, the message list (with one line per message, with one message selected), and the text of the selected message. You can drag the boundaries of these three panes to reallocate the space occupied by each. The three panes are shown in Figure 23-3.

If the author rated the message as Urgent, an exclamation point (!) appears on the left side of its entry on the list of messages. If you have decided to flag the message, a little flag appears. If the message has an attachment, a paper clip appears to the left of

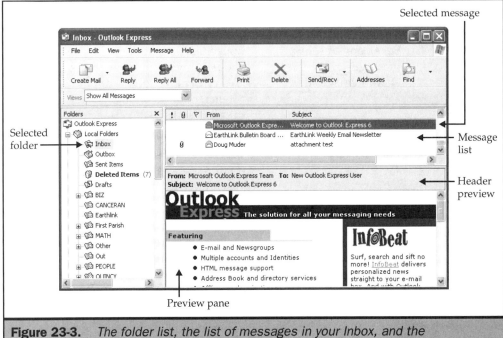

Selected message

Selected folder

Message list

Header preview

Preview pane

Figure 23-3. *The folder list, the list of messages in your Inbox, and the Outlook Express welcome message*

its entry. The currently selected message is highlighted. Unread messages have a closed-envelope icon next to them; read messages have an open-envelope icon.

To read messages, find and click the folder that contains the message in the folder list of the Outlook Express window. (The folder list works just like the Folders Explorer Bar in Windows Explorer.) Then find the message you want to read in the message list in the upper-right pane. Double-click to read the message in its own window, or single-click to read the message in the preview pane of the Outlook Express window.

Customizing the Message List

You can sort the messages in a folder according to any of the columns in the message list. This feature works just like the Details view in an Explorer window: click the label above any of the columns. Click once to sort in ascending order, twice for descending order.

To choose what columns are displayed in the message list, right-click the row of column headings and choose Columns from the shortcut menu. The Columns dialog box appears, listing the possible columns Outlook Express can display. Check the columns you want. You may also use this dialog box to rearrange the columns by selecting a column name and clicking the Move Up or Move Down button. You can switch the order of the columns by dragging the header left or right. You can use the Columns dialog box to fix the widths of the columns in the message list as well, but dragging the boundaries between the columns in the message list itself is simpler.

Opening Attached Files

Messages with attached files have a paper clip icon in the message list. When you select the message, a larger paper clip icon appears in the title bar of the preview pane. When you open the message, attached files appear as icons just below the subject line. Images from attached image files are appended to the bottom of the message automatically; you don't have to decide to open them.

Clicking the large paper clip icon produces a list of the attached files; selecting one of the files from this list opens the file. Similarly, selecting an attached-file icon from the bottom of the message window opens the file.

 Attached files are a major source of e-mail viruses. Don't open an attachment unless you know what it is. Never open an attachment if you can't identify its icon, if you don't know the sender, or if you weren't expecting to receive it.

You can save an attached file either before or after opening it. Click the paper clip icon and select Save Attachments, or select File | Save Attachments from the menu. A Save Attachments window opens listing all the attachments. All the attachments are selected by default, but you can unselect any that you don't want to save right now. Enter a destination for the attached files in the Save To box, or click the Browse button.

 Outlook Express hangs on to attachments for as long as you want it to, but a file attached to an ancient message is very hard to find. If you intend to keep an attached file for any length of time, save it into your regular file system.

Composing Messages

When you click the Create Mail, Reply, Reply All, or Forward button on the Outlook Express toolbar (or give the equivalent commands), Outlook Express opens a message window like this:

(Screenshot of the Outlook Express message composition window titled "Does this work?" with toolbar buttons: Send, Cut, Copy, Paste, Undo, Check, Spelling, Attach, Priority, Sign, Encrypt, Offline. To: winxptcr@gurus.com, Cc:, Subject: Does this work? Message body: "Dear Complete Reference folks, Is this working or what? a reader")

If you are composing a plain text message, you are limited (naturally) to plain text, but if you are composing in HTML you can use different fonts, inserted images, and other fancy formatting. You can choose an attractive background for your HTML messages by selecting one of Outlook Express' stationeries. Choose Format | Apply Stationery menu in the New Message window, and choose from the menu of stationery. If you are replying, Outlook Express can be set up to either include or not include the original text (see "Configuring Outlook Express to Include the Original Message in Your Reply" later in this chapter).

When you reply to a message that has an attachment, the attachment is not included in the reply (because presumably the person doesn't want another copy of the file). When you forward a message with an attachment, the forwarded message includes the attachment.

Configuration Options for Composing Messages

Table 23-2 shows the most important settings in the Options dialog box for composing messages. (Table 23-1 earlier in this chapter listed other settings.) Choose Tools | Options to display the Options dialog box.

Tab	Setting	Description
Receipts	Request a Read Receipt for all sent messages	Specifies that your outgoing messages include return receipt requests so you know when the person opened the message.
Receipts	Secure Receipts	Opens the Secure Receipts Options dialog box, from which you can specify whether your outgoing messages include a request for a *secure receipt* (return receipt for a digitally signed message) and how to respond to requests for secure receipts.
Send	Automatically put people I reply to in my Address Book	Adds entries to your Address Book for each person to whom you send a reply. If you reply to many messages from strangers to whom you are unlikely to write again, deselect this check box.
Send	Include message in reply	Specifies that replies contain the text of the original message in a quoted format.

Table 23-2. *Message Composition Settings of the Options Dialog Box*

Tab	Setting	Description
Send	Reply to messages using the format in which they were sent	Composes replies to HTML formatted messages using HTML formatting, and composes replies to plain text messages using plain text.
Send	Mail Sending Format: HTML/Plain Text	Specifies whether your e-mail messages are sent as HTML or as plain text.
Compose	Compose Font: Mail	Specifies how unformatted messages appear on your screen when you are composing them.
Compose	Stationery: Mail	Specifies what stationery (standard formatting) your new messages will use. Rather than specifying mail stationery here, turn it on only for occasional messages (by choosing Format | Apply Stationery when composing a message).
Signatures	Signatures	Enables you to create one or more *signatures*—a few lines of text that are appended to messages you send.
Spelling	Always check spelling before sending	Specifies that Outlook Express automatically run its spell checker when you send each message (this option is available only if you have a compatible spell-checker installed, such as the ones used by Microsoft Works or Microsoft Office). Other settings on this tab control whether it suggests correct spellings and which words to skip.
Security	Digitally sign all outgoing messages	Adds a digital signature to all messages that proves that you sent the messages. Click Advanced Settings to specify the type of digital signature.
Security	Encrypt contents and attachments for all outgoing messages	Encrypts (encodes) all outgoing messages so that they cannot be read unless the recipient has the encryption key. Click Advanced Settings to specify the type of encryption.

Table 23-2.   *Message Composition Settings of the Options Dialog Box* (continued)

WINDOWS XP HOME ON THE INTERNET

Configuring Outlook Express to Include the Original Message in Your Reply

One advantage e-mail has over paper mail is that you can indicate exactly what part of an e-mail message you are responding to. To make Outlook Express automatically include the original message in any reply, select Tools | Options to open the Options dialog box, select the Send tab, check the Include Message In Reply check box, and click OK.

By doing this, whenever you click the Reply or Reply All buttons, the body of the message window contains a divider, with the original message below the divider. The text of the original message is indented, with a > at the beginning of each line.

To remove the indentation or change the indentation character, open the Send tab of the Options dialog box and click either the Plain Text Settings button or the HTML Settings button in the Mail Sending Format section, depending on whether or not you use HTML to compose messages. If you click Plain Text Settings, check the Indent The Original Text With check box at the bottom of the Plain Text Settings dialog box to indent the original text. The drop-down list next to the check box lets you choose a different indentation character. If you click HTML Settings, check the Indent Message On Reply check box at the bottom of the HTML Settings dialog box.

You can use the original text in two ways. You can type your message at the beginning of the message, leaving the original message at the end for reference. Or, you can edit the original message, deleting the parts irrelevant to your reply, and then type your reply in parts (each part immediately below the portions of the message to which you are responding). If you don't want to include any of the original text for a particular message in your reply (but don't want to change the option), just press CTRL-A to select all the text in the message body window and then either press DELETE or just start typing your message.

Completing the Header

The header section of the message window consists of four lines (though Bcc may not appear unless View | All Headers is checked):

- **To**   If there is more than one recipient, separate the e-mail addresses with commas. Click the open book icon to look up addresses in the Address Book. If you are replying to a message and addresses appear automatically, you may add more addresses or delete some of them (see "Storing Addresses in the Address Book" later in this chapter).

- **Cc (Carbon Copy)**   Type the e-mail addresses of secondary recipients (if any).

- **Bcc (Blind Carbon Copy)**   Type the e-mail addresses of other secondary recipients, if any. The recipients listed in the To and Cc boxes can see the list of other recipients listed in the To and Cc boxes, but not those listed in the Bcc box. If one of the To or Cc recipients replies to your message with Reply All, the recipients on your Bcc list will not receive the reply.

■ **Subject** Be specific—the subject line helps both you and your recipients to keep track of the message in your files. If you are replying to another message, Outlook Express automatically uses the original subject line, preceded by Re. If you are forwarding, Outlook Express uses the original subject line, preceded by Fw.

Inserting Text Files into a Message

If what you want to say is already contained in a text file, you don't have to retype the text or even cut-and-paste the text out of the file. To incorporate the text into your message, move the cursor to the place in the text of your message that you want the text file inserted and select Insert | Text From File. When the Insert Text File window opens, browse to find the text file you want and click Open.

Attaching a File to a Message

You can send any file—a picture, a spreadsheet, a formatted text document—along with your message as an attachment. Click the Attach button on the message window toolbar or select Insert | File Attachment. When the Insert Attachment window appears, browse to find the file you want to attach, and click OK.

 Most ISPs or e-mail services limit the size of attachments. One megabyte is a popular limit. Hotmail's limit is 1.5MB.

When sending plain text messages, Outlook Express encodes file attachments using *MIME (Multipurpose Internet Mail Extensions)*, the most widely used method of attaching files to messages. Most e-mail programs, including Netscape, Eudora, and AOL's mail program, can deal with MIME attachments. However, some e-mail programs can't do this, especially LAN e-mail programs that weren't originally designed to work with the Internet. You can switch to a different encoding method called *uuencode*: Select Tools | Options and click the Plain Text Settings button on the Send tab of the Options dialog box. Now click the Uuencode radio button in the Plain Text Settings dialog box.

When Outlook Express is set up to send HTML messages, the situation is reversed: Uuencode is the default, and you can switch to MIME using the HTML Settings button in the Options dialog box.

 If you are attaching a large file or several small ones, create a compressed folder (ZIP file) that contains the file(s) and attach the compressed folder instead (see Chapter 8).

Creating a Signature

You can give your e-mail messages some style by adding a *signature*, a text or HTML file that is appended to your messages. Because you don't have to retype them each time, you can make your signature a bit more ornate than just your name. (However, we recommend that you don't go wild; signatures that contain some elaborate design or clever quotation are charming the first time you see them, but they quickly become annoying.) Your signatures should contain your name and e-mail address, and should be no more than four lines long.

To create a signature, choose Tools | Options to open the Options dialog box and go to the Signatures tab. Click New to create a signature, then type the text in the Edit Signature box. You can create as many signatures as you like. If you have more than one, use the Rename button to give each a recognizable name. Select one and click the Set As Default button to select the default signature.

Check the Add Signatures To All Outgoing Messages check box to automatically append the default signature to every message. Or, you can choose a signature for individual messages by selecting from the Insert | Signature menu in a new message window. Click the Advanced button to define different default signatures for different e-mail accounts.

Receipts

You can ask for an e-mail message to be sent to you automatically when your recipient opens your message. When you get the receipt message, you can be sure that your message has been received. However, if you *don't* get a receipt, don't assume that the message wasn't read; few e-mail programs send return receipts.

The time to make the receipt request is when you are composing the message. From the composing window, choose Tools | Request Read Receipt. This is a toggle switch, so you can change your mind by checking it again.

You can automatically request receipts on all the messages you send. To do this, choose Tools | Options from the main menu of Outlook Express. When the Options dialog box opens, go to the Receipts tab and check the Request A Read Receipt For All Sent Messages check box.

The recipient can refuse to send the requested receipt, however. If you don't want people to be able to know when you've seen their messages, you can set up Outlook Express not to respond to receipt requests. (And your recipients can do the same.) To do this, go to the Receipts tab of the Options dialog box. You have three choices:

- Never send a read receipt
- Notify me for each read receipt request
- Always send a read receipt

We recommend the Notify setting. You don't want spammers to get receipts verifying that your e-mail address is active, and there may be times when you don't want anyone to know that you're reading your e-mail at all (like when you're on vacation). But it's only polite to allow a receipt to be sent if a friend or coworker asks for one.

Composing in HTML

You can compose messages in HTML, the language in which web pages are written. Using HTML, you can insert pictures or hyperlinks into your messages and use a variety of fonts. You can even write your message on *stationery*—an attractive background image designed to resemble paper stationery. Writing in HTML has two disadvantages:

- Your recipient may not have an e-mail program that reads HTML, in which case they may not be able to decipher what you wrote. Probably they will receive your message either as gibberish or as an HTML attachment to a text message.

- If you include a lot of images and other fancy features in your message, the size of the message file increases. If your recipient has a slow Internet connection, your message may take some time to download.

To control whether your messages are in HTML, do one or both of the following:

- Choose Tools | Options, click the Send tab of the Options dialog box, and click the HTML radio button in the Mail Sending Format section.

- Check the Reply To Message Using The Format In Which They Were Sent check box on the Send tab of the Options dialog box.

 We recommend that you do both of the above if you intend to compose in HTML at all. People who write to you in plain text probably don't want to receive replies in HTML.

When Outlook Express is composing in HTML rather than plain text, the message box contains the following toolbar (called the *formatting toolbar*) just below the header:

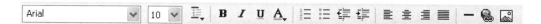

Most of the tools on the formatting toolbar are familiar if you have used a word processor. The rightmost three tools are

- **Insert Horizontal Line**   Draws a dividing line across your message.
- **Create a Hyperlink**   Links text in your message to web addresses (see the next section).
- **Insert Picture**   Inserts any image file into your message (see "Inserting Pictures" later in this chapter).

Linking to the Web

If your message mentions a web page, or if a web page reference would back up the point you are making, why not link to it? If your recipients have HTML-reading e-mail programs, they'll be able to open the page with their web browsers just by clicking the hyperlink in your message.

To insert a hyperlink into a message you are composing in HTML,

1. Select the text you want to link to the Web.

2. Click the Create A Hyperlink button on the formatting toolbar, located below the header. The Hyperlink dialog box opens.

3. Select the web address prefix from the Type drop-down list of the Hyperlink dialog box.

4. Type the web address into the URL box of the Hyperlink dialog box.

5. Click OK.

The selected text should now appear in a different color from the rest of the message.

Inserting Pictures

You can insert photographs, diagrams, charts, or other image files into any message you compose in HTML. These objects then appear in the body of the message the way that photographs appear in a newspaper, not as file attachments.

1. Move the insertion point to the place in your message that you want the picture to be located.

2. Click the Insert Picture button on the formatting toolbar, below the header. The Picture dialog box appears.

3. Type the location of the image file into the Picture Source box or click the Browse button and find the file with a Browse window.

4. Type into the Alternate Text box the text that recipients will see if the picture (for whatever reason) is not displayed.

5. Choose the alignment from the drop-down list. This controls where the picture appears relative to the text.

6. Type a number into the Border Thickness box. This defines the width (in points) of a border surrounding the image.

7. Type numbers into the horizontal and vertical spacing boxes. These numbers define the width (in points) of a region of empty space surrounding the image.

8. Click OK. You see the image inserted into the message window.

If you want to change any of these decisions before you send the message, select the image in the message window and click Insert Picture on the formatting toolbar. The Picture dialog box opens with all your current choices. Change anything you want to and click OK.

Saving and Filing Your Messages

Outlook Express keeps the messages that you send and receive until you tell it to delete them. Messages that you receive are stored in your Inbox folder unless you have created filters to send them somewhere else automatically (see "Filtering Your Mail with Message Rules" later in this chapter). Under the default settings, messages that you send wind up in your Sent Items folder and remain there until you either delete them or move them to another folder (see "Organizing Your Correspondence" later in this chapter).

Configuration Options for Saving Messages

Even though Outlook Express saves your messages automatically, you need to be aware of four issues:

- **Outlook Express folders and the messages in them are separate from the overall filing system of your computer.**   You may have a folder called Mom in Outlook Express, but no Mom folder exists on the folder tree you see in Windows Explorer. If you want a message to be a file in your computer's filing system, you have to save that message as a file. You can drag a message out of the Outlook Express window and drop it onto the desktop or into an Explorer window. Or, you can select the message in the Outlook Express message list window, and select File | Save As, and give the new file a name. Either way the message is saved in a text file with the extension .eml. To read these files on a system that doesn't have Outlook Express, use Notepad.

- **Unfinished messages are lost when you close Outlook Express unless you save them.**   You don't have to start and finish a message in one sitting. If you want to put the message away and work on it later, select File | Save to save the message in your Drafts folder. If you want the unfinished message to be in an Outlook Express folder other than Drafts, save it to Drafts first, and then drag it to another folder.

- **Your mail files should be backed up as often as (or perhaps more often than) any other files on your system.**   The simplest method is to back up the entire folder in which you told Outlook Express to store your messages. The default folder is called Outlook Express and lies inside the C:\Documents and Settings\ *user name*\Local Settings\Application Data\Identities*GUID*\Microsoft folder (*user name* is your user account name, as described in Chapter 6, and *GUID* is your user account's *globally unique identifier*, a long unintelligible code).

- **You can prevent Outlook Express from automatically saving your outgoing messages.**   Select Tools | Options to open the Options dialog box. Go to the Send tab and uncheck the Save Copy Of Sent Messages In The 'Sent Items' Folder check box.

Deleting and Recovering Messages

Delete a message by clicking it in the message list and pressing DELETE. The message is sent to the Deleted Items folder, which functions within the Outlook Express filing system as a kind of Recycle Bin.

You can still examine messages from the Deleted Items folder by opening them, and you can move them to another folder if you change your mind about deleting them. However, if you delete an item from the Deleted Items folder, it is gone permanently.

Outlook Express can be set up to empty the Deleted Items folder automatically when you exit the program as follows: Check the Empty Messages From The 'Deleted Items' Folder On Exit checkbox on the Maintenance tab of the Options dialog box. Otherwise, choose Edit | Empty 'Deleted Items' Folder when the folder gets large.

Sending Messages

Once you are satisfied with the message you've composed, click the Send button in its message window. One of the following two things then happens:

- Outlook Express connects to your ISP, finds your outgoing mail server, and sends the message.

- The message is placed in your Outbox and is not sent until you press the Send and Receive button.

This behavior is governed by the Send Messages Immediately check box on the Send tab of the Options dialog box.

Even if Send Messages Immediately is selected, you can move a message to your Outbox without sending it immediately to your outgoing mail server by selecting File | Send Later. This option is handy if you are temporarily unable to connect to the Internet— if your computer is not currently online, for example.

As long as the message is sitting in your Outbox, you can still intercept it. You can either delete it from the Outbox or move it to Drafts or some other folder for editing.

Storing Addresses in the Address Book

Computers have long been used to store lists of names and addresses, and Address Book keeps track of almost anything you would want to keep track of and provides a space for notes. The ideal address book program would be accessible from every program on your computer, so you'd never need to maintain redundant information about your contacts. The Windows XP Address Book utility is accessible from Internet Explorer, Outlook Express, and NetMeeting. Unfortunately, Microsoft Exchange, Microsoft's e-mail server, has its own address book, so that your addresses may be stored in two separate places.

You can use the information from the Windows Address Book in Windows Messenger; only available contacts are listed. You may be able to use Address Book from older versions of Outlook, but not Outlook XP.

 If you don't mind editing the Registry, you can configure Outlook Express to share Outlook XP's contacts (see Chapter 38). If you make this change, Outlook Express displays only Outlook's contacts, and you don't see the contacts that were stored in your Windows Address Book. After making a backup of the Registry, go to the HKEY_ CURRENT_USER\Software\Microsoft\WAB\WAB4 key. Right-click the WAB4 key, choose New | DWORD, and name the new value UseOutlook. Double-click the new key and set its value to 1.

Running Address Book

You can access Address Book either from another program (like Outlook Express), or by choosing Start | All Programs | Accessories | Address Book. You see the Address Book window, as shown in Figure 23-4.

The window lists the people you have entered into the address book (which the Address Book calls *contacts*) with the name, e-mail address, and phone numbers for each person. It also lists people who are on your Windows Messenger list and are logged on and available for chat.

Contacts are sorted according to identities (see "Identities" earlier in this chapter). However, this is convenience, not a security feature. You can see contacts for all identities by selecting File | Show All Contents from the menu.

Entering Information into Address Book

You can get information into Address Book in three ways: importing information from your current address book program into Outlook Express (described in the section

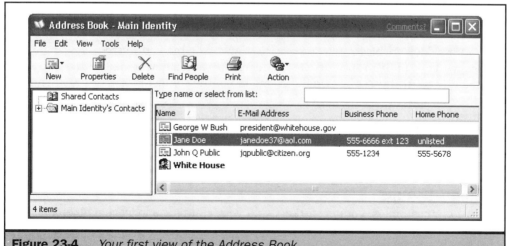

Figure 23-4. *Your first view of the Address Book*

"Importing Addresses from Other Mail Programs" earlier in this chapter), capturing information automatically from Outlook Express, or entering information by hand. Once you have a list of contacts in your Address Book, you can organize them into groups.

Capturing E-mail Addresses from Outlook Express

If you use Outlook Express as your e-mail program, you can set it up to add names and e-mail addresses to Address Book automatically whenever you reply to a message. To do this, open Outlook Express' Options dialog box by selecting Tools | Options from the Outlook Express menu. On the Send tab of the Options dialog box, check the box Automatically Put People I Reply To In My Address Book.

 This command can fill your address book with addresses you'll never need again for people you don't know or remember.

Entering Information by Hand

Information about a contact can be entered or edited from the contact's Properties dialog box, shown in Figure 23-5.

To enter a new contact into Address Book, click the New button on the toolbar and choose New Contact, or select File | New Contact from the menu bar. (You can also enter a new contact from Outlook Express by selecting File | New | Contact.) A blank Properties dialog box appears. Type in any information you want recorded, and leave blank any lines you want.

To open the Properties dialog box for an existing contact, select the contact on the contacts list and click the Properties button, or right-click the contact on the contacts list and select Properties from the shortcut menu.

 The Properties box displays a Summary tab that you didn't see when you were entering a new contact. This tab is just for reference; each piece of information on this tab can be edited on some other tab. Any web page listed on the Summary tab has a Go button next to it; clicking this button opens your web browser and displays the web page.

Address Book enables you to keep track of several e-mail addresses for a single person, with one of them specified as the default. To add a new e-mail address, type it into the E-Mail Addresses box on the Name tab of the contact Properties box. Then click the Add button. The new e-mail address appears in the list just below the E-Mail Addresses box.

To set one of a person's e-mail addresses as the default, select it from the list of e-mail addresses on the Name tab of the Properties dialog box associated with that person's name. Then click the Set As Default button.

Defining Groups

Having your customers, your coworkers, and your child's piano teacher all on one big alphabetical list can be confusing. Address Book enables you to give your contact list

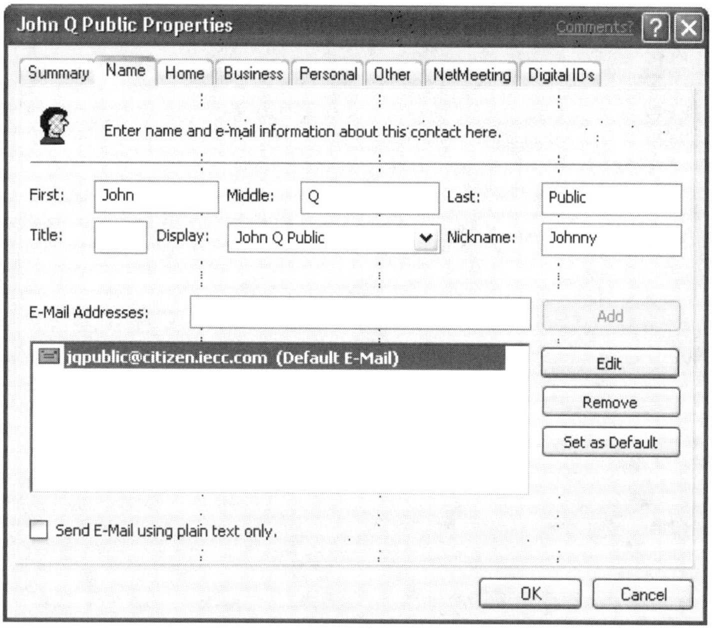

Figure 23-5.   *Detailed information about a contact*

some structure by defining groups of contacts that have something in common. An individual contact can appear in any number of groups.

To define a group:

1. Click the New button on the Address Book toolbar and choose New Group from the menu that appears. A group Properties dialog box opens, shown in Figure 23-6.

2. Type a name for the group into the Group Name box.

3. Click the Select Members button. A Select Group Members window appears. Your contacts list is in its left pane; its right pane contains the members of the new group.

4. One by one, select names in the left pane and click the Select button to add this name to the group. You can add an existing group to the new group in the same way.

5. When you have finished selecting group members, click OK to return to the group Properties dialog box. The members you have selected are listed.

If you want to add new members to or remove them from an existing group, open the group's Properties dialog box. You can do this from Address Book by selecting the

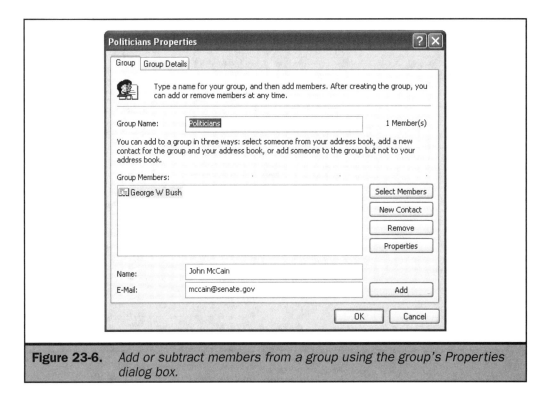

Figure 23-6.   *Add or subtract members from a group using the group's Properties dialog box.*

group from the address list and clicking the Properties button. Or, you can do it from either Address Book or the Contacts pane of Outlook Express by right-clicking the group's name in the Contacts list and selecting Properties from the shortcut menu. If you want to remove names from the list, select the names in from the Group Members list in the Properties dialog box and click Remove. Include new members from your Contacts list by clicking Select Members button. If you want to add people who aren't already in your Address Book, type the name and address into the Name and E-Mail boxes at the bottom of the dialog box, and then click the Add button. (Names that you add in this way will not be added to your contacts list as individuals, but only as part of the group.)

To enter information about the group as a whole—like the address of its headquarters or the URL of its web page—go to the Group Details tab of its Properties dialog box.

Looking Up Information in Address Book

When you open Address Book, the first thing you see is the contacts list, as shown in Figure 23-4. Address Book offers you the same choice of views that Windows Explorer does: Large Icon, Small Icon, List, and Details. Choose among them on the View menu.

Sorting the Contacts List

In any of the views, you can sort contacts according to any of the information displayed. In Small Icons, Large Icons, and List views only the name is shown, so contacts can be listed according to first or last name, in ascending or descending order. Make these choices by choosing View | Sort By.

In Details view, you can list contacts according to name, e-mail address, home phone number, or business phone number. As in the Details view in Windows Explorer, click the head of any column to list contacts according to that column in ascending order. To list in descending order, click the column head a second time. To tell Address Book whether the Name column should be ordered according to first name or last name, choose View | Sort By.

Looking Up Detailed Information

Each contact has a Properties dialog box associated with it, as shown in Figure 23-5. To view the Properties dialog box for a contact, double-click the person's entry in the contact list. Most of the tabs are self-explanatory. The entries on the NetMeeting tab refer to the conferencing server and address used with the NetMeeting program described in Chapter 25. The entries on the Digital ID tab enable you to send and receive encrypted information from the person.

Finding People

If you have a lot of contacts in your Address Book, you don't want to have to scan the whole list to find a particular entry. You can search the Address Book in three ways:

- From Address Book, click the Find People button on the toolbar, choose Edit | Find People from the menu, or press CTRL-F.

- From Outlook Express, select Edit | Find | People from the menu or press CTRL-E.

- From the desktop, choose Start | Search | People.

In any case, you see the Find People window, shown here:

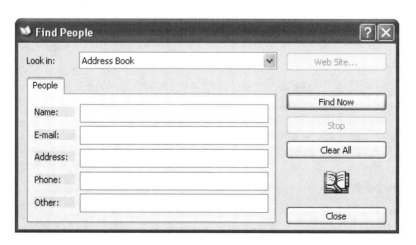

Make sure the Look In box is set to Address Book, type in what you know about the person, and then click Find Now. Any fragment of information helps to narrow down the search. If, for example, you remember the phone number has a 456 in it somewhere, enter 456 in the Phone line of the Find People box. Or, if you recall entering "wears red ties" as a note on the Other tab of the Contact Properties box, you can find the contact by typing **wears red ties** in the Other line of the Find People box.

You can also use the Find People box to search other address directories.

Contacting People

To send e-mail to a person or group on your contacts list, select the recipient(s) from the address list, click the Action button on the toolbar, and choose Send Mail from the menu that appears; or, choose Tools | Action | Send Mail. (To address a message to several people, choose them by holding down the CTRL key while you select them.) Your default e-mail program should start to compose a message to the people that you selected. To send a message to one member of a group in your Windows Address Book, open the group, right-click the person's name, and choose Action | Mail.

If you regularly send e-mail to the same collection of addresses, define them as a group. Right-click the group name and select Action | Send Mail from the shortcut menu to address mail to all the members of the group simultaneously.

Printing Information from Address Book

You can print information from the Address Book in three formats:

- **Memo** Prints all the information Address Book has about the selected contact(s).
- **Business Card** Prints only the information from the Business tab of the contact(s) Properties box.
- **Phone List** Prints a list of phone numbers of the selected contact(s).

To print:

1. Select contacts from the contacts list. Select blocks of names by holding down the SHIFT key while you click the names. Select individuals scattered throughout the list by holding down the CTRL key while you click the names. Select a group by clicking its name in the contacts list (not the group list). Select all contacts by choosing Edit | Select All. If you don't select any contacts, Address Book prints them all.

2. Click the Print button on the toolbar. A Print dialog box appears.

3. Select the Memo, Business Card, or Phone List from the Print dialog box, and then click OK.

To print addresses in any other format, export them (as described in the next section) to a database or word processing program that can print the format you want.

Exporting Names and Addresses from Address Book

You can also export names and addresses from Address Book in Microsoft Exchange Personal Address Book format, in Windows Address Book format, in a comma-delimited text file, or as vCards:

- **Windows Address Book format**   Choose File | Export | Address Book, choose the folder and filename to use (with the extension .wab), and click the Save button.

- **Microsoft Exchange Personal Address Book format**   Choose File | Export | Other Address Book and then select Microsoft Exchange Personal Address Book from the Address Book Export Tool window. Click the Export button. (If you're exporting to Outlook, you may be better off to export as vCards.)

- **Business card or vCard**   Select the person whose information you want to export, and then choose File | Export | Business Card (vCard). Specify the name and folder where you want to store the business card and click Save.

- **Text file**   Choose File | Export | Other Address Book, choose Text File (Comma Separated Values) from the list that appears, and click Export. The CSV Export Wizard runs. Specify the name of the file in which you want to store the exported addresses, and then click Next. Select the information you want to include for each person, and then click Finish.

Searching Additional Directory Services

When you choose Start | Search | People, you see the Find People window. In addition to searching Address Book entries, you can search other *directory services*—listings of names, e-mail addresses, and other information. These directory services may be public, such as the web-based services Yahoo! People Search and Bigfoot (at **people.yahoo.com** and **www.bigfoot.com**, respectively). Or, they may be private, such as the employee directory for a large organization or the active directory used by your network logon server.

Windows XP comes with a number of public directory services already set up—click the Look In box in the Find People window to see a list. When you choose a directory service, the boxes in the Find People window adjust to match the types of entries the directory service can accept.

You can configure Windows to use other directory services, for example, for your organization. Windows can work with any LDAP-compatible directory service. (*LDAP* stands for *Lightweight Directory Access Protocol*.) To configure Windows to work with an additional directory service, run Address Book or Outlook Express, and then choose Tools | Accounts. (In Outlook Express, click the Directory Service tab.) You see the Internet Accounts window listing the directory services Windows knows about. To add a new directory service, click the Add button in the Internet Accounts window. The Internet Connection Wizard runs and asks for the information it needs to configure the new service.

To remove a directory service you no longer use, select the service in the Internet Accounts window and click the Remove button.

Organizing Your Correspondence

A mail program is more than just a way to read and write messages, it is also a filing system. Over time, the records of your correspondence may become a valued asset. Although you can leave all of your mail in your Inbox, it's a lot easier to find messages if you file messages by sender or topic.

Working with Folders

The Outlook Express filing system resembles the filing system that Windows itself uses, but the Outlook Express files and folders can't be seen by other programs—you must use Outlook Express to manipulate them.

Creating, Deleting, and Renaming Folders

To create a new folder in Outlook Express, right-click the Local Folders icon in the folder list and select New Folder from the shortcut menu. When the Create Folder window appears, give the new folder a name and use the folder list in the lower part of the window to choose a location for the folder.

To delete a folder, right-click its icon in the folder list of the Outlook Express window and select Delete from the shortcut menu. To rename a folder, right-click its icon in the folder list of Outlook Express and select Rename from the shortcut menu. Type the new name into the Rename Folder window.

Moving and Copying Messages

The easiest way to move a message to a new folder is to drag its envelope icon from the message list of its current folder and drop it on the icon of the destination folder in the folder list. To move a folder, drag-and-drop its icon on the folder list to the desired location.

To copy a message to another folder, right-click its icon in the message list and select Copy To Folder, then select its new home from the folder list in the Copy window that appears.

You can move several messages or folders at the same time by holding down the CTRL key while you select the items to move.

Tip	*Each Outlook Express mailbox is actually a file with a .dbx extension. The Inbox, for example, is the file Inbox.dbx. One way to back up a mailbox is to make a copy of its file; you don't even need to open Outlook Express to do this. The files are a little hard to find, however, because they live many layers inside the hidden folder C:\Documents And Settings\username\Application Data. The best way to find them is to use the advanced Search option Search Hidden Files And Folders.*

Finding Messages in Your Files

A filing system isn't worth much unless you can find what you put there. Outlook Express gives you a search tool that lets you search for messages based on

- The sender
- The recipient
- The subject
- A word or phrase in the message body
- Whether the message has attachments
- Whether the message is flagged
- The date received
- A folder containing the message

Begin your search by selecting Edit | Find | Message. The Find Message dialog box appears, as shown in Figure 23-7. Enter as much information as you know about the message and click Find Now. Outlook Express lists at the bottom of the window all the messages that fit the description you've given. Open any message on this list by double-clicking it.

Type any string of characters into the From, To, Subject, or Message lines of the Find Message dialog box. This restricts your search to messages whose corresponding parts contain those character strings.

To specify the date of a message, check either the Received Before or Received After check box. Enter a date in MM/DD/YY format into the corresponding line or click the drop-down arrow to locate the date you want on a calendar. (Change months on the calendar by clicking the left or right arrows at the top of the calendar.) You can use Before and After together to specify a range of dates.

The Look In box specifies a folder in which to search. Click the Browse button to locate a new folder to look in. The Include Subfolders check box does just what it says— if the box is checked, the search includes all the subfolders of the specified folder; if it is not checked, the subfolders are not included.

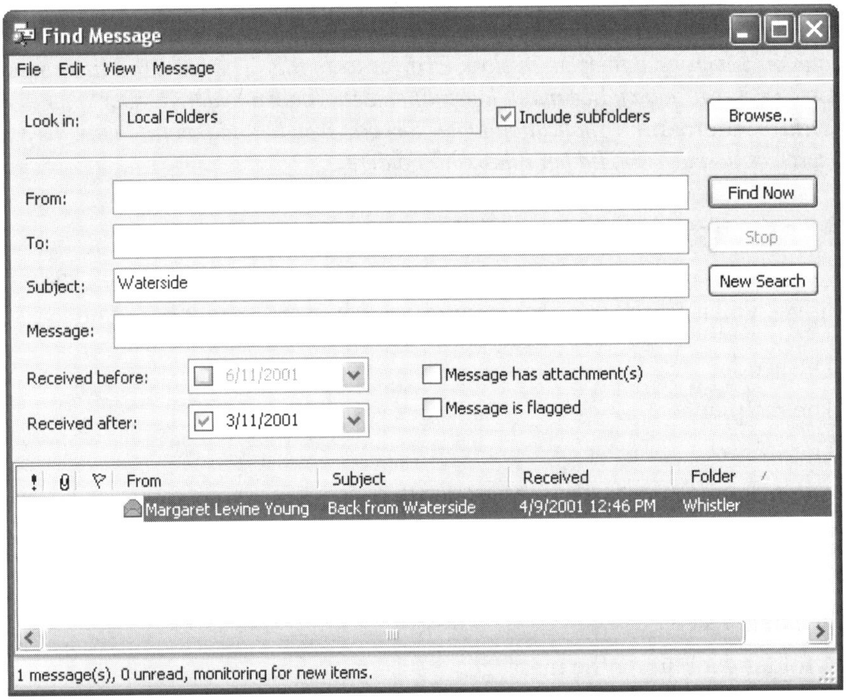

Figure 23-7.   *The Find Message dialog box*

If the message you wanted didn't show up, check the View | Current View menu in the Find dialog box. Make sure it is set to Show All Messages.

Tip   *If you know you're going to want to find a particular message in the future, flag it. Select the message, and then choose Message | Flag Message from the menu. A little flag appears next to the message's entry on the message list.*

Filtering Your Mail with Message Rules

Outlook Express can do some secretarial work to help you manage your POP e-mail messages automatically. It can do the following:

- File messages to the appropriate folders, rather than letting them pile up in the Inbox
- Forward messages to another e-mail address
- Send a stock reply message
- Delete unwelcome messages so that you never have to look at them

Tip *An easy way to delete messages from a particular person automatically is to add his or her name to your Blocked Senders list (see "Throwing Away Spam by Blocking Senders" later in this chapter).*

You tell Outlook Express to do these things by establishing *message rules* or *mail rules*, which specify a kind of message and a type of action to take when such a message arrives. To establish a message rule for your e-mail, select Tools | Message Rules | Mail. The Message Rules dialog box appears, as shown in Figure 23-8. (If there are no current message rules, the New Mail Rule dialog box opens as well, as shown in Figure 23-9.)

Note *You can't use message rules with IMAP mail accounts, or web-based mail accounts that don't also have POP servers.*

The upper portion of the Message Rules dialog box lists the rules you have created. A rule is active if its check box is checked, and inactive otherwise, so turning a rule on and off is easy. The lower portion of the dialog box gives a description of the currently selected rule. Some parts of the description are underlined in blue; these are links to other dialog boxes that allow you to edit these particular portions of the rule. In Figure 23-8,

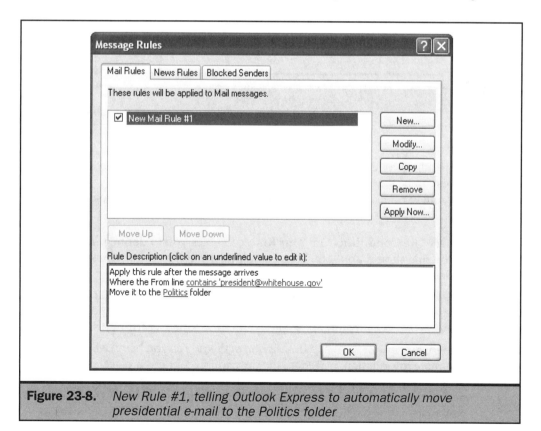

Figure 23-8. *New Rule #1, telling Outlook Express to automatically move presidential e-mail to the Politics folder*

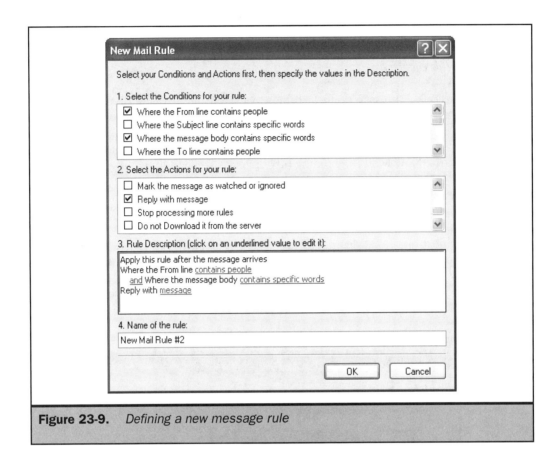

Figure 23-9.   *Defining a new message rule*

"Contains 'president@whitehouse.gov'" is linked—clicking it opens a box in which new addresses can be chosen.

To define a new rule, click the New button in the Message Rules dialog box. This opens the New Mail Rule dialog box, shown in Figure 23-9. This box has four sections.

- 1. **Select The Conditions For Your Rule**   Enables you to define the messages that the rule should apply to. These conditions are vague, but you specify their details in the Rule Description section.

- 2. **Select The Actions For Your Rule**   Enables you to specify what Outlook Express should do when such messages arrive. As in the first section, these actions are also vague, but are spelled out in the Rule Description section.

- 3. **Rule Description**   Gives a description of the rule as you have defined it so far; when more information is needed, the description contains a placeholder phrase that is linked to a dialog box for specifying the information. In Figure 23-9, for example, the phrases "contains people," "contains specific words," and "message" are all placeholders. Clicking these phrases opens additional dialog boxes that allow you to specify which people, which words, and what message. The word "and" is also linked; clicking it opens the And/Or dialog box, described in the next section.

■ **4. Name Of The Rule**   Enables you to specify a name for your rule. Otherwise, the rule will be numbered, such as in New Mail Rule #1 in Figure 23-8.

Defining Conditions for Message Rules

You define conditions for your message rules by checking the appropriate boxes in the Select Conditions For Your Rule section of the New Mail Rule dialog box. As you check boxes, the text next to those boxes appears in the Rule Description section, in which you click the linked phrases to specify any additional information that the condition requires.

If you check more than one box, the conditions are connected with an "and"—in other words, all checked conditions need to be true before the action you specify is taken. You can change this "and" to an "or" by clicking the corresponding "and" in the rule description and selecting the Messages Match Any One Of The Criteria radio button. There is no way to create more complicated conditions than to mix "ands" and "ors."

You can choose from 12 conditions listed in section one of the New Mail Rule dialog box:

■ **For All Messages**

■ **Where The From Line Contains People, Where the To Line Contains People, Where the CC Line Contains People, and Where The To Or CC Line Contains People**   Any of these four conditions requires you to specify which people the condition applies to. Click the phrase "contains people" in the Rule Description section to display the Select People dialog box. Add people to your list either by typing their e-mail addresses into the top line and clicking the Add button, or by clicking the Address Book button and selecting them from your address book. By default, the rule applies to a message in which any of the selected people are included in the specified line. You can require that the condition apply only if *all* of the people are included or if *none* of the people are included by clicking the Options button and choosing the appropriate radio button in the Rule Condition Options dialog box.

■ **Where The Subject Line Contains Specific Words and Where The Message Body Contains Specific Words**   Either of these conditions requires you to specify which words or phrases the rule is looking for. Click the phrase "contains specific words" in the Rule Description section. When the Type Specific Words dialog box appears, type a word or phrase and click the Add button. If you specify more than one word or phrase, click the Options button to specify whether all words/phrases must be present or just one of them.

■ **Where the Message Is Marked As Priority, Where The Message Is From The Specified Account, Where The Message Size Is More Than Size, Where The Message Has An Attachment, and Where The Message Is Secure**   These five conditions require you to specify which priority, which account, what size, and what kind of security. Click the highlighted phrase in the Rule Description section and choose the appropriate radio button from the dialog box that appears.

Specifying Actions for Message Rules

By setting conditions in the Select The Conditions For Your Rule section of the New Mail Rule dialog box, you have picked out a particular class of messages. Now you need to tell Outlook Express what to do with those messages by filling out the Select The Actions For Your Rule section. Select actions by checking the check boxes. You may select as many actions as you like. You have 12 choices:

■ **Move It To The Specified Folder** or **Copy It To The Specified Folder**   Either of these actions requires you to specify a folder to put the message into. Click the word "specified" in the Rule Description section and choose a folder from the dialog box that appears.

■ **Forward It To People**   This action requires you to specify which people to forward the message to. Click the word "people" in the Rule Description section and enter an e-mail address into the Select People dialog box, or click the Address Book button to choose an address from your Address Book.

■ **Delete It**, **Flag It**, **Mark It As Read**, **Do Not Download It From The Server**, and **Delete It From The Server**   These actions are self-explanatory. No highlighted words or phrases appear in the Rule Description.

■ **Stop Processing More Rules**   If more than one rule applies to a message, the message may get processed twice, and may even be duplicated. If you find this happening, you can add Stop Processing More Rules to the rules that are causing the problem.

■ **Highlight It With Color**   After you select this check box, click the word "color" in the Rule Description section and make your choice from the Select Color dialog box.

■ **Mark The Message As Watched Or Ignored**   Click "watched or ignored" in the Rule Description and choose the Watch Message or Ignore Message radio button. Outlook Express *watches* a message by displaying an icon (a pair of glasses) by it, and *ignores* a message by flagging it with the international "forbidden" icon.

■ **Reply With Message**   This action requires you to tell it which message to use as your automatic reply. Click the word "message" and identify a message file when the Open dialog box appears. (Prior to defining the rule, you should compose your reply and select File | Save As to save it as an .eml file.)

Throwing Away Spam by Blocking Senders

You can't stop annoying people or organizations from writing to you, but you can have Outlook Express send their e-mail messages straight to the Deleted Items folder or refuse to display their newsgroup messages. Make this happen by adding their names to the blocked senders list as follows:

1. Select Tools | Message Rules | Blocked Senders List from the Outlook Express menu bar. The Message Rules dialog box appears with the Blocked Senders tab on top, as shown in Figure 23-10.

2. Click the Add button. The Add Sender dialog box appears.

3. Enter the e-mail address that you want to block in the Address field. If you want to block all messages from an entire Internet domain (the part of the address after the @), type only the domain name.

4. Choose whether to block e-mail messages, newsgroup messages, or both by clicking the appropriate radio button.

5. Click OK. The Blocked Senders list now includes the new entry, with check boxes that say whether the blocking applies to the sender's e-mail or newsgroup messages.

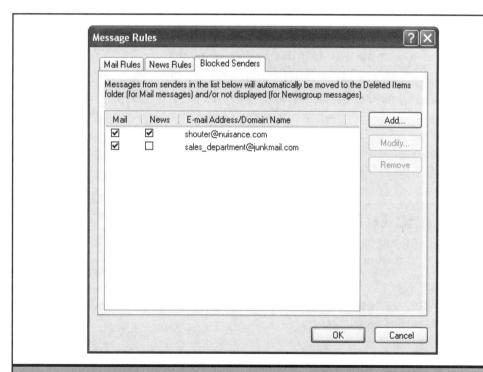

Figure 23-10.   *Blocking a few selected senders can lower your blood pressure.*

Remove a sender from your Blocked Senders list by choosing Tools | Message Rules | Blocked Senders List, selecting the sender in the Message Rules dialog box, and clicking the Remove button.

Managing Your Message Rules

All your message rules are listed by name in the upper section of the Message Rules dialog box. Outlook Express only applies rules whose check boxes are checked, so you can turn rules on and off easily by checking or unchecking their boxes. When you click a rule's name, its description appears in the Rule Description section of the dialog box. You can edit any of the highlighted phrases in the rule description, or you can rewrite the rule completely by clicking the Modify button. The Edit Mail Rule dialog box appears; it behaves in the same manner as the New Rule dialog box.

You can put the rules into a different order by selecting rules in the Message Rules dialog box and clicking the Move Up or Move Down button. To get rid of a rule completely, select its name and click Remove.

Using Message Rules to Sort Old Messages

Message rules are applied automatically to new messages as they arrive, but you can also apply message rules to the messages stored in a folder. This technique can help you organize your correspondence. To do this:

1. Select the rule you want to apply by clicking it (not its check box) on the Mail Rules tab of the Message Rules dialog box. If the rule you want does not already exist, you can create it as described earlier in this chapter.

2. Click the Apply Now button. The Apply Message Rules Now dialog box opens.

3. Select the folder that the rule should be applied to. Inbox is the default, but if you want to apply the rule to a different folder you can click the Browse button and find the folder you want.

4. Click the Apply Now button. Outlook Express opens a confirmation box to tell you when it has finished.

Usenet and Other Newsgroups

Newsgroups provide another way for you to use your computer and the Internet to communicate with the outside world. Unlike e-mail, however, a newsgroup is a public medium. When you send a message to a newsgroup, the message is available to anyone who wants to look at it—it's as if you have tacked up a notice on a public bulletin board. You never know who—if anyone—reads your message. The Internet-based system of newsgroups is called *Usenet*.

Newsgroups are organized by topic. Because there are tens of thousands of newsgroups, topics can be very specific. When you have something to say about the topic of a newsgroup, you can use a *newsreading program*, such as Outlook Express, to compose a message (which may be many pages or only one line) and send it to your *news server*, a computer on the Internet that supports *NNTP (Network News Transfer Protocol)*, which makes your message available to other news servers. People who want to read the recent contributions to this newsgroup (including your message) can use a newsreading program (not necessarily the same as yours) to download messages from their own news servers.

Most ISPs provide a news server for their subscribers, providing access to Usenet newsgroups, which are open to the public. Many organizations provide news servers for their own newsgroups, which may be public or private. For example, Microsoft runs a public news server called msnews.microsoft.com. It carries newsgroups about Microsoft's various products. It also runs a private news server with newsgroups that are accessible only to people who are testing forthcoming Microsoft products (products in "beta test"). To connect to a private news server, you need a logon and password.

Setting up accounts, sending, and receiving messages from newsgroups in Outlook Express is similar to working with e-mail. The following sections note the differences.

 For more information about Usenet newsgroups, see the Internet Gurus site at **net.gurus.com/usenet**.

Reading and Posting to Newsgroups

Before you can read and post to newsgroups with Outlook Express, you must set up a *news account* in Outlook Express by choosing Tools | Accounts, clicking the News tab, clicking Add, and choosing News (see "Setting Up Your Accounts" earlier in this chapter). A news account includes the information that allows Outlook Express to connect to a news server and subscribe to newsgroups—it's not an account on a news server. (To use most news servers, you don't need an account, logon, or password.) Once you create an account for a news server (for example, msnews.microsoft.com), its folder appears in the folder list of the Outlook Express window, just below your mail folders. To begin reading the newsgroups on a news server, click its icon.

 You can read and post to newsgroups using a web browser rather than a newsreader. The Google Groups web site at **groups.google.com** *gives you access to a large number of newsgroups.*

Notice that a news folder has a different icon than a mail folder, and that selecting a news folder rather than a mail folder changes the Outlook Express toolbar. Many of the news buttons resemble the mail buttons in name and function, but some do not. You can choose which buttons should be on the toolbar in the same way that you can with Windows Explorer—right-click the toolbar and choose Customize from the shortcut menu.

Configuration Options for Reading and Posting to Newsgroups

Table 23-3 shows configuration settings that affect newsgroup reading and posting. Choose Tools | Options to display the Options dialog box that shows these settings. (Tables 23-1 and 23-2 earlier in this chapter describe other settings in the Options dialog box.)

Tab	Setting	Description
General	Default Messaging Programs: This application is the default News handler.	Clicking the Make Default button specifies that when you click the URL of a newsgroup, Outlook Express opens to display the newsgroup messages.
Read	Get *xx* headers at a time	Specifies how many message headers to download when you read a newsgroup.
Read	Mark all messages as read when exiting a newsgroup	Specifies that when you are done reading a newsgroup, Outlook Express marks the unread messages as read, so that they don't show up as unread the next time you read the newsgroup.
Send	News Sending Format: HTML/Plain Text	Specifies whether your newsgroup postings are sent as HTML or as plain text (see "Composing in HTML" earlier in this chapter). Always set this option to Plain Text, because very few newsgroups tolerate HTML-formatted postings

Table 23-3.   *Configuration Settings for Newsgroup Reading and Posting*

Tab	Setting	Description
Compose	Compose Font: News	Specifies how unformatted messages appear on your screen when you are composing them.
Compose	Stationery: News	Specifies what stationery (standard formatting) your news messages will use. *Never use stationery for newsgroup messages, because it uses HTML formatting.*
Maintenance	Delete news messages *xxx* days after being downloaded	Specifies whether old news messages are deleted automatically, and if so, after how many days. Because of the volume of messages in many newsgroups, you are unlikely to want to save all the messages you receive.

Table 23-3.   *Configuration Settings for Newsgroup Reading and Posting* (continued)

Subscribing to Newsgroups

When you read newsgroups, Outlook Express looks at the list of newsgroups to which you subscribe and checks your news server to see whether those newsgroups have any new messages. The first step, then, in using Outlook Express as a newsreader program is to find some interesting newsgroups and subscribe to them.

To practice reading newsgroups, create an account for Microsoft's public news server, msnews.microsoft.com, and subscribe to the newsgroups about Windows XP. Start with microsoft.public.windowsxp.basics. Or, create an account for your ISP's news server (for example, news.earthlink.com) and choose interesting-looking newsgroups.

Downloading the List of Available Newsgroups

The first time that you click your news account icon, Outlook Express informs you that you are not subscribed to any newsgroups, and asks whether you want to download a list of available newsgroups from your news server. Most news servers carry thousands and thousands of newsgroups, so downloading the whole list with a dial-up Internet connection takes some time. Fortunately, you have to do this only once for each news account you establish. From time to time you will want to update this list, but updating does not take nearly as long.

Searching for Interesting Newsgroups

Once you have downloaded a news account's list of available newsgroups, you can view it by selecting the account in the left pane of the Outlook Express window and clicking the Newsgroups button on the toolbar. The Newsgroup Subscriptions window appears, as shown in Figure 23-11.

In the early days of the Internet, you could choose the newsgroups to which you wanted to subscribe just by scanning the list of available groups. Now, the number of groups has grown so large that this method is like wandering through the stacks of a poorly organized library. Scrolling down the list of newsgroups can be an entertaining way to give yourself an idea of the kinds of things that are available, but it is not an efficient way to look for a particular kind of newsgroup.

Fortunately, the Newsgroup Subscriptions window gives you a few tools to aid in your search. This window has three tabs:

- **All**   Shows the complete list of newsgroups available on this server.
- **Subscribed**   Lists the (much smaller) list of newsgroups to which you have chosen to subscribe.

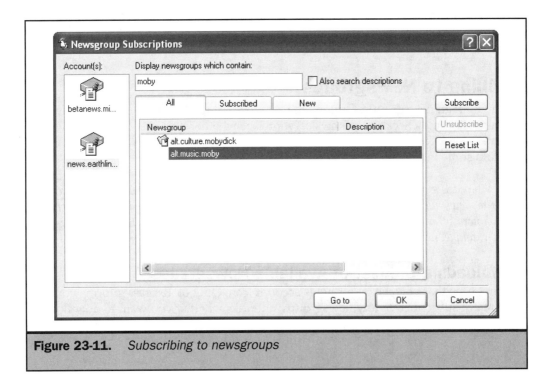

Figure 23-11.   *Subscribing to newsgroups*

■ **New**   Shows the newsgroups that your server has added since the previous time you updated the newsgroup list.

Above each of these tabs is the Display Newsgroups Which Contain line. When this line is blank, a tab lists all the newsgroups appropriate to it. (That is, the All tab lists all newsgroups.) Typing something onto this line restricts the list to newsgroups containing what you have typed. In Figure 23-11 for example, the All tab lists all newsgroups that have "moby" somewhere in their names—one (alt.culture.mobydick) about the novel *Moby Dick* and another (alt.music.moby) about the musician Moby.

So, for example, if you want to know whether there is a newsgroup devoted to your favorite author or entertainer, go to the All tab of the Newsgroup Subscriptions window and type his or her last name into Display Newsgroups Which Contain. If you already did that search last week, but want to know whether there are any new newsgroups you should look at, do the same thing with the New tab.

Subscribing to a Newsgroup (or Not)

Once you have found a newsgroup you want to try out, select its name in the Newsgroup Subscriptions window and click the Subscribe button. The newsgroup appears on the Subscribed tab of the Newsgroup Subscriptions window, and a folder corresponding to the newsgroup is automatically created as a subfolder of the news account folder. Whenever the newsgroup appears in the Newsgroup Subscriptions window, it has a newsgroup icon next to it. For example, in Figure 23-11, alt.culture .mobydick has been subscribed to.

To unsubscribe, right-click the newsgroup in the folder list of the main Outlook Express window and choose Unsubscribe from the shortcut menu. Or you can select the newsgroup in the Newsgroup Subscriptions window and click the Unsubscribe button.

You can examine a newsgroup without subscribing to it by selecting it in the Newsgroup Subscriptions window and clicking the Go To button rather than the Subscribe button. Outlook Express downloads the headers of recent articles on a one-time-only basis. When you stop looking at the newsgroup, Outlook Express asks whether you want to subscribe.

Reading a Newsgroup

Outlook Express displays newsgroups in a format that is similar to the way it displays mail folders: the left pane contains a folder list, the upper-right pane contains a message list for the currently selected newsgroup, and the lower-right pane previews the currently selected message. (You can alter this layout in a variety of ways.) Most newsgroup messages are sufficiently short that the preview pane is all you'll really need (see "Choosing a Layout for the Outlook Express Window" earlier in this chapter).

Unread articles are displayed in bold in the message list, and their icons are slightly brighter than the icons of messages that have been read. Newsgroups containing unread messages are displayed in bold on the folder list, with the number of unread messages in parentheses next to the name.

The message list groups all the messages that reply to a particular message. A plus box appears in the margin next to the original message; when clicked, it changes to a minus sign, and the replies are displayed underneath (and slightly indented from) the original message.

Reading a Newsgroup Online

If you are online, selecting a subscribed newsgroup from the folder list causes Outlook Express to download the headers of the messages on that newsgroup. In other words, the message list window fills up automatically. The messages themselves, however, are not downloaded until you select them in the message list. (The point of this is to save both download time and disk space on your computer.) When you find an intriguing header in the message list, click it to see its text in the preview pane, or double-click it to give the message a window of its own.

Reading a Newsgroup Offline

To read a newsgroup while spending the minimum amount of time online, download the headers as in the preceding section, and then disconnect by choosing File | Work Offline. You can then examine the headers of messages offline. When you find one you want, select it in the message window and then choose Tools | Mark For Offline | Download Message Later. The next time you are online and synchronize your new account, Outlook Express downloads all the marked messages, which you can then read either online or offline.

Using Message Rules to Filter a Newsgroup

Message rules for newsgroups work very much like message rules for e-mail (see "Filtering Your Mail with Message Rules" earlier in this chapter). They instruct Outlook Express to handle certain kinds of messages automatically. In particular, you can tell Outlook Express not to display messages written by particular people by adding them to your Blocked Senders list (see "Throwing Away Spam by Blocking Senders" earlier in this chapter). Applying message rules to a newsgroup also gives you a more focused list of headers and saves download time.

Conceptually, establishing a new message rule has two basic steps: you list the criteria that define a class of messages, and you tell Outlook Express what to do with the messages in that class. More precisely, you follow these steps:

1. Select Tools | Message Rules | News. The Message Rules dialog box opens with the News Rules tab on top. (If you have no other rules defined, Outlook Express may open the New News Rule dialog box as well; if so, you can skip step 2.)

2. Click the New button. The New News Rule dialog box opens.

3. Check boxes in the Select Conditions For Your Rule section of the New News Rule dialog box. These boxes correspond to criteria that describe messages. You may need to choose several of these boxes to get the exact messages you want to act on. When you check a box, the corresponding text appears in the Rule

Description section of the New News Rule dialog box. Most of the criteria need some other piece of information to make sense. For example, Where The From Line Contains People needs you to specify *which* people the rule should apply to. In these cases, the phrase that needs to be specified appears in blue. You'll insert this extra information in step 5. (A more detailed description of how to work with these criteria is contained in the section "Filtering Your Mail with Message Rules," earlier in this chapter.)

4. Check boxes in the Select The Actions For Your Rule section of the New News Rule dialog box. These boxes correspond to the actions you want Outlook Express to perform on the messages described in step 3. Like the Conditions in step 3, the Actions contain phrases that may require additional specification. For example, Highlight It With Color doesn't say which color should be used. You'll insert this extra information in step 5.

5. Examine the Rule Description section of the New News Rule dialog box. If any word or phrase is highlighted in blue, click it. A dialog box appears to allow you to insert the extra information needed to make the phrase specific.

6. When you have specified all the highlighted phrases in the Rule Description section, type a name into the Name Of The Rule section of the New News Rule dialog box.

7. Click OK. The Message Rules dialog box returns. Your new rule is included in the list of message rules. If you are done defining rules, click OK.

| Tip | *Mark all messages from yourself as watched so that you can easily spot replies to them.* |

You can turn a message rule on or off by choosing Tools | Message Rules | News and then checking or unchecking the rule's check box in the Message Rules dialog box. To remove a rule, select it from the list in the Message Rules dialog box and click Remove. To edit a rule, select it from the list in the Message Rules dialog box and click Modify.

You can use a rule to organize newsgroup messages that you have already downloaded, in the same way that you can use a rule to organize downloaded mail messages (see "Using Message Rules to Sort Old Messages" earlier in this chapter).

Saving Messages

By default, Outlook Express saves the text of downloaded news messages only for five days after you download them. When you close Outlook Express, messages older than that are thrown away, unless you save them by selecting File | Save As. Messages are saved in text files with the extension .nws that you can read with Notepad. You can drag news messages that you want to keep to your mail folders. Alternatively, you can tell Outlook Express to save messages longer—choose Tools | Options, click the Maintenance tab, and set the Delete News Messages *xx* Days After Being Downloaded setting.

Participating in a Newsgroup

Many people read a newsgroup for years and never respond to it in any way, neither writing e-mail messages to the authors of the messages they read, nor posting messages of their own. This is called *lurking*, and is a widely accepted practice. In fact, even if you do intend to post your own messages to a group eventually, we recommend that you lurk for a while first to learn the social norms of the group.

*To avoid asking obvious questions that a newsgroup's regular readers are sick of seeing, find out if the question is already answered in the newsgroup's Frequently Asked Questions (FAQ). You can look up the FAQs of many newsgroups at the International FAQ Consortium at **www.faqs.org/faqs**. A search engine at this web site will help you find the FAQ you are looking for.*

One alternative to lurking is to examine the archives of the newsgroup, or to browse the last week or two of messages. Many newsgroups are archived at Google Groups **groups.google.com** or (for a fee) at **www.supernews.com**.

Very few newsgroups tolerate posting HTML formatted messages or messages with attachments. Be sure to post messages as plain text.

Replying to Authors

Replying to the author of a newsgroup message is no different from replying to the author of a mail message. Just select the message and click the Reply button on the toolbar. Outlook Express opens a mail message window with the author's e-mail address entered automatically in the recipient list. You can create and edit this message just as you would any other mail message. To send your reply to the entire newsgroup rather than just the author(s), use the Reply Group button.

Posting a Message to a Newsgroup

To begin creating a newsgroup message, select a newsgroup from the folder list of the Outlook Express window, so that the Outlook Express News toolbar replaces the Mail toolbar. Then click the New Post button to start a message from scratch, or select a message from the message list of a newsgroup and click the Reply Group button on the toolbar. (Clicking the Reply button creates a mail message addressed to the author of the selected message and does not create a message to the newsgroup. Clicking Forward also creates an e-mail message rather than a newsgroup message.)

In either case a New Message window opens. Like an e-mail message window, it has a header and a body, as shown here:

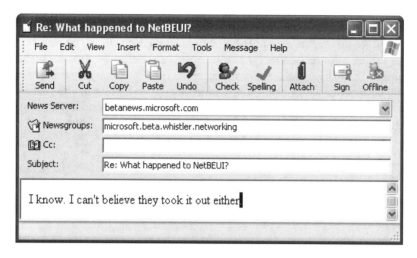

A news message header has three (or possibly four) lines:

- **News server**   Lists the news server the message will be sent through. If you have only one news server account, this line does not appear.

- **Newsgroups**   Lists the newsgroup(s) to which the message is to be posted. If you are replying to a message, Outlook Express inserts the newsgroup of the original message automatically. If you are composing a new message, Outlook Express inserts the currently selected newsgroup. To add newsgroups to the list, click the icon on the Newsgroups line of the header. The Pick Newsgroups dialog box appears.

- **Cc**   If you want your message sent (as e-mail) to other people, list their e-mail addresses in the Cc line of the header. Click the index card icon if you want to choose an address from the Address Book, or type your best guess and then click the Check Names button on the toolbar, just as you would for an e-mail message.

- **Subject**   Give your message a short, specific title. If you are replying or forwarding, the subject line is automatically the same as the original message, preceded by Re or Fwd.

After you have completed the header of your message, type the text into the body of the New Message window. You can use the Check Spelling button to check your spelling, just as you would in an e-mail message.

When you have the message exactly the way you want it, click the Send button. The message is then sent to your Outbox.

If you want to test your newsgroup-posting ability, you can use a newsgroup that Microsoft set up for that very purpose. It lives on the msnews.microsoft.com news server, which (unlike most news servers) anyone can access. Set up an msnews.microsoft.com account in Outlook Express, and then subscribe to the newsgroup microsoft.public .test.here. Send your message to this newsgroup and see if it appears. You can also post test messages to the test.test newsgroup on most public news servers. Don't send test messages to other newsgroups—you'll get irate responses.

Chapter 24

Web Browsing with Internet Explorer and MSN Explorer

Windows XP includes Internet Explorer 6, the latest version of the world's most popular web browser, as well as MSN Explorer, a simplified front-end for Internet Explorer that pulls MSN's free services together into a convenient package similar to AOL's interface. You also have the option of using other, non-Microsoft browsers, which have their various advantages and disadvantages.

This chapter describes how to configure Internet Explorer, remember your favorite web sites, and search for new sites. We also explain how to tell Internet Explorer to fill web forms in automatically, set colors, set your start page, and control privacy settings. Although Windows XP doesn't come with a web page editor, its Web Publishing Wizard can help you upload files to the Web.

Web Browser Concepts

A *web browser* (or simply *browser*) is a program that your computer runs to communicate with web servers on the Internet so that it can download the web pages you ask for and display them. At a bare minimum, a browser has to be able to understand HTML and display text. In recent years, however, Internet users have come to expect a lot more. A state-of-the-art browser provides a full multimedia experience, complete with pictures, sound, video, and even 3-D imaging.

HTML, XML, and URLs

Hypertext Markup Language (*HTML*) and *Extensible Markup Language* (*XML*) are the universal computer languages of the Web.

HTML is the original and still most popular web language. It describes how to lay out pages displaying all the diverse kinds of information that the Web contains. A browser, at the most basic level, is a program that reads and interprets HTML. You can see the HTML that makes up a web page by choosing View | Source in Internet Explorer.

XML is a newer and more powerful language that allows authors to describe not just how a page should *look*, but what the data in the page should *mean*. HTML, for example, can tell your browser how to display a web page with rows and columns of numbers. XML can tell your browser that these numbers are parts of a spreadsheet that relate to each other in various ways. So far, programmers and web site designers have barely scratched the surface of what XML can do, but many technology seers and soothsayers are predicting that it will lead to a whole new generation of advanced web services.

While various software companies own and sell HTML and XML reading and writing programs, no one owns the languages themselves. They are international standards, maintained and updated by a complicated political process that so far has worked remarkably well. The World Wide Web Consortium (W3C), at **www.w3.org**, manages the standards for both HTML and XML.

URLs and HTTP

When the pieces of a document are scattered all over the world, but you want to display them seamlessly to a person who could be anywhere else in the world, you need a very good addressing system. Each file on the Internet has an address, called a *Uniform Resource Locator* (*URL*), also sometimes called an *Internet address* or *web address*. For example, the URL of the ESPN web site is **http://espn.go.com**. The first part of a URL (the part before the first colon) specifies the *transfer protocol*, the method that a computer needs to use to access this file. Most web pages are accessed with the *Hypertext Transfer Protocol* (*HTTP*, the language of web communication), which is why web addresses typically begin with http (or its secure, encrypted versions, https or shttp). The http:// at the beginning of a web page's URL is so common that it is assumed as the default protocol by modern browsers. If you simply type **espn.go.com** into the address window of Internet Explorer, the browser fills in the **http://** for itself. In common usage, the http:// at the beginning of a URL is left out (we omit it from the URLs shown in this book).

The rest of the address denotes the web page, but might not tell you where its files are actually located. Whether ESPN's web server is in Los Angeles or Bangkok is invisible from its URL. Information about which web server is responsible for answering requests for which URLs is contained in a huge database that the web servers themselves are constantly updating. As users, we don't need to deal with this level of detail, and that's a good thing. The World Wide Web would be much less usable if sports fans had to learn a new set of URLs every time ESPN got a new computer.

Browser Plug-Ins

Plug-ins are programs that are independent of your browser but "plug in" to it in a seamless way, so that you might not even be aware that you are using software that is not part of the browser. Typically, plug-ins arise when a software company develops a way to display a new type of data over the Web such as 3-D animation or streaming audio. Rather than create a whole new browser with this additional capability, the software company writes a plug-in for popular browsers like Netscape Navigator or Internet Explorer. Users who want to extend the capabilities of their browser in this particular way can install the plug-in, which then operates as if it is part of the browser.

Typically, installing a plug-in is fairly painless. Web pages that contain content requiring a special plug-in usually include instructions for downloading and installing the plug-in. The main inconvenience is the length of time necessary to download the plug-in (which is not even that long if you have a broadband Internet connection). Installing the plug-in is usually a simple matter of clicking a few buttons and perhaps registering with the company that makes the plug-in. You can find a wide variety of plug-ins at the Tucows web site at **www.tucows.com**.

As with any kind of software, downloading and installing a plug-in requires faith in whoever created and distributed it. A plug-in can introduce viruses into your system, modify files without your consent, or transmit data from your machine without your knowledge. Plug-ins from reputable software companies are as safe as any other kind of Internet software, but you should be cautious about downloading plug-ins from web sites that you know nothing about.

The Default Web Browser

The *default web browser* is the application that Windows uses to open a web page when you haven't told it what browser to use—for example, when you click a web link in an e-mail message or choose a web page from the Favorites menu. Initially, Internet Explorer is the default browser, but you can choose another browser to be the default if you want (see "Changing the Default Browser" later in this chapter).

You can, of course, open any browser you want and use it to browse the Web, whether it is the default browser or not. You can even have several browsers running at the same time—for example, Internet Explorer and Netscape Navigator.

What's Going On With Java?

Java is a computer language that is used for writing *applets*, small computer programs that a browser can download, run, and throw away when it is done with them. Many web pages are much less interesting if your browser is not set up to run Java applets, and some web pages won't load at all.

Depending on when you acquired Windows XP and whether or not you installed Service Pack 1, you may or may not have a *Java virtual machine*, (or JVM) the software you need to run the Java applets on web pages. If you have Service Pack 1, you probably have Microsoft's Java virtual machine. If you don't, you may get an error message when you try to load a web page that contains a Java component.

What's going on? This is all part of a legal battle between Microsoft and Sun, the company that created Java. It's not really your concern, and it's silly that the dispute has gotten to the point where it inconveniences you. But here's what you should do:

If you don't run into any problems, do nothing. You probably have the Microsoft JVM, which is good enough for most practical purposes.

If you don't have the Microsoft JVM, the easiest way to get it is to get Service Pack 1 for Windows XP. You can buy it on a CD for about $10 or download it free from Microsoft's web site **www.microsoft.com**. It fixes a lot of bugs in Windows XP, and you really should have it anyway—the JVM is just a bonus.

But if you want the best, most up-to-date version of Java—or if you want to use Java with some browser other than Internet Explorer—get Sun's JVM, not Microsoft's. You can download it free from Sun's web site **java.sun.com/getjava**. You can also get Sun's JVM in the Java versions of Netscape Navigator, Mozilla, or Opera. The download of the JVM by itself is about 9MB, so if you have a dial-up connection you may want to get it on a CD-ROM. The cheapest way we've found to do that is to order the CD of Netscape Navigator for around $10. Order it from **cd.netscape.com**.

Which Browser Should You Use?

Windows comes with two applications you can use to browse the Internet: Internet Explorer and MSN Explorer. But many other browsers exist, and most of them can be downloaded free from the Internet. Each browser has its advantages and disadvantages.

 Don't be afraid to try out a new browser. All browsers work more or less the same way. For an Internet Explorer user to use Netscape Navigator, Mozilla, or Opera is about as difficult as a GM driver driving a Ford or Chrysler.

Which browser is best for you depends on what you do on the Web and how sophisticated a computer user you are.

■ Inexperienced users who want a simple interface to basic web services and don't want to make a lot of choices should use MSN Explorer. See "MSN Explorer" and "Getting Started with MSN Explorer" later in this chapter.

■ Most people should use either Internet Explorer or Netscape Navigator (see "Netscape Navigator" later in this chapter), which are the most popular, most full-featured browsers. The choice between them is largely a matter of taste, and the fact that Internet Explorer is already installed on any Windows system usually tips the balance in its favor. The bulk of this chapter is about using Internet Explorer.

■ If you are a fan of the open-source software movement, you should definitely try Mozilla. It gives you almost all the features of Netscape in a less commercial package. See the "Mozilla" section later in this chapter.

■ Sophisticated users who don't mind looking up how-to instructions on the Web should consider Opera. See the "Opera" section later in this chapter.

Internet Explorer

Internet Explorer (which we'll sometimes abbreviate as IE) is far and away the most popular browser. According to some surveys, Internet Explorer is used by 95% of the people who browse the Web. Following an antitrust agreement between the government and Microsoft, computer manufacturers have the option of hiding Internet Explorer and making some other browser the default, but in all probability your computer arrived ready to use Internet Explorer. (If not, you can restore it as follows: Go to the Add Or Remove Programs section of the Control Panel, click the Set Program Access And Defaults link, expand the Custom option, and select the Internet Explorer radio button.)

Internet Explorer has a lot going for it: It's free. It's already installed. It supports the full range of features. It looks just like Windows Explorer, which you have to learn to use anyway. It's what everybody else uses. Microsoft is not going to go out of business or stop supporting it. Some web sites (especially Microsoft web sites) are designed to work better with Internet Explorer. It interfaces nicely with other Microsoft applications like Windows Media Player and Windows Messenger.

WINDOWS XP HOME
ON THE INTERNET

Why wouldn't you use Internet Explorer? Here are a few reasons:

- **Security** Hackers design viruses to attack the most popular software packages, so using the same browser that everybody else uses is not a great idea from a security standpoint. Also, Microsoft historically has had a lax attitude toward security, though it claims it is trying to change. ActiveX controls (which only IE uses) are a security nightmare. Finally, a security flaw in a browser that is fully integrated into the operating system (as IE is) is in a position to do a lot more damage than a similar flaw in a stand-alone application like Netscape or Opera.

- **Internet Explorer's features for handling cookies and pop-up ads are not the best** Opera and Mozilla do better in this area.

- **Political reasons** IE's domination of the browser market gives Microsoft a lot of power over the future of the Internet, and a lot of opportunities to create new monopolies and co-opt existing standards. If you don't think this is a good thing, using an alternative browser is a painless way to express yourself.

MSN Explorer

Microsoft offers a number of free web-based services through its MSN division—Hotmail e-mail accounts, MSN Calendar for keeping track of your appointments, MSN Photos for sharing your photographs online, as well as the usual services you expect from any web portal, like news headlines, stock prices, and weather reports.

MSN Explorer is a simplified front end to Internet Explorer that integrates all these web services with other Windows applications like Windows Media Player and Windows Messenger. Microsoft has announced that it will begin charging a subscription fee for the next version of MSN Explorer (version 8). But MSN Explorer 7 is a free component of Windows XP.

| **Note** | *You don't have to subscribe to the MSN Internet service to use MSN Explorer.* |

If you're looking for an AOL-like experience without using AOL, MSN Explorer is your best bet. It's simple and unintimidating. It combines most of the services people look for from the Internet into one interface. If you already use a number of MSN's services, or if you just want services that work and don't want to be faced with dozens of choices every time you try to do something, then you should take a good look at MSN Explorer.

The downside of MSN Explorer is that it does not allow the same security controls that Internet Explorer does. The MSN Explorer Security Statement says: "If you have chosen security settings that will interfere with MSN Explorer, then your security settings are temporarily changed to allow MSN Explorer to work properly. In addition, while MSN Explorer is active on your computer, the special settings for MSN will apply to any Microsoft Internet Explorer window you may have open." Frankly, the idea that some program is mucking around with our security settings behind the

How Can Browsers Be Free?

Web browsers are large, complicated applications that require a huge amount of effort to create and maintain. And yet somehow all the major browsers are free (or, in the case of Opera, have a free version). How can this be? How do all the people who work on these browsers get paid?

The answer is different for different browsers. Internet Explorer, MSN Explorer, and Netscape Navigator are free because the companies that make them (Microsoft, Microsoft, and AOL/Time-Warner, respectively) use the browsers to direct you to their other commercial web services. Internet Explorer, for example, is set up with MSN as its default home page and numerous Microsoft web sites on its Links bar, while Navigator has Netcenter as its default home page and bookmarks to various AOL web sites like CNN. With the touch of a toolbar button, MSN Explorer sends you to its shopping web site, or to a web site from which you can order prints of your photos.

The free version of Opera is supported directly by advertising displayed next to the toolbar.

Mozilla is free because it is an open-source project. In other words, a network of computer programmers from around the world build and maintain Mozilla as a sort of hobby, without expecting to be paid. It is amazing that such a project works in a modern, money-driven economy, but open-source projects have produced several high-quality free applications, including Mozilla, the Linux operating system, and the GIMP image processor.

scenes gives us the willies. For this reason, we do not use MSN Explorer, no matter how cute and convenient it is.

If you decide to use it, see "Getting Started with MSN Explorer" later in this chapter.

Other Browsers You Can Use

In spite of Internet Explorer's near monopoly, dozens of other browsers exist, and we find at least three worth considering: Netscape Navigator, Opera, and Mozilla. To check out dozens of other browsers, go to **download.cnet.com**.

Netscape Navigator

Navigator dominated the browser market before Microsoft made Internet Explorer a free component of Windows. The tactics by which Internet Explorer took the market away from Navigator became the source of the famous Microsoft antitrust lawsuit (which is still unresolved as we write this book).

Netscape 7 matches Internet Explorer feature for feature and we like its security and privacy features better than Internet Explorer. Plus (to us, at least), it just looks cooler. The free way to get Netscape involves a huge download, however, and if you don't have a broadband connection it is probably not worth the effort. (The setup program is deceptively small at 228 kilobytes, but depending on the choices you make during setup, it downloads an additional 9–32MB. On a dial-up Internet connection it could take all day.) You can get Netscape to send you a CD-ROM for about $7. Either download the setup program or order the CD from **cd.netscape.com**.

Opera

Rather than try to compete feature for feature with IE and Netscape, the Opera browser focuses on being small and quick. It is widely regarded as the fastest browser at downloading and displaying web pages (though claims like these are hard to prove), and because it has a smaller program, it takes considerably less time to download and install than Netscape. The non-Java version is 3.4MB, while the Java version is 11MB. To download Opera, go to **www.opera.com**.

Opera has two main disadvantages compared to either Internet Explorer or Netscape:

- It's not free. You either have to accept a small advertising bar or pay $39 for the advertising-free version. (It sometimes goes on sale for $20.) On the other hand, after you pay for Opera you have a browser that is considerably less commercial than either Netscape or Internet Explorer: It lets you easily kill pop-up advertising windows and is not constantly trying to steer you towards the web sites of its commercial parents or partners.

- Finding and installing plug-ins for special kinds of web content can be tricky. In general, any plug-in that works with Netscape Navigator can be set up to work with Opera also, but the process is not always transparent. However, the Opera web site contains good instructions for most things you might want to do.

Mozilla

Mozilla is the open-source project on which the Netscape browser has been based since Netscape 6. There's a historical connection: the Mozilla project was started in 1998 by Netscape, which contributed the source code of Netscape Communicator.

Consequently, the Mozilla and Netscape browsers share a lot of code and look the same "under the hood." Netscape, however, is a commercial company (part of AOL Time Warner), and Mozilla is an organization with no revenues, salaries, or profits. In essence, Netscape makes each new version of its browser by taking the latest Mozilla code (which anyone is free to do) and commercializing it: adding proprietary features (like Netscape Radio), slick interfaces, links to AOL web sites, and so on. Occasionally they take a feature out, like Mozilla's easy way of avoiding pop-up advertisements.

As a matter of personal taste, we find Mozilla's noncommercial interface refreshing. Download it from **www.mozilla.org**. Netscape Radio is cool, but we'd rather zap the pop-up ads.

Getting Started with Internet Explorer

Internet Explorer is installed automatically when you install Windows XP. Its icon is a blue letter *e* at or near the top of the Start menu, on the Quick Launch toolbar, or on the desktop. Or, choose Start | All Programs | Internet Explorer. When you start Internet Explorer for the first time, it attempts to display its start page. This may cause it to attempt to connect to the Internet, which in turn may invoke the New Connection Wizard (see Chapter 22).

Explorer Windows in Internet Explorer

Internet Explorer displays web pages in Explorer windows (see Chapter 7, section "The Anatomy of Windows Explorer"). Explorer window menus and toolbars work in the same way whether they are being used by Internet Explorer to display a web page or by Windows Explorer to display a folder. As explained in Chapter 7, you can display as many or as few of the elements of the Explorer window as you like, and you can reconfigure the toolbars to your taste.

The only difference between the windows used by Windows Explorer and Internet Explorer is in the configuration of the Standard Buttons toolbar. Internet Explorer's default Standard Buttons toolbar has more buttons and looks like this:

Left to right the buttons are Back, Forward, Stop, Refresh, Home, Search, Favorites, Media, History, Mail, Print, and Edit. The menu and keyboard equivalents of buttons not already listed in Table 7-1 in Chapter 7 are given in Table 24-1.

Button	Menu Equivalent	Keyboard Equivalent
Stop	View	Stop	ESCAPE
Refresh	View	Refresh	F5
Home	View	Go To	Home Page	ALT-HOME
Favorites	View	Explorer Bar	Favorites	CTRL-I
Media	View	Explorer Bar	Media	None
History	View	Explorer Bar	History	CTRL-H
Mail	Tools	Mail and News	None
Print	File	Print	CTRL-P
Edit	File	Edit	None

Table 24-1.   *Default Internet Explorer Buttons That Are Not Default Windows Explorer Buttons*

You may add or remove buttons from this toolbar (see Chapter 7, section "The Standard Buttons Toolbar"). Changes that you make to the Standard Buttons toolbar in Internet Explorer do not affect the Standard Buttons toolbar in Windows Explorer, and vice versa. Some buttons you might want to consider are as follows:

- **Related**   Produces a Related Links Explorer bar, which gives a list of web pages that might be related to the current page. The menu equivalent is Tools | Show Related Links.

- **Full Screen**   Maximizes the viewing area by stretching the Internet Explorer window to the full size of your monitor while shrinking all the other features of the Internet Explorer window. Click it again to return to the previous configuration. It is equivalent to View | Full Screen on the menu or F11 on the keyboard.

- **Print Preview**   Shows a page-by-page view of what you would get if you printed out the current web page. The menu equivalent is File | Print Preview.

- **Disconnect**   Breaks your Internet connection.

Browsing the Web

On a standard web page, text phrases that are links to other web pages are displayed in underlined blue type. If you have recently displayed the web page to which the text is linked, the text is usually displayed in maroon. When you are exploring a web site, this feature lets you know where you've been and keeps you from going in circles. In Internet Explorer you can also define the color a link turns when the cursor is above it (the default is red). You can change these colors (see "Choosing Colors" later in this chapter).

When you pass the mouse pointer over a linked object (including a linked text phrase), the pointer changes from an arrow to a hand, and the URL of the web page that the object is linked to is displayed in the status bar of the browser window (if you have the status bar enabled). Not all links on a page are obvious; a small picture, for example, might just be an illustration, or it might be linked to a larger version of the same picture. Passing the mouse pointer over an object is the easiest way to tell whether it is linked.

While files are being downloaded to your browser, the mouse pointer changes to an hourglass. However, it is still functional—you can push buttons or scroll the window with an hourglass pointer. Most important, you can use it to click the Stop button if a link is taking longer to download than you're willing to wait.

Try right-clicking items on web pages—Internet Explorer provides shortcut menus of useful commands. Shortcut menus are available for links, images, backgrounds, and other parts of web pages.

Opening Files on Your System

You can use Internet Explorer to view HTML files that are stored on your hard drive or elsewhere on your system. You can also view images stored in several different image formats, such as JPEG or GIF. Select File | Open and then either type the file address into the Open dialog box that appears, or click the dialog box's Browse button and find the file in the window that appears. The default entry in the Files Of Type drop-down list is HTML files; be sure to change it if you are looking for a file that isn't HTML.

Opening Web Pages

You can open a web page in Internet Explorer by using any of the following methods:

- **Entering its URL into the Address box** The most direct way is to type the URL; but if you have the URL in a file or a mail message, you can copy it and paste it. The Paste command on the Edit menu might not work when the cursor is in the Address box, but you can always paste by pressing CTRL-V. Internet Explorer has an auto-complete feature that tries to guess what URL you are typing and finishes it for you, based on similar URLs that you've visited before. A list of its guesses appears under the Address box as you type. If one is correct, click it and press ENTER.

- **Selecting it from the list that drops down from the Address box** The Address box remembers the last 25 URLs that you have typed into it.

- **Clicking a link to it from another web page**

- **Clicking a link to it from a mail message or newsgroup article** Many mail and messaging programs, including Outlook Express and MSN Messenger, automatically link the URLs in a message to the corresponding web pages (see Chapter 23). Clicking the URL opens the default browser, which displays the web page. If the browser can't find the page, try copying and pasting the URL into its Address box and making sure it looks right (remove spaces and line breaks from the URL, for example).

- **Selecting it from History** Internet Explorer maintains records of the web pages you have viewed in the past 20 days (or as many days as you select). You can display these records and return to any of the web pages with a click (see "Examining History" later in this chapter).

- **Selecting it from the Favorites menu** Accessing a Favorite from the Internet Explorer Favorites menu opens it in Internet Explorer, no matter what the default browser is.

- **Opening an Internet shortcut** Opening an Internet shortcut from Windows Explorer starts the default browser (even if another browser is already running), connects to the Internet, and displays the web page to which the shortcut points.

| Tip | *To retrieve and display the same page again, click Refresh on the toolbar or press F5. Refresh a web page when it looks like it didn't load properly or if you think that the information on the page has changed since you loaded it (for example, if you are monitoring sports scores that change minute by minute).* |

Printing Web Pages, Frames, and Individual Images

Start the print job by selecting File | Print; then make your choices from the Print dialog box. Web pages are not usually paginated, so it's a good idea to look at the print preview before printing. Select File | Print Preview. The preview allows you to see how many pages the document requires and decide which pages are worth printing.

To print just one frame of a web page, right-click the item you want to print and select Print from the shortcut menu. To print a picture from a web page, rest the cursor over the picture and wait for the image toolbar to appear in the upper-left corner of the picture:

The image toolbar (a row of four small icons) appears (unless the picture is small). Click the Print button on the image toolbar.

Saving Web Page Files

You can save a web page in four ways. All of them begin by selecting File | Save As. When the Save Web Page dialog box appears, make one of the following four choices from the Save As Type drop-down list:

- To save all the files that make up a web page in a folder, select Web Page Complete. In a page with a number of pictures and advertisements, this can turn into a quite a file. When we saved the home page of Major League Baseball (**mlb.com**), the folder had 62 files in it.

- To save the entire web page as a single file of type MHTML, select Web Archive.

- To save only the HTML file, without the images, sounds, animations, and other supporting files, select Web Page HTML Only. If you do this, you should look at the saved file before you leave the web page. Sometimes we have been surprised by how little the HTML file actually contains.

- To save only the text from a web page, select Text File.

- To save a picture from a web page, rest the mouse pointer on the picture, wait for the image toolbar to appear, and click the Save button. Or right-click the picture and choose Save Image.

You can save a file from a web page that links to it by right-clicking the link and selecting Save Target As from the shortcut menu.

Managing Internet Explorer's Windows

Internet Explorer allows you to open as many windows as you like, which can be handy when you are comparing the web sites of two car companies or checking a sports scoreboard occasionally while you research something else.

To open a new window, choose File | New or press CTRL-N on the keyboard. The new window opens displaying the same web page as the previous window. If you want to open a link on a web page without losing the page you are displaying, right-click the link and select Open In New Window from the shortcut menu.

Web sites frequently open new Explorer windows on their own, usually to display advertisements. These are called *pop-up windows*, and most people consider them a nuisance. Internet Explorer doesn't give you any way to prevent unwanted pop-ups, though there are several software utilities that can work with Internet Explorer to solve this problem. If pop-ups annoy you, consider downloading Smasher (**www.popupstop.com**) or Power Popup Killer (**www.lnc-soft.com**).

 The browser that handles pop-up windows most easily is Opera. All you have to do is select File | Quick Preferences | Refuse Popup Windows from its menu. In Mozilla things are almost as simple: In the Advanced | Scripts and Windows section of its Preferences dialog box, just uncheck the Open Unrequested Windows check box. We also like Mozilla's ability to display multiple pages in a single window, displaying a separate tab for each window: just press CTRL-T to create a new tab.

Getting Started with MSN Explorer

MSN Explorer (described in the section "MSN Explorer" earlier in this chapter) is a utility that pulls together several of the free online services offered by the Microsoft Network (MSN). It is a web browser as well as a front end for Microsoft's Hotmail web-based e-mail. Its icon is a butterfly, which you can probably find on the taskbar. (If not, check the Start | All Programs menu.)

When you start MSN Explorer, the first thing you see is this dialog box:

If you click Yes, MSN Explorer becomes your default browser and e-mail program and appears at the top of the Start menu. If you are just experimenting with MSN Explorer and aren't ready to commit to it, click No—you'll get another chance to click Yes the next time you open MSN Explorer. Once MSN Explorer is your default browser, it's hard to get rid of it.

Figure 24-1. *MSN Explorer pulls together MSN's free services.*

A wizard then leads you through the process of creating a Microsoft Passport, (which you can avoid if you already have one). You also have the opportunity to sign up for MSN Internet service through the wizard, though it is not necessary.

The wizard also urges you to set your privacy setting to the default, if they are not already. This also seems not to be necessary; we clicked No and continued to maintain settings that block third-party cookies without running into any obvious problems.

When MSN Explorer is running, as shown in Figure 24-1, you are one click away from your Hotmail e-mail account, your local weather report, quotes on your stock portfolio, the appointments you have listed on MSN Calendar, and many other services. You do not have to get your Internet access from MSN to use these services—you can continue to use your existing ISP account.

Remembering Where You've Been on the Web

Internet Explorer provides a variety of ways to remember which web sites you've already visited and how to get back to them.

Covering Your Tracks and Tracking Others

Most of the time it's convenient that Internet Explorer remembers the web sites you've been viewing. But you are leaving a trail other people can follow if they have access to your computer and user account. Conversely, you may want to see what other people (your children, for example) have been viewing on the Web.

This is the trail that you may want to erase or follow:

- **The History Explorer bar** keeps track of every web page Internet Explorer sees for 20 days. You can erase this record selectively or completely. See "Examining History" later in this chapter.

- **The Address box** keeps a drop-down list of the last 25 addresses that have been typed into it. It remembers even more addresses than this. You can test whether Internet Explorer has seen a web site recently by starting to type its URL into the Address box. If it has, the auto-complete feature will finish the address for you. Clearing History clears this record also.

- **Temporary Internet Files** is a folder of web pages and other files that Internet Explorer has cached so that it won't have to download them again. It is not affected when you clear the History folder. It mostly contains cookies, icons, and images from recently visited web sites. To edit or delete the contents of this folder see "Managing the Cache of Web Pages" later in this chapter.

- **The Back menu**—don't forget about this one. If you walk away from your computer without closing Internet Explorer, anyone could hit the Back button and see where you've been browsing. Closing Internet Explorer clears the Back menu.

If you find yourself covering your tracks frequently, you can get software to do it for you. Check out the Web Washer utility from Webroot Software (**www.webroot.com**).

The two simplest are

- **The Back menu**   The Back button has a drop-down menu of the last several web pages you have looked at during the current session. To access this menu, click the arrow on the right side of the Back button. After you use the Back button, the Forward button becomes active and has a similar drop-down menu listing the web pages you have "backed over."

- **The Address box**   If you remember the beginning of the URL you are looking for, start typing it into the Address box. As you type, Internet Explorer's autocomplete feature generates a menu of URLs, based on the URLs you have visited recently. If the URL you want appears, you can choose it from the menu. In addition, Internet Explorer maintains a drop-down list of the last 25 URLs that you have typed into the Address box. You can select an entry off the drop-down list, and the browser fetches the corresponding web page.

To keep track of more sites, use the History and Favorites features.

Examining History

Internet Explorer stores your recently viewed web pages as Internet shortcuts inside a hierarchy of folders capped by the History folder. You can turn History off, wipe the History folder clean, or edit it selectively, removing only the web pages you don't want recorded.

Clicking the History button on the toolbar (the one with the turn-back-the-clock icon) or selecting View | Explorer Bar | History opens the History Explorer bar, shown here:

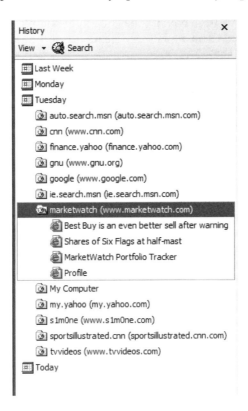

Clicking the History button again (or the X in the upper-right corner) causes the History pane to disappear.

The History folder is organized into subfolders—one for each day of the current week and one for each previous week, going back 20 days. (You can use the steps listed in the following paragraphs to change the number of days History remembers.) Selecting a closed folder expands the tree to show its contents; selecting an open folder compresses the tree to hide its contents. Each day's folder contains one subfolder for each web site visited. Inside the web site folders are Internet shortcuts to each of the pages viewed on that web site.

Delete a shortcut or a subfolder from the History folder by right-clicking it and selecting Delete from the shortcut menu.

Internet Explorer's History settings are controlled from the General tab of the Internet Options dialog box, shown in Figure 24-2. Choose Tools | Internet Options to display it.

To delete all the entries in the History folder, click the Clear History button on the General tab of the Internet Options dialog box.

Each user has his/her own History folder with its own settings. This folder is located at C:\Documents And Settings*username*\Local Settings\History (assuming that Windows is installed on C:—replace *username* with your user account name, as described in Chapter 6). Local Settings is a hidden folder, so you can only see it if you have set Windows Explorer to display hidden files and folders.

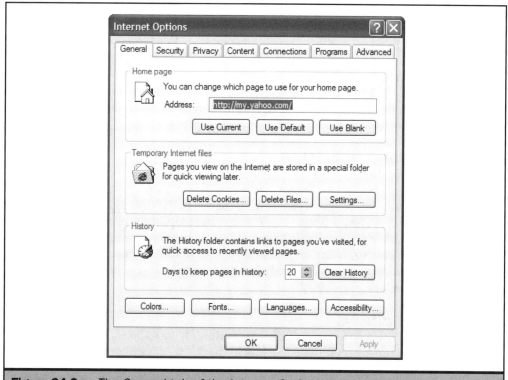

Figure 24-2.   *The General tab of the Internet Options dialog box*

Using Favorites, Links, and Internet Shortcuts

Favorites and Internet shortcuts are ways to keep track of web sites that you think you will want to come back to.

An *Internet shortcut* is a small file (of type URL) that contains the Internet address of a web page. Opening an Internet shortcut causes Windows to connect to your Internet provider (if necessary), open your default browser, and display the web page that the shortcut points to.

Favorites is a folder of Internet shortcuts. This folder is accessible from the Favorites menu in Internet Explorer, and you can add Favorites to the Start menu as well. Selecting an entry from the Favorites menu has the same effect as opening an Internet shortcut that points to that web page. When Favorites are chosen from the Start menu, they open in the default browser, but choosing a web page from the Favorites menu of Internet Explorer opens the page in Internet Explorer, even if another browser is the default browser.

The Links folder is a subfolder of Favorites. The items in the Links folder appear on the Links toolbar.

Adding Favorites and Links

Adding a web page to the Favorites menu automatically creates an Internet shortcut pointing to that web page. If a web page is displayed in Internet Explorer, you can add it to Favorites by dragging its icon from the Address box to the Favorites menu or the Favorites Explorer bar, or you can invoke the Add Favorites Wizard by selecting Favorites | Add To Favorites.

To add a web page to the Links toolbar, either drag its icon from the Address box to the place on the Links bar where you want it, or drag it into the Links folder on the Favorites Explorer bar or on the Favorites menu.

Creating Internet Shortcuts

To create an Internet shortcut on your desktop, open the page to which you want to create a shortcut and choose File | Send | Shortcut To Desktop.

You can also create shortcuts in Windows Explorer or the desktop. From Windows Explorer, choose File | New | Shortcut. From the desktop, right-click and choose New | Shortcut. Either way, a Create Shortcut box opens. Type the URL of the web page into the Create Shortcut box, or if you have copied the command line from some other document, paste it into Create Shortcut by pressing CTRL-V. Click Next, give the shortcut a name, and click Finish.

Organizing Favorites

If you have only a few web pages, your favorites don't have to be well organized, but as time goes by, favorites accumulate like knick-knacks. It saves time to reorganize them once in a while and toss out the ones that are obsolete.

The Favorites list is actually a folder (C:\Windows\Profiles*username*\Favorites), and each of the entries on the Favorites list is a shortcut pointing to the URL of the corresponding web page. Consequently, one way to organize Favorites is to use the same techniques you would use to organize any other folder in Windows Explorer. You can choose Favorites | Organize Favorites from any Explorer or Internet Explorer window. An Organize Favorites box opens. Move, rename, or delete entries on your Favorites list by selecting the entries and clicking the corresponding buttons in the Organize Favorites box.

Importing and Exporting Favorites and Bookmarks

When you install Internet Explorer on a computer that already has Netscape Navigator, the Navigator bookmarks are automatically imported to the Favorites list. Conversely, there is no need to convert the Favorites folder to Navigator bookmarks, as long as you are using both on the same computer: The Bookmarks | Imported IE Favorites menu in Navigator displays an up-to-date list of the entries in the Favorites folder.

To import bookmarks to Internet Explorer after installation, select File | Import And Export to start the Import/Export Wizard. This wizard provides the best way to convert between Internet Explorer's Favorites (a folder of Internet shortcuts) and Navigator's bookmarks (an HTML file of links).

Adding Favorites to the Start Menu

Having the Favorites menu appear under Start is a convenient way to eliminate one step in the process of opening a favorite web page. Rather than starting a browser and then choosing the web page, you can choose the web page directly from the Start | Favorites menu, and the default browser starts automatically.

If Favorites doesn't appear on your Start menu, you can add it as follows:

1. Right-click the Start button and select Properties from the shortcut menu. The Taskbar And Start Menu Properties dialog box appears with the Start Menu tab selected (see Chapter 10). The tab contains two radio buttons: Start Menu (the default setting) and Classic Start Menu. One of the buttons is selected, and the Customize button next to this choice is active.

2. Click the active Customize button on the Start Menu tab. Either the Customize Start Menu or the Customize Classic Start Menu dialog box appears.

3. Check the Favorites Menu check box on the Advanced tab of the Customize Start Menu dialog box, or the Display Favorites check box on the Customize Classic Start Menu dialog box.

Searching for Web Pages

Internet Explorer gives you three ways to search the Web: Simple convenient searches can be done from the Address box; more complex searches using a variety of search engines are possible from the Search Companion Explorer bar; and you can always do your searches from the web site of whatever search engine you like.

Search Engines

The Web is not well organized. It is not like an encyclopedia, in which articles of uniform quality are arranged in alphabetical order. It's also not like a library, where books are shelved according to topic. The Web would be practically unusable if not for *search engines*: web sites that contain vast databases of what words appear in which web pages. If you put a collection of words into a search engine, it outputs a list of web pages that contain those words. The best search engines have techniques for guessing which of the web sites on the list are most likely to be what you are looking for, and give you the list in ranked order. So, for example, entering "New York Times" into the Google search engine (**www.google.com**) produces a list of almost four million web pages, but the home page of *The New York Times* (**www.nytimes.com**) is the first entry on the list.

Internet Explorer's default search engine is MSN (**search.msn.com**), but you can change it to be any from a list of ten popular search engines. The choice is largely a matter of personal taste.

Different search engines have different ways for you to describe what you are looking for. Some (like **ask.com**) are expecting you to ask a question in everyday English, while others let you construct complex Boolean expressions describing exactly what you want and don't want to see. Any search engine will respond to a list of keywords (like: "campground Vermont lake").

Many search engines try to direct you to the web sites of their commercial partners. In MSN, for example, searching for "New York Times" produces the correct www.nytimes.com as the first choice, but the second and third choices are the competing Microsoft-owned web sites of MSNBC and Slate. One reason we prefer Google is that it tells you which links have been sponsored by advertisers.

Searching from the Address Box

The simplest way to search the Web is to type a question mark followed by a word or phrase into IE's Address box and press ENTER. (Be sure to leave a space after the question mark.) The word or phrase is sent to Internet Explorer's default search engine, and the results are displayed in the viewing area.

Using the Search Companion Explorer Bar

The Search Companion Explorer bar allows you to search not just for web pages, but for addresses, businesses, maps, words, pictures, and newsgroups. It is the same Explorer bar that you use to search for files and folders with Windows Explorer. The general aspects of the Search Companion Explorer bar are discussed in "Searching For Files and Folders" in Chapter 8.

When you click the Search button in Internet Explorer, you enter the Search Companion Wizard (shown in Figure 24-3) at a different point than when you select Start | Search or click the Search button in Windows Explorer.

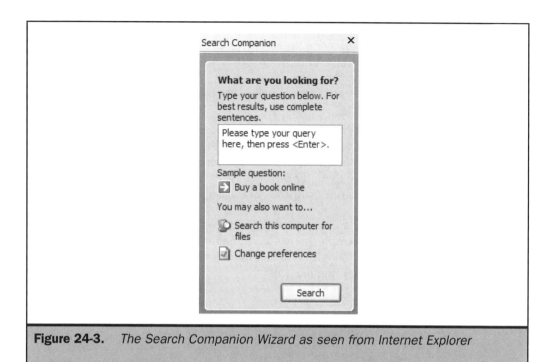

Figure 24-3.   *The Search Companion Wizard as seen from Internet Explorer*

To look for a web page, type a question or some keywords into the What Are You Looking For box and click the Search button in the Explorer bar. The word or phrase is sent to Internet Explorer's default search engine, and the results are displayed in the viewing area. After the results are displayed, the Explorer Bar offers suggestions for refining your search.

Changing Internet Explorer's Default Search Engines

By default, Internet Explorer uses the MSN search engine for searches from either the Address box or the Explorer bar. You can change search engines as follows from the Search Companion Explorer bar. Click Change Preferences and then Change Internet Search Behavior. Click the With Classic Internet Search radio button and choose a new search engine from the list (we recommend Google).

   No matter what search engine Internet Explorer wants to use, you can always go to the web site of your favorite search engine and use it directly.

Adding Custom Search Prefixes

You can add *search prefixes* that you can use when typing in the Address bar. For example, you can add the search prefix "kb" to facilitate searching the Microsoft Knowledge Base (MSKB): typing **kb Q123456** searches the MSKB web site. You can make a search prefix called "g" that performs an advanced search at Google, or one called "nyt" that searches the *New York Times* web site for back articles. You can add as many search prefixes as you want to speed up using the sites you search most often.

When you create a search prefix, you provide two pieces of information:

1. **Name**   The characters you'll type when using the search prefix to search; for example, "g" or "nyt."

2. **URL**   The web address to perform the search. Type **%s** in place of the search term: Internet Explorer will replace "%s" with the search word or phrase that you type in the address box after the search prefix. For example, if you type **g Vermont** then Internet Explorer replaces "%s" with "Vermont" when it performs the search. Include "http://" at the beginning of the URL.

To find the URL to use to search a web site, go to the site, perform a search, and copy the resulting URL. For example, go to Google (**google.com**), type a word to search for (like your first name), click Google Search, and look at the URL that appears in the Address box, which looks something like this:

```
http://www.google.com/search?hl=en&ie=UTF-8&oe=UTF-8
&q=Margy&btnG=Google+Search
```

(This URL resulted from searching for "Margy".) Replace your search term ("Margy" in this case) with "%s".

| Tip | *You can usually shorten the URL from the one that the web site generates. The automatically generated URL usually includes lots of unnecessary specifications, separated by semicolons or ampersands. Try shortening the URL and seeing what you get.* |

Windows stores the search prefixes in the Registry, in the key HKEY_Current_User\ Software\Microsoft\Internet Explorer\SearchUrl. Each search prefix is stored in a separate subkey of this key. You can create, edit, and delete search prefixes by editing the Registry directly (see Chapter 38). However, it's much easier to create and maintain your search prefixes by using TweakUI (see Chapter 1, section "Using TweakUI to Change the Windows Interface").

To add search prefixes using TweakUI:

1. Run TweakUI, as described in Chapter 1.

2. In the left pane, click the Internet Explorer plus box to display the categories indented below it. Click the Search category. You see a list of the existing search prefixes (probably blank).

3. Click Create to display the Search Prefix dialog box.

4. Type the name of the search prefix (for example, "kb") and the URL. Click OK.

5. Click Apply to make the changes to the Registry.

Here are some useful search prefixes:

- **Microsoft KnowledgeBase, by article number**   http://support.microsoft.com/default.aspx?scid=kb;en-us;%s

- **Microsoft KnowledgeBase, by keyword, with 100 results per page**   http://search.support.microsoft.com/search/default.aspx?KeywordType=ALL&maxResults=100&Query=%s

- **Google, with 100 results per page**   http://www.google.com/search?as_q=%s&num=100

- **Microsoft's public newsgroups, by keyword, with 100 results per page, newest first**   http://groups.google.com/groups?as_q=%s&ie=UTF-8&oe=UTF-8&as_ugroup=microsoft.public*&lr=&num=100&as_scoring=d&hl=en

- **Downloads.com by program name (Windows programs only)**   http://download.com.com/3120-20-0.html?qt=%s&tg=dl-2001

   We've crashed Internet Explorer by including more than one occurrence of "%s" in the search prefix URL.

Interacting with Web Sites Automatically

Web sites that provide some personalized service typically ask you to fill out a registration form when you first establish a relationship with the site and to log in by giving a user name and password when you return to the site in the future. Filling out forms and typing in passwords are precisely the kinds of repetitive, mindless work that computers are supposed to do for us, so Internet Explorer provides a way to do these small tasks automatically.

Caution   *Give some thought as to whether to let the browser remember passwords and which passwords to entrust to it. Once a browser has been allowed to remember a password for a personal account on a web site, anyone who uses your user account can get into that web account.*

Remembering Forms and Passwords Automatically

If you want Internet Explorer to remember forms and passwords for you, open the AutoComplete Settings dialog box by choosing Tools | Internet Options, clicking the Content tab, and clicking the AutoComplete button to open the AutoComplete Settings dialog box, as shown here:

The check boxes in this box control how Internet Explorer handles forms and passwords. Check the User Names And Passwords On Forms check box if you want Internet Explorer to insert the user names and passwords it has memorized into the appropriate logon forms for web pages.

If you check the Prompt Me To Save Passwords check box, Internet Explorer will ask you whether you want it to memorize any new password that it sees. If Internet Explorer already knows all the passwords you want it to know, leave this box unchecked.

Check the Forms box if you want Internet Explorer to remember forms that you fill out. When this box is checked, AutoComplete works for any box on any web form the way that it works in the Address box: As you start to type something into the box, AutoComplete lists previously typed entries that begin with the letters you have typed. If the list includes what you want to type, you can select it from the list rather than finishing the typing.

When these settings are in place, you will encounter the following dialog box every time you enter a new password:

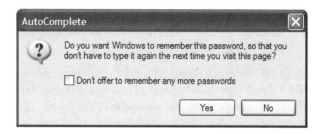

Click Yes if you want the password remembered. Checking the Don't Offer To Remember Any More Passwords check box has the same effect as unchecking the Prompt Me To Save Passwords box on the AutoComplete Settings dialog box: Internet Explorer remembers and continues to use the passwords it knows but stops asking whether it should remember new passwords.

Occasionally you click Yes to remember the password and then later regret it. Unfortunately, there is no way to instruct Internet Explorer to forget one or two of your passwords but remember the others. If you want Internet Explorer to forget all the passwords it knows, open the AutoComplete Settings dialog box (as in the previous steps) and click the Clear Passwords button.

Similarly, you may find that AutoComplete remembers items from web forms that you don't want it to remember—like credit card numbers. Click the Clear Forms button in the AutoComplete Settings dialog box to make it forget.

Using Internet Explorer's Profile Assistant

Profile Assistant is Internet Explorer's tool for filling out web forms automatically. You fill out a profile form similar to the Windows Address Book contact form. Information from this profile is used to fill out web forms that ask for things like your address or phone number. (No information is transmitted automatically. You have an opportunity to review forms and delete or change information before submitting forms.) Internet Explorer can fill in web forms with the information from the Address Book only when the names of the boxes on the form match the pieces of information that are entered in the Address Book—items like name, ZIP code, and phone.

■ How you set up your profile depends on whether you already have your own information stored as an entry in your address book. If you do, click the Select An Existing Entry From The Address Book To Represent Your Profile radio button, and do just that: select an entry from the list in the dialog box. Click OK, and your profile is established.

- If you do not want to use an existing Address Book entry to establish your profile, click the Create A New Entry In The Address Book To Represent Your Profile radio button and click OK. A Properties dialog box opens, showing a form from the Windows Address Book. Fill out as much or as little of it as you like, using the Name, Home, Business, and Personal tabs. Click OK, and your profile is established.

Your profile is stored as an entry in the Shared Contacts section of the Windows Address Book (see Chapter 23, section "Storing Addresses in the Address Book"). You can add or change information in your profile either by editing it from Windows Address Book or by clicking the My Profile button on the Content tab of the Internet Options dialog box.

To tell Internet Explorer to use your profile information to fill out forms, open the AutoComplete Settings dialog box by clicking the AutoComplete button on the Content tab of the Internet Options dialog box.

Changing How Web Pages Look

Internet Explorer allows you to change the fonts and colors that it uses to render web pages, and even the alphabets. You can also decide to save downloading time by telling Internet Explorer not to download pictures or other multimedia content.

These preferences are controlled from the Internet Options dialog box (shown in Figure 24-2), which you access by opening the Internet Options icon on the Control Panel, or by choosing Tools | Internet Options from Internet Explorer's menu bar.

 From its name, you might think that the Internet Options dialog box controls settings for any browser or other Internet program, but it doesn't. Changes you make in the Internet Options dialog box only affect Internet Explorer and programs that use it to display HTML (like Microsoft Word). They don't affect other browsers (like Netscape, Mozilla, or Opera).

Choosing Fonts

To make Internet Explorer display text in a different size, use the View | Text Size menu. There are five choices, from smallest to largest. The default size is Medium, which for the Latin-based alphabet means 12 point variable-width fonts and 10-point fixed-width fonts.

To make more fundamental changes in the fonts Internet Explorer uses, click the Fonts button on the General tab of the Internet Options dialog box. The Fonts dialog box opens, shown in Figure 24-4. This dialog box has three basic elements:

- A drop-down list of alphabets, labeled Language Script. The English language script is Latin Based.

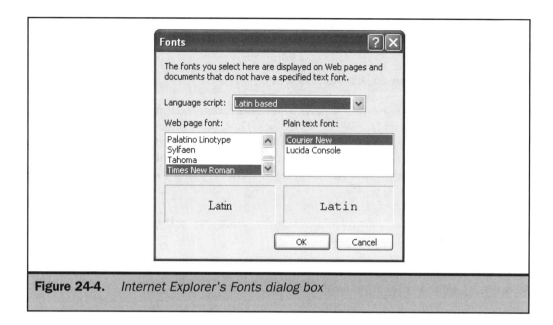

Figure 24-4.   *Internet Explorer's Fonts dialog box*

■ Two lists specifying the web page (or variable-width) font and the plain text (or fixed-width) font for the selected alphabet. Change either font by picking a new one from the corresponding list.

Sometimes a web page specifies a font, and that specification overrides the choices you make in the Fonts dialog box. To make your font choices override those of the web page, click the Accessibility button on the General tab of the Internet Options dialog box and check either the Ignore Font Styles Specified On Web Pages check box or the Ignore Font Sizes Specified On Web Pages check box.

Choosing Colors

You can change the colors Internet Explorer uses to display text, backgrounds, and links. To change the color of the text and background, click the Colors button on the General tab of the Internet Options dialog box.

The default is to use Windows colors—that is, the colors defined on the Appearance tab of the Display Properties dialog box (see Chapter 11, section "Choosing a New Color Scheme"). If you don't want to use the Windows colors, take the following steps:

1. Remove the check from the Use Windows Colors check box.

2. Click the colored button next to the Text or Background labels. A palette of colors appears.

3. Click the color you want for the Text or Background and click OK to make the palette disappear. The button next to Text or Background should now be the color you selected.

4. Click OK to close the Colors dialog box.

Changing the colors used for links is a similar process, except that you don't need to remove the check from Use Windows Colors. The Colors dialog box also allows you to define a *hover color*, a color that links change to when the cursor *hovers* over them.

If you get the urge to change the background color of the toolbar, you can do so by using the TweakUI program (see Chapter 1, section "Using TweakUI to Change the Windows Interface").

 We suggest you leave the colors alone, except perhaps for making the background color white (if it's not white already).

Internet Explorer has other accessibility features for the visually impaired (see Chapter 16, section "Making Internet Explorer Accessible").

Changing Language Preferences

Some web pages are available in multiple languages, and your browser picks the one that matches your preferences. To define or change your language preferences in Internet Explorer, click the Languages button near the bottom of the General tab of the Internet Options dialog box (shown in Figure 24-2, earlier in this chapter) to open the Language Preference dialog box:

The purpose of this dialog box is to maintain a list of favored languages in order, with your preferred language on top. Add a language to the list by clicking the Add button and selecting a language from the list that appears. Remove a language from the Language list by selecting it and clicking the Remove button. Reorder the Languages list by selecting a language on the list and clicking the Move Up or Move Down buttons. Some sites (such as MSN.com) display pages based on your first language.

Choosing Whether to Download Images, Audio, and Video

Many web pages have pictures or other graphics on them. These are more time consuming to download than text, so if your connection is slow, you may decide not to bother downloading graphics. Multimedia content such as audio, video, or animation is even slower to download, and you can tell your browser to ignore them, too. To do this, go to the Advanced tab of the Internet Options dialog box, shown in Figure 24-5. Scroll down until you see the Multimedia heading. Remove the check from each box next to any type of content that you want to ignore.

Note   *This setting affects programs that use Internet Explorer to display HTML content, including Microsoft Word, Microsoft Money, and Quicken.*

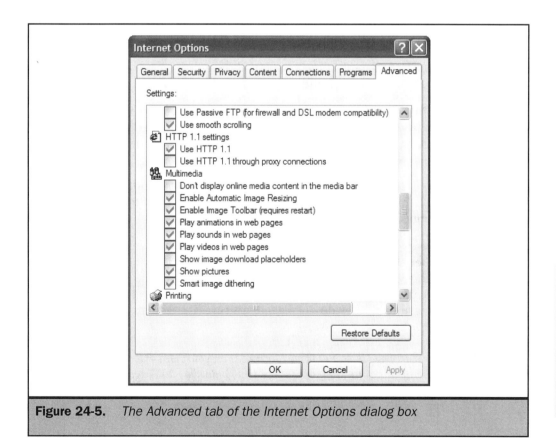

Figure 24-5.   *The Advanced tab of the Internet Options dialog box*

WINDOWS XP HOME
ON THE INTERNET

Managing Internet Explorer's Behavior

Internet Explorer is intended to be simple enough for novice users. For this reason, most of what it does is invisible. Some choices that IE makes for you, however, have implications for your system's use of disk space or its security—implications that more advanced users may want to consider. Internet Explorer allows you some limited opportunities to "get under the hood" and make choices for yourself about your start page, blocking offensive content, caching web pages, and the default mail and news applications. You can even decide that Internet Explorer should not be the default browser.

Choosing and Customizing Your Start Page

Your browser's home page (also called a *start page*) is the web page that the browser loads when you open the browser without requesting a specific page. You can also see the browser's home page by clicking the Home button on its toolbar. (Don't confuse this use of "home page" with the home page of a web site.)

Microsoft promotes its MSN web site by making it the default home page of Internet Explorer. In general, this not a bad home page, and many people never change it. However, you can select any web page or file that you want to be your browser's home page.

To change Internet Explorer's start page, choose Tools | Internet Options to display the Internet Options dialog box with the General tab on top (as you saw in Figure 24-2). You can type the URL of the new home page into the Home Page box on this tab, or you can click one of the following buttons:

- **Use Current**   The page currently displayed by Internet Explorer becomes the home page. (If Internet Explorer is not open, this button is grayed out.) This can be any page on the Web, or even an HTML document on your hard drive.

- **Use Default**   You get a personalizable MSN home page at **www.msn.com**.

- **Use Blank**   The home page is blank. This is handy if you want Internet Explorer to start up as quickly as possible and don't necessarily want to invoke your Internet connection.

Lots of web sites would like to be your home page, because they can sell advertising based on the number of viewers they get. Many (including the default MSN page) allow you to customize the page to get local weather, headlines in your areas of interest, scores for your favorite teams, quotes for the stocks you own, and so on. None of them charge a fee for this service, though they do display advertising. The industry leader is Yahoo (**my.yahoo.com**).

Setting your start page to be an HTML document on your hard drive makes Internet Explorer start up more quickly than if it has to download a start page from the Internet.

Blocking Offensive Web Content

Internet Explorer includes Content Advisor, which can block access to web sites based on their level of potentially offensive content. Unfortunately, this system does not work very well, and we cannot recommend it.

Content Advisor is based on a voluntary rating system devised by the Recreational Software Advisory Council for the Internet at **www.rsac.org**. It works like this: web site managers fill out a questionnaire about their sites, and these sites then get a numerical rating for each language, nudity, sex, and violence. These ratings are attached to the web sites with codes that browsers can read, but usually do not display. When you set up Content Advisor, you specify the numerical ratings you will accept, and web sites that with ratings beyond your specifications are blocked.

The RSACi rating system has been in place for several years now, and it has become clear that the vast majority of web sites (whether they contain potentially objectionable content or not) will never be rated. This leaves you with the following choice: You can block all unrated sites, which makes the web almost useless to you, or you can allow access to unrated sites, many of which contain the kind of content you had hoped to block.

If you want to block access to offensive content, we recommend buying a program specifically designed for that purpose. We can't recommend one, however, because your definition of "offensive" might be different from ours. Seek recommendations from people and organizations who share your values.

In general, no automatic content blocking is as good as parental supervision. And don't forget that you can always look at the History folder to see where your children have been on the Internet—until they become sophisticated enough to cover their tracks (see "Covering Your Tracks and Tracking Others" earlier in this chapter). See the Peacefire web site at **www.peacefire.org** for information about problems with web site blocking programs.

Managing the Cache of Web Pages

Internet Explorer stores some of the pages that you view so that they can be redisplayed quickly if you return to them. In general, this speeds up the browsing experience, but if you are running short of disk space, you may decide to limit or eliminate these caches. They are stored in a folder named Temporary Internet Files, which is inside the hidden folder C:\Documents And Settings*username*\Local Settings (assuming that Windows is installed on drive C:). The easiest way to examine and edit this folder is by clicking the Settings button on the General tab of the Internet Options dialog box and then clicking the View Files button when the Settings dialog box appears.

Delete all your temporary Internet files at once by clicking the Delete Files button on the General tab of the Internet Options dialog box. To set limits on the amount of disk space that can be devoted to temporary Internet files, click the Settings button to open the Settings dialog box. Move the slider to raise or lower the percentage of your hard drive that the Temporary Internet Files folder is allowed to use. Click OK to apply your changes.

Changing the Default Browser

When you install Windows XP, Internet Explorer is set as the default browser. (If you bought a computer with Windows XP already installed, it is possible that the manufacturer has set up another browser as the default.) After you install another browser, however, you can decide to make that browser the default. Possibly the browser's installation wizard will ask whether it should be the default browser, or the browser itself will ask whenever you run it. If not, follow the more detailed instructions shown here.

To make Netscape or Mozilla the default browser, select Edit | Preferences from the menu bar, expand the Advanced menu of the Preferences dialog box and select System. On the System tab of the Preference dialog box, click the check boxes of the protocols and file types you want Navigator to be the default program for. (The http protocol is the most important one to check.)

To make Opera the default browser, choose File | Preferences from the Opera menu bar. When the Preferences dialog box appears, select Default Browser in the left column. Check the file types and protocols you want Opera to be the default for or else just check the Check If Opera Is Default Browser On Startup check box, close Opera and restart it.

If Internet Explorer is no longer your default browser, you can easily restore it to this role. In most cases, all you have to do is open IE, and it asks whether you want it to be the default browser. If it doesn't ask, do the following: Choose Tools | Internet Options from the Internet Explorer menu bar. When the Internet Options dialog box appears, click the Programs tab. Click the check box labeled Internet Explorer Should Check To See Whether It Is The Default Browser. The next time you open IE it asks whether you want it to be the default browser.

 You can open any browser by choosing Start | All Programs or by opening its icon on the desktop, whether it is the default or not. Once a browser is running, you can use it to open any web page.

Setting Your Mail and Newsreading Programs

You can tell Windows which mail and newsreading programs to run with Internet Explorer; these are the programs that Internet Explorer runs when you click a mail or news link. Choose Tools | Internet Options to open the Internet Options dialog box. On the Programs tab, the Mail and News boxes show the default programs that Internet Explorer runs; both are set to Outlook Express when you install Windows. See Chapter 23 for how to use Outlook Express.

Not all non-Microsoft e-mail and newsreading programs show up on the drop-down lists of the Programs tab of the Internet Options dialog box. If the program that you want to make your default e-mail client or newsreader isn't on the appropriate list, consult the documentation that came with the program or the web site of the manufacturer.

Internet Explorer's Privacy Settings

You should keep two risk factors in mind when you use the Web:

- ■ Web sites may be collecting information about you and your browsing habits using small files called *cookies* that are stored on your computer.

- ■ The scripts and applets that allow web sites to offer more complex content and services may also make your computer more vulnerable to viruses or hackers.

This section discusses the tools and options that Internet Explorer provides for dealing with these risks. Also see the section "Managing Which Files Internet Explorer Downloads" in Chapter 32.

Controlling Cookies

Internet Explorer 6 gives you much more control over cookies than previous versions of Internet Explorer did. Unfortunately, the new privacy level settings make the situation seem much more complicated than it is, and none of them is a very good cookie policy. However, you can override Internet Explorer's automatic cookie-handling system to set up a simple, sensible cookie policy.

The next few sections explain what cookies are and how the P3P privacy protection system works. If you don't care about that and just want to know what to do, skip ahead to the "Setting Cookie Policy" section.

 For more information about cookies, see the Cookie Central web site at *www.cookiecentral.com.*

How Cookies Work

A *cookie* is a small (at most 4KB) file that a web server can store on your machine. Its purpose is to allow a web server to personalize a web page, depending on whether you have been to that web site before and what you may have told it during previous sessions. For example, when you establish an account with an online retailer or subscribe to an online magazine, you may be asked to fill out a form that includes some information about yourself and your preferences. The web server may store that information (along with information about when you visit the site) in a cookie on your machine. When you return to that web site in the future, the retailer's web server can read its cookie, recall this information, and structure its web pages accordingly.

Much has been written about whether cookies create a security or privacy hazard for you. If your browser is working properly, the security hazard is minimal. It is, at first glance, unsettling to think that web servers are storing information on your hard drive without your knowledge. But cookies are not executable programs. They cannot, for example, search for and accumulate information from elsewhere on your system. They simply record information that you have already given to the web server.

The privacy issue is real, however. Cookies do make it easier for advertising companies to gather information about your browsing habits. For example, a company that advertises on a large number of web sites can use cookies to keep track of where you have seen its ads before, and which ads (if any) you clicked. In this way advertisers can learn your interests and perhaps deduce more about you than you would want them to know.

Cookies are of two basic kinds: first-party cookies and third-party cookies. (You are considered to be the second party.) First-party cookies come directly from the web site you are browsing. For example, if you register with Yahoo and personalize a Yahoo start page, the cookie that Yahoo sets is a first-party cookie. Third-party cookies come from web servers that you may not realize you are dealing with. For example, the Yahoo start page may contain an advertisement that comes from the web server of an advertising agency like DoubleClick. The cookie that the advertising agency sets is a third-party cookie.

The Platform for Privacy Preferences (P3P)

The Platform for Privacy Preferences (P3P) is a new open standard (which Internet Explorer 6 supports) for web sites to specify their privacy policies in a form that can be read by computers. The idea is that you can decide once and for all how high to set your privacy standards, and your browser can compare your decisions to the privacy policies of the web sites you visit, warning you if your standards are about to be violated.

Here's how it works: The people who create web sites fill out a multiple-choice form about what information their web site collects, what it does with that information, and how long it keeps the information. Their answers get codified into tags that get attached to their web pages–tags that browsers like Internet Explorer 6 can read but typically don't display. You set one of five privacy levels that Internet Explorer offers, and it blocks cookies and issues privacy warnings accordingly.

The benefit of the system is that the multiple-choice questions at least pin down the web sites. Before P3P, most web sites either did not have privacy policies or wrote them in impenetrable legalese. It has been completely impractical to read the privacy policies of all the web sites you visit and make individual judgments about them.

The system has several weaknesses, however, and at the moment it is unclear whether it will do any good. First, it's voluntary—web sites don't have to fill out the questionnaire, and if very few do, the system will be useless. (This is what happened to the PICS system for rating the sex-and-violence content of web sites. See "Blocking Offensive Web Content" earlier in this chapter.) Second, it's nobody's job to verify that the web sites have answered the questions honestly. Finally, you have to count on the browser makers to implement P3P in a way that lets you do what you want to do in a simple, understandable fashion. Since Microsoft is a major player in e-commerce and web advertising, its sympathies are at least as much with the advertisers as with you, and they have designed Internet Explorer accordingly.

You can read more about the Platform for Privacy Preferences (P3P) at **www.w3.org/P3P**.

How Internet Explorer Implements P3P Privacy Policies

The Privacy tab of the Internet Options dialog box (displayed by choosing Tools | Internet Options) contains a slider that you can set to one of six levels from Accept All Cookies to Block All Cookies. The default level is Medium. The descriptions of these levels are phrased using technical terms like *personally identifiable information*, *implicit consent*, *explicit consent*, and *compact privacy policy*. What follows is our interpretation of what these levels actually mean.

- **Block All Cookies**   At this level you are unable to log in to access Hotmail, or a Yahoo home page, or to use a subscription to the online *The Wall Street Journal*. You could make this setting livable if you could create exceptions for your favorite web sites, but Microsoft has disabled the exception-making capability for this setting.

- **High**   Cookies are only accepted from web sites that offer P3P information, and then only if that information says that they don't make keep track of information that would identify you personally (like your name, for example, or your phone number) unless you've explicitly given them permission to do so. At this level we could log into Hotmail and Yahoo, but not *The Wall Street Journal*.

- **Medium High**   Same as High, except that first-party cookies are accepted from web sites that use personally identifiable information without your explicit consent, if they somehow allow you to opt out of this usage. (In general, we don't like opt-out processes. They require too much alertness and diligence on your part.) At this level we could see *The Wall Street Journal*.

- **Medium**   Allows third-party cookies that let you opt out of their use of personally identifiable information. Restricts first-party cookies that use personally identifiable information without letting you opt out. (We have no idea what the difference between "restrict" and "block" is.)

- **Low**   Accepts all first-party cookies. Restricts third-party cookies from web sites that don't offer P3P information or that don't let you opt out of their use of personally identifiable information.

- **Accept All Cookies**   Accepts all cookies without asking you.

A Sensible Cookie Policy

First we'll tell you what you don't want: You don't want to block all cookies, because you give up too much of the functionality and convenience of the Web. You also don't want Internet Explorer to ask you what to do every time a web site wants to set a cookie, because you'll spend more time deciding about cookies than you'll spend reading web pages.

You *do* want to make a distinction between first-party and third-party cookies, because third-party cookies benefit only the advertisers, not you.

The cookie policy we'd like to have is Medium High for first-party cookies, and block third-party cookies altogether. This does not seem to be possible with Internet Explorer. Given that fact, we recommend the following policy: accept all first-party cookies and block all third-party cookies. This isn't one of the six levels on the slider, but you can configure Internet Explorer to do it.

Another reasonable option (but somewhat more difficult to set up) is to select the High level and then create exceptions to unblock cookies for a few favorite web sites. This policy allows a few more third-party cookies and a few less first-party cookies than the policy suggested in the previous paragraph. However, this option stops many shopping sites from working, because the sites use shopping-cart programs hosted on third-party web sites. (Another option is to use Netscape instead of IE, because of its more flexible cookie policies.)

Setting Cookie Policy

Cookie policy is controlled from the Privacy tab of the Internet Options dialog box. If you want one of the settings described in the previous section, move the slider to that setting and click OK.

If you want to set up our recommended cookie policy (allow first-party and block third-party cookies), do the following:

1. Select Tools | Options to open the Internet Options dialog box.

2. Select the Privacy tab of the Internet Options dialog box (see Figure 24-6).

3. Click the Advanced button on the Privacy tab. The Advanced Privacy Settings box appears.

4. Check the Override Automatic Cookie Handling box.

5. Select the Accept radio button under First-Party Cookies and the Block radio button under Third-Party Cookies.

If a particular web site is not working because its cookies are being blocked, you can choose to create an exception for it without changing your settings for other web sites. (For reasons that escape us, Microsoft has made this option unavailable if you have chosen the Block All Cookies setting.) Do the following:

1. Select Tools | Options to open the Internet Options dialog box.

2. Select the Privacy tab of the Internet Options dialog box.

3. Click the Edit button on the Privacy tab. The Per Site Privacy Actions box opens.

4. Type the URL of the web site into the Address Of Web Site line.

5. Click the Allow button and click OK in both open dialog boxes.

If you want to block the cookies on a particular web site when your overall policy would allow them, do the previous steps, but click the Block button in step 5.

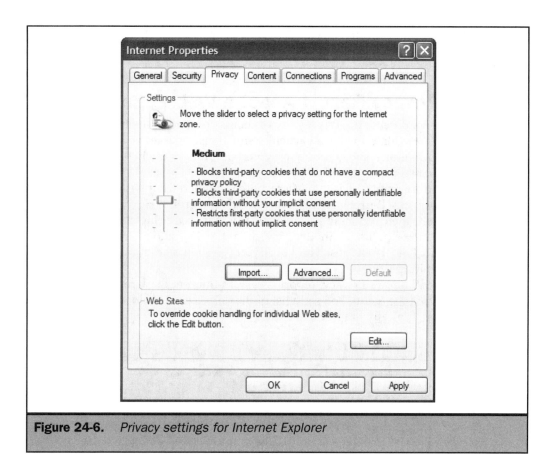

Figure 24-6.   *Privacy settings for Internet Explorer*

You can also make exceptions from the Privacy Policy box associated with a particular web site. See "Displaying a Privacy Report About a Web Page" later in this chapter.

 The setup program of MSN Explorer asks you to move your privacy setting down to Medium. We recommend that you ignore this request, go about your business, and see if anything fails to work. In our experience, any setting other than Block All Cookies was fine for anything we wanted to do on MSN Explorer.

Managing the Cookies You Have

Windows stores your cookies in two folders:

- C:\Documents And Settings*username*\Cookies
- C:\Documents And Settings*username*\Local Settings\Temporary Internet Files

Reading a cookie in Notepad or some other text program probably will not tell you much, though it may set your mind at ease to realize just how little information is there. Delete individual cookies from your system by deleting the corresponding text files, or nuke them all by clicking the Delete Cookies button on the General tab of the Internet Options dialog box.

Displaying a Privacy Report About a Web Page

New for Internet Explorer 6, the Privacy Report helps you determine how much information you are willing to give a particular site. It also enables you to determine what kind of information a site is storing on your computer and whether the site complies with its own privacy policy.

The primary drawback here is that Microsoft has aligned itself with TRUSTe (at **www.truste.org**), a self-proclaimed privacy watchdog group. However, TRUSTe predominantly sells their services as a site evaluator, only requiring sites to post a *privacy policy*. Posting a policy, no matter how good it looks, is no guarantee that it will be adhered to. Only trust those you know you can trust, and don't leave the trusting up to a third party.

Accessing the Windows Privacy Report is easy. In Internet Explorer, choose View | Privacy Report from the menu. You see a list of the objects that are loaded on the page you are looking at, typically graphics, like this:

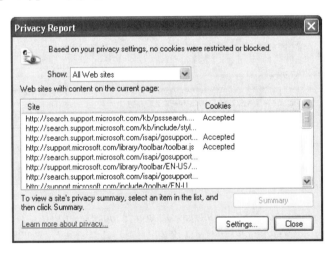

If any of the listed web sites have placed a cookie on your computer, the word "accepted" appears in the right column. To see a privacy report on any of the web sites listed, select it from the list and click the Summary button. You see a report like this:

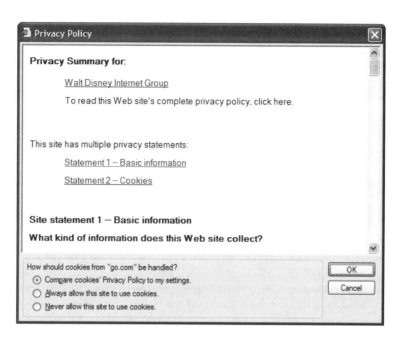

The radio buttons at the bottom of the window let you make a special policy for the cookies from this web site. You can also do this from Privacy tab of the Internet Options dialog box, as described in "Setting Cookie Policy" earlier in this chapter.

Creating Your Own Web Pages

Previous versions of Windows came with a web page editor called FrontPage Express. Windows XP doesn't come with a web page editor, although you can create web pages using Notepad if you learn all the HTML codes to include. If you have Microsoft Word or Corel WordPerfect, you can save documents as web pages, a much easier way to make pages. Web pages created by Microsoft Word tend to be huge, including an enormous number of unnecessary codes, but they work for quick-and-dirty pages that you plan to replace later. Better options are these:

- **CoffeeCup HTML Editor**   This program is an easy way for beginners to create their first sites. Information is available from CoffeeCup Software at **www.coffeecup.com**. You can also download the CoffeeCup Free HTML editor from the site.

- **HomeSite**   This program is a full-featured, reasonably priced web page editor from Macromedia Software at **www.macromedia.com/software/HomeSite**. You can download an evaluation version.

- **Netscape and Mozilla Composer**   Netscape Communicator (Netscape's suite of programs that includes Netscape Navigator) comes with a web page editor called Netscape Composer. See **home.netscape.com**. Mozilla (**www.mozilla.org**) comes with a similar version of Composer.

To make your web pages and picture files available on the Web, you must upload files from your computer to a web server. You can use Web Folders to drag-and-drop web pages to your web server, or you can use the Windows FTP program for uploading, but it uses arcane commands (see Chapter 26). Netscape Composer has a Publish button on its toolbar that makes uploading files easy. Windows XP comes with a Web Publishing Wizard, another way to upload files to a web server.

To run the Web Publishing Wizard, put the files that you want on the Web into one folder, and click Publish This Folder To The Web from the Task pane. The wizard lets you select the files from the current folder to include, select a web server from one of the web hosting companies which Microsoft has decided to offer (including MSN Groups), and (for pictures) choose whether to resize the pictures to reduce their file size (see Figure 24-7). When the wizard is finished, it displays the URL of the page you have just created. Save this URL (using cut-and-paste to a Notepad file or other file) so that you can tell other people to visit your page.

If you decide to upload your files to MSN Groups, the Web Publishing Wizard creates a My Groups folder inside My Network Places.

Xdrive, a widely used web hosting company, is one of the web servers that the wizard offers. Note that its web sites are no longer free. Unfortunately, your ISP, which probably offers free web space as part of your Internet account, might not be one of the wizard's options. You need to use Web Folders or FTP to upload your web pages.

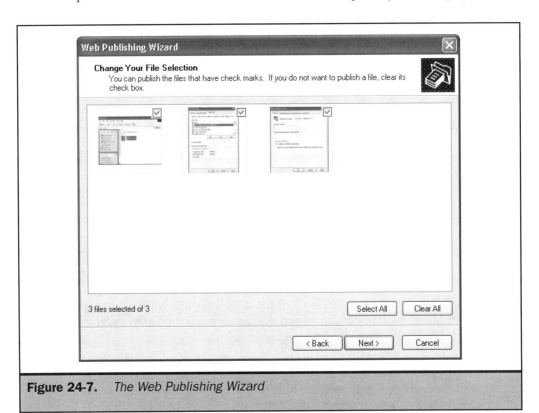

Figure 24-7. *The Web Publishing Wizard*

The Complete Reference

Windows XP

Chapter 25

Internet Conferencing with Windows Messenger and NetMeeting

W indows XP comes with two programs for chatting and conferencing over the Internet:

■ **Windows Messenger** lets you instantly communicate with anyone else online who is also using Windows Messenger. Microsoft has added audio and video features to its basic text chat capabilities, so Windows Messenger completely replaces Microsoft Chat and largely replaces NetMeeting.

■ **Microsoft NetMeeting** lets you use the Internet as a long-distance phone service, including videoconferencing, typed chat, and even sharing programs over the Internet. Microsoft isn't updating NetMeeting any more, so the main reason to use it is to converse with other people who have NetMeeting but not Windows Messenger.

This chapter describes how to use both programs. You can download other Internet chat and conferencing programs from the Internet itself; Chapter 26 tells you how.

Chatting Online with Windows Messenger

Windows Messenger enables you to chat with friends or coworkers who are online at the time that you want to chat. It's quicker than e-mail, and multiple people can take part in the conversation. Windows Messenger also enables you to speak to other users and send messages to pagers. Windows Messenger is useful for meetings or in circumstances when you might otherwise be sending e-mail messages back and forth. It's a great way to have an electronic conversation when everyone is connected to the Internet. Windows Messenger also allows you to exchange files, to let other people in your meeting see what's on your screen, and even let someone else take over your computer to help fix a problem.

Windows Messenger is usually loaded automatically when Windows starts up. If the Windows Messenger icon appears in the notification area of the taskbar, click it to display the Windows Messenger window. If it's not on the taskbar, run Windows Messenger by choosing Start | All Programs | Windows Messenger. Windows Messenger may ask whether you want to download updates to the program. This chapter describes Messenger 4.7, which comes with Windows XP SP1. The version that shipped with the original Windows XP (4.6) and updated versions of Windows Messenger should be similar.

Note *AOL Instant Messenger (AIM, available from **aim.aol.com**) has long been the king of instant messaging programs, and other popular instant messaging programs include ICQ (**www.icq.com**) and Yahoo Messenger (**messenger.yahoo.com**). Unfortunately, these instant messaging systems don't all talk to each other: people on one system can't send and receive messages from the others. However, you can easily run more than one instant message program at the same time. Or use an IM program that can communicate with multiple systems: Trillian (from Cerulean Studios, at **www.trillian.cc**) enables you to chat with people who use AIM, ICQ, Yahoo Messenger, and Windows Messenger.*

Getting Rid of Windows Messenger

If you don't want Windows Messenger to run automatically when you start Windows, you can prevent it, but it's not easy. Outlook Express runs Windows Explorer unless you configure it not to. Follow these steps:

1. In Windows Messenger, choose Tools | Options and click the Preferences tab.

2. Clear the Run This Program When Windows Starts check box and click OK.

3. In Outlook Express, choose Tools | Options and click the General tab.

4. Clear the Automatically Log On To Windows Messenger check box and click OK.

5. Restart Windows and check that no Windows Messenger icon appears in the notification area of the taskbar.

When you run Outlook Express, the program may load but not connect. Opening the Contacts pane in Outlook Express may cause Windows Messenger to connect.

If you want Windows Messenger not to load when you Outlook Express, you have to edit the Registry (see Chapter 38). After making a backup of the Registry, follow these steps:

1. Locate the key HKEY_LOCAL_MACHINE\Software\Policies\Microsoft.

2. Right-click the Microsoft key and choose New | Key. Type **Messenger** as the name of the new key (its full name is HKEY_LOCAL_MACHINE\ Software\Policies\Microsoft\Messenger). The Registry Editor also creates a value named (Default) in the new Messenger key.

3. Right-click the new Messenger key and choose New | Key. Type **Client** as the name of the new key (its full name is HKEY_LOCAL_MACHINE\Software\Policies\Microsoft\Messenger\ Client). It receives a blank value named (Default), too.

4. Right-click the new Client key and choose New | DWORD Value. Type **PreventRun** as the name of the new value.

5. Double-click the new PreventRun value to display the Edit DWORD Value dialog box. Type **1** in the Value Data box and click OK.

Now running Outlook Express doesn't load Windows Messenger.

For more information, go to **support.microsoft.com** and search for article Q302089.

Signing In to Windows Messenger with Your .NET Passport

If you haven't used Windows Messenger before, you need to establish a Microsoft .NET Passport—an ID used for Microsoft web sites and services. (Microsoft uses Windows Messenger as one way to get lots of people to sign up for a Microsoft .NET Passport, which will enable them to sell their .NET e-commerce services more effectively. Windows Messenger is a cornerstone of Microsoft's emerging .NET services.) The .NET Passport Wizard windows pops up the first time you run Windows Messenger and steps you through the process of telling it about your existing Microsoft Passport or creating a new one:

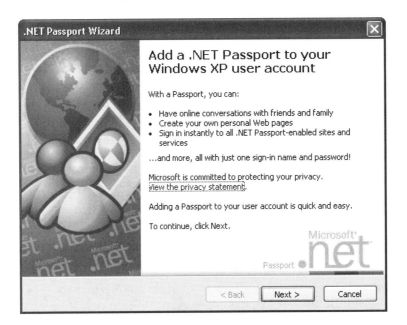

You get a Microsoft .NET Passport by creating a Hotmail (Microsoft's web-based e-mail service, at **www.hotmail.com**), by creating an MSN e-mail account, or by telling it about another e-mail address. When creating a new Microsoft .NET Passport, you provide a password, as well as a secret question and answer that you can use if you forget your password. You must also provide your location (country and state or province). The .NET Passport system doesn't let you log onto Windows Messenger until you have received its confirmation message (this ensures that the e-mail address that you typed is really yours).

 Be sure to use an address that you check often, because Windows Messenger users may send you e-mail if you aren't online when they try to send you an instant message.

If you have trouble creating a .NET Passport without creating a Hotmail account, go to MSN.com, click .NET Sign In at the top, then click the Get a .NET Passport link. (Because web site designs change constantly, these links may move.) You can also go to **www.passport.com** to create or get help with a .NET Passport.

When you have created a .NET Passport for yourself, you can sign in:

You can select the Sign Me In Automatically check box to avoid having to sign in each time you use the program.

Once you have a Microsoft .NET Passport, you see the Windows Messenger window, shown in Figure 25-1. The window lists your contacts—those who are online and those who are not. Of course, if you've never used Windows Messenger, you don't have any contacts listed (yet).

The Windows Messenger window includes an entry showing how many new e-mail messages are in your MSN or Hotmail mailbox, if you have one. If you don't have any new messages, you see a Go To My E-mail Inbox link. To read your MSN or Hotmail messages, click the E-mail Message (or xx New E-mail Messages) link: Your browser starts and displays the mail web site. There's no way to configure Windows Messenger to display how many messages are in mailboxes other than your Hotmail or MSN mailbox (Microsoft owns Hotmail and MSN, and they use Windows to promote it).

If you connect to the Internet via a LAN (as described in Chapter 31) and you have trouble connecting with Windows Messenger, choose Tools | Options, click the Connection tab, and clear the I Use A Proxy Server check box if it is selected. For details about getting Windows Messenger to work over a LAN, see the Microsoft support article on this topic at **www.microsoft.com/windowsxp/pro/techinfo/deployment/natfw**.

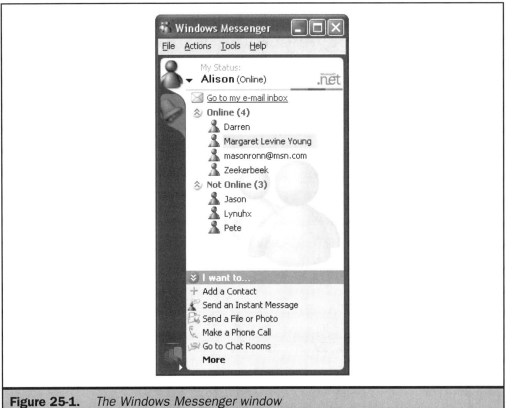

Figure 25-1. *The Windows Messenger window*

Note *Messenger functionality may be impaired by firewalls or routers: you may not be able to connect, or you may connect but not be able to send or receive files or use voice or video conferencing. For example, if you use the ZoneAlarm firewall program, you must enable outgoing traffic to the e450.voice.microsoft.com server. Check your firewall or router manufacturer's web site for instructions for enabling Windows messenger. Or, go to the Microsoft KnowledgeBase at **support.microsoft.com** and search for "Windows Messenger firewall" or read articles Q324243, Q320783, and Q324214.*

For answers to frequently asked questions about Windows Messenger and .NET Passports, go to **support.microsoft.com** and search for article Q316660. If you have trouble connecting with Windows Messenger, search for article Q307294.

If you have Outlook 2002 and your friends used their real e-mail addresses for .NET Passport, their online statuses appear in Outlook 2002. When someone sends you e-mail, you can see if the person is online, and you can IM the sender from the e-mail message. If you use your real e-mail address for your .NET Passport, other Outlook 2002 users can contact you from e-mail messages you send.

Configuring Your Contacts

Before you can begin to chat, you have to have someone to chat with. The easiest way is to ask your friends if they use Windows Messenger and, if so, what their e-mail address is (at least, the e-mail address they use for messaging—some people use a different address to avoid getting messages at the regular e-mail address). Once you know a person's e-mail address, add it to your contacts by clicking Add A Contact (or Add on the toolbar in Windows Messenger 4.6). You see the Add A Contact dialog box, shown here:

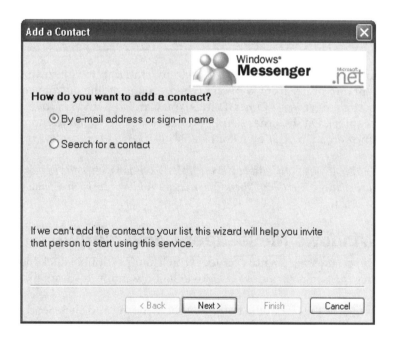

Choose By E-mail Address Or Sign-In Name, click Next, enter the person's e-mail address, and click Next again. Windows Messenger adds the person to your contact list if that person has a Microsoft .NET Passport. In case the person does not have a .NET Passport, you can send them an e-mail message telling them how to get up and running with Windows Messenger.

If you think someone has a .NET Passport but you don't know the person's e-mail address, choose Search For A Contact from the Add A Contact dialog box. Enter the information you know about the person and click Next. You see a list of people who meet your search criteria-select one and click Next. If the person has a .NET Passport, Windows Messenger adds the person to your contacts.

When someone adds your e-mail address as a contact, the Windows Messenger system notifies you with a message like this:

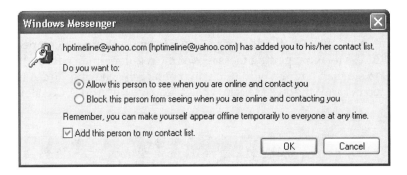

If you don't know the person (or are acquainted and don't want further contact), you can prevent him or her from knowing when you are online or from contacting you via Windows Messenger (see "Other Things You Can Do with Windows Messenger" later in this chapter). On the other hand, if the message is from a friend or coworker, you can add the person to your own contact list.

 You can disable this notification. Choose Tools | Options, click the Privacy tab, and make sure that the Alert Me When Other Users Add Me To Their Contact Lists check box is selected.

Starting a Windows Messenger Conversation

To exchange typed messages with a contact who is online, double-click his or her name in the Windows Messenger window. A Conversation window appears like the one in Figure 25-2.

Type messages in the box at the bottom of the window and click Send or press ENTER. If you have a sound card, microphone, and speakers, and the person you're chatting with does also, click Start Talking to speak with them.

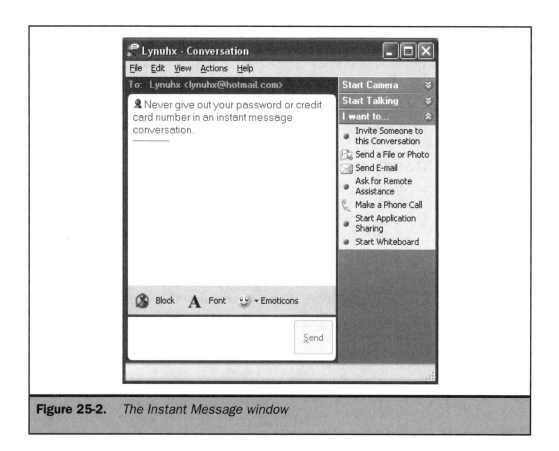

Figure 25-2.   *The Instant Message window*

When someone starts a conversation with you, a little box pops up from the notification area (right end) of the Windows taskbar, like this:

Click the box to switch to a conversation with the person. After a few seconds, this box disappears.

You can invite other contacts to join in the chat by clicking Invite Someone To This Conversation from the I Want To options. Up to five people (including you) can participate in a conversation. You can block the person you are talking to from contacting you in the future by clicking Block. (If you want to unblock someone, right-click the person's name in your contact list and select Unblock.)

Holding Voice Conversations

Once you have opened a Conversation window with someone, you can switch to a voice chat, assuming that you and the other person have microphones and speakers attached to your computers. The first time you click Start Talking in the Conversation window, Windows runs the Audio And Video Tuning Wizard to check your microphone and speakers.

When you click Start Talking in the Conversation window (or click a contact name in the Windows Messenger window and click Call), Windows Messenger sends an invitation to the other person to have a voice conversation. The Start Talking link is replaced by these settings, which you can use to adjust your volume, mute your microphone, and end the voice conversation:

Video Conferencing

If your computer has a video camera, you can use it to transmit a picture to the person with whom you are having a conversation. Click the Start Camera link in the Conversation window to start receiving video images from the other person. The video image appears in the upper-right part of the Conversation window. Click Stop Camera to stop receiving video data.

Sending Files to Others in a Conversation

To send a file to someone with whom you are having a conversation, click Send A File in the Conversation window. Otherwise, right-click the name of the contact in the

Windows Messenger window and choose Send A File Or Photo from the I Want To options. Select the file and click Open. The contact has to accept the file for the transfer to occur.

When you receive a file, Windows usually stores it in the My Received Files subfolder of your My Documents folder.

Sharing a Whiteboard

You can share a whiteboard—a drawing window on which everyone in the conversation can draw—as part of a Windows Messenger conversation. Choose Start Whiteboard from the I Want To options. The other people in the conversation receive an invitation to start using Whiteboard. If they click Accept, you (and they) see a Sharing Session window, like this:

The Sharing Sessions window shows the shared items that Windows Messenger supports: Application Sharing (described in the next section) and Whiteboard.

Then you see a Whiteboard window, as shown in Figure 25-3. The whiteboard works similarly to Microsoft Paint (see Chapter 18, section "Creating and Editing Images with Microsoft Paint"). To see what a tool does, hover your mouse pointer over it. When you are finished with the drawing, close the Whiteboard window (choose File | Save As first if you want to save your joint work).

Sharing Control of a Program

If you would like to show the other people in a conversation how a program works, or write a document as a group, you can use Windows Messenger's Application Sharing feature. You can let the other people take control of the program and give commands, even if they don't have the program installed on their computers.

Showing a Program on Everyone's Screen

In the Conversation window, choose Invite | To Start Application Sharing. Windows Messenger sends the other people in the conversation an invitation to share an application

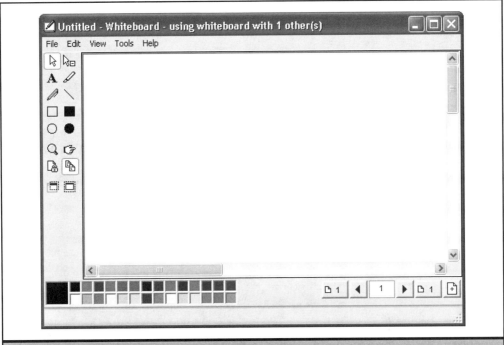

Figure 25-3.   *When you share a whiteboard with Windows Messenger, everyone in the conversation can draw on it.*

with you. If they click Accept, the Sharing Session window appears (pictured in the previous section), and then you see the Sharing window shown in Figure 25-4.

In the Sharing window, choose the program that you want to allow the other people in the conversation to share. For example, to edit a document as a group, choose to share a word processing program that is open with the document loaded. If you want to show the other people a presentation or some web pages, choose a presentation program or your browser. Then click Share.

Once you have selected a program to share, the program window appears on the screens of the other people in the Windows Messenger conversation. Bring the window to the front (that is, click in it to make it active) so that other windows don't obscure it on the other people's screens. The other people can see what you do, but can't give commands themselves.

Here are a few pointers when sharing a program:

■ Before you start to share an application, be sure to agree on a screen resolution for everyone to use. Using the same resolution as the rest of the people in the conversation prevents the screen from jumping around as the cursor and mouse pointer move in the shared application.

■ Others in the conversation can see only as much of the program's window as you can see on your screen; when you click another window that overlaps the window that is editing the file, the obscured part of the window disappears on everyone else's screen, too.

■ Unless you and everyone else in the conversation have fast Internet connections (faster than dial-up), displaying windows with a shared program can take a long time—a minute or two. Everyone in the conversation needs to wait for the shared window to appear, or everyone's screens will get hopelessly confusing. This feature works best for users connected by a high-speed LAN.

Enabling Others to Control the Program

If you want other people to be able to control the application (giving commands and controlling the mouse), switch back to the Sharing window and click the Allow Control button. When someone else double-clicks in the window that displays your program, you see a Request Control window, indicating who wants to control the application. Click Accept or Reject to give or deny control to that person. The other person controls

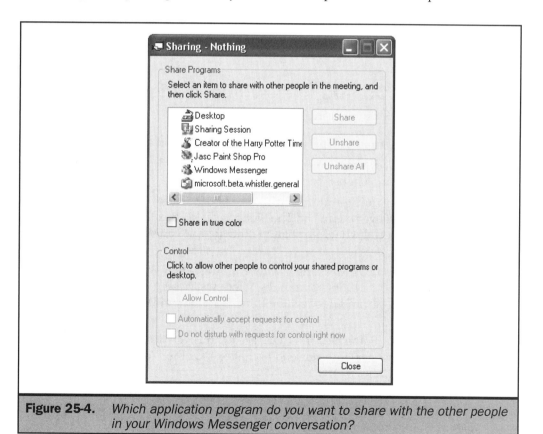

Figure 25-4. *Which application program do you want to share with the other people in your Windows Messenger conversation?*

the mouse and keyboard for that application until you press a key. When you are finished sharing control of the application, switch back to the Sharing window and click the Prevent Control button. When you are done sharing the application, close the Sharing window (and the application, if you like).

While you are sharing control, you can select the Automatically Accept Request For Control check box in the Sharing window to skip having to accept requests for control. Alternatively, to temporarily disable control-sharing, select the Do Not Disturb With Requests For Control Right Now check box.

Here are some tips about sharing control of a program:

- If you share Windows Explorer, all Explorer windows are shared with the other callers, including windows that you open after clicking the Share button.

- If you are going to edit a file collaboratively, make a backup copy of the file first, just in case. When you have finished editing the file collaboratively, only the person who originally shared the file can save or print the file. If other callers want copies of the finished file, the owner of the file can send the file to the other callers.

- Each person in the call does not need to have the program that the call is sharing; mouse clicks and keystrokes are transmitted to the program owner's computer.

Other Things You Can Do with Windows Messenger

You can use Windows Messenger in a few other ways, too:

- **Block someone from calling you**   Right-click a contact and choose Block.

- **Changing the way your name appears to others**   Click your own name in the list of contacts and choose Personal Settings.

- **Changing other configuration settings**   Choose Tools | Options from the Windows Messenger menu bar. The Options dialog box that appears contains settings that control what information other people can see about you and how the program runs.

- **Preventing Windows Messenger from running when Windows starts up**   Choose Tools | Options from the Windows Messenger menu bar, click the Preferences tab, and deselect the Run This Program When Windows Starts check box.

- **Playing games**   Some new Internet-based games are designed to work with Windows Messenger, and can send invitations to other Windows Messenger users to join a game.

- **Getting help with your computer**   If you choose Ask for Remote Assistance in the Conversation window, Windows runs the Remote Assistance program, described in "Allowing a Friend to Control Your Computer" in Chapter 36.

Conferencing with Microsoft NetMeeting

The newest version of Windows Messenger has all of NetMeeting's features, but if you are working with someone who is not using Windows XP and Windows Messenger 4.*x* you may want to use NetMeeting to chat, talk, videoconference, or share applications or a Whiteboard.

 **Note**   *If there is a firewall (like the Internet Connection Firewall) between you and the Internet, you will not be able to use many of NetMeeting's features.*

NetMeeting lets you connect only with other people who use NetMeeting: it doesn't conform to Internet conferencing standards (such as the H.323 standard). For example, you can't join a meeting with people who use Internet Relay Chat (IRC), CU-SeeMe, PowWow, Internet Phone, or other online chat programs. For more information about NetMeeting, try the Meeting By Wire web site at **www.meetingbywire.com**. You can also use Outlook Express to read the microsoft.public.internet.netmeeting and microsoft.public.windows.inetexplorer.ie5.netmeeting.chat newsgroups at msnews.microsoft.com. (See Chapter 23 for how to read newsgroups.)

Note   *This section describes NetMeeting version 3.01, the same version that shipped with Windows Me. Microsoft is no longer developing NetMeeting because Windows Messenger replaces it.*

Running and Configuring NetMeeting

If you upgraded from Windows Me, NetMeeting may be on the Start | All Programs | Accessories | Communications menu. To add NetMeeting to your menu, right-click the Start menu, choose Open, double-click Programs, right-click a blank space in the Explorer window, choose New | Shortcut from the menu that appears, type **C:\Program Files\ NetMeeting\Conf.exe** as the location of the new menu item, and type **NetMeeting** as the command to appear on the All Programs menu. To start NetMeeting without adding it to the Start menu, choose Start | Run, type **conf** (for "conferencing"), and press ENTER. If you haven't already configured NetMeeting, you see a series of windows that tell you about the program and ask for the following information:

- **Your name, e-mail address, location, and comments**   You don't have to enter your real name or address; consider using an alias if you are planning to talk to people you don't know.

- **Which directory server to use**   The default is Microsoft Internet Directory, which is the same directory you see when you use Windows Messenger. A number of other public directory servers are also available. You can find a list of them at the DevX NetMeeting Zone web site at **www.devx.com/netmeeting/ bestservers.asp**. If your organization uses NetMeeting, you may use a private directory server.

■ **Connection speed**   Choose the speed of your modem or specify that you are connected via a LAN (see Chapter 27). NetMeeting uses this information when sending you audio or video data.

■ **Shortcuts**   If you use NetMeeting often, you might want to add a shortcut to the desktop or to the Quick Launch toolbar on your taskbar.

NetMeeting runs the Audio And Video Tuning Wizard to make sure that your speakers are working, for use in audio chats (don't worry if you don't have a microphone—NetMeeting is still useful). When it finishes, the configuration program displays the NetMeeting window, as shown in Figure 25-5.

You can make changes to your configuration by choosing Tools | Options.

Connecting to a Directory Server

Once you see the NetMeeting window (as shown in Figure 25-5), you can start a meeting by clicking the Place Call button (the yellow telephone) if you know the e-mail address

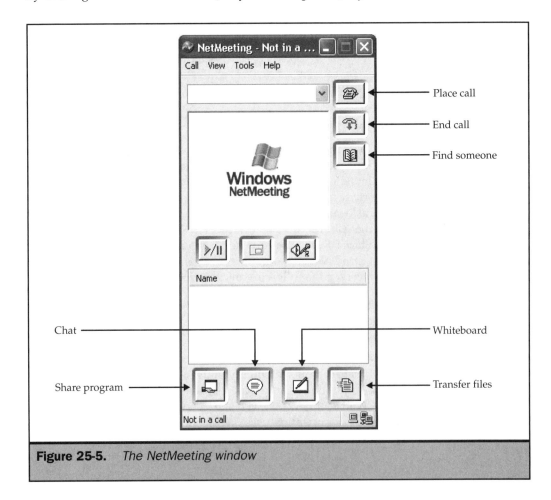

Figure 25-5.   *The NetMeeting window*

of the person you want to talk to. However, unless you know the person's IP address or have called them before, you usually need to start the call by selecting the person from a directory.

When you click the Find Someone In A Directory button (the little open book) when you are connected to a directory server, you see the Find Someone window (if your computer isn't connected to the Internet, you see a message first: click Connect). Set the Select A Directory to the directory to which you want to connect. If you want to use the Microsoft Internet Directory, you may need to click a link to log in using your Microsoft .NET Passport name and password. Then you see a list of the people who are on your contacts list (this is the same list that appears in Windows Messenger), as in Figure 25-6.

If you want to talk to someone who isn't on your Windows Messenger contact list, you and the other person need to connect to the same directory server. See the DevX NetMeeting Zone web site at **www.devx.com/netmeeting/bestservers.asp** for a list of servers to use. Choose Tools | Options from the NetMeeting window's menu bar, type the server name (usually ils.*domainname*) into the Directory box, and click OK. Now, when you click the Find Someone In A Directory button, a list of people on the

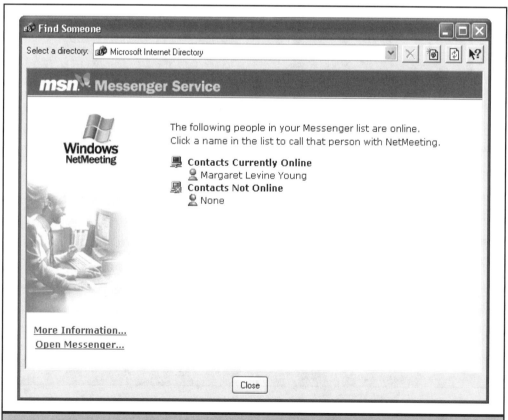

Figure 25-6.   *You can use the Microsoft Internet Directory to see your Windows Messenger contacts.*

server appears, with a little PC icon to the left of each person's e-mail address (as shown in Figure 25-7). An icon with a blue screen and red twinkle means that the person is currently in a call, whereas a gray icon means that the person is not in a call. A little yellow speaker icon indicates that the person can communicate via audio. A little gray camera icon means that the person can communicate via video. On the listing of people, click the column headings to sort by that column; sorting by last name or e-mail address makes finding the person you want easier.

 When you are connected to a public server and your name is listed, you are likely to get unwanted calls.

Making or Receiving a Call

To call someone, double-click the person's name on the contact or directory list, or type the name in the box and click the Call button. If you are using Microsoft Internet Directory, then the person is contacted through Windows Messenger: if they accept your invitation,

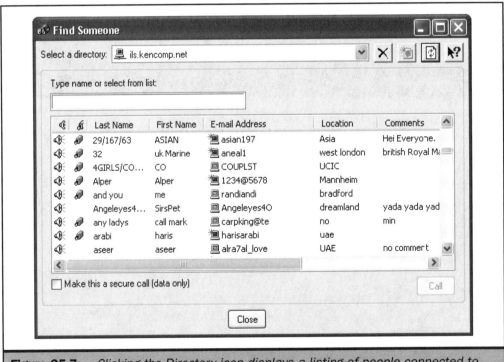

Figure 25-7. *Clicking the Directory icon displays a listing of people connected to your directory server.*

Windows Messenger takes over on your computer, too. If you use another directory server, NetMeeting contacts the directory server to make the connection and displays a dialog box on that person's computer screen, asking them whether they want to connect with you. If the person accepts your call, the NetMeeting window lists the people who are in your current call.

When you are done with the call, click the Hang Up button. NetMeeting maintains its connection with the directory server but disconnects from the call.

Once You Are Connected

Once you are connected to at least one other person, you can communicate using most of the same features that Windows Messenger offers:

- **Text chat**   Click the Chat button to display a window in which you can type messages to the other people in the chat.

- **Voice chat**   If both of you have microphones and speakers, you can just begin talking. Speak slowly, one at a time (as though you were using a walkie-talkie—over!). Unless you have a very fast connection, you may experience "breaking up"—the sound may be interrupted and "staticky." Keep your microphone away from the speakers, or use headphones, to avoid feedback.

- **Videoconferencing**   If other people in your call have video cameras (even if you don't have one), you can see video from one of their cameras (one at a time) in your NetMeeting window. The video appears in the Remote Video window, a small box on the right side of the window when the Current Call icon is selected. If you don't see the video, click the button at the bottom of the Remote Video window. To set your video options, choose Tools | Options and click the Video tab. You can tell NetMeeting to enable your video camera automatically when you make a call; set the size of the video image; choose between faster, low-quality video and slower, high-quality video; and specify the properties of your camera. If you have a camera, be sure to light your face (or whatever the camera points at) from the front. You can't see more than one person at a time; to switch the person in the call you can see, choose Tools | Switch Audio And Video and choose the name of the person whom you want to see.

- **Sharing a whiteboard**   If you and the other participants in your call want to draw diagrams or pictures that are visible by everyone in the call, use the Whiteboard feature. When you click the Whiteboard button near the bottom of the NetMeeting window, you see a window that works similarly to Microsoft Paint (see Chapter 18, section "Creating and Editing Images with Microsoft Paint"). When anyone in the call makes a change to the Whiteboard window, everyone in the call sees the change.

- **Sending and receiving files**   Choose Tools | File Transfer or click the File Transfer button at the bottom of the NetMeeting window to open the File Transfer window. Click the Add Files button and specify which file you want to send. Alternatively, drag the name of the file from Windows Explorer onto the File Transfer window. Click the Send All button to send the files. To send a file to one caller, rather than to everyone in the call, select the person from the drop-down list at the top right of the File Transfer window. If someone sends you a file, NetMeeting automatically receives the file, storing it in the C:\Program Files\ NetMeeting\Received Files folder (assuming that Windows is installed on C:). You see a window telling you about the arrival of the file. To open the file with the default application for the type of file you received, click the Open button.

Caution   *Beware of viruses in executable files and of generally offensive material when receiving files from people you don't know.*

- **Sharing programs**   You and the other people in your meeting can share the windows of a running program that one member has on his or her screens. For example, you could show a group around your web site by running a browser on your machine and sharing the browser window so that the other callers can see the contents of the browser window on their screens, too. This feature works like Windows Messenger's application-sharing (see "Sharing Control of a Program" earlier in this chapter).

Hosting a Meeting or Joining an Existing Meeting

In addition to calls, you can communicate in *meetings*, calls that are scheduled in advance. Hosting a meeting allows you to define some properties for the meeting. To host a meeting, let everyone invited to the meeting know when the meeting will take place and how to call you using NetMeeting. At the time the meeting is scheduled to begin, choose Call | Host Meeting and choose the options you want from the Host A Meeting dialog box, shown in Figure 25-8. When you click OK, you return to the NetMeeting window, with only you listed as a caller. When the other callers connect, you see a dialog box asking whether they can join; click Accept or Ignore.

Because you are the host of the meeting, the meeting ends when you hang up. Other participants can come and go without ending the meeting. As the host, you can also

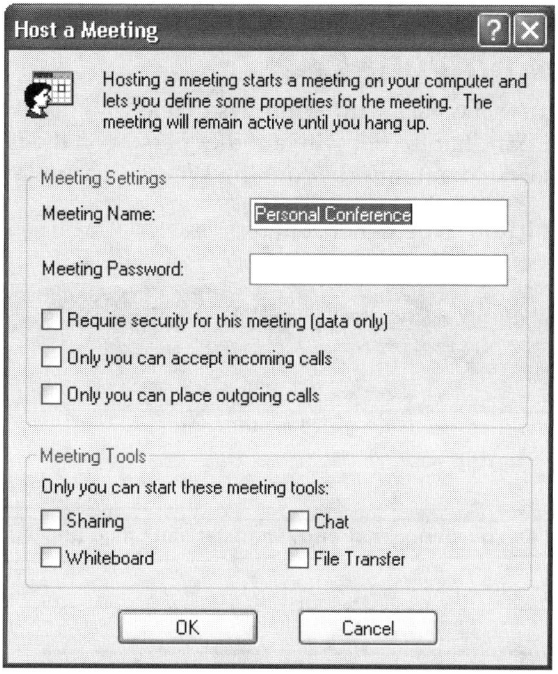

Host a Meeting

Hosting a meeting starts a meeting on your computer and lets you define some properties for the meeting. The meeting will remain active until you hang up.

Meeting Settings

Meeting Name: Personal Conference

Meeting Password:

☐ Require security for this meeting (data only)
☐ Only you can accept incoming calls
☐ Only you can place outgoing calls

Meeting Tools

Only you can start these meeting tools:

☐ Sharing   ☐ Chat
☐ Whiteboard   ☐ File Transfer

OK   Cancel

Figure 25-8.   *The Host A Meeting dialog box*

throw people out of your meeting: right-click the person's name on the list of callers and choose Remove from the menu that appears.

To join an existing meeting, call someone who is in the meeting. You see a message that the person is currently in a meeting, asking whether you want to try to join the meeting; click Yes. When the person you called leaves the meeting, you leave too, so it's best to call the person who is hosting the meeting.

If you don't want anyone else to join the meeting (or any NetMeeting call), choose Call | Do Not Disturb. Remember to choose the same command again when you want to reenable receiving calls.

Using WinChat to Chat with Other Users on your LAN

WinChat is a program that comes with Windows that allows users on a LAN to chat with each other. Use WinChat to chat with another person on the LAN. In order to receive a message, the recipient must be running WinChat, as follows:

1. Choose Start | Run, type **winchat** and press ENTER. You see the Chat window:

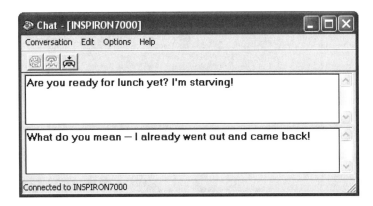

2. Click the first button on the toolbar and type the computer's name or select from the list. (To find the name of your computer open the Start menu, right-click My Computer, select Properties, and click the Computer Name tab.) The recipient needs to click the second button on the toolbar in order to chat with you.

3. Type in Chat window—the other user sees text as you type and can respond.

4. When finished, click the third button on the toolbar to hang up.

Chapter 26

Using Other Internet Programs with Windows XP

W indows XP comes with lots of Internet-related programs. In addition to the automated sign-up software, the New Connection Wizard, and dial-up connections (all described in Chapter 22), you get lots of Internet applications—which are described in the other chapters in this part of the book.

Windows also comes with these other useful Internet programs:

- **HyperTerminal** acts as a terminal emulator and lets you log into text-based systems, either over the Internet (like telnet) or by dialing directly.

- **Telnet** can also do terminal emulation over the Internet, faster but not as nicely as HyperTerminal.

- **Web folders** can display folders stored on FTP or web servers and enable you to copy, rename, and delete files using Explorer windows.

- **Ftp** lets you transfer files to or from FTP servers.

This chapter describes how to use these programs. You can also download other Internet programs from the Internet itself; at the end of this chapter we recommend some programs that complement those that come with Windows and suggest where to find the programs on the Web.

Logging into Text-Based Systems with HyperTerminal

HyperTerminal is useful for connecting to computers that are designed to talk to terminals, including UNIX shell accounts and bulletin board systems (see Chapter 22). The computer you connect to by using HyperTerminal is called the *remote computer* (as opposed to your own *local computer*).

You can use HyperTerminal in three ways:

- **Dial-up connections**   You can use HyperTerminal to call another computer over a modem and phone line. No other communications program or account is involved. You use this method when connecting directly to a bulletin board system, UNIX shell account, or other text-based system that works with terminals. You tell HyperTerminal what modem to use to make the connection, along with the country, area code, and phone number to dial.

- **Direct network connections**   You can use HyperTerminal to connect to a computer to which your computer is connected by a cable. You tell HyperTerminal the communications port (COM1 or COM2) to which the cable is connected. Alternatively, you can use a direct connection in the Network Connections window (see Chapter 27).

- **Telnet connections**   If you have an Internet account (or other TCP/IP-based connection), you can use HyperTerminal as a *telnet* program, a terminal program that works over the Internet. First, you connect to the Internet and then you connect to a computer over the Internet by using a HyperTerminal telnet connection—you "telnet in." You tell HyperTerminal to connect using TCP/IP (Winsock), along with the port number and host address of the computer to which you want to connect. The standard *port number* (a number that tells an Internet host computer whether you are connecting for e-mail, the Web, telnet, or another Internet service) is 23. The *host address* is the Internet host name of the computer you want to telnet in to.

Secure Telnet Connections with SSH

Many Internet host computers no longer accept telnet logins, so you can't use HyperTerminal to connect. Instead, they use a more secure system called *SSH* (secure shell), which encrypts messages between your computer and the host computer.

If you need to connect to a host that requires SSH, get a free program called PuTTY, which was written by Simon Tatham in the U.K. You can download this small program from its web site at **www.chiark.greenend.org.uk/~sgtatham/putty/**, or from various mirror sites, including **putty.bhni.net**.

When you run PuTTY, you see its Configuration window:

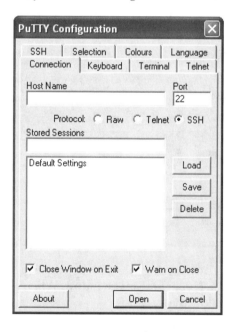

Click SSH to select a secure connection and type the host computer's name in the Host Name box. If you plan to connect to this host again, type a name for this computer in the Stored Sessions box and click Save. Then click Open. The first time you connect to a computer using SSH, PuTTY asks if you want to cache (store) the host key (used for encrypting messages) in your computer's Registry. Click Yes. You then see a terminal window that is similar to HyperTerminal's.

To dial up and connect to a computer, HyperTerminal creates a *HyperTerminal connection*, a configuration file with the specifications for the connection. HyperTerminal connection files have the extension .ht.

Windows XP comes with HyperTerminal 5.1, which is very similar to the version that shipped with Windows Me/9x.

Running HyperTerminal

To run HyperTerminal, choose Start | All Programs | Accessories | Communications | HyperTerminal. If HyperTerminal isn't already your default telnet program, you see a dialog box asking whether Windows should do so. The HyperTerminal window appears, and the Connection Description window also opens to help set up a new first HyperTerminal connection.

Configuring HyperTerminal for Your Account

The first time you run HyperTerminal, it displays the Connection Description dialog box:

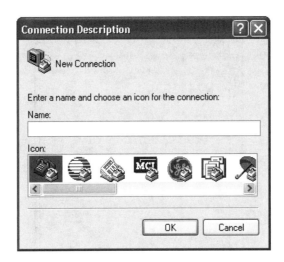

You can also display it by choosing File | New Connection or clicking the New button on the toolbar of the HyperTerminal window. When you see the Connection Description dialog box, follow these steps:

1. Type the name you want to use for the connection, choose an icon, and click OK. You see the Connect To dialog box, asking for information about how to dial the phone to connect to the computer:

2. The options you see on this dialog box depend on what you've selected for the Connect Using setting. For a dial-up connection, set the Connect Using box to the modem to use for the connection, choose the country, type the area code, and type the phone number to dial. For a direct cable connection, set the Connect Using box to your modem or to COM1 or COM2 (the communications port to which the modem is connected). For a telnet connection, set the Connect Using box to TCP/IP (Winsock, that is, your Internet connection) and fill in the host address and port number (usually 23).

3. Click OK. For dial-up connections, you see the Connect dialog box (for telnet connections, skip to step 6):

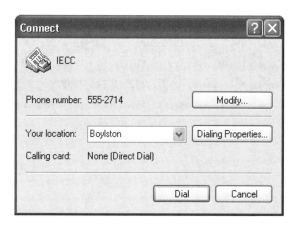

4. If you want to change your dialing location (where you are dialing from) or use a calling card, click the Dialing Properties button and use the New and Edit buttons to change the way the connection is dialed (see Chapter 21, section "Configuring Windows for Dialing Locations").

5. To connect, click Dial. (If you click Cancel, HyperTerminal remembers the connection information you entered, but doesn't make the connection.) For dial-up connections, HyperTerminal dials the phone. For telnet connections, if you're not already online, your dial-up connection may display its dialog box to get you connected to your Internet account; if so, click Connect. When HyperTerminal has established a connection with the remote computer, you see the HyperTerminal window, shown in Figure 26-1.

6. Log in and use the remote computer, typing the commands that the remote computer requires. For example, if the remote computer displays a UNIX command line, you must type UNIX commands. You can use the scroll bar along the right side of the HyperTerminal window to see the *backscroll buffer*, which stores the last 500 lines of text that have scrolled up off the top of the terminal window (you can configure the buffer to be larger).

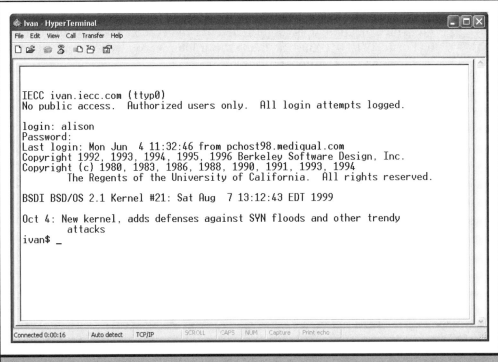

Figure 26-1.   *HyperTerminal connected to another computer*

Tip   *If you are trying to telnet into a host computer and the connection is refused (or if a firewall is blocking telnet connections), you may need to use SSH, the secure version of telnet. See the sidebar "Secure Telnet Connections with SSH" earlier in this chapter.*

7. When you are done using the remote computer, log off by using the commands that it requires. HyperTerminal disconnects, too. If you have trouble getting disconnected, tell HyperTerminal to hang up by choosing Call | Disconnect from the menu bar or by clicking the Disconnect icon on the toolbar.

8. When you exit HyperTerminal, it asks whether you want to save the session (connection) you just created. Click Yes. (If you never plan to connect to this remote computer again, click No to throw away the connection information you entered.) HyperTerminal creates an icon for the connection in the C:\Program Files\Accessories\HyperTerminal folder.

Connecting with HyperTerminal

You can connect to a computer for which you've already created a HyperTerminal connection in two ways:

- Open the C:\Program Files\Accessories\HyperTerminal folder (replace C with the drive letter on which Windows is installed if it's not C). Then double-click the icon for the connection.

- Choose Start | All Programs | Accessories | Communications | HyperTerminal. When the HyperTerminal window appears, click Cancel to close the Connection Description dialog box. Choose File | Open or click the Open button on the toolbar and choose the connection.

HyperTerminal runs and displays the Connect dialog box; click Dial to make the connection. If you are using a telnet connection and you are not already connected to the Internet, your dial-up connection displays its window to prompt you to get online; click Connect.

Changing Information About a Connection

If the phone number for a remote computer changes or you need to change the modem (or other information about the connection), run HyperTerminal by using the connection, or choose File | Open to open the connection. Click Cancel if you don't want to connect yet. Then click the Properties button on the toolbar or choose File | Properties to display the connection Properties dialog box, as shown in Figure 26-2. You can also display the Properties dialog box when you are using the connection. The settings on the Properties dialog box depend on the type of connection (dial-up, direct cable connection, or telnet).

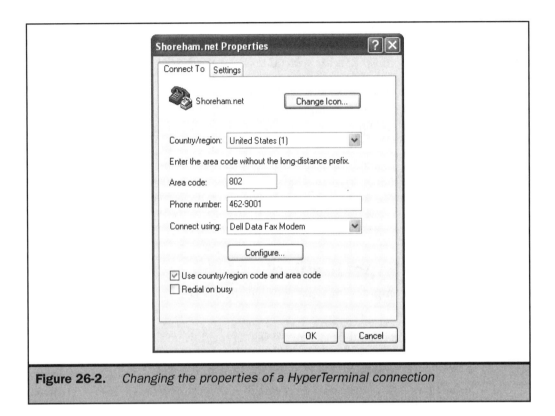

Figure 26-2.   *Changing the properties of a HyperTerminal connection*

In the Properties dialog box for the connection, you can set these types of options:

- **Connect using**   On the Connect To tab, you specify the icon and how to connect: via modem, via cable (connected to your modem, COM1, or COM2 port), or via TCP/IP (for a telnet connection). For dial-up connections, you also specify the phone number. For TCP/IP connections, you also specify the host address and port number (the default is 23, telnet's usual port). If you have Virtual Private Networking installed, VPN appears as an option (see Chapter 28).

- **What keys do**   On the Settings tab, you specify whether the function keys, cursor motion keys, and CTRL key combinations are transmitted to the other computer or are interpreted by Windows. You can also control the actions of the BACKSPACE key.

- **Terminal emulation**   On the Settings tab, you tell HyperTerminal what type of terminal to emulate (act like). Most remote computers are configured to work with certain standard terminal types. HyperTerminal can emulate many of the most commonly used terminal types: ANSI, ANSIW, Minitel, TTY, Viewdata, VT100, VT100J, VT52, and VT-UTF8. If you set the Emulation box to Auto Detect, HyperTerminal tries to figure out what type of terminal to emulate, based on information from the remote computer. If you click the Terminal Setup button, you can further configure HyperTerminal's actions, including how the cursor looks, what keys on the keypad do and whether the terminal window displays 80 or 132 columns.

■ **Character set** On the Settings tab, click the Terminal Setup button to control settings that are specific to the type of terminal that you are emulating. Click the ASCII Setup button to control the characters that HyperTerminal sends and receives, including which character(s) HyperTerminal sends at the end of each line, whether HyperTerminal displays the characters you type or waits to display them until the remote computer echoes them back, and whether HyperTerminal waits a fraction of a second after each character or line it sends.

■ **Other settings** You can specify how many lines of the text the backscroll buffer stores and whether HyperTerminal beeps when connecting and disconnecting.

Transferring Files

HyperTerminal can send files from your computer to the remote computer or receive files from the remote computer. A number of standard file transfer protocols exist; HyperTerminal can send and receive files by using the Xmodem (regular or 1K), Kermit, Ymodem, Ymodem-G, Zmodem, and Zmodem With Crash Recovery protocols. Choose a protocol that the remote computer can also handle. If you have a choice, use Zmodem With Crash Recovery.

Sending a File to the Remote Computer

To send a file to the remote computer:

1. Connect to the remote computer. If applicable, move to the directory on the remote computer in which you want to store the file.

2. If the file transfer protocol you plan to use requires you to give a command on the remote computer to tell it to expect a file, do so. For example, when transferring a file to a UNIX system by using Xmodem, you type the command **rx** *filename* on the remote computer. When transferring a file by using Zmodem (with or without Crash Recovery), no command is required; the UNIX system can detect when the file begins to arrive and stores it automatically.

3. Click the Send button on the toolbar or choose Transfer | Send File. You see the Send File dialog box, shown here:

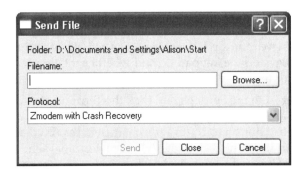

4. In the Filename box, type the name of the file you want to send or click the Browse button to select the file.

5. Set the Protocol box to a file transfer protocol that the remote computer can use when receiving files.

6. Click the Send button. You see a window displaying the status of the file transfer. How much information the window displays depends on which file transfer protocol you use. You can click the Cancel button to stop the file transfer. Click the cps/bps button to control whether you see the transfer speed in characters per second (cps) or bits per second (bps). When the window disappears, file transfer is complete.

Receiving a File from the Remote Computer

To receive a file from the remote computer:

1. Connect to the remote computer. If applicable, move to the directory on the remote computer in which the file is stored.

2. Give the command on the remote computer to tell it to send the file. For example, to tell a UNIX system to transfer a file to your system by using Xmodem, you type the command **sx** *filename* on the remote computer.

3. If you are using Zmodem (with or without Crash Recovery), HyperTerminal detects that a file is arriving and begins receiving the file automatically (skip to step 8). Otherwise, click the Receive button on the toolbar or choose Transfer | Receive File. You see the Receive File dialog box.

4. In the Place Received File In The Following Folder box, type the pathname of the folder into which you want to store the file or click the Browse button to change the pathname.

5. Set the Use Receiving Protocol setting to the file transfer protocol that the remote computer is using to send the file.

6. Click the Receive button.

7. For some protocols, HyperTerminal may need additional information. For example, when using Xmodem, the sending computer doesn't include the filename with the file, so HyperTerminal asks you what to name the file it receives. Type the additional information and click OK.

8. HyperTerminal displays a status window showing the progress of the file's transfer. You can click the Cancel button to stop the file transfer. Click the cps/bps button to control whether you see the transfer speed in characters per second (cps) or bits per second (bps). When the window disappears, the file transfer is complete.

Sending Text Files

You might want to send text to the other computer as though you were typing it. For example, if the remote computer asks a question to which you have an answer stored in a small text file, you can send the text file rather than retyping it—the remote computer doesn't realize that you are sending a file, and accepts the text as though you typed it. You can also send text that is displayed by some other program; for example, you might want to send a number that is displayed in your spreadsheet program.

You can send small amounts of text by using either of two methods:

■ **Copy and paste it**   Display the text file in another program and copy it to the Windows Clipboard (see Chapter 5, section "Sharing Data Through the Windows Clipboard"). In HyperTerminal, choose Edit | Paste To Host.

■ **Transfer it**   Choose Transfer | Send Text File. When you see the Send Text File dialog box, choose the file to send. (Make sure that it's a small text file; large files, or files that contain nontext information, rarely arrive intact.) HyperTerminal sends the contents of the file to the remote computer in the same way that it sends characters that you type.

| Note | CTRL-C *and* CTRL-V *may not work for cut-and-paste in HyperTerminal, depending on whether these keystrokes are used by the terminal that HyperTerminal is emulating. Choose Edit | Paste To Host from the menu bar instead, or right-click and choose Copy or Paste To Host.* |

Capturing Text from the HyperTerminal Window

If the remote computer displays interesting information in the HyperTerminal window, you may want to save it. You can use these three methods to save text:

- **Copy-and-paste it**   Select the text and choose Edit | Copy from the toolbar. You can use the scroll bar to see and select text that has already scrolled up off the top of the HyperTerminal window. HyperTerminal copies the text to the Windows Clipboard (see Chapter 5, section "Sharing Data Through the Windows Clipboard"). You can paste this text into the Windows Notepad, WordPad, your word processing program, or any other program that accepts blocks of text.

- **Capture it**   Choose Transfer | Capture Text. When you see the Capture Text dialog box, type the folder name and filename of the file into which you want to store the text. (Click Browse to select the folder.) Then click Start. All the text that appears in the terminal window from this point forward is also stored in the file. To stop capturing text, choose Transfer | Capture Text | Stop. To stop temporarily, choose Transfer | Capture Text | Pause; to restart the text later and capture into the same file, choose Transfer | Capture Text | Resume. While HyperTerminal is capturing text to a file, the word Capture appears on the status bar along the bottom of the HyperTerminal window.

- **Print it**   To tell HyperTerminal to print the information as it arrives in the terminal window, choose Transfer | Capture To Printer from the menu bar. As the remote computer sends text to your computer and HyperTerminal displays it, the text is printed. To stop printing, choose Transfer | Capture To Printer again. While HyperTerminal is printing all incoming text, the message Print Echo appears on the status bar.

- **Print the whole session**   To print the entire session with the remote computer, starting at the beginning of the backscroll buffer, choose File | Print.

Accepting Incoming Calls

If you are expecting a remote computer to dial into your computer, you can set your modem and HyperTerminal to answer the phone. Choose Call | Wait For A Call. The words Waiting For Calls appear on the status line. If an incoming call arrives on the phone line to which your modem is connected, your modem answers the phone, and

HyperTerminal tries to connect to a computer on the other end of the phone line. To turn off auto-answer, choose Call | Stop Waiting.

Logging into Other Computers Using Telnet

Windows XP also comes with a Telnet program. Unlike HyperTerminal, it can connect only over the Internet; the Telnet program can't dial the phone (see "Logging into Text-Based Systems with HyperTerminal" earlier in this chapter). If you do much telnetting, HyperTerminal is a nicer program to use because it can remember the settings for multiple host computers, transfer files, and emulate a wider variety of terminals. The only advantage of the Windows XP Telnet program is that it's faster over a LAN connection.

To run Windows built-in Telnet program:

1. Choose Start | Run, type **telnet**, and click OK. You see the Telnet window, shown in Figure 26-3.

2. To see a list of telnet commands, type **?** and press ENTER.

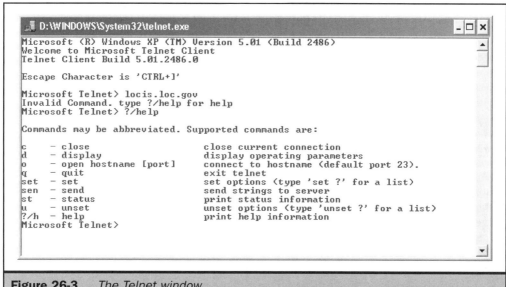

Figure 26-3.   *The Telnet window*

Working with FTP and Web Servers Using Web Folders

FTP (File Transfer Protocol) is a system for transferring files over the Internet. An *FTP server* stores files, and *FTP clients* can log into FTP servers either to upload (transfer) files to the FTP server or (more commonly) to download files from the FTP server. To use FTP, you must have an FTP client program.

Most web browsers, including Internet Explorer and Netscape Navigator, include an FTP client program that you can use to download and upload files (see Chapter 24). Web editors, including Netscape Composer (which is part of Netscape Communicator) include an FTP program for uploading your finished web pages to a web server.

Previous versions of Windows came with an FTP client (described in the section "Transferring Files Using Ftp" later in this chapter), but Windows XP has built an FTP client right into Windows Explorer. Using a feature called *Web Folders*, you can see the contents of FTP server folders in the same Explorer windows you use to manage the files on your own computer. Some web servers also support Web Folders.

> **Note**   *To create a Web Folder for a web server, the web server must support Microsoft's WebDAV extensions. (All FTP servers work with Web Folders.) Also, you need an account on the web or FTP server that gives you read and write access to the folders on the server. Many sites provide you with free web and FTP server space, including MSN Groups (formerly called MSN Communities) at **groups.msn.com**, Yahoo Geocities at **geocities.com**, Angelfire at **angelfire.lycos.com**, and Envy.nu at **www.envy.nu**. Not all web servers work with Web Folders. Windows steers you toward Microsoft's service, MSN Communities, which does.*

Creating a Web Folder

To work with the files on a web or FTP server, you create a Web Folder by adding an icon for it to your My Network Places window. Choose Start | My Network Places to open the My Network Places window, and click Add A Network Place from the Task pane to run the Add Network Place Wizard.

> **Note**   *If the Task pane isn't displayed, we don't know of a way to run the wizard. (See the Tip at the end of this section for a way to open a Web Folder without the wizard). Display the Task pane by choosing Tools | Folder Options from the menu bar and clicking the Show Common Tasks In Folders radio button. If you still don't see it, and the Folders Explorer bar appears, click the Folders button on the toolbar to remove the Folders Explorer bar, and the Task pane may appear.*

The Add Network Place Wizard asks several questions (click Next to move to the next question):

■ **Where Do You Want To Create This Network Place**   The wizard lists the web servers and FTP servers that Microsoft offers (currently only MSN Groups, which this wizard still calls MSN Communities). Click one, or click Choose Another Network Location to type the URL of an FTP or web server. If you choose MSN Communities, you are done: the wizard creates an MSN Communities account for you, along with a Web Folder icon with which you can access it.

■ **What Is The Address Of This Network Place**   If you choose to specify your own FTP or web server, type the URL into the Internet Or Network Address box. The URL must start with **http://** (for a web server) or **ftp://** (for an FTP server), as shown in Figure 26-4.

■ **User Name And Password**   If you plan to download files from a public FTP server to which you don't have write access (and on which you don't have an account), leave the Log On Anonymously check box selected. If you have an account on the FTP or web server and want to be able to upload files and use files that aren't available to the public, click the check box to deselect it. Type your account name in the User Name box.

■ **What Do You Want To Name This Place**   Type a name for the icon that the wizard will create for the FTP or web server.

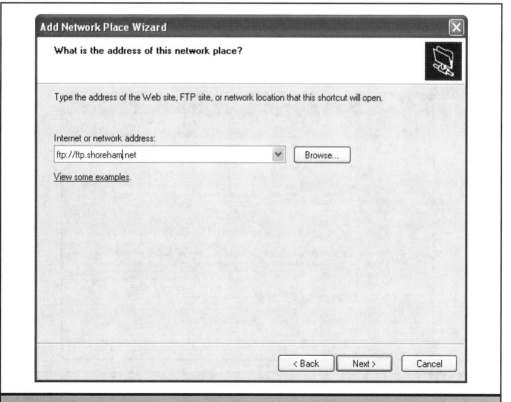

Figure 26-4.   *Specifying the address of a web or FTP server*

When the wizard exits, the My Network Places window is divided into two sections: Local Network (with icons for shared folders on the LAN) and The Internet (with icons for Web Folders). In the latter, you see a new icon for your Web Folder.

If you chose MSN Communities, the icon is called My Communities. Windows uses your Microsoft .NET Passport user name, e-mail address, and password to create a new account for you (see Chapter 25, section "Signing In to Windows Messenger with Your .NET Passport").

 *Here's a way to open a Web Folder without running the wizard: Open an Explorer window and type a URL in the Address box. For example, type **ftp://rtfm.mit.edu** to connect to an FTP server that contains the FAQs (lists of frequently asked questions and their answers).*

Working with Web Folders

Double-click the Web Folder icon to connect to the FTP or web server. When Windows tries to display the files on the server, you may see the Log On As dialog box, as shown in Figure 26-5. (For an MSN Communities Web Folder, Windows logs you on automatically using your .NET Passport.) Type the password for the FTP or web server. If you want Windows to remember this password so that you don't have to type it each time you view the contents of this Web Folder, select the Save Password check box. If you don't

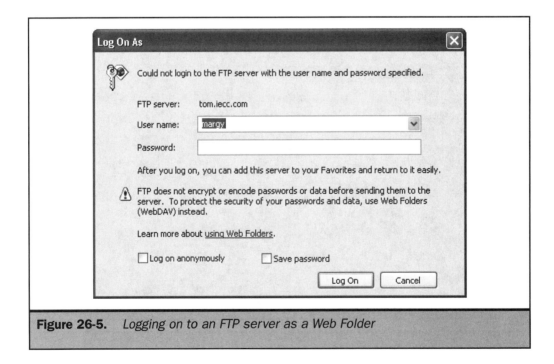

Figure 26-5.   *Logging on to an FTP server as a Web Folder*

have an account on the server, select the Log On Anonymously check box (not all servers allow anonymous FTP). Then click Log On.

Once you are logged onto the FTP or web server, your files on the server appear in an Explorer window. Move from folder to folder, copy, rename, delete, and view files just as you would with files on your own computer. To copy files to or from your computer, open a second Explorer window by choosing Start | My Computer, and drag files or folders from one Explorer window to the other.

Transferring Files Using Ftp

Another way to transfer files to or from an FTP server is by using a separate FTP client program. Windows XP comes with a basic command-driven FTP client program called Ftp. If you plan to do much file transfer, especially uploading, you'll want to use Web Folders (as described in the section "Working with FTP and Web Servers Using Web Folders" earlier in this chapter) or a better FTP client program, such as WS_FTP (see "Downloading, Installing, and Running Other Internet Programs" later in this chapter).

Basics of FTP

To run the Windows XP FTP program, choose Start | Run. Type **ftp** *serverhost*, where *serverhost* is the host name of the FTP server (for example, **rtfm.mit.edu**), and click OK. If you are not connected to the Internet and you see your dial-up connection window, click Connect. You see the Ftp window, as shown in Figure 26-6.

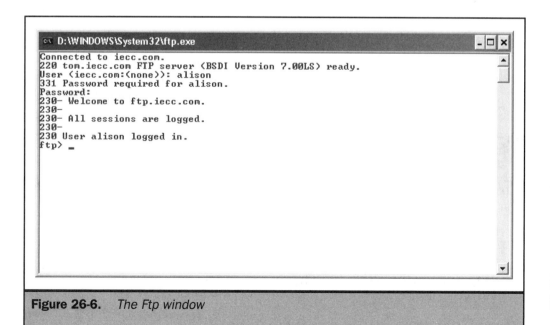

Figure 26-6.   *The Ftp window*

When the FTP server asks for your user name, you have two choices:

■ If you have an account on the FTP server, log in with your user name and password. You can access all the files that your user name gives you permission to use.

■ If you don't have an account on the FTP server, the server may accept connections from guests. Connection without an account on the FTP server is called *anonymous FTP*. To use anonymous FTP, type **anonymous** for the user name and your own e-mail address as the password. Thousands of FTP servers on the Internet allow you to use anonymous FTP to download files, although some are so busy that it may be hard to get connected.

Note *UNIX, the operating system of choice among Internet servers, is sensitive to the case of the names of files, unlike Windows. Be aware of capitalization in filenames.*

Once you are connected to an FTP server, it displays lots of messages to let you know what's going on. These messages start with three-digit numbers, which you can ignore. For example, when you have transferred a file, you see the message "226 Transfer Complete."

When you transfer a file—by either uploading or downloading—you must choose between two modes:

■ **ASCII mode**   When transferring text files, use ASCII mode. Different computer systems use different characters to indicate the ends of lines. In ASCII mode, the Ftp program automatically adjusts line endings for the system to which the file is transferred.

■ **Binary or Image mode**   When transferring files that consist of anything but unformatted text, use Binary mode. In Binary mode, the Ftp program does not make any changes to the contents of the file during transfer. Use Binary mode when transferring graphics files, audio files, video files, programs, or any kind of file other than plain text.

Tip *At the Ftp prompt, type **?** to see a listing of the commands that Ftp can perform.*

Navigating the Folder Trees

The following are the most common FTP tasks:

■ To see a list of files and subdirectories in the current directory on the FTP server, type **dir**. The exact format of the listing depends on the FTP server's operating system. Figure 26-7 shows a typical listing. You can use wildcards (*) to limit the list. If you want to see filenames only, with no other information, you can use the **ls** (list) command.

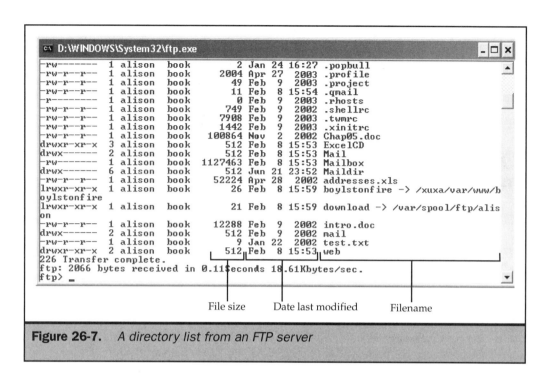

Figure 26-7. *A directory list from an FTP server*

- To change directories, type **cd** (for "change directory"), followed by the name of the directory to which you want to move.

- To find out the name of the current directory, type **pwd** (for "print working directory").

On many publicly accessible FTP servers, all the downloadable files are in a directory called pub. Here are a few tips for moving to the directory you want:

- To move to the parent directory of the current directory, type **cd ..** (that is, the **cd** command followed by a space and two dots).

- To move to the top-level directory on the FTP server, also called the root directory, type **cd /** (that is, the **cd** command followed by a forward slash). Most FTP servers run the UNIX operating system, which uses forward slashes (as opposed to the backslashes used in Windows).

- You can move directly to a directory by typing its full pathname, starting at the root; the full pathname starts with a / to represent the root directory.

- If the FTP server runs the UNIX operating system, capitalization is important. When typing directory or filenames, be sure to use the correct capitalization—most names use lowercase.

■ To change the current local directory (the folder from which Ftp can upload files and to which it can download files), type **lcd** (local directory), followed by the name of the folder on your computer. If the pathname of the folder contains spaces, enclose the pathname in quotes. To move to the parent folder of the current folder, type **lcd ..** (the **lcd** command followed by a space and two dots).

■ When you have finished transferring files, type **quit** or **bye** to disconnect from the FTP server. A message confirms that you have left the FTP server.

*If you want to disconnect from the FTP server and connect to a different server, you don't have to exit the Ftp program. Instead, type **close** or **disconnect** and press ENTER to disconnect from the FTP server. Next, type **open**, followed by a space, and then the host name of another FTP server; press ENTER to connect to the other server.*

Uploading Files

You use the **put** command to upload the files. To upload a group of files, you can use the **mput** command.

You can upload files only if you have write permission in the directory on the FTP server. Most anonymous FTP servers don't accept uploads, or they accept them into only one specific directory. Read the welcome message to find out the rules for the FTP server you are using.

To upload a file, follow these steps:

1. Connect to the FTP server, move to the directory on the FTP server in which you want to store the file, and set the current local directory to the folder on your computer that contains the files you want to upload.

2. If the file or files you want to upload contain anything but unformatted ASCII text, type **binary** to select Binary mode (see "Basics of FTP" earlier in this chapter). To switch back to ASCII mode to transfer text files, type **ascii**.

3. Type **put**, a space, the filename on your computer, a space, and the filename to use on the FTP server. Then press ENTER. For example, to upload a file named draft13.doc and call the uploaded version report.doc, you would type **put draft13.doc report.doc**.

4. You see a series of messages; the message Transfer Complete appears when the file transfer is done.

Caution

*If a file with the name that you specify already exists on the FTP server, the **put** command may overwrite the existing file with the uploaded file. You can use the **dir** or **ls** command to check for the existence of a file with the same name.*

5. If you want to check that the file is really on the FTP server, type **dir** to see a listing of files in the current directory.

You can copy a group of files to the FTP server by typing **mput** (multiple put). Type **mput**, followed by a wildcard pattern that matches the names of the files you want to upload. The pattern * indicates that all files in the current directory on your computer should be copied. For example, to upload all the files with the extension .html, you would type **mput *.html**.

As it copies the files, **mput** asks you about each file. Type **y** to upload the file or **n** to skip it.

*If you don't want **mput** to ask you about each file before uploading it, type the **prompt** command first before giving the **mput** command. The **prompt** command turns off filename prompting.*

Downloading Files

To download files from the FTP server to your computer, follow these steps:

1. Connect to the FTP server, move to the directory on the FTP server that contains the file that you want to download, and set the current local directory to the folder on your computer in which you want to store the files you download.

2. If the file or files you want to download contain anything but unformatted ASCII text, type **binary** to select Binary mode (see "Basics of FTP" earlier in this chapter). To switch back to ASCII mode to transfer text files, type **ascii**.

3. Type **get**, a space, the filename on the FTP server, a space, the filename to use on your computer. Then press ENTER. (You can't use filenames with spaces.) For example, to download a file named bud9812.doc and call the downloaded version budget.dec1998.doc, the command is **get bud0412.doc budget.dec2003.doc**.

4. You see a series of messages; the message Transfer Complete appears when the file transfer is done. To interrupt the file transfer, press CTRL-C. Sometimes that doesn't work, and the only way to interrupt the transfer is to close the FTP window.

5. If you want to check whether the file is really downloaded, use Windows Explorer to see a listing of files on your computer.

You can copy a group of files to the FTP server by typing **mget**, followed by a wildcard pattern that matches the names of the files that you want to download. The pattern * means that all files in the current directory on your computer should be copied. For example, to download all the files whose names start with *d*, you would type **mget d***.

As it copies the files, **mget** asks you about each file. Type **y** to download the files or **n** to skip it.

*If you download a nontext file that is unusable, you probably forgot to issue the **binary** command before downloading the file.*

Downloading, Installing, and Running Other Internet Programs

Once you have established a dial-up connection to the Internet, you can run any Winsock-compatible program (see Chapter 22). Although Windows comes with some good Internet applications, you can supplement (or replace) them with other programs. For example, the Ftp program that comes with Windows is not particularly powerful or easy to use and Web Folders lack a few features; we prefer the excellent shareware WS_FTP program, which shows you the contents of the local and remote directories, and lets you transfer files by clicking buttons rather than typing commands. (Read on to find out how to get it.)

Where to Get Internet Programs

Lots of Winsock-compatible Internet programs are available for downloading from the Internet itself. Some are *freeware* programs that are entirely free to use; some are *shareware* programs that require you to register the program if you decide that you like it; some are demo programs that let you try a partially disabled version of the program before you decide whether to buy the real program; and some are commercial programs that ask you to pay before downloading.

Many web-based libraries offer all types of programs. Here are our favorites:

- **The Ultimate Collection of Windows Software (TUCOWS)** at **www.tucows.com**   Classifies programs by operating system and type. It has lots of mirror sites (identical web sites) all over the globe, so it's rarely a problem to begin downloading even very popular programs. It's particularly easy to browse a long list of programs of a given type (browsers or e-mail programs, for example) and compare reviews.

- **The CWApps List** at **cws.internet.com**   This is the original Winsock library, and it is still excellent. Forrest Stroud set up this site when shareware and freeware Internet software were starting to become available.

- **CNET Shareware.com** at **shareware.cnet.com**   Offers lots of non-Internet-related programs.

- **Download.com** at **download.com.com**   Has thousands of downloadable programs organized by category. (Yes, that URL has *.com* in it twice.)

Installing and Running Internet Programs

Once you've downloaded a program from the Internet, it's a good idea to check it for *viruses*, self-replicating programs that may infect other programs on your computer. Windows doesn't come with a virus checker, but you can download a good one from any of the software libraries in the preceding section (see Chapter 32, section "Preventing Infection by Viruses"). We like McAfee's and Symantec's Norton antivirus programs, too (commercial software downloadable from McAfee's web site at **www.mcafee.com** and Symantec's web site at **www.symantec.com/nav**). To monitor outgoing and incoming transmissions, check out ZoneAlarm at **www.zonealarm.com**.

Most downloaded programs arrive as self-installing files; in Windows Explorer, run the file you downloaded. The program usually installs itself, asking you configuration questions along the way. Most programs either add themselves to the Start | All Programs menu or add an icon to the desktop (or both). Other downloaded programs arrive in ZIP (compressed) files, which the Windows compressed folders feature can uncompress (see Chapter 8, section "Working With Compressed Folders (ZIP Files)").

The first time you run a program, you might need to configure it further; check any documentation files that are installed along with the program. Look for a Tools | Options command or an Edit | Preferences command, as these usually display configuration or preference dialog boxes.

The
Complete
Reference

Part VI

Home and Office Networking with Windows XP Home

Chapter 27

Designing a Windows-Based Local Area Network

If you have more than one computer, consider connecting them with a local area network (LAN) so you can share printers, files, and your Internet connection. Windows XP Home Edition provides all the features needed to connect your computer to a LAN—no other software is required (although you will probably need some hardware). This chapter introduces LANs, including what a network is and why you might want one. Most new networks use Ethernet technology, either with cables or wireless links. This chapter also describes what you need to do to install a LAN, including buying and installing cards and cables.

This chapter provides the background for the specifics covered in the rest of the chapters in Part V, which cover connecting two computers without a LAN (Chapter 28), configuring Windows for a LAN (Chapter 29), sharing disks and printers (Chapter 30), sharing an Internet connection (Chapter 31), and network security (Chapter 32).

This chapter covers setting up your network from scratch. However, if you are adding a Windows XP computer to an existing peer-to-peer network or upgrading a computer on a network from an earlier version of Windows to Windows XP, the steps you need to follow are also found in this chapter (see the sidebar on "Adding to an Existing Network" and "Upgrading a Computer on an Existing Network").

Purposes of Networks

A network provides a connection between computing resources, a way to share hardware and files, and a paperless way to communicate. A *local area network (LAN)* is a network limited to one building or group of buildings. A LAN can be as useful in a home or small office of two or three computers as it is in a large office.

Larger networks also exist. *Wide area networks (WANs)* connect computers that are geographically dispersed, and the Internet—the biggest network of them all— is a worldwide network of interconnected networks, including LANs and WANs.

Sharing Hardware

Without a network, each *resource* (hard disk, CD-ROM drive, printer, or other device) is connected to only one computer. You may have a hard drive on which your small company's main database or your family's collection of digital photos is stored, the color printer everyone wants to use, and the CD-RW drive on which nightly backups are made. Without a network, you can use a resource only from the computer to which the resource is attached. With a network, anyone using a computer attached to the network can print to the color printer or open the database, and the computer with the tape drive can access all the hard disks on various machines that need to be backed up.

The cheapest way to share resources is what some techie types call *sneakernet*— take a removable disk, copy the file you need to print or share, and jog over to the computer with the printer or the person who needs to use the file. But sneakernet isn't very efficient—in the long run you save time and hassle (which of those 12 floppies or Zip disks has the current version of that file?) with a network. At home or in a small office, using a network and only one printer—to which everyone can print—is more cost effective.

Sharing Files

If you want to share files without the danger of creating multiple versions, you need a network, so every person who accesses the file uses the same copy. Some software (notably database software) enables multiple users to use one file at the same time. Other software warns you when a file is being used by someone else on the network and may even notify you when the file is available for your use.

When you work with files that are too large to fit on a floppy disk, moving them to other computers can be cumbersome without a network (unless both computers have a Zip, Jaz, CD-R, or CD-RW drive).

Sharing an Internet Connection

If everyone in your home or office wants to access the Internet—to send and receive e-mail, browse the Web, or other Internet applications—it's silly for each computer to have its own modem, phone line, and Internet account. Instead, one computer on the LAN can have a fast Internet connection (perhaps a DSL or cable Internet) and serve as the gateway to the Internet. Or, you can use a specialized device called a *router*, which connects a LAN to an Internet connection.

Chapter 31 describes how to use Windows XP Internet Connection Sharing to connect a LAN to the Internet.

Peer-to-Peer vs. Domain-Based Networks

Networks are either peer-to-peer or client-server. Windows XP Home Edition can connect only to peer-to-peer networks. However, the next two sections describe both types of networks, so you understand the difference and can determine whether you need to upgrade to Windows XP Professional.

Clients and Servers

A *client* is a computer that uses resources on the network. A printer client, for instance, is a computer that uses a network printer. A *server* is a computer (or a device with a computer hidden inside) that has resources used by other devices on the network. For instance, a file server is a computer that stores files used by other computers; a print server is a computer with a printer attached to it—the print server lets other computers on the network send print jobs to the printer. The server makes a resource available to the network, and a client uses the resource. It's possible and often useful for a computer to act as both a client and a server—for example, sharing files on its large disk but using a printer on another computer.

Peer-to-Peer (Workgroup-Based) Networks

In a *peer-to-peer network*, all computers are equal and can function as both clients and servers. Security and permissions are administered from each computer in the network. Each computer in a peer-to-peer network can both request resources from other computers and share its own resources with other computers in the network. You can also configure the network so that some computers only share their resources and others only use resources. Even in this situation, however, the network is still a peer-to-peer network because each computer on the network is administered individually.

Versions of Windows since Windows 3.11, including Windows XP Home Edition, have included support for peer-to-peer networks. Microsoft calls a group of computers on a peer-to-peer network a *workgroup*, and a the network itself a *workgroup-based* network. When you configure Windows to connect to a workgroup-based LAN, you tell it the name of the workgroup (we like to use the name WORKGROUP).

A peer-to-peer workgroup-based network is relatively easy to set up—any home or small office with more than one computer can create a small peer-to-peer network by using Windows to share printers and files. Only a small amount of hardware is required. The rest of this chapter explains how to choose, install, and configure the hardware to create a peer-to-peer network, and Chapter 29 describes how to configure Windows XP for a LAN.

Note   *Windows XP Home Edition is limited to connecting to up to six computers. So a peer-to-peer LAN with Windows XP Home Edition computers is limited to seven computers, unless not all computers need to communicate with each other. For example, you might need to install Windows XP Professional on the computer with the large hard disk and fast printer so that more than six Windows XP Home Edition computers can share its hard disk and printer.*

Client-Server (Domain-Based) Networks

In a *client-server network*, server computers provide resources for the rest of the network, and client computers (also called *workstations*) use these resources. Client-server networks typically are more difficult and expensive to set up and administer than peer-to-peer networks, but they also have many advantages: they can handle more computers, they provide more-sophisticated administration and security options, and all resources are managed centrally on dedicated servers.

Client-server networks require a *network operating system (NOS)*—Windows .NET Server, Windows 2000 Server, Windows NT, Novell Netware, Linux, and UNIX are common NOSs—as well as a greater initial outlay of time and money for setup and equipment, and a network administrator to create and maintain user IDs and permissions.

Microsoft's client-server network system uses domains to organize the large numbers of computers that can be on corporate networks. A *domain* (when used in reference to

	Peer-to-Peer (Workgroup-Based)	**Client-Server (Domain-Based)**
Size	Good for small networks (under 12 computers, depending on the uses for the network). Keeping track of available resources and passwords for each resource becomes difficult on a large peer-to-peer network.	Good for medium-to-large networks. Because administration of network resources is central, the user can access all available resources with only one password (more passwords may be necessary if the network has more than one server).
Hardware	No dedicated file server is needed.	At least one computer must be a server.
Operating system	Windows XP Home Edition or Professional, Me/9x, NT Workstation, or 2000 Professional on all computers.	Requires a network operating system (NOS) on the server. Workstations can run Windows XP Professional, but not XP Home Edition.
Administrator training	Little training needed for users to administer their own computers' resources for all users on the network.	System administrator must be trained.

Table 27-1.   *Differences Between Peer-to-Peer and Client-Server Networks*

Microsoft LANs) is a group of user accounts administered together. Microsoft calls a client-server network a *domain-based* network.

Table 27-1 lists differences between peer-to-peer and client-server networks. To set up your Windows computer on an already-existing Novell or Windows NT network, contact your LAN administrator. You may need to upgrade your Windows XP Home Edition to Windows XP Professional. For information on creating your own domain-based network with Windows .NET Server, read *Windows .NET Server: The Complete Reference*, by Kathy Ivens (published by Osborne/McGraw-Hill).

Steps for Setting Up a Peer-to-Peer LAN

Setting up a network consists of four major tasks:

- Choosing the network technology (the type of cabling, cable connections, and adapter cards for your computers). These choices are described in the next few sections of this chapter.

- Choosing and buying the hardware (see "Buying Network Hardware" later in this chapter).

- Installing the hardware (see "Installing Your Network Hardware" later in this chapter).

- Configuring Windows to use the network (see Chapter 29).

Adding to an Existing Network

If you're adding a computer to an existing network, you can skip the sections regarding choosing a network technology and a topology—someone has already made those choices for you. If your computer doesn't come with a network adapter, buy one for the computer you want to add to the network. Also, if no leftover cable is on hand, buy the correct kind of cable for your network. Once you've done these things, you can dive into the section "Installing Your Network Hardware" later in this chapter.

Upgrading a Computer on an Existing Network

If you are upgrading the operating system of a computer on an existing network from an earlier version of Windows to Windows XP, you may find your network works right away—open the My Network Places icon on the desktop to see whether other computers on the network appear. If your computer doesn't appear to be communicating on the network, skip ahead to Chapter 29.

While you needn't be a network engineer to set up a small peer-to-peer network, you do need to have some knowledge about your computer. You need to be able to install a *network adapter* or *network interface card* (*NIC*) in each computer that will be on the LAN (unless your computers came with NICs, or they have already been installed), and to use Windows to configure each computer to communicate on the LAN. If you don't feel comfortable installing network cards (or attaching USB NICs to USB ports) and configuring Windows, you can hire someone to install your hardware and configure your network. Make sure you tell the installer that you want a small, peer-to-peer, workgroup-based network. Otherwise—read on.

Choosing Between Cabled and Wireless LANs

Before you buy hardware for your network, you need to decide how to connect the computers on your network. Almost all new cabled networks use *Ethernet* cards and cabling. Although there are topologies other than Ethernet (such as IBM Token Ring), the majority of new LAN installations are some form of Ethernet because the components are widely available and cheap. Because it's so widely used, Ethernet network interface boards are relatively cheap and are also available as PC Cards that fit most laptops.

If you are setting up a new network, you need to choose between regular Ethernet cabling, Ethernet-based wireless equipment, and phone or power line Ethernet.

Ethernet Cable and NICs

There are three speeds of Ethernet. Original Ethernet has a speed of 10 Mbps (megabits/ second). *Fast Ethernet* has a speed of 100 Mbps. An even faster version, *Gigabit Ethernet*, is available and can transmit data at a maximum speed of 1 Gbps (gigabits/second), or ten times the Fast Ethernet standard.

The *topology* of a network determines the pattern of cabling you use to connect the computers. In a *star topology* network, each computer is connected by a cable to a *hub*, the computer in the center of the star. One end of the cable plugs into a computer's network interface card, and the other end plugs into the hub, which provides a central connection point for the network cabling. Hubs vary in size (with different numbers of ports), and more advanced hubs can connect both 10- and 100-Mbps Ethernet. Ethernet *switches* serve the same function as hubs but offer higher network performance by permitting several data transfers to occur simultaneously. Figure 27-1 shows a diagram of a network using star topology.

In the past, you chose from star and bus topology (see the "Bus Topology" sidebar in this chapter). However, most new networks use star topology. This configuration uses more cable and more hardware than a bus topology network, but it's easier to manage and less likely to fail. Star topology is easy to set up, and the network is easier to troubleshoot than a bus network because a damaged cable affects only one computer.

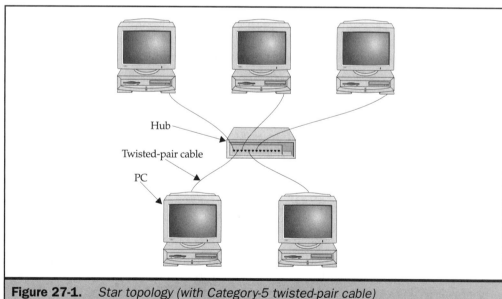

Figure 27-1.   *Star topology (with Category-5 twisted-pair cable)*

The cable used in Ethernet star topology is usually *unshielded twisted-pair* (also called *Category-5* or *Cat-5*). The connectors on the ends of the cables are *RJ-45 connectors*, which look like large phone connectors. You can also use *Cat-5e* (enhanced), which is rated for higher speeds.

Wireless LANs

In a *wireless LAN* there are no network cables. Instead, each computer has a wireless network adapter, allowing the computers to communicate via radio waves. Wireless LANs enable you to put computers as far as 300 feet away from each other, depending on what walls and furniture are between them. The adapters include scrambling or encryption to prevent other computers from listening in on your data transmissions or adding themselves to your LAN.

A wireless LAN can either be arranged as an *infrastructure* or an *ad hoc* LAN. An infrastructure LAN is a star topology LAN, with an *access point* as the hub of the star. The access point is a box that contains a radio transceiver, hardware and software for communications and encryption, and an Ethernet port that lets you connect it to a cabled LAN, if you have one. The rest of the computers on the LAN have wireless LAN adapters that contain a radio transceiver, which communicates with the access point. An ad hoc wireless LAN has no access point, just the adapters in each computer. Ad hoc LANs save the cost of the access point but require that every computer in the LAN be within radio range of every other, usually in a single room, while with an infrastructure LAN the access point is put in a central location and each computer need only be within radio range of the access point, not of the other computers.

Two standards for wireless LANS exist to ensure that wireless adapters from different manufacturers can communicate with each other. The most popular is *IEEE 802.11b*, also known as *Wi-Fi*, which uses the 2.4GHz radio band and can communicate at 11 Mbps, as fast as slower cabled networks. The newer *802.11a* uses the 5GHz band and can communicate at up to 54 Mbps over shorter distances than 801.11b. For more information about these standards, see **www.80211-planet.com**.

For instructions for configuring Windows to work with your wireless LAN, see the section "Adding Your Computer to a Wireless LAN" in Chapter 29.

Phone and Power Line Networking

Two recent additions to the networking world are HomePNA and HomePlug. HomePNA (Home Phoneline Networking Alliance) is a version of Ethernet that uses your existing phone wiring as its network cabling, sharing it with regular phones and DSL. It runs at up to 10 Mbps, depending on distance and the condition of the wire. HomePlug uses your power wiring as its network wiring and runs at up to 14 Mbps, depending on distance and the way your power wiring is arranged.

Both HomePNA and HomePlug connect to computers like an Ethernet, using Category-5 cable and an RJ45 connector. See the section "Connecting to a Phone Line or Power Line LAN " in Chapter 29.

Making the Choice—or Choosing More than One

The cabling technology you choose determines the hardware you buy. Each standard has advantages and disadvantages. However, if you are starting a network from scratch, choose the cheaper and more common Fast Ethernet. If cabling would be a problem (for example, people using laptops will be moving around the building, or the architecture of the building would make cabling expensive), consider a wireless LAN or perhaps HomePNA.

You may decide that you need several types of networks. For example, within your home office, you may need to connect your three computers with cables for reliability and speed. But you may also want to install a wireless access point on one of the office computers to communicate with laptops in the rest of your house, so your kids can get online (see Figure 27-2 for what this might look like). Or, you might have wired network hubs in two parts of the house, and use HomePNA between the two.

If your networks don't already have hubs that you can cable together, you can buy devices called *bridges* that connect two kinds of Ethernet into one network. Or, Windows XP can connect several Ethernet networks together via software *bridging*. Chapter 29 describes how to bridge networks.

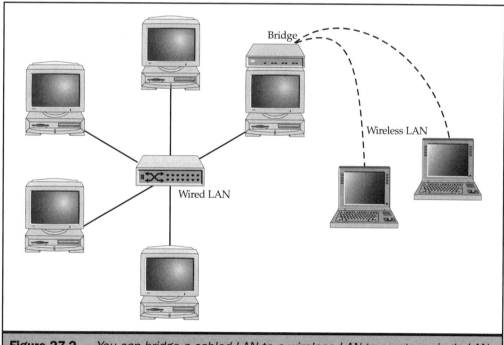

Figure 27-2.   *You can bridge a cabled LAN to a wireless LAN to create a single LAN.*

Bus Topology

Older networks used the *bus topology*, in which the *bus* is the main cable to which all the other computers are attached. (Communication within a computer also happens along a bus.) A *coaxial cable* (or *coax*) cable is connected from one computer to the next, in a long line, until all computers are connected. A network using bus topology looks like this:

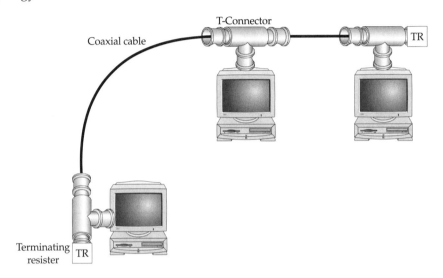

Unless you're adding computers to an existing small bus topology network, we recommend you use a star topology. Network interface cards with coaxial cable connectors are becoming hard to find. To migrate from a bus network, you can buy a network hub that has a coax connection for your old network, in addition to the ports for the twisted-pair cables.

From here on, this chapter discusses setting up an Ethernet network. However, the steps outlined here don't differ much for setting up a wireless or phone-wiring network—instead of buying NICs, cabling, and a hub, you buy wireless LAN adapters and a wireless access point.

Buying Network Hardware

You need the following hardware to set up your network:

Cabled LAN	Wireless LAN
A network interface card for each computer in the network.	A wireless LAN adapter with an antenna for each computer in the network.
A connection among all the computers, most commonly, copper wires, but can also be fiber-optic cable, infrared, radio waves, or a mixture. The amount and type of cable you need depends on the topology you choose for your network.	Nothing.
A hub.	A wireless access point for one computer.

If you are connecting only two computers with no plans to add additional computers, you may not need a hub or access point. You can use a crossover cable to connect the two computers. The crossover cable takes the place of a hub and two network cables.

Take inventory of every computer that will be on the LAN. For cabled LANS, check whether they have a RJ-45 jack or built-in wireless adapter. If not, make a note of the type of slot each has available—you have to buy a network interface card (NIC) or wireless LAN adapter that fits a slot in each computer. The easiest way to determine slot types is to check the documentation for each computer. PCI slots are most common for desktop computers. Laptops usually have PC Card slots (also called PCMCIA) that look like they fit a credit card. Both laptops and desktops may have Universal Serial Bus (USB) ports (a narrow rectangular plug) that may be used for some models of network cards, especially wireless NICs. You may be able to tell what kind of slot your computer has by taking the cover off and looking, and then describing the slot to your local computer store expert. However, it's safer to check your documentation for the type of architecture the motherboard has for each computer that will be on the LAN. You can and probably will mix cards of different slot types so long as the network type is consistent. For example, one of our networks has PCI and PC Card interface cards connected to a 100 Mbps Fast Ethernet.

For a cabled network, the hardware is not expensive to install—often less than $25 per PC on the network. You may be able to buy a network kit with all the hardware you need to set up a small network: network interface cards, cable, and a hub. For a wireless network, look into the wireless kits that are readily available at office supply and computer stores.

Buying Network Interface Cards (NICs)

Many new computers come with network interface cards preinstalled. Check the back of the computer for a RJ-45 connector, which looks like a large phone jack. If you have to buy NICs, choose cards that

- Match the speed you chose for your Ethernet LAN—the two most common speeds are 10 Mbps and 100 Mbps. A good choice is a *10/100Base-T* card, which can handle both speeds and autonegotiates to choose the right one.

- Fit the cable you are using—usually Category-5 wire with a RJ-45 jack on the end that plugs into the computer.

- Fit the computer you buy it for—computers with PCI, ISA, PC Card, or other slots. If a computer doesn't have any available slots, consider a USB or parallel-port based–network adapter, if either of those ports is free. Contact your computer's manufacturer if you're not sure.

All the NICs in each computer in the network must support the same standard—in an Ethernet network, for instance, all network interface cards must be Ethernet cards. Decide whether you want a speed of 10 Mbps or 100 Mbps (or expensive Gigabyte) and buy cards that are all the same speed (most people base their decision on price). You should be able to find 10/100Base-T cards for desktop computers for under $20 and for laptops for under $50 in the United States.

Buying a Hub

If you've chosen a standard Ethernet network—star topology with Category-5 cable—you need a *hub*, a small box with lots of cable connectors. Buy a hub with enough connections for all the computers on your network. You may want a few extra connections, so you can add additional computers to the network later. Hubs are widely available with 4, 8, 16, or 24 ports. Instead of a hub, you can install a *switch*, although the extra performance is usually wasted in a small network. A cheap four-port hub can cost less than $50. If you plan to connect a small LAN to a DSL line, consider a router, which combines a hub with a small computer that provides Internet connection sharing (see Chapter 27, section "Sharing an Internet Connection").

Caution *Although it's tempting, you cannot take a twisted-pair cable and connect two computers directly, unless you get a crossover cable. You need to connect the cable into a hub because the hub manages which pairs of wires inside your cable are used for transmitting and receiving data. If you try to connect two computers directly with a standard cable, the transmit and receive wires will be incorrect on one end, and your connection won't work. Even if you only have two computers, an inexpensive hub may be a good investment to ease network debugging and future upgrades.*

Buying Wireless LAN Adapters and Access Points

If you are planning a wireless LAN, decide whether you need the cheaper and more popular 802.11b WiFi or faster but more expensive 802.11a network. WiFi adapters are available as PCI cards (for desktop computers), PC Cards (for laptops), or USB. We've had good luck with all three, but as a general rule, the larger the antenna on the adapter, the greater its range. An infrastructure wireless LAN needs one access point (base station) as its hub. An access point costs about $100, and each computer's wireless LAN adapter costs from $50 to $80.

Buying Ethernet Cable

For a standard cabled Ethernet network, you need twisted-pair or Category-5 cable (as shown in Figure 27-1). The ends of these cables have RJ-45 connectors, which look like telephone cord connectors (the ones that plug into a telephone wall jack), but are about twice as big. When using twisted-pair cable, plug one end of each cable into a network interface card installed in a PC and plug the other end into the hub that's at the center of the star topology.

A general rule is not to run a cable more than 150 meters between computers (although the actual specifications for different types of cable in different types of networks may be greater). If you are connecting computers that are not close to each other, you need to do some research on how to create a network over medium distances.

To determine how much cable you need, decide where you are going to place the hub, and then measure from each computer to the hub's location. Remember to allocate extra cable to go around furniture and out of the way of office traffic, and add some slack to allow you to move the computer around—like pulling it away from the wall for repairs.

 When you buy your cable, remember string it so people don't trip over the cable. Measure carefully and allow extra—you can always hide cable that's too long. If your cable is too short, you'll have to go shopping again.

Buying Phone Line or Power Line Adapters

Be sure that any phone line network hardware you buy has the HomePNA logo and any power line network hardware has the HomePlug logo so you can be sure they interoperate. Given a choice, HomePNA will probably be more reliable because there's far less electrical noise on phone lines than on power lines.

Installing Your Network Hardware

Now that you have all your parts—an NIC (or wireless LAN adapter) for each computer, enough cabling (or none, for a wireless LAN), and a hub (or wireless access point), you're ready to put it all together to create the physical network. This procedure is best done when the computers aren't in use and when you have a good chunk of time to devote to it—on a weekend.

Installing Network Interface Cards or Wireless LAN Adapters

The first step to installing your network hardware is to install a network interface card (or wireless LAN adapter) in each computer that will be on the network. Turn off each computer, take the cover off, install the NIC, and put the cover on again. For a laptop, this is usually as easy as sliding the card into the PC slot. For a desktop computer, this requires installing the card in a slot on the motherboard according to the manufacturer's installation instructions.

Once the NIC or wireless LAN adapter is installed, start the computer. Windows should detect the new hardware and ask you to install the adapter drivers for it (see Chapter 13).

Installing the Hub, Switch, or Wireless Access Point

Put the hub, switch, or wireless access point in a location where it won't be disturbed. It doesn't have to be near any computers—in a house, you might want to put a hub in the basement or attic, because it's easy to run all your cables there. You can have more than one hub, too; you might want one in the basement, with a cable from each room to the basement, and another hub in the office, to connect all the computers in the office. (This is more efficient than running a separate cable from each computer in the office to the basement.) You can *cascade* hubs by connecting one of the jacks on one hub to the uplink port of the other hub.

A wireless access point should be in a central location to minimize the distance and the number of walls between it and each of the computers with which it has to communicate. If you have a large house or office, you can have multiple access points and cable them all to a hub.

 Be sure to label each cable, so that when you are troubleshooting later, you can tell which cable goes to which computer. We use indelible laundry marker: paper labels may rip, mold, or fall off. When you buy your Ethernet cable, you can choose different-colored cables.

Stringing Cable

For a cabled network, once the NIC and its driver are installed, you can connect the cabling. The computers can be turned on when you connect the cables.

Cabling can be a simple job or an extravagant one, depending on your needs and how much time, effort, and money you're willing to invest. A home office network that consists of two computers close together probably means cables running on the floor around the edge of the room and behind furniture. Cabling for an office probably means cables hidden by conduit, running inside walls, and running above dropped ceilings. You may want to hire someone if you have many computers to connect and want it done neatly. If you put cable inside ceilings or walls, be sure the installation conforms to fire and electrical codes.

When planning your wiring job, plan for the future. If you're wiring your office, add extra cables while the walls and ceiling are open. (We ran two Category-5 cables to each room in the house while we were doing some construction.) Put network jacks in the walls of any room that you think might have a computer in it some day. Plan your network cabling in the same manner you would plan phone extensions. Doing all the wiring now can make adding a computer to your network much easier in the future.

Connecting the cables to the hub and to the computers is easy—just plug the cable into the RJ-45 jacks on the NIC and the hub as you would plug a phone wire into a phone jack.

 Don't run twisted-pair cable in a bundle with electrical power cable because the electromagnetic interference can adversely affect the network—a short-circuit between power and network cables could cause injury or fire.

Once you complete the construction phase, you need to sit at each computer and configure Windows so it knows about the network, as described in the next chapter.

The Complete Reference

Chapter 28

Networking without LANs

Nearly all computers these days come with a network card, so if you frequently need to use resources on other computers, you can carry a crossover cable and create a quick peer-to-peer LAN. A LAN is the best way to use resources on another computer; however, you may find yourself in a situation where you want to share resources but you don't have a LAN, a network card, or the cable needed to connect to one. Or, you may be physically distant from the computer you want to connect to. This chapter presents some alternatives for those times when you don't have a LAN but need to connect two computers.

All the connection options in this chapter are accessed though the New Connection Wizard, which you run by clicking Create A New Connection in the Task pane of the Network Connections window (see Chapter 29). One way to display the Network Connections window is to choose Start | My Network Places, then click the View Network Connections link.

When you connect computers without a LAN, you need to set up one computer to accept a connection from the other computer by creating an *incoming connection* in the Network Connections window. An incoming connection tells Windows how the other computer can connect (by phone, by cable, or over the Internet) and who is authorized to connect (which user accounts can log in using the connection).

Connecting Two Computers with Direct Network Connection

When you don't have a network card, you can create a one-way network with a serial, parallel, or FireWire cable and a *direct network connection* (called a *direct cable connection* in previous versions of Windows). If both computers have infrared ports, you don't even need a cable. FireWire is supported by Windows XP and Me, but not in earlier versions of Windows.

A direct network connection has a *host computer* with resources you want to use, and a *guest computer* that you give access to those resources. A direct network connection is one-way: The guest computer can see and use any shared resources on the host computer, and it can access any shared network resources the host can access. However, the host computer cannot see the guest computer.

To create the direct connection, you need a cable with connectors that fit the computers you want to connect. If you're using serial ports, get a *null-modem cable*, LapLink cable, Serial PC-to-PC File Transfer cable, or InterLink cable. If you're using parallel ports, look for a DirectParallel cable. If both computers have FireWire ports (which are faster than serial or parallel ports), get a regular FireWire cable.

Connect the cable, and power up the two computers. Open the Network Connections window and click Create A New Connection from the Task pane to start the New Connection Wizard (see Chapter 29). Choose Set Up An Advanced Connection, choose Connect Directly To Another Computer, and then configure the computer according to whether it is the host or the guest, and the ports you've used for the cable.

Once you have created connections on both the guest and the host computers, open the new connection in the Network Connections window on the guest computer.

To access the shared resources on the host computer from the guest computer, open the My Network Places folder on the guest computer. To close the connection, right-click the connection icon in the Network Connections window or in the notification area of the taskbar and choose Disconnect.

 If you're having trouble, check that both computers are members of the same workgroup.

Connecting Two Computers by Using a Dial-Up Connection

Dial-up connections are most frequently used to connect computers to the Internet (see Chapter 22). However, you can also create one to connect your computer to another Windows computer through a modem.

The computer that dials in is called the *remote client*. The computer you call using a dial-up connection is called the *remote access server*. When the remote access server computer is also attached to a LAN, the remote client becomes a *remote node* on the network, meaning the client computer's connection to the LAN works exactly as it would if you were in the building and attached to the LAN (see Figure 28-1). From the remote client computer, you can use resources on the network, and other computers on the network can see the shared resources on your computer. For example, you might set up your desktop computer on your home office LAN as a remote node and set up your laptop as a remote client, so you can call into your LAN when you are away from home and get access to the files and printers on the LAN.

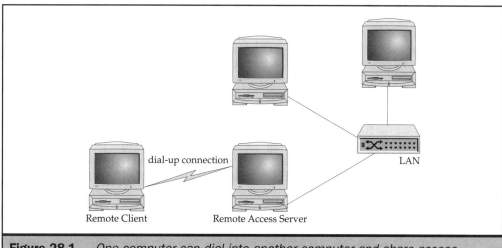

Figure 28-1. *One computer can dial into another computer and share access to a LAN.*

You create connections on both the remote access server and the remote client, as follows:

- **Create a dial-up incoming connection on the remote access server** Open the Network Connections window, click Create a New Connection, select Set Up An Advanced Connection, select Accept Incoming Connections, and choose the modem as the device for incoming calls (see Chapter 29). You can select more than one device if you have more than one modem. For accepting dial-up connections, it doesn't matter whether you choose to allow virtual private connections (described in the next section). Select the users you want to allow to connect. Deselect any components that you don't want used. (Generally, no changes are necessary.) Click Finish. Windows creates an icon called Incoming Connections in the Incoming section of your Network Connections window. If you already have an Incoming Connections icon, its properties are edited to allow dial-in access.

- **Create a dial-up outgoing connection on the client computer** In the Network Connections window, select Connect To The Network At My Workplace, select Dial-up Connection, and complete the information required to create the connection. You can create additional dial-up connections by repeating these steps. When you double-click the connection, Windows dials the phone, and if the host computer answers, you are asked to log in.

Once you establish the connection, you can use My Network Places on the remote client computer to use resources on the remote access server. When you want to close the connection, click the Disconnect button on the dialog box.

Connecting Computers with Virtual Private Networking

Virtual Private Networking (*VPN*) provides a way for an authorized computer on the Internet to *tunnel* through the firewall and connect to a LAN. VPN allows you to connect over the Internet rather than needing to dial in directly, as described in the previous section. A VPN can allow you to connect to a single computer or to a LAN connected to the Internet, as shown in Figure 28-2.

Home users may find VPN useful when they need the resources available on another computer, or even on a remote network. You may use VPN to tunnel into a LAN at work, or you may use it to access your home computer when you are away from home. In either case, be sure that you have configured the server and tried it out before you are in a situation where accessing it is crucial! Once you have tunneled in with VPN you can use disks, printers, and other resources as if you were there using the host computer. If you're accessing a LAN, the LAN doesn't have to use TCP/IP as its protocol: an IPX/SPX network is also accessible through VPN once you're tunneled in.

A VPN network using Windows XP uses one of two protocols to connect through a firewall: PPTP (Point-to-Point Tunneling Protocol) or L2TP (Layer Two Tunneling Protocol).

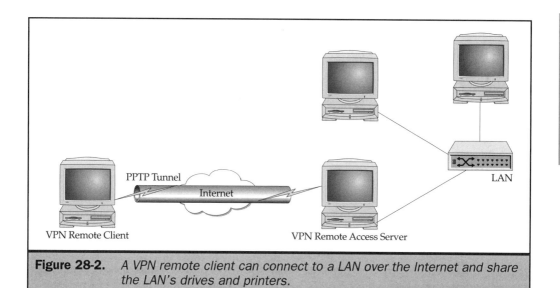

Figure 28-2.   *A VPN remote client can connect to a LAN over the Internet and share the LAN's drives and printers.*

When you are connecting to a LAN with a firewall, the firewall must support one of these protocols. The LAN administrator must have set up the firewall and a *VPN server*, the program that provides PPTP or L2TP. Both the *VPN client* (the computer making the connection) and the VPN server must have Internet connections.

To connect to an existing VPN server (for example, you are tunneling into your company's computer from home), you don't have to worry about configuring the server: you just have to configure your computer as a VPN client. Contact your organization's system administrator to find out the host name or numeric IP address of the VPN server. However, if you are creating both the VPN client and the server (for example, you want to be able to tunnel into your home LAN over the Internet when you are traveling), then you need to complete the steps in both of the following sections to configure both the VPN client and the VPN server.

The following sections describe using Windows XP's built-in VPN feature. You can also buy and install third-party VPN software, like Cisco's VPN Client.

    Windows XP Home Edition includes VPN server software that can accept only one incoming connection at a time. If you need more than one simultaneous VPN connection to your server, upgrade to Windows .NET Server. (Windows XP Professional is also limited to one incoming connection.)

Configuring the VPN Client

If you want to be able to connect to your company's (or other) LAN over the Internet using VPN, you need to configure your computer as a VPN client.

Creating the VPN Connection on the Client Computer

Follow these steps for creating a VPN connection on the client computer:

1. Connect to the Internet.

2. Open the Network Connections window (see Chapter 29).

3. Click Create A New Connection in the Network Tasks part of the Task pane to run the New Connection Wizard. Click Next to move from window to window.

4. For the Network Connection Type, select Connect To The Network At My Workplace.

5. For the Network Connection, select Virtual Private Network Connection.

6. For the Connection Name, type a name for the connection in the Company Name box (like "VPN" or the name of your organization or the location of the VPN server). Click Next.

7. For the Public Network, specify which Internet connection to use to connect to the Internet. (If you have a broadband connection you may not see this window.) If you'd prefer to make the Internet connection yourself, rather than allowing the VPN connection to initiate a connection, or if you don't have a dial-in connection, choose Do Not Dial The Initial Connection.

8. For the VPN Server Selection, shown in Figure 28-3, type the host name or numeric IP address of the VPN server (for example, **pptp.microsoft.com** or **123.45.67.89**). If you are connecting to an organization, get this information from your organization's system administrator.

9. If the wizard asks who can use this VPN connection, choose Anyone's Use (for all users on this computer) or My Use Only (for only the current user).

10. You see a window confirming that you have created a VPN connection. Choose whether you want to add a shortcut for the connection to the desktop. Click Finish.

The VPN connection appears in a new Virtual Private Network section of the Network Connections window.

Configuring the VPN Client Connection

You can see and configure the properties of the VPN connection. In the Network Connections window, right-click the VPN connection and choose Properties from the menu that appears. The Properties dialog box for a VPN client connection is shown in Figure 28-4.

The administrator of the remote access server to which you are connecting should provide you with the configuration settings required to connect. If you are connecting to a domain-based (corporate) LAN, click the Options tab and select the Include Windows Logon Domain check box. If the remote access server to which you are connecting requires encryption, click the Security tab and make sure that the Require Data Encryption check box is selected (it's selected by default).

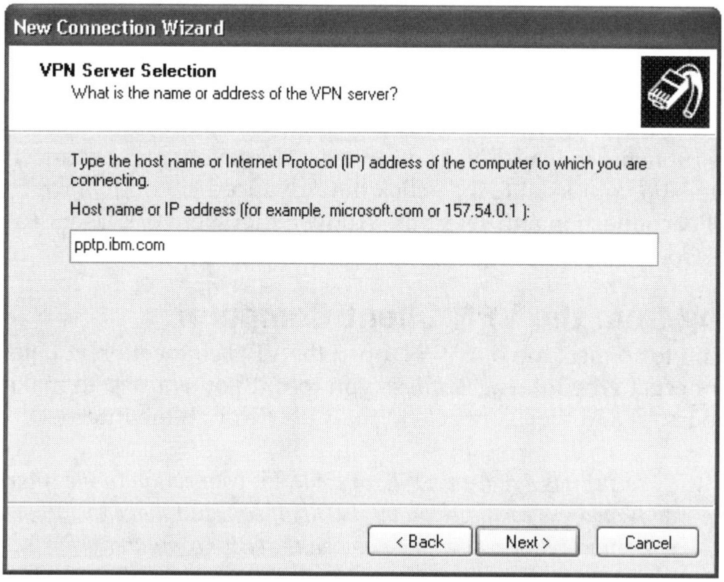

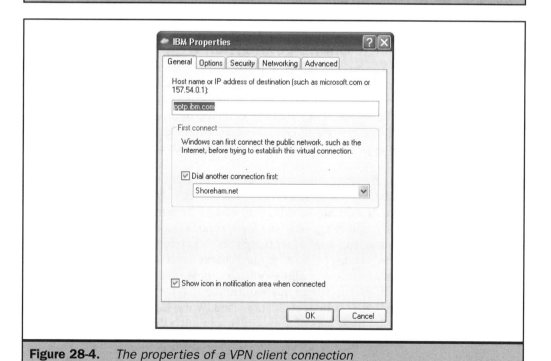

Figure 28-3.   *Specifying the name of your VPN server*

Figure 28-4.   *The properties of a VPN client connection*

On the General tab, you can change the host name or IP address of your company's VPN server or the Internet connection to use. The Advanced tab allows you to enable the Internet Connection Firewall, and to share the VPN connection.

You can also configure whether Windows redials your Internet connection if the connection is lost and whether to display an icon in the notification area of the taskbar when you are tunneled in via VPN. You can even share your VPN connection with other computers on your local LAN—click the Advanced tab of the Properties dialog box for the VPN connection and select the Allow Other Network Users To Connect Through This Computer's Internet Connection check box.

Connecting from the VPN Client Computer

When you want to connect to your VPN, open the VPN connection you just created. Windows connects to the Internet (unless you told it you wanted to make the connection yourself) and then connects to the VPN through the Internet.

If your VPN server has a dial-in, DSL, or cable TV connection to the Internet, it may be issued a new IP address each session by its ISP. If so, you'll have to adjust the address on the VPN connection's Properties dialog box on the client computer before each connection.

Once you have tunneled in to the remote access server, you can share disks and printers just as if you were on the LAN. For example, if you connect from home to your office LAN, you can edit files on your office computer's disk drives, and print documents on your office printers. (With luck, they won't be out of paper.)

Troubleshooting VPN Client Connections

When connected via VPN, you may not be able to browse the Internet. To fix this problem, display the Properties dialog box for the Internet connection (not the VPN connection), click the Networking tab, choose Internet Protocol (TCP/IP) from the list of installed items, click Properties, click Advanced on the Internet Protocol (TCP/IP) Properties dialog box that appears, and clear the Use Default Gateway On Remote Network check box that appears on the General tab of the Advanced TCP/IP Settings dialog box that appears.

If you can connect to the remote access server but you can't browse the LAN (that is, view the drives on other computers), you may need to change the way your VPN connection is assigned an IP address when it connects to the remote access server. Right-click the VPN connection in the Network Connections window, choose Properties from the menu that appears, click the Networking tab, choose Internet Protocol (TCP/IP) from the list, and click Properties. Make sure that Obtain An IP Address Automatically is selected. If the remote access server allows you to choose your own address, select Use The Following IP Address and type in an address in the format *xx.xx.xx.xx*. The IP address must be in the same subnet as the one used by the LAN to which you are connecting (that is, the first three sets of numbers must match the addresses used on the LAN).

Some ISPs block VPN communication—check with your ISP if you suspect that this is so. For more information about configuring VPN client connections, go to the Microsoft support web site at **support.microsoft.com** and search for article Q314076.

Configuring the VPN Server

When you configure your Windows XP computer as a remote access server, you configure it to accept incoming VPN connections. These connections can come from other computers running Windows XP or any computer that can connect to the Internet and is running a VPN client program.

The VPN server needs a fixed IP address, or at least you need to be able to find out the VPN server's address at the moment that you want to connect from the VPN client. If you want to set up a VPN server on a computer that connects via dial-up, DSL, or a cable Internet connection, the IP address may change each time you connect.

To find out a computer's IP address, right-click the Internet connection in the Network Connections window, choose Status from the shortcut menu, and click the Details tab. The following blocks of IP addresses are reserved and not used on the Internet, so a computer with one of these numbers cannot be used in VPN: 10.0.0.0 through 10.255.255.255, 172.16.0.0 through 172.31.255.255, and 192.168.0.0 through 192.168.255.255.

Finding out the current IP address of the VPN server requires that someone be at the VPN server each time the client connects, to communicate the IP address to the user at the client computer. Another solution is to use a service like DNS2Go (**dns2go.deerfield.com**) or TZO (**www.tzo.com**) that can issue you a static IP address by installing a small utility on your remote access server.

| Note | *The VPN server must have a routable IP address—that is, it must be directly on the Internet. If the computer you want to connect to shares an Internet connection, it is not accessible using VPN. Computers inside a firewall on a company LAN and those otherwise sharing an Internet connection (using ICS, for instance) do not have routable IP addresses.* |

Creating the Incoming Connections Icon on the VPN Server

To configure a computer as a remote access server—that is, to accept VPN connections—you need an Incoming Connections icon in the Network Connections folder. If you already have this icon, double-click it to display the Incoming Connections Properties dialog box. Check that the Virtual Private Network option is selected (Allow Others To Make Private Connections To My Computer By Tunneling Through The Internet Or Other Network).

| Note | *To create or modify an Incoming Connections icon, you must be logged in as an administrative user (see Chapter 6).* |

If you do not have the Incoming Connections icon, follow these steps to create it and configure your computer to accept incoming VPN connections. (Make sure that you've already configured the computer to connect to the Internet.)

1. Open the Network Connections window (see Chapter 29).

2. Click Create A New Connection to start the New Connection Wizard. Click Next to move from window to window.

3. For the Network Connection Type, select Set Up An Advanced Connection.

4. For the Advanced Connection Options, select Accept Incoming Connections.

5. If the Devices For Incoming Connections screen appears, it doesn't include an option for the Internet, which is the actual device you'll be using. Deselect all modems and ports.

6. For the Incoming Virtual Private Connection (VPN) Connection, select Allow Virtual Private Connections.

7. The User Permissions screen shows a list of the users on the system, including some hidden users you might not have known about (like HelpAssistant and Support), Select the users you want to allow to connect.

8. For Networking Software, deselect any protocols that you don't want used. Generally, no change to this page is necessary as long as TCP/IP is one of the selected protocols.

9. Click Finish. The wizard creates an icon called Incoming Connections in the Incoming section of your Network Connections window. If you already have an Incoming Connections icon, its properties are changed to support VPN.

If your VPN server uses the Internet Connection Firewall, the New Connection Wizard configures the firewall to allow VPN connections (see Chapter 22). However, if you use another firewall, you may need to reconfigure your firewall to allow PPTP (on port 1723) or L2TP connections (on port 1701).

Once you configure a computer as a VPN server, be sure to read the section "Networking Security Issues" later in this chapter.

Configuring the VPN Incoming Connection

In the Network Connections window, right-click the VPN incoming connection and choose Properties from the menu that appears. The properties for clients and servers are different—the Properties dialog box for a VPN incoming (server) connection is shown in Figure 28-5.

You can make changes to the options you selected with the New Connection Wizard. You can turn VPN on or off, display an icon in the notification area of the taskbar, and add and remove allowed users. To require that VPN clients use encryption, click the Users tab and select the Require All Users To Secure Their Passwords And Data check box.

Figure 28-5. *The properties of a VPN server connection*

Troubleshooting VPN Incoming (Server) Connections

If you can connect to the remote access server but you can't browse the LAN (that is, view
the drives on other computers), you may need to change the IP address of your VPN
connection. Double-click the Incoming Connections icon in your Network Connections
window to display the Incoming Connections Properties dialog box. Click the
Networking tab, select Internet Protocol (TCP/IP) from the network components list,
and click Properties. You see the Incoming TCP/IP Properties dialog box:

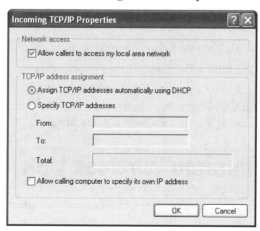

Make sure that the Allow Callers To Access My Local Area network check box is selected. Choose Assign TCP/IP Addresses Automatically Using DHCP, unless you have a reason to specify an address for incoming VPN connections.

Networking Security Issues

When a computer is configured as a server that accepts dial-in or VPN connections, it is open to abuse by unauthorized users. Damage can include reading and destroying files on shared drives, as well as introducing viruses.

Be sure to disable Incoming Connections when you don't expect any. Here's how:

1. Open the Network Connections window (see Chapter 29).

2. Double-click the Incoming Connections icon to display the Incoming Connections Properties dialog box.

3. On the General tab, deselect the modem and port check boxes in the Devices box to disable dial-up connections. Deselect the Virtual Private Network check box to disable VPN.

4. Click OK.

Because networking does you no good when it's turned off, take some additional prudent security measures for the times you need it enabled:

■ For dial-up connections, keep your modem's phone number a closely guarded secret.

■ Use strong passwords that can't be easily guessed and change them regularly.

■ If your computer is a remote access server, you have the option of enabling *callback*. When callback is enabled, the caller logs in. Then, if login is accepted, the server disconnects and calls the client back at a specified phone number.

Enable callback by following these steps:

1. In the Network Connections window, double-click the Incoming Connections icon to display the Incoming Connections Properties dialog box.

2. Click the Users tab.

3. Select the user for whom you want to enable callback. Click Properties.

4. Click the Callback tab on the user's Properties dialog box.

5. Choose either to Allow The Caller To Set The Callback Number or to Always Use The Following Callback Number (and enter the user's phone number with any additional digits, such as 9, to get an outside line).

Creating an Infrared Wireless Link

If you have an infrared device installed on your computer, you can create an infrared link for file transfer. Infrared links are often used to transfer photos from a digital camera to a computer.

To configure your infrared link, choose Start | Control Panel and choose Wireless Link (an icon that appears if your computer has an infrared port). On the File Transfer tab of the Wireless Link dialog box, select Allow Others To Send Files To Your Computer Using Infrared. If you do not want to allow file transfer using infrared, be sure that this option is not selected. On this tab you can also set the default location for transferred files. The Infrared tab allows you to choose whether or not to display a Wireless Link icon on the taskbar and the default location for storing files you receive over the link (the default is your desktop). The Image Transfer tab gives you options for transferring photos.

To make a connection with infrared, just point the infrared transceivers of the two computers (or other devices) point at each other. The Wireless Link icon appears in the notification area of the taskbar and on your desktop:

The icon turns into an hourglass when data is flowing. To find out the status of the infrared link, move your mouse pointer to the icon without clicking.

To send files to another computer or device over the infrared link, select the file(s) in an Explorer window and drag them to the Wireless Link icon on the desktop. Or, click the Wireless Link icon on the taskbar to display the Wireless Link dialog box and specify the file(s) you want to send.

For more information go to Microsoft's support web site at **support.microsoft.com** and search for article Q305551.

The Complete Reference

Chapter 29

Adding Your Computer to a LAN

If your home or office has up to six computers and they all run some version of Windows (any version since 3.11), you can set up a peer-to-peer local area network (LAN) using Windows as your network operating system. You don't need a separate server: Windows XP Home Edition and all previous versions of Windows back to 3.11 contain all the networking software you need. Read the previous chapter for how to choose a cabling technology, a cabling topology, and network interface cards, as well as how to install the necessary hardware.

Once the network interface cards are installed and the cable is strung, you still need to configure the networking software. You need to make sure that Windows' networking components are installed and then configure the components. The easiest way to configure your computer to communicate over a LAN is usually to run the Network Setup Wizard and then to test your network connection using the Ping program and the My Network Places window. Windows comes with some network troubleshooting tools, described at the end of this chapter. Once your computer can communicate over the LAN, read the next chapter to learn how to share folders and printers with other computers.

> **Note**   *This chapter describes how to connect your computer to a new or existing peer-to-peer (workgroup-based) LAN. Windows XP Home Edition can't connect to a domain-based corporate LAN: you need Windows XP Professional for that. (In fact, the ability of Windows XP Professional to connect to corporate LANs is the key feature that forces corporations to buy Professional instead of Home Edition.) Also, Windows XP Home Edition can connect to up to six other computers, limiting your network to seven computers.*

If you are looking for additional information about Windows networking, check out PracticallyNetworked.com (**www.practicallynetworked.com**) and Small Net Builder (**www.smallnetbuilder.com**).

Windows Networking Components

To configure Windows for a peer-to-peer LAN, you use these network components:

- **Client**   Specifies the type of network to which you are attaching—a Windows-compatible peer-to-peer network.

- **Protocol**   Identifies the way information is passed between computers on the network. TCP/IP is the protocol used by the Internet, for example. The most commonly used protocols are described in the next section.

- **Service**   Enables you to share resources on the computer (for example, file or printer sharing).

Network Protocols

The *protocol* is the language your computer uses on the network. More than one protocol may be installed on a single computer because computers can speak more than one language. Windows networks usually use one of these three protocols:

- **TCP/IP (Transmission Control Protocol/Internet Protocol)**   The language spoken by computers on the Internet. Any computer using the Internet through a direct connection needs to have TCP/IP installed. Microsoft is standardizing on this protocol for all networking. See the next section for more details.

- **IPX/SPX (Internetwork Packet eXchange/Sequenced Packet eXchange)**   Used primarily by Novell in its NetWare operating system. IPX/SPX also works well for peer-to-peer networks. Using IPX/SPX, rather than TCP/IP, for sharing files on networks that connect to the Internet provides more security.

- **NetBEUI (NetBIOS Extended User Interface)**   Microsoft's older peer-to-peer networking product. NetBEUI is fast and requires almost no configuration—it's by far the simplest protocol to use and configure. That simplicity has a drawback, however. NetBEUI is *nonroutable*, which means it works only on simple networks where routing devices aren't used to connect multiple segments of networks. On previous versions of Windows, NetBEUI was the default protocol.

Generally, you can use TCP/IP for everything, eliminating all other protocols from your network. However, if you are adding a new computer to an existing NetBEUI- or IPX/SPX-based network, you may not want to reconfigure all the other computers: instead, you can install these additional protocols on your Windows XP computer.

IP Addressing

When you use TCP/IP on a LAN, the network interface card in each computer on the LAN has an IP address on the LAN. IP addresses are in the format *xxx.xxx.xxx.xxx*, where each *xxx* is a number from 0 to 254. IP addresses are used on the Internet to identify Internet host computers and on LANs to identify the computers on the LAN. When you connect directly to the Internet, you also use TCP/IP, and your computer has an IP address to identify it to other computers on the Internet.

On a LAN that uses TCP/IP, computers usually use "private" IP addresses that are not used on the Internet. Several ranges of IP addresses have been set aside for private use. The most commonly used private IP addresses are in the format 192.168.0.*xxx*, where *xxx* is a number from 1 to 253. If one computer on the LAN provides a gateway to the Internet, that computer has the address 192.168.0.1, and the rest of the computers have addresses from 192.168.0.2 up to 192.168.0.253. Figure 29-1 shows a LAN with an IP address assigned to each computer.

Displaying the Network Connections Window

Because you'll be using the Network Connections window frequently if you use any of the connection options in this chapter, we recommend that you add the Connect To command to the Start menu, if it isn't there already. Follow these steps:

1. Right-click the Start menu and choose Properties to display the Start Menu tab of the Taskbar And Start Menu Properties dialog box.

2. Click the Customize button to display the Customize Start Menu dialog box.

3. Click the Advanced tab.

4. Scroll down in the Start Menu Items box until you see Network Connections. Choose either Display As Connect To Menu or Link To Network Connections Folder. Either of these options will make it easy to open the Network Connections window from the Start menu.

5. Click OK to close the two dialog boxes.

Now you can choose Start | Network Connections or Start | Connect To | Show All Connections to display the Network Connections window, depending on which option you chose in step 4.

If you choose not to add the Connect To command to the Start menu, you can open the Network Connections folder in one of the following ways:

■ Choose Start, right-click My Network Places, and choose Properties from the shortcut menu.

■ Open the Control Panel, click Network And Internet Connections, then click Network Connection.

■ Open My Network Places and click View Network Connections. (My Network Places is one of the options in the Task pane on most Explorer windows.)

How are IP addresses assigned? You can use one of three methods:

■ **Static IP addressing** You can assign the IP addresses yourself, using addresses in the format 192.168.0.*xxx*. You need to keep track of which addresses you've assigned, so that you don't give two computers the same address. Another problem is that ICS (Windows' Internet Connection Sharing program, described in Chapter 31) doesn't always work with static IP addressing.

■ **Automatic private IP addressing (APIPA)** This Windows system assigns IP addresses to the computers on a LAN automatically (called *dynamic addressing*). The addresses are in the format 169.254.*xxx.xxx*, where each *xxx* can be a number from 1 to 253. You can't use APIPA addresses with ICS or on LANs that use DHCP addressing.

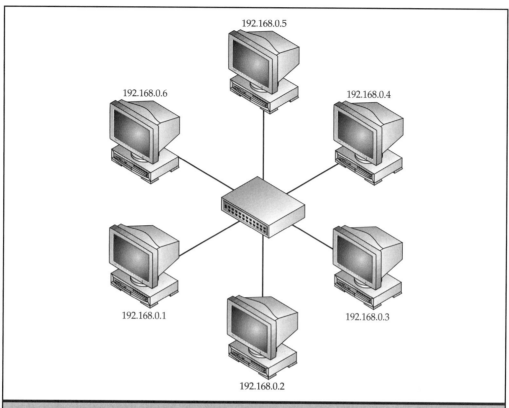

192.168.0.5

192.168.0.6

192.168.0.4

192.168.0.1

192.168.0.3

192.168.0.2

Figure 29-1.   *Assigning IP addresses to computers on a LAN*

- **DHCP (Dynamic Host Configuration Protocol) addressing**   A *DHCP server* is software that assigns IP addresses for the LAN. Like APIPA, DHCP assigns an IP address to your computer automatically, but it is designed to work with much larger LANs. ICS, which is part of Windows XP, includes a DHCP server. Most Internet routers include a DHCP server, too. Microsoft's TCP/IP networking systems generally use DHCP addressing.

When you connect directly to the Internet, you don't have a choice about your address; your ISP assigns it for you. In the early days of dial-up connections, ISPs issued a static IP address with each Internet account. Now, most ISPs run DHCP-like servers that issue your computer an IP address each time you connect.

When setting up a LAN that uses TCP/IP, you must choose among these IP addressing methods. Use static addressing only for very small LANs (with fewer than 10 computers) that don't use ICS. If you plan to share an Internet connection using ICS or a router, it includes a DHCP server (see Chapter 31).

If your computer has more than one TCP/IP connection, it needs more than one IP address. For example, your computer might have a network interface card that connects it to the LAN and another card that connects to a DSL modem that connects to the Internet. Each network interface has one TCP/IP address.

The section "Configuring the TCP/IP Protocol" later in this chapter describes how to configure Windows to communicate using TCP/IP.

Identifying the Computer

For your computer to communicate with the other computers in your workgroup, you need to give the computer a unique name, identify the workgroup, and, optionally, provide a description:

- **Computer name** Naming your computer lets the users of other computers to refer to your computer by name. Each computer on the LAN needs a unique name. If you are adding your computer to an existing LAN, check the names of the other computers and choose one that's not already in use.

- **Workgroup** The *workgroup* is a group of computers on your network. Large LANs may have a different workgroup for each department, but on a small LAN (fewer than 20 computers), all the computers on the LAN need to have the same workgroup name. For a new LAN, the default name is MSHOME (although we prefer to use WORKGROUP as the name).

- **Computer description** Optionally, you can enter a description of the computer. Windows doesn't use this description during logon, but it does display it in the My Network Places window.

For example, a small network of five computers may all belong to the same workgroup called WORKGROUP. Within the workgroup, the computers might be named Office, Playroom, JohnsRoom, SarahsRoom, and Kitchen or Accounting, Sales, Marketing, Administration, and Shipping. We recommend not using people's names as computer names, because people tend to switch computers, or move desks, or go off to college and get new computers. It's confusing when Ted regularly uses a computer named Mary.

Larger networks use domains to centralize network administration and require a computer running Windows .NET Server, Windows 2000 Server, or Windows NT Server. Windows XP Home Edition can't connect to server-based (domain-based) networks.

When you configure your LAN using the Network Setup Wizard (described in the next section), the wizard asks you for the computer name, workgroup, and computer description. You can also change them later (see "Changing the Computer Name, Workgroup, or Domain" later in this chapter).

Windows XP Home Edition and Domain-Based LANs

Windows XP Professional can connect to a domain-based corporate LAN, but Windows XP Home Edition cannot. Either version can, however, dial into a company's domain-based network using a dial-up connection and your company's Remote Access Server (RAS); see Chapter 15, section "Accessing Other Computers with Remote Desktop." If your office uses the Microsoft Exchange Server for e-mail, you can use Exchange's web interface to read your mail. Check with your company's LAN administrator for instructions. Windows XP Home Edition can also connect to an Exchange server by using Outlook to send and receive mail without logging in to the domain.

Adding Your Computer to a TCP/IP Peer-to-Peer LAN

Windows XP installs most networking components automatically, either when you install Windows or when it detects a network interface card among your computer's hardware. The Network Setup Wizard can step you through the rest of the process of configuring your computer to communicate on your LAN, including setting up ICS (described in Chapter 31). The wizard can also create a floppy disk containing a configuration program that you can use to configure other Windows systems to work with your network (to use this feature, you need a blank floppy disk). Once your computer is connected to the LAN, you can use the Network Connections window to see your connections and the My Network Places window to see folders on other computers (see Chapter 22).

 In order to run the Network Setup Wizard or make any of the configuration changes described in this chapter, you must be logged in with an administrative user account (see Chapter 6).

Running the Network Setup Wizard

After installing your network interface card (if it's not already installed) and attaching a cable to connect your computer to the LAN, follow these steps:

1. Connect to the Internet, if you have an Internet connection. Turn on all printers on the network, so that the wizard can detect them.

2. Start the Network Setup Wizard by choosing Start | All Programs | Accessories | Communications | Network Setup Wizard. Alternatively, choose Start | Control Panel, click Network And Internet Connections, click Network Connections, and click Set Up A Home Or Small Office Network in the Task pane. You see the Network Setup Wizard window.

3. Follow the instructions the wizard displays, clicking Next to move from screen to screen. Tell it whether you dial into the Internet directly from this computer, you want to connect to the Internet over the LAN, or you don't connect to the Internet.

4. Provide a computer name for your computer (see Figure 29-2). On the wizard's next screen, type the workgroup name. If you are attaching to an existing network, use the same name as the rest of the computers on the LAN. If you are setting up a new workgroup, use WORKGROUP or MSHOME as the workgroup. All computers that will share files on a small network need to use the same workgroup name.

5. If you want the wizard to create a Network Setup Disk with a LAN configuration program that you can run on Windows Me, 2000, 9x, and NT computers on your LAN, insert a blank floppy disk into the drive when the wizard prompts you. Choose to create the disk if you are setting up a new network that includes computers running previous versions of Windows; otherwise, don't bother.

The wizard installs the Client For Microsoft Networks, the TCP/IP protocol, and the File And Printer Sharing service to enable your computer to communicate on the LAN.

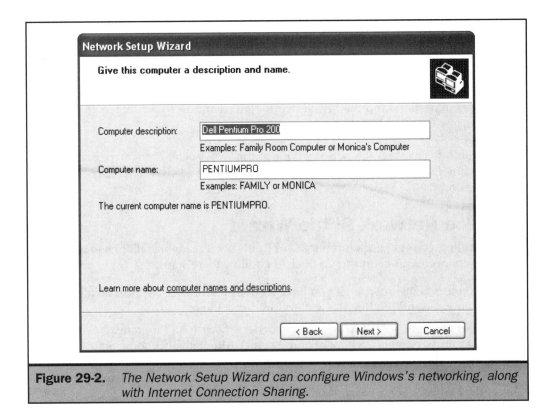

Figure 29-2.   *The Network Setup Wizard can configure Windows's networking, along with Internet Connection Sharing.*

If you tell the Network Setup Wizard that you dial directly into the Internet and you want to share your Internet connection with other computers on the LAN, the wizard installs ICS (see Chapter 31 for more information).

Viewing Network Resources with the My Network Places Window

When the Network Setup Wizard finishes, My Network Places should appear on the right side of your Start menu. My Network Places also appears as a choice in the Task pane of many Explorer windows and Open dialog boxes, enabling you to access shared folders on the network easily. When you choose Start | My Network Places, you see the My Network Places window, which is an Explorer window with shortcuts to network resources, as shown in Figure 29-3.

Note   *If My Network Places doesn't appear on the Start menu, Windows may not have found your network interface card. Check that it's listed and working by using the Device Manager (see Chapter 13, section "Managing Your Hardware Components with the Device Manager"). Or you may need to run the Network Setup Wizard as described in the previous section.*

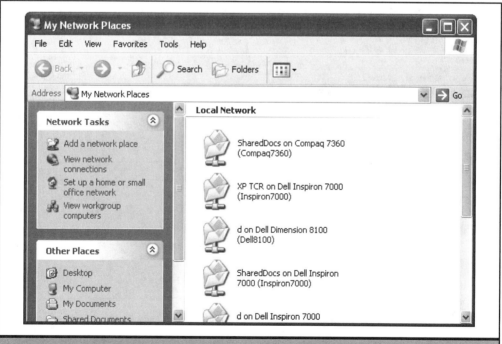

Figure 29-3.   *My Network Places lists shared disks and printers.*

The My Network Places window should list shared folders you can use. Click a shortcut to see the contents of the folder. Chapter 30 describes how to add folders on your computer to the list of folders that other people on your LAN can share and how to share printers. My Network Places can also include shortcuts to web and FTP servers on the Internet.

 If you want a My Network Places icon to appear on your desktop, click Start, right-click My Network Places, and choose Show On Desktop from the menu that appears.

Viewing Your Network Connections

To configure the network, you use the Network Connections window, shown in Figure 29-4. Choose Start | Control Panel, click Network And Internet Connections, and click Network Connections. Another way to display this window is by clicking Start, right-clicking My Network Places, and choosing Properties. Alternatively, if Connect To appears on the Start menu, choose Start | Connect To | Show All Connections.

The Network Connections window displays your LAN and Internet connections and lists network-related tasks. To check whether your computer can communicate with other computers on the LAN, click View Workgroup Computers on the Task pane. You should see a list of the other computers in your workgroup or domain.

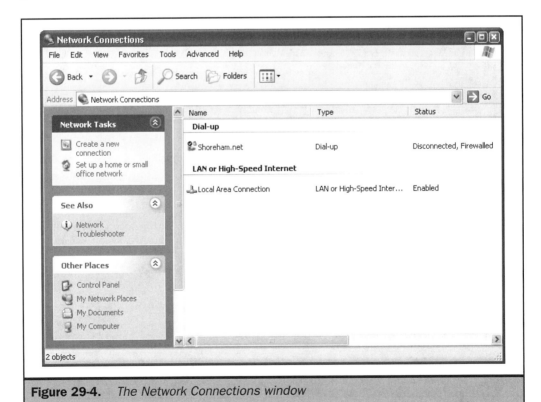

Figure 29-4.   *The Network Connections window*

You also use the Network Connections window to configure Windows to communicate with an Internet account.

Reconfiguring Windows Me/98, 2000, and NT Systems to Use TCP/IP

You can use the Network Setup Wizard to configure computers on your LAN, even if they don't run Windows XP. If you created a Network Setup Disk when you ran the Network Setup Wizard (as described in section "Running the Network Setup Wizard" earlier in this chapter), you can run the Network Setup Wizard on Windows 2000, Me, NT, or 9x computers on your LAN by putting the floppy disk in the drive, choosing Start | Run, typing **a:setup** in the Open box, and clicking OK. The wizard configures the computers to use TCP/IP and may need to restart each computer after it runs.

If you didn't create a Network Setup Disk, you can run the wizard from the Windows XP CD-ROM. Follow these steps:

1. Put the Windows XP CD-ROM in the computer's CD drive. If the Welcome To Microsoft Windows XP window doesn't appear, choose Start | Run and type **d:setup** (where *d* is the letter of your CD drive) to display it.

2. Choose Perform Additional Tasks.

3. Choose Set Up A Home Or Small Office Network.

4. Follow the wizard's instructions, clicking Next to move from window to window.

Adding Your Computer to a NetBEUI Peer-to-Peer LAN

Starting with Windows XP, Microsoft no longer supports NetBEUI. However, you can still add your Windows XP computer to a NetBEUI-based peer-to-peer LAN. You have two options:

■ **Install TCP/IP on the rest of the computers**   The world is switching to TCP/IP, and you might want to convert your existing LAN to TCP/IP. This method requires configuring each existing computer on the LAN to use TCP/IP. If the computers run Windows 98, Me, NT, or 2000 (not 95 or 3.1), you can follow the steps in the previous section to run the Windows XP Network Setup Wizard on each computer, converting it to TCP/IP.

■ **Install NetBEUI on the Windows XP computer**   Although Windows XP defaults to using TCP/IP as the network protocol, you can install NetBEUI on Windows XP. Windows XP doesn't come with NetBEUI installed, but you can install it from the Windows XP CD-ROM, as described in the section "Installing a Protocol" later in this chapter.

If your computer uses NetBEUI to communicate on a LAN and TCP/IP only for Internet communication, unbind the TCP/IP protocol from File And Printer Sharing For Microsoft Networks. Follow the steps in the section "Setting the Order of Your Protocols" later in this chapter, and deselect the Internet Protocol (TCP/IP) check box for the File And Printer Sharing For Microsoft Networks service.

Adding Your Computer to a Wireless LAN

If your computer has a wireless LAN connection (see Chapter 27, section "Wireless LANs"), it appears as a local area connection in the Network Connections window (choose Start | Control Panel, click Network And Internet Connections, and click Network Connections). Right-click the connection and click View Available Wireless Networks to configure the connection, as shown in Figure 29-5.

 Every wireless network should have a WEP (Wireless Equivalent Privacy) network key (password) to prevent unauthorized connections to the network. Otherwise, people in nearby houses and offices, and even people driving by in a car with a laptop (called "wardriving") can connect to your network and potentially have access to all the resources on all your computers. Older network adapters and access points provide 40-bit keys, while newer ones provide 104-bit keys.

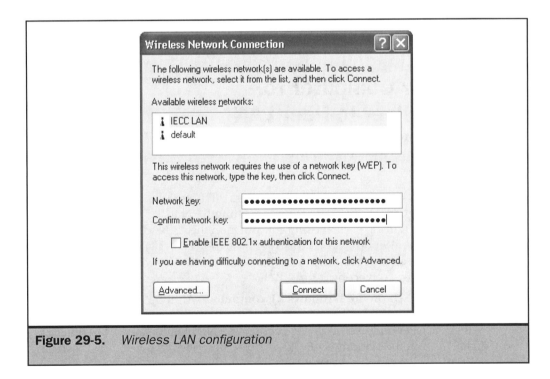

Figure 29-5. *Wireless LAN configuration*

If your wireless network setup offers you a "default" network, don't use it because that network would have no security at all.

Connecting to a Wireless Access Point

If your network has an access point, you should already have installed and configured the access point, including settings the network's name (also known as its SSID) and the WEP network key. The Wireless Network Connection window displays the network name. Follow these steps:

1. In the Wireless Network Connection window, select the network and type the network key. If the network has a 40-bit key, you enter the key either as a five text characters or 13 hex digits. If the network has a 104-bit key, you enter it as 13 text characters or 26 hex digits.

2. Don't check the IEEE 802 1.x box, which applies only to more complex networks.

3. Click Connect.

4. If your network name doesn't appear in the list, click Advanced to get the Connection Properties window; then click the Refresh button to look for available networks. Your network should appear; then click OK.

5. You should see the Wireless Network Connection window. If you don't, check that the access point is operating correctly, and that the wireless network adapter is in a place where it can contact the access point.

Connecting to an Ad Hoc Network

Setting up an ad hoc network is a little more complicated than connecting to an access point. The first computer that connects to the network has to define the network name and WEP key. Then other computers can connect to the ad hoc network.

On the first computer, follow these steps:

1. Open the Wireless Network Connection window, then click Advanced to open the Wireless Network Connection Properties window.

2. Click the Add button in the Preferred networks area to open the Wireless Network Properties window, as shown in Figure 29-6.

3. Enter a network name, something descriptive that won't be the same as the name of any other nearby network.

4. Check the Data Encryption check box.

5. Uncheck The Key Is Provided For Me Automatically.

6. Enter a password for the network key: five characters if any of your network adapters only support 40-bit encryption, 13 characters otherwise.

7. Click OK.

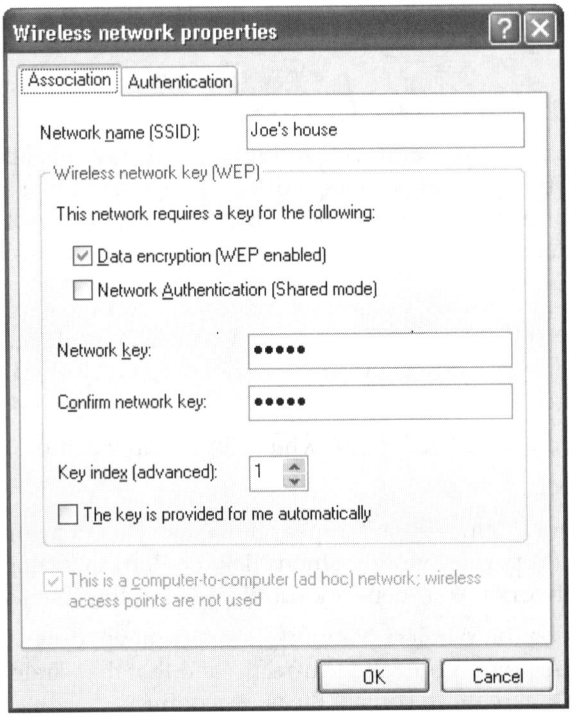

Figure 29-6.   *Defining an ad hoc wireless LAN*

Once you have defined the ad hoc network on one adapter, you can connect to it from all the adapters in the network just like you can to an access point, as shown in Figure 29-7. The icon next to an ad hoc network is a little network card rather than the little radio tower for an access point. Select the network name, enter the key twice if it's not already present, and click OK.

Wireless Network Properties

If you have more than one wireless network available—for example, if you have two access points in different parts of the house or office—you can configure your network adapter to use them automatically. Open the Wireless Network Connection Properties window as described in the previous section. All of the access points your computer can contact appear in the Available Networks window. For each network you want to use, select the network and click Configure to open the Properties window where you can enter the access key.

The available networks also appear in the Preferred Networks window. You can select a network: click the Move Up and Move Down buttons to have your computer try the network before or after other networks, or click Remove not to use the network at all. If you have an ad hoc network but someone else's nearby access point appears in

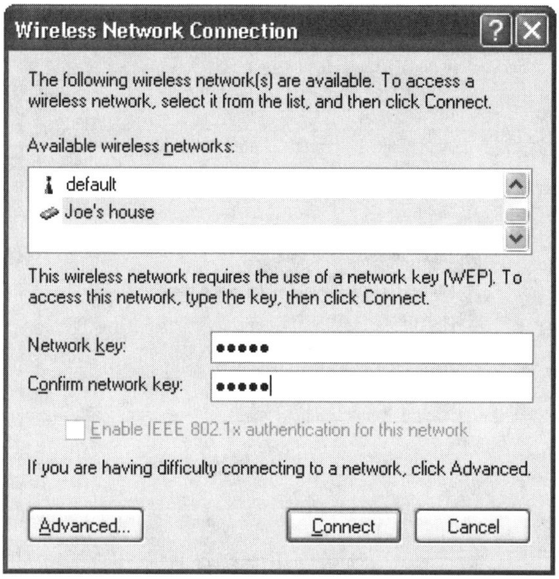

Figure 29-7. *Connecting to ad hoc wireless LAN*

the menu or vice versa, click Advanced to open a menu where you can specify to use only access point or only ad hoc networks.

Connecting to a Phone Line or Power Line LAN

Phone line and power line LANs connect to your computer like any other wired Ethernet (see Chapter 27, section "Phone and Power Line Networking"). No special setup is necessary. If you have both a phone line or power line LAN and an Ethernet or wireless LAN, you may want to bridge the two networks together as described later in this chapter.

Installing and Configuring Network Components

Running the Network Setup Wizard is usually all you need to do to set up a TCP/IP-based peer-to-peer network or attach your PC to an existing LAN. However, if you are connecting to a NetBEUI- or IPX/SPX-based network, or if your network connection isn't working properly, you may need to install, configure, or uninstall network components yourself.

For each networking connection listed in the Network Connections window, you can see its properties by right-clicking the connection and choosing Properties from the menu that appears. Figure 29-8 shows the properties of a LAN connection.

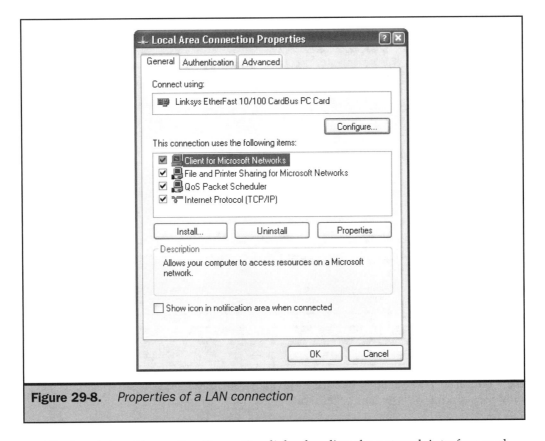

Figure 29-8.   *Properties of a LAN connection*

The Local Area Connection Properties dialog box lists the network interface card that connects your computer to the LAN. It also lists the clients, protocols, and services used for this network connection. The network interface card appears at the top, in the Connect Using box. The clients, protocols, and services are listed in the This Connection Uses the Following Items box, with icons that identify the different types of components:

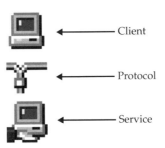

For a standard TCP/IP LAN, these four components should be installed (they should appear in your Local Area Connection Properties dialog box) and enabled (each check box contains a check mark):

- **Client For Microsoft Networks**   Client that enables the computer to communicate with other Windows computers.

- **File And Printer Sharing For Microsoft Networks**   Service that shares files and printers. This service should be enabled only on a LAN connection, not on an Internet connection. The Internet Connection Firewall blocks this service.

- **QoS Packet Scheduler**   Service that determines the precedence of information packets on the LAN based on Quality of Service (QoS) standards.

- **Internet Protocol (TCP/IP)**   Protocol used on the Internet and many LANs (see "Network Protocols" earlier in this chapter).

If your LAN connection has these four components and your LAN uses TCP/IP, you probably don't need to install any other network components. Skip down to the section "Checking Your Network Connection" later in this chapter.

Installing and Configuring an Adapter

Chapter 13 described how to install a network interface adapter if your computer doesn't already have one. The *adapter* is the software driver that allows your PC to communicate with the network interface card in your PC. (Network interface cards are also called *network adapters*.) Every model of network interface card has its own driver, which must be installed so the client software knows how to package information and send it to the network interface card.

Your network adapter appears in the Connect Using box of the Local Area Connection Properties dialog box (Figure 29-8). Click the Configure button to see the Properties dialog box for the network interface card (see Chapter 13, section "Hardware Drivers").

Installing a Client

The next step is to install the client component, which identifies the type of network on which your computer will be. When you configure your network connection (or when Windows finds your Plug and Play network interface card), Windows also installs the Client For Microsoft Networks. If a client is installed, it appears in the This Connection Uses The Following Items dialog box in the Local Area Connection Properties dialog box (Figure 29-8).

Because you are installing a peer-to-peer Windows network, the Client For Microsoft Networks is the one you need. (It is similar to the Workstation service that came with Windows NT 4.0 Workstation.) If you mistakenly deleted your Client For Microsoft Networks, or if you need the Client Service For NetWare (which also comes with Windows XP), follow these steps:

1. Display the Local Area Connection Properties dialog box (by clicking Start, right-clicking My Network Places, choosing Properties, right-clicking Local Area Connection, and choosing Properties). Click the General tab (if it's not already selected).

2. Click the Install button. You see the Select Network Component Type dialog box:

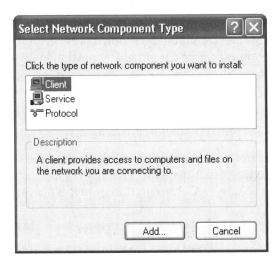

3. Select Client as the type of network component you want to install and click the Add button. You see the Select Network Client dialog box.

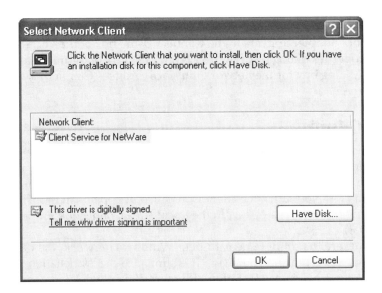

4. Choose the network client. If you have a floppy disk or CD with software for another type of client, insert it now and click Have Disk.

5. Click OK. You return to the Local Area Connection Properties dialog box, with the client you just defined listed. You may be prompted to insert the Windows XP CD-ROM.

6. Click OK to save your changes.

Installing a Protocol

When you install Windows, it automatically installs the TCP/IP protocol, in case you want to use TCP/IP for Internet communication. We recommend that you use TCP/IP if you are setting up a new network, since it's the standard. Windows XP also comes with support for NetBEUI (Microsoft's older protocol) and NetWare's IPX/SPX protocol.

Copying NetBEUI Files

Before you can install the NetBEUI protocol, you need to follow these steps to copy the files from the Windows XP CD-ROM:

1. Put the Windows XP CD-ROM in the drive. Choose Perform Additional Tasks from the menu that appears, and then Browse This CD.

2. In the Explorer window that appears, locate the Valueadd\msft\net\netbeui folder on the CD.

3. Copy the Nbf.sys file into the C:\Windows\System32\Drivers folder (assuming that Windows is installed in C:\Windows).

4. Copy Netnbf.inf into the C:\Windows\Inf folder.

After copying the files, you can install NetBEUI, as described in the next section.

 You may need to configure Windows Explorer to display hidden files in order to see the copied files. In an Explorer window, choose Tools | Folder Options, click the View tab, and select the Show Hidden Files and Folders check box in the Advanced Settings list.

Installing NetBEUI or IPX/SPX

Installing a protocol is similar to installing other network components. Follow these steps to install NetBEUI or IPX/SPX:

1. Display the Local Area Connection Properties dialog box (by clicking Start, right-clicking My Network Places, choosing Properties, right-clicking Local Area Connection, and choosing Properties). Click the General tab (if it's not already selected). It looks like Figure 29-8, shown earlier in this chapter.

2. Click the Install button to display the Select Network Component Type dialog box.

3. Select Protocol and click the Add button. You see the Select Network Protocol dialog box:

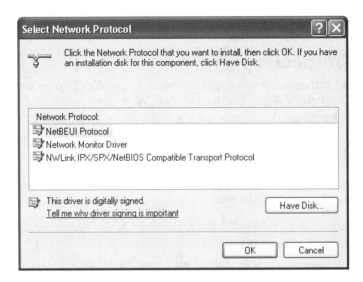

4. Select the protocol and click OK. (For IPX/SPX, select NWLink IPX/SPX/NetBIOS Compatible Transport Protocol.)

5. You return to the Local Area Connection Properties dialog box, with the protocol you just defined listed and enabled for this local area connection. You may be prompted to insert the Windows XP CD-ROM.

6. Click Close to save your changes.

Setting the Order of Your Protocols

When you install a protocol, Windows "binds" the new protocol to all the clients and services you have available—usually File And Printer Sharing For Microsoft Networks and Client For Microsoft Networks. A *binding* tells Windows to use a specific protocol with a specific client or service.

You might not want to use all of your installed protocols to work with all your installed clients and services. You can control which protocols work with which clients and services, and which protocol Windows should try first, by opening the Network Connections window (choose Start | Control Panel, click Network And Internet Connections, and click Network Connections) and choosing Advanced | Advanced Settings from the menu bar. You see the Advanced Settings dialog box, shown in Figure 29-9. Click the Local Area Connection in the Connections box (if it's not already selected). The lower part of the Adapters And Bindings tab shows your client and services for that connection, with your installed protocols listed under each client or service.

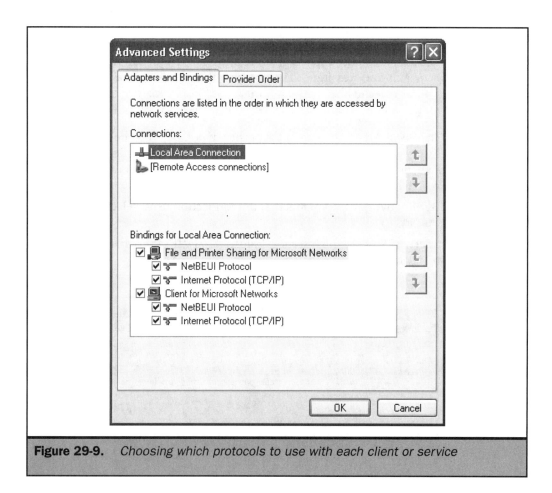

Figure 29-9. *Choosing which protocols to use with each client or service*

You can switch the order of the protocols, so that the one you plan to use most often appears first. Click the protocol and click the up- or down-pointing arrow button to move it. If you don't plan to use a protocol with a particular service, deselect the check box by the protocol.

Tip *If you connect to the Internet through a hub or router than doesn't provide a firewall between your computers and the Internet, don't use TCP/IP for your file and printer sharing. Instead, on each computer on your LAN, install the NetBEUI or IPX/SPX protocol, as described in "Installing a Protocol" earlier in this chapter. Then use the Advanced Settings dialog box on each computer to disable Internet Protocol (TCP/IP) for File And Printer Sharing For Microsoft Networks. Leave NetBEUI or IPX/SPX enabled, so that all the computers can use that protocol for file and printer sharing. Leave TCP/IP installed for communications with the Internet.*

Configuring the TCP/IP Protocol

On a TCP/IP-based LAN, you need to assign an IP address to your computer's network interface card, using static addressing or DHCP (see "IP Addressing" earlier in this chapter). For a laptop, you can also use an alternate configuration, for when the computer isn't connected to its regular network. Follow these steps:

1. Display the Local Area Connection Properties dialog box (by clicking Start, right-clicking My Network Places, choosing Properties, right-clicking Local Area Connection, and choosing Properties). Click the General tab (if it's not already selected).

2. On the list of network components that the connection uses, select Internet Protocol (TCP/IP).

3. Click Properties. You see the Internet Protocol (TCP/IP) Properties dialog box, shown in Figure 29-10.

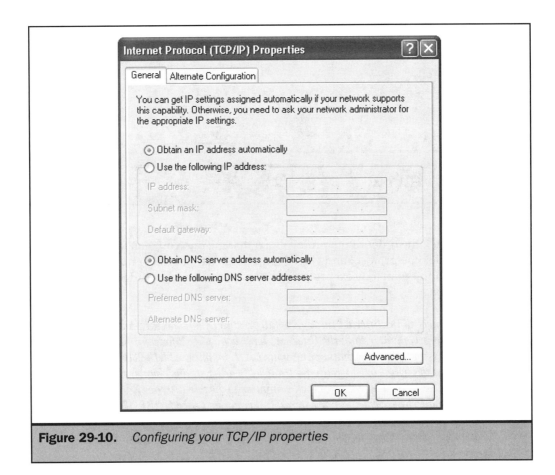

Figure 29-10.   *Configuring your TCP/IP properties*

4. To assign a static IP address, click Use The Following IP Address. In the IP Address box, type the IP address you've chosen. Windows supplies the dots that separate the four parts of the address.

5. In the Subnet Mask box, type **255.255.255.0**.

6. To use DHCP or APIPA (systems that assign an IP address to your computer when Windows starts up), select Obtain An IP Address Automatically. If your LAN has a DHCP server, Windows will get IP addresses from the server each time you start Windows. If not, Windows will assign itself an address.

7. If you have a laptop that connects to a LAN in a different way when you are not at your desk, click the Alternate Configuration tab. Your IP addressing choices are Automatic Private IP Address (APIPA) or User Configured (a static address).

8. Click OK in each dialog box.

On rare occasions, the TCP/IP protocol installation may get damaged. You can reset TCP/IP by following these steps:

1. Open a Command Prompt window by choosing Start | All Programs | Accessories | Command Prompt (or Start | Run, type **cmd**, and press ENTER).

2. Type the following command and then press ENTER:

```
netsh int ip reset ipreset.log
```

3. If you want to read the contents of the log file created by the command, you can type the command **type ipreset.log** and press ENTER.

4. Type **exit** and press ENTER to close the Command Prompt window.

Installing a Service

A service is the last network component you install. It also is the only optional component. Your network can work fine without a service, but no one on the network will be able to share resources, such as hard disks, CD-ROM drives, files, or printers. If you don't want to share resources, don't install any services.

Note	*Even when a service has been defined, you can add some security measures (see Chapter 30).*

On a peer-to-peer network of Windows computers, you need the File And Printer Sharing For Microsoft Networks service. The Network Setup Wizard installs this service automatically. If you need to install it (or another service) yourself, follow these steps:

1. Display the Local Area Connection Properties dialog box (by clicking Start, right-clicking My Network Places, choosing Properties, right-clicking Local Area Connection, and choosing Properties). Click the General tab (if it's not already selected).

2. Click the Install button to display the Select Network Component Type dialog box.

3. Select Service and click the Add button. You see the Select Network Service dialog box:

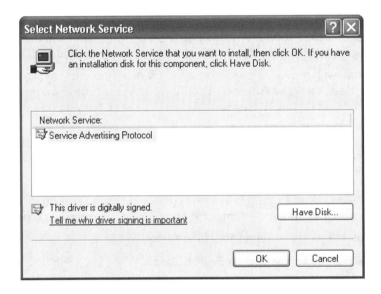

4. Select the service you want and click OK.

5. You return to the Local Area Connection Properties dialog box, with the protocol you just defined listed. You may be prompted to insert the Windows XP CD-ROM.

6. Click Close to save your changes.

Changing the Computer Name, Workgroup, or Domain

To see or change your computer's name and which workgroup or domain it is in, follow these steps:

1. Click Start, right-click My Computer, and choose Properties from the menu that appears. You see the System Properties dialog box.

2. Click the Computer Name tab, shown in Figure 29-11.

3. Type a description of the computer in the Computer Description box. This description appears in the My Network Places window.

4. To change the computer name or workgroup, click the Change button to display the Computer Name Changes dialog box:

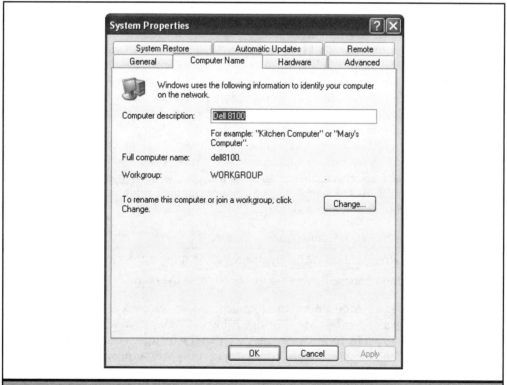

Figure 29-11. *Each computer needs a unique name and the name of the workgroup to which it belongs.*

5. In the Computer Name box, type a unique name for the computer.

6. In the Workgroup box, type the workgroup name. Use the same workgroup name as the other computers in the LAN.

7. Click OK. You may see a message telling you to restart Windows for your changes to take effect.

Displaying a LAN Icon in the Notification Area

If you would like to see an icon for the LAN connection in the notification area (the right end of the taskbar, next to the clock), display the Local Area Connection Properties dialog box, click the General tab, and select the Show Icon In Notification Area When Connected check box.

Bridging Networks

If you have two or more network interface cards that connect your computer to different networks, your computer can *bridge* (connect together) networks. You can create a bridge among LANs that are logically organized as Ethernets, including real Ethernets, wireless, phone line, power line, and IEEE1394 (FireWire) networks. You can't bridge to a VPN, dial-up, or direct cable connection.

When networks are bridged, all of the computers on all of the bridged networks are effectively on a single LAN, and any of them can communicate directly with any other. You can't bridge a connection that has the Internet Connection Firewall or ICS enabled. (See the sidebar "Why Bridge When You Can Plug?" for some advice on using bridges and ICS together.) Network bridges are most often used for connecting an ad hoc wireless or phone wire LANs to your regular cable-based LAN. A computer can have only one bridge, but it can connect as many different networks as you want.

If you have multiple LANs when you run the Network Setup Wizard, it'll offer to bridge them for you. If that's appropriate (they're all internal networks, not connections to the outside), you can let it do so. Otherwise, when it tells you that your computer has multiple connections, check the box to let you choose your own connections, and select the networks (if any) to bridge. Or, you can create the bridge yourself.

To create a bridge, follow these steps:

1. Display the Network Connections window.

2. Select the two (or more) LANs by dragging the mouse around their icons.

3. Right-click and choose Bridge Connections from the menu

Windows creates a bridge among the connections you selected, as in Figure 29-12. The bridge appears as a virtual "MAC Bridge Miniport" adapter, and all of the bridged adapters are logically part of it. Once you've created a bridge, you can configure it by right-clicking the Bridge icon and configuring it the way you would any other network adapter, installing services, clients, and protocols. You can also add and remove adapters to the bridge. Right-click the adapter and select Add To Bridge or Remove From Bridge. Although Windows demands at least two adapters to create a bridge, the bridge works fine with only a single adapter under its control. This can be useful if you need to disconnect a network temporarily.

 Don't try to bridge anything to an Internet connection. It won't work, because your Internet provider isn't expecting to see your other computers on its network.

Using Bridging with Internet Connection Sharing

It's frequently useful to use bridging in connection with ICS. For example, suppose you have a home office with several computers connected to an Ethernet hub. One of those computers has a DSL or dial-up Internet connection, as well as a wireless LAN card used to communicate with a laptop via an ad hoc network. How can you give Internet access to all your computers? First, create a bridge connecting the wired LAN and the wireless LAN into one logical network. Then enable ICS on the DSL or dial-up Internet connection.

The bridge acts as the LAN side of the shared Internet connection, providing Internet access to the other computers both on the wired LAN and on the wireless LAN. Since the bridge makes the two LANS into one network, computers on the wireless LAN can also use resources such as printers on other computers on the wired LAN.

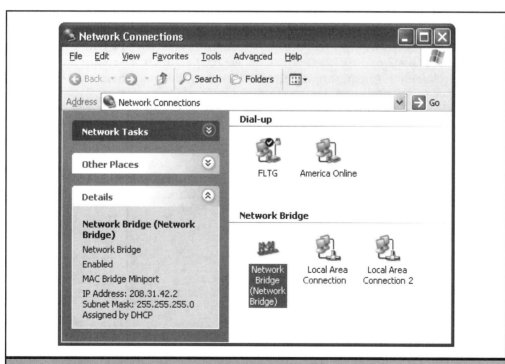

Figure 29-12.   *Bridged network connections*

Why Bridge When You Can Plug?

Bridging two networks is the software equivalent of physically plugging the two networks together. If you can connect the two networks with a cable, it's usually better to do that than to bridge using Windows, both to save a network adapter and to keep the whole network from depending on a single computer. If you bridge two wired LANs, you can generally connect them by running a regular network cable from the uplink port on one hub to a regular port on the other. Similarly, if you use a wireless hub, the hub invariably has an Ethernet port you can connect to your wired network hub using a regular Ethernet cable.

Checking Your Network Connection

The Network Setup Wizard usually installs and configures your network components correctly. This section describes how to discover your computer's IP address and how to try rudimentary network communication.

Checking Your TCP/IP Address

Windows can display your computer's IP address and other TCP/IP settings. In the Network Connections window (choose Start | Control Panel, click Network And Internet Connections, and click Network Connections), right-click a connection and choose Status from the menu that appears. You see a window like this:

Click the Support tab to see your IP address:

You can also see where the IP address came from (in this example, it was assigned by a DHCP server). For details, click the Details button. You can click Repair to re-request an IP address from the DHCP server.

Another way to see your IP address and other information is by running the Ipconfig program. Choose Start | All Programs | Accessories | Command Prompt to open a Command Prompt window (see Chapter 4, section "The Command Prompt Window"). Then type **ipconfig /all** and press ENTER. You see a listing like this:

```
Windows IP Configuration

        Host Name . . . . . . . . . . . . : inspiron7000
        Primary Dns Suffix  . . . . . . . :
        Node Type . . . . . . . . . . . . : Hybrid
        IP Routing Enabled. . . . . . . . : No
        WINS Proxy Enabled. . . . . . . . : No

Ethernet adapter Local Area Connection:

        Connection-specific DNS Suffix  . : mshome.net
        Description . . . . . . . . . . . : EtherFast 10/100 PC Card
        Physical Address. . . . . . . . . : 00-E0-98-04-47-15
        Dhcp Enabled. . . . . . . . . . . : Yes
        Autoconfiguration Enabled . . . . : Yes
        IP Address. . . . . . . . . . . . : 192.168.0.4
```

```
Subnet Mask . . . . . . . . . . . : 255.255.255.0
Default Gateway . . . . . . . . . : 192.168.0.1
DHCP Server . . . . . . . . . . . : 192.168.0.1
DNS Servers . . . . . . . . . . . : 192.168.0.1
Lease Obtained. . . . . . . . . . : Tuesday, July 31, 2001
Lease Expires . . . . . . . . . . : Wednesday, August 01, 2001
```

The Dhcp Enabled line tells you whether your computer got its IP address from a DHCP server, and if so, the Lease Obtained line tells when your computer got the address. If your computer uses ICS, the Default Gateway, DHCP Server, and DNS Servers entries are 192.168.0.1 (see Chapter 31).

Testing Your TCP/IP Connection

Once you've installed and configured the network components for a computer, you need to see whether your network works. Sit down at any of the computers on the network and follow these steps:

1. Use the Ping program (described in Chapter 22) to ping yourself—that is, ping your own computer's IP address. In the Network Connections window (choose Start | Control Panel, click Network And Internet Connections, and click Network Connections), right-click your LAN connection, choose Status, and click the Support tab to find out your own computer's IP address. If this step doesn't work, TCP/IP isn't correctly installed on your computer, or it's not getting an IP address. (The Ipconfig program described in the previous section pings your own computer to get some of the information the Ipconfig displays.)

2. Ping another computer on the LAN to see whether information can travel from your computer to another. Follow the instructions in the previous section first to determine the IP address of a computer on the LAN to ping. (Trying pinging your default gateway, which is frequently at 192.168.0.1.) If this step fails, your LAN cable or connection may not work.

3. Open the My Network Places window (choose Start | My Network Places) to see what appears. Shortcuts to shared folders on the other computers should appear automatically. Otherwise, you can click Add A Network Place to add shortcuts to folders (see Chapter 30, section "Using Network Drives with My Network Places"). If this step doesn't work, your workgroup name may not be set correctly.

4. If you don't see shortcuts in the My Network Places window, there's another way to connect to other computers on the LAN. Click View Workgroup Computers in the Task pane of the My Network Places window. You see the names of all the computers in the workgroup. Open an icon (click or double-click it, depending on how you have Windows configured) to see the folders and printers that are available on that computer. If you see Entire Network as an entry, open it. Then open Microsoft Windows Network and open your workgroup. The computers in your workgroup should appear.

5. If you still don't see icons for the other computers on the network, read through the section "Troubleshooting Your Network" later in this chapter to find and fix the problem. If you see only your own computer in the workgroup, or the Entire Network window is blank, communication has broken down with the other computers. It could be physical, like a bad cable, or it could be a problem with your software configuration, such as using the wrong protocol.

Once your network is working, the next step is to use it to share resources (see Chapter 30).

Viewing LAN Resources with the Net Command

You can see a list of the shared resources of a computer on the LAN by using a command-line program called NET VIEW (actually, it's the NET program with the VIEW command-line argument). Open a Command Prompt window by choosing Start | All Programs | Accessories | Command Prompt. Then type **net view** *\\computername* and press ENTER. Replace *computername* with the name of a computer on the LAN. For example, the command **net view \\dell8100** might produce this listing:

```
Shared resources at \\dell8100

Dell Dimension 8100

Share name     Type        Use as    Comment
---------------------------------------------
D              Disk
SharedDocs     Disk
PRINTER        Print
The command completed successfully.
```

If the computer has no shared resources, you see the message "There are no entries in the list." If you don't have permission to view the shared resources on that computer, you see the message "Access is denied." If you see the message "System error 53 has occurred," the computer name is wrong, the computer is not on the LAN, or File And Printer Sharing For Microsoft Networks isn't running on that computer.

You can see a list of all the shared resources on your own computer by typing **net share**.

 *The **NET VIEW** command works with all installed protocols. Ping works only with TCP/IP.*

Viewing LAN Usage

If you are worried that your LAN is slowing down because it can't handle the volume of data, Windows can display a graph of LAN utilization. Press CTRL-ALT-DELETE to see the Windows Task Manager window (see Chapter 35). Click the Networking tab (see Figure 29-13).

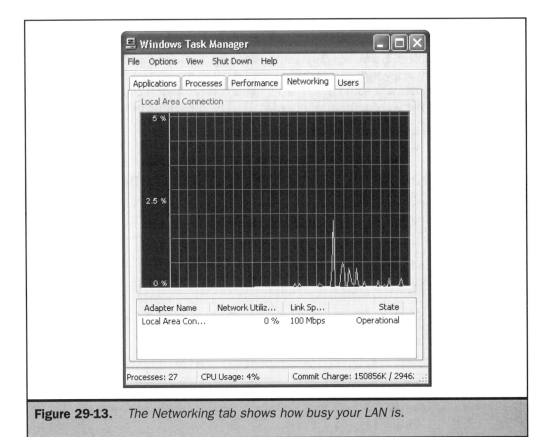

Figure 29-13. *The Networking tab shows how busy your LAN is.*

The graph shows network usage over time, as a percentage of the amount of data that it could carry. Unless you are copying huge files (for example, if you do backups over the LAN), the percentages usually stay amazingly low.

Troubleshooting Your Network

Although Windows networking generally works well, you may have trouble with one computer or all of the computers on the network, especially when you first set up the network. This section recommends some steps to take to solve your problems.

If you have trouble with the IP addresses on the LAN, use the Networking (TCP/IP) Troubleshooter. Choose Start | Help And Support, click Fixing A Problem in the Pick A Help Topic list, click Networking Problems, and click Home And Small Office Networking Troubleshooter. Another useful program is Network Diagnostics.

To use it, type **Network Diagnostics** in the Help and Support Center window's Search box and press ENTER.

The solutions to some common problems and solutions follow:

- **The "Local Area Network: A Network Cable Is Unplugged" message appears**   If you see this message in a pop-up window from the notification bar of the taskbar, the message is probably right—the cable from your computer to the LAN hub is unplugged or damaged, or for a wireless LAN, the SSID or network key is wrong. When you fix the connection, the message goes away.

- **Computer can't log onto a domain**   You can't log onto a domain-based LAN if you use Windows XP Home Edition; only Windows XP Professional can log on to a domain.

- **Computers do not appear in My Network Places**   If a computer doesn't appear in your My Network Places window when you click View Workgroup Computers, it may have a loose cable connection, a bad cable, or a network interface card that isn't working properly. Check all of the cable connections. Occasionally, cables become damaged, so you might want to try replacing a suspect length of cable with one you know is good. Use Ping to see if the computer can communicate (see Chapter 22).

- **Shared folders don't appear in My Network Places**   The My Network Places window contains shortcuts to shared folders on the LAN, but these shortcuts can be deleted. If a shared folder you need doesn't appear in My Network Places, click Add A Network Place in the Task pane (see Chapter 30, section "Using Network Drives with My Network Places"). Try searching for the computer name by choosing Start | Search and choosing Computers Or People at the What Do You Want To Search For prompt (if you don't see that prompt, click More Advanced Options and then Other Search Options).

- **Bad or missing protocol**   A protocol may be missing or incorrectly configured. Check to see that your computer is speaking the same language as all the others. If the other computers are using NetBEUI and you are using TCP/IP, you will not be able to communicate with them. Open the Network Connections window, right-click the Local Area Connection icon, and choose Repair from the menu that appears. Windows will try to reinstall any missing components. Also, check which protocols the other computers are using to communicate, and install that protocol on the computer that is incommunicado.

- **Network interface card problem**   You may have a hardware conflict. Use the Device Manager to see whether there's a problem with the network interface card. If the network interface card appears with a yellow exclamation point, the card isn't working properly. Check the installation instructions for your card.

- **Password problems**   If Windows asks for a password when you try to use a shared folder or printer, you may need to find out the password for that resource or have your user account name added to the list of users who can address the resource. See Chapter 30 for more information on sharing resources.

The Complete Reference

Chapter 30

Sharing Drives and Printers on a LAN

If you have a LAN, you probably have resources that you want to share. Perhaps you have three computers and only one printer or one Internet connection. Perhaps several people use a database from different computers, and you want to make sure that they're always working with updated information. Whatever the reason, your LAN isn't much good if you don't know how to share your hardware and files.

This chapter tells you how to share disks and folders on your own computer, use shared disks and folders on other computers, and choose which of your own disk drives to make available to other people on your LAN. We also describe how to share the printers on your system and how to use printers on other people's systems.

Note	*This chapter assumes that you have connected your computer to a workgroup-based LAN and have installed file-sharing and printer-sharing services (see Chapters 27 and 29).*

Network drives (also called *shared drives*) are disk drives that have been configured to be available for use from other computers on the LAN. Similarly, *shared folders* are folders that have been configured to be usable by other computers on the LAN. For a disk drive or folder to be shared by other people on a LAN, it must be configured as sharable. Once a drive or folder is sharable, other people can read and write files on the disk drive or in the folder. Microsoft makes sharing a whole drive a little more difficult than sharing just a folder because of the security risks involved.

Enabling Hardware Sharing

To share your hardware—disk drives and printers—with others on the LAN, you need to make sure that sharing is enabled. For a workgroup-based, peer-to-peer network, see "Installing a Service" in Chapter 29 to install File And Printer Sharing For Microsoft Networks.

Installing file and printer sharing does not automatically share your printer and disk drives—that could compromise security. Instead, you choose exactly which resources to share on your computer by using the commands covered in this chapter.

Tip	*You can't share files or printers through a network connection that uses the Internet Connection Firewall (see Chapter 22). You should enable ICF on any connections to the outside world, so outsiders can't snoop on your network, but do not use ICF on connections to your LAN, which would prevent sharing resources with other computers on the LAN. If you use the Network Setup Wizard to configure your LAN, it automatically enables ICF on external connections but not on internal ones.*

User Accounts and LAN Security

Chapter 6 describes how you can set up user accounts on a computer to allow several people to be able to use the computer, storing separate settings for each person. The section "Keeping Files Private" describes how to set up public and private folders for each user.

User accounts are also useful on a peer-to-peer LAN, even if each computer is normally used by only one person. Windows XP Home Edition doesn't support the security provided by Microsoft's domain-based LANs. However, you have the following security options:

- **Read-only drives and folders files**   When you share a drive or folder on the LAN, you can designate it to be read-only, so that people on other computers can't change your files. For example, on a home LAN you might have a folder that contains your family's photos. You might want to share the folder with family members on other computer, but you set it as read-only so that other people can't accidentally delete pictures (or deliberately delete pictures in which their hair looks funny).

- **Non-shared drives**   You can set some drives not to be accessible over the LAN. We recommend that you separate your programs and documents into two separate partitions, and share only the documents partition (see Chapter 33). (Few programs run off of partitions on other computers, so there's no point sharing your Windows and program partition.)

- **Private folders**   You can use Windows XP's user accounts to create private folders (see Chapter 6, section "Keeping Files Private").

Using Shared Drives from Other Computers

You can access a shared drive or shared folder in one of two ways:

- If you use the drive or folder only occasionally, you can use My Network Places to access the drive.

- If you use the drive or folder frequently, you can *map* the drive or folder, which means that you assign the drive or folder a letter so that it appears on the drop-down list of drives in Open and Save As dialog boxes and as a disk in My Computer.

Using Network Drives with My Network Places

You can see a list of the shared drives and folders to which you have access. The My Network Places window, shown in Figure 30-1, lists *network shortcuts* to all the shared drives and folders available to you on the LAN. Choose View | Details to display all the information about each shared drive.

The name of each shared drive or folder appears, along with its UNC (Universal Naming Convention) address—the path name you use when referring to that shared drive or folder. The UNC address consists of two backslashes, the name of the computer, another backslash, and the share name of the drive or folder (see "Sharing Your Disk Drives and Folders with Others" later in this chapter).

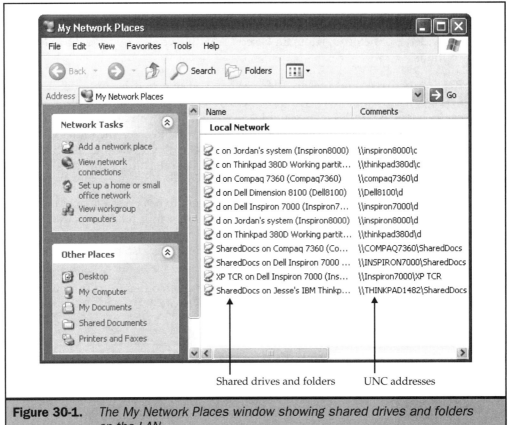

Figure 30-1.   *The My Network Places window showing shared drives and folders on the LAN*

To display the My Network Places window, use one of these methods:

- Choose Start | My Network Places.

- Open any folder (such as My Computer or My Documents) and click the My Network Places link in the Task pane on the left.

- Use Windows Explorer (where the folder tree is showing) and click My Network Places near the bottom of the folder tree.

If you don't see a list of shared folders, consider troubleshooting your network (see Chapter 29, section "Troubleshooting Your Network"). If one or two shared folders are missing, click Add A Network Place in the Task pane to add it. This command is also useful for adding web servers and FTP servers to your My Network Places window (see Chapter 26, section "Working with FTP and Web Servers Using Web Folders").

Another way to see all the shared folders on the system in the My Network Places window is by clicking the Entire Network plus box, the Microsoft Windows Network plus box, and the plus box for your workgroup (which is usually named MSHOME). You see a list of the computers on the LAN. Click a computer's plus box to see its shared drives and printers.

| Tip | *You can change the name of a shared drive or folder as it appears on your computer. For example, if a drive appears as "data drive on Dell" and you'd rather see the name "Accounting Data," you can rename it by right-clicking the shared drive or folder in an Explorer window and choosing Rename from the shortcut menu that appears. Renaming a shared drive or folder on your computer doesn't change its real name on the computer on which it's stored, just how it appears in your Explorer windows.* |

Opening and Saving Files on Shared Drives and Folders

You can see the folders and files on a shared drive by opening the drive or folder in the My Network Places window. Once you see the drive, you can work with it as you do any drive on your own computer (see Chapter 7).

My Network Places is also available from dialog boxes of any applications you use. It appears in the Places bar on the left side of the dialog box (see Chapter 1). If the dialog box doesn't have a Places bar down the left side, click the Save In or Look In box at the top of the dialog box and choose My Network Places from the drop-down menu. Once you have opened My Network Places, move to the folder and file you want. A few programs don't allow saving to a network drive unless you assign it a drive letter, which is covered in the next section.

Mapping a Shared Drive or Folder to a Drive Letter

If you use a shared drive or folder frequently, you can assign it a drive letter. When you want to find or save a file to the shared drive or folder, you don't have to spend so much time navigating through My Network Places to find it. For example, if you frequently use files in a shared folder on another computer, you can map drive letter S: to that folder. Drive S: appears as a disk drive on your computer, even though it's actually on the server.

Here's the easiest way to map a shared drive or folder to a drive letter:

1. Run Windows Explorer (choose Start | My Computer) to display an Explorer window.

2. Choose Tools | Map Network Drive from the menu bar. You see the Map
   Network Drive dialog box, shown here:

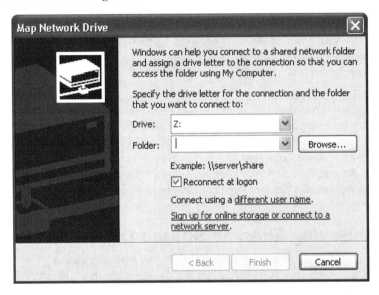

3. Choose a drive letter, clicking the Drive drop-down list to see the available
   letters. Letters that are mapped to drives on your own computer don't appear.
   Letters that are already mapped to shared drives or folders appear with the
   name of the resource to which they are mapped.

4. In the Folder box, type the UNC address of the shared drive or folder you want
   to Map. Better yet, click the downward-pointing arrow at the right end of the
   Folder box and choose from the UNC addresses that appear or click the Browse
   button and navigate to the drive or folder. The list includes all the drives and
   folders on the LAN that have been configured to be sharable.

5. If you want to continue to map this drive or folder to this drive letter each time
   you restart Windows, leave the Reconnect At Logon check box selected.

6. Click Finish to close the dialog box. If the shared drive or folder requires
   a password, Windows prompts you to type it.

 *To display a Map Network Drive button on the Windows Explorer toolbar, right-click
the toolbar, choose Customize from the shortcut menu that appears, click Map Drive
from the Available Toolbar Buttons list, click Add, and click Close.*

Once you have mapped a drive, it appears in the folder tree with your local drives,
and in Windows Explorer you see it when you open My Computer. You can access
a mapped network drive in the same way that you access a local drive from any
dialog box.

> **Note** To map a drive letter to a folder, the folder itself must be defined as shared. It is not enough to share the drive on which the folder resides.

You can map a drive letter to a shared folder on a domain-based corporate LAN if the server has a fixed IP address or domain name: see the sidebar "Using NET USE to Connect to Domain Servers."

Using NET USE to Connect to Domain Servers

Windows XP Home Edition isn't supposed to be able to connect to domain-based corporate LANs, but there is a way to do so. If you need to access files on a shared folder on your company's domain-based LAN, and if the folder is stored on a computer that has a static IP address or an Internet-style host name (ask your organization's LAN administrator), you can map that shared folder to a drive letter on your computer and then access your files. Follow these steps:

1. Connect to the Internet.

2. Choose Start | All Programs | Accessories | Command Prompt to open a Command Prompt window (see Chapter 4, section "The Command Prompt Window").

3. Type

   ```
   net use d: \\xxx.xxx.xxx.xxx\\sharename
   ```

   and press ENTER. Replace *d:* with any drive letter you aren't currently using. Replace *xxx.xxx.xxx.xxx* with the host name or IP address of the computer on which the shared folder is stored. Replace *sharename* with the share name of the folder. For example, you might type one of these commands to map your drive T: to the shared Helpdesk folder at work:

   ```
   net use t: \\215.26.128.137\helpdesk
   net use t: \\server.mycompany.com\helpdesk
   ```

4. When you see a prompt for your user name and password, type the user name and password that you use when you log on to the domain. After a pause, during which the domain server authenticates your password, you connect. Now, drive T: (or whatever letter you used) on your computer is the shared folder on the computer at your office.

   You can also use the NET USE command if you like to use the DOS command prompt or batch files (lists of commands) that create or delete mappings (see Chapter 4, section "Running Batch Files"). For more NET USE options, type this command:

   ```
   net use /?
   ```

Tips for Mapping Shared Folders and Drives

When you map a drive letter, you only map it for only one computer at a time. If you want the drive letter mapped for other computers on the LAN, you need to sit down at each of them and repeat the steps in the preceding section. That is, if you want all the computers in your home or small office to be able to use the drive letter F to refer to the Family Finances folder on the Kitchen computer, you must map the Family Finances folder to the F drive on each computer on the LAN.

If you use a shared drive or folder from more than one computer, you might want to spend a moment considering which drive letter to use. You will find it more convenient if the shared network drive has the same drive letter on each computer on the LAN—that way you won't have to refer to "the C drive on the computer in the corner near the door—the one called Bambi." Instead, you can just call it the F drive (the exception, of course, is the person who uses the computer called Bambi, for whom it's just the C drive). Choose a letter that people can remember—for example, map the disk drive on the playroom computer to drive P, or the drive with your accounting data to drive Z. Before you assign the drive letter, make sure that letter is available on the other computers on the LAN (letters up to about G are frequently already occupied by hard disks, CD-ROM drives, Zip drives, and other devices).

You may have noticed the Reconnect At Logon check box on the Map Network Drive dialog box. When this option is selected, your computer checks that the shared resource is available each time you log on. Reconnecting at logon slows down the log on process slightly, but means that using the drive the first time is quicker, because the drive is already connected. If you are mapping a drive only temporarily (you need it only for the next twenty minutes, for example), or if the computer that drive is on gets rebooted or turned off often, turn off the Reconnect At Logon option.

Unmapping a Drive Letter

If you want to "unmap" a drive letter, you can do so by disconnecting it: right-click the drive in Windows Explorer and choose Disconnect from the shortcut menu or choose Tools | Disconnect Network Drive, choose the drive to disconnect, and click OK. The drive remains accessible through My Network Places, but a drive letter is no longer mapped to it. (To make a drive inaccessible even through My Network Places, you must disable sharing from the computer that owns the resource.)

Sharing Your Disk Drives and Folders with Others

You might want to share the files stored on your computer's disk drives in a number of ways. You might want to permit all the computers on the LAN to access a Zip drive, Jaz drive, or CD-R or CD-RW writer, so that you don't have to buy a drive for each computer. You can permit other people to read files in specific folders on your hard drive. For instance, you can give read-only access to the folder that contains your family's collection of digital photos and music, so that you don't waste space on each computer saving the same files (and time updating numerous copies of the files). Maybe there is one shared folder on your hard drive that you want other people to be able to use. Maybe you just want to share everything—you want to allow everyone on the LAN to read and write to your hard drive.

Before anyone else can read or write files on your disk drives, you must configure either the entire drive or specific folders as sharable. You choose a *share name* for the drive or folder—the name that you want to appear in Windows Explorer as *name* on *computer name*. For example, if your computer is named Laptop, and you share your CD-ROM (your drive D) with the share name CD-ROM Drive, it appears as "CD-ROM Drive On Laptop" in Windows Explorer on other people's computers. You can provide a comment to further identify a shared drive or folder. The comment is visible only when the properties are displayed.

When you make a drive or folder sharable, you also decide what access to specify, within the limits of what Windows XP Home Edition allows. There are alternatives to sharing a whole drive with full read and write access:

- You can share just a folder.
- You can specify read-only rights.

By default, Windows XP enables *Simple File Sharing*, which means that when you share a drive or folder, you share it with everyone in your network workgroup (see Chapter 6, section "Simple File Sharing").

> **Note** *If you need more flexible security, enabling specific people read and write access to specific folders, consider upgrading to Windows XP Professional and setting up a domain-based LAN, which has more powerful LAN security features. In Windows XP Professional, you can disable Simple File Sharing to display a Security tab on file and folder Properties dialog boxes, on which you can specify permissions for individual users.*

Making a Drive Sharable

Follow these steps to share a drive or folder:

1. Run Windows Explorer (choose Start | My Computer) and display the name of the drive or folder you want to share with others.

> **Note** *If you open the folder you want to share, you can use the Share This Folder link in the Task pane to share it.*

2. Right-click the drive or folder you want to share and choose Sharing And Security from the shortcut menu. (If you don't see Sharing And Security, you need to install File And Printer Sharing For Microsoft Networks from the Network dialog box.) You see the Properties dialog box for the drive or folder, with the Sharing tab selected. If you have chosen to share a whole drive, you will see a link warning you that sharing the root of the drive is risky. Click the link to see Figure 30-2.

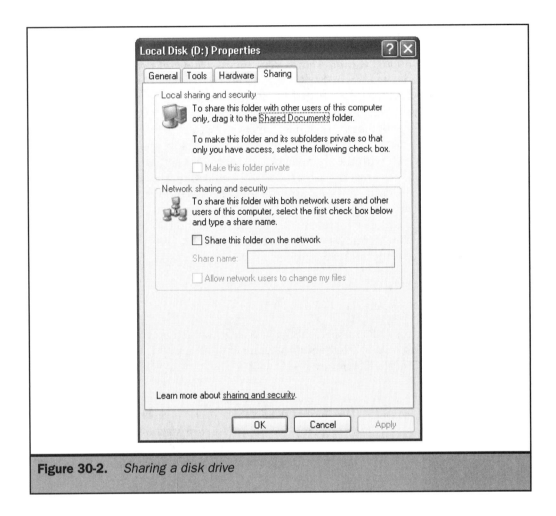

Figure 30-2. *Sharing a disk drive*

The Local Sharing And Security section of the Sharing tab is for sharing files with other users of your own computer, not users on other computers (see Chapter 6, section "Sharing Files with Other Users").

3. Click the Share This Folder On The Network check box.

4. Type the share name into the Share Name box. A share name can be from one to 12 characters long, including spaces.

5. If you want the drive or folder to be available to everyone in your workgroup, click OK to close the dialog box.

6. Clear the Allow Network Users To Change My Files check box to make files on the shared resource read-only—other users will be able to open files, but not save changes to your drive. Select this check box if you want other users to be able to save changes to files on your disk.

When you close the dialog box, you see a tiny hand as part of the drive or folder icon, signifying that the resource is shared. Other users can use your files by navigating to them through My Network Places. If they use the drive or folder often, they have the option of mapping the drive. If you decide to stop sharing of the drive, open the Properties dialog box for the drive and select the Do Not Share This Folder radio button or deselect the Share This Folder On The Network check box on the Sharing tab.

If you make a folder sharable, the shared folder looks like a whole drive from other computers on the LAN, but other people can see and use only the shared folder.

 *To hide shared folders, add a dollar sign ($) to the end of the share name (for example, type **Docs$** in the Share Name box). Other people can still use this shared folder by mapping it to a drive letter.*

Controlling Access to Files and Folders on NTFS Volumes

If a shared folder is on an NTFS volume, you can set individual files and folders to be read-only even if the folder is read-write. You can also mark files and folders as hidden so they don't normally appear in Explorer windows. Right-click the file or folder, select Properties, and check or uncheck the Read-Only or Hidden check box. When you close the Properties dialog box for a folder, Windows asks whether you want the changes to apply to the files and folders within the folder, or just to the folder itself.

Sharing Printers on a LAN

Sharing a printer on a LAN has two steps. First you sit at the computer that is directly attached to the printer and configure the printer to be a *network printer* or *shared printer* so that other computers on the network can print to it. Then you configure the other computers on the LAN so that they know about the network printer—with luck, Windows on each computer automatically detects the existence of the newly sharable printer and installs the new printer driver itself.

 Not all printers come with printer drivers that work for sharing the printer on a LAN.

Making Your Printer Sharable

If you want other people on the LAN to be able to print on your printer, first install the printer on your own computer and make sure that you can print to it (see Chapter 14, section "Setting Up a Local Printer"). Once the printer is correctly installed, you can share it.

The computer that the printer is attached to is called a *print server*. The print server can also be someone's PC, the usual arrangement on a small network, or a computer that does nothing else. You give the printer a share name, the name that other people will see when they connect to the printer. The share name can be the type of printer (for example, HP1100A), the group that uses the printer (for example, Accounting), or some other name. A straightforward name makes it easier for others on the network to figure out which printer they are using.

To share the printer so that other computers on the LAN can print to it, follow these steps:

1. Choose Start | Printers And Faxes to see the Printers And Faxes folder. (If this command doesn't appear on your Start menu, choose Start | Control Panel | Printers And Other Hardware | Printers And Faxes.)

2. Right-click the printer you want to share and choose Sharing from the Shortcut menu (or select the printer icon and click Share This Printer in the Task pane). You see the Properties dialog box for the printer, with the Sharing tab displayed, as shown in Figure 30-3. (Depending on what type of network you use, you might see different settings.)

3. Click the Shared This Printer radio button.

4. Give your printer a share name.

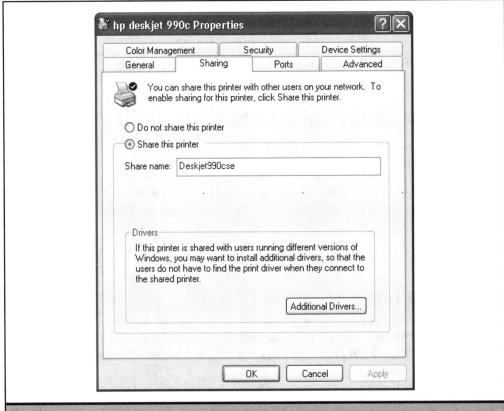

Figure 30-3. *Giving the printer a name and description when you share it*

5. Close the printer's Properties dialog box. The icon for the printer you just shared now has a tiny hand under it, indicating that the printer is shared.

To turn sharing off, open the Properties dialog box for the printer and select the Do Not Share This Printer radio button on the Sharing tab.

Printing to a Network Printer from Another Computer

When Windows detects a shared printer on another computer on the LAN, it tries to install the printer's driver automatically. When you print from an application, check the list of available printers—the list may already include shared printers on other computers. To see the list of printers you can use, choose Start | Printers And Faxes (or Start | Control Panel | Printers And Other Hardware | Printers And Faxes) to display the Printers And Faxes folder. The icon for a shared printer has a cable beneath it.

If the printer doesn't appear on the list, you need to install a driver for the printer. Here's how:

1. Open the Printers And Faxes window.

2. Click Add A Printer. You see the Add Printer Wizard. The wizard asks the following:

   - **Whether you're installing a local or network printer**   You're installing a network printer.

   - **The network path for the printer**   Unless you can type the path for the printer from memory, use the Browse button to find it. To find the printer, first find the computer to which it is attached by expanding the My Network Places hierarchy; click My Network Places, then Entire Network, then the computer to which the printer is attached, then the name of the printer.

   - **Which driver to install**   If you already have a driver installed for this type of printer, the wizard asks whether you want to keep the existing driver or install a new one (one of these options will be recommended). If you don't have a driver installed, the wizard prompts you to install one—you'll probably need your Windows XP CD-ROM or a printer driver from another source (many can be found at the printer manufacturers' web site).

   - **What name you want to call the printer**   This should be a name that enables you to identify the printer. If you have three DeskJets on your network, you probably don't want to call it just "DeskJet"—instead, you might want to call it "Cindy's DeskJet" since it's attached to Cindy's machine. That way, when you print to this printer, you'll know where to go to pick up your printout.

   - **Whether you want this printer to be your default printer**   If you want to print automatically to this printer every time you print, then the answer is Yes. If you usually want to print to another printer, choose No.

Once you've completed these steps, the printer appears in your Printers And Faxes window, like this (this figure shows the shortcut menu that appears when you right-click a printer, too):

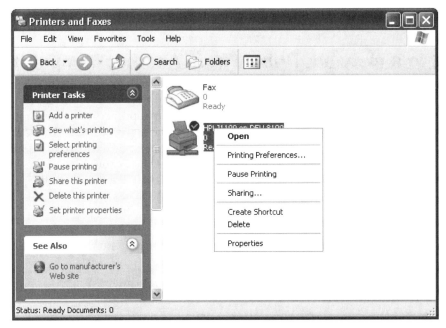

You can print to the shared printer from this computer any time you want. If you defined the shared printer as your default printer, then anything you print automatically goes to that printer. If you didn't define the network printer as the default printer, then you have to choose it from the list of defined printers before you print. This is usually done on the Print dialog box of the application you are using.

If the network printer is unavailable, any print jobs will be held on your computer until the printer is again available.

A quick way to connect to a network printer is by using the Run dialog box. Choose Start | Run and type UNC path of printer. For example, if the printer is called DeskJet900 and it's attached to a computer called Inspiron8000, type **\\Inspiron8000\DeskJet900** *as the UNC path. When you click OK, your computer connects to the printer.*

If you need to print to a network computer from DOS programs, you can type the **NET USE** command in a Command Prompt window (see Chapter 4). At the command prompt, type:

```
net use lp2 \\computername\printername
```

This command maps the LP2 (second parallel printer) port to the printer you specify.

For more information about printing, installing and configuring a printer and changing the default printer, refer to Chapter 14.

The Complete Reference

Chapter 31

Connecting Your LAN to the Internet

813

I f you have a LAN, connecting the whole LAN to the Internet makes more sense than giving each individual computer on the LAN a separate connection. By connecting the LAN to the Internet, all of the PCs on the LAN can share one Internet account and one phone line or cable connection. Large companies have connected their internal networks to the Internet for years, and small offices and home LANs can do the same. In fact, sharing an Internet connection is a good reason to connect your computers into a LAN.

For the PCs on a LAN to use the Internet, you must configure each PC to communicate using TCP/IP, the Internet's communication protocol (see Chapter 29, section "IP Addressing"). Then a program or device must route the TCP/IP information between the LAN and the Internet; you can use a dedicated device (a router) or a gateway program running on a PC.

Windows XP comes with Internet Connection Sharing (ICS), a gateway program that can route information between a LAN and the Internet. This chapter describes how to configure the ICS server program on the computer connected to the Internet and the ICS client settings on the other computers on the LAN. Once ICS (or another gateway) is installed, everyone on the LAN can send and receive e-mail, browse the Web, and use other Internet programs at the same time. Windows comes with troubleshooting tools for making sure that your ICS system works.

If you have more than one LAN in your home or office (for example, a cabled LAN and a wireless LAN), you can connect them together via bridging, a service that ties two physical LANs together into one larger LAN. Bridging is a simpler service than ICS; we discuss the differences in this chapter.

 Virtual Private Networking (VPN) is a system that lets your organization extend a private LAN over the Internet. Windows comes with a VPN program that enables your computer to connect to a virtual private network.

Methods of Connecting a LAN to the Internet

Communication on the Internet uses the TCP/IP protocol; messages are addressed to other computers using numeric IP (Internet Protocol) addresses. To share an Internet connection, the computers on your LAN must be able to communicate with TCP/IP. The computers can also communicate on the LAN with another protocol (for example, a LAN might use NetBEUI for file and printer sharing on the LAN and TCP/IP for Internet Connection Sharing).

The device or program that connects your LAN to the Internet acts as a *gateway*, passing messages between the computers on the LAN and computers on the Internet, and possibly controlling what types of information can pass.

What Does a Gateway Do?

An Internet gateway can perform the following tasks:

- **Routing packets of data between the LAN and the Internet**   The most basic function of a gateway is to pass packets of data from computers on your LAN out to the Internet and vice versa.

- **Translating between the IP address on the LAN and the IP addresses on the Internet**   Computers on a LAN usually use private, LAN-only IP addresses, assigned by a DHCP server on the LAN. Computers on the Internet use publicly visible IP addresses that are usually assigned by your ISP. A gateway accepts packets (messages) from the LAN, replaces the private IP address with its own ISP-supplied IP address, and passes the packet along to the Internet. When a reply returns, the gateway figures out which computer on the LAN the reply is intended for, replaces the gateway's address with that of the real destination, and sends the reply along to the computer that made the request. To the rest of the Internet, all packets from the LAN appear to be from the gateway. This service is called *Network Address Translation* (*NAT*). All gateways to networks that use private addresses must perform this task.

- **Address assignment**   NAT gateways invariably include a DHCP server to assign private addresses to the other computers on the LAN.

- **Controlling the types of information that can flow between the Internet and your LAN**   The gateway can act as a *firewall* and control what services on internal computers are visible to hosts on the Internet (see Chapter 32). This adds an important level of security, since outsiders cannot exploit security holes in services that they can't see. Computers on small LANs usually offer no services at all to outside users. A few peer-to-peer applications such as online chat require that the user's computer act as a server to its peers; you'll have to adjust the firewall settings if you use them.

- **Caching**   The gateway can store information that has been requested from the Internet so that if a user requests the same information, the gateway can provide it without having to get it from the Internet again.

- **Logging usage of the Internet**   The gateway can log all packets that pass between the LAN and the Internet so you can have a record of who has access to your LAN from the Internet and what Internet services your LAN users have used.

ICS provides address translation and DHCP and can optionally use the Windows XP Internet Connection Firewall. Other gateway programs, called *proxy servers*, also provide caching (storing web pages and other information for reuse) and logging (so you can track what people are using the Internet for).

Devices That Can Act as Gateways

Three kinds of devices are commonly used as gateways, connecting LANs to the Internet:

- **Routers**   A "black box" that connects to your LAN hub or switch and to a phone line (dial-up, ISDN line, DSL line, or cable modem connection). NAT, DHCP, and firewall software are built into the router. All you have to do is cable it to your LAN, connect your phone line or cable modem, plug it into power, and your LAN is on the Internet. Routers can be the simplest and most effective way to connect your LAN to the Internet. You connect your Internet connection (phone line or cable Internet cable) to the router and run a LAN cable from the router to the LAN's hub or switch.

- **UNIX or Linux systems**   Because the Internet was built on UNIX systems, lots of excellent TCP/IP communication software comes with most UNIX and Linux systems. Some "black box" routers are actually computers running UNIX or Linux, but you can often set up your own on an old PC. (A 133-MHz Pentium is plenty fast to be a router.) You can run a wide variety of firewall software, as well as web server, POP (e-mail) server, or other Internet server software on the UNIX or Linux system. The UNIX or Linux system needs two connections: an Internet connection (phone line or cable Internet cable) and a LAN connection (cable to the LAN's hub or switch).

- **Windows systems running connection-sharing software**   A Windows XP, Me, 98, 2000, or NT 4 system can act as a router, running a gateway program. The Windows system connects to the Internet over a phone line or cable connection, and the gateway program provides the IP address translation. If you run proxy server or firewall programs, the Windows system also provides security: Windows XP comes with a built-in firewall (Internet Connection Firewall, described in Chapter 22).

> **Caution**   *Even though DSL and cable Internet connections use the same cabling as a LAN, don't plug the DSL or cable Internet cable into your LAN's hub or switch. The DSL or cable Internet must connect to a PC or router so that you have a gateway between the Internet and the LAN. (If your hub includes router functions, this warning doesn't apply.)*

Should You Use ICS or a Hardware Router?

Several vendors such as Linksys and D-Link sell dedicated routers for homes and small offices. These physically resemble network hubs, with one Ethernet jack for the connection to the outside world (cable modem or DSL), in addition to the Ethernet jacks for the computers on your LAN. Built-in software provides the same features as ICS, including NAT, DHCP, firewall, and even PPPoE if your DSL line requires it. For the most part, they're self-configuring, but you can control them through your browser if you need to adjust something.

We've seen these routers advertised for as little as $40, probably less than you'd pay for a hub and a second Ethernet card for the computer running ICS. At that price, we'd suggest getting the router and forget ICS if you're sharing a cable Internet or DSL connection. With a router, you don't have to leave the ICS server computer on all the time (or at least whenever any computer needs Internet access).

Software and Hardware for a Windows-Based Gateway

If you use a Windows system running NAT (Network Address Translation), proxy server, or firewall software, the system has two connections: one to the LAN (using a network interface card) and the other to the Internet (using a modem for dial-up or another network interface card or USB port for DSL or cable Internet connection). Previous versions of Windows needed third-party gateway software, but Windows XP comes with Internet Connection Sharing and Internet Connection Firewall, which are easy to install and set up and are adequate for a gateway for small LANs.

More sophisticated gateway software is available from third-party vendors such as Deerfield **www.deerfield.com**, Ositis **www.winproxy.com**, and Sygate **soho.sygate.com**.

 *Test the security of your LAN's Internet connection by going to the Gibson Research Corporation's web site at **grc.com**. Follow the links to his Shields UP! service, which can check how vulnerable your computer is to attack from the Internet.*

Installing and Using Internet Connection Sharing

Windows XP's Internet Connection Sharing (or ICS) provides routing and NAT, and doesn't provide caching or logging. ICS allows one computer—the *ICS server*—to provide an Internet connection for all the computers on a LAN. The ICS host runs the ICS server program. The other computers—the *ICS clients*—on the LAN can run Windows Me, 9*x*, 2000, NT, older Windows versions, or other operating systems, as long as they support TCP/IP.

ICS uses private IP addresses in the range 192.168.0.*xxx*. ICS includes a DHCP (Dynamic Host Configuration Protocol) server, which runs on the ICS server and assigns IP addresses to the rest of the computers on your LAN automatically (see Chapter 29, section "IP Addressing"). ICS assigns the address 192.168.0.1 to the ICS server itself. You can manually assign static addresses in the 192.168.0.*xxx* range to computers on your LAN if you want, setting the network gateway and DNS server to 192.168.0.1, but there's no reason not to let the DHCP server do the work. (We've had trouble getting ICS to work reliably with static IP addresses.)

Figure 31-1 shows a LAN with five computers, including the ICS server computer, with private IP addresses from 192.168.0.1 to 192.168.0.5. The ICS server has a separate IP address for communicating with the Internet over a cable modem; this address is assigned by the ISP (in the figure, it has the address 24.62.168.33).

ICS includes these components:

- **DHCP Allocator**   Assigns IP addresses to ICS client computers on the LAN
- **DNS Proxy**   Translates between IP addresses and Internet host names (like www.yahoo.com), using your ISP's DNS server

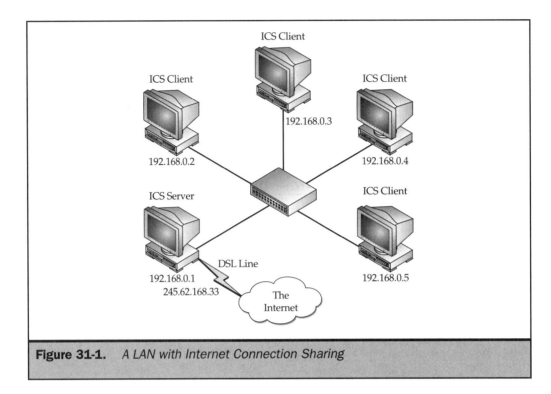

Figure 31-1. *A LAN with Internet Connection Sharing*

■ **Network Address Translation (NAT)**   When passing packets of information between the LAN and the Internet, replaces the private IP address with the ICS server's IP address, and vice versa

The next section describes how to install ICS on the ICS server and how to configure the rest of the computers on the LAN to share the connection.

Installing ICS on the ICS Server

One computer on your LAN, the ICS server, runs the ICS program. This computer must connect to the Internet with a dial-up account, ISDN line, DSL line, cable modem, or other Internet connection—make sure that you have this Internet connection working (see Chapter 22).

The Network Setup Wizard can't set up your computer as an ICS server if it's not connected to the Internet or to a LAN. It also doesn't work if another computer is already acting as the Internet gateway for the LAN, running a DHCP server, or is using the IP address 192.168.0.1.

Configuring the ICS Server Using the Network Setup Wizard

The easiest way to install and configure ICS is by running the Network Setup Wizard (see Chapter 29, section "Adding Your Computer to a TCP/IP Peer-to-Peer LAN").

The wizard can create a floppy disk with a client version of the wizard that you can use to configure the other Windows Me, 9*x*, 2000, and NT computers on the LAN. You can also use your Windows XP CD-ROM instead of a floppy to configure the other computers.

On the computer that has the Internet connection, run the Network Setup Wizard by choosing Start | All Programs | Accessories | Communications | Network Setup Wizard or choose Start | Control Panel, click Network And Internet Connections, click Network Connections, and click Set Up A Home Or Small Office Network in the Task pane. As the wizard asks you questions, make these choices:

- **Select A Connection Method** Choose This Computer Connects Directly To The Internet. You must already have created a dial-up, DSL, ISDN, or cable connection.

- **Select Your Internet Connection** The wizard displays a list of the connections (both Internet and LAN connections) on your computer. Choose the connection to the Internet, as shown here:

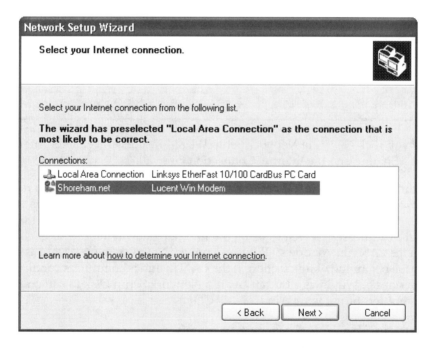

- **Give This Computer A Description And Name** Type a description of your computer in the Computer Description box and a unique name for your computer in the Computer Name box. The boxes may already be filled in if you entered this information when you installed Windows or when you set up your LAN.

- **Name Your Network** In the Workgroup Name box, type the name of your workgroup. The workgroup name must match the workgroup name of the other computers on the LAN. When you click Next, the wizard confirms your settings, like this (the Internet Connection Firewall is turned on by default):

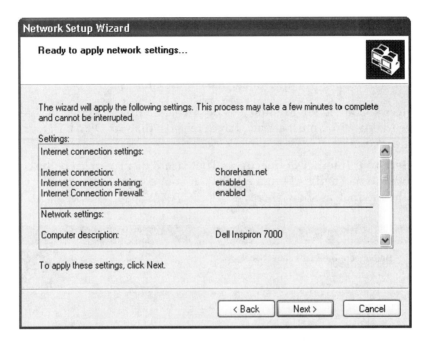

When you click Next, the Network Setup Wizard installs and enables Internet Connection Sharing and the Internet Connection Firewall.

■ **You're Almost Done**   If you haven't already set up your LAN, you need to configure each other computer on the LAN to work with the settings you've just installed (that is, your ICS server computer is the DHCP server that hands out IP addresses, as well as being the Internet gateway). If the other computers on the LAN run Windows XP, you can run the Network Setup Wizard as described at the beginning of this section. If the LAN includes computers running older versions of Windows, you can create a Network Setup Disk to run on those computers or use your Windows XP CD.

Configuring the ICS Server Manually

If your LAN and Internet connections both work, there's a quicker way to turn on Internet Connection Sharing. On the computer that has the Internet connection, follow these steps:

1. Open the Network Connections window (choose Start | Control Panel | Network And Internet Connections | Network Connections).

2. Click the Internet connection (not the LAN connection).

3. Click Change Settings Of This Connection in the Network Tasks listed in the Task pane. You see the Properties dialog box for the Internet connection.

4. Click the Advanced tab. You see the Internet Connection Firewall and Internet Connection Sharing settings, shown in Figure 31-2. The settings are as follows:

- **Protect My Computer And Network By Limiting Or Preventing Access To This Computer From The Network**   Select this check box to turn on the Internet Connection Firewall, which we recommend for all Internet connections (see Chapter 22).

- **Allow Other Network Users To Connect Through This Computer's Internet Connection**   Select this check box to turn on ICS or clear the check box to turn ICS off.

- **Establish A Dial-Up Connection Whenever A Computer On My Network Attempts To Access The Internet**   If you don't have an always-on connection, select this check box to enable dial-on-demand.

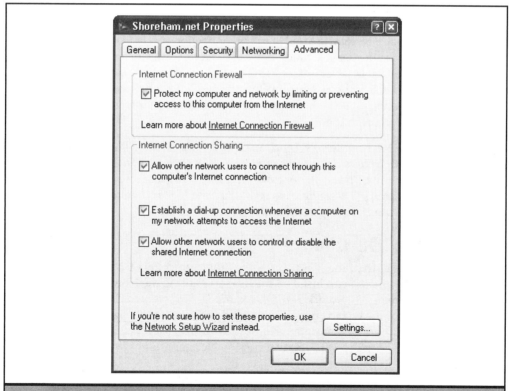

Figure 31-2.   *Checking your Internet Connection Sharing settings*

■ **Allow Other Network Users To Control Or Disable The Shared Internet Connection**   Select this check box to allow other people on the LAN to disconnect the Internet connection (hang up) or reconnect (if dial-on-demand is turned off).

5. Click OK to put the changes into effect.

Testing the ICS Server

To test whether your computer is working as the ICS server, try connecting to the Internet from the ICS server—you should connect as if ICS weren't installed. Browsing, e-mail, and other Internet services should be unaffected. Right-click the Local Area Network connection in the Network Connections window and choose Status to see whether the LAN is working and confirm that your IP address is 192.168.0.1.

ICS Server Configuration Details

Make sure that the Internet connection works. To test it on the ICS server, connect to the Internet and browse the Web or send and receive e-mail.

Make sure that the ICS server is set to connect to the Internet whenever it receives a request to connect. To set your Internet options to dial the Internet on demand, choose Start | Control Panel | Network And Internet Connections and click Internet Options to display the Internet Properties dialog box (see Chapter 22). Click the Connections tab and choose Always Dial My Default Connection so that Windows can connect to the Internet on demand. Click the Settings button and make sure that your user name and password are entered so that the ICS server can connect to the Internet without waiting for you to type this information.

If you ran the Network Setup Wizard, take a look at the Nsw.log file, which is stored in your C:\Windows folder (or whatever folder Windows is installed in). Open it in Notepad or any other text editor or word processor. It lists the actions that the wizard took when installing and configuring your LAN and ICS, including searching your system for networking components and deciding which to use.

Configuring the ICS Clients

You must configure each of the ICS *clients*—the other computers that share the ICS connection to the Internet. If you installed the ICS server using the Network Setup Wizard and you chose to create a Network Setup Disk, the wizard created a floppy disk that contains a version of the wizard program with which you can configure the ICS clients. The wizard configures only computers running Windows Me, 9x, 2000, or NT 4. For ICS clients running Windows XP, you can run the Network Setup Wizard that is part of Windows.

When you configure a computer as an ICS client, you add TCP/IP as a network protocol, if it's not already installed, and set the computer to get its IP address from a DHCP server (the one that is running on the ICS server).

Configuring an ICS Client with the Network Setup Wizard

To configure your computer as an ICS client, insert the floppy disk that the Network Setup Wizard created, choose Start | Run, type **a:setup**, and click Open. Or, insert your Windows XP CD-ROM into the client's CD drive, and in the Welcome screen click Perform Additional Tasks and then Set Up A Home Or Small Office Network. Or, if your computer runs Windows XP, choose Start | All Programs | Accessories | Communications | Network Setup Wizard. Depending on your version of Windows, the wizard may have to install some drivers and reboot before proceeding.

As the wizard asks you questions, make these choices:

- **Select A Connection Method**   Select This Computer Connects To The Internet Through Another Computer On My Network Or Through A Residential Gateway.

- **Give This Computer A Description And Name**   Type a unique name for your computer and a description (this description doesn't have to be unique and appears only in the My Network Places window).

- **Name Your Network**   Type the name for your workgroup (see Chapter 29, section "Identifying the Computer"). Use the same workgroup name you entered for the ICS server. When you click Next, the wizard confirms your settings, like this:

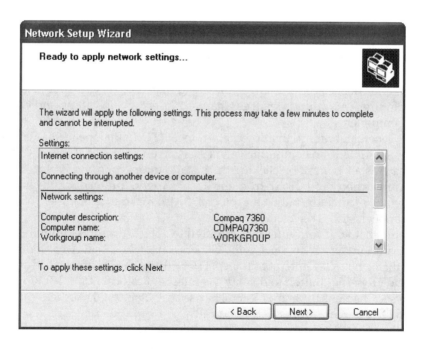

As the wizard completes, it may instruct you to insert the setup disk for the version of Windows running on the client (Windows 98, for example) so it can install some driver files and will then probably reboot.

Testing Your Internet Connection from an ICS Client

When you ask a browser or other Internet program to display a web page or send or receive e-mail on an ICS client computer, Windows passes your the Internet request along to the ICS server, which connects to the Internet on your behalf. If the ICS server was already logged into the Internet, you should see your web page or e-mail right away; if the ICS server has to connect, there's the usual delay in logging in. Once the ICS server and clients are configured correctly, users on all ICS servers and clients can use the Internet connection simultaneously.

To test your connection from an ICS server, try these actions:

- Run Internet Explorer (or another browser) and try to display a web page.

- Run the Ping program and try to ping the ICS server at 192.168.0.1 (see Chapter 22). If that works, try pinging a computer on the Internet, like **www.yahoo.com**.

ICS Client Configuration Details

Here are ways you can check the configuration of your ICS client.

Check that your computer is configured to communicate over the LAN using TCP/IP. Choose Start | Control Panel | Network And Internet Connections | Network Connections to display the Network Connections window. Right-click your Local Area Connection and choose Properties from the menu that appears to display the Properties dialog box for the LAN connection (see Chapter 29, section "Installing and Configuring Network Components").

On the General tab, check that Internet Protocol (TCP/IP) appears and is selected so that your computer can communicate via TCP/IP on the LAN. If the TCP/IP entries don't appear, install TCP/IP by clicking the Install button, choosing Protocol, clicking the Add button, choosing TCP/IP from the list of network protocols, and clicking OK (see Chapter 29, section "Installing a Protocol"). Also make sure that the QoS Packet Scheduler appears and is selected.

Make sure that your computer is configured to get its IP address from the DHCP server that runs on the ICS server. On the General tab of the Local Area Connections Properties dialog box, click Internet Protocol (TCP/IP) on the list of installed components and click the Properties button to display the Internet Protocol (TCP/IP) Properties dialog box (see Chapter 22). On the General tab, select Obtain An IP Address Automatically and Obtain DNS Server Address Automatically.

Check the TCP/IP settings on the ICS client by opening the Network Connections window, right-clicking the Local Area Connection, and choosing Status from the menu that appears. Click the Support tab, shown here:

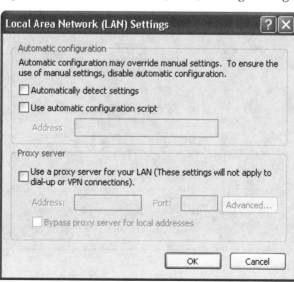

The settings should be the same as those in this illustration, except for the IP Address, which may end with a number other than 2.

Check to see that your computer is not configured to connect to the Internet directly. Choose Start | Control Panel, click Network And Internet Options, and click Internet Options. On the Connections tab of the Internet Properties dialog box, select either Never Dial A Connection or Dial Whenever A Network Connection Is Not Present. (If no connections appear in the Dial-Up And Virtual Private Network Settings box, the Never Dial A Connection setting is gray, but it's still selected.)

Click the LAN Settings button on the Connections tab of the Internet Properties dialog box to display the Local Area Network (LAN) Settings dialog box, shown here:

These are settings you might need to use if you connect to the Internet using a proxy server other than ICS. None of the check boxes should be selected for use with peer-to-peer LANs that use ICS.

Using Internet Connection Sharing

Once you've configured the ICS server and the ICS clients, ICS works unobtrusively. From either the server or a client, run a browser, e-mail program, or other program that works with the Internet. When the program sends information to or requests information from the Internet, the ICS server connects to the Internet to provide the Internet connection.

To see how many people are sharing the Internet connection on the ICS server, double-click the ICS icon on the notification area of the taskbar (or click it and choose Status from the menu that appears). A small dialog box pops up, telling you how many computers are sharing the connection, including the ICS server itself.

Controlling ICS from Client Computers

If you checked the box to allow other network users to control the shared Internet connection, you can use the Internet Gateway program on each client computer. You run it by choosing Start | All Programs | Accessories | Communications | Internet Gateway. The exact appearance varies depending on the version of Windows; this is what it looks like on Windows 98:

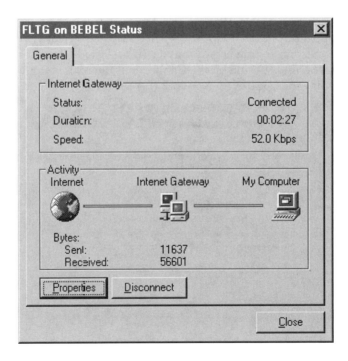

If the shared connection is always on, one button is Enable or Disable—to turn the shared connection on and off. If it's dial-up or PPPoE, it's Connect or Disconnect.

Click Properties in the Internet Gateway program to see a Properties window. A check box lets you put an icon for the connection in the System Tray so you can right-click and select Connect or Disconnect there. The Services tab in the Properties window lets you control the firewall on the ICS server (see Chapter 22). (To control the firewall on the client computer, open the connection on the Network Connections menu, although if you have a firewall on the server, there's little advantage to a second firewall on the client.)

Recovering from Server Restarts

If you reboot your ICS server, the DHCP server will probably not reassign client addresses in the same order as it did originally. This will cause clients to act as though their network connections have failed. Fortunately, it is easy to have the clients get their new addresses. Open a Command Prompt window, and type

```
IPCONFIG /RELEASE
IPCONFIG /RENEW
```

The first command discards the old address, and the second command gets the new address from the DHCP server.

On clients running older versions of Windows, run WINIPCFG and click its Release and Renew buttons.

Troubleshooting ICS

If you can't get connected to the Internet from an ICS client computer, here are some things to try.

- Give the ICS server time to connect to the Internet, especially if it uses a dial-up phone line. The program on the ICS client may time out before the ICS server gets connected to your Internet account and ICS passes your request along.

- If you have restarted the ICS server since you restarted the ICS client, restart the client computer.

- Test your Internet connection from the ICS server (as described in "Testing the ICS Server" earlier in this chapter) and test your LAN connection from an ICS client (as described in "Testing Your Internet Connection from an ICS Client " earlier in this chapter).

- Run the Internet Connection Sharing Troubleshooter on the ICS server and at least one ICS client. Choose Start | Help And Support to display the Help And Support Center window, click Fixing A Problem, click Networking Problems, and click Internet Connection Sharing Troubleshooter.

Using NAT with Internet Applications

Network Address Translation (NAT) works invisibly with most Internet applications, including web browsing and e-mail. A few applications have trouble, either because the computer on the LAN has to act as a server, or because the application is sensitive to the TCP/IP port number used for the connection.

For applications that act as servers (peer-to-peer file transfer and chat, mostly), you'll have to adjust the firewall settings on the ICS server to enable the port number(s) that the application uses (see Chapter 22).

For applications that are sensitive to port numbers, either the NAT software has to be aware of the application and translate appropriately, or the application has to work with the NAT server. FTP falls into the first category; although FTP is sensitive to port numbers, every NAT server can do the necessary translations in a way that's invisible to the FTP client. You may have to tell your FTP program to use *passive data transfers* for the NAT translations to work.

Other applications can use *NAT Traversal* to deal with NAT translation issues. This is a facility based on UPnP that lets applications communicate with the NAT process on the gateway computer or router to detect and control the translations that NAT performs. NAT Traversal was invented in mid 2001 and is only slowly being adopted. ICS provides NAT Traversal, and client programs running on Windows XP. It's also available to applications running on Windows Me/98 if you've run the Network Setup Wizard and installed Internet Explorer 6.0.

Deleting Internet Connection Sharing

To delete ICS, you need to delete and install the driver for the network interface card (NIC). Click Start and right-click My Computer to display the System Properties dialog box. Click the Hardware tab and the Device Manager button. Delete the network adapter entry. Restart Windows, and Windows should detect and reinstall the NIC driver without ICS. You may need to reconfigure your LAN settings.

The Complete Reference

Chapter 32

Network, Internet, and Web Security

Communication security ensures that the data you transmit and receive through the Internet or an intranet is sent to and received from the actual systems with which you intend to communicate, as opposed to another system impersonating the desired system. It also ensures that messages are sent and received without being intercepted or spied upon.

This chapter discusses viruses and how to avoid catching them, how to control what Internet Explorer downloads when you browse the Web, browsing secure web sites, and how to send and receive secure e-mail messages. Windows XP includes an Internet Connection Firewall that you can turn on to protect your computer from malicious Internauts (see Chapter 22).

Note *User accounts and passwords for multiple people using the same computer are described in Chapter 6. Security settings for people sharing files over a LAN are described in Chapter 30.*

For more information about Windows security, see the Microsoft Security web site at **www.microsoft.com/security** and the Microsoft TechNet web site at **www.microsoft.com/ technet/security**. A good check list is available at LabMice.net (**www.labmice.net/articles/winxpsecuritychecklist.htm**).

The Microsoft Baseline Security Advisor

Microsoft has written a program that can check your computer for incorrect security settings. Go to **www.microsoft.com/technet/security/tools/Tools/ mbsahome.asp** to download the Microsoft Baseline Security Advisor. Or go to Microsoft's support site at **support.microsoft.com** and search for article Q320454. The program is small—about 2.5MB. It can scan the computer on which it is running or other computers on a LAN or the Internet. It displays a security report like this:

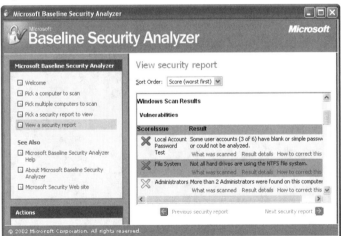

The report includes security information about user accounts, file systems, Windows updates, Internet Explorer settings, and other configuration options.

Protecting Your System from Viruses and Worms

A *virus* is a self-reproducing program that can infect files on one computer but needs help in order to find other systems to infect (like people sharing programs). A *worm* is a self-reproducing program that can send itself to other systems (e-mail viruses are actually worms). Some viruses and worms are just annoying, taking up space on your system or displaying an annoying message, but many others are destructive, deleting or altering files or clogging up Internet e-mail systems with thousands of unwanted messages. The sidebar "How Viruses Spread" contains more information.

Types of Virus Files

Viruses and worms can be stored in several types of files:

- **.exe, .com, .bat, .msi, .mso, or .pif (program files); scraps; or shortcuts**   These viruses and worms run when they are opened (clicked or double-clicked in Windows Explorer or Outlook Express, for example). If Windows is configured not to show file extensions, you may not be able to tell easily which files have these extensions. (Tell Windows to display filename extensions by choosing Start | My Computer, choosing Tools | Folder Options, clicking the View tab, and deselecting the Hide Extensions For Known File Types check box.)

- **.doc (Word documents), .xls (Excel spreadsheets), or .mdb (Access databases)**   These files may contain viruses and worms written in Microsoft Word, Excel, or Access macro languages. The macros (customized automation instructions) usually run when you open the file. Because Word and Excel are the most popular programs that run macros, Word documents and Excel spreadsheets are the most common macro virus carriers.

- **.vbs (Visual Basic Script files)**   These viruses and worms are written in Visual Basic and run when you click or double-click them. Visual Basic is a programming language used, among other things, to write macros for the Office suite of applications, including Outlook 2002.

For a more complete list of file types that might contain viruses, see article Q262631, "Information About the Outlook E-mail Security Update" in Microsoft's Knowledge Base: go to **support.microsoft.com** and search for the article number.

 *Scraps, a Windows file type created by cut-and-paste operations, can contain executable files (including viruses and worms) that appear to be other types of (harmless) files. An article on this issue is on the Web at **pc-help.org/security/scrap.htm**.*

How Viruses Spread

The commonly cited psychological reasons for individuals to open suspicious e-mails are fear, greed, and sex. The notorious Melissa worm by David Smith was started by simply being posted to the **alt.sex** newsgroup. Smith asked that the file not be circulated, so of course, it was. That single posting to a newsgroup was the only action that Smith performed to spread his worm throughout the world, causing millions of dollars in damages and, in some cases, days of mail server downtime for some major companies.

A new tactic is to appeal to the recipient's ego. The SirCam worm drew in the viewer by asking for sage advice on the "subject" included in the attached "message." The attachment was the worm in disguise. Recent viruses forge their return addresses so the message appears to be from a friend, and some send text found in your outbox.

So, the moral of the story is: If you receive a message from someone you don't know, or from someone you know but didn't expect to receive a file from, approach it with caution. If it has an attachment, just delete it. If you're not sure, let it sit unopened in your inbox for a few days, while you check the antivirus and e-mail hoax web sites. A one-day delay in opening an attachment might be enough for you to hear about the danger of the virus.

Preventing Infection by Viruses

The best prevention for viruses is to avoid getting infected in the first place (practice safe computing). If you do get infected, tools are available to clean your system.

Avoiding Getting Infected

The generally accepted method of preventing viruses from successfully attacking your computer is the use of antivirus software that detect known viruses before they run and infect your computer. Of course, there is the tried-and-true method of not downloading or opening anything that you cannot verify, validate, or otherwise determine the source of.

Note *The Internet isn't the only way to catch viruses. If you commonly move files from one place to another using removable media (for example, floppy disks, writable CD-ROMs, Zip disks, or Jaz disks) then you need to be careful. The data on a disk, whether it be from school, office, or library, likely came from the Internet. This simple fact makes it possible for the disk to contain a virus. Office networks are typically more secure, because your LAN administrator has probably installed antivirus software, but don't take that for granted. School networks can be less secure because of insufficient staffing resources. Public access points like ones in libraries, copy shops, or cyber cafés are a mixed bag. Your best bet is to be wary of any data coming to your computer from the outside. Even commercial software has been known to be a transmission source for viruses.*

When in doubt, wait at least 24 hours before opening attachments, and check an antivirus web site in the meantime (see "Sources of Antivirus Information" later in this chapter). And back up your entire system regularly, as described in Chapter 9!

Antivirus Programs   Do *not* wait until you have contracted a virus to install an antivirus program. An antivirus program can't prevent infection if it's not running. Buying and installing an antivirus application is a small price to pay, compared to losing all of your work for a week, all of your carefully collected bookmarks, the hours that you spent making all of your CDs into MP3 files, your family pictures from last year's picnic in Hawaii—whatever your most treasured files include. Here are two of the most popular and effective antivirus programs:

- **Symantec Norton AntiVirus, at (www.symantec.com/nav)**   Norton AntiVirus is a complete solution. You can go with the simple Norton AntiVirus or pop for the complete Internet Security Family Edition suite of security applications— the Family Edition is a particularly good deal, including a personal firewall that is particularly well suited to protecting broadband (cable and DSL) users.

- **McAfee VirusScan, at www.mcafee.com**   McAfee has lately turned many of their programs into online applications—online information services that are updated 24 hours a day. They also offer an application update service that tracks what you have and sends you updates as they become available.

After you install an antivirus program, arrange to get regular updates. Good antivirus programs update themselves by downloading lists of viruses from the manufacturer's web site automatically. You can also visit the manufacturer's web site and download new virus lists yourself. An antivirus program won't protect you from the latest virus if your virus lists are months old.

Once you have an antivirus program installed, configured, and running according to the documentation that came with the program, the antivirus program scans all incoming files (via e-mail and Web) for viruses. For example, the antivirus program might display a dialog box while you are retrieving your e-mail, reporting that a message contains a worm and offering to delete it for you. Some antivirus programs also scan your hard disk regularly to look for viruses that might have sneaked through. If the program sees a virus, it displays a message telling you what to do.

Practicing Safe Computing Online   Here's a brief list of ways to protect yourself when you're online:

- Do not open an attachment that you either did not specifically request or that would not normally be unexpected. If a colleague sends you a file that you asked for, it's likely to be safe. However, if someone named GaToR I RoTaG or something similar sends you a file, or if a colleague sends you a file that you weren't expecting and doesn't look related to your work, don't touch it. Similarly, if someone you know (whose address book you are likely to be in) sends a file you aren't expecting, write back and ask about it *before* opening the file.

■ Before opening an attachment, wait a few hours or days. In the meantime, check an antivirus web site for news of new viruses and worms.

■ Do not download files from sources you are not familiar with. Stick to known, reputable web-based software libraries like ZDNet (**www.zdnet.com**), Tucows (**www.tucows.com**), Stroud's CWSApps (**cws.internet.com**), and C I Net (**www.cnet.com**) or the web sites of well-known hardware and software manufacturers, as sources for downloadable software. Many pornographic sites require you to download a viewer program: think twice, since these programs have been known to contain dangerous viruses.

■ Do not accept any file that is offered unsolicited. If you receive an e-mail notifying you that you have won a contest and you can click a URL in the message to download your prize, think again. Did you sign up for a contest? Legitimate sources invariably draw from an existing customer base and rely on word of mouth and advertising campaigns to get new customers, not random free give-aways.

■ Ask friends and family not to forward too many jokes to you (or choose *one* friend to be your Internet joke source). This reduces your potential for infection, as well as cutting down on your e-mail volume.

Avoiding Outlook and Outlook Express   Many people believe that your computer can't get infected by a virus simply by opening an e-mail message that has no attachments. This used to be true, but is no longer. Formatted e-mail messages can carry viruses, too, because some versions of Outlook and Outlook Express automatically open and display attachments. Many viruses have been written specifically to exploit security holes in Outlook and Outlook Express. Microsoft has issued many security patches to close security holes, but new vulnerabilities keep appearing. As Microsoft finds new security problems, they usually respond quickly with patches. Be sure to use Windows Automatic Updates to download and install these patches (see Chapter 36).

Tip *One simple solution to this and many other worms is not to use older versions of Outlook or Outlook Express. The most recent versions, Outlook 2002 and Outlook Express 6, respectively, have vastly improved handling of known viruses. If you use Eudora, an excellent and widely-used e-mail program from Qualcomm, Inc. (at www.eudora.com), or Pegasus Mail, a popular free mail program (at www.pmail.com) you can avoid most viruses by not opening attached files.*

Chapter 23 contains information on how to configure Outlook Express to avoid some viruses (see Chapter 23, section "Protecting Yourself from E-Mail Viruses").

Knowing When You're Infected   You may find out that your system is infected when you see a strange message telling you that you're a victim. Some other ways of telling are as follows (although all but the last can be signs of other Windows problems):

- Your system slows down (especially programs loading).
- Files disappear.
- Programs crash unexpectedly.

Dealing with an Infected Windows System

If you have already been infected with a virus, follow these steps:

1. If an unfamiliar dialog box, error message, or something else unfamiliar appears, make a note of the message or other symptom. Unplug the modem or network cable, and then shut down the computer. Continuing to use an infected computer is a bad idea for several reasons. Depending on what type of virus or worm you have, additional damage can be done. With the speed of today's systems, a virus or worm can delete or write over gigabytes of data in a matter of minutes. Also, some viruses exploit functions in Microsoft Outlook and Outlook Express that can cause your computer to forward a copy of the virus to all entries in your address book.

2. Do not try to repair or otherwise contain the damage or effects of a virus or worm using software that was not specifically designed to do so. In other words, don't run Norton Speed Disk to try and solve the problem.

3. Do not install antivirus software *after* you discover a virus or worm. Unless you are sure that the virus is nondestructive, leave the computer turned off until you find out how to get rid of the specific virus that your system has contracted.

4. Locate a computer that is not infected. Go to a virus resource web site and find out how to fix it. Try the web site of one of the most popular antivirus programs (listed in a previous section) or one of the virus information sites listed in the next section. Look for step-by-step instructions for removing the virus. Companies like Symantec and McAfee often develop scripts that aid in the removal of recently discovered viruses and publish of the details about what that virus has done or can do, so that they can be safely removed.

5. Once you know which virus you have, follow the steps to disinfect your system (that is, remove the virus). If the virus has deleted or overwritten files, it might not be possible to get the files back, but you can at least prevent further damage to your system and infection of other systems.

6. If you can't find identify the virus or find a procedure for getting rid of it, call technical support for your computer (or your local technical support person). Explain to them what happened and that you would like some assistance in removing the virus, or at least in taking steps to minimize the damage.

7. Once you are sure that the virus is gone, buy and install an antivirus program. Don't make the same mistake twice!

Another approach is to back up all your data files (but none of your programs), reformat your hard disk, reinstall Windows and your applications, restore your data files, and buy and install an antivirus program to prevent reinfection. However, leaving your computer running while you make the backups can give the virus time to delete more files.

 After you have cleaned up a virus, back up, reformat, and reinstall your system. Many viruses and the resulting repairs leave your system unstable, and parts of virus files may still be lying around.

If you make regular backups, check the backups that you made within at least 72 hours of discovering the infection (see Chapter 9). Your system may have been infected for days (or longer) before you realized it.

Sources of Antivirus Information

Here is a quick list of applications and sites that you should investigate long before you need them:

- **Doug Muth's Anti-Virus Help Page, at www.claws-and-paws.com/virus** A fantastically deep collection of information regarding computer viruses with lots of helpful papers, reports, and links to additional resources. One thing that makes this site great is that it's not tied to any commercial concern.

- **Symantec AntiVirus Research Center (SARC), at www.sarc.com** An easy enough domain name to remember, especially when you need fast access to the latest virus alerts. Doug's page is great, but the SARC team is fast, which is one of the benefits of commercial relations.

- **McAfee Virus Information Library, at vil.nai.com/vil** This encyclopedic listing of viruses is one of the first places you should look to get help or find out what's going on.

- **Vmyths (formerly the Computer Virus Myths page), at www.vmyths.com** Myths and news about viruses and hoaxes.

Please take our advice and make sure you're covered.

Managing Which Files Internet Explorer Downloads

Internet Explorer can retrieve a wide variety of files and objects, ranging from innocuous plain text files and images to potentially destructive executable programs. Some web pages increase the amount of interactivity they can offer by downloading small programs to run on your computer. For example, rather than transmitting the individual frames of an animation over the Internet, a web server may send an animation-constructing program that runs on your computer. A financial web site may download a program that displays a scrolling stock ticker. Typically, this process is invisible to the user—the interaction or the animation just happens, without calling your attention to how it happens.

While these programs are useful, they also create security issues. If web sites can put useful programs on your computer and run them without informing you, precautions must be taken to make sure that they can't also put harmful programs on your computer. Internet Explorer takes certain precautions automatically and allows you the option to choose additional precautions.

Internet Explorer's downloaded object security allows you to decide, based on both the web site where an object came from and the type of object, whether to retrieve an object, and once it's retrieved, what to do with it. Internet Explorer defines three levels of object access (low, medium, and high) to give varying amounts of access to your computer. You can also define custom access permissions, if the three standard settings don't meet your needs.

Java, JavaScript, VBScript, and ActiveX

Java is a language for sending small applications (called *applets*) over the Web so that they can be executed by your computer. *JavaScript* is a language for extending HTML to embed small programs called *scripts* in web pages. *VBScript*, a language that resembles Microsoft's Visual Basic, can be used to add scripts to pages that are displayed by Internet Explorer. Anything that VBScript can do, JavaScript (which Microsoft calls JScript) can do, too and vice versa.

ActiveX controls, like Java, are a way to embed executable programs into a web page. Unlike Java and JavaScript, but like VBScript, ActiveX is a Microsoft system that is not used by Navigator or most other browsers. When Internet Explorer encounters a web page that uses ActiveX controls, it checks to see whether that particular control is already installed and if it is not, IE installs the control on your machine.

 ActiveX controls are considerably more dangerous than JavaScript or VBScript scripts or Java applets. Java applets and JavaScript scripts are run in a "sandbox" inside your browser, which limits the accidental or deliberate damage they can do; and VBScript scripts are run by an interpreter, which should limit the types of damage they can do. However, ActiveX controls are programs with full access to your computer's resources.

Internet Explorer's Zones

Internet Explorer's security policy is based on trust, and the decisions that you make involve who to trust and who not to trust. For example, when a web page wants to run an ActiveX control on your machine, IE verifies who wrote the control (Microsoft, for example) and that it hasn't been tampered with. It doesn't consider what the control intends to do or what privileges it requests on your system (rewriting files, for example). Instead, it asks you whether you trust its author.

To determine who to trust, Internet Explorer divides the world into four *zones*:

- ■ **Internet** Includes all sites that are not in one of the other three zones. Objects from this zone generally are given the medium level of access to your computer.

- ■ **Local Intranet** Contains computers on your local network. They're usually considered fairly trustworthy, and objects are given a medium level of access to your computer.

- **Trusted Sites**   Includes the sites that you or Microsoft have listed as trustworthy. Objects from this zone generally are given the high level of access to your computer.

- **Restricted Sites**   Includes the sites that you have listed as untrustworthy. Objects from this zone are given the low level of access to your computer. Don't change the access level of this zone to grant higher access.

Downloaded ActiveX controls and other executable objects can and should be signed by their authors using a certificate scheme similar to that used for validating remote servers.

For each of the four zones into which a web page can fall, you can set the security to high, medium, medium-low, or low. For each zone, you can set exactly which remote operations you're willing to perform. To prevent downloading and running software that might infect your system with a virus, see the section "Preventing Infection by Viruses" earlier in this chapter.

Controlling Your Download Security

The rules governing scripts and applets are set zone by zone on the Security tab of the Internet Options dialog box. To examine or change these settings:

1. Open the Internet Options dialog box by selecting Tools | Internet Options from the Internet Explorer menu bar.

2. Click the Security tab of the Internet Options dialog box (as shown in Figure 32-1).

3. Select the security zone you want to examine or change. The rest of the information on the Security tab changes to show the settings for that zone.

4. If you want to change the general security setting of the zone without specifying how to handle specific web page elements, move the slider on the Security tab of the Internet Options dialog box. (The slider doesn't appear if the zone has been given custom settings. To reset such a zone to one of the standard settings, click the Default Level button. When the slider reappears, you can move it to the desired setting.)

5. If you want to specify how to handle specific web page elements, click the Custom Level button to display the Security Settings dialog box, shown in Figure 32-2. Scroll through the settings until you see the item you want to change. Change an item by selecting or deselecting its check box or by selecting a different radio button than the current selection.

6. Click OK to close each open dialog box. Click Yes in the confirmation box that asks if you want to change the security settings.

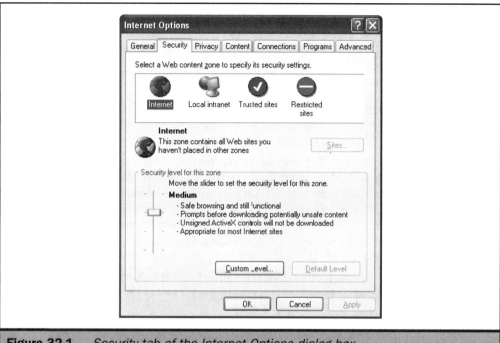

Figure 32-1. *Security tab of the Internet Options dialog box*

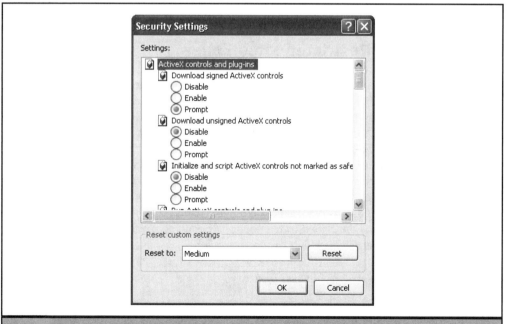

Figure 32-2. *Enabling and disabling web page elements for a security zone*

Controlling Which Web Sites Are in the Local Intranet Zone

The Local Intranet Zone normally contains sites on your own local area network and is set up that way by your network administrator when he or she sets up the network. When you click the Sites button on the Security tab, Windows displays the Local Intranet Zone dialog box, with these three check boxes:

- **Include All Local (Intranet) Sites Not Listed In Other Zones**   Select this check box to include all other sites on the same local area network in the Local Intranet Zone. This check box is usually checked.

- **Include All Sites That Bypass The Proxy Server**   Many organizations have a *proxy server* that mediates access to sites outside the organization. Select this check box to include sites outside your organization to which your organization lets you connect directly in the Local Intranet zone. You can see a list of the sites that bypass the proxy server by displaying the Internet Properties or Internet Options dialog box, clicking the Connections tab, and clicking the Advanced button.

- **Include All Network Paths (UNCs)**   Select this check box to include all the sites with UNC addresses (Universal Naming Convention addresses), which apply only to computers on your LAN.

You can also click the Advanced button to add sites individually, as for Trusted and Restricted sites. See Chapter 31 for more information on how networks connect to the Internet.

Controlling Which Web Sites Are in the Trusted and Restricted Sites Zones

The Trusted and Restricted Sites zones start with no web sites listed; you must specify the web sites to include in these zones. To specify sites, select the zone to which you want to add sites and click Sites on the Security tab of the Internet Options dialog box. You see the Trusted Sites or the Restricted Sites dialog box, the first of which is shown in Figure 32-3. To add a new site, type its full address, starting with **http://** or **https://**, into the Add This Web Site To The Zone box and click Add. The web site appears in the Web Sites list. To remove a site, select it in the Web Sites list and click Remove. You can require a verified secure connection to all sites in this zone by clicking the Require Server Verification (https:) For All Sites In This Zone check box at the bottom of the dialog box; when selected, this setting prevents you from adding any sites that don't support HTTPS, which is described in the section "Securing Your Web Communication with Encryption and Certificates" later in this chapter.

Managing Java and JavaScript

The security settings that affect how Internet Explorer deals with Java and JavaScript programs are in the Microsoft VM and Scripting sections of the Security Settings dialog box. Follow these steps:

1. On the Security tab of the Internet Options dialog box, click the zone for which you want to change or see the settings.

2. Click the Custom Level button to display the Security Settings dialog box, shown in Figure 32-2.

3. You may change what these applets and scripts are allowed to do on your computer, or even disable Java or JavaScript entirely, by choosing Disable (Internet Explorer does not run this type of program downloaded from this zone), Enable (IE does run this type of program downloaded from this zone), or Prompt (ask before running the program).

Managing ActiveX Controls

We have never been big fans of ActiveX controls. They allow web sites to have too much power over your system and are hard to monitor. If you should happen to download and install a rogue ActiveX control by mistake, it could (on its own) download and install lots more rogue ActiveX controls—which would then be permanent parts of your software environment, even when you are offline. None of this would appear the least bit suspicious to any virus-detecting software you might own. They have the same status as applications that you install yourself.

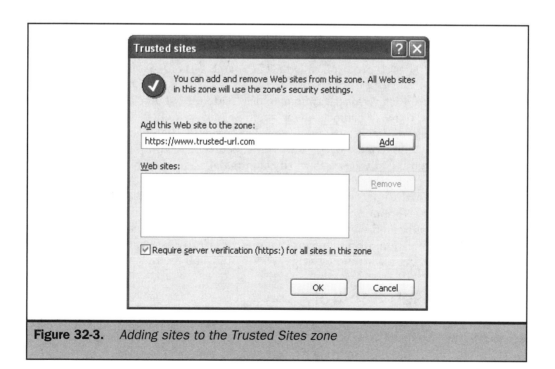

Figure 32-3.   *Adding sites to the Trusted Sites zone*

Disabling ActiveX controls is one option, as described in the previous section. However, if you frequent Microsoft web sites like MSN or MSNBC, you will be exposed to numerous temptations to turn them back on. (We finally gave in to the excellent portfolio-tracking services at MSN Moneycentral.) We suggest the following compromise: Disable ActiveX controls everywhere but in the Trusted Sites security zone. (Do this from the Security Settings dialog box, following the steps in the previous section.) When you find a Microsoft web site that offers some wonderful service involving ActiveX controls, move that site into the Trusted Sites security zone.

ActiveX controls are stored in the folder C:\Windows\Downloaded Program Files (if Windows is installed in C:\Windows). If you use Internet Explorer, you should check this file periodically to see what applications Internet Explorer has downloaded. Dispose of an ActiveX control by right-clicking its icon and selecting Remove from the shortcut menu.

Securing Your Web Communication with Encryption and Certificates

Browsers store *certificates*, cryptographic data that can identify your computer to remote computers or vice versa. Certificates are issued by *certificate authorities*, each of which has its own certificate. Internet Explorer comes with about 30 *authority certificates* that they can use to check that the certificates presented to your computer by other sites are, in fact, issued by known certificate authorities. To provide secure communication with a remote web site, Internet Explorer uses *SSL* (Secure Sockets Layer) to provide a variation of the standard HTTP Web protocol, called *HTTPS*. Web servers that use HTTPS are called *secure servers*.

You can also acquire a *personal certificate* to use to identify yourself when Internet Explorer or another browser contacts a web site. The most widely used authorities for personal certificates are VeriSign, at **www.verisign.com** and Thawte (which is owned by VeriSign) at **www.thawte.com**. See RSA Data Security's list of questions and answers at their web site at **www.rsasecurity.com/rsalabs/faq** for more information about certificates.

New applets usually are digitally signed by their authors, that is, each applet includes certificate information that identifies the applet's author and verifies that the applet wasn't tampered with since the author signed it. Unfortunately, the cost of Microsoft's certification process means that many perfectly safe applets won't be signed and will trigger a warning message when you install them.

Browsing the Web Securely

Internet Explorer handles communication security by using SSL (Secure Sockets Layer) to encrypt messages sent to and from remote servers and certificates to verify who the party is at the other end of a connection. For example, you use this type of security when you place a credit card order with a web-based retailer that uses a secure web server. For the most part, SSL works invisibly, with all the security validation happening automatically. Internet Explorer, by default, warns you when you switch between secure and normal pages with dialog boxes like this:

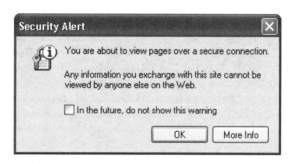

(We find these warnings annoying and turn them off.) You can tell whether the current page is secure in the following ways:

■ Look at the URL for the page in the browser's Address or Location box to see whether the page's address starts with **https://** rather than **http://**.

■ Look at the status bar at the bottom of the browser window to see whether a little lock icon appears, indicating that the connection is secure.

Whenever your browser opens an HTTPS connection to a server that supports SSL, the server presents a certificate to your computer. If the certificate is validated by one of the authority certificates known to your browser, and the name on the certificate matches the name of the web site, the browser uses the connection and displays web pages as usual. If either of those checks fails, the browser warns you and gives you the option to continue. You see a Security Alert or similar dialog box when your browser can't validate a remote site's certificate. If you trust the source of the file that you are downloading, you can tell Windows to continue and use the connection despite the warning.

Using Object Certificates When Downloading Files

Whenever Internet Explorer retrieves a web page that uses a hitherto unknown ActiveX or Java applet, Internet Explorer checks to see whether your download security settings permit you to download it (see "Controlling Your Download Security" earlier in this chapter). If your settings don't permit the download, Internet Explorer warns you and doesn't download the file. You see the dialog box shown here:

Unless a site is in the Trusted Zone (in which case Internet Explorer accepts the applet without question), Internet Explorer checks the certificate with which the program is signed and displays the Security Warning dialog box, as shown in Figure 32-4. You see who the signer is and who verified the signature. If the signer is someone you're inclined to trust, such as a large reputable organization or someone you know personally, click Yes to accept the applet. If you expect always to accept applets from this signer, click the Always Trust Content From *ThisSigner'sName* check box at the bottom of the dialog box to tell Internet Explorer not to ask about signatures from this signer in the future. (If you check the box and later change your mind, the list of signers you've checked is in the Internet Properties dialog box; click the Content tab and click Publishers to examine and change the list.)

Managing Certificates from Certificate Publishers

If you expect to download many programs (or display web pages that contain applets), you will end up with a collection of certificates with which Internet Explorer can verify the sources of the programs. You can see lists of the certificates that you have received. Click the Content tab on the Internet Options dialog box. Click the buttons in the Certificates section of the dialog box.

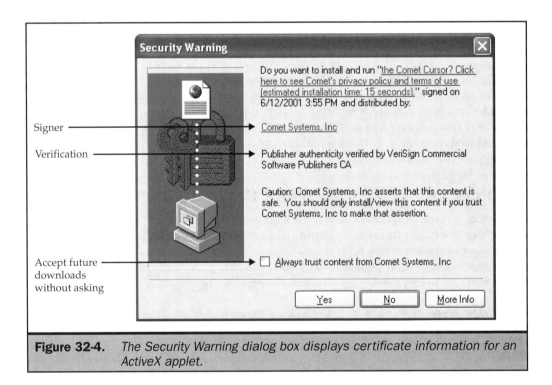

Figure 32-4. *The Security Warning dialog box displays certificate information for an ActiveX applet.*

In Internet Explorer, choose Tools | Internet Options from the menu to see the Internet Options dialog box. Clicking the Content tab and then the Publishers button displays the Certificates dialog box, as shown in Figure 32-5. Click the Trusted Publishers tab to see certificates for software publishers that you have told your browsers to trust (by clicking the Always Trust Content From check box in the Security Warning dialog box, shown in Figure 32-4). New certificates are added when you download authenticated software from the Internet. You can delete a certificate from this list by selecting it and clicking Remove.

Managing Your Personal Certificates

You can get your own certificate to identify yourself to secure remote web servers that demand user certificates for identification. See "Sending and Receiving E-Mail Securely" later in this chapter for how to get your own certificate for use both on the Web and in sending and receiving secure e-mail.

To see what personal certificates are installed in Internet Explorer, choose Tools | Options, click the Content tab, and click the Certificates button to display the Certificates dialog box with the Personal tab selected, shown in Figure 32-6. You see a list of the certificates you have installed on your computer that you can use to identify yourself.

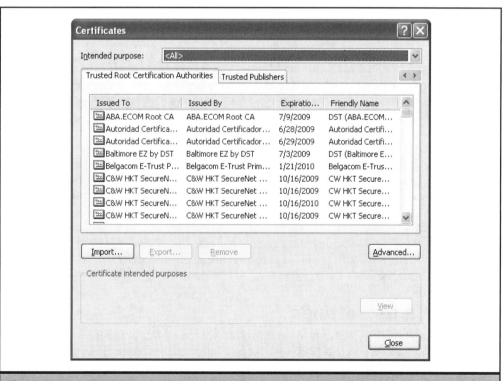

Figure 32-5.   *Viewing certificates from software publishers*

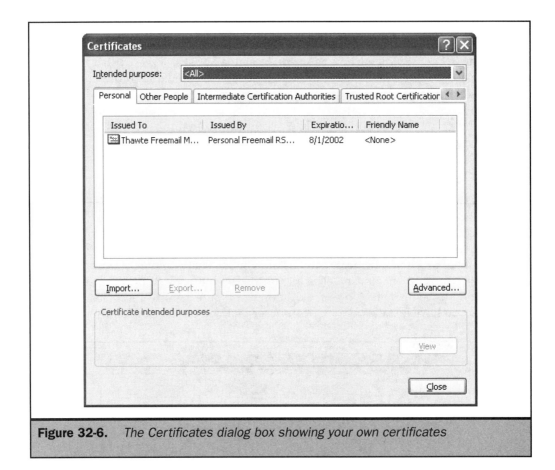

Figure 32-6. *The Certificates dialog box showing your own certificates*

If you receive a certificate and store it on your disk, click Import to read the certificate and include it on the list in this dialog box. Windows can read certificates stored in personal certificate files (with the extension .pfx). You can export a certificate and its associated information to a personal certificate file; select the certificate from the list on the Certificates dialog box and click Export.

 If you get a certificate in Internet Explorer, you can export it to a file and then import the certificate from that file into any other certificate-capable web browser (like Netscape) or vice versa.

Other IE Security Settings

A few additional security settings appear on the Advanced tab of the Internet Options dialog box (shown in Figure 32-7): choose Tools | Internet Options in IE, click Advanced, and scroll down to the Security section of the list of settings. Click the What's This button (the blue question mark near the right end of the title bar) and click a setting to see an explanation of the setting.

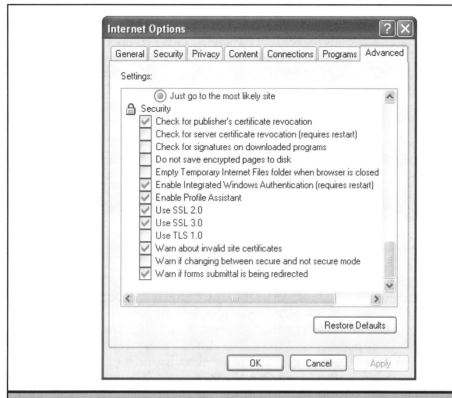

Figure 32-7. *Additional security settings in IE*

MSN Explorer May Compromise Security

MSN Explorer is a program that works with Internet Explorer and provides access to a bunch of MSN services like Hotmail (see Chapter 24, section "MSN Explorer"). It's pretty cute. But we found the following line in the MSN Explorer Security Statement:

If you have chosen security settings that will interfere with MSN Explorer, then your security settings are temporarily changed to allow MSN Explorer to work properly. In addition, while MSN Explorer is active on your computer, the special settings for MSN will apply to any Microsoft Internet Explorer window you may have open.

If Internet security is important to you, you may prefer to forego using MSN Explorer.

Sending and Receiving E-mail Securely

E-mail programs offer two kinds of security: signatures and encryption. Both depend on certificates that serve as electronic identity keys. The security system that Microsoft provides with Outlook Express, *S/MIME*, uses certificates issued by third parties, such as VeriSign and Thawte. Another popular security system, *Pretty Good Privacy* (or *PGP*), lets each user generate his or her own keys (PGP add-ins are available for Eudora and Outlook Express). Both are forms of *public-key cryptography*. Each certificate consists of a *public key* (or *digital* ID), a *private key*, and a *digital signature*. You keep your private key and digital signature secret, while you provide your public key to anyone with whom you exchange secure mail, either directly or via a generally available key server.

Signatures allow you to add to your mail a *signature block*, generated with your private key, that verifies the author is indeed you, and that the message was not modified in transit. Anyone who wants to validate your signature can check it by using your public key. The signature is added as an extra block at the end of the message, without modifying the other contents, so that the recipient can read your message, whether he or she validates your signature or not.

Encryption scrambles a message so that only the recipient can decode it. A message encrypted with someone's public key can be decrypted only with that person's private key. You encrypt a message with the recipient's public key, and the recipient uses his or her private key to decode it. Anyone else looking at the message would see only unreadable gibberish. It's possible both to *digitally sign* and encrypt the same message, so that only the designated recipient can decode the message and the designated recipient can then verify that the message is really from you.

Mail security depends on a *key ring* of keys. On your key ring, you need your own private key and digital signature and the public key of everyone with whom you plan to exchange secure mail. Outlook Express security keeps your private key and digital signature as one of the properties of your Mail account and keeps other people's public keys in the Address Book.

Outlook Express and other Microsoft e-mail programs provide a certificate-based system (called S/MIME) for signing and encrypting mail. *Signed* mail uses your own certificate to prove to the recipient that the author of the message is you and that the message arrived without tampering (these are the same type of certificates described in the preceding sections for authenticating material you download from the Web). *Encrypted* mail uses the recipient's certificate to protect the message's contents so that only the intended recipient can read the messages. A single message can be both signed and encrypted.

Note   *For more information about encryption and signature, see RSA Security's web site at **www.rsasecurity.com** and the PGP Corporations' Pretty Good Privacy web site at **www.pgp.com**. These sites describe how to use encryption with various e-mail programs.*

Getting a Certificate

The only source of certificates is a certificate authority, and for a certificate to be useful, the authority has to be one that is widely accepted. The best known certificate authority is VeriSign, at **www.verisign.com**, who also owns Thawte, at **www.thawte.com**. It provides a variety of certificates at various prices, usually including a free two-month trial of a personal certificate suitable for signing e-mail. The certificate authority's web site walks you through the process of getting a certificate. Details vary, but, generally, the steps include the following:

- You enter basic information, including your e-mail address, into a form on the authority's web site.

- Your browser automatically downloads your private key, part of the security information from the authority.

- The authority e-mails a confirmation code to the address you give. This ensures that the address you provide is really yours.

- You run Outlook Express and receive the message. It contains the URL of a page that will finish the registration and a unique code to identify yourself when you get there. Use Windows cut-and-paste tool to copy the code from your mail program to the browser window, rather than trying to retype it.

- The authority generates the public key that matches your private key and downloads it as well.

Note *This process of obtaining a certificate only verifies your e-mail address, not any other aspect of your identity. VeriSign offers more secure certificates with more careful identity checks, but the vast majority of certificates in use are the simplest kind.*

Sending Signed Mail

Once you have a certificate, sending signed mail is simple. While you're composing a message in Outlook Express, click the Digitally Sign Message button (the one with the little orange seal) to tell Outlook Express to sign the message as it's sent. Signed messages appear with the orange seal in the list of messages, as shown in the next illustration.

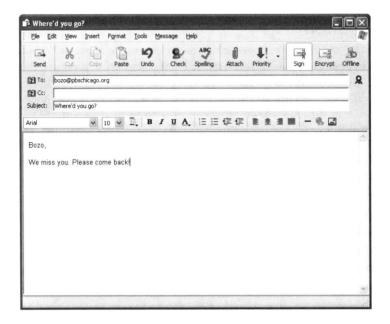

Sending Encrypted Mail

Sending encrypted mail is only slightly harder than sending signed mail. The difference is that before you can send signed mail to someone, you have to have that recipient's digital ID (public key) in your Windows Address Book (see Chapter 23, section "Storing Addresses in the Address Book"). Once you have the digital ID, create the message as usual in Outlook Express and click the Encrypt Message button (the envelope with the little blue lock) before sending the message. The encrypted mail icon looks like this:

There are three common ways to obtain someone's digital ID: from a signed message he or she sent, from an online directory, or from a file obtained elsewhere, such as a web-based lookup system.

Getting a Digital ID from Incoming Mail

Any time someone sends you a digitally signed message, you can get that person's digital ID from the message and add it to your Address Book. (Note that the digital ID is the equivalent of the sender's public key; the corresponding private key is not disclosed.) Open the message, select File | Properties and click the Security tab; you see the View Certificates dialog box shown in Figure 32-8. Assuming that the signature is valid, click Add To Address Book. The Address Book opens, creating a new entry for your correspondent (if one does not already exist). Click the Digital IDs tab and observe that a digital ID is listed; then click OK to update the Address Book.

Getting a Digital ID Through LDAP Search

If you know that your correspondent has a digital ID and you know which certificate authority issued it, you can look it up in that authority's directory.

In Outlook Express, open the Address Book and click the Find button to open the search window, shown in Figure 32-9. In the Look In box, select the directory to search, which is most likely VeriSign for personal digital IDs. Enter the person's name or e-mail address and click Find Now.

Figure 32-8.   *Getting a digital ID from a mail message*

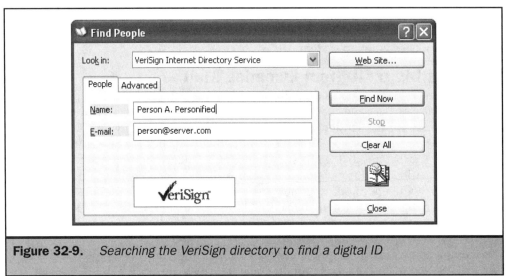

Figure 32-9. *Searching the VeriSign directory to find a digital ID*

The directory returns a list of entries that match your request. Double-click any entry in the list to see the details, which are arranged like an address book entry, to be sure it's the person you want. If it is, click Add To Address Book to turn it into an Address Book entry, edit as desired (adding more personal info, usually) and click OK to update the Address Book.

Getting a Digital ID from a File

Digital IDs can be stored in certificate files, usually with the extension .cer (see "Securing Your Web Communication with Encryption and Certificates" earlier in this chapter). Someone can mail you a third party's ID as a file, or you might download the file from a web-based search system.

To add the digital ID to your Address Book, open the Address Book and create an entry for the person, including his or her e-mail address. (The e-mail address has to match the one to which the certificate is assigned.) Then click the Address Book's Digital IDs tab, shown in Figure 32-10. Click the Import button and select the file containing the ID. The Address Book reads the digital ID and adds it to the Address Book entry.

If you want to store someone's digital ID in a file to transfer it to another computer or send it to a third person, open the Address Book entry for that person, click the Digital IDs tab, click Export, and specify the file to create.

Don't try to export your own digital ID this way; bugs in Windows keep it from working. Remember, you can send anyone your digital ID by sending a signed e-mail message.

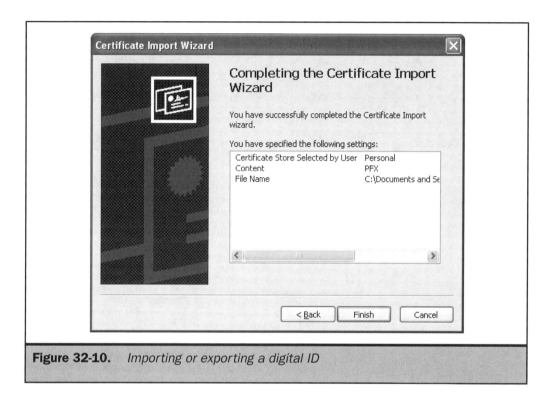

Figure 32-10. *Importing or exporting a digital ID*

Receiving Encrypted or Signed Mail

Outlook Express automatically handles incoming encrypted or signed mail. Signed messages have a little orange seal at the right end of the Security line of the message headers; encrypted messages have a little blue lock. When you open the message, Outlook Express automatically validates the signature or decrypts the message. The first time it does so, it displays a special window in place of the actual message, telling you what it did. Scroll down and click Continue to see the actual message. If you'd rather not see the special window in the future, a box above the Continue button lets you avoid the window in the future.

The
Complete
Reference

Windows
XP

Part VII

Windows and Disk Housekeeping

Chapter 33

Formatting and Partitioning Disks

H ard disks can be *partitioned*—divided into one or more logical sections—using a Disk Management or compatible program. (Most disks have only one partition.) Both hard disks and removable disks must be formatted with a *file system*, the information that keeps track of which files are stored where on the disk. Windows XP supports three file systems: FAT (the file system used in DOS and Windows 95), FAT32 (file system introduced with Windows 95 OSR2 and used in Windows 98, 98SE, and Me), and NTFS 5.0 (the latest version of the file system designed for Windows NT/2000).

On computers with Windows preinstalled, the hard disk has already been partitioned (usually into a single large partition) and formatted. However, if you install an additional hard disk or replace the original hard disk, you have to partition and format the new disk. Some disks (both hard disks and removable disks) come preformatted and some don't. Whether or not a disk is preformatted, you can reformat it to remove any existing files and make it a "clean" empty disk.

Each disk drive, including floppy disks, other removable disks (like Zip drives), and CD drives, has a drive letter assigned to it by Windows, but you can change these letters, or assign drive letters to folders, if you must. You can also check how much free space is on any disk and look at the properties of a disk.

This chapter describes how to partition and format hard disks; how to decide whether to use FAT, FAT32, or NTFS (and how to convert partitions to NTFS); how to assign drive letters to disk drives; how to check for free space; and how to control the way in which Windows uses CD-ROMs. It also covers how to format and copy floppy disks.

 For information on dividing your hard disk into separate partitions for Windows XP and other operating systems, see the section "Creating Dual-boot Installations" in the Appendix.

Partitions, File Systems, and Drive Letters

Partitions and file systems determine how and where Windows stores information on your hard disk. Drive letters refer to the various disks on your computer. Before you can decide which file system to use on your partitions, you need to know the differences among FAT, FAT32, and NTFS.

Hard Disk Partitions

A *partition* is a section of a hard disk. Normally, a disk is set up as a single large partition spanning the entire disk, but sometimes using more than one partition makes sense. When you partition a disk, you allocate a fixed amount of space to each partition.

 If your disks contain only one partition each, you can use the terms "disk drive" and "partition" interchangeably. Neither CDs nor floppy disks can contain multiple partitions.

Types of Partitions

The partitions used by DOS and Windows have historically been called *primary partition* and *extended partition*. One disk drive can store either four primary partitions, or three primary partitions and one extended partition. An extended partition can contain many *logical drives*, which are also partitions—extended partitions provide a way to have more than four partitions on a disk. An extended partition can also contain free space, which isn't allocated to a logical drive. Disks can also contain unallocated space, which doesn't belong to any partition. Other operating systems, such as Linux and OS/2, have their own types of partitions.

When you are running Windows XP, it also designates partitions as system, boot, and active:

- **System partition**   Has the files needed to start up the computer, stored in the root (main) folder. May be FAT, FAT32, or NTFS. For a multiboot system with Windows Me/9*x*, the system partition must be FAT or FAT32. The system partition can be small because only a few files are needed. The files needed to start the computer are Ntldr (the NT boot loader, the most important startup file), Boot.ini (which contains the operating system menu for multiboot systems), and Ntdetect.com.

- **Boot partition**   Has the files that contain the Windows XP operating system. May be formatted with the FAT (not recommended), FAT32, or NTFS (recommended) file system (see "The FAT, FAT32, and NTFS File Systems" later in this chapter). The boot partition must be large enough for the Windows XP program files and lots of extra space, since other programs usually install in the same partition and Microsoft encourages users to store data there, too— your boot partition should be at least 2GB. If you have other operating systems installed on your computer, each one has a separate boot partition containing its system files.

- **Active partition**   The current boot partition. If you have several operating systems installed on your computer, each one has a boot partition. You can mark a partition as active so that the next time you restart your computer, this partition will be used as the boot partition (see "Selecting the Active Partition" later in this chapter). The active partition must be on disk 0 (the first hard disk attached to the computer).

Note   *We find it confusing that your computer boots off the system partition, while the operating system is stored in the boot partition. Just remember that the names are backward.*

The system and boot partitions can be the same partition, or they can be different. If you have one hard disk with one partition, it's both the boot and system partition. If they are different, the computer reads the files from the system partition first when it starts up, then switches to the boot partition to load Windows XP.

You can see what partitions your hard disks contain, what types of partitions they are, and which are your system, active, and boot partitions, by using the Disk Management program (see "Displaying Information about Drives and Partitions" later in this chapter).

 Windows also refers to partitions as volumes. Volumes can be disk partitions or they can be on storage media other than hard disks, such as tape drives.

The Master Boot Record (MBR)

When your computer starts up, the computer's BIOS (Basic Input/Output System, which is stored on ROM chips on the system board) performs various self-tests. Then it searches for the very first sector on your hard disk(s)—cylinder 0, head 0, sector 1 of the first hard disk—which contains the *master boot record* (*MBR*).

The MBR tells the computer where your active partition is stored. The computer reads the first sector of the active partition (the *boot sector*) to look for a *boot loader*, a program that begins loading an operating system (like Windows or UNIX). For Windows XP, the boot loader is stored in the Ntldr file. When your computer runs Ntldr, it begins to load the Windows XP program from the boot partition.

Partitions for Multiple Operating Systems

If you run more than one operating system on your computer, you can create a partition for each operating system and then start the computer from the partition that contains the operating system you want to use (see the Appendix, section "Creating Dual-boot Installations"). With Windows Me/9*x*, using multiple partitions to switch between different Windows versions was hard, because they all started from the same primary partition. (PartitionMagic, a program you can purchase separately, enables you to install more than one version of Windows.) Windows NT and 2000 included the NT Boot manager, which made dual-boot systems easier to set up (see the sidebar "Managing Partitions with PartitionMagic").

Managing Partitions with PartitionMagic

PartitionMagic is a program from PowerQuest Corporation (**www.powerquest.com/partitionmagic**) that enables you to create, resize, move, and delete all types of partitions. The Windows XP setup program can set up a separate partition for Windows XP, and the Windows Disk Management window can create and delete partitions, but it still can't do everything that we use PartitionMagic for, such as expanding, shrinking, copying, and moving partitions. Also, PartitionMagic can move and resize partitions without losing the data stored in the partitions: Windows XP loses your files when you make changes to partitions.

Because all of our data is stored separately on drive D:, backups can be smaller and faster, including only data and not programs. Backing up is easy when all you have to do is specify all files on D:.

Windows XP has partitioning built in, and its setup program can create a separate partition for it, leaving other versions of Windows alone. It can display a list of the installed operating systems (each in its own boot partition). However, PartitionMagic is still useful for moving and resizing partitions.

The FAT, FAT32, and NTFS File Systems

A *file system* is the information that keeps track of which files and folders are stored where in a partition, and what disk space is free. The Windows file system includes a *FAT (File Allocation Table)* or *Master File Table*, which stores information about each *sector*, or physical block of storage space, on the disk. Windows XP supports three different file systems: FAT, FAT32, and NTFS:

- **FAT** Also known as FAT16, FAT was introduced with the OSR2 update to Windows 95. Partitions are limited to 4GB. Files are limited to 2GB. Works on floppy disks. Readable by DOS, OS/2, and all versions of Windows. Does not work with domains (server-based network security) (see Chapter 27, section "Peer-to-Peer vs. Domain-Based Networks"). Not recommended unless you need to share data with a DOS, OS/2, or Windows 95 system.

- **FAT32** Partitions can be from 512MB to 2 terabytes, although Windows XP can format a FAT32 only as large as 32GB. Files are limited to 4GB. Readable by Windows 95 OSR2, 98, Me, NT, 2000, and XP. Does not work with domains. Recommended for home systems with no security needs, and for systems that need to share data with a Windows 98 or Me system.

- **NTFS** (NT file system) A more mature version of FAT32 that was originally designed for use with Windows NT and Windows 2000 for server applications. Partition size can be from 520MB to 2 terabytes (larger sizes are possible, but not recommended). Files are limited only to the size of the partition. Can't be used on floppy disks. Readable by Windows 2000 and XP, and by Windows NT 4.0 with Service Pack 4 or later. Required for domains. Enables encrypted folders and files, permissions for individual folders and files, and disk quotas by user. Windows XP uses NTFS 5.0 (it was called 5.1 during product testing), a very slight upgrade from the version used in Windows 2000. Recommended for systems with security needs, large hard disks, and LAN connections.

Each partition on a hard disk and each removable disk must be formatted with FAT, FAT32, or NTFS, but it's possible (and often desirable) to have some disks with one format and some with the other format on the same system. Both FAT32 and NTFS are designed for large partitions and disks and offer no significant benefits when used on smaller disks. However, with XP's rather significant system requirements it will be unlikely to see a system available with less than 10GB of hard drive space, making FAT largely useless.

NTFS 5.0 offers all of the advantages of FAT32 as well as the following:

- **More efficient use of space** NTFS can allocate as little as 2KB of disk space to a file, reducing wasted disk space.

- **On-the-fly compression**   Individual files can be compressed and decompressed as needed. Entire drives can be reduced in size without affecting overall performance.

- **Encryption**   In Windows XP Professional, files and folders can be encrypted with a user's password (see Chapter 8, section "File and Folder Attributes"). However, Windows XP Home Edition doesn't support file and folder encryption.

> **Note**   *NTFS 5.0 was introduced with Windows 2000. The original NTFS that was used by Windows NT does not have the same features as NTFS 5.0. Partitions made with Windows NT need to be converted for Windows XP to use them. Windows XP automatically converts Windows 2000 to the slightly updated version of NTFS that it uses. Older versions of disk utilities (like PartitionMagic) don't work with Windows XP NTFS partitions: be sure to get the latest versions.*

Why Divide Your Hard Disk into Partitions?

Most often, you allocate all the space on a hard disk to one partition, which Windows treats as a single logical disk drive using a single drive letter (drive C: for the first hard disk). You can also allocate some of the space to the primary partition and some to an extended partition, which can, in turn, be subdivided into multiple logical disks.

As a general rule, a single partition is all you ever need. However, here are circumstances where more than one partition will be useful:

- **Compatibility with older operating systems**   If you want a disk to be usable from DOS, Windows 3.1, or Windows 95, you need to make a FAT16 partition that is less than 2GB. If you want a disk to be usable from Windows 98 or Me, make a FAT32 partition.

- **Scratch areas**   In some cases, it's useful to have a separate partition to use as a scratch area that you can quickly reformat to wipe out its contents and start fresh.

- **Multiboot systems**   The boot manager built into Windows (or PartitionMagic) can dynamically reassign active partitions so that you can effectively have more than one operating system on a large drive (see the sidebar "Managing Partitions with PartitionMagic").

- **Data partitions**   We recommend creating a separate partition for your data— all your documents, spreadsheets, databases, and other files. You should back up your data partition regularly. You needn't back up your programs as often because you can restore them from your program CDs.

- **Quotas**   You can set quotas for each user, limiting the amount of space that each user can use on a partition (see Chapter 6, section "Setting Quotas for Disk Usage").

We recommend that you set up two partitions: one primary NTFS partition (which appears as drive C:) for Windows XP and one primary or extended partition (drive D:) for data. Use drive C: for Windows and programs, and use drive D: for data—all documents, spreadsheets, e-mail, and other files that you create or edit. You can configure Windows to store your Documents And Settings folder on D: (see the section "Changing the Location of the Entire User Profile" in Chapter 6). You can also configure your programs (where possible) to store their program configuration files on D:—for example, Microsoft Word's template files and Netscape or Mozilla's bookmark files.

Keeping all your data and personal configuration settings in a separate partition has several advantages:

- **Backups**   Making backups is easier when all your files are stored together. Whether you use Windows Explorer, the Backup Utility, or another backup program, it's easy to specify that you want to back up all the files on D: (see Chapter 9).

- **Reinstalling Windows**   If Windows starts acting oddly or you decide to start fresh when you upgrade to a new version of Windows, you can reinstall Windows without disturbing your data files. (Make a backup of all your data before reinstalling or upgrading Windows, though, just in case!) You can wipe out the files on C: without deleting the files on D:.

- **Multiboot systems**   If you need to switch between two operating systems (for example, Windows XP and Linux), you can access your data files from either one. You might want to store Windows XP on C:, Linux on D:, and your data on E:. Make your data partition an NTFS partition unless you have a dual-boot system with Windows 9*x*/Me system.

Tip   *Don't slice your disk into too many partitions—we rarely use more than three. Unlike folders, when you create a partition, you must decide in advance how much disk space to devote to that partition. You are bound to run out of space in one partition while you still have plenty of space in another.*

Partition and Drive Letters

Every partition, logical drive, and removable disk available to Windows has a *drive letter*. Whether your computer has floppy drives or not, drives A: and B: are reserved for floppy disk drives. Hard disk partitions and drives for *removable disks* (such as CD-ROMs, CD-R/W drives, Zip, and Jaz drives) are assigned letters starting with C:. Any remaining letters can be used for network drives.

Note   *Windows XP has an annoying habit of assigning drive letters in the order in which drives and partitions are added to the system, so that the drive that contains the Windows XP program itself may not be C:, and hard disk drive letters may follow CD-ROM drive letters. You can reassign drive letters if necessary (see "Choosing Your Own Drive Letters" later in this chapter).*

Displaying Information about Drives and Partitions

Windows stores a set of properties for each installed disk drive and partition and allows you to manage them from one program, Disk Management. You can also look at the properties of individual drives and partitions.

The Disk Management Window

To use the Disk Management program, right-click My Computer and select Manage. In the Computer Management window that appears, click the Disk Management item under the Storage heading in the left pane. The Computer Management window with Disk Management selected, as shown in Figure 33-1, includes everything that you ever wanted to know about your disk drives in an easy-to-read format.

The top part of the Disk Management pane (or the right half of the Computer Management window), lists the volumes (partitions and volumes stored on other devices) on your computer. It lists all disks, drives, and partitions that are loaded,

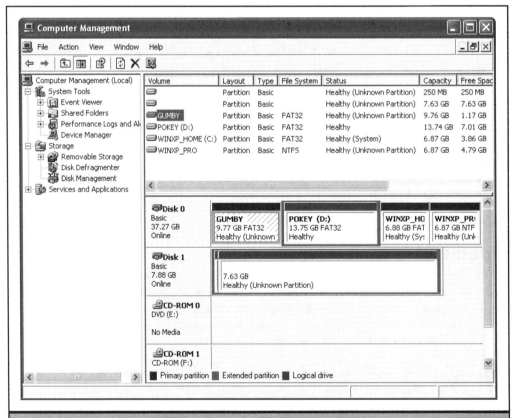

Figure 33-1. *Viewing information about drives and partitions*

mounted, and recognized by Windows XP. It doesn't include removable storage like floppy, CD, CD-R/W, or DVD drives. The columns that run across the top of the volume list are

- **Volume**   The label name applied to the volume.
- **Layout**   Generally a partition. For server computers that provide large-scale storage to networks of computers, other types of volumes may be listed.
- **Type**   Identifies whether the volume is Basic or Dynamic. A *dynamic disk* is formatted so that volumes can be changed on-the-fly (dynamically)—*dynamic volumes*. Dynamic disks aren't supported in Windows XP Home Edition.
- **File System**   Indicates whether the volume is FAT, FAT32, or NTFS. A blank entry indicates a file system *other* than one developed by Microsoft, such as EXT2 (Linux extended), NFS (Network File System, from Sun Microsystems), or HFS (Hierarchical File System, from Apple).
- **Status**   Shows the state of the volume and its relationship to the operating system. Typical states are Healthy, Healthy (At Risk), Initializing, and Failed.
- **Capacity**   Shows the overall capacity for the volume.
- **Free Space**   Shows the space that is free on the volume.
- **% Free**   Shows said free space in percentage format.

The last items (Fault Tolerant and Overhead) are for *RAID* (redundant array of independent disks) and spanned disks only, which are not supported by Windows XP Home Edition.

The bottom half of the Disk Management pane lists the hard disk, CD-ROM, CD-R/RW, and DVD drives on your computer. To the right of each disk name is a diagram of the partitions that are stored on that drive. You see the same partitions that appear in the volume list, in the approximate positions where they are stored on the drives (the sizes of the partitions aren't accurately depicted, though). This diagram includes *hidden partitions* (partitions with file systems that Windows XP can't read), even though you cannot access them or their files.

 Another way to see and manage your disk partitions is by using the Recovery Console's DISKPART command (see Chapter 2, section "Managing Your Disk Partitions with DISKPART").

Properties of Drives and Partitions

Each item on your system with a drive letter—each hard disk partition, floppy disk, and removable disk—also has properties. You can display these properties from an Explorer window (choose Start | My Computer); right-click the drive and choose Properties from the menu that appears or from the Disk Management pane of the Computer Management window, right-click the partition or drive and choose Properties. Figure 33-2 shows the Properties dialog box for a partition (the dialog boxes for other kinds of disk drives look similar, but may have different tabs).

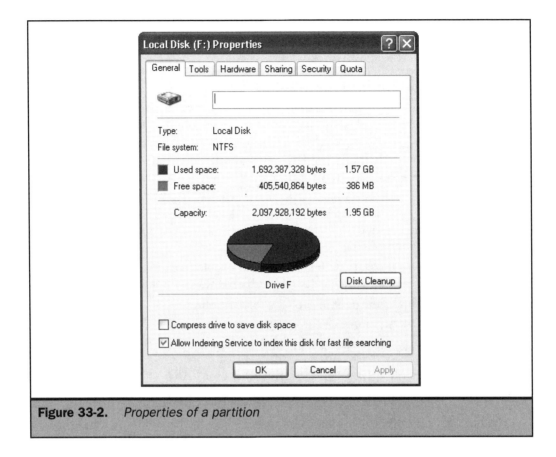

Figure 33-2. *Properties of a partition*

The tabs that appear on the Properties dialog box for a disk drive or partition include the following:

■ **General** Appears for all drives and partitions, showing used and free disk space, type, and file system.

■ **Tools** Contains buttons for error checking, defragmenting, and backing up the drive. This tab doesn't appear for disks you can't write on, such as CD-ROM drives.

■ **Hardware** Lists disk drives and displays the manufacturer, location, and status for the selected drive. You can click the Troubleshoot button on the Hardware tab for device-specific troubleshooting and the Properties button for the drive's properties.

■ **Sharing** Enables you to share the drive or partition with other computers on a LAN.

■ **Quota** Provides settings for disk quotas for user accounts (see Chapter 6).

- **AutoPlay**   For CD-ROM, CD-R, and CD-RW drives, controls what happens when you put a CD into the drive, depending on the type of files it contains (see "Configuring CD Drives" later in this chapter).

- **Recording**   For CD-R and CD-RW drives, displays the write speed and location of the temporary files used during CD burning (see "Configuring CD-R and CD-RW Drives" later in this chapter).

If you have installed a hard-disk housekeeping program like Norton Utilities, additional tabs may appear.

Properties of Hard Disk Drives

The Properties dialog box for a disk drive (shown in Figure 33-3) contains information about the hard disk drive itself, rather than about the partitions stored on the drive. To display the dialog box from the Disk Management pane of the Computer Management window, right-click a disk drive from the list in the lower part of the window and choose

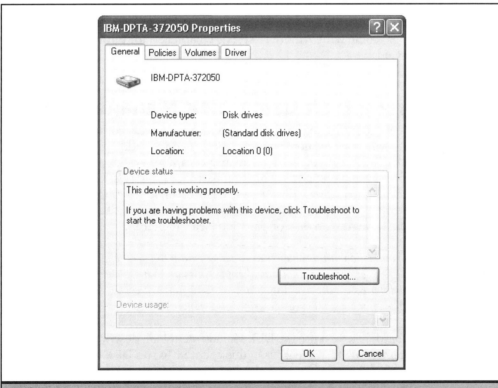

Figure 33-3.   *The properties of a hard disk drive*

Properties from the menu that appears. Or, choose Start | My Computer, right-click any drive or partition, select Properties from the menu that appears (you see the properties of that partition), click the Hardware tab, select the drive you are interested in, and click the Properties button.

The tabs on a hard disk drive Properties dialog box are as follows:

- **General**   Shows the manufacturer, model number, and status of the drive. The Location setting shows the drive's physical device number. (The first hard disk is Location 0.) Click the Troubleshoot button if the drive is not working properly.

- **Policies**   Enables the write cache, which on some drives improves performance.

- **Volumes**   Click the Populate button to display a list of the partitions stored on this drive. This tab also shows the disk number Windows assigns to the drive. The first disk attached to the first disk controller is disk 0. Floppy disk, CD-ROM, and DVD drives don't have disk numbers. The Type is Basic (for hard disks), CDRom, Removable (for Zip, Jaz, and similar disks), and DVD. The Partition Style setting shows how the disk is partitioned, usually MBR (master boot record). Other styles are GPT (GUID Partition Table).

- **Driver**   Shows the source and date of the driver used for this disk drive; many drivers come with Windows XP. See Chapter 13 for information about device drivers.

Partitioning a Disk Using Disk Management

When you buy a new computer or hard disk, you receive it ready for use—already partitioned (usually with one partition) and formatted. If you are adding new unformatted, unpartitioned disk drives or if you want to create a computer system that can run one of several operating systems—such as switching between Windows XP and UNIX or Linux—you may need to partition a disk yourself. However, formatting destroys the data in the areas of the disk it partitions, so be sure to make a backup copy of all the information on your disk before formatting a disk or partition (see Chapter 9).

Note   *Most of the commands in this chapter are available only to users who have administrator user accounts—user accounts that give them permission to make changes to the system itself (see Chapter 6). Before working with partitions and drives, be sure to back up the important files on your system (as described in Chapter 9).*

To partition a hard disk, you use the Disk Management tool, described in the section "The Disk Management Window" earlier in this chapter. To run Disk Management, choose Start, right-click My Computer, and select Manage from the menu that appears. When you see the Computer Management window, click the Disk Management item listed underneath the Storage heading. You then see the main Disk Management pane in the right side of the Computer Management window, as shown in Figure 33-1 earlier in this chapter.

Many computer systems have only one hard disk and one CD-ROM (CD-R/RW, DVD, or what have you), which appear as Disk 0 and CD-ROM 0 in the left column of the lower pane. Figure 33-1 shows two hard disks, Disk 0 and Disk 1, and two removable storage drives, CD-ROM 0 (which is actually a DVD drive) and CD-ROM 1.

 The Disk Management program replaces the Fdisk program that was part of previous versions of Windows.

Creating a New Partition

If you have unallocated space (which appears as an Unknown Partition in the Disk Management diagram), you can create a new partition in some or all of that space. To create a new partition, right-click the part of the diagram that represents the unallocated space (unallocated space has a black stripe running along the top), and choose New Partition from the menu that appears. To create a new logical drive in an extended partition that contains free space (free space has a light green strip along the top), right-click the free space and choose New Logical Drive from the menu that appears. Either way, you see the New Partition Wizard.

The New Partition Wizard asks you to specify the following:

- **Type**   Primary, extended, or logical partition. A disk drive can contain up to four primary partitions or three primary partitions and one extended partition. The logical partition type is available only if you choose to create the new partition in an extended partition with some free space. Choose a primary partition if you are created a partition in which you will install an operating system (an unusual situation). Choose extended if you plan to create several logical partitions within it.

- **Size**   The wizard displays the minimum and maximum size for the partition, based on its type and the space where it will be stored. You can use the entire available space or leave room for other partitions. Windows XP doesn't provide a way to resize partitions later, but you can use a third-party program like PartitionMagic to do so (see the sidebar "Managing Partitions with PartitionMagic").

- **Drive letter or path**   The wizard offers the next available drive letter, but you may select any unused letter. To use the Mount In The Following Empty NTFS Folder option, you must have an NTFS partition with a drive letter on the same machine. If you plan on installing more than one operating system on your computer, you may select the Do Not Assign A Drive Letter Or Drive Path option and let Windows assign a letter later. We usually take the default drive letter assignment.

■ **File system**   The default is NTFS, but you can feel good about using FAT32 as well. Both efficiently utilize space on large drives, but NTFS has more security features, better recovery capabilities after a crash, and file-level compression built in. If you select NTFS, you are also given the option to enable compression. Leave the Allocation unit size as Default.

■ **Label**   Type a name for the partition, indicating what you will use it for.

Figure 33-4 shows the final screen of the New Partition Wizard, summarizing your choices before Windows creates the partition. Formatting a new partition can take several minutes (see "Formatting a Disk" later in this chapter).

Selecting the Active Partition

If you partition your disk among multiple operating systems, one of the partitions is the active partition, the partition from which your computer starts. If you run Windows only, the primary partition is always active. In Windows XP you can change this behavior manually by selecting another partition as active using the Disk Management pane in the Computer Management window. Right-click the disk or partition that you want to make active and select Mark Partition As Active from the menu that appears. You can

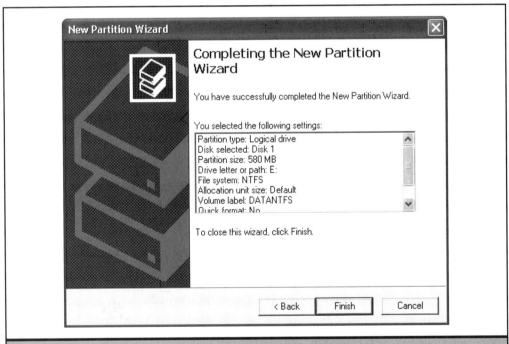

Figure 33-4.   *Creating a new partition with the New Partition Wizard*

only make this change to primary partitions. Extended partitions and logical drives cannot be made active. Only one partition is active at a time—and make sure it's a partition that contains a bootable operating system!

Deleting a Partition

You can delete a partition using the Disk Management pane of the Computer Management window. Right-click the partition and choose Delete Partition (for a primary or extended partition) or Delete Logical Drive (for a logical drive). If you want to delete an extended partition, you first have to delete all the logical drives in the partition.

 When you delete a partition, all the files and folders on the partition are deleted for good—they don't go to the Recycle Bin. There's no way to get them back (unless you have a backup copy).

Repartitioning a Disk

Repartitioning a disk with Windows XP is unpleasant at best. Windows can only create and delete partitions—it can't move, resize, or copy them, and converting them requires using a DOS command. To rearrange the partitions on your system using only the Windows Disk Management program, you delete the partitions that are the wrong size or in the wrong location. Then create new partitions. Follow these steps:

1. Back up all the files on the partitions that you need to delete (see Chapter 9).

2. Open the Disk Management pane in the Computer Management window—choose Start, right-click My Computer, choose Manage, and click Disk Management under the Storage heading in the Computer Management window. You see the Disk Management pane shown in Figure 33-1.

3. Delete the partitions that are in the wrong place or are the wrong size by right-clicking each one and choosing Delete Partition or Delete Logical Drive from the menu that appears.

4. Create new ones by right-clicking the unallocated space (or free space in an extended partition) and choosing New Partition or New Logical Drive from the menu that appears.

5. Reload the backed up data.

Third-party disk utilities, such as PartitionMagic, make this process safer and easier and permit many kinds of changes without backing up and reloading everything. PartitionMagic can move, copy, and resize partitions without deleting them (it's amazing, actually). Utilities such as Drive Image make it easy to create a copy of a partition so you can reload it later. If you plan to use multiple partitions, we recommend you look into third-party partitioning programs (see the sidebar "Managing Partitions with PartitionMagic" earlier in this chapter).

Converting Partitions to NTFS

Windows comes with a Convert command that can convert a FAT or FAT32 partition to NTFS (the Convert command can't convert anything to FAT or FAT32). To convert a partition to NTFS (after backing it up!), follow these steps:

1. Choose Start | All Programs | Accessories | Command Prompt to open a Command Prompt window (see Chapter 4, section "Starting and Exiting DOS Programs").

2. Type **convert** *n:* **/FS:NTFS** and press ENTER, replacing *n:* with the drive letter of the partition you want to convert. If you want verbose mode, in which you see extra explanatory messages, type **/v** at the end of the command.

If you need to convert to a file system other than NTFS, try PartitionMagic. Be sure to get the latest version, since earlier versions don't support NTFS 5.0, which is new in Windows XP.

Choosing Your Own Drive Letters

Windows assigns a drive letter to each partition, logical drive, and removable disk that it can read. Whenever possible, we recommend you use the drive letters Windows assigns (see "Partition and Drive Letters" earlier in this chapter). If you can't, (for example, you are using an antiquated program that expects files to be on certain drives or you install an application that reassigns drive letters willy-nilly), you have a few options: change the letters, assign letters to folders, or assign pathnames to drives or partitions.

When assigning or changing drive letters, you can use any unassigned letter from C: to Z: (inclusive). Letters A: and B: are reserved for floppy disk drives. If a program is using the files on a drive or partition when you try to change its letter, Windows displays an error message.

Changing Drive Letters

You can tell Windows to assign different drive letters to most of your drives and partitions. You cannot, however, change the drive letter of the boot partition (the one that contains the Windows XP program files). You can alternatively add new drive letter assignment or, if you're using NTFS, assign special folders to act as conduits to drives.

To change the drive letter for a partition, follow these steps:

1. Choose Start, right-click My Computer, and choose Manage from the menu that appears. In the Computer Management window, click the Disk Management item under the Storage heading (as shown in Figure 33-1 earlier in the chapter). The Disk Management pane appears in the right part of the Computer Management window.

2. Locate the partition whose letter you would like to change in the upper-right pane of the Computer Management console (the volume list) or the lower-right pane (the list of drives and the diagram of partitions on each drive).

3. Right-click the partition and select Change Drive Letters And Paths from the menu that appears. You see the dialog box shown in Figure 33-5.

4. Click the Change button to modify the existing letter assignment. You see this dialog box:

5. Type or choose a letter in the Assign The Following Drive Letter box and click OK. You return to the Computer Management window, with updated drive letters for the partition.

You can't add a second drive letter to a partition—each partition has only one drive letter at a time. You can remove the drive letter, though, by clicking the Remove button in the Change Drive Letter And Paths dialog box. Windows warns you not to proceed

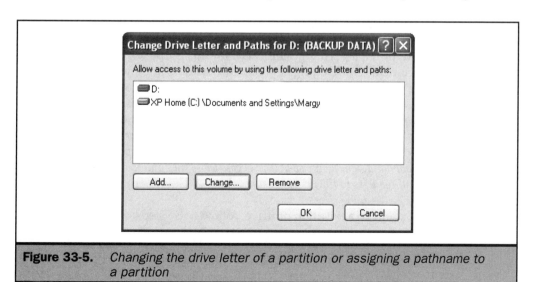

Figure 33-5.   *Changing the drive letter of a partition or assigning a pathname to a partition*

if the drive letter is in use. If you click the Add button, Windows assumes that you want to assign a pathname to the partition, as described in the next section.

Don't change the drive letters of the boot partition (which contains Windows XP itself— Windows XP shouldn't allow you to, anyway). Watch out when changing the drive letter of a partition that contains programs. With a different drive letter, existing references to the program files on that partition would be wrong. Changing the drive letter does not update references to the files on that partition.

Assigning Pathnames to Partitions

You can assign a pathname—like C:\My Documents or D:\Budget Workarea—to a partition. The partition still has its usual drive letter (unless you remove it), but it also has a second name—a pathname. This technique is called *mounting a partition.*

Any space allocated to a specific file system is called a partition, whether it is a small partition on a large drive or a single partition that takes up an entire drive.

Before you mount a partition (that is, assign it a pathname) you choose two things:

- **The partition to mount**   It continues to have its original drive letter, unless you delete the drive letter. The partition can contain files and folders, which will not be disturbed by assigning a pathname to the drive.

- **The pathname to assign to the partition**   The pathname must refer to an existing, empty folder on an NTFS partition. After you assign the pathname to the partition (mount the partition), Windows will redirect references to that folder to the partition instead.

For example, rather than storing all your user's settings and files in the C:\Documents And Settings folders and their subfolders, you might want to store them on a separate partition. You could format a partition with NTFS for this purpose. Move the entire contents of C:\Documents And Settings to the new partition, and mount this partition at the pathname C:\Documents And Settings.

Be sure to empty the folder in which you are about to mount a partition. In the C:\Documents And Settings example, move the contents of C:\Documents And Settings before issuing the command to mount the partition at the pathname. After issuing the command, you won't be able to access those files and folders—Windows will redirect all requests to the new partition.

To assign a pathname to a partition or drive, follow these steps:

1. In an Explorer window, create an empty folder (choose New | Folder from the menu) in a partition formatted with NTFS. Or, empty out an existing folder. If

you have a blank NTFS partition, you can use the root folder. (In the C:\Documents And Settings example, you might use a partition currently named D:.)

2. Choose Start, right-click My Computer, and choose Manage from the menu that appears. In the Computer Management window, click the Disk Management item under the Storage heading (as shown in Figure 33-1 earlier in the chapter).

3. Right-click the partition that you want to mount and choose Change Drive Letter And Paths from the menu that appears. You see the dialog box shown in Figure 33-5. (In our example, right-click the D: partition.)

4. Click the Add button to create a new pathname for the partition. You see this dialog box:

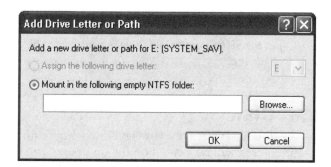

5. In the Mount In The Following Empty NTFS Folder box, type the pathname that you want to assign to the partition, or click the Browse button and navigate to the empty folder you identified in step 1. (In our example, browse to C:\ Documents And Settings.)

6. Click OK.

 You can also assign a drive letter to a network drive or a folder stored on a network drive (see Chapter 30, section "Mapping a Shared Drive or Folder to a Drive Letter").

Assigning Drive Letters to Folders

You can use the DOS SUBST command to assign new drive letters that correspond to folders on existing disks. Follow these steps:

1. Open a Command Prompt window by choosing Start | All Programs | Accessories | Command Prompt.

2. Type the SUBST command in the following format (press ENTER after typing the command):

SUBST N: C:\MYAPP

This command makes the drive letter N a synonym for the folder C:\Myapp. You can use any unused drive letter and the address (pathname) of any folder.

3. Type **exit** to close the Command Prompt window.

The new substituted drive letter is available immediately.

 If the path of your folder uses long names, then in the SUBST command, you have to use the MS-DOS name equivalent, as shown by the DOS DIR command (see Chapter 4, section "DOS Filenames").

To disconnect a SUBSTed drive letter, type the following:

SUBST N: /D

 The SUBST command lists only until you restart Windows. If you use a SUBSTed drive on a regular basis, put the SUBST command in your Autoexec.nt file so that it's available every time you start Windows.

Formatting a Disk

Formatting a disk writes the file system, the low-level structure information needed to track where files and folders will be located on the disk (see "The FAT, FAT32, and NTFS File Systems" earlier in this chapter). Generally, you need to format disks only when you want to clean off a floppy disk or other removable disk (like a Zip or Jaz disk) for reuse, if you repartition your hard disk and create a new partition, or if you have a disaster with Windows and want to reinstall it from scratch. CD-R and CD-RW disks don't need to be formatted before use.

 Formatting a disk—hard disk or removable—deletes all the information from the disk, so proceed with care!

Formatting a Hard Disk

Before formatting your hard disk (or one partition on a hard disk), be sure you make a backup copy of any files you want to keep (see Chapter 9). To format a hard disk, follow these steps:

1. Open My Computer and locate the drive you want to format.

2. Right-click the icon for the drive and choose Format in the menu that pops up. You see the Format dialog box shown in Figure 33-6. Almost none of the fields in the window, except for the volume label, apply to hard disks—leave them with their default settings.

3. Type a drive label in the Volume Label box (if the box is blank or if you want to change the existing label) and click the Start button in the Format dialog box.

4. If the drive contains files or folders, Windows asks whether you really want to reformat the disk because existing files will be lost. Assuming you want to format the disk, choose Yes to do so. Formatting can take several minutes—the process involves reading the entire disk to check for bad spots.

  You can't format the disk from which you are running Windows; Windows displays an error message saying the disk contains files Windows is using. You can't format a CD-ROM either.

Formatting a Removable Disk

Formatting a removable disk (like a floppy disk, Zip disk, or Jaz disk) is like formatting a hard disk, except more format options are available. If you only want to erase the files on a previously formatted disk without rechecking for bad spots, select Quick Format or Quick (Erase) on the Format dialog box shown in Figure 33-6. Then click the Start button in the Format dialog box.

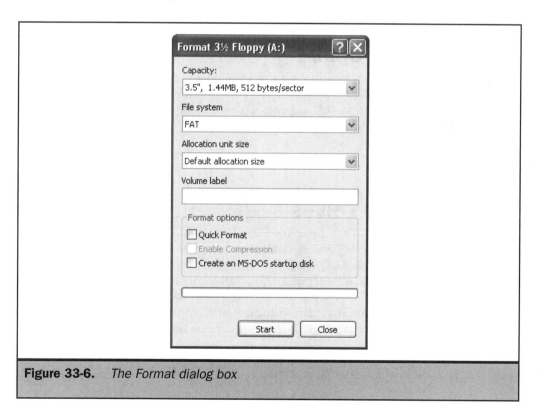

Figure 33-6. *The Format dialog box*

When you format a disk, Windows may report bad sectors on the disk. Windows marks the sectors as unusable to prevent programs from trying to write information there. If a floppy disk has any bad sectors, throw it away and use a new one—floppy disks are too cheap for you to fool around with the possibility of losing data.

Copying a Floppy Disk

To copy a floppy disk (that is, to copy all the information from one floppy to another while erasing the previous contents of the disk you are copying into), right-click the floppy disk in an Explorer window and choose Copy Disk from the shortcut menu that appears. Click Start and follow the prompts to insert first the original disk and then the disk onto which you want to copy.

 *If you copy floppy disks often, create an icon on your desktop for the Copy Disk command. Right-click a blank space on the desktop and choose New / Shortcut from the shortcut menu that appears. In the Type The Location Of The Item box on the Create Shortcut dialog box that appears, type **diskcopy a: a:** (the DOS command that copies a floppy). Click Next. In the Type A Name For This Shortcut box, type a name like **Copy Floppy**. Click Next, choose an icon and click Finish.*

Checking Free Space

You can easily see how much free space is available on any partition. Choose Start | My Computer and select the partition (or drive). Right-click the partition or drive and select Properties from the menu that appears. You see a Properties dialog box with a pie chart like the one in Figure 33-2 (if the General tab isn't selected, click it).

 Click the Disk Cleanup button to look for and delete unneeded files (see Chapter 34).

Configuring CD Drives

Because CD-ROMs (data CDs) and audio CDs (CDs containing sound, or CD-DAs) are prerecorded, no preparation is needed to use them. Just insert them in the drive, and Windows recognizes them. If a CD-ROM contains an *AutoRun* program (that is, a file named Autorun.inf in the root folder of the CD-ROM, containing instructions for what program to run), Windows runs it. For audio CDs, Windows usually runs the Windows Media Player application automatically, turning your computer into a CD player (see Chapter 19, section "Playing Audio CDs")—useful if you like background music while you work.

 If you don't want the AutoRun program on a CD-ROM to run, or you don't want Windows to start playing an audio CD, open the drive, insert the disk and hold down the SHIFT key while closing the drive—keep the SHIFT key down until you are sure no program has started.

If the CD-ROM that you insert contains audio or video files (that is, MP3 or AVI video), a dialog box may appear asking what you would like to do with the media contained on the disk. Your options are to either play the files or to open an Explorer window displaying the items. Checking the Always Do The Selected Action check box causes Windows to either play or display the files for that disk.

You can control what happens when you put an audio or data CD in the drive:

1. In an Explorer window, right-click the CD drive, choose Properties, and click the AutoPlay tab on the Properties dialog box that appears (see Figure 33-7).

2. Set the Select Content Type drop-down menu to the type of files on the CD. For audio CDs, choose Music CD.

3. Choose the action that you want Windows to perform when it detects this type of CD in the drive. The list of actions depends on the type of CD you chose in the previous step.

4. Or, choose the Prompt Me Each Time To Choose An Action option. This setting tells Windows that each time you put a CD in the drive, you want to see a dialog box with this list of options.

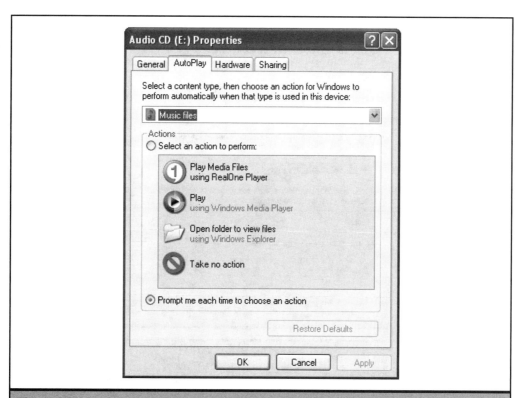

Figure 33-7. *Specifying what to do when you put a CD in the drive*

Configuring CD-R and CD-RW Drives

Recordable CD disks include CD-Rs (which can be recorded once) and CD-RWs (which can be written, erased, and written again). Neither type of CD needs to be formatted before use (or can be formatted, for that matter). See the section "Making Your Own CDs" in Chapter 8 for how to burn data CDs and section "Creating Your Own Music CDs" in Chapter 19 for how to burn music CDs.

Most CD burners are CD-RW drives, which can burn both CD-R and CD-RW disks. Some older systems have CD-R drives that can burn only CD-R disks. The Properties dialog box for a CD-R or CD-RW drive includes the Recording tab shown in Figure 33-8. The tab includes these settings:

■ **Enable CD Recording On This Drive**   Normally, this check box is selected. If you have more than one CD-R or CD-RW drive on your system, only one can be enabled.

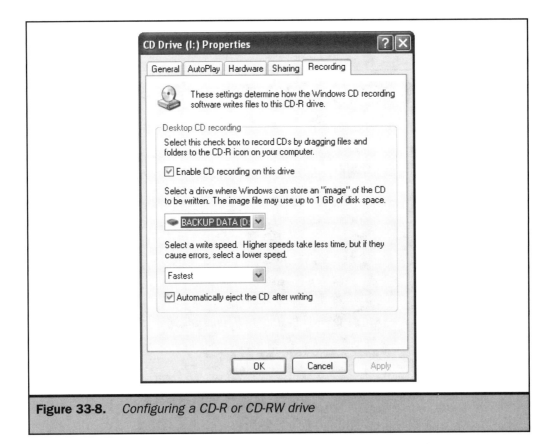

Figure 33-8.   *Configuring a CD-R or CD-RW drive*

- **Select A Drive Where Windows Can Store An Image Of The CD To Be
  Written**   Before burning a CD, Windows copies all the files to a temporary
  storage space, converting file formats as necessary for the CD. Normally, this
  drive is the one where Windows is installed, but you can switch to another
  drive with more free space. An audio CD can take up to 70MB of disk space,
  while a data CD can use up to 700MB.

- **Select A Write Speed**   This setting defaults to Fastest (the fastest speed that
  the CD-R or CD-RW drive supports). However, if you have trouble with the
  CDs that you burn, try setting this to a lower speed.

- **Automatically Eject The CD After Writing**   If you like to test your CD right
  after you burn it, you may want to turn this off. We like to select this check box,
  because the sound of the CD drawer opening is our signal that the CD is finished.

Tip   *If you have trouble burning CDs, or if the CDs you burn can't be played in CD players
or other computers, see the section "Troubleshooting Burning CDs" in Chapter 8
for ideas. For audio CDs, see the section "Troubleshooting Burning Audio CDs" in
Chapter 19.*

WINDOWS AND DISK
HOUSEKEEPING

Chapter 34

Keeping Your Disk Safe

In addition to the files and folders on a disk, some of the space on each disk is used to store the structure of the disk, including a table of the parts of the disk that are free (available for storing new information), a table of the files and folders on the disk, and a list of which blocks on the disk store the information in which file.

If this structural information gets corrupted, you can lose some or all of the information on the disk. It's wise to check the structure of the information on each hard disk regularly by using a Windows program called ChkDsk—which not only checks the disk structure, but can also fix most of the errors that it finds.

Another disk problem arises when you create and delete many files over a long period of time. Files are stored in a series of sectors on your disk, and the sectors are not necessarily next to each other. While this is more of a problem for FAT32 partitions, NTFS partitions can also become fragmented after time. To fix this problem, you can run the Disk Defragmenter utility that comes with Windows. Disk Defragmenter moves the information on your disk around to speed up access.

Many programs create temporary or backup files, which are not always deleted when they are no longer needed. The Disk Cleanup program can delete stale temporary files for you.

Note *If you need to restore your Windows system files to the way they were before you installed an upgrade or before your system started having problems, try the System Restore program. For information about your system and repairing Windows system files, see Chapter 2, section "Returning Your System to a Predefined State with System Restore".*

Windows File Protection

Windows XP comes with a feature called *Windows File Protection*, or *WFP*. WFP is running whenever Windows is running, monitoring the files that make up Windows itself. Whenever a program replaces one of the Windows system files, WFP checks whether the new file was accompanied by a "signed" (verified and encrypted) file from Microsoft. If not, or if an earlier version of a file has replaced a later version, WFP replaces the file with its own copy (from the WFP collection of duplicate files at C:\Windows\System32\dllcache, if Windows is installed on C:).

You don't have to turn WFP on, and there's no way to turn it off. WFP doesn't display any messages when it decides to replace a system file with its own version, but it may prompt you to insert the Windows XP CD-ROM to reinstall a file.

Testing Your Disk Structure with ChkDsk

The ChkDsk (Check Disk) program can both diagnose and repair errors on a wide variety of devices, including hard disks, floppy disks, RAM drives, removable disks, and laptop memory cards. ChkDsk doesn't work on CD-R or CD-RW disks. ChkDsk can check the physical surface of disk drivers for bad sectors and possibly recover lost data, and it checks the file allocation table (FAT), the directory structure, and the long filenames associated with many files.

 If Windows crashes or you turn off the computer without shutting down, Windows typically runs ChkDsk when you restart to check your hard disk for errors resulting from the unexpected termination. There are some occasions when ChkDsk will not run.

Running ChkDsk

Certain ChkDsk functions, like fixing disk errors and recovering lost sectors, are not accessible while Windows is running. This is because the repairs cannot be completed while there are open files on the disk to be fixed. When you try to run ChkDsk, Windows might need to schedule the program to run the next time you restart Windows instead.

To run ChkDsk, follow these steps:

1. Right-click the disk drive in an Explorer window and choose Properties.

2. On the Properties dialog box for the disk, click the Tools tab and click the Check Now button. You see the Check Disk dialog box:

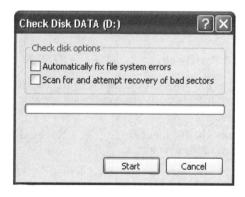

3. Select both check boxes to perform a full disk check and click Start. You usually see a message saying that Windows can't run the program until the next time you start Windows.

4. Click Yes. The next time Windows starts, you see a message that the disk check has been scheduled, and displaying the results as the program runs, which can take several minutes (depending on the size of the disk). When ChkDsk runs, you see its results before Windows displays your logon screen or desktop.

 You can also run ChkDsk at the DOS command prompt (see Chapter 4, section "The Command Prompt Window"). Choose Start | Run and type **chkdsk** *at the command prompt. Then press* ENTER. *To tell ChkDsk to fix any errors it finds, type* **chkdsk /f** *instead.*

Other ChkDsk Options

ChkDsk can do a number of other things if you run it at the command prompt. To see your options at the command line, type the following at the prompt in a Command Prompt window:

```
chkdsk /?
```

or type **help chkdsk**. When you press ENTER, you see information about ChkDsk's options, which are also listed in Table 34-1. Some switches work only on NTFS partitions, and some work only on FAT32 partitions.

Switch or Argument	FAT32 Partitions	NTFS Partitions
volume	Specifies the drive to be acted on. Enter the drive letter as the letter and a colon (such as, c:, d:, x:) or as a volume name (such as, CRUNCHY, DRV012).	
filename	Specifies specific files to be checked for fragmentation.	Not used.
/F	Fixes errors on the specified disk. If no disk is specified, ChkDsk checks the boot disk and fixes it as needed.	
/V	Displays the full filename and path of every file on the disk. This is not recommended unless you have a lot of free time.	Not used.

Table 34-1. *ChkDsk Command Switches*

Switch or Argument	FAT32 Partitions	NTFS Partitions
/R	Locates and attempts to recover the data in lost sectors. This command also implicitly applies an /F command.	
/L:*size*	Not used.	Changes the file size of the operations log to the specified amount (in KB: 1MB = 1024KB).
/X	Causes a mounted volume to be forcibly dismounted before performing the implicit /F command. This switch cannot be used on the boot volume.	Not used.
/I	Not used.	Performs a less complete index check.
/C	Not used.	Skips checking directory structure cycles.

Table 34-1.   *ChkDsk Command Switches* (continued)

Defragmenting Your Disk

Windows stores information on your disks in sectors, which can be anywhere from 2 to 32 kilobytes (KB) in size. Files are stored in as many sectors as requires to fit (for example, a 64KB file would take two sectors on a disk with 32KB sectors). These sectors do not need to remain sequential: Windows keeps track of which sectors are used for which files, no matter where they are on the disk. Sectors for a single file can be located just about anywhere on the disk.

Fragmentation occurs when you add and remove files from your computer. When you delete a file, Windows marks the sectors as available and uses them the next time you create a file. If a file gets larger and contiguous space isn't available, Windows uses other available sectors to store the new part of the file. As you continue to use your computer, your files can become more and more fragmented. When you save a new file, if no contiguous space is large enough, Windows writes the new file using sectors that aren't together—the file is fragmented right from the start.

Fragmentation slows down your disk access and, subsequently, your computing efficiency because Windows has to spend more time finding the parts of each file. The more chunks a file is split into, the slower Windows accesses the file because the file system has to move all over the disk to find pieces of the file.

Fortunately, Windows comes with a program that moves the contents of files around on your hard disk so that each file is stored as one contiguous string of sectors—Disk Defragmenter. Run the Disk Defragmenter utility when you plan on not using your computer for some time, because it can take an hour or so and has to restart if you change any files.

In this day of ultra-cheap, gargantuan drives (80GB and beyond) with superfast access times (7,200 RPM standard and 10,000 RPM becoming more common), fragmentation doesn't affect speed nearly as much as it did on older hard disks. One reason is that newer disks read an entire *track* (concentric circle of information) at a time from the disk into the disk's buffer memory, so it matters less if the sectors of the track contain information in the wrong order. If your disk has lots of free space, your files are less likely to be badly fragmented.

Even though Disk Defragmenter moves data about on your drive, no files or folders appear to move. How you organize your files and such are really an illusion anyway. Which folder you put your copy of the next Great American Novel has nothing to do with where it's stored in the disk itself.

Running Disk Defragmenter

Follow these steps to run Disk Defragmenter.

1. Choose Start | All Programs | Accessories | System Tools | Disk Defragmenter, or right-click the disk drive in an Explorer window and choose Properties. On the Properties dialog box for the disk, click the Tools tab and click the Defragment Now button. You see the Disk Defragmenter window, shown in Figure 34-1.

2. Choose the drive you want to defragment by right-clicking the drive from the list that appears. (They're listed by the partition's location on the drive and not by drive letter.) The list of drives includes physical drives (actual disk drives or partitions of drives) and removable drives. The list does not include networked drives on other systems (see Chapter 30).

3. Click Analyze. Disk Defragmenter starts to work and displays the results of its analysis, as shown in Figure 34-1. The colored bar in the Estimated Disk Usage Before Defragmentation box shows the usage of the sectors on the disk. The meanings of the colors are shown at the bottom of the window.

4. If the analysis reveals that the volume should be defragmented, the same dialog box offers to start the process. Click the Defragment button if it appears: if it doesn't, your disk doesn't need defragmentation.

5. While Disk Defragmenter is running, you see two disk usage maps: the upper one the analysis of your hard disk, and the lower one an estimate of what it will look like following the defragmentation. When Disk Defragmenter is done, a message asks whether you want to exit the program; click Yes.

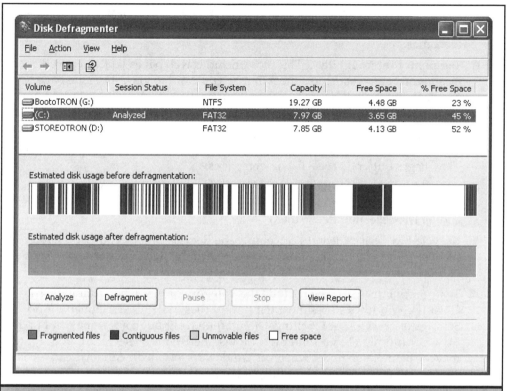

Figure 34-1.   *Disk Defragmenter analyzing your disk for file fragmentation.*

Deleting Temporary Files with Disk Cleanup

When Windows notices that there's not much free space left on the disk on which Windows is installed (usually C:), it offers to run Disk Cleanup, a program that can delete unneeded temporary files from your hard disk. Some programs create temporary files and then don't delete the files when they are through with them. If a program, or Windows itself, exits unexpectedly (or "crashes"), temporary files can be left on your hard disk. Deleting these files from time to time is a good idea, not only because they take up space, but also because their presence can confuse the programs that created them.

Types of Temporary Files That Disk Cleanup Can Delete

Disk Cleanup may suggest deleting these categories of unnecessary files:

■ **Downloaded Program Files**   These files are downloaded when you browse the Web and encounter web pages that include ActiveX controls or Java applets.

If you need these files again, your browser will download them automatically, so it's safe to delete them. You can click the View Files button to see a list of filenames.

■ **Temporary Internet Files**   This *cache* includes web pages you've viewed recently. You browser stores them in case you want to view the same page again. They are always safe to delete. You can click the View Files button to see a list of filenames.

■ **Offline Web Pages**   Your browser can store web pages so that you can look at them when you are offline (not connected to the Internet). You can click the View Pages button to see a list of web pages.

■ **Old Chkdsk Files**   When Chkdsk finds misallocated disk sectors, it puts them in files. Unless you plan to look in these files for missing information, go ahead and let Disk Cleanup delete them.

■ **Recycle Bin**   Disk Cleanup can empty the Recycle Bin for you (see Chapter 7, section "Using the Recycle Bin"). You can click the View Files button to see a list of filenames.

■ **Temporary Files**   Always include this category of files when running Disk Cleanup. Windows stores most temporary files in the C:\Documents And Settings*username*\Local Settings\Temp folder, although a few may end up in the C:\Windows\Temp folder (if you installed Windows in a different folder, they are in the Temp folder wherever Windows is installed). Windows can become confused if this folder contains lots of temporary files that should have been deleted automatically but weren't.

■ **WebClient/Publisher Temporary Files**   These are temporary files created when you use Web Folders (see Chapter 26, section "Working with FTP and Web Servers Using Web Folders"). They are seldom large.

■ **Compress Old Files**   On NTFS disks, Windows can compress files that you rarely used, using NTFS compression (not ZIP files). The files aren't deleted. Click the Options button to specify what files are compressed: you enter the number of days within which the files must not have been accessed.

■ **Catalog Files For The Content Indexer**   The Indexing Service speeds up searches for files but creates temporary files in the process (see Chapter 8, section "Using Indexing Service"). You can safely delete them.

Caution   *Disk Cleanup may recommend deleting files that haven't been used in months, without regard to type. When you click some categories in the Disk Cleanup dialog box, a View Names button appears. Take a look at the names of the files it recommends deleting to make sure that they don't include important documents that you haven't used in months but want to keep.*

Running Disk Cleanup

Here's how to run Disk Cleanup any time, not just when Window notices that space is running low:

1. Choose Start | All Programs | Accessories | System Tools | Disk Cleanup.

2. The Disk Cleanup program runs and asks which disk you want to clean up. Choose a disk drive and click OK. The Disk Cleanup program checks the disk for unnecessary files and displays a window, shown in Figure 34-2, that tells you how much disk space you can reclaim by deleting temporary files right now. Of course, this may include temporary files that your programs are currently using!

3. Click the box for each type of temporary file you want Disk Cleanup to delete. For more information on a type of temporary file, click the description; the program displays an explanation of what the files are and what folders Disk Cleanup will delete them from.

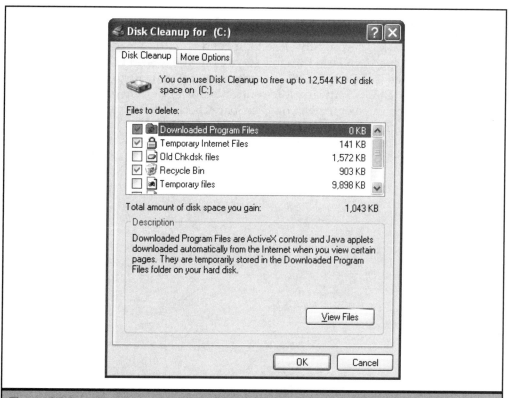

Figure 34-2.   *The Disk Cleanup's list of temporary files to delete*

4. For additional options, click the More Options tab. Three buttons provide other ways to free up disk space, including deleting Windows components you don't use, uninstalling programs, and reducing the amount of space used by the System Restore program (see Chapter 2, section "Returning Your System to a Predefined State with System Restore"). Click the corresponding button to try any of these methods.

5. If you want to see the names of the files that will be deleted (in a separate Explorer window), select the type of files to be deleted and click the View Files button.

6. To begin deleting files, click OK. The program asks whether you are sure you want to delete files. Click Yes.

Note   *The programs shown on the More Options tab that can free up disk space are one-time operations. If you schedule the Disk Cleanup program to run on a regular basis (using Scheduled Tasks), these other programs do not run (see Chapter 1, section "Running Programs on a Schedule Using Scheduled Tasks").*

Disabling Low Disk Space Notification

If your Windows disk is chronically close to full and you don't want Windows to check for low disk space, you can turn this service off. You'll need to edit the Registry to make this change (see Chapter 38). After backing up your Registry, open the HKEY_CURRENT_USER/Software/Microsoft/Windows/CurrentVersion/Policies/Explorer key. Set the value of the NoLowDiskSpaceChecks key to 1. If there is no key by that name, right-click the Explorer key, choose New | DWORD Value from the menu that appears, name the new key NoLowDiskSpaceChecks, and press ENTER. Double-click the new key and type **1** for its value. Restart Windows to complete the change.

The
Complete
Reference

Chapter 35

Tuning Windows XP for
Maximum Performance

Windows XP automatically sets itself up to give you adequate performance. Several tools enable you to enhance performance, primarily disk performance:

- **The Performance Options dialog box**   Shows you display, processor, and memory settings that affect performance.
- **The Task Manager program**   Displays the system resources of your computer.
- **The System Monitor**   Displays graphs of system usage.

Another important way to speed up Windows is to tune your hard disk to speed up disk access. Finally, be sure to check what programs Windows is running automatically on startup—you may be running AOL Instant Messenger and Quicken BillMinder without knowing it, slowing down your system (see Chapter 2, section "Stopping Programs from Running at Startup").

Don't make a lot of performance changes at once. Change one or two settings and then wait a day to judge the effects.

On the other hand, in our experience, few tuning techniques make a noticeable difference on a balanced system with adequate memory and disk, although they do make some difference on small systems with slow disks. The best ways to improve system performance are to add more memory and a faster disk, in that order. Microsoft recommends at least 128MB of RAM, but adding more (so you have at least 256MB) speeds up computing considerably.

Tuning Your Computer's Performance with the Performance Options Dialog Box

To look at and change settings that affect Windows performance, you use the Performance Options dialog box. Click Start, right-click My Computer and choose Properties to display the System Properties dialog box, which contains information about many aspects of your computer system. Click the Advanced tab (shown in Figure 35–1) and then click the Settings button in the Performance section (the top part). You see the Performance Options dialog box (shown in Figure 35–2).

Tuning Your Display Settings

The Visual Effects tab of the Performance Options dialog box lists about a dozen effects that make your screen display look snazzy but that also require processing power

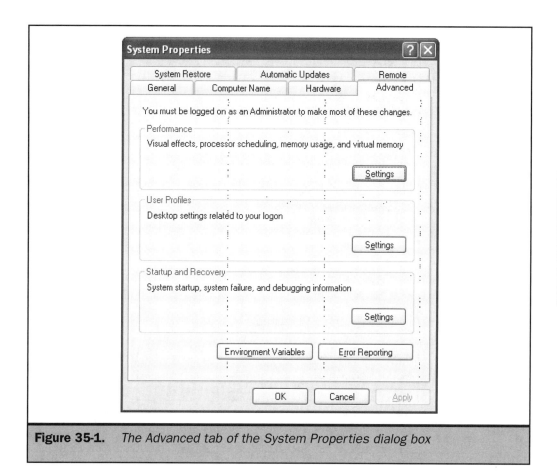

Figure 35-1. *The Advanced tab of the System Properties dialog box*

almost every time your computer updates the screen. The top part of the dialog box shows four options:

- **Let Windows Choose What's Best For My Computer**   Windows decides which effects to make active (or inactive) based on the system resources you have available. Newer, faster systems have most, if not all, effects selected.

- **Adjust For Best Appearance**   Turns all effects on.

- **Adjust For Best Performance**   Turns all effects off, possibly speeding up your system.

- **Custom**   Enables you to select which effects you want active.

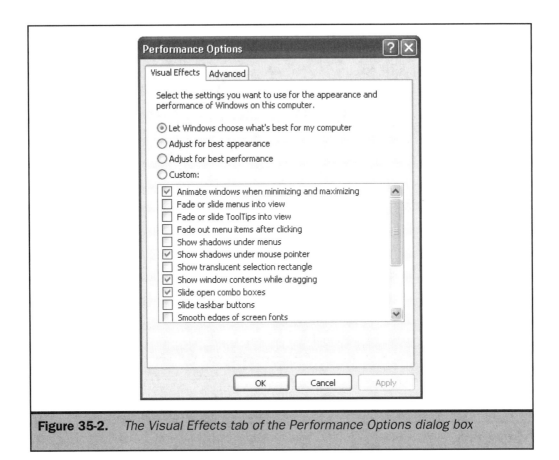

Figure 35-2. *The Visual Effects tab of the Performance Options dialog box*

The list of screen effects appears in the lower part of the dialog box with check boxes to show which effects are active. If you select Custom, you can override Windows settings. Most of the effects do exactly what their names say they do, but two names defy comprehension:

- **Use Common Tasks In Folders** Toggles on and off the Task pane that appears by default in all Explorer windows. (We find the Task pane useful, so we leave this check box selected.)

- **Use Visual Styles On Windows And Buttons** Toggles on and off the default Windows XP appearance. If you use a utility like WindowBlinds (**www.windowblinds.net**) from Stardock Corporation to customize your Windows screen, be sure to uncheck this item, or else the Windows XP appearance will conflict with your WindowBlinds skins.

Tuning Your Processor and Memory Settings

A few settings affect how Windows allocates its resources. These settings appear on the Advanced tab of the Performance Options dialog box (see Figure 35–3).

■ **Processor Scheduling** Controls how Windows allocates processor time to processes. You can elect to favor either Programs (applications) or Background Services (processes that Windows runs behind the scenes). If your computer provides file, printing, or Internet connection services for other computers on a network, you may wish to select Background Services to give requests from other computers higher priority. Otherwise, leave it at Programs. You can use the computer even if Background Services is selected, though your programs may run slowly.

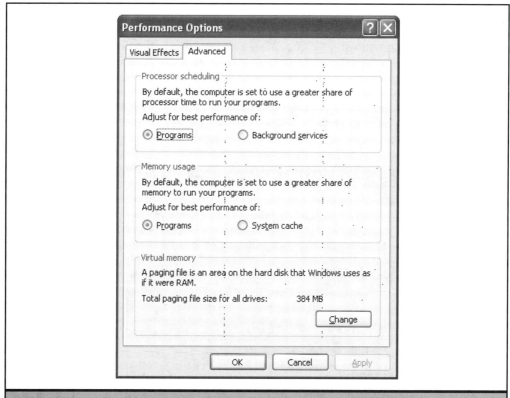

Figure 35-3.   *The Performance Options dialog box showing the Advanced tab*

■ **Memory Usage**   This setting, which controls how Windows allocates your computer's memory, is interesting. Normally, leave this setting at its default, Programs, to give your programs as much memory as they need. However, if you tend to load a few applications and then run them without loading other applications, you may be better served by selecting the System Cache option. Specifically designed for web and network servers, this setting can also assist users who frequently access large files. The System Cache has priority over the disc cache, and is faster.

Tuning Your Swap File Size

Windows automatically manages program storage by using *virtual memory*, which moves chunks of program and data storage between disk and memory automatically, so individual programs don't have to do all their own memory management.

Normally, Windows manages virtual memory automatically, but in a few cases you may want to change its parameters. Click the Change button in the Virtual Memory part of the Advanced tab of the Performance Options dialog box to see the Virtual Memory dialog box, as shown in Figure 35-4. You can specify the disk drive on which Windows stores its *swap file* (the file to which virtual memory is copied), along with the

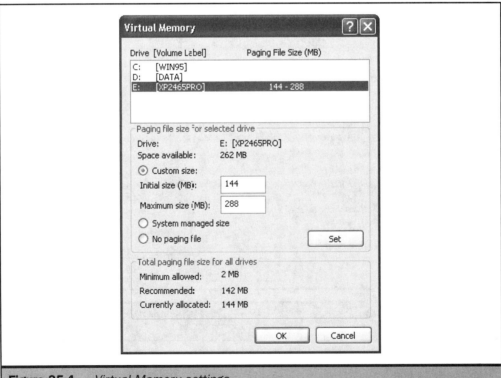

Figure 35-4.   *Virtual Memory settings*

minimum and maximum sizes of the swap file. Click a drive to see the settings for any swap file stored on it.

You might want to set your own virtual memory settings in two cases:

- If you have more than one disk, Windows normally puts the swap file on the boot partition (the partition or drive from which Windows loads). If you have another partition or drive that is larger or faster, you might want to tell Windows to store the swap file there, instead.

- If you are extremely short of disk space, you can decrease the amount of virtual memory and, hence, the disk space that Windows allocates. If you decrease virtual memory too far, programs may fail as they run out of memory. Generally, there's no advantage to increasing the amount of virtual memory beyond the default because extra virtual memory doesn't make the system run any faster.

You can also disable virtual memory altogether, which is usually a bad idea unless you have an enormous amount of RAM.

Tracking System Resources

To keep Windows running smoothly, it helps to know when your system resources are running low. Windows XP deals with *system resources*—memory used by Windows applications—on a much more sophisticated level than Windows Me/9x. Because it is based on Windows 2000/NT, Windows XP inherits its foreparents' technological edge in memory management and does not succumb to the same resource limitations as Windows Me/9x.

Windows XP runs each application in its own protected memory space. If a program crashes, XP is far more likely to be responsive than Windows Me was because other programs and Windows itself are not affected by the crash. The protected memory space also allows you to restart a crashed application safely, which rarely worked in Windows Me/9x. Of course, Windows XP has its own liabilities.

If you push Windows XP to the limit of its resources—by running too many programs at the same time—it behaves unreliably, just as Windows Me/9x did. This is because Windows XP requires access to global system resources just like all other versions of Windows, so the benefits of protected memory do not apply in the event of a general system overload. If you only have a 64MB system but have 256MB appetites, your system will operate unreliably, if at all. The best thing to do is to monitor your system to see where your computer's cycles are going. (A *cycle* is a process in which the CPU completes one string of instructions.)

Monitoring System Use with the Task Manager

Windows, like any computer system, can monitor many aspects of its own operation, including CPU use, the software disk cache, disk operations, serial port operations, and network operations. Sometimes, when system performance is unacceptable, you can monitor key aspects and determine where the bottleneck is occurring. This helps determine whether the most effective improvements would be through software reconfiguration or a hardware upgrade, such as adding more memory. The Task Manager is a utility that comes with Windows and displays performance data, running applications, system-level processes, and network operability (see Figure 35–5).

You can run the Task Manager by right-clicking the taskbar and selecting Task Manager or pressing CTRL-ALT-DEL. The Task Manager loads a small icon in the notification area of the task bar, with bars that indicate at what percentage the CPU is being used.

The Processes tab lists all the processes that are currently running. If you want to see only your applications programs, rather than all the Windows-related background processes that take up most of the processes list, click the Application tab. The Networking tab displays information about your network connection, if any (see Chapter 29). The Users tab (which doesn't appear if Fast User Switching is disabled) shows what user accounts are in use (see Chapter 6).

The Performance tab, as shown in Figure 35-6, reveals a plethora of technical information, the same as the equivalent tab in Windows 2000.

The important item to note is the CPU Usage bar graph in the upper-left corner. Even when the computer is idle (meaning that no applications are doing anything significant), you still see some activity. However, if the meter spikes and mouse movement

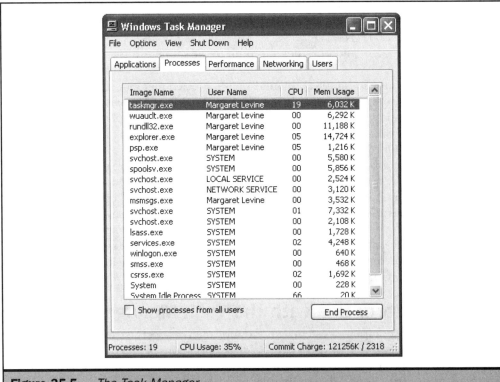

Figure 35-5.   *The Task Manager*

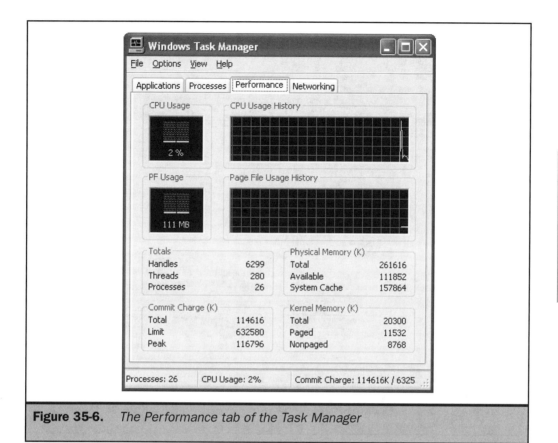

Figure 35-6.   *The Performance tab of the Task Manager*

is sluggish, a culprit application is probably causing havoc. Switch to the Processes tab (as shown in Figure 35-5) and look in the CPU column. (You can click a column heading to sort by the values in that column—click the CPU heading twice to list the highest CPU values at the top of the list.) The System Idle Process item should have a number from 0 to 99 in the CPU column. If a process is using a lot of CPU cycles, try closing the program that created it. You can also end (kill) a process by selecting it and clicking End Process. If that doesn't work, you may be forced to shut down and restart the computer to stop the rogue process.

Viewing Graphs in the System Monitor

Older versions of Windows came with a program called System Monitor, which graphed various measures of system performance. Windows XP also has this program—its version is shown in Figure 35-7. You can run it by choosing Start | Control Panel | Performance And Maintenance | Administrative Tools and running the Performance icon. The meanings of the items on the graph are listed below the graph. You can use the toolbar buttons to change the format of the graph and add data to it.

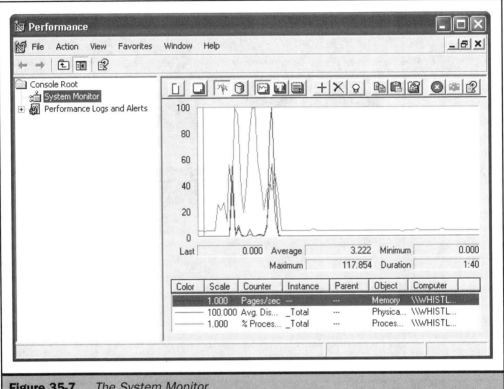

Figure 35-7. *The System Monitor*

Tuning Your Hard Disk's Performance

The most effective way to speed up most Windows systems, short of adding extra memory or a faster drive, is to optimize your hard disk. Try these two Windows utilities:

- **Disk Defragmenter** The most important Windows tuning program is the Disk Defragmenter (see Chapter 34, section "Defragmenting Your Disk"). As it defragments your disk, this program can also rearrange your executable programs so they can start and run faster.

- **Disk Cleanup** As time passes, your computer's hard disk gathers junk (such as unneeded files). Windows slows down and may act strangely if too many of these unneeded files have accumulated, especially if they are in your temporary storage folder (usually C:\Documents And Settings*username*\Local Settings\ Temp). The Disk Cleanup utility deletes these troublesome files (see Chapter 34, section "Deleting Temporary Files with Disk Cleanup").

Tip *The biggest space waster of the bunch is Internet Explorer, which is usually configured to occupy as much as 100MB of your hard disk with temporary files. Two options can help to reduce this waste. First, reduce the amount of space that Internet Explorer uses for its temporary files. Choose Start | Control Panel | Network And Internet Connections and open the Internet Options icon. Or choose Tools | Internet Options from the Internet Explorer menu bar. You see the General tab of the Internet Properties or Internet Options dialog box. In the Temporary Internet Files section of the dialog box, click the Settings button and reduce the space allocation to something more reasonable, like 50MB. Click OK. Second, click the Advanced tab of the Internet Properties or Internet Options dialog box and scroll down to the Security section of the settings. Select the Empty Temporary Internet Files Folder When Browser Is Closed check box to tell Internet Explorer to remove all old files automatically.*

Disabling Unnecessary Services

Windows has dozens of *services*—special programs running in the background that other programs (including Windows itself) rely on. Most of the services are vital parts of the operating system, but some aren't. For example, if your computer isn't on a LAN, you don't need to run the Computer Browser service, which maintains an updated list of the computers on your LAN.

To see and configure the services running on your computer, choose Start | Control Panel | Performance And Maintenance | Administrative Tools and running the Services icon. Or, choose Start | Run, type **services.msc**, and press ENTER. Either way, you see the Services window, as shown in Figure 35-8. Maximize the window and enlarge the columns so you can read the names and descriptions of the services. Click the Extended tab at the bottom of the window if it's not already selected, so that you see information about the selected service. To read all the information about a service, double-click it so that its Properties dialog box appears.

Services that don't say "Started" in the Status column aren't running, so skip them. Look at each service that is running. If you don't understand what it does, don't stop it.

If a process on the Processes tab of the Windows Task Manager window is taking large amounts of CPU time, a program may be running out of control. To check whether it's a service, note the name of the program and search the Services window for the program name (it appears in the Path To Executable box on the service's Properties dialog box).

You can stop or pause a service by double-clicking the service and clicking the Stop or Pause button on the General tab of the Properties dialog box that appears. To restart a stopped service, click the Start button. Click Resume to restart a paused service. You can also control when the service starts by setting the Service Type on that General tab to Manual (you have to start the service), Automatic (the service starts when Windows starts), or Disabled (the service never starts).

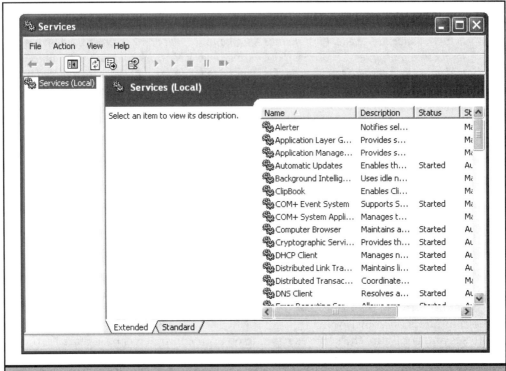

Figure 35-8.   *The Services window lists the services running in the background of your computer.*

To disable a service so that it doesn't restart when you restart Windows, set its Service Type to Manual. Or, use the System Configuration Utility: Choose Start | Run, type **msconfig**, and press ENTER. Click the Services tab to see a list of Services. To disable a service whenever you start Windows, clear its check box.

The
Complete
Reference

Chapter 36

Windows Update, Remote Assistance, and Other Windows XP Resources

Microsoft updates Windows constantly to accommodate new hardware and software and to enhance features already found in the system. To stay up to date with these changes, you can run the Windows Update program to scan your system and look for outdated drivers and programs, or you can configure the Automatic Updates program to download and install updates automatically.

If you run into trouble or want more information about Windows XP, you can ask a friend to take a look at your system right over the Internet, using Remote Assistance. You can consult online help, check the information that Microsoft provides on the Internet, and do your own sleuthing.

This chapter explains how to update your computer by using Windows Update and Automatic Updates, how to use Remote Assistance, and how to locate information about Windows from Microsoft and other sources.

Updating Your Computer with Windows Update

If your computer is on the Internet, Windows Update can examine your computer and give you a list of device drivers and other files that can be updated based on information from Microsoft's Internet-based servers. When the scan is complete, it presents a list of available updates, and you can choose which update(s) you want to install.

You can run Windows Update at any time to see whether new updates are available. It is especially important to run Windows Update after you install a new piece of hardware or a new software program to be sure you have the drivers and files that you need on your system.

Note *You must be logged in with an administrator user account to use Windows Update or Auto Update. (See Chapter 6.)*

Windows Update uses a wizard that guides you through the screens to complete the setup. The first time you run Windows Update, you may be asked to register as a Windows user and supply some personal information, such as your name, location, and e-mail address. Windows Update uses Internet Explorer and your Internet settings to connect you to the Microsoft site on the Web. Before you start Windows Update, be sure your computer is connected or is ready to connect to the Internet. Also, close all your other programs, since some updates require restarting Windows.

Scanning for Updates

To run Windows Update and update your Windows installation, follow these steps:

1. Choose Start | All Programs | Windows Update, or run Internet Explorer and choose Tools | Windows Update. The Help And Support Center home page has a link to Windows Update, too. Or, choose Start | Control Panel, run Add Or Remove Programs, click Add New Programs, and click the Windows Update button.

2. If your computer is not already connected to the Internet, you may see the Dial-Up Connection dialog box; if so, enter your user name and password and click Connect. Windows Update connects to the Microsoft server over the Internet and displays a web page like the one shown in Figure 36-1. The Windows Update page shows options that you can use to update Windows, get answers to technical support questions, or send your feedback about the Update page to Microsoft. (Since this page is on the Web, Microsoft may change its design at any time, but similar options will probably be available.)

Note *The Windows Update site works only with Internet Explorer, not with other browsers.*

3. Click the Scan For Updates button to check for updates. You see a catalog of available updates from which you can choose those appropriate for your system.

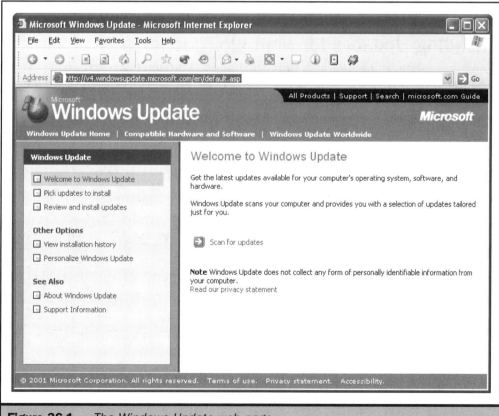

Figure 36-1. *The Windows Update web page*

4. Click the Critical Updates link in the Task pane section of the web page. Be sure to download all the Critical Update items. Windows Update lists the items it found.

5. For each update you want to download, click the Add button.

6. When you've chosen the updates you want, click the Review And Install Updates link in the Task pane section of the web page. You see a list of the updates you've selected.

7. Click the Install Now button to download and install the updates.

8. If an update requires you to agree to a license, you see a dialog box with the license agreement. Click Accept if you agree to the license agreement.

9. Windows displays a status dialog box to let you know about its progress.

10. Some updates require restarting Windows: if so, Windows Update asks before restarting.

To see a list of the updates that you have installed, go to the Windows Update web site as described in step 1 and click View Installation History.

Downloading Updates for Multiple Machines

If you have several computers at your home or office, you don't have to download Windows updates over and over for each computer. Instead, you can download the updates once, store them on a network drive, and install them on each computer. Follow these steps:

1. Display the Windows Update web site in Internet Explorer as described in the previous section.

2. Click Personalize Windows Update under Other Options.

3. Click the first check box, which is called Display The Link To The Windows Update Catalog Under See Also. Click the Save Settings button. Now a new Windows Update Catalog link appears in the See Also section of the web page.

4. Click the new Windows Update Catalog link.

5. Follow the instructions to choose updates to download, clicking the Add button for each update you want to download.

6. Click the Go To Download Basket link.

7. Type the pathname of the folder in which you want to store the updates, or click Browse to select it.

8. Click Download Now. If you see a dialog box with a license agreement, read the agreement and click Accept if you accept it. (If you don't, you can't download the updates.) Windows downloads one file for each update you selected. It usually creates folders in the location you specified. For example, if you are downloading updates to D:\Temp, Windows may create a folder named D:\

Temp\Software\en\com_Microsoft.WindowsXP\x86WinXP to contain the updates, and this folder may contain a folder name Com_Microsoft.Q*xx* for each update, where *xx* is the Microsoft Knowledge Base article number about the update. Each update folder contains an Internet shortcut to a page about the update and an .exe file.

9. For each update, on each computer you want to update, display the update folders in an Explorer window and double-click the .exe file to install the update.

Updating Your Computer Automatically with Automatic Updates

When you install Windows XP, within a few days it displays an Update Reminder balloon above the notification area on the taskbar, asking you to configure Windows to update itself automatically over the Internet. This message comes from Automatic Updates, a Windows feature that contacts Microsoft over the Internet, checks for Windows updates, downloads them, and installs them. You can configure Automatic Updates to ask you before downloading or installing updates.

Configuring Automatic Updates

You have two ways to configure Automatic Updates:

■ If the Automatic Updates icon or balloon appears in the notification area of the taskbar, click it to see the Updates dialog box. Click Settings to configure Automatic Updates, Remind Me Later if you want the Update Reminder Box to appear later, or choose Next to view the license for Windows Updates and to turn the feature on.

■ Otherwise, choose Start | Control Panel, click Performance And Maintenance, and click System to display the System Properties dialog box. (Another way to display this dialog box is to click Start, right-click My Computer, and choose Properties from the menu that appears.) Click the Automatic Updates tab, shown in Figure 36-2.

You see a check box that enables Automatic Updates, and three notification options:

■ **Notify Me Before Downloading Any Updates And Notify Me Again Before Installing Them On My Computer**   Windows checks to see whether updates are available. If they are, an icon appears in the notification area of the taskbar, and a reminder box asks whether you want to download and install them, as described later in this section. Double-click the icon to see the list of updates and click the check boxes so that a check mark appears next to each update you want to download.

■ **Download the Updates Automatically And Notify Me When They Are Ready To Be Installed**   When Automatic Updates downloads a group of updates, you can choose which ones to install.

■ **Automatically Download The Updates And Install Them On The Schedule That I Specify**   After Automatic Updates downloads updates, it installs them without asking you first. You can specify when it installs the updates (the default is the middle of the night, when you are unlikely to be using the computer).

We recommend against choosing the third option. Some updates require restarting Windows, and the system might restart without you having saved your work.

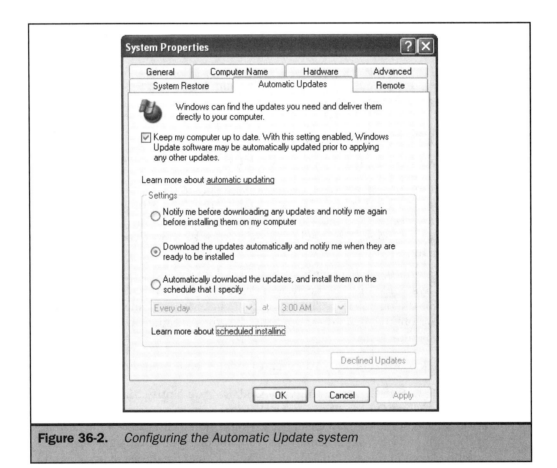

Figure 36-2.   *Configuring the Automatic Update system*

Choosing Which Updates to Install

If Automatic Updates are enabled and new updates are available for you to download an install, an icon appears in the notification area on the taskbar, and a balloon appears, like this:

Click the icon or balloon to display the Automatic Updates Ready To Install dialog box (shown in Figure 36-3), which asks whether you want to install them. Click the Details button to see a list of the downloaded updates. For each update, click the Read

Figure 36-3. *Automatic Updates has downloaded an update to Windows and asks whether you want to install it.*

More link to display a window that explains what the update does and how to uninstall it if it creates problems. Click Install to install the updates you choose. Click Remind Me Later if now is not a convenient time to install them (for example, you don't want to restart Windows).

If you decide not to install an update you've downloaded, Windows deletes it from your hard disk. However, you can decide to install it later. From the Automatic Updates tab of the System Properties dialog box, click the Declined Updates button to display a list of the updates that you decided not to install. You can choose which items you want to install after all. The next time Automatic Updates checks the Microsoft site for updates, it includes the items you specify.

Some updates are categorized as Critical, but most are just Recommended. We suggest that you install all critical updates, which usually relate to security holes in Internet-related features of Windows or its bundled programs. Decide whether to install other updates depending on whether you use the program that it updates and whether you've had the problem it fixes. Updates sometimes break Windows or applications, so there's no point installing unneeded noncritical updates.

Uninstalling Updates

You can uninstall most updates (the Read More window about each update explains whether it can be uninstalled, and how). For most updates, choose Start | Control Panel, run Add Or Remove Programs, and click the Change Or Remove Programs tab if it's not selected. You see a list of the programs you've installed, with updates at the bottom. Most appear as "Windows XP Hotfix" followed by the Microsoft Knowledge Base article number that contains details about the update. Choose the update to uninstall and click Change/Remove.

Allowing a Friend to Control Your Computer

Programs have been available for years that allow someone to control another computer over the phone or the Internet. PcAnywhere (at **www.symantec.com/pcanywhere**) and Carbon Copy (at **www.altiris.com/products/carboncopy**) are popular programs with support technicians because these programs allow them to look at and fix a computer without having to visit the office where the computer sits. Windows XP comes with Remote Desktop, which provides this same functionality (see Chapter 15, section "Accessing Other Computers with Remote Desktop"). Remote Assistance is a special version of Remote Desktop that enables you to invite someone to control your PC to help you solve a software problem.

With Remote Assistance, you invite a specific person to take control of your computer. You can contact the person via Windows Messenger or by e-mail. If the person agrees to help, then the helper can control the mouse pointer and type as if he or she were at your computer. You can also chat by typing or talking (if you have microphones and speakers), and send files.

Inviting a Friend to Help

To invite someone to take control of your PC:

1. Open the Help And Support Center window by choosing Start | Help And Support.

2. Click Support in the toolbar and click Ask A Friend To Help in the Support task list. Click Invite Someone To Help You in the window that appears.

3. Choose whether to contact your helper by using Windows Messenger or e-mail, identify the person, and click Invite. Then type the message you'd like to send with the invitation (something more specific than "Help!" is useful). In the Set The Invitation To Expire box, specify how long to leave the invitation open.

4. Leave the Require The Recipient To Use A Password check box selected; otherwise, anyone who gets ahold of the invitation can take complete control of your computer while the invitation is open. Type a password in the Type Password box that the helper will have to type when taking control.

5. Click Send Invitation.

6. If you use Outlook Express for your e-mail program and Outlook Express is configured to let you know whenever another program tries to send e-mail (a useful antivirus feature), you see a warning about it—click Send (refer to Chapter 23, section "Protecting Yourself from E-Mail Viruses").

7. Communicate the invitation password to your helper by Windows Messenger, e-mail, phone, or other medium.

8. Wait for your helper to get the invitation and to respond. When your helper receives the invitation and types in the password in response to your invitation, you see a dialog box with the helper's name and the message "Do you want to let this person view your screen and chat with you?"

9. Click Yes to proceed. You see the Remote Assistance window shown in Figure 36-4. The left side of the window is where you can chat with your helper.

10. Send a message explaining the problem to your helper by typing in the Message Entry area in the lower-left part of the Remote Assistance window.

Once Windows makes the Remote Assistance connection, you can do the following:

- **Share control of your computer**   When the helper clicks Take Control, you see a dialog box asking whether you want to let the helper share control of your computer. Click Yes to do so. While the helper is using your computer, keep your hands off the mouse and keyboard—it's terribly confusing when two people try to control the mouse pointer or type at the same time! Press ESC (or any key combination with ESC) to end sharing control or click Stop Control.

- **Send a file** Click Send A File and specify the filename.
- **Voice chat** Click Start Talking, if you and your helper have speakers and microphones on your computers, to start a voice chat. Click Settings to set the audio quality. If the helper clicks Start Talking first, you see a message asking whether you'd like to start a voice chat.

Click Disconnect when you are done being helped, unless the helper disconnects first.

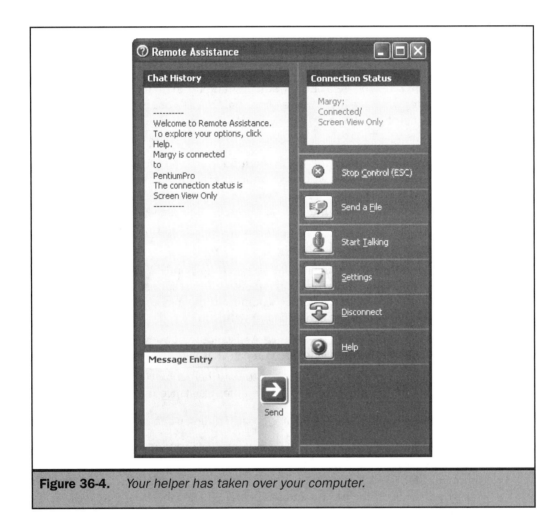

Figure 36-4. *Your helper has taken over your computer.*

Responding to an Invitation for Remote Assistance

If you receive an invitation to help someone by using Remote Assistance, you get an e-mail or Windows Messenger message with the subject "YOU HAVE RECEIVED A REMOTE ASSISTANT INVITATION FROM: *xx*." The message says something like this:

> Fred H. would like your assistance. You can easily provide assistance from your computer by following the instructions at: http://windows.microsoft.com/RemoteAssistance/en/RA.htm Caution: * Accept invitations only from people you know and trust. * E-mail messages can contain viruses or other harmful attachments. * Before opening the attachment, review the security precautions and information at the above address.

The message includes an attached file named rcBuddy.MsRcIncident. (The first part of the file name may be different.) Click the link in the message to read a web page about how Remote Assistance works. (This web page works only in Internet Explorer.)

Follow these steps when you receive an invitation and password from someone you know and want to help:

1. Make sure that you are either connected to the Internet or (if both computers are on the same LAN) to the LAN.

2. Open the attached file. Your e-mail program may display a warning that attached files may contain viruses. Go ahead and open the file. You see the Remote Assistance dialog box:

WINDOWS AND DISK
HOUSEKEEPING

3. Type the password and click Yes to connect. Remote Assistance makes the connection over the LAN or the Internet. You see a Remote Assistance window similar to Figure 36-4, but with an image of the other computer screen in the right side of the window. The left side of the window is where you can chat with the other person.

4. Type messages in the Message Entry area in the lower-left part of the Remote Assistance window and click Send to send the message to the other computer.

If someone sends you an invitation to help from a computer that has a higher screen resolution than your computer, you won't be able to see much of the other person's screen in your Remote Assistance window (if you click Scale To Window, it will be unreadable). Set your screen resolution as high as you can.

Once Windows makes the Remote Assistance connection, you can do the following:

■ **Control the other person's computer**   Click Take Control and wait for the other person to give permission for you to proceed. When you see a message indicating that you are sharing control, click in the right side of the Remote Assistance window, where the image of the other person's computer screen appears. While your mouse pointer is in that part of the window, its movements also move the mouse pointer on the other computer. However, the other person can also use the mouse and keyboard, and it gets confusing if you both try to do so at the same time. You can click Scale To Window if the image of the other computer screen doesn't fit in the Remote Assistance window, but it usually becomes unreadable: click Actual Size to display the other computer screen at actual size. Press ESC (or any key combination with ESC) to end sharing control, or click Release Control.

■ **Send a file**   Click Send A File and specify the filename.

■ **Voice chat**   Click Start Talking to start a voice chat. If the other person clicks Start Talking first, you see a message asking whether you'd like to start a voice chat. Both computers need microphones and speakers.

Click Disconnect when you are done helping, unless the other person disconnects first.

If you can't make a connection, one of the computers may be behind a firewall, and you may need to ask the network administrator to enable the port used by Remote Assistance (port 3389).

Microsoft's Support Resources

Microsoft provides a wealth of support information about Windows XP, including the Help And Support Center, the Microsoft web site, and newsgroups.

The Help And Support Center

The Help And Support Center is a set of web pages about Windows and the programs and accessories that come with it. The pages are stored on your hard disk and are displayed by a special Internet Explorer window. Other programs you install may also come with their own online help.

To see the Help And Support Center window (shown in Figure 36-5), choose Start | Help And Support. The toolbar shows many of the same icons you see in any Explorer window, including Back, Forward, Home, Favorites, and History. You also see Index, Support, and Options commands. The Task pane (left side of the window) shows a list of topics from which to choose. The rest of the window displays the help information you request from the Task pane.

When the Help And Support Center window first appears, you see lists of help topics and tasks (click Home on the toolbar to return to it). Click a topic to see a detailed list of subtopics in the left pane. When you see a plus box to the left of a topic, click the plus box to see its subtopics. When you see a topic with a question mark icon to its left, clicking the topic displays an explanation, and steps to follow, in the right pane. If a word or phrase becomes underlined when you move your mouse pointer over it, click it to see information about that topic.

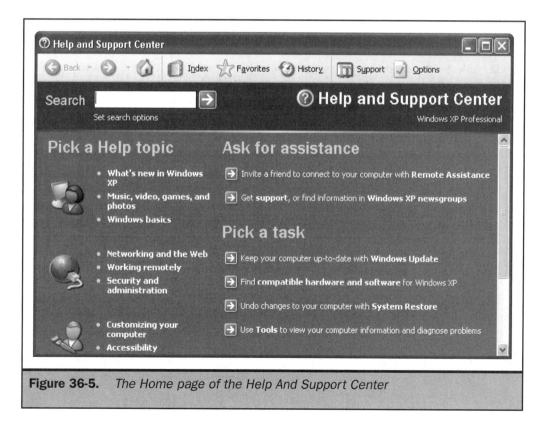

Figure 36-5.   *The Home page of the Help And Support Center*

If your computer is connected to the Internet, Windows automatically updates the home page of the Help And Support Center with news and updates, which appear in the lower-right corner of the window.

When you search for a topic in the Help And Support Center window by typing in the Search box, a list of topics appears in the left pane in three sections:

- **Suggested Topics**   Pages that Microsoft recommends about this topic.
- **Full-Text Search Matches**   Pages that contain the word(s) in the Search box.
- **Microsoft Knowledge Base**   Pages in the web-based Microsoft Knowledge Base, which is a huge searchable database of articles about all Microsoft products, at **support.microsoft.com**.

Click the heading to see the list of matches in that category, and then click a match to display its information in the right pane.

   You can copy the error text from many error dialog boxes with CTRL-C, *which is helpful when asking for help in a forum. Paste the error text into your message.*

Getting Help from Microsoft Online

You can get helpful information over the Internet about Windows. In the Help And Support Center window, click Support on the toolbar to see a list of your options:

- **Ask A Friend To Help**   Using Remote Assistance, you can ask a knowledgeable friend to take control of your computer via an Internet connection (see "Allowing a Friend to Control Your Computer"earlier in the chapter).
- **Get Help From Microsoft**   If your PC is online, you can sign up for a Microsoft .NET Passport, which identifies you to Microsoft, and get information from the Microsoft web site (see Chapter 25, section "Signing In to Windows Messenger with Your .NET Passport"). Once you sign in with your .NET Passport name and password, you can contact a Microsoft support technician for help, check on the status of problems you've submitted or download and install software that enables Microsoft to upload files from your computer to resolve a software issue.
- **Go To A Windows Web Site Forum**   Participate in online newsgroups about Windows XP. Your browser runs and displays the **www.microsoft.com/ windowsxp/expertzone/newsgroups** site. For more information about reading newsgroups, see Chapter 23.

You must be connected to the Internet to use these Internet-based resources.

   If you are asking for help from Microsoft or on a newsgroup, you may be asked for information about your computer system. In the Help And Support Center window, click Support and then click My Computer Information in the lower part of the Task pane to see information about your hardware and software.

Microsoft's Web Resources

Microsoft maintains a number of useful web sites with information about Windows XP:

■ **Microsoft Product Support Services web site at support.microsoft.com**   Support information for all Microsoft products (see Figure 36-6). Use the searchable Knowledge Base to find articles about problems and solutions, known bugs, and overviews of how products work. You can also get to this page by clicking the Support link on the Windows Update web page. The Knowledge Base is a huge searchable database on articles, including bugs and fixes, about all Microsoft products. To search, type the product name and some keywords into the Search The Knowledge Base box (for example, "Windows XP CD burning"). Each article has an article number consisting of the letter Q followed by a six-digit number; if you know the article number, search for it.

Note   *When you read a Microsoft Knowledge Base article, look just below the title of the article to make sure that it pertains to Windows XP Home Edition. The Knowledge Base includes articles about other versions of Windows, too.*

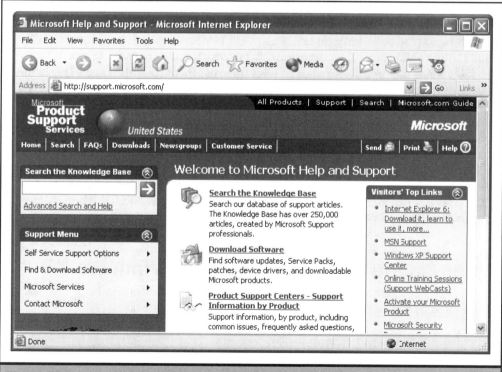

Figure 36-6.   *The Microsoft Product Support Services web site, where you can search the Microsoft Knowledge Base (MSKB)*

- **Windows XP home page at /www.microsoft.com/windowsxp** A good resource for general announcements and information about Windows XP. You can also check the general Windows site at **www.microsoft.com/windows**.

- **Windows XP Service Pack 1 page at www.microsoft.com/insider/pf/ windowsxp_servicepack1.asp** Installation information about SP1.

- **Microsoft TechNet at www.microsoft.com/technet** Free technical support site with background articles for corporate IT (information technology) professionals.

- **Internet Explorer home page at www.microsoft.com/windows/ie** Each component included with Windows has its own page at the Microsoft web site. From the Internet Explorer page, click Features to see an overview of the new features incorporated as part of Internet Explorer.

- **Computing Central at computingcentral.msn.com/software/OS** Microsoft's consumer-oriented web site about computers has a section about Windows.

Microsoft's Public Support Newsgroups

Microsoft hosts over a thousand discussions on its news server, with newsgroups about its major products in a variety of languages (two-letter country codes appear in the newsgroup names, like *br* for Brazil or *fr* for France). Choose Start | Help And Support to see the Help And Support Center window, click Get Support Or Find Information In Windows XP Newsgroups, and click Go To A Windows Web Site Forum in the Task pane. Or, go to the web page **communities.microsoft.com/newsgroups** and choose Windows XP as the product, or start at **www.microsoft.com/windowsxp/expertzone/ newsgroups**.Then follow the instructions on the web page (see Chapter 23, section "Usenet and Other Newsgroups").

You can also use Outlook Express to read the newsgroups. To add a Microsoft news server to your list of servers in Outlook Express, run Outlook Express. Select Tools | Accounts and click the News tab. Click Add, choose News, and follow the prompts as the wizard walks you through the steps to add the news server. The public Microsoft news server is named **msnews.microsoft.com**. After you add the server, download all the newsgroups so that you can see a list of what's available on the server. Many newsgroups discuss Windows and its components.

Other Online Information about Windows XP

Windows is a popular topic on the Internet. A number of Windows-related web sites and newsgroups are not connected to or sponsored by Microsoft.

Web Sites

These web sites provide information on a variety of computer-related issues, including Windows:

- **CNET.com at www.cnet.com** Current news on all things related to computers.

- **Free Study Resources for MSCE/MSCA Exam at mcmcse.com/windows_xp/ guides** Tutorials for people studying for the Microsoft Certified Engineer exam in Windows XP.

- **Internet Gurus at net.gurus.com/winxptcrhome** Our own web site for readers of the book. As we find useful information about Windows, we'll post it.

- **James A. Eshelman's Favorite Freeware at aumha.org/freeware.htm** Good collection of useful utilities.

- **John Savill's Windows /NT/2000 FAQ at www.ntfaq.com** Questions and answers from Windows & .NET Magazine Network, as well as discussion forums.

- **Paul Thurrott's SuperSite for Windows at www.winsupersite.com** FAQs (frequently asked questions and their answers), reviews, and news about upcoming Windows releases.

- **SysInternals Freeware at www.sysinternals.com** Information about the internals of all recent versions of Windows, by Mark Russinovich and Bryce Cogswell.

- **Window Planet at www.windowplanet.net** Articles, reviews, and discussion boards.

- **WinPlanet at www.winplanet.com/winplanet** Articles, tutorials, and downloads of utilities and drivers.

- **ZDNet: Windows at www.zdnet.com/windows** Articles on a variety of computer topics, including articles from *PC Magazine*.

Usenet Newsgroups

Usenet newsgroups are public discussion arenas on the Internet. In addition to the newsgroups hosted by Microsoft, some Usenet newsgroups, unaffiliated with Microsoft, discuss Windows topics (see Chapter 23, section "Usenet and Other Newsgroups").

To find Usenet newsgroups about Windows, run Outlook Express or your favorite newsreader, connect to your ISP's news server, and search for newsgroups with **win** in the newsgroup name. Most should be in the **comp** (computing) hierarchy, but you may find them in the **alt** or other hierarchies as well.

WINDOWS AND DISK HOUSEKEEPING

When you are searching for newsgroups, you can enter as few or as many characters as you like. The more characters you enter, the narrower the search. For example, a search for "Windows" will not show newsgroups with "WinXP" in the title.

If you can't find the type of discussion you want in the newsgroups listed on your ISP's news server, use the Google Groups web site **groups.google.com** as a resource for newsgroup information. This site lets you search past newsgroup articles. You can search for newsgroup messages containing a word or phrase, or you can read messages from newsgroups that do not appear on your news server.

Only one newsgroup is dedicated to Windows XP—**alt.os.windows-xp**. You might also want to read **comp.os.ms-windows.nt.misc**, **comp.os.ms-windows.networking .misc**, and **comp.os.ms-windows.misc**.

The Complete Reference

Part VIII

Behind the Scenes:
Windows Internals

The Complete Reference

Chapter 37

Windows XP Configuration Files

W indows stores its configuration information in a variety of files of different formats, including files for configuring Windows itself, as well as for running Windows and DOS programs. Windows comes with the System Configuration Utility (or Msconfig, for short) to help make controlled changes to some of its configuration files. This chapter explains the configuration files used by Windows XP, as well as how to run the System Configuration Utility program. The last section offers some pointers for running both Windows and another operating system (such as UNIX or Linux) on the same computer.

Note   *Most Windows and application configuration information is stored in the Registry (described in Chapter 38).*

Types of Windows XP Configuration Files

Other than the Registry, most of Windows' control information is stored in text files that you can open with Notepad or any other text editor. Although changing these files is usually a bad idea unless you're quite sure you know what you're doing, looking at their contents is entirely safe—and provides fascinating glimpses into how Windows works.

Making Configuration Files Visible

Most of the control information is stored in hidden, system, and read-only files (see Chapter 8, section "File and Folder Attributes"). Hidden and system files are like any other files, except that they don't normally appear in file listings when you use Windows Explorer to display a folder that contains them. (Any file can be hidden, but only a couple of required files in the root folder of the boot drive are system files.) If you try to delete a read-only file, you see a warning asking whether you really want to delete it.

You can tell Windows to show you all the hidden files on your computer. In an Explorer window, select Tools | Folder Options and click the View tab. The list of Advanced Settings includes a Hidden Files And Folders category. Click the Show Hidden Files And Folders check box so a check appears. This setting reveals hidden files in all folders, not just the current folder. Hidden files appear listed with regular files, but their icons are paler than regular files. To reveal the hidden files that Windows considers "special," uncheck the Hide Protected Operating System Files (Recommended) check box. Click Yes in the warning dialog box. Click OK when you have finished making changes in the Folder Options dialog box to make the changes active.

You can change a file's hidden or system status by right-clicking the file and selecting Properties. Click the Hidden and Read-only check boxes at the bottom of the Properties dialog box to select or deselect these attributes.

Tip   *We recommend that you leave hidden and system folders and files hidden unless you plan to look at them. They can be distracting during normal work. If you do decide to display them, you can tell hidden and system files from normal files by their dimmed appearance.*

What Is %SystemRoot%?

You may see pathnames that include "%SystemRoot%" in a dialog box setting or in a configuration file. SystemRoot is a global system variable that tells Windows where the Windows program is stored. Windows replaces "%SystemRoot%" with the current location of Windows (usually C:\Windows).

Why is this useful? Because if you create a configuration file for your computer and then give it to a friend, your friend's Windows system may be installed somewhere else (for example, F:\Windows on a dual-boot system in which the C: partition is used by a previous version of Windows). Your Windows system could be installed on C: but theirs could be F: or L: or Z:. Using %SystemRoot% in a configuration file allows it to work on any system, regardless of circumstance.

Windows Initialization Files

Since Windows 95, Microsoft has moved most Windows initialization information into the Registry, but some programs still use two initialization files from earlier versions of Windows: Win.ini and System.ini. Some Windows 3.1 applications stored their setup information in individual *INI files* (initialization files), such as Progman.ini for the Windows 3.1 Program Manager. Other Windows 3.1 programs used sections in the general-purpose Win.ini file.

All INI files have the file extension .ini, and nearly all reside in the folder in which Windows is installed (usually C:\Windows). All INI files have a common format, of which the following is a typical example (it contains configuration information for the WS_FTP file transfer program):

```
[WS_FTP]
DIR=F:\Program Files\WS_FTP
DEFDIR=F:\Program Files\WS_FTP
GROUP=WS_FTP Pro
INSTOPTS=4

[Mail]
MAPI=1
```

An INI file is divided into sections, with each section starting with a section name in square brackets. Within a section, each line is of the form *parameter=value*, where the value may be a filename, number, or other string. Blank lines and lines that start with a semicolon are ignored.

In general, editing the Win.ini or System.ini file is a bad idea, but if you need to do so, use the System Configuration Utility (see "Configuring Windows XP with the System Configuration Utility" later in this chapter). You can take a look at the contents of the files using this program, too.

While Windows may not make much use of the Win.ini and System.ini files, third-party software publishers make wide use of application-specific INI files to retain their program settings. Take a peek into the program folders for a few of your applications, and you'll almost certainly find an INI file.

The Win.ini File

In Windows 3.1, nearly every scrap of setup information in the entire system ended up in the Win.ini file in C:\Windows, meaning that if any program messed up Win.ini, the system could be nearly unusable. More recent versions of Windows alleviate this situation by moving most configuration of the information into the Registry, but Win.ini is retained to offer support for 16-bit applications. You'll typically find sections for a few of your application programs in Win.ini, plus a little setup information for Windows itself.

 You can use Notepad to edit Win.ini, but it's dangerous. Instead, use the System Configuration Utility to edit the Win.ini file (see "Configuring Windows XP with the System Configuration Utility" later in this chapter).

The System.ini File

In Windows 3.1, the System.ini file in C:\Windows listed all the Windows device and subsystem drivers to be loaded at startup. In Windows XP the vast majority of the driver information is in the Registry, but System.ini still contains driver configuration information for 16-bit applications. Use the System Configuration Utility (rather than Notepad) to edit the System.ini file (see "Configuring Windows XP with the System Configuration Utility" later in this chapter).

The Registry

The Windows Registry contains all of the configuration information not in an INI file, including the vast majority of the actual information used to control Windows and its applications. Use the Registry Editor to examine and manage the Registry (see Chapter 38).

Configuring Windows XP with the System Configuration Utility

Microsoft provides the System Configuration Utility to help you make controlled changes to the various configuration files described earlier in this chapter. To run the System Configuration Utility, choose Start | Run, type **msconfig** in the Open box, and click OK. You see the System Configuration Utility window, shown in Figure 37-1.

The System Configuration Utility includes a tab for each configuration file, along with the Startup tab, which lists information from the Registry about programs to be run at startup time. Changes you make don't take effect until the next time Windows restarts, so when you close the System Configuration Utility, it asks whether you want to save the changes you've made; if you click Yes, it offers to reboot Windows for you.

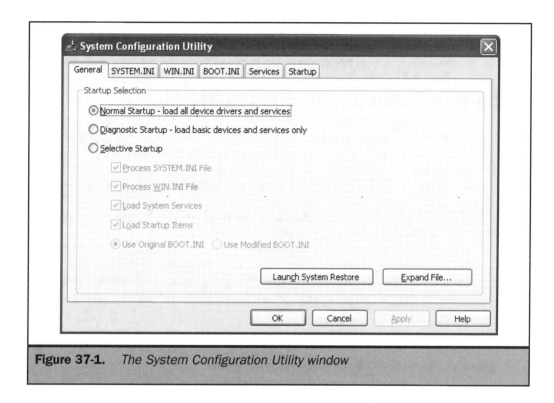

Figure 37-1.   *The System Configuration Utility window*

Restarting Windows with Selected Startup Options

The General tab of the System Configuration Utility window can help you restart Windows in a startup mode that helps diagnose problems (see Chapter 2, section "Starting Windows in Other Startup Modes"). The three startup items are as follows:

- **Normal Startup**   The default mode. You'll not likely switch back to this if things are running smoothly.

- **Diagnostic Startup**   Essentially the same as Safe Mode. This option limits loading device drivers and system services that may interfere with normal operation.

- **Selective Startup**   Enables you to select which startup items to load. A good plan when you experience system instability is to turn all your startup items off, reboot, and then turn one on at a time. If that doesn't help, try different combinations. You'd be surprised how much instability can come from a little icon like AOL or Palm Desktop in the notification area of the Windows taskbar.

If you want to restart Windows and tell it to process only specific configuration files, click the Selective Startup setting on the General tab of the System Configuration Utility window and choose the files to process. When you click OK, Windows asks whether you want to reboot your computer. Click Yes. Windows restarts and processes only the files you specified. To save your changes without restarting Windows, click Apply (the changes to the files are saved, but don't go into effect until you reboot). The next section describes the changes you can make to your startup configuration.

Changing Your Services and Startup Settings

The Services and Startup tabs in the System Configuration Utility window (Figure 37-2) show the services and applications that run when Windows starts up, including the startup programs listed in the Registry and the programs in your StartUp folder (usually stored in the C:\Documents And Settings*username*\Start Menu\Programs\ StartUp folder). You can disable loading a service or program at startup by deselecting its check box.

Unlike in previous versions of Windows, no essential Windows services appear on the Startup tab (they have moved to the Services tab). Many startup programs are "helpers" that are installed along with applications. For example, the AOL startup program asks you whether you want to sign onto AOL the moment you log into your computer. If you don't want the help that the startup program provides, you can usually disable the startup program without affecting the operation of the main program.

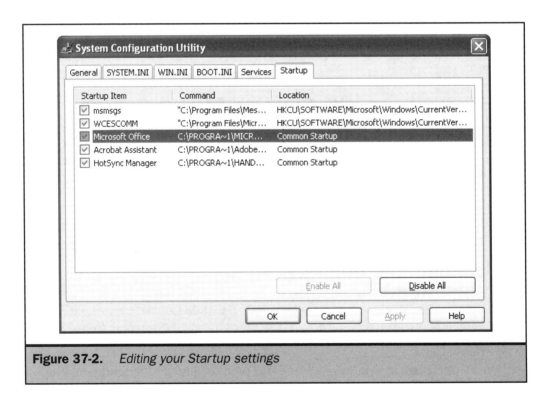

Figure 37-2.   *Editing your Startup settings*

Programs that appear on the Startup tab that you may want to disable include

- **Aim**   AOL Instant Messenger
- **Billminder**   Quicken's Billminder feature
- **Evntsc**   Part of the RealPlayer
- **Microsoft Office (OSA9.exe)**   Office's background speedup program
- **Mozilla**   Mozilla's fast-load option
- **Msmsgs**   Windows Messenger
- **Navapw32**   Norton Antivirus virus scanner
- **Quicken Startup**
- **Ypager**   Yahoo Messenger

For a long list of programs that may appear on your Startup tab, see Paul Collins' Start-Up Applications list at **www.pacs-portal.co.uk/startup_pages/startup_full.htm**.

Check the program's options or preferences settings to see whether you can disable automated startup. Disabling startup from with the program is usually more effective than removing the program from the Startup tab of the System Configuration Utility window.

The Services tab lists Windows' built-in services—programs running in the background that are used by other programs. Click the Status column heading to sort the services with running services first, then stopped services. You can disable a service by clearing its check box.

You usually don't need to change anything on the Services tab. When installed as a workstation or home system, most of these services are already disabled, so unchecking them results in no change of functionality anyway. The Startup tab, which lists application programs, is where you should concentrate your debugging efforts.

Replacing a Corrupted Windows File

Occasionally, one of the program files that make up Windows is deleted or corrupted (perhaps by a virus). The Expand File on the General tab of the System Configuration Utility window provides an easy way to extract a single file from the Windows XP CD-ROM (or any other CAB file) and replace it on your system. The program extracts a file from a CAB file (Windows Cabinet file, the format in which program files are stored on the Windows XP CD-ROM). You need to know which file is bad and which CAB file contains the replacement for the file.

If you know what file you want to replace and the location of the CAB file that contains a good copy, follow these steps:

1. Click the Expand File button on the General tab of the System Configuration Utility window. You see the Expand One File From Installation Source dialog box, shown here:

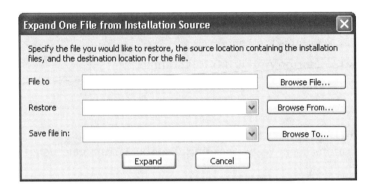

2. Click the Browse File button and navigate to the problem file. When you have it selected in the Open dialog box, click OK.

3. Click the Browse From button and select the CAB file on the CD-ROM that contains the file you want to replace.

4. Click the Browse To button and navigate to the directory that the replacement file should be stored in.

5. Click Expand.

The program doesn't give you any help in figuring out which CAB file on the Windows XP CD-ROM contains the file you need. Also, CAB filenames are not known for their readability. You may have quite a time locating the one you need. Finally, there's no indicator that you have or have not successfully extracted the file. One way to know is to keep an Explorer window open on the desktop showing the contents of the folder into which you are storing the replacement file. If a file is added, it will appear in that folder within 30 seconds or so.

Changing Your System.ini and Win.ini Files

The System Configuration Utility window's System.ini tab, shown in Figure 37-3, and Win.ini tab (which looks similar) show a list of the sections in the System.ini and Win.ini files. To see the individual lines within a section, click the plus box to the left of the section name. To disable an entire section, deselect the check box to the left of the section name (or select it and click the Disable button). To disable an individual line, deselect the check box to its left (or select it and click the Enable button). If you want to add a new setting, select the line after which you want to add the setting and click the New button. The program adds a new blank line: type the contents (in the

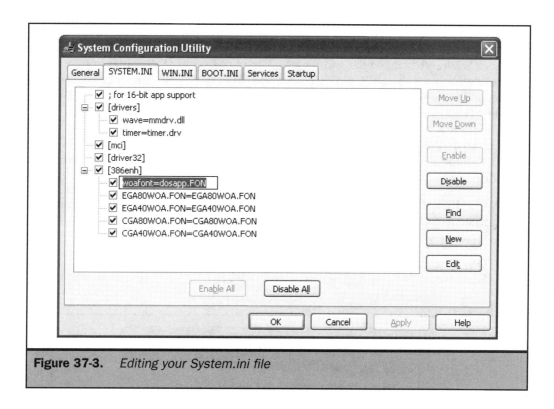

Figure 37-3.   *Editing your System.ini file*

format *parameter=value*) and press ENTER. You can also reorder the items by selecting them and clicking the Move Up and Move Down buttons.

Changing Your Boot.ini File

Windows XP, like Windows NT and Windows 2000 before it, was designed as a multiuser operating system. It was also designed to allow more than one operating system to be installed at a time on one computer. It is this capability you see when you start your computer and are asked whether you would like to boot Windows XP or another operating system in another partition (in some cases, whether or not you have another OS installed). This multiboot feature stores your list of bootable partitions in the Boot.ini file.

You can edit the Boot.ini file by clicking the Boot.ini tab in the System Configuration Utility window or by using the System Properties dialog box (see the Appendix, section "Setting Boot Options").

Changing Your Environment Settings

DOS and early versions of Windows used *environment variables* to store some settings. Environment variables can be changed while Windows is running by using the DOS SET command. When Window or a DOS VM start up, the variables must be *initialized* (that is, set to their initial values).

To see or set your environment variables, click Start, right-click My Computer and select Properties from the shortcut menu. On the System Properties dialog box that appears, click the Advanced tab and then click the Environment Variables button. You see the Environment Variables dialog box (shown in Figure 37-4). The upper part of the dialog box shows user variables (which store information about the current user account). The lower part shows system variables (which store information about Windows itself).

The two default user variables are TEMP and TMP. Both define where Windows stores its temporary files. The default system variables, which you should not remove or modify, are as follows:

- **COMSPEC**   Location of the Command Prompt program (usually C:\Windows\System32\Cmd.exe). See Chapter 4 for how to use the Command Prompt program.

- **NUMBER_OF_PROCESSORS**   For single-CPU computers, 1.

- **OS**   The name of your OS. Though a bit odd for more than one reason, Windows XP's name appears as "Windows_NT."

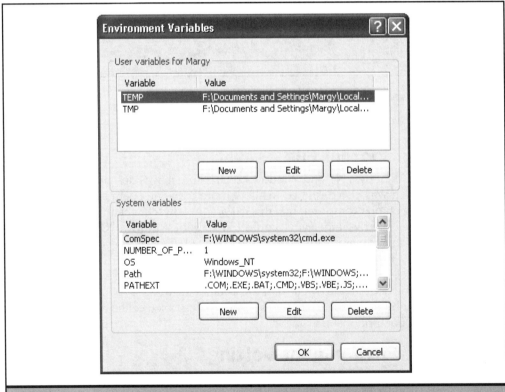

Figure 37-4.   *User and system environment variables*

- **PATH**   Where Windows looks for executable programs for launching applications from the command prompt (usually a list of pathnames including C:\Windows\System32 and C:\Windows. If you install service applications that are designed to be called as utilities from other applications, you may need to add the paths to the service applications' folders.

- **PATHEXT**   Which extensions are recognized as executable when launching from the command prompt (usually a list of extensions including COM, BAT, CMD, VBS, VBE, JS, JSE, WSF, and WSH).

- **PROCESSOR_ARCHITECTURE**   Usually "x86", the types of processors designed and sold by Intel.

- **PROCESSOR_IDENTIFIER**   Description of your computer's CPU. Ours shows "x86 Family 6 Model 8 Stepping 6, GenuineIntel".

- **PROCESSOR_LEVEL**   Stepping level in the PROCESSOR_IDENTIFIER.

- **PROCESSOR_REVISION**   Revision number of the processor. Ours is "0806."

- **TEMP**   Where to store temporary files (usually "C:\Windows\Temp").

- **TMP**   Where to store temporary files (usually "C:\Windows\Temp").

- **WINDIR**   Location of the system directory (usually "C:\Windows").

 Do not remove or modify these system variables unless you are sure you understand the consequences of doing so.

Changing Your International Settings

Most of the Windows international and regional settings appear in the Regional And Language Options dialog box (see Chapter 12, section "Windows' Regional Settings"). Set the Language box to the language of your choice—Windows updates the rest of the settings on the tab to match. Don't edit the individual settings unless you know what you are doing.

Configuring DOS and Older Windows Programs to Run Under Windows XP

Most previous versions of Windows ran "on top" of DOS —that is, DOS loaded first, and then Windows loaded, continuing to run DOS for basic operating system functions. Windows XP doesn't load DOS; it performs these operating system functions itself.

You rarely need to run DOS itself. All recent versions of Windows programs are designed to work directly with Windows rather than requiring DOS. However, some older *legacy programs* that were written when DOS ran "beneath" Windows require DOS to run. Legacy programs include programs written to run directly under DOS, and Windows programs that call on DOS for operating system services. (Many older games are legacy programs.) Like Windows 2000, Windows XP comes with a DOS

Virtual Machine (VM), which simulates DOS, displaying the DOS prompt and responding to DOS commands (see Chapter 4). See the section "Configuring the DOS Environment" in Chapter 4 for how to configure DOS and Windows 3.1 programs to run under Windows XP.

Disk Formats and Coexisting with Other Operating Systems

Windows can share a hard disk with some other operating systems. Because different operating systems format the disk differently, sharing a disk requires splitting it up into partitions.

Partitioning Disks

One way for multiple operating systems to be installed on a single hard disk is for each system to be assigned one or more partitions on the disk and use its partition(s) when running (see the Appendix, section "Creating Dual-boot Installations"). Windows can share a disk with OS/2 or UNIX this way. Windows uses a Primary partition (which used to be called a Primary DOS partition). Most other operating systems also use a single partition. Windows can create FAT32 and NTFS partitions and respects partitions created by other systems, but cannot itself create a partition for any other system (see Chapter 33, section "Partitioning a Disk Using Disk Management").

Here are ways to partition a disk between Windows and another system:

- *Install Windows first.*   When installing Windows, tell the Setup Wizard to use only as much of the disk as you want to assign to Windows and leave the rest of the disk unassigned. Once Windows is installed, shut Windows down and install the other system, which generally creates its own partition using the rest of the disk.

- *Install the other system first.*   Most other operating systems can usually create a Primary partition for Windows at the same time they create their own partitions by using an included utility. Once the other system is installed, shut the system down and install Windows, which automatically uses the existing Primary partition.

- *Use a partitioning program like PartitionMagic to create the partitions.*   There are utility programs designed for creating, modifying, and copying partitions of all types (see Chapter 33, section "Managing Partitions with PartitionMagic"). Windows XP's built-in partitioning doesn't allow you to resize or move partitions without data loss, while PartitionMagic can.

A few systems offer other ways to coexist with Windows or DOS. For example, some versions of Linux (a popular clone of UNIX) can create a large file in a DOS partition and use that file as the Linux partition. This makes it possible to install Linux, even on a system that has Windows preinstalled and assigns the entire disk to the DOS partition.

Note *If you share your computer with Windows Me/9x, and you install Windows Me/9x last, it will only boot the computer to Windows Me/9x. (You can use fdisk to force it to reboot from another partition, but that's rather inconvenient.) The easiest way around this is to install Windows Me/9x first if you plan to install it at all, followed by UNIX or Linux. Install Windows XP last: its boot loader detects the existing operating systems and adds them to its boot menu to create a multiboot installation (see the Appendix, section "Creating Dual-boot Installations"). Windows 9x/Me must be on the first partition, and requires the FAT32 (not NTFS) file system.*

Other Operating Systems and Windows Files

Windows XP can't read or write files in partitions that are formatted with any file system other than DOS FAT, FAT32, or NTFS. Fortunately, nearly every other operating system that runs on a PC can deal with Windows files. Most UNIX and Linux systems, for example, can logically mount a DOS FAT partition so that it appears to be part of the UNIX file system. Consult the documentation for your other operating system to find out how to give it access to your Windows files.

Note *If you are creating a dual-boot system with Windows XP and Windows Me/9x and you use NTFS for your Windows XP partition, Windows Me/9x running on this computer won't be able to read the files in the Windows XP partition. Solve this problem by creating an additional FAT or FAT32 partition that contains no operating system, only data. Windows Me/9x computers on a network can access shared NTFS partitions that are stored on computers running Windows XP or 2000.*

Chapter 38

Displaying and Editing the Windows XP Registry

The Windows Registry stores configuration information about the your desktop, taskbar, folder options, and other settings, as well as configuration settings for the programs you run. It also includes configuration information for each program, service, window, icon, and user account on your system. You can use the Registry Editor program to edit the Registry, but do so with caution! (This chapter describes Registry Editor versions 5 and 5.1.)

Registry Concepts

Early versions of Windows scattered configuration settings among dozens of different files. Many settings were stored in C:\Windows\Win.ini and C:\Windows\System.ini, but programs were as likely to use their own INI files as the standard ones, and there was no consistency in the way that INI files were created and maintained (see Chapter 37, section "Windows Initialization Files"). In Windows 95, Microsoft created the *Registry*, a single centralized database in which programs keep their setup information. The Registry contains all of the information that the INI files contained, as well as other settings from around the system. All subsequent versions of Windows store configuration information settings in the Registry, and the win.ini and system.ini files remain only for backward compatibility with older programs.

The Registry contains configuration settings for Windows itself, as well as for most programs you have installed. It also includes user profile information and information about each hardware component.

Most of the time, the Registry works automatically in the background, but in a few circumstances, you may want to edit it yourself.

You can assign permissions to Registry keys so that other users can't make changes to the Registry. Some keys are locked by Windows.

Where the Registry Is Stored

The Registry is stored in a group of files in your C:\Windows\System32\Config folder (assuming that Windows XP is installed on C:). The files with no extension (Default, Software, System, Sam, Security, Userdiff) contain the actual Registry entries. The .sav files are copies of the corresponding files made when you installed Windows. User profile information is stored in files named Ntuser.dat in the user's folder in C:\Documents And Settings.

Although the Windows XP Registry Editor looks and works the same as the Windows Me/9x Registry Editor, the location and format of the Registry files are quite different. The Windows XP Registry system is based on Windows 2000/NT and is much larger than its Windows Me/9x equivalent.

Registry Keys and Root Keys (Hives)

The Registry is organized much like the Windows file system. The Registry contains a set of *keys*, which are like folders. Additional keys can be stored within keys. Each key defines a setting or behavior for Windows or an installed application. Key pathnames are written with reverse slashes between them, much like filenames, so a typical key name is

```
HKEY_LOCAL_MACHINE\System\CurrentControlSet\Services\Sysaudio
```

The top-level key is called the *root key* (also sometimes called a *hive*). The root key of this key is HKEY_LOCAL_MACHINE, which contains a key named System, which in turn contains a key named CurrentControlSet, which contains a key named Services, which contains a key named Sysaudio.

The Registry's root keys, stored directly under the My Computer entry in the Registry are as follows:

- **HKEY_CLASSES_ROOT**   File associations for file types. It's actually another name for HKEY_LOCAL_MACHINE\Software\Classes. This key is sometimes abbreviated HKCR, and contains file associations (what programs are associated with what file extensions).

- **HKEY_CURRENT_USER**   Configuration information for the current user account. It's actually another name for the HKEY_USERS subkey for the current user. This key is sometimes abbreviated HKCU.

- **HKEY_LOCAL_MACHINE**   Configuration information about the computer, for all users. This key is sometimes abbreviated HKLM. It contains the subkeys Hardware (with hardware configuration data), Sam (with user account security data), Security (with general security policies), Software (with configuration information for installed applications), and System (with device drivers, hardware profiles, recovery, and other data).

- **HKEY_USERS**   Configuration information for all user accounts. This key is sometimes abbreviated HKU. It contains subkeys for each user account on the system, including .Default (the default settings for new user accounts) and hidden accounts. User accounts are hard to identify, because they are named using *SIDs* (security IDs) instead of user names. To make changes, log on as the user and make changes to the HKEY_CURRENT_USER keys.

- **HKEY_CURRENT_CONFIG**   Hardware profile information for the hardware profile that your computer uses at startup. It's actually another name for HKEY_LOCAL_MACHINE\System\CurrentControlSet\Hardware Profiles\Current.

BEHIND THE SCENES: WINDOWS INTERNALS

Key Values

Each key has one or more *values*, each of which consists of a name, a data type, and some data. A key at any level can contain any number of values, so in the example, values can be associated with HKEY_LOCAL_MACHINE\System\CurrentControlSet\ Services or HKEY_LOCAL_MACHINE\System. Every key has at least one key, called

(Default) (including the parentheses), which is frequently empty (not set). Most of the useful values are stored at the lowest level or next lowest level key.

The data type of a value can be one of the following:

- **REG_BINARY or Binary**   A series of binary or hexadecimal digits—for example, "80 00 01 00".

- **REG_DWORD or DWORD**   A four-byte (double word) numeric value that can be displayed in binary, hexadecimal, or decimal format—for example, 15 (or 0000000F hex).

- **REG_SZ or String**   Fixed-length human-readable *string* or text—for example, "System" or "Margy".

- **REG_EXPAND_SZ or Expandable String**   Variable-length string—for example, "C:\Documents and Settings\Margy".

- **REG_MULTI_SZ or Multi-String**   List of strings, separated by spaces, commas, or other punctuation—for example, "C:\Windows\System 32\query.dll, C:\Windows\System32\ciadmin.dll, C:\Windows\System32\ixsso.dll" (except that the strings are separated by line-ending characters instead of by commas).

- **REG_FULL_RESOURCE_DESCRIPTOR**   Larger grouping of information for storing a resource list, usually for a hardware driver—for example, a table of interface types, resources, descriptions, and devices.

- **REG_LINK**   A link to another part of the Registry tree. You can't create these links in Registry Editor, but Windows uses these links to create additional names for keys. For example, HKEY_CURRENT_USER is a link to the current user's key in HKEY_USERS.

You never change the data type of a value: you change the data. (But only if you are sure you know what you are doing!)

Restoring the Registry

If the Registry is damaged, you can restore it from a backup. Follow these steps:

1. Save your files and close all your programs.

2. Choose Start | Turn Off Computer | Restart. Windows shuts down and restarts.

3. When you see the message Please Select The Operating System To Start, press F8. Windows displays a list of options (see Chapter 2).

4. Press the UP-ARROW or DOWN-ARROW until you highlight the Last Known Good Configuration option, and press ENTER. (If the arrow keys don't work, press NUM LOCK to enable them.)

5. Choose the operating system (Windows XP Home Edition). Windows then restores your most recently backed up values for the HKEY_LOCAL_MACHINE\System\CurrentControlSet key in the Registry, and restarts Windows.

If the Registry entries for an application get damaged, consider uninstalling and reinstalling the program. If restoring a backup of the Registry still doesn't fix your problem, you may have to back up your data, reformat the disk (or partition) on which Windows is installed, and reinstall Windows and all your programs.

System Restore can also restore a previous version of the Registry (see Chapter 2, section "Returning Your System to a Predefined State with System Restore").

Editing the Registry

You rarely need to edit the Registry directly. When you configure Windows or other programs, the configuration is usually stored automatically in the Registry by the program. Occasionally, however, a bug fix or parameter change requires a change to the Registry. If you're interested in how Windows works, you can also spend as much time as you want nosing around the Registry with the Registry Editor program.

Never make changes to the Registry without first making a backup! Better yet, include the Registry in your daily backups (see Chapter 9).

Running Registry Editor

Registry Editor lets you edit anything in the Registry. To run Registry Editor, select Start | Run, type **regedit**, and press ENTER. (You can type **regedt32** instead of **regedit**, but they both run the same program. Microsoft combined the features of the 32-bit version with the regular program.)

Registry Editor has almost no built-in checks or validation, so be very sure that you make any changes correctly. Incorrect Registry entries can lead to anything from occasional flaky behavior to complete system failure.

Registry Editor has a two-part window, shown in Figure 38-1, much like Windows Explorer. Each key is shown as a folder in the left pane of the Registry Editor window. When you select a key in the left pane, the name and data of each of its values appear in the right pane.

You can identify the current key by its open folder icon and by the full key name that appears in the status bar at the bottom of the Registry Editor window. You can expand and contract parts of the name tree by clicking the plus box and minus box in the key area. Select any key to see the names and data of the values, if any, associated with that key.

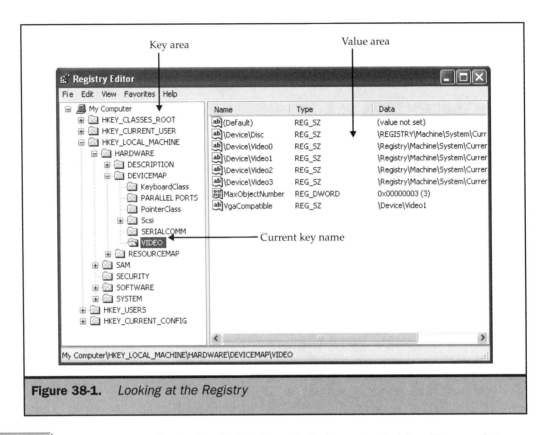

Figure 38-1. *Looking at the Registry*

Note *Windows XP Professional and .NET Server include remote Registry editing so that a systems administrator can edit your Registry over a LAN. Windows XP Home Edition doesn't support remote Registry editing: In Registry Editor, you can give the File | Connect Network Registry command, but you can't actually open the other computer's Registry files.*

There's a REG command you can use in the Command Prompt window to edit the Registry. In a Command Prompt window, type **reg /?** and press ENTER to see information.

Finding Registry Entries

If you know the name of the key you want, you can navigate through the key names similar to the way you navigate through files in Windows Explorer. In addition, you can type a letter to move to the next subkey that starts with that letter. Press RIGHT ARROW to open a key and see its subkeys. Press LEFT ARROW to close the subkey listing for a key or to move up one level.

If you don't know the name of the key, you can search for it by choosing Edit | Find (or pressing CTRL-F). You can search for any combination of keys, value names, and value data. For example, if you mistyped your name at the time you set up Windows and want to correct it, search for the mistyped name as value data. Press F3 to step from one match to the next.

As you edit Registry entries, Registry Editor makes the changes right away—there's no Save, Cancel, or Undo command. You can edit the Registry and leave the Registry Editor window open while you check whether your changes produce the desired effect. Some programs aren't affected by Registry changes until they or Windows itself are restarted; others reflect the changes immediately.

When you run Registry Editor again, it displays the key that you were looking at when you last exited the program, so it's easy to continue making changes to the same key.

If you find that you return frequently to edit the same Registry key, add it to your Registry Favorites by selecting the key in the left pane and choose Favorites | Add To Favorites. You can choose Favorites from the menu bar to see a menu of your favorite keys.

Backing Up Registry Keys, Just in Case

We suggest that you export the keys that you plan to edit before making any changes, so that you can reimport them if the changes cause problems. To export a key (and all its subkey and values), select the key and choose File | Export to export the keys as a text file. Leave the Save As Type box set to Registration Files (*.reg). When you specify a name and click Save, Registry Editor writes the data into the new file, which may take a few minutes. You can export the entire Registry by choosing the top-level My Computer entry at the top of the tree in the left pane.

If you need to import the exported keys later, to replace errors that you made while editing, choose File | Import. Or, double-click the .reg file in an Explorer window. The keys and values in the imported file replace the corresponding keys and values in the Registry, restoring the keys to their previous state.

If you created any new keys or values, reimporting the keys doesn't delete them.

Adding and Changing Registry Entries

You can add, edit, and delete Registry entries (but be sure you back them up first):

- **Changing the value data**   Double-click the name of the value (in the Name column of the right pane of the Registry Editor window). Registry Editor displays a dialog box in which you can enter the new data for the value.

You see an Edit dialog box, which looks different depending on the data type of the value you are changing:

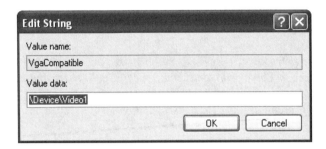

You can't change the type of a value, so you have to enter a text string, a numeric value, or a string of hexadecimal digits, depending on the type of the data.

- **Renaming a key or a value**   Right-click its name and choose Rename from the menu that appears. (Don't rename a value that Windows or another program uses, because Windows won't be able to find the key under its new name.)

- **Creating a new key**   In the left pane, right-click the folder (key) into which you want to add the new key and choose New | Key from the menu that appears. As in Windows Explorer, the new key is created with a dummy name. Type the name you actually want and press ENTER.

- **Creating a new value**   In the left pane, right-click the key in which you want store the new value, choose New from the menu that appears, and choose the type of value (String Value, Binary Value, DWORD Value, Multi-String Value, or Expandable String Value). Once you've created a value, double-click the value's name to enter its data.

- **Deleting a value or key**   Select the value or key and press DELETE.

Here are a few Registry editing tips:

- If you're not absolutely sure about deleting a key, rename it. Add an underscore or number to the end, so that the Registry doesn't recognize it, but you will if you need to change it back later.

- You can rename and delete keys and values by using the Edit menu.

- If you want to remember the name of a Registry key—or tell a friend about it—you can copy it to the Clipboard. Select the key whose complete name you want, and choose Edit | Copy Key Name from the menu bar. Or, right-click the key and choose Copy.

- If you can't edit a Registry key, it may have been assigned permissions that exclude you. Right-click the key and choose Permissions from the menu that appears. Add your user account and make sure that the Allow check box is selected for Full Control. Now you can edit the key. If you don't have full permissions for a key, you may not be able to see the key's subkeys and values.

Throughout this book you will find information about Registry keys that you can change in order to customize Windows and the programs that come with it.

Editing the Registry as a Text File

Another way to edit the Registry is to export all or part of the Registry to a text file, edit the text file, and then import the changed values back into the Registry. You can export and import the entire Registry or one "branch" of the Registry's tree of keys. Registry Editor stores the exported Registry entries in a *registration file* with the extension .reg.

A registration file consists of a series of lines that look like this:

```
[HKEY_CLASSES_ROOT\.bfc\ShellNew\Config]
"NoExtension"="Temp"
```

The first line is the name of the key (enclosed in square brackets) and the lines that follow are the values in the key, in the format *"name"="value"*.

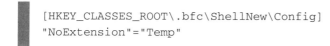 *Windows XP (like Windows NT and2000) exports the Registry using Unicode rather than plain text. If you want to export keys from the Windows XP Registry and import them into a Windows Me/9x Registry, set the Save As Type box in the Export Registry File dialog box to Win9x/NT4 Registration Files.*

Follow these steps to edit the Registry by using a text editor:

1. Select a key in the left pane, choosing one that contains all the keys that you want to edit. To export the entire Registry, select the My Computer item at the root of the Registry tree.

2. Choose File | Export to write the text file. Registry Editor asks you for the folder and filename to use for the registration file. Then it writes the data into the new file, which may take a few minutes.

3. Edit the registration file in any text editor. (Notepad works fine.) Right-click the .reg file in Windows Explorer and choose Edit from the shortcut menu that appears. Notepad runs (or another text editor, if you choose it). If you want to delete a key, add a minus sign after the first bracket (for example, [-HKEY_CURRENT_USER/…]). Make as few changes as possible to the file and save the file.

4. In Registry Editor, choose File | Import to read the edited file back into the Registry. Or, double-click the .reg file in an Explorer window. The keys and values in the imported file replace the corresponding keys and values in the Registry. Note that if you delete a key or value in the text file, importing the file doesn't delete the key or value in the Registry.

The Registry is quite large—an exported version of the whole thing can be 30MB or more. If you do plan to edit it, export only the branch you plan to work on.

Registry Keys That Run Programs on Startup

You can tell Windows to start a program automatically when Windows starts up by including a shortcut to it in the Startup folder of your Start Menu (see Chapter 1, section "Starting Programs When You Log In").

In addition, two places in the Registry can contain entries that run programs at Windows startup. Look in these two keys:

```
HKEY_LOCAL_MACHINE\Software\Microsoft\Windows\Current Version
HKEY_CURRENT_USER\Software\Microsoft\Windows\Current Version
```

These keys can contain keys named Run, RunOnce, or RunOnceEx, which contain values that start programs when Windows starts. To stop the program from running, remove or rename the key.

The
Complete
Reference

Windows XP

Appendix

Installing or Upgrading to Windows XP

This appendix explains your installation options for Windows XP Home Edition and details how to install, upgrade to, and uninstall it. You'll also find out how to check your installation, how to install optional Windows components, how to upgrade to Windows XP Service Pack 1 (SP1), and other installation tips.

The Windows Setup Wizard installs Windows in three phases:

- **File Copy phase**   The wizard copies program files from the CD onto your hard disk, then reboots.

- **Text Mode phase**   The screen displays information in text mode (plain text only). It checks your system's hardware and installs the basic files, then reboots again.

- **GUI Mode phase**   The wizard completes the installation, including prompting you for information.

After installation, Microsoft's new product activation system requires you to check in with Microsoft so that your copy of Windows XP can be "locked" to your particular computer. If you are replacing an old computer with a new one, you may want to use the Files And Settings Transfer Wizard to move your files. If you want to create a dual-boot installation, this appendix has instructions, along with information about the Boot.ini file, which controls which partition your system boots from.

Windows XP Installation Requirements

To install Windows XP, you need the following:

- A Windows XP CD-ROM and a CD-ROM or DVD drive

- A Pentium II, Celeron, or compatible CPU running at a speed of at least 233 MHz

- At least 128MB of RAM memory (you can install Windows XP with only 64MB, but it's not reliable). Windows XP can use up to 4GB of RAM.

- A hard disk with at least 2GB total space, with at least 1.5GB free, depending on which options you choose to install (see "Disk Space Requirements" later in this appendix).

- A VGA or better monitor

- A keyboard and mouse (or other pointing device)

- CD-ROMs, floppy disks, or files on your hard disk with hardware drivers for devices needing drivers that don't come with Windows

Windows itself is stored in compressed format in a group of *cabinet files* (*CAB* files) with the extension .cab on the CD-ROM. The setup program copies and decompresses the Windows programs during installation.

 Installation Options

You can install Windows in one of the following ways:

- **From scratch**   Install Windows on a blank, formatted hard disk or on a blank partition of a hard disk.

- **Upgrade**   Install Windows XP Home Edition over Windows Me or 98, replacing your previously installed operating system. You can't install Windows XP Home Edition as an upgrade to Windows NT or Windows 2000; for that upgrade, you need Windows XP Professional. When you upgrade, you can decide whether to install Windows XP over your existing Windows version, leaving the program and data files intact, or delete everything and start with a clean partition or disk.

- **Dual-boot**   Create a dual-boot installation with Windows 95, 98, Me, 2000, or NT, or with Linux, Unix, or another operating system. A dual-boot installation allows you to choose to start your computer in either Windows XP or your previously installed operating system.

Each of these methods is described in detail later in this appendix. We don't recommend upgrading an existing system, since most installation problems happen using this method. Instead, install Windows XP from scratch.

 If you install Windows XP Home Edition, you can upgrade to Windows XP Professional later.

Dynamic Update

An option during Windows XP setup offers to communicate with Microsoft over the Internet to check for updated Windows program files. You can choose to enable Windows Update if you have a working Internet connection, or disable it if you don't—or if you'd rather install the Windows program as it appears on your CD.

Choosing Your File System

When you install Windows XP on a new, blank partition, you need to choose the file system for the partition (see Chapter 33, section "The FAT, FAT32, and NTFS File Systems"). If you don't plan a multiboot system (that is, Windows XP will be the only operating system on the computer), choose NTFS, which provides more features than the older FAT32. If you are setting up a dual-boot system on which older versions of Windows will need access to the partition, choose FAT32.

Service Pack 1 (SP1)

Windows XP Service Pack 1 (SP1) is a collection of upgrades and bug fixes for Windows XP. Copies of Windows XP (or computers with Windows XP preinstalled) acquired after the fall of 2002 come with SP1. You can get SP1 to update earlier versions of Windows XP. Refer to section "Windows XP Service Pack 1" in the Introduction to this book for a list of the new features in SP1—few are vital. The main purpose of SP1 is to package all the bug fixes and security updates to Windows XP in one package.

You can use SP1 to upgrade either Windows XP Home Edition or Windows XP Professional. Consult the Windows XP web site at **windowsupdate.microsoft.com** for the latest updates, including SP1. The upgrade is available as a large downloadable file or as a CD-ROM. Microsoft insists that you use Internet Explorer when downloading updates. You can also download it from its home page at **www.microsoft.com/ WindowsXP/pro/downloads/servicepacks/sp1**, which also includes installation details.

When you install SP1 on a Windows XP system, it asks whether you want to archive the files that it will replace, so that you can uninstall SP1 later. The archive will occupy about 140MB of space on the hard disk on which Windows is installed. The installation program keeps a log of events, warnings, and errors in C:\Windows\Svcpack.log (assuming that Windows is installed on C:), which you can view in Notepad. You don't have to reactivate an activated copy of Windows after installing SP1.

If you are using a corporate, no-activation-required version of Windows XP (which many bootleggers distribute), then SP1 may refuse to install on your system. If your copy of Windows XP has been activated and has a legal product key, installing SP1 won't require you to reactive Windows. See "More Information on Windows Product Activation" later in this appendix.

Disk Space Requirements

The Windows Setup Wizard tells you how much disk space it will need, anywhere from 850MB to 1.5GB during installation. It refuses to install if it doesn't find enough space. The amount of space required depends on the following:

- What operating system, if any, is already installed.

- Whether you choose to save the previous operating system (if any) to enable you to uninstall Windows XP later. This optional uninstall file can be up to 100MB. You can delete this backup later (see "Checking Your System After Installing Windows" later in this appendix).

- How many optional programs you install along with Windows. Windows comes with dozens of utilities and applications that aren't needed to run Windows, but may come in handy.

If you don't have enough space to install Windows, try emptying your Recycle Bin, deleting your browser's cache (or the temporary file caches of other application programs), and deleting all .tmp and .bak files. Exit all programs and delete all the files in C:\ Windows\Temp (or other temporary file folders) except those dated within the past few days. If you still don't have enough space, you can uninstall programs and reinstall them later when Windows XP is running. However, Windows XP requires a lot of elbow room; if your disk space is tight, consider buying a larger hard disk.

If your system has more than one hard disk or partition, the free space Windows requires must be on the drive that contains your Windows program folder (usually C:\Windows).

Windows Product Activation (WPA)

In addition to entering a 25-character product key, Microsoft requires you to *activate* your copy of Windows XP, Office 2002, and Visio 2002. (If you bought a computer with Windows XP preinstalled, it usually comes already activated, so you don't have to do anything.) Windows XP allows you 30 days of use before requiring activation. When the 30 days expires, if you haven't activated Windows, it won't let you log on until you activate it.

 Activation is different from product registration, in which you give Microsoft your name and contact information so that they can contact you with upgrades and other support information. Activation doesn't send Microsoft any personally identifying information.

How Activation Works

Many of the components inside any computer have unique serial numbers that Windows can read. The Windows Setup Wizard collects data about the hardware components of your computer as it installs drivers for the hardware you have installed in your system. Specifically, it records information about the first device of each the following types:

- Display adapter
- SCSI adapter
- IDE (disk) adapter
- Network adapter
- Amount of RAM memory
- CPU type
- CPU serial number
- Hard disk type
- Hard disk volume serial number (VSN), which is changed when you reformat the disk or convert it from FAT32 to NTFS
- CD-ROM, CD-RW, and DVD-ROM
- Docking station, and whether the computer is a laptop

APPENDIX

WPA then creates an individually identifiable *activation ID* that it applies to your computer. When you activate Windows XP, Windows sends a license request with your activation ID over the Internet to Microsoft's database, where the information is stored, and Microsoft's activation server sends a certificate ID that "unlocks" (activates) your copy of Windows. The activation information is stored in C:\Windows\System32\Wpa.dbl, with a backup file in Wpa.bak (assuming that Windows is installed on drive C:).

The activation ID cannot be decoded to point directly to a particular machine, so Microsoft can't figure out (using only your activation information) who you are or what your are doing with your computer. However, future efforts could conceivably reveal a way to exploit the information about your computer that is contained in the activation ID.

If your computer isn't on the Internet, you need to call Microsoft on the phone to activate Windows XP. The Windows XP Setup program displays your activation ID as a 50-digit number on the screen. You call Microsoft's activation hotline (which is toll-free in many countries), read this activation ID to the operator, get a confirmation ID (a 42-digit number), and type it in.

If you decide not to activate Windows right away (we recommend waiting a few days), a balloon appears from an icon in the notification area of the taskbar once a day, reminding you how many days you have left before you must activate the program. You can click the balloon to run the Activate Windows program.

If you haven't yet activated Windows and want to run the Activate Windows program, choose Start | Run, type \windows\system32\oobe\msoobe /a, and press ENTER. *You can also run this program to check whether you've activated Windows.*

Each time you start Windows, it compares your activation hardware information in the Wpa.dbl file against the hardware in your computer to make sure that nothing has changed. If the hardware is substantially different from the information recorded in the file, you have to re-active Windows (see "Activation and Changes to Your PC's Hardware" later in this appendix).

You can't install the same copy of Windows XP on several different computers, because they have different hardware serial numbers. If you try, when the activation ID is checked against your original activation ID, they won't match, so Microsoft won't allow you to activate Windows XP. In addition, you can't *clone* (copy an entire disk partition) an installation of Windows XP from one computer to another. If you do, when Windows starts up, it will notice that the hardware doesn't match the activation ID. This is how Microsoft's product activation prevents casual piracy.

Reinstalling Windows after Activation

If you format your hard disk and reinstall Windows XP, you must reactivate it, and Microsoft checks that the activation ID hasn't changed. Product activation does not limit the number of times you can reinstall Windows XP on a single machine. Installing SP1 doesn't force you to reactivate.

Activation and Changes to Your PC's Hardware

Replacing more than a specified number of hardware components in your machine causes the software to require reactivation. Only changes to the hardware components listed in the "How Activation Works" section count. The number of hardware components that can be changed depends on whether the computer is a desktop, laptop, or laptop with docking station, and whether it has a network adapter:

	Network adapter that has not changed	No network adapter (or a changed network adapter)
Desktop (or laptop with no docking station)	5	3
Laptop with docking station	8	6

Changing the same hardware component multiple times counts as a single change (for example, you could try 10 different sound boards without triggering activation). Adding a new hardware component that didn't exist when you activated Windows XP doesn't count as a change (for example, adding a game controller or CD-RW drive). A swappable hard disk (a drive bay that enables you to swap hard disks easily) doesn't affect activation as long as it's not your primary hard disk. If you get a new motherboard, you usually have to reactivate Windows, because the motherboard usually includes the CPU, IDE disk adapter, display adapter, and RAM.

When Windows decides that you have made too many changes to your hardware, and that you may have installed it on an entirely different system, you have to call Microsoft to get permission to continue to use the product. Microsoft has toll-free product activation phone numbers in many countries. If you cannot activate the product by then, you will not able to log on to Windows. You can call Microsoft to explain what has happened so that you can get your product activated. The original version of Windows XP required you to reactivate before you could run Windows again; Windows XP Service Pack 1 gives you a three-day grace period during which you can use Windows without reactivation.

After 120 days, the activation server assumes that you might be moving your copy of Windows XP to a new computer, and allows you to install the same product key on different hardware. If it has been at least 120 days since you last activated your Windows license and you install Windows XP on another computer using the same product key, activation succeeds over the Internet. The server knows the hardware doesn't match, but allows activation to succeed anyway.

 When you use Windows Update or Automatic Updates, Windows transmits your product key to Microsoft's site. Only Windows installations with legal product keys get updated.

Identifying Which Product Key You Used

When you install Windows, you type the 25-character product key. Windows uses the product key when it activates the software. If you need to reinstall Windows later and you have more than one copy of Windows, you may need to know which product key you used for which Windows installation. Unfortunately, Windows won't display the product key you typed in.

You can download and run Alex Feinman's GetProdKey program to find out what your product key is. Go to **tools.alexfeinman.com/getprodkey.htm** to download the program, which arrives in a ZIP file (compressed ZIP folder). Copy the program file, GetProdKey.exe, from the compressed folder into your C:\Windows folder (if Windows is installed on C:). Open a Command Prompt window (described in Chapter 4) by choosing Start | Run, typing **cmd**, and pressing ENTER. Type **getprodkey** and press ENTER. The GetProdKey program displays the first five and last five characters of the product key you used when you installed Windows on this computer.

If you want to use a different product key for a system, you can change it. Follow these steps:

1. Make a backup copy of C:\Windows\System32\Wpa.dbl (assuming that you installed Windows on drive C:). Copy it onto a floppy disk or rename it as Wpa backup.dbl.

2. Reboot your computer. (Restarting Windows isn't enough.) Windows should notice that the activation information is missing and should tell you that you need to activate Windows. A balloon should appear from the Activation icon (two keys) in the notification area of the taskbar, telling you how many days you have left before Windows will stop working (usually 29 days).

3. Click the Activation icon in the toolbar to open the Active Windows window.

4. Choose Yes I Want To Telephone A Customer Service Representative To Activate Windows and click Next. Windows generates a new activation ID based on your old product key and existing hardware. You see the Activate Windows By Phone window.

5. Click the Change Product Key button at the bottom of the window and type your product key in the window that appears. Click Update.

6. Click Back to return to the first Activate Windows window to activate normally (either over the Internet, by phone, or later).

More Information on Windows Product Activation

For the latest information on product activation or any other Windows XP-related news, check these web pages:

- Microsoft Windows XP Product Activation web page at **www.microsoft.com/ windowsxp/pro/evaluation/overviews/activation.asp**, with links to other Microsoft pages on the subject

- Microsoft's Piracy Basics: Product Activation web page at **www.microsoft.com/ piracy/basics/activation**

- What's New with Product Activation for Windows XP Service Pack 1 web page at **www.microsoft.com/piracy/basics/activation/windowsxpsp1.asp**

- Technical Details On Microsoft Product Activation web page: Start at **www.microsoft.com/technet** and search for "Windows XP activation"

- Alex Nichol's article about activation at **www.aumha.org/a/wpa.htm**

- Internet Gurus Windows XP Home Edition Completer Reference web site at **net.gurus.com/winxphometcr**

Preparing to Install Windows

Here are some tips, including suggestions from Microsoft, for a smoother installation:

- **Virus-checking**   Run a virus-checker on your system before installing Windows, so that no viruses interfere with the installation. You can download several good virus-checkers from the Internet, including those from McAfee (at **www.mcafee.com**) and Symantec (at **www.symantec.com**). Then disable your virus-checker before installing Windows.

 Some computers have antivirus programs stored in the computer's BIOS (Basic Input/ Output System). In this case, the Setup Wizard won't run. If you see an error message reporting an antivirus program, check your system's documentation for instructions on how to disable virus checking.

- **Disk errors**   Run ScanDisk or ChkDsk (if you use Windows) to clean up any formatting errors on your hard disk.

- **Backups**   Make a complete backup of your system. If that's not possible, make a backup of all of your data files (see Chapter 9). Be sure to use a backup program that you'll be able to reinstall after upgrading to Windows XP, so that you'll be able to restore your files later. Or, copy your data files to a removable disk or burn them to a CD-R or CD-RW.

- **Unused programs**   Uninstall programs you rarely use.

- **Program installation disks**   Make sure that you have the program disks (CDs or floppies) for all the programs you want to install. If you downloaded programs, make backups of the installation files.

- **Disk space**   Make sure that you have enough free space on the hard disk on which your Windows program folder will be stored (see "Disk Space Requirements"earlier in this appendix). You need from 850MB to 1.5GB of space, and more if you plan to install many optional programs.

APPENDIX

■ **Hardware problems** If you have problems with hardware or software on your system, fix the problems first or uninstall the hardware or software.

■ **Other utilities** Disable any non-Microsoft disk-caching programs, such as the caching programs that come with the Norton Utilities and PC Tools. Turn off other utilities that might interfere with installation, such as CleanSweep (which monitors software installations). Exit from all programs.

■ **Network information** If your computer is on a network, contact your network administrator before upgrading to Windows XP. Ask whether the computer is part of a domain, and if so, ask for the domain name and your computer's name on the domain. If your network uses static IP addresses (your network administrator will know), ask for your computer's IP address. If your computer isn't part of a domain (that is, it's on a peer-to-peer network as described in Chapter 29), ask for the name of the workgroup. Make sure that your computer is connected to the network during installation, because the Setup Wizard can detect many LAN and Internet settings and configure your computer automatically.

■ **System BIOS** Check that you have the latest updates to your system's BIOS (Basic Input/Output System, which is stored on a chip on the motherboard). Go to the web site of your computer manufacturer for information. For example, if you are upgrading a Dell computer, go to **support.dell.com**, sign in with your computer's serial number or "service tag," and click Upgrades.

Tip *You can check your system for compatibility with Windows XP by running the Upgrade Advisor. You can download it from **www.microsoft.com/windowsxp/ pro/howtobuy/upgrading/advisor.asp**, but the file is large (50MB). If you have the Windows XP CD, you can run the Upgrade Advisor by starting the Windows Setup Wizard, choosing Check System Compatibility, and choosing Check My System Automatically.*

Starting the Installation

Before starting the installation process, you need to take a few steps, depending on whether you are installing on a blank hard disk, upgrading an existing Windows installation, or creating a dual-boot system.

Installing Windows on a Blank Hard Disk

The Windows XP CD-ROM is bootable; that is, it contains startup operating system files so that you can use it to start your computer. However, your computer must be configured to boot from the CD-ROM. Your computer may look first in the floppy drive and then on the hard drive for operating system files at startup. Try putting the Windows XP CD-ROM in the CD drive and starting your computer to see if the computer loads the Setup Wizard from the CD-ROM. If not, follow the instructions in the rest of this section.

To tell your computer to look on the CD-ROM during startup, you need to change your computer's BIOS setup. The method to do this varies from computer to computer, and you should check your computer's documentation. Generally, you press a key (usually F2, F6, F10, or DELETE) during startup, while the computer manufacturer's logo is on the screen, before you see the Windows logo. Some computers display a prompt to tell you what to press (for example, "Press <Del> key if you want to run setup").

Once you press the correct key, you see your computer's BIOS configuration screen. Follow the instructions on the screen (or in your computer's documentation) to change the boot sequence (or boot order) to start with the CD-ROM. Then follow the instructions to save your changes and reboot with the Windows XP CD-ROM in the drive. The Setup Wizard should run. Follow its instructions to install Windows XP (see "Answering the Windows Setup Wizard's Questions" later in this appendix).

*If your system can't boot from a CD, but can boot from floppy disks, you can create a set of six boot floppies from which you can start the installation. See the Microsoft.com Download Center at **www.microsoft.com/downloads/release.asp?ReleaseID=33290**, or go to the Microsoft support web site at **support.microsoft.com** and search for article Q310994.*

Upgrading to Windows XP

When you upgrade to Windows XP, the Windows Setup Wizard can save your old operating system's files and settings, so that you don't need to reinstall all of your programs. If you run Windows 95, Windows 3.1, or DOS, installation replaces your old operating system entirely, and you must reinstall and restore all your programs and files.

If you want to be able to run either another operating system or Windows XP when you start the computer, you can set up a dual-boot configuration (see the next section).

If your hard disk has become full of junk, or your Windows installation is unreliable, you may want to start from scratch anyway, rather than installing Windows on top of what you already have on the hard disk. A *clean install* reduces problems with older incompatible program files and with unneeded files that waste disk space. You can save the data files you want to keep, reformat the hard disk, install Windows, install the programs you want to use, and restore your data files. The Windows Setup Wizard can even do the reformatting for you. A clean install usually saves time in the long run, even though you need to reinstall your programs.

We prefer to make a separate partition for data (usually D:), move our data files there, and use the C: partition for only Windows and programs (see Chapter 33, section "Partitions, File Systems, and Drive Letters"). This allows us to reinstall Windows any time we like without disturbing our data.

To upgrade from a previous version of Windows, start your current version of Windows. When you put the Windows XP CD-ROM in the CD-ROM drive, you should see the Welcome To Microsoft Windows XP window. If you don't, use Windows Explorer to look at the contents of the CD-ROM and run the Setup.exe program. Another way to run the program is to choose Start | Run, type **d:\setup**, and press ENTER (if your CD-ROM drive is drive D:).

Follow the instructions that the Windows Setup Wizard displays (see "Answering the Windows Setup Wizard's Questions" later in this appendix). The Setup Wizard creates an upgrade report that lists hardware and software issues that may arise.

The Windows Setup Wizard asks in which folder to install Windows XP (usually C:\ Windows). If you choose a different folder than the one in which the previous version of Windows was installed, you must reinstall all of your application programs, and possibly all of your hardware drivers.

Creating Dual-boot Installations

A *dual-boot* or *multiboot installation* is an installation of Windows that leaves another operating system intact on your computer. When you start your computer, you can decide which operating system to run. In order to keep the versions of Windows separate, you install each in a separate partition. If one of the operating systems is Windows 9x/Me, it must be on the first partition.

The Windows Setup Wizard can create a new partition if your hard disk has unused, unpartitioned space. It can install Windows XP into this new partition, leaving your existing operating system intact. You do not need to use a third-party partitioning program.

However, you will probably want to get a third-party partitioning program like PartitionMagic (from PowerQuest Corp., at **www.powerquest.com/partitionmagic**) or BootIt NG (from TeraByte Unlimited, at **www.terabyteunlimited.com**) to adjust the sizes of your existing partitions to make space for Windows XP. We like to create a separate partition for each operating system, plus one for our data. This arrangement enables us to switch or reinstall operating systems without disturbing our data (see Chapter 33, section "Managing Partitions with PartitionMagic").

Another way to create a dual-boot system is to make a copy of your old Windows partition, and upgrade the copy to Windows XP, leaving the original partition intact. This method is tricky, however: copying (or *cloning*) a Windows partition requires editing the Registry and startup files to fix all the drive letter references. We don't recommend it. Instead, install Windows XP in a blank partition.

Yet another way to create a multiboot system is to use a virtual machine (VM) manager. VMware (**www.vmware.com**) enables you to run one operating system within another. For example, you can install Windows XP, and then run Windows 98 (or Linux) in a window. These VM programs enable you to switch operating systems without restarting.

Note *For more information about creating multiboot systems, go to the Microsoft support web site at **support.microsoft.com** and search for article Q306559.*

Dual-booting with Windows 2000, Unix, or Linux

You can't use the Windows Setup Wizard to create a dual-boot system with Windows 2000 and Windows XP unless Windows 2000 is installed in a FAT32 partition. This is because the wizard will upgrade Windows 2000's NTFS partition to Windows XP's slightly newer NTFS format, and Windows 2000 will no longer be able to read its own partition. However, PartitionMagic, BootIt NG, and similar third-party partitioning programs provide a way to create a dual-boot system with Windows 2000. Use a third-party partitioning program to create a new partition for Windows XP and to hide the Windows 2000 partition. Then install Windows XP on the new, blank partition. This method also works for creating a dual-boot system with Unix or Linux.

Dual-booting with Windows Me or 9*x*

To create a dual-boot system with Windows XP and Windows Me or 9*x*, install the older version of Windows first, and then install Windows XP. During the installation process, Windows XP creates a file named Boot.ini in C:\, listing the bootable partitions and which partition is the default. When the Setup Wizard displays the Setup Options window, click the Advanced Options button and select the I Want to Choose the Install Drive Letter and Partition During Setup check box. This setting causes the Setup Wizard to display a list of your partitions and enables you to choose the partition in which you want to display Windows XP. You also have the option of deleting existing partitions and creating new ones. The next section steps through the installation process.

Once you have both versions of Windows installed in separate primary DOS partitions, you can switch back and forth by using the boot menu that Windows XP displays:

```
Please select the operating system to start:

Microsoft Windows XP Home Edition
Microsoft Windows

Use the up and down arrow keys to move the highlight to your choice.
Press ENTER to choose.
Seconds until highlighted choice will be started automatically: 30
```

Windows Me, 98, and 95 appear simply as "Microsoft Windows." You can change the text and entries in this boot menu, as described in the "Setting Boot Options" section later in this appendix.

Note *On a dual-boot system with Windows NT or Windows 3.1, you can't use FAT32 for your data partition, because Windows NT and Windows 3.1 don't support FAT32 (as Windows 2000, Me, 98, and XP do)—see Chapter 33 for information about the FAT32 and NTFS file systems. On a dual-boot system with Windows Me or 9x, you can't use an NTFS partition for your data partition, since these versions of Windows can't read it.*

Windows Setup Wizard Versions and Command-Line Options

When you start the Windows XP Setup Wizard from the CD-ROM, you are running the program Setup.exe stored in the root folder of the CD. The CD contains two other versions of the Setup Wizard, stored in the I386 folder. These two versions enable you to supply configuration information when you start the Setup Wizard, in the form of command-line options. The Winnt.exe program runs on DOS and Windows 3.1 systems, Winnt32 runs on Windows 9*x*, 98, and Me systems. (If you're not sure, try Winnt32 first.)

You can run the Setup Wizard with command-line options by typing **D:\i386\winnt32** followed by the command-line options (replace D with the drive letter of your CD-ROM drive, if it's not D). . Then press ENTER. You type this command at the DOS command prompt, in the Run dialog box (choose Start | Run), or in the Target box in the Properties dialog box of a shortcut. For example, to check whether your system is compatible with Windows XP (assuming that the Windows XP Setup CD is in drive D:), type

  d:\i386\winnt32 /checkupgradeonly

Table A-1 lists some of the command-line options you can use with Winnt32. For more information about installation options, go to **www.microsoft.com/technet**, search

Command-line Option	Description
/checkupgradeonly	Verifies that your system is compatible with Windows XP. Doesn't install Windows XP. Creates a report named Upgrade.txt or Ntcompat.txt in C:\Windows, C:\Winnt, or wherever the existing version of Windows is installed.
/cmdcons	Adds the Recovery Console to your boot menu (see Chapter 2, section "Using The Recovery Console"). Doesn't install Windows XP.

Table A-1. *Some Command-line Options for Winnt32*

Command-line Option	Description
/debug*level:filename*	Creates a log file containing errors messages from the Windows installation. Replace *level* with 0 (for severe errors only), 1 (for all errors), 2 (for warnings and all errors), or 3 (for informational messages, warnings, and errors). Replace *filename* with the name of the log file to create (if you omit the colon and filename, the log file is C:\Windows\Winnt32.log, if you are installing Windows in C:\Windows).
/dudisable	Disables Dynamic Update (see "Dynamic Update" earlier in this appendix).
/makelocalsource	Copies all the installation source files from the CD to your hard disk before beginning to install.
/s:*foldername*	Looks in *foldername* for the installation files rather than looking on a CD or the same folder that contains Winnt32.exe.

Table A-1.   *Some Command-line Options for Winnt32* (continued)

for "Windows XP Winnt32," and look for the "Unattended Installations" article. For information about how to use the /unattend option to install Windows XP unattended (with no questions on the screen during the installation), go to **support.microsoft.com** and search for the article Q291997.

Answering the Windows Setup Wizard's Questions

Follow the steps outlined in this section to install Windows once you have started the Windows Setup Wizard and you see the Welcome To Microsoft Windows XP window, shown in Figure A-1. (The second option, Install Optional Windows Components, appears only when you run the program on a system that is already running Windows XP.) You

APPENDIX

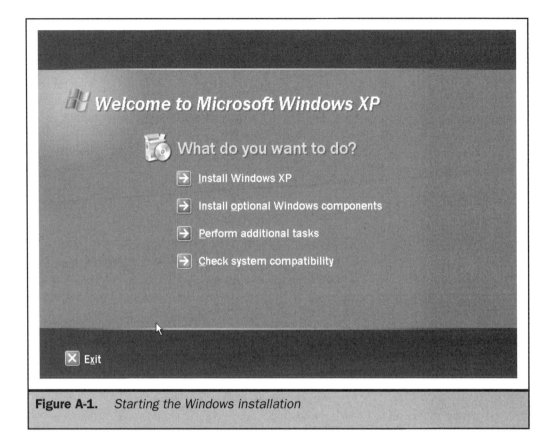

Figure A-1.   *Starting the Windows installation*

can press ESC at any time to cancel your installation. Click Next to move from one screen of the Setup Wizard to the next.

1. Before starting the installation, click Check System Compatibility. The Microsoft Windows Upgrade Advisor checks your system for incompatibilities with Windows XP and displays a window like the following:

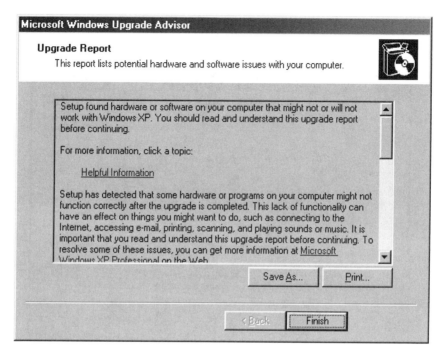

If your system includes hardware or software that Windows can't handle or that needs to be upgraded, you can click Details for a list. Microsoft's online hardware compatibility list is also on the Web at **www.microsoft.com/hcl**. For an installation on a blank disk, this includes information only about your hardware, since the Upgrade Advisor has no way of knowing what software you plan to install later. If the Upgrade Advisor finds Blocking Issues, you can't proceed to upgrade. If it lists only Helpful Information, you are good to go.

2. To start the installation, click Install Windows XP. The Windows Setup Wizard checks your computer for installed operating systems, and tells you whether you can upgrade or need to install Windows XP from scratch.

APPENDIX

3. In the Windows Setup dialog box, set the Installation Type to either Upgrade or New Installation:

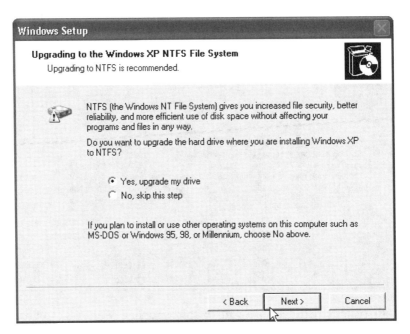

Choose New Installation to install to a new, blank partition (Setup can reformat a partition or disk for you), or Upgrade to update your Windows 98, Me, NT 4.0 Workstation, or 2000 installation. You won't see the Upgrade option if your existing version of Windows is too old (Windows 95 or earlier).

4. After you agree to the license agreement, the Setup Wizard prompts for your product key, a 25-character license number that appears on the Windows XP CD box. We suggest that you write this number right on the CD-ROM, using a fine-point permanent marker, on the same side that the printing appears on the disk. *Don't write on (or touch) the other (bottom) side of the disk.*

5. If you choose Upgrade, the Setup Wizard displays the Upgrade Report screen, which asks how much information you want on the upgrade report that it creates: hardware issues only, all issues, or no report at all. Don't choose Do Not Show Me The Report, since hardware issues may prevent Windows XP from running correctly, even if your hardware worked fine with a previous version of Windows. If you have enough disk space, the Setup Wizard stores a compressed version of your old version of Windows so that you can uninstall Windows XP later (see "Uninstalling Windows XP and SP1" at the end of this appendix).

6. If you choose New Installation, you see the Setup Options screen.

- If you want to copy the installation files from the CD to hard disk, click Advanced Options and select the Copy All Installation Files From The Setup CD (this option is useful if you plan to install Windows options later and want to do so without needing to put the Windows XP CD-ROM into the drive). Click OK.

- If you are creating a dual-boot installation, click Advanced Options and select the I Want To Choose The Install Drive Letter And Partition During Setup check box. We recommend that you select this option if your system has more than one partition or hard disk. Don't change the To This Folder On My Hard Drive box to an entry other than \WINDOWS unless you have a good reason. Microsoft recommends that Windows XP be installed in the \Windows folder. Click OK.

- If you are installing from a network drive, or somewhere other than your CD, you can specify a pathname where the installation files are stored. Click Advanced Options and set the Copy Installation Files From This Folder box (click the Browse button to navigate to the folder). Click OK.

- If you have vision problems, click the Accessibility Options button. You can choose to enable the Microsoft Magnifier (if you want the contents of the screen magnified) or Microsoft Narrator (which can read the screen aloud) while the Setup Wizard runs. Click OK.

- Change the language if you want Windows to be installed with screens in another language (this option doesn't change the Setup Wizard). Click OK.

7. If you chose New Installation in step 3 and the disk partition to which you are installing Windows XP doesn't already use the NTFS file system, you see the Upgrading To The Windows XP NTFS File System screen, shown in Figure A-2 (see "Choosing Your File System" earlier in this appendix). Of course, the Setup Wizard may not yet know on which partition you plan to install Windows—it's just guessing. If you plan to use only Windows XP on your computer, choose Yes. If you are creating a dual-boot system and you want older versions of Windows to be able to read files on the disk, choose No.

8. On the Get Updated Setup Files screen, you choose whether to use Dynamic Update to connect to the Internet to check the Microsoft web site for updated Windows XP files. If you have a working Internet connection on the computer, choose Yes; otherwise, choose No. If you choose No, or if the Setup Wizard can't get through to the Microsoft Windows Update site, you can update your Windows XP installation later using Windows Update (see Chapter 36, section "Updating Your Computer with Windows Update").

9. The Setup Wizard analyzes your computer, figures out which files you need to install, and copies them from the CD-ROM to your hard disk. It reboots and begins the Text Mode (nongraphical) phase of the installation.

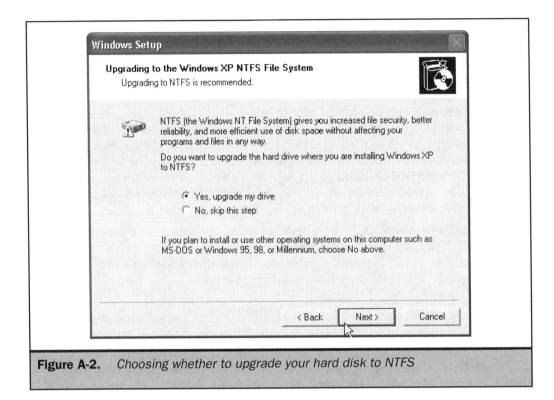

Figure A-2.   *Choosing whether to upgrade your hard disk to NTFS*

10. If you selected the I Want To Choose The Install Drive Letter And Partition During Setup check box in step 6, you see several menus.

- If your system already contains an installation of Windows XP, a menu asks whether you would rather repair it or install a fresh copy of Windows. Press ESC to install a fresh copy of Windows (either on the same partition or a different one).

- Then you see a list of your partitions, as shown in Figure A-3. You can select a partition and delete it, if it contains a version of Windows you no longer want. You can create a new partition in unpartitioned space. Don't choose a partition that already contains a version of Windows. If you are replacing your existing Windows installation, delete the partition that contains Windows and create a new partition in its place for Windows XP (just make sure that you have a backup of any files on that partition that you want to keep!).

- If you create a partition, you can specify how much of the unpartitioned space to use (in kilobytes). Make the partition at least 2GB to leave room for Windows.

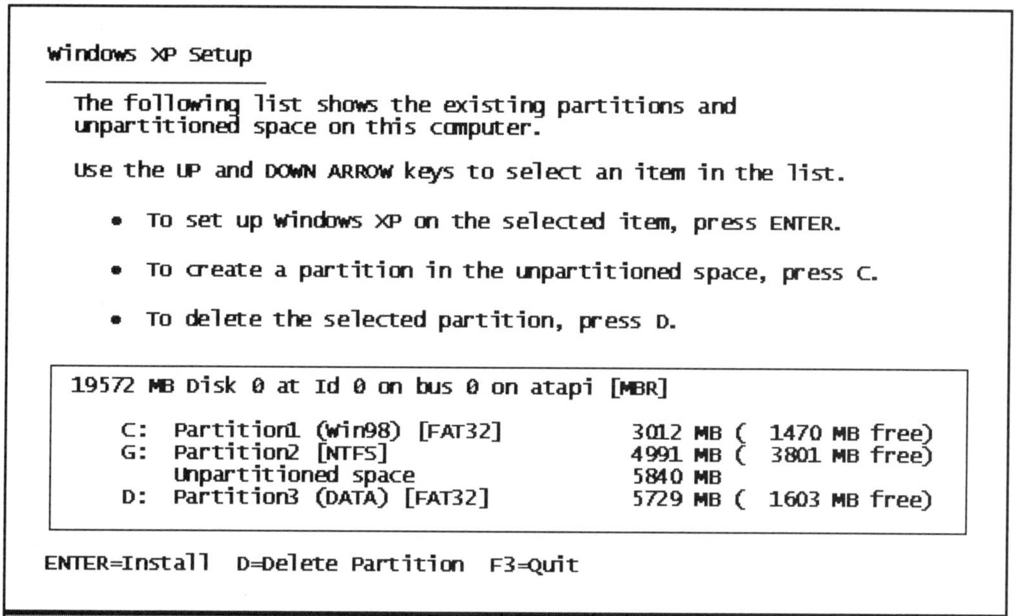

```
Windows XP Setup

    The following list shows the existing partitions and
    unpartitioned space on this computer.

    Use the UP and DOWN ARROW keys to select an item in the list.

        •  To set up Windows XP on the selected item, press ENTER.

        •  To create a partition in the unpartitioned space, press C.

        •  To delete the selected partition, press D.

    ┌──────────────────────────────────────────────────────────────┐
    │  19572 MB Disk 0 at Id 0 on bus 0 on atapi [MBR]               │
    │                                                                │
    │      C:  Partition1 (win98) [FAT32]        3012 MB ( 1470 MB free) │
    │      G:  Partition2 [NTFS]                 4991 MB ( 3801 MB free) │
    │          Unpartitioned space               5840 MB              │
    │      D:  Partition3 (DATA) [FAT32]         5729 MB ( 1603 MB free) │
    └──────────────────────────────────────────────────────────────┘

 ENTER=Install   D=Delete Partition   F3=Quit
```

Figure A-3.   *Choosing the partition in which to install Windows*

■ When you are finished, select the partition on which to install Windows XP and press ENTER. Then choose whether to use FAT32 or NTFS for the partition (use NTFS unless you have a specific reason for using FAT32). Don't choose the Quick Format options—let the Setup Wizard make sure that the hard disk has no bad sectors or other problems.

11. Windows reboots again and displays a graphical screen during the final GUI phase of the installation. (This step can take more than half an hour.)

12. If you chose New Installation rather than Upgrade in step 3, the Setup Wizard asks you a series of questions. (If you are upgrading, the wizard can get this information from your old version of Windows.) It asks about the following:

■ **Regional and Language Options**   You can change the way dates, numbers, and money are displayed. You can also change these settings later (see Chapter 12, section "Windows' Regional Settings").

■ **Text Input Languages**   You can choose your default language and keyboard layout (see Chapter 12, section "Changing Language Properties").

■ **Name and Organization**   Applications can get your name and company name from Windows (for example, Outlook Express does this). You can change your name in most applications, but getting it right the first time is more convenient.

APPENDIX

- **Computer name**   This is the name you want to use for your computer. If your computer is connected to a local area network (LAN), the LAN administrator might want to issue your computer a name.

- **Administrator password**   This is the password you'll type when you log onto Windows with the Owner or Administrator user account. Don't leave it blank.

- **Country, area code, and outside line number**   Windows uses these numbers when configuring dial-up connections to the Internet.

- **Date and time**   Set your clock, and remember to set the time zone. When you connect to the Internet, it will automatically update your clock to the correct time for your area. If Windows thinks you are in the wrong time zone, the time will be wrong!

- **Network settings**   If the Setup Wizard detects a network adapter, it asks whether to create LAN connections using TCP/IP (the protocol used on the Internet and many LANs) and Client For Microsoft Networks (Microsoft's LAN client program). You can click Custom Settings to use a different protocol (like IPX/SPX) or client (like NetWare). See Chapter 27 for more information.

- **Workgroup or domain name**   This is the name of the workgroup or domain your computer is part of, if your computer is on a LAN. Ask your LAN administrator for the workgroup or domain name (Windows suggests MSHOME). See Chapter 29 if your computer is part of a workgroup.

13. When Windows is installed, it prompts you to help it set up your computer. The exact order of the next couple of steps depends on whether your computer is connected to a LAN or the Internet, and whether you are upgrading or doing a new installation.

14. If the Setup Wizard detects a LAN connection, it asks whether you connect to the Internet via the LAN or connect directly.

15. When you see the Ready To Activate Windows screen, you can choose whether to activate Windows now or later. You must activate Windows—you can put it off, but after a 30-day grace period, Windows won't let you log in if you haven't activated it (see "Windows Product Activation" earlier in this appendix). You don't need to register though (registration gives Microsoft your name, address, and other information; activation gives Microsoft only the technical "signature" of your computer and your Windows XP serial number). Windows tries to connect to the Internet, and if it can't, it reminds you to activate later. If you don't have an Internet connection, you can activate Windows over the phone.

Tip   *Wait a few days before activating, to make sure that the system works and that you are happy with the hardware. When you activate, the activation ID records the current state of the computer's hardware, and if you change it significantly, you'll need to call Microsoft later when you install the new hardware.*

16. If the Setup Wizard hasn't already figured out how you connect to the Internet (if you have a LAN connection), you see the Let's Get On The Internet screen. Microsoft suggests that you sign up for their MSN Internet service. If you have another account, choose Create A New Internet Account After I Finish Setting Up Windows. If the Setup Wizard detects a modem, it may offer to call the Microsoft Referral Service to suggest one of the ISPs that has signed up with its referral program. If so, click Skip to set up your Internet account yourself after the setup is finished (choose Start | Internet and refer to Chapter 22).

17. On the Who Will Use This Computer screen, type the names of up to five people who will use this computer, so that the Setup Wizard can create user accounts for each one. If you will be the only user, type just your name (first, last, both, or whatever you would like your user account name to be). If you want to create more than five user accounts, you can add them later (see Chapter 6, section "Creating New User Accounts"). Windows sets up administrator accounts for each name you specify, or for Owner if you don't specify any names.

18. After you click Finish on the Setup Wizard's last screen, you may see the Password Creation dialog box, which lists the user accounts that were created during installation, not counting the names you typed in the previous step. Windows creates an additional hidden user named Administrator that you use only when you start Windows in Safe Mode or the Recovery Console (see Chapter 2). Type a password to use for all the accounts listed. You can change these passwords later (see Chapter 6, section "Adding or Removing Passwords").

19. You see the Windows logon screen. Choose a user name you specified in step 17 and type the password you specified in step 18 to log on. (If Windows didn't ask you for a password in step 18, it shouldn't ask for one now, either.)

You see the Windows desktop. You are ready to test Windows and install your programs!

 To see the release notes for Windows XP, start the Windows XP Setup program from the CD, choose Perform Additional Tasks, choose Browse This CD, and open the Readme.htm file (click or double-click the filename to display it in Internet Explorer or on your default browser).

Checking Your System After Installing Windows

Here are things to do after Windows is installed:

- **Configure your hardware**   Check that all of your hardware was correctly detected by Windows, including your modem, network card, and printer. Choose Start, right-click My Computer, and choose Properties. Then click the Hardware tab of the System Properties dialog box and click the Device Manager button (see Chapter 13, section "Managing Your Hardware Components with the Device Manager"). If any of the computer components listed in the Device Manager window have exclamation marks on their icons, something is wrong.

> **Tip** *You can print a summary of your Windows configuration. Choose Start | All Programs | Accessories | System Tools | System Information. Then choose File | Print.*

- **Check your network connection** If your computer is connected to a LAN, check that the network communication is functioning normally. If it's not, see "Troubleshooting Your Network" in Chapter 29.

- **Check your user account passwords** Windows XP sets up user accounts whether you plan to use them or not, and it's important for your computer's security for your accounts to have passwords. Otherwise, if your computer connects to the Internet, some hacker may think of a way to break into your computer. Choose Start | Control Panel and click User Accounts. In the User Accounts window, choose each of the existing accounts, click Create A Password, and specify a password for the account. If "Guest account is off" doesn't appear, click it and turn it off.

- **Reinstall programs** If you didn't reformat your hard disk to install Windows from scratch, and if you installed Windows XP in the same folder as your previous version of Windows, you shouldn't need to reinstall the application programs that were installed on your hard disk. The Setup Wizard looks for installed programs and installs them in Windows XP, too. Otherwise, get out your installation CDs and start installing programs.

- **Set up your Internet connection** The Setup Wizard offers to help only with MSN Internet access and with ISPs who have signed up with their referral program. Choose Start | Internet to run the New Connection Wizard to set up other Internet connections (see Chapter 22, section "Running the New Connection Wizard").

- **Update your antivirus program** If you have antivirus software (and you should if your computer connects to the Internet), check whether it is compatible with Windows XP. Go to the program's web site and check whether you need to upgrade the antivirus program. Also make sure that you have an up-to-date virus database.

- **Check your documents and settings** If you updated from a previous version of Windows, check that your documents and program settings are intact. If your My Documents folder is empty, the files may be in another user's folder. In Windows Explorer (My Computer), check the C:\Documents And Settings folder (assuming that Windows is installed on C:), which should contain a folder for each user account. In each user's folder is a My Documents folder, one of which should contain your files.

Troubleshooting Windows XP Installation

Most Windows installations go smoothly, but there are many things that can go wrong. Here are a few ideas for troubleshooting installation problems:

- **Insufficient disk space**   If you didn't start with at least 1.5GB of free disk space, the installation can fail. Free up some space and try again. You may need to uninstall programs and reinstall them after Windows XP is installed.

- **Incompatible hardware**   Windows XP isn't compatible with every possible piece of PH hardware, and hardware problems can cause the Setup Wizard to hang in the GUI phase of the installation. Check the Hardware Compatibility List at **www.microsoft.com/hwdq/hcl**. Set the In box to the type of hardware component you want to know about and click Search Now. If possible, remove questionable hardware during the installation and add it back later.

- **File-copying errors**   If you receive the message that Setup cannot copy a file, you may have a problem with the CD or your CD-ROM drive. Try copying the \I386 folder from the Windows XP CD to your hard disk and running the Setup.exe program from there.

- **Log files**   The main log file is called Setupact.log and is stored in C:\Windows (or wherever you are installing Windows XP).

- **Outdated BIOS**   If the Setup Wizard hangs after the first reboot (the beginning of the Text Mode phase), your computer's BIOS may be incompatible. Go to your computer manufacturer's web site for updates.

- **Virus-scanners**   If you use virus-scanning software, uninstall it and try installing Windows XP again. If may be incompatible with Windows XP. Check its compatibility before reinstalling it.

- **Clean-booting your computer**   If you are upgrading from a previous version of Windows, it may be running background programs that interfere with Windows XP installation. In Windows Me or 98, choose Start | Run, type **msconfig.exe**, and press ENTER. On the General tab of the System Configuration Utility window, click Selective Startup and clear all the check boxes that appear under it. (In Windows Me, also click the Startup tab and click the StateMgr check box.) Close the System Configuration Utility window and click Yes to restart the computer. Run Msconfig again and check that the Selective Startup check boxes are still clear: if any are disabled or are selected, consult the program manufacturer to find out how to disable the program from running at startup.

Note *If you have upgraded from Windows 9x/Me, programs that used to start automatically may not do so if they don't appear on Windows XP's list of "known good programs." Choose Start | Run, type* **msconfig**, *press* ENTER, *and click the Startup tab to see a list of the programs that run when Windows starts up. A Restore Startup Programs button appears if programs were disabled during the upgrade. Click it, select the programs you want to run at startup, and click OK. However, before reinstating a program, make sure that it is compatible with Windows XP by consulting the program's web site.*

For more troubleshooting ideas, go to the Microsoft Support web site at **support.microsoft.com** and search for article Q310064.

Deleting the Backup of Your Previous Version of Windows

If you upgraded to Windows XP, the Setup Wizard may have kept a backup copy of your previous operating system, which can occupy 50MB or more of disk space. If you are sure that you will never want to uninstall Windows XP, follow these steps to delete the previous operating system files:

1. Choose Start | Control Panel | Add Or Remove Programs.
2. If Windows XP Uninstall appears in the Currently Installed Programs list, there is a backup copy of your previous operating system.
3. Click Windows XP Uninstall. Additional information appears.
4. Click the Change/Remove button. You see the Uninstall Windows XP dialog box.
5. Click Remove The Backup Of My Previous Operating System, and then click Continue. Windows deletes the unneeded file.

Transferring Your Data Files and Windows Configuration Settings

If you get a new computer that runs Windows XP, you can transfer your data files and some of your configuration settings from your old computer to your new one. You can move the files over a LAN, over a direct cable connection (serial null-modem cable), on floppy disks, or on other removable disks (like Zip or Jaz disks).

Tip *If you have Zip, Jaz, or other large-capacity removable disks, you can use the Files And Settings Transfer Wizard to back up your configuration and settings before you upgrade to Windows XP, and then restore them after you upgrade.*

What to Transfer

You can choose to transfer your Windows settings, your data files (specifying the folders where they are stored, or all files with specific file extensions), or both. The Files And Settings Transfer Wizard can transfer the configuration settings for Windows itself, including your desktop and taskbar setup, screen saver, folder settings, dial-up connections, regional settings, accessibility settings, and fonts, as well as the settings for Internet Explorer, Outlook Express, Windows Messenger, MSN Explorer, Windows Media Player, Windows Movie Maker, and Microsoft Office. Passwords are not transferred. The wizard works with some third-party programs as well; for a list, go to the Microsoft support web site at **support.microsoft.com** and search for article Q304903.

If you plan to use floppies to transfer your settings, you'd better have a lot of them! If you want to transfer your files, chances are that you'll have too many files to fit on floppies.

You will need to reinstall your application programs from their installation CDs or floppies (see the sidebar "Moving Programs from One Computer to Another" if you don't have the program CDs). We recommend that if you installed Windows from scratch, you reinstall your programs first. Then run the Files And Settings Transfer Wizard to transfer the program settings (the settings can't be transferred if the programs aren't already installed on the new computer).

If your old and new computers are connected over a network, you can transfer your files and settings from one computer to the other over the network. Make sure that you can access the old computer's hard disk from the new computer over the network.

When you move programs from one computer to another with the Files And Settings Transfer Wizard, you must move them to a drive with the same letter. For example, if your programs are on D: on the old computer, the wizard moves them to drive D: on the new computer.

Running the Transfer Wizard

To transfer your files or Windows settings, run the Files And Settings Transfer Wizard first on your old computer and then on your new one. The wizard runs under previous versions of Windows as well as Windows XP. There are three ways to run the wizard:

- Put the Windows XP CD-ROM into the CD drive on your old computer and run the Setup program. It may run automatically, or you may need to choose Start | Run, type **d:setup.exe** (replacing *d* with your CD drive letter), and press ENTER. You see the Welcome To Microsoft Windows XP window (shown earlier in Figure A-1). Click Perform Additional Tasks, and then click Transfer Files And Settings.

- In Windows XP, choose Start | All Programs | Accessories | System Tools | Files And Settings Transfer Wizard. Or choose Start | Run and type **migwiz**.

■ Run the wizard on another computer and create a Wizard Disk that contains the wizard program. (To create the Wizard Disk, run the wizard, choose New Computer, and choose I Want To Create A Wizard Disk In The Following Drive.) Run the wizard from that floppy disk by running the A:\Fastwiz.exe program.

After you start the wizard, you see the Files And Settings Transfer Wizard window. Click Next to move from screen to screen. Tell the wizard whether this is the new computer or the old one (as shown in Figure A-4, how you are going to transfer the files (cable, network, floppies, or other disks), and whether you want to transfer settings, files, or both. If you are transferring via floppies or other disks, the wizard determines how much data is to be transferred and stores it on floppies or other removable disks, prompting for additional disks as needed. If you are transferring your files as well as your settings, the transfer may take several minutes.

Note *If you run a firewall program that detects outgoing traffic, such as Zone Alarm, it may notify you that the wizard is setting up a server process. You must approve the wizard's activities for it to work. (But it's nice to know that the firewall noticed!)*

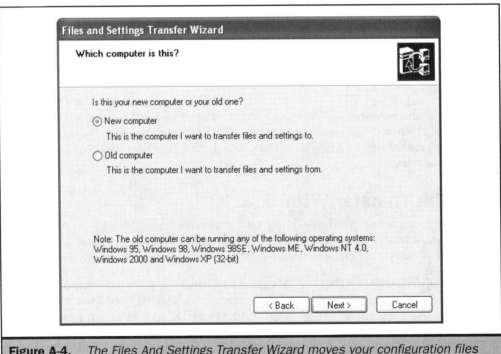

Figure A-4. *The Files And Settings Transfer Wizard moves your configuration files and documents from your old computer to your new one.*

The wizard packages your files and settings into DAT files with names like Img00001.dat. The DAT files can be up to 2GB, so when the wizard fills one file it starts a new one.

Answering the Transfer Wizard's Questions

On your old computer, make these choices:

- Choose Old Computer.
- Choose how you plan to move the files: Direct Cable (see the next section for details), Home Or Small Office Network (LAN), Floppy Drive Or Other Removable Media, or Other. Sometimes the LAN option is unavailable (this is a bug). If so, choose Other to store the files on a network drive that both computers can access.
- Choose what you want to transfer—settings, files, or both.

On your new computer, make these choices:

- Choose New Computer.
- When the wizard asks whether you need to create a Wizard Disk to run on the old computer, choose the last option, because you have already collected the information to transfer from the old computer.
- Choose where the wizard can find the data from the old computer: Direct Cable, Floppy Drive Or Other Removable Media, or Other.
- When the wizard prompts to you log off so that the transferred Windows settings can take effect, click Yes.

Transferring Files via Direct Cable Connection

If you are using a cable to transfer files, you need a *null-modem cable,* a type of serial cable that connects two computers together via their serial ports. Follow these steps:

1. On the old computer, run the wizard, choose Old Computer, choose Direct Cable, and choose what you want to transfer.

2. When you see the Set Up Your Serial Connection screen, connect the cable to the two computers.

3. On the new computer, run the wizard, choose not to create a Wizard Disk, and choose Direct Cable. You see the same Set Up Your Serial Connection screen.

4. On both computers, choose Autodetect. The two wizards make a connection over the cable.

5. Click Next. The wizards transfer your files, settings, or both.

APPENDIX

Moving Programs from One Computer to Another

You should have the installation CD, or downloaded installation program file, for each program that you own. But what if you've lost your installation CD, and you want to install it on your new computer? You may not be out of luck. Try following these steps:

1. Copy the program's folder from the old computer to the new computer. For example, copy C:\Program Files*programname* (assuming that Windows is installed on C: on your old computer). A few programs run entirely from files stored in this folder. If yours doesn't, read on.

2. Most programs require DLLs in C:\Windows or C:\Windows\System32, as well as Registry settings that contain configuration information (see Chapter 38). To copy Registry settings, run the Registry Editor on both computers (after making a backup of the Registry).

3. In the old computer, search the Registry for keys for the program. Choose Edit | Find to search for the program name or software company name. Also look in \HKEY_LOCAL_MACHINE\ Software and \HKEY_CURRENT_USER\Software.

4. If you find keys that appear to belong to the program, export by choosing the key, choosing File | Export, and specifying a filename for the .reg file.

5. Import the .reg file into the Registry Editor on the new computer by choosing File| Import. If you copied the program folder (in step 1) to a different location (for example, it's C:\Program Files*programname* on the old computer and D:\Program Files*programname* on the new computer), edit each Registry value that contains pathnames that have changed.

6. Try running the program again to see if the new Registry keys provide the information it needs.

7. If you see error messages that DLL files are missing, make a note of the filenames and copy the files from the old computer to the new one, into the same locations. Many DLL files are in C:\Windows\System32, and need to be in this folder to work.

8. When you have the program working, create shortcuts to it in your Start menu or desktop.

Note   *Just because it's possible to copy a program from one computer to another make it legal. Use this procedure only to move a program to a new computer, erasing the program from the old computer.*

Installing Additional Programs

The Windows XP CD-ROM contains a number of additional programs. You can install a few of them by running the Setup program on the CD and choosing Perform Additional Tasks from the Welcome To Microsoft Windows XP window. You can choose the following:

- Set Up Remote Desktop Connection (see Chapter 15, section "Accessing Other Computers with Remote Desktop").
- Set Up A Home Or Small Office Network (see Chapter 29, section "Adding Your Computer to a TCP/IP Peer-to-Peer LAN").
- Browse This CD, to see the files on the CD in an Explorer window.

The Valueadd folder on the CD contains more programs. Valueadd\Msft contains Microsoft programs, and Valueadd\3rdparty contains programs from other companies.

Setting Boot Options

Windows XP includes support for multiple partitions and multiple operating systems (it inherits this ability from Windows NT/2000). The boot program (Ntldr) is stored in the root folder of the first partition on the first disk. Ntldr reads the Boot.ini file, which is stored in the same folder, to find out which partitions you might want to boot from, which partition to use as the default, what to display in the boot menu, and how long to wait before loading the operating system from the default partition. If the boot menu contains only one option, you won't see it—Ntldr simply boots from that partition.

 Ntldr and Boot.ini are hidden, protected system files. To see them in an Explorer window, choose Tools | Folder Options, click the View tab, and deselect the Hide Protected Operating System Files check box. Also choose Show Hidden Files And Folders.

Understanding the Boot.ini File

A typical Boot.ini file looks like this:

```
[boot loader]
timeout=30
default=multi(0)disk(0)rdisk(0)partition(2)\WINDOWS
[operating systems]
multi(0)disk(0)rdisk(0)partition(2)\WINDOWS=
"Microsoft Windows XP Home Edition" /fastdetect
C:\="Microsoft Windows"
```

The [boot loader] section lists the timeout (the number of seconds that it waits before loading from the default partition) and the default (which partition is the default). The [operating systems] section lists all of the partitions that contain operating systems from which you can boot.

Lines that specify partitions tell the boot program (Ntldr) exactly where to find the Windows system folder for any version of Windows, like this:

```
multi(0)disk(0)rdisk(r)partition(p)\windowsfolder
```

The "multi" in this line means that Ntldr relies on the computer's BIOS to load the system files. *R* is the number of the disk attached to the hard disk adapter (0 for the first disk, 1 for the second disk, and so forth). *P* is the number of the partition on that hard disk (1 for the first partition, 2 for the second partition, and so forth). Partitions are numbered starting with primary partitions, then logical partitions. Unused space and MS-DOS Extended partitions (which you are unlikely to have) are omitted.

If you have a SCSI disk, the line looks like this: (see Chapter 13, section "Disk Controllers: IDE, EIDE, and SCSI Devices").

```
scsi(a)disk(s)rdisk(lun)partition(p)\windowsfolder
```

A is the number of the SCSI adapter, *s* is the SCSI ID of the disk, *lun* is the logical unit number of the disk (usually 0), and *p* is the partition number on that list. (For more information about booting from SCSI disks, see article Q102873 in the Microsoft Knowledge Base at **support.microsoft.com**.)

In the [operating systems] section, each partition is followed by an equal sign and the string (text) that will appear in the boot menu. Previous versions usually appear simply as "Microsoft Windows," but you can edit this to specify the version of Windows or other information about the partition. For example, you might have "Windows XP Pro Test" and "Windows XP Pro Daily Use."

You can add a few switches to the end of partition lines in the [operating systems] section. (In the example in this section, one of the lines includes the /FASTDETECT switch.) The following are some of the switches that you can use for Windows XP, 2000, and NT 4.0 partitions:

- **/BASEVIDEO**   Starts up in Enable VGA Mode, which is useful for diagnosing video driver problems (see Chapter 2, section "Starting Windows in Other Startup Modes").

- **/MAXMEM:*n***   Allows Windows to use only a maximum of *n* kilobytes of RAM, which is useful if you suspect memory problems.

- **/FASTDETECT**   Skips checking of parallel and series communications devices.

In the [boot loader] section, set the timeout to 0 if you don't want Ntldr to display the menu. Set it to –1 if you want Ntldr to wait forever.

Editing Boot.ini

You can edit the Boot.ini file by using one of three Windows programs: The System Properties dialog box (which provides fewer choices), the System Configuration Utility (which displays the whole file for editing), or Notepad.

 From the Recovery Console, you can also use the Bootcfg program to edit Boot.ini (see Chapter 2, section "Using The Recovery Console"). See article Q291980 in the in the Microsoft Knowledge Base at **support.microsoft.com.**

Editing Boot.ini from the System Properties Dialog Box

To display the System Properties dialog box, click Start, right-click My Computer, and choose Properties from the menu that appears. In the System Properties dialog box, click the Advanced tab. Click the Settings button in the Startup And Recovery section. You see the Startup And Recovery dialog box, shown in Figure A-5.

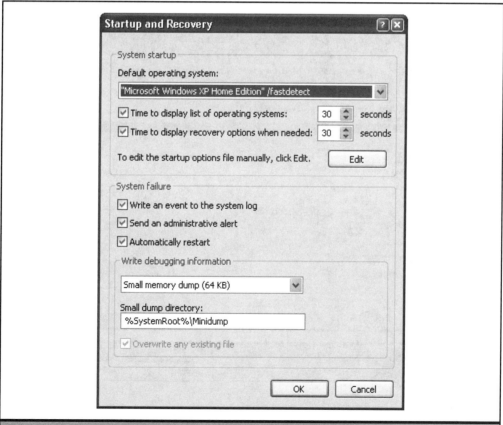

Figure A-5. *You can edit the Boot.ini file by changing settings in the System Startup section.*

The settings in the System Startup section of the dialog box control part of the contents of the Boot.ini file. You can change the default operating system and the timeout by changing the first two settings. Don't deselect these check boxes, or you won't have time to make a selection from the boot menu. You can also click the Edit button to display and edit the Boot.ini file in Notepad—but proceed with care!

 The third setting in the System Startup section of the Startup And Recovery dialog box controls how long you have to choose to use the Recovery Console in the event that Windows won't start, if you have previously installed the Recovery Console. See Chapter 2 for details on the Recovery Console.

Editing Boot.ini from the System Configuration Utility

To see more of your Boot.ini options, run the System Configuration Utility by choosing Start | Run, typing **msconfig**, and pressing ENTER. Then click the BOOT.INI tab, as shown in Figure A-6 (see Chapter 37, section "Configuring Windows XP with the System Configuration Utility").

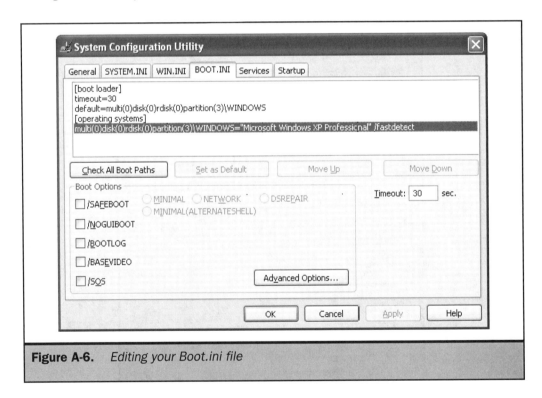

Figure A-6.   *Editing your Boot.ini file*

The BOOT.INI tab is divided into two parts. The top part shows the actual contents of the current Boot.ini file. The lower part offers options that you can use to change the file. The options that appear in the lower part of the window enable you to start up in various startup modes (see Chapter 2, section "Starting Windows in Other Startup Modes"). The options work as follows:

- **/SAFEBOOT**   Boots in one of Windows startup modes. When you select the /SAFEBOOT check box, you can choose from Minimal to start in Safe Mode, Network to start in Safe Mode With Network, or Minimal (Alternateshell) to start in Safe Mode With Command Line.
- **/NOGUIBOOT**   Boots into Windows XP without displaying the XP splash screen.
- **/BOOTLOG**   Enables the verbose boot logging feature, which displays messages that can help you track down deeply embedded glitches.
- **/BASEVIDEO**   Boots in the standard VGA Mode, which can operate with 99 percent of the video cards on the market.
- **/SOS**   Displays all drivers and services that are loading as they load. This can be helpful if you can't finish booting.
- **Timeout**   Indicates how long the menu appears before automatically selecting the default item.

You can click the Advanced Options button to display the BOOT.INI Advanced Options dialog box, with these additional settings:

- **/MAXMEM**   Enables you to limit the amount of RAM that the system sees on startup.
- **/NUMPROC**   Enables you to define a finite number of processors that are recognized by the system. This setting works only on multiprocessor machines.
- **/PCILOCK**   Locks assigned PCI resources to already installed hardware to assist in avoiding conflicts.
- **/DEBUG**   For programmers only; provides debugging features. (This option offers no benefit to even the most advanced user.)

Most of these options should never be used without direction from a qualified technician, if you plan on retaining a stable XP installation.

Checking Your Boot.ini Entries

If you reinstall Windows or other operating systems, or copy or delete partitions, you may end up with Boot.ini entries for partitions that aren't really there. The System

APPENDIX

Configuration Utility can check the entries in your Boot.ini file and delete those that no longer refer to an installed operating system (see Chapter 37, section "Configuring Windows XP with the System Configuration Utility"). Follow these steps to check your Boot.ini file:

1. Choose Start | Run, type **msconfig**, and press ENTER.

2. Click the BOOT.INI tab.

3. Click Check All Boot Paths.

4. If an entry no longer refers to the location of a valid operating system, Windows displays a message asking whether to delete the line from Boot.ini.

5. Click Yes to remove the line (so the operating system won't appear on your boot menu) or No to leave it.

Uninstalling Windows XP and SP1

If you upgraded to Windows XP from a previous version of Windows, the Setup Wizard may have backed up your current operating system. (The backup files are named Backup.cab and Boot.cab and are stored in C:\Undo, assuming that Windows is stored on C.) If so, you can uninstall Windows XP and return to that operating system. Be sure to make a backup of your data files before uninstalling Windows XP.

| Note | *If you have changed your partitions or drives since installing Windows XP, you usually can't uninstall it.* |

To uninstall Windows XP, follow these steps:

1. Choose Start | Control Panel | Add Or Remove Programs.

2. If Windows XP Uninstall appears in the Currently Installed Programs, you can uninstall it.

3. Click Windows XP Uninstall. Additional information appears.

4. Click the Change/Remove button. You see the Uninstall Windows XP dialog box.

5. Choose Uninstall Windows XP and click Continue.

6. Follow the directions on the screen. When the uninstall process is finished, your computer restarts and runs your previous operating system.

Uninstalling Windows doesn't delete your data files. However, any programs that you installed after you installed Windows XP probably won't work. To fix this, just install them again. If you created any documents or files, they may still be stored in C:\Documents And Settings*username*\.

If you upgraded your version of Windows XP with Service Pack 1 (SP1) and you choose to keep backup files, you can uninstall SP1. Choose Start | Control Panel | Add Or Remove Programs, choose Windows XP Service Pack 1 from the list of programs, and click Remove.

Index

Symbols and Numbers

* (asterisk), 208
16-bit applications, 9
32-bit applications, 9

A

Accelerated Graphics Port
　(AGP), 334
access points
　　connecting to, 777
　　installing, 748
　　wireless LANs and, 742, 747
accessibility options
　　cursors, 405
　　FilterKeys, 399-400
　　for hearing-impaired,
　　　402-403
　　High Contrast, 404-405
　　input devices, 409, 411-412
　　installing, 397
for Internet Explorer, 415
Keyboard tab, 397-398
Magnifier, 405-407
Microsoft Narrator, 407-408
MouseKeys, 410-411
On-Screen Keyboard,
　401-402
StickyKeys, 398-399
ToggleKeys, 400-401
turning on/off, 412-414
for visually impaired,
　403-409
Accessibility Options
　dialog box, 414
Accessibility Wizard, 397
account setup, Outlook Express,
　599-601
accounts. *See also* Internet
　accounts; user accounts
　　administrator, 124, 125
　　cable accounts, 558
　　domain, 122
　　group, 123
guest, 125, 140
news, 599, 637
ACPI (Advanced Configuration
　and Power Interface), 384
activation ID, WPA, 956
active partition, 859, 870-871
ActiveX, 837, 840-842
Actual Size tool, Windows Picture
　And Fax Viewer, 436
ad hoc LANs, 742, 777-778
adapter cards, 334-335, 781.
　See also network adapters
Add Hardware Wizard, 340-344
Add New Hardware Wizard, 326
Add Or Remove Programs
　　installing programs, 66-67
　　removing orphaned entries,
　　　79-80
　　uninstalling programs,
　　　78-80
Add/Remove Windows
　Components button, 69-71
Address bar, Windows
　Explorer, 164

Address Book, 620-628
   accessing, 621
   capturing addresses, 622
   contacts list, 624-625
   entering information
      manually, 622
   exporting names and
      addresses, 627
   finding and contacting
      people, 625-626
   groups, 622-624
   printing from, 626-627
   searches, 627-628
Address box, Internet Explorer
   navigating with, 178
   overview of, 661-662
   searching from, 666-669
Address toolbar, 166, 269
addresses. *See also* IP addresses
   capturing for Address
      Book, 622
   I/O addresses, 335
   importing into Outlook
      Express, 602-603
   types of, 163-164
administrator accounts, 124, 125
Advanced Appearance dialog box,
   290-291
Advanced Audio Properties
   dialog box, 462
Advanced Configuration and
   Power Interface (ACPI), 384
Advanced Dial-Up dialog box, 579
Advanced Power Management
   (APM), 384
Advanced Streaming Format
   (ASF), 511
AGP (Accelerated Graphics
   Port), 334
AIM (AOL Instant Messenger), 688
albums, Media Player, 477
alerts, 59
All Programs option, 254
ALT-PRINT SCREEN, 111
America Online (AOL), 556, 558
animated screen characters, 205
anonymous FTP, 726
antivirus. *See also* viruses
   programs, 833
   resources, 836
AOL (America Online), 556, 558
AOL Instant Messenger (AIM), 688
APIPA (automatic private IP
   addressing), 768

APM (Advanced Power
   Management), 384
appearance
   Advanced Appearance
      dialog box, 290-291
   Appearance tab, 289
   Display Properties
      dialog box, 276-277
applets, Java, 650
APPLICATION key, 23
application logs, 58
Archive attribute, files and
   folders, 193
area code rules, 539-541
arithmetic calculator, 427-428
Arrange Icons menu, 293-294
ASCII files, 420
ASCII mode, FTP, 726
ASF (Advanced Streaming
   Format), 511
.asf files, 511
ASR (Automated System
   Recovery), 221
asterisk (*), 208
.asx files, 511
ATTRIB command, 49
attributes, file and folder, 193-194
audio. *See* sound
audio CDs
   AutoPlay, 485-486
   burning, 494-495, 497
   compared with data CDs,
      493-494
   Media Player configuration,
      484-485, 488-490,
      496-497
   overview of, 493
   play order, 484
   playing, 483-484
   ripping, 488-491
   selected tracks, 484
   troubleshooting, 497
   web sites, 498
audio devices
   built-in support for, 458
   list of, 458
   viewing status of, 463
audio files
   downloading, 675
   organizing, 474
   playing, 471-473
audio input/output drivers,
   460-463
audio jacks, 333

audio players, 486. *See also*
   Windows Media Player
Auto Update feature, Media
   Player, 470
AutoComplete Settings, Internet
   Explorer, 669-671
autoexec.bat, 92, 104-105
Automated System Recovery
   (ASR), 221
automatic private IP addressing
   (APIPA), 768
Automatic Updates
   choosing which updates to
      install, 911-912
   configuring, 909-910
   uninstalling, 912
AutoPlay, audio CDs, 485-486
.avi files, 508

B

Back buttons, Windows
   Explorer, 178
Back menu, Internet Explorer, 661
back ups. *See also* Backup Utility
   backup jobs, 221-222,
      226-227, 236-237
   frequency of, 220
   LAN back up, 219-220
   media storage, 220
   media types, 220
   removable storage, 222-223
   types of files to back up,
      218-219
   with Windows Explorer,
      223-224
background, 278-283
   color selection, 279-280
   creating images for, 279
   Display Properties dialog
      box, 276-277
   selecting image or
      pattern, 279
   using Web page as, 280-283
backup media pool, 222
Backup Or Restore Wizard
   backup destination, 229-231
   backup type, 231
   creating backup job,
      226-227
   file selection, 228-229
   how to back up, 231-232
   settings, 234
   when to back up, 232

Backup tab, 232-236
Backup Utility
    backup destination, 229-231
    backup jobs, 226-227,
        236-237
    Backup tab approach,
        232-236
    command line backups,
        241-244
    compared with Windows
        Explorer back ups, 224
    configuration options,
        239-241
    excluding files from
        backups, 237-239
    how and when to back up,
        231-232
    installing, 224-225
    main window, 234
    overview of, 221
    restoring files, 244-248
    running, 225
    selecting files, 228-229
    type of back up, 231
balance controls, 463-465
balloon tips, 264
.bat files, 91, 831
batch files, 91-92
battery status, laptops, 387-388
Best Fit tool, Windows Picture
    And Fax Viewer, 436
Bigfoot, 627
binary (Bin) numbers, 429
Binary mode, FTP, 726
bitmaps, 361
.bkf extension, 230
.bks files, 236
blocked senders list, Outlook
    Express, 635-636
.bmp files, 442
bookmarks, importing/
    exporting, 665
boolean searches, 666
boot
    information, 51
    loader, 860
    options, 981-986
    partitions, 859
boot floppies, 51-53
    DOS, 52-53
    quick boot, 51-52
    XP Setup, 52
BOOTCFG command, 49-50

Boot.ini file
    checking entries, 985-986
    editing, 49-50, 983-985
    example of typical, 981-982
    msconfig and, 933
bridges, network, 560, 743
bridging, 790-792
    compared with direct
        connection, 792
    ICS and, 791
    process, 790-791
briefcases. See Windows Briefcase
broadband connections, 559
Browse dialog box, 24
browsers. See web browsers
buffer, audio, 460
burning audio CDs, 494-495
bus topology, 744
buttons, Classic Style, 289
buttons, mouse, 315-316

C

.cab (cabinet) files, 345, 952
cable accounts, 558
cable modems, 551-552
    advantages of, 551
    configuring Windows
        for, 552
    connecting to, 552
    installing, 345
    overview of, 344
cabling, network
    installing, 748-749
    overview of, 740-741
    unshielded twisted pair, 742
calculators. See Windows
    Calculator
call waiting, 536
callback, 762
calling cards
    creating, 542-546
    information needed for
        using, 541-542
    setting up, 542
    using, 546
Carbon Copy, 912
Cascading windows, 19
case sensitivity, 208
cassette tapes, 491
Category-5 (Cat-5) cable, 742, 747
Category View, Control Panel, 21
cd command, 48, 727

CD-DA (Compact Disk Digital
    Audio), 493
CD-ROM (Compact Disk
    Read-Only Memory), 493
CD-Rs
    burning, 210, 212-214
    disks, 210
    drives, 210-211, 880-881
    settings, 496
CD-RWs
    burning, 210, 212-214
    disks, 210
    drives, 210-211, 880-881
    erasing files, 214
    settings, 496
CD Writing Wizard, 495
CDs
    audio. see audio CDs
    as backup media, 220
    burning, 210-211
    burning from Media
        Player, 214
    burning from Windows
        Explorer, 212-214
    drive configuration, 878-879
    storing backup, 221
    troubleshooting burning,
        214-216
cell phones, 492
central processing unit (CPU), 328
certificate authorities, 842
certificates
    getting, 849
    managing, 844-845
    object certificates, 843-844
    personal certificates,
        845-846
Challenge Handshake
    Authentication Protocol
    (CHAP), 573
Change Icon button, 203
Change permissions, 153
CHAP (Challenge Handshake
    Authentication Protocol), 573
Character Map, 361, 431-432
character sets, HyperTerminal, 717
chats, online. See NetMeeting;
    WinChat; Windows Messenger
ChkDsk (Check Disk), 49, 885-887
Classic Windows style
    double click, 6
    logon screen, 130
    Start menu, 262-264
    windows and buttons, 289

clean install, 953, 960-961

ClearType, 292

CLI (command-line interface), 84

click-and-drag, 179

ClickLock feature, 317

client/server (domain-based) networks
  overview of, 737
  vs. peer-based, 738-739
  XP Home Edition and, 771

clients
  FTP, 722
  ICS, 822-826
  LANs, 781-783
  network, 737
  Remote Desktop, 378-379
  VPNs. *see* VPN clients

Clipboard
  ClipBook Viewer and, 109-111
  compared with OLE, 112
  cut, copy, and paste techniques, 108-109
  DOS programs and, 89-90
  drag and drop techniques, 109
  screen capture, 111

ClipBook Viewer, 109-111

clock, hiding, 267

.clp files, 109

cmd command, 86

CNET Shareware, 730

color
  256 colors, 31
  compatibility and, 31
  desktop profiles, 300-301
  desktop quality settings, 299-300
  DOS settings, 96
  Microsoft Paint and, 442, 445
  schemes, 286-289
  web pages and, 673-674

Color dialog box, 287-289

.com files, 10, 88, 831

com ports, 329

command line
  backups, 241-244
  DOS and, 84
  Winnt/Winnt32 options, 964-965

command-line interface (CLI), 84

command prompt, 149-151

Command Prompt window
  DOS commands, 87-88
  opening, 86-87
  properties, 93-95
  running command when opens, 97

commands
  DOS, 47-49, 87-88
  for repairing Windows, 49-51
  selecting from menus, 22-23

communication security. *See* security, of web communications

Compact Disk Digital Audio (CD-DA), 493

Compact Disk Read-Only Memory (CD-ROM), 493

compatibility mode
  DOS options, 102
  settings, 31-33
  troubleshooting compatibility issues, 33

components. *See also* network components
  hardware, 326-328
  ICS, 817-818
  Windows, 70-71

Compressed attribute, files and folders, 194

compressed folders
  adding passwords, 199
  creating, 198
  treating as files, 175
  types of, 196-197
  working with files in, 198-199

compression, graphics and, 434

CompuServe, 558

Computer Management MMCs, 36, 57. *See also* MMC (Microsoft Management Console)

computers
  adding to phone line networks, 779
  adding to wireless LANs, 776-779
  changing name of, 788-790
  hangs on shutdown, 44
  identifying in workgroups, 770
  sharing. *see* sharing computers

conferencing. *See* NetMeeting; Windows Messenger

config.sys, 92, 104-105

configuration
  Control Panel, 20-21
  property settings, 20

configuration files
  editing with Notepad, 423
  initialization files, 927-928
  making visible, 926-927
  registry and, 928

connections, Remote Desktop, 379-380

connectors, 329-334
  audio and video jacks, 333
  display ports, 332
  FireWire ports, 333
  network ports, 332
  parallel ports, 330
  PC cards, 334
  PS/2, 331
  serial (com) ports, 329
  telephone, 332
  USB, 330-331

contacts list
  in Address Book, 621
  finding and contacting people, 625-626
  grouping contacts, 623
  looking up detailed information, 625
  sorting, 624-625

contacts, Windows Messenger, 693-694

container files, OLE, 112

Content Advisor, Internet Explorer, 677

context menus. *See* shortcut menus

Control Panel, 20-21

cookies, 679-684
  how cookies work, 679-680
  managing, 683-684
  P3P and, 680-681
  policy for, 681-683

Cool Edit, 492

copy backups, 231

COPY command, 48-49

copy (CTRL-C), 108

copying and moving, files and folders, 182-184

copying music
  from cassette tapes, 491
  from CDs, 488-491
  from LP records, 491

correspondence, 628
counter logs, 59, 60
cover-page faxes, 367
CPU (central processing unit), 328
Create New Extension
  dialog box, 76
Create New Folder button, 26
Create Shortcut Wizard, 195-196
cropping, Microsoft Paint, 446
CTRL-ALT-DEL, 53, 145, 795
CTRL-C (copy), 108
CTRL-click, 179
CTRL-P (printing), 426
CTRL-V (paste), 108
CTRL-X (cut), 108
CTRL-Z (undo), 182
Currently Installed Programs list,
  79-80
cursors, 396, 405
Curve tool, Microsoft Paint, 444
Customize Start Menu
  dialog box, 260
cut-and-paste, Remote
  Desktop, 382
cut, copy, and paste techniques,
  Clipboard, 108-109
cut (CTRL-X), 108
CWApps, 730

D

daily backups, 231
data CDs, 493-494
data sharing. *See* Clipboard;
  OLE (Object Linking and
  Embedding)
data types, registry, 896
databases, backing up, 218
Date and Time Properties
  dialog box, 324
date, setting, 323-324
DB-15 connectors, 332
dBpowerAMP Music
  Converter, 492
debuggers, 61-62
Debugging Mode, 45
decimal (Dec) numbers, 429
default web browser, 650, 678
defragmenting disks, 887-889
DEL command, 49
DELETE key, 181, 295
desktop
  appearance, 290
  backgrounds, 278-283

Classic style, 289
color, 286-289, 299-301
display settings, 276-277,
  302-305
fonts, 290-292, 301-302
function of, 4
icons, 10, 293-296
illustration of, 5
notification area, 5-6
reducing clutter, 296
screen resolution, 299
screen savers, 284-286
sound effects, 297-298
start button, 6
synchronizing files with
  laptops, 373, 375-376
task buttons, 4-5
taskbar, 4
themes, 103, 277-278
visual effects, 296
Desktop Cleanup Wizard, 296
Desktop folder, 163
Desktop toolbar, 269
Details view
  Recycle Bin, 184-185
  Windows Explorer, 171-172
device drivers
  audio input/output,
    460-463
  displaying driver
    information, 338
  DOS, 104
  installing, 340
  modems, 546
  printers, 353
  signed vs. unsigned, 339
  troubleshooting, 347
  TWAIN, 449
  updating, 338
  video, 33
Device Manager
  list of computer hardware
    in, 326-327, 391
  managing hardware,
    326-328
  modem conflicts and, 547
  resolving configuration
    problems, 346-348
DHCP (Dynamic Host
  Configuration Protocol),
  549, 769
DHCP servers, 769
Diagnostic Startup, 45, 55, 929
diagnostic tools, 348-349

dial-up connections, 530-536
  area code rules, 539-541
  creating, 566
  dialing locations and,
    536-539
  HyperTerminal and, 710
  logon scripts, 573-574
  settings, 569-572, 574-577
  TCP/IP connection
    and, 573
  troubleshooting, 546-547
dial-up Internet accounts, 557
dial-up modems, 344, 345
dial-up networks, 559, 753-754
dialing locations
  adding, 536-537
  default, 538-539
  displaying, 536
  editing, 538
  using, 539
Dialing Rules tab, Phone
  And Modem Options
  dialog box, 536
dialog boxes, 24-27
differential backups, 231
digital cameras
  downloading images from,
    447-449
  importing files into Movie
    Maker, 514-515
  linking to programs,
    449-450
  media for, 447
  setting up, 446-447
digital IDs, 851-853
digital images, 439-441
digital music, 492
digital signal processor (DSP), 508
digital signatures, 848
Digital Subscriber Line (DSL)
  dial-up Internet accounts,
    557-558
  modems, 344-345, 549-551
Digital Versatile Disk or Digital
  Video Disk. *See* DVDs (Digital
  Versatile Disk or Digital
  Video Disk)
digital video cameras, 508
dir command, 47-48, 726
direct cable connection. *See* direct
  connection networks
direct connection networks,
  752-753

direct memory access (DMA)
    channels, 336
directory contents, listing, 47-48
directory servers, NetMeeting,
    702-704
directory services, 627-628
Directory Services Restore
    Mode, 45
DirectPC, 554
DirectX, 508
Disk Cleanup, 889-892, 902
disk controllers, 337
Disk Defragmenter, 887-889, 902
disk drives
    CD drives, 878-879
    CD-R and CD-RW drives,
        880-881
    checking free space, 878
    checking integrity of, 49
    ChkDsk and, 885-887
    defragmenting, 887-889
    deleting temporary files,
        889-892
    disabling low disk space
        notification, 892
    floppy drives, 878
    formatting hard disks,
        876-877
    formatting removable
        disks, 877-878
    listing with MAP
        command, 47
    multiple operating systems
        and, 936-937
    properties of, 865-867
    repartitioning, 871
    sharing. see sharing drives
    Windows XP space
        requirements, 954-955
Disk Management window,
    864-865
disk partitions. See partitions
disk quotas, 146-149
DISKPART command, 50-51
display adapters
    adding, 302
    compatibility problems, 305
    DB-15 connectors, 332
    dual display adapters, 302
display ports, 332
Display Properties dialog box,
    276-277, 298-300

displays. See also screen
    accessibility options,
        396-397
    color profiles, 300-301
    color quality settings,
        299-300
    magnification, 301-302
    multiple, 302-304, 393
    problems, 304-305
    properties, 276-277
    screen resolution, 299
    tuning, 894-896
distribution files, 64
DMA (direct memory access)
    channels, 336
DNS server, 573
.doc files, 10, 831
docking stations
    docking/undocking, 389
    features for, 388
    hardware profiles and,
        389-393
documents
    backing up, 218
    My Documents folder,
        133-134, 163
    privacy of, 138-140
    recent on Start menu, 262
    Shared Documents
        folder, 143
    starting programs by
        opening, 10-11
domain accounts, 122
domain-based networks. See
    client/server (domain-based)
    networks
domains. See also client/server
    (domain-based) networks
    changing, 788-790
    defined, 738-739
    domain accounts, 122
DOS
    basics, 84-85
    batch files, 91-92
    boot floppy disk, 52-53
    Clipboard and, 89-90
    color settings, 96
    Command Prompt window,
        86-87, 93-95
    commands, 47-49, 87-88
    compatibility options, 102

configuring to run under
    XP, 935-936
executable and shortcut
    properties, 96-101
filenames and extensions,
    85, 88
font selection, 95
icons, 102-103
initialization files, 92-93
installing/configuring DOS
    programs, 104-105
memory settings, 102
mouse and, 89-90
printing from DOS
    programs, 90-91
prompt, 84
running DOS programs,
    88-92
screen settings, 89
starting/exiting
    programs, 89
window settings, 95-96
Windows XP themes
    and, 103
WordPad and, 423-424
DOS Protected-Mode (DPMI), 102
DOS Virtual Machine (DOS VM), 84
dotted lines, Windows Explorer, 177
double click
    mouse speed and, 316
    vs. single click, 6-7
DOWN-ARROW key, 178
Download.com, 730
downloads
    FTP files, 729
    Internet Explorer options
        for, 675
    security of. see security, of
        downloads
    updates, 908-909
DPMI (MS-DOS Protected-
    Mode), 102
Dr. Watson, 36, 61-62
drag-and-drop techniques
    arranging desktop
        icons, 293
    Clipboard and, 109
    creating shortcuts, 195
    editing Start menu, 263
    embedding OLE objects,
        113-114

moving and copying files
and folders, 182-183
moving Start menu
items, 256
moving toolbars, 167
drawing, with Microsoft Paint, 444
drive letters
assigning to folders,
875-876
changing, 872-874
mapping shared drives and
folders to, 803-806
partitions and, 863
unmapping, 806
drivers. *See* device drivers
drives. *See* disk drives
drwtsn32, 62
DSL (Digital Subscriber Line)
dial-up Internet accounts,
557-558
modems, 344-345, 549-551
DSP (digital signal processor), 508
dual-boot installation, 953, 962-963
dual display adapters, 302
DualView, 393
DVD decoders, 520-521
DVDs (Digital Versatile Disk or
Digital Video Disk), 520-523
drives, 211
DVD decoders, 520-521
Parental Control feature,
521-523
playing, 521
dynamic addressing, 768
dynamic disks, 865
Dynamic Host Configuration
Protocol (DHCP), 549, 769
dynamic update, XP installation
and, 953

E

e-mail, 607-620
attaching files to, 615
backing up files, 218-219
capturing addresses from
Outlook Express, 622
composing in HTML, 617
configuration options,
608-609
headers, 614-615
how it works, 595-596
including original message
in replies, 614
inserting pictures, 618
inserting text files into
messages, 615
Internet Explorer and,
678-679
message composition
settings, 612-613
overview of, 607-608
receipt notification, 616
saving and filing messages,
619-620
security. *see* security,
of e-mail
sending messages, 620
services, 596-597
sharing pictures, 454-455
showing e-mail programs
on Start menu, 261
signing, 615-616
viewing incoming mail,
609-611
virus protection, 605-607
Web links, 617-618
e-mail attachments
adding to messages, 615
opening, 611
restrictions on, 605-606
spreading viruses via, 605
e-mail programs, 261, 595
EBD (emergency boot disk). *See*
boot floppies
Edit File Type dialog box, 77-78
Effects dialog box, 296
EFS (Encrypting File System), 122
EIDE (Enhanced IDE)
controllers, 337
embedded objects, 112. *See also*
OLE (Object Linking and
Embedding)
emergency boot disk (EBD).
See boot floppies
EMS (expanded memory), 84, 102
Enable Boot Logging, 45
Enable VGA Mode, 45
Encrypting File System (EFS), 122
encryption
EFS (Encrypting File
System), 122
overview of, 848
receiving encrypted
mail, 853
sending encrypted mail,
850-853
Enhanced IDE (EIDE)
controllers, 337
environment variables, 933-935
error reporting, 54
Ethernet
cable, 747
cards, 740
types of, 741
Eudora e-mail programs, 595,
601-602
event logs, 57-58
Event Viewer, 57-58
.exe files
DOS programs and, 88
installing programs from, 68
program filenames and, 10
viruses and, 605-606, 831
executable, DOS programs, 96-101
EXPAND command, 48-49
expanded memory (EMS), 84, 102
expansion slots, 328
Explorer bar, 169-170
Explorer windows, 165-166,
655-656
extended memory (XMS), 84, 102
extended partitions, 859
Extensible Markup Language
(XML), 648

F

Fast Ethernet, 741
Fast User Switching, 122, 128
FAT (File Allocation Table),
152-155, 861-862
FAT32, 152-155, 861-862
favorites, 664-665
Fax Configuration Wizard, 365-366
Fax Console
archiving faxes, 369
configuring, 365-367
default dialing
locations, 538
receiving faxes
automatically, 368
receiving faxes
manually, 368
Fax Properties dialog box, 366
faxes
archiving, 368-369

calling cards and, 546
configuring Fax Console,
    365-367
cover-page, 367
dialing locations and, 538
faxing from applications, 367
receiving automatically, 368
receiving manually, 368
File Allocation Table (FAT),
    861-862
file associations
    creating, 76-77
    editing, 75-78
    folder options and, 75-77
    registry and, 73-74
    when opening files, 74-75
file attachments. *See* e-mail
    attachments
file extensions
    associating with programs.
        see file associations
    changing file type, 191
    DOS programs and, 88
    indicating file type, 190-191
    making visible, 191
File Folder. *See* folders; folders
file system
    defined, 861
    FAT, FAT32, and NTFS,
        861-862
    partitions, 861-862
    selecting during
        installation, 953
    structure of, 162-163
File Transfer Protocol. *See* FTP
    (File Transfer Protocol)
filenames
    DOS filenames, 85
    starting programs from, 10
files
    addresses, 163-164
    associating with programs.
        see file associations
    attributes, 49, 193-194
    backing up, 218-219,
        228-229, 237-239
    in compressed folders,
        198-199
    copying, 48-49, 182-184
    creating, 179
    deleting, 49, 181-182
    extracting, 48-49
    file system and, 162-163

formats, 423-424
graphic, 439
hidden, 199-200
listing contents of, 47-48
naming/renaming, 180-181
navigating, 177-179
opening, 180, 656-657
password protecting, 124
permissions, 151-157
printing to, 358-359
properties, 192-193
Recycle Bin and, 184-185
searching for. *see* Search
    Companion
selecting, 179-180
sharing, 737
shortcuts, 194-196
storing, 38
types, 77-78, 190-191
undoing last action, 182
Files and Settings Transfer Wizard
    answering questions, 979
    direct cable connection
        and, 979
Files And Settings Transfer Wizard
    moving settings between
        computers, 599
    running, 977-979
Files of Type box, 26
Filmstrip view, Windows Explorer,
    172-173, 435
FilterKeys, 396, 399-400
Find Compatible Hardware and
    Software, 33
Find Message dialog box, 629
firewalls
    ICF vs. third party
        options, 585
    NetMeeting and, 701
    port configuration for,
        584-585
    turning on, 584
FireWire ports, 333
FIXBOOT command, 51
FIXMBR command, 51
floppy disks, 220, 878. *See also*
    boot floppies
Folder Options dialog box, 7, 76
folder templates, 201-202
folder tree
    dialog boxes, 25
    navigating, 177-179
    structure of, 162

folders, 200-203
    assigning drive letters to,
        875-876
    attributes, 193-194
    cd command and, 48
    copying, 182-184
    creating, 179
    deleting, 181-182
    file system and, 162-163
    hidden, 199-200
    icons, 202-203
    naming/renaming, 180-181
    navigating, 177-179
    opening, 180
    overview of, 200-201
    permissions, 151-157
    privacy, 138-140
    properties, 192-193
    Recycle Bin and, 184-185
    searching for. *see* Search
        Companion
    selecting, 179-180
    settings, 174
    sharing. *see* sharing folders
    templates, 201-202
    thumbnail icon, 202
    undoing last action, 182
folders, Outlook Express, 628-629
    creating, deleting,
        renaming, 628
    moving and copying,
        628-629
fonts, 290-292
    deleting, 364-365
    DOS, 95
    finding similar, 365
    installing, 363-364
    magnification options,
        301-302
    Open Type, 363
    printers and, 362
    size of, 290-292
    smoothing edges of, 292
    substituting, 362
    TrueType, 361-362
    web pages and, 672-673
formats
    audio, 458-460
    files, 423-424
    graphic, 434
    IP addresses, 767
    Media Player, 502
    Microsoft Paint, 442

multiple operating systems and, 936-937
for numbers, 323
video, 508
formatting
hard disks, 876-877
removable disks, 877-878
WordPad documents, 424-425
Forward button, 178
Found New Hardware Wizard, 354
fragmentation, 887-889
frames, printing with Internet Explorer, 658
Free-Form Select tool, Microsoft Paint, 443-444
free media pool, 222
freehand tools, Microsoft Paint, 444
freeware programs, 730
FTP clients, 722
FTP (File Transfer Protocol), 722-725
basic operation of, 725-726
downloading files, 729
navigating folder trees, 726-728
overview of, 710, 722
uploading files, 728-729
Web Folders, 722-725
FTP servers, 722, 727
Full Control permissions, 153, 155

G

game controllers, 319-321
games, Windows Messenger, 700
gateways
functions of, 814-815
gateway devices, 815-816
network connections and, 560
Windows-based, 817
get command, 729
GetProdKey program, 958
.gif files, 442
Gigabit Ethernet, 741
GIMP (GNU Image Manipulation Program), 442
GNU Image Manipulation Program (GIMP), 442
Go To Last Folder Visited button, 25
GoldWave, 492, 502

Google search engine, 665
graphic equalizers, Media Player, 486-488
graphical user interface (GUI), 84
graphics
adding information to digital images, 439-441
creating/editing with Microsoft Paint, 442-446
downloading, 675
downloading from digital cameras, 447-449
downloading from scanners, 449
images, pixels, and compression, 434
linking scanners/digital cameras to programs, 449-450
printing images, 450-453
setting up scanner/digital cameras, 446-447
sharing pictures, 453-455
slide shows, 438-439
tools, 434-435
viewing images, 435-438
graphs, System Monitor, 901-902
groups
Address Book, 622-624
group accounts, 123
guest accounts
enabling/disabling, 140
generated during installation of XP, 125
guest computers, 752
GUI (graphical user interface), 84

H

handwriting recognition, 312-313
hangs, computer, 44
hard disks
as backup media, 220
formatting, 876-877
partitions, 858-861
playing video files from, 509-510
properties, 867-868
tuning, 902-903
hardware
adapter cards, 334-335
Add Hardware Wizard, 340-344

compatibility issues, 346
configuration problems, 346-348
configuring Windows for, 339-340
connectors, 329-334
diagnostic tools, 348-349
disk controllers, 337
drivers, 338-339
installing on networks, 747-749
integrated vs. separate peripherals, 328
managing with Device Manager, 326-328
memory (RAM), 338, 349-350
modems, 344-345
network requirements, 744-747
parameters, 335-337
PC Cards and hot-swabble devices, 340
Safe Mode and, 348
sharing, 800
sharing on networks, 736-737
troubleshooting, 345-349
WPA and, 957
hardware profiles, 389-393
creating, 389-392
defined, 388
modifying, 393
overview of, 389
switching between, 392
headers, e-mail, 614-615
hearing-impaired, accessibility options, 402-403
help. See support services
Help and Support Center, 37, 917-918
hexadecimal (Hex) numbers, 429
Hibernate Mode, 7, 387
hidden files and folders, 193, 199-200
High Contrast option, 396, 404-405
History Explorer bar, 661, 662-663
hives, registry, 940-941
HKEY_CLASSES_ROOT, 895
HKEY_CURRENT_CONFIG, 895
HKEY_CURRENT_USER, 895
HKEY_LOCAL_MACHINE, 895
HKEY_USERS, 895

home page, 676
HomePlug, 742, 747
HomePNA, 742, 747
host computers, 752
hot docking, 388
hot swapping
    devices, 340
    FireWire, 333
    USB, 331
Hotmail, 596-597, 690-691
HSV (hue, saturation, and
    luminescence) coordinates, 288
HTML (Hypertext Markup
    Language), 648, 617
HTTP (Hypertext Transfer
    Protocol), 596, 649
hubs, 741, 746, 748
hue, HSV, 288
hung programs, 52-54
hyperlinks, 618
HyperTerminal, 547-548
    capturing text, 720
    configuring, 712-715
    connecting with, 715
    connection information,
        715-717
    incoming calls, 720-721
    overview of, 710
    receiving files from remote
        computer, 718-719
    running, 712
    sending files to remote
        computers, 717-718
    sending text files, 719
    ways of using, 710-712
Hypertext Markup Language
    (HTML), 617, 648
Hypertext Transfer Protocol
    (HTTP), 596, 649

I

I/O addresses, 335
ICF (Internet Connection
    Firewall), 584-585
icons, 293-296
    arranging automatically,
        293-294
    choosing new, 294
    deleting and recovering,
        295-296
    Display Properties dialog
        box and, 276-277

DOS, 102-103
folder icons, 202-203
folder thumbnails, 202
renaming, 295
single click vs. double
    click, 6-7
size of, 260, 293
small icons on Start
    menu, 264
spacing, 293-294
starting programs with, 10
Icons view, Windows Explorer,
    170-171
ICS (Internet Connection Sharing)
    bridging networks and, 791
    components of, 817-818
    configuring ICS clients,
        822-824
    configuring ICS server,
        818-821
    installing, 818
    testing ICS clients, 824-826
    testing ICS server, 822
    troubleshooting, 827
    using, 826-827
IDE (Integrated Device
    Electronics), 337
identities, Outlook Express,
    600-601
IEEE 1394, 333
IEEE 80211a, 742
IEEE 802.11b, 742
i.Link, 333
images
    adding information to
        digital, 439-441
    annotating, 439-441
    creating/editing, 434
    downloading, 447-449
    formats, 434
    overview of, 434
    printing, 450-453, 658
    viewing, 435-438
IMAP (Internet Message Access
    Protocol), 596
import media pool, 222
incremental backups, 231
Indexed attribute, files and
    folders, 194
Indexing Service, 209
information sharing. *See*
    Clipboard; OLE (Object
    Linking and Embedding)

infrared wireless links, 762-763
infrastructure LANs, 742
initialization (INI) files, 927-928
    DOS, 92-93
    System.ini, 928
    WIN.ini, 928
input devices, 409, 411-412
Input Languages dialog box, 312
Input Method Editor, 44
installation files, 64
installation programs, 67
installation, Windows XP
    adding programs
        following, 981
    boot options, 981-986
    checking system following,
        973-975
    clean install, 960-961
    dual-boot installation,
        962-963
    dynamic update and, 953
    file system selection, 953
    optional methods, 953
    preparing for, 959-960
    product key and, 958
    removing back up copy of
        previous version, 976
    repairing corrupted
        installation, 43
    requirements, 952, 954-955
    Service Pack 1, 954
    Setup Wizard and, 965-973
    transferring data files and
        configuration settings,
        976-980
    troubleshooting, 975-976
    uninstalling, 986
    upgrade installation,
        961-962
    user accounts, 125-126
install.exe, 64
instant messaging, 688
Integrated Device Electronics
    (IDE), 337
Integrated Services Digital
    Network. *See* ISDN (Integrated
    Services Digital Network)
interface, Windows, 23
international settings, 935
Internet
    addresses, 164
    configuring Media Player
        for, 481

playing streaming audio
from, 480-481
Remote Desktop use of, 378
shortcuts, 664
Internet accounts
cable accounts, 558
dialing automatically,
578-580
dialing manually, 580-582
disconnecting from, 582-583
online services and, 558-559
PPP accounts, 557-558
Internet conferencing.
See NetMeeting;
Windows Messenger
Internet Connection Firewall
(ICF), 584-585
Internet Connection Sharing.
See ICS (Internet Connection
Sharing)
Internet connections. *See also*
network connections
account types and, 557-559
dial-up settings. *see* dial-up
connections
displaying IP addresses,
586
DSL modems, 549-550
firewalls, 584-585
ISPs, 563-565
netstat utility and, 591-592
sharing, 737
streamlining, 578
testing, 587-589
tracing packets over,
589-591
Internet Explorer
accessibility options, 415
advantages/disadvantages,
651-652
AutoComplete Settings,
669-671
blocking offensive web
content, 677
changing default browser
and, 678
cookies, 679-683
download options, 675
download security. *see*
security, of downloads
Explorer window, 655-656
favorites and links, 664-665

History button, 662-663
Internet shortcuts on
desktop, 664
mail and newsreading
programs, 678-679
navigation aids, 660-662
opening system files,
656-657
opening web pages, 657
printing with, 658
Privacy Report, 684-685
Profile Assistant, 671-672
saving web pages, 658
searches with, 666-671
security settings, 846-847
security zones, 837-838
start page, 676
web browsing with,
651-652, 656
web page appearance,
672-675
web page cache, 677-678
window management,
658-659
Internet Message Access Protocol
(IMAP), 596
Internet Options dialog box, 663
Advanced tab, 675
color selection, 673-674
font selection, 672-673
language preferences,
674-675
Security tab, 838-839
Internet programs
FTP. *see* FTP (File Transfer
Protocol)
HyperTerminal. *see*
HyperTerminal
running, 730-731
telnet, 721
where to find, 730
Internet Protocol (TCP/IP)
dialog box, 573
Internet Service Providers. *See* ISPs
(Internet Service Providers)
Internet settings, Media Player, 499
Internetwork Packet eXchange/
Sequenced Packet eXchange
(IPX/SPX), 767, 783-784
interrupts (IRQs), 335-336, 348
IP addresses
assigning, 768-769

displaying, 586
format of, 767
Internet connections and, 586
TCP/IP and, 573
ipconfig, 586, 793-794
IPX/SPX (Internetwork Packet
eXchange/Sequenced Packet
eXchange), 767, 783-784
IRQs (interrupts), 335-336, 348
ISDN (Integrated Services Digital
Network)
availability, 553
configuring Windows for,
553-554
connecting to, 552-553
creating, 567-568
dial-up Internet
accounts, 557
modems, 552-554
ISPs (Internet Service Providers)
Microsoft
recommendations,
564-565
MSN account, 565
New Connection Wizard,
563-564
signing up for, 563

J

Java, 650, 837, 840-842
Java applets, 650
Java virtual machine (JVM), 650
JavaScript, 837, 840-842
.jpeg files, 442
JVM (Java virtual machine), 650

K

Kermit, 717
Keyboard Properties dialog box,
308-309
keyboard shortcuts
for commands, 22
list of, 409
selecting files and
folders, 179
switching between layouts
or languages, 312
for use with Narrator, 408
Keyboard tab, 397-398

keyboards
configuring, 308
handwriting and speech
recognition features,
312-313
language options, 309-312
properties, 308-309
PS/2 ports, 331
WINDOWS key, 314
keys, registry, 940-941
backing up, 899
root keys (hives), 940-941
values, 941-942

L

L2TP (Layer Two Tunneling
Protocol), 754
Language bar, 269, 312
language preferences, web pages,
674-675
language properties, keyboards,
309-312
LANs (local area networks)
adding computers to,
771-775
backing up, 219-220
cabled vs. wireless, 740-744
changing computer name,
workgroup, or domain,
788-790
defined, 736
gateways. *see* gateways
hardware installation,
747-749
hardware requirements,
744-747
ICS and. *see* ICS (Internet
Connection Sharing)
LAN icon in notification
area, 790
NAT and. *see* NAT
(Network Address
Translation)
network connections, 559
Remote Desktop and, 378
setting up, 739-740
sharing resources, 800.
see also sharing drives;
sharing printers
troubleshooting, 796-797
users accounts, 800-801
viewing resources, 795

viewing usage, 795-796
WinChat and, 708
Windows Briefcase and,
373-374
Windows Messenger
and, 691
wireless LANs, 742
laptops. *See also* Remote Desktop
battery status, 387-388
coordinating files with
Windows Briefcase,
372-376
docking station
features, 388
docking/undocking, 389
DualView, 393
hardware profiles, 389-393
Hibernate Mode, 387
power schemes, 387-388
printing away from home,
376-377
Standby Mode, 386
Last Know Good Configuration, 45
Layer Two Tunneling Protocol
(L2TP), 754
lcd command, 728
LDAP (Lightweight Directory
Access Protocol), 627
legacy programs, 935-936
library, Removable Storage, 222
licensing issues, digital music, 492
Lightweight Directory Access
Protocol (LDAP), 627
limited user accounts, 124-125
Line tool, Microsoft Paint, 444
linked objects, 112. *See also* OLE
(Object Linking and
Embedding)
links
adding, 665
e-mail messages and, 618
Internet Explorer, 664-665
Links dialog box, 118
Links toolbar, 166, 169, 269
Linux, 816, 963
List Folder Contents, 156
List view, Windows Explorer,
171-172
.lnk extension, 194
Local Area Connection Properties
dialog box, 780-781
local drives, Remote Desktop,
382-383

Local Internet Zone, 840
local printers, 353-355
locking Windows, 142
log files, 423, 549
Log Off button, 142
logarithmic functions, 430
logical drives, 859
logical functions, 430
logon
automatic, 130-131
controlling, 130
scripts, 573-574
to shared computers, 141
starting programs during,
14-15
logs, 58-61
application logs, 58
counter logs, 59-60
event logs, 57-58
system logs, 58
trace logs, 59
Long Distance tab, 545
Look In pull-down menu, 24
Low disk space notification, 892
LP records, 491
ls (list) command, 726
luminescence, HSV, 288
Luna theme, 103

M

Magnifier, 396, 405-407, 413
Magnifier tool, Microsoft
Paint, 444
mail programs. *See* e-mail
mail rules. *See* message rules
mail servers, 595
mainboard, 328
mandatory user profiles, 122
manifest, Luna theme, 103
MAP command, 47
Map Network Drive
dialog box, 804
mapping to drive letters, 803-806
master boot record (MBR), 860
Maximized, window states, 17
MBR (master boot record), 860
McAffee VirusScan, 731, 833
.mdb filename extensions, 11
media, backup, 220
Media Center Edition, 523-526
My Music, 525-526
My Pictures, 526

My TV, 524-525
My Video and Play
  DVD, 526
overview of, 523-524
Media Guide web site, 480, 512
Media Library
  configuring, 478
  creating, 474-476
  file categories, 476
  updating, 477
  video files in, 509
Media Player. *See* Windows
  Media Player
media pools, Removable
  Storage, 222
Melissa worm, 832
memory
  addressees, 336-337
  DOS settings, 102
  RAM, 338, 349-350
  tuning, 897-898
menus
  Programs menu. *see*
    Programs menu
  selecting commands from, 22
  Send To menu, 183-184
  shortcut menus, 22-23
  Start menu. *see* Start menu
message boxes, 290
Message Rule dialog box, 631-633
message rules
  actions, 634
  conditions, 633-634
  filtering mail with, 630-633
  filtering newsgroups,
    642-643
  managing, 636
  sorting old messages
    with, 636
messages, Outlook Express.
  See also e-mail
  composing in HTML, 617
  composition settings,
    612-613
  folders, 603-604
  importing, 601-602
  list of, 610
  receipt notification, 616
  storing, 603
mget command, 729
mice. *See* mouse
Microsoft
  ISPs recommended by,
    564-565

legal battle with Sun, 650
newsgroups, 920
removing Microsoft
  programs from
  Start menu, 273
support, 916-920
web resources, 919-920
Microsoft Baseline Security
  Advisor, 830
Microsoft Help and Support
  Center, 917-918
Microsoft Hotmail, 596-597,
  690-691
Microsoft Knowledge Base, 692
Microsoft Management Console.
  See MMC (Microsoft
  Management Console)
Microsoft Narrator, 396, 407-408
Microsoft NetMeeting. *See*
  NetMeeting
Microsoft Paint, 442-446
  adding text, 445-446
  coloring objects, 445
  cropping, 446
  drawing, 444
  flipping, rotating, and
    stretching, 446
  magnifying and
    enlarging, 444
  opening and saving files,
    442-443
  overview of, 434
  selecting objects, 443-444
  shapes, 444-445
  window anatomy, 443
Microsoft Passport, 660
Microsoft Windows Upgrade
  Advisor, 346
Microsoft Windows versions.
  See under Windows
middleware, Windows, 71-73, 273
MIDI (Musical Instrument Digital
  Interface), 458, 460
Minimized, window states, 18-19
minus box (-), Explorer bar, 177
MKDIR command, 48
MMC (Microsoft Management
  Console), 57-61
  diagnosing system
    problems, 57
  Event Viewer, 57-58
  Performance Logs and
    Alerts, 58-61

Modem Configuration dialog box,
  535-536
modems
  area code rules, 539-541
  cable connections, 551-552
  dial-up connections,
    530-536
  dialing locations, adding,
    536-537
  dialing locations, default,
    538-539
  dialing locations,
    displaying, 536
  dialing locations,
    editing, 538
  dialing locations, using, 539
  dialing manually, 547-548
  DSL connections, 549-551
  installing, 345
  ISDN connections, 552-554
  log files, 549
  satellite connections, 554
  telephone connections
    for, 332
  troubleshooting dial-up
    connections, 546-547
  types of, 344
Modify permissions, 156
monitors. *See* displays
motherboard, 328
mouse
  accessibility options, 397, 409
  buttons, 315-316
  ClickLock feature, 317
  configuring, 313-315
  DOS programs and, 89-90
  hover, 318
  pointer options, 316-317
  PS/2 ports, 331
  speed options, 316-317
  tweaks, 318-319
  wheel mice settings,
    317-318
  windows activation and, 319
Mouse Properties dialog box, 315
MouseKeys, 397, 410-411
movies. *See* Windows Movie Maker
Mozilla, 651, 654, 678
Mozilla Mail, 595
MP3s
  burning, 497
  portable players, 492
  ripping CDs, 491
  web sites, 498

.mpeg, 508
mput command, 728-729
MS-DOS. *See* DOS
MS-DOS Protected-Mode
    (DPMI), 102
msconfig. *See* System
    Configuration Utility
.msi files, 67, 831
MSN Explorer
        getting started with,
            659-660
        overview of, 652-653
        security concerns with, 847
MSN (Microsoft Network)
        home page, 676
        as online service, 559
        signing up for, 565
MSN search engine, 666-667
.mso, 831
multiboot installation. *See*
    dual-boot installation
multiboot systems, 863
multiple displays, 302-304
multiple users
        disk quotas, 146-149
        logon, 130-131
        managing from command
            prompt, 149-151
        managing logged-in users,
            145-146
        User Accounts window,
            128-130
music
        burning audio CDs, 494-498
        copying from cassettes and
            LPs, 491
        copying from CDs, 488-491
        licensing digital music, 492
        playing. *see* Windows
            Media Player
        playing music files on
            stereo, 478
        sources of music files, 473
Musical Instrument Digital
    Interface (MIDI), 458, 460
My Computer, 163
My Documents, 133-134, 163
My Music, 471, 525-526
My Network Places
        listing shared disks and
            printers, 773-774
        as special folder, 163
        viewing shared drives and
            folders, 801-803
        Web Folders and, 722, 724

My Pictures, 434
My Pictures, Media Center, 526
My TV, Media Center, 524-525
My Video and Play DVD, Media
    Center, 526

N

Narrator, 396, 407-408, 413
NAT (Network Address
    Translation), 817, 828
NAT Traversal, 828
navigating FTP folder tree, 726-728
navigating Windows Explorer
    folder tree
        Address box, 178
        Forward/Back buttons, 178
        opening new windows for
            each folder, 178-179
        UP-ARROW/DOWN-
            ARROW keys, 178
navigation aids, Internet Explorer,
    660-662
.NET Passport, 690-692
.NET Passport Wizard, 690
NET USE command, 805
net user command, 149-151
net view command, 795
NetBEUI (NetBIOS Extended
    User Interface)
        adding computers to
            NetBEUI LAN, 775-776
        installing, 783-784
        as network protocol, 767
NetBIOS Extended User Interface,
    NetBEUI (NetBIOS Extended
    User Interface)
NetMeeting, 701-707
        connecting to directory
            servers, 702-704
        features and options,
            705-706
        making/receiving calls,
            704-705
        overview of, 688, 701
        posting/joining meetings,
            706-707
        running and configuring,
            701-702
Netscape Navigator
        bookmarks, 665
        browser selection and, 651
        changing default
            browsers, 678

e-mail programs and, 595
    ordering, 650
    overview of, 653-654
Netstat, 591-592
network adapters, 740, 781
Network Address Translation
    (NAT), 817, 828
network bridges, 560, 743.
    See also bridging
network components, 779-790
        clients, 781-783
        network adapters, 781
        overview of, 779-781
        protocols, 783-785
        services, 787-788
        TCP/IP, 786-787
        Windows, 766
network connections
        creating for existing
            account, 566
        dial-up, 566
        displaying, 560-562
        HyperTerminal, 710
        ISDN, 567-568
        renaming, copying,
            deleting, 577
        TCP/IP, 792-795
        types of, 559-560
        viewing, 774
Network Connections window,
    560-562, 768
network drives. *See* sharing drives
network interface cards (NICs),
    740, 746, 748
Network News Transfer Protocol
    (NNTP), 637
network operating systems
    (NOS), 738
network ports, 332
network printers, 90-91, 353
Network Setup Wizard, 771-773,
    818-820, 823-824
network shortcuts, 801
Networking (TCP/IP)
    Troubleshooter, 796-797
networks. *See also* LANs (local area
    networks); VPNs (virtual
    private networks)
        adding to existing, 740
        cabled vs. wireless, 740-744
        dial-up connections,
            753-754
        direct connections, 752-753
        Ethernet and, 741-742

hardware installation, 747-749

hardware requiements, 744-747

peer-based vs. domain-based, 737-739

phone and power line, 742

protocols, 767

sharing files, 737

sharing hardware, 736-737

sharing Internet connections, 737

upgrading computer on existing, 740

viewing resources, 773-774

WANs, 736

wireless LANs, 742

New Area Code Rule dialog box, 540

New Connection Wizard, 563-564

New Partition Wizard, 869-870

news accounts, 599, 637

news servers, 637

newsgroups, 636-637

configuration options, 638-639

downloading list of, 639-640

participating in, 644-646

reading from, 641-643

searching for, 640-641

subscribing to, 639-641

support services, 920-922

newsreading programs, 637, 678-679

NICs (network interface cards), 740, 746, 748

NNTP (Network News Transfer Protocol), 637

normal backups, 231

Normal Startup, 55, 929

Norton Anti-Virus, 137, 731, 833

NOS (network operating systems), 738

Notepad, 420-423

notification area

as desktop object, 5-6

hiding, 268

LAN icon, 790

Volume icon, 463

ntbackup, 224-225, 242-244

NTFS (NT File System)

compressed folders, 196-197

converting partitions to, 872

drives, 155-156

overview of, 861-862

volumes, 809

null-modem cable, 752, 979

number pad, MouseKeys and, 410

number systems, Scientific Calculator and, 429

numbers, format for, 323

O

object certificates, 843-844

Object Linking and Embedding. See OLE (Object Linking and Embedding)

objects, OLE, 112

octal (Oct) numbers, 429

Office Clipboard, 109

OLE (Object Linking and Embedding), 111-119

combining output from different applications, 111-112

compared with Clipboard, 112

dragging and dropping, 113-114

editing linked or embedded objects, 115-117

maintaining links, 117-118

overview of, 111-113

Paste Special command, 114-115

scraps, 119

On-Screen Keyboard, 396, 401-402, 413

online chats. See NetMeeting; Windows Messenger

Online Print Ordering Wizard, 435, 451-453

online resources, 920-922

Microsoft, 919-920

newsgroups, 921-922

web sites, 921

online security, 833-834

online services, 558-559

OnNow power option, 9

Open dialog box, 24

Open Type fonts, 363

Open With dialog box, 11

Opera

browser selection and, 651

default browsers and, 678

handling of pop-up windows by, 659

overview of, 654

operating systems

other systems reading Windows files, 937

partitions for multiple, 860, 936-937

Outlook Express

account setup, 599-601

advantages of, 594

blocked senders list, 635-636

configuration options, 608-609

importing addresses, 602-603

importing files, 601-602

newsgroups. see newsgroups

overview of, 607-608

preventing other programs from sending e-mail via, 606

security of, 594-595, 833-834

security zones, 607

signatures, 615-616

storing addresses. see Address Book

viewing incoming mail, 609-611

Web links, 617-618

window, 597-599, 604-605

working with folders, 628-629

Outlook Express Import Wizard, 601-602

Outlook Express messages

attachments to, 605-606, 615

composition settings, 612-614

headers, 614-615

including original message in replies, 614

inserting pictures into, 618

inserting text files into, 615

message rules, 630-634, 636

receipt notification, 616

saving and filing, 619-620

searching for, 629-630

sending, 620

storing message folders, 603-604

Outlook security, 833-834
Outpost Firewall, 585
owner account, 125

P

P3P (Platform for Privacy
Preferences), 680-681
packages, OLE, 112
Paint Shop Pro, 442
panes, window, 16
PAP (Password Authentication
Protocol), 573
parallel ports, 330
parameters, hardware, 335-337
Parental Control feature, DVDs,
521-523
PartitionMagic, 860
partitions
assigning pathnames,
874-875
converting to NTFS, 872
creating new, 869-870
deleting, 871
Disk Management and,
864-865
drive letters and, 863,
872-874
files systems and, 861-862
free space on, 878
hard disks, 858-861
listing with MAP
command, 47
managing with DISKPART,
50-51
multiple operating systems
and, 936-937
properties of, 865-867
reasons for partitioning,
862-863
repartitioning a disk, 871
selecting active, 870-871
Windows XP installation
and, 971
Password Authentication Protocol
(PAP), 573
password hints, 124
password reset disks, 124
passwords
adding/removing, 137-138
adding to compressed
folders, 199
Internet Explorer
remembering, 669-671
user accounts, 124, 128

paste (CTRL-V), 108
Paste Special command, 114-115
pathnames, 163-164, 874-875
PC Cards, 334, 340, 745
PcAnywhere, 912
PCI (Peripheral Connect Interface)
cards, 334
PCI (Peripheral Connect Interface)
slots, 745
PCMCIA cards. See PC Cards
PDA (personal digital assistant), 492
Peacefire web site, 677
peer-to-peer (workgroup-based)
networks, 738-739, 766. See also
LANs (local area networks)
Performance Logs and Alerts,
58-61
Performance Options dialog box,
896, 897
Performance tab, Media Player, 510
performance tuning, 894-904
disabling unnecessary
services, 903-904
display settings, 894-896
hard disks, 902-903
monitoring resource use,
899-901
processor and memory
settings, 897-898
swap file size, 898-899
System Monitor graphs,
901-902
Peripheral Connect Interface (PCI)
cards, 334
Peripheral Connect Interface (PCI)
slots, 745
peripherals, 328
permissions, 151-157
FAT32 drives, 152-155
file and folder, 151-152
function of, 152
NTFS drives, 155-156
setting, 156-157
personal certificates, 842, 845-846
personal digital assistant (PDA), 492
Personal License Update
Wizard, 489
PGP (Pretty Good Privacy), 848
Phone And Modem Options
dialog box, 531, 536-538
phone line networks, 742, 779
Photo Album templates, 435-436
Photo Printing Wizard, 435,
451-452

Picture and Fax Viewer. See
Windows Picture And
Fax Viewer
pictures. See also images
adding to e-mail
messages, 618
importing files, 514
Pictures templates, 435-436
.pif files, 92, 831
PIN numbers, calling cards, 542
ping utility, 587-589
pinned programs, Start menu, 254
pixels
color and, 300
overview of, 434
screen resolution and, 299
Places bar, 24, 26-27
Platform for Privacy Preferences
(P3P), 680-681
playing music. See Windows
Media Player
playlists
adding to, 479
creating and editing,
478-479
Media Library and, 475
Plug and Play (PNP), 326, 354
plug-ins, web browsers, 649-650
plus box (+), Explorer bar, 177
PNP (Plug and Play), 326, 354
Point-to-Point Protocol (PPP),
557-558
Point-to-Point Tunneling Protocol
(PPTP), 754
pointer options, 316-317
pointer schemes, 313
policy settings, 123
POP (Post Office Protocol), 596
pop-up menus. See shortcut menus
pop-up windows, 659
port replicators, 388. See also
docking stations
portable players, 492-493
ports. See also connectors
displays, 332
firewalls, 584-585
FireWire, 333
modems, 547
network, 332
parallel, 330
printer, 90
PS/2 (keyboard and
mouse), 331
serial (com) ports, 329
Post Office Protocol (POP), 596
power line networks, 742, 779

power management, 385-388
    battery status (laptops), 387-388
    Hibernate Mode, 387
    power schemes, 387-388
    standards, 384
    Standby Mode, 386
Power Meter tab, 388
Power Option Properties dialog box, 386
Power options, OnNow, 9
Power Popup Killer, 659
power schemes, 387-388
PowerDVD (CyberLink), 521
PPP (Point-to-Point Protocol), 557-558
PPPoE (PPP over Ethernet), 549
PPTP (Point-to-Point Tunneling Protocol), 754
Pretty Good Privacy (PGP), 848
primary partitions, 859
Print Control window, 360
print (CTRL-P), 426
Print dialog box, 357-358
print jobs
    changing order of, 360
    pausing or canceling, 360
    queueing, 353
    scheduling, 361
PRINT SCREEN, 111
Printer And Faxes folder, 352-353, 811-812
printers
    changing description of, 377
    configuring, 355-357
    drivers, 353
    fonts and, 362
    local, 354-355
    options, 357-358
    ports, 90
    Remote Desktop and, 382
    sharing. see sharing printers
    testing and troubleshooting, 357
    types of, 353-354
printing
    from Address Book, 626-627
    away from home, 376-377
    from DOS programs, 90-91
    to files, 358-359
    images or photographs, 450-453
    with Internet Explorer, 658
    WordPad documents, 424-425

privacy of files and documents, 138-140
Privacy Report, 684-685
privacy settings, Internet Explorer
    cookies and, 679-683
    Privacy Report and, 684-685
private keys, 848
processors, tuning, 897-898
product key, Windows XP, 958
Profile Assistant, 671-672
Program Compatibility Wizard, 31
Program Files folder, 66
programs
    Add Or Remove Programs, 66-67, 78-80
    Add/Remove Windows Components button, 69-71
    associating with file extensions. see file associations
    exiting, 15-16
    hiding Windows middleware, 71-73
    installation or distribution files, 64
    installing, 65-69
    killing hung programs, 53-54
    legacy programs, 935-936
    moving between computers, 980
    running out of space for, 66
    scheduling. see Scheduled Tasks
    sharing, 697-700, 706
    Start menu and, 254, 260
    starting by opening documents, 10-11
    starting from Run dialog box, 13-14
    starting when logging in, 14-15
    starting with shortcut keys, 11-13
    stopping from running at startup, 55-57
    switching, 15
    uninstalling, 78-81
    ZIP and .exe files and, 68
Programs menu
    adding programs to, 256
    overview of, 254
    scrolling, 263
    shortcuts, 257

properties
    command prompt, 93-95
    dial-up connections, 569
    displays, 276-277
    DOS executable and shortcut, 96-101
    faxes, 366
    file and folder, 192-193
    hard disks, 867-868
    keyboards, 308-309
    languages, 309-312
    modems, 533-535
    mouse, 315
    partitions and drives, 865-867
    printers, 355-356
    settings, 20
    sound and audio devices, 297
    Start menu, 260-264
    system, 895
    Taskbar, 265-268
    wireless LANs, 778-779
protocols
    installing network, 783-784
    setting order of, 784-785
PS/2 (keyboard and mouse) ports, 331
public-key cryptography, 848
public keys, 848
put command, 728
PuTTY, 711
pwd command, 727

Q

.qt files, 508
question mark (?), filename searches, 208
quick boot disk, 51-52
Quick Launch toolbar
    adding programs to, 69
    editing, 270-271
    overview of, 268
QuickTime, 508
Quota Entries dialog box, 148-149
quotas, disk usage, 146-149

R

radio stations, 481-483
RAM (random access memory)
    adding, 349-350
    Clipboard use of, 109

overview of, 338
requirements for Fast User
    Switching, 128
random access memory. *See* RAM
    (random access memory)
rated movies, 521-523
Read & Execute permissions, 156
Read-only attribute, files and
    folders, 193
Read permissions, 153, 156
RealAudio, 482
RealOne Player, 511
RealVideo, 511
Recovery Console
    commands for repairing
        Windows, 49-51
    DOS family commands,
        47-49
    entering, 45-46
    overview of, 36
Recreational Software Advisory
    Counsel, 677
Recycle Bin
    eliminating confirmation
        box, 181-182
    emptying, 185
    finding files and
        folders, 184
    permanent deletes without
        sending to, 181
    resizing, 186-187
    retrieving files and folders,
        184-185
    as special folder, 163
    turning off, 187
refresh rate, 305
regedit/regedt32, 897. *See also*
    Registry Editor
Regional and Language Options
    dialog box, 322
regional settings, 322-323
registry, 940-948
    adding/changing entries,
        899-901
    backing up keys, 899
    configuration files and, 928
    data types and, 896
    editing as text file, 901-902
    file associations and, 73-74
    finding entries, 898-899
    key values, 941-942
    keys and root keys (hives),
        940-941
    keys that run programs on
        startup, 948

overview of, 940
restoring, 942-943
running Registry Editor,
    943-944
startup programs in, 55
where stored, 940
Registry Editor
    adding/changing registry
        entries, 899-901
    backing up keys, 899
    finding registry entries,
        898-899
    running, 943-944
remote access servers, 753-754
Remote Assistance, 912-916
    asking for help, 913-914
    overview of, 912
    responding to invitation
        for remote assistance,
        915-916
remote clients, 753
remote computers, 717-719
Remote Desktop
    capabilities and options,
        382-384
    configuring clients for,
        378-379
    connecting via, 379-380
    overview of, 377-378
    settings, 385-388
    web connections, 380-382
Remote Desktop Connection
    dialog box, 385
remote nodes, 753
removable disks, 863, 877-878
Removable Storage, 222-223,
    249-250
resizing windows, 19
resources. *See* online resources
resources, network. *See also*
    sharing drives; sharing printers
    sharing, 736, 800
    viewing, 773-774, 795
Restart option, 7
Restore And Manage Media tab,
    246-248
restore points
    automatic, 38-39
    creating, 41
    restoring to, 41-42
    undoing restorations, 42-43
Restore Wizard, 245-246
Restored, window states, 18
restoring files, 244-248

RGB (red, green, and blue)
    coordinates, 288
Rich Text Format (.rtf), 423
right click, context menus, 22-23
rights, group accounts, 123
ripping CDs, 488-491
RJ-11 connectors, 332
RJ-45 connectors, 742, 747
roaming user profiles, 122, 134
root folders, 164
root keys (hives), 940-941
rotation tools, Windows Picture
    And Fax Viewer, 437
routers
    connecting LANs to
        Internet, 737
    as gateway device, 815-816
    ICS vs. hardware routers, 816
Rover, 205
RSACi rating system, 677
.rtf files, 423
Run As dialog box, 143-144
Run dialog box, 13-14

S

S/MIME, 848
S/PDIF jacks, 333
Safe Mode
    display problems and, 304
    file and folder permissions,
        151-152
    folder permissions by user,
        156-157
    hardware, 348
    overview of, 36
    startup options, 44
    user permissions for FAT32
        drives, 152-155
    user permissions for NTFS
        drives, 155-156
Safe Mode With Command
    Prompt, 44
Safe Mode With Networking, 44
satellite modems, 554
saturation, HSV, 288
Save As dialog box, 24
Save Movie button, 519
Save Web Page dialog box, 658
Scanner And Camera Wizard,
    434-435, 448
Scanner And Printer Wizard, 449
scanners
    downloading images
        from, 449

linking to programs, 449-450
setting up, 446-447
Scanners And Cameras window, 447
Scheduled Task Wizard, 29
Scheduled Tasks
    backup jobs, 237-238
    batch files, 91-92
    canceling, 29
    configuring, 29-30
    information specified by, 27-28
    passwords and, 137
    scheduling programs, 28-29
    tracking, 30-31
scheduling print jobs, 361
Scientific Calculator, 428-431
    button operation on, 428
    functions, 430-431
    number systems and angle measures, 429-430
scraps
    OLE, 119
    viruses and, 831
screen resolution, 32, 299
screen savers
    configuring, 286
    installing, 285-286
    requiring logon, 142
    selecting, 284-285
screen shots, 111
screens. *See also* displays
    capturing with Clipboard, 111
    DOS programs and, 89
SCSI (Small Computer System Interface), 337
Search Companion, 203-209
    advanced options, 208-209
    case sensitivity, 208
    Indexing Service and, 209
    saving and retrieving searches, 209
    search criteria, 206-208
    standard vs. advanced, 204-206
    starting, 203
    wildcards, 208
Search Companion Explorer bar, 666-667
search criteria, 206-208
search engines, 666-667
search prefixes, 667-669

searches, 666-671
    from Address box, 666
    advanced options, 208-209
    criteria, 206-208
    saving and retrieving, 209
    Search Companion Explorer bar, 666-667
    search engines, 666-667
    search prefixes, 667-669
    Start menu and, 264
secure servers, 842
secure shell (SSH), 711
Secure Sockets Layer (SSL), 842-843
security
    Internet Explorer and, 652
    levels in XP Home Edition, 138-140
    logs, 58
    MSN Explorer and, 847
    Outlook Express and, 594-595
    user account options, 801
    VPNs and, 762
    XP features not in Me/9x, 122-123
security identifier (SID), 140
security, of downloads, 836-842
    controlling, 838-840
    IE zones, 837-838
    Java, JavaScript, VBScript, and ActiveX, 837, 840-842
    overview of, 836-837
security, of e-mail, 848-853
    getting certificates, 849
    overview of, 848
    receiving encrypted mail, 853
    sending encrypted mail, 850-853
    signing mail, 849-850
security, of web communications, 842-847
    certificate management, 844-845
    IE security settings, 846-847
    object certificates, 843-844
    personal certificates, 845-846
    web browsing, 842-843
security zone, Outlook Express, 607
security zones, Internet Explorer
    Local Internet Zone, 840

overview of, 837-838
    Trusted and Restricted Sites zone, 840
Select All, 179
Select Network Client dialog box, 782
Select Network Component Type, 782
Select Users or Group dialog box, 154
Selective Startup, 45, 56-57, 929
Send And Receive button, Outlook Express, 607
Send Fax Wizard, 367
Send/Receive options, Outlook Express, 608-609
Send To menu, 183-184
serial (com) ports, 329
Serial Line Internet Protocol (SLIP), 557-558
SerialKey, 397, 411-412
servers
    DHCP, 769
    FTP servers, 722, 727
    mail, 595
    NetMeeting directory, 702-704
    network, 737
    news, 637
    remote access, 753-754
    Remote Desktop, 378
    secure, 842
    time, 323
servers, VPNs. *See* VPN servers
Service Pack 1 (SP1)
    hiding nonremovable features, 64, 71
    JVM and, 650
    uninstalling, 986
    XP installation and, 954
services
    changing with msconfig, 930
    disabling unnecessary, 903-904
    installing network, 787-788
Set Program Access And Defaults, 71-72, 273
setup information files, 423
setup programs, 67
Setup Wizard
    disk space requirements, 954-955
    installation phases, 952

questions, 965-973
repair option, 36
repairing corrupted
    installation, 43
versions and command-line
    options, 964-965
setup.exe, 64
SFS (Simple File Sharing), 123,
    127-128
shape tools, Microsoft Paint,
    444-445
share names, 807
Shared Documents folder, 143
shareware programs, 730
sharing computers, 140-144.
    See also user accounts
    log off, 142
    logging on as another user,
        143-144
    logon, 141
    resuming work after
        locking Windows, 142
    screen saver logon, 142
    sharing files, 143
    switching users, 142
sharing drives, 801-806
    accessing, 801
    making drive sharable,
        807-809
    mapping to drive letters,
        803-806
    opening and saving files, 803
    overview of, 806-807
    viewing, 801-803
sharing files, 143, 151-157
sharing folders
    controlling access to, 809
    controlling from Safe Mode,
        151-157
    defined, 800
    making folder sharable,
        807-809
    mapping to drive letters,
        803-806
    opening and saving files, 803
    viewing, 802
sharing pictures, 453-455
    e-mailing, 454-455
    publishing on the Web,
        453-454
sharing printers, 809-812
    making printer sharable,
        809-811
    printing with, 811-812

sharing programs
    NetMeeting, 706
    Windows Messenger,
        697-700
SHIFT-click, 179
SHIFT-delete, 181
shortcut keys, 11-13
shortcut menus, 22-23
shortcuts. *See also* keyboard
    shortcuts
    adding to desktop, 69
    creating, 195-196
    to Device Manager, 327
    for DOS programs, 104-105
    to Internet from desktop, 664
    network shortcuts, 801
    overview of, 194-195
    using, 196
    viruses and, 831
    working with, 194-195
ShowSounds, 396, 403
shrpubw, 156
shutdown
    hangs on, 44
    options, 8-9
SID (security identifier), 140
signatures, digital, 848
signed e-mail, 615-616, 848-850
Simple File Sharing, 807
Simple File Sharing (SFS), 123,
    127-128
Simple Mail Transfer Protocol
    (SMTP), 595
single click, vs. double click, 6-7
skins, Media Player, 499-501
slide shows
    controlling, 438-439
    Movie Maker, 518
    selecting images, 438
SLIP (Serial Line Internet
    Protocol), 557-558
Small Computer System Interface
    (SCSI), 337
Smasher, 659
SMTP (Simple Mail Transfer
    Protocol), 595
snapshots. *See* restore points
sneakernet, 736
sound
    accessibility options, 396
    adding to movies, 516-517
    converting WAV files,
        505-506

copying music from
    cassettes and LPs, 491
copying music from CDs,
    488-491
creating own music,
    494-498
editing WAV files, 504
formats, 458-460
importing files, 514
input/output drivers,
    460-463
playing music. *see* Windows
    Media Player
playing WAV files, 502-503
portable players, 492-493
recording WAV files, 503
selecting Windows sounds,
    465-467
viewing device status, 463
volume and balance
    controls, 463-465
Sound And Audio Devices
    Properties dialog box, 297
sound effects, 297-298
Sound Forge, 492
Sound Recorder, 492, 502-503
sound schemes, 297, 467
sound settings, Media Player,
    486-488
Sounds And Audio Device
    Properties dialog box,
    460-464, 467
SoundSentry, 396, 403
soundtracks, 516-517
spam, 635
special characters, 431-432
special permissions, 156
speech recognition, 312-313
spooling, printers, 353
SSH (secure shell), 711
SSL (Secure Sockets Layer),
    842-843
Standard Buttons toolbar, 167-169
    list of buttons, 167-168
    managing buttons, 168-169
    moving, 166
Standard Calculator, 428
standards
    HTML and XML, 648
    power management, 384
    wireless LANs, 742
Standby Mode, 7, 386
star topology, 741, 742
Starband, 554

start button, 6
Start menu, 254-264
    adding favorites to, 665
    adding programs to, 69
    Classic style, 262-264
    configuration options, 136
    customizing with
        TweakUI, 272
    dragging and dropping
        items within, 256
    editing, 258
    moving commands and
        submenus, 256-258
    possible changes to, 256
    removing Microsoft
        programs from, 273
    searching, 264
    starting programs with, 10
    structure of, 254-255
    XP-style, 260-262
start page, Internet Explorer, 676
Start | Run command, 67
starting Windows XP, 7-8
startup folder, 14, 55
startup modes, 44-45
startup options, 929-931
startup problems, 43-45. See also
    Recovery Console
static IP addressing, 768
statistical functions, 430
status bar, Windows Explorer,
    176-177
StickyKeys, 396, 398-399
Storyboard view, Movie Maker,
    515-516
streaming audio, 458-460, 480-483
streaming video, 511
subnet masks, 587
subscribing, to newsgroups,
    639-641
Sun, 650
support services
    Help and Support Center,
        917-918
    newsgroups, 920-922
    web sites, 919-921
Suspend Mode, 7
swap file size, 898-899
switches
    installing, 748
    network, 741
    purchasing, 746
switching programs, 15
switching users, 142

system board, 328
system checkpoints, 39
system clock, 267
System Configuration Utility
    (msconfig), 928-935
    boot.ini file, 933
    environment settings,
        933-935
    international settings, 935
    overview of, 928
    replacing corrupted
        Windows file, 931-932
    running, 55
    service settings, 930
    startup options, 929-931
    System.ini and Win.ini files,
        932-933
    troubleshooting with,
        348-349
system logs, 58
System Menu button, 93
System Monitor, 901-902
system partitions, 859
system problems, 57-61
System Properties dialog box, 895
system resources, 899-902
System Restore, 37-43
    automatic restore points,
        38-39
    configuring, 39-40
    creating restore points, 41
    files stored by, 38
    functions of, 39
    overview of, 36
    restoring to restore point,
        41-42
    tips and warnings, 38
    undoing restorations, 42-43
system state, 58-61
system tray. See notification area
System.ini files, 928, 932-933
%SystemRoot%, 927

T

tapes, storing backup, 221
task buttons, 4-5
Task Manager
    accessing with
        CTRL-ALT-DEL, 795
    canceling programs, 16
    killing hung programs, 53
    monitoring resource use,
        899-901

overview of, 36
vs. task buttons, 5
Windows versions and, 145
Task pane, Windows Explorer, 170
Taskbar
    adding/removing toolbars,
        268-269
    allowing to be covered by
        windows, 267
    controlling look of
        toolbars, 270
    creating toolbars, 271-272
    customizing with
        TweakUI, 272
    as desktop object, 4
    editing Quick Launch
        toolbar, 270-271
    enabling changes, moving,
        sizing, 265
    grouping buttons on, 267
    hiding, 266
    hiding clock, 267
    hiding notification area, 268
    moving toolbars, 269-270
    properties, 265-268
TCP/IP (Transmission Control
    Protocol/Internet Protocol)
    addresses, 792-794
    as communication
        protocol, 556
    configuring, 786-787
    configuring Windows
        clients to use, 774
    dial-up settings, 573
    as network protocol, 767
    testing connection, 794-795
telephone connections, 332
telnet
    HyperTerminal
        connections, 710-711
    overview of, 710
    running, 721
    SSH and, 711
Temporary Intranet Files, 661,
    677, 890
terminal emulation, 558, 716-717
text, adding to Microsoft Paint
    graphics, 445-446
text chats, NetMeeting, 705
text files
    capturing with
        HyperTerminal, 720
    displaying contents of, 48
    editing registry as, 901-902

reading with Notepad, 414
sending with
    HyperTerminal, 719
text services, 32
Text Services And Input
    Languages dialog box, 308
Text tool, Microsoft Paint, 445-446
Thawte, 849
themes
    color, 277
    desktop, 103, 276-278
    visual, 103
The Ultimate Collection of
    Windows Software
    (TUCOWS), 649, 730
thumbnail icon, folders, 202
Thumbnail views, Windows
    Explorer, 172-173, 435
.tiff files, 442
Tiles view, Windows Explorer,
    170-171
tiling windows, 19
time servers, 323
time, setting, 323-324
Timeline view, Movie Maker,
    515-516
title bars, 290
titles, Movie Maker, 519
ToggleKeys, 396, 400-401
toolbar buttons, Media Player,
    468-470
toolbars, taskbar
    adding/removing, 268-269
    controlling look of, 270
    creating, 271-272
    editing Quick Launch
        toolbar, 270-271
    moving, 269-270
    types of, 268-269
toolbars, Windows Explorer,
    166-167
topology
    bus topology, 744
    networks, 741
    star topology, 741, 742
trace logs, 59
trace route (tracert), 589-591
tracert (trace route), 589-591
tracks, of albums, 477
trails, pointer, 316
transitions, movies, 518

Transmission Control
    Protocol/Internet Protocol. *See*
    TCP/IP (Transmission Control
    Protocol/Internet Protocol)
trigonometric functions, 430
Trillian, 688
troubleshooters, 37
troubleshooting
    CD burning, 214-216, 497
    compatibility issues, 33
    dial-up connections,
        546-547
    hardware, 345-349
    ICS, 827
    LANs, 796-797
    printers, 357
    VPN clients, 758-759
    VPN servers, 761-762
    XP installation, 975-976
troubleshooting tools, 36-37
TrueType fonts, 361-362
TRUSTe, 684
Trusted and Restricted Sites
    zone, 840
TUCOWS (The Ultimate
    Collection of Windows
    Software), 649, 730
tuning performance. *See*
    performance tuning
TWAIN drivers, 449
TweakUI
    changing Windows
        interface, 23
    customizing Start menu
        and Taskbar, 272
    mouse settings, 315, 318-319
    search prefixes, 668-669
.txt files, 423. *See also* text files
TYPE command, 48
typefaces. *See* fonts

U

UNC (Universal Naming
    Convention), 164, 801
Undo command, Windows
    Explorer, 182
undo (CTRL-Z), 182
Unicode format, 424
Uniform Resource Locators
    (URLs), 649

uninstall programs, 80
uninstall.exe, 80
unique names, 770
Universal Naming Convention
    (UNC), 164, 801
Universal Plug and Play
    (UPnP), 326
universal serial bus. *See* USB
    (universal serial bus)
UNIX, 816, 963
UNIX shell account, 558
unshielded twisted pair, 742
Unwise.exe, 80
UP-ARROW key, 178
Up One Level button, 25
updates. *See* Automatic Updates;
    Windows Update
upgrade installation, 953, 961-962
upgrade report, 967
uploading, FTP files, 728-729
UPnP (Universal Plug and
    Play), 326
.url extension, 196
URLs (Uniform Resource
    Locators), 649
USB (universal serial bus)
    connections, 330-331
    hubs, 331
    ports, 745
Usenet, 636-637. *See also*
    newsgroups
user accounts
    adding/removing
        passwords, 137-138
    configuration options, 127
    created by Windows during
        installation, 125-126
    creating new, 131-132
    deleting, 140
    Fast User Switching, 128
    guest accounts, 140
    multiple users, 128-131
    overview of, 123-124
    privacy of files and
        documents, 138-140
    profile settings, 126-127
    security options, 801
    settings, 132-136
    Simple File Sharing, 127-128
    types of, 124-125
    window, 128-130

user passwords, 124
user permissions
    FAT32 drives, 152-155
    NTFS drives, 155-156
user profiles, 126-127, 134-136
Utility Manager, 413

V

.vbs files, 831
VBScript, 837, 840-842
VeriSign, 849
video, 508-526
    downloading files, 675
    DVDs, 520-523
    importing files, 514
    Media Center, 523-526
    movies. *see* Windows Movie
        Maker
    playing streaming video, 511
    playing video files from
        hard disk, 509-510
    updating drivers, 33
    Windows and, 508
video capture devices, 508
video cards. *See* display adapters
video jacks, 333
videoconferencing
    NetMeeting, 705
    Windows Messenger, 696
View Menu button, 26
views, Windows Explorer
    changing, 174
    List and Details views,
        171-172
    Thumbnails and Filmstrip
        views, 172-173
    Tiles and Icons views,
        170-171
virtual machines, 84-85
virtual memory, 898-899
virtual printers, 353
viruses
    avoiding infection, 832-835
    dealing with infected
        systems, 835-836
    defined, 831
    downloading programs
        and, 730
    e-mail and, 605-607
    file types and, 831
    information sources for, 836
    restore points and, 41

spread of, 832
    XP installation and, 959
visual effects, 296
visual themes, 32
visually impaired, accessibility
    options, 403-409
VMware, 962
voice chats, NetMeeting, 705
voice communication, DSL and, 551
voice conversations, Windows
    Messenger, 696
volume control, 463-466
volume settings, Media Player,
    486-488
VPN clients, 755-759
    configuring, 756-758
    connecting from, 758
    creating connection, 756
    troubleshooting, 758-759
VPN servers, 759-762
    configuring incoming
        connection, 760-761
    creating Incoming
        Connections icon,
        759-760
    troubleshooting, 761-762
VPNs (virtual private networks),
    754-762
    client configuration,
        755-759
    connection configuration,
        756-758
    creating connections, 756
    network connections, 559
    overview of, 754-755
    Remote Desktop use of, 378
    security issues, 762
    server configuration,
        759-762

W

W3C (World Wide Web
    Consortium), 648
.wab files, 603
wallpaper. *See* background
WANs (wide area networks), 736
.wav files, 467
WAV sound
    converting to other formats,
        505-506
    editing, 504
    overview of, 492

playing, 502-503
    recording, 503
web browsers, 648-654
    choosing, 651
    concepts, 648-649
    default, 650, 678
    free, 653
    Internet Explorer. *see*
        Internet Explorer
    Java and, 650
    Mozilla, 654
    MSN Explorer, 652-653
    Netscape Navigator,
        653-654
    Opera, 654
    plug-ins, 649-650
    showing on Start menu, 261
web browsing
    with Internet Explorer, 656
    security of, 842-843
web communication security.
    See security, of web
    communications
Web Connection, Remote Desktop,
    380-382
web content, blocking
    offensive, 677
Web Folders
    creating, 722-724
    overview of, 710
    working with, 724-725
web forms, 669-671, 671-672
web links, 617-618
web pages
    adding Web content to
        desktop, 281-282
    caching, 677-678
    color selection, 673-674
    creating, 685-686
    fonts selection, 672-673
    language preferences,
        674-675
    opening with Internet
        Explorer, 657
    printing with Internet
        Explorer, 658
    recently viewed, 662-663
    saving, 658
    updating desktop, 283
    working with on desktop,
        282-283
Web Publishing Wizard, 435, 686
web service, 11

Web, sharing pictures via, 453-454
web sites
    automatic interaction with,
      669-672, 669-672
    online resources, 921
    support services,
      919-920, 921
web style, 6
WebView pane, 170
Welcome screen, 130, 141
WEP (Wireless Equivalent
  Privacy), 776
WFP (Windows File
  Protection), 884
wheel mouse settings, 317-318
whiteboard
    NetMeeting, 705
    Windows Messenger, 697
wildcards, 208
WinAmp, Media Player, 499
WinChat, 708
windows
    activation settings, 319
    allowing Taskbar to be
      covered by, 267
    arranging, 19
    Classic Style, 289
    DOS settings, 95-96
    minimizing, 18-19
    moving and resizing, 19
    parts of, 16-17
    states of, 17-18
    view settings, 174
Windows 2000
    configuring to use
      TCP/IP, 775
    dual-booting with XP, 963
    as gateway device, 816
    security compared with
      Windows Me/9x, 122
Windows 3.x, 84
Windows 95/98, 84
Windows 9x
    configuring to use
      TCP/IP, 775
    dual-booting XP with, 963
    as gateway device, 816
    security compared with
      XP, 122
Windows Briefcase, 372-376
    overview of, 372-373
    synchronizing files from
      desktop to laptop, 373
    synchronizing files from
      laptop to desktop,
      375-376

    using files in, 374-375
    using with/without a LAN,
      373-374
Windows Calculator, 427-431
    overview of, 427
    Scientific Calculator,
      428-431
    Standard Calculator, 428
Windows Components Wizard,
  70-71
Windows Error Reporting, 54
Windows Explorer
    Address bar, 164
    back ups with, 223-224
    CD burning from, 212-214
    changing view settings, 174
    compared with Backup
      Utility, 224
    compared with Internet
      Explorer, 655-656
    Explorer bar, 169-170
    Links toolbar, 169
    List and Details views,
      171-172
    moving toolbars, 166-167
    sorting/arranging folder
      content, 175-176
    Standard Buttons toolbar,
      167-169
    status bar, 176-177
    structure of, 164-166
    Task pane, 170
    Thumbnails and Filmstrip
      views, 172-173
    Tiles and Icons views,
      170-171
    viewing images in an
      Explorer window,
      435-436
Windows File Protection
  (WFP), 884
Windows files
    other operating systems
      reading, 937
    replacing corrupted,
      931-932
Windows Installer, 67
WINDOWS key, 10, 314
WINDOWS-L, 142
Windows Me
    configuring to use
      TCP/IP, 775
    DOS Virtual Machine, 84
    dual-booting with XP, 963
    as gateway device, 816

    security compared with
      XP, 122
    WebView pane, 170
Windows Media Player, 468-488
    CD burning from, 214
    configuring for creating
      CDs, 496-497
    configuring for Internet, 481
    configuring for playing
      CDs, 484-485
    configuring for ripping
      CDs, 488-490
    customizing, 498-499
    file format selection, 502
    Internet settings, 499
    Media Library, 474-478
    My Music folder, 471
    older versions, 470
    playing audio files, 471-473
    playing CDs, 483-486
    playing DVDs, 521
    playing streaming audio,
      480-483
    playlists, 478-479
    skins, 499-501
    toolbar buttons, 468-470
    volume, graphic
      equalization, and sound
      settings, 486-488
    window, 468
Windows Messenger, 688-700
    contact configuration,
      693-694
    getting rid of, 689
    options, 700
    overview of, 688
    sending files to
      conversation
      participants, 696-697
    sharing programs, 697-700
    signing in with .NET
      Passport, 690-692
    starting conversations,
      694-696
    videoconferencing, 696
    voice conversations, 696
    whiteboard, 697
Windows middleware, hiding,
  71-73
Windows Movie Maker, 512-520
    adding sound, 516-517
    composing movies, 515-516
    editing movies, 518-519
    importing files, 514-515
    overview of, 512
    previewing movies, 517

saving movies, 519-520
window, 513-514
Windows NT, 775, 816
Windows Picture And Fax Viewer
annotating images with, 439-441
overview of, 434
viewing images with, 436-438
Windows Product Activation. *See* WPA (Windows Product Activation)
Windows Sockets (Winsock), 562
Windows sounds, 465-467
Windows Task Manager. *See* Task Manager
Windows Update, 906-909
downloading updates, 908-909
overview of, 906
scanning for updates, 906-908
Windows XP
as gateway device, 816
installing. *see* installation, Windows XP
security compared with Windows Me/9x, 122
Windows XP CD-ROM, 69-71
Windows XP Home edition
domain-based LANs and, 771
security features compared with Professional edition, 122-123
security levels, 138-140
Service Pack 1 and, 954
Windows XP Professional edition, 122-123, 954

Windows XP Service Pack 1. *See* Service Pack 1
Windows XP Setup Wizard. *See* Setup Wizard
WinDVD (Intervideo), 521
Win.ini files
initialization files, 928
msconfig and, 932-933
startup programs in, 55
winmodems, 530
Winnt/Winnt32, 964-965
Winsock (Windows Sockets), 562
WinZip, 68
Wireless Equivalent Privacy (WEP), 776
wireless LANs, 742
adding computer to, 776-779
installing adapters, 748
properties, 778-779
purchasing adapter cards, 747
wireless links, infrared, 762-763
Wireless Networks Connection Properties, 778-779
WMA files, 490-491
word wrap, Notepad, 422
WordPad
features and options, 426-427
file formats, 423-424
formatting documents with, 424-425
printing documents, 424-425
workgroups, 738, 770, 788-790
workstations, 738
World Wide Web Consortium (W3C), 648

worms, 605, 831
WPA (Windows Product Activation)
hardware changes and, 957
how it works, 955-956
latest information on, 958-959
reinstalling following, 956
Write permissions, 156

X

XML (Extensible Markup Language), 648
Xmodem, 717
XMS (extended memory), 84, 102
XP-style properties, 260-262

Y

Yahoo, 676
Yahoo Messenger, 688
Yahoo! People Search, 627
Ymodem, 717

Z

ZIP compressed folders, 197. *See also* compressed folders
Zip disks, 220
ZIP files, 68
ZipMagic, 68
Zmodem, 717
Zone Alarm, 585, 731
zoom in/out, Windows Picture And Fax Viewer, 436

INTERNATIONAL CONTACT INFORMATION

AUSTRALIA
McGraw-Hill Book Company Australia Pty. Ltd.
TEL +61-2-9900-1800
FAX +61-2-9878-8881
http://www.mcgraw-hill.com.au
books-it_sydney@mcgraw-hill.com

CANADA
McGraw-Hill Ryerson Ltd.
TEL +905-430-5000
FAX +905-430-5020
http://www.mcgraw-hill.ca

GREECE, MIDDLE EAST, & AFRICA
(Excluding South Africa)
McGraw-Hill Hellas
TEL +30-1-656-0990-3-4
FAX +30-1-654-5525

MEXICO (Also serving Latin America)
McGraw-Hill Interamericana Editores S.A. de C.V.
TEL +525-117-1583
FAX +525-117-1589
http://www.mcgraw-hill.com.mx
fernando_castellanos@mcgraw-hill.com

SINGAPORE (Serving Asia)
McGraw-Hill Book Company
TEL +65-863-1580
FAX +65-862-3354
http://www.mcgraw-hill.com.sg
mghasia@mcgraw-hill.com

SOUTH AFRICA
McGraw-Hill South Africa
TEL +27-11-622-7512
FAX +27-11-622-9045
robyn_swanepoel@mcgraw-hill.com

SPAIN
McGraw-Hill/Interamericana de España, S.A.U.
TEL +34-91-180-3000
FAX +34-91-372-8513
http://www.mcgraw-hill.es
professional@mcgraw-hill.es

UNITED KINGDOM, NORTHERN,
EASTERN, & CENTRAL EUROPE
McGraw-Hill Education Europe
TEL +44-1-628-502500
FAX +44-1-628-770224
http://www.mcgraw-hill.co.uk
computing_neurope@mcgraw-hill.com

ALL OTHER INQUIRIES Contact:
Osborne/McGraw-Hill
TEL +1-510-549-6600
FAX +1-510-883-7600
http://www.osborne.com
omg_international@mcgraw-hill.com